A PERSONAL N...
FROM HARLEY HAHN

This book will change your life.

That's a strange thing to say about a computer book but, as sure as you are reading this introduction, your life will be different by the time you finish the book. You will think differently and you will approach problems differently.

You see, your computer is not a lifeless piece of machinery. It is a dynamic tool that interacts with your very thought processes. Whenever you use a computer it becomes, for better or for worse, an extension of your mind. This means that, over an extended period of time, the computer system you use changes how you think. Indeed, we might classify systems as mentally "good" or "bad" depending on how they affect the minds of their users. In this sense, Unix is, without a doubt, the very best computer system ever invented (and Linux is a type of Unix).

When you use Unix, you are not working with a machine. You are working with the people who designed Unix. Every line and every picture you see on your monitor was put there by a person. Every tool you use was invented by a person. Every technical term and every concept you learn was created by a person. When you use Unix, you are interacting with these people, just as surely as you are interacting with me as you read this page.

Unix and Linux are wonderful because they were developed by bright, creative people who delighted in thinking well. These people were not only very, very smart; they knew what they were doing and they loved their work. This means that, whenever you use a Unix or Linux system, you are forging a mental relationship with some of the smartest, most accomplished (and satisfied) programmers and computer scientists who ever lived. Such a partnership can't help but have a positive effect on you.

The fact is it really doesn't matter why you want to learn Unix or Linux, or why you picked up this book. Perhaps you love computers and you have a burning desire to learn. Perhaps you are taking a class and this will be your textbook. Perhaps you have a job and you are required to use Unix or Linux. It doesn't matter.

You are about to begin a long, complex, and very rewarding journey. In the days, weeks, and months to come, you will encounter new ideas and build new skills, far beyond anything you can imagine at this moment. As you do, your mind will change for the better, your thought processes will improve, and your way of looking at the world and at yourself will change.

This is not your average computer book. (I'm sure you realize that by now.) Aside from a large amount of technical material, there are hints, jokes and a lot of plain-spoken advice. I did the very best I could to show what you really need to know. This is not a computer manual. This is not a compendium of impersonal details. This is one person (me) talking to another person (you).

I will make you a promise. As you teach yourself Unix, I will be with you, every step of the way. What you are holding in your hand is my guide to learning Unix and Linux, and now it is yours.

Are you ready?

Good. Turn to page 1 and start reading.

HARLEY HAHN

HARLEY HAHN'S

GUIDE TO
UNIX AND LINUX

Harley Hahn

 **McGraw-Hill
Higher Education**

Boston   Burr Ridge, IL   Dubuque, IA   New York   San Francisco   St. Louis
Bangkok   Bogotá   Caracas   Kuala Lumpur   Lisbon   London   Madrid   Mexico City
Milan   Montreal   New Delhi   Santiago   Seoul   Singapore   Sydney   Taipei   Toronto

HARLEY HAHN'S GUIDE TO UNIX AND LINUX

1 2 3 4 5 6 7 8 9 0 DOC/DOC 0 9 8

ISBN 978–0–07–313361–4
MHID 0–07–313361–2

Global Publisher: Raghothaman Srinivasan
Director of Development: Kristine Tibbetts
Developmental Editor: Darlene M. Schueller
Senior Project Manager: Kay J. Brimeyer
Lead Production Supervisor: Sandy Ludovissy
Associate Design Coordinator: Brenda A. Rolwes
Cover Designer: Lee Anne Dollison, and Studio Montage
(USE) Cover Image: Harley Hahn
Copy editing / Page Layout: Lydia Hearn
Compositor: Lachina Publishing Services
Typeface: 10/12 Minion Regular
Printer: R. R. Donnelley Crawfordsville, IN

Library of Congress Cataloging-in-Publication Data

Hahn, Harley, 1952-
  Harley Hahn's Guide to Unix and Linux / Harley Hahn. -- 1st ed.
    p. cm.
  Includes index.
  ISBN 978–0–07–313361–4 — ISBN 0–07–313361–2 (hbk. : alk. paper) 1. UNIX (Computer file)
  2. Linux. 3. Operating systems (Computers) I. Title. II. Title: Guide to Unix and Linux.
  QA76.76.O63H3378 2009
  005.4'32--dc22
                              2007052525

ABOUT THE AUTHOR

Harley Hahn is a writer, computer expert, philosopher, humorist, artist and musician. In all, he has written 32 books, which have sold more than 2 million copies. This is his 7th Unix book.

The book *Harley Hahn's Internet Yellow Pages* was the first Internet book in history to sell more than 1,000,000 copies. Two of his other books, *Harley Hahn's Internet Insecurity* and *Harley Hahn's Internet Advisor* have been nominated for a Pulitzer Prize. These books, along with others, have made Hahn the best-selling Internet author of all time.

Hahn has written numerous articles, essays and stories on a wide variety of topics, including romance, philosophy, economics, culture, medicine and money. Much of his writing is available on his Web site `www.harley.com`.

Hahn's work — including a complete set of his books — is archived by the Special Collections Department of the library at the University of California at Santa Barbara.

Hahn has a degree in Mathematics and Computer Science from the University of Waterloo (Canada), and a graduate degree in Computer Science from the University of California at San Diego. He also studied medicine at the University of Toronto Medical School. Hahn has been the recipient of a number of honors and awards, including a National Research Council (Canada) post-graduate scholarship and the 1974 George Forsythe Award from the ACM (Association for Computing Machinery).

Hahn enjoys writing computer books, because "I get to sleep in, and I like telling people what to do."

To Linda, for patience and encouragement.

LIST OF CHAPTERS
AND APPENDIXES

TABLE OF CONTENTS

LIST OF FIGURES

NOTE TO TEACHERS

I designed this book very carefully to help you teach Unix and Linux. My goal is to support your teaching no matter what the length of your course, and no matter which topics you choose to present to your class.

To do so, I offer you a long book that covers every important topic a student needs to master to understand and use basic Unix. I designed the book as a comprehensive reference that can be read from beginning to end, in order. However, I also designed it to give you maximum flexibility. My intention is for you to look at the Table of Contents and see what the book has to offer. Then choose which topics you want to teach directly, and which ones you want to assign for self-study.

This approach will work well for you, because I wrote every chapter so it can be studied independently. Moreover, every section within a chapter is designed so that the student can teach himself. In order to make this possible, I used several techniques.

First, we know that, in any area of study, one of the most important things a student must learn is the relevant terminology. There are 622 technical terms explained in this book, and each term is explained explicitly. Moreover, no term is used until it is explained.

To support this effort, there is an extensive glossary at the end of the book. If you assign a chapter or section out of order, your students can simply use the glossary to look up concepts with which they are unfamiliar. (Please encourage them to do so.) For further help, each glossary definition is followed by the number of the chapter in which the student can find a detailed discussion of the topic.

Second, as the student reads, he or she is led from one idea to the next by the careful use of examples. Indeed, this book contains well over a thousand examples fully integrated into the text. Most commands and ideas are coupled with sample input and output, which allows the book to stand on its own. This makes it possible for the student to fully understand what he is reading, even if he is not working in front of his computer at the time.

Third, all the examples in this book were tested on Linux, FreeBSD and Solaris systems. In most cases, each example was also tested under four different shells: Bash, the Korn Shell, the Tcsh, and the C-Shell. Thus, no matter which type of Unix or Linux your students use, what they read in the book will work for them. Where there are important exceptions, I note them. Thus, if the student is following along at his computer, what he sees will be similar to what is printed in the book.

Finally, as a student reads a particular section, there is no assumption that he has read the previous section or that he will read the next section. This allows you to teach whatever you want in whichever order makes sense to you. (For more thoughts on choosing what to teach, see the discussion on the Unix Model Curriculum below.)

What makes this possible is the liberal use of forward and backward references to other parts of the book. Thus, whenever a topic depends upon ideas discussed elsewhere, the student will find it easy to take a moment and fill the gap in his knowledge.

UNIX AS A PART OF COMPUTER SCIENCE

One of the most interesting aspects of teaching Unix is that, unlike other areas of computer science, there is no standard curriculum. This, in spite of the fact that Unix is a mature area of study, having been taught for well over two decades.

This seeming paradox is explained by the observation that, for many years, Unix was considered to be merely a technology, rather than a part of computer science. As such, instruction in Unix was confined mostly to explaining how to carry out various tasks such as using the shell, entering commands, manipulating files, running programs, and so on. For programming students, Unix was presented only as a vehicle for writing and testing programs. To be sure, some operating systems teachers considered Unix to be a classical system, important enough to be studied from a historical point of view. To suggest, however, that Unix should be recognized as a legitimate topic within computer science was, for many years, considered to be far-fetched.

Today, however, this viewpoint is changing with the realization that the study of Unix and Linux form an important part of the computer science curriculum. There are several reasons for this change.

First, the history of Unix is the best example we have of a well-designed computing system that has evolved and survived for more than a (human) generation. There are, indeed, many people using Unix whose fathers and mothers used Unix.

Second, most parts of Unix were designed by computer scientists or programmers well versed in basic computer science. Thus, a proper study of Unix affords the student a chance to see computer science in action. This naturally leads to the study of more mainstream topics, such as data structures and number systems. For example, see the discussion of trees in Chapters 9 and 23; of stacks in Chapter 8 and 24; and of the hexadecimal, octal and binary number systems in Chapter 21.

Finally, the Unix culture was the crucible from which Linux and the Open Source movement emerged in the 1990s. Thus, the study of Unix affords the student the background necessary to understand, appreciate, and (perhaps) contribute to these important international efforts.

To promote the teaching of Unix and Linux in this way, this book is structured around what is called the "Unix Model Curriculum". The intention is that teachers will use this curriculum to help plan their courses. For more information, see the section called "Support for Teachers" below.

A UNIX-NEUTRAL APPROACH

One of the goals of this book is to ensure that students become comfortable using any type of Unix or Linux, in their own language, anywhere in the world. This goal is promoted in several ways.

First, it is a core belief of mine that students should be educated generally enough as to be able to use any major type of Unix as well as the most important shells. Specifically, students should be comfortable, not only with Linux, but with System V-based Unix (such as Solaris), and BSD-based Unix (such as FreeBSD and Mac OS X). Moreover, students should understand the basic operation of the most important shells: Bash (the default Linux shell); the Korn shell (the modern version of the Bourne shell); and the Tcsh (the modern version of the C-Shell). After all, in the course of a lifetime, one will be called upon to use a variety of Unix and Linux systems. Thus, it behooves us to consider the student's long-term needs, regardless of which system happens to be available at your particular school.

Toward this end, this book introduces Unix and Linux by using a set of basic principles common to all Unix-like operating system. Where significant differences exist, they are taught as variations of the standard, ensuring that the student becomes comfortable with the most important, most enduring concepts.

A similar didactic approach is used with the shells. The student is introduced to the idea that there are the two main families of shells, each of which is explained in terms of the appropriate historical and technical background. The Korn shell and Bash are then introduced as members of the Bourne Shell family, while the C-Shell and the Tcsh are taught as being members of the C-Shell family. Because some of the details are complex, the book has numerous tables and explanatory notes that act as a reference, should the student need to switch from one operating system to another, or from one shell to another (as we all must do from time to time).

The second way in which a Unix-neutral teaching environment is developed concerns internationalization. In the early days (1970s and 1980s), all Unix systems were derived from either System V or BSD (see Chapter 2), both of which were U.S.-centric systems, based on the ASCII code.

Today, Unix and Linux systems are used widely, well beyond the United States. Indeed, the Linux kernel and the various Linux distributions are developed by volunteers from around the world. As a result, Unix has evolved into a true international operating system that supports much more than U.S. English and ASCII. For the beginner, the most significant concepts related to internationalization are locales, collating sequences, and character classes. These topics are discussed in detail as part of the treatment of filters (Chapter 19) and regular expressions (Chapter 20).

It is my feeling that establishing and maintaining a Unix-neutral approach in our teaching leads the student to internalize the idea that Unix and Linux are global systems. In this way, the student develops the knowledge and skills to become conversant with any type of Unix or Linux he or she may be called upon to use.

SUPPORT FOR TEACHERS: THE UNIX MODEL CURRICULUM

The Unix Model Curriculum is a detailed plan for teaching all the important concepts necessary for an introductory course for Unix or Linux. The Unix Model Curriculum was designed to help you decide which topics to teach and the order in which to teach them.

You can learn about the Unix Model Curriculum by visiting either of the following Web sites. First, a special site I have set up for Unix teachers and students:

`www.harley.com/unix`

Second, a teaching support site sponsored by McGraw-Hill Higher Education specifically for teachers who use this book:

`www.mhhe.com/harleyhahn`

On this Web site, you will find a great deal of useful material, including answers to all the exercises, a discussion of the Unix Model Curriculum, and a variety of teaching aids.

To access the McGraw-Hill site, you will need a password, which you can obtain at no charge, either from your sales rep or from the McGraw-Hill Higher Education marketing department.

ACKNOWLEDGEMENTS

This is a large book, and if you are going to read it all, you have a lot of work ahead of you. As such, you might be asking yourself if you should take the time to read the acknowledgements. I think you should, for two important reasons.

First, if you are a student, this might be the only part of the book you will not cover in class. For a few minutes, then, you can relax and enjoy yourself, knowing that what you read here will never appear on a test.

Second, although the information in this section is somewhat esoteric, you never know when it will come in handy. For example, later in this section, you will find out that Professor Sanjiv Bhatia of the University of Missouri, St. Louis, was one of my reviewers. One day, you may be visiting St. Louis and, as you are walking around the university, you might actually run into Professor Bhatia. "Dr. Bhatia," you will say, "it is such a pleasure to meet you. I hear you did an excellent job helping Harley Hahn with his book." Upon which, he shakes your hand and invites you to the Faculty Club for tea.

So are you ready? Good. Let's push on.

MY TEAM (AND WELCOME TO IT)

This book was a long time in the making and, during that time, a lot of people helped me. I produced the book myself, which means I hired and supervised the people who did most of the work so, to start, let me introduce the members of my team.

First, Lydia Hearn. Lydia and I have worked together on books for a long time, and I have found her to be a truly remarkable person. Her skill, energy and enthusiasm is virtually boundless. For this book, Lydia did the copy editing and the page layout. However, to call Lydia a mere "copy editor" or "layout artist" is like calling the Grand Canyon a hole in the ground. The reason this book looks so good is that Lydia spent many, many hours painstakingly making every single page look as good as possible. She is a tireless perfectionist with a devotion to quality that would be difficult to overpraise. And just between us, Lydia Hearn is the only person in the world I will let make changes in what I write.

Lydia, by the way, is an accomplished academic in her own right. She is a tenured professor at De Anza College in Cupertino, California, where she teaches English. She has served as Academic Senate President and Dean of Language Arts, and has been recognized by the college as a Distinguished Educator. I am lucky to have her.

Next, my art director, Lee Anne Dollison. Lee Anne brought her many years of publishing experience to the project. Over many months, she helped Lydia and me create an attractive, easy-to-read book. Lee Anne was responsible for the interior design, the front cover*, and the illustrations. She was also our resident layout expert, patiently finding answers to the many technical questions that come with producing a book of this complexity. Actually, except for one thing, Lee Anne would be perfect. She doesn't have a PC; she only has a Macintosh. Still, maybe it's all for the best. If she did get a PC, she would be perfect, and it is not easy to work with a perfect person. (Just ask any of my editors.)

The indexes for the book (there are more than one) were created by Cheryl Lenser. Cheryl is a very talented, highly experienced indexer, who has indexed several of my books. She is always my first choice, and I was lucky to get her for this project.

Next, Alan Jones, one of the smartest people I know, prepared the production budget, and helped solve a variety of important problems.

Finally, the snazzy photo of me and Little Weedly (my cat) on the back cover was taken by Dan Sullivan, a professional photographer based in Santa Barbara, California.

REVIEWERS

As I wrote the book, I had help from a number of extremely smart people who read and critiqued every chapter as I finished it. I had two types of reviewers: professors who teach Unix courses and technical experts who use Unix or Linux in their work. Because there are 26 chapters, each of these people had to go through the process 26 times, which is a lot of work, so they all deserve a special mention. First, here are the professors:

Ron Thomson:	Central Michigan University
Don Southwell:	Delta College, Michigan
Damarra Mulholland:	Delta College, Michigan (retired)
Eugene Eberbach:	Rensselaer Polytechnic Institute, Connecticut
James Heliotis:	Rochester Institute of Technology, Rochester NY
Ivan Bajic:	San Diego State University, California
Sanjiv Bhatia:	University of Missouri, St. Louis

The experts are:

Andrew Eberbach:	IBM Software Engineer, Research Triangle Park
Susan Pierce:	Santa Barbara Linux Users Group (SBLUG)
Michael Schuster:	Solaris Kernel Engineer, Sun Microsystems
Tammy Cravit:	Taylored Software
Stephanie Lockwood-Childs:	VCT Labs; President, SBLUG

---

*In case you are wondering, the green design on the left side of the front cover was taken from one of my paintings. To see more, take a look at **www.harley.com/art**.

TABLE OF CONTENTS COMMENTATORS

This book was three years in the making. However, before I even started writing, I created a proposed Table of Contents for the book. The next group of people contributed by looking at my original plans for the book and sharing generously with their comments and suggestions:

Dave Spence:	BBC, England
Ronald Czik:	Boston University, Massachusetts
Mark Hutchenreuther:	Cal Poly, San Luis Obispo, California
John Connely:	Cal Poly, San Luis Obispo, California
Seung Bae Im:	California State University, Chico
Tulin Mangir:	California State University, Long Beach
Jay Harris:	Clemson University, South Carolina
Riccardo Pucella:	Cornell University, Ithaca, New York
Nathaniel Nystrom:	Cornell University, Ithaca, New York
Pamela Williams:	Fayetteville State University, North Carolina
Mike Smith:	Harvard University, Cambridge, Massachusetts
Ancelin Shah:	Houston Community College, Texas
Don Lopez:	Idaho State University, College of Technology
Weldon Hill:	Idaho State University, College of Technology
Ashvin Mahajan:	Iowa State University
Brian Davison:	Lehigh University, Pennsylvania
Peter McDervitt:	New Brunswick Community College, Canada
Gordon Goodman:	Rochester Institute of Technology, Rochester NY
Ivan Bajic:	San Diego State University, California
Thuy Le:	San Jose State University, California
Marty Froomin:	San Jose State University, California
Ka-Cheong Leung:	Texas Tech University, Lubbock, Texas
Adrienne Decker:	University at Buffalo, State University of NY
Charlie Shub:	University of Colorado, Colorado Springs
Frank Ducrest:	University of Louisiana, Lafayette
Robert Morris:	University of Massachusetts Boston
Iren Valova:	University of Massachusetts, Dartmouth
Fred Hosch:	University of New Orleans, Louisiana

EXPERTS WHO ANSWERED QUESTIONS

As I was working on the book, there were times when I needed to contact various experts to ask questions. Most everyone was kind enough to write me back and, in some cases, provide valuable historical information that you will not find elsewhere. In particular, I am happy to thank:

Richard Stallman, one of the seminal figures in the world of open source software. Stallman is the founder of the Free Software Foundation (see Chapter 2) and a highly accomplished programmer.

Matthias Ettrich, founder of the KDE desktop environment project (see Chapter 5.)

John Mashey, who worked at Bell Labs in the early days of Unix. Mashey is the creator of the Mashey/PWB shell (see Chapter 11).

Doug McIlroy, who also worked at Bell Labs on the early versions of Unix. It was McIlroy who first suggested the idea of pipes (see Chapter 15).

Mark Nudelman, the creator of the **less** pager (see Chapter 21).

Charles Haley, who worked with Bill Joy at U.C. Berkeley in the mid-1970s (see Chapter 22). Haley and Joy created the **ex** text editor. Haley also contributed to the original version of the **vi** text editor.

This is also a good place to mention the members of the Santa Barbara Linux Users Group, who patiently answered many questions: Stephanie Lockwood-Childs and Susan Peirce (both mentioned above), Ron Lockwood-Childs, Chad Page, Tom King, Nick Lockwood, Ron Jeffries and Marc Provett. Thanks also to Skona Brittain, who read and commented on an early version of the first five chapters of the book.

PEOPLE WHO PROVIDED SERVICES

As you read through this book, you will see well over a thousand examples. Each of these examples had to be tested on several different Unix and Linux systems using all four major shells. (Shells are explained in Chapter 11.) For access to such systems, I am grateful to the following people.

First, Patrick Linstruth, co-founder of QNET, a high-quality, personalized Southern California Internet Service Provider. Pat arranged for me to have access to a FreeBSD system, as well as important Web and FTP services. Thanks also to Pat's brother and QNET co-founder Chris Linstruth, and to the staff of the Austin Cafe: Lana, Melanie and Austin.

Next, Helmut vom Sondern, a Service and Support Engineer for Sun Microsystems in Germany. Helmut very generously provided me with access to a state-of-the-art Solaris system, which I used for as a test system virtually every day for well over two years.

For other Sun-related resources, I thank the following Sun Microsystems employees. In the Netherlands: Antoon Huiskens, Support Engineer. In California: Angel Camacho, Senior Technical Product Manager, and Neha Sampat, Group Manager in Product Marketing.

At Apple, I am grateful to Ernie Prabhaker (Unix Product Manager) and Farman Syed (Software QA Engineer) for arranging for me to evaluate a Macintosh laptop computer running OS X (which runs on Unix).

As I mentioned earlier, the front cover image was created by my art director, Lee Anne Dollison. The back cover and spine were created by Jenny Hobein, a cover designer who proved herself to be both talented and patient (two traits that are crucial for anyone working with me).

Finally, Jake Warde of Warde Publishers, a pleasant, skillful, freelance developmental editor, assisted the original publisher, Alan Apt, during the first part of this project.

HOW THIS BOOK WAS DEVELOPED

Since this is such a long, complex book and since I supervised the production myself, it occurred to me that you might be interested in how such a book was created.

To start, I created a preliminary Table of Contents, planning the chapters and some of the topics. As you might expect, in the course of the writing, many of the details changed. Still, one needs to start somewhere. Using the Web, I showed the preliminary Table of Contents to 28 Unix and Linux teachers from around the country. I asked them all to fill in a form with their comments and suggestions. This helped me enhance my overall plan. I then began to write the book, one chapter at a time.

For each chapter, I started doing my research and compiling notes. I then talked to Susan Pierce (a very experienced Unix/Linux expert) about my plans. Susan and I brainstormed various ideas. What should be in the chapter? What should be omitted? I then started to write the chapter, testing ideas and examples constantly. Indeed, almost every example you see in this book — and there are over 1,000 of them — was tested on Linux, Solaris and FreeBSD using a variety of shells. (Shells are explained in Chapter 11.)

After the first draft of the chapter was finished, I posted it on a secret Web site, and notified my reviewers. Each chapter was read by 12 different Unix professors and experts (see the Acknowledgments on page xxx). Each reviewer used a special Web page to answer questions about the chapter, send me their comments, make suggestions, and point out mistakes. Since there are 33 chapters and appendixes, the reviewers and I went through this time-consuming process 33 times. After each round, I would revise the chapter .

I then sent the revised chapter to Lydia Hearn for copy editing, while I moved on to the next chapter. At the same time, my art director, Lee Anne Dollison, created the illustrations and tables for the chapter. After the editing was complete, Lydia (who is multi-talented) created the actual book pages. In this way, the entire book — chapters, appendixes, glossary, and indexes — was built carefully and slowly, one step at a time.

You might ask, why did I decide to produce the book myself?

Producing the book myself enabled Lydia, Lee Anne, and me to have complete control over the final product. It was a *lot* of work but I hope, by the time you finish reading the book, you will agree that the extra effort was worth it.

CHAPTER 1

INTRODUCTION TO UNIX

This book is about using Unix: a family of operating systems that are used throughout the world and that run on virtually all types of computers. This book is also about Linux, a type of Unix.

We'll talk about the details in Chapter 2. For now, all you have to know is that an operating system is a master control program that runs a computer.

There are many types of Unix: some are Linux; some aren't. As a general rule, all types of Unix are similar enough so that, for practical purposes, if you know how to use one type of Unix, you know how to use them all.

The first Unix system was developed in 1969 by a programmer at AT&T's Bell Labs so that he could run a program called Space Travel*. Today, Unix is nothing less than a worldwide culture, comprising many tools, ideas and customs.

Modern Unix in its entirety is very large and complicated. Indeed, there is no single person who knows everything about Unix in general or even everything about one specific type of Unix. In fact, there is no single person who knows even most of Unix.

I realize this might seem strange. After all, if Unix is that complex, how did it come to exist at all? Who creates and enhances Unix? And who changes it and fixes problems when things go wrong?

I'll answer these questions in Chapter 2, when we talk a bit about the history of Unix and about how Unix is maintained today.

For now, what I want you to appreciate is that Unix is much more than an operating system: it is nothing less than a culture. So as you read this book and think about what you are learning, realize that you are doing more than simply learning how to use yet another computer tool. You are becoming a member of the global Unix community, the largest collection of smart people in the history of the world.

If you have never used Unix before, you are in for some pleasant surprises. Unix is not easy to learn, but it is well-designed, extremely powerful, and – once you get used to it – a great deal of fun.

---

*Space Travel simulated the movements of the Sun and planets, as well as a spaceship that you could land in various locations. The programmer in question was Ken Thompson who, with various other people at Bell Labs, went on to develop the first full-fledged Unix operating system (presumably, after they got tired of Space Travel).

As with all computer systems, there will be times when you are puzzled by a problem whose solution is not obvious. There will also be times when you will be frustrated or discouraged. However, no matter what happens, I can promise you one thing: you will never be bored.

WHY USE UNIX?

The Unix culture, which you are about to enter, contains an enormous number of tools for you to learn about and use. You can create and manipulate information – text files, documents, images, music, video, databases, spreadsheets, and so on – in more ways than you can imagine; you can access the Internet to use the Web, email, file transfer, and discussion groups; you can play games; you can design your own Web pages and even run your own Web server; and you can write computer programs using a variety of different languages and programming tools.

Of course, you can do all these things using other operating systems, such as Windows, so why learn Unix?

There are lots of reasons but, at this point, they will seem rather technical, so let me give the four most important reasons to learn Unix.

The first is choice. With Unix, *you* will decide how you want to use your computer and how deep you want to get into the details. You are not stuck with using your computer the way anyone else (such as Microsoft or IBM or your mother) thinks you should use it. You can customize your system as you see fit, and you can choose from many well-designed tools and applications.

Second, using Unix will change how you think, and for the better. I believe that if you learn how to read Shakespeare, listen to Mozart, or appreciate the paintings of Van Gogh, you will, in some sense, be a better person. The same is true for learning how to use Unix.

At this point, I don't blame you if you don't believe me, but when you have finished the book, come back to this chapter, reread this section, and see if I am not right.

Third, as a member of the global Unix community, you will learn how to use some of the best tools ever invented by human beings.

In addition, you will be working with a computer system that can run for months without rebooting. You won't have to worry about your computer crashing, freezing or stopping unexpectedly, and – unless you are administering a large network – you won't need to care about such irritations as computer viruses, spyware, programs that run amok, or mysterious rituals that must be carried out to keep your computer running smoothly.

Finally, if you are a programmer (or if you want to learn how to be a programmer), you will find a wonderful selection of Unix-based tools to develop, test and run programs: text editors with language-specific plugins, script interpreters, compilers, cross-compilers, debuggers, emulators, parser generators, GUI builders, software configuration managers, bug-tracking software, build managers, and documentation tools. Moreover, for most types of programming, there are active communities with their own Web sites, mailing lists and discussion groups, as well as comprehensive software archives.

Of course, I can't teach you all the details of the Unix culture in one book. If I tried, both of us would be overwhelmed. Rather, I will teach you the basics. By the time you finish this book, you will understand the most important concepts, and you will be able to use the most important tools. You will also be able to teach yourself whatever else you want to know as the need arises. To start, all you need is access to any computer that runs some type of Unix (such as Linux), an Internet connection, and a lot of time and patience.

And, oh yes, one more thing: in most cases, everything – including software upgrades – is free.

THE UNIX LANGUAGE

Around the world, the first language of Unix is American English. Nevertheless, Unix systems and documentation have been translated into many other languages, so it is not necessary to know English, as long as your system works in your language. However, as you explore the worldwide Unix-based community, you will find that much of the information and many of the discussion groups are in English.

In addition, the Unix community has introduced many new words of its own. In this book, I will pay particular attention to such words. Every time I introduce a new word, I will use CAPITAL LETTERS. I will make sure to explain the word and show you how it is used. For easy reference, all the definitions are collected into a glossary at the end of the book. When I come to a name with a particularly colorful history, I will give a special explanation like this.

WHAT'S IN A NAME?

Unix

In the 1960s, a number of researchers from Bell Labs (a part of AT&T) worked at MIT on a project called Multics, an early time-sharing operating system. Multics was a collaborative effort involving programmers from MIT, GE and Bell Labs. The name Multics was an acronym for "Multiplexed Information and Computing Service". ("Multiplex" refers to combining multiple electronic signals into a single signal.)

By the late 1960s, the management at Bell Labs decided not to pursue Multics and moved their researchers back into the lab. In 1969, one of these researchers, Ken Thompson, developed a simple, small operating system for a PDP-7 minicomputer. In searching for a name, Thompson compared his new system to Multics.

The goal of Multics was to offer many features to multiple users at the same time. Multics was large and unwieldy and had many problems.

Thompson's system was smaller, less ambitious and (at least at the beginning) was used by one person at a time. Moreover, each part of the system was designed to do only one thing and to do it well. Thompson decided to name his system Unics (the "Uni" meaning "one", as in unicycle), which was soon changed to Unix.

In other words, the name Unix is a pun on the name Multics.

Throughout the book, I print certain names in boldface, usually the names of commands. This allows you to see immediately that a word is a special Unix term. Here is an example:

"To copy a file, you use the Unix **cp** command. To remove (delete) a file, you use the **rm** command."

HINTS FOR LEARNING UNIX

As you read this book, you will notice many hints for learning Unix. These are ideas and shortcuts I have found to be important for newcomers and experienced users alike. To emphasize these hints, I present them in a special format that looks like this:

HINT
Unix is fun.

PEOPLE WHO DON'T KNOW THEY ARE USING UNIX

What type of person uses Unix?

Taken literally, there is no definitive answer to this question. Unix systems are used by a vast number of people around the world, so it would be very difficult to generalize. However, that never stopped me, so let's have a go at it.

Broadly speaking, we can divide the world of Unix users into two parts: those who know they are using Unix and those who don't.

Most of the people who use Unix don't know they are doing so. This is because Unix is used with many different types of computer systems, and those systems work so well that the people using them aren't even aware they are using Unix.

For example, most Web servers run some type of Unix. When you visit Web sites, more often than not you are using Unix, at least indirectly. Unix is also used by many businesses, schools, and organizations. When you have occasion to use their computer systems, say, to make a reservation, look up information, control a machine, register for a class, or do office work, you are also using Unix without even knowing it.

In addition, Unix is used to run all kinds of machines: not only computers of all sizes (from the largest mainframes to the smallest handheld devices), but embedded or real-time systems, such as appliances, cable modems, cell phones, robots, karaoke machines, cash registers, and so on.

Finally, most of the machines that support the Internet run Unix. For example, the computers that pass data from one point to another (routers) all use some type of Unix, as do most mail servers (which store email) and Web servers (which send out Web pages). Once you understand Unix, a lot of the idiosyncrasies that you find while using the Net will make sense. For example, you will understand why you must pay attention to case – that is, small letters and capital letters – when you type Web addresses. (Most Web servers run under some type of Unix and, as you will see, Unix is case sensitive.)

To me, the most interesting group of people who use Unix without knowing it are the Macintosh users. Millions of people using a Mac with OS X have no idea that, underneath, OS X is actually based on a type of Unix called FreeBSD. (We'll talk more about OS X in Chapter 2.) This is one reason Macs are so reliable, especially when compared to PCs running Windows (which is definitely *not* based on Unix).

PEOPLE WHO DO KNOW THEY ARE USING UNIX

What about the people who do know that they are running Unix? In other words, what type of person voluntarily chooses to learn Unix?

In my experience, such people (like you and I) have four basic characteristics.

First, Unix people are smarter than average, in most cases, a lot smarter than average.

Second, Unix people are both lazy and industrious. They don't like to do busy work for no reason, but when they have a problem that interests them, they will work hour after hour looking for a solution.

Third, Unix people like to read. In a world in which most people have trouble mustering up an attention span longer than five minutes, Unix people will actually *read* the manual when they have a problem.

Finally, when Unix people use a computer, they want to be in control of the experience; they don't want to feel as if the computer is controlling them.

Are you wondering about yourself? If so, don't worry. The fact that you are reading this book and have gotten this far qualifies you as a Unix person.

GETTING THE MOST FROM THIS BOOK

I have designed this book to make it easy for you to find what you need quickly. Before you start, take a moment to examine the various parts of the book. (I know when I say that, most of you won't want to do it, but please do it anyway.)

First, look at the Quick Index of Unix Commands on the inside back cover. This is a list of the most important commands covered in the book and where to look for the discussion and examples.

Next, take a look at the glossary. This will give you an overview of the important concepts I will be teaching you in this book. Notice there is a lot to learn.

Third, take a glance at the Quick Index for the **vi** Text Editor. Once you learn how to use the program (Chapter 22), you will find this index especially helpful.

Now take a look at the general index. Spend a few minutes skimming it (always a good idea with a new book). This will give you a rough feeling for the new ideas you will encounter as well as the concepts I will be emphasizing.

Aside from the glossary and the indexes, there are two summaries of Unix commands, also at the back of the book. These summaries contain one-line descriptions of each command I cover in the book.

One summary lists the commands in alphabetical order; the other summary groups the commands by category. These summaries are a good place to check if you want to do something and are not sure what command to use. Once you have found your command, check with the Quick Index of Unix Commands (inside back cover) to see what page to read.

If you want to find the discussion of a particular topic, you can, of course, use the general index. Alternatively, you can look up the appropriate term in the glossary. Along with each definition, you will find a reference to the chapter in which that term is explained. Once you know the chapter you want, a quick look at the table of contents will show you what section to read.

WHAT I ASSUME IN THIS BOOK

In this book, I make two important assumptions as to what type of Unix system you are using.

First, as you will see in Chapter 2, there are many versions of Unix. Today, the most popular Unix systems are of a type called Linux. Most Unix systems contain the same basic elements so, for the most part, it doesn't matter what type of Unix you are using. However, at times, there will be a choice between Linux or non-Linux functionality. In such cases, I will lean toward the Linux conventions as these are the most popular.

Second, as you will see in Chapter 4, the program that reads and interprets the commands you type is called the "shell". In Chapter 11, I will explain that there are various shells you might choose to use. Almost all the time, it doesn't really matter what shell you use. However, in those few places where it does matter, I will use a particular shell named "Bash". If you want to use another shell, that is fine. A few details may be different, but you won't have any real problems.

WHAT I DO NOT ASSUME IN THIS BOOK

If you are an experienced computer user who wants to learn about Unix, this book will get you started and provide you with a firm background in all the important areas.

However, I do not assume that you have any prior experience. It's okay if you have never really used a computer. You do not need to know anything about Unix. You do not need to be a programmer, nor do you need to know anything about electronics or mathematics.

I will explain everything you need to know. Work at your own speed and enjoy yourself.

HOW TO USE THIS BOOK

Before we start, it is important to realize that the world of Unix is bursting with information. To get started, read the first seven chapters of the book. They will introduce you to Unix and teach you the basic skills.

After you are oriented to Unix, and you know how to start and stop a work session, enter commands, and use the keyboard, you can read the rest of the book in any order you want.

HINT

It is impossible to learn everything about Unix. Concentrate on what you need and what you think you will enjoy.

Although every effort has been made to make each chapter as independent as possible, you should realize that each topic is dependent on other topics. There is no perfect place to start learning Unix and no perfect order in which to study the various topics.

For example, say that you want to customize your work environment. Naturally, it would make sense to start by reading about the Unix working environment (Chapter 6). You then need to understand what we call the "shell" (Chapter 11), as well as the details of using the shell (Chapters 12, 13 and 14). At this point, you can customize your work environment by modifying certain files.

However, in order to modify files, it is handy to already know how to use a text editing program (Chapter 22). Since you need to save these files, you should already understand the file system (Chapter 23), the commands to display your files (Chapter 21), and the commands to manipulate your files (Chapters 24 and 25). And, of course, before you can type in messages, you need to understand how to start a work session (Chapters 4 and 5) and how to use the keyboard with Unix (Chapter 7).

Obviously, this sort of approach leads nowhere fast, but it does underscore the most important principle that you need to understand at the outset: Unix was not designed to be learned; Unix was designed to be used. In other words, it can be confusing and time-consuming to learn Unix. However, once you have mastered the skills you need for whatever work you want to do, working with Unix is fast and easy.

If you think back to when you learned how to drive a car, you will remember that it was anything but simple. Once you had some experience, though, your actions became smooth and automatic. By now, you can probably drive all day with one hand on the wheel as you listen to the radio and talk to other people.

Let us embody this idea as the following hint:

> **HINT**
>
> Unix is easy to use, but difficult to learn.

Remember, once you have read the first few chapters of this book, you can teach yourself any topic in any order. If you come across an idea or skill you do not yet understand, you can either pause for a quick look at another chapter, or skip the part that confuses you and learn it later. This is how people learn Unix in real life: a bit at a time, depending on what they need at the moment.

Don't worry about memorizing every detail. In some chapters, I treat topics in depth. Learn what seems interesting and useful to you and just skim the rest. If you know the basics and you have an idea as to what is available, you can always return to the details when you need them.

> **HINT**
>
> Start by learning the basics. Then learn whatever you want, in whatever order you want.

CHAPTER 1 EXERCISES

REVIEW QUESTIONS

1. When was the first Unix system developed? Where was the work done?

2. What are four important reasons to learn Unix?

3. What is the origin of the name "Unix"?

FOR FURTHER THOUGHT

1. Prior to 2001, the operating system used by Apple for Macintosh desktop computers was completely proprietary. In 2001, Apple introduced a new operating system (OS X) based on Unix. What are three advantages to changing to a Unix-based operating system? What are three disadvantages?

WHAT IS LINUX? WHAT IS UNIX?

What is Unix and what is Linux? The short answer is Unix is a type of computer system, and Linux is the name of a particular family of Unix systems.

That answer should be good enough if your grandmother happens to ask "What is all this Unix stuff you are learning?" For practical purposes, however, you need to know more.

In this chapter, I'm going to explain the most important ideas that underlie Unix in general and Linux in particular, and I'm going to do it for two reasons. First, I think you will find the discussion interesting. To me, Unix is the most wonderful computer system ever invented, and I'd like you to share that feeling.

Second, once you have a basic understanding of Unix, you'll have a context for what I will be teaching in this book. In that way, when we get into the heavy-duty technical stuff, you'll find it a lot easier to remember the details.

By the end of the chapter, I will have given you a good, serviceable definition of both Unix and Linux. However, before I can do that, I'm going to have to explain a number of important concepts. To lay the groundwork, I'm going to start with a discussion of the fundamental component of any computer system: the operating system.

WHAT IS AN OPERATING SYSTEM?

Computers perform tasks automatically by following instructions. A list of instructions is called a PROGRAM. As the computer follows the instructions, we say that it RUNS or EXECUTES the program. In general, programs are referred to as SOFTWARE, while the physical components of the computer are referred to as HARDWARE. The hardware includes the system board, disk drives, keyboard, mouse, display, screen, printers, and so on.

An OPERATING SYSTEM (which is software) is the complex master control program that runs the computer. The principal function of an operating system is to make efficient use of the hardware. To do so, the operating system acts as the primary interface to the hardware, both for you as you are working, and for your programs as they are executing.

Whenever your computer is up and running, the operating system is there, waiting to serve you and to manage the resources of your computer.

For example, say you type a command to display the names of your files. It is the operating system that handles the details of finding the names and displaying them on your screen. When you are running a program that needs to open a new file, it is the operating system that sets aside the storage space and handles all the details.

More precisely, the most important functions of an operating system are to:

- Take control of the computer and initialize itself each time the machine starts or restarts. This initialization is part of the BOOTING process.

- Support the interface (text or graphical) that you use to interact with the computer.

- Provide an interface for programs as they need to use the computer's resources (disk space, file allocation, processing time, memory, and so on).

- Manage the computer's memory.

- Maintain and manage a file system.

- Schedule work to be done.

- Provide accounting and security services.

In addition, all operating systems are packaged with a large variety of programs for you to use. For example, there are programs to help you create, modify and manage files; to manage your work environment; to communicate with other people; to use the Internet; to write programs; and on and on. Unix comes with more than a thousand such programs, each of which is a tool to perform one specific job.

As a family, Unix operating systems all share two important characteristics: multitasking and multiuser. MULTITASKING means that a Unix system can run more than one program at a time. MULTIUSER means that Unix can support more than one user at a time. (Microsoft Windows, by the way, is a multitasking, single-user operating system.)

WHAT'S IN A NAME?

Booting
The term "booting" is short for bootstrapping, which refers to the old saying "pulling yourself up by the bootstraps". For example, "After Bartholomew lost all his money, he was poor for a long time. However, by working hard, he was able to pull himself up by the bootstraps and become a successful groatcakes merchant."

Obviously, it is physically impossible to pull yourself up by straps that are attached to your own boots. The idea is that a difficult, complex goal can often be accomplished by starting with one small action and then, using that as a foundation, building one step at a time until the desired goal is reached.

A computer system starts in just this way. When you turn on the power (or restart the computer) a single, small program is run automatically. That program starts another, more elaborate program, and so on. Eventually, the operating system (a very complex program) takes control and finishes the initialization.

WHAT IS THE KERNEL?

When a computer is started, it goes through a sequence of actions that comprise the booting process. The final act in this process is to start a very complex program called the KERNEL.

The job of the kernel is to take control of the computer and to act as the core of the operating system. As such, the kernel is always running. Indeed, it does not stop until you shut down the system. In this way, the kernel is constantly available to provide essential services as they are needed.

The kernel, being the heart of the operating system, is *very* important, so I want to take a moment to tell you a few details. I'm going to get a bit technical, so if you are at all confused, just nod your head wisely and pretend you understand.

Although the nature of a kernel can vary from one operating system to another, the essential services it provides are pretty much the same from one system to another. They are:

- Memory management (virtual memory management, including paging)

- Process management (process creation, termination, scheduling)

- Interprocess communication (local, network)

- Input/output (via DEVICE DRIVERS, programs that perform the actual communications with physical devices)

- File management

- Security and access control

- Network access (such as TCP/IP)

If these technical terms mean something to you, fine. If not, don't worry about it. Only the most nerd-like programmers actually care about the internal details of a kernel. For people like you and me, the crucial thing is to appreciate that the kernel is the most important part of the operating system. In fact, as we will see later, the main difference between Linux and other types of Unix is that Linux uses a particular kernel that is different from other Unix kernels.

There are a variety of different types of kernels, but basically they can be divided into large ones called MONOLITHIC KERNELS and small ones called MICROKERNELS.

A monolithic kernel consists of one very large program that does everything by itself. A microkernel is a much smaller program that can carry out only the most basic tasks. To perform the rest of its functions, a microkernel calls upon a set of other programs called SERVERS.

The advantage of a monolithic kernel is that it is fast: everything is done within a single program, which is efficient. The disadvantage is that monolithic kernels are large and unwieldy, which makes them difficult to design and maintain.

A microkernel is slower, because it must call upon servers to do most of its work, which is less efficient. However, because of the modular design, microkernels are a lot easier for programmers to understand, and they can be modified to work on new systems relatively quickly. Microkernels also have the advantage in that they are easier to customize than are monolithic kernels.

For example, say you are creating an operating system for a mobile phone or a robot. Storage space is at a premium, so a small kernel is better than a large one. Moreover, with a special purpose device, you may not need all the functionality of a monolithic kernel. In this case, a microkernel with a carefully selected set of servers may be the best bet.

When a new operating system is being created, the designers have a choice. They can use either a single large monolithic kernel or a small minimal microkernel with servers. Most Unix systems use some type of monolithic kernel. However, as we will see, some Unixes, such as the Macintosh Unix (called OS X), use a microkernel.

WHAT'S IN A NAME?

Kernel

Imagine a pistachio nut. The outside is a hard shell. The inside is a soft, edible seed which, in biology, is called the kernel. Thus, if we want to be precise, we can say that, when we eat pistachio nuts, we crack open the shell in order to eat the kernel.

If we think of Unix as a nut, the inside would be the kernel, and the outside would be the shell; and indeed, that is the case.

The kernel, which we just discussed, is what we call the core of the operating system. The SHELL (which we will discuss in Chapter 11) is the name we give to a special type of program (a command processor) that "surrounds" the kernel and acts as our personal interface into the system.

UNIX = KERNEL + UTILITIES

I have explained that the kernel is the central part of the operating system. The kernel is always running, and its job is to perform the essential tasks.

But what about everything else?

With Unix, "everything else" consists of a large number of auxiliary programs that are included as part of the Unix package. These programs fall into a number of different categories.

The most important programs are the ones that provide an interface for you to use the computer. They are the shells and GUIs. A shell is a program that provides a text-based interface: you type commands, one after another; the shell reads your commands and does what is necessary to carry them out. A GUI (graphical user interface) is a more elaborate program, which provides a graphical interface with windows, a mouse pointer, icons, and so on. We will talk about shells and GUIs in Chapters 5 and 6, and shells in detail in Chapter 11 so, for now, all I will do is mention that they exist.

The other programs are called the Unix UTILITIES, of which there are hundreds. Each utility (that is, each program) is a separate tool. All Unix systems come with hundreds of such tools as part of the operating system. Some of these are for programmers, but many of them are useful to anyone, even casual users. Moreover, as we will discuss in Chapter 15, Unix provides ways to combine existing tools to solve new problems as they arise. This wealth of tools, which is part of every Unix system, is the main reason why Unix is so powerful.

Unix utilities work pretty much the same on every Unix system. This means that, for practical purposes, if you know how to use one type of Unix, you know how to use them all. Indeed, most of this book is devoted to teaching you how to use the most important Unix utilities. My goal is that, by the time you have finished this book, you will be familiar with the most important tools, which means you will feel comfortable using Unix on a day-by-day basis.

So, what is Unix?

A good answer would be that Unix is a type of operating system that uses a Unix kernel and comes with the Unix utilities and a Unix shell. In fact, most (but not all) Unixes come with a selection of shells and at least one GUI.

In informal speech, we often use the term "utilities" to include the shell, so at this point, we can define Unix as follows:

Unix = a Unix kernel + the Unix utilities

"UNIX" USED TO BE A SPECIFIC NAME

In Chapter 1, I described how the first primitive Unix system was developed in 1969 by a single programmer, Ken Thompson. The work was done at Bell Labs, the research arm of AT&T. Since then, a large number of people have developed Unix into a modern family of operating systems. But who owns the actual name "Unix"?

For years, it was owned by AT&T, which insisted that Unix must always be spelled with capital letters: UNIX. More precisely, the AT&T lawyers specified that "The trademark UNIX must always appear in a form that is typographically distinct."

In addition, the lawyers decreed that you could not talk about UNIX in its own right. You had to talk about UNIX operating systems. ("The trademark UNIX may not be used as a noun, but must always be used as an adjective modifying a common noun as in 'UNIX operating system.'")

For many years, Bell Labs remained one of the centers of Unix development, and the silliness continued. In 1990, AT&T formed a new organization to take over Unix. The new organization was called Unix Systems Laboratory (USL). In June 1993, AT&T sold USL to Novell Corporation. In October 1993, Novell transferred the rights to the name "UNIX" to an international standards organization called X/Open. Finally, in 1996, X/Open merged with the Open Software Foundation (a consortium of computer companies) to form The Open Group. Thus, the UNIX trademark is now owned by The Open Group.

So what does The Open Group say that UNIX means? They say that "UNIX" is a brand that refers to any operating system that has been certified by them as complying with their so-called "Single UNIX Specification".

The details are horrible, so let's move on.

"UNIX" IS NOW A GENERIC NAME

The Open Group (and AT&T and USL and Novell and X/Open) notwithstanding, the word "Unix" has, for years, been used informally to refer to any operating system that is Unix-like. In this sense, there are many, many different types of Unix, with more being developed every year.

However, all of this begs the question, what does it mean to be Unix-like?

There are two answers, neither of which is exact. The first answer is that an operating system is Unix if (1) it consists of a Unix kernel and the Unix utilities and, (2) it can run Unix programs that run on other Unix systems.

The second answer is that an operating system is Unix if people who understand Unix say that it is Unix.

I realize that to a purist – such as Socrates or an Orthodox Rabbi – such an informal definition is not satisfying. However, in the real world (the place we live when we are not in school), it is not always possible to be completely precise.

Consider, for example, the very interesting United States Supreme Court case of *Jacobellis v. Ohio, 378 U.S. 184 (1964)*. This case involved an appeal by the manager of a movie theater who was convicted of showing an obscene film. In the official written judgment, Mr. Justice Potter Stewart discusses the question of obscenity. What, in fact, is it?

He writes, "I shall not today attempt further to define the kinds of [hard-core pornography] material I understand to be embraced within that shorthand description; and perhaps I could never succeed in intelligibly doing so. But I know it when I see it, and the motion picture involved in this case is not that."

So, I know I am in good company if I tell you the truth: If you want to get really technical, I can't tell you what Unix is – perhaps no one can – but I know it when I see it. (And, one day, you will too.)

THE FREE SOFTWARE FOUNDATION

Now that you know what Unix is, I'd like to answer the next question: What is Linux? To do so, I need to start by talking about the Free Software Foundation and the idea of open source software.

Imagine you enjoy this book so much that you would like all your friends to have a copy. How could you do so? You could buy a whole set of books and give them out to your friends (which isn't a bad idea, especially if you are trying to impress everyone you know). Of course, that would cost a lot of money. However, each person would receive an actual printed book, and at least you would feel you were getting something for your money.

Alternatively, you could make copies of the book. For example, you could photocopy, say, 30 copies of the book and give away the copies. This would save you some money but, compared to the original, the copies would be far from perfect. Moreover, it would take a lot of time and effort to photocopy, collate, bind and distribute the copies, and when your friends received them, they would know they were getting an inferior product. Even worse, if a friend wanted to make copies of his own, the quality would be worse because a photocopy of a photocopy is not nearly as good as the original.

Now, suppose you were reading an electronic version of this book, and you wanted to share the book with your friends. All you would have to do is copy some files and email them to your friends or burn them onto a CD and give it away. Not only would it be cheap to do so (maybe even free), but the copies would be identical to the original. Furthermore, your friends could easily make copies of the copies.

To be sure, it would be illegal to make such copies, but forget legal for a moment. Morally, is it right or wrong to copy and distribute electronic data (books, software, music, videos, and so on)?

There is no easy answer here. It all depends on your point of view, and there are good arguments on each side. One thing I can tell you: because electronic copying is so cheap and reliable, we tend to devalue anything that is in electronic format. For example, think of what you paid for this book. Would you feel comfortable paying the same amount of money for a CD that contained the book? Or for access to a Web site where you could read the book online?

Because it is so easy to copy (or steal) electronic data, people tend to feel that electronic data isn't worth much. For this reason, software companies have traditionally been wary about releasing programs without strict license agreements that prohibit copying and modification.

However, what if you could convince a lot of talented programmers to distribute their software in such a way that it *encouraged* copying? Would it change the world for the better? In the early 1980s, a visionary named Richard Stallman asked himself that question.

Stallman had been working in the MIT Artificial Intelligence (AI) Lab since 1971. The AI Lab had a long history of sharing software with anyone, not only inside the lab, but in other organizations. In 1981, however, conditions changed, and many of the AI Lab people left to join a startup company. The main computer was changed and the operating system was replaced with a proprietary system. Stallman now found himself working in an environment in which he and his coworkers had lost the right to look inside the operating system and modify it.

It happened that Stallman was more than an expert programmer. He was also a thoughtful social critic, who saw the change to a proprietary operating system as a restriction on his social rights as a creator. In his words, a "proprietary-software social system, in which you are not allowed to share or change software", was not only "antisocial", it was "unethical" and "wrong". Such systems, he observed, create unhealthy power struggles between programmers and software companies.

The solution was to create a large body of well-written, useful software that, from the beginning, was designed to be freely distributed.

In January 1984, Stallman quit his job to devote himself to the project. Within a short time, he had attracted a small number of other programmers and, in 1985, they started an organization called the FREE SOFTWARE FOUNDATION or FSF. Stallman's guiding principle was "Computer users should be free to modify programs to fit their needs, and free to share software, because helping other people is the basis of society." Stallman believed that programmers, by their nature, like to share their work and, when they do, everyone benefits.

It is important to understand that when Stallman talked about "free software", he was not referring to cost; he was referring to freedom. Free software can be examined, modified, shared and distributed by anyone. However, according to Stallman, there is nothing wrong if someone charges for their services or makes other people pay for software distribution. The way Stallman explained it is to think in terms of "free speech, not free beer".

Since the word "free" can refer to both freedom and cost, there is some ambiguity. So, to avoid any possible confusion, free software is now called OPEN SOURCE SOFTWARE.

(The name comes from a programming term. When a programmer creates a program, the actual instructions he writes are called the SOURCE CODE or, more simply, the SOURCE or the CODE.

(For example, let's say that you are talking to the Queen of England, and she is complaining that the program she uses to rip music from CDs keeps crashing. "If I only had the code", she says, "I could get Charles to fix the bug." "Don't worry," you answer. "I know where to get the source. I'll email Chuck the URL.")

Since the heart of any computer is the operating system, Stallman's first major goal for the FSF was to create an operating system that could be shared freely and modified by anyone. In order for the new operating system to be freely distributable, Stallman realized that it would have to be written from scratch.

Stallman wanted the FSF's products to fit smoothly into the prevailing programming culture, so he decided that the new operating system should be compatible with Unix in the sense that it should look just like Unix and should be able to run Unix programs. In the tradition of the programming community in which he worked, Stallman chose a whimsical name for the as-yet unbuilt operating system. He called it GNU.

WHAT'S IN A NAME?

GNU

GNU is the name Richard Stallman chose to describe the Free Software Foundation's project to develop a full Unix-like operating system. The name itself is an acronym meaning "GNU's Not Unix" and is pronounced "ga-new". (It rhymes with the sound that you make when you sneeze.)

Notice that, within the expression "GNU's Not Unix", the word GNU can be expanded indefinitely:

```
        GNU
       (GNU's Not Unix)
      ((GNU's Not Unix) Not Unix)
     (((GNU's Not Unix) Not Unix) Not Unix)
    ((((GNU's Not Unix) Not Unix) Not Unix) Not Unix)
```

and so on. Thus, GNU is actually a recursive acronym. (RECURSIVE refers to something that is defined in terms of itself.)

EXCERPTS FROM THE GNU MANIFESTO

As I mentioned in the last section, Richard Stallman, the founder of the Free Software Foundation, was more than a programmer. He was an educated social critic, and his vision of the future was to have an enormous impact on the world.

Shortly after founding the FSF, Stallman wrote a short essay in which he explained his reasons for promoting the idea of free software. He called the essay the GNU MANIFESTO.

His basic idea – that all software should be shared freely – is, at best, naïve. However, with the rise of the Internet, the development and distribution of open source software (what Stallman called "free software") has become an important economic and social force in our world. There are literally tens of thousands of programs available for free, and their contribution to the world at large (and to the happiness of their programmers) is beyond measure.

We will discuss this idea more in the next section. Before we do, I'd like to take a moment to show you a few passages from the original 1985 essay.

As a philosopher, Stallman was not a heavyweight. His public declaration was not as sophisticated as other well-known manifestos, such as *95 Theses* (Martin Luther, 1517), *Manifesto of the Communist Party* (Karl Marx and Frederick Engels, 1848), or *The Playboy Philosophy* (Hugh Hefner, 1962-1966). Still, the work of the Free Software Foundation was very important and, to this day, it continues to make an important contribution to our culture. For this reason, you may be interested in reading a few excerpts from Stallman's 1985 essay.

(Quick aside: When Stallman was working at MIT, he created the Emacs text editor. If you have access to a GNU version of Emacs, which is the case if you use Linux, you

---

EXCERPTS FROM THE GNU MANIFESTO

"I consider that the golden rule requires that if I like a program I must share it with other people who like it. Software sellers want to divide the users and conquer them, making each user agree not to share with others. I refuse to break solidarity with other users in this way. I cannot in good conscience sign a nondisclosure agreement or a software license agreement. For years I worked within the [MIT] Artificial Intelligence Lab to resist such tendencies and other inhospitalities, but eventually they had gone too far: I could not remain in an institution where such things are done for me against my will.

"So that I can continue to use computers without dishonor, I have decided to put together a sufficient body of free software so that I will be able to get along without any software that is not free. I have resigned from the AI lab to deny MIT any legal excuse to prevent me from giving GNU away...

"Many programmers are unhappy about the commercialization of system software. It may enable them to make more money, but it requires them to feel in conflict with other programmers in general rather than feel as comrades. The fundamental act of friendship among programmers is the sharing of programs; marketing arrangements now typically used essentially forbid programmers to treat others as friends. The purchaser of software must choose between friendship and obeying the law. Naturally, many decide that friendship is more important. But those who believe in law often do not feel at ease with either choice. They become cynical and think that programming is just a way of making money...

"Copying all or parts of a program is as natural to a programmer as breathing, and as productive. It ought to be as free...

"In the long run, making programs free is a step toward the post-scarcity world, where nobody will have to work very hard just to make a living. People will be free to devote themselves to activities that are fun, such as programming, after spending the necessary ten hours a week on required tasks such as legislation, family counseling, robot repair and asteroid prospecting. There will be no need to be able to make a living from programming..."

---

can display the entire GNU Manifesto by starting Emacs and entering the command <Ctrl-H> <Ctrl-P>.)

THE GPL AND OPEN SOURCE SOFTWARE

Over the years, Stallman and the many other programmers who supported the Free Software Foundation worked hard to create a huge body of open source software. In fact, as I mentioned, Stallman was the original author of the Emacs text editor.

Today, the FSF is not the only organization to promote open source software; indeed, there are many. However, the FSF has always been one of the leaders, not only with Emacs, but with a C compiler (**gcc**), a C++ compiler (**g++**), a powerful debugger (**gdb**), a Unix shell (Bash), and many, many other tools. All of this software – which is part of the GNU project – is used around the world and is considered to be of the highest quality.

In the late 1980s, Stallman had some experiences that showed him if he was going to create a large body of free software, he was going to need an appropriate license under which he could distribute that software. For this purpose, he invented the idea of the COPYLEFT. (The name came from a friend of Stallman's who, in the mid-1980s, sent Stallman a letter in which several witty sayings were written on the envelope. Among these was "Copyleft — all rights reversed.")

Within the software community, traditional copyrights were used to restrict the use of the software. The purpose of the copyleft was to do the opposite. In Stallman's words, "The central idea of copyleft is that we give everyone permission to run the program, copy the program, modify the program, and distribute modified versions – but not permission to add restrictions of their own."

To implement the idea of copyleft, Stallman wrote the GENERAL PUBLIC LICENSE or GPL, which he released in 1989. The GPL itself is rather complicated, so I won't go into the details. Basically, when applied to software, the GPL says that anyone may distribute the software, view the source code, modify it, and distribute the changes. Furthermore – and this is the crucial part – no one who redistributes the software, including modified versions, can take away any of the freedoms or add any restrictions of his own.

The GPL ensures that, whenever anyone uses free software to create a new product, the new product cannot be distributed except under the GPL. In practical terms, this means that if someone starts with free software, changes it, and redistributes it, he must also release the source code.

The GPL became popular and, over the years, a variety of similar licenses have been developed. Indeed, the combination of copyleft licenses and the Internet (allowing programmers around the world to share and to work together) has led to an enormous flourishing of shared creativity, the so-called OPEN SOURCE MOVEMENT.

The open source movement is so important that it would be difficult to overstate its impact within the world of programming and on the world at large. By way of illustration, if all open source software were to vanish, the Internet as we know it would disappear in an instant. (For example, most of the Web servers in the world are run by an open source program called Apache.)

In the world of Unix, the effects of the open source movement have been momentous. There are many reasons for this, not least of which is that if it hadn't have been for the FSF and the GPL, and the changes they made in the programming culture, you and I probably would never have heard of Linux.

UNIX IN THE 1970S: FROM BELL LABS TO BERKELEY

At the beginning of Chapter 1, I explained that the first version of Unix was developed at AT&T's Bell Labs, in New Jersey, in 1969. In the early 1970s, Unix was rewritten and enhanced by a handful of people, all from Bell Labs.

In 1973, a Unix development support group was formed. Later that year, Ken Thompson (one of the two principal Unix developers) delivered the very first paper on Unix at a conference of computer professionals. This sparked an interest in Unix, and within six months, the number of sites running Unix increased from 16 to 48.

In July 1974, Thompson and Dennis Ritchie (the other principal Unix developer) published a paper, "The UNIX Time-Sharing System", in *Communications of the ACM**, the most widely read computer science journal in the world. It was the first time that Unix was described to the world at large, and the world at large began to respond. Academics at universities and researchers inside companies requested copies of Unix and began running it on their own computers. In some cases, they PORTED Unix (that is, they adapted it) to run on new types of hardware.

Outside Bell Labs, the most important nexus of Unix development was the Computer Science Department at the University of California at Berkeley. In 1974, a professor at Berkeley, Bob Fabry, procured a copy of AT&T's UNIX version 4, and Berkeley students started making major enhancements. In 1975, Ken Thompson went to Berkeley for a one-year sabbatical, which acted as a catalyst for Berkeley's Unix development.

In the same year, AT&T formally started licensing UNIX to universities. (As you will remember, AT&T insisted that "UNIX" must always be spelled in capital letters, and I will do just that when I am referring specifically to AT&T UNIX.)

Around this time, Bill Joy, a Berkeley graduate student, became very interested in Unix. Although no one knew it at the time, Joy's work was to have far-reaching effects.

What Joy was doing set the stage for Berkeley to become a major player in the Unix world, creating and distributing their own version of Unix. Indeed, several of today's important Unixes are direct descendents of Berkeley Unix and the work of Bill Joy.

In addition, Joy was a skillful and prolific programmer who, over the course of a few years, single-handedly created a great deal of important software. Even today, there

---

*One month later, in August 1974, the same journal published my first technical paper. At the time, I was an undergraduate student at the University of Waterloo, in Canada, and I had won the ACM's George E. Forsythe Student Paper Competition. The name of the paper was "A New Technique for Compression and Storage of Data".

(In case you are wondering, the ACM is the principal professional association for computer scientists. The name, which dates back to 1947, stands for Association for Computing Machinery.)

Here is something interesting. If you check out the back copies of the *CACM* (as the journal is usually called), you will find that the July 1974 issue with the original UNIX paper is often missing, no doubt the result of overenthusiastic souvenir hunters. The August 1974 issue (the one with my paper), however, is always available.

exists no Unix system in the world that is not significantly influenced by the work Joy did in Berkeley from 1975 to 1982. In 1982, Joy became one of the cofounders of Sun Microsystems which, in its time, was one of the most important Unix companies in the world.

Perhaps I can illustrate the importance of Joy's work in this way. It has been more than 20 years since Joy worked at Berkeley, and yet, there are several chapters of this book in which we discuss programs that Joy developed at that time: the **vi** editor (Chapter 22) which was written in 1976, and the C-Shell (Chapters 11-14) which was written in 1978.

(While I am musing, let me mention the startling fact that the two most popular Unix text editors, still in wide use today, were both written a very long time ago: **vi** by Bill Joy in 1976, and Emacs by Richard Stallman in 1975.)

In 1977, Bill Joy shipped the first version of Berkeley's Unix. This was the same year in which I started using Unix. (At the time, I was a computer science graduate student at U.C. San Diego.)

The system that Bill Joy shipped was referred to as the Berkeley Software Distribution, later abbreviated as BSD. In all, Joy ended up shipping about 30 copies to users outside of Berkeley. Although this seems like a small number, it was considered a success, and in mid-1978, Joy shipped the next version, 2BSD.

In 1979, AT&T finally acknowledged the potential of UNIX and announced that they were going to start selling it as a commercial product. The first commercial version was called UNIX System III ("System Three"). In time, it was replaced by UNIX System V ("System Five").

By 1979, all BSD users were required to buy a license from AT&T and, every year, AT&T increased the price of that license. More and more, the BSD programmers were chafing under the yoke of the AT&T restrictions.

UNIX IN THE 1980S: BSD AND SYSTEM V

The first version of Linux was developed in 1991, and we'll get to it in a moment. However, to understand how Linux fits into the overall picture, we need to look at what happened to Unix in the 1980s. In particular, I want to explain how it came to pass that, by the end of the 1980s, there were two principal branches of Unix: BSD and System V.

By 1980, there was a dichotomy between East Coast Unix (AT&T UNIX) and West Coast Unix (BSD), and it was growing quickly.

The Berkeley programmers and BSD users resented having to pay money to AT&T just to install BSD. AT&T, on the other hand, was determined to make UNIX a successful commercial product, one that was oriented towards the needs of companies who were willing to pay a lot of money for a license.

In 1980, Bob Fabry, the Berkeley professor I mentioned earlier, received a large contract from DARPA (the U.S. Defense Advanced Research Projects Agency) to develop Unix. DARPA had set up a nationwide computer network connecting all their major research centers. As such, they wanted an operating system that could run on different types of hardware. The purpose of the Berkeley grant was to develop Unix for this purpose.

(Quick aside: DARPA was the same agency that from 1965 through 1988 funded the research that led to the creation of the Internet. Before 1972, the name of the agency was ARPA. Thus, the ancestor of the Internet was called the Arpanet, a name you may have heard. The Arpanet as a separate entity was shut down in 1989.)

Once Fabry got the DARPA contract, he set up an organization called the Computer Systems Research Group or CSRG. Although Fabry couldn't have known it at the time, the CSRG was to last until 1994 and, during those years, was to have a major influence on BSD and on the growth of Unix throughout the world.

In 1980, however, all Fabry cared about was developing BSD, and that was the task to which the CSRG devoted itself. Over the years, they released a number of versions, all of which were highly regarded within the academic and research communities. The number of BSD users began to grow. By 1982, 4.1BSD supported TCP/IP, the system which was to become the basis of the Internet. In 1983, 4.2BSD was released and was considered very popular, being used in almost 1,000 installations around the world.

In the commercial world, AT&T was pushing in a different direction. AT&T's goal was to market UNIX as a commercial product. In 1982, they released UNIX System III, the first public release of UNIX outside of Bell Labs. In 1983, they released System V, the first version that came with official support. At the same time, AT&T combined three internal groups to create the UNIX System Development Lab.

By the end of the year, System V had an installed base of 45,000. In 1984, when System V Release 2 (SVR2) was introduced, there were 100,000 UNIX installations.

Thus, by 1985, there were two main Unix streams of consciousness. To be sure there were other forms of Unix, but all of them were derived from either BSD or System V.*

In the world of Unix, the late 1980s was characterized by two phenomena: the growth of Unix in general, and the proliferation of different types of Unix.

Figure 2-1 shows the most important commercial Unixes that were used during the 1980s and beyond. (A few of these operating systems are still being sold today.) Every one of these Unixes, without exception, was based on either BSD or System V or both.

Although all the important Unixes were derived from either BSD or System V, there came to be many different versions and, for several years, there was enormous infighting and contention.

During the last half of the 1980s, I was a writer and a consultant, and I remember the intrigue and the confusion. The world of Unix was characterized by the various companies making alliances, breaking alliances, forming consortiums, disbanding consortiums, and offering one technical proposal after another, all in an attempt to "standardize" Unix and dominate the market.

In the meantime, in the universities and research institutions, Unix users were growing restless. Many of them were using some variant of BSD, and they were not happy that

---

*Indeed, this situation was to last well into the 1990s, until the growing influence of Linux and the open source movement was to change the world of Unix permanently.

For example, in the first two editions of this book (1993 and 1996), I taught that Unix had basically two variations: BSD and System V.

NAME	COMPANY	BSD OR SYSTEM V?
AIX	IBM	BSD + System V
AOS	IBM	BSD
A/UX	Apple	BSD + System V
BSD/OS	Berkeley Software Design	BSD
Coherent	Mark Williams Company	System V
Dynix	Sequent	BSD
HP-UX	Hewlett-Packard	System V
Irix	Silicon Graphics	BSD + System V
MachTen	Tenon Intersystems	BSD
Nextstep	Next Software	BSD
OSF/1	Digital Equipment Corp	System V
SCO Unix	Santa Cruz Operation (SCO)	System V
Solaris	Sun Microsystems	BSD + System V
SunOS	Sun Microsystems	BSD
Ultrix	Digital Equipment Corp	BSD + System V
Unicos	Cray Research	System V
UNIX	AT&T	System V
Unixware	Novell	System V
Xenix	Microsoft/SCO/Altos/Tandy	System V

FIGURE 2-1: The most important types of commercial Unix

AT&T had partial control over what they were doing. The solution was to rewrite, from scratch, the parts of BSD that were based on AT&T UNIX.

It took a long time, but the Berkeley programmers worked diligently, replacing the UNIX parts of BSD one component at a time. Creating a completely independent version of BSD was a noble goal, but it was not to happen until 1992.

UNIX IN 1991: WAITING FOR...

By 1991, PCs had been around for 10 years. Still, there was no PC operating system that was attractive to hackers, the type of programmers who like to take things apart and modify them just for fun. DOS (for PCs) was simple and unsatisfying. The Apple Macintosh operating system was better, but the machine itself was too expensive for hobbyists.

Unix would have been fine. After all, some of the best hackers in the world had been working on it for years. However, BSD (as yet) didn't run on a PC, and commercial versions of Unix were prohibitively expensive.

Computer science professors had a similar problem. AT&T UNIX would be a good tool to use for teaching operating systems courses except that, in 1979, AT&T changed their policy. Starting with what they called UNIX Seventh Edition, no one outside AT&T was allowed to look at the UNIX source code.

AT&T's new policy meant that, unfortunately, UNIX could no longer be used for teaching, because operating systems students need to be able to look at the source code to see how the system works.

What computer science professors needed was a free, readily available operating system, one that was suitable for teaching and for which source code was readily available.

One such professor was Andrew Tanenbaum, who taught at the Vrije Universiteit in Amsterdam. He bought an IBM PC and set out to build his own operating system from scratch. The new operating system was a lot like Unix, but was much smaller, so Tanenbaum called it Minix ("minimal Unix").

Minix contained no AT&T source code whatsoever, which meant that Tanenbaum could distribute the new operating system as he wished. The first version of Minix, released in 1987, was designed to be compatible with UNIX Seventh Edition. It was used primarily for teaching and, as teaching tools go, it was a good one (but not perfect).

For several years, Minix was the best tool available for programmers who wanted to learn about operating systems and to experiment. People around the world began to use it, especially in universities. At the same time, a great number of enthusiastic volunteers began to modify Minix on their own.

Still, Minix did not meet people's expectations. A lot of programmers liked it and wanted to enhance the official version, but the copyright was held by Tanenbaum who vetoed most of the requests. Minix, he insisted, should remain a simple operating system, suitable for teaching.

Minix users were disgruntled. When Richard Stallman had founded the Free Software Foundation in 1985, he had inspired programmers around the world, and they yearned for a robust, free operating system on which they could vent their collective energy.

Now, Stallman had planned a free, Unix-compatible operating system as his first major project. He even had a name for it, GNU. By 1991, Stallman and the FSF had created a great deal of high-quality, free software, but GNU itself was nowhere near ready.

As we discussed earlier, there are two types of programs that make up Unix: the kernel and everything else, which we called the "utilities". By the end of the 1980s, the FSF had programmed a lot of the important utilities, including a shell. However, they did not have a finished kernel (the core of the operating system).

Stallman and the FSF programmers had been working for some time, but the GNU kernel, which he called HURD, was far from ready. In fact, work on HURD had really only started in 1990 and, for years, programmers around the world had been crying themselves to sleep every night, plaintively singing, "Someday, my HURD will come..."

So to put it all together: By 1991, PCs had been available for 10 years, and thousands of programmers, students and computer scientists shared a strong desire for an open-source, Unix-like operating system.

AT&T, however, had commercialized UNIX up the wazoo. BSD was available, but it was encumbered by the AT&T license. Minix was okay, but far from perfect. Although the source code was readily available, it still required a license and it couldn't be shared freely.

GNU, on the other hand, was distributed under the auspices of the GPL copyleft, which was great. However, the kernel – the most important part of the operating system – was a long way from being finished.

As fate would have it, a young student in Finland named Linus Torvalds had just started a project: just for fun, he decided to write his own operating system kernel.

Little did Torvalds know that, within a decade, his personal operating system would grow into the most important open source undertaking in history, an innovative project that, in the fullness of time, would engage hundreds of thousands of programmers and, literally, change the world.

WHAT'S IN A NAME?

Hurd

In our discussion of kernels, I explained that most operating systems use either a monolithic kernel (a single large program) or a microkernel combined with a number of smaller programs called servers. For GNU, Richard Stallman chose to use a microkernel called Mach, combined with a group of servers which he called "the Hurd". (The name was coined by Thomas Bushnell, the main kernel programmer.)

Strictly speaking, the GNU kernel should be described as the Hurd (servers) running on top of Mach. However, in common usage, the entire kernel is usually referred to as Hurd.

You already know that when Stallman chose a name for the Free Software Foundation's version of Unix, he decided to call it GNU: a recursive acronym for "GNU's not Unix". When it came to naming the kernel, Stallman one-upped himself.

The name Hurd stands for "HIRD of Unix-Replacing Daemons". (In Unix, a "daemon" is a program that runs by itself in the background.) The name HIRD stands for "HURD of Interfaces Representing Depth".

Thus, Hurd is an indirectly recursive acronym. (Hopefully, the only one you will ever meet in your life).

...MR. RIGHT, LINUS TORVALDS

Linus Torvalds is the quintessential right guy with the right idea in the right place at the right time.

In 1991, Linus (pronounced "Lee'-nus") was a second-year computer science student at the University of Helsinki. Like tens of thousands of other programming students who loved to tinker, Linus had read Andrew Tanenbaum's book *Operating Systems: Design and Implementation*, which explained the principles behind the design of Minix. As an appendix to the book, Tanenbaum had included the 12,000 lines of source code that comprised the operating system, and Linus spent hours studying the details. (At this point, you may want to take a moment to think about what it would take to read through 12,000 lines of code, and compare that to the type of information you find in the appendices of this book.)

Like many other programmers, Linus wanted a free (open source) version of Unix. Unlike the other programmers, Linus didn't want to wait.

LINUS TORVALDS ANNOUNCING HIS NEW PROJECT...

```
From: torvalds@klaava.Helsinki.FI (Linus Benedict Torvalds)
Newsgroups: comp.os.minix
Subject: What would you like to see most in minix?
Summary: small poll for my new operating system
Date: 25 Aug 91 20:57:08 GMT
Organization: University of Helsinki


Hello everybody out there using minix -
I'm doing a (free) operating system (just a hobby,
won't be big and professional like gnu) for
386(486) AT clones. This has been brewing since
april, and is starting to get ready. I'd like any
feedback on things people like/dislike in minix,
as my OS resembles it somewhat (same physical
layout of the file-system (due to practical
reasons) among other things).


I've currently ported bash(1.08) and gcc(1.40),
and things seem to work. This implies that I'll
get something practical within a few months, and
I'd like to know what features most people would
want. Any suggestions are welcome, but I won't
promise I'll implement them :-)


Linus (torvalds@kruuna.helsinki.fi)


PS. Yes - it's free of any minix code, and it has
a multi-threaded fs [file system]. It is NOT
protable (uses 386 task switching etc), and it
probably never will support anything other than
AT-harddisks, as that's all I have :-(.
```

On August 25, 1991, Linus sent a message to the Usenet discussion group that was used as a Minix forum (**comp.os.minix**). In retrospect, this short message is considered to be one of the historical documents in the world of Unix, so I will show it to you in its entirety. When you read it, remember that English was Linus's second language, and that he was writing informally.

Clearly, Linus was just trying to have fun by building his own operating system. He recognized that his main job would be to write a kernel because, for the most part, the utilities were already available from the Free Software Foundation in a form that he could adapt for his own use when the time came.

In September 1991, Linus released the first version of his kernel, which he called LINUX. Linux was distributed over the Internet, and within a short time, Linus began to release one new version after another. Programmers around the world began to join Linus: first by the tens, then by the hundreds, and, eventually, by the hundreds of thousands.

Interesting note: Linus chose to design Linux using a monolithic kernel. Minix, written by Andrew Tanenbaum, used a microkernel. Soon after Linux began to attract attention, Tanenbaum (a well-known professor) publicly excoriated Linus (a more-or-less unknown student) for that design decision. Even today, after the Linux kernel has become the basis for the most successful form of Unix in history, Tanenbaum still criticizes Linus for using a monolithic kernel. (Personally, I have read Tanenbaum's arguments, and I think he is wrong.)

Eventually, Linux became so popular as to run on every type of computer: not only PCs, but everything from handheld devices with their small built-in processors, to massively parallel supercomputing clusters, the fastest, most powerful systems in the world. Indeed, by 2005, virtually every niche in the world of computing would come to be occupied by machines running some type of Linux, and Linux would be the most popular operating system in the world. (Windows is more widespread, but Linux is more popular.)

Why was Linux so successful? There are four reasons, and they all have to do with Linus himself.

First, Linus Torvalds was an extremely skillful and knowledgeable programmer. He was a fast worker, and he loved to program. In other words, he was exactly the type of guy whose idea of fun would be writing his own operating system kernel.

Second, Linus was an endless perfectionist. He was dedicated to his work and, when a problem fell into his lap, Linus would not rest until he had come up with a solution. In the early days of Linux, it was not unusual for Linus to make modifications so quickly that he would sometimes release a new kernel more than once a day!

Third, Linus had a pleasing personality. People describe him as a low-key, unassuming fellow: a genuinely nice guy (see Figure 2-2). In person or online, Linus pretty much gets along with everyone because he is so easygoing. As he once observed in an interview, "Unlike Richard Stallman, I really don't have a message."

Fourth – and most important – Linus had a genius for using the Internet to tap into a wellspring of programming talent: the thousands and thousands of people who would volunteer their efforts to modify and extend the Linux kernel.

How large is Linux? Today, the Linux kernel in its entirely consists of well over 17,000 files and millions of lines of code. Every day, volunteer programmers submit hundreds of patches (changes or corrections). (It is interesting to compare this to the very first kernel, version 0.01, which consisted of 83 files. In all, there were a bit fewer than 9,000 lines of code.)

Having so many people on the job also gave Linus unusual opportunities because he had the brain power to handle any new problem that came along. When a new piece of hardware came out, for example, there was always somebody somewhere who was knowledgeable enough to write the code to make the new device work under Linux.

FIGURE 2-2: Linus Torvalds

In 1991, Linus founded a project to create a new operating system kernel, which we now call the Linux kernel. The Linux kernel is the basis for the various Linux operating systems, making Linus' undertaking one of the most important software projects in history. As you can see from the photo, Linus does not take himself too seriously.

Early on, Linus made a strategic decision to release the Linux kernel under the auspices of the GNU GPL. This decision proved to be crucial, as it encouraged programmers to volunteer their time. They knew that everything they worked on would be shared freely with the rest of the world. Moreover, the GPL ensured that any operating system that ultimately used the Linux kernel would itself fall under the auspices of the GPL and, hence, would be freely distributable.

From the start, Linus released new versions of the kernel as often as he could. Normally, programmers like to hold onto new software, so they can test it thoroughly and fix as many bugs as possible before the program is released to the public.

Where Linus' genius came in is in realizing that, since he was releasing software to a vast audience, he would have so many people testing and reading the new code, that no bug could hide for long. This idea is embodied in what is now called LINUS'S LAW: "Given enough eyeballs, all bugs are shallow."

Linus released new versions of the kernel far more often than anyone had ever done before, and bugs were identified and fixed quickly, often within hours. The result was that work on Linux progressed faster and better than any major software project in the history of the world.

WHAT'S IN A NAME?

Linux

The proper way to pronounce Linux is to rhyme with "Bin'-ex".

From the beginning, Linus Torvalds used the name Linux informally, "Linux" being a contraction of "Linus' Minix". However, he actually planned to use the name Freax ("free Unix") when he released the first public version of the kernel.

As it happened, another programmer, Ari Lemmke, had convinced Linus to upload the files to a server Lemmke ran, so they could be accessed easily via a system called "anonymous FTP". Lemmke was not happy with the name Freax, so when he set up a directory to hold the files, he called the directory `linux`, and the name stuck.

LINUX DISTRIBUTIONS

Strictly speaking, what Linus Torvalds and the Linux project created was a kernel, not a complete operating system (and this is still the case). When the kernel was first released, you needed to be a Unix expert in order to use it because you had to find all the necessary bits and pieces and put them together to form an operating system.

Within 5 months of Linus' first kernel release, however, other people were offering free operating systems that were based on the Linux kernel. Such an offering is called a Linux DISTRIBUTION (sometimes shortened to DISTRO).

As you can imagine, the first few distributions were welcomed by the Linux community but, unfortunately, they were not well-maintained. In July 1993, however, a programmer named Patrick Volkerding announced a new distribution he called SLACKWARE. The name comes from the word "slack", referring to the feeling of exhilaration and satisfaction that comes from achieving your personal goals. (For more information, look up the Church of the SubGenius.)

Slackware was a success because, over the years, Volkerding has always managed to maintain it. Today, it is the oldest Linux distribution still being actively developed. In fact, Slackware is so popular that it has spawned an entire family of distributions and supporting groups of its own.

Today's modern Linux distributions offer a complete product: the kernel, the utilities, programming tools, and at least one GUI. As I write this, there are literally hundreds of such distributions. (If you want, once you become proficient at Unix, you can make a Linux distribution of our own.)

Before we leave this section, I want to make sure you understand that the word "Linux" has two meanings: First, "Linux" refers to a kernel, the product of the countless programmers who work on the Linux project.

Second, "Linux" is the name of any operating system that is based upon the Linux kernel. This is the way most people use the word when they talk, and that is how we will use it in this book.

Most Linux distributions use the GNU UTILITIES from the Free Software Foundation. For this reason, the FSF insists that Linux-based operating systems should actually be called GNU/Linux. I don't know anyone who does this, but you might remember it in case you are hanging out at a Unix bar and you happen to run into Richard Stallman.

BSD DISTRIBUTIONS

As we discussed earlier, BSD was one of the two main streams of Unix during the 1980s. (The other was System V.) BSD was developed within the Computer Science Department at U.C. Berkeley and, since 1980, the development had been managed by the CSRG (Computer Science Research Group).

By the end of the 1980s, BSD aficionados had become disgruntled over AT&T's commercialization of Unix. Because BSD contained certain proprietary elements from AT&T UNIX, and because the CSRG released source code with the operating system, every BSD user was forced to buy an expensive source code license from AT&T.

For this reason, the CSRG set a goal for themselves: to completely rewrite all the AT&T-based parts of BSD. Doing so would free BSD from the clutches of the AT&T lawyers (and the AT&T marketing department) once and for all.

In 1989, the CSRG offered the first totally open source BSD distribution called Networking Release 1 (more formally, 4.3BSD NET/1). NET/1, however, consisted mostly of networking tools – which were independent of AT&T UNIX – and not the full BSD operating system.

To create a truly independent version of BSD would require rewriting hundreds of AT&T utilities and programming tools, but it had to be done. Using the Internet, the CSRG solicited help from outside programmers and, within a year and a half, all the AT&T utilities had been replaced with brand new programs.

A careful check of the code showed that everything in BSD was fine except for six kernel files. Rewriting these six files would have been a big job so, in 1991, the CSRG released a new version of BSD that was almost UNIX-free. They called it NET/2.

In 1992, a programmer named Bill Jolitz rewrote the last six problematic files and used them to create a version of BSD for PCs. He called this operating system 386/BSD and began to distribute it over the Internet.

This was a huge achievement. After all these years, the holy grail of Berkeley – an operating system that was independent of AT&T UNIX – existed. Finally, BSD could be distributed freely as open source software to anyone in the world.

This was important because BSD contained some of the best Unix software ever written. To this day, there are very few Unixes in the world that don't contain BSD code. Indeed, most Linux distributions use a large number of BSD utilities. For this reason, the creation of 386/BSD is one of the milestones in the history of Unix.

Within a short time, 386/BSD became popular and an ever-increasing number of people began to maintain it. Jolitz, however, had a full-time job, and he was not able to keep up with all the incoming patches and enhancements. For this reason, a group of volunteers was formed to take over the job. The first thing the group did was to rename the operating system FreeBSD.

Initially, FreeBSD ran only on PC hardware, which was fine with most of the users. Some, however, wanted to run BSD on other types of machines, so a new group was formed, with the goal of porting FreeBSD to as many other types of computers as possible. The version offered by the new group was called NetBSD.

In the mid-1990s, the NetBSD group spawned yet another group that wanted to focus on security and cryptography. Their operating system was called OpenBSD.

As you can see, the world of BSD, which has only three main distributions (FreeBSD, NetBSD and OpenBSD), is a lot different from the world of Linux, where there are literally hundreds of different distributions.

By now, you are probably wondering, if FreeBSD is completely open source and is distributed for free over the Internet, how is it that Linux was the version of Unix that grew so popular?

There are two reasons. First, Linux was distributed under the auspices of the GNU GPL, which encourages sharing. Since the GPL prohibits anyone from using Linux to create and distribute a proprietary system, anything done with Linux belongs to the world at large.

The BSD license is far less restrictive than the GPL. Under the BSD license, it is allowable to use parts of BSD to create a new product without having to share it. When this happens, the world at large does not get the benefit of being able to use and modify the new product. For this reason, many programmers prefer to work with Linux.

(On the other hand, because the BSD license is so flexible, FreeBSD has been used widely in a large variety of machines and devices, as well as a great many Web servers around the world.)

The second reason Linux was more successful than FreeBSD had to do with timing. In retrospect, it was clear that, by the end of the 1980s, programmers around the world had a strong need for a completely open source version of Unix. Since Linus Torvalds released the Linux kernel in 1991, and 386/BSD was not released until 1992, Linux got a head start. As a result, Linus was able to attract a large number of programmers, who were just waiting to work on the world's first free version of Unix.

Now you know why this book is called *Harley Hahn's Guide to Unix and Linux*, not *Harley Hahn's Guide to Unix and FreeBSD*.

(And now you also know why I described Linus Torvalds as the right guy with the right idea in the right place at the right time.)

WHAT TYPE OF UNIX SHOULD <u>YOU</u> USE?

With all the different types of Unix, the questions arises, what type of Unix should *you* use?

The answers (there are several) are actually rather simple. However, before I proceed, let me tell you that, for practical purposes, basic Unix is basic Unix: if you know how to use one type of Unix, you know how to use them all. In particular, as you read this book, it really doesn't matter what type of Unix you are using (as long as you don't read with your mouth full).

I first used Unix in 1977, and everything I learned then still works the same way. If you had used Unix in 1977 and you fell into a time warp, emerging in 2006 in front of a Linux or FreeBSD computer, how would you feel? You would have to learn how to use some new tools, including a new, sophisticated GUI (graphical user interface). However, you wouldn't feel like you had woken up in a brand new world. Unix is Unix.

That said, here is my advice.

In many cases, you don't have a choice as to what type of Unix you must use. For example, you may work for a company that uses a commercial Unix such as AIX (from IBM) or Solaris (from Sun); or you may be taking a class where everyone has to use the same type of Linux; or you might be hacking with your grandmother, who insists on using FreeBSD because it reminds her of all the fun she had in Berkeley in the '70s. If this is the case, just go with the flow and don't worry. Unix is Unix.

If you are choosing your own Unix, here is how to decide:

1. If you are using Unix because you want to learn how it works, how to customize your environment, how to program, or you just want to have fun, use Linux.

To help you with your choices, Figure 2-3 shows the most important Linux distributions. All of these are readily available on the Internet. Most of the distributions can be downloaded at no cost. If you are not sure which one to use, use Ubuntu.

2. FreeBSD is very stable and reliable, and tends to work just out of the box. So, if you are working at a company, and you are looking for a system that needs as little attention as possible, use FreeBSD. Similarly, if you are working at home and want to run a server (such as a Web server), use FreeBSD.

If your system is not supported by FreeBSD, use NetBSD. If you are very interested in security, use OpenBSD. For completeness, Figure 2-4 shows the most important BSD distributions.

3. If you want to run Unix under Microsoft Windows, you can use a free product called Cygwin. Once Cygwin is installed, all you have to do is open a Cygwin window and, within that window, everything looks like Linux.

I love Cygwin. Even though I have several Unix computers, I use Windows a lot and, with Cygwin, I can access my favorite Unix programs whenever I want.

NAME
Debian
Fedora Core
Gentoo
Knoppix
Mandriva (used to be Mandrake)
MEPIS
Red Hat
Slackware
SuSE
Ubuntu
Xandros

FIGURE 2-3: The most important Linux distributions

NAME
FreeBSD
OpenBSD
NetBSD

FIGURE 2-4: The most important BSD distributions

4. Finally, if you want Unix, but you want it to look like Windows, get a Macintosh and run OS X.

OS X is the Macintosh operating system. Although it has a Mac-like look and feel, it is actually Unix under the hood. Specifically, OS X uses a microkernel based on Mach, the FreeBSD utilities, and a proprietary GUI named Aqua.

To access Unix directly under OS X, just open a Terminal window. (You will find Terminal in your Applications/Utilities folder.)

WHAT'S IN A NAME?

OS X

OS X (the Macintosh operating system) is pronounced "O-S-ten". The name is a pun.

The previous Mac operating system — which was not based on Unix — was called OS 9. Thus, the "X" stands for the Roman numeral 10, but it also makes you think of Unix.

HOW DO YOU GET LINUX OR FREEBSD?

Most of the time, Unix is installed from one or more CDs. To install Linux or FreeBSD, all you need to do is find a free downloading site (which is easy), download the files, burn the CDs, and then use the CDs to install the operating system.

Better yet, if you ask around, you may find someone who already has the CDs. Since both Linux and FreeBSD are free software, there is no problem borrowing CDs or even making your own copies to share with other people.

When you install Linux or FreeBSD in this way, the operating system resides on your hard disk. If your Unix system is the only operating system on your computer, the situation is simple. Whenever you turn on the computer, Unix will boot automatically.

Alternatively, you can install more than one operating system on your computer. You might, for example, want both Windows and Unix, which allows you to switch back and forth as you wish. However, you can only run one operating system at a time and, to switch from one to the other, you need to reboot. Such a setup is called a DUAL BOOT system.

When you use a dual boot system, you make use of a special program called a BOOT LOADER. The boot loader takes control every time you start or restart your computer. Its job is to show you a list of available operating systems, so you can choose the one you want. The boot manager then transfers control to the appropriate kernel, and the kernel starts the rest of the operating system. (As a general rule, if your PC takes a minute to boot, about 15 seconds is used by the boot loader, and about 45 seconds is used to load the operating system.)

The most common Linux boot loaders are GRUB (Grand Unified Bootloader) and LILO (Linux Loader). LILO was developed a long time ago as part of the Linux distribution, and it has been well maintained over the years. GRUB is newer and was developed as a part of GNU. Both boot loaders are fine but if you have a choice, use GRUB because it is more powerful and more flexible.

To set up your machine as a dual boot system, you must divide your hard disk into parts called PARTITIONS. To do so, you use what is called a PARTITION MANAGER. Each operating system must be installed using its own partition (or partitions, if more than one is required).

The most common type of dual boot system is one in which Windows coexists with some type of Unix. However, there is no reason why you can't partition your disk to use more than two operating systems on the same computer. For example, you might have Windows, Fedora Core Linux and FreeBSD. The boot loader will then offer you three choices, rather than two. In such cases, we would say that you have a MULTI-BOOT system.

A second way to run Unix is not to install it onto your hard disk. Instead, you can boot from a special CD called a LIVE CD.

A live CD is a CD-ROM that has been made bootable, and that contains everything necessary to run a full operating system: the kernel, the utilities, and so on. When you boot from a live CD, you bypass the hard disk. This allows you to use a second (or third or fourth) operating system whenever you want, without having to install anything on your disk.

For example, if you are a Windows user, you can experiment with Linux or FreeBSD without having to repartition and install a whole new operating system. Similarly, if you are a Linux user, you can try out, say, FreeBSD, without having to make changes to your system. Some people who don't know what type of Linux they want to use permanently will use live CDs to try out different distributions.

Live CDs are also useful when you are using a PC that does not belong to you. For example, if you work for a company that forces you to use Windows, you can use a live Linux CD to run Unix when no one is watching. Or, if you are fixing a friend's computer, you can boot your own operating system with your favorite tools without changing your friend's computer in any way.

To create a live CD, just pick the one you want, download the files, and burn the CD. You might even make several live CDs to experiment with different systems.

There are many different live CDs available on the Internet for free. To help you, Figure 2-5 lists the most important ones. If you are not sure which one to use, use Knoppix (pronounced "Nop'-pix").

HINT

If your computer boots from the hard disk even when you have a CD in the drive, check the BIOS settings.

You may have to modify a setting to tell the computer to look for a bootable CD before looking for a bootable hard disk.

How do you choose between a full hard disk installation and a live CD?

A full installation is a commitment as it requires you to make lasting changes to your hard disk. (Of course, you can undo these changes if you want.) The advantage of a full installation is that the operating system is on your disk permanently. Not only is this convenient, but you can customize your system and store files permanently.

With a live CD, there is less of a commitment. However, unless you set aside a special disk partition for the live CD to use for its data, you can't make permanent modifications or save Unix data files.

Moreover, running Unix from a live CD will decrease the performance of your computer a bit. Not only is it slower to boot off a CD than a hard disk, a live CD system will have to create a RAM disk to hold the files that would normally be on your hard disk. This will use up some of your memory. (A RAM disk is a part of memory that is used to simulate a real disk.)

A nice compromise is to install Unix to some type of removable storage device, such as a USB key drive (sometimes called a USB flash drive). This is a very small, portable device that plugs into a USB port and acts like a tiny hard disk.

Once you have installed Unix to a key drive, all you have to do is insert it into a USB port, turn on (or restart) the computer, and Unix will boot automatically. (You may need to change your computer's BIOS settings to tell it to boot from the key drive before the hard disk.)

By installing to a key drive, you get most of the benefits of a permanent Unix system without having to modify your hard disk. For example, when you boot from a key drive, you can modify your system, you can save files, and so on. Unlike a CD-ROM, which is only readable, a key drive is read/writeable. And whenever you want to use the operating system on your hard disk, all you have to do is remove the key drive and reboot.

Still, once you decide to use an operating system permanently, you will find it faster and more practical to install it on your hard disk. Flexibility is nice but, in the long run, as with most areas of life, commitment works better.

NAME
Damn Small Linux
FreeBSD
Kanofix
Knoppix
MEPIS
PCLinuxOS
SLAX
SuSE
Ubuntu

FIGURE 2-5: The most important Linux live CDs

> **HINT**
>
> Downloading and installing any type of Unix will take longer than you anticipate, so don't do it when you are in a hurry.
>
> For example, if it is your honeymoon night, and you have a half hour to kill while your wife changes her clothes and freshens up, starting a brand new Linux installation would be a bad idea.

WHAT IS UNIX? WHAT IS LINUX?

Before we leave this chapter, I'd like to summarize our discussion by, once again, answering the questions: What is Unix? and What is Linux?

Unix is a multiuser, multitasking operating system that consists of a Unix-like kernel, Unix-like utilities and a Unix-like shell. Linux is the name given to any Unix that uses the Linux kernel. (As we discussed, there is no good definition of the term "Unix-like". You just have to know it when you see it.)

However, there is another way to look at Unix.

Over the years, a great many very, very smart people have worked on Unix to build themselves the very best tools they could. As Unix users, you and I get to reap the benefits of that work.

To me, Unix is an an abstract idea: an actual applied philosophy that dictates a particular approach to problem solving. In using Unix, you will learn to approach and solve problems the Unix way. For example, you will learn how to combine simple tools, like building blocks, into elegant structures to solve complex problems; you will learn how to be self-reliant, teaching yourself most of what you need to know; and you will learn how to organize your thoughts and actions in a logical way that makes the best use of your time and effort.

As you do so, you will be following in the footsteps of giants, and your mind will be changed for the better. This may be hard to understand right now, but don't worry. Just stick with Unix long enough, and you will see for yourself.

For this reason, let me give you another definition of Unix. This is the best definition of Unix I know, and it is the one I would like you to remember as you read this book.

I'll give it to you in the form of a hint:

> **HINT**
>
> Unix is a set of tools for smart people.

CHAPTER 2 EXERCISES

REVIEW QUESTIONS

1. What is an operating system?

2. What is the kernel? Name four tasks performed by the kernel.

3. What is open source software? Why is it important?

4. What is Linux? When was the first version of Linux released? By whom?

FOR FURTHER THOUGHT

1. Would the Internet have been possible without Unix? Would Linux have been possible without the Internet?

2. When Richard Stallman founded the Free Software Foundation in 1985, he was able to tap into the energy of many programmers around the world who wanted to work on a free operating system. Later, in the early 1990s, Linux Torvalds was also able to find programmers to help him, in this case, to develop the Linux kernel. Why are so many programmers willing to work a long time on a difficult project and then give away the fruits of their labor for free? Is this more common with young programmers than old programmers? If so, why?

3. Traditionally, lawyers are expected to offer a certain amount of work free as a public service, such work being described as *pro bono publico* (Latin: "for the public good"). Should the programming profession have a similar expectation of its members? If so, why? If not, why not?

C H A P T E R 3
THE UNIX CONNECTION

Being able to connect to different types of computers has always been an integral part of Unix. Indeed, the fact that Unix has this capability is one of the main reasons there are so many computer networks in the world. (The Internet, for example, has always depended on Unix connections.)

In this chapter, we'll discuss the basic concepts that make it possible to connect to other computers: on the Internet and on local networks. Along the way, you will learn how these concepts underlie the most fundamental Unix connection of all: the one between you and your computer.

HUMANS, MACHINES AND ALIENS

I'd like to start by talking about an idea that is rarely discussed explicitly. And yet, it is such an important idea that, if you don't understand it, a lot of Unix is going to seem mysterious and confusing. The idea concerns human beings and how we use machines.

Think about the most common machines in your life: telephones, cars, TVs, radios, and so on. Because you and the machine are separate entities, there must be a way for you to interact with it when you use it. We call this facility an INTERFACE.

Consider, for example, a mobile phone. The interface consists of a set of buttons, a speaker or ear plug, a small video screen, and a microphone. Consider a car: the interface consists of a key, the steering wheel, the accelerator pedal, the brake pedal, a variety of dials and displays, and a gaggle of levers, knobs and buttons.

The point is every machine that is used by a human being can be thought of as having two components: the interface and everything else.

For example, with a desktop computer, the interface consists of the monitor, the keyboard, the mouse, speakers and (possibly) a microphone. "Everything else" consists of the contents of the box: the hard disk, the CD drive, the processors, the memory, the video card, the network adapter, and so on.

In Unix terminology, we call the interface the TERMINAL (I'll explain why later), and we call everything else the HOST. Understanding these concepts is crucial, so I am going to talk about them in detail.

Since the terminal provides the interface, it has two main jobs: to accept input and to generate output. With a desktop computer, the input facility consists of the keyboard, mouse and microphone. The output facility consists of the monitor and the speakers.

To capture these ideas, we can describe any computer system by the following two simple equations:

COMPUTER = TERMINAL + HOST

TERMINAL = INPUT FACILITY + OUTPUT FACILITY

Has it ever occurred to you that, as a human being, you also consist of a terminal and a host? In other words, these same two equations describe you and me and everyone else.

Your "terminal" (that is, your interface to the rest of the world) provides your input facility and your output facility. Your input facility consists of your sense organs (eyes, ears, mouth, nose, and skin). Your output facility consists of the parts of your body that can make sounds (your mouth) and can create change in your environment (your hands and arms, your legs, and the muscles of facial expression).

What is your "host"? Everything else: your brain, your organs, your muscles and bones, your blood, your hormones, and so on.

It might seem artificial and a bit ludicrous to separate your "host" from your "terminal" because you are a single, self-contained unit. But think about a laptop computer. Even though all the components are built-in, we can still talk about the terminal (the screen, the keyboard, the touch pad, the speakers, and the microphone) and the host (everything else).

Imagine two aliens from another planet watching you use a laptop computer. One alien turns to the other and says, "Look, there is a human being who is using his interface to interact with the interface of a computer."

To the aliens, it doesn't matter that your interface is built-in because the laptop's interface is also built-in. The aliens, being from another planet, see what you and I don't normally see: as you use a computer, your interface communicates with the computer's interface. Indeed, this is the *only* way in which you can use a computer (or any other machine, for that matter).

However, what if the aliens happened to come from a Unix planet? After the first alien made his comment, the second alien would respond, "I see what you mean. Isn't it interesting how the human's terminal interacts with the computer's terminal?"

IN THE OLDEN DAYS, COMPUTERS WERE EXPENSIVE

In Chapter 1, I mentioned that the very first version of Unix was developed in 1969 by Ken Thompson, a researcher at Bell Labs, New Jersey. (At the time, Bell Labs was part of AT&T.) Thompson had been working on a large, complex project called Multics, which was centered at MIT. When Bell Labs decided to end their support of Multics, Thompson returned full-time to New Jersey, where he and several others were determined to create their own, small operating system. In particular, Thompson had a game called Space Travel that he had developed on Multics, and he wanted to be able to run the program on a system of his own.

At the time, there were no personal computers. Most computers were large, expensive, temperamental machines that required their own staff of programmers and administrators. (We now call such machines MAINFRAME COMPUTERS.)

Mainframe computers required their own special rooms, referred to whimsically as "glass houses". There were three reasons for glass houses. First, the machines were somewhat fragile, and they needed to be in an environment where the temperature and humidity could be controlled. Second, computers were *very* expensive, often costing millions of dollars. Such machines were far too valuable to allow just anyone to wander in and out of the computer room. A glass house could be kept locked and closed to everyone but the computer operators.

Finally, computers were not only complex; they were relatively rare. Putting such important machines in glass houses allowed companies (or universities) to show off their computers, especially to visitors. I have a memory as a young college student: standing in front of a huge computer room at the University of Waterloo, looking through the glass with awe, intimidated by the large number of mysterious boxes that comprised three separate IBM mainframe computers.

Multics ran on a similar computer, a GE-645. The GE-645, like most mainframes, was expensive to buy, expensive to lease, and expensive to run. In those days, computer users were given budgets based on real money, and every time someone ran a program, he was charged for processing time and disk storage. For example, each time Thompson ran Space Travel on the GE-645, it cost about $75 just for the processing time ($445 in 2008 money).

Once Bell Labs moved Thompson and the others back to New Jersey, the researchers knew there was no way they would be able to get their hands on another large computer. Instead, they began looking around for something smaller and more accessible.

In those days, most computers cost well over $100,000, and coming up with a machine for personal research was not easy. However, in 1969, Thompson was looking around Bell Labs and he found an unused PDP-7.

(The PDP-7, made by DEC, the Digital Equipment Corporation, was a so-called MINICOMPUTER. It was smaller, cheaper and much more accessible than a mainframe. In 1965 dollars, the PDP-7 cost about $72,000; the GE-45 mainframe cost about $10 million. The name PDP was an abbreviation for "Programmed Data Processor".)

This particular PDP-7 had been ordered for a project that had floundered, so Thompson was able to commandeer it. He wrote a lot of software and was able to get Space Travel running. However, the PDP-7 was woefully inadequate, and Thompson and several others lobbied to get another computer.

Eventually, they were able to acquire a newer PDP-11, which was delivered in the summer of 1970. The main advantage of the PDP-11 was that its base cost was only(!) $10,800 ($64,300 in 2008 money). Thompson and a few others began to work with the PDP-11 and, within months, they had ported Unix to the new computer. (You can see Thompson and Dennis Ritchie, his Unix partner, hard at work in Figure 3-1.)

Why am I telling you all of this? Because I want you to appreciate that, in the late 1960s and early 1970s, computers cost a lot and were difficult to use. (The PDP-11 was expensive and inadequate. The PDP-7 was very expensive and inadequate. And the GE-645 was very, very expensive and inadequate.) As a result, there was an enormous need to make computing, not only easier, but cheaper.

One of the biggest bottlenecks was that, using the current software, the PDP-11 could only run one program at a time. This meant, of course, that only one person could use the machine at a time.

The solution was to change Unix so that it would allow more than one program to run at a time. This was not easy, but by 1973 the goal had been achieved and Unix became a full-fledged multitasking system. (The old name for multitasking is MULTIPROGRAMMING.)

From there, it was but a step to enhance Unix to support more than one *user* at a time, turning it into a true multiuser system. (The old name is a TIME-SHARING SYSTEM.) Indeed, in 1974, when Thompson and Ritchie published the first paper that described Unix (see Chapter 2), they called it "The UNIX Time-Sharing System".

However, in order to make such a change, the Unix developers had to come to terms with a very important concept, the one you and I discussed earlier in the chapter: human beings could only use a machine if the machine had a suitable interface. Moreover, if

FIGURE 3-1: Ken Thompson, Dennis Ritchie, and the PDP-11

Ken Thompson (sitting) and Dennis Ritchie (standing) and the Bell Labs' PDP-11 minicomputer. Thompson and Ritchie are using two Teletype 33-ASR terminals to port Unix to the PDP-11.

more than one person were to use a computer at the same time, each person would need a separate interface.

This only makes sense. For example, if two people wanted to type commands at the same time, the computer would have to be connected to two different keyboards. However, in the early days of Unix, computer equipment was expensive and hard to come by. Where could Thompson and Ritchie come up with the equipment they needed to run a true multiuser system?

The answer to this question proved to be crucial, as it affected the basic design of Unix, not only for the very early Unix systems, but for every Unix system that ever existed (including System V, BSD, Linux, FreeBSD and OS X).

HOST AND TERMINALS

It was the early 1970s, and Ken Thompson and Dennis Ritchie had a problem. They wanted to turn Unix into a true multitasking, multiuser operating system. However, this meant that each user would need his own interface. Today, high quality color video monitors, keyboards and mice are cheap. In those days, however, *everything* was expensive. There was no such thing as a separate keyboard; there were no mice; and the cost of a separate computer monitor for each user was prohibitive.

As a solution, Thompson and Ritchie decided to use a machine that was inexpensive and available, even though it had been designed for a completely different purpose. This machine was the Teletype ASR33 (ASR stood for Automatic Send-Receive).

Teletype machines were originally developed to send and receive messages over telegraph lines. As such, the machines were called teletypewriters ("Teletype" was a brand name).

The original experimental teletypewriters were invented in the early 1900s. Throughout the first half of the twentieth century, teletypewriter technology became more and more sophisticated, to the point where Teletype machines were used around the world. AT&T (Bell Lab's parent company) was heavily involved in such services. In 1930, AT&T bought the Teletype company and, indeed, the name AT&T stands for American Telephone and Telegraph Company.

Thus, it came to pass that, in the early 1970s, Thompson and Ritchie were able to use Teletype machines as the interfaces to their new PDP-11 Unix system. You can see the actual machines in Figure 3-1 above, and a close-up view in Figures 3-2 and 3-3.

As an interface, all the Teletype had was a keyboard for input and a wide roll of paper for printed output. To store programs and data, there was a paper tape punch that could make holes in a long, narrow band of paper, and a paper tape reader that could read the holes and convert them back to data.

Compared to today's equipment, the Teletype was primitive. Except for the power supply, everything was mechanical, not electronic. There was no video screen, no mouse and no sound. Moreover, the keyboard was uncomfortable and difficult to use: you had to depress a key about half an inch to generate a character. (Imagine what typing was like.)

What made the Teletype so valuable was that it was economical and it was available.

Here's where it all comes together. Thompson and Ritchie wanted to create a true multiuser system. Computing equipment was expensive. All they had were some Teletypes for the interfaces, and a single PDP-11 minicomputer to do the processing.

Like the aliens I mentioned above, Thompson and Ritchie realized that they could, conceptually, separate the interface from the rest of the system, and this is the way they designed Unix.

There would be a single processing element, which they called the host, along with multiple interface units, which they called terminals. At first, the host was the PDP-11 and the terminals were Teletypes. However, that was merely for convenience. In principle, Unix could be made to work with any host and any type of terminal. (It would take work, but not too much work.)

This design decision proved to be prescient. From the beginning, the connection that Unix forged between a user and the computer was dependent upon a specific *design principle*, not upon specific hardware. This meant that, year after year, no matter what new equipment happened to come along, the basic way in which Unix was organized would never have to change.

As terminals became more sophisticated, an old one could be thrown away and a new one swapped in to take its place. As computers became more complex and more powerful, Unix could be ported to a new host and everything would work as expected.

FIGURE 3-2: Teletype 33-ASR

A Teletype 33-ASR, similar to the ones used by Ken Thompson and Dennis Ritchie with the very early Unix systems.

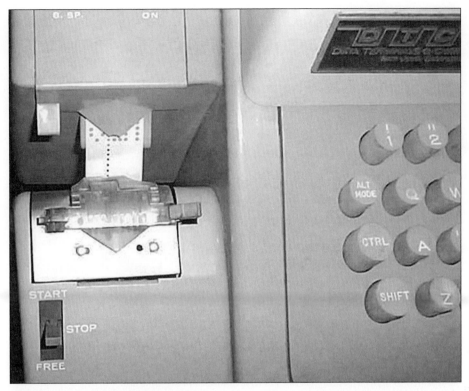

FIGURE 3-3: Close-up of a Teletype 33-ASR

A close-up view of a Teletype 33-ASR. Notice the tall, cylindrical keys. A key had to be depressed about half an inch to generate a character. To the left, you can see the paper tape punch/reader. The tape is 1-inch wide.

Compare this to Microsoft Windows. Because Windows was created specifically for single-user PCs, Microsoft never completely separated the terminal from the host. As a result, Windows is inelegant, inflexible, and is wedded permanently to the PC architecture. Unix is elegant, flexible, and can be made to work with *any* computer architecture. After all these years, the Unix terminal/host paradigm still works marvelously.

TERMINAL ROOMS AND TERMINAL SERVERS

As I explained, Unix was designed as a multiuser system. This meant that more than one person could use a computer at the same time, as long as (1) each person had his own terminal, and (2) that terminal was connected to a host.

So, imagine a room full of terminals. They are not computers. In fact, they are not much more than a keyboard, a monitor, and some basic circuitry. At the back of each terminal is a cable that snakes down into a hole in the floor and, from there, makes its way to an unseen host computer.

The room is occupied by a number of people. Some of them are sitting in front of a terminal, typing away or looking at their screens and thinking. These people are using the same host computer at the same time. Other people are patiently waiting for their turn. It happens to be a busy time, and there are not enough terminals for everyone.

The picture I just described is what it was like to use Unix in the late 1970s. At the time, computers – even minicomputers – were still expensive, and there weren't enough to go around. Terminals, however, were relatively inexpensive.

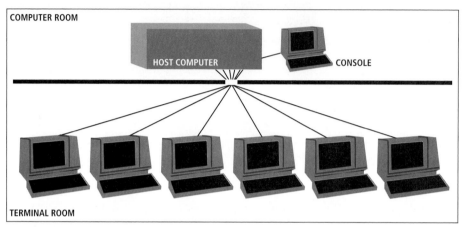

FIGURE 3-4: Terminals in a terminal room

In the late 1970s, when computers were still expensive and terminals weren't, it was common to see terminal rooms, in which multiple terminals were connected to the same host.

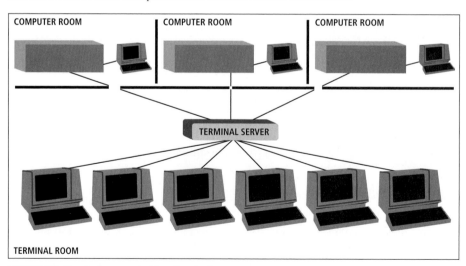

FIGURE 3-5: Terminals connected to a terminal server

In the late 1970s, some organizations could afford to have more than one computer available for their users. It was common to have all the terminals in the organization connect to a terminal server which would act as a switch, allowing a user to access any of the host computers from any terminal.

Since Unix was designed to support multiple users, it was common to see TERMINAL ROOMS filled with terminals, each of which was connected to a host. When you wanted to use the computer, you would go to the terminal room, and wait for a free terminal. Once you found one, you would log in by typing your user name and password. (We'll talk about this process in detail in Chapter 4.)

This setup is conceptualized in Figure 3-4.

Some organizations, such as university departments or companies, could afford more than one host computer. In this case, it only made sense to allow people to use any host from any terminal. To do so required a TERMINAL SERVER, a device that acted as a switch, connecting any terminal to any host.

To use a terminal server, you entered a command to tell it which computer you wanted to use. The terminal server would then connect you to that host. You would then enter your user name and password, and log in in the regular manner.

You can see such a system in Figure 3-5. In this drawing, I have shown only six terminals and three hosts. This is a bit unrealistic. In large organizations, it was common to have many tens of terminals, all over the building, connected to terminal servers that allowed access to a number of different hosts.

THE CONSOLE

Out of all the terminals that might be connected to a host, there is one terminal that is special. It is the terminal that is considered to be part of the computer itself, and it is used to administer the system. This special terminal is called the CONSOLE.

To give you an example, I'd like to return, for a moment, to the late 1970s. We are being given a tour of a university department, and we see a locked room. Inside the room there is a PDP-11 minicomputer with a terminal next to it. The terminal is connected directly to the computer. This is the console, a special terminal that is used only by the system administrator. (You can see the console in Figure 3-4 above.) Down the hall, there is a terminal room with other terminals. These terminals are for the users, who access the computer remotely.

Now, let's jump forward in time to the present day. You are using a laptop computer on which you have installed Linux. Although Linux can support multiple users at the same time, you are the only person who ever uses the computer.

Do you have a console?

Yes, you do. Because you are using Unix, you must have a terminal. In this case, your terminal is built-in: the keyboard, the touch pad, the screen, and the speakers. That is also your console.

Typically, the console is used by the system administrator to manage the system. In the first example, when the system administrator wanted to use the console of the PDP-11, he would need to go into the computer room and sit down in front of the actual console. With your laptop, you are the administrator, and there is only one (built-in) terminal. Thus, any time you use your Linux laptop, whether or not you are actually managing the system or just doing work, you are using the console.

Why do you need to know about consoles and regular terminals? There are three reasons. First, Unix systems have always distinguished between consoles and regular terminals and, when you are learning about Unix and come across a reference to the "console", I want you to know what it means.

Second, if you are a system administrator (which is the case when you have your own Unix system), there are certain things that can only be done at the console, not from a remote terminal.

(Here is an example. If your system has a problem that arises during the boot process, you can only fix the problem from the console. This is because, until the system boots, you can't access it via a remote terminal.)

Finally, from time to time, a Unix system may need to display a very serious error message. Such messages are displayed on the console to ensure that the system administrator will see them.

Having said so much about consoles and why they are important, I'd like to pose the question: Are there computers that don't have consoles?

You betcha. There are lots of them. However, before I explain how a system can work without a console, I need to take a moment to talk about Unix and networks.

THE UNIX CONNECTION

As we have discussed, Unix is designed so that the terminal (that is, the interface) is separate from the host (the processing unit). This means that more than one person can use the same Unix system at the same time, as long as each person has his or her own terminal.

Once you understand this idea, it makes sense to ask, how far apart can a terminal be from the host? The answer is as far as you want, as long as there is a connection between the terminal and the host.

When you run Unix on a laptop computer, the terminal and the host are connected directly. When you run Unix on a desktop computer, the terminal is connected to the host by cables. (Remember, the terminal consists of the keyboard, monitor, mouse, speakers, and microphone.)

What about a larger distance? Is it possible to connect a terminal to a host over a local area network (LAN)? Yes, it is.

For example, let's say you use a PC that is connected to a LAN on which there are many computers, three of which are Unix hosts. It is possible to use your PC as a terminal to access any one of the three Unix hosts. (Of course, before you can use any Unix host, you must have authorization to use that computer.)

When you use your computer to connect to a remote Unix host, you run a program that uses your hardware to EMULATE (act like) a terminal. This program then connects over the network to the remote host.

You can do this from any type of computer system: a Windows computer, a Macintosh, or another Unix computer. Typically, the terminal program runs in its own window, and you can have as many separate windows as you want.

For example, you might have three windows open at the same time, each running a terminal program. Each "terminal" can be connected to a different Unix host over the network. In this case, you would be working on four computers simultaneously: your own computer, and the three Unix hosts.

You can see this illustrated in Figure 3-6.

In Figure 3-6, the network connections between the PC and the three Unix hosts are via cables, as in a traditional network. However, any type of network connection will do. In particular, you can use a wireless connection.

Here is an example. Let's say you have three geeky friends, Manny, Moe and Jack. Each of you has a laptop computer that runs Unix. You use Debian Linux; Manny uses Fedora Core Linux; Moe uses Gentoo Linux; and Jack uses FreeBSD. (Jack always was a bit odd.)

You get together for a Unix party (that is, computers, caffeinated drinks, and junk food), and you decide that each person should have access to the other three computers. First, each of you creates user accounts on your own computer for the other three people. (I won't go into the details here, but it's not hard.)

Then, you all use either the **iwconfig** command or the **wiconfig** command to configure your computers in such a way as to allow them to connect, wirelessly, into a small network.

Once the network is established, you each open three terminal windows on your own computer. Within each window, you connect to one of the three other computers.

You now have four people in the same room, each running a different type of Unix on his laptop computer, each of which also has access to the other three computers. Could anything be cooler?

So, we have talked about a terminal directly connected to a host (a laptop computer), a terminal connected to a host by cables (a desktop computer), a terminal connected to

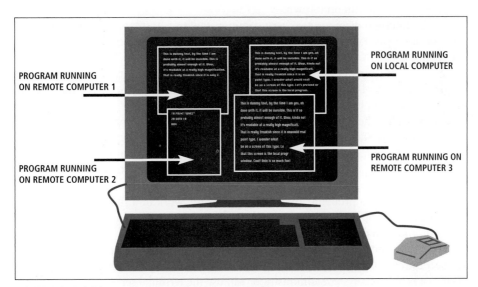

FIGURE 3-6: Unix/Linux computer on a local area network

A computer on a local area network, running four terminal programs, each in its own window. Three of the "terminals" are connected, via the network, to different remote hosts. The fourth "terminal" is running a program on the local computer.

a host over a regular LAN, and a terminal connected to a host over a wireless LAN. Can we go further?

Yes. By using the Internet to connect a terminal to a host, we can have a connection that can reach anywhere in the world. Indeed, I regularly use the Net to connect to remote Unix hosts from my PC. To do so, I open a terminal window and connect to the remote host. And, as long as I have a good connection, it feels as if I were working on a computer down the hall.

HOSTS WITHOUT CONSOLES

I mentioned earlier that there are many Unix host computers in the world that are not connected to terminals. This is because, if a computer can run on its own, without direct input from a human being, there is no need for a terminal. Such computers are referred to as HEADLESS SYSTEMS.

On the Internet, there are many Unix hosts that run just fine without terminals. For instance, there are millions of headless systems acting as Web servers and mail servers, silently doing their job without any human intervention. Many of these servers are running Unix, and most of them are not connected to a terminal.

(A WEB SERVER responds to requests for Web pages and sends out the appropriate data. A MAIL SERVER sends and receives email.)

If the need arises to directly control such a host computer – say, to configure the machine or to solve a problem – the system administrator will simply connect to the host over a network. When the system administrator is done, he simply disconnects from the host and leaves it to run on its own.

On the Internet, there are two very common types of hosts that run automatically without terminals. First, there are the servers, such as the Web servers and mail servers I mentioned above. We'll talk about them in a moment.

Second, there are the ROUTERS: special-purpose computers that relay data from one network to another. On the Internet, routers provide the connectivity that actually creates the network itself.

For example, when you send an email message, the data will pass through a series of routers on its way to the destination computer. This will happen automatically, without any human intervention whatsoever. There are millions of routers, all around the world, working automatically, 24 hours a day, and many of them are Unix hosts without a console.

What if there is a problem? In such cases, it is the work of a moment for a system administrator to open a terminal window on his PC, connect to the router, fix the problem, and then disconnect.

Some large companies with many Unix servers use a different approach. They will connect the console of every host computer to a special terminal server. That way, when there is a problem, a system administrator can use the terminal server to log in directly to the computer that has the problem. I have a friend who once worked at a company where 95 different Unix hosts were connected to a set of terminal servers that were used only for system administration.

THE CLIENT/SERVER RELATIONSHIP

In computer terminology, a program that offers a service of some type is called a SERVER; a program that uses a service is called a CLIENT.

These terms, of course, are taken from the business world. If you go to see a lawyer or an accountant, you are the client and they serve you.

The client/server relationship is a fundamental concept, used in both networks and operating systems. Not only are clients and servers used extensively on the Internet, they are an important part of Unix (and Microsoft Windows, for that matter). Consider the following example.

As I am sure you know, to access the Web you use a program called a BROWSER. (The two most important browsers are Internet Explorer and Firefox. Internet Explorer is used more widely, but Firefox is much better.)

Let's say you decide to take a look at my Web site (`http://www.harley.com`). To start, you type the address into the address bar of your browser and press the Enter key. Your browser then sends a message to my Web server. (I'm skipping a few details here.) Upon receiving the request, the Web server responds by sending data back to your browser. The browser then displays the data for you in the form of a Web page (in this case, my home page).

What I have just described is a client/server relationship. A client (your browser) contacts a server on your behalf. The server sends back data. The client then processes the data.

Let's take another example. There are two ways to use email. You can use a Web-based service (such as Gmail), or you can run a program on your computer that sends and receives mail on your behalf. I'd like to talk about the second type of service.

When you run your own email program, it uses different systems for sending and receiving. To send mail, it uses SMTP (Simple Mail Transport Protocol). To receive mail, it uses either POP (Post Office Protocol) or IMAP (Internet Message Access Protocol).

Let's say you have just finished composing an email message, and your email program is ready to send it. To do so, it temporarily becomes an SMTP client and connects to an SMTP server. Your SMTP client then calls upon the SMTP server to accept the message and send it on its way.

Similarly, when you check for incoming mail, your email program temporarily becomes a POP (or IMAP) client, and connects to your POP (or IMAP) server. It then asks the server if there is any incoming mail. If so, the server sends the mail to your client, which processes the messages appropriately.

My guess is that, even if you have sent and received email for years, you may have never heard of SMTP, POP and IMAP clients and servers. Similarly, you can use the Web for years without knowing that your browser is actually a Web client. This is because client/server systems generally work so well that the clients and servers are able to do their jobs without bothering the user (you) with the details.

Once you get to know Unix and the Internet, you will find that there are clients and servers all over the place. Let me leave you with three such examples.

First, to connect to a remote host, you use a client/server system called SSH. (The name stands for "secure shell".) To use SSH, you run an SSH client on your terminal, and your SSH client connects to an SSH server running on the host. Second, to upload and download files to a remote computer, you use a system called FTP (File Transfer Protocol). To use FTP, you run an FTP client on your computer. Your FTP client connects to an FTP server. The client and the server then work together to transfer the data according to your wishes.

As you become an experienced Unix or Linux user, you will find yourself working with both these systems. As you do, you will come to appreciate the beauty and power of the client/server model.

Finally, you may have heard of Usenet, the worldwide system of discussion groups. (If you haven't, go to `http://www.harley.com/usenet`.) To access Usenet, you run a Usenet client, called a newsreader. Your newsreader connects to a Usenet server called a news server. (I'll explain the names in a minute.)

All of these examples are different, but one thing is the same. In each case, the client requests a service from the server.

Strictly speaking, clients and servers are programs, not machines. However, informally, the term "server" sometimes refers to the computer on which the server program is running.

For example, suppose you are taking a tour of a company and you are shown a room with two computers in it. Your guide points to the computer on the left and says, "That is our Web server." He then points to the other computer and says, "And that is our mail server."

WHAT'S IN A NAME?

Newsreader, News server

The Usenet system of worldwide discussion groups was started in 1979 by two graduate students at Duke University, Jim Ellis and Tom Truscott. Ellis and Truscott conceived of Usenet as a way to send news and announcements between two universities in North Carolina (University of North Carolina and Duke University).

Within a short time, Usenet spread to other schools and, within a few years, it had blossomed into a large system of discussion groups.

Because of its origin, Usenet is still referred to as the NEWS (or sometimes NETNEWS), even though it is not a news service. Similarly, the discussion groups are referred to as NEWSGROUPS, the clients are called NEWSREADERS, and the servers are called NEWS SERVERS.

WHAT HAPPENS WHEN YOU PRESS A KEY?

As you now understand, Unix is based on the idea of terminals and hosts. Your terminal acts as your interface; the host does the processing.

The terminal and the host can be part of the same computer, such as when you use a laptop or a desktop computer. Or the terminal and host can be completely separate from one another, as when you access a Unix host over a LAN or via the Internet.

Regardless, the terminal/host relationship is deeply embedded into the fabric of Unix. Having said that, I want to pose what seems like a simple question: "What happens when you press a key?" The answer is more complex than you might expect. Let's say you are using a Unix computer and you want to find out what time it is. The Unix command to display the time and date is **date**. So, you press the four keys: <d>, <a>, <t>, <e>, followed by the <Enter> key.

As you press each letter, it appears on your screen, so it's natural to assume that your terminal is displaying the letters as you type them. Actually, this is not the case. It is the host, not the terminal, that is in charge of displaying what you have typed.

Each time you press a key, the terminal sends a signal to the host. It is up to the host to respond in such a way that the appropriate character is displayed on your screen.

For example, when you press the <d> key, the terminal sends a signal to the host that means "the user has just sent a **d** character". The host then sends back a signal that means "display the letter **d** on the screen of the terminal". When this happens, we say that the host ECHOES the character to your screen.

The same thing happens when you use a mouse. Moving the mouse or clicking a button sends signals to the host. The host interprets these signals and sends instructions back to your terminal. Your terminal then makes the appropriate changes to your screen: move the pointer, resize a window, display a menu, and so on.

In most cases, it all happens so fast that it looks as if your keyboard and mouse are connected directly to your screen. However, if you are using a long-distance connection, say over the Internet, you may occasionally notice a delay between the time you press the key and the time you see the character appear on your screen. You may also see a delay when you move your mouse or press a mouse button and the screen is not updated right away. We refer to this delay as LAG.

You might ask, why was Unix designed so that the host echoes each character? Why not have the host silently accept whatever it receives and have the terminal do the echoing? Doing so would be faster, which would avoid lag.

The answer is that when the host does the echoing, you can see that what you are typing is being received successfully, and that the connection between your terminal and the host is intact. If the terminal did the echoing and you had a problem, you would have no way of knowing whether or not your connection to the host was working. This, of course, is most important when you are using a host that is physically separate from your terminal.

Aside from dependability, there is another reason why the Unix designers chose to have the host do the echoing. As I will discuss in Chapter 7, there are certain keys (such as <Backspace> or <Delete>), that you can press to make corrections as you type. Unix was designed to work with a wide variety of terminals, and it made sense for the operating system itself to handle the processing of these keypresses in a uniform way, rather than expect each different type of terminal to be able to do the job on its own.

HINT

When you use Unix, the characters you type are echoed to your screen by the host, not by the terminal. Most of the time, the lag is so small that you won't even notice it. However, if you are using a distant host over a slow connection, there may be times when there will be a delay before the characters you type are displayed on your screen.

Unix allows you to type ahead many characters, so don't worry. Just keep typing, and eventually, the host will catch up. In almost all cases, no matter how long the lag, nothing will be lost.

CHARACTER TERMINALS AND GRAPHICS TERMINALS

Broadly speaking, there are two classes of terminals you can use with Unix. How you interact with Unix will depend on which type of terminal you are using.

Take a moment to look back at Figures 3-2 and 3-3, the photos of the Teletype ASR33. As we discussed, this machine was the very first Unix terminal. If you look at it carefully, you will see that the only input device was a rudimentary keyboard, and the only output device was a roll of paper upon which characters were printed.

Over the years, as hardware developed, Unix terminals became more advanced. The keyboard became more sophisticated and a lot easier to use, and the roll of paper was replaced by a monitor with a video screen.

Still, for a long time, one basic characteristic of Unix terminals did not change: the only form of input and output was characters (also called TEXT). In other words, there were letters, numbers, punctuation, and a few special keys to control things, but no pictures.

A terminal that only works with text is called a CHARACTER TERMINAL or a TEXT-BASED TERMINAL. As PC technology developed, a new type of terminal became available, the GRAPHICS TERMINAL. Graphics terminals had a keyboard and mouse for input and, for output, they took full advantage of the video hardware. Not only could they handle text; they could display just about anything that could be drawn on a screen using small dots: pictures, geometric shapes, shading, lines, colors, and so on.

Obviously, graphics terminals are more powerful than character terminals. When you use a character terminal, you are restricted to typing characters and reading characters. When you use a graphics terminal, you can use a full-fledged GUI (graphical user interface), with icons, windows, colors, pictures, and so on.

For this reason, you might think that graphics terminals are always better than character terminals. After all, isn't a GUI always better than plain text?

This is certainly true for PCs using Microsoft Windows and for Macintoshes. From the beginning, both Windows and the Macintosh operating systems were designed to use a GUI; in fact, they depend upon a GUI.

Unix is different.

Because Unix was developed in an era of character terminals, virtually all the power and function of the operating system is available with plain text. Although there are Unix GUIs (which we will discuss in Chapter 5) and you do need to learn how to use them, a great deal of what you do with Unix – including everything I teach you in this book – requires only plain text. With Unix, graphics are nice, but not necessary.

What does this mean in practical terms? When you use Unix on your own computer, you will be working within a GUI (using a mouse, manipulating windows, and so on). This means your computer will be emulating a graphics terminal.

However, much of the time, you will find yourself working within a window that acts as a character terminal. Within that window, all you will type is text, and all you will see is text. In other words, you will be using a character terminal. In the same way, when you connect to a remote host, you usually do so by opening a window to act as a character terminal.

When you find yourself working in this way, I want you to take a moment to think about this: you are using Unix in the same way that the original users used Unix back in the 1970s. What's interesting is that, over thirty years later, the system still works well. Most of the time, text is all you need.

THE MOST COMMON TYPES OF TERMINALS

Over the years, Unix was developed to work with literally hundreds of different types of terminals. Today, of course, we don't use actual standalone hardware terminals: we use computers to emulate a terminal.

I have mentioned the idea of opening a window to emulate a character terminal. In most cases, the emulation is based on the characteristics of a very old terminal, called the VT100, which dates from 1978. (The VT100 was made by the Digital Equipment Corporation, the same company that made the PDP-11 computers we discussed at the beginning of the chapter.) Although actual VT100s haven't been used for years, they were so well-designed and so popular, they set a permanent standard for character terminals. (You can see an actual VT100 in Figure 3-7 below.)

Graphics terminals, of course, have a different standard. As you will see (in Chapter 5), Unix GUIs are all based on a system called X Window, and the basic support for X Window

FIGURE 3-7: VT100 Terminal

The most popular Unix terminal of all time, the VT100, was introduced in 1978 by the Digital Equipment Corporation. The VT100 was so popular that it set a permanent standard. Even today, most terminal emulation programs use specifications based on the VT100.

is provided by a graphics terminal called the X TERMINAL. Today, the X terminal is the basis of graphics terminal emulation, the same way that the VT100 is the basis of character terminal emulation.

Thus, when you connect to a remote host, you have two choices. You can use a character terminal (the most common choice), in which case you will be emulating a VT100 or something like it. Or, if you want to use GUI, you can use a graphics terminal, in which case you will be emulating an X terminal.

Although I won't go into the details now, I'll show you the two commands you will use. To connect to a remote host and emulate a character terminal, you use the **ssh** (secure shell) command. To emulate an X Window graphics terminal, you use the **ssh -X** command.

CHAPTER 3 EXERCISES

REVIEW QUESTIONS

1. What type of machine was used as the very first Unix termina and why was it chosen?

2. What are terminal rooms? Why were they necessary?

3. What is a headless system? Give two examples of headless systems that are used on the Internet to provide very important services.

4. What is a server? What is a client?

FOR FURTHER THOUGHT

1. In 1969, Ken Thompson of AT&T Bell Labs was looking for a computer to create what, eventually, became the first Unix system. He found an unused PDP-7 minicomputer, which he was able to use. Suppose Thompson had not found the PDP-7. Would we have Unix today?

2. In the 1970s, computers (even minicomputers) were very expensive. Since no one had their own computer, people had to share. Compared to today, computers in the 1970s were slow, with limited memory and storage facilities. Today, every programmer has his own computer with very fast processors, lots of memory, lots of disk space, sophisticated tools, and Internet access. Who had more fun, programmers in the 1970s or programmers today? How about programmers 20 years from now?

CHAPTER 4
STARTING TO USE UNIX

When you take your very first lesson on how to use Unix, what you need to learn depends on how you will be accessing Unix. Will you be using Unix as part of a shared, multiuser system, say, at school or on the job? Or do you have a Unix computer of your own, in which case you will control the computer and be the only user?

In this chapter, we'll discuss the first situation: what it's like to use a Unix system that is maintained by someone else. I'll show you how to start and stop a work session, and I'll explain the basic concepts, such as system administrators, passwords, userids, users and superusers. As I explain ideas to you, I will assume that you are using a straightforward text-based interface.

In Chapter 5, we'll talk about the more complex situation, in which you are using your own Unix system installed on your own computer. In that chapter, we'll talk about the ideas underlying a graphical interface.

What if you are never planning to use Unix as part of a shared system? What if you will only be using your own computer and a graphical interface? Do you still need to read this chapter?

The answer is yes. No matter how you use Unix, the skills and ideas we are going to cover in this chapter are basic to Unix and important for everyone. (Besides, you don't want to miss the story about the Hotdog-bun Boy.)

THE SYSTEM ADMINISTRATOR

In the broadest sense, there are two ways in which you can access a Unix system. First, you might have your own Unix computer, in which case you are the only user and you are in charge of managing the system.

Alternatively, you might use a shared multiuser system – at school or at work – in which case you will be only one of the users. If this is the case, someone else will be in charge, so you don't have to worry about maintaining the system. However, you will have to follow some rules and work within certain limitations.

Of course, you may be able to access Unix in both ways. For example, you might use a shared system at school and your own PC at home.

Although having your own Unix computer sounds simpler, it actually isn't. The truth is it's easier to use a shared system. Because you don't own the system, someone else manages it for you, which is a very big deal.

All Unix systems require administration and maintenance. The person who performs these duties is called the SYSTEM ADMINISTRATOR, often abbreviated as SYSADMIN or ADMIN. (The old term, not used much anymore, is SYSTEM MANAGER.)

If the computer you use is owned by an organization – such as a university or a company – the admin will probably be a paid employee. Indeed, within organizations that have networks of Unix computers, system administration is a full-time job that calls for a great deal of specialized knowledge. There may be many admins with a staff of assistants.

Before the mid 1990s, it was very unusual for someone to have his or her own Unix computer. Most everyone who used Unix did so by accessing a shared system. Unix systems were maintained by an organization (usually a school or a company), and there were rules that all the users were required to follow.

Most of the time, people accessed Unix remotely, either by using a terminal or by using a PC to emulate a terminal (see Chapter 3). As such, the most common way to use Unix was with a text-based interface, using only a keyboard and a monitor (as we will be doing in this chapter). It was only a minority of users who used Unix with a graphical interface.

When you have your own personal Unix computer, you are, for better or for worse, your own admin. At best, administering your system is a highly fulfilling activity, which will build your skills and confidence, making you feel that you are truly in control of your computing destiny. At worst, you will, at times, feel frustrated and confused.

To use Unix well, you need to understand a number of basic concepts: the file system, text editors, the shell, and so on, all of which I will teach you in this book. To be an effective administrator of a large system or a network, you need a lot more. You will have to master a great many esoteric skills, many of which are, alas, beyond the scope of this book. To manage your own personal system is a lot easier. All you will need is basic Unix skills and a thoughtful attitude.

Regardless, no matter how long it takes to learn to manage your own Unix computer well, I can assure you that system administration is always a learning experience. (If nothing else, you will, at least, learn patience.)

In the meantime, let's move ahead and see what life is like when someone else is managing the system for you.

USERIDS AND PASSWORDS

Before you can use a Unix computer, the system administrator must give you a name that you will use to identify yourself to the system. This name is called your USERID. The word userid is a contraction of "user identification", and is pronounced "user-eye-dee".

Along with the userid, you will also get a PASSWORD, which you will have to type in each time you start a work session.

Once you have permission to use a Unix system, we say that you have an ACCOUNT on that computer. Even though you aren't paying real money for your account, Unix will keep track of how much you use the system. (Unix comes with a lot of built-in accounting, which your system administrator can use to keep records of who is doing what.) In addition, your account will probably come with certain predefined limits, such as how much disk space you are allowed for your files, or how many pages you can print.

If you are a student, one limit you are likely to encounter is an expiration date on your account. For example, your account may terminate automatically at the end of the semester, which only makes sense.

What will your userid be? In most cases, your system administrator will choose a userid for you. One common method is to base the userid on the person's real name. For example, for the name Harley Q. Hahn, the userid might be **harley**, **hahn**,**hhahn**, **harleyh** or **hqh**.

Alternatively, your userid may reflect some completely objective criteria. For example, if you are a student and you are the 25th person in the CS110 class to ask for a Unix account, you might be assigned the userid **cs110-25**.

Each time you start a Unix session, you must enter your userid. From then on, this name is used by Unix to identify you. For example, when you create files, they will not belong to you; they will be "owned" by your userid. (We'll talk about this distinction later in the chapter.)

It is important to understand that userids are not secret. For example, if you use Unix for email, your userid will be part of your address. Moreover, at any time, it is easy for anyone to display all the userids that are currently using the system and – if you know what you are doing – you can even display a list of all the userids that are registered with the system.

Security, of course, is important, but it does not require that userids be secret. Rather, security is maintained by making sure that passwords are secret. In this way, everyone can find out who else uses the computer, but access to the system is controlled.

Your password will probably be a meaningless group of characters, such as **H!lg%12**, something which is difficult for someone else to guess. Later in the chapter, I'll explain how to change your password if you don't like it, and what types of passwords are good to use.

LOGGING IN (STARTING WORK WITH UNIX)

When you sit down in front of your terminal, the process you go through to start work is called LOGGING IN. Although the idea is simple, the terminology is a bit tricky.

When we talk about the idea as a verb, we write two words, "log in". When we express the same idea as a noun or an adjective, we use a single word LOGIN.

For example, "In order to log in, you need to learn the login procedure." Or, "We need a larger computer. Our current one gets over 500 logins a day; there are too many people trying to log in at the same time."

The actual login process is straightforward. All you need to do is type your userid and your password. Here is how it works.

When a Unix program wants you to type something, it displays a PROMPT, a short message indicating that you must enter input from the keyboard. When Unix wants to show that it is waiting for you to log in, it displays the following prompt:

```
login:
```

Unix is saying, "Type your userid and press the <Return> key."

Although this seems straightforward, I would like to pause for a moment to answer an important question: What, exactly, is the <Return> key?

In Chapter 7, you will learn that Unix uses a set of special keys that do not necessarily correspond to the exact same physical keys on every keyboard. We'll talk about the details then. For now, all I want you to know is that Unix has a special key that you press to indicate you have finished typing a line of input. This key is called the <Return> key. When you press the <Return> key, it sends Unix a signal called a newline.

If your keyboard has an actual <Return> key, pressing it will send the newline signal. (This is the case with a Macintosh.) Otherwise, you send the newline by pressing the <Enter> key (which is the case with PCs). Thus, throughout this book, when I tell you to press <Return>, use either the <Return> key or the <Enter> key, whichever you have on your particular keyboard.

Once you have typed your userid and pressed <Return>, Unix asks for your password by displaying the following prompt:

```
Password:
```

As you type, you will notice that your password is not echoed. This is to prevent other people from seeing your password if they happen to be looking over your shoulder. (Remember, in Unix, userids are not secret but passwords are, which is why, when you log in, userids are echoed but passwords are not.)

Notice also that, unlike Windows, when you type a password, the system does not display an asterisk for each character. This means that if someone is watching you, he not only can't see your password, but also he doesn't even know how many characters you typed.

After you have typed your password, press <Return> once again. Unix will check to confirm the password is valid. If it is, Unix will complete the login process and you will be ready to start work.

If either your userid or password was incorrect, Unix will display:

```
Login incorrect
```

and let you try again. If you are connecting remotely, some systems will disconnect you if you log in incorrectly too many times. This is to make it difficult for someone who is trying to break into the system to keep guessing passwords indefinitely. (Typically, you get 3-5 tries. The exact number is controlled by the system administrator.)

As you type your userid and your password, there are three important things I would like you to remember.

• Be sure not to mix up small letters and capital letters. For example, if your userid is "harley", type **harley**, not **Harley**.

• Be careful not to confuse the number **0** (zero), with the capital letter **O** (oh).

• Be careful not to confuse the number **1** (one), with the small letter **l** (el).

Before we finish this section, I want to point out a curious thing that very few people notice. On virtually all Unix systems, the login program displays **login:** with a small "l" and **Password:** with a capital "P". No one knows why.

HINT

Whenever you type a userid, Unix always asks for a password, even if that particular userid is invalid. This makes it more difficult for evil-minded people to guess userids.

For example, if someone enters the userid **harley**, he or she will always be asked for a password, even if there is no such userid registered with the system.

Of course, this also means that if you mistype your userid or your password, you won't know which one was wrong. You will just be told that your login was incorrect.

WHAT'S IN A NAME?

The <Return> key

Today, most keyboards have an <Enter> key, not a <Return> key. Why, then, does Unix use the name <Return>?

The use is traditional. As I explained in Chapter 3, for many years Unix was accessed from terminals, not from PCs, and it happened that all terminals had a <Return> key. Even though there are now countless PC keyboards with <Enter> keys, the Unix terminology has not changed.

The name "Return" comes from typewriters. In the olden days, the part of a mechanical typewriter that held the paper was called the "carriage". Each time you put in a new piece of paper, the carriage would start at the far right. As you typed, the carriage would move to the left one character at a time.

When you came to the end of a line, you would use your left hand to push a lever that would move the carriage back to the right. At the same time, the lever would also move the paper up one line. In this way, the paper would be positioned at the start of a new line.

The first Unix terminals were Teletype ASR33 machines (see Chapter 3). Unlike typewriters, they did not have a movable carriage. However, while printing text, changing from the end of one line to the beginning of the next did involve two separate motions. These motions were analogous to what happened when you pushed the lever on a typewriter, so they were described using typewriter terminology and referred to as CARRIAGE RETURN and LINEFEED. (These two terms are still important in the world of Unix, and you will meet them time and again.)

Figure 4-1 shows a photo of the Teletype ASR33 keyboard. Notice that there is both a <Linefeed> key and a <Return> key. This is why, to this day, Unix still refers to the key that terminates a line of text as the <Return> key.

WHAT HAPPENS AFTER YOU LOG IN?

After you log in successfully, Unix will display some informative messages, followed by an invitation to enter a command. You can then start your work session by entering one command after another.

The informative messages you see will vary, depending on how the system administrator has configured your system. Figure 4-2, for example, has a typical example from a FreeBSD system:

The first line shows us the last time we logged into this computer using the current userid. At the end of the line, we see **ttyp1**, which is the name of the terminal that was used at the time.

Whenever you log in, take a minute to check this line; it is here for security reasons. If the time you see is more recent than you remember, someone else may have been using your account without your permission. If so, change your password immediately. (I'll explain how to do so later in the chapter.)

The next three lines contain copyright information. As you will recall from Chapter 3, FreeBSD is based on work done at U.C. Berkeley, so it is understandable that the University of California is named as the copyright holder.

The second to last line shows we are using FreeBSD version 4.9. The date and time show that the kernel was "built" – that is, generated – on March 8, 2006 at 4:26 PM. (Unix uses a 24-hour clock.)

Finally, the last line is a welcome greeting put there by a friendly FreeBSD programmer.

What happens after the login message is displayed depends, in part, on how your system was set up. As part of the login process, Unix executes a list of predefined commands that are kept in special initialization files. Some of these files are controlled by the system administrator, so he can ensure that specific tasks are carried out each time someone logs in. For example, he may want to display a specific message to all the users whenever they log in.

FIGURE 4-1: Keyboard of the Teletype ASR33

The keyboard of the Teletype ASR33, the very first device used as a Unix terminal. Notice the <Linefeed> and <Return> keys (on the far right of the second row).

```
Last login: Sat Jun 28 17:02:18 on ttyp1

Copyright 1980, 1983, 1986, 1988, 1990, 1991, 1993, 1994
The Regents of the University of California.
All rights reserved.

FreeBSD 4.9-RELEASE: Wed Mar 8 16:26:07 PDT 2006

Welcome to FreeBSD!
```

Figure 4-2: Login Messages

After you login successfully, you will see welcome messages. In this example, we see typical messages displayed by a FreeBSD system.

Aside from the general initialization files, each userid has its own personal initialization files which can be customized. The first time you log in, your initialization files will contain whatever default commands your system administrator has put in it. As you become more experienced, you can modify these files to suit your preferences. For example, you might have Unix execute a certain program each time you log in.

We'll talk about these files in Chapter 14, after we discuss the details and basic concepts involved in using the shell. (As I mentioned in Chapter 2, the shell is the program that reads and processes your commands.)

GETTING DOWN TO WORK: THE SHELL PROMPT

Once the initialization commands have finished executing, you are ready to start work. Unix will start the shell and pass control to it. The shell will then display a prompt – called the SHELL PROMPT – and wait for you to enter a command. To do so, you type the command and press the <Return> key. The shell will then process the command appropriately, usually by running a program.

For example, if you enter the command to start your email program, the shell will see that the program starts properly and will give it control. When the email program terminates, control will return to the shell, which will display a new prompt and wait for another command.

Eventually, when you have no more commands to enter, you will end your work session by logging out (explained below), at which time the shell will stop running.

It is very important to know when the shell is waiting for you to enter a command. For this reason, the shell prompt is chosen to be particularly distinctive.

Within the world of Unix, there are many different shells, and the actual prompt depends on which shell you are using. The three most popular shells are (in this order) Bash, the C-Shell, and the Korn Shell. I'll talk about each of them in detail later in the book (Chapters 12-14). For now, all I want you to know is what the basic shell prompt looks like for each particular shell.

For Bash and for the Korn shell, the prompt is a dollar sign:

$

For the C-Shell, the prompt is a percent sign:

`%`

If your system administrator has customized your environment, the prompt may be somewhat different. For instance, it may show the name of the machine you are logged into such as:

nipper$

In this case, the prompt shows us that we are logged into the machine called **nipper**. As you get more advanced, you can customize your shell prompt in many different ways. However, one thing that you should never change is the very last character of the prompt (the **$** or the **%**). This character is a reminder that the shell is running and that it is waiting for you to type in a command. And, because the various shells use different prompts, this character is also a reminder of what shell you are running. (It is true that both Bash and the Korn shell use the **$** prompt, but it's not difficult to remember which shell you are using so, for practical purposes, there is no real ambiguity.)

Regardless of which shell you are using, once you see the prompt, you can type any command you want and press the <Return> key. If you are logging in for the first time and you would like to practice, try the **date** command to display the time and date; the **whoami** command to display your userid; or the **who** command to display the userids of all the people who are currently logged in. If you want to snoop a bit more, try the **w** command. It tells you who is logged in and what they are doing.

LOGGING OUT (STOPPING WORK WITH UNIX): `logout`, `exit`, `login`

When you are finished working with Unix, you end your session by LOGGING OUT. (When we refer to this idea as a noun or adjective, we use a single word, LOGOUT.) You log out to tell Unix that you are finished working under the current userid. Once your logout is complete, Unix will stop your shell and end your work session.

It is important that you never forget to log out when you are finished working with a Unix system. If you were to just pick up and leave with your terminal (or computer) logged in, anyone could come by and use the Unix system under the auspices of your userid.

At the very least, you run the risk of someone fooling around under your userid. At the other extreme, some mischievous person might erase files (including yours) and cause all types of trouble. If this happens, you will bear some responsibility: leaving a terminal logged in in a public place is like leaving your car unlocked with the keys in the ignition.

There are several ways to log out. First, you can wait until you see the shell prompt and then press <Ctrl-D>. (Hold down the <Ctrl> key and press the <D> key at the same time.)

When you press <Ctrl-D>, it sends a signal called **eof** or "end of file". Essentially, this tells the shell that there is no more data coming. The shell terminates, and Unix logs you out. (We will discuss the Unix keyboard in detail in Chapter 7.)

As you will find out later, the end-of-file signal has other uses, and it is altogether possible that you might press <Ctrl-D> once too often and inadvertently log yourself out.

For this reason, there is a safeguard. Most shells have a way for you to specify that you do not want to log out by pressing <Ctrl-D>. Rather, you must enter a special command. In this way, it is impossible to log out accidentally.

It may be that your system administrator has set up your system so that, by default, you cannot log out by pressing <Ctrl-D>. If this is the case, you must use one of the specific logout commands. They are **logout** and **exit**.

To find out how you must log out with your system, try pressing <Ctrl-D>. If it works, fine. If not, your shell was set up to ignore <Ctrl-D>, and you may see a message like this:

```
Use "logout" to logout.
```

In this case, use the **logout** command. (Type "logout" and press the <Return> key.) If, instead, you see a message like this:

```
Use "exit" to logout
```

you will need to use the **exit** command.

One final way to log out is to use the **login** command. This tells Unix to log you out and then get ready for a new person to log in. After you are logged out, Unix will ask for a new userid by displaying the original prompt:

```
login:
```

This command is handy if you want to log out but leave your computer or terminal ready for someone else to log in.

HINT

On some systems, the **login** command will not disengage you completely. Instead, **login** will change the userid temporarily but, officially, you will still be logged in under your original name. When the new person logs out, he will find himself back in your original session.

If this is the case on your system, you should not use **login** because it could allow someone else to end up logged in under your userid.

You can find out how your version of **login** works by testing it. Enter the **login** command. Then log in and log out, and see if you are back in your original session. If so, it is not safe to use **login** for logging out. Use **logout** or **exit** instead.

UPPER- AND LOWERCASE

Unix distinguishes between small letters and capital letters. For example, when we discussed possible userids, I used the examples **harley** and **hahn**, both of which start with a small "h". At the same time, I suggested a possible password, **H!lg%12**, which contains two small letters and one capital letter.

Some operating systems are designed to ignore the differences between small and capital letters, a notable example being Microsoft Windows. Unix (which is much older) was written to be more precise.

For convenience, we refer to small letters as LOWERCASE and capital letters as UPPERCASE. The names come from typewriter terminology. When you use an old-fashioned typewriter, pressing the <Shift> key moves the "upper" case into position to print capital letters.

> **HINT**
>
> The idea of upper- and lowercase applies only to the letters of the alphabet, not to punctuation, numbers or any special characters.

Within Unix, when you type names or commands, you must be sure to be exact. For example, if your userid is **harley**, you must type all lowercase letters when you log in. If you type **Harley**, Unix considers it to be an entirely different userid. Similarly, when you log out, you must type **logout**, not **Logout**.

When a program or an operating system distinguishes between upper- and lowercase, we say that it is CASE SENSITIVE. Thus, we can say that Unix is case sensitive, and Windows is not.

Since Unix considers uppercase letters to be different from lowercase letters (as, indeed, they are), it is possible for a system administrator to assign two different userids that differ only in the case of the letters, for example, **harley** and **Harley**. In practice, however, you would never see such userids, because it would be too confusing. In fact, it is the custom to use only lowercase letters for userids.

In order to maintain scrupulous accuracy in this book, I will not capitalize command names, even when they come at the beginning of a sentence. For example: "**logout, exit** and **login** are three commands that you can use to log out."

Please appreciate that the distinction between upper- and lowercase applies only when you are logging in and entering Unix commands. When you use a program that works with regular textual data – for example, if you are using a word processor to create a document – you type in the regular manner.

A SAMPLE SESSION WITH UNIX

Figure 4-3 shows a short session with Unix. This example was created using a shared system on which several userids were logged in at the same time.

The session starts by logging in using userid **harley**. Notice that Unix does not echo the password.

After the userid and password are accepted, the Unix system identifies itself. In this example, you can see that we are using Linux on a computer named **weedly**.

The rest of the numbers show information about the kernel. The version of the kernel is **2.6.22-14-generic**; it was built on June 24 at 4:53 PM. (Remember, Unix uses a 24-hour clock.)

Next come two messages regarding Ubuntu, which is the name of this particular Linux distribution.

After the Ubuntu messages is a line showing the last time we logged in under the same userid. The login was on September 20 at 8:33 AM, and the connection was made from a computer named **nipper.harley.com**.

Finally, the preliminaries are over, and we are presented with the shell prompt. In this case, the prompt is configured to display the name of the userid (**harley**), the name of the computer (**weedly**), and the **$** character.

The **$** indicates that we are using Bash for our shell, and that the shell is ready for us to enter a command.

We enter the **date** command, which displays the current time and date. (Unix does have a **time** command, but it does not display the time. Rather, it times how long it takes to execute a specified command.)

After the **date** command has displayed its output, we see the shell prompt again. We then enter the **who** command. This displays a list of all the userids that are currently logged in to the system.

The first column shows the userids. Notice that **tammy** (who happens to be the system administrator) is logged in from two terminals.

The second column – **tty1**, **pts/0**, **pts/1**, and so on – are the names of the terminals that are in use.

The third column shows the time that the userid logged in.

```
login: harley
Password:

Linux weedly 2.6.22-14-generic Tue Jun 24 16:53:01 2008

The programs included with the Ubuntu system are free
software; the exact distribution terms for each program
are described in the individual files in
/usr/share/doc/*/copyright.

Ubuntu comes with ABSOLUTELY NO WARRANTY, to the extent
permitted by applicable law.

Last login: Sat Sep 20 08:33:17 from nipper.harley.com

harley@weedly:$ date
Mon Sep 29 10:34:36 PDT 2008

harley@weedly:$ who
tammy   tty1    Sep 28 21:25
linda   pts/0   Sep 29 07:13 (static)
tammy   pts/1   Sep 29 09:31 (coco)
casey   pts/2   Sep 29 10:07 (luna)
alex    pts/4   Sep 29 10:27 (alpha.taylored-software.com)
harley  pts/3   Sep 29 10:34 (nipper.harley.com)

harley@weedly:$ logout
Connection to weedly.wordsofwonder.net closed.
```

FIGURE 4-3: Sample Unix work session

The final column shows the computers from which the users logged in. The first three computers (**static**, **coco**, **luna**) are on the same network as **weedly**. The last two are on remote networks, which is why we are shown longer names.

After the **who** command finishes, we see another shell prompt. We type the **logout** command, ending the session.

As I mentioned, userid **tammy** is logged in twice. Unix allows you to log in as many times as you want without logging out. However, you would normally use only one terminal at a time. In our example, **tammy** is the system administrator, so it's okay.

However, if you ever enter the **who** command and see yourself logged in to more than one terminal, you should figure out what is happening. You may have inadvertently finished a previous work session without logging out. Or, you may be running more than one X session (see Chapter 6), and each such session shows up as a separate terminal. Alternately, the explanation may not be so benign: someone may be using your userid without your permission.

CHANGING YOUR PASSWORD: `passwd`

When your Unix account is set up, the system administrator will assign you a userid and a password. System administrators usually have their own ways of organizing things, and you may not be able to get the userid you want.

For example, you may want to use your first name as a userid, but the system administrator may have decided that all userids should be last names. Don't fight with your system administrator. He or she has a great deal of responsibility – Unix systems are hard to manage – and is probably massively overworked.

You can change your own password. Indeed, some system administrators use a facility called PASSWORD AGING to force you to change your password regularly for security reasons. (Password aging may also be used to prevent you from changing your password too often.) For example, you might be required to change your password every 60 days. If your system has password aging and your password has expired, you will be notified when you log in. You will then be forced to select a new password.

Aside from password aging, you can change your password voluntarily whenever you want (as long your system manager has no restrictions). To change your password, use the **passwd** command.

Once you enter the command, **passwd** will ask you to enter your old password. This proves you are authorized to make the change. Otherwise, anyone who walks by a terminal or computer that was left logged in could change your password.

Next, **passwd** will ask you to type the new password. Some systems require all passwords to meet certain specifications. For example, your password may need to be at least eight characters. If your new password does not meet the local criteria, you will be so informed and asked to enter a new choice.

Finally, **passwd** will ask you to retype the new password. Entering your new password a second time ensures that you did not make a mistake.

As you type the password, the characters will not be echoed. This prevents anyone from reading your new password over your shoulder.

WHAT'S IN A NAME?

passwd

To change your password, you use the **passwd** command. Obviously, **passwd** is a contraction of "password", so why isn't the command named **password**?

The answer is that Unix people like short names. As you learn Unix, you will encounter this tradition repeatedly. For example, the command to list your files is **ls**; the command to copy files is **cp**; and the command to show the status of processes (programs that are running) is **ps**. There are many more such names.

At first, leaving out a few letters seems unnecessary and even a bit odd, but once you get used to it, you will find the brevity to be comfortable.

CHOOSING A PASSWORD

The reason we use passwords is to make sure that only authorized people are able to access Unix accounts. As you might imagine, there are always a number of bright people who take pleasure in trying to break into a system. Such people are called CRACKERS. (Note: You will often see troublemakers referred to as hackers. There is a difference, which I will explain below.)

Some crackers want only to match wits against the Unix security system to see if they can log in on the sly. Other crackers enjoy causing real damage.

Thus, it behooves you to (1) never tell your password to anyone, and (2) choose a password that is not easy to guess. Remember, if you give your password to someone who damages the computer system, you are responsible.

When you first get your Unix account, the system administrator will choose a password for you. Whenever you want, you can use the **passwd** command to change your password.

The rules for choosing a password are actually guidelines for what not to choose:

• Do not choose your userid (such as **harley**), or your userid spelled backward (**yelrah**). This is like hiding the key to your house under the mat.

• Do not choose your first or last name, or any combination of names.

• Do not choose the name of a loved one or friend.

• Do not choose a word that is in the dictionary, any dictionary.

• Do not choose a number that is meaningful to you, such as a phone number, important date (such as a birthday), social security number and so on.

• Do not choose a password that is even remotely related to Harry Potter, Star Wars, Monty Python, The Hitchhiker's Guide to the Galaxy, or any other part of the popular culture.

• Do not choose a keyboard sequence, such as **123456**, **qwerty**, or **1q2w3e4r**. There are password-guessing programs that look for this type of pattern.

- Do not use the password **fred**. Many people pick this password because it's easy to type, but it's also one of the first ones a cracker will try.

In addition, there are several routine precautions you should practice:

- Never write down your password on a piece of paper. (Someone is bound to find it after you lose it.)

- Change your password regularly (once a month works well).

Within the cracker community, there are programs that exist to guess passwords. Such programs not only make intelligent guesses (such as your first name, last name and so on), but they use large lists of probable passwords to see if any of them will work. For example, there are lists of dictionary words, first and last names, movie actors, movie titles, Internet addresses, U.S. zip codes, and much, much more, including words from foreign languages.

Thus, if you think of an idea that is well-known and amusing, chances are that the crackers have been there ahead of you. This is especially true for passwords that relate to popular movies, books, and TV shows. For example, if you are a college student, both Star Wars and Monty Python were cool long before you were born, and there is probably no name or term that you could use that is not in a widely distributed cracker's list.

Password cracking programs are far more successful than you would imagine, so protect yourself (and your files) by choosing wisely. The best idea is to make up a pattern of meaningless characters. For good measure, mix in uppercase, lowercase, numbers and punctuation. (Some systems will force you to use such mixtures.) As an example, consider the password **H!lg%12**, which I used earlier in the chapter. Such a password would be hard to guess.

If you suspect that someone knows your password, change it right away. If you are using a shared system and you forget your password, all you need to do is tell your system administrator. He or she can assign you a new password without knowing the old one. You can then change the new password to whatever you want.

An ideal password is one you can remember without writing down, but that no one will ever guess and that will never appear on a cracker's word list. One good idea is to start with a phrase or sentence that makes sense to you and create an abbreviation. Here are some examples:

```
dontBL8   ("Don't be late")
tHd-bBic  (the Hotdog-bun Boy* is cool)
2b||~2b   (for C programmers: "To be or not to be")
wan24NIK8? (random meaningless phrase)
```

---

*The Hotdog-bun Boy came home from school one day. His mother looked at him and said, "You look so unhappy. Did something go wrong in school today?"

"Yes," he answered. "I hate history class."

"Why is that?" asked the Hotdog-bun Boy's mother.

"Because we read and read, and we listen to the teacher talk, and we have to memorize so many facts, but we never learn anything about Hotdog buns."

"Now son," said the mother, "how many times do I have to tell you? History is written by the wieners."

You get the idea. Just be sure that, in the excitement of creating a totally cool password, you resist the temptation to tell someone just to show off how clever you are.

WHAT'S IN A NAME?

Hacker, Cracker

There are two types of people who spend a lot of time programming: hackers and crackers. A HACKER is someone who spends his or her time working on useful (or at least benign) programming projects.

The word HACK is often used as a verb to indicate a larger-than-life devotion to programming. For example, "Elmo spent all weekend hacking at his file-sharing program."

Thus, the term "hacker" is often used in a positive sense, to describe someone who is capable of massive amounts of nerd-like effort. Similarly, "hacker" also refers to a clever person who knows how to utilize a computer to solve problems creatively.

Hackers are socially useful people, though rarely cool. The most financially successful hacker in the world is Bill Gates.

A CRACKER is a bad guy: someone who enjoys breaking into computer systems and doing things that people in authority do not want him to do. (Notice I say "him". For some reason – perhaps a genetic deficiency – virtually all crackers are male.)

A cracker is someone you would not want your sister to marry. A hacker in the family would be okay. It's just that everyone would receive their wedding invitations by email and, during the honeymoon, you would receive a daily email update of what the happy couple is doing, along with a Web address where you can find the latest photos of their trip and updated blog entries.

CHECKING IF SOMEONE HAS BEEN USING YOUR UNIX ACCOUNT: last

Whenever you log in, look carefully at the initial message; most systems will tell you the time and date you last logged in. If you don't remember logging in at this time, somebody might be using your account.

To check further, you can use the **last** command. Simply enter **last** followed by your userid. For example, if you are logged in as **harley**, enter:

last harley

You will see some information telling you the last time, or last several times, you logged in. If you accidentally enter the command without a userid:

last

you will see information about all the userids on the system. This may go on for some time, so if you want to terminate the command, press <Ctrl-C>. (Hold down the <Ctrl> key and press <C> at the same time.)

You might think it would be fun to enter the **last** command without a userid and spy on all the other people by seeing when they logged in. Well, you can if you want, but it gets boring real fast. If you have nothing to do, you will probably have more fun using one of the programs I describe in Chapter 8.

```
$ who
tammy   tty1    Jun 28 21:25
tlc     pts/0   Jun 29 07:13  (static)
tammy   pts/1   Jun 29 09:31  (coco)
casey   pts/2   Jun 29 10:07  (luna)
harley  pts/3   Jun 29 10:52  (nipper.harley.com)
alex    pts/4   Jun 29 14:39  (thing.taylored-soft.com)
```

FIGURE 4-4: Output of the who command

USERIDS AND USERS

A USER is a person who utilizes a Unix system in some way. However, Unix itself does not know about users: Unix knows only about userids.

The distinction is an important one. For example, if someone logs in using your userid, Unix has no way of knowing whether or not it is really you (which is why you need to protect your password).

In the world of Unix, only userids have a real identity. Userids, not users, own files, run programs, send email, log in, and log out. This means that if someone is able to log in using your userid, he will have the same rights as you do. He will be able to change your files, send email under your name, and so on.

Earlier in this chapter, we saw a sample session in which we used the **who** command to find out who was logged in. Figure 4-4 shows the output from that command.

Notice that you see only userids, not people's names. This is because Unix systems are populated by userids, not users.

THE SUPERUSER USERID: root

Within Unix, all userids are more or less equal, with one notable exception.

From time to time, it becomes necessary for the system administrator to have special privileges. For example, he or she may need to add a new user to the system, change somebody's password, update some software, and so on.

Toward this end, Unix supports a special userid, called **root**, that has extraordinary privileges. A person who has logged in using the **root** userid is allowed to do anything he or she wants. (Obviously, the **root** password is a closely guarded secret.) When someone logs in as **root**, we refer to him or her as the SUPERUSER.

At first, the name **root** may not make any sense. However, in Chapter 23, you will see that the basis of the entire Unix file system is called the "root directory". Thus, the name **root** refers to a very important part of Unix.

Most of the time, the system administrator will use his regular userid for regular work and will change to superuser only to do work that requires special privileges. Once the special job is done, the system administrator will change back to his regular userid. This prevents the power of the superuser from causing damage inadvertently.

For example, if you make a mistake entering the **rm** (remove) command, it is possible to erase files accidentally. If you are logged in under your own userid, the worst that you can do is erase your own files. If you are logged in as **root**, an ill-formed **rm** command could create widespread damage by erasing files all over the system.

HINT

When the shell is ready to accept a command from you, it displays a prompt. The final character of the prompt shows you which shell you are using. For example, the Korn shell and Bash use a **$** character. The C-Shell uses a **%** character.

Regardless of which shell you are using, when you log in as superuser, your prompt will change to the **#** character. When you see the **#** prompt, be careful: the superuser has a lot of power.

HAVING FUN WHILE PRACTICING SAFE COMPUTING

From its early days, Unix was designed for people working together who needed to share programs and documents, and who enjoyed helping one another. The basic design of the system assumes that everybody is honest and of good will. Even modern Unix, with its passwords and security measures, is not 100 percent bulletproof, nor is it meant to be. People who use Unix are supposed to respect other users.

Since Unix is so complex, there are always a few crackers who get a kick out of trying to beat the system. In some environments, young programmers who figure out how to break into a system and perform clandestine acts are tolerated, perhaps even admired for their ingenuity.

Not so in the Unix community. Crackers and troublemakers are tracked down and punished. For example, I mentioned earlier that there exist programs that are used to guess people's passwords. In some schools, just being caught running such a program is grounds for immediate expulsion.

However, the wonderful thing about Unix is that there are so many challenging and pleasant diversions. It is unlikely that you (as one of my readers) will ever become bored enough to get into real mischief. Nevertheless, if you are ever so tempted, please remember that system administrators are always overworked, and they have little patience with willful people who create unnecessary trouble.

If you find that you like Unix and you do have extra time on your hands, you can get a great deal of pleasure out of teaching and helping other people, two of the most important Unix traditions.

CHAPTER 4 EXERCISES

REVIEW QUESTIONS

1. What is the difference between a user and a userid?

2. What are four different ways to log out?

3. You suspect that someone has been using your Unix account without your permission. How do you check to see if this is the case? Suppose you find out someone has been using your account, but you don't know who it is. How do you stop them?

4. What is the userid of the superuser?

APPLYING YOUR KNOWLEDGE

1. Being able to change your password is a basic skill you must master before you start using Unix. Whenever you change your password, you should immediately test to make sure it works properly. Use **passwd** to change your password to **dontBL8** ("Don't be late"). Log out and back in again to make sure it works. Then change your password back to what it was originally. Test again to make sure it worked.

FOR FURTHER THOUGHT

1. Unix is case sensitive; that is, it distinguishes between lower case (small letters) and upper case (capital letters). Microsoft Windows is not case sensitive. For example, in Unix, **harley** and **Harley** are two completely different names. With Windows, they are the same. Why do you think the original Unix developers chose to make Unix case sensitive? Why did Microsoft choose to make Windows case insensitive? Which do you prefer, and why?

2. When you use **passwd** to change your password, the program requires you to type the new password twice. Why?

3. Why is it important to have a superuser?

C H A P T E R 5
GUIs: Graphical User Interfaces

There are two ways in which you can interact with Unix: you can use a text-based interface or you can use a graphical interface. In Chapter 4, I introduced you to using Unix by explaining what it is like to use a shared system that has a text-based interface. In this chapter, I am going to explain graphical interfaces: what they are, how and why they were developed, and which ones are in common use today. In Chapter 6, we'll talk about both types of interfaces, and I'll show you the details of how to manage your work sessions.

Before we do, I want to introduce you to the basic concepts about graphical interfaces: how to think about them and their place in the Unix universe. Along the way, I have a few treats for you: a few jokes you will probably get; one joke you probably won't get; a true/false test to see if you are a KDE or a Gnome person (you'll see); and some sound advice on how to create a Grandmother Machine.

WHAT IS A GUI?

A GRAPHICAL USER INTERFACE or GUI is a program that allows you to interact with a computer using a keyboard, a pointing device (mouse, trackball or touchpad), and a monitor. Input comes from the keyboard and the pointing device; output is displayed on the monitor. The design of the interface is such that it uses not only characters but windows, pictures and icons (small pictures), all of which you can manipulate.

When it comes to displaying information, there are, broadly speaking, two types of data, text (characters) and graphics (images), hence the name graphical user interface. Both Microsoft Windows and the Macintosh use GUIs, so I am sure you are familiar with the idea.

HINT

When you talk about GUIs, there are two ways to pronounce "GUI": either as three separate letters "G-U-I", or as a word in itself, "gooey".

Choose whichever pronunciation best fits your temperament and your audience. (I'm a "G-U-I" man, myself.)

Because of cultural inertia, most GUIs today follow the same basic design. Compared to Windows and the Mac, when you take a look at the various Unix GUIs, you will see some important differences. Perhaps the most basic one is that, in the world of Unix, no one believes that one size fits all. As a Unix user, you have a lot of choice.

To work with a GUI, there are several basic ideas you need to understand and several skills you have to master. First, you need to learn to use two input devices cooperatively: the keyboard and a pointing device.

Most people use a mouse but, as I mentioned above, you may also see trackballs, touchpads, and so on. In this book, I will assume that you are using a mouse, but the differences are minor. (I prefer a trackball, by the way.)

Typically, as you move the mouse, a pointer on the screen follows the motion. This pointer is a small picture, often an arrow. With some GUIs, the pointer will change as you move from one region of the screen to another.

Pointing devices not only move the on-screen pointer, but they also have buttons for you to press. Microsoft Windows requires a mouse with two buttons; the Mac requires only a single button. Unix GUIs are more complex. Most of them are based on a system called X Window (explained in detail below). X Window uses three mouse buttons, although it is possible to get by with two.

By convention, the three buttons are numbered from left to right. Button number 1 is on the left, number 2 is in the middle, and number 3 is on the right. GUIs are designed so that you use button 1, the left button, most often. This is because, if you are right-handed and the mouse is on your right, the left button is the easiest one to press (using your right index finger). If you are left-handed, it is possible to change the order of the buttons, so you can move the mouse to your left and use it with your left hand.

With a GUI, the screen is divided into a number of bounded regions called WINDOWS. As with real windows, the boundary is usually, but not always, a rectangle. Unlike real windows, GUI windows can overlap on the screen, and you can change their sizes and positions whenever you want. (You can see this in Figures 5-3 and 5-4 later in the chapter.)

Each window contains the output and accepts input for a different activity. For example, you might be using five different windows, each of which contains a different program. As you work, it is easy to switch from one window to another, which allows you to switch back and forth from one program to another. If you don't want to look at a window for a while, you can shrink it or hide it, and when you are finished with it, you can close it permanently.

In Chapter 4, we talked about what it is like to use Unix with a text-based interface, one that emulates a character terminal. In such cases, you can only see one program at a time. With a GUI, you can see multiple programs at once, and it is easy to switch from one to another. In fact, one of the prime motivations behind the development of X Window – and of windowing systems in general – was to make it as easy as possible for people to work with more than one program at the same time.

There are other important ideas and skills that you need to understand in order to work with a Unix GUI, and we will discuss them in Chapter 6. In this chapter, we'll talk about the most important ideas relating to such systems. We'll start with the software that forms the basis for virtually all Unix GUIs: X Window.

X WINDOW

X Window is a system that provides services to programs that work with graphical data. In the world of Unix, X Window is important in three ways. First, it is the basis of virtually all the GUIs you will encounter. Second, X Window allows you to run programs on a remote computer, while displaying full graphical output on your own computer (see Chapter 6). Third, X Window makes it possible for you to use a wide variety of hardware. Moreover, you can use more than one monitor at the same time.

Imagine yourself working at your computer and, in front of you, you have five open windows. Three of them are running programs on your computer; the other two are running programs on remote computers. All of them, however, are displaying the graphical elements that come with a GUI: icons, scroll bars, a pointer, pictures, and so on. It is X Window that makes this all possible. It does so by working behind the scenes to provide the supporting structure, so that programs needing to display graphical data and receive input from a mouse or keyboard don't have to bother with the details.

For convenience, we usually refer to X Window as X. Thus, you might ask a friend, "Did you know that most Unix GUIs are based on X?" (I know X is a strange name, but you will get used to it quickly if you hang around the right type of people.)

The roots of X extend back to MIT (Massachusetts Institute of Technology) in the mid-1980s. At the time, MIT wanted to build a network of graphical workstations (powerful, single-user computers) for teaching purposes. Unfortunately, what they had was a mishmash of mutually incompatible equipment and software from a variety of different vendors.

In 1984, MIT formed PROJECT ATHENA, a collaboration between researchers at MIT, IBM (International Business Machines Corporation) and DEC (Digital Equipment Corporation). Their goal was to create the first standardized, networked, graphical operating environment that was independent of specific hardware. This environment would then be used to build a large, campus-wide network called Athena.

To build Athena, MIT needed to connect a large amount of heterogeneous computing hardware into a functioning network, and it all had to be done in a way that would be suitable for students. This required the Athena developers to replace the complex gaggle of vendor-specific graphical interfaces with a single, well-designed interface: one that they hoped would become the industry standard.

Because of the demands of such an ambitious undertaking, they decided to name the project – and the network itself – after Athena, the Greek goddess of wisdom. (Athena was also the goddess of strategy and war which, in 1984, made her an important ally for anyone trying to connect computing equipment made by different vendors.)

Ultimately, Project Athena was successful in two important ways. First, the Athena programmers *were* able to create a vendor-neutral, network-friendly graphical interface, which they called X Window. X Window grew to achieve wide acceptance and, indeed, did become an industry standard (although not the only industry standard). Second, the programmers were able to build the Athena network and deploy it successfully, servicing hundreds of computers within the MIT community.

The first version of X Window (called X1) was released in June 1984. The second version (X6) was released in January 1985, and the third version (X9) was released the following September. (I am sure the numbering scheme made sense to someone.) The first popular version of X Window was X10, which was released in late 1985.

By now, X had started to attract attention outside of MIT. In February 1986, Project Athena released X to the outside world. This version was called X10R3: X Window version 10 release 3. The next major release was X11, which came out in September 1987.

Why am I telling you all this? To illustrate an interesting point. When a complex software product is new, it has yet to gather many users. This means that the developers can change the product radically without inconveniencing a lot of people or "breaking" programs that use that product. Once the product acquires a large installed base, and once programmers have written a large amount of software that depends on the product, it becomes a lot more difficult to make significant changes.

The more popular a product becomes, the more its development slows. This only makes sense: as more and more people – and more and more programs – come to depend on a piece of software, it becomes inconvenient to make major changes.

Thus, it came to pass that, in its first five years, X Window went through five major versions (X1, X6, X9, X10 and X11). X10 was the first popular version and X11 gathered an even bigger audience. X11 was so successful that it slowed down the development of X enormously. In fact, over 20 years later, the current version of X is still X11!

To be sure, X11 has been revised. After all, over a period of more than 20 years, hardware standards change and operating systems evolve. These revisions were called X11R2 (X Window version 11 release 2), X11R3, X11R4, X11R5 and X11R6, culminating in X11R7, which was released on December 21, 2005 (my birthday, by the way). However, none of the revisions was significant enough to be called X12.

Since 2005, X11R7 has been the standard. Again, there have been revisions, but they were relatively minor: X11R7.0, X11R7.1, X11R7.2, X11R7.3, and so on. There are people who talk about X12, but it's not going to happen anytime soon.

One way to make sense out of all this is by quoting the principle I mentioned above: a large user base retards future development. This is certainly true, and is something worth remembering, because it is one of the important long-term principles of software design that most people (and most companies) fail to appreciate.

However, there is another way to look at X Window development. You could say that the original MIT programmers designed such a good system that, almost 20 years later, the basic principles still work well, and the main changes that have had to be made are in the details: fixing bugs, supporting new hardware, and working with new versions of Unix.

What the X programmers showed is that, when you develop an important product and you want it to last a long time, it is worthwhile to take your time at the beginning. A flexible, well thought-out design gives a product enormous longevity. This too is a programming principle that many people fail to appreciate.

WHAT'S IN A NAME?

X Window, X

The roots of X Window lie in a particular operating system that was developed at Stanford University. This system, called V, was developed by the Distributed Systems Group at Stanford University from 1981 to 1988.

When a windowing interface was developed for V, it was called W. Some time later, the W program was given to a programmer at MIT who used it as a basis for a new windowing system, which he called X.

Since then, the name has stuck, perhaps for two reasons. First, names of Unix systems often end in "x" or "ix", and X Window is used mostly with Unix. Second, if they kept changing the name, they would reach the end of the alphabet in just two more letters.

Notice, by the way, that the proper name for the system is X Window, not X Windows.

WHO IS IN CHARGE OF X WINDOW?

By 1987, X was becoming so popular that MIT wanted to relinquish the responsibility for running the show. (After all, they were a school, not a company.) At first, a group of vendors who wanted X development to remain neutral talked MIT into remaining in charge. Eventually, however, MIT stood firm and the responsibility for X was passed on: first to one organization (the MIT X Consortium), then to another (the X Consortium), and then to yet another (the Open Group).

Today, X is maintained by a fourth organization, an independent group called X.Org. (I bet you can guess their Web address.) X.Org was formed in January 2004, and has supervised the maintenance of X since X11R6.5.1.

In 1992, a project was started by three programmers to work on a version of X for PCs. In particular, they were working with PCs that used an Intel 386 processor, so they called their software XFree86. (The name is a pun, because "XFree86" sounds like "X386".)

Because XFree86 supported PC video cards, it came to be used with Linux and, as Linux grew in popularity, so did XFree86. During the late 1990s and early 2000s, when official X development had slowed to a crawl, the XFree86 developers took up the slack. Indeed, XFree86 became so widespread that, at one time, if you were using a PC with Unix and a GUI, you were probably using XFree86.

However, in 2004, the president of the XFree86 organization decided to make a change in the distribution license. His idea was to force people to give credit to the XFree86 development team whenever certain parts of the software were distributed.

It sounds like a noble idea, and XFree86 was still open source software. That idea never changed. However, the new license was incompatible with the standard GNU GPL distribution license (see Chapter 2). This bothered a lot of programmers as well as most of the Unix companies, because it would have resulted in terrible logistical problems.

The ultimate solution was for X.Org to take over the development of X, which they did, starting with the most recent version of XFree86 that was unencumbered by the new license. As a result, the XFree86 project lost most of its volunteer programmers, many of whom switched to X.Org.

I mention all of this for two reasons. First, from time to time, you will come across the name XFree86, and I want you to know what it means. Second, I want you to appreciate that, when open source software is distributed, the details of the license can be crucial to the future of the software. The more popular the software, the more important the license be in harmony with previous licenses. We will see this again, later in the chapter, when we talk about a system called KDE.

LAYERS OF ABSTRACTION

As I have explained, X Window is a portable, hardware-independent windowing system that works with many different types of computing equipment. Moreover, X can run on virtually any type of Unix as well as certain non-Unix systems (such as Open VMS, originally developed by DEC).

How can this be? How can a graphical windowing system work with so many operating systems and so many different types of computers, video cards, monitors, pointing devices, and so on?

As we discussed earlier, X was developed as part of Project Athena with the goal of providing a graphical operating environment that would run a variety of software on many different types of hardware. Thus, from the beginning, X was designed to be flexible.

To achieve this goal, the designers of X used what computer programmers call LAYERS OF ABSTRACTION. The idea is to define a large overall goal in terms of layers that can be visualized as being stacked from the bottom up, one on top of the next. Each layer is designed to provide services to the layer above and to request services from the layer below. There is no other interaction.

Let's take a quick, abstract example, and then we'll move onto something concrete. Let's say that a computing system is made up of five layers: A, B, C, D and E. Layer E is at the bottom; layer D is on top of E; layer C is on top of D; and so on. Layer A is on top.

Programs running in Layer A call upon programs in Layer B (and only Layer B) to perform various services; Layer B programs call upon programs in Layer C (and only Layer C); and so on.

If such a system is designed well, it means that a programmer working on, say, Layer C, does not have to know about all the other layers and how they function. All he has to know is how to call upon Layer D for services, and how to provide services for Layer B. Because he is concerned only with the details of his own layer, he doesn't care if someone makes changes to the internals of Layer A or Layer E.

THE WINDOW MANAGER

To cement the idea of layers of abstraction, let's consider a real example.

From the beginning, X Window was designed to be a standardized interface between a GUI and the hardware. In itself, X does not furnish a graphical interface, nor is there any specification that describes what the user interface should look like. Providing the actual GUI is the job of another program called the WINDOW MANAGER.

The window manager controls the appearance and characteristics of the windows and other graphical elements (buttons, scroll bars, icons, and so on). What X does is bridge the gap between the window manager and the actual hardware.

For example, say that the window manager wants to draw a window on the screen of a monitor. It sends the request to X along with the relevant specifications (the shape of the window, the position of the window, the thickness of the borders, the colors, and so on). X causes the window to be drawn and sends back a message to the window manager once the task is completed.

In this way, the window manager doesn't have to know anything about how to draw a window. That is X's job. Similarly, X doesn't have to know anything about how to create an actual GUI. That is the window manager's job.

Thus you see the importance of levels of abstraction. A programmer working on one level can ignore the internal details of all the other levels. In this case, the window manager resides in a layer above X Window. When the window manager needs to display something, it calls upon X Window to do the job.

When Project Athena released X10 – the first popular version of X – they included a rudimentary window manager named **xwm** (the X Window Manager). With X10R3, they included a new window manager, **uwm**. With X11, the first very successful version of X, there was another new window manager, **twm**.

(The name **uwm** stood for Ultrix Window Manager, Ultrix being DEC's version of Unix. Later, the name was changed to the Universal Window Manager. The name **twm** stood for Tom's Window Manager, because it was written by Tom LaStrange. Later, the name was changed to the Tab Window Manager.)

The **twm** window manager became very popular. In fact, it is still included with X11 and can be considered the default window manager; it is certainly the most influential. Over the years, **twm** has spawned a number of derivative products written by programmers who modified it to create window managers of their own. (Remember, all of X Window is open source, and anyone can change any part of it to create their own version of whatever they want.)

I mention **xwm**, **uwm** and **twm** because they are important for historical reasons, so you should know the names. Since then, there have been many other window managers written for X, each with its own special features, advantages, and disadvantages. However, out of the many new window managers that have been created, there are only two I want to mention: Metacity and **kwm**.

These are particularly important window managers. However, before I can explain why, I need to discuss the next layer of abstraction, the one that sits on top of the window manager: the desktop environment.

THE DESKTOP ENVIRONMENT

As we discussed, it is the job of a window manager to provide a basic graphical interface. As such, it is the window manager that enables you to create windows, move and size them, click on icons, maneuver scroll bars, and so on.

However, using a modern computer system requires a lot more than a basic GUI. You need a well thought-out, *consistent* interface. Moreover, you want that interface to be attractive, sensible and flexible (just like the people in your life).

The power of a GUI comes from being able to provide a work environment in which you can manipulate the various elements in a way that makes sense and serves your needs well. Your interface needs to have an underlying logic to it, one that will allow you to solve problems from moment to moment as you work.

In the early days of X, people would interact directly with the window manager. However, the basic GUI provided by a window manager can only go so far. What it can't do is help you with the complex cognitive tasks associated with using a modern computer. This is the job of a more sophisticated system called the DESKTOP ENVIRONMENT and, sometimes, the DESKTOP MANAGER.

The name comes from the fact that, as you are working, you can imagine the screen of your monitor as being a desktop on which you place the objects with which you are working. The metaphor was chosen in the olden days, when graphical interfaces were still new, and GUI designers felt that it would be intuitive to untrained users to consider the screen as a desktop. Personally, I think the metaphor is misleading and confusing. I wish it would have been discarded a long time ago*.

The desktop environment allows you to answer such questions as: How do I start a program? How do I move or hide a window when I don't want to look at it? How do I find a file when I can't remember where it was? How do I move an icon from one place to another? How do I prioritize my files and programs so that the most important ones are easier to find?

Here is a specific example. Where a window manager might process our mouse movements and display icons and windows, a desktop environment would allow us to use the mouse to drag an icon and drop it on a window. In doing so, it is the desktop environment that brings *meaning* to the idea of dragging and dropping.

HINT

Never let yourself be fooled into thinking that a computer interface should be so "intuitive" as to be immediately useful to a beginner. Complex tasks require complex tools, and complex tools take time to master.

In some cases, it is possible for designers to dumb down an interface so much that people with no experience can use it immediately. However, what's easy to use on the first day will not be what you want to use once you are experienced. In the long run, easy-to-learn interfaces are much more frustrating than powerful tools that take time to master.

When we use tools that are designed primarily to be easy to learn, we end up with systems in which the *computer* is in control. When we use well-designed, powerful tools that take time to learn, we end up with systems in which the *user* is in control.

That is the case with Unix.

---

* However, when it comes to metaphors I am a lot more picky than other people. Consider, for example, the American humorist Will Rogers who used to say, "I never met-a-phor I didn't like."

LAYERS OF ABSTRACTION: REVISITED

To continue with our layers of abstraction model, we can say that the window manager sits on top of X Window, and the desktop environment sits on top of the window manager.

You can see this in Figure 5-1, which shows the layers of abstraction that support a typical Unix GUI. Notice there are several layers I have not mentioned. At the bottom, X Window calls upon the operating system's device drivers to do the actual communication with the hardware. At the top, the user and the programs he or she runs call upon the desktop environment as needed.

There are two important concepts I want to emphasize about this model. First, as we discussed, the details of what is happening at any particular level are completely independent of any other level. Second, the only communication that exists takes place between adjacent levels, using a well-defined interface.

For example, the window manager communicates only with X Window below and the display environment above. This is adequate because the window manager doesn't care about the details of anything that is happening on any other level. It lives only to respond to requests from the level above (the desktop environment) and, in turn, it calls upon the level below (X Window) to service its own requests.

HOW THE UNIX COMPANIES BLEW IT

When X Window was first developed, there were only window managers which, by today's standards, offered primitive GUIs. The idea that people might want a full-featured desktop environment developed over time, as programmers learned more about designing and implementing interfaces. Although there is no exact moment when window managers were replaced by desktop environments, here is more or less how it happened.

By 1990, the world of Unix was fragmented because there were a number of different Unix companies, each with its own type of Unix. In spite of promises to cooperate, there

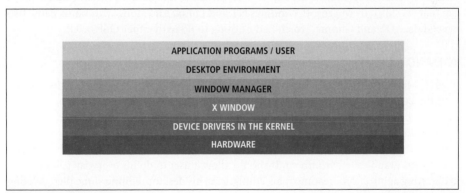

Figure 5-1: Layers of abstraction

Within Unix, a graphical working environment can be thought of as a system consisting of various levels of programs and hardware At the top level, we have our application programs (including utilities), as well as the user. One level down is the desktop environment. Below the desktop environment is the window manager, and so on. At the very bottom is the actual computer. Philosophically, we can think of the entire system as a means of bridging the gap between human hardware and computing hardware.

was a great deal of competitive sniping, and most companies were much more interested in dominating the marketplace than in working together. In the same way that young boys who fight in the playground will choose up sides, the Unix companies formed two umbrella organizations, each of which purported to be developing the one true Unix.

As we discussed in Chapter 2, by the mid-1980s, most types of Unix were based either on AT&T's UNIX or Berkeley's BSD or both. In October 1987, AT&T and Sun Microsystems announced their intention to work together on unifying UNIX and BSD once and for all. This upset the other Unix vendors and in May 1988, eight of them formed the OPEN SOFTWARE FOUNDATION (OSF) in order to develop their own "standard" Unix. The eight vendors included three of the most important Unix companies: DEC, IBM, and HP (Hewlett-Packard).

The formation of the OSF scared AT&T and Sun. They decided that, if they were to compete against OSF, they too needed their own organization. So in December 1989, they corralled a few smaller companies and formed UNIX INTERNATIONAL (UI).

Thus, by the early 1990s, there were two rival organizations, each of which was trying to create what it hoped would become the one true Unix. As part of their work, both OSF and UI developed their own window managers. OSF's was called **mwm** (Motif window manager), and UI's was called **olwm** (Open Look window manager). This meant that X Window users now had three popular choices for their window managers: **mwm**, **olwm**, and **twm** (which I mentioned earlier).

However, where **twm** was a plain vanilla window manager, both **mwm** and **olwm** were more complex and powerful. In fact, they were the ancestors of today's sophisticated desktop environments.

So, why aren't Motif and Open Look the most important GUIs today? The answer is that their sponsors, OSF and UI, spent so much time fighting that they lost their leadership in the Unix world. The details are incredibly boring, so I won't go into them*. What is important is that, by the mid-1990s, there was a big gap in the world of Unix, a gap that was filled by Microsoft Windows NT and Linux. And along with Linux came two new GUIs, KDE and Gnome, which had nothing to do with either OSF or UI.

KDE AND GNOME

In 1996, Matthias Ettrich, a German student at the University of Tübingen, was dissatisfied with the current state of Unix GUIs. On October 14, 1996, he sent out a Usenet posting in which he proposed to remedy the problem by starting a new project called the Kool Desktop Environment (KDE). (See Figure 5-2.)

Ettrich argued that the current window managers were deficient, that "a GUI should offer a complete, graphical environment. It should allow a user to do his everyday tasks with it, like starting applications, reading mail, configuring his desktop, editing some files, deleting some files, looking at some pictures, etc. All parts must fit together and work together."

---

* If you really want to know what happened, just go to a Unix programming conference, find an old person, and invite him for a drink. Once he gets settled in, ask him to tell you about the "Unix Wars".

If you are not sure whom to ask, just walk around the conference until you see someone with a ponytail and a faded Grateful Dead T-shirt.

Ettrich had noticed these deficiencies when he was configuring a Linux system for his girlfriend. He realized that, in spite of all his expertise, there was no way for him to put together a GUI that was integrated well and was easy for his girlfriend to use. He asked people to volunteer to work on KDE, promising that "one of the major goals is to provide a modern and common look & feel for all the applications." *

FIGURE 5-2: Matthias Ettrich, founder of the KDE project

Matthias Ettrich founded the KDE project in October, 1996. Eventually, KDE would become so successful that Ettrich can be considered the Father of the Desktop Environment.

---

* Presumably, Ettrich's girlfriend was not as technically inclined as he was, leading him to realize that the current GUIs, while tolerated by programmers, did not work well for regular people. Eventually, the KDE project inspired by Ettrich's experience would produce the very first integrated desktop environment, changing forever the way people thought about GUIs.

One can only wonder: If Ettrich's girlfriend had been, say, a tad less pretty and a tad more nerd-like, how long would it have taken to develop a true desktop environment? Since KDE would come to have a profound influence on the acceptance of Linux around the world, is this not, then, an argument that more of society's resources should be devoted to encouraging beautiful women to date programmers?

More specifically, Ettrich asked people to help create a control panel (with "nice" icons), a file manager, an email client, an easy-to-use text editor, a terminal program, an image viewer, a hypertext help system, system tools, games, documentation, and "lots of other small tools". Ettrich's invitation was answered by a variety of programmers, and the KDE project was formed.

One of Ettrich's major complaints was that none of the popular Unix applications worked alike or looked alike. The KDE programmers worked hard and, by early 1997, they were releasing large, important applications that worked together within an integrated desktop environment. In doing so, they produced a new, highly functional GUI that began to attract a great deal of interest.

Within a few months, however, a number of programmers within the Linux community began to voice concerns about KDE. Ettrich had chosen to build the new desktop environment using a programming toolkit called Qt. Qt had been written by a Norwegian company, Trolltech, which had licensed it in such a way that it was free for personal use, but not for commercial use.

To the KDE programmers, this was fine: from the beginning, they saw KDE as a non-commercial product. Other people, however, felt that Trolltech's licensing arrangement was not "free" enough. In particular, the programmers who were associated with the GNU project and the Free Software Foundation wanted a less restrictive license for KDE, either that, or an alternative to KDE that would be licensed under the GNU GPL. (See the discussion of free software in Chapter 2.)

In August 1997, two programmers, Miguel de Icaza and Federico Mena, started a project to create just such an alternative, which they called GNOME. Although KDE was already well-established, the Gnome project attracted a lot of attention and, within a year, there were about 200 programmers working on Gnome.

(You may remember that, earlier in the chapter, I mentioned two window managers, Metacity and **kwm**. At the time, I said that, out of the many window managers that are available, these two are important enough that I wanted you to know the names. The reason they are important is that Metacity is the window manager for Gnome, and **kwm** is the window manager for KDE.)

WHAT'S IN A NAME?

KDE, Gnome

The project to build KDE, the first X-based desktop environment, was started by a German university student, Matthias Ettrich. At the time Ettrich proposed the project, he suggested the name KDE, which would stand for Kool Desktop Environment. Later, however, this was changed to K Desktop Environment.

In the same way that X Window became X, the letter K is often used to stand for the KDE desktop environment. For example, within KDE, the native Web browser is called Konqueror; the CD ripper is KAudioCreator; the calculator program is called KCalc; and so on. In perhaps the most egregious use of the letter K, the KDE terminal emulator is called Konsole.

Within Gnome – and the GNU project in general – you see the same thing with the letter G. For example, the Photoshop-like program is called Gimp (GNU Image Manipulation Program); the instant messaging program is Gaim; and the calculator program is Gcalctool; and so on.

(continued...) The name Gnome stands for GNU Network Object Model Environment. "Gnome" is pronounced either "Guh-nome" or "Nome". In my experience, programming geeks pronounce GNU with a hard G ("Guh-new") and Gnome with a soft G ("Nome").

CDE AND TOTAL COST OF OWNERSHIP

By 1999, there were two popular, well-designed desktop environments: KDE and Gnome. Both GUIs enjoyed widespread support within the Linux community (and, to this day, they are used widely around the world).

In the meantime, the commercial Unix companies were still in business and, by now, they realized the importance of desktop environments. The Open Group organization I mentioned earlier had taken over development of the Motif window manager. In the early 1990s, they had started work on a new proprietary desktop environment – CDE (Common Desktop Environment) – based on Motif. After a large, multi-company effort, CDE was introduced in 1995. By 2000, CDE had become the GUI of choice for commercial Unix systems, such as AIX from IBM, HP/UX from HP, Unix from Novell, and Solaris from Sun.

You may wonder why there was a need for CDE? Why would so many computer companies pay to develop a proprietary product when both KDE and Gnome were available at no cost? On a larger scale, why was there a need for commercial Unix at all? After all, Linux was available for free and the licensing terms were liberal. Why didn't every company simply switch to Linux and use either KDE or Gnome?

The answer has to do with one of the fundamental differences between the commercial and consumer markets, and the principle is so important that I want to take a moment to explain it.

As consumers, you and I want two things out of our software. First, it should be inexpensive (free, if possible); second, it should work. We realize that when we have problems, we are on our own. We can read the documentation, we can look for help on the Internet, or we can ask someone else for help. If we get desperate we can pay someone to help us but, in most cases, there is no great urgency. If we have to wait for a solution, it is inconvenient but not devastating.

In a company, especially a large company, the situation is different. Even a simple software problem can affect hundreds or thousands of people. Waiting for a solution can be very expensive, both to the company and to its customers. Because large companies can't afford serious problems, they employ full-time computer personnel to maintain networks, servers, and personal computers. For this reason, when companies evaluate a product – software or hardware – they don't focus on initial cost. They look at what is called the TOTAL COST OF OWNERSHIP or TCO.

To calculate the total cost of ownership, a company must answer the question: If we decide to use this product, what is it going to cost us in the long run?

Calculating the TCO for something as complex and as fundamental as a desktop environment is not simple. For you or me, the initial cost is the only cost. If we can get KDE or Gnome for free, that's all we care about. Software problems can be bothersome but, as I said, it's more a matter of inconvenience than money.

A large company looks at it differently. Although they do evaluate the initial purchase cost or licensing fees, they also perform a more complicated, long-term analysis. The details of such calculation are beyond the scope of this book, but the ideas are important to understand, so I will give you a quick summary.

Before a company adopts a significant hardware or software system, their financial analysts look at what are called direct costs and indirect costs. The direct costs include both hardware and software: initial purchase or lease expenses, operations, tech support, and administration. The indirect costs have to do with lost productivity. They include the amount of time employees spend learning how to use the system; the amount of time some employees will lose because they are helping other employees (something that happens everywhere); and the cost of downtime due to failure and scheduled maintenance.

Once all these costs are estimated, they are converted to annual expenditures, a calculation that includes the depreciation and the cost of upgrades. The annual expenditures are then integrated into the company-wide budget, which is reconciled with the company's plan for long-term growth.

In most cases, when total cost of ownership for software or hardware is calculated, what we find is counter-intuitive: the initial costs are not that significant. In the long run, what counts the most are the ongoing expenditures and indirect costs.

Thus, when a company is thinking about adopting new software, they don't ask how much it costs to buy or license the product. They ask, how well will this software integrate into our existing environment? How does it fit into our long-term plans? How well does it serve our customers? How much will it cost to maintain on an ongoing basis?

Once these questions are answered, it becomes clear that, for *corporate use*, the best software is usually not free software that has been designed for individual or educational use. Business software must have features that are suitable for business. There must be a large family of well-maintained programming tools; there must be a well-defined, long-term development plan tailored to the needs of businesses, not individuals; most important, there must be excellent documentation and high-quality tech support. This is why most large businesses prefer to stick to commercial software. It is also why, in the corporate world, Linux has not replaced Microsoft Windows and probably never will.

This is not to say that large companies never use free software. They do when it makes sense to do so. For example, IBM offers not only their own version of Unix (AIX), but Linux as well. However, when a company like IBM offers an open source ("free") software product, they put a *lot* of money into it, supporting and enhancing that product. IBM, for example, has spent millions of dollars on Linux development and support. The truth is, for a large company, nothing is free.

To return to the desktop, you can see why, in the 1990s, it was so important for the corporate world to have its own desktop environment. Although both KDE and Gnome worked well, they didn't have the type of features and support that were needed by businesses.

That is why the Open Group was set up and why they developed CDE. And that is also why, at the end of the 1990s, CDE – not KDE or Gnome – was the desktop environment of choice for corporate users.

In the 2000s, as free software became more and more important, Unix companies started to offer their own versions of Linux as well as their own proprietary Unix. For example, IBM offers both AIX and Linux; Sun offers both Solaris and Linux; HP offers both HP-UX and Linux; and so on.

As you might expect, this also means that Unix companies also offer KDE and Gnome. For example, IBM offers their AIX users a choice of CDE, KDE and Gnome; Sun offers both CDE and Gnome; and HP offers both CDE and Gnome.

Of course, these versions of Linux, KDE and Gnome are not the same distributions that you or I would download for free from the Net with no support. They are commerical-quality products that come with commerical-quality tech support (at a price).

CHOOSING A DESKTOP ENVIRONMENT

When you use Unix, you get a strong feeling that the desktop environment is separate from the actual operating system. This is not the case with Windows or Mac OS, because Microsoft and Apple try hard to convince people that every important program that comes with the computer (including the browser, the file manager and the media player) is part of the operating system.

The truth is it isn't: it's just packaged that way. Because you are a Unix user, you can make the distinction between the operating system and everything else, which leaves you free to ask yourself, "What do I want on *my* desktop?"

Many companies and schools standardize on computer tools. If you work for one of these companies or go to one of these schools, you will have to use whichever desktop environment they tell you to use. However, if you are running Linux on your own computer – or if your organization gives you a choice – you will be able to decide for yourself what GUI to use.

So which desktop environment is best for you?

If you use Linux, there are many free desktop environments, so you have a lot of choice. (To see what I mean, just search on the Internet for "desktop environment".) However, virtually all Linux distributions come with either KDE or Gnome or both, and it is my advice that – unless you have a reason to choose otherwise – you start with one of these two GUIs. (See Figures 5-3 and 5-4. When you look at these pictures, please focus on the appearance and organization of the GUI – the windows, the icons, the toolbar, and so on – rather than on the content within the windows.)

So let's narrow down the question: With respect to KDE and Gnome, which one is right for a person like you?

To start, take a look at the following five statements. Mark each statement either True or False, with respect to your personal preferences. We will then evaluate your answers to choose the desktop environment that's best for you.

1. I would rather drive a car with manual transmission than a car with automatic transmission.

2. I am more comfortable in a home that is simple and organized than a home that is decorated and has comfortable clutter.

3. When I have a personal discussion with my girlfriend/boyfriend or wife/husband, it is important to me that we take the time to figure out who is right.

4. After I bought my DVD player, I read at least part of the manual.

5. When I use Microsoft Windows or a Macintosh, I generally leave things the way they are. I don't mess around with the colors, the backgrounds, and so on.

Before we interpret your answers, I want you to appreciate that all desktop environments are merely a way of using the same underlying computing environment. So no matter which desktop environment you pick, it will be fine. Having said that, you will be more comfortable using a desktop environment that is suited to your personality, so let's move on with the analysis.

Regardless of your technical skill or your interest in computers, if you answered True 3, 4 or 5 times, use Gnome; if you answered True 0, 1 or 2 times, use KDE.

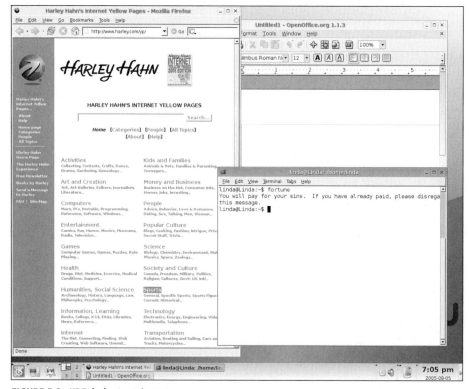

FIGURE 5-3: KDE desktop environment

The project to create KDE, the first real desktop environment, was started in 1996 by Matthias Ettrich. His goal was to create "a complete, graphical environment" in which "all parts fit together and work together".

Notice that I said that your choice should not depend on how much you know about computers. Some very technical people prefer KDE; others prefer Gnome. Similarly, many non-technical people choose KDE, while others like Gnome.

The dichotomy has more to do with how you see the world, rather than how much you know. Gnome people thrive on simplicity and order. They want things to be logical. If necessary, they are willing to put in as much effort as it takes to make something work in a way that makes sense to them.

A Gnome person would agree with the dictum "form ever follows function", an idea expressed by the American architect Louis Sullivan in 1896. Sullivan observed that the appearance of natural objects was influenced by their function. Gnome people want the world to behave in a rational way, and they prefer tools whose appearance directly reflects their purpose.

Whereas Gnome people like to control how things work, KDE people like to control how things *look*. This is because they care less about "being right" than they do about living in a way that makes them emotionally comfortable.

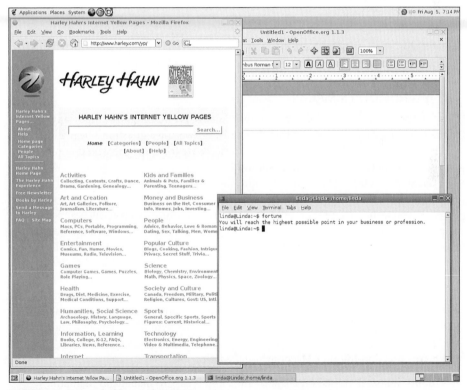

FIGURE 5-4: Gnome desktop environment

The Gnome project was started in 1997 by Miguel de Icaza and Federico Mena in order to create an alternative to KDE that would be distributed with more liberal licensing terms.

KDE people see the world as a place filled with color, variation and, at times, confusion. They are inclined to accept much of life as it is, rather than putting in a lot of effort to fix small details. When they feel motivated to spend time customizing their working environment, they tend to makes things that look nice and act nice.

Now, take another look at your answers to the true/false questions. Are you a KDE person or a Gnome person?

A question arises. We have two different desktop environments, each of which was created by its own group of people from around the world, working together. How could it be that there are personality traits that differentiate KDE people from Gnome people?

The answer lies in the genesis of each group. As we discussed earlier, the KDE group was started by people who were not satisfied with the status quo. They wanted to create a complete working environment that worked better and looked better than the window managers of the day.

The Gnome group was started by people who were dissatisfied with KDE because of an abstract legal problem related to licensing terms, a deficiency that – let's face it – most people would have ignored (as all the KDE people did). However, to a Gnome person – or, more precisely, to a Free Software Foundation-type of person – what's right is right and what isn't isn't, and that's all there is to it. (See the discussion of Richard Stallman in Chapter 2.)

Does it not make sense, then, that each group would create a desktop environment suitable for their type of person? Perhaps people who design consumer products (including software) should pay more attention to the KDE/Gnome dichotomy.

THE GRANDMOTHER MACHINE

Now that we have discussed the most important GUIs and the most important types of Linux (Chapter 2), I want to end this chapter by answering a question I hear a lot:

"I am putting together a system using free software for someone who doesn't know a lot about computers. What software should I use?"

I call such a computer the Grandmother Machine, because it is the type of machine you might create for your grandmother.

When you set up a Grandmother Machine, you must realize that you will bear permanent responsibility because, whenever your grandmother has a problem, she will call you. So you should use software that is dependable, easy to install, and easy to update. You also want a system that you can configure to make it easy for a beginner to access the Web, check email, and (in some cases) use word processing, spreadsheets, presentation graphics, and so on.

Here are my recommendations. When you read them, remember that conditions change over time. New software comes along and old software grows to become bloated and unusable. So concentrate on the general principles behind my choices, and not just the specific selections.

To create a Grandmother Machine, use the following:

- Ubuntu Linux: It's based on Debian Linux and is easy to install and maintain.

- Gnome: The Gnome desktop environment is simple to use, but robust enough that a beginner won't mess it up.

If the grandmother in question is a very KDE-like person, you can give her KDE. However, please stick with either Gnome or KDE. Regardless of your personal preferences, don't mess around with the less common desktop environments.

When you set up the GUI, be sure to take some time to make it as easy as possible for your grandmother to start her favorite applications. The best idea is to create a few icons on the control panel. (At the same time, you can remove the icons she will never use.)

- Firefox: The Firefox browser is easy to use and powerful. For email, get her a Web-based account (such as Google's Gmail) and let her use her browser to communicate.

  Firefox is wonderful, but do plan on taking some time to show your grandmother how to use it. In addition, plan on answering questions over the phone until she gets used to using the Web. (The best way to avoid unnecessary questions is to create a link to Google, and to show your grandmother how to use it. When you do, be sure to take a few moments to explain how to make sense out of the search results.)

- Open Office: A suite of free productivity software (word processor, a spreadsheet program, and so on), compatible with Microsoft Office.

One last piece of advice: I have a lot of experience helping people choose computer systems, and there is a general principle I have noticed that rarely gets mentioned.

When you choose a computer for someone, it doesn't work well to base your advice on what I might call their "hardware needs". What works best is to choose a system based on their psychological needs. This idea is so important that I will embody it in the form of a hint.

HINT

Harley Hahn's Rules for Helping Someone Choose a Computer

1. When you are choosing a computer for someone to use as their personal machine, choose a system that meets their psychological and emotional needs.

   In most cases, the person will not be able to articulate their needs, so you must figure them out for yourself. During this process, do not allow yourself to be sidetracked into long discussions of hardware specifications or other trivia.

2. When you choose a computer for someone who is working for a company, choose a system that is in harmony with the psychology of the person who will be approving the expenditure.

   Within a corporate environment, people come and go, so don't choose a system based on the needs of a particular user. Choose a system that suits the *company*.

   The best way to do this is to look for a computer that meets the psychological and emotional needs of the person writing the check, not the person who will be using the machine. This is especially true when you are dealing with a small business.

CHAPTER 5 EXERCISES

REVIEW QUESTIONS

1. When it comes to displaying information, there are, broadly speaking, two types of data. What are they?

2. What is the name of the system that supports most Unix graphical user interfaces (GUIs)? Where and when was it first developed? Name three important services it provides.

3. What are layers of abstraction? Name the six layers in a typical Unix GUI environment.

4. What is total cost of ownership? Who uses the concept and why? When total cost of ownership is calculated, how important are the initial costs?

5. What is a desktop environment? In the Linux world, what are the two most popular desktop environments?

FOR FURTHER THOUGHT

1. As a general rule, when using a GUI, windows are rectangular. Why is this? When might it make sense to use a round window?

2. You work for a large company that uses PCs running Windows. The company has standardized on Microsoft Office products (Word, Excel, Powerpoint, and so on). You are at a meeting where a young, newly graduated programmer proposes that the company change from Office to the free software alternative, Open Office. Why is this a bad idea? Does it bother you to recommend that the company stick with Microsoft products? If so, why?

C H A P T E R 6
THE UNIX WORK ENVIRONMENT

As I explained in Chapter 3, Unix was developed using a text-based interface. Later, as more sophisticated hardware became available, graphical interfaces were created. Although the Unix interfaces were based on hardware, they were created with more in mind than their appearance and basic function. They were designed to provide a complex working environment that is particularly well-suited to the human mind.

In this chapter, I'm going to show you how to use a combination of the text-based and graphical interfaces. My goal is to teach you enough so you can organize your work in a way that suits your thought processes and your temperament. Along the way, I'm going to cover other topics that are important to mastering the Unix work environment, such as how to copy and paste data, how to work as superuser, and how to shutdown and reboot your system.

Throughout this chapter, I will be building on ideas from Chapters 4 and 5. So before you continue reading, please make sure you are comfortable with the following concepts:

- From Chapter 4: userids, passwords, logging in and logging out, the shell prompt, upper- and lowercase letters, the system administrator, the superuser.

- From Chapter 5: GUIs, desktop environments.

As you read this chapter, a lot of what you have already learned will come together, as you start to use Unix in the way it was intended to be used.

DOING MORE THAN ONE THING AT A TIME: PART I

In Chapter 3, I explained that Unix systems are multitasking, which means they can run more than one program at the same time.

"Multitasking" is a technical term but, these days, it is fashionable to use the word to describe the type of mental processing that allows people to concentrate on more than one thing at a time. For example, one hears, "Women are better at multitasking than men," or, "It's okay if I talk on the phone while I drive, because I am good at multitasking."

The truth is neither computers nor human beings can actually perform two similar tasks at the same time. This realization has important implications when it comes to learning how to use the Unix interfaces so, before we move on, I'd like to take a moment to talk about multitasking. We'll start with computers.

Within a computer system, what looks like multitasking is, in reality, a very fast machine performing tasks so quickly that they look as if they are happening at the same time.

In Unix, instead of talking about programs executing, we talk about PROCESSES executing. A process is a program that is loaded into memory and ready to run, along with the program's data and the information needed to keep track of that program*.

At all times, Unix systems have many active processes, each of which requests processor time in order to run. (Although you may not be aware of it, there are processes running in the background.) However, a processor can execute only one process at a time. This means that a one-processor computer can honor only one request at a time. A multi-processor computer may be able to handle more than one request, but even then, it is not nearly enough to service all the processes at the same time.

To manage so many overlapping processor requests, Unix uses a system in which each process in turn is allowed to use the processor for a very short interval, called a TIME SLICE. A typical time slice would be 10 milliseconds (10 thousandths of a second).

Once the time slice is over, the current process is put on hold and a special service called the SCHEDULER decides which process to execute next. Because time slices are so short and processors are so fast, and because the Unix scheduler handles the whole thing so artfully, it looks to you and me as if Unix is doing more than one thing simultaneously. Thus, the illusion of multitasking is created.**

Now let's talk about humans. In certain circumstances, we can all do more than one thing at a time. For example, when we eat, we can smell, taste and chew at the same time. Similarly, we can talk while we walk, play an instrument while we sing, or listen to sound as we watch a movie. However, what we *can't* do is think about two things at the same time.

We can, of course, switch back and forth between mental activities and, if we do it fast enough, it looks as if the activities are happening at the same time. For example, say you are instant messaging with four different people. As long as you answer each person within a reasonable amount of time, they have no way of knowing that you are not talking to them exclusively.

This sounds a bit like what Unix does when it multitasks. However, there are important differences. First, compared to computers, human beings change from one task to another very slowly. (The next time you are instant messaging, try switching from one conversation to another every 10 milliseconds.)

Second, human minds are much more complex than computers†, and the type of tasks people carry out are much more complicated than what a computer does.

Third, as Unix switches from one process to another, it needs to keep track of only a small amount of information. When you change from one task to another, you need to

---

*The idea of a process is fundamental to Unix. Indeed, within a Unix system, every object is represented by either a file or a process. In simple terms, files hold data or allow access to resources; processes are programs that are executing.

Processes can be divided into smaller units called threads, a thread being a set of instructions that runs within the environment of a process. It is possible to structure programs so that, within a process, more than one thread can run at the same time.

In Chapter 26, we will talk more about processes and how to control them. For now, I'll tell you that if you want to see how many processes are active on your system right now, use the **top command. (Note: This command is not available on all systems.)

†The most complex piece of matter in the known universe is the human brain.

reorient yourself in a much more complicated manner. Consider, for example, what must be happening in your mind as you switch from using your Web browser, to checking your email, to answering the phone, to returning to your Web browser, to eating a jelly donut. Although you aren't consciously aware of your mental processes, they are much more complex than what Unix does as it juggles multiple processes. (Moreover, even the latest versions of Linux don't know what to do with a jelly donut.)

The biggest difference, however, between computers and humans is that we have free will. From moment to moment, we can think about whatever we want. This means that, as we use a computer, we form momentary strategies as to how we will do what needs to be done, and the operating system must support such strategies. Because there is no way of knowing in advance exactly how a person will think in a particular situation, an operating system must be flexible when it comes to providing a work environment.

Within reason, every computer user should be allowed to structure his work environment according to his needs. Moreover, he should be able to change that environment whenever he wants, from one moment to the next, as his mental processes evolve. What's more, as a user becomes more experienced, there should be more sophisticated tools for him to use.

For example, a beginner (or a dull person) will typically do only one thing at a time on his computer. He will expand one window to take up the entire screen, and he will control what is happening by using the mouse almost exclusively (and not the keyboard). As a result, he will be unable to carry out any but the simplest tasks.

An experienced person (especially one who is smart and creative) will use multiple windows, will use the keyboard as much as possible, and will structure his moment-to-moment work so that it moves quickly and efficiently. If you have ever watched someone work who is a master at using his computer, you know what I mean.

When people design user interfaces systems, they must take into account that, when it comes to thinking, humans have important limitations. For example, it is very difficult for us to remember much of what happens from one moment to the next* and, conventional wisdom notwithstanding, we are incapable of concentrating on two things at the same time.

What we *can* do is reorient ourselves within a fraction of a second as conditions change. This is why mothers can watch a toddler, hold the baby, talk on the phone, and cook dinner, all at the same time. (It is also why people *think* they can talk on the phone and drive safely at the same time.)

Our limited memory and our ability to reorient ourselves mean that a good user interface must allow us to juggle as many tasks as we want, and it should do so in such a way that we feel comfortable, once we are used to the interface.

Moreover, the user interface should be able to support our growth. That is, no matter how skillful we become, our interface should still be able to meet our demands.

It is my contention that the text-based and graphical interfaces that come with Unix are so well-designed and so flexible that, when they are combined well, they are able to meet all these demands and then some. For this reason, I want you to consider two important ideas as you read this chapter.

*Can you close your eyes and remember what you read ten seconds ago?

First, I want you to understand that what you are about to read is more than a mere description of how things work. The system I am about to show you has evolved by trial and error, and has been designed by some of the smartest people who have ever lived. The goal of this system is to overcome the limitations of both the computers and the humans who use them, in such a way that the human thinks that both he and the computer are actually multitasking.

Second, I want you to take some time to practice and master the interfaces you will meet in this chapter. The real power of Unix comes when you are able to combine the text-based interfaces with the graphical interfaces.

I believe that, overall, Unix has the best system of user interfaces that has ever existed (including Microsoft Windows and the Macintosh). By the time you finish this chapter, I expect you to agree with me.

THE GUI AND THE CLI

From time to time, I have referred to two different Unix interfaces, text-based and graphical. The time has come to give them formal names.

The graphical interface is, of course, the GUI (graphical user interface) we discussed at length in Chapter 3. Unix GUIs are created by a combination of X Window, a window manager and a desktop environment.

The text-based interface is usually referred to as the COMMAND LINE INTERFACE (CLI). Here is why.

As you know from Chapter 4, the basic Unix text-based interface is simple. The shell (command processor) displays a prompt. You type a command. The shell does what's necessary to carry out the command. Once the command has been processed, the shell displays another prompt, you type another command, and so on.

The entire process uses only text (plain characters), and the line on which you type your commands is called the COMMAND LINE. Thus, we have the name "command line interface".

I want you to know the term CLI, because it is the counterpart of GUI, and you will see it a lot in your reading, especially on the Internet. However, when people talk, they don't say CLI; they say "command line". For example, you might read the following on a Web site: "Although the Groatcake Software Package was designed for a GUI, there is also a CLI version."

When people talk about interfaces in person, however, you are more likely to hear, "I started with the GUI version of the Groatcake Software Package, but now I prefer using the command line version." Even more common would be, "I prefer to use the Groatcake Software Package from the command line."

In other words, when you read or hear "command line" or when you read "CLI", it tells you that someone is typing a command, not selecting a choice from a menu.

GUI programs are important. For example, just about everyone uses the GUI programs for Web browsers and office software, so I expect that you too will spend a lot of time using your GUI.

However, most of the power of Unix lies with the command line, because it provides a fast and simple way to use the hundreds of different Unix commands. Indeed, once we leave this chapter, we will be concentrating on using command line programs for the rest of the book.

> **HINT**
>
> As a Unix user, the basic skill you need is the ability to solve problems by using the command line to enter one command after another.

LOGGING IN AND LOGGING OUT WITH A GUI

In Chapter 4, we discussed what happens when you log in with a traditional Unix text-based system. You see the prompt **login:** and you type your userid. You then see the prompt **Password:** and you type your password. The system completes the login process, starts your shell, and leaves you at the shell prompt. When you are finished, you log out.

With a GUI, it's more complicated. I'll explain what happens with Linux. If you are using another type of Unix, things may be a bit different, but you should be able to figure it out.

After you turn on the computer, Linux will start. When the system is ready for you to log in, you will see a login screen. The exact appearance varies depending on what Linux distribution you are using. However, most distributions will show you the same basic elements.

First you will see a small box with the label "Username:". This box corresponds to the **login:** prompt. You are being asked to enter your userid.

Before you enter your userid, take a moment to look around. You will see several other choices: Language, Session, Reboot and Shutdown. To select a choice, you can either click on it with your mouse or press what is called an ACCELERATOR key.

To figure out what the accelerator key is for a particular choice, look carefully at the word. One letter will be underlined. To select that choice, hold down the <Alt> key and press that letter. For example, let's say that, in the word "Session", the letter "S" is underlined. This means that the accelerator key for Session is <Alt-S>.

> **HINT**
>
> Accelerator keys are a standard feature of GUIs, and you will find them on many menus and dialog boxes. For example, within most GUI-based programs, you can display the File menu by pressing <Alt-F>, the Edit menu by pressing <Alt-E>, the Help menu by pressing <Alt-H>, and so on.
>
> Do take time to look for accelerator keys, as they can make your work easier. You will find that, when you want to make a selection, it is a lot easier to press a simple key combination than it is to take one hand off the keyboard to move your mouse and click a button.

To return to the login screen, the four choices are used as follows:

- Language: To change the language that Linux will use for this particular work session.

- Session: To select what type of work session you want.

Normally, you would not have to change either the language or type of session, because the default will be what you want.

- Reboot: To reboot the computer.
- Shutdown: To shutdown the computer.

Once you enter your userid, you will be prompted to enter your password. Linux will then proceed with the login process and start your desktop environment.

When you are finished working, you log out by selecting the "Logout" item from the main menu. You will then be asked to confirm that you want to end your work session. (Depending on what desktop environment you are using, you may also be given a choice to shutdown or restart the computer.)

Once you confirm that you want to log out, Linux will terminate your desktop environment and return you to the login screen. At this point, you can either log in again or select Reboot or Shutdown.

RUNLEVELS

You now know that Unix can boot as either a GUI-based system or as a CLI-system. Before we continue our discussion of interfaces, I'd like to take a few minutes to explain to you how Unix can offer such flexibility. The concepts are not only interesting, but they will also show you a lot about the type of thinking and organization that makes Unix such a good operating system.

When a computer system, a program or a device can be in one of several states, we use the term MODE to refer to a particular state. For example, we might say that you can use Unix either in text mode (with a CLI) or in graphics mode (with a GUI).

The concept of modes is so basic to computing that computer people often use the term whimsically to refer to states of mind. For instance, one programmer might tell another, "Sorry I didn't come to visit you yesterday. I was in cleaning mode, and I spent all afternoon vacuuming the house."

The reason I mention this idea is because Unix was designed to be flexible when it boots. This is done by having the capability of running Unix in one of several different modes. These modes are called RUNTIME LEVELS or, more simply, RUNLEVELS.

The strict definition of a runlevel is somewhat technical: a runlevel is a system software configuration that allows a specified group of processes to exist. This is a tough definition, so let's be a bit more informal. A runlevel specifies which fundamental services Unix will provide. At different runlevels, Unix provides different sets of services*.

Each time a Unix system boots, it goes through a complex process and, as part of that process, the runlevel is set. Setting the runlevel controls the mode in which Unix will run. Figure 6-1 shows the runlevels that are used with most Linux distributions.

* The runlevel system that is used in Linux was originally introduced in System V. Within the BSD world (including FreeBSD), runlevels are not used. Instead, the system boots into either single-user mode or multiuser mode. Thus, the discussion of runlevels in this chapter applies to Linux, but not to FreeBSD. (For information about System V and BSD, see Chapter 2.)

In most cases, Linux will boot, by default, into either runlevel 3 or runlevel 5. If your system is set to boot into runlevel 3, you will see a text-based login screen, and you will log in and log out in the manner we discussed in Chapter 4. Once you log in, you will work with a basic CLI.

If your system boots into runlevel 5, Linux will start your default GUI. You will log in using a graphical login screen (as I described earlier in the chapter), and you will work with a desktop environment.

Most people want to use a desktop environment so runlevel 5 is the default. However, when a system administrator needs to solve a problem with a server – such as a Web server or mail server – he will usually want runlevel 3, because the CLI allows him to do what he wants quickly and easily. (Most system administration is done by typing commands, not by making selections from menus.) For this reason, desktop systems are usually set to boot into runlevel 5, and servers are set to boot into runlevel 3.

Runlevel 1 is a holdover from the old days, when most Unix systems were shared by a number of users and managed by a system administrator. From time to time, the admin would have to do some work that required that no one else be logged in to the system. In other words, for a short period of time, the admin would have to turn a multiuser user system into a single-user system.

To do this, the admin would send a notice to all the users that the system would be going down in, say, 5 minutes. When the interval had passed, he would reboot Unix into what, today, is runlevel 1. This would place the system in what used to be called SYSTEM MAINTENANCE MODE and is now called SINGLE USER MODE. The admin could now do his work, knowing that no one else would be able to log in. Once his work was finished, he would reboot into multiuser mode (runlevel 3 or 5), and the users would, once again, be allowed to log in to the system.

Today, runlevel 1 is not used much. This is because modern Unix systems are so flexible that admins can do a lot of work – even upgrades and maintenance – while other users are logged in. (This was not true in the old days.) The only times admins need to boot the system into runlevel 1 occur when there are very serious problems, such as when a hard disk becomes corrupted.

RUNLEVEL	DESCRIPTION
0	Halt (Shutdown)
1	Single-user mode: command line
2	Not standardized
3	Multiuser mode: command line
4	Not standardized
5	Multiuser mode: GUI
6	Reboot

FIGURE 6-1: Typical Linux runlevels

TECHNICAL HINT

If you would rather use the basic CLI rather than a GUI (as many people do), you can change your system so that by default it boots to runlevel 3 instead of runlevel 5. If you use a computer at a company or school, just ask your system administrator* to make the change for you.

If you maintain your own computer, you'll have to do it yourself. I won't go into the details, as they lie beyond the scope of the book, but I'll give you the general idea.

First, make the system boot automatically to runlevel 3 by changing the value of `initdefault` to **3** in the `/etc/inittab` file. Then examine the symbolic links in the `rc3.d` directory, and make sure the GUI is not started automatically for this runlevel.

Hint: If you are using a CLI at runlevel 3 and you want to start the GUI, you can use the `startx` command.

Before we leave this section, here are two questions to ponder. However, let me warn you, don't actually make the changes I am about to describe, or you will be sorry. Just think about them.

1. What would happen if you set the value of `initdefault` to **0** (Halt)?
2. Would would happen if you set it to **6** (Reboot)?

DOES MICROSOFT WINDOWS HAVE RUNLEVELS?

Because so many people use Microsoft Windows, it is instructive to compare it to Unix and ask: Does Windows have runlevels? (If you don't care about Windows, just skip this section.)

There are two answers to this question. First, Windows does have boot options that look like runlevels, but really aren't. Second, Windows has a facility that does offer runlevels, but it is hidden so well hardly anyone knows it exists.

To begin, Windows has a special startup menu that you can display as the system initializes. (With Windows XP, hold down <F8> as the system starts.) The menu is called the Windows Advanced Options Menu, and it gives you a number of different choices, which you can see in Figure 6-2.

These choices do allow Windows to boot into different modes. However, unlike Unix runlevels, the Windows startup options are not configurable, and they do not offer a great deal of flexibility. To get very technical for a moment, the Windows boot modes are more like Unix kernel boot options than runlevels. (If this makes no sense to you, don't worry about it.)

Still, Windows does have a system that can work the same way as runlevels, in that you can decide which system services you want to run. It is possible to create what are called "hardware profiles". (Right-click on "My Computer", and select "Properties". Click on the "Hardware" tab, and then click on the "Hardware Profiles" button.)

Hardware profiles were intended to let you boot a computer using different sets of devices. For example, with a laptop computer, you may want different hardware configurations when the machine is docked than when you are using it on its own.

This much is common knowledge (at least among the type of people who care about stuff like this). What is less well known is that, once you have created a hardware profile,

---

* "Real admins understand runlevels." ~Stephanie Lockwood-Childs

STARTUP OPTIONS FOR MICROSOFT WINDOWS
Safe Mode
Safe Mode with Networking
Safe Mode with Command Prompt
Enable Boot Logging
Enable VGA Mode
Last Known Good Configuration
Debugging Mode
Start Windows Normally

FIGURE 6-2: Windows XP Pro: Startup options

you can choose which system services you want enabled and disabled for that profile. This is very similar to Unix runlevels.

Seeing as this is not a Windows book, I won't go into the details. However, if you are interested in exploring on your own, here's what to do with Windows XP Professional.

Start by creating one or more hardware profiles. Then, from the Control Panel, click on "Administrative Tools", and then "Services". Right-click on any service, select "Properties", and then click on the "Log On" tab. You will now be able to enable or disable this service for the various hardware profiles.

An example of when you might want to do this would be if you have a special hardware profile for a laptop when it is not connected to a network. In such a situation, you would want to disable all the network-related services.

LEARNING TO USE A GUI

My guess is that, even if you have never used Unix, you have some experience with GUIs, either with Microsoft Windows or with a Macintosh. However, before we discuss how to integrate the Unix GUI and CLI in your work, I want you to be completely comfortable with the basic concepts, so I'm going to take a few minutes to discuss the most important ideas.

Learning to use a graphical user interface is easy. Learning to use it well is not so easy. So even if you are a veteran GUI user, do take a few moments to skim this part of the chapter. I bet you'll find something you don't know.

Although the various desktop environments have a lot of commonality, there are small but important differences, and it is difficult to write down a single set of instructions that will work for all the different interfaces. In addition, virtually every part of a GUI can be customized. The first time you use a particular GUI, you will find that the default settings look and act in a specific way. Once you become a veteran user, you should take some time to customize your system according to your own needs and preferences.

In the following three sections, I will discuss the basic ideas that you must understand to use a GUI. This will be enough to get you started. After you have finished reading, please set aside some time to read the built-in help that comes with your specific desktop environment. In particular, look for a list of the shortcut keys. Learning how to use them well is the single most important thing you can do to master any GUI.

In Chapter 5, I have already covered the first few important ideas:

• A GUI allows you to work with windows.

• A window is a bounded area of the screen, usually a rectangle.

• Windows can overlap.

• As the need arises, you can change the size of a window, or move it from one part of the screen to another.

Let's move on.

OF MICE AND MENUS

On your screen will be a small, movable image called a POINTER. You use a pointing device, usually a mouse, to move the pointer around the screen. The shape of the pointer may change, depending on what you are doing and where it is on the screen.

To initiate an action, you move the pointer to a specific position on the screen and then press a button. Your mouse may have either one, two or three buttons. X Window is designed to work with a 3-button mouse, which means – as a general rule – that Unix desktop environments use a 3-button mouse. These buttons are referred to as the LEFT, MIDDLE and RIGHT BUTTONS.

HINT

Unix GUIS are designed to work with a 3-button mouse. If your mouse only has two buttons, you simulate the middle button by pressing the left and right buttons at the same time. (Pressing two mouse buttons at the same time is called CHORDING.) Alternatively, if your mouse has a scroll wheel, pressing the wheel may simulate the middle button.

For Macintosh users: If you are using OS X with a one-button mouse, you simulate a right-click by using Control-Click, and you simulate a middle-click by using Option-Click.

That is, to right-click, hold down the <Control> key and click the mouse button. To middle-click, hold down the <Option> key and click the mouse button.

There are only two things you can do with a mouse button: click or hold.

When you press it and let go, we say that you CLICK the button. If you press the button twice in rapid succession, we say that you DOUBLE-CLICK. On rare occasions, you may have to TRIPLE-CLICK, that is, press a button three times quickly.

When you click the left button, we say that you LEFT-CLICK. This is the most common type of click. Similarly, you can RIGHT-CLICK (less common) and MIDDLE-CLICK (least common).

When you see the word "click" by itself, it always means left-click. For example, you might read, "To pull down the Groatcakes Menu, click on the icon of a groatcake."

This means to left-click on the icon of a groatcake. (An ICON is a tiny picture that represents something.)

Aside from clicking, you can press a button and HOLD it. Most of the time, you hold down a button when you want to move something. For example, to move a window, you position the pointer onto the TITLE BAR (the horizontal area at the top of the window that has the name of the program). Hold down the left button and move the mouse. The window will follow your movement. Once the window is where you want it, release the mouse button.

When we move an object in this way, we say that we DRAG it. Thus, we can say that to move a window, you drag its title bar to a new location.

Much of the time, you make choices by selecting an item from a list called a MENU. There are two types of menus: pull-down menus (more common) and pop-up menus (less common).

A PULL-DOWN menu is a menu that appears when you click on a particular word or icon. For example, most windows have a horizontal list of words near the top of the window (the MENU BAR). If you move the pointer to one of these words and click, a list of related items will appear below the word. You can then select an item from the list.

The most important pull-down menu is the WINDOW OPERATION MENU, which you will find in virtually every window. To display the Window Operation menu, click on the tiny icon at the top-left of the window (at the left edge of the title bar). Doing so will display a list of actions that pertain to the window itself, the most important of which are: Move, Resize, Minimize, Maximize and Close. You can see this in Figures 6-3 (KDE) and 6-4 (Gnome).

HINT

As I mentioned earlier in the chapter, you can also pull down a menu by pressing its accelerator key. For example, you can pull down the File menu by pressing <Alt-F>.

Using accelerator keys saves you the trouble of taking your hand off the keyboard in order to move the mouse and click a button.

Whenever you pull down a menu, take a careful look at the choices. Some of them will have the name of a key or a key combination next to them. These are called SHORTCUT KEYS. By pressing the shortcut key, you can select the particular actions without having to go to the trouble of pulling down the menu.

A few shortcut keys are standardized – that is, they are the same for all windows within most GUIs – and are worth memorizing. The most important such shortcut key is <Alt-F4>. Pressing it will close the current window.

Make sure you memorize <Alt-F4>. Using it will make your work with a desktop environment a lot smoother. If you don't learn to use it, every time you want to close a window, you have to use the mouse, which is awkward and slow. Personally, I use <Alt-F4> many times a day.

The second type of menu, the POP-UP MENU, appears out of nowhere after some action has occurred, often a right-click. By convention, right-clicking on an item will display what is called a CONTEXT MENU, that is, a group of actions that relate to the item itself. To try this for yourself, position your pointer over anything you want – for example, within a window that contains a program – right-click and see what happens.

RESIZING, MINIMIZING, MAXIMIZING AND CLOSING WINDOWS

It is possible to change the size of the windows you are using to suit your minute-to-minute preferences. When you do this, we say that you RESIZE the window. The details can vary from one GUI to another. However, there are two standard methods.

First, you can use your mouse to change the borders of a window. Move the pointer to the border you want to change. Then hold down the left button and drag the border to a new location. You can also start with the pointer at a corner of the window. Dragging the corner changes two adjacent sides at the same time. (Try it.)

Second, you can use the keyboard to move the borders of the window. Pull down the Window Operation menu and select "Resize". You can then use the arrow keys (<Left>, <Right>, <Up> and <Down>) to change the size of the window. (Many people don't know about this feature.)

Similarly, you can move a window by selecting "Move" from the Window Operation menu, and then using the arrow keys to move the window however you want. When you are finished, press <Return> (or <Enter>).

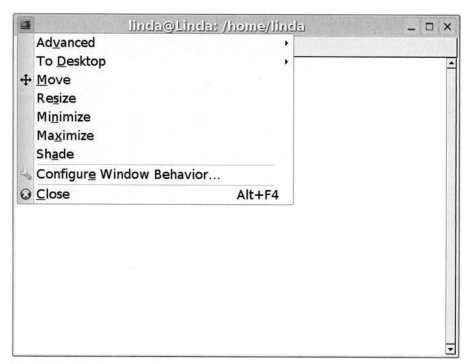

FIGURE 6-3: KDE window operation menu

The Window Operation menu displays a list of actions pertaining to the current window. This is the KDE version of that menu.

Aside from changing the size of a window or moving it, there will be times when you want the window to vanish temporarily. You don't want to close the window (which would stop the program). You just want it out of the way until you need it.

In such cases, you MINIMIZE or ICONIFY the window. This causes it to vanish from the main part of the screen. At the same time, a small representation of the window (an icon) appears on the TASKBAR, the horizontal bar at the bottom of the screen.

When a window is minimized, the program inside the window keeps running. So, for example, you might have seven windows, four of which are open, and three of which are minimized to the taskbar. However, even though only four windows are visible, all seven programs are still running.

Once a window is minimized, you can expand the window back to its original size and position whenever you want. When you do, we say that you RESTORE the window.

I'll tell you how to minimize and restore in a moment. Before I do, I want to mention two more things you can do with a window. First, you can CLOSE a window permanently, which stops the program running in the window and makes the window disappear.

Second, you can MAXIMIZE a window, which expands it to take up the entire screen. This is handy when you want to concentrate on only one task. Maximizing the window allows you to concentrate on that task without being visually distracted by other windows.

So, how do you minimize, restore, close and maximize windows? There are several ways. Before I explain, I want to take a moment to discuss what I call the "window controls".

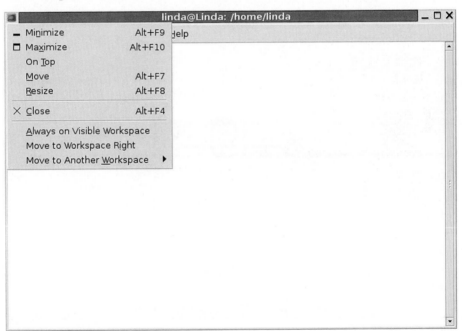

FIGURE 6-4: Gnome window operation menu

The Window Operation menu displays a list of actions pertaining to the current window. This is the Gnome version of that menu.

If you look at the top right-hand corner of a window, you can see three small boxes (see Figure 6-5). From right to left, there is a CLOSE BUTTON (it looks like an "X"), a MAXIMIZE BUTTON (a small rectangle) and a MINIMIZE BUTTON (an underscore). The use of these buttons is straightforward:

- Click on the Minimize Button to minimize the window to the taskbar.

- Click on the Close Button to close the window and stop the program running in the window. (This is the same as pressing <Alt-F4>.)

- Click on the Maximize Button to maximize the window. This enlarges the window to take up the entire screen (although you will still see the taskbar).

However, you don't have to click on these buttons. There is an alternative that you may prefer: you can select the same actions from the Window Operation menu. Display the menu by clicking on the small icon in the top-left corner of the window and select either "Minimize", "Maximize" or "Close".

Once a program is minimized to the taskbar, you can restore it by clicking on the representation of the window in the task bar. This will cause the window to be expanded back to its original size and position.

FIGURE 6-5: Window controls

In the top-right of most windows, you will see three window controls. The right control ("X") closes the window; the middle control (the rectangle) maximizes the window; the left control (the underscore) minimizes the window to the taskbar.

FIGURE 6-6: Window controls showing the Unmaximize Button

When a window is maximized, the Maximize Button changes into an Unmaximize Button. Here we see three window controls. The right control ("X") closes the window; the middle control (the overlapping rectangles) unmaximizes the window; the left control (the underscore) minimizes the window to the taskbar.

When you maximize a window, it expands to fill the entire screen. When this happens, the middle of the three window control buttons changes from a maximize button to an UNMAXIMIZE BUTTON. (See Figure 6-6.) To change the window back to its original size and location, simply click on this button. Alternatively, you can pull down the window operation menu and select the appropriate action.

CONTROLLING THE FOCUS: TASK SWITCHING

With a GUI, you can have as many windows as you want, each of which contains its own program. However, when you type on the keyboard, or click, or hold down a mouse button, the input will go to only one specific window. The window to which your input goes is said to have the FOCUS and is called the ACTIVE WINDOW. The window that has the focus is highlighted in some way. Typically, its title bar will be a different color than the other windows. (See Figure 6-7 later in the chapter.)

From one moment to the next, you can change which window has the focus, according to your needs. For example, over the course of a few minutes, you might change from a Web browser, to an email program, to a word processor, and back to the browser.

There are several ways to change the focus. First, if the window is open, just click on it. Alternatively, you can click on the name of the window in the taskbar.

In either case, the focus will be brought to the window you select, and the keyboard will be connected to the program that is running in that window. In addition, if the window is partially obscured by another window, the window with the focus will be redrawn to be on top and will become completely visible.

Another way to change the active window is to use what is called TASK SWITCHING. Each program that is running in a window is called a TASK. To see all the tasks that are currently running, just look at the task bar (usually at the bottom of the screen). Each task will have its own small button. As I mentioned, if you click on one of these buttons, it sends the focus to that window.

This works fine, but there is an easier way. Pressing <Alt-Tab> allows you to switch from one task to another without having to take your hands away from the keyboard.

When you press <Alt-Tab>, your GUI will highlight a specific task. (You will see small pictures in the center of your screen. It will be obvious.) Press <Alt-Tab> again and the next task is highlighted.

All you have to do is hold down the <Alt> key, and keep pressing <Tab> until you get to the task you want. Release the keys and the window for that task will be given the focus.

HINT

To switch from one task to another, press <Alt-Tab> repeatedly. At first, this can be a bit slow, so here is a trick.

Hold down the left <Alt> keys with your left thumb. Without letting go, press the <Tab> key repeatedly with the middle finger of your left hand. (Take a moment to try it now.)

To cycle through the tasks in the opposite order, simply press <Alt-Shift-Tab> instead of <Alt-Tab>. (Give it a try.)

Do take a few moments and master the <Alt-Tab> and <Alt-Shift-Tab> key combinations. Not only will they speed up your task switching, but they are so handy that they will change the way you organize your work environment.

MULTIPLE DESKTOPS / WORKSPACES

When you are using a GUI, the basic space in which you work is called your DESKTOP. As we discussed in Chapter 5, the name is a metaphor. As such you can imagine your windows open on the desktop like pieces of paper on a real desk.

The desktop metaphor runs out of steam quickly, so we won't push it. Instead, I want you to consider your desktop as an abstract environment in which you can organize your work. The desktop has characteristics that reach well beyond the physical reality of the screen. Understanding those characteristics is crucial if you are to master the Unix working environment*.

---

*In the *Yoga Sutras*, written about 2,000 years ago, the ancient sage Patañjali addresses this very concept. In Book II, Verse 21, he writes (in the original Sanskrit): *Tadartthah eva drsyasya atma*.

This can be translated as "The nature and intelligence of the Unix desktop exist solely to serve the user's true purpose, emancipation."

The most important idea is that you can have more than one desktop, each of which has its own background, its own windows, its own taskbar, and so on. Switching from one desktop to another is easy and, when you do, it feels as if you are switching to a totally new system.

WHAT'S IN A NAME?

Desktop, Workspace

Within a GUI, the desktop is the basic working environment. The desktop contains the background, the windows, the task bar, and so on.

Most desktop environments allow you to use multiple desktops. This has the advantage of being able to create what look and feel like multiple graphical work environments.

The name "desktop", however, can be confusing, because it is often used to refer to the desktop environment itself, that is, the GUI as a whole. For this reason, you will often see desktops referred to as WORKSPACES, which makes a lot more sense.

For example, when you work with KDE, you use "desktops". When you work with Gnome, you use "workspaces". Regardless of what they are called, they are the same thing and, minor details aside, work the same way.

There are two ways to switch from one desktop/workspace to another. You can use your mouse or your keyboard.

To use your mouse, look at the bottom of the screen near the taskbar. You will see a set of small squares, one for each desktop. For example, if you have four desktops, there will be four squares. You can see this in Figure 6-7 (later in the chapter). To change to a desktop, just click on its square. Although this sounds a bit vague, it's easy once you get the hang of it. Just experiment a bit.

To use your keyboard to switch from one desktop to another, there are shortcut keys. These keys can vary from one desktop environment to another, so the best thing is to check the documentation under "Shortcut Keys". (Look for a Help icon.)

With KDE, the desktop shortcut keys are <Ctrl-Tab> and <Ctrl-Shift-Tab>.

With Gnome, they are <Ctrl-Alt-Left>, <Ctrl-Alt-Right>, <Ctrl-Alt-Up> and <Ctrl-Alt-Down>. (That is, hold down <Ctrl> and <Alt> and press an arrow key.)

Using the desktop shortcut keys is so simple that you will probably master it quickly and never have to use your mouse to switch from one desktop to another.

As a general rule, desktop environments offer four different desktops by default. However, it is possible to add more if you want. To do so, right-click on one of the small desktop squares at the bottom of the screen. This will pop up a context menu. Look for a menu item like "Preferences" or "Desktop Configuration".

Before we leave this section, I want to bring up an idea that we will revisit at the end of the chapter. So far, I have shown you how the Unix work environment makes it possible to do more than one thing at the same time. Within each desktop, you can open multiple windows, each of which runs a separate program. You can have multiple desktops, each of which has its own set of windows. Moreover, using shortcut keys, it is easy to move from one desktop to another and, within a desktop, from one window to another.

What I want you to think about is, given all these resources, what is the best way for you to organize your work? As you will come to see, how you answer this question is very important to your total Unix experience.

HINT

As you organize your work, you can move a window from one desktop to another.

Right-click on the window's title bar. This will pop up a menu that will let you move the window to the desktop of your choice.

TERMINAL WINDOWS

In Chapter 3, we talked about terminals, and how they were used in the old days to access multiuser Unix systems using a CLI or command line interface. We discussed how, today, we don't use actual terminals. Instead, we run a program that emulates (acts like) a terminal. When we run such a program under a GUI, the program emulates an X terminal (the graphics terminal we discussed at the end of Chapter 3).

As I have explained, most of the power of Unix lies in using the CLI. This means that most of what you will be doing as you read this book is entering commands at the shell prompt, one command after another, as well as working with text-based programs. In order to do this, you will need access to a terminal.

Obviously, we don't use real terminals. Instead, we use terminal emulators. So the question arises, how do we access a terminal emulator?

With modern Unix systems, there are two ways, both of which are important. We'll discuss one now (terminal windows) and the other (virtual consoles) in the next section.

Within your desktop environment, all your work is done within windows, so it only makes sense that you would run a terminal emulation program within a window.

Doing so is easy. All desktop environments come with a simple way to start a terminal program. Just open the main menu and look for it. Within Gnome, for example, if you look in the System Tools submenu, you will see "Terminal". Within KDE, if you look at the System submenu, you will find two such programs: "Terminal" and "Konsole". (I'll explain why there are two in a moment.)

When you start such a program, a window will appear on your screen. Within that window, you have a standard CLI. As an example, take a look at Figure 6-7, where you will see two terminal windows.

As you remember from Chapter 4, the shell is the command processor. It displays a prompt and waits for you to enter a command. It then processes the command. When the command is done, the shell displays another prompt, and waits for the next command.

In our example, at the first shell prompt, I entered the **date** command (to display the current time and date). The shell processed this command, and then displayed another prompt.

Since the terminal emulator runs in a window, and since you can have as many windows as you want, you can have multiple terminals running at the same time. Although you may wonder why you would want to do so, the time will come – once you are an experienced

Unix user – when it will be commonplace for you to have a variety of command-line programs working for you at the same time, each one in its own terminal window.

HINT

Most desktop environments have a collection of icons that allow you to start frequently used programs. (You will find these icons at either the top or bottom of your screen.) If you right-click in this area, you will see a pop-up menu that will allow you to add and delete programs by creating an icon for them.

My suggestion is to add your favorite terminal program. That way you can open a new terminal window whenever you want, just by clicking on an icon.

This is so important that I suggest you take a moment and do it now. At the same time, you can reduce the clutter by deleting the icons for programs that you won't be using.

As I mentioned earlier, KDE gives you a choice of two terminal programs. Actually, the need to emulate a terminal has been around for so long that there are many different terminal programs, and most desktop environments give you a choice as to which one you want to use.

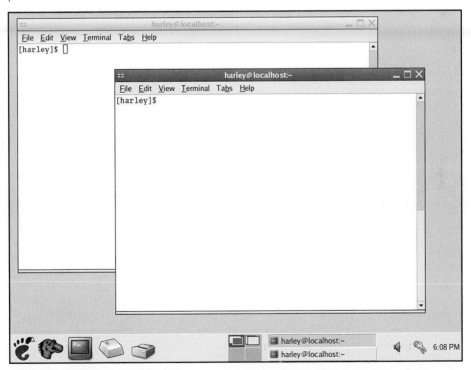

FIGURE 6-7: Multiple terminal windows

Within your desktop environment, you can open as many terminal windows as you want. Inside a terminal window, you enter commands using the standard Unix CLI (command line interface). In this example, there are two open terminal windows. The active window, with the focus, has the darker title bar.

Some desktop environments let you choose the terminal program you want directly from the menu. (This is the case with KDE, which is why you see two choices.) Other desktop environments have only one Terminal item in the menu, but you can change it to refer to whichever terminal program you want. (This is the case with Gnome.) To see the choices, right-click on Terminal item and select "Properties".

So which terminal program should you use? Strictly speaking, it doesn't really matter all that much, because all terminal programs offer the same basic functionality: providing a CLI within a window. However, if you want to get fancy, the Konsole program is a particularly good one, in that it has a number of useful features not found in other terminal programs.

For example, you can run multiple CLI sessions in the same window, each session having its own tab. You can then switch from one session to another by clicking on a tab or by using the shortcut keys <Shift-Right> and <Shift-Left>. (That is, hold down the <Shift> key and press the right-arrow key or the left-arrow key.) You will find these keys particularly handy.

My advice is to use Konsole if it is available on your system. It is a common program and it may be installed on your computer even if you are not using KDE. Once you start using Konsole, do take some time to read the built-in help. It's easy to understand, and doing so will help you a lot.

WHAT'S IN A NAME?

xterm, xvt, Konsole

When X Window was first developed, it came with a terminal program named **xterm**, which emulated the VAXstation 100 (VS100) graphics terminal. (See Chapter 3 for a discussion of graphics terminals.) The original version of **xterm** was developed in the summer of 1984 by Mark Vandevoorde, a student at MIT.

(Interestingly enough, Vandevoorde developed **xterm** as a standalone terminal emulator: it had nothing to do with X. Within a short time, however, **xterm** was recast and ported to the new X Window system, where it has lived ever since. For this reason, it made sense to keep the name **xterm** for the X Window terminal.)

The modern version of **xterm** can emulate both a character-based terminal (the old DEC VT-102, very similar to a VT-100) and a graphics terminal (the Tektronix 4014). For a long time, **xterm** was the main terminal program available with X.

In 1992, John Bovey of the University of Kent, wrote **xvt**, a new terminal emulator to replace **xterm**. Although **xvt** was more or less compatible with **xterm**, the new program was faster and required less memory (a big deal in those days). One reason was that it was only a basic VT-100 emulator; it did not include Tektronix 4014 support. (Thus, the name **xvt**, X Window VT-100 emulator.)

Since the 1990s, many X Window-based terminal programs have been written, and almost all of them have been based on either **xterm** or **xvt**. In 1998, a German programmer Lars Doelle released Konsole, a brand new terminal program. Konsole was part of the KDE project and, over the years, it has been enhanced so that, today, it is one of the most powerful terminal emulators around.

Konsole, by the way, is the German word for "console". This is a happy coincidence because, as I mentioned in Chapter 5, it is the custom that KDE programs should have names that begin with K.

VIRTUAL CONSOLES

It's 1980 and we are at a major East Coast university, visiting the Most Important Professor on campus. The MIP has a fancy office with a large desk and seven different terminals, all of which are connected to a powerful Unix system. (See Figure 6-8.)

The MIP is showing us around his office. "Six of these terminals are character devices, offering the standard command-line interface," he explains. "In fact, this particular terminal over here is the console."

Wait a second, we say. Isn't the console supposed to be near the computer or, at the very least, in the system administrator's office?

"In most cases, yes," says the MIP, "but I'm a very important person. The six character terminals are for me to use however I want. It often happens that I need to work on more than one project at a time, so having all the terminals all to myself is very convenient. If the system breaks, let the admin come to *my* office to use the console."

How kind of you, we say. But do you really use all six terminals?

"You bet I do. I'm important. I need a lot of terminals. However, I do let my secretary* use one of them from time to time."

Finally, the MIP points to the seventh terminal, off to one side. "This is a graphics terminal, very special" he says. "It's true; there are only a limited number of programs that run on such a terminal but, since I am so important, I must, of course, have one."

FIGURE 6-8: Multiple terminals for one user

In the year 1980, this was the desk of the Most Important Professor in the university. The MIP was so important he had seven terminals just for his own use: six text-based terminals and one graphics terminal (the one on the right). Today, when you use your own Linux computer, you have a much better facility: the 7 built-in virtual consoles. (See text for details.)

---

*A secretary was a mammalian version of a personal digital assistant. Secretaries flourished in the university environment from the 1930s to the late 1980s.

Compared to PDAs, university secretaries were unreliable, difficult to control, not upgradable, and often had memory problems. Moreover, because of licensing restrictions in the 1980s and 1990s, many secretaries were impossible to discard, even if they were performing poorly.

In 1996, secretaries were put on the endangered species list and, since 1998, they have been considered extinct. The last sighting of an actual university secretary was in late 1998 at the University of North Dakota, Fargo. However, the sighting was not confirmed, and most authorities believe the "secretary" was actually a reference librarian (also on the endangered list).

Let's move forward 25 years. You have just read about the Most Important Professor, and you are thinking wistfully, "Imagine having seven terminals all to yourself. Wouldn't that be wonderful? I wish I were that important."

Actually, if you have your own Unix computer, you *are* that important. All modern Unix systems allow you to use multiple terminals at the same time, one of which is a graphics terminal.

Moreover, you don't have to clutter your desk with more than one monitor and keyboard. Unix will use the same monitor and keyboard for each terminal. All you have to do is press a shortcut key to switch from one terminal to another.

Here is how it works with Linux (other systems are similar).

When you start Linux, your GUI – that is, your desktop environment – starts automatically. What you may not know is that, at the same time, Linux actually starts seven different terminal emulation programs running on your behalf. They are called VIRTUAL CONSOLES. (Unfortunately, the name is a bit misleading, as I will discuss in the next section.)

Virtual consoles #1-6 are full-screen, text-based terminals for using a CLI. Virtual console #7 is a graphics terminal for running a GUI. In fact, when your desktop manager starts, what you are looking at is actually virtual console #7. The other six virtual consoles are invisible.

To switch from one virtual console to another, all you need to do is press a special key combination. For virtual console #1, press <Ctrl-Alt-F1>. (That is, hold down the <Ctrl> and <Alt> keys and press <F1>.) For console #2, press <Ctrl-Alt-F2>; for console #3, <Ctrl-Alt-F3>; and so on.

When you press one of these key combinations, you will instantly see a full-screen CLI terminal. You have six of them to use however you want. To return to the GUI (your desktop environment), just press <Ctrl-Alt-F7>. (Remember, the 7th virtual console is the graphics terminal.)

HINT

The shortcut keys to switch from one virtual console to another are actually <Alt-F1> (terminal #1) through <Alt-F7> (terminal #7). However, within most GUIs, these keys have other uses, so you must hold down the <Ctrl> key as well.

For example, say you are working with your GUI (terminal #7). To switch to terminal #3, you press <Ctrl-Alt-F3>.

You are now at a CLI. To switch to terminal #4, press <Alt-F4>; to switch to terminal #1, press <Alt-F1>; and so on. To switch back to terminal #7 (the GUI), press <Alt-F7>.

So why would you want to use <Alt> by itself instead of <Ctrl-Alt>? It's simpler and quicker, and Unix people like it when things are as simple and as quick as possible.

When you switch away from a virtual console, the program that is running in it keeps running. For example, you start a program in terminal #4 to perform a lengthy job (such as compiling a large program or downloading a lot of files from the Internet). You can then press <Alt-F5> and switch to terminal #5 to work on something else. Later, you can press <Alt-F4> to return to terminal #4 and see how your program is doing.

The question arises, why bother with the six text-based virtual consoles? Why not just stay in the GUI and use terminal windows and multiple desktops? There are several reasons.

First, the text-based virtual consoles use the entire screen, and display characters using a monospaced (constant width) font typeface. Overall, this is a particularly pleasing way to use a CLI, much more so than a terminal window under a GUI, even a maximized window. (Try it and see.)

Second, it is cool to press <Alt-F1>, <Alt-F2>, and so on, to switch from one command line to another. (Again, try it and see.)

Third, if you ever have a serious problem with your desktop environment, it's handy to be able to switch to a virtual console in order to solve the problem. For example, if your GUI freezes, you can usually press <Ctrl-Alt-F1> to get to another terminal. You can then log in to fix the problem or reboot the system.

To complete our discussion, let me explain why I told you the story about the Most Important Professor. There are two reasons.

First, I want you to realize how powerful modern Unix really is. If you used Unix in 1980, you would have had to share terminals, usually by going to a terminal room and waiting your turn. If you somehow managed to acquire your own personal terminal, it would have been a very big deal.

The truth is, in 1980, computing equipment was so expensive that even the most important person at a university wasn't important enough to have several terminals in his office, let alone seven. And yet, today, that's exactly what you have on your desktop when you use Linux on a PC. (FreeBSD actually gives you eight.)

Second, I want you to notice that the idea of multiple virtual consoles is a software implementation of a hardware reality from over a quarter century ago. How many computing paradigms that old are still so valuable? So far, in this book, we have met two: the system of clients and servers (Chapter 3), and the flexible, open-ended design of X Window (Chapter 5). To these two, we can now add another basic principle.

Unix is based on the idea of using terminals to access a host computer, an idea so powerful that – long after the actual terminals were gone – the system they inspired is still thriving.

WHAT'S IN A NAME?

Virtual

Within computing, the term "virtual" is used to describe something that exists because it is simulated by software. For example, the virtual consoles we discussed in this chapter are not real, in the sense that they do not have an independent physical existence. They exist only because they are created by software.

A more important example is the idea of virtual memory, a method of simulating more memory than physically exists in the computer. For example, if a computer has 2 GB of memory, the operating system may simulate, say, an extra 4 GB of virtual memory by using the hard disk to hold the excess data. (Unix, by the way, uses virtual memory.)

The term "virtual" comes from optics, a branch of physics. Imagine you are looking at a candle in front of a mirror. When you look at the actual candle, a physicist would say you are looking at the "real" image. When you look at the candle in the mirror, you are looking at the "virtual" image.

THE ONE AND ONLY CONSOLE

In Chapter 3, we talked about the idea of the console. This term can be a bit confusing, so let's take a moment to get it straight.

In the old days, most Unix computers were connected to a number of terminals. When someone wanted to use the system, he or she would find an unused terminal and log in.

One of the terminals, the console, was special because it was used by the system administrator to manage the system. In most cases, the console was kept in a locked room, either next to the host computer or in the admin's office.

Physically, the console looked like other terminals, but there are two things that made it different. First, when Unix needed to display a very important message, that message was sent to the console.

Second, when the system was booted into single-user mode – for maintenance or problem solving – only the console would be activated. In this way, other users would not be able to log in until the system was rebooted into multiuser mode.

Today, the word "console" is often used as a synonym for terminal, which can be confusing. For example, the virtual consoles we just discussed are not real consoles. It would make a lot more sense to call them "virtual terminals".

Similarly, consider the Konsole terminal emulation program I mentioned earlier in the chapter. The program was written by a German programmer, and Konsole is the German word for "console". Still, the name is incorrect. When you run Konsole you get a terminal window, not a console.

SELECTING AND INSERTING

When you are working with multiple windows, each of which contains its own program, there will be times when you will want to copy or move information from one window to another. If you have used Microsoft Windows or a Macintosh, you are probably familiar with copying and pasting.

With Unix, there are two different ways to copy data. First, X Window allows you to select and insert text from one window to another or within the same window. Second, many GUI-based programs support the Windows-type of copy/paste facility (<Ctrl-C>, <Ctrl-V> and so on).

These two systems are completely separate and they work differently, so you need to learn how to use them both. Let's start with the X Window system, as it is simpler.

The X Window select/insert facility works only with text, that is, characters. To start, you select some text with your mouse (more on that in a moment). You then move the mouse to where you want to insert the text and click the middle button. That's all there is to it. As soon as you click the middle button, the selected text will be inserted. If your mouse doesn't have a middle button, click the right and left buttons at the same time.

To select text, position the mouse pointer at the start of the text. Then hold down the left mouse button while you drag the pointer over the text. As you drag the pointer, the selected text will be highlighted. (Open a terminal window and try it.)

Alternatively, you can select text in two other ways. If you double-click, a word will be selected; if you triple-click, the entire line will be selected. (Try it. It takes a bit of practice.)

Although the instructions might sound a bit complicated when you read them, selecting and inserting text is actually quick and easy once you get the hang of it. If you are in front of your computer, I suggest that you take a few moments now to open two windows and practice selecting and inserting. If possible, have someone show you how it works.

HINT

Since it is X Window that provides the select/insert facility, you can only use it within your GUI. You can't use it with the virtual consoles.

There is, however, a program called Linux **gpm** that extends this functionality to text-based virtual consoles (#1-6). With FreeBSD, there is a similar program called **moused**.

If **gpm** or **moused** is installed on your system (as they often are by default), you can select and insert within the text-based virtual consoles in the same way that you do within your GUI. The only difference is that, to insert text, you may have to right-click rather than middle-click.

COPYING AND PASTING

As I explained in the previous section, you can use the X Window select/insert facility to copy text within a window or between two windows. In addition to selecting and inserting, many – but not all – GUI-based programs also support a completely different system called copying and pasting.

The Unix copy/paste facility works the same way as it does with Microsoft Windows. It even uses the same keys and menus. Unlike Windows, however, not all GUI-based Unix programs use copy/paste. You will have to check for yourself.

Before we get into the details, here is a brief summary: To start, you "copy" or "cut" data to the "clipboard". You can then "paste" the contents of the clipboard anywhere it makes sense to do so. Most of the time you will be copying text, that is, characters. However, you can also copy graphics, as long as it makes sense to do so with the programs you are using.

To work with copy/paste, you need to understand four basic ideas:

- The CLIPBOARD is an invisible storage area.

- When you COPY to the clipboard, the original data is not changed.

- When you CUT data to the clipboard, the original data is deleted.

- To copy data from the clipboard, you PASTE it into a window.

Thus, to *copy* data from one place to another, you copy and paste. To *move* data from one place to another, you cut and paste.

Whenever you copy or cut, the current contents of the clipboard are replaced, and you can't get them back. For example, let's say the clipboard contains 50 paragraphs of text. You then copy one single character to the clipboard. The clipboard now contains only the one character; the 50 paragraphs of text are gone.

On the other hand, when you paste data, the contents of the clipboard do not change. This means that the contents of the clipboard remain unchanged, until you perform another copy or cut. This allows you to paste the same data over and over. (Of course, the contents of the clipboard are lost when you reboot or when you shutdown the system.)

So how do you copy, cut and paste? To start, you must select the data you want to go to the clipboard. There are two ways to do this.

First, you can use the mouse. Position the mouse pointer at the start of the data you want to copy or cut. Then hold down the left mouse button while you drag the pointer over the text. As you drag the pointer, the selected text will be highlighted.

Alternately, if you are working with data that can be typed, you can select using the keyboard. Position the cursor at the beginning of the text you want to copy, and hold down the <Shift> key. While you are holding it down, use any of the cursor control keys to move the cursor. The text it passes over will be selected.

Once you have selected your data, you can copy or cut it in three different ways. You can press <Ctrl-C> to copy and <Ctrl-X> to cut; or you can right click to pop up a menu and select "Copy" or "Cut"; or you can pull down the Edit menu and select either "Copy" or "Cut".

Similarly, you can paste in three different ways. Move the cursor to where you want the data inserted and press <Ctrl-V>; or right-click and select "Paste"; or pull down the Edit menu and select "Paste".

HINT

If you make a mistake when you cut or paste, you can cancel the last operation by pressing <Ctrl-Z> or by selecting "Undo" from a menu.

With some programs, you can cancel more than one operation by pressing <Ctrl-Z> more than once.

WORKING AS SUPERUSER: su

In order to maintain security, Unix is designed so that each userid has a limited set of privileges. For example, you can delete your own files, but you can't delete someone else's files unless he gives you explicit permission. Similarly, as a regular user, you cannot make changes or run programs that could affect the integrity of the system.

In Chapter 4, we discussed the idea that, from time to time, it becomes necessary for the system administrator to log in as superuser, in order to have privileges beyond those of a regular user. For example, an admin may need to add a new user to the system, change somebody's password, update or install software, and so on.

As I explained, there exists a special userid, **root**, that has such privileges. When you log in as **root**, you are the superuser and you can do pretty much whatever you want. (Obviously, the **root** password is a very important secret.)

If you are using a shared system, say, at school or at work, someone else will take care of the system administration, so you don't have to worry about it. If you forget your password, for example, you have someone to ask for help. However, when you use your own Unix system, such as a PC running Linux or FreeBSD, *you* are the admin and, as such, you must know how to work as superuser.

In order to become superuser, you need the superuser password, usually referred to as the **root** password. If you installed Unix on your computer, you will have chosen the **root** password as part of the installation process.

HINT

Some Linux distributions are set up so that a **root** userid is not created during the installation process. In such cases, use your regular password as the superuser password.

HINT

On any Unix system, the **root** password is the single most important piece of information you possess. Thus, it makes sense to memorize it rather than writing it down. However, if in the course of human events, you happen to forget the **root** password for your own computer, it is a big, big deal.

In the olden days, there was not a lot you could do other than reinstall Unix. With modern systems, there is a way out. For the details, see Appendix G, *What to Do If You Forget the* **root** *Password*.

Once you know the **root** password, there are two ways to become superuser. First, at a login prompt, you can log in as **root**. You can do this when the system first starts, or by using a virtual console.

Alternatively, if you are already logged in as a regular user, you can use the **su** (substitute userid) command to change to superuser.

The purpose of the **su** command is to allow you to change temporarily to another userid. Just type **su** followed by the new userid. Here is an example.

You are logged in as **harley**, and here is what the shell prompt looks like:

```
[harley]$
```

(In this example, we are using the Bash shell. The shell prompt has been set to show the current userid. We will discuss the shell prompt in detail in Chapter 13.)

You now enter the **su** command to change to userid **weedly**. You are then prompted for **weedly**'s password. Once you enter the password, your current shell is put on hold and a new shell is started for **weedly**.

```
[harley]$ su weedly
Password:
[weedly]$
```

When you are finished working as **weedly**, all you need to do is end the current shell. To do this, you type **exit**. Once you end the new shell, you will be returned automatically to your original shell as userid **harley**:

```
[weedly]$ exit
[harley]$
```

Although you can use **su** to change to any userid (if you have the password), it is mostly used to change to superuser. Before we get into the details, I want to explain one more thing.

Whenever you log in, Unix runs certain commands to set up an environment specific to your userid. (Later in the book, when we talk about shells, I'll show you how to customize the process.) Let's say you are logged in as **harley**, and you enter the following command:

```
su weedly
```

You have changed your userid to **weedly**, but you are still working under the **harley** environment. If you want to change both your userid and the environment, type a – (hyphen) after the command name. Notice there is a space on each side of the hyphen.

```
su - weedly
```

You are now working as **weedly** within the **weedly** environment. When you type **exit**, you will go back to working as **harley** within the **harley** environment.

I know this all sounds a bit mysterious but, I promise you, one day it will make sense. The reason I mention it now is that I am about to show you how to use **su** to change to superuser. When you do, it is important that you work under the superuser environment, not your own environment.

To change to superuser, use the **su** command with the userid **root**. Remember not to leave out the hyphen.

```
su - root
```

You will now be asked for a password. Once you enter the password, your current shell will be put on hold, and a new shell will be started. Within the new shell, your userid will be **root**, and you will have full superuser privileges.

```
[harley]$ su - root
Password:
#
```

Notice that the shell prompt has changed to **#**. As I explained in Chapter 4, this indicates you are the superuser.

When you are finished doing whatever you need to do as superuser, type **exit** and you will be returned to your old shell:

```
# exit
[harley]$
```

As a convenience, if you use the **su** command without a userid, the default is **root**, which is what you want most of the time anyway. Thus, the following two commands are equivalent.

```
su -
su - root
```

One last word. If your system is shared by a number of people, you must be careful what you do as superuser. There's a lot I could say, but it all boils down to two basic rules:

1. Respect the privacy of others.

2. Think before you type.

IMPORTANT HINT

When you are logged in as **root**, you can do anything that can be done, which can lead to mistakes. The best way to guard against accidentally causing a problem (or a catastrophe!) is to be the superuser for as short a time as necessary.

For example, on my system, I am normally logged in as **harley**. When I need to perform a system administration task, I use **su** to become superuser just long enough to do what I have to do. I then return to **harley** as soon as possible. There is no need to stay logged in as **root**, because I can become superuser again whenever I want.

In other words, spend most of your time as Clark Kent, not as Superman.

ENTERING A SINGLE COMMAND AS SUPERUSER: sudo

As I mentioned in the last section, it can be dangerous to spend too much time as superuser: you might inadvertently type something that will cause trouble. There is, in addition, another potential problem.

Let's say you are logged in as **root**, and you happen to get hungry. You walk away from your computer for a moment to get some hot buttered groatcakes. While you are gone, you unexpectedly get into an argument with someone about whether or not the water in a sink in the Southern Hemisphere flows out in the opposite direction than the water in a sink in the Northern Hemisphere*. When you get back, you find that – while you were gone – some wiseguy took over your machine and, acting as superuser, deleted hundreds of files.

Of course, you should never walk away from your computer while you are logged in under any userid. That's like leaving your car unlocked with the keys hidden under the seat. However, leaving your computer while you are logged in as **root** is like leaving the car unlocked with the engine running and the door open.

The best defense against these types of inadvertent errors is to use the **sudo** command.

The job of **sudo** is to allow you to execute a single command as another userid. (The name **sudo** means: "substitute the userid, then do something".) Like **su**, the default is to assume userid **root**. Thus, to run a specific command as superuser, type **sudo** followed by the command:

sudo *command*

For example, to run the **id** command as **root**, you would use:

sudo id

(The **id** command displays your current userid.)

---

*It doesn't.

When you use **sudo** to run a command as **root**, you will be asked to enter your password (not the superuser password).

As superuser, you run any command you want*. Here is a simple example showing how the userid changes when you run the **id** command as **root**. Don't worry about understanding all the output right now. All I want you to notice is how the name of the userid (**uid**) changes.

```
[harley]$ id
uid=500(harley) gid=500(harley) groups=500(harley)
[harley]$ sudo id
Password:
uid=0(root) gid=0(root) groups=0(root)
```

As a convenience, once you have entered the superuser password correctly, you can run **sudo** for a certain amount of time without having to enter the password again. The default on most systems is 5 minutes, although it can vary. This means that, if you use the **sudo** command more than once within a 5 minute interval, you will only have to enter the password once.

WHAT'S IN A NAME?

su, sudo
The **su** (substitute userid) command allows you to change to another userid. The **sudo** (substitute the userid and do something) command allows you to run a single command under the auspices of another userid.

The name **su** is pronounced as two separate letters: "ess-you". The name **sudo** is pronounced phonetically to sound like "pseudo". In fact, the first few times you hear someone talk about **sudo**, you will be confused as it sounds as if they are saying "pseudo".

It is the custom to use **su** and **sudo**, not only as names, but as verbs. For example, let's eavesdrop on two Unix people who have had a bit too much to drink.

Person 1: "I have an idea. Let's edit the password file just for fun. All we have to do is pseudo the **vipw** command."

Person 2: "Ahh, that's too lame. Let's ess-you instead. I like to live dangerously."

CONFIGURATION FILES

We have discussed how, from time to time, it is necessary to become superuser in order to carry out certain tasks. Certainly this is true often enough if you are managing a system with multiple users ("I forgot my password"). But how often is this the case when you are the only user, running Linux or FreeBSD on your own PC?

---

* You might be wondering if this is a security problem. As I mentioned, when you use the **sudo** command, you are asked for your own password, not the superuser password. Does this mean that, on a shared system, anyone would be allowed to use **sudo** to run a command as superuser?

The answer is no, because not everyone is allowed to use **sudo**. You can only use **sudo** if your userid is on a special list. This list is kept in the file **/etc/sudoers**, and it can be changed only by the superuser. (The name of this file will make sense after we talk about the Unix file system in Chapter 23.)

The answer is when you have your own system you don't need to become superuser all that often. However, there are times when it is necessary. In particular, there is one important function you will want to perform that does require special privileges.

Most Unix programs are written so they can be customized by editing a CONFIGURATION FILE. The configuration file contains information that is read by the program, usually when it starts. This information affects how the program does its work.

For example, earlier in the chapter, we discussed the startup process, when Unix boots into a particular runlevel. This process depends on information in a specific configuration file named **inittab** (see below).

Configuration files are particularly important when you are installing new software. Most likely, the software uses a configuration file and, if you want to set certain options, you will need to modify the file. In most cases, the details will be explained in the documentation that comes with the software.

With some software, there are easy-to-use programs that help you to change a configuration file. For example, within your desktop environment, there are menu-based programs that you can use to select preferences and specify options. What you may not know is that all of these preferences and options are stored in a configuration file somewhere. When you "apply" the changes, all the program is doing is updating the configuration file according to your instructions.

Although this is a convenient way to modify a configuration file, it is important that you learn how to edit such files on your own, for several reasons.

First, most programs don't come with a menu-based configuration program so, if you want to make changes, you'll have to do it for yourself.

Second, changing a configuration file yourself is faster (and more fun) than using a program to do it for you.

Third, even if there is a menu-driven program, it may not allow access to all possible options and preferences. To really know what is available, you will have to look inside the configuration file.

Finally, when you look inside a configuration file, it gives you insight into how the underlying program functions. It is common for programmers to put comments in such files and, sometimes, the only way you can actually understand the more subtle aspects of the program is by reading the comments.

HINT

In Unix, you are encouraged to look inside any system file you want, including configuration files.

Before you can edit a configuration file safely, you must fulfill several requirements. First you must be comfortable working as superuser.

Second, you must be able to use a text editor well. The best choices are either **vi** (which I will teach you in Chapter 22) or Emacs.

Finally, you must, in a general sense, know what you are doing. This will come in time.

You may be wondering, how do Unix configuration files compare to what is done in Microsoft Windows? Within Windows, programs store configuration information in two places: in the Registry and, sometimes, in `.ini` files. Windows users are encouraged to leave the Registry alone. This is because if you screw up the registry, you can cause yourself big trouble. Moreover, the contents of the Registry are poorly documented. Indeed, many of the entries are not documented at all.

Unix has a very different philosophy. There is no central Registry. Instead, every program is allowed to have its own configuration file. Moreover, the contents of that file are documented. Users are encouraged to read the file and (when appropriate) make changes.

Of course, if you change a configuration file incorrectly, you might cause a problem. However, it will be confined to that particular program and, in most cases, it will be easy to fix.

> **HINT**
>
> Before you edit any important file, such as a configuration file, make a backup copy. That way, if something goes wrong, you can restore the original. (You will learn how to work with files in Chapters 23, 24 and 25.)
>
> Here is an example to show you how I do it. Let's say I want to edit a file called **harley**, and that date happens to be December 21, 2008. Before I start, I would make a copy of the file and call it **harley-2008-12-21**. Then, if I have a problem, I can copy the file back to its original name.
>
> Why don't I use a name such as **harley-** or **harley-original** or **harley-old**? It would work, but sometimes I want to leave the backup file around after I finish my work. By embedding the date in the file name, I know exactly when the backup file was created.

LOOKING INSIDE A CONFIGURATION FILE

In the previous section, I told you not to edit a configuration file until you know what you are doing. However, there's no reason why you can't look inside a file, just to see what's there.

Below is a list of several interesting configuration files. To look inside, you use a program called **less**. The job of **less** is to display the contents of a file, one screenful at a time.

We will discuss **less** in detail (including its name) in Chapter 21. For now, I'll tell you that to display the contents of a file you type **less** followed by the name of the file. For example, to examine the file named **/etc/passwd**, you use the command:

```
less /etc/passwd
```

Once **less** starts, it shows you the first screenful of information. To move forward, you press <Space>; to move back, press <b>; for help, press <h>; to quit, press <q>. That's all you'll need for now.

Here is a list of configuration files you may find interesting. You don't need to be superuser to look at them (just to change them).

Don't worry if you don't understand what you see. Eventually, you will. In particular, the file name will make sense to you after you read Chapter 23. (Note: These files are found on most Linux systems. If you use a different type of Unix, some of the files may have different names.)

/boot/grub/menu.lst: Information about the operating systems that can boot on your computer.

/etc/hosts: A list of hostnames and IP addresses that are known to the system.

/etc/inittab: Definition of the various runlevels.

/etc/passwd: Basic information about each userid. (The actual passwords are encrypted and kept elsewhere.)

/etc/profile: Commands that are executed automatically when a userid logs in.

/etc/samba/smb.conf: Configuration information for Samba, a facility that allows Unix systems to share files and printers with Windows systems.

SHUTTING DOWN AND REBOOTING: `init, reboot, shutdown`

At the beginning of the chapter, we talked about what happens when you log in. It's now time to talk about what to do when you are finished working.

Basically, you have two choices. You can SHUTDOWN, which stops Unix and turns off the computer; or you can REBOOT (also called RESTART), which stops Unix and then starts it again. You can perform both of these actions by making a selection from a menu, or by typing commands.

From within your desktop environment, you shutdown or reboot by opening the main menu and selecting "Logout" (or something similar). As part of the logout process, you may have a choice to shutdown or reboot. If not, you can click on "Shutdown" or "Reboot" when you find yourself back at the login screen.

Using GUIs, however, is rather boring. It's a lot more interesting to shutdown or reboot by typing commands. Before I teach you the commands, let me recall to your memory the idea of runlevels. If you look back at Figure 6-1, you will see that there are 6 different runlevels, each of which causes Unix to run in a particular way.

Normally, a runlevel is chosen as part of the startup process in order to boot the system. For example, runlevel 5 boots Linux in multiuser mode with a GUI.

However, there are two runlevels that have special meanings. Runlevel 0 halts the system (that is, causes it to shutdown), and runlevel 6 reboots the system. Thus, when you choose "Shutdown" from a menu, it's like changing to runlevel 0; and when you choose "Reboot", it's like changing to runlevel 6.

As you might have guessed by now, almost anything that you can do in Unix by using a menu, you can also do by typing a command. The command to change runlevels is called **init**.

In order to use **init**, you need to be superuser. Once you are superuser, type the command followed by the runlevel to which you want to change. For example, you can reboot the system by changing to runlevel 6:

```
sudo init 6
```

To shutdown the system, you can change to runlevel 0:

```
sudo init 0
```

If you feel brave, try changing to another runlevel and see what happens.

Although you can use **init** to reboot or shutdown, it is not designed for everyday use. Instead, we normally use two other commands, **reboot** and **shutdown**.

The reboot command is straightforward. Just type it and your system will change to runlevel 0:

```
sudo reboot
```

The **shutdown** command is a bit more complex, because you have to specify when you want to shutdown. The are various choices, but the simplest one is to use the word **now**:

```
sudo shutdown now
```

Typing this command tells the system to change to runlevel 0 right away.

WHAT HAPPENS WHEN THE SYSTEM STARTS OR STOPS? `dmesg`

During the booting and shutdown processes, Linux displays a lot of messages on the console. Most of these messages relate to finding and configuring the hardware components of your system. Other messages have to do with starting or stopping the services that are involved in the boot process, and the processes that will run in the background once the system has booted.

A discussion of all the details is beyond the scope of this book. However, it is interesting to look at these messages, just to see what's there.

As the system boots, many of the messages go by so fast you won't have time to read them, let alone figure out what they mean. Once you have logged in, however, you can display the boot messages at your leisure. Just go to a command line and enter:

```
dmesg | less
```

Although the boot messages look cryptic, you will eventually be able to understand them*.

The job of the **dmesg** command is to display the boot messages. However, there are so many that, if you enter the command by itself, most of the output will scroll off your screen before you can read it. (Try it.)

Instead, use the three-part command above **dmesg**, followed by the **|** (vertical bar) character, followed by **less**. This runs **dmesg** and sends the output to **less**, which will

---

*If you are a guy and you have a special someone in your life, here is an especially good way to impress her.

Invite your special someone over on a Friday night and, when she arrives say, "You are in for a real treat." Then show her the output of the **dmesg** command. If you are knowledgeable enough, invite her to pick any message and offer to explain it to her.

According to my research, this technique works especially well when combined with pizza and non-caffeinated beverages.

display the output one screenful at a time. The vertical bar creates what is called a "pipeline". (We'll talk about pipelines in Chapter 15; we'll talk about **less** in Chapter 21.)

DOING MORE THAN ONE THING AT A TIME: PART II

We started this chapter by talking about the characteristics of people and computers. I explained that, as human beings, we have imperfect memories and cannot concentrate on more than one thing at a time. What we *can* do is work with complex mental ideas and, whenever necessary, change from one idea to another within a fraction of a second.

Computers can store and recall data much faster and much more accurately than can humans. Computers can also perform straightforward tasks extremely quickly and, while they are doing so, they can change from one task to another within milliseconds.

While human beings can think and plot strategies, computers can do many things quickly without mixing up the details. In this way, machines are able to make up for the shortcomings of our minds, and our minds are able to complement the astounding capabilities of the machines. The result – when we do it right – is a melding of human being and computer in such a way as to produce something that is neither one nor the other, but far greater than the sum of its parts.

The glue that holds together the man/machine partnership is the user interfaces. In Unix, we have two of them, the GUI (your desktop environment) and the CLI (the command line).

For the rest of this book, we will be concentrating on the CLI. In other words, we will be typing commands and learning how to use text-based programs. In order to do this well, you must become proficient in using terminal windows, regular windows, virtual terminals and multiple desktops/workspaces – all at the same time.

The ultimate goal is to be able to conceive of doing something and then – without thinking – to make it happen. You already know how to do this when you drive a car, play a musical instrument, or cook a meal. What I want is for you to be able to carry out the same type of actions when you are sitting in front of your computer, using Unix to work on mental tasks.

Since we are all different, I can't teach you how to conceive of your moment-to-moment mental strategies. You will have to develop those skills for yourself. What I can do is focus your attention, right now, by reminding you of the wonderful tools that are at your disposal. To do so, I will summarize the default Linux work environment.

Within Linux, you have 6 text-based virtual consoles, each of which has its own CLI. In addition, you have a 7th virtual console that contains your desktop environment (the GUI).

Within your desktop environment, you have 4 different desktops/workspaces, each of which can have as many windows as you want, including terminal windows.

You are able to copy and paste text from one window to another, and from one virtual console to another. Moreover, you can work as either a regular user or as superuser.

To manipulate your work environment, you can use the following shortcut keys:

In KDE, to change from one desktop to another:
    <Ctrl-Tab>, <Ctrl-Shift-Tab>

In Gnome, to change from one workplace to another:
    <Ctrl-Alt-Left>, <Ctrl-Alt-Right>, <Ctrl-Alt-Up>, <Ctrl-Alt-Down>

Within a desktop or workspace, to change from one task to another:
    <Alt-Tab>, <Alt-Shift-Tab>

Within your GUI, to change to a text-based virtual console:
    <Ctrl-Alt-F1>... <Ctrl-Alt-F6>

From a text-based virtual console, change to another virtual console:
    <Alt-F1>... <Alt-F7> (<Alt-F7> changes to the GUI

To copy text within the GUI:
    Select with mouse, then middle-click

To copy text between virtual terminals:
    Select with mouse, then right-click

Within GUI-based programs, to copy, cut and paste data:
    <Ctrl-C>, <Ctrl-X>, <Ctrl-V>

HINT

Unix has the best system of user interfaces that has ever existed.

CHAPTER 6 EXERCISES

REVIEW QUESTIONS

1. What is a time slice? What is a typical length for a time slice?

2. What is the Unix CLI? What is the GUI?

3. What is a runlevel? At this very moment, Fester Bestertester is sitting at the back of a lecture hall listening to a boring lecture on animal husbandry. To keep himself awake, Fester is playing a GUI-based game on his Linux laptop. What is the runlevel on Fester's computer? Across the campus, a Unix system administrator has brought down the system and rebooted, so he can solve an important hardware problem. What is the runlevel on the admin's computer?

4. Which person acts as superuser on your particular Unix system?

5. What is a virtual console? How do you switch from one virtual console to another?

APPLYING YOUR KNOWLEDGE

1. The **who** command (which we will discuss in Chapter 8), displays a list of all the userids that are currently logged into the system. If a userid is logged in more than once, **who** will show that. Log in on each of your virtual consoles, one by one. Then switch to your GUI, open a terminal window, and enter the **who** command. What do you see?

2. Being able to switch from one desktop to another and being able to copy and paste quickly are important skills. Within your GUI, open two terminal windows, each in its own desktop. In the first desktop, enter the command **date** (to display the time and date) into the terminal window. Copy that command into the clipboard. Now change to the second desktop and paste the command into the other terminal window. Now repeat the exercise using two text-based virtual consoles. Which set of copy and paste procedures is more comfortable to you? Why?

FOR FURTHER THOUGHT

1. Some Linux distributions are set up so that a root userid is not created during the installation process.In such cases, your regular password serves as the superuser password. Why would a distribution be set up in this way? What are the advantages? What are the disadvantages?

2. Why do so many people believe they can think about more than one thing at a time? What effect do fast, multitasking computer systems like Unix have on such beliefs? Is this healthy or unhealthy? Do you, personally, think it is okay to talk on the phone or text message while you are driving? What about when other people do it?

CHAPTER 7
USING THE KEYBOARD WITH UNIX

In Chapter 6, we talked about the differences between the GUI (graphical user interface) and the CLI (command line interface). Starting with this chapter, and for the rest of the book, we will be concentrating on the CLI, the traditional way to use Unix.

There are several ways in which you can use the CLI. When you work with your own computer, you can use a virtual console or a terminal window (including the Konsole program). We discussed the details in Chapter 6. When you work with a remote host, you can connect via the **ssh** program, which will act as a terminal emulator for you. Regardless of how you get to a Unix command line, once you are there, it always works the same way (more or less).

If you are using a GUI-based system, I would like you to be familiar with several topics from Chapter 6 before you read this chapter: virtual consoles, terminal windows, and how to select and paste. With a GUI, understanding these ideas is crucial to using the CLI well.

THE FIRST UNIX TERMINALS

When Unix was first developed by Ken Thompson and Dennis Ritchie (see Chapter 2), they used Teletype ASR33 terminals (see Chapter 3). The Teletype ASR33 was an electromechanical device, originally developed to send and receive text messages. It had a keyboard for input and a built-in printer for output. It also had a paper tape punch, which could store data by punching holes on paper tape, as well as a paper tape reader, which could read data from punched tape.

The ASR33's capabilities made it suitable to use as a computer terminal. In fact, from the mid-1960s to the mid 1970s, virtually all non-IBM computer systems used an ASR33 for the console. This was true of the PDP minicomputers used by Thompson and Ritchie, so it was natural that these devices should become the very first Unix terminals (see box).

The keyboard of the ASR33 was originally designed to send and receive messages, not to control the operation of a computer. As such, Thompson and Ritchie had to adapt Unix to work with the ASR33 keyboard. What is interesting is that the basic system they devised worked so well, it is still used today.

THE TELETYPE ASR33

The ASR33, manufactured by the Teletype Corporation, was introduced in 1963. There were three Teletype 33 models: the RO, KSR and ASR. Of the three Teletype 33s, the ASR was by far the most popular.

The RO (Receive-Only) had a printer but no keyboard. As such, it could receive messages, but not send them.

The KSR (Keyboard Send-Receive) had both a printer and a keyboard, and could send and receive messages. The outgoing messages were typed by hand on the keyboard.

The ASR (Automatic Send-Receive) had a printer, a keyboard, and a paper tape punch/reader. Like the KSR, the ASR could send and receive messages. However, with the ASR the outgoing text could be generated in two ways. It could be typed at the keyboard by hand, or it could be read automatically from pre-punched paper tape (hence the name "Automatic"). It was these combination of features that made the ASR33 useful as a computer terminal.

The Teletype ASR 33 terminal weighed 56 pounds, including a 12-pound stand. If you had bought one from DEC in 1974, it would have cost you $1,850, plus a $120 installation fee and $37/month maintenance. In 2008 dollars, that's $8,400 for the machine, $550 for the installation, and $170/month for maintenance.

You can see photos of an ASR33 in Chapter 3. Figures 3-1 and 3-2 show the machine. Figure 3-3 is a close-up of the paper tape punch/reader.

As you would expect, the keyboard of the Teletype contained keys for the 26 letters of the alphabet, the digits 0-9, as well as the most common punctuation symbols. However, there were also a few special keys that were used to provide the functions necessary to send and receive messages (see Figure 7-1). The most important such keys were <Esc>, <Ctrl>, <Shift>, <Tab> and <Return>.

The <Ctrl> (Control) key was especially useful because, like the <Shift> key, it could be combined with other keys to form new combinations. For example, by holding down the <Ctrl> key and pressing one of the letters or numbers, you could send a signal such as <Ctrl-A>, <Ctrl-B>, <Ctrl-C>, and so on.

What Thompson and Ritchie did was to incorporate the use of these keys into their basic design of the operating system. To do this, they wrote Unix so that certain signals could be used to control the operation of a program as it was running. For example, the signal called `intr` (interrupt) was used to terminate a program. To send the `intr` signal, you pressed <Ctrl-C>.

In technical terms, when there is an equivalence between two things, we say that there exists a MAPPING between them. When we create such an equivalence, we say that we MAP one thing onto the other. For example, if we say that A is mapped onto B, it means that, when we use A, it is the same as using B.

The idea of mapping is an important concept, one that you will meet again and again as you use computers. In this case, we can say that, within Unix, the <Ctrl-C> character is MAPPED onto the `intr` signal. This is the same as saying that when we press <Ctrl-C>, it has the effect of sending the `intr` signal.

In a moment, we'll talk about the Unix signals in detail. In fact, my main goal in this chapter is to explain the important signals and their keyboard mappings. First, however, I want to take a moment to talk about nomenclature.

TELETYPES AND THE UNIX CULTURE

As you use Unix, you will find that many conventions are based on the technology of the 1970s, the time during which the first versions of Unix were developed. In particular, the world of Unix abounds with ideas that are based on the characteristics of the early terminals. This is why I have made a point of talking about Teletypes (the original terminals) and VT100s (the most popular terminals), both in this chapter and in Chapter 3.

In this section, I'd like to take a quick detour to mention two such conventions that you will encounter a great deal.

The first convention to which I want to draw your attention is the abbreviation "tty" (pronounced "tee-tee-why"). During the many years that Teletype machines were in use, they were referred to as TTYs. This custom was adopted into Unix and, even though it has been a long time since Teletypes were used, the word "tty" is often used as a synonym for a Unix terminal. In particular, you will see this term a lot in Unix documentation and in the names of programs and commands. Here are some examples:

- Within a Unix system, each terminal has its own name. The command to display the name of your terminal is **tty**. (Try it and see what you get.)

- The **stty** ("set tty") command can be used to display or change the settings of your terminal.

- The **getty** ("get tty") program is used to open communication with a terminal and start the login process.

The second convention I want to mention relates to the idea of printing. Teletype terminals had two ways to output data. They could print data on a continuous roll of

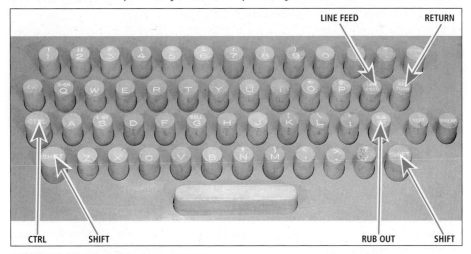

FIGURE 7-1: Keyboard of the Teletype ASR33

For our purposes, the most interesting keys on the Teletype ASR33 keyboard are as follows. In the second row from the top, the RETURN key is on the far right. The LINE FEED key is to the left of RETURN. In the second row from the bottom, the RUB OUT key is third from the right. The CTRL key is on the far left. In the bottom row, the two SHIFT keys on either end. Note that there is no backspace key.

8½ inch paper for a human to read*, and they could punch data on 1-inch wide paper tape for a machine to read. If you take a look at Figure 3-2 in Chapter 3, you can see both the roll of printer paper (in the center) and the roll of paper tape (to the left).

Because output was printed, it became the custom within Unix to use the word PRINT to describe the outputting of information. At the time, this made sense because output was, literally, printed on paper. What is interesting, however, is that, even when more modern terminals became available and data was displayed on monitors, the word "print" was still used, and that is still the case today.

Thus, within Unix documentation, whenever you read about printing data, it almost always refers to displaying data. For example, the **tty** I mentioned above displays the internal name of your terminal. If you look up this command in the Linux version of the online Unix manual (see Chapter 9), you will see that the purpose of **tty** is to "print the file name of the terminal connected to standard input".

Here is another example. As you work within the Unix file system, the directory in which you are working at the current time is called your "working directory". (We'll cover these ideas in Chapter 23.) The command to display the name of your working directory is **pwd**, which stands for "print working directory".

At this point, it only makes sense to ask: If "print" means "display", what term do we use when we really mean print?

There are two answers to this question. First, in some cases, "print" is used to refer to real printing and the meaning is clear by context.

At other times, you will see the term "line printer" (itself an anachronism) or the abbreviation "lp". When you see this, you can consider it a synonym for "printer". For example, the two most important commands to print files are named **lp** and **lpr**. (**lp** comes from System V; **lpr** comes from Berkeley Unix.)

TERMCAP, TERMINFO AND `curses`

As I explained in Chapter 3, Unix was designed as a system in which people used terminals to access a host computer. One of the most important problems that Unix developers had to overcome was that each type of terminal had its own characteristics and used its own set of commands. For example, although all display terminals have a command to clear the screen, the command may not be the same for all terminals.

So, what do you do if you are writing a program and at a particular point, you need to clear the screen of the user's terminal? How would you know what command to send to the terminal, when the actual command depends on what type of terminal is being used?

It doesn't make sense to require every program to know every command for every type of terminal. This would be an enormous burden for software developers.** Moreover, what would happen when a new terminal was introduced? How could it be made to work properly with existing programs?

---

*In case you are curious, Teletypes printed output on continuous rolls of 8½ inch paper, which could be up to 5 inches in diameter. The machine printed 10 characters/inch, with a maximum line length of 72 characters. The vertical spacing was 6 lines/inch. The printing was in one color, normally black.

**Even as long ago as 1980, most terminals supported well over 100 different commands.

The solution was to collect descriptions of all the different types of terminals into a database. Then, when a program wanted to send a command to a terminal, it could be done in a standardized manner by using the information in the database. (We'll talk more about how it works in a moment.)

The first system of this nature was created by Bill Joy, one of the fathers of Berkeley Unix (see Chapter 2). In 1977, when Joy was a graduate student and he put together 1BSD, the first official version of Berkeley Unix, he included a system for managing the display screen of various types of terminals. In mid-1978, he released 2BSD with a more elaborate version of this system, which he named TERMCAP ("terminal capabilities"). The first important program to use Termcap was the **vi** editor (see Chapter 22), also written by Joy.

Using Termcap from within a program was a lot of work. To make it easier, another Berkeley student, Ken Arnold, developed a programming interface he called **curses**. (The name refers to "cursor addressing".) **curses** was designed to carry out all the functions that were necessary to manage a screen display, while hiding the details from the programmer.

Once a programmer learned how to use **curses**, he could write programs that would work with any type of terminal, even those that had yet to be invented. All that was required was that the terminal should have an entry in the Termcap database. The first program to use Termcap was a popular text-based game called Rogue (see box).

In order to work effectively, the Termcap database had to contain technical information for every variation of every terminal that might be used with Unix, and all this data was

---

THE FIRST USE OF CURSES AND TERMCAP: THE GAME OF ROGUE

The first program to use **curses** and Termcap to control the display screen was Rogue, a single-player, text-based fantasy game in the genre of Dungeons & Dragons.

To play Rogue, you would take on the role of an adventurer in an enormous dungeon. At the beginning of the game, you are at the top level of the dungeon. Your goal is to fight your way to the bottom of the dungeon, where you can pick up the Amulet of Yendor. You must then return to the top, bringing the amulet with you. Along the way, you encounter monsters, traps, secret doors and treasures.

At the time Rogue was developed, there was another single-player fantasy game, Adventure, that was very, very popular among programmers. (In fact, I remember playing it on an old Texas Instruments print terminal, connected to a Unix computer over a slow phone line.) Adventure was the same each time you played it but, with Rogue, the dungeon and its contents were generated randomly. This meant that the game was always different. In addition, because Rogue used **curses**, it was able to draw simple maps, something Adventure was not able to do.

The authors of Rogue were Michael Toy, Glenn Wichman and, later, Ken Arnold. The first version of the game was written for Berkeley Unix and, in 1980, Rogue was included with 4.2BSD. 4.2BSD was so popular that, within a short time, Rogue was available to students around the world.

If you were to look at the first version of Rogue, you would find it incredibly primitive. However, it was much more sophisticated than any previous computer game and, at the time, was considered to be *very* cool. Eventually, Rogue was ported to a variety of other systems, including the PC, Macintosh, Amiga and Atari ST.

Today, Rogue is still around and, in its modern incarnation, is played by people around the world. If you are interested in taking a look at one of the more interesting legacies from the early days of Unix, search for "Rogue" on the Internet.

---

contained in a single file. Over the years, as many new terminals became available, the Termcap file grew so large as to become unwieldy to maintain and slow to search.

At the time, **curses** was being enhanced by the programmers at Bell Labs for System III and, later, for System V Release 1 (see Chapter 2). To improve the performance of **curses**, the Bell Labs programmers replaced Termcap with a new facility called TERMINFO ("terminal information"). Terminfo stored its data in a series of files, one for each terminal type. The files were organized into 26 directories named **a** through **z**, all of which were kept in a single Terminfo directory. (This will make sense after you read Chapter 23.) The Terminfo design was so flexible that it is still used today. For example, within Linux, the information for the generic VT100 terminal is stored in the file named:

```
/usr/share/terminfo/v/vt100
```

The location of the master Terminfo directory can vary from one system or another. In case you want to look for it on your system, the most common names are:

```
/usr/share/terminfo/
/usr/lib/terminfo/
/usr/share/lib/terminfo/
/usr/share/misc/terminfo
```

The biggest problem with Terminfo was that AT&T, which owned Bell Labs, would not release source code (see Chapter 2). This meant that, although System V had Terminfo and a better version of **curses**, the hacker community did not have access to it. They had to make do with the older, less powerful Termcap-based facility.

To overcome this limitation, in 1982, a programmer named Pavel Curtis began to work on a free version of **curses**, which he called **ncurses** ("new **curses**"). **ncurses** had very limited distribution until it was taken over by another programmer, Zeyd Ben-Halim, in 1991. In late 1993, Ben-Halim was joined by Eric Raymond, and together they began to work on **ncurses** in earnest.

Throughout the early 1990s, **ncurses** had a lot of problems. However, in time, as other people joined the effort, the problems were solved and **ncurses** and Terminfo emerged as an enduring standard.

Today, Terminfo has replaced Termcap permanently. However, to maintain compatibility with very old programs, some Unix systems still have a Termcap file, even though it is obsolete and its use is deprecated*.

Would you like to see what Termcap or Terminfo information looks like? The Termcap database is easy to display because it consists of plain text, stored as one long file. If your system has a Termcap file, you can display it by using the following command:

```
less /etc/termcap
```

---

*If something is deprecated, it means that, although you can use it, you shouldn't, because it is obsolete.

You will often see the term "deprecated" in computer documentation, especially in the programming world, where things change quickly. When you see such a note, you should take it as a warning that the feature may be eliminated in future versions of the product.

The **less** program displays a file, one screenful at a time. We will talk about **less** in detail in Chapter 21. For now, I'll tell you that, once **less** starts:

- To move forward one screenful, press <Space>.
- To move backward one screenful, press <B>.
- To quit, press <Q>.
- To display help, press <H>.
- To jump to the Termcap entry for the VT100, type **/^vt100** and press <Return>.

(The **/** (slash) character means "search", and the **^** (caret) character means "at the beginning of a line".)

Terminfo data is compiled (that is processed into a non-textual format), which means that you can't look at it directly. Instead, you must use a special program, called **infocmp**, to read the data and render it into plain text. (If your system doesn't recognize the **infocmp** command, it probably means that **ncurses** is not installed.)

To use **infocmp**, just specify the name of the terminal whose information you want to see. For example, to display the Terminfo data for the VT100 terminal, use the command:

```
infocmp vt100 | less
```

The **|** (vertical bar) character sends the output of the command to **less**, in order to display the output one screenful at a time.

To display the Terminfo data for whatever terminal you are currently using, use the command name without a terminal name:

```
infocmp | less
```

If you are running Linux on a PC, you will see one of two possibilities. From a terminal window, such as the Konsole program (see Chapter 6), you will have a terminal of type **xterm**, an X Terminal. From a virtual console (also see Chapter 6), you will have a terminal of type **linux**, which is like a VT220, the color version of the VT100.

HOW DOES UNIX KNOW WHAT TYPE OF TERMINAL YOU ARE USING?

As you can see from the preceding discussion, it is important that Unix know what type of terminal you are using. Before the late 1990s, that could be a problem. There were a lot of different terminals and, it was up to you to tell the system exactly which type you were using. Doing so required you to learn how to use various technical commands.

Today that is not necessary for two reasons. First, many people use Unix on their own PC. When you do so, the "terminal" is built into the computer, and Unix knows about it as a matter of course.

When you connect to a remote host — over a local network, the Internet, or via a phone line — you use a terminal emulation program, not a real terminal. These days, such programs are able to tell the remote host what terminal they are emulating, so you don't have to worry about the details.

Although it would be possible for a program to emulate any type of terminal, in practice there are only four types you will see today. The two most common are the

VT100 and **xterm**. The VT100 is the well-known text-based terminal we discussed at length in Chapter 3. **xterm** is an X Terminal, the standard graphics terminal also discussed in Chapter 3. To a lesser extent, you may see two other terminals emulated: the VT220, a color version of the VT100; and the 3270, used with IBM mainframes. (If you use Linux, you may see a terminal type of "linux". This is essentially a VT220.)

To keep track of what type of terminal you are using, Unix uses what is called a ENVIRONMENT VARIABLE. A environment variable is an entity with a name and a value, which is always available to the shell and to any programs you may run. In particular, there is a global environment **TERM** whose value is set to the type of terminal you are using.

At any time, you can display the value of any environment variable by using the command **echo**, followed by a **$** (dollar sign) character and the name of the variable. For example, to see the value of the **TERM** variable, enter:

echo $TERM

This will show you the type of terminal you are using right now.

We will discuss environment variables in more detail in Chapter 12. For now, if you are curious, here is a command you can use to display the values of all the environment variables within your shell.

printenv

The name of this command, **printenv**, stands for "print environment variables". You will remember that, earlier in the chapter, I explained that it is the custom in Unix to use the word "print" as a synonym for "display".

HINT

You will remember that, as I explained in Chapter 4, Unix distinguishes between lower- and uppercase letters. For example, in Unix, the name **harley** is completely different than the name **Harley**.

Because lowercase is easier to type, it is the custom to use it almost exclusively for names, including userids, commands, and files. This is why, for example, although you may see the userid **harley**, you will never see **Harley** or **HARLEY**.

The main exception to this rule is with respect to environment variables. It is the tradition that, within the shell, environment variables are given uppercase names, such as **TERM**. This allows us to tell at a glance that what we are looking at is, indeed, an environment variable.

THE MODIFIER KEYS; THE <CTRL> KEY

The <Ctrl> key (the name stands for "Control") was a feature on the early Teletype terminals I mentioned at the beginning of the chapter. In the picture of a Teletype keyboard in Figure 7-1, the <Ctrl> key is the leftmost key in the second row from the bottom. As the name implies, this key was used to control the operation of the Teletype. When Unix was created, the <Ctrl> key was adopted by the Unix developers and integrated into the system in several important ways, which we will discuss in a moment.

To use the <Ctrl> key, you hold it down (like the <Shift> key) and press another key, usually a letter. For example, you might hold down <Ctrl> and press the <A> key.

There are 26 such combinations based on the alphabet — <Ctrl>+<A> through <Ctrl>+<Z> — as well as a couple of others that you might run into. Because it is awkward to write "Ctrl" over and over again, the Unix community uses a shorthand notation: the character ^ (the caret). When you see this character next to another character, it means "hold down the <Ctrl> key". For example, **^A** means hold down <Ctrl> and press the <A> key. You might also see the notation <Ctrl-A> or **C-a**, which means the same thing.

By convention, we always write a <Ctrl> combination using an uppercase letter. For instance, we write **^A**, never **^a**. Using uppercase letters makes such combinations easy to read: compare, for example, **^L** to **^l**. However, it's not a real uppercase letter so, when you use a <Ctrl> combination, do not press the <Shift> key.

To get used to this notation, take a look at the following example. This is part of the output from an **stty** command we will meet later in the chapter.

```
erase   kill   werase   rprnt   flush   lnext
^H       ^U      ^W        ^R      ^O       ^V


susp    intr    quit    stop    eof
^Z/^Y    ^C      ^\      ^S/^Q    ^D
```

The output of the **stty** command tells us which keys to press to send certain signals. The details aren't important for now. What I want you to notice is the notation. In this example, we see that to send the **erase** signal you use **^H**. That is, you hold down <Ctrl> and press <H>. For the **kill** signal, you use **^U**; for **werase**, you use **^W**; and so on.

The <Ctrl> key is an example of what are called MODIFIER KEYS. These are keys that you hold down while you press another key. For example, when you type **^H**, the <Ctrl> key "modifies" the <H> key.

On a standard PC keyboard, the modifier keys are <Shift>, <Ctrl> and <Alt>. <Shift> is used for two purposes: to type uppercase letters, and to type the top character on a two-character key. For example, to type the **&** (ampersand) character on a U.S. keyboard, you press <Shift-7>. <Ctrl> is used to type special signals, in the way I explained above. The <Alt> key is the newest of the modifier keys. Since it was not around when Unix was developed, it is not a part of the standard Unix keyboard. Thus, you don't need it to use the standard Unix CLI (command line interface). However, as we discussed in Chapter 6, the <Alt> key is used by the GUI.

THE UNIX KEYBOARD SIGNALS

The original Unix design assumed that people used terminals to connect to a host computer. More than three decades later, that is still the case, even when you are running Unix on your own PC*. Over the years, there have been many different types of terminals with many different types of keyboards, and Unix has been able to work with them all.

---

*As we discussed in Chapter 6, when you run Unix on your own computer, each virtual console and each terminal window is a separate terminal, all of which are connected to the same host computer.

This is because Unix uses a system of keyboard mappings that is so flexible, it can be made to work with any particular keyboard.

To control the operation of programs as they run, Unix uses a set of keyboard signals. Although the signals are standard, the actual keys you press to send the signals can be changed as necessary. That is what creates the flexibility. For example, there is a signal called **intr** (interrupt) that tells a process to abort. If you enter a command that takes a long time to finish, you can stop it by sending it the **intr** signal.

The concept of the **intr** signal is built into the definition of Unix. What is not built into Unix is the actual key that you press to send this signal. In theory, you could use any valid key or key combination, and it can vary from one terminal to another.

With most terminals, **^C** (Ctrl-C) is mapped to the **intr** signal. In other words, to stop a program, you would press **^C**. With a few terminals, the <Delete> key is mapped to the **intr** signal. With one of these terminals, you would press <Delete> to abort a program. In either case, if you don't like the keyboard mapping, you can change it.

Normally, you wouldn't change the Unix keyboard mappings, but you *can*, and that is what makes the system so adaptable. In the next few sections I will describe the important keyboard signals and how you use them. I will then show you how to find out which keys are used on your particular terminal, and how you can change them if you want.

Understanding the keyboard signals and how to use them is one of the basic skills you need to use the Unix CLI.

SIGNALS TO USE WHILE TYPING: `erase`, `werase`, `kill`

There are three keyboard signals you can use as you are typing: **erase**, **werase** and **kill**. **erase** deletes the last character you typed; **werase** deletes the last word you typed; **kill** deletes the entire line.

To send the **erase** signal, you press either the <Backspace> or <Delete> key, depending on your keyboard and its mappings. Take a look at the large key in the top right-hand corner of the main part of your keyboard. In almost all cases, this will be the key that is mapped to **erase**. As you are typing, you can erase the last character you typed by pressing this key.

With most terminals and with a PC, you would use the <Backspace> key. With a Macintosh, you would use the <Delete> key. If you are using a Sun computer whose keyboard has both keys next to one another, use the <Delete> key (the one on top).

HINT

With most keyboards, you press <Backspace> to send the **erase** signal. With a Macintosh, you press <Delete>. The important thing is that you use whichever key works on your particular keyboard.

You may remember that, in Chapter 4, I mentioned that some keyboards have an <Enter> key while others have a <Return> key. It's the same idea. Unix only cares about the signal that is sent when you press the key. As long as you press the right key, Unix doesn't care what it is named.

Throughout this book, when I refer to the <Backspace> key, I mean either <Backspace> or <Delete>, whichever is used on your system. Similarly, when I refer to the <Return> key, I mean either <Return> or <Enter>, whichever is on your keyboard.

Here is an example of how to use the **erase** signal. Say that you want to enter the **date** command (to display the time and date), but you spell it wrong, **datx**. Before you press the <Return> key, press <Backspace> (or <Delete>) to erase the last letter and make your correction:

datx<Backspace>**e**

On your screen, the **x** will disappear when you press <Backspace>. If you want to delete more than one character, you can press <Backspace> as many times as you want.

The next signal, **werase**, tells Unix to erase the last word you typed. The **werase** key is usually **^W**. This key is useful when you want to correct one or more words you have just typed. Of course, you can always press <Backspace> repeatedly, but **^W** is faster when you want to erase whole words.

Here is an example. You are a spy and you want to use the **less** program to display the contents of three files named **data**, **secret** and **top-secret**. The command to use is:

less data secret top-secret

You type the command but, before you press the <Return> key, you notice that another spy is standing behind you, casually looking over your shoulder. You decide that you had better not display the **secret** and **top-secret** files. Press **^W** twice to erase the last two words:

less data secret top-secret^W^W

On your screen, first the word **top-secret** and then the word **secret** will disappear. You can then press <Return> to run the command.

The third signal to use while typing is **kill**. The **kill** key is usually **^X** or **^U**, depending on how your system is set up. This signal tells Unix to erase the entire line.

For example, let's say that you are just about to display the contents of the three files I mentioned above. You type the command but, before you press <Return>, someone runs in the room and tells you they are giving away free money at the bank. Thinking quickly, you erase the command by pressing **^X** (or **^U**):

less data secret top-secret^X

On your screen, the entire line disappears. You can now log out and run to the bank. (Of course, you would never leave your terminal logged in, even to rush out to get free money.)

For reference, Figure 7-2 summarizes the keyboard signals to use when typing.

SIGNAL	KEY	PURPOSE
erase	<Backspace>/<Delete>	erase last character typed
werase	^W	erase last word typed
kill	^X/^U	erase entire line

FIGURE 7-2: Keyboard signals to use while typing

> **HINT**
>
> The **kill** keyboard signal does not stop programs. It only erases the line you are typing. To stop a program, use the **intr** signal, which will be either **^C** or <Delete>.

THE STRANGENESS OF <BACKSPACE> AND <DELETE>

As I mentioned earlier, Unix was designed to use the basic keys that were available on the early Teletype terminals: the letters of the alphabet, numbers, punctuation, the <Shift> keys, a <Return> key, and the <Ctrl> key. Indeed, to this day, you can still use the Unix CLI with only these basic keys.

Modern keyboards have other keys, such as <Backspace>, <Alt>, <PageUp>, <PageDown>, the function keys, the cursor control (arrow) keys, and so on. The most interesting of these keys is the <Backspace> key (<Delete> on a Macintosh). To understand why this key is so interesting, we need to take a trip back in time to revisit our old friend, the Teletype ASR33, the very first Unix terminal. Along the way, we'll prepare ourselves to solve The Case of the Mysterious **^H**.

As you will remember, the Teletype had more than a keyboard and printer; it also had a paper tape punch and a paper tape reader. The punch was used to punch holes in the tape, and the reader was used to read holes and interpret them as data.

Paper tape was 1-inch wide and came in rolls 1,000 feet long. Each position on the tape could store 1 byte (8 bits) of data by punching holes in any of 8 positions. The tape could hold 10 bytes per inch. When the tape was read, the presence or absence of holes was interpreted as a binary (base 2) number: a hole was a one; no hole was a zero. (If you don't understand binary arithmetic, don't worry about it.)

By now you may be asking yourself, why is this important to a modern-day Unix system? The answer is: the physical configuration of the paper tape in 1970 had a direct influence on how the <Backspace> key works today on your computer. Here is why.

Imagine you are using a Teletype machine, and you are typing information that is being punched onto paper tape. Each time you type a character, the machine punches a combination of holes onto the tape. These holes correspond to the ASCII code (see Chapter 19) for the character you typed. You are doing fine until you accidentally make a mistake. Now what do you do?

With a modern PC, you would simply press the <Backspace> key. The cursor on your monitor would then move back one position, and the character you just typed would be erased from the screen. However, life isn't so simple when you have just punched the wrong pattern of holes in a piece of paper.

The solution had two parts and involved special Teletype commands. First, you would press <Ctrl-H> which would send a BS (backspace) command to the paper tape punch. This caused the punch to move back to the previous line where the error occurred. Then you pressed the <Rubout> key which sent the DEL command. This caused the punch to make holes in every one of the 8 positions.

The reason this worked is that the paper tape reader was programmed to skip over any characters that had all 8 holes punched. In the language of base 2, we would say that the paper tape reader ignored any binary patterns consisting of all ones.

Thus, by overpunching a character with 8 holes — that is, by turning whatever binary code happened to be there into 8 ones — you effectively erased the character. This is why the key to do this was named "Rubout". (You can imagine making a mistake with a pencil and rubbing it out with an eraser.)

Thus, to the early Unix developers, there were two different operations that went into erasing a mistake: backspacing with **^H** and rubbing out with <Rubout>. The question they faced was, which key should be mapped to the **erase** signal, **^H** or <Rubout>? They chose **^H**.

Within a short time, computer companies started to make terminals with a <Backspace> key. For convenience, this key was programmed to be the same as pressing **^H** so, when you made a typing mistake, you could erase it by pressing either <Backspace> or **^H**, both of which were mapped to the **erase** signal.

In later years, the name of the <Rubout> key was changed to <Delete>, which only made sense. Eventually, some Unix companies (notably Sun Microsystems) decided to add an actual <Delete> key to their keyboards. Like the old <Rubout> key, <Delete> generated the DEL code (the one that was originally used to "erase" a character on paper tape). These same companies then decided to use the DEL code, instead of **^H**, for backspacing.

Thus, it came to pass that, with some keyboards, you pressed <Backspace> to erase a character while, with others, you pressed <Delete>. In the first case, <Backspace> was the same as **^H**, the key that, on a Teletype, sent the BS code. In the second case, <Delete> was the same as <Rubout>, the key that, on a Teletype, sent the DEL code.

To make matters more confusing, there was a problem when Unix documentation was written. There was an easy way to represent the BS code, **^H**, but there was no easy way to represent the DEL code. To solve this problem, the designation **^?** was chosen to represent DEL.

Unlike **^H**, however, **^?** is not a real key combination. That is, you can't hold down the <Ctrl> key and press **?** (question mark). **^?** is simply a two-character abbreviation that means "whichever key on your keyboard that sends the code that used to be called DEL".

To make things even more confusing, in later years some Unix systems were configured so that the <Backspace> key works the same as **^?** (DEL), not **^H** (BS). In such cases, **^?**, not **^H**, is mapped to **erase**.

So here is the situation. If you have a <Backspace> key on your keyboard, it will be mapped to **erase**. This is the case with PCs. If you do not have a <Backspace> key, you will have a <Delete> key that will be mapped to **erase**. This is the case with Macintoshes.

If you are using a Sun computer with both a <Backspace> and <Delete> key, the <Backspace> key will be the same as **^H**, and the <Delete> key will be the same as **^?**. One of these keys will be mapped to **erase**. Try both and see which one works.

In order to get around the **^H/^?** confusion, some Unix systems define an extra signal called **erase2**. This is the case with FreeBSD, for example.

erase2 has the same effect as **erase**. That is, it erases the last character you typed. The difference is that **^H** maps to one of the signals — **erase** or **erase2** — and **^?** maps to the other. In this way, your <Backspace> key will always work properly, regardless of whether it sends **^H** or **^?**.

HINT

When the first IBM PC was introduced in August 1981, it came with a brand new keyboard. This keyboard (which is almost the same as the one we use today), had several new keys, such as <Insert>, <Delete>, <PageUp>, <PageDown>, and so on.

It is important to realize that the <Delete> key on the PC keyboard is *not* the same as the <Delete> key on the old terminals, or on the Macintosh or Sun computers. It is a completely different key.

If you have a PC, you can prove this to yourself. Type something at the Unix command line, but don't press the <Return> key. Now press <Backspace> a few times. Notice that the last few characters are erased. This is because, on your computer, <Backspace> is the same as either **^H** or **^?**, whichever one happens to be mapped to **erase**.

Now press <Delete> (the key next to <Insert>). It does not erase the previous character, because it is not mapped to the **erase** signal.

THE CASE OF THE MYSTERIOUS ^H

You are using your PC to connect to a remote Unix host over a network. You are typing and, all of a sudden, someone throws a red and white Betty Boop doll at your head. This startles you and, when you look back at the screen, you notice you have made a typing mistake.

You press <Backspace> a few times but, instead of erasing the last few characters, you see:

```
^H^H^H
```

You look at the screen with amazement. Why did the <Backspace> display **^H** instead of erasing? After all, isn't **^H** mapped to the **erase** signal?

The answer is, on your computer, <Backspace> is the same as **^H**, and **^H** *is* mapped to **erase**. This is why, on your machine, <Backspace> works fine.

On the remote host, however, **^?** is mapped to **erase**. When you press the <Backspace> key, you are sending **^H** which, on the remote host, is meaningless. That is why, on the remote host, <Backspace> does not work.

You have four choices. First, you can use other keys to fix your typing mistakes. Instead of using <Backspace> to erase one character at a time, you can use **^W** to erase an entire word, or **^X**/**^U** to erase the entire line.

Second, you can look for a key that will send **^?** to the remote host. On many systems, <Ctrl-Backspace> will do the job. Try it and see if it works. (If you are using a Macintosh, try <Option-Backspace>.)

Third, you can change the configuration of the program you are using to make the connection. Most communication programs will let you control whether <Backspace> sends **^H** or a **^?**. If your program lets you do this, you can configure it so that, whenever you connect to this particular host, <Backspace> sends **^?** instead of **^H**.

Finally, you can change the mapping on the remote host itself so **^H**, not **^?** maps to the **erase** signal. Once you do this, <Backspace> will work just fine. This is usually the best solution, especially if you are going to use the remote host a lot.

To make the change, all you need to do is place one specific command in the initialization file that gets executed each time you log in to the remote host. Here is the command.

```
stty erase ^H
```

(We will discuss the **stty** command in more detail later in the chapter.)

The name of the file in which you put this command varies depending on what shell you are using. If you use Bash (the default shell for Linux systems) or the Korn Shell, put the command in your **.profile** file. If you use the C-Shell, put the command in your **.login** file. In both cases, the "." (period) is part of the file name. (We'll discuss these files in Chapter 14.)

STOPPING A PROGRAM: `intr`

There are several signals that you can use to stop or pause a program. These signals are **intr**, **quit**, **stop** and **susp**. We will discuss each one in turn. Interestingly enough, as you will see, the **stop** signal isn't the one that stops a program.

On most systems, the **intr** key is **^C**. On some systems, you use the <Delete> key instead. Try both and see which one works for you.

The **intr** (interrupt) signal actually has two uses. First, you can use it to stop a program dead in its tracks. For example, say you enter a command that is taking so long to finish that you decide to stop waiting. Just press **^C**. The remote command will abort, and you will be back at the shell prompt.

Some programs are programmed to ignore the **intr** signal. In such cases, there will always be a well-defined way to end the program (some type of "quit" command). By ignoring the **intr** signal, the program keeps you from causing damage by pressing **^C** inadvertently. We say that the program TRAPS the **intr** signal.

For example, consider what happens if you are editing a file with the **vi** text editor (Chapter 22) and you press **^C**. **vi** traps the **intr** signal and does not stop. In order to stop the program you need to use the **vi** quit command. If **vi** had not trapped the **intr** signal, pressing **^C** would abort the program, and you would lose all the data that was not yet saved.

Note: You may sometimes see the **intr** key referred to as the "break" key. If you use a PC, you may know that **^C** acts as a break key under Microsoft Windows for command line programs. As you can see, this idea (along with many others) was taken from Unix.

The second use for the **intr** signal arises when you are typing a Unix command at the shell prompt. If you are typing a command and you change your mind, you can press **^C** instead of <Return>. Pressing **^C** will cancel the command completely.

Be sure that you do not confuse the **intr** key (**^C**/<Delete>) with the **kill** key (**^U**/**^X**). When you are typing a command, **intr** cancels the command, while **kill** erases all the characters on the line. Effectively, this has the same result: whatever you were typing is discarded, and you can enter a new command.

However, only **intr** will stop a program. In spite of its name, **kill** will not kill.

ANOTHER WAY TO STOP A PROGRAM: `quit`

Aside from **intr** (**^C**), there is another keyboard signal, **quit** that will stop a program. The **quit** key is usually **^** (<Ctrl-Backslash>).

What is the difference between **intr** and **quit**? Not much. In the olden days, **quit** was designed for advanced programmers who needed to abort a test program. When you pressed **^**, it not only stopped the program, but it also told Unix to make a copy of the contents of memory at that instant. This information was stored in a CORE FILE, that is, a file with the name of **core** (the old name for computer memory). A programmer could then use special tools to analyze the core file to figure out what went wrong.

Today, programmers have better tools to debug programs and, on most systems, the **quit** signal does not generate a core file, although core files are still used within some programming environments to help debugging. If you are not actively debugging a program and a file named **core** mysteriously appears in one of your directories, it means that a program you were running aborted with a serious error*. Unless you really want the file, you can erase it. In fact, you should erase it, because core files are rather large and there is no reason to waste the space.

WHAT'S IN A NAME?

Core file

In the early days of computing, computer memory was constructed from electro-mechanical relays and, later, vacuum tubes. In 1952, a new technology called CORE MEMORY was first used in an experimental version of the IBM 405 Alphabetical Accounting Machine. (The 405, which was IBM's high-end tabulator, was a very old device, dating back to 1934.)

The new type of memory was constructed using tiny, round, hollow magnetic devices called CORES, measuring about 0.25 inch (6.4 mm) in diameter (see Figure 7-3). A large number of cores were arranged in a lattice with several electrical wires running through each core. By changing the current in the wires, it was possible to modify the magnetic properties of individual cores to either "off" or "on". This made it possible to store and retrieve binary data.

Over the years, magnetic core memory was improved and, by the 1960s, it was the mainstay of the IBM's flagship System/360. Eventually, technology advanced, and magnetic core memory was replaced by semiconductors (transistors) and integrated circuits, leading to today's fast, high-density memory chips. However, because the first modern computers used core memory, the word CORE became a synonym for "memory", a term that has survived to this day.

In the olden days, debugging was a particularly difficult process, especially when a program aborted unexpectedly. One technique programmers used was to have the operating system print a copy of the contents of memory used by a program at the time the program aborted. This was called a CORE DUMP, and was printed on paper. A core dump could take up many pages of paper and took great skill to interpret.**

When Unix was developed, this technique was continued. However, instead of printing a core dump on paper, Unix saved the data in a special file with the name of **core**. If you were

---

*The most common cause is a segmentation fault. This occurs when a program attempts to access memory that is not allocated to the program, for example, by the improper use of a pointer. (A pointer is a variable that points to something else.)

** As an undergraduate at the University of Waterloo, Canada, I worked as a systems programmer at the Computing Center, which maintained two, large IBM mainframes. From time to time, I would watch the more experienced system programmers use a large, multi-page core dump to track down an elusive bug. To my young, untutored eye, the process of reading a core dump was both mysterious and awe-inspiring.

(*cont'd...*) testing a program, you could force it to abort and create a core file by pressing ^\
(the **quit** key). Although the old-time Unix programmers had to learn how to interpret core
files, they are rarely used today because much better debugging tools are available.

PAUSING THE DISPLAY: stop, start

When a program writes a line of output to the bottom of your screen and all the other
lines move up one position, we say they SCROLL upward. If a program produces output
too fast, data will scroll off the top of the screen before you can read it.

If you want to see an example of this, use one of the following commands. The **dmesg**
command, which we met in Chapter 6, shows you all the messages that were displayed when
the system booted. Alternatively, you can use the **cat** command to display the Termcap file:

```
dmesg
cat /etc/termcap
```

FIGURE 7-3: Magnetic core memory

*A close-up photo of the first magnetic core memory, used in an experimental version of the IBM 405
Alphabetical Accounting Machine in 1952. The individual cores were tiny, having a diameter of about
0.25 inch (6.4 mm). Over the years, core memory was improved and, during the 1960s, it was the
mainstay of IBM's flagship line of computers, the IBM System/360. Eventually, core memory was
replaced by semiconductors, which were themselves replaced by modern integrated circuits.*

The **cat** command, which we will meet in Chapter 16, concatenates data and sends it to the default output location, or "standard output". In this case, **cat** copies data from the file **/etc/termcap** to your display. However, the copying is so fast that most of the data scrolls off the screen before you can read it, which is the purpose of this example.

In such cases, you have three choices. First, if the lost data is not important, you can ignore it. Second, you can restart the program that generates the data and have it send the output to a so-called paging program like **less** (Chapter 21) that will display the output one screenful at a time. This is what we did earlier in the chapter when we used the command:

```
less /etc/termcap
```

With **dmesg**, we would use a different command that makes use of the **|** (vertical bar) character. This is called the "pipe symbol", and we will discuss it in Chapter 15. The idea is to reroute the output of **dmesg** to **less**.

```
dmesg | less
```

Finally, you can press the **^S** key to send the **stop** signal. This tells Unix to pause the screen display temporarily. Once the display is paused, you can restart it by pressing **^Q** to send the **start** signal. To remember, just think of "S" for Stop and "Q" for Qontinue.

Using **^S** and **^Q** can be handy. However, you should understand that **^S** only tells Unix to stop displaying output. It does not pause the program that is executing. The program will keep running and will not stop generating output.

Unix will store the output so that none will be lost and, as soon as you press **^Q**, whatever output remains will be displayed. If a great many lines of new data were generated while the screen display was paused, they will probably whiz by rapidly once you press **^Q**.

By the way, you might be wondering, why were **^S** and **^Q** chosen to map to the **start** and **stop** signals? It does seem like an odd choice. The answer is, on the Teletype ASR33, <Ctrl-Q> sent the XON code, which turned on the paper tape reader; <Ctrl-S> sent the XOFF code, which turned it off.

HINT

If your terminal ever locks up mysteriously, try pressing **^Q**. You may have pressed **^S** inadvertently and paused the display.

When everything seems to have stopped mysteriously, you will never cause any harm by pressing **^Q**.

THE END OF FILE SIGNAL: eof

From time to time, you will work with programs that expect you to enter data from the keyboard. When you get to the point where there is no more data, you indicate this by pressing **^D** which sends the **eof** (end of file) signal.

Here is an example: In Chapter 8, I discuss the **bc** program which provides the services of a built-in calculator. Once you start **bc**, you enter one calculation after another. After each calculation, **bc** displays the answer. When you are finished, you press **^D** to tell **bc** that there is no more data. Upon receiving the **eof** signal, the program terminates.

THE SHELL AND THE eof SIGNAL

In Chapter 2, I explained that the shell is the program that reads your Unix commands and interprets them. When the shell is ready to read a command, it displays a prompt. You type a command and press <Return>. The shell processes the command and then displays a new prompt. In some cases, your command will start a program, such as a text editor, that you will work with for a while. When you end the program, you will be returned to the shell prompt.

Thus, in general terms, a Unix session with the CLI (command line interface) consists of entering one command after another.

Although the shell may seem mysterious, it is really just a program. And from the point of view of the shell, the commands you type are just data that needs to be processed. Thus, you can stop the shell by indicating that there is no more data. In other words, you can stop the shell by pressing **^D**, the **eof** key.

But what does stopping the shell really mean? It means that you have finished your work and, when the shell stops, Unix logs you out automatically. This is why it is possible to log out by pressing **^D**. You are actually telling the shell (and Unix) that there is no more work to be done.

Of course, there is a potential problem. What if you press **^D** by accident? You will be logged out immediately. The solution is to tell the shell to trap the **eof** signal. How you do this depends on what shell you are using. Let's take each shell in turn — Bash, the C-Shell, and the Korn Shell — and you can experiment with your particular shell.

BASH: TRAPPING THE eof SIGNAL

Bash is the default shell with Linux. To tell Bash to ignore the **eof** signal, you use an environment variable named **IGNOREEOF**. (Notice there are two **E**s in a row, so be careful when you spell it.) Here is how it works.

IGNOREEOF is set to a particular number, which indicates how many times Bash will ignore **^D** at the beginning of a particular line before logging you out. To set IGNOREEOF, use a command like the following. (You can use any number you want instead of 5.)

```
IGNOREEOF=5
```

To test it, press **^D** repeatedly, and count how many **^D**s are ignored until you are logged out.

When **IGNOREEOF** is set and you press **^D**, you will see a message telling you that you can't log out by pressing **^D**. If you are working in the login shell (that is, the shell that was started automatically when you logged in), you will see:

```
Use "logout" to leave the shell.
```

If you are working in a subshell (that is, a shell that you started after you logged in), you will see:

```
Use "exit" to leave the shell.
```

If, for some reason, you want to turn off the **IGNOREEOF** feature, just set it to 0:

```
IGNOREEOF=0
```

To display the current value of **IGNOREEOF**, use:

```
echo $IGNOREEOF
```

To set **IGNOREEOF** automatically each time you log in, put the appropriate command in your **.profile** file (see Chapter 14).

KORN SHELL: TRAPPING THE eof SIGNAL

The Korn shell is the default shell on various commercial Unix systems. In addition, the default shell for FreeBSD is almost the same as the Korn shell.

To tell the Korn Shell to ignore **^D**, you set a shell option named **ignoreeof**. (Notice there are two **e**s in a row, so be careful when you spell it.) To do this, use the command:

```
set -o ignoreeof
```

Once you do, if you press **^D**, you will see a message telling you that you can't log out by pressing **^D**:

```
Use "exit" to leave shell.
```

If, for some reason, you want to turn off the **ignoreeof** option, use:

```
set +o ignoreeof
```

To display the current value of **ignoreeof**, use:

```
set -o
```

This will show you all the shell options and tell you whether or not they are off or on.

To set **ignoreeof** automatically each time you log in, put the appropriate **set** command in your **.profile** file (see Chapter 14).

C-SHELL: TRAPPING THE eof SIGNAL

To tell the C-Shell to ignore **^D**, you set a shell variable named **ignoreeof**. (Notice there are two **e**s in a row, so be careful when you spell it.) To do this, use the command:

```
set ignoreeof
```

Once you do, if you press **^D**, you will see a message telling you that you can't log out by pressing **^D**. If you are working in the login shell (that is, the shell that was started automatically when you logged in), you will see:

```
Use "logout" to logout.
```

If you are working in a subshell (that is, a shell that you started after you logged in), you will see:

```
Use "exit" to leave csh.
```

(**csh** is the name of the C-Shell program.)
If, for some reason, you want to turn off the **ignoreeof** feature, use:

```
unset ignoreeof
```

To display the current value of **ignoreeof**, use:

```
echo $ignoreeof
```

If **ignoreeof** is set, you will see nothing. If it is not set, you will see:

```
ignoreeof: Undefined variable.
```

To set **ignoreeof** automatically each time you login, put the **set** command in your **.cshrc** file (see Chapter 14).

DISPLAYING KEY MAPPINGS: stty -a

So far, I have mentioned a number of keyboard signals, each of which corresponds to some key on your keyboard. These are shown in Figure 7-4. The key mappings I have shown are the most common ones, but they are changeable.
To display the key mappings on your system, use the following command.

```
stty -a
```

stty is the "set terminal" command; **-a** means "show me all the settings".
The **stty** command displays several lines of information about your terminal. The only lines we are interested in are the ones that show the keyboard signals and the keys to which they are mapped. Here is an example from a Linux system:

SIGNAL	KEY	PURPOSE
erase	<Backspace>/<Delete>	erase last character typed
werase	^W	erase last word typed
kill	^X/^U	erase entire line
intr	^C	stop a program that is running
quit	^\	stop program & save **core** file
stop	^S	pause the screen display
start	^Q	restart the screen display
eof	^D	indicate there is no more data

FIGURE 7-4: Summary of important keyboard signals

```
intr = ^C; quit = ^\; erase = ^?; kill = ^U;
eof = ^D; eol = <undef>; eol2 = <undef>;
start = ^Q; stop = ^S; susp = ^Z; rprnt = ^R;
werase = ^W; lnext = ^V; flush = ^O;
```

And here is an example from a Free BSD system:

```
discard = ^O; dsusp = ^Y; eof = ^D; eol = <undef>;
eol2 = <undef>; erase = ^?; erase2 = ^H; intr = ^C;
kill = ^U; lnext = ^V; quit = ^\; reprint = ^R;
start = ^Q; status = ^T; stop = ^S; susp = ^Z; werase = ^W;
```

Notice that the FreeBSD example has an **erase2** signal.

As you can see, there are several signals I did not cover. Most of these are not important for day-to-day work, and you can ignore them.

> **HINT**
>
> In Chapter 26, we will discuss how to pause and restart programs that are running. At the time, you will see that you can pause a program by pressing **^Z**, which is mapped to the **susp** (suspend) signal. Once you pause a program with **^Z**, it stops running until you restart it by entering the **fg** (foreground) command.
>
> So if you are ever working and, all of a sudden, your program stops and you see a message like **Suspended** or **Stopped**, it means you have accidentally pressed **^Z**.
>
> When this happens, all you have to do is enter **fg**, and your program will come back to life.

CHANGING KEY MAPPINGS: stty

If you would like to change a key mapping, use the **stty** command. Just type **stty**, followed by the name of the signal, followed by the new key assignment. For example, to change the **kill** key to **^U**, enter:

```
stty kill ^U
```

Important: Be sure to type the <Ctrl> key combination as two separate characters, not as a real <Ctrl> combination; **stty** will figure it out. For example, in this case, you would type the ^ (caret) character, followed by the **U** character. You would not type <Ctrl-U>.

When you use **stty** with the name of a <Ctrl> character, it is not necessary to type an uppercase letter. For instance, the following two commands will both work:

```
stty kill ^u
stty kill ^U
```

Just remember to type two separate characters.

Strictly speaking, you can map any key you want to a signal. For example, you could map the letter **K** to the **kill** signal. Either of these commands will do the job:

```
stty kill k
stty kill K
```

Of course, such a mapping would only lead to problems. Every time you pressed the <K> key, Unix would erase the line you were typing! What an interesting trick this would be to play on a friend.*

Normally, we use only <Ctrl> combinations for mappings. In fact, in almost all cases, it's better to leave things the way they are, and stick with the standard key assignments.

Here is one situation, however, where you may want to make a change. Let's say you often connect to a remote host over a network and, on that host, the **erase** key is **^?**. However, your Backspace key sends a **^H**. To make life more convenient, you map **^H** to **erase**. This allows you to press <Backspace> to delete a character.

```
stty erase ^H
```

Here is the opposite example. You connect to a remote host on which **^H** is mapped to **erase**. However, your <Backspace> (or <Delete>) key sends **^?**. Use **stty** to change the mapping as follows:

```
stty erase ^?
```

Remember, the notation **^?** does not refer to an actual <Ctrl> key combination. **^?** is a two-character abbreviation for "whichever key on your keyboard sends the DEL code".

If you decide to mess around with keyboard mappings, you can use the command I described above to check them:

```
stty -a
```

Alternatively, you enter the **stty** command by itself:

```
stty
```

This will display an abbreviated report, showing only those mappings that have been changed from the default.

COMMAND LINE EDITING

As you type on the command line, the cursor points to the next available location. Each time you type a character, the cursor moves one position to the right.

What do you do when you make a mistake? As we discussed earlier in the chapter, you press the <Backspace> key, erase one or more characters, and type the new ones.

However, what happens if you want to fix a mistake at the beginning of the line, and you have already typed 20 characters after the mistake? Certainly you can press <Backspace> 21 times, fix the mistake, and retype the 20 characters. However, there is an easier way.

With most (but not all) shells, you can simply use the left-arrow key, which I will call <Left>. Each time you press this key, it moves your cursor to the left without erasing anything. You can then make the changes you want and press <Return>.

Try this example, using the **echo** command. (**echo** simply displays the value of whatever you give it.) Type the following:

---

*You didn't read it here.

```
echo "This is a test!"
```

Now press <Return>. The shell will display **This is a test!** Now type the following, but do not press <Return>:

```
echo "Thus is a test!"
```

Before you press <Return>, you need to change **Thus** to **This**. Your cursor should be at the end of the line, so press <Left> repeatedly until the cursor is just to the right of the **u** in **Thus**. Press <Backspace> once to erase the **u**, and then type **i**. You can now press <Return>, and you should see the correct output.

This is an example of what is called COMMAND LINE EDITING, that is, changing what is on the command line before you send it to the shell. Notice that you did not have to move the cursor to the end of the line before you pressed <Return>.

HINT

When you press <Return>, the characters that are on the command line are sent to the shell to be interpreted. Because the cursor does not generate a character, the shell doesn't care where the cursor is when you send it a command.

This means that, when you are command line editing, you can press the <Return> key from anywhere in the line. The cursor does not have to be at the end of the line.

All modern shells support some type of command line editing, but the details vary from one shell to another. For that reason, we will leave the bulk of the discussion to later in the book, when we talk about each individual shell. For now, I'll teach you the three most important techniques. Try them and see if they work with your particular shell.

First, as you are typing, you can use the <Left> and <Right> arrow keys to move the cursor within the command line. This is what we did in our example above.

Second, at any time, you can press <Backspace> to erase the previous character. With some shells, you can also use the <Delete> key to erase the *current* character. (The <Delete> key I am talking about is the one you find on a PC keyboard, next to the <Insert> key.)

Third, as you enter commands, the shell keeps them in an invisible "history list". You can use the <Up> and <Down> arrow keys to move backward and forward within this list. When you press <Up>, the current command vanishes and is replaced by the previous command. If you press <Up> again, you get the command before that.

Thus, you can press <Up> one or more times to recall a previous command. If you go too far, press <Down> to move down in the list. You can then edit the line to your liking, and resubmit it by pressing <Return>.

WHAT'S IN A NAME?

Destructive backspace, Non-destructive backspace

When you press the <Backspace> key, it moves the cursor one position to the left while erasing a character. When you press the <Left> arrow key, it moves the cursor to the left without erasing a character.

(*cont'd...*) In a sense, the two actions are similar in that they both move the cursor backwards. The only difference is whether or not anything is erased. To capture this idea, you will sometimes see the terms "destructive backspace" and "non-destructive backspace" used.

A DESTRUCTIVE BACKSPACE occurs when the cursor moves back and characters are erased. This is what happens when you press the <Backspace> key.

A NON-DESTRUCTIVE BACKSPACE occurs when the cursor moves back but nothing is changed. This is what happens when you press the <Left> key.

RETURN AND LINEFEED

Earlier in the chapter, we discussed how the way in which Unix handles the <Backspace> key can be traced back to the original Unix terminal, the Teletype ASR33. More specifically, there were two Teletype codes (BS and DEL) that were involved in erasing a character on paper tape. The Unix developers chose one of these codes to use for the **erase** signal.

Interestingly enough, they had the same type of choice when it came to deciding what should happen with the <Return> key. Moreover, the decision they made regarding the <Return> key turned out to be much more important than the one they made with the <Backspace> key. This is because the code they chose is used — not only with the <Return> key — but as a special marker that goes at the end of every line in a text file. To begin our discussion, we need to, once again, go back in time to the Teletype ASR33.

The Teletype ASR33 had a print head that used a ribbon to print characters on paper. As characters were printed, the print head moved from left to right. When the print head got to the end of a line, two things had to happen. First, the paper had to be moved up one line; second, the print head, which was attached to a "carriage", had to be returned to the far left.

To make the Teletype perform these actions, there were codes embedded in whatever data was being printed. The data could come from the keyboard, from an incoming communication line, or from the paper tape reader.

The first code, CR (carriage return), returned the carriage to its leftmost position. The second code, LF (linefeed), caused the paper to be moved one line. Thus, the sequence CR-LF performed the actions necessary to prepare to print a new line.

From the keyboard, you would send a CR code by pressing either the <Return> key or **^M**. (They were equivalent.) You would send the LF code by pressing either the <Linefeed> key or **^J**. (If you look at Figure 7-1 earlier in the chapter, the <Return> key is at the far right of the second row from the top. The <Linefeed> key is one position to the left.)

When the Unix developers came to use the Teletype as a terminal, they created two signals based on the CR and LF codes. The CR code became the RETURN signal. The LF code became the LINEFEED signal.

So now, let us ask a question: When you type at a Unix terminal, what happens when you press the <Return> key? Before I can answer that, I need to talk a bit about how Unix organizes plain text into files.

Chapter 7

THE IMPORTANCE OF NEWLINE

As we have discussed, Unix uses two signals based on the old Teletype: return and linefeed. From the keyboard, you send return by pressing **^M** and linefeed by pressing **^J**.

Since return and linefeed are really the same as **^M** and **^J**, we usually refer to them as characters, rather than signals. Here is how they are used in three different situations.

First: When files contain textual data, we usually divide the data into lines. In Unix, we use a **^J** character to mark the end of each line. When we use **^J** in this way, we refer to it as a NEWLINE character, rather than linefeed. Thus, when a program reads data from a file, it knows it has reached the end of a line when it encounters a newline (that is, a **^J** character).

Second: When you are typing characters at a terminal, you press <Return> at the end of the line. Doing so sends the return character, that is, **^M**.

Third: When data is displayed, it is sent to your terminal one line at a time. At the end of each line, the cursor must be moved to the beginning of the next line. As with the Teletype, this involves two separate actions: a "carriage return" to move the cursor to the beginning of the line, followed by a "line feed" to move the cursor down one line. For the "carriage return" Unix sends a return character (that is, **^M**). For the "linefeed", Unix sends a linefeed character (that is, **^J**). Thus, when data is displayed, each line must end with **^M^J**.

One of the most elegant features of Unix is that data typed at the keyboard is treated the same as data read from a file. For example, say you have a program that reads a series of names, one per line. Such a program can read the names either from a file on your disk or from the keyboard. The program does not need to be written in a special way to have such flexibility. This feature, called "standard input", is built into Unix. Standard input allows all Unix programs to read data in the same way, without having to worry about the source of the data. (We will discuss this idea in Chapter 15.)

In order for standard input to work properly, every line of data must end with a newline. However, when you type characters at the keyboard, they come in with a return at the end of the line, not a newline. This creates a problem.

Similarly, when Unix programs output data, they can make use of "standard output". This allows all programs to write data in the same way, without having to worry about where the data is going.

When data is written to a file, each line must end with a newline character (that is, **^J**). However, when data is written to the terminal, each line must end with return+newline (**^M^J**). This creates a second problem.

These problems are reconciled in two ways. First, as you type, whenever you press <Return>, Unix changes the return into a newline. That is, it changes the **^M** into **^J**.

Second, when data is being written to the terminal, Unix changes each newline to a return+linefeed. That is, it changes **^J** to **^M^J**.

Here is a quick summary to help you make sense of all this:

1. return = **^M**.

2. linefeed = newline = **^J**.

3. In general, every line of text must end with a newline.

4. When you press the <Return> key, it sends a return character, which Unix automatically changes to a newline.

5. To display data on a terminal, each line must end with the sequence of characters: return+linefeed. Thus, as data is sent from a file to the terminal to be displayed, Unix automatically changes the newline at the end of each line to return+linefeed.

At first, this may seem a bit confusing. Eventually, you will come to see that it all makes perfect sense, at which time you will know that you have finally started to think in Unix.

HINT

Within text files, Unix marks the end of each line with a **^J** (newline) character. Microsoft Windows, however, does it differently. Windows marks the end of each line with a **^M^J**. (In Unix terms, that would be return+linefeed.)

Thus, when you copy text files from Unix to Windows, each **^J** must be changed to **^M^J**. Conversely, when you copy files from Windows to Unix, each **^M^J** must be changed to **^J**.

When you use a program to copy files between two such computers, the program should know how to make the changes for you automatically. If not, there are utility programs available to do the job.

AN IMPORTANT USE FOR ^J: `stty sane`, `reset`

Unless you are a programmer, it is not really necessary to master all the technical details regarding return and newline. Just remember to press <Return> at the end of each line and let Unix do the work.

However, there are some situations in which understanding these ideas is helpful. On rare occasions, the settings for your terminal may become so messed up that the terminal does not work properly. In such cases, there are two commands you can use to reset your terminal settings to reasonable values: **stty sane** or **reset**.

In rare cases, you may find that when you try to enter one of these commands by pressing <Return>, the return to newline conversion will not work, and Unix will not accept the command. If this happens, simply press **^M** instead of <Return>. This will work because the two keys are essentially the same.

The solution is to press **^J** (the same as newline), which is all Unix wants anyway. Thus, when all else fails, typing one of the following commands may rejuvenate your terminal. Be sure to type **^J** before and after the command. You can try it now if you want; it won't hurt anything.

<Ctrl-J>**stty sane**<Ctrl-J>
<Ctrl-J>**reset**<Ctrl-J>

You might ask, if that is the case, can you press **^J** instead of <Return> to enter a command at any time? Of course — try it.

To show you how useful these commands can be, here is a true story.

I have a friend Susan who was helping someone with a Linux installation. They were working with a program that allows you to choose which options you want included in the kernel. The program needed a particular directory that did not exist, so Susan pressed **^Z** to pause the program. She now had an opportunity to create the directory.

However, it happened that the program — in order to keep the display from changing — had disabled the effect of the return character. This meant that, whenever Susan entered commands, the output would not display properly.

(Remember, when Unix writes data to the terminal, it puts return+linefeed at the end of every line. What do you think happens when only the linefeed works?)

Susan, however, is nothing if not resourceful. She entered the **reset** command and, in an instant, the terminal was working properly. She then created the directory she needed, restarted the installation program, and lived happily ever after.

THE FABLE OF THE PROGRAMMER AND THE PRINCESS

A long time ago, there lived a young, handsome, charming programmer (you can tell this is a fable), who won the love of a beautiful princess. However, the night before their wedding, the princess was kidnapped.

Fortunately, the princess had the presence of mind to leave a trail of pearls from her necklace. The programmer followed the trail to a remote corner of the lawless Silicon Valley, where he discovered that his love was being held captive in an abandoned technical support center by an evil Vice President of Marketing.

Thinking quickly, the programmer took a powerful magnet and entered the building. He tracked down the princess and broke into the room where the VP of Marketing stood gloating over the terrified girl.

"Release that girl immediately," roared the programmer, "or I will use this magnet and scramble all your disks."

The VP pressed a secret button and in the blink of an eye, four more ugly, hulking vice presidents entered the room.

"On the other hand," said the programmer, "perhaps we can make a deal."

"What did you have in mind?" said the VP.

"You set me any Unix task you want," answered the programmer. "If I do it, the princess and I will go free. If I fail, I will leave, never to return, and the princess is yours."

"Agreed," said the VP, his eyes gleaming like two toady red nuggets encased in suet. "Sit down at this terminal. Your task will have two parts. First, using a single command, display the time and date."

"Child's play," said the programmer, as he typed **date** and pressed the <Return> key.

"Now," said the VP, "do it again." However, as the programmer once again typed **date**, the VP added, "—but this time you are not allowed to use either the <Return> key or **^M**."

"RTFM, you ignorant buffoon!" cried the programmer, whereupon he pressed **^J**, grabbed the princess, and led her to his waiting Ferrari and a life of freedom.

CHAPTER 7 EXERCISES

REVIEW QUESTIONS

1. Why is it a Unix convention to use the abbreviation "tty" to refer to terminals?

2. Why is it a Unix convention to use the word "print" to refer to displaying data on a monitor?

3. What does the term "deprecated" mean?

4. How does Unix know which terminal you are using?

5. Which key do you press to erase the last character you typed? The last word? The entire line?

APPLYING YOUR KNOWLEDGE

1. By default, the **erase** key is the <Backspace> key (or on a Macintosh, the <Delete> key). Normally, this key is mapped to **^H** or, less often, **^?**. Use the **stty** command to change the **erase** key to the uppercase letter "X". Once you do this, you can erase the last character you typed by pressing "X". Test this. What happens when you press a lowercase "x"? Why? Now use **stty** to change the **erase** key back to the <Backspace> (or <Delete>) key. Test to make sure it worked.

FOR FURTHER THOUGHT

1. One way to logout is to press **^D** (which sends the **eof** signal) at the shell prompt. Since you might do this by accident, you can tell the shell to ignore the **eof** signal. Why is this not the default? What does this tell you about the type of people who use Unix?

2. In Chapter 1, I mentioned that the first version of Unix was developed by Ken Thompson, so he could run a program called Space Travel. In this chapter, I explained that the first program to use Termcap (terminal information database) and **curses** (terminal manager interface) was a text-based fantasy game called Rogue, written by Michael Toy and Glenn Wichman. Creating a new operating system and experimenting with a brand new set of interfaces are both extremely time-consuming, difficult tasks. What do you think motivated Thompson and, later, Toy and Wichman to take on such challenging work for what seem to be such trivial reasons? If you were managing a group of programmers, what motivations do you think they would respond to (aside from money)?

PROGRAMS TO USE RIGHT AWAY

When you enter a command at the shell prompt, you are actually telling the shell to run the program by that name. For example, when you enter the **date** command, you are asking the shell to run the **date** program*.

Unix has literally thousands of different programs, which means there are thousands of different commands you can enter. Many of these programs require that you understand some theory. For instance, before you can use the file system commands you need to learn about the file system. Other programs are so complex as to require a great deal of time to master. This is the case, for example, with the two principal Unix text editors, **vi** and Emacs. These are very useful programs, but extremely complicated. In fact, in this book, I devote an entire chapter to **vi**.

There are, however, programs that require no special knowledge and are not especially difficult to use. These are the programs that you can use right away and, in this chapter, we'll take a look at some of them.

Of the many, many Unix programs, I have chosen a few that I feel are particularly useful, interesting, or fun. I have two goals. First, I want you to know about the programs, as they really *are* useful, interesting or fun. Second, after talking so much about general principles earlier in the book, I want to give you a chance to get used to the Unix CLI (command line interface). Traditionally, one of the ways in which people learn Unix is by having a good time while they are learning. Let's, you and I, carry on that tradition.

FINDING A PROGRAM ON YOUR SYSTEM: which, type, whence

As we discussed in Chapter 2, Unix is not a specific operating system. It is a family of operating systems: Linux, FreeBSD, Solaris, AIX, and on and on. Moreover, even Linux itself is not one system. The name "Linux" refers to any Unix system that uses the Linux kernel, and there are literally hundreds of different Linux distributions.

---

*Strictly speaking, this is not the entire story. Some commands are "built into" the shell, which means they are not actually separate programs.

At this point, however, the distinction between separate programs and built-in programs is not important.

Although the various Unixes have a lot in common, they don't all come with the exact same set of programs. For example, there are programs you will find in the Berkeley Unixes (FreeBSD, NetBSD and OpenBSD) that you won't find in Linux systems. Moreover, even when you compare two computers that are running the same version of Unix, you may find different programs. This is because, during a Unix installation, there is a lot of choice as to which programs should be installed, and not everyone makes the same choices.

It is true that basic Unix is basic Unix, and most systems have all of the important programs. Still, no matter what type of Unix you are using, there may be programs in this chapter (or elsewhere in the book) that are not available on your system.

For this reason, there are two important questions I would like to consider now: How do you know if a particular program is available on your system? If it isn't, is there anything you can do about it?

The easiest way to see if you have access to a program is to type its name at the shell prompt. (Remember, the job of the shell is to interpret your commands.) If the program exists on your system, something will happen. If not, the shell will tell you that it can't find that program. Don't worry about experimenting in this way. If you enter a non-existent command, it won't cause a problem. All that will happen is that you will see an error message.

A more precise way to check if a program is available is to use the **which** command. The purpose of **which** is to have the shell answer the question: If I were to enter a specific command, which program would be run? If there is an answer to this question, the program is installed on your system and you can use the command. If not, the command is not available.

To use **which**, type the command followed by the names of one or more programs, for example:

```
which date
which date less vi emacs
```

Here is the output for the first command:

```
/bin/date
```

In this case, **which** is telling you that, if you were to enter the **date** command, the shell would run the program stored in the file **/bin/date**. If you don't understand the Unix file system (which we will discuss in Chapter 23), this name will not make sense to you just yet. Don't worry about it. The important thing is that **which** has found a program to run, which tells you that **date** is a valid command on your system.

What happens if you ask **which** about a program that does not exist? For example:

```
which harley
```

There are two possibilities depending on your version of **which**. First, nothing may happen. That is, there will be no output. This means **which** could not find the program you specified. This is a characteristic of many Unix programs: if they don't have anything to say, they don't say it. (If only more people had the same philosophy.)

The second possibility is that you will see an error message. Here is a typical one:

```
/usr/bin/which: no harley in (/usr/local/bin:/usr/bin:
  /bin:/usr/X11R6/bin:/home/harley/bin)
```

What **which** is telling you is that it can't find a program named **harley** anywhere in your search path. We'll talk about search paths when we discuss the various shells. For now, the important thing is to realize that, because **which** cannot find a program named **harley**, you can't use the **harley** command on your system.

So what do you do if you want to try one of the programs in this chapter, and it doesn't seem to be on your system? As obvious as it might seem, the first thing to check is your spelling. Smart people make spelling mistakes all the time, and you and I are no exception*.

If you have spelled the command correctly and it just can't be found, you have several choices. First, you can forget about it. This chapter has a variety of programs to try and most of them will be available on your system.

Second, if you have access to other Unix systems, you can try them to see if they have the command.

Third, if you are using a shared system, you can ask the system manager if he or she could please install the program on your system. System managers are very busy people but, for a knowledgeable person, it doesn't take long to install a new program, so if you are polite and charming you may get what you want.

Finally, if you are using your own Unix computer, you can install the program for yourself. The details of how to do so vary with one type of Unix to another and are, alas, beyond the scope of this chapter. Perhaps you can find a local nerd who might be able to help you with your particular system.

If you use Bash for your shell (see Chapter 12), there is an alternative to the **which** command, **type**, for example:

```
type date
```

If you use the Korn shell (see Chapter 13), you can use the **whence** command:

```
whence date
```

The **type** and **whence** commands will sometimes display more detailed information than **which**. This can be useful in certain circumstances. However, for practical purposes, **which** will be fine most of the time.

Before we leave this section let me ask you, what do you think would happen if you use the **which** command on itself. In other words, which which is which? When you have a moment, give it a try:

```
which which
```

---

*In fact, seeing as you and I are smarter than most other people, we probably make more spelling mistakes because our minds work so quickly.

If you use Bash, try:

```
type which
which type
type type
```

HOW DO YOU STOP A PROGRAM?

Most Unix commands carry out one task and then stop automatically. For example, in the next section, we will meet the **date** command. All it does is display the time and date. It then stops and returns you to the shell prompt.

Other commands are more complex. When you start them, they put you in an environment in which you interact with the program itself by entering one command after another. When you are finished working with the program, you enter a special command to quit the program, at which point the program stops and you are returned to the shell prompt.

An example of this type of command is **bc**, a calculator program we will discuss later in the chapter. When you use **bc**, you start it and then enter one calculation at a time for as long as you want. When you are finished, you must tell **bc** that you are ready to quit. To do so, you enter the **quit** command.

With such programs, there will always be a special command that you can use to quit the program. The command will often be **q** or **quit**. To find out for sure, you can read the documentation for the program in the online Unix manual (which we will discuss in Chapter 9).

Aside from a special quit command, you can often stop a program simply by telling it there is no more data. To do so, press **^D** (<Ctrl-D>), the **eof** key (see Chapter 7). This is often the easiest way to stop a program. For example, when you are using **bc**, just enter **^D** and the program stops.

If all else fails, you may be able to stop a program by pressing the **intr** key, which will be either **^C** or <Delete> (again, see Chapter 7).

HINT

Most programs that have their own interactive environment come with some type of built-in help. To access the help facility, try typing **help** or **h** or **?** (a question mark).

DISPLAYING THE TIME AND DATE: `date`

The **date** command is one of the most useful of all the Unix commands. Simply enter:

```
date
```

and Unix will display the current time and date. Here is some sample output. Notice that Unix uses a 24-hour clock.

```
Sun Dec 21 10:45:54 PST 2008
```

If you live in a place that uses daylight savings time, Unix knows how to spring forward and fall back at the appropriate times. The example here shows Pacific Standard Time. In the summer, it would be Pacific Daylight Time.

Notice that **date** gives both the time and date, so this is the command to use when you want to know what time it is. There is a **time** command, but it does not display the time. It measures how long it takes to run a program.

Internally, Unix does not really run on local time. All Unix systems use Coordinated Universal Time (UTC), which is the modern name for Greenwich Mean Time (GMT). Unix silently converts between UTC and your local time zone as necessary. The details about your local time zone are specified at the time Unix is installed.

Sometimes it is handy to see what time it is in UTC. To display the time in UTC, enter:

`date -u`

You will see a time and date like this:

`Sun Dec 21 18:45:54 UTC 2008`

This time, by the way, is the UTC equivalent of the time in the previous example.

For more information, see Appendix H, in which I explain all about time zones, 24-hour time, and UTC. I also show you how to convert from one time zone to another, illustrating it all with a few practical examples.

DISPLAYING A CALENDAR: `cal`

One of the nice things about Unix is that it was not designed by a committee. When a Unix programmer decided he wanted a new tool, he could write it himself and add it to the system. A good example of this is the **cal** command, which displays a calendar.

To display the calendar for the current month, enter:

`cal`

To display a calendar for a particular year, just specify the year. For example:

`cal 1952`

When you specify a year, be sure to type all four numbers. For example, if you enter **cal 52**, you will get the calendar for 52 A.D. If you want 1952, you need to use **cal 1952**. You can use any year between 1 and 9999.

HINT

When you display a full-year calendar, the output is so long it may not fit on your screen.

If the top part of the calendar scrolls out of sight before you get a chance to read it, you can display the output one screenful at a time, by sending it to the **less** program. For example:

`cal 1952 | less`

(We will talk about **less** in Chapter 21.)

To display a calendar for a particular month, specify that month as a number between 1 and 12 (1 = January), as well as the year. For example, to display the calendar for December 1952, enter:

`cal 12 1952`

You will see:

```
      December 1952
Su Mo Tu We Th Fr Sa
       1  2  3  4  5  6
 7  8  9 10 11 12 13
14 15 16 17 18 19 20
21 22 23 24 25 26 27
28 29 30 31
```

If you want a specific month, you must always specify both the month and the year. For instance, if you want a calendar for July 2009, you must enter:

`cal 7 2009`

If you enter:

`cal 7`

you will get a calendar for the year for 7 A.D.

If, instead of displaying dates, you want to see the numbers of the days of the year, from 1 to 365 (Jan 1 = 1; Jan 2 = 2; and so on), the **cal** program can oblige. Just type **-j** after the name **date**. Here is an example.

`cal -j 12 2009`

The output is:

```
       December 2009
Sun Mon Tue Wed Thu Fri Sat
            335 336 337 338 339
340 341 342 343 344 345 346
347 348 349 350 351 352 353
354 355 356 357 358 359 360
361 362 363 364 365
```

Suppose you want to figure out whether or not a particular year is a leap year. A non-Unix person would check if the year is divisible by 4 and, if so, say that it is a leap year*. However, as a Unix person, you have an alternative. All you have to do is display the numbers of the

---

*The only exception is that centenary years are leap years only if they are divisible by 400. For example, 2000 was a leap year, while 900 was not.

days for December of that year. If December ends on day 366, you have found a leap year. Otherwise, it's not a leap year. Try these commands and see for yourself:

```
cal -j 12 2000
cal -j 12 2008
cal -j 12 1776
```

By the way, the **-j** stands for Julian, the name of our modern calendar that has 365 or 366 days per year. For more information, see the box.

THE JULIAN AND GREGORIAN CALENDARS

The idea that we should have 365 days during regular years and 366 days during leap years is derived from the Julian Calendar, which was introduced by Julius Caesar in 46 B.C.*

But how long, exactly, is an average year? If three out of four years have 365 days and the fourth year has 366 days, a year would be an average of 365.25 days. However, nature is not always cooperative, and this value is too long by a matter of 11 minutes, 10 seconds. By the sixteenth century, this small error had accumulated into about 10 days, which meant that the calendar everyone was using did not match the motions of the sun and stars.

To solve the problem, Pope Gregory XIII decreed in 1582 that the world should modify its calendar so that not all centenary years (1600, 1700, 1800, and so on) should be leap years. Only the centenary years that are divisible by 400 (such as 1600 or 2000) would be leap years. This scheme is called the Gregorian or New Style Calendar. To calibrate the current calendar, Gregory further decreed that 10 days should vanish mysteriously.

If we want to be especially precise, we can say that the modern (Gregorian) calendar is based on a cycle of 400 years, with an average year being 365.2425 days. (An interesting fact is that, under this calendar, one nanocentury is approximately π seconds.)

The Pope delivered his decree in 1582. By 1587, the Catholic European countries had implemented the change. The Protestant countries, however, did not follow for some years, the last holdout being Great Britain, which did not make the change until 1752.

As Great Britain changed, so did the American colonies but, by this time, the error had increased to 11 days. Thus, if you enter the command:

```
cal 9 1752
```

you will see that between September 2 and September 14, 1752, there is a gap of 11 days. This gap is necessary for the sun and stars to work properly (at least in Great Britain and America).

THE UNIX REMINDER SERVICE: `calendar`

The **cal** program we just discussed displays a calendar. Unix does have a command named **calendar** but it is completely different. The **calendar** program offers a reminder service based on a file of important days and messages that you create yourself.

All you need to do is make a file named **calendar**. The **cal** program will look for this file in the current directory. (We will discuss the current directory in Chapter 24.) Within this file, you put lines of text in which each line contains a date, followed by a tab character, followed by a reminder note. For example:

---

*Actually, the calendar was developed by a graduate student, but Caesar put his name on the paper.

```
October 21<Tab>Tammy's birthday
November 20<Tab>Alex's birthday
December 3<Tab>Linda's birthday
December 21<Tab>Harley's birthday
```

Since tabs are invisible, you won't see them when you look at the file:

```
October 21      Tammy's birthday
November 20     Alex's birthday
December 3      Linda's birthday
December 21     Harley's birthday*
```

Once your **calendar** file is set up, you can enter the **calendar** command whenever you want:

calendar

When you do, the program will check your **calendar** file and display all the lines that have today's or tomorrow's date. If "today" is a Friday, **calendar** will display three days worth of reminders.

The intention is that, from time to time, you should add lines to your **calendar** file, until your life is completely organized. Of course, before you can create such a file, you must know how to use a text editor program. The most important text editors are **vi** (Chapter 22) and Emacs.

If you want to run the **calendar** command automatically each time you log in, put it in your **.profile** file (Bash or Korn Shell), or your **.login** file (C-Shell). See the individual shell chapters for details.

Some Unix systems come with a built-in **calendar** file that contains a lot of interesting entries. So, even if you don't want to create your own file, you may want to run the **calendar** command from time to time, just to see what happens. Try it right now.

For more information about **calendar** and the format of the information file, take a look at the entry for **calendar** in the online Unix manual (see Chapter 9). The command to use is:

man calendar

INFORMATION ABOUT YOUR SYSTEM: uptime, hostname, uname

There are several commands you can use to display information about your system. To start, the **uptime** command displays information about how long your system has been up (that is, running continuously):

uptime

Here is some typical output:

---

*Gifts are accepted until the end of January.

```
11:10AM   up 103 days, 6:13, 3 users,
   load averages: 1.90, 1.49, 1.38
```

In this case, the system has been up for 103 days, 6 hours and 13 minutes, and there are 3 userids currently logged in. The last three numbers show the number of programs that have been waiting to execute, averaged over the last 1, 5 and 15 minutes respectively. These numbers give you an idea of the load on the system. The higher the load, the more the system is doing.

To find out the name of your computer, use the **hostname** command. This can come in handy if you are in the habit of logging in to more than one computer. If you forget what system you are using, just enter:

```
hostname
```

The **uname** command shows you the name of your operating system. For example, you might enter:

```
uname
```

and see:

```
Linux
```

To find out more details about your operating system, use **-a** (all information):

```
uname -a
```

Here is some sample output:

```
Linux nipper.harley.com 2.6.24-3.358 #1
Mon Nov 9 09:04:50 EDT 2008 i686 i686 i386 GNU/Linux
```

The most important information here is that we are using the Linux kernel, in this case, version 2.6.24-1.358.

INFORMATION ABOUT YOU: whoami, quota

The **whoami** command displays the userid you used to log in. This command is handy if you have a variety of userids and you forget which one you are currently using. Similarly, if you come upon a computer that someone has left logged in, **whoami** will show you the current userid. Just enter:

```
whoami
```

The **whoami** command is also useful if you are suddenly struck by amnesia and forget your name. Looking at your userid may give you a clue.

If your system doesn't have a **whoami** command, try entering the following as three separate words:

```
who am i
```

The last command to show you information about yourself is **quota**. On shared systems, the system manager will sometimes impose a limit as to how much disk storage space each user is allowed to use. To check your limit, enter:

```
quota
```

Note: Unix measures disk space in KB or kilobytes; 1 KB = 1024 bytes (characters).

INFORMATION ABOUT OTHER USERS: `users, who, w`

In the olden days, Unix computers were shared and, most of the time, a system would have multiple users logged in simultaneously. Indeed, very large Unix computers could support tens — or even several hundred — users at the same time. To find out who was currently logged in, there were several commands you could use. These commands are still useful today if you are sharing a system with other users.

The simplest command is **users**. Just enter:

```
users
```

and you will see a list of all the userids that are currently logged in, for example:

```
alex casey harley root tammy
```

You will remember from Chapter 4 that, within a Unix system, only userids have a real identity. Real people — that is, users — are represented by their userids. Thus, you won't see the names of real people, only userids.

The **users** command is useful if you use a shared system. I can tell you from my experience that being aware that other people are using the same system as you is a pleasant feeling, especially when you are working by yourself, late at night, in an office or terminal room. Just knowing that there is someone else out there makes you feel connected. Unfortunately, many people have no idea what this feels like because their only experience is that everyone has his or her own computer. They don't know what it feels like to share a system.

You might ask, is there any point in using the **users** command if you use Unix on your own computer? Most of the time the answer is no: it's not all that exciting to see that you are the only person logged in. However, when you use multiple terminal windows or virtual consoles (see Chapter 6), you are logged in to each one separately and, if you run the **users** command, your userid will show up more than once. Similarly, if you log into virtual consoles using several different userids, they will all show up. So, at the very least, if you get lonely, you can pretend there are other people on the system.

The next command is the **who** command that we discussed in Chapter 4. This command shows more information than does **users**. For each userid, **who** will show you the name of the terminal, the time that the userid logged in and, if appropriate, the remote computer from which the userid has connected to your system.

Here is the output from a **who** command that was run on a system to which people connect remotely:

```
tammy    tty1     Nov 10 21:25
root     tty2     Nov 11 15:12
casey    pts/0    Nov 11 10:07  (luna)
harley   pts/1    Nov 11 10:52  (nipper.harley.com)
alex     pts/2    Nov 11 14:39  (thing.taylored-soft.com)
```

In this example, userid **tammy** is logged in using terminal **tty1**, and **root** (the superuser) is logged in on terminal **tty2**. These are virtual consoles on the main computer. As I mentioned in Chapter 7, the name **tty** is often used as an abbreviation for "terminal". In this example, it happens that a user named Tammy is the system administrator, and she is currently logged in twice: once using her personal userid and once as superuser.

To continue, we see that another userid, **casey** is logged in from a computer named **luna**, which is on the local network. Finally, two other userids, **harley** and **alex**, are logged in remotely via the Internet.

If you want to find out even more information about the userids on your system, you can use the **w** command. The name stands for "Who is doing what?" Here is some sample output:

```
8:44pm up 9 days, 7:02, 3 users,
   load average: 0.11, 0.02, 0.00
USER    TTY      FROM LOGIN@ IDLE   JCPU   PCPU   WHAT
tammy   console  -    Wed9am 2days  2:38   0.00s  -bash
harley  pts/1    -    12:21  0:00          0.01s  w
alex    ttyp0    luna 13:11  20:18 43.26s  1.52s  vi birdlist
```

The first part of the output shows the system statistics, which we saw earlier in the chapter in our discussion of the **uptime** command. In this case, the system has been up for 9 days, 7 hours and 2 minutes, and there are 3 userids currently logged in. The last three numbers show the number of programs that have been waiting to execute, averaged over the last 1, 5 and 15 minutes respectively. These numbers give you an idea of the load on the system. The higher the load, the more the system is doing.

Following the first line, we see eight columns of information, as follows.

USER: The userids that are currently logged into the system. In this case, they are **tammy**, **harley** and **alex**.

TTY: The names of the terminals used by the various userids.

FROM: The name of the remote computer from which the userid has logged in. In our example, **tammy** and **harley** logged in directly on the host computer. **alex**, however, has logged in from another computer named **luna**.

LOGIN@: The time that the userid logged in.

IDLE: How long it has been since the user last pressed a key. This is called IDLE TIME. In this case, **tammy** has been idle for about 2 days, and **alex** has been idle for 20 minutes and 18 seconds. If you are waiting for a time-consuming job to finish and you are not typing while you are waiting, the **w** command will show you being idle.

JCPU: The processor time used by all processes since login. The "J" stands for "jobs".

PCPU: The processor time used by the current process. The "P" stands for "process".

Processor time is expressed either in seconds (for example, **20s**) or in minutes and seconds (for example, **2:16**). These numbers were more valuable in the days when computers were expensive and processor time was considered a valuable commodity.

WHAT: The command that is currently running. In our example, **tammy** is running the Bash shell; **alex** is using the **vi** editor (see Chapter 22) to edit a file named **birdlist**; and **harley** is running the **w** command.

Putting this all together, we can infer that **tammy** has been logged in at the console, with a shell prompt, without doing anything for about 2 days. Perhaps this is the system administrator, who likes to stay logged in at all times. We also see that **alex** is editing a file but has not done anything for over 20 minutes. Perhaps he or she has been taking a break.

Notice that, whenever you run the **w** command, you will see yourself running the **w** command. In our example, this is the case with **harley**.

By default, the **w** command shows you information about all the userids logged into the system. If you want information about just one userid, you can enter the name along with the command. For example, let's say you have just logged in and you enter the **users** command to see who else is logged in. You see:

```
alex casey harley tammy weedly
```

If you want to see what **weedly** is doing, enter:

```
w weedly
```

WHAT'S IN A NAME?

CPU

In the days of the large mainframe computers, the "brain" of the computer — what we would now call the processor — was big enough to require a large box, which was called the central processing unit or CPU.

Today, even though most people don't use mainframe computers, we still use the term CPU as a synonym for "processor".

LOCKING YOUR TERMINAL TEMPORARILY: lock

As I mentioned in Chapter 4, it is a bad idea to walk away from your computer while you are logged in. Someone can come along and, by entering commands under the auspices of your userid, cause a lot of trouble. For example, a mischievous person might delete all your files, send rude email to the system manager in your name, download pornography, and so on.

However, if you do need to step away from your terminal for just a moment, it is irritating to have to log out and in again. This is especially true if you are using one or more terminal windows to log in to remote hosts or you have a whole working environment set up just the way you like it.

Instead, you can use the **lock** command. This tells Unix that you want to lock your terminal temporarily. The terminal will remain locked until you enter a special password. To use this command, just enter:

lock

Unix will display:

Key:

Enter the password that you want to use to unlock the terminal. This password can be anything you want; it has nothing to do with your login password. If fact, it is better to not use your login password. Unix will not echo the password as you type, just in case someone else is looking at your screen. After you enter the password, Unix will display:

Again:

This is asking you to retype the password, to ensure that you did not make a mistake.

As soon as you have entered and re-entered the special password, Unix will freeze your terminal. Nothing will happen, no matter what anyone types on the terminal, until you enter the password. (Don't forget to press the <Return> key.) As soon as you enter the password, Unix will reactivate your terminal and you can go back to work.

HINT

If you are logged into one or more remote hosts, you should lock each session separately.

If you are working in a place where you must share computers and there are people waiting, it is considered bad form to lock your terminal and leave for more than a very short time, say, to eat dinner. Since Unix was developed in an environment based on sharing, the **lock** command has a built-in limitation: the terminal will unlock automatically after a specific amount of time.

By default, **lock** will freeze a terminal for 15 minutes. However, if you want to override this default, some versions of **lock** will let you specify an alternate time limit when you enter the command. After the name of the command, leave a space, and then type **-** (a hyphen), followed by a number. For example, to lock your terminal for 5 minutes, enter:

lock -5

You might ask, what happens if someone locks a terminal and then leaves for good? Eventually, the command will time out and unlock. If the terminal needs to be reactivated before the lock times out, the system manager can enter the **root** (superuser) password. **lock** will always accept the **root** password, sort of like a master key.

Remember though, if you lock your terminal and don't come back, someone will come along eventually and find your terminal reactivated and logged in under your userid. Whatever trouble they cause under your userid will be your responsibility.

ASKING UNIX TO REMIND YOU WHEN TO LEAVE: `leave`

As you know, working on a computer can be engrossing, and it is easy to lose track of the time. To help you fulfill your worldly obligations, just enter the command:

```
leave
```

As the name implies, you can use **leave** to remind you when it is time to leave. You can also use it to remind you when it is time to take a break. For example, if you like to get up and stretch every so often, you can ask for a reminder in, say, 20 minutes.

When you enter the command, **leave** will ask you for a time:

```
When do you have to leave?
```

Enter the time that you want to leave in the form *hhmm* (hours followed by minutes). For example, if you want to leave at 10:33, enter **1033**.

You can enter times using either a 12-hour or 24-hour system. For instance, **1344** means 1:44 PM. If you enter a number of hours that is 12 or fewer, **leave** assumes that it is within the next 12 hours. For instance, if it is 8:00 PM and you enter **855**, **leave** will interpret it to mean 8:55 PM, not 8:55 AM.

An alternate way to enter the **leave** command is to enter the time right on the command line. After the name of the command, leave a space and type the time. For example, to leave at 10:30, enter:

```
leave 1030
```

If you need to leave after a certain time interval, type a **+** (plus sign) followed by the number of minutes. For example, if you need to leave in 15 minutes, use:

```
leave +15
```

Be sure not to leave a space after the **+** character.

HINT

When you log out, Unix discards a pending **leave** command. Thus, if you use **leave**, but then log out and in again, you will have to run the program again.

Once you have entered the **leave** command, Unix checks periodically to see how much time is left. When it is five minutes before the time you specified, Unix will display:

```
You have to leave in 5 minutes.
```

When there is one minute left, you will see:

```
Just one more minute!
```

When the time is up, Unix displays:

```
Time to leave!
```

From that point on, Unix will keep nagging you with reminders, once a minute, until you log off:

You're going to be late!

Finally, after ten such reminders, you will see:

You're going to be late!
That was the last time I'll tell you. Bye.

Perhaps this program should have been named **mother**.

HINT

You can run the **leave** command automatically when you log in, by putting the command in your initialization file (**.profile** for Bash or the Korn Shell and **.login** for the C-Shell).

This means that, each time you log in, you will be asked for the time (or length of time) you want to work. This way, you don't have to keep an eye on the clock: Unix will do it for you.

If you use **leave** in this way and you don't want it to run for the current session, just press <Return> at the first prompt and the program will abort.

HINT

The **leave** program is handy when you need to do something in a short time, and you need a reminder. For example, let's say that, as you are working, you like to get up and stretch every 15-20 minutes. However, you get too immersed in your work to remember to take a break. Simply enter the command:

leave +20

In 15 minutes (5 minutes early), **leave** will get your attention with a warning. Over the next 5 minutes, **leave** will display several more warnings.

After your break, enter the command again, and you'll get another reminder in 15 minutes*.

A BUILT-IN CALCULATOR: bc

One of the most useful (and least appreciated) Unix programs is **bc**, a full-fledged, programmable scientific calculator. Many people do not bother learning how to use **bc**. "I spit on **bc**," they sneer. "Nobody uses it." Don't be misled. Once you learn how to use **bc**, you will find it invaluable for quick calculations.

---

*The distinguished doctor Janet G. Travell (1901-1997), who held the office of Personal Physician to U.S. Presidents John Kennedy and Lyndon Johnson, was an expert on the pain and dysfunction of skeletal muscles, as well as on the treatment of chronic pain.

While working on her classic book, *Myofascial Pain and Dysfunction: The Trigger Point Manual*, Dr Travell found that, in order to maintain her comfort and well-being, she needed to take a short break every 15-20 minutes. During this break, she would stand up, move around, and stretch.

You will find that, while you are working, taking such a break will make you feel a lot more comfortable, especially if you suffer from headaches, backaches or eyestrain. Just use the command **leave +20** to remind you when to move around and stretch. Once you start this practice, you will feel an improvement in your comfort level within hours. (Another example of how using Unix is good for your well-being.)

If you use a desktop environment (Chapter 5), you will most likely find some type of GUI-based calculator program to use. These programs look nice — they actually draw a picture of a calculator on your screen — but, for minute-to-minute work or for extensive calculation, **bc** is much better. Moreover, **bc** is text-based, which means you can use it from the command line at any terminal.

To explain **bc**, I will start with a short technical summary. If you don't understand all the mathematical and computer terms, don't worry. In the next few sections, I will explain how to use **bc** for basic calculations (which is easy) along with a few examples.

The technical summary: **bc** is a fully programmable mathematical interpreter, which offers extended precision. Each number is stored with as many digits as necessary, and you can specify a scale of up to 100 digits to the right of the decimal point. Numeric values can be manipulated in any base from 2 to 16, and it is easy to convert from one base to another.

You can use **bc** either by entering calculations from the keyboard, which are interpreted immediately, or by running programs stored in files. The programming syntax of **bc** is similar to the C programming language. You can define functions and use recursion. There are arrays, local variables, and global variables. You can write your own functions and store them in a file. You can then have **bc** load and interpret them automatically.

bc comes with a library that contains the following functions: sin, cos, arctan, ln, exponential and Bessel function. (Everybody who knows what a Bessel function is, raise your hand...)

For more information, you can display the online manual description of the **bc** by using the command:

```
man bc
```

(We will discuss the online Unix manual in Chapter 9.)

USING bc FOR CALCULATIONS

Most of the time, you will use **bc** for routine calculations, which is simple. To start the program, enter:

```
bc
```

If you want to use the built-in library of mathematical functions (see below), start the program using the **-l** (library) option:

```
bc -l
```

Once you start **bc** there is no specific prompt; just enter one calculation after another. Each time you press <Return>, **bc** evaluates what you have typed and displays the answer. For example, if you enter:

```
122152 + 70867 + 122190
```

bc will display:

```
315209
```

OPERATOR	MEANING
+	addition
–	subtraction
*	multiplication
/	division
%	modulo
^	exponentiation
sqrt(x)	square root

FIGURE 8-1: bc: Basic operations

You can now enter a new calculation. If you want to enter more than one calculation on the same line, separate them with semicolons*. **bc** will display each result on a separate line. For example, if you enter:

```
10+10; 20+20
```

you will see:

```
20
40
```

When you are finished working with **bc**, stop the program by telling it there is no more data. To do this, press **^D**, the **eof** key (see Chapter 7). Alternatively, you can enter the **quit** command.

Figure 8-1 shows the basic operations available with **bc**. Addition, subtraction, multiplication, division and square root are straightforward and work as you would expect. Modulo calculates the remainder after a division. For example, **53%10** is **3**. Exponentiation refers to taking a number to a power. For example, **3^2** means "3 to the power of 2", which is **9**. The power must be a whole number but can be negative. If you use a negative power, enclose it in parentheses, for example, **3^(-1)**.

bc follows the general rules of algebra: multiplication, division and modulo take precedence over addition and subtraction; exponentiation has precedence over everything. To change the order of evaluation, use parentheses. So, **1+2*3** is **7**, where **(1+2)*3** is **9**.

Aside from the basic operations, **bc** has a number of useful functions in a special library. These functions are shown in Figure 8-2.

If you want to use the functions in this library, you need to start **bc** using the command:

```
bc -l
```

When you use this command, **bc** automatically sets the scale factor to **20** (see below).

---

*As you will see in Chapter 10, when you are working at the shell prompt, you can type more than one Unix command on the same line, by separating the commands with semicolons.

FUNCTION	MEANING
s (*x*)	Sine of *x*; *x* is in radians
c (*x*)	Cosine of *x*; *x* is in radians
a (*x*)	Arctangent of *x*; *x* is in radians
ln (*x*)	Natural logarithm of *x*
j (*n*,*x*)	Bessel function of integer order *n* of *x*

FIGURE 8-2: bc: Mathematical functions

As I mentioned earlier, **bc** can compute to arbitrary precision. That is, it will use as many digits as necessary to perform a calculation. For instance, you can ask it to add two 100-digit numbers. (I tested this.)

However, by default, **bc** will assume you are working with whole numbers. That is, **bc** will not keep any digits to the right of the decimal point. If you want to use fractional values, you need to set a scale factor to tell **bc** how many digits you want to keep to the right of the decimal point. To do this, set the value of **scale** to the scale factor you want.

For example, to ask for three digits to the right of the decimal point, enter:

```
scale=3
```

From now on, all subsequent calculations will be done to three decimal places. Any extra digits will be truncated.

If at any point you want to check what the scale factor is, simply enter:

```
scale
```

and **bc** will display the current value.

When you start **bc**, the value of **scale** is set automatically to **0**. One of the most common mistakes is to start calculations without setting a scale factor. For instance, let's say that you have just started **bc**, and you enter:

```
150/60
```

bc displays:

```
2
```

You now enter:

```
35/60
```

bc displays:

```
0
```

Finally, you figure out what the problem is. Your results are being truncated, so you need to set an appropriate scale factor:

```
scale=3
```

Now **bc** will display what you want to see. (Try it.)

Remember, when you use the mathematical library, **bc** automatically starts with a scale factor of **20**. For this reason, many people always start **bc** by using **bc -1**, even if they do not want to use the mathematical library. (I do this all the time.)

USING VARIABLES WITH bc

bc is a lot more than a calculator. It is actually a full-featured mathematical programming language. Like all programming languages, **bc** allows you to set and use variables.

A variable is a quantity with a name and a value. Within **bc**, variable names consist of a single lowercase letter; that is, there are 26 variables, from **a** to **z**. (Make sure that you do not use uppercase letters; these are used when working with bases — see below.)

To set the value of a variable, use an **=** (equal sign) character. For example, to set the value of the variable **x** to **100**, enter:

```
x=100
```

To display the value of a variable, just enter its name. For example:

```
x
```

bc will display the current value of that variable. By default, all variables are assumed to be zero unless you set them otherwise.

You will find that using variables is straightforward and adds a lot of power to your work with **bc**. Here is an example that illustrates the basic principles.

The Maharaja of Gaipajama has been impressed with your facility in Unix. As a token of his esteem, he offers you twice your weight in rubies, worth $1,000 a pound, and one third of your weight in diamonds, worth $2,000 a pound. (The Maharaja of Gaipajama buys his gems wholesale.)

You weigh 160 pounds. How much is the Maharaja's gift worth? To solve this problem, start **bc** and enter:

```
w=160
r=(w*2)*1000
d=(w/3)*2000
r+d
```

The answer is displayed:

```
426000
```

Thus, your gift is worth $426,000.

But wait: once the Maharaja realizes how much his promise will cost him, he says, "Did I say I would give you gems based on your weight in pounds? I should have said kilograms."

Since 1 kilogram is 2.2 pounds, you make a quick calculation to convert the value of the **w** variable to kilograms:

```
w=w/2.2
```

Now you re-enter the calculations for the value of rubies and diamonds:

```
r=(w*2)*1000
d=(w/3)*2000
r+d
```

The new answer is displayed:

```
192000
```

Thus, by adhering to the metric system, the Maharaja* has saved $234,000. At the same time, he has allowed you to demonstrate how to set a new value for a variable, based on its old value, in this case, **w=w/2.2**.

USING bc WITH DIFFERENT BASES

As you would assume, **bc** normally uses base 10 arithmetic. (If you don't know what a base is, you can skip this section with impunity.) However, there will be times when you may want to calculate using another base. For example, in computer science, it is sometimes necessary to use base 16 (hexadecimal), base 8 (octal) or base 2 (binary). (We will discuss these number systems in Chapter 21.)

bc allows you to specify different bases for input and for output. To do so, there are two special variables that you can set: **ibase** is the base that will be used for input; **obase** is the base that will be used for output.

For example, if you want to display answers in base 16, enter:

```
obase=16
```

If you want to enter numbers in base 8, use:

```
ibase=8
```

In the last section, I said that, by default, variables have a value of zero until you set them. **ibase** and **obase** are exceptions: they are automatically initialized to **10** so you can work in base 10. If you want to work in another base, you can set either of the variables to any value from **2** to **16**.

You should appreciate that the values of **ibase** and **obase** do not affect how **bc** manipulates numbers internally. Their only effect is to specify how numbers should be translated during input or output.

To work with bases larger than 10, **bc** represents the values of 10, 11, 12, 13, 14 and 15 as the uppercase letters **A, B, C, D, E** and **F**, respectively. Always remember to use uppercase; if you use lowercase, **bc** will think you are referring to variables, and the result will not be what you intended.

For convenience, you can use these uppercase letters regardless of what input base you have set. For instance, even if you are working in base 10, the expression **A+1** will have the value **11**.

---

*For more information about the Maharaja of Gaipajama, see *Cigars of the Pharaoh* by Hergé.

As with all variables, you can find out the current values of **ibase** and **obase** by entering the names by themselves:

```
ibase; obase
```

However, you must be careful. Once you set **obase**, all output will be displayed in that base, and you may have trouble interpreting what you see. For instance, if you enter:

```
obase=16
obase
```

you will see:

```
10
```

This is because all output is to be displayed in base 16 and, in base 16, the value of "16" is expressed as **10**.

Similarly, once you change **ibase**, you must be careful what you type as input. For example, say that you set:

```
ibase=16
```

You now want to set **obase** to base 10, so you enter:

```
obase=10
```

However, you have forgotten that input is now in base 16, and **10** in base 16 is really "16". Thus, you have just set **obase** to base 16.

To avoid such errors, use the letters **A** though **F**, which retain the same value regardless of the **ibase** value. Thus, if things become confusing, you can always reset the bases by entering:

```
obase=A; ibase=A
```

Here are two examples of changing bases. In the first, you want to add two hexadecimal (base 16) numbers, **F03E** and **3BAC**. Enter:

```
obase=16
ibase=16
F03E + 3BAC
```

bc displays the answer:

```
12BEA
```

In the second example, you want to convert the hexadecimal number FFC1 to binary (base 2). Reset the bases:

```
obase=A; ibase=A
```

Then enter:

```
obase=2; ibase=16
FFC1
```

bc displays the answer:

```
1111111111000001
```

> **HINT**
>
> **bc** is a lot more than a calculator program. It is a sophisticated mathematical programming system with its own built-in programming language. In this chapter, I have explained only the most basic features. However, if you have some time, I suggest that you explore **bc** and learn more about what it can do for you.
>
> The best way to do so is to read the online manual page for **bc**. The command to do so is:
>
> ```
> man bc
> ```
>
> (We will discuss the online Unix manual in Chapter 9.)

REVERSE POLISH NOTATION

Originally, the **bc** program was based on a program called **dc** (desk calculator). **dc** is among the oldest Unix programs, even older than the C programming language. In fact, the original version of **dc** was written in 1970 using the programming language B, the ancestor of C. In a moment, we'll talk more about the relation of **bc** to **dc**. For now, though, I'd like to teach you a bit about **dc** — a very interesting tool in its own right — because, like **bc**, it is a program you can use right away.

Let's start with a technical description: **dc** is an interactive, arbitrary precision calculator that emulates a stack machine using Reverse Polish notation.

Obviously, **dc** is not the type of program that will appeal to everyone: if you have no interest in mathematics or computer science, please feel free to skip this discussion. However, if you are technically inclined, **dc** is important for you to understand for several reasons.

First, as I mentioned, **dc** uses what is called Reverse Polish notation. Although the idea may mean nothing to you now, it is an important concept you should appreciate if you are studying mathematics, engineering or computer science.

Second, to learn about **dc**, you need to understand the idea of a stack (which I will explain), a concept that is important to computer scientists and programmers.

Finally, the type of thinking that is required to use **dc** is the same type of thinking that is required to use Unix. Thus, taking a few moments to learn about **dc** and — if you are so inclined — teaching yourself how to use it, will bring you that much closer to becoming a Unix person.

We will start our discussion of **dc** with an explanation of Reverse Polish notation. In the next section, we will move on to the concept of a stack. Once you understand these two fundamental ideas, you will be able to teach yourself how to use **dc** by using the online documentation.

In 1920, a Polish mathematician named Jan Lukasiewicz (1878-1956) observed that the way in which we write arithmetical expressions can be made more compact by placing the operators before the operands. In doing this, we are able to write complex expressions without using parentheses or brackets. A short example will illustrate the idea.

Say you want to add 34 to 25 and then multiply the sum by 15. Using standard notation, you would write:

```
(34 + 25) * 15
```

Because the operators — in this case **+** (the plus sign) and ***** (the multiplication sign) — are placed in between the operands, we call this INFIX NOTATION.

Lukasiewicz's system uses PREFIX NOTATION in which we write the operators first followed by the operands. For example:

```
* + 34 25 15
```

To evaluate prefix notation, we process the elements, one at a time, from left to right. In this example, we start with the ***** operator, which tells us to perform a multiplication as soon as we get two numbers. We then encounter the **+** operator, which tells us to perform an addition as soon as we get two numbers.

Next, we see two numbers in a row, **34** and **25**, so we perform the addition operation, which gives us a sum of **59**. Remembering the **59**, we keep going and encounter the number **15**. We can now perform the multiplication, **59*15**, to get the final answer **885**.

In honor of Lukasiewicz — who was a renowned mathematician, logician and philosopher — prefix notation is often referred to as POLISH NOTATION*. For computer scientists, Polish notation is important because it is compact, straightforward, and can be evaluated efficiently.

In 1957, the Australian computer scientist Charles Hamblin wrote two papers in which he proposed using a variation of Polish notation with a stack-based computing system. (We'll talk about stacks in the next section.) The variation he described was to put the operators *after* the operands, using what is called POSTFIX NOTATION.

To illustrate postfix notation, let's reconsider the expression above. In postfix notation it would look like this:

```
34 25 + 15 *
```

To evaluate, we process the elements from left to right. First, we see the two numbers **34** and **25**, which we must remember. Next, we see the **+** operator, which tells us to add the last two available numbers. In this case, we add **34** and **25** to get **59**, which we must remember.

Next, we see the number **15**, which we also remember. Finally, we see the ***** operator, which tells us to multiply two numbers. In this case, the numbers are **59** and **15**, which we multiply to get the final answer **885**.

---

*Jan Lukasiewicz was born on December 21, 1878 in the city of Lwow in Galicia, the largest and most northern province of Austria. Galicia was created as a result of the First Partition of Poland in 1772. Although, technically, Lukasiewicz was Austrian, he was an ethnic Pole by birth and the town of Lwow was dominated by Poles. Today, Lwow is known by the name of Lviv and is the largest city in Western Ukraine.

Here is something interesting: As a young man, my grandfather Irving Hahn (1895-1986) lived in Lwow where he apprenticed to be a barber. Moreover, my birthday is December 21.

Postfix notation is particularly suitable for automated computation because expressions can be evaluated in a straightforward manner, from left to right, by remembering numbers and applying operators as they are encountered. With infix notation, the parentheses and other types of precedence — for instance, multiplication must be done before addition — often require that operations be delayed until other operations are completed. This is not the case with postfix notation.

In honor of Lukasiewicz, postfix notation is often referred to as REVERSE POLISH NOTATION or RPN. Over the years, both Polish notation and Reverse Polish notation have been used in a variety of computer systems. For example, Polish (prefix) notation is used in the Lisp programming language and the Tcl scripting language. Reverse Polish (postfix) notation is used in the Forth programming language and the PostScript page description language.

Perhaps the most well-known use of RPN is as the basis for the HP calculators that have been used for years by scientists and engineers. The first such calculator was the HP 9100, which was introduced in 1968.

Since then, RPN calculators have become very popular because, once you understand RPN, it is much faster and easier to use than the traditional infix notation. For example, when you use an RPN calculator, the results of each computation are displayed immediately. This means that you see the partial results as you enter the calculation, making it much easier to catch errors. This is not the case with a calculator that uses traditional infix notation. If you enter an expression that uses the standard rules of precedence, the results cannot be displayed until the entire calculation is finished.

In 1970, a researcher at Bell Labs, Robert Morris, inspired by the HP calculator, used RPN to develop a Unix-based, interactive calculator program, which he called **dc** (desk calculator). **dc** was a wonderful tool, but it did require users to learn how to use RPN.

A few years later, Morris and another researcher, Lorinda Cherry, wrote another program called **bc**, which allowed users to write calculations using the more traditional infix notation. **bc** worked by converting its input to RPN and then calling upon **dc** to do the actual work. In other words, **bc** was a "front-end" to **dc**. This allowed people to use whichever system they preferred: postfix notation with **dc** or infix notation with **bc**.

Years later, as part of the GNU Project (see Chapter 2), **bc** was completely rewritten as an independent program. Because many types of modern Unix (including Linux and FreeBSD) use the GNU utilities, chances are that, when you use **bc** today, you are using a standalone program that does not depend upon **dc**. **dc**, of course, is still available on its own.

THE STACK-BASED CALCULATOR: dc

Consider the following example of RPN (postfix) notation:

```
34 25 + 15 *
```

dc evaluates this expression in the manner I described in the last section, one element at a time, reading from left to right. Each time **dc** encounters a number, the value of that number must be remembered. Each time **dc** encounters an operator, the appropriate operation must be performed and the result must be remembered.

The question arises, how does **dc** keep track of the various quantities that must be remembered? The answer is, by using what we call a stack.

Within computer science, there are a variety of different DATA STRUCTURES used to hold data. Each type of data structure is capable of storing and retrieving data according to its own set of precise rules. The most common types of data structures are lists, linked lists, associative arrays, hash tables, stacks, queues, deques (double-ended queues), as well as a variety of tree-based structures. In this section, we'll concentrate on stacks because that's what **dc** uses.

A STACK is a data structure in which data elements are stored and retrieved, one at a time, according to a procedure called "last in, first out" or LIFO. Here is how it works.

The stack starts out empty. To store a data element, you PUSH it onto the stack. The data now resides on the TOP of the stack. You can push as many data elements as you like onto the stack, one at a time. Each time you do so, all the elements on the stack are pushed down one level. Thus, at any time, the top of the stack contains the data that was most recently pushed onto the stack. You can retrieve data from the stack only by taking it off the top. When you do, we say that you POP the stack.

In other words, when you pop the stack, you retrieve the last value pushed on the stack. This is why stacks are described as LIFO (last-in, first-out).

For a concrete example of a stack, imagine a spring-loaded column of plates in a cafeteria. The plates are pushed onto the "stack", one at a time. When you want a plate, you must pop the top one off the stack. You have no access to any of the other plates. If, for some reason, you wanted the bottom plate, you would have to pop off all the others, one at a time.

The **dc** program uses a stack in just this manner to interpret arithmetic expressions that are expressed in RPN. To do so, **dc** follows a simple procedure: Read the expression from left to right, one element at a time. If a numeric value is encountered, push it onto the stack. If an operator is encountered, pop the appropriate number of elements off the stack, perform the operation, and push the answer onto the stack.

To illustrate this, let's consider the previous example:

34 25 + 15 *

Here is a step-by-step description of what **dc** does to interpret this expression:

1. Read the value **34** and push it onto the stack.
   The stack contains: **34**

2. Read the value **25** and push it onto the stack.
   The stack contains: **25 34**

3. Read the **+** (addition sign). In order to perform addition, two values are needed so...

4. Pop **25** and **34** off the stack and add them. Push the result (**59**) onto the stack.
   The stack contains: **59**

5. Read the value **15** and push it onto the stack.
   The stack contains: **15 59**

6. Read the ***** (multiplication sign). In order to perform multiplication, two values are needed so...

7. Pop **15** and **59** off the stack and multiply them. Push the result (**885**) onto the stack. The stack contains: **885**.

If you don't get the hang of RPN right away, don't worry about it. You can always figure it out by practicing with **dc**. In fact, the best way to really understand RPN is by experimenting.

In our example, I showed you the contents of the stack at each step of the way. With **dc**, you don't see the stack. However, at any time you can display the top of the stack by using the **p** (print) command*. To show how this works, start **dc** and enter the following two lines. (Don't forget to press <Return> at the end of each line.)

```
34 25 + 15 *
p
```

After you enter the first line, **dc** performs the calculation. However, you don't see anything. Once you enter the second line (the **p** command), **dc** displays the value of the element at the top of the stack, in this case, **885**, which is the result of the previous calculation.

If you would like to see the entire stack, use the **f** command:

```
f
```

Why doesn't **dc** automatically print the value of the top of the stack each time you enter a new line? The answer is that if **dc** printed something every time you entered a line, it would clutter up your screen. Instead, **dc** (like most Unix programs) is as silent as possible. It is up to you to look at the top of the stack as the need arises.

To help you get started with **dc**, Figure 8-3 contains a summary of the most important **dc** commands. Aside from this summary, the best way to teach yourself how to use **dc** is to read the online manual (see Chapter 9) and experiment. The command to look at the **dc** manual page is:

```
man dc
```

The number of digits that **dc** keeps after the decimal point is called the "precision". The default is **0** digits. To change this, push the number of digits you want onto the stack and then enter the **k** command. This value can be as large as you want. For example, to change the precision to **14** digits, use:

```
14 k
```

---

*As I explained in Chapter 7, because the old Unix terminals printed their output on paper, the term "print" is often used as a synonym for "display". Thus, the **dc** print command displays the value on the top of the stack. This convention is used with many Unix programs.

To display the current precision, use the **K** (uppercase "K") command. This will push the current precision onto the top of the stack. You can then use the **p** command to display the actual value:

K p

Finally, to stop **dc** you can either press **^D** to indicate that there is no more data, or you can use the **q** (quit) command.

HINT

If you like mathematical or scientific thinking, you should find it fun to play around with **dc**. As you do, you will find that **dc** is more than a diversion. In order to learn how to use the program, you will need to master the ideas of Reverse Polish notation and how to use a stack, both of which are difficult concepts. However, once you do master these ideas, you will find that **dc** is an efficient, well-designed tool that is easy to use.

If you look back at the very end of Chapter 1, you will see that I made two general comments about Unix: Unix is easy to use, but difficult to learn. Start by learning the basics, then learn whatever you want, in whatever order you want.

Can you see that **dc** fits into the exact same paradigm? It is easy to use, but difficult to learn. And, to start, you learn the basics (by reading this chapter), and then experiment on your own as you see fit.

So, if you take the time to practice with **dc**, you will not only be learning how to use an interesting tool, you will be training your mind to think in the way Unix minds should think.

COMMAND	MEANING
q	Quit
p	Print top of stack
n	Pop stack and print value
f	Print entire contents of stack
c	Clear (empty) the stack
d	Duplicate top value of stack
r	Reverse (swap) top two values on stack
+	Pop two values, add, push sum
−	Pop two values, subtract, push difference
*	Pop two values, multiply, push product
/	Pop two values, divide, push quotient
%	Pop two values, divide, push remainder
~	Pop two values, divide, push quotient, push remainder
^	Pop two values, second to power of first, push result
v	Pop one value, take square root, push result
k	Pop one value, use it to set precision

FIGURE 8-3: dc: The most important commands

CHAPTER 8 EXERCISES

REVIEW QUESTIONS

1. Describe three different ways that are used to stop a program.

2. Which program do you use to display the time? The date?

3. What is the difference between the **cal** and **calendar** programs?

4. How do you display the name of the computer you are using? Your operating system? Your userid?

APPLYING YOUR KNOWLEDGE

1. Mickey Mouse was born on November 18, 1928. Display the calendar for that month. What day of the week was Mickey born on? What number day within the year was it (Jan 1 = 1, Dec 31 = 366)?

2. The element lutetium is a very heavy, rare, silvery white metal. It is considered to be the most expensive metal in the world. The Maharaja of Gaipajama wants you to babysit with his son. The fee will be 1 gram of lutetium for every 2 hours, and he wants you to work for 5 hours. Assume that gold costs $25.42 (U.S.) per gram, and 1 gram of lutetium is worth 6 grams of gold. Use the **bc** program to calculate how much your babysitting fee worth in U.S. dollars. The answer must be accurate to 2 decimal places. (Once you are finished, look up the Maharaja of Gaipajama on the Internet.)

FOR FURTHER THOUGHT

1. At the beginning of the chapter, I made the comment, "Traditionally, one of the ways in which people learn Unix is by having a good time while they are learning." This is usually not the case with other operating systems, such as Microsoft Windows. Why?

2. The **users**, **who** and **w** programs all display information about the userids that are currently logged into the system. Do we need three different programs?

DOCUMENTATION: THE UNIX MANUAL AND INFO

Within the world of Unix, there are many different documentation systems, each with its own characteristics. Some are used widely; some serve a particular niche. In general, all such systems have two common goals: to make it easy for programmers to document their work, and to make it easy for users to learn how to use the tools created by the programmers.

In this chapter, I am going to teach you how to use the two most important Unix documentation systems: the online Unix manual, a facility that comes with every Unix system; and Info, the official documentation system of the GNU project.

Both of these tools are designed to be used with the Unix CLI (command line interface). The reason is that graphical programs are self-documenting, in the sense that they almost always have their own built-in help facility. Thus, when you want help with a GUI-based program, you don't use the online manual or Info. You look within the program itself, usually by pulling down a Help menu.

THE UNIX TRADITION OF TEACHING YOURSELF

As we discussed in Chapter 2, Unix was developed in the early 1970s in New Jersey, at Bell Labs (then a part of AT&T). Soon after Unix was created, it became popular with programmers and researchers, first within Bell Labs and later in the computer science departments at a handful of research universities.

As Unix grew in popularity, more and more people needed to learn how to use the system. However, the Bell Labs programmers were busy people who did not have the time, nor the inclination, to teach new users how to use Unix. Moreover, the prevailing culture encouraged anyone to create new tools and share them with other users. Thus, from one month to the next, the amount of material that one might need to learn increased, as did the number of new users.

In response to these needs, the Unix developers adopted a two-part solution. First, they created an online manual, built into Unix itself, which contained information regarding every Unix tool. Since the Unix manual was itself part of Unix, it was available to all users all the time. This meant, for example, when a user at a far-away location had a question in the middle of the night, he or she would be able to turn to the manual for help.

The second part of the solution was to encourage a work environment in which all Unix users — both new and experienced — were expected to try to answer their own questions before they asked for help. To be precise, what we might call the Unix tradition requires you to teach yourself and try to solve your own problems. However, if you have tried your best and you still have a problem, other Unix people will be glad to help you. The converse of this is that, once you are experienced, *you* are expected to help others.

This Unix tradition was important for two reasons. First, it provided an efficient way for Unix to spread. Since people would only ask for help if they really needed it, experienced people were not called upon to waste their time helping others unnecessarily. Second, by making people responsible for teaching themselves, the Unix developers encouraged the type of independent thinking and personal creation that caused Unix to flourish. In fact, the Unix tradition bred a generation of users who were smart, independent, and willing to help others (when necessary), all working within an atmosphere of cooperative creativity.

For example, if a programmer wanted a new tool, he was encouraged to create it for himself. Once the program was finished, it would be added to the general Unix system. The programmer would then write the relevant documentation, which would be added to the online manual. The new tool would be announced to the general Unix community, with the understanding that anyone who wanted to learn how to use it would read the online manual, experiment, and teach himself. If a user found a bug or had a serious problem, he or she was free to contact the author of the program.

Thus, you can see the Unix tradition is based on two main ideas: Try your best to teach yourself before you ask for help; when others ask you for help, give willingly of your time. These ideas proved to be so important that they become embodied in a single, very odd word: RTFM.

WHAT'S IN A NAME?

Online

In the old days, the word ONLINE was used to describe the idea of being connected to a specific computer system. For example, when you were logged into a system, we would say you were online.

When we talk about the online Unix manual, we are using the word in this way. The manual is "online" because it is available to all the users of a particular Unix system.

Today, we also use the term "online" to indicate that a resource or a person is connected to the Internet, not to a specific computer system. For example, once you are connected to the Net, you can use online banking, online bill paying, and even participate in an online relationship.

Thus, as a Unix user, you are online in two different ways: you are logged into a particular Unix system, and you are connected to the Internet.

RTFM

The word RTFM is unique in several ways. First, it is the longest verb in the English language without vowels. Second, it is usually spelled with all uppercase letters. Finally, because RTFM has no vowels, the word is pronounced as four distinct letters ("R-T-F-M"), even though it is not an acronym.

As I mentioned, RTFM is a verb. (I'll explain its origin in a moment.) We use it to embody the idea that, before you ask for help or information, you must try to solve the problem or find the information for yourself.

The word RTFM can be used in two ways. First, you can tell someone not to bother you for help until he has tried to help himself. For example, if someone says, "Can you show me how to use the **whatis** command?" you might reply, "RTFM." In this case, RTFM means, "Don't ask for help until you have checked with the online Unix manual."

Second, you can also use RTFM to indicate you have tried to solve a problem on your own before asking for help. For example, you might email a message to a friend: "Can you help me get my Linux system to share files with a Windows PC? I have RTFM'd for two days now, and I still can't get it to work without having to reboot Windows every few hours."

Since the early days, the idea of RTFM has been an integral part of the Unix culture. Today, its use is also widespread on the Internet, especially within Usenet and the open source community. (See Chapter 2 for a discussion of the open source movement.) As the use of RTFM has expanded, so has its meaning. Today, the doctrine of RTFM requires you to look for information — not only in the online Unix manual — but on the Internet as well.

Thus, it is a good idea not to ask for help until you have at least used a search engine, such as Google, to look for relevant Web sites. With respect to Usenet, if you are a newcomer to a discussion group, it is expected that you will read the FAQ (frequently asked question list) for that group before you send in your first posting. This too is considered RTFMing.

HINT

When you are looking for solutions to Unix problems, don't forget Usenet, the worldwide system of discussion groups.

The easiest way to search Usenet is to use the Google Usenet archive, called Google Groups. I have often found answers to even the most obscure questions by searching the Usenet archive.

If after all your searching, you can't find what you want, you can post a request in the appropriate discussion group. If you do, be sure to mention that you have already RTFM'd.

WHAT'S IN A NAME?

RTFM, RTFM'd

RTFM is a verb, indicating the idea that, when you need information or you are working on a problem, you should spend some time trying to find what you need on your own before you ask someone else for help.

When we talk about already having performed such actions, we use the past participle of the verb, which is spelled RTFM'd, not RTFMed. Thus, you might say, "I have RTFM'd for the last two hours, and I can't figure out how to connect my cat to the Internet."

Like many technical words, RTFM started life as an acronym. In the early days of Unix, RTFM stood for "Read the fucking manual,"* referring, of course, to the online Unix manual. Today, however, RTFM is not an acronym, but a legitimate word in its own right.

---

* Sometimes you will see RTFM explained by using the euphemism "Read the fine manual". However, as you know, it is my practice within this book to explain things as they really are. In this case, as you can see, the original meaning of RTFM used profanity, and I think you should know the truth. Thanks for not being offended.

(*cont'd...*) This is not unusual. The same can be said for many other technical words, such as radar ("radio detection and ranging"), laser ("light amplification by stimulated emission of radiation"), and scuba ("self-contained underwater breathing apparatus"); as well as various proper nouns, such as Nato ("North Atlantic Treaty Organization"), and collective nouns, such as yuppie ("young urban professional").

The biggest difference between RTFM and other such words is that RTFM is normally spelled with uppercase letters. This only makes sense as RTFM is much more important to our culture than radar, laser, scuba, Nato or yuppies.

WHAT IS THE UNIX MANUAL? man

The UNIX MANUAL, often referred to as the ONLINE MANUAL or, more simply, the MANUAL, is a collection of files, each of which contains documentation about one specific Unix command or topic. The manual is available on every Unix system, where it is accessible to any user at any time. To use the manual, you enter a simple command (which we will discuss in a moment). The information you requested is then presented to you, one screenful at a time.

In the olden days (of mainframe computers), most computer systems came with a large amount of highly technical, printed documentation, which was kept in a central location, such as a computer room or a terminal room. Not only was the documentation awkward to use, it was often out of date, and it was common to have to deal with a stack of printed updates. For this reason, the old-time computer manuals were stored in large, unwieldy holders that could be opened to insert new pages, but were generally awkward to use or to move from one place to another.

Unix was different. From the beginning, the documentation was always online, which meant that it was convenient for any user to read whatever he needed, whenever he wanted, on his own terminal. Moreover, because the online manual was stored as a collection of disk files, it was a simple matter to add new material by adding a new file, or update existing material by modifying a file. In the very early days, Unix systems did have a printed manual as well as the online manual. However, the information in the printed manual was the same as what was already available online.

Accessing the Unix manual is easy. All you need to do is type the word **man**, followed by the name of the command you want to know about. Unix will display the documentation for that command.

For example, to display the documentation about the **cp** (copy a file) command, enter:

```
man cp
```

Suppose you want to learn about the **man** command itself. Just enter:

```
man man
```

HINT

The **man** command is the single most important Unix command, because you can use it to learn about any other command.

If you want to learn about more than one command name, just enter all the names on the same line. For example:

```
man cp mv rm
```

Unix will display the documentation for each command in turn. These three commands, by the way, are used to copy, rename [move], and delete [remove] files. We will meet them more formally in Chapter 25.

WHAT'S IN A NAME?

The Manual

Unix manuals have always been important. Indeed, at one time, when Unix was primarily a product of AT&T's Bell Labs, successive versions of Unix were named after the current edition of the manual: Unix Sixth Edition, Unix Seventh Edition, and so on.

Although there are many Unix books and references, when a Unix person refers to "the manual", you can assume that he or she is talking about the one and only online Unix manual. For example, say you are reading an email message from your system administrator describing a new program he has just installed on the system. At the end of the message, he says, "For more information, check the manual." You can assume, without asking, that he wants you to use the **man** command to read the appropriate entry in the online manual.

To a Unix user, there is never any doubt as to which manual is The Manual.

MAN PAGES

In the very early days, Unix users used slow terminals that printed output on paper. Since there were no monitors, when someone wanted to learn about a command, he or she would have to print the relevant pages of the online manual. This wasn't as inconvenient as it might sound because, at the time, there weren't that many entries in the manual, and many of them were designed to fit on a single page.

Today, the Unix manual has a large number of entries, many of which are much longer than a printed page. Still, it is the custom to refer to a single entry, no matter how long it is, as a PAGE or, more formally, as a MAN PAGE. For example, the documentation for Bash, the default Linux shell (which we will meet in Chapter 12), runs to well over 4,500 lines. Still, it is considered to be a single man page.

Consider this example of word usage. You are in a Unix bar, quaffing down a glass of caffeinated chocolate milk, and you happen to overhear two programmers talking. The first one says, "I can't decide what to get my girlfriend for Valentine's Day. Do you have any ideas?" to which the other programmer replies, "Why not print her a copy of the Bash man page?"

DISPLAYING MAN PAGES

Virtually all the entries in the online manual are longer than the number of lines on your screen. If an entry were displayed all at once, most of it would scroll off the screen so fast that you would not be able to read the text.

This is a common situation for which Unix has a good solution: send the output to a program that displays the output more carefully, one screenful at a time. There are three such programs, called paging programs, that are commonly used on Unix systems. Their names are **less**, **more** and **pg**. The best — and most widely used — paging program is **less**, which we will talk about in detail in Chapter 21. For now, I will give you a brief overview, so you will know enough to be able to read the online manual.

If you want to practice as you are reading, enter one of the following commands, each of which displays information about a particular shell: Bash, the Korn shell, or the C-Shell:

```
man bash
man ksh
man csh
```

My suggestion is to display the man page for the shell that you plan on using or that most people use on your system. If you are not sure, just pick one — it's only for practice.

The job of a paging program is to display data one screenful at a time. After each screenful, the program pauses and displays a prompt at the bottom left-hand corner of the screen. The prompt differs depending on what paging program is being used.

The **less** and **pg** programs display a colon:

```
:
```

On some systems, **less** displays a message instead of the colon. For example:

```
byte 1357
```

In this case, **less** is telling you that it has just displayed character number 1357. (Each byte holds one character.) As you page through the file, this number will increase, giving you a rough idea of how far you are from the beginning.

The **more** program displays a prompt that contains the word "More". For example, you might see:

```
--More--(10%)
```

This means that there is more to come and that you are 10 percent of the way through the page.

Once you see the prompt, you can display the next screenful of information by pressing the <Space> bar. (With **pg**, you press <Return>.) When you are finished reading, press **q** (the letter "q") to quit.

As you are reading a man page, there are many commands you can use. Normally, however, you won't need them. Most of the time, you will simply press <Space>, reading one screenful after another. When you reach the end of the page, or when you find what you want, you will press **q** to quit.

From time to time, you may want to use some of the other commands, so I'm going to take a moment to describe the ones that I find most useful. These commands are summarized in Figure 9-1. As I mentioned, there are many others, more than you will ever need. Note: The commands in Figure 9-1 are for systems that use **less**. If your system uses **more** or **pg**, there will be some differences. If you have a problem, use the **h** command for help.

GENERAL COMMANDS	
q	quit
h	display help information
READING A MAN PAGE	
<Space>	display next screenful
<PageDown>	display next screenful
f	display next screenful
<PageUp>	display previous screenful
b	display previous screenful
SEARCHING	
/pattern	search down for specified pattern
?pattern	search up for specified pattern
/	search down for previous pattern
n	search down for previous pattern
?	search up for previous pattern
N	search up for previous pattern
MOVING AROUND WITHIN A MAN PAGE	
<Return>	move down one line
<Down>	move down one line
<Up>	move up one line
g	go to top of page
G	go to bottom of page

FIGURE 9-1: Reading a man page: Important commands

With any program, the most important command is the one that displays the help information. In this case, all you need to do is press **h** (the letter "h"). When you do, the man page information will be replaced by a summary of all the paging commands. When you are finished reading the help information, press **q** to quit and return to the man page. Note: The summary is quite long and, just as with the man page itself, you will have to press <Space> to work your way through the information. However, the most important commands will be near the top of the summary.

The commands I am about to discuss are for the **less** paging program, because it is used with most Unix systems. If your **man** command uses either **more** or **pg**, all you have to do is press **h**, to get the help summary for that particular paging program. My suggestion is that, as you read, follow along at your computer, trying the various commands.

To start, if you are looking for a specific pattern, press the **/** (slash) character, type the pattern, and then press <Return>. For example:

/output<Return>

This example tells the paging program to skip forward to the next line that contains the word "output". Once you have specified a pattern, you can search for it again by entering the **/** character by itself:

/<Return>

If you search for a pattern, but it's not the line you want, you can keep searching for the same pattern, over and over, until you find what you do want. Just keep pressing **/**<Return>*.

Alternatively, you can press **n** (next) to search for the same pattern, either once or more than once.

To search backward, use **?** instead of **/**. For example:

?output<Return>

To search backward for the same pattern, use **?** by itself:

?<Return>

Alternatively, you can press **N** (next) to search backward for the same pattern.

To move down one screenful, as you already know, you press <Space>. You can also press **f** (for forward). To move up one screenful, press **b** (for backward). Alternatively, you can move down and up by pressing <PageDown> and <PageUp>.

To move down one line at a time, press the <Return> key or the <Down> key (that is, the down-arrow key). To move up one line at a time, press the <Up> key (that is, the up-arrow key).

To jump to the top of the page, press **g** ("go to top"). To jump to the bottom of the page, press **G** ("go to bottom").

TWO USEFUL MAN PAGE TECHNIQUES

The way in which you read man pages – so far as we have discussed it – is conceptually simple. You use the **man** command to display information about a particular topic. You then look at the information, one screenful at a time, until you find what you want.

This is the common way to read man pages using the standard Unix CLI (command line interface). However, if you put the **man** command together with the Unix working environment, you can access man pages in a more sophisticated way.

As we discussed in Chapter 6, you can use the CLI in two ways, with a terminal window or with a virtual console. My suggestion is to learn how to use two terminal windows at the same time, one for doing your work and the other for displaying man pages. For example, let's say you are working within one terminal window, editing a file with the **vi** text editor (see Chapter 22). You need some help, so you decide to look at the **vi** man page. If you do so by displaying the page in a second terminal window, you can look at both the man page and the original window at the same time. You can see this in Figure 9-2.

To become a skillful Unix user, you need to master the skill of using more than one window at a time. More precisely, you must be able to answer the questions: When should

---

*This feature is taken from the **vi** editor, which we will meet in Chapter 22.

I use a single window? When should I use two windows? When should I use more than two windows? When do I want to forget about windows and use virtual consoles?

The answers to these questions aren't obvious, and you will find your skills growing with your experience. The trick is to never allow yourself to get into a rut. For example, don't always use one window, or don't always use two windows in the exact same way.

To further add to your bag of tricks, I'd like to teach you one more tool to use while reading a man page.

As you are reading a man page, if you type an **!** (exclamation mark), you can follow it with a shell command. The **man** program will send the command to the shell, which will run it for you. When the command is finished, you can press <Return> to go back to the **man** program.

To see how this works, display a man page and type:

!date<Return>

In this case you are entering the **date** command from within the **man** program. The result is that you see the time and date. Once the **date** command is finished, simply press <Return> and you will be back where you were within the **man** program.

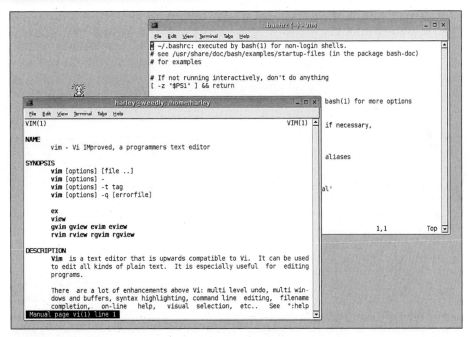

FIGURE 9-2: Displaying a man page in its own terminal window

*By displaying a man page in its own terminal window, you can use it as a reference while you are working in another window. In this example, the man page for the **vim**, a version of the **vi** editor is on the left. On the right is a terminal window in which **vim** is running.*

As you might imagine, being able to enter a shell command whenever you want can be very useful. What is particularly handy is that you can use this technique to display one man page while you are reading another, without having to switch to a separate window. Here is how it works.

Let's say that you are reading the man page about the **man** command:

```
man man
```

As you are reading the page, you see that there are several other related commands, among them **whatis** (which we will discuss later in this chapter). At this point, you decide that you'd like to pause what you are doing and read about **whatis**. Just enter:

!man whatis<Return>

When you are finished reading about **whatis**, press **q** to quit. You will then be asked to press <Return> and, once you do, you will be back in the original man program, reading about the **man** command.

WHAT'S IN A NAME?

Bang

As a Unix user, you will, from time to time, use the **!** (exclamation mark) character in a special way. Usually it will change the mode of what you are doing, so you can pause the current program and send a command to the shell. (See Chapter 6 for a discussion of the idea of modes.)

As an example, as you are reading a man page, you can display the time and date by entering:

!date<Return>

When the **!** character is used in this way – as a command and not as a punctuation symbol – it is given a special name. We call it a BANG CHARACTER or, more simply, a BANG. Thus, a Unix person might say, "If you are reading a man page and you want to display the time and date, just type 'bang-d-a-t-e' and press <Return>."

The name "bang" is a slang term that has been used within the printing and typesetting professions for a long time. Its origins are unknown.

ALTERNATIVES TO man: xman AND THE WEB

As I have explained you can use the **man** command to display pages from the online Unix manual. Aside from this command, there are two alternatives I want you to know about.

First, the man pages for most Unix systems are available as Web pages on the Internet. This means that, whenever you want, you can use your browser to find and display a specific page. The advantage to reading man pages on the Web is that they will often have links that allow you to jump from one page to another. Regular man pages (using the **man** command) are plain text with a bit of highlighting, not hypertext with links.

The easiest way to find the man page you want on the Web is to use a search engine such as Google to search for "man" followed by the name of a command, for example:

```
"man whatis"
```

Be sure to include the quotation marks.

Alternatively, you can find a more general resource by searching for "man pages" followed by the name of your type of Unix, for example:

```
"man pages" Linux
"man pages" FreeBSD
"man pages" Solaris
```

Again, don't forget the quotation marks.

> **HINT**
>
> When you get a moment, find some Web sites that offer the man pages for the type of Unix or Linux you are using. Choose one site that you particularly like, and save the URL (Web address) so you can access it quickly whenever you want.
>
> My suggestion is to save the URL as a button on the Links bar within your browser. That way, it will always be visible and easy to use. However, you can also save the URL as an icon on your desktop or as an entry in your Bookmarks/Favorites list. See what works best for you.

An alternative to using Web-based man pages is **xman**, a GUI-based program that acts as a man page browser. (The "x" indicates that the program is written for X-Window based GUIs; see Chapter 5.) If **xman** is available on your system, it is well worth your while to take a few moments to experiment and learn how to use it.

To start **xman**, type the following at the command line:

```
xman&
```

Using the **&** (ampersand) character tells the shell to start running the program on its own in the background.

When **xman** starts, it displays a simple window with three large buttons labeled Help, Quit, and Manual Page (see Figure 9-3). It is much easier for you to read the instructions than for me to explain the full complexity of the program, so I'll restrict myself to giving you only two hints.

First, to start, click on the Help box and read the instructions. when the focus is on an **xman** window, you can press **^S** (<Ctrl-S>) to display a small search box. This makes it easy to find what you want (see Figure 9-3). Try it, so you can see what I mean.

HOW THE UNIX MANUAL IS ORGANIZED

The best way to think about the online manual is to imagine a gargantuan reference book that lives somewhere inside your Unix system. The book is like an encyclopedia in that it contains many entries, in alphabetical order, each of which covers a single topic.

You can't turn the pages of this book; hence, there are no page numbers and no formal table of contents or index. However, there are several layers of organization that are appropriate to an electronic book.

Traditionally, the entire manual is divided into eight sections, numbered 1 through 8. These classic divisions are shown in Figure 9-4. From one system to another, the actual names may vary but, for the most part, all Unix manuals tend to follow the same general

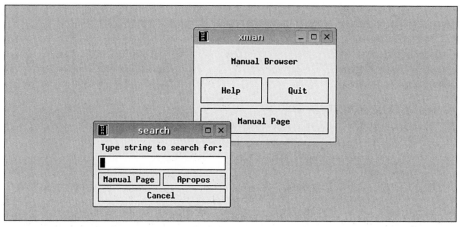

FIGURE 9-3: xman program

xman *is a GUI-based program for browsing man pages. In the top right, you see the initial window. To get started, click on "Help". In the bottom left, you see the search box, which you can display at any time by pressing <Ctrl-S>.*

organization. Although the manual on your system may be a bit different, it should be close enough so that, when you read the following discussion, it will make sense to you.

The most important part of the manual is section 1. This section contains the man pages for the bulk of the Unix commands. In fact, unless you are a programmer or a system administrator, you can probably get by with just this section of the manual.

If you are a programmer, you will also be interested in Sections 2 and 3. Section 2 contains the man pages for system calls, used within programs to request the kernel to perform a specific action. Section 3 documents library functions, sometimes called subroutines. These are standardized tools, not involving the kernel directly, that are used within programs to perform specific tasks.

Section 4 discusses special files, a type of file that usually represents a physical device. You will also find information about device drivers (programs that act as an interface to a device). This section is used primarily by programmers.

1. Commands
2. System calls
3. Library functions
4. Special files
5. File formats
6. Games
7. Miscellaneous information
8. System administration

FIGURE 9-4: Eight sections of the online Unix manual

Section 5 describes the important file formats used by the system, including configuration files. This section is used by both programmers and admins.

Section 6 contains man pages for whatever games are installed on the system. In the olden days, there were lots of text-based games and diversions that users could use from the command line. An example is the the game of Rogue that we discussed in Chapter 7. In those days, Section 6 was an important part of the manual. Today, most systems omit the text-based games and, more often than not, this section of the manual will be empty. To be sure, there are many GUI-based games but, as I mentioned at the beginning of the chapter, such programs have their own built-in help, so they don't need man pages.

This doesn't mean there are no Unix text-based games. There are many of them, including a variety of wonderful diversions, and you can install them on your system if you want. If you are using a shared system and the system administrator has not installed the games (or if he has removed them), Section 6 of the manual may be empty. This is because most admins do not want to handle complaints from users who can read about the games, but can't use them (sort of like Moses standing on Mount Pisgah, gazing down wistfully at the Promised Land).

Section 7, the Miscellaneous Information section, contains a grab-bag of information. The contents of Section 7 vary greatly from one system to another, so there's not a lot I can say about it, except that, like most of the other sections, it is primarily of interest to programmers and admins.

Finally, Section 8 contains the man pages for all the special commands that system administrators use to carry out their work. In other words, these are the commands that can be used only by the superuser. (See Chapter 4 for a discussion of system administration and the superuser.)

If you use a shared system, you probably won't care about Section 8 of the manual, because someone else is doing the system administration. However, if you are running Unix on your own computer, you are the admin and, from time to time, you will need to use some of the commands from this section of the manual.

HINT

Except for Section 1 (Commands) and Section 6 (Games), the bulk of the Unix manual is of interest only to programmers and system administrators.

The idea of organizing the Unix manual into these specific eight sections was derived from the earliest Unix implementations and has, for the most part, remained intact over the years. However, the modern manuals cover much more material than their venerable ancestors. Thus, on your system, you may see different, more comprehensive sections, possibly with different names.

You may also find that a particular section contains specialized sub-sections. For example, on some Linux systems, if you look within Section 3 (Library functions), you will find several sub-sections: Section 3c, for standard C functions; Section 3f for Fortran functions; Section 3m for mathematical functions; Section 3s for standard I/O functions; and Section 3x for special functions.

SPECIFYING THE SECTION NUMBER WHEN USING THE man COMMAND

So far, we have seen how to use the Unix manual by typing **man** followed by the name of a command. For example, to learn about the **kill** command (see Chapter 26), which can stop a runaway program, you would enter:

```
man kill
```

This command displays the man page for **kill** from Section 1 of the manual.

However, it happens that there is also an entry for **kill** in Section 2 of the manual (System Calls). If this is what you really want, you can specify the section number before the name of the command:

```
man 2 kill
```

This tells Unix that you are only interested in a particular section of the manual.

If you are using a type of Unix that is derived from System V (see Chapter 2), the form of the command is a bit different: you have to type **-s** before the section number. This is the case, for example, with Solaris:

```
man -s 2 kill
```

If a section is divided into subsections, you can be as specific as you want.

For example, on some systems there is an entry for **kill** in Section 3f, the part of the manual that documents Fortran subroutines. To display this man page, enter:

```
man 3f kill
```

As I mentioned earlier, you can ask for more than one part of the manual at a time. For instance, if you want to see all three entries for **kill**, you can enter:

```
man 1 kill 2 kill 3f kill
```

When you do not specify a section number, Unix starts at the beginning of the manual (Section 1) and works its way through until it finds the first match. Thus, the following two commands have the same result:

```
man kill
man 1 kill
```

HINT

Most of the time, you will be interested in Section 1 of the manual (Commands), so it is not necessary to specify a section number. You only need to use a section number when you are looking for information related to programming (sections 2, 3, 4, 5 and 7) or system administration (sections 4, 7 and 8).

To orient you to the various parts of the manual, each section and subsection contains a page called **intro** that acts as a brief introduction. A good way to become familiar with the contents of a section is to read its **intro** page.

Here are some examples of commands that display such pages:

```
man intro
man 1 intro
man 1c intro
man 6 intro
```

As you know, **man** will assume, by default, that you want to reference Section 1; thus, the first two examples are equivalent.

HINT

If you are a beginner, the best way to learn about the online manual is by using the following two commands:

```
man intro
man man
```

HOW MAN PAGES ARE REFERENCED

When you read about Unix, you will often see the name of a command followed by a number in parentheses. This number tells you what section of the manual to look in for information about that particular command.

For example, here is part of a sentence taken from a BSD (Berkeley) version of the man page for the **chmod** command (which you will meet in Chapter 25). For now, don't worry about what the sentence means, just look at the reference:

"...but the setting of the file creation mask, see **umask(2)**, is taken into account..."

The citation "**umask(2)**" tells us that the man page for **umask** can be found in Section 2 of the manual. To read it, you would use:

```
man 2 umask
```

Since we know that Section 2 describes system calls, we can guess that we would only care about this reference if we were writing a program.

At the end of the same **chmod** man page, however, are the following two lines:

```
SEE ALSO
ls(1), chmod(2), stat(2), umask(2), chown(8)
```

Here is a reference to five other commands related to **chmod**. As you can see, three of the references are in Section 2 and are for programmers. The last reference is in Section 8 and is for system administrators.

The first reference, however, refers to a command, **ls** whose man page lies in Section 1. Since Section 1 describes general commands, there is a good chance that this reference will be of interest. To display this man page, we can use either of the following commands:

```
man ls
man 1 ls
```

(By the way, the purpose of **ls** is to display the names of files. We will meet this command in Chapter 24.)

> **HINT**
>
> When you are looking for information or working on a problem, and you see a reference to a command in Section 1 of the manual, you should take the time to follow up the reference. Even if the information is not exactly what you need at the moment, it will come in handy later.
>
> If you see references to other sections, however, you can ignore them, unless the information looks particularly interesting.

THE FORMAT OF A MANUAL PAGE

Each man page explains a single topic, most often a command, system call or library function. Some pages are short, while others are quite long. For example, the man pages that describe the various shells are long enough to be reference manuals in their own right. To see what I mean, try one of the following commands:

```
man bash
man ksh
man csh
```

For convenience, every man page, regardless of size, is organized according to a standard format, in which the page is divided into a number of parts, each with its own heading. The most common headings are shown in Figure 9-5. Interestingly enough, these headings are the same ones that were used many years ago in the original Unix manual as it was developed at Bell Labs. (Of course, the content has changed radically since then.)

Not all man pages have each of these headings,; some man pages have headings not in this list. For example, I have encountered **Examples**, **Reporting Bugs**, **Copyright**, **History** and **Standards**. However, regardless of the actual design, the basic format is the same from one man page to another. Indeed, every man page I have ever seen has started with the same three headings: **Name**, **Synopsis** and **Description**.

To help you, Figure 9-6 contains a sample man page. This man page is actually from an older Unix system, and it's likely that the equivalent page on your system will be a lot longer. I have used this particular example, however, because it is short enough to print, easy to understand, and contains all the important elements of a typical man page.

Note: As you read the man page in Figure 9-6, remember that the word "print" usually refers to displaying text on your terminal, not actual printing (see Chapter 7).

To begin our discussion, let's take a quick tour of each of the basic headings. As I mentioned, you may see other headings from time to time, but once you get a bit of experience you won't have any trouble understanding the variations.

NAME: This is a one-line summary of the command or feature. Be aware that some summaries are vague; if you are confused, you may have to do a bit more RTFMing.

SYNOPSIS: This section shows the syntax of the command. This is the official explanation of how to enter the command. I describe command syntax in detail in Chapter 10, so we'll leave most of the discussion till then. For now, I just want to draw your attention to one point.

In general, when you enter a command, you type a name, followed by options, followed by parameters. We'll discuss the technical details in Chapter 10, so don't worry about them for now. All I want you to understand is that you will see two variations of how the **Synopsis** section shows the options.

First, you may simply see the word **OPTION**. In this case, the actual options are listed and explained in the **Description** section below. Here is an example, taken from the Linux man page for the **ls** command:

```
ls [OPTION]... [FILE]...
```

This convention is used with the man pages that come with the GNU utilities (see Chapter 2). Since the GNU utilities are used with virtually all Linux systems, this is what you will see on many of the Linux man pages.

Here are two more examples. The first is taken from the FreeBSD manual; the second is from the Solaris manual.

```
ls [-ABCFGHLPRTWabcdfghiklmnopqrstuwx1] [file...]
ls [-aAbcCdeEfFghHilLmnopqrRstux1@] [file...]
```

In this case, the actual options are specified. (This is also the case with the sample man page you see in Figure 9-6.) As with the example above, the details are explained in the **Description** section. The job of the **Synopsis** is to provide a quick summary of the command.

DESCRIPTION: This section is the largest one and usually takes up the bulk of the man page. Its purpose is to explain most of the details you need to know, including how to use the options. On some systems, the full explanation is divided into two separate sections: **Description** and **Options**.

As you read, it helps to remember that you are looking at a reference manual, not a teaching guide. Be prepared to find that many descriptions are difficult to understand until you know what you are doing. This is normal. If you have trouble, keep reading

HEADING	MEANING
Name	name and purpose of the command
Synopsis	syntax of the command
Description	full description (may be long)
Environment	environment variables used by the command
Author	name of the programmer
Files	list of files important to this command
See also	where to look for related information
Diagnostics	possible errors and warnings
Bugs	mistakes, shortcomings, warnings

FIGURE 9-5: Standard headings used in a man page

```
MAN(1)                          USER COMMANDS                          MAN(1)


NAME
     man - display reference manual pages; find reference pages by keyword

SYNOPSIS
       man [-] [section] title ...
       man -k keyword ...
       man -f filename ...

DESCRIPTION
       Man is a program which gives information from the programmer's manual. It
       can be asked for one-line descriptions of commands specified by name, or
       for all commands whose description contains any of a set of keywords. It
       can also provide on-line access to the sections of the printed manual.

       When given the option -k and a set of keywords, man prints out a one-
       line synopsis of each manual section whose listing in the table of
       contents contains one of those keywords.

       When given the option -f and a list of names, man attempts to locate
       manual sections related to those files, printing out the table of
       contents lines for those sections.

       When neither -k or -f is specified, man formats a specified set of manual
       pages. If a section specifier is given man looks in that section of the
       manual for the given titles. Section is either an Arabic section number
       (3 for instance), or one of the words "new","local", "old" or "public".
       A section number may be followed by a single letter classifier (for
       instance, 1g, indicating a graphics program in section 1). If section is
       omitted, man searches all sections of the manual, giving preference to
       commands over subroutines in system libraries, and printing the first
       section it finds, if any.

       If the standard output is a teletype, or if the flag - is given, man
       pipes its output through more(1) with the option -s to crush out useless
       blank lines and to stop after each page on the screen. Hit a space to
       continue, a control-D to scroll 11 more lines when the output stops.

FILES
     /usr/man            standard manual area
     /usr/man/man?/*     directories containing source for manuals
     /usr/man/cat?/*     directories containing preformatted pages
     /usr/man/whatis     keyword database

SEE ALSO
     apropos(1), more(1), whatis(1), whereis(1), catman(8)

BUGS
     The manual is supposed to be reproducible either on a photo-typesetter
     or on an ASCII terminal.  However, on a terminal some information
     (indicated by font changes, for instance) is necessarily lost.
```

FIGURE 9-6: Sample page from the Unix manual

until you run out of patience: some of what you read will stick. When you learn more, you can try again.

Realize also that there are some descriptions (such as those for the various shells) that you will probably *never* understand completely. If this bothers you, remind yourself that the people who do understand everything in the Unix manual are much less attractive and socially adept than you.

FILES: This section shows the names of the files that are used by this command. If the information in this section makes no sense to you, you can ignore it. (We will discuss file names in detail in Chapter 23.)

SEE ALSO: This is an important section. It shows you other places to look in the manual for more information. In particular, you will see commands that are related in some way to the command under discussion. Following up these references is a good way to learn. Concentrate on the references to the Section 1 man pages.

ENVIRONMENT: Before I can explain this section, I need to lay a bit of groundwork with respect to the idea of variables.

A variable is an entity with a name and a value. Within Unix, there are certain variables whose values are available to all programs and shell scripts. (A shell script is a file containing a list of commands that can be executed automatically.) Such variables are known by several different names depending on the context: environment variables, global variables, or shell variables (see Chapter 12). By convention, environment variables and global variables are given names consisting of all uppercase letters.

This section of the man page describes the environment variables that are used by the program. For example, the man page for the **date** command refers to an environment variable named **TZ**, which shows what time zone should be used.

AUTHOR: The name of the person or persons who worked on the program. You will often see this section when you are looking at a man page for one of the GNU utilities. This is because the Free Software Foundation, which runs the GNU Project (see Chapter 2), likes to give credit to programmers.

DIAGNOSTICS: This section can contain two types of information. First, there may be an explanation of possible error messages. Second, there may be a list of error codes that a command can return upon completion.

Error codes are important for programmers who want to call upon a command from a program or shell script and then test to see if the command completed successfully. If the command was successful, the error code will have the value **0** (zero). Otherwise, the error code will be non-zero.

BUGS: All programs have two kinds of bugs: the ones you know about and the ones you don't know about. The original developers of Unix recognized that no program is perfect and users deserve to know about the imperfections. Thus, many man pages contain a section devoted to documenting known problems.

Some commercial Unix vendors have decided that a section named **Bugs** gives the paying customers the wrong idea. Thus, you may see this section living under an assumed name, such as **Notes** or **Limitations**. Don't be fooled, bugs are bugs and, if you use the program, you have a right to know about them.

A QUICK WAY TO FIND OUT WHAT A COMMAND DOES: whatis

When you enter the **man** command, Unix displays the entire manual page. Sometimes, however, you only want a quick description. In such cases, you have an alternative.

As I explained above, the **Name** section of a man page contains a one-line description. If all you want to see is this single line, type **man -f**, followed by the names of one or more commands. For example:

```
man -f time date
```

In this form of the **man** command, the **-f** is called an option. (We will discuss options in Chapter 10.) The letter **f** stands for the word "files". Each man page is stored in a separate file; when you use the **-f** option, you are telling **man** which files to look at.

As a convenience, you can use the command **whatis** as a synonym for **man -f**. For example, if you want to display the time, but you are not sure whether to use **time** or **date**, enter either of these commands:

```
whatis time date
man -f time date
```

You will see something like this:

```
date (1) - print or set the system date and time
time (1) - run programs & summarize system resource usage
time (3) - get date and time
time (7) - time a command
```

You can ignore the last two lines as they do not refer to Section 1 of the manual. Looking at the first two lines, you see that the command you want is **date**. The **time** command actually measures how long it takes for a program or command to execute.

As you know, when you enter the **man** command, you can specify a particular section number (such as **man 1 date**). With **man -f** or **whatis**, you cannot be so specific. Unix will always search the entire manual.

Thus, a good way to find out what your manual contains is to enter:

```
whatis intro
```

You will see quick summaries of each of the **intro** pages. (Try it.)

Note: For the **whatis** command to work properly, the man pages must be preprocessed in a certain way. This involves collecting all the one-line descriptions and storing them in specific files. It is these files that **whatis** searches, not the actual manual (that would be far too slow). If the preprocessing has not been carried out, **whatis** will not return useful information. If this is the case on your system, talk to your system administrator.

SEARCHING FOR A COMMAND: `apropos`

When you want to learn about a specific command, you can use **man** to display the man page for that command. What if you know what you want to do, but you are not sure which command to use?

The solution is to use **man** with the **-k** option. This searches for commands whose NAME sections contain specified keywords. (The letter **k** stands for "keyword".) For example, say you want to find all the entries in the manual that have something to do with the manual itself. Enter:

```
man -k manual
```

As a convenience, you can use the single word **apropos** as a synonym for **man -k**:

```
apropos manual
```

Note: When you pronounce **apropos**, the accent is on the last syllable, and the "s" is silent: a-pro-poe'. This is because the name comes from a French expression and, in French, an "s" at the end of the word is normally not pronounced*.

The **apropos** command searches through all the one-line command descriptions, looking for those that contain the same string of characters you specified. To make the command more powerful, Unix does not distinguish between upper- and lowercase.

Here is some sample output from the previous example.

```
catman (8) - create the cat files for the manual
man (1)    - displays manual pages online
man (5)    - macros to format entries in reference manual
man (7)    - macros to typeset manual
route (8c) - manually manipulate the routing tables
whereis (1) - locate source, binary, or manual for program
```

Notice there are two commands of interest, **man** and **whereis**, as they are the only ones in Section 1. Notice also that the **route** command was cited because the characters "manual" happened to appear in its description.

You might ask, why don't **apropos** and **whatis** appear in this list? After all, both commands help you access the online manual. To answer this question, enter:

```
whatis apropos whatis
```

You will see that the word "manual" does not appear in these descriptions:

```
apropos (1) - locate commands by keyword lookup
whatis (1) - display command description
```

The lesson here is: The **apropos** command is not magic – all it can do is search blindly for character strings – so if you can't find what you want, try asking in a different way.

---

*French people are good at spelling, but bad at pronouncing.

HINT

Most commands are actually programs. For example, the **man** command is really a program named "man". However, some of the most basic commands, called builtin commands, are carried out by the shell itself. These commands will be documented within the man page for the shell. They will not have their own separate entries in the manual.

If you are looking for a command that you know exists, but you cannot find it under its own name, check the man page for your shell:

```
man bash
man ksh
man csh
```

If you are a Bash user, there is a special man page that will list all the builtin commands:

```
man builtin
```

WHAT'S IN A NAME?

Apropos

In Unix, the **apropos** command is a synonym for **man -k**. The word comes from the French expression *à propos* meaning "related to". In English, "apropos" is a preposition meaning "concerning" or "with reference to". For example, you might read the following passage in a novel:

"...Amber raised her eyebrows and reached over to touch the tall, handsome programmer lightly on the lips. As she shook her long blond hair, she felt a frisson of desire travel through her lean, lissome body. 'Apropos to your proposal,' she cooed seductively, batting her eyelashes, 'I'd love to be the Mistress of Ceremonies at your Unix bachelor party. But does Christine know about the invitation?'..."

FOO, BAR AND FOOBAR

There are two marvelous words you will see from time to time: FOO and BAR. These words are used as generic identifiers by programmers. You will see them, not only throughout the world of Unix and Linux, but on the Web and in Usenet discussion groups.

The idea is that whenever you want to refer to something without a name, you can call it "foo"; when you want to refer to two things without a name, you call them "foo" and "bar". Nobody knows for sure how this tradition got started, but it is used a lot.

For example, here is an excerpt from the Linux man page for the **exec** command. (Don't worry about the meaning.)

"...Most historical implementations were not conformant in that **foo=bar exec cmd** *did not pass* **foo** *to* **cmd**..."

From time to time, you will also see the word FOOBAR used in the same way. For example, the following is a question written by a well-known Unix professor for one of his final exams. (Again, don't worry about the meaning.)

"...Give a Unix command, and the equivalents in **sed** *and* **awk** *to achieve the following: Print the file named* **foobar** *to standard output, but only lines numbered 4*

through 20 inclusive. Print all the lines in file **foobar**, *but only columns numbered 10 through 25 inclusive..."*

WHAT'S IN A NAME?

Foo, Bar, Foobar

In the world of Unix and on the Internet, the words foo, bar and foobar are commonly used as generic terms to represent unnamed items within a discussion or exposition. Where do these strange words come from?

The word "foobar" derives from the acronym FUBAR, which was popular during World War II. FUBAR means "fouled up beyond all recognition"*.

The word "foo" seems to have a more robust history. No doubt foo owes much of its popularity to foobar. Nevertheless, foo seems to have been used on its own even earlier. For example, in a 1938 cartoon, Daffy Duck holds up a sign that reads "Silence is Foo" (which is absolutely correct). Some authorities speculate that foo might have roots in the Yiddish "feh" and the English "phoo".

THE INFO SYSTEM

INFO is an online help system, separate from the Unix manual, which is used to document the GNU utilities (explained in Chapter 2). Since many types of Unix – including virtually all Linux systems – use the GNU utilities, most people find it useful to understand how to use both the online manual and Info. Indeed, you will find that many of the Linux man pages refer you to Info for more information.

Superficially, Info is a bit like the online manual. Information is stored in files, one topic per file, just like man pages. The files are called INFO FILES and, to read them, you use the **info** program. Just type **info** followed by the name of a command.

Consider the following two examples. The first displays the man page for the **date** command. The second display the Info file for the same command:

```
man date
info date
```

Like the online manual, **info** will show you information one screenful at a time. As is the case with the manual, you press <Space> to move from one screenful to the next, and you press **q** to quit. However, as you will see in a moment, that is where the similarity ends.

If you have trouble starting Info, you can check to see if it is on your system by looking for the **info** program. Any of the following commands will do the job (see Chapter 7):

```
which info
type info
whence info
```

Alternatively, you can look for an **info** man page:

```
man info
```

---

*Actually, the F in fubar doesn't really stand for "fouled". However, I thought it might be offensive to use the word "fuck" twice in the same chapter (see the discussion on RTFM).

I'm sure you understand.

If your system does not have the **info** program or an **info** man page, you can assume that you don't have Info (which means you can skip the rest of this chapter secure in the knowledge that your life is not passing you by).

As you know, all Unix and Linux commands have a man page. However, many commands do not have an Info file. For this reason, if you try to display the Info file for a command that doesn't have one, Info will simply show you the man page instead. For example, the **man** command does not have an Info file. See what happens when you enter:

```
info man
```

There are three main differences between Info and the online manual. First, Info files contain not just information, but links to other Info files. Thus, reading an Info page is similar to reading a Web page in the sense that you can use a link to jump to another file.* This is not the case with man pages.

Second, as you are looking at an Info file, there are a *lot* of commands you can use, many more than are available with the online manual. This makes for a much more powerful environment. For this reason, some people prefer to look at man pages using **info** instead of **man**.

Finally, as I described earlier in the chapter, the online manual was designed by the original Unix developers at Bell Labs. Their goal was to keep things simple, for the programmers who would create documentation and for the users who read it. Info was created by the developers of the Emacs text editor. The chief architect was Richard Stallman, the founder of the Free Software Foundation and the GNU Project (see Chapter 2).

Stallman trained at the MIT Artificial Intelligence Lab in the early 1970s, where there was a much different environment than Bell Labs. One of the most important differences was that MIT tended to build large, complex powerful systems, while the Unix programmers (who had a much smaller budget) valued simplicity. Compare, for example, Multics vs. Unix (see Chapter 1).

Although Stallman was not your typical MIT programmer, he did tend to write programs that were very powerful, idiosyncratic, and had a great many esoteric commands. To a large extent, you can see these characteristics within both Emacs and Info.

So, as you read the rest of this chapter and as you practice with Info, remember that it was brought to you by the same people who created Emacs. If you feel a bit confused, take solace in the fact that so does everyone else the first time they try to use Info.

As complex as Info is, it is actually part of something larger called TEXINFO, the official documentation system for the GNU project. Texinfo is a sophisticated set of tools that allows you to use a single information file to generate output in a variety of formats: Info format, plain text, HTML, DVI, PDF, XML and Docbook.

For our purposes, all we need to know is that GNU documentation starts life as Texinfo files, which are then used to generate Info files. For this reason, you will sometimes see Info referred to as Texinfo. For example, if you ask someone a question and he asks, "Have you checked with Texinfo?" he is telling you to use Info.

---

*Unlike Web pages, Info files contain only plain text with very little formatting and no pictures. Thus, as you use Info, you can see what it was like to use the Web in its early days, when it was a primitive, text-based system.

Since Info is so complex, we can't cover everything, nor would we want to. Instead, I will confine myself to three main goals, showing you: how to use Info to display what you want, how to maneuver around the Info system, and how to display the Info help information. Once you have these three skills, you can RTFM as necessary, and teach yourself whatever you need to know.

WHAT'S IN A NAME?

Texinfo

When you first look at the name Texinfo, you might think that it should be Textinfo. After all, it is the name of a text-based information system. Actually, the spelling of Texinfo is correct: it comes from TeX, a typesetting system created by the eminent computer scientist Donald Knuth (pronounced "kuh-NOOTH").

The name TeX comes from the Greek word *techni*, from which we get the English word "technical". *Techni* refers to an art, a craft or, more generally, the end result of someone's effort. Thus, the letters TeX are not the English letters T-E-X; they are actually the Greek letters Tau, Epsilon and Chi, the first three letters of *techni*. If you want to be pedantically accurate, you should pronounce the Chi as the "ch" in the Scottish word "loch" or the name "Bach". Most computer people, however, pronounce the Chi as a "K".

So how should *you* pronounce Texinfo? You have four choices.

First, if you like being pedantically accurate you should say "Te[ch]info", where [ch] is the funny sound I described above.

If you are a programmer and you want to look like an insider, say "Tekinfo".

If you want to fit in with the non-technical crowd, say "Texinfo", which is what most people do who read the word literally.

Finally, if you want to be a leader within your social circle, tell everyone that it is obvious the name should really be "Textinfo". Explain that the second "t" must have been left out accidentally, and it is about time someone fixed the mistake. (Actually, you might be correct: just because someone invents something, doesn't mean he has the right to give it a foolish name just to show how clever he is.)*

INFO AND TREES

You may remember that, in Chapter 8, we discussed the idea of data structures, a basic concept of computer science. A data structure is an entity used to store and retrieve data according to a set of precise rules. At the time, I mentioned that the most common types of data structures are lists, linked lists, associative arrays, hash tables, stacks, queues, deques (double-ended queues), as well as a variety of tree-based structures.

In Chapter 8, we discussed stacks, so you could understand how the **dc** calculator handles reverse Polish notation. In this section, we are going to discuss trees, because that is the data structure Info uses to store and retrieve Info files. Once you understand trees, you can make sense out of the commands you use to control Info. If you don't understand what a tree is, you can certainly use Info, but it won't be fun and it won't be easy.

---

*In my time, I have met both Donald Knuth, who named TeX, and Richard Stallman, who named GNU. If you put them in a room together, probably the only point they would agree on is that both TeX and GNU are good names.

When a computer scientist talks about a tree, he is referring to a family of complex data structures. So, to make life simple, let's start with a simple metaphor.

Let's say you decide to go on a hike. You start at the trailhead and find there are several possible paths to follow. You choose one of them. You follow that path until you come to a fork, at which point you have a choice of several new paths. Again, you make a choice and keep walking until you come to another fork and are forced to make another choice. And so on. Once in a while, you follow a path that leads to a dead end. When this happens, you need to go back to a previous fork and make a different choice.

In the language of computer science, we call each fork a NODE. The main node (the trailhead in our example) is called the ROOT. The path that joins one node to another is called a BRANCH. When a branch leads to a dead end, it is a special type of node we call a LEAF.

Here is the technical definition: To a computer scientist, a TREE is a collection of nodes, leaves, and branches, organized in such a way that there is, at most, one branch between any two nodes.*

Although all of this sounds a bit complicated, it is similar to what we see when we look at a real tree. As an example, look at the sample tree in Figure 9-7. Notice that, unlike a real tree, a computer tree is usually drawn with the root at the top.

Within computer science, there are a variety of different types of trees, each with its own characteristics. The type of tree I have just described is the data structure Info uses to store information.

Each Info file is broken into parts and stored as a series of nodes. As you read a file, you move from one node to another. This allows you to read an entire file from beginning to end, one node at a time. As you are looking at a particular node, we say that you are VISITING that node. Many nodes also contain LINKS that allow you to jump to other, related files (just like links on a Web page).Using Info requires three basic skills. You need to understand how to:

1. Use the **info** command to start Info.
2. Move from one node to the next, in order to read through an entire file.
3. Use links to jump from one file to another.

We will now discuss each of these skills in turn.

STARTING INFO: `info`

To start the Info system, you use the **info** command. There are two variations. First, if you want to display information about a specific command, type **info** followed by the name of the command. For example:

---

*The ideas behind computer trees are taken from a part of mathematics called graph theory. Mathematical trees are similar to computer trees. However, the terminology is different.

Within graph theory, a node is called a "vertex" (plural "vertices"), and a branch is called an "edge". Thus, if you ever meet a graph theorist, you can expect him to say things like, "Strictly speaking, the Info system uses a data structure that isn't a real tree. Since some vertices are joined by more than one edge, you should really describe it as a connected graph in which tree-like objects are embedded." (Now you see why Unix people tend to not invite graph theorists to parties.)

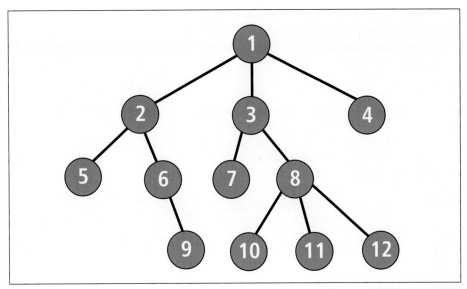

FIGURE 9-7: Example of a tree

A tree is a data structure consisting of a number of nodes that are joined by branches. The top (main) node is called the root of the tree. Terminal nodes (dead-ends) are called leaves. In this example, the Node 1 is the root. Nodes 4, 5, 7, 9, 10, 11 and 12 are leaves. The Info system uses trees in which each node holds information, and each branch is a link from one node to another.

```
info date
info bc
info info
```

If you are not sure which command you want to learn about, or if you want to browse the system, enter the **info** command by itself:

```
info
```

When you start Info in this way, it displays a special node called the DIRECTORY NODE. The Directory Node contains a list of major topics, so you can consider it to be the main menu for the entire Info system.

LEARNING ABOUT INFO

Info has a fair amount of help information you can read to get started. Before you do, be sure to read to the end of this chapter.

The place to begin your journey is the **info** man page. Either of the following commands will do the job:

```
info --help | less
man info
```

Notice that, in the first command, there are two hyphens and no spaces before the word **help**. We will discuss what this means in Chapter 10.

Once you have read the man page, you can display a short introductory Info file, by entering the command:

```
info info
```

Next, you should read the Info tutorial. To do so, start Info and press the **h** (help) key. It may be a bit confusing, but if you have read this chapter, you'll do okay.

Once you have finished the tutorial, take a moment to display the Info command summary and skim the list of commands. You can display this summary by pressing the **?** (question mark) key.

HINT

At any time, from within any Info file, you can display the built-in tutorial (by pressing **h**) or the command summary (by pressing **?**). As you read these files, don't worry about understanding everything. Just learn the basic commands, and add to your repertoire as the need arises.

When it comes to Info, no one knows (or needs to know) everything.

As you are using Info, you are always looking at a node. If you want to leave that node and return to the last node you were reading, press **l** (the letter "L").

For example, say you are reading the node that contains help for the **date** command. You press **?** to display the command summary (a new node). To return to the **date** node, all you need to do is press **l**. Don't press **q**, or you will quit Info completely and end up back at the shell prompt.

As you read the command summary, you will see <Ctrl> keys referred to using the notation **C-x**, instead of **^X** or <Ctrl-X>. (This is an Emacs convention.)

You will also see the notation **M-x**. The **M-** stands for Meta key, a very important concept in Emacs. For now, I'll just say that to use the Meta key, you can either hold down the <Alt> key while you press the second key; or press <Esc>, let it go, and then press the second key.

For example, let's say you want to press **M-x**. You can use either <Alt-X>, or press <Esc> followed by <X>.

READING AN INFO FILE

There are a great many commands you can use within the Info system. I have summarized the most important commands in Figure 9-8, and I will discuss them in the next few sections. As you read, it will help a lot if you start Info and follow along by testing the commands as we discuss them. When you are finished reading, you can use Figure 9-8 as a reference.

Each Info file is structured as a small tree consisting of a linear series of nodes. The purpose of each file is to cover one main idea, such as how to use a particular command; each node covers a single topic. When you start reading a file, you are placed at the root of the tree for that file. Within Info, the root of a tree is called the TOP NODE.

As a general rule, the Top Node contains a summary of the topic under discussion, as well as a list of the topics covered in the file. The list is in the form of a menu.

You can read the file in two ways. First, you can read the nodes in order, one after the other, from the Top Node to the last node. Alternatively, you can use the menu to jump directly to a particular node, if you want to read about a specific topic.

The simplest way to read a file is to start with the Top Node and read the entire file straight through. All you have to do is press <Space>, which will display one screenful of

General Commands	
q	quit
z	start help tutorial
?	display command summary
Reading a node	
<PageDown>	display next screenful
<Space>	display next screenful
<Space>	(at bottom of node) go to next node
<PageUp>	display previous screenful
<Backspace>	display previous screenful
<Delete>	display previous screenful
<Backspace>	(at top of node) go to previous node
<Delete>	(at top of node) go to previous node
Moving around within a node	
b	jump to beginning of current node
<Up>	move cursor up one line
<Down>	move cursor down one line
<Right>	move cursor one position right
<Left>	move cursor one position left
Jumping around from one to another within a file	
n	jump to next node in file
p	jump to previous node in file
t	jump to Top Node (first node in file)
Jumping from one file to another	
<Tab>	move cursor down to next link
M-<Tab>	move cursor up to previous link
<Return>	follow a link to a new node or file
l	jump to previous (last viewed) node
d	jump to Directory Node (main menu)

FIGURE 9-8: Info: Important Commands

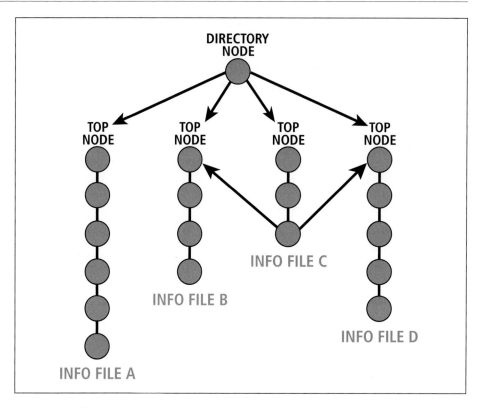

FIGURE 9-9: Info tree

Here is a highly simplified rendition of how Info files are stored as nodes in a tree. At the root of the tree1 is the Directory Node. In our example, the Directory Node has links to four Info files, which I have called A, B, C and D. Each file is stored as a sequence of nodes. The first node in the sequence is called the Top Node. Notice that file C has links to the Top Nodes of files B and D.

information after another. When you get to the end of a node, pressing <Space> will take you to the beginning of the next node in the tree. Thus, you can traverse the entire tree by starting at the Top Node and pressing <Space> repeatedly.

To move backwards one screenful at a time, press either <Backspace> or <Delete>. If you are at the beginning of a node and you press one of these keys, you will be taken to the previous node. (Try it.)

As a convenience, you can also use <PageDown> and <PageUp> to move within a node. However, unlike the other keys, <PageDown> and <PageUp> will move only within a node, they will not move to the next or previous mode. Thus, they are handy when you want to move up and down without leaving the current node.

As a convenience, you can jump to the beginning of the current node whenever you want by pressing the **b** key.

Finally, for small movements, you can use the arrow (cursor) keys. <Down> moves the cursor down one line; <Up> moves the cursor up one line. Similarly, <Right> and <Left> move the cursor one position to the right or left respectively.

To help you visualize how Info nodes and files are connected, take a look at Figure 9-9, which shows how the Info tree is organized. At first, the organization may seem complicated. However, taking a moment to understand the connections will make your work with Info a lot easier.

HINT

The simplest way to read an Info file is to start at its Top Node and press <Space> repeatedly. In this way, you will work your way through the file, one node at a time.

JUMPING FROM ONE NODE TO ANOTHER

As you are reading an Info file, there are several commands you can use to jump from one node to another, either within the same file or in a completely different file.

To jump to the next node in the current file, press **n**; to jump to the previous node, press **p**. To jump to the Top Node (the beginning) of the current file, press **t**.

Many nodes, especially Top Nodes, contain a list of topics in the form of a menu. Each topic is actually a link, which you can follow. Some links jump to another node within the file; other links jump to a completely different file.

You will recognize links because they have a specific format: an asterisk (*), followed by the name of the topic, followed by a colon (:). After the colon, you will see a short description of the topic. Sometimes, there will also be an informative comment.

Here are two examples taken from the Info tutorial I discussed above. The examples were designed to show what typical menu items look like*:

```
* Foo: Help-FOO. A node you can visit for fun.
* Bar: Help-BAR. A second way to get to the same place.
```

The actual link is the part of the menu item between the asterisk and the colon (inclusive). It is similar to a link on a Web page. To follow a link, just move your cursor to it and press <Return>.

The easiest way to do so is to press <Tab>, which moves down to the next link in the node; or **M-**<Tab>**, which moves up to the previous link in the node. Alternatively, you can use the arrow keys (<Down>, <Up>, <Right> and <Left>).

Regardless of how you get to a link, once you are there, all you have to do is press <Return> to make the jump.

---

*These examples, taken directly from the Info tutorial, show how the words "Foo" and "Bar" are used as generic names. See the discussion earlier in the chapter.

** As I explained earlier, **M-** refers to the Meta key. To use **M-**<Tab>, you can use either <Alt-Tab>, or press <Esc> followed by <Tab>.

Aside from following a link, there are two other ways to jump. As we discussed earlier, each Info file is organized as a simple tree consisting of a sequence of nodes. The entire Info system, in fact, is actually one huge tree, with branches that reach – directly and indirectly – to every file and every node in the system. You can jump to the root of this very large tree – the Directory Node – by pressing **d**. Since the Directory Node acts as the main menu for the entire system, the **d** command is worth memorizing.

The last way to jump is to press **l** (the letter "L") to leave the current node and return to the last node you visited. For example, let's say you have followed a link to jump from file A to file B. If you press **l**, you will jump back to file A.

The **l** command is useful, because you can press it repeatedly to retrace all of your steps throughout the tree. This allows you to move backwards, one step at a time. Like the **d** command, the **l** command is worth memorizing.

HINT

Although the Info system is complicated, there are only seven really important commands:

1. <Space>: display next screenful
2. <Backspace>: display previous screenful
3. <Tab>: move cursor down to next link
4. <Return>: follow a link
5. **d**: jump to the Directory Node
6. **l**: jump to last node you visited
7. **q**: quit

If you memorize these seven commands and commit yourself to learning more as the need arises, you will do just fine.

CHAPTER 9 EXERCISES

REVIEW QUESTIONS

1. What are the two principle Unix documentation systems? What commands do you use to access each system?

2. When you are reading a man page, how do you enter a single shell command?

3. When you are looking at an Info node, which commands do you use to display the help tutorial, display the command summary, display the next screenful, jump to the beginning of the current node, jump to the next node, jump to the Top Node, jump to the Directory Node?

APPLYING YOUR KNOWLEDGE

1. Use the **man** command to display the man page for your default shell (**man sh**). Once the page is displayed, perform the following operations: display the next screenful of information; jump to the end of the page; jump to the beginning of the page; search for the word "variable"; search forward several times for the next occurrence of the same word; search backwards several times for the same word; display a command summary; quit.

2. If you are using Linux or FreeBSD, use the **info** command to display information about the Info system itself (**info info**). Once the first node is displayed, perform the following operations: display the next screenful of information; jump to the end of the current node; jump to the beginning of the current node; jump to the Top Node; jump to the Directory Node; display a command summary; quit.

FOR FURTHER THOUGHT

1. The doctrine of RTFM requires people to try to help themselves by reading the documentation before asking for help. What are two advantages of this guideline? What are two disadvantages?

CHAPTER 10
COMMAND SYNTAX

As you use the Unix CLI (command line interface), you enter one command after another. When you enter a command, the entire line you type is called the COMMAND LINE. When you press <Return> at the end of the line, the contents of the command line are sent to the shell to be processed.

As you enter a command, there are two things to understand. First, you must type the command properly according to certain rules. How to do so is the subject of this chapter. Second, you must understand what happens as the shell processes the command. This is an important topic, which we will discuss later in the book when we talk about the shell.

There are literally hundreds of commands, and as long as you work with Unix, you will never stop learning new ones. For that reason, you need to be able to teach yourself from the online manual as the need arises. In order to use the manual well, you need to understand the formal rules that describe how a command must be entered.

ENTERING MORE THAN ONE COMMAND AT A TIME

In most cases, you will type only one command on the command line. However, you should know that it is possible to enter more than one command at a time. All you need to do is separate the commands with semicolons.

Here is an example. You are on the phone planning a party with one of your friends. You want to display today's date, as well as the calendar for the current month. The commands to do this are **date** and **cal** (see Chapter 8). Of course, you can enter the two commands separately:

```
date
cal
```

However, you can do it all in one line by using a semicolon as a command separator:

```
date; cal
```

Notice that you do not need a semicolon at the end of the command line.

Here is another example using the **cp** command to copy a file (see Chapter 25), the **ls** command to list information about a file (Chapter 24), and the **rm** command to erase (remove) a file (also Chapter 25).

Your goal is to make two copies of a file named **data**. The copies will be called **backup1** and **backup2**. After you make the copies, you want to erase the original file. You then list all your files to see what you have. The commands look like this:

```
cp data backup1
cp data backup2
rm data
ls
```

Don't worry about the details. We will cover these commands later in the book. The important point here is that, instead of typing the commands on four separate lines, we can enter them on one line by separating them with semicolons:

```
cp data backup1; cp data backup2; rm data; ls
```

You might ask, what's the point of entering all the commands on one line? After all, you have to type the same number of characters either way.

The answer is that, in the long run, you will use Unix more effectively if you learn how to think ahead more than one step at a time, much like a chess player does as he decides on his next move. Although this may not seem like a big deal now, it will become important as you become more experienced.

In Chapters 15 through 19, I will show you how to put together commands and tools to form complex command lines. To do this well, you need to develop your skills as a Unix problem solver. For now, I'd like you to start thinking in this way by seeing how many opportunities you can find to enter multiple commands on the same command line.

> **HINT**
>
> The difference between a good Unix user and a great Unix user is the ability to solve problems as they arise by putting together tools and ideas quickly, creatively, and with a minimum of fuss. In fact, some people would say that this is the essence of using Unix well.

WHAT HAPPENS WHEN YOU ENTER A COMMAND?

To enter a command, you type the name of the command, possibly followed by other information. For example, consider the following **ls** command line.

```
ls -l -F file1
```

This command has four parts: the name of the command, **ls**, followed by **-l**, **-F** and **file1**. (I'll be more specific in a moment about what these other parts are called.)

When you press the <Return> key, the shell processes your command. The actual details are a bit complex, and we will leave the discussion to later chapters. For now, here is a simplified description that works well for most people most of the time.

The shell processes a command line by assuming that the first part of the line is the name of a command you want to run. The shell then searches for and executes the program by that name. For example, if you were to enter the previous **ls** command, the shell would find and run the **ls** program.

If you enter the name of a command that the shell can't find, it will display an error message. For example, let's say you enter:

```
harley
```

Although it's hard to believe, Unix doesn't have a **harley** command, so you will see:

```
harley: not found
```

When the shell does find the program you want, it runs it. At that time, the shell sends a copy of the entire command line to the program. It is up to the program to figure out what to do with all the information. In the example above, it would be up to the **ls** program to figure out what to do with **-l**, **-F** and **file1**.

COMMAND SYNTAX

A Unix command must be typed just so, according to well-defined rules. Putting a punctuation mark in the wrong place or spelling a word incorrectly can invalidate the entire command. Most of the time, you will see an error message and the command will be ignored. However, in the worst case, a mistyped command will execute incorrectly and cause problems. Thus, it is important that you learn how to enter commands correctly. The formal description of how a command should be entered is called its COMMAND SYNTAX or, more informally, its SYNTAX.

How do you learn the syntax for a command? It's easy. Once you understand the general rules and conventions, you can teach yourself how to use any command by looking up its syntax in the manual or in the Info system (see Chapter 9).

If you are a beginner, you know that there are many commands that, right now, are beyond your capabilities. Indeed, there are some commands you will never understand (or never need to understand). Regardless, my goal is that, by the time you finish this chapter, you should be able to understand the syntax of *any* command you happen to encounter, even if you don't understand the command itself*.

As a general rule, Unix command syntax can be expressed as follows: You type the name of the command, followed by any "options", followed by any "arguments":

command-name options arguments

---

*This is not as odd as it sounds. For example, when you learn a foreign language, it doesn't take long to get to the point where you can read sentences you can't understand. The same is true for Unix. By the time you finish this chapter, you will be able to understand the syntax of any Unix command. However, until you get more experience, most commands will still be a mystery to you.

My goal is to make sure you have a firm grasp of the basic principles, such as command syntax. This will allow you to fill in the gaps by practicing regularly and taking the time to teach yourself. For example, whenever you have a question, I encourage you to take a moment to use the manual or the Web to find yourself an answer. (If this sounds like fun to you, you are a lucky person.)

Options allow you to control how a command should do its job, while arguments specify the data you want the command to use.

Consider the example:

```
ls -l -F file1 file2 file3
```

The command name is **ls**. The options are **-l** and **-F**. The arguments are **file1**, **file2** and **file3**.

Now, let's move on to the details.

OPTIONS

When you type a command, you use OPTIONS to modify how the command should do its job. When you read Unix documentation, you will sometimes see options referred to as SWITCHES or FLAGS, so you should know those words as well.

As the name implies, the use of options is optional. Most commands have at least a few, but some commands have so many that you wonder how anyone can ever know them all. The answer is no one does. Even experienced people depend on the manual to look up obscure options.

Within the command line, options come directly after the command name. An option consists of either a hyphen followed by a single letter, or two hyphens followed by a word. For example:

```
ls -l -F file1 file2 file3
ls --help
```

In the first command, there are two options, **-l** and **-F**. In the second command, there is one option, **--help**.

The job of an option is to allow you to control the actions of the command. In our example, for instance, the **-l** option tells the **ls** command to display the "long" listing. Normally, the **ls** command lists only the names of files. When you use the **-l** option, **ls** lists extra information about each file, as well as the names.

Occasionally, you will see an option that is a number, such as:

```
ls -1 file1 file2 file3
```

You will have to be careful. For example, in this case, do not confuse **-l** (the lowercase letter "L") with **-1** (the number 1).

When you use more than one single-character option, you can combine them by using a single hyphen. Moreover, you can specify options in any order. Thus, all of the following commands are equivalent:

```
ls -l -F file1
ls -F -l file1
ls -lF file1
ls -Fl file1
```

As with all Unix commands, you must make sure that you use upper- and lowercase exactly. For example, the **ls** command has both **-F** and **-f** options and they are different. However, as a general rule, most options are lowercase. (As I explained in Chapter 4, almost everything in Unix is lowercase.)

> **HINT**
>
> When you look up a command in the manual, you will see an explanation for each individual option. However, the man page will not tell you that single-character options can be combined. For example, **-l -F** can be combined into **-lF**. This is basic Unix, and it is assumed that you already know it.

At this point, an interesting question arises: When you talk about an option, how do you pronounce the hyphen?

In the olden days, it was pronounced as "minus", probably because it is easier to say than "hyphen". For example, an older person would pronounce **ls -l** as "L-S-minus-L".

Within the Linux culture, however, it has become common for people to refer to the hyphen as "dash", especially among younger users. Thus, a Linux person would probably pronounce **ls -l** as "L-S-dash-L". Similarly, "ls --help" would be pronounced "L-S-dash-dash-HELP".

The distinction between "minus" and "dash" is not important when you type a command. However, when you are talking, what you say out loud can have important social implications.

For example, let's say your teacher calls upon you during class, and asks you, "How do you tell the **ls** command to display a long file listing?" For most students, the answer would be, "Use the dash-L option." However, if you think your teacher learned Unix before the mid-1990s, show respect for an elderly person by saying, "Use the minus-L option." (Remember, one day you will be old yourself.)

DASH OPTIONS AND DASH-DASH OPTIONS

When it comes to options, the single dash format is the older one. It dates back to the earliest Unix system (see Chapter 2), when programmers desired brevity on the command line. Many of the command names were only two or three letters, and all of the options were only a single letter.

Years later, when the GNU utilities were being developed (see Chapter 2), the designers wanted to be able to use longer options. However, the longtime conventions dictated that all options should only be one letter, and that options could be combined as I explained above. For example, what do you think would happen if the shell encountered the following command?

```
ls -help
```

Since multiple options can be combined, **-help** would refer to four separate options, **-h**, **-e**, **-l** and **-p**.

Of course, it would be possible to modify the rules, but that would be a drastic change that would invalidate many existing programs, and force too many people to change their habits. Instead, it was decided that longer options would be allowed, as long as they were preceded by two hyphens, instead of one. In that way, the system could be expanded without compromising what already existed.

Since Linux uses the GNU utilities, you will see both types of options if you are a Linux user. With most other systems, you will see only single-character options.

The chief purpose of what we might call the dash-dash options is to use longer option names, which makes them easier to understand and remember. On the other hand, longer options are slower to type and a lot easier to misspell. For this reason, many commands give you a choice by giving the same option a short and a long name. This allows you to use whichever one you want.

For example, the **ls** command (which lists file information) has a **-r** option, which causes the command to list the files in reverse order. With Linux, the command also has a **--reverse** option, which does the same thing. Thus, the following two commands are equivalent:

```
ls -r
ls --reverse
```

Within the world of dash-dash options, there are two options that you will often encounter when you use the GNU utilities. If you are a Linux user, these options are worth memorizing.

First, many commands will display a summary of the command's syntax if you use the **--help**. Typically, you would use this option by itself. For example:

```
ls --help
date --help
cp --help
```

In many cases, the summary is so large that most of it will scroll off your screen before you can read it. If this happens, send the output to the **less** program, which will display the information once screenful at a time. To do so, type a **|** (vertical bar) followed by **less**. For example:

```
ls --help | less
date --help | less
cp --help | less
```

(See Chapter 21 for a discussion of **less**.)

The second common dash-dash option is **--version**:

```
ls --version
date --version
cp --version
```

This option displays information about what version of this particular program is installed on your system. Normally, this is not information that you would need. However, if you are having a problem, it sometimes helps to know what version of the program you are running.

> **HINT**
>
> The rules for typing options are the same for virtually all Unix commands: each option starts with either one or two hyphens; single-character options may be combined. However, there are a few exceptions.
>
> Some commands use options without a hyphen. Other commands will accept a hyphen, but don't require it. Finally, some commands will not allow you to combine single-character options.
>
> Fortunately, the exceptions are rare. However, if you have any problems with a command, check with the man page. It is the definitive reference.

ARGUMENTS

I mentioned earlier that the general syntax of a Unix command can be expressed as follows: the name of the command, followed by any options, followed by any arguments:

command-name options arguments

We have already talked about command names and options, so let us move on to discuss how to use arguments.

ARGUMENTS are used on the command line to pass information to the program you want to run. Consider this example, which we looked at earlier during our discussion of options:

`ls -l -F file1 file2 file3`

The command is **ls**, the options are **-l** and **-F**, and the arguments are **file1**, **file2** and **file3**.

The meaning of an argument will vary from one command to another. Typically, the arguments specify the data upon which the program will perform an action. In our example, we are specifying the names of three files.

Consider another example:

`man date`

The command name is **man**, there are no options, and the argument is **date**. In this command, we are telling **man** to display the man page for **date**.

One last example:

`passwd weedly`

Here we are using the **passwd** (change password) command with one argument, **weedly**. In this case, we are indicating that we want to change the password for userid **weedly** (see Chapter 4).

WHAT'S IN A NAME?

Argument

The general syntax of a Unix command is:

command-name options arguments

The word "option" only makes sense because command line options give you a choice as to how the command should execute. However, what about the word "argument"? Obviously, it does not indicate an intellectual conflict or "a connected series of statements intended to establish a proposition"*.

Actually, the computer term "argument" is borrowed from mathematics, where it indicates an independent variable. For example, in the equation $f(x) = 5x + 17$, the argument is x. In this sense, an argument is something upon which a command or a function operates.

In English, the word "argument" comes from the Latin word *arguere*, which means to clarify or to make clear.

WHITESPACE

When you enter a command, you must make sure to separate each option and argument. To do so, you must type at least one space or tab between each separate part. For example, here are several ways of entering the same command. Notice that I have explicitly indicated where I pressed the <Space> bar and <Tab> key:

```
ls<Space>-l<Space>-F<Space>file1
ls<Tab>-l<Tab>-F<Tab>file1
ls<Space><Tab>-l<Space>-F<Tab><Tab><Tab>file1
```

Normally, of course, you would put a single space between each part of the command. In fact, with some shells, you can only use spaces, because tabs have a special function (called command completion). However, the idea of using spaces and tabs as separators is important enough to have its own name: whitespace.

This idea will come up repeatedly as you use Unix, so let me give you a formal definition. Within a command line, WHITESPACE refers to one or more consecutive spaces or (with some shells) tabs. In other situations, whitespace may refer to one or more consecutive spaces, tabs or newlines. (See Chapter 4 for a discussion of the newline character.)

If you are a Windows or Macintosh user, you will have seen file names that contain spaces. For example, Windows systems use folders (directories) with names like "Program Files", "My Documents", and so on. Within Unix, spaces in the command line are considered to be whitespace. As such, you should never use spaces in the name of a file. Similarly, you will never see a Unix command with a space in its name.

** If you don't recognize this quotation as coming from the Monty Python sketch "The Argument Clinic", you have a significant gap in your cultural training. My advice is to take a moment right now and correct this deficiency. (Hint: Use the Web to search for: `"monty python" "argument clinic"`.)

WHAT'S IN A NAME?

Whitespace

The term "whitespace" refers to consecutive spaces and tabs that are used to separate two items. The name derives from the earliest Unix terminals that printed on paper. As you typed a command, there was real white space between each word.

The Unix shell (command processor) was designed to be flexible; it didn't care how much space there might be between parts of the command line, as long as the parts were separated. Thus, the term "whitespace" came to mean any number of spaces and tabs.

Later, for certain applications, the term was extended to mean any number of spaces, tabs or newlines. (You will remember from Chapter 4 that a newline is the character generated when you press the <Return> key.)

ONE OR MORE; ZERO OR MORE

In the next section, I will discuss the formal method for describing commands. Before I do, however, I need to define two important expressions: "one or more" and "zero or more".

When you see the expression ONE OR MORE, it means that you must use at least one of something. Here is an example.

In Chapter 9, I explained that you can use the **whatis** command to display a short description of a command, based on its entry in the online manual. When you use **whatis**, you must specify one or more command names as arguments. For instance:

```
whatis man cp
whatis man cp rm mv
```

The first example has two arguments; the second example has four arguments. Because the specifications for this command call for "one or more" names, we must include at least one — it is not optional.

The expression ZERO OR MORE, on the other hand, means that you can use one or more of something, but it is also okay to leave it out.

For instance, I said earlier that the **ls** command, along with the **-l** option, lists information about the files you specify. The exact format of the command requires you to specify zero or more file names. Here are three examples:

```
ls -l
ls -l file1
ls -l file1 file2 data1 data2
```

Whenever you see a specification that requires zero or more of something, you should ask, "What happens if I don't use any?" Frequently, there is a DEFAULT — an assumed value — that will be used.

With **ls**, the default is the set of files in your "working directory" (explained in Chapter 24). Thus, if you do not specify any file names — as in the first example — **ls** lists information about all the files in your working directory. When you specify one or more file names, **ls** displays information only about those particular files.

> **HINT**
>
> Whenever you are told that you can use zero or more of something, ask, "What is the default?"

THE FORMAL DESCRIPTION OF A COMMAND: `syntax`

A good approach to learning a new command is to answer the following three questions:

* What does the command do?
* How do I use the options?
* How do I use the arguments?

To learn what a command does, use the **man** command to look it up the command in the online manual (see Chapter 9) and read the summary. If you need more information, take a look at the full description.

When you check the man page, you will see the command syntax: the exact, formal specification for using the command. Informally, you can think of the syntax as the "official" description of how to use the command.

Within Unix, command syntax follows seven rules. The first five rules are the most basic, so let's start with those. We'll cover the other two rules in a moment.

1. Items in square brackets are optional.

2. Items not in square brackets are obligatory.

3. Anything in boldface must be typed exactly as written.

4. Anything in italics must be replaced by an appropriate value.

5. An argument followed by an ellipsis (. . .) may be repeated any number of times.

Here is an example to show how it all works. The following is the syntax for the **ls** command on one particular Unix system:

ls [**-aAcCdfFgilLqrRstu1**] [*filename...*]

From looking at the syntax, what can we say about this command?

• The command has 18 different options. You can use **-a**, **-A**, **-c**, **-C** and so on. Since the options are optional, they are enclosed in square brackets. In other words, you can use zero or more options.

• There is one argument, *filename*. This argument is optional, as it too is enclosed in square brackets.

• The name of the command and the options are printed in boldface. This means that they must be typed exactly as they appear.

• The argument is in italics. This means that you must replace it with an appropriate value. (In this case, the name of a file or a directory.)

• The argument is followed by "...", which means that you can use more than one argument (to specify the name of more than one file). Since the argument is itself optional, we can be precise and say that you must specify zero or more file names.

Based on this syntax, here are some valid **ls** commands. Remember, single-hyphen options can be typed separately or grouped together with a single hyphen:

```
ls -l
ls file1
ls file1 file2 file3 file4 file5
ls -Fl file1 file2
ls -F -l file1 file2
```

Here are some invalid **ls** commands. The first command is invalid because it uses an unknown option (**-z**):

```
ls -lz file1 file2
```

The next command is invalid because the option comes after an argument:

```
ls file1 -l file2
```

This example is tricky, and it shows why you must follow the syntax exactly.

As a general rule, options must come before arguments (although there can be exceptions, which I will mention in a moment). Since the word **file1** does not begin with a hyphen, **ls** assumes it is an argument, as is anything else that follows. Thus, **ls** thinks you are specifying the names of three files: **file1**, **-l** and **file2**. Of course, there is no file named **-l**, so the results of this command will not be what you intended.

The last two syntax rules cover more complicated situations.

> 6. If you see a single option grouped with an argument, the option and argument must be used together.

The following example (a simplified version of the Linux **man** command) illustrates this rule:

man [**-P** *pager*] [**-S** *sectionlist*] *name...*

In this case, if you want to use the **-P** option, it must be immediately followed by the argument *pager*. Similarly, if you want to use the **-S** option, it must be immediately followed by the argument *sectionlist*.

As you can see, this type of syntax is an exception to the general guideline that all options come before the arguments. In this case, it is possible for the *pager* argument to come before the **-S** option.

Finally, here is the last syntax rule.

> 7. Two or more items separated by a | (vertical bar) character, indicates that you are to choose one item from a list.

This is illustrated by the next example, which shows the syntax of the Linux version of the **who** command:

who [**-abdHilmpqrstTu**] [*file* | *arg1 arg2*]

In this case, the syntax tells us that we can use either a single argument named *file* or two arguments named *arg1* and *arg2*.

Here are two examples. The first specifies *file*; the second specifies *arg1* and *arg2*:

```
who /var/run/utmp
who am i
```

Don't worry about the details*. What I want you to notice is how the vertical bar is used to specify alternatives when you have more than one choice.

---

*If you read the man page for **who**, you will see that the first argument (*file*) is the location of the file from which **who** draws its information. You can specify your own file instead of the default. This is not something you would normally do, but the idea is straightforward.

The other two arguments (*arg1* and *arg2*) are more interesting. You may recall from Chapter 8 that you can display the name of the userid that is currently logged in by entering:

```
who am i
```

Interestingly enough, the **who** command will respond in this way no matter what you type, as long as you specify two arguments. For example, you can type:

```
who are you
who goes there
```

Or, if you are brave:

```
who is god
```

Why do you think the command was programmed in this way?

LEARNING COMMAND SYNTAX FROM THE UNIX MANUAL

When you read printed material (such as this book), it is easy to see which words are in boldface and which are in italics. However, when you look at the online manual on your monitor, you may not see the special typefaces.

On some systems, you will see boldface and italics; on others, you will not. On systems that don't show italics, you will often see underlining instead. Regardless, you will have to get used to your particular system so you can deduce, from context, exactly which words are arguments. Most of the time, this is not difficult.

A typical man page will explain each possible option and argument. However, within the syntax summary, some versions of the manual use a simplified form in which the individual options are not listed. Rather, they are represented by the word "options". Here is an example. Earlier I showed the syntax for one version of the **ls** command:

ls [**-aAcCdfFgilLqrRstu1**] [*filename...*]

Using the simplified system, the syntax would be:

ls [**options**] [*filename...*]

Not to worry. Whether or not you see the options in the syntax summary, they will all be enumerated — and explained — within the detailed command description.

HOW CAN YOU LEARN SO MANY OPTIONS?

You will have noticed that in the example we have been using, the **ls** command has 18 different options. Actually, some versions of the **ls** command have even more options, many of which are the so-called dash-dash options. The question arises, how can you learn so many options?

The answer is you don't. Nobody remembers all the options for every command, even for the commands they use regularly. The best idea is to memorize only the most important options. When you need to use other options, look them up — that is what the online manual is for.

One of the characteristics of Unix programmers is that they tend to write programs with many options, most of which you can safely ignore. Moreover, it is not uncommon to find that different versions of Unix offer different options for the same command.

The **ls** command we have been using is from one particular type of Unix. Other systems will have **ls** commands that have a different number of options. However, the most important options — the ones you will use most of the time — rarely vary much from one system to another.

In this book, I explain many Unix commands. As I do, I will make a point to describe only the most important options and arguments, the ones you will need most of the time. If you are learning about a command, and you are curious as to all the possible options and arguments, all you have to do is take a moment to check with the manual on your system.

Consider the syntax for the **man** command as I described it in Chapter 9:

```
man [section] name...
man -f name...
man -k keyword...
```

Since this command can be used in three different ways, it is easiest to show its syntax using three different descriptions.

The first way to use **man** is with an optional *section* number and one or more *name* values. The second way is to use the **-f** option and one or more *name* values. The third way is to use the **-k** option and one or more *keyword* values.

These are not the only options that **man** uses, just the most important ones. On some systems, **man** has a large number of options. However, for most day-to-day work, **-f** and **-k** are the only ones you will need. If you want to know more about what is available on your system, just check the manual.

To conclude this chapter, here is one final example. As I explained in Chapter 9, you can use the **whatis** command instead of **man -f**, and the **apropos** command instead of **man -k**. The syntax for these two commands is:

```
whatis name...
apropos keyword...
```

The syntax shows us that, to use either of these commands, you enter the command name (**whatis** or **apropos**) followed by one or more arguments.

HINT

Some commands have minor differences from one version of Unix to another. In this book, I generally use the GNU/Linux version of the command. Most of the time, this will be fine, as the most important options and arguments tend to be the same in most types of Unix.

However, if you have a problem, the definitive source for how a program works on *your* system is your online manual, not this book (or any book).

CHAPTER 10 EXERCISES

REVIEW QUESTIONS

1. How do you enter more than one command on the same line?

2. The syntax of a Unix command can be expressed in the form: command-name options arguments. What are options? What are arguments?

3. What are dash options and dash-dash options? What is each type used for?

4. What is whitespace?

5. When you learn the syntax of a new program, what are the three basic questions you should ask?

APPLYING YOUR KNOWLEDGE

1. It is often desirable to enter more than one command on the same line. Create a short summary of your system's status by typing the following three commands on a single line: **date** (time and date), **users** (userids that are logged in), and **uptime** (how long your system has been up).

2. Write the syntax for the following program. The command name is **foobar**. There are three options **-a**, **-b** and **-c**. The **-c** option takes an optional argument named **value**. Finally, there must be one or more instances of an argument named **file**.

FOR FURTHER THOUGHT

1. Many of the GNU utilities (used with Linux and FreeBSD) support both the traditional, abbreviated **-** (dash) options, as well as the longer **--** (dash-dash) options. Why did the GNU developers feel it was necessary to introduce a new style of options? What are the advantages? What are the disadvantages?

# CHAPTER 11

THE SHELL

As you know, the shell is the program that reads and interprets your commands. From the very beginning, the shell was designed to be a regular program, one that requires no special privileges to do its job. In this sense, it is like any other program that might run on a Unix system.

Because of this basic design, it is possible for anyone with the requisite programming skill to design his own shell, which he can then share with other Unix users. Over the years, this is exactly what has happened and, today, there are a large number of shells in use. Your Unix system will have at least a few, and you can use whichever one you want. You can even switch back and forth from one shell to another. If you want to try a shell that is not installed on your system, there are a variety of shells you can download from the Internet for free.

In this chapter, I will answer several questions: What is the shell, and why is it important? What are the most popular shells? Which shell should you use? In the following chapters, I will teach you how to use the most important shells: Bash, the Korn shell, the C-Shell, and the Tcsh.

WHAT IS A SHELL?

Once you start using Unix, you will hear a lot of talk about the shell. Just what is this "shell" thing, anyway? There are several answers.

The short technical answer is that a SHELL is a program that acts as a user interface and script interpreter, allowing you to enter commands and, indirectly, to access the services of the kernel.

To be a bit less technical, let me give you a more elaborate, two-part description of a shell. First, a shell is a COMMAND PROCESSOR: a program that reads and interprets the commands that you enter. Every time you type a Unix command, the shell reads it and figures out what to do. Most shells also offer facilities to make your minute-to-minute work more convenient. For instance, you can recall, edit and re-enter previous commands.

In addition to being a command interpreter, a shell also supports some type of programming language. Using this language, you can write programs, called SHELL SCRIPTS, for the shell to interpret. These scripts can contain regular Unix commands, as well as special shell programming commands. Each type of shell has its own specific programming language and rules. As a general rule, however, shells within the same "family" use similar programming languages. (We will talk about the two main families of shells later in the chapter.)

Just between you and me, none of these explanations really captures the *je ne sais quoi* — that certain something — that surrounds the idea of the shell. You see, the shell is your main interface into Unix. Since there are a variety of shells, you have a choice as to which interface you use and, your choice affects how Unix feels to you as you use it.

As you can imagine, there are all kinds of arguments among the cognoscenti as to which shells are best and which shells should be avoided at all costs. Until you are an experienced Unix user, however, it doesn't really matter which shell you use. The differences, though important, are not significant to beginners: you might as well use whichever shell is the default on your system. Once you get more experience, you can choose the shell you like the best and then use it to create a highly customized work environment for yourself.

At that point — once you know how to deliberately manipulate your work environment — you will begin to understand the mysterious feeling people have for the shell. You can't see it and you can't touch it, but it is always there, waiting to serve your every need in the way that works best with your individual thinking process. (If you are a pantheist, this will make perfect sense.)

HINT

Becoming proficient with the shell you are currently using is far more important than spending a lot of time trying to choose the "right" shell, or trying to convince a busy admin to install a new shell on your system.

"If you can't use the shell you love, love the shell you use." — Harley Hahn

---

WHAT'S IN A NAME?

Shell

There are three ways to think about the name "shell". First, a Unix shell provides a well-defined interface to protect the internals of the operating system. In this sense, a shell acts like the shell of an oyster, shielding its vulnerable parts from the harsh realities of the outside world.

Alternatively, you can visualize a seashell that winds around and around in a spiral. When you use a Unix shell, you can pause what you are doing and start another shell or another program whenever you want. Thus, you can put as many programs as you want on hold, each one "inside" its predecessor, just like the layers of the real seashell.

My advice, however, is to refrain from asking the question, What does the name "shell" mean? Instead, think of the word "shell" as a brand new technical term (like RTFM or foo), and let its meaning come solely from your experience with Unix over the years.

THE BOURNE SHELL FAMILY: `sh`, `ksh`, `bash`

The shell is a program and, like all programs, it is known by the name of the command you type to run it. The very first shell was written in 1971 by one of the original creators of Unix, Ken Thompson, two years after Unix was invented. (See Chapter 2 for the history of Unix.) In keeping with the tradition of giving programs short names, Thompson named the shell **sh**.

Let's pretend that you are an early user in the early 1970s. Here is how you would use the **sh** program. To start, you log into the system by typing your userid and password (see Chapter 4). Once your password is validated and the various startup procedures have been carried out, Unix runs the **sh** program on your behalf, which begins your work session.

The **sh** program displays a shell prompt (see Chapter 4) and waits for input. Each time you enter a command, **sh** does whatever is necessary to process it; once the command is finished, **sh** displays a new shell prompt and waits for another command. Eventually, you tell **sh** there is no more input data by pressing **^D** to send the **eof** [end of file] signal (see Chapter 7). Upon trapping this signal (again, see Chapter 7), **sh** terminates and you are logged out, ending your work session.

Today, using the shell is basically the same experience as it was in 1971. To be sure, modern shells are a lot more powerful than the original **sh** program, but they still act as your interface by reading one command after another and terminating when there is no more data. (This is why the shell is called the CLI, command line interface.)

The very first shell, which we might call the Thompson shell, was used from 1971 to 1975, being distributed with Unix First Edition (Version 1) through Unix Sixth Edition (Version 6). In 1975, a new shell was written by a group of Bell Labs programmers led by John Mashey. This new shell was released in 1976 as part of a special version of Unix called the Programmer's Workbench or PWB. Because the Mashey Shell (also called the PWB Shell) was designed to replace the original shell, it was also named **sh**.

The advantage of keeping the same name for a new shell is that, as a user, you don't have to do anything special when the new shell is introduced. One day, you run the **sh** program and you get the old shell; the next day, you run the **sh** program and you get the new shell. As long as the new shell is compatible with the old shell, everything works fine. You can do everything you did in the old shell *and*, if you want, you can take advantage of the enhanced features of the new shell.

When a new program relates to an old program in this way, we say that the new program is BACKWARDS COMPATIBLE with the old program. For example, the Mashey Shell was backwards compatible with the original Thompson Shell.

Because the shell was designed to be a regular program, anyone who had enough expertise could change an existing shell to their liking, or even write their own shell*. In 1976, another Bell Labs programmer, Steve Bourne, started work on a brand new shell. Because it was designed to replace the older Thompson shell, the BOURNE SHELL was also named **sh**.

Both the Mashey and Bourne shells offered important improvements, particularly in the area of programming and, within a short time, both shells had gained a significant following within Bell Labs. However, although they were both backwards compatible with the existing **sh** program, they were incompatible with one another. This led to an

---

*John Mashey once described to me what it was like at Bell Labs in those days. "At one point, our department of 30 people probably had 10 different flavors of shell. After all, we were all programmers, and the source was all there, and it was an ordinary user program, so anyone who felt like it 'fixed' things. This got crazy, and we got it under control later..."

internal debate as to which shell should become the standard Unix shell. The result of this debate was important, for it changed the course of Unix for years to come.

At three successive Unix user meetings, Mashey and Bourne each discussed their shells. In between the meetings, they both worked hard to enhance their shells by adding new functionality. To settle the problem once and for all, a committee was formed to study the issue; they chose the Bourne shell.

Thus, with the release of Unix Seventh Edition (Version 7), the Bourne shell became the default shell for all Unix users. In fact, the Bourne shell was so stable and so well-designed that, for many years, it was the standard Unix shell. From time to time, new versions of the shell were released and, each time, the shell kept its backwards compatibility and the name **sh**. The Bourne shell became so widely used that, today, all compatible shells — older and newer — are considered to be members of the BOURNE SHELL FAMILY.

In 1982, another Bell Labs scientist, David Korn, created a replacement for the Bourne shell, called the KORN SHELL or **ksh**. The new shell was based on tools that Korn and other researchers had been building over the last several years. As such, it represented a vast improvement over the standard Bourne shell. In particular, the new Korn shell offered a history file, command editing, aliasing, and job control (all of which we will discuss later in the book).

Korn ensured that the **ksh** program was backwards compatible with the current **sh** program, and within a short time, the Korn shell became the de facto standard within Bell Labs. With the next release of Unix, the Korn shell was distributed to the world at large, and it soon became a permanent replacement for the Bourne shell. Since then, there have been two new major releases of the Korn shell: Ksh88 in 1988, and Ksh93 in 1993.

In the early 1990s, a great deal of pressure grew to standardize Unix (see Chapter 2). This pressure led to two different movements, one controlled by organizations and committees, the other arising from popular demand. Each movement had its own solution to the question: How can we standardize the Unix shell once and for all?

The "official" movement created a large set of specifications called POSIX (pronounced "pause-ix"), a blueprint for standardizing operating systems. For practical purposes, you can think of POSIX as an organized attempt by commercial interests to standardize Unix.

WHAT'S IN A NAME?

POSIX
The project to standardize Unix was initiated under the mantle of an organization called the IEEE. At first, the project was called IEEE-IX, but since this was such a bad name, the IEEE tried to come up with something better. They had trouble doing so and, at the last minute, Richard Stallman, founder of the Free Software Foundation (see Chapter 2), suggested the name POSIX. Stallman chose the name as an acronym for "Portable Operating System Interface". The adventitious "X" was added to make the name look more Unix-like.

An important part of the POSIX standard was the specification for the basic features of a shell. Over the years, this standard has had several names including IEEE 1003.2

and ISO/IEC 9945-2*. For companies, governments and other organizations, the 1003.2 standard was an important benchmark in that it gave anyone who worked on shell development a well-defined baseline target for which to aim. For example, the Ksh93 shell was designed to conform to the 1003.2 standard.

The 1003.2 standard, however, was not readily available to individuals. Indeed, it cost money to get a copy of the technical details**. Among most Unix programmers, the prevailing ethic was not to follow one universal standard such as POSIX, but to create free software that could be modified and enhanced by anyone. As we discussed in Chapter 2, the free software movement led to the development of the Free Software Foundation and to the creation of Linux. The Korn shell, however, could not be distributed with Linux. The problem was that the Korn shell, being part of Unix, was a commercial product that belonged to AT&T. As such, it was not available to the general public.

In 2000, AT&T finally allowed the Korn shell to become an open source product, but it was too late. In the 1990s, a number of free, open source shells were created, the most important of which were the FreeBSD shell, Pdksh, the Zsh, and Bash. All of these shells complied with the 1003.2 standard, making them adequate replacements for the Korn shell.

The FREEBSD SHELL, as the name implies, is the default shell for FreeBSD. In keeping with tradition, it is known as **sh**, the standard name for a member of the Bourne shell family. (In other words, if you are using FreeBSD and you run the **sh** program, you get the FreeBSD shell.)

PDKSH is a modern clone of the Korn shell. Pdksh was written to provide a Korn shell without restrictive licensing terms; hence the name "public domain Korn shell". The best way to think of Pdksh is as a modern Korn shell that is free in both senses of the word (no cost + open source). The original Pdksh was written in 1987 by a programmer named Eric Gisin, who based his work on a public domain version of the Unix Seventh Edition Bourne shell written by Charles Forsyth†. Over the years, many people contributed to Pdksh. Since the mid-1990s, however, the shell has stabilized and remained mostly unchanged. This is because (1) it works well, and (2) most people in the open source community are using Bash (see below). Still, many Linux systems do include Pdksh as one of the installed shells so, if it is available on your system, you may want to give it a try.

The next important member of the Bourne shell family is the Zsh, pronounced "zee-shell" (even in England and Canada, where the letter Z is normally pronounced "zed"). The name of the Zsh program is **zsh**.

The ZSH was developed by Paul Falstad in 1990, when he was an undergraduate at Princeton University. His philosophy was to "take everything interesting that I could

*If you like acronyms, here they are: IEEE is the Institute of Electrical and Electronics Engineers. ISO is the International Organization for Standardization. (The name ISO is not an acronym. It comes from the Greek word *isos* meaning "equal".) Finally, IEC is the International Electrotechnical Commission.

This is still the case with the ISO. With the IEEE, however, you can view the 1003.2 standard online as part of a larger specification called IEEE 1003.1. On the Net, go to **www.unix.org and look for a link to the "Single UNIX Specification". The part you want is called "Shell & Utilities".

†In the 1970s, I was an undergraduate at the University of Waterloo (Canada) studying math and computer science. For a short time, I actually shared an apartment with Charles Forsyth. He was quiet, easy going, a bit odd, and very, very smart. Perhaps the best way I can describe him is that, as a young programmer in the mid-1970s, he seemed like the type of guy who would, one day, write his own shell.

get my hands on from every other shell". As he explained, "I wanted a shell that can do anything you want". The result is a shell that offers all of the important features of the other Unix shells, as well as new capabilities that are not widely available. For example, you can tell the Zsh to notify you when a particular userid has logged in.

So where does the name come from? When Falstad was working on the shell, there was a teaching assistant, Zhong Shao, whose Unix userid was **zsh**. Falstad figured that would be a good name for a shell, and appropriated it for his new creation.

Within a short time of being released, the Zsh developed a cult following around the world and became popular among programmers and advanced Unix users. Today, the Zsh status is much like that of Pdksh: it works, it's stable, and it's a great shell. However, since the mid-1990s, new development has slowed to a crawl.

Of all the members of the Bourne shell family, the most important, by far, is BASH. Bash was originally created by Brian Fox (1987) and later (starting in 1990) maintained by Chet Ramey, all under the auspices of the Free Software Foundation. Today, Bash is supported by a community of programmers around the world. The name of the actual program, as you might guess, is **bash**.

Bash extends the capabilities of the basic Bourne shell in a manner similar to the Korn shell. Bash is not only a command processor with a powerful scripting language; it supports command line editing, command history, a directory stack, command completion, filename completion, and a lot more (all of which will make sense to you eventually).

Bash is free software, distributed by the Free Software Foundation. It is the default shell for Linux, as well as Unix-based Macintoshes, and is available for use with Microsoft Windows (running under a Unix-like system called Cygwin). In fact, every important Unix system in the world either comes with Bash or has a version of Bash that can be downloaded for free from the Internet. For all these reasons, Bash is the most popular shell in history, being used by millions of people around the world.

WHAT'S IN A NAME?

Bash
The name Bash stands for "Bourne-again shell", a name that is an acronym and a pun. The idea is that — literally and spiritually — Bash is based on a resurrected ("born again") version of the standard Unix shell.

Notice that, although we talk about the Korn shell or the C-Shell or the Zsh, we never say the Bash Shell. We always say "Bash".

THE C-SHELL FAMILY: csh, tcsh

As I described above, the original Bourne shell was introduced in 1977. A year later, in 1978, Bill Joy, a graduate student at U.C. Berkeley developed a brand new shell, which he based on the Unix Sixth Edition **sh** program, the predecessor of the Bourne shell.

However, Joy did more than copy the existing functionality: he added many important improvements, including aliases, command history, and job control. In addition, he completely revamped the programming facilities, changing the design of the scripting syntax so that it resembled the C programming language. For this reason, he called his new shell the C-SHELL, and he changed the name of the program from **sh** to **csh**.

During the late 1970s and throughout the 1980s, the C-Shell became very popular. You might wonder, why should this be the case when there were already other good shells? There were several reasons.

First, the C-Shell offered major improvements over the standard Unix shell. Second, the C-Shell was included as part of the BSD Unix distribution (see Chapter 2), which itself was very popular. Finally, the C-Shell was created by Bill Joy, one of the most important Unix programmers of all time. Joy's tools, such as the **vi** editor , were extremely well-designed and tended to be used by a lot of people. (For a discussion of Joy's contributions to Unix, see Chapter 2.)

For a long time, the C-Shell was the shell of choice of Unix users at universities and research organizations, where it was usually the default shell. I first used Unix in 1976, and the C-Shell is the shell I started with. To this day, it is still close to my heart.

There were, however, two important problems with the C-Shell. One was solvable; the other, unfortunately, was not, and it led to the C-Shell falling out of favor among experienced users.

First, because of BSD's licensing terms, the C-Shell could not be distributed and modified freely, which was a big issue for many programmers. For this reason, in the late 1970s, a programmer named Ken Greer from Carnegie-Mellon University, began work on a completely free version of the **csh**, which he called **tcsh**. In the early 1980s, the responsibility for the TCSH (pronounced "Tee sea-shell") was passed on to a small number of programmers led by Paul Placeway at Ohio State.

The Tcsh was wonderful. Not only was it free (it was distributed in the public domain), but it enhanced the C-Shell by offering a number of advanced features, such as filename completion and command line editing. The Tcsh was attractive to a great many users and, over time, a large group of volunteers formed to maintain and extend it.

However, there was a problem that could not be solved: both the C-Shell and the Tcsh were not as good for programming as the Bourne family shells. Although the C-like syntax was fine for writing C programs, it wasn't as suitable for writing shell scripts, especially when it came to I/O (input/output). Moreover, both the C-Shell and the Tcsh had a number of design flaws, too esoteric to mention, which bothered the type of programmers who care about esoterica.

By the 1990s, all the popular shells were available on all Unix systems, and a general debate arose as to which shell was the best. Like a young lady whose dress was a bit too meretricious for her own good, the C-Shell began to lose its reputation without knowing why. Among hard-core Unix users and their wannabes, it became trendy to say, "I like using the C-Shell for regular work, but I use the Bourne shell for programming."

A watershed occurred in 1995, when Tom Christiansen, a highly respected Unix programmer and one of the fathers of the Perl programming language, wrote a widely circulated essay entitled "Csh Programming Considered Harmful". The title was taken from a very well-known computer paper, "Go To Statement Considered Harmful", a short essay by the Dutch programmer Edsger Dijkstra*. In 1968, Dijkstra's paper had changed the world of programming, leading to the popularization of what became known as structured programming. In 1995, Christiansen's paper, though not as seminal, led to the eventual abandonment of both the C-Shell and the Tcsh for programming.

Today, the C-Shell and the Tcsh are not used nearly as widely as they once were and, since the mid-1990s, Tcsh development has slowed to a virtual standstill. Still, the C-SHELL FAMILY is held in high regard by many advanced Unix users and, for that reason, I have devoted a chapter of this book to show you how to use the shell, should you wish to do so.

On some systems, **csh** and **tcsh** are two separate programs. On many Unix systems, however, **tcsh** has completely replaced **csh**. That is, if you run **csh**, you will actually get **tcsh**. You can tell if this is the case on your system by looking at the **csh** man page (see Chapter 9).

Even today, the C-Shell is still important. Indeed, when you read about other shells, you will often see that they contain features taken from the C-Shell that Bill Joy designed so many years ago. For example, on the Web site for the Zsh, you will read, "Many of the useful features of **bash**, **ksh** and **tcsh** were incorporated into **zsh**."

WHAT'S IN A NAME?

C-Shell, Tcsh

The name C-Shell comes from the fact that Bill Joy designed the shell's programming facilities to work like those of the C programming language. I imagine that Joy liked the name "C-Shell" because it sounds like "sea shell", and everyone likes sea shells.

But what about the Tcsh?

When Ken Greer wrote the original Tcsh for Unix, he was also using an operating system called TENEX on a PDP-10 computer from DEC. The TENEX command interpreter used very long command names because they were easy to understand. The commands, however, were a bother to type, so TENEX had a facility, called "command completion" to do a lot of the work. All you had to do was type a few letters and press the <Esc> key. The command interpreter would then expand what you had typed into the full command.

Greer added this feature to the new C-Shell, and when it came time to name the shell, he called it **tcsh**, the "t" referring to TENEX.

WHAT'S IN A NAME?

C, C++, C#

Both the C-Shell and the Tcsh are named after the C programming language. But how did such an odd name arise for a language?

In 1963, a programming language called CPL was developed in England as part of a project involving researchers from Cambridge and the University of London. CPL stood for

---

Communications of the ACM (*CACM*), Vol. 11, No. 3, March 1968, pp 147-148. When you get a moment, read this paper. (It's easy to find on the Internet.) As you do, think about the fact that this short, 14-paragraph essay changed the world of programming more than any single act before or since. If you are intrigued, take a look at Dijkstra's seminal book, *A Discipline of Programming* (Prentice-Hall PTR, 1976).

By the way, the title of Dijkstra's paper (and hence, Christiansen's) was actually made up by Niklaus Wirth, not Dijkstra. Wirth, the creator of the Algol W, Pascal and Modula-2 programming languages, was editor of *CACM* at the time.

(*cont'd...*) "Combined Programming Language" and was based on Algol 60, one of the first well-designed, modern programming languages.

Four years later, in 1967, a programmer at Cambridge named Martin Richards created BCPL, "Basic CPL". BCPL itself gave rise to yet another language, known by the single letter, B.

The B language was taken to Bell Labs, where Ken Thompson and Dennis Ritchie made modifications and renamed it NB. In the early 1970s, Thompson (the original Unix developer) used NB to rewrite the basic part of Unix for its second edition. Up until then, all of Unix had been written in assembly language. Not long afterwards, the NB language was extended and renamed C. C soon became the language of choice for writing new Unix utilities, applications and even the operating system itself.

People asked, where did the name C come from? Was it the next letter after B in the alphabet, or was it the second letter of BCPL? This question had philological implications of cosmic importance: would the successor to C be named D or P?

The question proved to be moot when, in the early 1980s, Bjarne Stroustrup (also of Bell Labs) designed the most popular extension of C, an object-oriented language, which he called C++, pronounced "C-plus-plus". (In the C language, **++** is an operator that adds 1 to a variable. For instance, to add 1 to the variable **total**, you can use the command **total++**.)

In 2002, Microsoft created a special version of C++ as part of their .NET initiative. They called the new language C#, which is pronounced "C sharp" (like the music term). If you want, you can imagine two small "++" designations, one on top of the other, to form the "#" symbol.

Thus, when you see the names C, C++ or C#, you can recognize them as examples of those wonderful programming puns that make people scratch their heads and wonder if Man is really Nature's last word.

WHICH SHELL SHOULD YOU USE?

There are tens and tens of different Unix shells, of which we have discussed the most important ones: the Bourne shell, the Korn shell, the FreeBSD shell, Pdksh, the Zsh, Bash, the C-Shell, and the Tcsh.

For reference, Figure 11-1 shows each of these shells along with the name of its program.*
To run the shell, if it exists on your system, just type in the name, for example:

```
bash
ksh
tcsh
```

On some Unix systems, the various shells are all installed under their own names. The **sh** program is different from **ksh** or **bash**, and **csh** is different from **tcsh**. So if you want to use an old Bourne shell, you type **sh**; if you want to use Bash, you type **bash**. Similarly, you can use either **csh** (the standard C-Shell) or **tcsh** (the enhanced C-Shell).

On many systems, however, the newer shells have replaced the old ones, and you won't find the Bourne shell or the C-Shell. Instead, if you type **sh**, you will get either Bash or the Korn shell; and if you type **csh**, you will get the Tcsh. To see if this is the case on your system, just look at the man page for the shell in question. For example, on Linux systems,

---

*There are two other common names you might encounter that look like regular shells but are not: **ssh** and **rsh**. The **ssh** program is the "Secure Shell", used to connect to a remote computer. The **rsh** program is the "Remote Shell" — an old program whose use is deprecated — used to run a single command on a remote computer.

SHELL	NAME OF THE PROGRAM
Bash	**bash** or **sh**
Bourne Shell	**sh**
C-Shell	**csh**
FreeBSD Shell	**sh**
Korn Shell	**ksh** or **sh**
Pdksh	**ksh**
Tcsh	**tcsh** or **csh**
Zsh	**zsh**

FIGURE 11-1: The Unix shells

There are a large number of Unix shells. This table shows the most popular shells, along with the names of the actual shell programs.

if you ask for the **sh** man page, you get the **bash** man page; if you ask for the **csh** man page, you get the **tcsh** man page.

To display the man page for a particular shell, use the **man** command (Chapter 9) with the name of the appropriate program. For example:

```
man sh
man csh
```

Since shells are so complex, the man page will actually be the size of a small manual. Don't be overwhelmed: a lot of what you see is reference material for advanced users.

So, which shell should you use? If you are a beginner, it really doesn't matter, as all shells have the same basic functionality. However, as you begin to progress as a Unix user, the details do begin to matter and you need to make a commitment.

If you like to go with the flow, stick with the default and use whatever you get on your system when you type **sh**. Most likely this will be Bash with Linux, the FreeBSD shell with FreeBSD, and the Korn shell with a commercial Unix system.

NAME OF SHELL	SIZE OF MAN PAGE	RELATIVE COMPLEXITY
Bourne Shell	38,000 bytes	1.0
FreeBSD Shell	57,000 bytes	1.5
C-Shell	64,000 bytes	1.7
Korn Shell	121,000 bytes	3.2
Tcsh	250,000 bytes	6.6
Bash	302,000 bytes	7.9
Zsh	789,000 bytes	20.8

FIGURE 11-2: Relative complexity of various shells

One way to estimate the complexity of a program is to look at the size of its documentation. Here are statistics showing the relative complexity of the most popular Unix shells.

If you are adventurous, however, there are many shells for you to try. For example, although the C-Shell is no longer a default shell, many people do enjoy using it, and you may find that **tcsh** or **csh** is already available on your system. If you want to go further afield, just search the Internet for Unix or Linux shells, and I guarantee you'll find something new to try. (If you are adventurous and you can't make up your mind, try the Zsh.)

HINT

For day-to-day work, you can use whichever shell takes your fancy, and you can change whenever you like.

However, if you write shell scripts, you should stick with the standard Bourne shell programming language to ensure that your scripts are portable enough to be used on other systems.

In a moment, I am going to show you how to change your shell. Before I do, I'd like to answer an interesting question: How complex are each of the shells? A complicated program will have a lot of capability, but it will also demand more of your time to master. Moreover, like many Unix programs, the shells have a lot of esoteric features and options that you will never really need. These extra facilities are often a distraction.

One crude way to measure the complexity of a program is by looking at the length of the documentation. The table in Figure 11-2 shows the approximate number of bytes (characters) in the manual pages for each of the shells. For comparison, I have normalized the numbers, assigning the smallest number a value of 1.0. (Of course, these numbers change from time to time as new versions of the documentation are released.)

From these numbers, it is easy to see that the C-Shell and FreeBSD shell provide a nice middle ground between the older, less capable Bourne shell and the other, more complex shells.

Of course, one can argue that none of this matters, because all modern shells are backwards compatible, either with the Bourne shell or with the C-Shell. If you don't want the added features, you can ignore them and they won't bother you.

However, documentation is important. The manual pages for the more complex shells take a long time to read and are very difficult to understand. In fact, even the manual page for the Bourne shell is too large for a normal human being to peruse comfortably. So take another look at the numbers in Figure 11-2, and think about the following questions:

Assuming that the FreeBSD shell, Bash, and the Zsh have most of the modern features knowledgeable Unix users require, what can you say about the type of person who chooses to use FreeBSD and the FreeBSD shell?

What about a person who chooses to use Bash because it is the default on his system?

And what sort of person, do you think, enjoys downloading, installing and learning about a tool as complex as the Zsh (which is not the default on any system)?

CHANGING YOUR SHELL TEMPORARILY

Whenever you log in, a shell will be started for you automatically. This shell is called your LOGIN SHELL. An important question to answer is, which particular shell is your login shell? Is it Bash, the Korn shell, the C-Shell, the Tcsh?

Unless you have changed the default, your login shell will be whichever shell is assigned to your userid. If you use Linux, your login shell will probably be Bash. If you use a commercial Unix, your login shell will probably be the Korn shell. If you use FreeBSD, it will probably be the Tcsh.

If you use a shared system, your system administrator will have set your login shell. As you know, on your own computer, you are the admin (see Chapter 4), so unless you have changed the default shell, it will be whatever was set automatically when you installed the system.

There are two ways in which you might change your shell. You may want to use a different shell temporarily, perhaps to experiment with it. Or, you may find that you like a new shell better than your current shell, and you want to make a permanent change.

Let's say, for example, you decide to try the Zsh. You download it from the Internet and install it on your system. From time to time, you change to the Zsh temporarily just for fun. Eventually, you come to like the Zsh so much that you want it to be your permanent login shell. In this section, I'll show you how to change your shell temporarily. In the next section, I'll show you how to do it permanently.

To start, remember that a shell is just a program that you can run like any other program. This means that, at any time, you can pause your current shell and start another one simply by running the new shell. For example, let's say you have just logged in, and your login shell is Bash. You enter a few commands, and then you decide you want to try the Tcsh (assuming it is available on your system). Just enter:

```
tcsh
```

Your current shell (Bash) is paused and the new shell (the Tcsh) starts. You can now do whatever you want using the Tcsh. When you are ready to switch back to Bash, just press **^D** (see Chapter 7) to indicate that there is no more data. The Tcsh shell will now end, and you will be returned to your original Bash shell. It's that easy.

If you want to experiment, you can see what shells are available on your system by using the following command:

```
less /etc/shells
```

We'll discuss this command in the next section.

If you are experimenting, and you get confused as to which shell you are using, you can use the following command at any time to show you the name of the current shell:

```
echo $SHELL
```

> **HINT**
>
> It is possible to start a new shell, and then another new shell, and then another new shell, and so on. However, when it comes time to end your work session, you can only log out from the original login shell.
>
> Thus, if you have started one or more new shells, you must work your way back to the login shell before you can log out.

THE PASSWORD FILE: CHANGING YOUR LOGIN SHELL: `chsh`

Unix uses two files to keep track of all the userids in the system. The first file **/etc/passwd** — the PASSWORD FILE — contains basic information about each userid. The second file **/etc/shadow** — the SHADOW FILE — contains the actual passwords (encrypted, of course).

When you log in, Unix retrieves information about your userid from these files. In particular, the **/etc/passwd** file contains the name of your login shell. Thus, to change your login shell, all you need to do is make a simple change in the **/etc/passwd** file. However, you don't do this directly. It would be too risky, as screwing up the **/etc/passwd** file can wreak havoc with your system. Instead, you use a special command, which I will explain in a moment.

Before I do, I want to say a word about file names. The way in which I have written the names of the two files I just mentioned is called a "pathname". A pathname shows the exact location of a file within the file system. We will discuss this idea in detail when we talk about the Unix file system in Chapter 23. For now, all you need to know is that the pathname **/etc/passwd** refers to the **passwd** file within the **/etc** directory. A directory is what a Windows or Mac user would call a folder. (This idea, like many others, was taken from Unix.)

When you change your shell, you need to specify the name of the shell program as a pathname. The pathnames of the available shells are stored in a file named **/etc/shells***. To display this file, use the **less** command (which we will meet formally in Chapter 21).

```
less /etc/shells
```

Here is some typical output:

```
/bin/sh
/bin/bash
/bin/tcsh/bin/csh
```

From this output, you can see that (in this case) there are four available shells: **sh**, **bash**, **tcsh** and **csh**.

To change your login shell, you use the **chsh** (change shell) command. The syntax* is:

chsh [**-s** *shell*] [*userid*]

where *userid* is the userid for which you want to make the change; *shell* is the pathname of the new login shell.

Notes: (1) You can only change the shell for your own userid. To change the shell for another userid, you must be superuser. (2) On some systems, **chsh** will not allow you to change to a shell unless it is listed in the **/etc/shells** file. On other systems, **chsh** will allow you to make such a change, but it will give you a warning. Thus, if you

---

*The **/etc/shells** file is used with Linux and FreeBSD, but not with certain commercial Unix systems such as AIX and Solaris.

download and install a shell on your own, it behooves you to put the pathname of the shell in the **/etc/shells** files.

By default, **chsh** assumes that you want to change your own login shell, so you don't have to specify the userid. For example, to change your login shell to **/bin/tcsh**, use:

```
chsh -s /bin/tcsh
```

If you leave out the **-s** option and the name of the shell, **chsh** will prompt you (ask you) for it. For example, say you are logged in as **harley**, and you enter:

```
chsh
```

You see:

```
Changing shell for harley.
New shell [/bin/bash]:
```

At this point **chsh** is telling you two things. First, you are about to change the login shell for userid **harley**. Second, the current login shell is **/bin/bash**.

You now have two choices. If you enter the pathname of a new shell, **chsh** will make the change for you. For example, to change your login shell to the Tcsh, enter:

```
/bin/tcsh
```

If you simply press <Enter> without typing anything, **chsh** will not make a change. This is a good way to see the name of your current login shell.

With Linux, the **chsh** command has another option that is useful. To display a list of all the available shells, you can use the **-l** (list) option:

```
chsh -l
```

Some Unix systems don't have a **chsh** command. Instead, you change your login shell by using a variation of the **passwd** command (which we discussed in Chapter 4). For example, with AIX, you use **passwd -s**; with Solaris, you use **passwd -e**. For more details, see your **passwd** man page.

If you are a system administrator, and you are called upon to change someone else's login shell, you can use the **usermod -s**. Again, see the man page for details.

> **HINT**
>
> When you change your login shell, you modify the **/etc/passwd** file. Thus, whatever change you make will not take effect until the next time you log in (just as when you change your password).

---

*Throughout this book, I will be teaching you how to use a great many commands. Each time I describe a new command, I will begin by showing you its syntax. When I do, I will only show you the most important options and arguments. If you need more information, you can always get it from the man page (see Chapter 9).

As I explained in Chapter 10, some commands have minor differences from one version of Unix to another. In this book, I generally use the GNU/Linux version of a command. Most of the time, this will be fine, as the important options and arguments tend to be the same in most types of Unix. If you have a problem, however, I want you to remember that the definitive source for how a program works on your system is your online manual.

HINT

In certain situations, if your system is in critical shape and you need to log in as superuser (**root**) to make repairs, some shells may not be able to run properly. For this reason, the login shell for **root** must be the type of shell that will always run, no matter what.

Thus, unless you really know what you are doing, do *not* change the login shell for userid **root**. If you do, you run the risk that, one day, you will have a broken system with no way to log in.

CHAPTER 11 EXERCISES

REVIEW QUESTIONS

1. What is a shell?

2. What are the two principal shell families? Name the most commonly used shells in each family.

3. What does "backwards compatible" mean? Give an example of a shell that is backwards compatible with another shell.

4. What is POSIX? How is it pronounced?

5. How do you change your shell temporarily? How do you change your shell permanently?

APPLYING YOUR KNOWLEDGE

1. Check which shells are available on your system. Display the name of your default shell.

2. Change your default shell to another shell. Log out and log in again. Check to make sure your default shell has been changed. Change your default shell back to what it was. Log out and log in again. Check to see that your default shell was changed back correctly.

FOR FURTHER THOUGHT

1. Over the years, many different Unix shells have been created. Why is this necessary? Why not just have one main shell that can be enhanced from time to time?

2. Program A has been replaced by program B. What are the advantages if program B is backwards compatible with program A? What are the disadvantages?

CHAPTER 12
USING THE SHELL: VARIABLES AND OPTIONS

Many people do not take the time to learn how to use the shell well. This is a mistake. To be sure, the shell — like all complex Unix programs — has many features you do not really need to understand. However, there are a number of fundamental ideas that are of great practical value. Here is my list:

- Interactive Shells
- Processes
- Environment Variables
- Shell Variables
- Shell Options
- Metacharacters
- Quoting
- External Commands
- Builtin Commands
- Search Path
- Command Substitution
- History List
- Autocompletion
- Command Line Editing
- Aliases
- Initialization Files
- Comments

If you look at this list and feel overwhelmed, I understand. You may even feel like asking, "Do I really need to learn all this stuff?"

The answer is yes, and it will take a bit of time, but don't worry. First of all, I will spread the material over three chapters, so you won't get too much at once. Second, I will make sure that we cover the topics in a way that each one leads to the next, so you won't feel confused. (In fact, we will be covering the topics in the order you see in the list.) Finally, as you come to appreciate the beauty of the shell, and it all starts to make sense, you will find yourself having a good time as we move from one idea to the next.

As you know, there are two shell families: the Bourne family (Bash, Korn shell) and the C-Shell family (C-Shell, Tcsh). When you learn how to use a shell, some of the details vary depending on which shell you are using, and that will be reflected in what I will be teaching you. Nevertheless, a basic aspect of being skilled with Unix is understanding and appreciating how each of the shell families approaches certain problems.

Thus, as you study the next three chapters, I'd like you to read all the sections and look at all the examples, regardless of which shell you use. Some people only study the shell they happen to be using at the time, but that is a mistake. My goal is for you to be comfortable with *all* the major shells. The way to do this is by paying attention to the basic principles, not by memorizing the esoteric details of one particular shell.

As you read this chapter, you will need to know what shell you are currently using. If you are not sure, you can display the name of the shell that started when you logged in by using the following command (which will make sense later in the chapter):

```
echo $SHELL
```

If you have temporarily changed to a different shell (see Chapter 11), you will, of course, know what shell you are using.

One last point before we start. Chapter 11 covers shells in general. If you have not already read that chapter, please take a few moments to look at it before you continue.

INTERACTIVE AND NON-INTERACTIVE SHELLS

An INTERACTIVE program is one that communicates with a person. When you run an interactive program, the input comes from your keyboard or your mouse, and the output is sent to your monitor. For example, when you use a word processor or a Web browser, you are using an interactive program.

A NON-INTERACTIVE program runs independently of a person. Typically, it will get its input from a file and write its output to another file. For example, when you compile a program (process it so it can be run), you are using a non-interactive program, the compiler.

At times, the lines between interactive and non-interactive programs can blur a bit. For instance, an interactive program might send output to a file or to a printer. Similarly, a non-interactive program might ask you to enter a bit of data at the keyboard, or might display a message on your monitor when something important happens.

Still, for practical purposes, it is usually simple to classify a program as being interactive (working with you) or non-interactive (working by itself). In general, interactive programs get their input from a person (keyboard, mouse) and send their output to a person (monitor, speakers). Non-interactive programs use input that comes from a non-human source (say, a file), and send their output to a non-human source (another file). So, the question arises, what is the shell: interactive or non-interactive?

The answer is, it can be both. You will recall from Chapter 11 that the shell can act as both a user interface and a script interpreter. To use the CLI (command line interface) you open a terminal window or use a virtual terminal (see Chapter 6). When you see the shell prompt, you enter a command. The shell processes your command and then displays another prompt. As you work in this way, the shell is your user interface, and we say that you are using an INTERACTIVE SHELL.

Alternatively, you can create a set of commands, called a SHELL SCRIPT, which you save in a file. When you run your script, the shell reads the commands from the file and processes them one at a time without your input. When this happens, we say that you are using a NON-INTERACTIVE SHELL.

It is important to understand that, in each case, you are using the same type of shell. This is possible because shells are designed to work either interactively or non-interactively.

When you log in, a shell is started on your behalf and set to be interactive. Similarly, when you manually start a new shell from the command line (say, by typing **bash** or **tcsh**), the new shell is also set to be interactive.

On the other hand, when you run a shell script, a new shell is started automatically and given the task of interpreting your script. This new shell is set to be non-interactive. Once the job is done — that is, when the script is finished — the non-interactive shell is terminated.

So how does a shell know if it should be interactive or non-interactive? It depends on the options it is given when it starts. We will discuss shell options later in the chapter.

WHAT'S IN A NAME?

Shell

In everyday life, we use the word "shell" in two different ways, which can be confusing. We can talk about the idea of the shell in general, or we can refer to an instance of a shell that is running.

For example, you are a young man who is invited to a sorority party where there are a lot of cheerleaders. Someone introduces you to the prettiest girl in the room and to break the ice you ask her, "What shell do you use?" After talking to you for a few minutes she says, "Football players bore me. I like a man who understands the shell. Why don't you come over to my place and help me fine tune my kernel?" In this example, you and the girl are talking about the shell in general.

The next day, you are sitting in a lecture in your Unix class and the professor says, "...After you log in, a shell is started to act as your user interface. If you type the **bash** command, a new shell is started. When you run a shell script, another shell is started..." In this case, the professor is not talking about the shell as a general concept. He is talking about actual shells that are running.

To make sure that you understand the distinction, see if the following sentence makes sense to you: "Once you learn how to use the shell, you can start a new shell whenever you want."

THE ENVIRONMENT, PROCESSES AND VARIABLES

In Chapter 6, during the discussion of multitasking, I introduced the idea that, within a Unix system, every object is represented by either a file or a process. In simple terms, files hold data or allow access to resources; processes are programs that are executing. Thus, a shell that is running is a process. Similarly, any program that is started from within the shell is also a process.

As a process runs, it has access to what is called the ENVIRONMENT, a table of variables, each of which is used to hold information. To make sense out of this idea, we need to start with a basic question: What are variables and what can we do with them?

Let's start with a definition. A VARIABLE is an entity used to store data. Every variable has a name and a value. The NAME is an identifier we use to refer to that variable; the VALUE is the data that is stored within the variable.

Here is an example. As we discussed in Chapter 7, Unix uses a variable named **TERM** to store the name of the type of terminal you are using. The idea is that any program that needs to know your terminal type can simply look at the value of **TERM**. The most common values for **TERM** are **xterm**, **linux**, **vt100** and **ansi**.

When you name your own variables, you have a lot of leeway: there are only two simple rules. First, a variable name must consist of uppercase letters (**A-Z**), lowercase letters (**a-z**), numbers (**0-9**), or the underscore character (**_**). Second, a variable name must start with a letter or an underscore; it cannot begin with a number. Thus, the variable names **TERM**, **path** and **TIME_ZONE** are valid; the name **2HARLEY** is not.

When you use a Unix shell, there are two different types of variables. They are called "shell variables" and "environment variables", and we will talk about them throughout the chapter. As a general rule, there are only four different things you can do with variables. You can create them, check their value, change their value, or destroy them.

Informally, it can help to think of a variable as a small box. The name of the variable is on the box. The value of the variable is whatever is inside the box. For example, you might imagine a box named **TERM** that contains the word **xterm**. In this case, we say that the variable **TERM** has the value **xterm**.

With most programming languages, variables can contain a variety of different types of data: characters, strings, integers, floating-point numbers, arrays, sets, and so on. With the shell, however, variables almost always store only one type of data, a CHARACTER STRING, that is, a sequence of plain-text characters. For instance, in our example the **TERM** variable stores a string consisting of 5 characters: **x**, **t**, **e**, **r** and **m**.

When you create a variable, you will often give it a value at the same time, although you don't have to. If you don't, we say the variable has a NULL value, which means it has no value. This is like creating a box with a name, but not putting anything inside the box. If a variable has a null value, you can always give it a value later, should the need arise.

Now let's see how variables, the environment and processes fit together. Consider the following scenario. You are at a shell prompt and you start the **vi** text editor (Chapter 22). In technical terms, we say that one process, the shell, starts another process, **vi**. (We'll talk about the details in Chapter 26.)

When this happens, is called the PARENT PROCESS or PARENT; the second process is the CHILD PROCESS or CHILD. In this case, the parent is the shell and the child is **vi**.

At the time the child process is created, it is given an environment which is a copy of the parent's environment. We say that the child INHERITS the parent's environment. This means that all the ENVIRONMENT variables that were accessible to the parent are now accessible to the child.

For instance, in our example, when **vi** (the child) is created, it inherits the environment of the shell (its parent). In particular, **vi** is now able to examine the value of the **TERM** variable in order to discover what type of terminal you are using. This enables **vi** to format its output properly for your particular terminal.

ENVIRONMENT VARIABLES AND SHELL VARIABLES

If you are a programmer, you will understand the difference between global and local variables. In programming, a LOCAL VARIABLE exists only within the scope in which it was created. For example, let's say you are writing a program and you create a variable **count** to use only within a function named **calculate**. We would say that **count** is a local variable. More specifically, we would say that **count** is LOCAL to the function **calculate**. This means that, while **calculate** is running, the variable **count** exists. Once **calculate** stops running, the variable **count** ceases to exist.*

A GLOBAL VARIABLE, on the other hand, is available everywhere within a program. For example, let's say you are writing a program to perform statistical operations upon a long list of numbers. If you make the list a global variable, it is available to all parts of the program. This means, for example, that if one function or procedure makes a change to the list, other parts of the program will see that change.

The question arises: when you use a Unix shell, are there global and local variables similar to those used by programmers?

The answer is yes. All shells use global and local variables, and you need to know how they work. First, there are the environment variables we have already discussed. Since environment variables are available to all processes, they are global variables and, indeed, we often refer to them by that name.**

Second, there are SHELL VARIABLES that are used only within a particular shell and are not part of the environment. As such, they are not passed from parent to child and, for this reason, we call them local variables.

As a general rule, local (shell) variables are used in one of two ways. First, they may hold information that is meaningful to the shell itself. For example, within the C-Shell and Tcsh, the **ignoreeof** shell variable is used to control whether or not the shell should ignore the **eof** signal when you press **^D** (see Chapter 7).

Second, shell variables are used in shell scripts in the same way that local variables are used in ordinary programs: as temporary storage containers. Thus, when you write shell scripts, you create shell variables to use as temporary storage as the need arises.

So far, this is all straightforward. Shell variables are local to the shell in which they are created. Environment variables are global, because they are accessible to any process that uses the same environment.

In practice, however, there is a problem. This is because, when it comes to shells, the line between local and global variables is blurry. For that reason, I want to spend a few minutes explaining exactly how the shell handles variables. Moreover, there are significant differences between the Bourne and C-Shell families, so we'll have to talk about them separately. These

---

*In this chapter, we will be talking about simple variables that store only one value at a time. If you plan to write shell scripts, you should know that both Bash and the Korn shell allow you to also use one-dimensional arrays. (An array is a variable that contains a list of values.) For more details, see the Bash man page (look in the "Arrays" section) or the Korn shell man page (look in the "Parameters" section).

**In a strict programming sense, environment variables are not completely global, because changes made by a child process are not propagated back to the parent.

There is a good reason for this limitation. Allowing child processes to change environment variables for parent processes would be a massive source of confusion, bugs, and security holes.

concepts are so important, however, that I want you to make sure you understand how variables work with both families, regardless of which shell you happen to use right now.

Before I start, let me take a moment to explain how variables are named. There is a tradition with some programming languages that global variables are given uppercase names and local variables are given lowercase names. This tradition is used with the C-Shell family (C-Shell, Tcsh). Environment variables have uppercase names, such as **HARLEY**; shell variables have lowercase names, such as `harley`.

The Bourne shell family (Bash, Korn shell) is different: both shell variables and environment variables are traditionally given *uppercase* names. Why this is the case will become clear in a moment.

With most programming languages, a variable is either local or global. With the shell, there is a strange problem: some variables have meaning as both local *and* global variables. In other words, there are some variables that are useful to the shell itself (which means they should be shell variables), as well as to processes that are started by the shell (which means they should be environment variables).

The Bourne shell family handles this problem by mandating that every variable is either local only, or both local and global. There is no such thing as a purely global variable. For example, you might have two variables **A** and **B**, such that **A** is a shell variable, and **B** is both a shell variable and an environment variable. You cannot, however, have a variable that is only an environment variable. (Take a moment to think about this.)

So what happens when you create a variable? Within the Bourne shell family, you are only allowed to create local variables. That is, every new variable is automatically a shell variable. If you want a variable to also be an environment variable, you must use a special command called **export**. The **export** command changes a shell variable into a shell+environment variable. When you do this, we say that you EXPORT the variable to the environment.

Here is an example. (Don't worry about the details, we'll go over them later in chapter.) To start, we will create a variable named **HARLEY** and give it a value of `cool`:

`HARLEY=cool`

At this point, **HARLEY** is only a shell variable. If we start a new shell or run a command, the new processes will not be able to access **HARLEY** because it is not part of the environment. Let us now export **HARLEY** to the environment:

`export HARLEY`

HARLEY is now both a shell variable **and** an environment variable. If we start a new shell or run a command, they will be able to access **HARLEY**.

So now you see why the Bourne shell family uses only uppercase letters for both shell variables and environment variables. Using uppercase makes the name stand out and, because there is no such thing as a pure environment variable, there is no easy way to distinguish between local and global. (Take another moment to think this through.)

As you can see, the way in which the Bourne shell family handles variables is bewildering, especially to beginners. In fact, the system used by these shells dates back to the first Bourne shell, developed in 1976 by Steve Bourne at Bell Labs (see Chapter 11). Two years later, in

1978, when Bill Joy was developing the C-Shell at U.C. Berkeley (also see Chapter 11), he decided to improve how variables were organized. To do so, he created a much simpler system in which there is a clear distinction between environment variables and shell variables.

In the C-Shell family, environment variables are created by the **setenv** command (described later) and are given uppercase names, such as **TERM**. Shell variables are created by the **set** command (also described later) and are given lowercase names, such as **user**.* For practical purposes, that's all there is to it.

However, the simplicity of the C-Shell system leaves one nagging problem. As I mentioned, there are certain variables that have meaning both within the shell and within all the child processes. The Bourne shell family avoids this problem by letting you use variables that are both local and global. The C-Shell family does not allow this.

Instead, the C-Shell family recognizes a handful of special quantities that need to be both local and global. The solution is to have a few special shell variables that are tied to environment variables. Whenever one of these variables changes, the shell automatically updates the other one.

For example, there is a shell variable named **home** that corresponds to the environment variable named **HOME**. If you change **home**, the shell will make the same change to **HOME**. If you change **HOME**, the shell will change **home**.

Of all the dual-name variables, only five are important for everyday use (see Figure 12-1). The **TERM** and **USER** variables should make sense to you now. The **PATH** variable will be explained later in the chapter. **PWD** and **HOME** will make sense after we have discussed the Unix file system (Chapter 23) and directories (Chapter 24).

SHELL VARIABLE	ENVIRONMENT VARIABLE	MEANING
cwd	PWD	your current/working directory
home	HOME	your home directory
path	PATH	directories to search for programs
term	TERM	type of terminal you are using
user	USER	current userid

FIGURE 12-1: C-Shell family: Connected shell/environment variables

With the C-Shell family, a few shell variables are considered to be the same as corresponding environment variables. When one variable of the pair is changed, the shell automatically changes the other one. For example, when **home** *is changed, the shell automatically changes* **HOME**, *and vice versa. See text for details.*

---

*For a long time, it has been fashionable to disparage the C-Shell, especially when comparing it to modern Bourne shells, such as Bash. I talked about this cultural belief in Chapter 11, when we discussed the essay *Csh Programming Considered Harmful* by Tom Christiansen.

The Bourne shells, however, inherited a number of serious design flaws that, in order to maintain backwards compatibility, cannot be changed. Consider, for example, the confusing way in which the Bourne shells handle local and global variables. The C-Shell, though it has its faults, reflects the insights of Bill Joy, a brilliant programmer who, in his youth, had an amazing flair for designing high-quality tools.

When it comes to choosing your own personal shell, don't let people influence you unduly. The modern version of the C-Shell (the Tcsh) is an excellent tool that, for interactive use, can hold its own against Bash and the Korn shell. (Perhaps it's time for someone to write a new essay called *Don't Bash the C-Shell*.)

DISPLAYING ENVIRONMENT VARIABLES: env, printenv

Although it is possible to create your own environment variables and shell variables, you won't need to do so unless you write programs. Most of the time, you will use the default variables.

But what are the default variables? To display them, you use the **env** command:

```
env
```

On many systems, there is another command you can use as well, **printenv**:

```
printenv
```

When you use **env** or **printenv**, there may be so many environment variables that they scroll off the screen. If so, use **less** to display the output one page at a time:

```
env | less
printenv | less
```

When you display your environment variables, you will notice that they are not in alphabetical order. If you want to sort the output, use the **sort** command (see Chapter 19) as follows:

```
env | sort | less
printenv | sort | less
```

This construction is called a "pipeline". We will talk about it in Chapters 15 and 16.

For reference, Figure 12-2 shows the most important environment variables and what they mean. The actual variables you see on your computer will vary depending on which operating system and which shell you are using. However, you should have most of the variables in the table. Don't worry if you don't understand everything: by the time you learn enough to care about using an environment variable, you will understand its purpose.

SHELLS	VARIABLE	MEANING
B K • •	CDPATH	directories searched by the **cd** command
B K • T	COLUMNS	width (in characters) of your screen or window
B K C T	EDITOR	default text editor
B K • •	ENV	name of environment file
B K • •	FCEDIT	history list: editor for **fc** command to use
B K • •	HISTFILE	history list: name of file used to store command history
B K • •	HISTSIZE	history list: maximum number of lines to store
B K C T	HOME	your home directory
• • • T	HOST	name of your computer
B • • •	HOSTNAME	name of your computer
B • • T	HOSTTYPE	type of host computer
B • • •	IGNOREEOF	number of **eof** signals (**^D**) to ignore before ending shell
B K C T	LOGNAME	current userid
B • • T	MACHTYPE	description of system
B K C T	MAIL	file to check for new mail
B K C T	MAILCHECK	how often (in seconds) the shell checks for new mail
B K • •	MAILPAT	files to check for new mail
B K • •	OLDPWD	your previous working directory
B • • T	OSTYPE	description of operating system
B K C T	PAGER	default program for displaying data (should be **less**)
B K C T	PATH	directories to search for programs
B K • •	PS1	your shell prompt (customize by changing this variable)
B K • •	PS2	special shell prompt for continued lines
B K C T	PWD	your working [current] directory
B K • •	RANDOM	random number between 0 and 32,767
B K • •	SECONDS	time (in seconds) since the shell was invoked
B K C T	SHELL	pathname of your login shell
B K C T	TERM	type of terminal you are using
B K • •	TMOUT	if you don't type a command, seconds until auto-logout
• K C T	TZ	time zone information
B K C T	USER	current userid
B K C T	VISUAL	default text editor (overrides **EDITOR**)

FIGURE 12-2: The most important environment variables

By default, Unix systems use a large number of environment variables. What you will find on your system depends on which operating system and which shell you are using.

The leftmost column shows which shells support each variable: B = Bash; K = Korn Shell; C = C-Shell; T = Tcsh. A dot indicates that a shell does not support that option.

DISPLAYING SHELL VARIABLES: `set`

To display all the shell variables along with their values, you use the **set** command with no options or arguments:

`set`

This command is simple and will work for all shells. There is, however, an important point you need to remember.

With the C-Shell family, the shell variables you see will all have lowercase names. By definition, they are local variables.

With the Bourne shell family, the shell variables all have uppercase names. However, you can't tell if a particular variable is a local or global variable just by looking at its name. If it is a shell variable only, it is local; if it is a shell variable and an environment variable, it is both local and global. (Remember, in the Bourne shell family, there are no purely global variables.) This means that when you use **set** to list your variables, there is no easy way to know which ones have not been exported to the environment.

> **HINT**
>
> Strange but true: The only way to determine which Bourne shell variables are not exported is to compare the output of **set** to the output of **env**. If a variable is listed by **set** but not by **env**, it is a shell variable. If the variable is listed by **set** *and* by **env**, it is both a shell variable *and* an environment variable.

Obviously, this is confusing. However, it doesn't matter a lot because shell variables aren't used much with the Bourne shell family. To be sure, when you write shell scripts you will create local (shell) variables as you need them. But for day-to-day interactive work, it is the environment variables that are important, not the shell variables.

In the C-Shell family, things are different. There are a large number of shell variables, many of which are used to control the behavior of the shell. Earlier, I mentioned several of these variables: **cwd**, **home**, **term** and **user**. For reference, Figure 12-3 shows you these four, as well as the others I consider to be the most important. For a comprehensive list, see Appendix G. (In fact, you might want to take a moment right now to sneak a quick look at Appendix G, just to see how many shell variables the C-Shell family actually uses.)

This leaves us with one last question. If the C-Shell family uses shell variables to control the behavior of the shell, what does the Bourne shell family use? The answer is: an elaborate system called "shell options", which we will talk about later in the chapter. First, however, we need to cover a few more basic concepts related to using variables.

DISPLAYING AND USING THE VALUE OF A VARIABLE: `echo`, `print`

If you want to display the values of all your environment variables at once, you can use the **env** or **printenv** command. If you want to display all your shell variables, you can use **set**. There will be many times, however, when you want to display the value of a single variable. In such cases, you use the **echo** command.

The job of the **echo** command is to display the value of anything you give it. For example, if you enter:

`echo I love Unix`

SHELLS		SHELL VARIABLE	MEANING
•	T	autologout	if you don't type a command, time (in minutes) until auto-logout
C	T	cdpath	directories to be searched by **cd**, **chdir**, **popd**
•	T	color	cause **ls -F** command to use color
C	T	cwd	your working [current] directory (compare to **owd**)
C	T	filec	autocomplete: enable
C	T	history	history list: maximum number of lines to store
C	T	home	your home directory
C	T	ignoreeof	do not quit shell upon **eof** signal (**^D**)
•	T	implicitcd	typing directory name by itself means change to that directory
•	T	listjobs	job control: list all jobs whenever a job is suspended; **long** = long format
•	T	loginsh	set to indicate a login shell
C	T	mail	list of files to check for new email
C	T	noclobber	do not allow redirected output to replace a file
C	T	notify	job control: notify immediately when background jobs finished
•	T	owd	your most recent [old] working directory (compare to **cwd**)
C	T	path	directories to search for programs
C	T	prompt	your shell prompt (customize by changing this variable)
•	T	pushdsilent	directory stack: **pushd** and **popd** do not list directory stack
•	T	pushdtohome	directory stack: **pushd** without arguments assumes home directory
•	T	rmstar	force user to confirm before executing **rm *** (remove all files)
•	T	rprompt	special prompt for right side of screen (hint: set to **%~** or **%/**)
•	T	savedirs	directory stack: before logout, save directory stack
C	T	savehist	history list: before logout, save this number of lines
C	T	shell	pathname of your login shell C T **term** type of terminal you are using
C	T	user	current userid
C	T	verbose	debug: echo each command, after history substitution only
•	T	visiblebell	use a screen flash instead of an audible sound

FIGURE 12-3: C-Shell family: The most important shell variables

With the C-Shell family, there are a great many shell variables that are used by the shell for special purposes. Here are the ones I consider to be the most useful. A more comprehensive list can be found in Appendix G.

The leftmost column shows which shells support each option: C = C-Shell; T = Tcsh. A dot indicates that a shell does not support that option.

You will see:

I love Unix

(Which, by now, should be true.)

To display the value of a variable, you use a **$** (dollar sign) character followed by the name of the variable enclosed in brace brackets (usually referred to as braces). For example, to display the value of **TERM**, you would enter:

echo ${TERM}

Try it on your system and see what you get. If there is no ambiguity, you can leave out the braces.

echo $TERM

This will be the case most of the time, but I'll show you an example in a moment where you would need the braces.

When we talk about using variables in this way, we pronounce the **$** character as "dollar". Thus, you might hear someone say, "If you want to display the value of the **TERM** variable, use the command echo-dollar-term."

The notation **$**_NAME_ is important so I want you to remember it. When you type a variable name alone, it is just a name; when you type a **$** followed by a name (such as **$TERM**), it refers to the _value_ of the variable with that name. Thus, the **echo** command above means, "Display the value of the variable **TERM**."

Consider the following example, similar to the previous one but without the **$** character. In this case, the **echo** command will simply display the characters **TERM**, not the value of the **TERM** variable:

echo TERM

You can use **echo** to display variables and text in any way you want. For example, here is a more informative message about the type of your terminal:

echo The terminal type is $TERM

If your terminal type is, say, **xterm**, you will see:

The terminal type is xterm

Within the shell, some punctuation characters called "metacharacters" have special meanings (we'll discuss this in Chapter 13). To keep the shell from interpreting metacharacters, you enclose them in double quotes. This tells the shell to take the characters literally. For example, to display the value of **TERM** within angled brackets. You might try:

echo The terminal type is <$TERM>.

The **<** and **>** characters, however, are metacharacters used for "redirection" (see Chapter 15), and the command won't work. (Try it.) Instead, you need to use:

echo "The terminal type is <$TERM>."

HINT

When you use the **echo** command to display punctuation, use double quotes to tell the shell not to interpret the punctuation as metacharacters.

When you use the **echo** command, you have a lot of flexibility. For example, you can display more than one variable:

```
echo $HOME $TERM $PATH $SHELL
```

If you want to use a variable such that it is not separated from its neighbors, you must use braces to delimit it. For example, say that the variable **ACTIVITY** has the value **surf**. The command:

```
echo "My favorite sport is ${ACTIVITY}ing."
```

will display:

My favorite sport is surfing.

HINT

If you write shell scripts, you will find yourself using the **echo** command a lot. Take a moment to check out the man page (**man echo**), where you will find a variety of options and features you can use to control the format and content of the output.

HINT FOR KORN SHELL USERS

All shells let you use the **echo** command to display text and variables. With the Korn shell, you can also use the **print** command:

```
print "The terminal type is $TERM."
```

The developer of the Korn shell, David Korn, (see Chapter 11) created **print** to replace **echo**. He did this because the two main versions of Unix at the time, System V and BSD (see Chapter 2), used **echo** commands that had slightly different features. This meant that shell scripts that used **echo** were not always portable from one system to another.

To solve the problem, Korn designed **print** to work the same on all systems. This is not as much of an issue today as it was in Korn's day. Still, if you are writing a Korn shell script that you know will be run on more than one computer, it is prudent to use **print** instead of **echo**.

BOURNE SHELL FAMILY: USING VARIABLES: export, unset

With the Bourne shell family, it is easy to create a variable. All you do is type a name, followed by an **=** (equal sign) character, followed by a value. The value must be a string of characters. The syntax is:

NAME=value

As I mentioned earlier, a variable name can use letters, numbers or an underscore (_). However, a variable name cannot start with a number.

Here is an example you can try (use your own name if you want). Be careful not to put spaces around the equal sign:

```
HARLEY=cool
```

When you create a variable in this way, we say that you SET it. Thus, we can say that the previous example sets the variable **HARLEY** and gives it a value of **cool**.

If you want to use a value that contains whitespace (spaces or tabs; see Chapter 10), put the value in double quotes:

```
WEEDLY="a cool cat"
```

Once a variable exists, you can use the same syntax to change its value. For example, once you have created **HARLEY**, you can change its value from **cool** to **smart** by using:

```
HARLEY=smart
```

Within the Bourne shell family, every new variable is automatically a shell variable. (See the discussion earlier in the chapter.) To export a variable to the environment, you use the **export** command. Type **export** followed by the name of one or more variables. The following example exports **HARLEY** and **WEEDLY**:

```
export HARLEY WEEDLY
```

Both **HARLEY** and **WEEDLY** have now been changed from shell variables to shell+environment variables.

As we discussed in Chapter 10, you can enter multiple commands on the same line by separating them with a semicolon. Because it is common to create a variable and export it immediately, it makes sense to enter the two commands together, for example:

```
PAGER=less; export PAGER
```

This is faster than entering two separate commands and you will see this pattern used a lot, especially in Unix documentation and in shell scripts. However, there is an even better way. The **export** command actually lets you set a variable and export it at the same time. The syntax is:

```
export NAME[=value]...
```

Here is a simple example:

```
export PAGER=less
```

Look closely at the syntax. Notice that **export** allows you to specify one or more variable names, each of which may have a value. Thus, you can do a lot with one command:

```
export HARLEY WEEDLY LITTLENIPPER
export PAGER=less EDITOR=vi PATH="/usr/local/bin:/usr/bin:/bin"
```

HINT

As a rule, the very best Unix users tend to think fast. As such, they favor commands that are as easy to type as possible. For this reason, the preferred way to set and export a variable is with a single command:

export PAGER=less

Although many people use two commands to set and export a variable, using a single command to do a double job marks you as a person of intelligence and distinction.

As I mentioned, when you create a variable, we say that you set it. When you delete a variable, we say that you UNSET it. You will rarely have to unset a variable, but if the need arises, you can do so with the **unset** command. The syntax is simple:

unset *NAME...*

Here is an example:

unset HARLEY WEEDLY

HINT

Interestingly enough, within the Bourne shell family, there is no easy way to remove a variable from the environment. Once a variable is exported, the only way to un-export it is to unset it.

In other words, the only way to remove a Bourne shell variable from the environment is to destroy it.*

C-SHELL FAMILY: USING VARIABLES: `setenv`, `unsetenv`, `set`, `unset`

As we have discussed, the C-Shell family — unlike the Bourne shell family — has a clear separation between environment variables and shell variables. In other words, the C-Shell clearly distinguishes between global and local variables. For this reason, you will find that working with variables is easier with the C-Shell family than with the Bourne shell family.

To set (create) and unset (delete) environment variables, you use **setenv** and **unsetenv**. To set and unset shell variables, you use **set** and **unset**.

The syntax of the **setenv** command is as follows:

setenv *NAME* [*value*]

where *NAME* is the name of the variable; *value* is the value to which you want to set the variable. Notice we do not use an = (equal sign) character.

Here are some examples in which we create environment variables. If you want to experiment, remember that, once you have created environment variables, you can display them using the **env** or **printenv** commands.

---

*Riddle: How is a Bourne shell variable like the spotted owl?

```
setenv PATH /usr/local/bin:/usr/bin:/bin
setenv HARLEY cool
setenv WEEDLY "a cool cat"
setenv LITTLENIPPER
```

The first three commands set a variable and give it a specified value. In the third example, we use double quotes to contain whitespace (the two spaces). In the last example, we specify a variable name (**LITTLENIPPER**) without a value. This creates the variable with a null value. We do this when we care only that a variable exists, but we don't care about its value.

To unset an environment variable, you use the **unsetenv** command. The syntax is:

unsetenv *NAME*

where *NAME* is the name of the variable.

For example, to unset (delete) the variable **HARLEY**, you would use:

unsetenv HARLEY

To set a shell variable, you use a **set** command with the following syntax:

set *name*[=*value*]

where *name* is the name of a shell variable; *value* is the value to which you want to set the variable.

Here are several examples:

```
set term=vt100
set path=(/usr/bin /bin /usr/ucb)
set ignoreeof
```

The first example is straightforward. All we do is set the value of the shell variable **term** to **vt100**.

The second example illustrates an important point. When you are using variables with the C-Shell family, there are times when you enclose a set of character strings in parentheses, rather than double quotes. When you do so, it defines a set of strings that can be accessed individually. In this case the value of **path** is set to the three character strings within the parentheses.

In the last example, we specify a shell variable without a value. This gives the variable a null value. In this case, the fact that the variable **ignoreeof** exists tells the shell to ignore the **eof** signal. This requires us to use the **logout** command to end the shell. (See Chapter 7.)

Once a shell variable exists, you can delete it by using the **unset** command. The syntax is:

unset *variable*

where *variable* is the name of a variable.

As an example, if you want to tell the shell to turn off the **ignoreeof** feature, you would use:

```
unset ignoreeof
```

Make sure you understand the difference between setting a variable to null and deleting the variable. Consider the following three commands:

```
set harley=cool
set harley
unset harley
```

The first command creates a shell variable named **harley** and gives it a value of **cool**. The second command sets the value of **harley** to null. The final command deletes the variable completely.

SHELL OPTIONS: `set -o, set +o`

As we discussed earlier, with the C-Shell family, we control various aspects of the shell's behavior by using shell variables. With the Bourne shell family, we use SHELL OPTIONS. For instance, it is shell options that control whether a shell is interactive or non-interactive.

Shell options act like on/off switches. When you turn on an option, we say that you SET it. This tells the shell to act in a certain way. When you turn off an option, we say that you UNSET it. This tells the shell to stop acting in that way.

For example, the shell supports a facility called "job control" to let you run programs in the background. (We'll talk about this in Chapter 26.) To turn on job control, you set the **monitor** option. If you want to turn off job control, you unset the **monitor** option. By default, **monitor** is turned on for interactive shells.

> **HINT**
>
> The words "set" and "unset" have different meanings depending on whether we are talking about shell options or variables.
>
> Shell options are either off or on; they do not need to be created. Thus, when we set a shell option, we turn it on. When we unset an option, we turn it off.
>
> Variables are different. When we set a variable, we actually create it. When we unset a variable, we delete it permanently.

There are two ways in which shell options can be set or unset. First, at the time a shell is started, options can be specified in the usual manner, by specifying one or more options with the command (see Chapter 10). For example, the following command starts a Korn shell with the **monitor** option set (turned on):

```
ksh -m
```

In addition to the standard command-line options, there is another way to turn shell options on and off, using a variation of the **set** command. Here is the syntax. To set an option, use:

```
set -o option
```

To unset an option, you use:

```
set +o option
```

where *option* is the "long name" of an option (see Figure 12-4).

For example, say the shell is running and you want to set the monitor option. Use:

```
set -o monitor
```

To unset the **monitor** option, use:

```
set +o monitor
```

Be careful that you type **o**, the lowercase letter "o", not a zero. (Just remember, **o** stands for "option".)

At first, it will seem strange to use **-o** to turn an option on and **+o** to turn it off. However, I promise you, it will make sense eventually.*

Every time a shell starts, the various options are either set or unset by default, according to whether the shell is interactive or non-interactive. The programmers who designed the shell knew what they were doing and, in most cases, the shell options are just fine the way they are. This means that you will rarely have to change a shell option.

However, if you do, you can use Figure 12-4 for reference: it shows the shell options that are the most useful with interactive shells. As with the environment variables we discussed earlier, don't worry if you don't understand everything. This list is for reference. By the time you learn enough to care about using an option, you will understand its purpose.

Aside from what you see in Figure 12-4, there are many other shell options, most of which are useful with non-interactive shells (that is, when you are writing shell scripts). In addition, if you use Bash, there is a special command called **shopt** ("shell options") that gives you access to yet more options.

I have collected the full set of shell options, plus some hints about **shopt** in Appendix G. Although you don't need to understand all this material right now, I'd like you to take a moment to look at Appendix G, just so you know what's available.

HINT

For definitive information about shell options, see your shell man page:

```
man bash
man ksh
```

With Bash, search for "SHELL BUILTIN COMMANDS". With the Korn shell, search for "Built-in Commands" or "Special Commands".

---

*Here is the short explanation. As you know from Chapter 10, the standard form of an option is a − (hyphen) character followed by a single letter. It happens that most of the time when you modify shell options, you will want to set them — that is, turn them on — not unset them. For this reason, the common syntax (**-o**) is used for "set", and the less common syntax (**+o**) is used for "unset".

Over time, as you gain experience, this type of reasoning will start to make sense to you. As that happens, something changes in your brain and using Unix becomes much easier. (Unfortunately, this same change also makes it harder to meet cheerleaders at sorority parties.)

SHELLS	OPTION	LONG NAME	MEANING
B K	-a	`allexport`	export all subsequently defined variables and functions
B •	-B	`braceexpand`	enable brace expansion (generate patterns of characters)
B K	-E	`emacs`	command line editor: Emacs mode; turns off **vi** mode
B K	-h	`hashall`	hash (remember) locations of commands as they are found
B •	-H	`histexpand`	history list: enable **!**-style substitution
B •		`history`	history list: enable
B K	-I	`ignoreeof`	ignore **eof** signal ^D; use **exit** to quit shell (see Chapter 7)
• K		`markdirs`	when globbing, append **/** to directory names
B K	-m	`monitor`	job control: enable
B K	-C	`noclobber`	do not allow redirected output to replace a file
• K		`nolog`	history list: do not save function definitions
B K	-b	`notify`	job control: notify immediately when background job is finished
• K		`trackall`	aliases: substitute full pathnames for commands
B K	-V	`vi`	command line editor: **vi** mode; turns off Emacs mode
• K		`viraw`	in **vi** mode: process each character as it is typed

FIGURE 12-4: Bourne Shell family: Summary of options for interactive shells

This table summarizes the shell options that are useful with an interactive shell. For more information, see the man page for your particular shell.

The leftmost column shows which shells support each option: B = Bash; K = Korn Shell. A dot indicates that a shell does not support that option. Notice that some options, such as **history***, have a long name but not a short option name.*

Notes: (1) Although Bash supports the **emacs** *and* **vi** *options, it does not use* **-E** *and* **-V***. (2) The Korn shell uses -h, but does not support the long name* **hashall***.*

DISPLAYING SHELL OPTIONS

The Bourne shell family uses shell options to control the operation of the shell. To display the current value of your shell options, use either **set -o** or **set +o** by themselves:

```
set -o
set +o
```

Using **set -o** displays the current state of all the options in a way that is easy to read. Using **set +o** displays the same information in a compact format that is suitable for using as data to a shell script or a program.

If the output is too long for your screen, send it to **less**, which will display it one screenful at a time:

```
set -o | less
set +o | less
```

If you would like to practice setting and unsetting options, try doing so with the **ignoreeof** option. As we discussed in Chapter 7, you can terminate a shell by pressing **^D** (the **eof** key). However, if the shell happens to be your login shell, you will be logged out.

Unfortunately, it is all too easy to press **^D** by accident and log yourself out unexpectedly. To guard against this you can set the **ignoreeof** option. This tells the shell not to end a shell when you press **^D**. Instead, you must enter **exit** or **logout**. To set this option, use the following command:

```
set -o ignoreeof
```

To unset the option, use:

```
set +o ignoreeof
```

Try experimenting by setting, unsetting and displaying the options. Each time you make a change, display the current state of the options, then press **^D** and see what happens.

HINT

Unless you are an advanced user, the only options you need to concern yourself with are **ignoreeof**, **monitor** and **noclobber**, and either **emacs** or **vi**.

The **monitor** option enables job control, which I discuss in Chapter 26. The **noclobber** option prevents you from accidentally removing a file when you redirect the standard output (see Chapter 15). The **emacs** and **vi** options are used to specify which built-in editor you want to use to recall and edit previous commands. This is explained later in the chapter.

These options are best set from within your environment file, an initialization file that is executed automatically each time a new shell is started. We will discuss this file in Chapter 14.

WHAT'S IN A NAME?

set

You will notice that, in just this one chapter, we have used the **set** command in several different ways, each with its own syntax. We have used **set** to display shell variables, to create shell variables, to turn shell options on and off, and to display shell options.

If you take a careful look, you can see that we are actually dealing with four different commands that happen to have the same name. Apparently, there is something about the name **set** that makes programmers want to use it a lot.

This is not as odd as it sounds. Did you know that, in English, the word "set" has more distinct meanings than any other word in the language? Check with a dictionary. I promise you will be amazed.

MACHINE-READABLE, HUMAN-READABLE

When a program displays complex output in a way that it can be used as data for another program, we say that the output is MACHINE-READABLE. Although this term conjures up the image of a robot reading like a person, all it means is that the output is formatted in a way that is suitable for a program to process. For example, you might have a table of census data formatted as lists of numbers separated by commas, instead of organized into columns. Although this would be awkward for you or me to read, it would be suitable input for a program.

When output is designed to be particularly easy to read, we sometimes say that it is HUMAN-READABLE. This term is not used much, but you will encounter it within the man pages for the GNU utilities which, as we discussed in Chapter 2, are used with many types of Unix, including Linux. In fact, many commands have options that are designed specifically to produce human-readable output.

As an example, in the previous section, I mentioned that the **set -o** command displays output in a way that is easy to read, while **set +o** displays output suitable for using as data for a shell script. Another way to say this is that **set -o** produces human-readable output, while **set +o** produces machine-readable output.

Of course, not everyone is the same. Just because something is supposed to be human-readable, doesn't mean you personally will like it better than the machine-readable counterpart. For example, I happen to like the output of **set +o** better than the output of **set -o**.*

CHAPTER 12 EXERCISES

REVIEW QUESTIONS

1. What is the difference between an interactive shell and a non-interactive shell?

2. The environment is a table of variables available to the shell and to any program started by that shell. What type of variables are stored within the environment? Give three examples. What type of variables are not part of the environment?

3. With the Bourne shell family (Bash, Korn shell), what command do you use to make a shell variable part of the environment?

4. How do you display the values of all your environment variables? Your shell variables? A single variable?

5. Explain the terms "machine-readable" and "human-readable".

APPLYING YOUR KNOWLEDGE

1. The environment variable **USER** contains the name of the current userid. Show three different ways to display the value of this variable.

---

*But then, I also like putting peanut butter on avocado.

2. Create an environment variable named **SPORT** and give it the value "surfing". Display the value of the variable. Start a new shell. Display the variable again to show that it was passed to the new shell as part of the environment. Change the value of **SPORT** to "running", and display the new value. Now quit the shell and return to the original shell. Display the value of **SPORT**. What do you see and why?

3. Within the Bourne shell family (Bash, Korn shell), the **ignoreeof** option tells the shell not to log you out when you press **^D** (the **eof** key). Start either Bash or a Korn shell. Check if **ignoreeof** is turned on or off. If it is off, turn it on. Press **^D** to confirm that you do not log out. Then turn **ignoreeof** off. Press **^D** again to confirm that you do indeed log out.

FOR FURTHER THOUGHT

1. Environment variables are not true global variables, because changes made by a child process are not propagated back to the parent. Supposing this was not the case. Show how a hacker might use this loophole to cause trouble on a multiuser system on which he has an account.

2. The C-Shell family has a clear separation between environment variables and shell variables. The Bourne shell family is not so clear, because a newly created variable is, by default, a shell variable. If it is exported, it becomes both a local and an environment variable. What are the advantages and disadvantages of each system? Which system do you think is better, and why? Why do you think the Bourne shell family has such a confusing way of dealing with variables?

# CHAPTER 13

USING THE SHELL: COMMANDS AND CUSTOMIZATION

In Chapter 11, we discussed the shell in general. In Chapter 12 we built on that foundation and discussed interactive shells, processes, environment variables, shell variables, and shell options. In this chapter, we will cover the rest of the fundamental concepts.

The time you spend reading this chapter will repay you well for two reasons. First, the ideas we are going to cover are crucial to using the shell well. Second, as you begin to integrate your knowledge of the shell, you will find that the skills you are about to learn will save you a lot of time in your day-to-day work.

METACHARACTERS

Using your keyboard, you can type letters, numbers, and a variety of other characters, such as punctuation and arithmetic symbols. In addition, you can use the <Space>, <Tab> and <Return> keys to generate the space, tab and newline characters (see Chapter 7).

Collectively, we refer to the letters and numbers as the ALPHANUMERIC characters. Using alphanumeric characters is straightforward: you type what you want, and what you see is what you get. However, when you use the shell, many of the other symbols have special meanings. We call such characters METACHARACTERS, and you need to be aware of how they work.

For example, as we discussed in Chapter 10, you can enter multiple commands on the same line by separating them with a semicolon. Because it has a special meaning to the shell, the semicolon is a metacharacter.

In a more abstract way, when you press <Space>, <Tab> or <Return>, you also are using metacharacters. The space and tab characters are used as whitespace to separate the various parts of a command (Chapter 10), while the newline character is used to mark the end of a line (Chapter 7).

If you try to memorize the purpose of all the metacharacters right now, it will be difficult because what you are memorizing won't make sense. Since each metacharacter is used to implement a particular service offered by the shell, it makes sense to learn about a metacharacter as you learn about the service it provides.

For example, I explained earlier that the **$** (dollar) character is used when you want to refer to the value of a variable (such as **$TERM**). As such, **$** is a metacharacter. But how

CHARACTER	ENGLISH NAME	UNIX NICKNAME
&	ampersand	—
'	apostrophe	quote, single quote
*	asterisk	star
@	at sign	at
`	backquote	backtick
\	backslash	—
{ }	brace brackets	braces, curly brackets
^	circumflex	carat
:	colon	—
,	comma	—
$	dollar sign	dollar
<Return>	enter, return	newline
=	equal sign	equals
!	exclamation mark	bang
>	greater-than sign	greater-than
–	hyphen, minus sign	dash, minus (see Hint)
<	less-than sign	less-than
#	number sign	hash, pound (see Hint)
( )	parentheses	—
%	percent sign	percent
.	period	dot
+	plus sign	plus
?	question mark	—
"	quotation mark	double quote
;	semicolon	—
/	slash	forward slash
<Space>	space	—
[ ]	square brackets	brackets
<Tab>	tab	—
~	tilde	—
_	underscore	—
		vertical bar	pipe

FIGURE 13-1: Non-alphanumeric characters used with Unix

*Here are all the non-alphanumeric characters we use with Unix. As part of the Unix tradition, most of the characters have nicknames that we use when we talk. For example, the exclamation mark is called a "bang"; **$TERM** is pronounced "dollar term"; and so on. If you want to sound like a Unix pro, use the nicknames.*

much sense would it have made to you if, when I told you that, you didn't yet understand about variables?

I am going to give you a list of all the metacharacters, but I don't expect you to understand them all now. You will learn about them later, one by one. For now, I just want to make sure that you recognize them when you see them, so you don't accidentally use them the wrong way.

For example, if you were to enter the following command, the shell would see the semicolon and interpret what you typed as two commands:

```
echo The search path is $PATH; the shell is $SHELL.
```

However, if you recognize that the semicolon is a metacharacter, you can tell the shell to leave it alone:

```
echo "The search path is $PATH; the shell is $SHELL."
```

When we protect metacharacters in this way, we say that we "quote" them.

We'll talk about quoting in a moment. Before we do, however, I'd like to introduce you to the full cast of metacharacters. To start, take a look at Figure 13-1. This shows all the non-alphanumeric characters that we use with Unix, not all of which are metacharacters. Then look at Figure 13-2, where you will see the metacharacters along with a short description of how they are used. For reference, I have included the chapter number in which we discuss each particular metacharacter.

Within Figure 13-2, you will notice that several of the metacharacters are used for filename expansion, which is also known as "globbing". Globbing has a whole set of rules for using metacharacters, and we will discuss it in detail in Chapter 24.

HINT

Two of the non-alphanumeric characters in Figure 13-1 have different names depending on how long ago you started to use Unix. This is because traditions changed in the mid-1990s as Linux began to be popular.

Hyphen(-): Young people call the hyphen "dash"; old people call it "minus".

Number sign(#): Young people call the number sign "hash"; old people call it "pound".

If you are a student, this is important when you are talking to professors who are over 30. Remember to say "minus" and "pound", and you will make an old person comfortable.

QUOTING AND ESCAPING

From time to time, you will want to use a metacharacter literally, with no special meaning. For example, you may want to use a semicolon as a semicolon, not as a command separator. Or you may want to use the | (vertical bar) but not have it act as a pipe*. In such cases, you must tell the shell to interpret the character literally. When you do so, we say that you QUOTE the character.

---

*As Freud once said, "Sometimes a vertical bar is just a vertical bar."

Chapter 13

There are three ways to quote characters: using a backslash, using a pair of single quotes, or using a pair of double quotes.

The most straightforward way to quote a metacharacter is to put a backslash (\) in front of it. This tells the shell to ignore any special meaning the character might have. For example:

```
echo It is warm and sunny\; come over and visit
```

In this example, we put a backslash in front of the ; (semicolon) character. If we hadn't, the shell would have interpreted the ; as a metacharacter, which would have led it to

CHARACTER	CHAPTER	NAME	PURPOSE
{ }	24	braces	brace expansion: generate a pattern of characters
|	15	pipe	command line: create a pipeline
<	15	less-than	command line: redirect input
>	15	greater-than	command line: redirect output
( )	15	parentheses	command line: run commands in a subshell
#	14	hash, pound	command line: start of comment, ignore rest of line
;	10	semicolon	command line: used to separate multiple commands
`	13	backquote	command line: command substitution
~	24	tilde	filename expansion: insert name of home directory
?	24	question mark	filename expansion: match any single character
[ ]	24	brackets	filename expansion: match from a set of characters
*	24	star	filename expansion: match zero or more characters
!	13	bang	history list: event marker
&	26	ampersand	job control: run command in background
\	12	backslash	quoting: escape the next character
'	12	quote, single quote	quoting: suppress all substitutions
"	12	double quote	quoting: suppress most substitutions
{ }	12	braces	variables: delimit a variable name
$	12	dollar	variables: substitute the value of a variable
<Return>	7	newline	whitespace: mark the end of a line
<Tab>	10	tab	whitespace: separate words within the command line
<Space>	10	space	whitespace: separate words within the command line

FIGURE 13-2: Metacharacters used with the shell

Many of the non-alphanumeric characters have a special meaning within the shell. These are the metacharacters. This table shows all the metacharacters, along with their Unix nicknames. Eventually, you will learn the exact rules for using each of the metacharacters. Note that braces are used in two different ways.

For reference, I have specified the chapter in which each particular metacharacter is discussed.

280 Harley Hahn's Guide to Unix and Linux

assume that you meant to type two separate commands, **echo** and **come**. Of course, this would produce an error.

HINT

When you want to quote a single character, be careful to use the backslash (\), not a regular slash (/). The regular slash has a completely different purpose. It is used within pathnames (see Chapter 23).

When you use a backslash to quote a single character, we call the backslash an "escape character". This is an important concept, so I want to spend a moment discussing it.

You may remember that, when we talked about runlevels in Chapter 6, we discussed the idea of a mode. Specifically, when a computer system, a program, or a device can be in one of several states, we use the term MODE to refer to a particular state. In Chapter 6, for example, I explained that your Unix or Linux system could boot in single-user mode or multiuser mode. Similarly, when we discuss the **vi** text editor in Chapter 22, you will see that, at any time, **vi**, is either in input mode or command mode.

When a program is in a specific mode and we do something to change to another mode, we say that we ESCAPE from one mode to another. When we change modes by pressing a particular key, we call it an ESCAPE CHARACTER*. When you are typing a command for the shell, the backslash is an escape character, because it tells the shell to change from one mode (pay attention to metacharacters) to another mode (don't pay attention to metacharacters). I want you to remember the idea of an escape character, because you will encounter it again and again, especially if you are a programmer.

Within Unix, the word "escape" is used in two ways. Most commonly, we talk about escaping from one mode to another. For example, when you use the **vi** text editor, you press the <Esc> key to escape from insert mode to command mode.

With the shell, we use the word "escape" a bit differently, as a synonym for quote. For example, consider this example:

```
echo It is warm and sunny\; come over and visit
```

We can say we are using a backslash to escape the semicolon. This is the same as saying we are using a backslash to quote the semicolon**.

If we had just the backslash to escape metacharacters, it would be enough, as we can use the backslash more than once in the same line. Consider the following command:

---

*Now you know why there is an <Esc> or <Escape> key on your keyboard. It was designed to be used by programs to change from one mode to another.

**To be precise, when we talk about escaping from one mode to another, we are using "escape" as an intransitive verb, that is, a verb that does not take an object. When we talk about escaping (quoting) a character, we are using "escape" as a transitive verb, a verb that takes an object.

Unless you went to school before the Beatles were popular, your English teacher may have forgotten to teach you grammar. If so, you won't know the difference between transitive and intransitive verbs, so here is another example to pique your interest.

When you say, "Feel the fabric and tell me if it is soft," you are using a transitive verb. The verb is "feel"; the object is "fabric".

When you say, "Do you feel lucky?", you are using an intransitive verb. The verb is "feel", and there is no object. (To be precise, "feel" is a copula verb, and "lucky" is a predicate adjective, acting as a subjective completion.)

Although you might find it hard to believe, stuff like this is important, especially if you want to be a writer.

```
echo It is warm (and sunny); come over & visit
```

This command won't work properly, because of all the metacharacters: **(**, **)**, **;** and **&**. To make the command work, we need to escape all four characters:

```
echo It is warm \(and sunny\)\; come over \& visit
```

We now have a valid command, one that will work just fine. However, it is much too hard to read. As an alternative, the shell allows us to use single quotes to quote a string of characters. Thus, instead of the example above, we can use:

```
echo 'It is warm (and sunny); come over & visit'
```

In this case, we have quoted everything between the single quotes. Of course, this includes all the characters, not just the metacharacters, but it doesn't hurt to quote alphanumeric characters. (Stop a moment, and think about why this should be the case.)

Thus, we have (so far) two ways to quote metacharacters: we can use a backslash to quote single characters or single quotes to quote a string of characters. If the need arises, you can combine both types of quoting in the same command:

```
echo It is warm '(and sunny);' come over \& visit
```

Most of the time, the backslash and single quotes will be all that you need. However, there will be situations when it will be more convenient to use a third type of quoting using double quotes. Here is an example.

From time to time, you may want to use the **$** character within a quoted string, usually to refer to the value of a variable. For example, the following command displays your userid and terminal type within angled brackets:

```
echo My userid is <$USER>; my terminal is <$TERM>
```

In this form, the command doesn't work, because the metacharacters **<**, **;** and **>** have a special meaning. (The **$** is okay; we want it to be a metacharacter.) The solution is to quote only those metacharacters we want to be taken literally:

```
echo My userid is \<$USER\>\; my terminal is \<$TERM\>
```

This works, but it is much too complicated. We could, of course, use single quotes instead of backslashes:

```
echo 'My userid is <$USER>; my terminal is <$TERM>'
```

This is easier to read, but it quotes *all* the metacharacters, including the **$**. This means that we will literally see **$USER** and **$TERM**, rather than the values of the variables. For situations like this, we use double quotes because all the **$** metacharacters retain their special meaning. For example:

```
echo "My userid is <$USER>; my terminal is <$TERM>"
```

Because we used double quotes, the **<**, **;** and **>** characters are all quoted, but the **$** is not. (Try it for yourself.)

Aside from **$**, double quotes also preserve the meaning of two other metacharacters, **** (backslash) and **`** (backquote). We'll talk about the backquote later. For now, all you have to know is that it has a special meaning that is preserved within double quotes, but not within single quotes.

To summarize:

- Use a backslash to quote a single character. (When you do this, we say that you *escape* that character.)

- Use single quotes to quote a string of characters.

- Use double quotes to quote a string of characters, but to keep the special meaning of **$** (dollar), **`** (backquote) or **** (backslash).

STRONG AND WEAK QUOTES

From the previous discussion, you can see that single quotes are more powerful than double quotes. For this reason, we sometimes refer to single quotes as STRONG QUOTES and double quotes as WEAK QUOTES. Here is an easy way to remember the names: single quotes are so strong, they only need a single symbol; double quotes are weaker, so they need a double symbol.

Actually, the backslash is the strongest quote of all (although we don't give it a special name). A backslash will quote *anything*, so if your single quotes ever fail you, try a backslash. For example, one day you may have to escape a single quote:

```
echo Don\'t let gravity get you down
```

The backslash is so powerful, it can even quote a newline character. (Take a moment to think about that.)

Let's say you type **\<Return>** at the end of a line. This generates **** followed by newline (see Chapter 7). The cursor will move to the next line but, since the newline character has lost its special meaning, it will not signal the end of a line. This means that whatever you type will be a continuation of the previous line.

Try this example, pressing <Return> at the end of each line:

```
echo This is a very, very long \
line that goes on and on for a \
very, very long time.
```

If you do it just right, you will type one long command, and you will see one long line of output.

Unlike the backslash, single and double quotes will **not** quote a newline. This being the case, what do you think happens if you press <Return> within a string that is quoted by a single or double quote? For example, say that you type the following:

```
echo 'This line ends without a second quote
```

When you press <Return> at the end of the line, the newline is not quoted, so it retains its special meaning: that is, it marks the end of the line. However, there is a problem because the single quote is unmatched.

If you are using the C-Shell or the Tcsh, you will get an error message telling you there is an unmatched ' character.

If you are using Bash or the Korn shell, the shell will simply wait for you to enter more input hoping that, eventually, you will type the second quote. (Bourne shells are more optimistic than C-Shells.) Once you type the second quote the shell will put everything together into one very long command with a newline in the middle.

As an exercise, type the following two lines, and see what your shell does:

```
echo 'This line ends without a matching quote
and here is the missing quote'
```

Can you explain what happened and why?

COMMANDS THAT ARE BUILT INTO THE SHELL: `type`

When you enter a command, the shell breaks the command line into parts that it analyzes. We say that the shell PARSES the command. The first part of each command is the name; the other parts are options or arguments (see Chapter 10).

After parsing the command, the shell decides what to do with it. There are two possibilities. Some commands are internal to the shell, which means the shell interprets them directly. These are the INTERNAL COMMANDS, often called BUILTIN COMMANDS or, more simply, BUILTINS. All the other commands are EXTERNAL COMMANDS, separate programs that must be run on their own.

When you enter a builtin command, the shell simply runs the command itself, within its own process. When you enter an external command, the shell searches for the appropriate program and then runs it in a separate process. As an analogy, let's say you call the customer service line for a large company. If the person who takes your call can answer your question, he does so himself (an internal command). Otherwise, he transfers you to the appropriate person (an external command).*

There are two ways to find out if a command is built into the shell. First, you can try to display a man page for the command. External commands have their own man page; builtins do not. Builtin commands are documented either within the man page for the shell, or on a special man page for all the builtin commands.

A faster way to check if a command is a builtin is to use the **type** command. The syntax is:

type *command...*

---

*To be a bit more precise, here is how an external command is handled. The shell forks to create a child process and then waits. The child process execs to run the actual program. When the program is done, the child process dies. Control then returns to the parent, which causes the child to vanish. The parent then displays a shell prompt, inviting you to enter another command. (For more details, see the discussion about processes in Chapter 12.)

For instance:

```
type date time set
```

The exact output depends on which shell you are using. For example, here is what I saw when I used this command with Bash:

```
date is /bin/date
time is a shell keyword
set is a shell builtin
```

Here is what I saw with the Korn shell, Tcsh and C-Shell:

```
date is a tracked alias for /bin/date
time is a reserved shell keyword
set is a special builtin
```

Although the output differs a bit, the results are the same: **date** is an external command; the others are builtins.

At this point, it is not important to understand what is meant by a "tracked alias". It is a technical distinction you can ignore. Similarly, we do not need to distinguish between builtins and keywords: they are both built into the shell. (Keywords are special internal commands used for writing shell scripts.) The important thing is to realize that **date** is an external command residing in its own file (**/bin/date** on one system, **/usr/bin/date** on the other).

Unix and Linux systems come with literally hundreds of external commands, but how many builtins are there? That depends on the shell you are using. As an interesting reference, Figure 13-3 shows the number of builtin commands for the shells we discussed in Chapter 11.

SHELL	BUILTIN COMMANDS
Bourne Shell	18
Korn Shell	47
C-Shell	55
Bash	69
Tcsh	87
FreeBSD Shell	97
Zsh	129

FIGURE 13-3: Number of builtin commands for various shells

There are hundreds of different Unix commands, most of which are external; that is, they exist as separate programs. Each shell, however, has a certain number of internal commands, the builtins, that it can run directly. The table in this figure shows the number of builtin commands, including keywords, for each shell. As an interesting comparison, I have also included the old version of the Bourne Shell as used by the early Unix users at Bell Labs.

LEARNING ABOUT BUILTIN COMMANDS

Part of the Unix tradition is that when someone creates a tool, he should document that tool for other users. Specifically, it is expected that, when a programmer writes a new command, he will furnish a man page for that command. Because the format of the online manual is well-established (see Chapter 9), it is not hard for a programmer to create a man page once the programming is done. In fact, virtually all Unix programs are distributed with a man page that acts as the official documentation.

This system works fine when it comes to external commands. Because each external command is a program in its own right, it comes with its own man page. But what about the builtin commands? As we discussed, builtins are not separate programs; they are part of the shell. Since there are so many builtin commands (see Figure 13-3), it is unrealistic to expect the programmers who work on the shell to create a separate man page for every builtin.

Instead, all the builtin commands are documented within the man page for the shell. For example, the Korn shell builtins are documented in the Korn shell man page. Thus, for information about the builtins for a particular shell, you need to look at the appropriate man page. You can use one of the following commands:

```
man bash
man ksh
man tcsh
man csh
```

Bear in mind, however, that man pages for shells are quite long, and you may have to search a bit to find what you want.

Some Unix/Linux systems have a separate man page for builtin commands. To see if this is the case on your system, you can use the **apropos** command (see Chapter 9):

```
apropos builtin
```

If your system has such a page, that is the place to look for a quick list of all the builtins. For Linux and FreeBSD, you can use:

```
man builtin
```

For Solaris, use:

```
man shell_builtins
```

Linux also has a **help** command you can use to display information from the **builtin** man page in several ways. The syntax is:

```
help [-s] [command...]
```

where *command* is the name of a command.

To start, you can display a one-line summary of all the builtin commands by entering **help** by itself. If the output is too long, you can send it to **less** (Chapter 21) to display the information one screenful at a time:

```
help
help | less
```

This is the command to use when you want to display a compact list of all the builtins, for example, when you are looking for a particular command.

You can also use **help** to display information about one or more specific commands, for example:

```
help set
help pwd history kill
help help
```

(As you can see, **help** itself is a builtin command.)

Finally, if you only want to take a look at the syntax for a command, you can use the **-s** (syntax) option:

```
help -s help
help -s pwd history kill
```

HINT

When you write a shell script, you use special builtin commands — **for**, **if**, **while**, and so on — to control the flow of your script. These commands are sometimes called KEYWORDS.

As you are working on a Bash script, the fastest way to check the syntax of a keyword is by using the **help** command. For example, to check syntax for all the Bash keywords, use:

```
help -s case for function if select time while until
```

If you need more information, leave out the **-s** option:

```
help case for function if select time while until | less
```

Notice that I have used **less** to make sure the output doesn't scroll off the screen.

EXTERNAL COMMANDS AND THE SEARCH PATH

If a command is not built into the shell — and most commands are not — the shell must find the appropriate program to execute. For example, when you enter the **date** command, the shell must find the **date** program and run it for you. Thus, **date** is an example of an external command.

How does the shell know where to look for external commands? It checks the **PATH** environment variable (see Chapter 12). As with all variables, **PATH** contains a string of characters, in this case a series of directory names, which we call the SEARCH PATH.

We won't discuss directories in detail until Chapter 24. For now, all I want you to know is that programs are stored in files, and every file resides in a directory*. The search path is the list of directories that contain the programs for all the external commands. Thus, one of the directories in the search path will contain the file that holds the **date** program.

If you would like to see your search path, just display the value of the **PATH** variable:

```
echo $PATH
```

Here is some typical output:

```
/bin:/usr/bin:/usr/ucb:/usr/local/bin:/home/harley/bin
```

In this case, the search path consists of five directories:

```
/bin
/usr/bin
/usr/ucb
/usr/local/bin
/home/harley/bin
```

Your search path may be a bit different from this example but, for the most part, Unix systems tend to use standard names for the directories that hold external commands. For example, every Unix system I have ever seen has had a **/bin** and a **/usr/bin** directory, and many have **/usr/ucb**.

The names will make more sense after we discuss directories in Chapter 24. For now, I'll just mention the name **bin** is used to indicate that a directory holds programs.

In our example, the first three directories — **/bin**, **/usr/bin** and **/usr/ucb** — hold programs that are used by all the users on the system. The first two directories are found on all Unix systems and are set up automatically when Unix is installed. The **/usr/ucb** directory is found on some systems. Its job is to hold programs derived from Berkeley Unix (see Chapter 2). (The name **ucb** is an abbreviation for University of California at Berkeley.)

The next two directories are for customization: **/usr/local/bin** is set up by the system manager to hold programs that he or she has installed specifically for local use; **/home/harley/bin** refers to a directory named **bin** within the home directory of userid **harley**. You can make such a directory for yourself, and use it to hold your own programs.

When the shell needs to find an external command, it checks each directory in the search path in the order they are specified. In our example, the shell would start by looking in **/bin**. If it couldn't find what it wanted, it would then look in **/usr/bin**, and so on down the line.

When the shell finds the external command, it stops the search and executes the program. If none of the directories contains the command, the shell will give up and

---

*To relate this to your experience, you can think of a Unix directory as being similar to a Windows or Macintosh folder. There are, however, subtle, but important, differences.

display an error message. For example, if you enter the command **weedly**, you will see a message similar to:

```
weedly: command not found
```

MODIFYING YOUR SEARCH PATH

On most systems, you don't have to define the search path yourself, because the **PATH** variable is set for you. However, in certain circumstances, which we will discuss in a moment, you may want to modify the search path, so I'm going to show you how to do so. The basic idea is to put the command that modifies the **PATH** variable in an initialization file that is executed automatically whenever you log in. (We'll talk about initialization files in Chapter 14.)

To start, let's talk about how to set the **PATH** variable to a particular value. We'll deal with the Bourne shell family separately from the C-Shell family, because the commands are a bit different.

With the Bourne shell family (Bash, Korn shell), you set **PATH** by using the export command (Chapter 12). Using **export** makes **PATH** an environment variable, which means it is available to the shell and all subsequent processes. Here is a typical command that will do the job:

```
export PATH="/bin:/usr/bin:/usr/ucb:/usr/local/bin"
```

The command itself is straightforward: it sets the value of **PATH** to a character string consisting of a list of several directory names. As you can see, the names are separated by colons, and there are no spaces on either side of the equal sign.

To set the value of **PATH** yourself, you put this command (or one like it) in your "login file", an initialization file that is executed automatically each time you log in. To make a change to the search path, you simply modify the login file. (All of this is explained in Chapter 14.)

With the C-Shell family (C-Shell, Tcsh), we use a somewhat different command, because we set the **path** shell variable rather than the **PATH** environment variable:

```
set path=(/bin /usr/bin /usr/ucb /usr/local/bin)
```

As you may remember from Chapter 12, whenever you change **path**, the shell resets **PATH** automatically. Thus, this command results in the same setting for **PATH** as did the earlier Bourne shell command.

Notice, however, the difference in syntax. In the Bourne shell command, we set the value of an environment variable (**PATH**) to a long string of characters. In the C-Shell command, we set the value of a shell variable (**path**) to a list of names. In C-Shell syntax, a list consists of one or more elements, separated by spaces and enclosed in parentheses.

A moment ago, I mentioned that the Bourne shell command to set **PATH** would go in your login file. The C-Shell command to set **path** goes in your "environment file", a different initialization file that is executed automatically every time a new shell starts. (Again, this is all explained in Chapter 14, where you will find examples.)

On most systems, the command to define the **PATH** variable is already set up for you, so you don't have to use commands like the ones we have been discussing. However, you may want to modify the default search path for your own use. For example, if you write your own shell scripts and programs, which you keep in your own personal **bin** directory (**$HOME/bin**), you will want to add the name of this directory to your search path.

Here are two commands to show you how to do it. The first command is for the Bourne shell family; the second is for the C-Shell family.

```
export PATH="$PATH:$HOME/bin"
set path = ($path $HOME/bin)
```

Take note of the syntax. It means "Change the value of the search path to be the old value followed by **$HOME/bin**." In other words, we append the name **$HOME/bin** to the end of the existing search path.

Alternatively, you may want to insert the new directory name at the beginning of the search path. The commands are:

```
export PATH="$HOME/bin:$PATH"
set path = ($HOME/bin $path)
```

As these examples show, it is possible to modify a variable based on its current value. This is an important idea, so don't just memorize the pattern. Take a moment to make sure you understand exactly what is happening.

Now that you know how to add your own directory to a search path, the question arises: should you put a directory of your own at the beginning or at the end of the list? It all depends on what you want.

If you put your personal directory at the end of the search path, the shell will check your directory last. If you put your directory at the beginning of the search path, the shell will check it first. For example, say that you write a program named **date**, which you put in **$HOME/bin**. You now enter:

```
date
```

If you put your directory at the beginning of the search path, the shell will run your **date** program, not the standard version. In this way, you can effectively replace any external command with a program of your own. Alternatively, if you put your directory at the end of the search path, the shell will run the standard **date** program, not your version. This keeps you from inadvertently replacing a program with a file of the same name. It is up to you to choose what works best for you.

As a programmer, there is one more directory name you may also wish to add to your search path. If you specify a dot (.) character, it adds your "working directory" to the search path. (Your working directory is the one in which you are currently working. We'll talk about it in Chapter 24.)

Here is an example that will help you clarify the concept. The following commands add both **$HOME/bin** and your working directory to the end of the current path (in that order). The first command is for the Bourne shell family; the second is for the C-Shell family:

```
export PATH="$PATH:$HOME/bin:."
set path = ($path $HOME/bin .)
```

This tells the shell that — when it looks for a program — the last directory to check is the one in which you are currently working.

A detailed discussion of search paths is beyond the scope of this book (and not all that necessary). Normally, you can just accept the search path that is set up for you by default, possibly with minor changes.

> **HINT**
>
> Unless you are an expert, play it safe by putting your personal directories at the *end* of the search path.

HOW A HACKER CAN USE THE SEARCH PATH

It's fine to put the working directory (.) in your own search path, but never do so for the superuser (**root**) or for any other userid with special privileges. Doing so can create a security hazard. For example...

You are a system administrator and, for convenience, you have put the working directory at the beginning of the **root** search path. One of your users — who is really a hacker* — asks you for help, so you log in as **root** and change to the user's home directory (a common occurrence). You then enter the **ls** command to list the contents of the user's directory (also a common occurrence).

What you don't know is that the hacker has created an alternate version of **ls**, which he has placed in his home directory. The spurious **ls** acts like the real thing but — when run by **root** — it has the side effect of creating a secret file with special privileges. Later, the hacker can use that file, called a BACK DOOR, to gain superuser access for himself.

Here is how it happens: The moment you change to the user's home directory, it becomes your working directory. When you enter the **ls** command, the shell looks in the working directory, finds the hacker's version of **ls**, and runs it. The next thing you know, the hacker has taken over your system, and your life is exposed as a total sham.

Actually, this is an old hacker's trick: finding a way to run a doctored program as **root** to create a back door that can be used later. The moral of the story? Think carefully before you modify the search path for any userid that is used for system administration.

> **HINT**
>
> Make sure that the search paths used by all the system administration userids (including **root**) do not contain the working directory, or any other directory to which users might have access.

---

*Of course, I am referring to a bad hacker — that is, a cracker — not a good hacker. For a discussion of good and bad hackers, see Chapter 4.

THE SHELL PROMPT

As you know, the shell displays a prompt whenever it is ready for you to enter a command. Should you so desire, it is possible to change this prompt. In fact, there is wide latitude in how prompts can be displayed, and some people have developed elaborate prompts that display colors, as well as various types of information. Let's start simple, and then move on to more complex customizations.

Originally, all shells had a two-character prompt: a single character followed by a space. The Bourne shell used a **$** (dollar) character; the C-Shell used a **%** (percent) character. Today, the tradition is maintained. Thus, if you use a member of the Bourne shell family (Bash, Korn shell), the simplest shell prompt you will see is:

```
$ date
```

I have typed the **date** command after the prompt so you can see the space that follows the **$**. The space is part of the prompt.

If you use the C-Shell or the Tcsh, the simplest shell prompt looks like this:

```
% date
```

Although tradition dictates that the **%** character be used for the C-Shell family, many Tcsh users use a **>** (greater-than) character instead as a reminder that they are using an extended C-Shell:

```
> date
```

The final tradition concerns the superuser. When you are logged in as **root**, your prompt will always be a **#** (hash) character, regardless of which shell you are using. The intention is that you should always remember you are superuser, so you can be extra careful:

```
# date
```

Before we move on, take a look at Figure 13-4 in which the basic prompts are summarized. There are only a few conventions, and I want you to memorize what they mean so,

SHELL	PROMPT CHARACTER
Bash	$
Korn Shell	$
C-Shell	%
Tcsh	% or >
Superuser	#

FIGURE 13-4: Standard shell prompts

By convention, the standard shell prompt consists of a single character, followed by a space. The Bourne Shell family uses a $ (dollar) character; the C-Shell family uses a % (percent) character. The only exception is that the Tcsh sometimes uses a > (greater-than) character. When you are logged in as superuser, you will see a # (hash) character, regardless of what shell you are using.

whenever you see a shell prompt, you can answer two questions instantly: (1) Are you logged in as superuser? (2) If not, what type of shell are you using?

MODIFYING THE SHELL PROMPT

As I explained in the last section, it is possible to modify your shell prompt by changing the value of a variable. With the Bourne shell family, you change an environment variable named **PS1***. With the C-Shell family, you change a shell variable named **prompt**.

Let's start with a simple example. Here is a command, suitable for the Bourne shell family, that sets the prompt to a **$** (dollar) character followed by a space:

```
export PS1="$ "
```

Similarly, here is a command, suitable for the C-Shell family, that uses the standard **%** (percent) character:

```
set prompt = "% "
```

If you are a Tcsh user, you should use the customary **>** (greater-than) character instead:

```
set prompt = "> "
```

Before we move on, I want to make sure you understand these commands by reviewing the basic concepts we covered in Chapter 12.

There are two types of variables, global and local: the global variables are called "environment variables". The local variables are called "shell variables".

All Bourne shells store the value of their prompt in an environment variable named **PS1**. To change the value of an environment variable, you use **export**. Hence, the **export** command above. Please pay attention to the syntax. In particular, you must not put a space before or after the **=** (equal sign) character.

All C-Shells store the value of their prompt in a shell variable named **prompt**. Within a C-Shell, you use **set** to modify a shell variable. Hence, the two **set** commands.

At this point, you might be wondering, is it significant that the Bourne shells use an *environment* (global) variable to hold the prompt, while the C-Shells use a *shell* (local) variable? In general, it's not all that important, as long as you make sure to use the appropriate command (**export** or **set**) if you want to change your shell prompt. The distinction is important, however, when we talk about initialization files, which help us set the prompt automatically each time we log in. We'll get to that in Chapter 14.

To continue, so far we have made only simple changes to the shell prompt. However, by manipulating the appropriate variable, you can set your shell prompt to be whatever you want. For example, you might set the prompt to display a cute message:

---

* The name **PS1** means "prompt for the shell, number 1". There are three other such variables — **PS2**, **PS3** and **PS4** — but you won't ever need to change them, so don't worry about them. If you are curious about the details, see the man page for your shell.

```
export PS1="Enter a command please, Harley$ "
set prompt = "Enter a command please Harley% "
```

Actually, cute shell prompts lose their appeal fast. Here is something more useful: a prompt that shows you the name of the shell as a reminder. (Choose the command for your particular shell.)

```
export PS1="bash$ "
export PS1="ksh$ "
set prompt = "csh% "
set prompt = "tcsh> "
```

Here are the prompts that are generated by these commands:

bash$
ksh$
csh%
tcsh>

This type of prompt is particularly handy for the superuser. For example, say that your **root** userid uses Bash as a default shell. If you set the prompt as follows:

```
export PS1="bash# "
```

The prompt will be:

bash#

The **#** will remind you that you are superuser, and the name will remind you which shell you are using.

Aside from using words and characters, there are three other ways to enhance your shell prompt. You can:

- Insert the value of a variable into the prompt.

- Use an escape character to make use of a variety of special codes.

- Insert the results of a command into the prompt. (This is called command substitution.)

Each of these techniques is important in its own right, and has a usefulness that goes far beyond modifying a shell prompt. For this reason, I am going to discuss each idea separately so you can understand the general principles.

USING THE VALUE OF A VARIABLE

As we discussed in Chapter 12, to use the value of a variable, you type a **$** (dollar) character followed by the name of the variable enclosed in brace brackets. For example:

```
echo "My userid is ${USER}."
```

For convenience, you can omit the braces if they are not necessary to separate a variable name from other characters. For example:

```
echo "My userid is $USER."
```

Using the value of a variable within your shell prompt is straightforward. For example, to insert your userid into the prompt, you can use:

```
export PS1="${USER}$ "
set prompt = "${USER}% "
```

(The first command is for a Bourne shell; the second is for a C-Shell.)

If your userid were **harley** (which would be way cool), these commands would generate the following prompts:

```
harley$
harley%
```

Which environment variables might you want to use in a shell prompt? You can find a list of the most important environment variables in Figure 12-2 in Chapter 12. In principle, you can use any variables you want. However, most of them are not suitable to use in a shell prompt. To help you narrow down your choices, Figure 13-5 shows the variables I think are most useful or interesting for shell prompts. To experiment, just use one of the following commands, whichever works with your shell, substituting a variable from Figure 13-5.

```
export PS1="${VARIABLE}$ "
set prompt = "${VARIABLE}% "
```

Most people like to use either **LOGNAME**, **PWD**, **SHELL** or **USER**. However, to me, the most interesting variables to see over and over are **RANDOM** and **SECONDS**. However, they are available only with Bash and the Korn shell. If you want to experiment, here are the commands:

```
export PS1='Your lucky number is ${RANDOM} $ '
export PS1='Working time: ${SECONDS} seconds $ '
```

SHELLS	VARIABLE	MEANING
B K C T	HOME	your home directory
• • • T	HOST	name of your computer
B • • •	HOSTNAME	name of your computer
B • • T	HOSTTYPE	type of host computer
B K C T	LOGNAME	current userid
B K C T	PWD	your working [current] directory
B K • •	RANDOM	random number between 0 and 32,767
B K • •	SECONDS	time (in seconds) since current shell started
B K C T	SHELL	pathname of your login shell
B K C T	USER	current userid

FIGURE 13-5: Environment variables that are useful within a shell prompt

One way to enhance your shell prompt is to include the value of a variable that is either useful or interesting. Figure 12-2 in Chapter 12 contains a list of all the important environmental variables. This table shows you the ones that are suitable for a shell prompt.

The leftmost column shows which shells support each variable: B = Bash; K = Korn Shell; C = C-Shell; T = Tcsh. A dot indicates that a shell does not support that option.

WHICH QUOTES TO USE WHEN QUOTING VARIABLES

Take a careful look at two examples from the previous section:

```
export PS1='Your lucky number is ${RANDOM} $ '
export PS1="${USER}$ "
```

Did you notice that one command uses single quotes and the other uses double quotes? This difference illustrates a subtle, but important, point I want you to understand, especially if you want to write shell scripts.

The reason we use two different types of quotes is that, of the two variables in question, one of them changes and the other doesn't. To be precise, the value of **RANDOM** is a random number that is different every time you look at it. The value of **USER** is your userid, which is always the same.

We quote **${USER}** with double quotes to allow the **$** character to be interpreted as a metacharacter. This means that the value of **USER** is fixed at the moment the command is processed, which is fine because the value of **USER** never changes.

We quote **${RANDOM}** using single quotes, which enables us to preserve the meaning of the **$** character for later use. This technique ensures that the value of **RANDOM** is not evaluated until the actual prompt is created. In this way, when it comes time to display a new prompt, the shell uses whatever value **RANDOM** happens to have at that moment.

At this point, it may help to recall our discussion about strong and weak quoting from earlier in the chapter. To summarize:

- Single quotes (`'...'`), also known as strong quotes, quote everything. Within single quotes, no characters have special meanings.

- Double quotes (`"..."`), also known as weak quotes, quote everything except the three metacharacters **$** (dollar), ` ` ` (backquote) and **** (backslash). Within double quotes, these three characters retain their special meaning.

Thus, when you use `'${VARIABLE}'` within a command, all the characters are taken literally, and the meaning of **$** is preserved to be used later. When you use `"${VARIABLE}"`, the **$** is interpreted as a metacharacter and the entire expression is replaced *at that moment* with the value of **VARIABLE**.

So when you need to quote a variable, just ask yourself: "Will the value of the variable change before I use it?" If the answer is yes, use strong quotes (that is, single quotes) to keep the **$** characters from being interpreted until you need them. Otherwise, use weak quotes (double quotes) to allow the **$** characters to be interpreted right away.

SPECIAL CODES THAT USE AN ESCAPE CHARACTER

So far, I have explained that your shell prompt can contain any characters you want, as well as the value of one or more variables. In this section, we'll discuss how to enhance your prompt by using special codes.

Of the four shells we have been discussing, only Bash and the Tcsh allow you to use such codes. The codes allow you to insert various types of information into your prompt: the name of your working directory, your userid, the hostname of your computer, and so on. If you want to spend time being creative, you can even incorporate colors, underlining and boldface, although most people don't bother.

For reference, Figure 13-6 shows the most useful codes. The full list is documented on the man page for your particular shell. If you are very ambitious and you have extra time on your hands, you may want to learn how to use colors and other such effects in your prompt. If so, you'll find the help you need by searching the Web. (Hint: Using such codes is complicated, so don't worry if you don't understand it right away.)

You will notice that each of the Bash and Tcsh codes in Figure 13-6 consists of an escape character followed by another character. (As we discussed earlier in the chapter, an escape character tells the shell to change from one mode to another.) With Bash, the shell prompt escape character is **** (backslash); with the Tcsh, it is **%** (percent).

As I mentioned, only Bash and the Tcsh use special codes. However, with the other shells, there is still a need to place such information within the shell prompt. In a few cases, it can be done by using commands and variables. For completeness, this is shown in Figure 13-6. (Compare to Figure 13-5.) You will notice that some of these variables are used within an expression containing backquotes. This syntax is explained later, in the section on command substitution.

Most of the shell prompt codes are easy to understand. However I will mention that the codes for your working directory will make sense once you understand directories (Chapter 24), and the codes for history event numbers will make sense once you learn about using the history list (later in this chapter.)

MEANING	BASH	TCSH	KORN SHELL	C-SHELL
working directory: ~ notation	\w	%~	•	•
working directory: basename only	\W	•	•	•
working directory: full pathname	•	%/	$PWD	•
hostname of your computer	\h	%m	`hostname`	`hostname`
current userid	\u	%n	$LOGNAME	$LOGNAME
name of the shell	\s	•	`basename $SHELL`	`basename $SHELL`
time: AM/PM notation	\@	%@	•	•
time: 24-hour notation	\A	%T	•	•
date	\d	•	•	•
day of week	•	%d	•	•
day of month	•	%D	•	•
month	•	%w	•	•
year	•	%Y	•	•
history list: event number	\!	%!	!	!

FIGURE 13-6: Special codes, commands, and variables to use within shell prompts

Bash and the Tcsh allow you to use special codes to insert information into your shell prompt. The table shows the most useful codes. For a full list, see the Bash or Tcsh man page. A dot indicates that a shell does not support a particular function.

The Korn Shell and C-Shell do not support such codes. However, for completeness, the table shows several ways in which a few of the codes can be simulated by using variables.

To show you how it all works, here are a couple of examples. To insert your userid into a prompt, you would use **\u** for Bash and **%n** for the Tcsh. Thus, the following two Bash commands have the same effect:

```
export PS1="\u$ "
export PS1="${USER}$ "
```

If your userid were **harley**, your prompt would be:

```
harley$
```

Similarly, the following two Tcsh commands have the same effect:

```
set prompt = "%n> "
set prompt = "${USER}> "
```

The codes in Figure 13-6 are straightforward so, when you get time, feel free to experiment. If you like, you can use more than one code at a time. For example, to display the date and time in the Bash prompt, you use:

```
export PS1="\d \@$ "
```

In the Tcsh prompt, you use:

```
set prompt = "%d %w %D %@> "
```

COMMAND SUBSTITUTION

In this section we will talk about one of the most fascinating and powerful features offered by the shell: command substitution. COMMAND SUBSTITUTION allows you to embed one command within another. The shell first executes the embedded command and replaces it by its output. The shell then executes the overall command.

Obviously, we are dealing with a complex idea, so I'll start with a few examples. I'll then show you a practical application: how to use command substitution within a shell prompt to display useful information that would otherwise be unavailable as part of a prompt.

Let's begin with the basic syntax. You embed a command within another command by enclosing the first command in ` (backquote) characters. For example:

```
echo "The time and date are `date`."
```

In this example, the **date** command is enclosed by backquotes. This tells the shell to execute the overall command in two stages. First, evaluate the **date** command and *substitute* its output into the larger command. Then execute the larger command (in this case, **echo**).

Let's say it happens to be 10:30 am on Monday, December 21, 2008, and you are in the Pacific time zone. The output of the **date** command would be:

```
Mon Dec 21 10:30:00 PST 2008
```

During the first stage, the shell substitutes this value for **date**, changing the original command to:

```
echo "The time and date are Mon Dec 21 10:30:00 PST 2008."
```

During the second stage, the shell executes the modified **echo** command to produce the following output:

```
The time and date are Mon Dec 21 10:30:00 PST 2008.
```

Although I have broken down my explanation into two parts, it all happens so quickly that, to you, it will look as if the shell is displaying the final output instantly.

Here is another example. The environment variable **$SHELL** contains the pathname of your shell program. For example, say you are using Bash and you enter:

```
echo $SHELL
```

You will see the following output (or something similar):

```
/bin/bash
```

This means that your shell is the **bash** program, which resides in the **/bin** directory. (We will discuss directories and pathnames in Chapter 24.)

The full specification **/bin/bash** is called a pathname. In this case, however, we don't care about the entire pathname, just the last part (**bash**). To isolate the last part of any pathname, we use **basename**, a command whose purpose is to read a full pathname and output the last part of it. For example, the output of the following command is **bash**:

```
basename /bin/bash
```

More generally, to display the name of your shell program without the rest of the pathname, you can use:

```
basename $SHELL
```

Now consider how this might be used as part of the shell prompt using command substitution. Say you want to display the name of your shell as part of the prompt. All you need to do is insert the output of the **basename** command within the command that sets the prompt:

```
export PS1="`basename ${SHELL}`$ "
set prompt = "`basename ${SHELL}`% "
set prompt = "`basename ${SHELL}`> "
```

The first command is for Bash or the Korn shell; the second is for the C-Shell; the third is for the Tcsh.

As you can see, command substitution is used to create functionality that would otherwise not exist. For instance, in the last section, we discussed using special codes to insert information into your shell prompt. However, these codes are available only with Bash and the Tcsh. What about the other shells? The solution is to use command substitution.

For example, in Figure 13-6, you can see that the codes to insert the hostname (name of your computer) into the shell prompt are **\h** for Bash and **%m** for the Tcsh. With the other shells, we can use command substitution instead.

The basic approach is always the same. Start by asking the question: What command will do the first part of the job? Then figure out the best way to substitute the output of this command into another command that will do the second part of the job.

In this case, you would ask yourself: What command displays the name of your computer? The answer is **hostname** (see Chapter 8). More specifically, depending on your version of Unix or Linux, you may or may not need the **-s** option. See which variation works best on your system:

```
hostname
hostname -s
```

Now all you have to do is substitute the output of **hostname** into the command to set the prompt. (Leave out the **-s** if you don't need it.)

```
export PS1="`hostname -s`$ "
set prompt = "`hostname -s`% "
```

The first command will work with a Bourne shell (Bash, Korn shell); the second one will work with a C-Shell (C-Shell, Tcsh).

One last example. In the same way that Bash and the Tcsh have codes to display your hostname within a shell prompt, they also have codes to display your userid (\u and %n respectively). However, as you know, there are no codes for the other shells.

One solution is to use the $USER variable within the shell prompt, as we did earlier in the chapter. Alternatively, you can use command substitution with the **whoami** command (Chapter 8):

```
export PS1="`whoami`$ "
set prompt = "`whoami`% "
```

To conclude this section, let me remind you of something we discussed earlier. When you use single quotes (strong quotes), nothing between the two quotes retains a special meaning. When you use double quotes (weak quotes), three metacharacters do retain their special meaning: **$** (dollar), **`** (backquote) and **** (backslash). Now you understand why the backquote is included in this list.

> **HINT**
>
> The backquote character is used only for command substitution. Be careful not to confuse it with the single quote or double quote. In spite of its name and appearance, the backquote has nothing to do with quoting. This is probably why many Unix people use the name "backtick" instead of "backquote".

TYPING COMMANDS AND MAKING CHANGES

Once you have used Unix for a while, you will know how frustrating it is to have to type an entire command over because you need to make a tiny change. This is especially bothersome if you are prone to making spelling mistakes (as I am). As a convenience, the shell has several features that make it easy to enter commands: the history list, command line editing, autocompletion, and aliasing. We'll cover these features one at a time throughout the rest of the chapter. The details vary from one shell to another so, when you need help, remember that the man page for your particular shell is always the definitive reference.

As long as there have been shells, people have been arguing about which ones are best. In my opinion, you can talk all you want about this feature or that, but the shells that make it easy to type (and retype) commands get my vote. As a general rule, the best features are available only in Bash and the Tcsh, which is why knowledgeable users prefer to use one of these two shells.

To start, let me remind you of the ideas we discussed in Chapter 7, with respect to correcting mistakes and editing the command line. We will then move on to new material.

- To erase the last character you typed, you would press <Backspace>. This will send the **erase** signal. (With some computers, such as a Macintosh, you would use <Delete> instead of <Backspace>.)

- To erase the last word you typed, you would press **^W** (<Ctrl-W>) to send the **werase** signal.

- To erase the entire line, you would press **^X** or **^U** (depending on your system) to send the **kill** signal.

- To display all the key mappings on your system, you would use the **stty** command.

With most (but not all) shells, you can also use the <Left> and <Right> cursor control keys to move around the command line. For example, let's say you mean to enter the **date** command but, instead, you type:

dakte

Your cursor is at the end of the line. Just press <Left> twice to move two positions to the left. Then press <Backspace> to erase the **k**. You can now press <Return> to enter the command. Note that you can press <Return> from anywhere in the line. You do not need to be at the end of the line.

In addition to changing the current line, you can press <Up>, to recall a previous command, which you can then modify and reenter. You can press <Up> more than once to find old commands, and you can press <Down> to go back to more recent commands.

You can use <Left>, <Right>, <Up> and <Down> in this way with Bash and the Tcsh, but not with the Korn shell and C-Shell. With Bash, you get a bonus: not only can you use <Backspace> to erase a character to the left, you can use <Delete> to erase a character to the right. This is a big deal once you get used to it. (Note: If <Delete> doesn't work on your system, you can use **^D** instead.)

HINT

Using <Left> and <Right> to move within the command line and <Up> and <Down> to recall previous commands is so handy that I urge you to practice until you find yourself using these keys without thinking about it.

When it comes to entering commands, your motto should be: Reuse; don't retype.

THE HISTORY LIST: fc, history

As you enter commands, the shell saves them in what is called your HISTORY LIST. You can access the history list in a variety of ways to recall previous commands, which you can then modify and reenter. For example, when you press <Up> and <Down> to recall commands, you are actually moving backwards and forwards through the history list.

<Up> and <Down>, however, allow you to see only one command at a time. A more powerful feature enables you to display all or part of the history list and then select a particular command. How this works depends on your shell. As a general rule, the Bourne shell family (Bash, Korn shell) uses the **fc** command, and the C-Shell (C-Shell, Tcsh) family uses the **history** and **!** commands. Most people find the C-Shell system easier and, for this reason, Bash allows you to use either system. Here are the details.

Within the history list, each command is called an EVENT, and each event is given an internal number called an EVENT NUMBER. The power of the history list is that it is easy to recall a command based on its event number. For example, you might tell the shell to recall command #24.

With the Bourne shell family, you display the history list by using the **fc** command with the **-l** (list) option. (I'll explain the name **fc** in a moment).

```
fc -l
```

With the C-Shell family, you use the **history** command:

```
history
```

The output of these commands consists of one event per line, prefaced by its event number. The event numbers are not part of the commands; they are displayed only for your convenience. Here is an example:

```
20   cp tempfile backup
21   ls
22   who
23   datq
24   date
25   vi tempfile
26   history
```

If your history list is so long that it scrolls off the screen, use the **less** command:

```
history | less
```

Notice that every command you enter is added to the history list, including commands with mistakes, as well as the **history** or **fc** commands themselves.

You can recall and execute a specific command by referencing its event number. With a Bourne shell, you type **fc** with the **-s** (substitute) option, followed by the number. For example, to re-execute command number 24, use:

```
fc -s 24
```

With a C-Shell, it is even easier. Just type a **!** (bang) character followed by the number. Note that you do not use a space after the **!**:

```
!24
```

A special case occurs when you want to repeat the very last command you entered. With a Bourne shell, you re-execute the previous command by using **fc -s** without a number:

```
fc -s
```

With a C-Shell, you type two **!** characters in a row:

```
!!
```

Both types of shells allow you to make small changes before you re-execute the command. With **fc**, the syntax is:

fc -s *pattern=replacement number*

With the C-Shell family, the syntax is:

! *number* **: s** */ pattern / replacement /*

In both cases, *pattern* and *replacement* refer to strings of characters, and *number* refers to an event number.

For example, in the previous example, event number 25 is a command that starts the **vi** editor with a file called **tempfile**:

```
25  vi tempfile
```

Say that you want to run the command again, but with a file named **data** instead. That is, you want to recall event number 25, change **tempfile** to **data**, and then re-execute the command. With a Bourne shell you would use:

```
fc -s tempfile=data 25
```

With a C-Shell, you would use:

```
!25:s/tempfile/data/
```

Once again, if you want to use the most recent command, the commands are simpler. For example, say that you want to run the **date** command, but by accident, you enter **datq**, which displays an error message:

```
$ datq
datq: Command not found.
```

You want to change the **q** to an **e** and re-execute the command. With **fc -s**, if you leave out the event number, the default is the previous command:

```
fc -s q=e
```

With a C-Shell, you use the syntax:

^pattern^replacement

For example:

```
^q^e
```

I know it looks odd, but it's quick and easy, and you will use it a lot, especially when you have a long command that needs a tiny change. For example, suppose you want to make a copy of a file named **masterdata** and call it **backup**. Using the **cp** command (Chapter 25) you type:

-Using the Shell: Commands and Customization

```
cp masterxata backup
```

You get an error message because, when you typed the first filename, you accidentally pressed **x** instead of **d**. To fix the mistake and re-run the command, just enter:

```
^x^d
```

HINT

When you use Bash, you get two important advantages over the other shells.

First, with respect to the history list commands, you get the best of both worlds. You can use either the **fc** command, or the **history/!** system, whichever you like better.

If you are not sure which one to use, start with the **history/!** system.

Second, Bash supports an extra feature using **^R**. (Think of it as the "recall" key.) Press **^R** and then start typing a pattern. Bash will recall the most recent command that contains that pattern. For example, to recall the most recent **ls** command, press **^R** and then **ls**.

If this is not the command you want, simply press **^R** again to get the next most recent command that contains the pattern. In our example, you would press **^R** again to get another **ls** command.

When you see the command you want, you can press <Return> to run it, or you can make a change and press <Return>.

WHAT'S IN A NAME?

fc

The Bourne shells (Bash, Korn shell) use the **fc** command to display and modify commands from the history list. **fc** is a powerful command with complicated syntax that can take awhile to master.

The name **fc** stands for "fix command". This is because, when you make a typing mistake, you can use **fc** to fix the command and then re-execute it.

HISTORY LIST: SETTING THE SIZE

The shell stores the history list in a file. This file can be saved automatically when you log out and can be restored when you log in. This is important, because it means that a record of what you do will be saved from one work session to the next.

With the Bourne shell family, the history file is saved and restored automatically. With the C-Shell family, your file will not be saved unless you set the **savehist** shell variable (see below).

The important thing to realize is that, when you examine your history list you are, in effect, looking back in time, possibly across separate work sessions. As with life in general, you will find that it is counterproductive to remember too much. For this reason, the shell lets you limit the size of your history list by setting a variable.

With the Bourne shell family, you set the **HISTSIZE** environment variable. For example, to specify that you want your history list to hold 50 commands (large enough for most people), use:

```
export HISTSIZE=50
```

With the C-Shell family, you set the **history** shell variable:

```
set history = 50
```

If you want to keep a longer record of your work, just set the variable to a larger number. If you don't set the size, it's okay. The shell will use a default value that will probably be fine.

As I mentioned above, if you want the C-Shell or Tcsh to save your history list when you log out, you must set the **savehist** shell variable. As with **history**, you must specify how many commands you want to save. For example, to save the last 30 commands from one work session to the next, use

```
set savehist = 30
```

HINT

If you want to set the size of your history list, the place to put the command is in an initialization file, so that the variable will be set automatically each time you log in. We will discuss how to do this in Chapter 14.

HISTORY LIST EXAMPLE: AVOID DELETING THE WRONG FILES

As we will discuss in Chapter 25, you use the **rm** (remove) command to delete files. When you use **rm**, you can specify patterns to represent lists of files. For example, the pattern **temp*** stands for any filename that begins with **temp** followed by zero or more characters; the pattern **extra?** refers to any filename that starts with **extra** followed by a single character.

The danger with **rm** is that once you delete a file it is gone for good. If you discover that you have made a mistake and erased the wrong file — even the instant after you press <Return> — there is no way to recover the file. (We will now pause for a moment, to allow Macintosh users to regain their composure.)*

Let's say you want to delete a set of files with the names **temp**, **temp_backup**, **extra1** and **extra2**. You are thinking about entering the command:

```
rm temp* extra?
```

However, you have forgotten that you also have an important file called **temp.important**. If you enter the preceding command, this file will also be deleted.

A better strategy is to first use the **ls** (list files) command using the patterns that you propose to use with **rm**:

---

*Believe it or not, the fact that the Unix **rm** command deletes files permanently is actually a good thing. Experienced Unix users rarely lose a file by accident, because they have trained themselves to think carefully before they act. Moreover, they learn to take responsibility for their actions, because they cannot depend on the operating system to compensate for their weaknesses. As you would imagine, such intelligence and self-reliance influence all aspects of life, which is why Unix people are, as a whole, so accomplished and fulfilled as human beings.

(We will now pause for a moment, once again, to allow Macintosh users to regain their composure.)

```
ls temp* extra?
```

This will list the names of all the files that match these patterns. If this list contains a file you have forgotten, such as **temp.important**, you will not enter the **rm** command as planned. If, however, the list of files is what you expected, you can go ahead and remove the files by changing the **ls** to **rm** and re-executing the command. With a Bourne shell, you would use:

```
fc -s ls=rm
```

With a C-Shell:

```
^ls^rm
```

You may ask, why reuse the previous command? Once you have confirmed that the patterns match the files I want, why not simply type the **rm** command using those same patterns?

You could, but when you reuse the **ls** command, you are guaranteed to get exactly what you want. If you retype the patterns, you may make a typing mistake and, in spite of all your precautions, still end up deleting the wrong files. Also, in many cases, it is faster to modify the previous command than it is to type a brand new one.

If you like this idea, you can make the process even easier by using an alias. I'll show you how to do so later in the chapter.

DISPLAYING EVENT NUMBER & WORKING DIRECTORY IN YOUR SHELL PROMPT

Earlier in the chapter, we discussed how to put various types of information into your shell prompt: your userid, the name of your shell, and so on. In this section, I'll show you how to display two items that change from time to time: the event number and the name of your working directory. Putting these items in your shell prompt helps you keep track of what you are doing.

To display the current value of the event number, you use a special code. The codes vary from one shell to another, so I have summarized them in Figure 13-7. Here are some examples that show how to do it for the four major shells. In the examples, I have placed the event number within square brackets*, which looks nice when it is displayed.

```
export PS1="bash[\!]$ "
export PS1="ksh[!]$ "
set prompt = "csh[\!]% "
set prompt = "tcsh[%\!]> "
```

Let's say, for example, the current event number is 57. The four prompts as defined above would look like this:

```
bash[57]$
ksh[57]$
```

---

*It happens that, with the C-Shell and Tcsh, a ! character followed by a right square bracket causes a problem. Thus, in these examples, I used a backslash to quote the !. The reason for this is obscure, so don't worry about it.

SHELL	CODE
Bash	\!
Korn Shell	!
C-Shell	!
Tcsh	%!

FIGURE 13-7: Displaying the history list event number in your shell prompt

To display the current value of the history list event number in your shell prompt, use the code for your particular shell. See text for examples.

```
csh[57]%
tcsh[57]>
```

As you might expect, the event number can be combined with other codes or with variables to construct a more elaborate prompt. For example, here are several prompts that display the name of the shell, the working directory (see Chapter 24), and the event number. (For information on displaying the name of your working directory in a shell prompt, see Figure 13-6.)

For readability, I have inserted some spaces, placed the name of the working directory in parentheses, and placed the event number in square brackets.

To start, here is the prompt for Bash. We use **\w** to display the working directory and **\!** to display the event number:

```
export PS1="(\w) bash[\!]$ "
```

The same prompt for the Korn shell is a bit trickier. Because the Korn shell has no code to display the name of the working directory, we use the **PWD** variable. However, because **PWD** changes from time to time, we must use strong quotes, rather than weak quotes. (See the discussion earlier in the chapter.)

```
export PS1='($PWD) ksh[!]$ '
```

Alternatively, we could use weak quotes, as long as we make sure to use a backslash to quote the **$** character:

```
export PS1="(\$PWD) ksh[!]$ "
```

Finally, here is the command to use with the Tcsh. We use **%~** to display the working directory and **%!** to display the event number.

```
set prompt = "(%~) tcsh[%\!]> "
```

What about the C-Shell? As you can see from Figure 13-6, there is no easy way to display the name of the working directory in a C-Shell prompt, so I have no example to show you. However, there is a more complicated way to do it using what are called "aliases". We'll talk about this idea later in the chapter.

AUTOCOMPLETION

One of the ways in which the shell makes it easier for you to enter commands is by helping you complete words as you type. This feature is called AUTOCOMPLETION.

For example, you are entering a command and you need to type the name of a very large file, such as:

```
harley-1.057-i386.rpm
```

If there are no other files with similar names, why should you have to type the entire name? You should be able to type just a few letters and let the shell do the rest for you.

With autocompletion, the shell carefully looks at everything you type. At any time, you can press a special key combination, and the shell will do its best to complete the current word for you. If it can't complete the word, the shell will beep. I'll give you an example just to show you the concept, and then we'll go over the details.

Let's say you have four files:

```
haberdashery
hardcopy
harley-1.057-i386.rpm
hedgehog
```

If you type **harl** and press the autocomplete key combination, there is no ambiguity. Since there is only one file that begins with **harl**, the shell will fill in the rest of the name for you.

However, what happens if you type **har** and then press the autocomplete key? There are two filenames that begin with **har**, so the shell beeps to indicate that what you have typed is ambiguous.

At this point, you have two choices. You can type a bit more and try again. Or, if you are not sure what to type, you can press a second autocomplete key combination and have the shell display a list of all possible matches.

With our example, if you type **har** and press the second key combination, the shell will display:

```
hardcopy
harley-1.057-386i.rpm
```

You can then type either a **d** or an **l**, and tell the shell to finish the job.

As you can see, to use the basic autocomplete facility, you only need to remember two different keys combinations. For historical reasons, these keys differ from one shell to another, so I have listed them in Figure 13-8. The first key combination tells the shell to try to complete the current word. The second key combination tells the shell to display a list of all possible completions that match what you have already typed.

To let you see how autocompletion works, I'll show you some examples that you can try at your own computer. Before we begin, however, I want to make sure autocompletion is turned on for your shell. For Bash, the Korn shell and the Tcsh, this is always the case.

SHELL	COMPLETE THE WORD	DISPLAY ALL POSSIBILITIES
Bash	<Tab>	<Tab><Tab>
Korn Shell	<Esc><Esc>	<Esc>=
C-Shell	<Esc>	^D
Tcsh	<Tab>	^D

FIGURE 13-8: Autocomplete keys

The basic autocompletion features use two different keys combinations. The first one tells the shell to try to complete the word you are currently typing. If this doesn't work, you can use the second key combination to have the shell display all possible completions that match your pattern.

However, for the C-Shell, you need to turn on autocompletion by setting the **filec** variable. The command to do so is:

```
set filec
```

The best place to put this command is in an initialization file, so the variable will be set automatically each time you start a new shell. I'll show you how to do this in Chapter 14.

To return to our examples, in order to experiment with autocompletion, we will need a few files that have similar names. To create them, we will use the **touch** command. The files will be **xaax**, **xabx**, **xacx** and **xccx***. Here is the command:

```
touch xaax xabx xacx xccx
```

(We'll talk about the **touch** command in Chapter 25. For right now, all you need to know is this is the easiest way to create empty files.)

We will now use the **ls -l** command, which lists file names along with other information, to demonstrate autocompletion. To start, let me show you what happens when you complete a filename. Type the following and then stop, without pressing <Return>:

```
ls -l xc
```

Now, look at Figure 13-8 and press the "Complete Word" key combination for your particular shell. That is, with Bash or the Tcsh, press <Tab>; with the C-Shell, press <Esc>; with the Korn shell, press <Esc> twice.

Since there is no ambiguity, the shell will complete the filename for you. You will see:

```
ls -l xccx
```

You can now press <Return> to enter the command.

This type of autocompletion is called FILENAME COMPLETION. There are several other types, which we will discuss later.

Now, let's see what happens when the shell cannot complete a file name. Type the following and then stop, without pressing <Return>:

```
ls -l xa
```

---

*In case you are wondering, I named these files after four of my ex-girlfriends.

Once again, press the "Complete Word" key combination for your shell (<Tab>, <Esc> or <Esc><Esc>). This time, the shell will beep, because there is no single filename that matches what you have typed. (In fact, there are three.) Type the letter **b** and then stop, without pressing <Return>. You will see:

```
ls -l xab
```

Now press the key combination again. This time, the shell will be able to make the completion for you, as there is only one filename that matches **xab** (**xabx**). Press <Return> to enter the command.

One final example. Type the following and then stop, without pressing <Return>:

```
ls -l xa
```

This time, look at Figure 13-8 and press the "Display Possibilities" key combination for your particular shell. That is, with Bash, press <Tab> twice; with the Korn shell, press <Esc>=; and with the C-Shell or the Tcsh, press **^D** (Ctrl-D). This tells the shell to list all possible matches.

The shell will display the matches and then retype your command for you, so you can complete it. You will see:

```
xaax   xabx   xacx
ls -l xa
```

You can now complete the command however you want and press <Return>.

Finally, when you are finished experimenting, you need to clean up after yourself by removing the four practice files:

```
rm xaax xabx xacx xccx
```

Here is one last example. At any time, the directory in which you are currently working is called your "working directory" (see Chapter 24). From time to time, you will want to change your working directory and, to do so, you will type the **cd** (change directory) command, followed by the name of a directory. There will be times when you find yourself typing long directory names, especially if you are a system administrator. When this happens, you are better off using autocompletion.

For example, let's say you are using a Linux system, and you want to change to the following directory:

```
/usr/lib/ImageMagick-5.5.7/modules-Q16/filters
```

You could type **cd** followed by the very long directory name. However, it is a lot easier to type the minimum number of characters and use autocompletion. In this case, with Bash, you could type:

```
cd /us<Tab>/li<Tab>/Im<Tab>/mo<Tab>/fi<Tab><Return>
```

If you use a different shell, the autocomplete key would be different, but the idea is the same: Why type a long name if the shell will do it for you?

AUTOCOMPLETION: BEYOND THE BASICS

In Chapter 11, when I explained where the names C-Shell and Tcsh came from, I mentioned that the creator of the original Tcsh, Ken Greer, had been working on a PDP-10 computer using the TENEX command interpreter (similar to a shell).

TENEX used very long command names because they were easy to understand, but it was a lot of bother to type the full commands. A facility called "command completion" was used to do a lot of the work. All you had to do was type a few letters and press the <Esc> key. The command interpreter would then expand what you had typed into the full command. Greer added this feature to the new C-Shell he was writing and, when it came time to name the shell, he called it the Tcsh, the "T" referring to TENEX.

In the last section, we used autocompletion to help us type the names of files, and this is how you will use it most of the time. However, as you can see from the Tcsh story, autocompletion is an old idea. Moreover, it can be used to complete more than just filenames. In fact, modern shells offer autocompletion for a variety of different types of names.

The details vary from shell to shell, and they are complex. In fact, most shells, particularly Bash and the Zsh (mentioned in Chapter 11), give you many more autocomplete features than you would ever use in three lifetimes. Most of the time, the techniques that we discussed in the last section will be all you need. In this section, I'll explain a bit more. If you want more details, display the man page for your particular shell and search for the word "completion".

In general, there are five types of autocompletion. Not all shells support every type, although all modern shells offer filename completion, which is the most important type of autocompletion. For reference, Figure 13-9 shows which types of autocompletion you can use with the various shells.

We have already discussed filename completion. COMMAND COMPLETION (Bash, Tcsh only) is similar. When you are typing the beginning of a line, you can use autocompletion to help you type the name of a command. This can be an external command, a builtin command, an alias, or a function.

SHELLS	AUTOCOMPLETION	COMPLETES NAMES OF...
B K C T	Filename completion	Files and directories
B · · T	Command completion	Commands, including pathnames
B · · T	Variable completion	Variables
B · C T	Userid completion	Userids on your system
B · · ·	Hostname completion	Computers on your local network

FIGURE 13-9: Types of autocompletion

Autocompletion allows you to type part of a name and have the shell complete it for you. In general, there are five different types of autocompletion, each of which completes a different type of name. See text for details.

The leftmost column shows which shells support which type of autocompletion: B = Bash; K = Korn Shell; C = C-Shell; T = Tcsh. A dot indicates that a shell does not support that feature.

For example, say you are using Bash or the Tcsh, and you want to enter the **whoami** command to display your userid (see Chapter 8). You start by typing:

whoa

You then press <Tab> and the shell will complete the command for you.

VARIABLE COMPLETION (Bash, Tcsh) comes into play whenever you start a word with a **$** character. The shell assumes you are about to type the name of a variable.

For example, you are using Bash and you want to display the value of an environment variable, but you forget its name. All you remember is that it begins with the letter **H**. Type the following:

echo $H<Tab><Tab>

With the Tcsh, you would type **$H** followed by **^D** (Ctrl-D):

echo $H^D

The shell lists all the variables whose names begin with **H**. For example:

```
HISTCMD     HISTFILESIZE   HOME        HOSTTYPE
HISTFILE    HISTSIZE       HOSTNAME
```

You recognize the variable you want as **HOSTTYPE**, so you type enough of the name so that it can be recognized and (with Bash) press <Tab> to finish the job:

echo $HOST<Tab>

With the Tcsh, you would use:

echo $HOST<Esc><Esc>

USERID COMPLETION (also called USER NAME COMPLETION) is available with Bash, the C-Shell and the Tcsh. It works like variable completion, except that you must start the word with a **~** (tilde) character. This is because the syntax *~userid* is an abbreviation for *userid*'s home directory.

Finally, HOSTNAME COMPLETION, available only with Bash, will complete the names of computers on your local network. Hostname completion is used when you start a word with the **@** (at sign) character. You will do this, for example, if you are typing an email address.

HINT

Autocompletion is particularly useful when you have an idea of what you want to type, but you can't remember the full name.

For example, if you are using Bash, and you want to enter a command that begins with **lp** but you can't remember which one, just type **lp**<Tab><Tab>. (With the Tcsh, use **lp^D**.)

Similarly, you can list the names of all your variables by typing **$**<Tab><Tab> (or **$^D**). Try it.

USING AUTOCOMPLETION FOR FUN AND PROFIT

You may remember *The Fable of the Programmer and the Princess* from Chapter 7. In this story, a handsome young programmer is able to rescue a beautiful princess by entering a command without pressing the <Return> key or **^M**. (He uses **^J**.) Here is something even cooler: how to use autocompletion to make a few bucks and (assuming you are a guy) impress women at the same time.

The next time you are at a gathering of Linux users, look around at all the geeks and find one who looks like he has a bit of money. Since this is a Linux geek, you know he will be using Bash. Offer a small bet (say, five dollars) that you can list the names of all his environment variables without pressing the <Return> key. When he takes the bet, enter:

env^M

He will now see how you tricked him, so offer to double the bet. This time, you promise not to use <Return> or **^M**. When he takes the bet, enter:

env^J

You are now ready to move in for the kill. Offer to triple the bet and, this time, you promise not to use <Return>, **^M** or **^J**. And, to make it harder, you won't even type a command.

By now, you will have attracted the attention of a lot of other Linux geeks who will want in on the action. Make them put their cash on the table and, once you have gathered all the bets you can, type:

$<Tab><Tab>

As you scoop up the money and walk away, look back at the geeks and say, "Haven't you guys ever heard of RTFM?"

COMMAND LINE EDITING: `bindkey`

In the past few sections, we talked about several interrelated topics: making changes as you type a command, using the history list, and using autocompletion. As you read these sections, you may have noticed two things. First, the three newer shells — Bash, Korn shell, and the Tcsh — offer significantly more features than the older C-Shell. Second, there seems to be an underlying thread tying all of this together.

This is indeed the case. The general principle at work here is called COMMAND LINE EDITING, and it is available only with the newer shells, not with the C-Shell. Command line editing is a powerful facility that allows you to use a large variety of commands to manipulate what you type on the command line, including the ability to use the history list and autocompletion.

You will remember my telling you several times that there are two main Unix text editors: **vi** (pronounced "vee-eye") and Emacs. Eventually, you must learn how to use at least one of the editors well. Indeed, I have devoted an entire chapter to **vi** (Chapter 22).

Both **vi** and Emacs offer a large, powerful set of commands that allow you to view and modify text files. These commands are so well-designed that they are suitable for editing any type of text in any situation. In particular, the shell lets you use either the **vi** commands or Emacs commands (your choice) to view and modify what you type on the command line as well as your history list.

It happens that the **vi** commands are very different from the Emacs commands, so the shell lets you use only one set at a time. By default, the shell assumes you want to use Emacs commands. We call this EMACS MODE. However, you can change to **vi** if you want. If you do, we say that the shell is in **vi** MODE.

The way in which you change from one command editing mode to another depends on your shell. With Bash and the Korn shell, you set a shell option, either **emacs** or **vi**. (Shell options are explained in Chapter 12.) Thus, you would use one of the following commands:

```
set -o emacs
set -o vi
```

With the Tcsh, you use the **bindkey** command. You can do so with either the **-e** (Emacs) or -v (**vi**) option:

```
bindkey -e
bindkey -v
```

The best place to put either of these commands is in an initialization file, so the command will be executed automatically each time you log in. I will show you how to do so in Chapter 14.

When it comes to editing regular text files, **vi** is the best choice for beginners. This is because, while **vi** is difficult to learn, Emacs is *very* difficult to learn. So, if you are a beginner, when the time comes to learn how to edit files, I will recommend that you start with **vi**, not Emacs.

However, when it comes to editing the history list and command line, Emacs is actually easier to use than **vi**. The reason is that, most of the time, you only need to move up and down within the history list or make small changes to the command line. With Emacs, this is straightforward. The **vi** editor is more complicated, because it has two different modes — command mode and insert mode — and before you can use **vi**, you need to learn how to switch back and forth from one mode to another. (We'll go into the details in Chapter 22.) For this reason, all the shells use Emacs mode as the default.

When I taught you how to use <Up> and <Down> to move within the history list, and how to make basic changes to your command line (earlier in the chapter), I was actually showing you simple Emacs commands. Thus, you have already been using Emacs for command line editing, even though you didn't realize it at the time. In fact, if your shell had been in **vi** mode, you would have found that the cursor movement keys would not have worked the way you expected.

Both **vi** and Emacs offer a very large number of ways to manipulate your history list and command line. However, none of this helps you at all until you learn how to use one of the editors. For this reason, I'm not going to explain the details of advanced command line editing. If you are so inclined, you can experiment with the **vi** or Emacs commands once you learn how to use them. At that time, come back to this chapter, and read the rest of this section. (For **vi**, that will be after you read Chapter 22.)

To teach yourself command line editing, start by using **set** or **bindkey** to put your shell in either **vi** or Emacs mode. Now, imagine you are working with an invisible file that contains the history list. At any time, you can copy one line from this file to your command line, where you can modify the text as you wish. Whenever you press <Return> to run a command, the contents of the command line are added to the bottom of the invisible file (that is, to the history list).

Keeping this image in mind, it is easy to experiment. All you have to do is use the **vi** or Emacs commands in a way that makes sense. Start by practicing the basic maneuvers: moving through the invisible file, searching for patterns, making replacements, and so on. You will find that, once you are comfortable with **vi** or Emacs, command line editing is straightforward and intuitive.

If you need a reference, take a look at the man page for your particular shell and search for information about command editing. You may find the instructions a bit confusing, but be patient. Rearranging your brain cells takes time.

ALIASES: `alias, unalias`

An ALIAS is a name that you give to a command or list of commands. You can use aliases as abbreviations, or you can use them to create customized variations of existing commands. For example, let's say you often find yourself entering the command:

```
ls -l temp*
```

If you give it an alias of **lt**, you can enter the command more simply by typing:

```
lt
```

To create an alias, you use the **alias** command. The syntax varies slightly depending on which shell you use. For the Bourne shell family (Bash, Korn shell), the syntax is:

alias [*name=commands*]

Be sure not to put a space on either side of the equals sign (the same as when you create a variable).

For the C-Shell family (C-Shell, Tcsh), the syntax is almost the same. The only difference is you leave out the equals sign:

alias [*name* commands]

In both cases, *name* is the name of the alias you want to create, and **commands** is a list of one or more commands.

An an example, let's create the alias I mentioned above. The first command is for a Bourne shell; the second command (which leaves out the equals sign) is for a C-Shell:

```
alias lt='ls -l temp*'
alias lt 'ls -l temp*'
```

Notice that I have enclosed the command in single quotes. This is because the command contains both spaces and a metacharacter (*****). In general, strong quotes (single quotes) work better than weak quotes (double quotes), because they preserve the meaning of the metacharacters until the alias is executed.

Here is an example that creates an alias for a list of two commands. Again, the first command is for a Bourne shell; the second is for a C-Shell:

```
alias info='date; who'
alias info 'date; who'
```

Once you have created this alias, you can enter **info** whenever you want to run these two commands.

Here is my favorite alias. It creates an abbreviation for the **alias** command itself:

```
alias a=alias
alias a alias
```

Once you create this alias, you can create more by using **a** instead of having to type the whole word **alias**. For example, once you define this alias, you could enter:

```
a info='date; who'
a info 'date; who'
```

If you want to change the meaning of an alias, just redefine it. For example, if **info** is an alias, you can change it whenever you want simply by using another **alias** command:

```
alias info='date; uname; who'
alias info 'date; uname; who'
```

To check the current value of an alias, enter the **alias** command with a name only. For example, to display the meaning of the alias **info**, use:

```
alias info
```

To display all your aliases at once, enter the **alias** command with no arguments:

```
alias
```

To remove an alias, you use the unalias command. The syntax is:

unalias *name*

where **name** is the name of an alias. For example, to remove the alias we just defined, you would use:

```
unalias info
```

If you want to remove all your aliases at once (say, if you are experimenting), use the **unalias** command with either the **-a** option (for a Bourne shell), or with a ***** character (for a C-Shell):

```
unalias -a
unalias *
```

Do you remember the **type** command, we discussed earlier in this chapter? (You specify the name of a command, and **type** tells you what type of command it is.) You can use **type** to find out if a particular command is an alias. For example, say you define the **info** alias as shown above. You then enter:

```
type info
```

You will see a message similar to this one:

```
info is aliased to 'date; who'
```

As you might imagine, you are likely to develop a whole set of aliases that you use all the time. However, it is bothersome to have to retype the alias commands every time you log in. Instead, you can put all your favorite alias definitions in an initialization file, which causes them to be executed automatically whenever you start a new shell. I'll show you how to do this in Chapter 14.

SUSPENDING AN ALIAS TEMPORARILY

One very common use for aliases is to make it easy to use the same options every time you run a particular command.

For example, the **ls** command (which we will discuss in Chapter 24) lists the contents of a directory. When you use **ls** by itself, you get a "short" listing; when you use **ls** with the **-l** option, you get a "long" listing.

Suppose you find that, almost all the time, you use **l** with the **-l** option. To save yourself having to type the option every time, you define the following alias:

```
alias ls="ls -l"
alias ls "ls -l"
```

(The first definition is for the Bourne shell family; the second is for the C-Shell family.)

Now, you can simply enter the command by itself. You don't have to type the option:

```
ls
```

This will produce a long listing, just as if you entered:

```
ls -l
```

When you use such aliases, you may find that, from time to time, you want to run the original command, not the alias. For example, you may want to run **ls** without the **-l** option.

To suspend an alias temporarily — for one command only — type a \ (backslash) character at the beginning of the command name:

```
\ls
```

This tells the shell to run the actual command, not an alias. In our example, the shell will ignore the **ls** alias, and you will get the (default) short listing.

ALIAS EXAMPLE: AVOID DELETING THE WRONG FILES

In this section, I will show you how to combine an alias with a command recalled from the history list to produce an exceptionally handy tool.

Earlier in the chapter, we discussed an example in which we were thinking about using the **rm** (remove) command to delete all the files whose names match a particular pattern. The example we discussed was:

```
rm temp* extra?
```

To make sure we don't make a mistake, we should check the pattern we are using *before* we perform the actual deletion. We do this by using the same pattern with the **ls** command:

```
ls temp* extra?
```

If **ls** lists the files we want, we proceed with the deletion. Otherwise, we can try again with a different pattern, until we get what we want. In this way, we ensure that **rm** does exactly what we want it to do. This is important because once Unix deletes a file it is gone forever.

So let's say the **ls** command finds the files we want to delete. We could simply enter the **rm** command using the same pattern. However, what if we make a typing mistake? We might end up deleting a wrong file after all. A better idea is to let the shell do the work for us. To do so, we recall the **ls** command from the history list, change **ls** to **rm**, and then execute the modified command.

With a member of the Bourne shell family (Bash, Korn shell), we use:

```
fc -s ls=rm
```

To make this command easy to use, we define an alias named **del**:

```
alias del='fc -s ls=rm'
```

With a member of the C-Shell family (C-Shell, Tcsh), we would normally use:

```
^ls^rm
```

However, for technical reasons I won't go into, this won't work within an alias. Instead, we need to use the following command:

```
rm !ls:*
```

Obviously, this is tricky. (Unix is full of tricky commands.) Informally, we are asking the shell to extract the arguments from the most recent **ls** command, and use them to run an **rm** command. The effect is to run the **rm** command with the same arguments as the **ls** command.

To make this command easy to use, we define an alias. Notice that we quote the **!** to preserve its meaning. (Does this make sense to you?)

```
alias del 'rm \!ls:*'
```

Once we have defined a **del** alias, we can use the following procedure to delete files that match a particular pattern. The nice thing is that the procedure is the same regardless of which shell we are using.

First, we enter an **ls** command with the pattern that describes the files you wish to delete. For example:

```
ls temp* extra?
```

If the pattern displays the names we expect, we enter:

```
del
```

That's all there is to it.

If the pattern does not work, we re-enter the **ls** command with a different pattern until we get what we want. Then we use **del**. In this way, it is impossible for us to delete the wrong files because of a mismatched pattern.

If you make a habit of using **ls** with a **del** alias in this way, I promise you that, one day, you will save yourself from a catastrophe. In fact, I have mathematical proof — using mathematical induction and hypergeometric functions — that this one trick alone is worth the price of this book. (Unfortunately, the explanation of the proof is beyond the scope of the book.)

ALIAS EXAMPLE: REUSING COMMANDS FROM THE HISTORY LIST

Earlier in the chapter, I explained that the Bourne shell family and the C-Shell family use different commands to access the history list. In particular, the Bourne shells (Bash, Korn shell) use the **fc** command, while the C-Shells (C-Shell, Tcsh) use the **history** and **!** commands.

The original history list facility was written for the C-Shell. It was a breakthrough at the time and, in fact, it is still useful and easy to use. Later, the Korn shell introduced a much more powerful system using the **fc** command. Unfortunately, the syntax of **fc** was designed poorly and the details of the command itself are awkward to remember and to use. However, by using aliases, we can make **fc** look like the C-Shell system.

To start, we define an alias named **history** that uses **fc** with the **-l** (list) option to display lines from the history list:

```
alias history="fc -l"
```

To make it even easier, we can abbreviate **history** to **h**:

```
alias h=history
```

This is one of my favorite aliases, and I use it with every shell, even the C-Shell and Tcsh. After all, who wants to type the word **history** over and over?*

Next, we define an alias **r** (recall) to take the place of **fc -s**, the command that recalls and re-executes a line from the history list:

```
alias r="fc -s"
```

Now, whenever we want, it is easy to re-execute the last command we entered. We just use the **r** alias:

```
r
```

If we want to make a change, we simply specify an old pattern and a new pattern. For example, suppose we just typed the command:

```
vi tempfile
```

This starts **vi** to edit a file named tempfile. We decide to run the command again to edit a file named **data**. All we need to type is:

```
r tempfile=data
```

Working with a specific line in the history list is just as easy. Just specify the event number (line number). For example, let's say your history list looks like this:

```
20  cp tempfile backup
21  diff backup backup1
22  whoami
23  date
24  vi tempfile
25  vi data
```

You are wondering what time it is, so you want to re-execute the **date** command, event number 23:

```
r 23
```

Next, you want to re-execute command 20. However, first you want to change **tempfile** to **data**:

```
r 20 tempfile=data
```

---

*For that matter, who wants to type the word **alias** over and over? This is why I suggest you create an alias for the **alias** command itself:

```
alias a=alias
```

If you specify one or more characters, the shell will re-execute the most recent command that starts with those characters. For example, to re-execute the last command that began with a **di** (in this case, number 21, the **diff** command), use:

```
r di
```

If you want to re-execute the **date** command, you can specify the last command that begins with **d**:

```
r d
```

With a little practice, such substitutions can save you a lot of time and effort.

To finish this section, let me give you some specific advice with respect to using the **history**, **h** and **r** aliases with your particular shell.

Bash: As I explained earlier in the chapter, Bash comes with both the **fc** command and the **history** and **!!** commands. However, you should create the **h** and **r** aliases for yourself:

```
alias h=history
alias r="fc -s"
```

Korn shell: The Korn shell uses **fc**, and it comes with the **history** and **r** aliases already defined, so you don't need to create them. For convenience, however, you should add the **h** alias:

```
alias h=history
```

C-Shell and Tcsh: As I explained earlier in the chapter, both these shells come with a **history** command as well as an easy way to modify and re-use commands from the history list. For convenience, all you need to add is the **h** alias:

```
alias h history
```

The beauty of these aliases is twofold: First, they make it easy to use the history list; second, they allow you to access the history list the same way regardless of which shell you are using.

ALIAS EXAMPLE: DISPLAYING NAME OF WORKING DIRECTORY IN SHELL PROMPT

The goal of this section is to solve a specific problem that pertains only to the C-Shell. However, we will be covering several concepts that are generally useful so, regardless of which shell you happen to use, I want you to read this section and think about the ideas that emerge from the discussion.

Earlier in the chapter, we talked about how to display the name of your working directory in your shell prompt. At the end of that discussion, I mentioned that the C-Shell does not have an easy way to do this. There is a complicated way to do so, however, that uses aliases, and that is what we are going to discuss here.

The discussion will involve directories, which we will cover in Chapter 24. For now, all you need to know is that directories hold files, and your "working directory" is the one in which you are currently working. You can change your working directory whenever you want and, when you do, it's handy to see the name of the new directory in your shell prompt, so you can keep track of where you are.

Displaying the name of your working directory in this way is easy with Bash (use **\w**), the Korn shell (use **$PWD**), and the Tcsh (use **%~**). Here are some sample commands that do the job. For readability, they display the name of the working directory in parentheses:

```
export PS1="(\w) bash$ "
export PS1='($PWD) ksh$ '
set prompt = "(%~) tcsh> "
```

The reason these commands work is that the shells automatically update the code or variable within the shell prompt whenever your working directory changes.

To be sure, the C-Shell has a **PWD** variable. However, if you put it in your shell prompt, you will find that the variable is not updated automatically. This is because the C-Shell is older than the other three shells, and it does not have this capability.

The approach to solving this problem is to use an alias that redefines the shell prompt every time you change your working directory. To start, we need to answer the question: Which command do we use to change our working directory? The answer is the **cd** (change directory) command.

We'll talk about **cd** in detail in Chapter 24. For now, I'll tell you that, to change to a new directory, you type **cd** followed by the name of the directory. For example, if you want to change to the **bin** directory, you would enter:

```
cd bin
```

You may remember from Chapter 12 that, at all times, the C-Shell maintains the name of your working directory in two different variables: **cwd** (a shell variable) and **PWD** (an environment variable). Whenever you use **cd** to change your working directory, these two variables are updated.

Thus, our plan is to create an alias to redefine **cd** so that it does two things: (1) Change the working directory according to whatever you specify, then (2) Use either the **cwd** or **PWD** variable to redefine the shell prompt to reflect the new working directory. The following alias does the job:

```
alias cd 'cd \!* && set prompt="($PWD)% "'
```

To understand how this works, you need to know that **&&** separates two commands. The meaning of **&&** is to run the first command and then, if it terminates normally, to run the second command. If the first command fails, the second command is not executed. In other words, if, for some reason, the **cd** command fails, there's no point in updating the prompt.

Our **cd** alias starts by executing the command:

```
cd \!*
```

The notation \!* refers to whatever arguments were typed on the original command line. In this way, the original arguments from the command line are passed to the **cd** command inside the alias. (This is a programming thing, so if this doesn't make sense to you, don't worry about it.)

If the first command terminates normally, the **PWD** variable will be updated by the shell automatically. We can then run the second command:

```
set prompt="($PWD)% "
```

This command changes the shell prompt to display the name of the working directory in parenthesis, followed by a % character, followed by a space. That's all there is to it.

The reason the whole thing works is that alias expansion is done *before* the shell parses and interprets the command line. For example, say we have defined the **cd** alias above and we enter:

```
cd bin
```

The first thing the shell does is expand the alias. Internally, the command line changes to:

```
cd bin && set prompt="($PWD)% "
```

Then the **cd** command is executed, followed by the **set** command.

Once you have the basic alias defined, you can make it more elaborate. For example, why not have the prompt display more than the working directory and a % character?

The following alias defines a more complex prompt in which we display the working directory in parentheses, a space, the name of the shell, the event number in square brackets, a % character, and a space:

```
alias cd 'cd \!* && set prompt = "($PWD) csh[\\!]% "'
```

A typical prompt defined in this way would look like this:

```
(/export/home/harley) csh[57]%
```

This is the type of alias you would put in an initialization file, so that your prompt will be updated for you automatically. We'll cover initialization files in Chapter 14.

One final comment. You will notice in the last example that the **!** character is quoted twice (by two backslashes). The first backslash quotes the **!** when it is parsed the first time, as part of the **alias** command. The second backslash quotes the **!** when it is parsed the second time, as part of the **set** command.

This is a concept I want to make sure you understand: when something is being parsed more than once, you may need to quote it more than once. Please take a moment to think about this until it makes sense to you.

CHAPTER 13 EXERCISES

REVIEW QUESTIONS

1. What is an alphanumeric character? What is a metacharacter? Name three metacharacters and explain what they are used for.

2. Within the world of Unix, some characters have nicknames. For example, an apostrophe is usually referred to as a "quote" or a "single quote". What are the nicknames Unix people use for the following characters: asterisk, enter/return, exclamation mark, period, quotation mark, vertical bar?

3. What are the three different ways to quote characters? How do they differ?

4. What is a builtin command? Where do you find the documentation for a builtin command?

5. What is the search path? How can you display your search path?

6. What is the history list? The simplest, most common use of the history list is to re-execute the previous command. How do you do this? Using Bash or the Tcsh, how would you recall, edit, and then execute the previous command?

7. What is autocompletion? How many different types of autocompletion are there? Explain briefly what each type of autocompletion does. Which type of autocompletion is the most important?

APPLYING YOUR KNOWLEDGE

1. How do you modify the Bash shell prompt to display your userid, the working directory, and the current time? How do you do the same for the Tcsh prompt?

2. What is command substitution? Use command substitution to create a command that displays "These userids are logged in right now:" followed by a list of the userids.

3. Enter the command:

   ```
   echo "I am a very smary person."
   ```

   Using a history list tool, change this command to correct the spelling of "smart".

4. Your working directory contains the following files (only):

   ```
   datanew   dataold   important   phonenumbers   platypus
   ```

   Using autocompletion, what are the minimum number of characters you need to type to reference each of the files?

FOR FURTHER THOUGHT

1. In this chapter, we have discussed several tools that help you enter commands quickly: the history list, autocompletion and aliases. These tools are complicated and take time to master. Some people can't be bothered to put in the time because, to them, it is not worth the effort. Other people embrace such tools with alacrity. What type of person has a strong need to enter commands as quickly as possible?

2. What are the advantages of creating a great many specialized aliases? What are the disadvantages?

CHAPTER 14

USING THE SHELL: INITIALIZATION FILES

This is the last of four chapters that deal with the shell. Chapter 11 discussed the shell in general; Chapters 12 and 13 covered the basic concepts needed to use the shell well.

In this chapter, we will discuss the last major topic, initialization files. You will like this chapter because, as you read it, everything you have already learned will come together. As it does, you will begin to appreciate the beauty of the shell.

INITIALIZATION FILES AND LOGOUT FILES

The Unix shells were designed by programmers who knew the value of letting users customize their working environments. Toward this end, all shells allow you to specify commands to be executed automatically on your behalf. Your job is to use these commands to set up your working environment exactly how you want it. Here is how it works.

To start, you create two special files, called INITIALIZATION FILES. In the first file, the LOGIN FILE, you put all the commands you want executed every time you log in. In the second file, the ENVIRONMENT FILE, you put the commands you want executed every time a new shell starts.

For example, you might use your login file to set specific variables each time you login. If you use a multiuser system, you might also run the **users** command to show you who else is logged in. And you might use your environment file to set specific shell options and define certain aliases every time a new shell starts.

Once you create your initialization files, the shell will look for them and run the commands automatically at the appropriate times. If your needs change, just change the files.

To provide a bit more customization, some shells also support a LOGOUT FILE. The logout file holds commands that are run automatically whenever you log out. For example, you might run the **date** command whenever you log out, to display the current time and date.

> **HINT**
>
> In the olden days, there was a cool program named **fortune**. Each time you ran the program it would display a joke or pithy saying, selected at random from a large collection of interesting diversions. Many people put a **fortune** command in their logout file, so they would see something interesting each time they logged out.
>
> Unfortunately, the **fortune** command is not included with most of today's Unix/Linux systems. However, it is readily available on the Net, and you might want to download and install it. If you do, you will find that **fortune** is an excellent command to put in your logout file.

Taken together, the login file, environment file, and logout file give you the power to cause any commands you want to be executed automatically at three different times: when you log in, whenever a new shell starts, and when you log out.

Can you see the elegance of this design? The ability to run commands at these three specific times gives you the control you need to set up your work environment exactly the way you want. If you are a beginner, the power of these files will not be obvious. However, once you have used Unix for a year or two, and you are good at setting variables, creating shell scripts, and defining aliases and functions, you will appreciate how important the initialization files are to your overall Unix experience. (We talked about aliases in Chapter 13; functions are beyond the scope of the book.)

The names of the three files differ from one shell to another. For example, with the C-Shell, the login file is called `.login`; the environment file is `.cshrc`; and the termination file is `.logout`. Figure 14-1 shows the standard names used with the various shells. Look closely and you will see that the Bourne shell family (Bash, Korn shell) uses a different pattern of filenames than the C-Shell family (C-Shell, Tcsh).

SHELL	LOGIN FILE	ENVIRONMENT FILE	LOGOUT FILE
C-Shell	`.login`	`.cshrc`	`.logout`
Tcsh	`.login`	`.tcshrc, .cshrc`	`.logout`
Bourne Shell	`.profile`	—	—
Korn Shell	`.profile`	`$ENV`	—
Bash (default)	`.bash_profile, .bash_login`	`.bashrc`	`.bash_logout`
Bash (POSIX)	`.profile`	`$ENV`	`.bash_logout`

FIGURE 14-1: Names of the initialization and logout files

Unix shells allow you to customize your working environment by placing commands in special files that are run automatically at certain times. There are two initialization files, the login file (run when you log in) and the environment file (run whenever a new shell starts). Some shells also allow you to use a logout file (run when you log out). As you can see from the table, the names of these files vary from one shell to another. The original Bourne shell, which I included for interest, used only a login file called `.profile`.

*Notes: (1) The Korn Shell and Bash (in POSIX mode), do not use a standard name for the environment file. Instead, you set the **ENV** variable to the name of whichever file you want to use. (2) If your shell does not support a logout file, it is still possible to use one by trapping the **EXIT** signal. (See text for details.)*

You will notice that all the initialization and logout files have names that begin with a . (dot) character. Such files are called "dotfiles", and we will discuss them later in the chapter and again in Chapter 24. For now, you only need to know three things. First, a dot (that is, a period) is a legitimate character in a filename. Second, a dot at the beginning of a name has a special meaning. Third, when you talk about a dotfile, you pronounce the "dot". For example, when you talk about the `.login` file, you say "dot-login"; when you talk about `.profile`, you say "dot-profile".

NAMES OF INITIALIZATION AND LOGOUT FILES

The names used by the C-Shell family for initialization and logout files are straightforward. The login file is `.login`; the environment file is `.cshrc` for the C-Shell and `.tcshrc` for the Tcsh; and the logout file is `.logout`. For backwards compatibility, if the Tcsh can't find a file named `.tcshrc`, it will look for one named `.cshrc`, which only makes sense.

The names used by the Bourne shell family take a bit of explanation. To start, we need to recall an important idea from Chapter 11. In the early 1990s, a set of specifications called POSIX 1003.2 was created to describe a "standard" Unix shell. For the most part, the POSIX standard was modeled after the Bourne shell family. Indeed, today's modern Bourne shells (Bash, Korn shell, FreeBSD shell) all conform to the 1003.2 standard.

The POSIX standard mandates that a shell should support both a login file and an environment file, but not necessarily a logout file. The name of the login file should be `.profile`. However, to retain flexibility, the name of the environment file is not fixed. Instead, an environment variable named **ENV** should hold the name of the environment file. For example, if you are a Korn shell user, you might set the value of **ENV** to `.kshrc`. (We'll talk about filenames later.)

If you look at Figure 14-1, you will see that the Korn shell follows the POSIX specification: The name of the login file is `.profile`, and the name of the environment file is stored in the **ENV** variable.

Bash is different because it was created by very clever programmers (see Chapter 11) who designed it to run in two different modes: default mode, for power and flexibility*, and POSIX mode for compatibility. In default mode, Bash supports enhancements over the POSIX standard; in POSIX mode, Bash strictly adheres to the 1003.2 standard.

In general, the Bash default mode is just fine, and that is what most people use most of the time. However, if you ever have a need for a POSIX-compliant shell, say, to run a special shell script, you can always run Bash in POSIX mode**.

---

*Of all the major shells, the only one that offers more flexibility than Bash is the Zsh (see Chapter 11).

**There are two ways to run Bash in POSIX mode. First, you can start it with the `--posix` option. This technique will work on all systems:

```
bash --posix
```

The second choice is simpler, but only works on some systems.

Some Unix systems are set up so that both the **bash** command and the **sh** command will start Bash. (This is generally the case with Linux.) On such systems, the **bash** command starts the shell in default mode, while the **sh** command starts the shell in POSIX mode.

In default mode — which is what you and I would normally use — Bash looks for a login file named either **.bash_profile** or **.bash_login** (use whichever one you want), and an environment file named **.bashrc**.

In POSIX mode, Bash follows the same rules as the Korn shell. The login file is named **.profile**, and the name of the environment file is stored in the **ENV** variable.

In both modes — the default mode and the POSIX mode — Bash uses a logout file named **.bash_logout**.

You should now be able to understand all of Figure 14-1, which means we can turn our attention to a very important question: What types of commands should you put in your initialization files and in your logout file?

Before I lay the groundwork for answering that question, I want to make two quick digressions, one to explain about dotfiles and **rc** files, the other to talk about what you need to know in order to create and edit a file.

DOTFILES AND rc FILES

When you look at the filenames in Figure 14-1, you will notice two odd things. First, all the names begin with a dot; second, the names of the environment files end with **rc**.

Files whose names start with a period are called DOTFILES or HIDDEN FILES. We will discuss them in Chapter 24 but, to help you now, here is a summary in advance.

There are many files that, for one reason or another, you want to ignore most of the time. Usually, these are configuration files that are used silently by some program or other. A good example of this are the shell initialization files we have been discussing.

As we will discuss in Chapter 24, the command you use to list your files is **ls**. As a convenience, **ls** will not list any names that begin with a dot unless you use the **-a** (all files) option. Thus, when you use **ls** in the usual manner, you won't see the names of any of your dotfiles.

This is why all the initialization and logout files have names that begin with a dot. Once you set up the files the way you want, there is no reason to think about them unless you want to make a change. In particular, you don't want to look at their names every time you list your files.

If you ever do want to list *all* your files, including the dotfiles, just use **ls -a**. To see how it works, take a moment to try both commands:

ENVIRONMENT FILE	PRONUNCIATION
.cshrc	"dot-C-shell-R-C"
.tcshrc	"dot-T-C-shell-R-C"
.bashrc	"dot-bash-R-C"

FIGURE 14-2: Pronouncing the names of rc files

Many Unix programs use initialization files whose names start with a dot (period) and end with the letters rc. The dot keeps the names from being displayed when you list your files; the rc is an abbreviation for "run commands". (See text for a full explanation.) This table lists the names of the most common shell environment files, along with the most common pronunciation for each name. Can you see the pattern?

```
ls
ls -a
```

Moving on, you will notice that the environment files have names that end with the letters **rc**: **.bashrc**, **.cshrc** and **.tcshrc**. This is a common convention used by Unix programs for naming initialization files. For example, the **vi** and **ex** editors (which are related) use an initialization file named **.exrc**; and the generic Unix email program, **mail**, uses an initialization file called **.mailrc**.

As you work with Unix over the years, you will encounter a great many **rc** files. As a general rule, such files are used to hold initialization commands and, almost always, they will be dotfiles to hide them from the **ls** command.

WHAT'S IN A NAME?

---

rc Files

Many Unix programs use configuration files whose names end in **rc**, for example, **.bashrc**, **.tcshrc** and **.exrc**. The designation **rc** stands for "run commands": commands that are run automatically each time a particular program starts.

The name derives from the CTSS operating system (Compatible Time Sharing System), developed at MIT in 1963. CTSS had a facility called "runcom" that would execute a list of commands stored in a file. Some of the early Unix programmers had used CTSS and, when they created configuration files, they chose names that ended in **rc**.

This was the start of a long-standing tradition among Unix programmers of naming initialization files by using dotfiles whose names end in **rc**. For example, if you wrote a program called **foo**, you would probably name the initialization file **.foorc**. That is why, earlier in the chapter, I suggested that, if you are a Korn shell user, you should name your environment file **.kshrc**.

When we talk about such files, we pronounce **rc** as two separate letters. For example, **.foorc** is "dot-foo-R-C". For reference, Figure 14-2 shows the pronunciations for the most common environment files. Knowing how to pronounce such names is important when you talk to other Unix people.

USING A SIMPLE TEXT EDITOR

In order to be a skillful Unix user, you must be able to edit (modify) text quickly. This is especially true if you are a programmer. Specifically, your login file, environment file, and logout file all contain text and, in order to create or modify these files, you need to be able to use a text editor program.

The two main Unix text editors are **vi** and Emacs and, eventually, you will need to master one of them. However, both **vi** and Emacs are complex. In fact, within this book, I have devoted an entire chapter to **vi** (Chapter 22). Reading this chapter, or teaching yourself Emacs, will take some time, so I have some alternatives for you. If you use a desktop environment such as Gnome or KDE (see Chapter 5), there will be a simple GUI-based editor you can use to create and modify small text files. If you use the CLI (command line interface), there will probably be a simple text-based editor you can use until you learn **vi** or Emacs.

Let's start with the desktop environment. There are two ways to access the GUI-based editor. First, you can start it from within the menu system. You will most likely find it listed under "Accessories". Second, you can start the program from a command line. Just open a terminal window (see Chapter 6), wait for the shell prompt, and enter the name of the program. With KDE, the GUI-based text editor is **kedit**; with Gnome, it is **gedit**.

Most Linux systems will have KDE or Gnome, but even if you don't use Linux, try running **gedit** anyway. It's part of the GNU utilities (Chapter 2) and, as such, you will find it on many different systems. For example, you can run **gedit** from a Solaris terminal window under JDS (the Java Desktop System).

If you don't have access to a GUI-based editor, there is a good chance your system will have a simple text-based editor. The most common ones are Pico and Nano. (They are pretty much the same; Nano is the GNU version of Pico.) To check if your system has one of these editors, see if you can display one of the man pages. If so, you can use the man page to teach yourself the basics:

```
man pico
man nano
```

Once you figure out how to use one of the simple text editors — either a GUI-based text editor or Nano/Pico — you can use it to create and edit your initialization and logout files. However, remember what I said: such programs are only for beginners. In the long run, you need to learn either **vi** or Emacs.

LOGIN SHELLS AND NON-LOGIN SHELLS

In Chapter 12, we talked about interactive and non-interactive shells. You use an interactive shell when you enter commands at the shell prompt; you use a non-interactive shell when you run a shell script. In order to understand how to use initialization files, we need to go a bit further in our analysis, because there are two different types of interactive shells.

Whenever you log in, the shell that starts is called a LOGIN SHELL. All other interactive shells are called NON-LOGIN SHELLS. The distinction is important because initialization files are processed differently for login shells than for non-login shells. Let's consider a few common situations.

1. Virtual consoles and terminal windows

When you use a desktop environment, such as Gnome or KDE, there are two ways to get to a shell prompt: you can open a terminal window, or you can change to a virtual console (see Chapter 6). When you use a virtual console — say, by pressing <Ctrl-Alt-F1> — you are required to log in. When you do, a login shell starts. On the other hand, if you simply open a terminal window, a non-login shell starts (because you did not log in).

2. Starting a new shell

At any time, you can start a new shell by entering its name. For example, say you are using Bash, and you want to try the Tcsh. Just enter the **tcsh** command. The new shell is a non-login shell (because you did not log in).

3. Using a remote host

To connect to a remote Unix host, you use the **ssh** (Secure Shell) program. Once **ssh** makes the connection for you, you must log in. Doing so starts a login shell.

WHEN ARE INITIALIZATION FILES EXECUTED?

Now that you understand the difference between a login shell and a non-login shell, we can discuss what happens when a new shell starts. The important question to answer is: Which initialization files are executed and when?

There are two general rules, with minor variations. Let's start with the rules.

1. A login shell executes your login file *and* your environment file.
2. A non-login shell only executes your environment file.

Here are the specific details, starting with the members of the Bourne shell family. As a shortcut, I will use **$ENV** to represent the file whose name is stored in the **$ENV** environment variable. For example, for the Korn shell, you might set the value of **$ENV** to be **.kshrc**.

Bash (default mode)
- Login shell: **.bash_profile**
- Non-login shell: **.bashrc**

Bash (POSIX mode)
- Login shell: **.profile**, then **$ENV**
- Non-login shell: **$ENV**

Korn shell
- Login shell: **.profile**, then **$ENV**
- Non-login shell: **$ENV**

Before we move on to the C-Shell family, let me make a few comments. First, you will notice that we can divide all the Bourne shells into two groups. Two of the three shells follow the POSIX convention of using **.profile** and **$ENV**. The exception is Bash in default mode. This is an important insight because, once you have used shells for a while, you will see that there is something different about Bash.

Bash reflects the attitudes of the young programmers who came of age in the mid- to late 1990s, during the growth of Linux and the open source movement (see Chapter 2). Emotionally, the open source programmers felt a bit like outlaws, rebelling against commercial Unix conventions, such as proprietary software and restrictive licensing agreements. For this reason, they opted to create an enhanced shell that was more than just a clone of the standard POSIX shell*. This is why, as a Bash user, you will encounter many situations in which Bash behaves differently than other shells.

For example, it is only the Bash login shell that executes a login file and not an environment file. With all other shells, a login shell executes *both* the login file and

---

*To be sure, the Bash programmers were not complete iconoclasts. They did create POSIX mode for situations that require strict conformity to community standards.

the environment file, in that order. This means that Bash users must put a special command in their login file to force it to execute the environment file. (I'll show you how to do this.)

Moving on, let's take a look at how the members of the C-Shell family use initialization files:

C-Shell
- Login shell: **.cshrc**, then **.login**
- Non-login shell: **.cshrc**

Tcsh
- Login shell: **.tcshrc**, then **.login**
- Non-login shell: **.tcshrc**

(For backwards compatibility, if the Tcsh can't find **.tcshrc**, it will look for **.cshrc**.)

This pattern is straightforward, except for one interesting anomaly. In the C-Shell family, login shells execute the environment file first. In the Bourne shell family, login shells execute the login file first. To understand why this is the case, we need to talk a bit about the history of initialization files.

A QUICK HISTORY OF SHELL INITIALIZATION FILES

(In this section, I am going to talk a bit about the history of the shell. For more details, see Chapter 11.)

The original Unix shell was written by Ken Thompson and used at Bell Labs in the early 1970s. This shell did not make use of a standardized initialization file. In the mid-1970s, Bell Labs programmers wrote two new replacement shells: the Mashey shell (also known as the PMB shell) and the Bourne shell. A programmer named Dick Haight added support for an initialization file (**.profile**) to the Mashey shell. Later, the same feature was added to the Bourne shell.

The **.profile** file was executed only once, when you logged in. In 1987, when Bill Joy developed the C-Shell at U.C. Berkeley, he enhanced the initialization process by using two files instead of one. The first file, **.cshrc**, ran every time a new shell started. The second file, **.login**, ran only when a login shell started. Thus, it made sense to execute **.login** after **.cshrc**, as its job was to run only those extra commands that were necessary at login time.

In 1982, David Korn of Bell Labs developed another replacement for the Bourne shell, the Korn shell. Korn adopted Bill Joy's idea of using two initialization files, what we now call an environment file (**.cshrc**) and a login file (**.login**). Because Korn worked at Bell Labs, which was a Bourne shell shop, he used the name **.profile** for the login shell. When it came time to name the environment file, Korn decided to let the users choose the name for themselves, by setting the **ENV** variable to the name of the environment shell. In this way, you could have more than one environment file for different purposes.

However, once he made this decision, Korn had to ensure that the login file executed **before** the environment file. Otherwise, there would be no way for a user to set the **ENV** variable.

That is why, to this day, Bourne family shells run the login file first, and the C-Shell family shells run the environment file first. In practice, this is usually not a big deal, but it is something to remember if you ever have a mysterious initialization problem that seems insolvable.

WHAT TO PUT IN YOUR INITIALIZATION FILES

We can now consider the questions I posed a while back: What should you put in your login file? What should you put in your environment file? Here are the answers.

Your login file has two jobs: to set up your environment and to initialize your work session. Thus, your login file should contain commands to (1) create or modify environment variables, and (2) perform all one-time actions.

The login file, then, is where you set variables such as **PATH**, **PAGER**, and so on, and use **umask** to set your file creation mask (Chapter 25). If the login file is for a remote host, you may also need to use **stty** to modify key mappings (Chapter 7). Finally, you may want to display a personal message or other information each time you log in.

As we discussed earlier in the chapter, the environment is automatically inherited by all child processes, including new shells. Thus, you only need to set environment variables (such as **PATH**) once, in your login file. It makes no sense to set an environment variable in your environment file, where it will be reset every time a new shell starts.

Your environment file has a different job: to set up whatever customizations cannot be stored in the environment, in particular, shell options, aliases and functions. Because these settings are *not* stored in the environment, they must be recreated every time a new shell starts.

DISPLAYING, CREATING AND EDITING YOUR INITIALIZATION FILES

You may already have one or more initialization files. On a shared system, such files are often created by the system administrator. On your own system, they may be generated automatically at the time your account was created. If you already have such files, you can modify them to suit your needs. If not, you can create the files yourself.

Initialization files are kept in your home directory (your personal directory; see Chapter 23). As we discussed earlier, all initialization files are dotfiles, which means their names start with a . (period). For reference, Figure 14-1, earlier in the chapter, contains the names of the standard initialization files.

As we discussed earlier, you display the names of all your dotfiles by using the **ls -a** command. (Without the **-a** option, **ls** won't show dotfiles.) If the list is too long, you can send it to **less**:

```
ls -a
ls -a | less
```

Once you see which initialization files you have, you can look at their contents by using **less**. One of the following commands should do the job:

```
less .bash_login
less .bash_logout
less .bash_profile
less .bashrc
less .cshrc
less .kshrc
less .login
less .logout
less .profile
less .tcshrc
```

To create or modify a dotfile, you need to use a text editor. If you already know **vi** or Emacs, great. If not, you can — for now — use one of the simpler editors we discussed earlier, **kedit** or **gedit**. Because these are GUI-based editors, you must use them from within a desktop manager. You can't use them from a virtual terminal or from a CLI connected to a remote host.

Starting from your GUI, open a terminal window and enter the name of the editor, followed by the name of the file you want to create or edit. With KDE, use **kedit**; with Gnome, use **gedit**. For example:

```
kedit .bash_profile
gedit .bash_profile
```

A new window will open. If the file already exists, it will be loaded, allowing you to modify the contents. If the file does not exist, you will have an empty window, allowing you to create the file.

COMMENTS IN SHELL SCRIPTS

The initialization files we have been discussing are actually shell scripts: programs that are written in the language of the shell and executed by the shell. In a moment, we will take a look at some sample scripts. Before we do, I want to explain an important point regarding shell scripts and programs in general.

Take a look at the initialization files in Figure 14-3, 14-4, 14-5 and 14-6. Although they are quite different from one another, you will notice they have one thing in common: many of the lines begin with a **#** (hash or pound) character. Such lines are called COMMENTS.

As a script is executed, the shell ignores all the comments. This allows you to put in notes to help you remember the logic and understand the script. If you have never programmed before, you might think comments should not be necessary when you write scripts for your own use. Surely, when you read a script at a future date, you will remember the logic behind the various commands. After all, you are the one who wrote the script in the first place.

The truth is, although your reasoning may be clear right now, when you read a shell script, or any program, even a few days later, you *will* have trouble remembering what you were thinking at the time. This is why all experienced programmers put lots of comments in everything they write.

Moreover, the time may come when someone else will need to read your scripts. In such cases, comments are invaluable. My advice is to document what you are doing, as you are doing it. Pretend that everything you write will have to be understood by another person. Later, you will be that person and, believe me, you will never be sorry you took the time to put in comments*.

Within a shell script, the actual definition of a comment is a **#** character and everything that follows it to the end of the line. Thus, a comment can take up all or part of a line. Consider the following example:

```
# Display the time, date, and current users
date; users
```

The first line is a comment; the second line contains two commands with no comments. When the shell executes these two lines, it will ignore the comment and run the commands on the second line. Now consider:

```
date; users  # Display time, date, and current users
```

In this case, we have a single line, containing two commands followed by a comment. When the shell executes this line, it will run the **date** command and **users** command, and ignore everything else on the line. Thus, when you write shell scripts, you have two ways to put in a comment: at the end of a line, or on a line by itself.

In the following few sections, we will take a closer look at the sample initialization files. As we do, think about how difficult it would be to understand these files if there were no comments.

BOURNE SHELL FAMILY: SAMPLE INITIALIZATION FILES

In the next two sections, we will discuss four sample initialization files. What you are about to see will tie together everything you have learned in the last three chapters: interactive shells, environment variables, shell variables, shell options, metacharacters, quoting, the search path, command substitution, the history list, command line editing, aliases, and comments. My intention is for you to adapt these files for your own use, making whatever changes and additions are necessary to serve your needs.

---

*When I was a computer science grad student at the University of California at San Diego, I was a teaching assistant for a course in systems programming, a very technical type of programming. At the same time, there was another teaching assistant named Peter.

Although Peter and I got along, there was one point on which we disagreed categorically. I felt we should teach the students to use lots of comments in their programs. Peter didn't like comments, and he didn't teach his students to use them. He said the comments got in the way of his reading the programs (which we had to grade).

After graduating, I went on to medical school and became a professional writer. To date, I have written 32 books which have sold over 2,000,000 copies and been translated into many languages. I live in Southern California with a beautiful, intelligent woman, in a house with an ocean view. We have loving families and we share wonderful friends and a variety of interests and accomplishments. Peter, on the other hand, most likely turned out to be a total failure.

The moral, I think, is obvious.

In this section, we will discuss initialization files that are suitable for a member of the Bourne shell family (Bash, Korn shell). In the next section, we will discuss initialization files for the C-Shell family. Regardless of which shell you happen to use right now, I'd like you to take a look at both sections. Over the course of your life with Unix and Linux, you will find yourself using a variety of systems, and it will help you to be familiar with the initialization files for both shell families.

Our goal in this section is to take a close look at a sample login file and a sample environment file. You will find the login file in Figure 14-3. I will remind you that this is the file that is executed automatically each time you log in. With Bash, your login file will be named **.bash_profile** or **.bash_login**. With the Korn shell, or Bash in POSIX mode, it will be **.profile**.

The environment file is in Figure 14-4. This file is executed every time a new shell starts. With Bash, your environment file is named **.bashrc**. With the Korn shell or Bash in POSIX mode, you can name the environment file anything you want by setting the **ENV** variable. My suggestion is to use **.kshrc** for the Korn shell and **.bashrc** for Bash.

With the Bourne shell family, the login file is run first, before the environment file, so we will discuss the login file first. (With the C-Shell family, the environment file is run first.)

By now, you should understand most of the commands, variables and options used in the sample files. I'll go over each section for you and, for reference, I'll tell you the chapter in which you can find more information should you need it.

Section 1 of the login file defines the environment variables. We set the size of the history list to 50 lines, the default paging program to **less**, and the default text editor to **vi**. We also add a specific directory to the end of the search path. (Chapter 12: variables; Chapter 13: history list, search path; Chapter 17: paging programs.)

Sections 2A and 2B define the shell prompt by setting the **PS1** environment variable. Section 2A is for Bash; section 2B is for the Korn shell. Use either 2A or 2B, but not both. (Chapter 12: variables; Chapter 13: shell prompt.)

Section 3 sets the file creation mask to control the default permissions for newly created files (Chapter 25: file permissions, **umask**).

Section 4 is used only for login files on a remote host. You do not need this section when you are using Unix or Linux on your own computer. The **stty** command sets the key mapping for the **erase** signal. I have given you two possible commands: use whichever one works best with your keyboard. (Chapter 7: **erase** signal, **stty**.)

Section 5 displays a welcome message. You can change this to whatever you want. (Chapter 8: **date**; Chapter 12: **echo**, command substitution.)

Section 6 displays interesting information about the system. (Chapter 4: **last**; Chapter 8: **whoami**, **users**, **uptime**; Chapter 12: **echo**, command substitution; Chapter 15: pipeline; Chapter 16: **head**.)

Sections 7A and 7B make sure the environment file is run. Section 7A is for Bash. It checks to see if a file named **.bashrc** exists. If so, it tells the shell to run the file. Section 7B is for the Korn shell. It sets the value of the **ENV** environment variable to the name of the environment file. Use either 7A or 7B, but not both. (Chapter 12: variables; Chapter 14: environment files.)

Section 8 is for the Korn shell only. By default, the Korn shell does not support a logout file, the file that is executed automatically each time you log out. However, you can simulate a logout file by trapping the **EXIT** signal, which is generated when you log out.

```
# ======================================
# Bourne Shell family: Sample login file
# ======================================

# 1. Environment variables
export HISTSIZE=50
export PAGER=less
export PATH="${PATH}:${HOME}/bin"
export VISUAL=vi

# 2A. Shell prompt - Bash
export PS1="(\w) `basename ${SHELL}`[\!]$ "

# 2B. Shell prompt - Korn Shell
export PS1="(\$PWD) `basename ${SHELL}`[!]$ "

# 3. File creation mask
umask 077

# 4. Terminal settings (for remote host only)
stty erase ^H
# stty erase ^?

# 5. Display welcome message
echo "Welcome Harley."
echo "Today is `date`."
echo

# 6. System information
echo "Last three logins:"; last `logname` | head -3
echo
echo "Current users: `users`"
echo
echo "System uptime:"; uptime
echo

# 7A. Environment file - Bash
if [ -f ${HOME}/.bashrc ]
then source ${HOME}/.bashrc
fi

# 7B. Environment file - Korn Shell
export ENV=${HOME}/.kshrc

# 8. Logout file - Korn Shell
trap '. ${HOME}/.logout; exit' EXIT
```

FIGURE 14-3: Bourne Shell family: Sample login file

The login file is executed automatically each time you log in. Here is a sample login file suitable for Bash or the Korn shell. Use this file as a template and adapt it for your own use. See text for details.

Here, we specify that when the **EXIT** signal occurs, the file named `.logout` should be executed. (Chapter 7: trapping a signal; Chapter 14: logout files.)

With the Bourne shell family, the environment file is simpler than the login file, because the login file does most of the work. All the environment file needs to do is re-create whatever is lost when a new shell is started: shell options, aliases and functions. Take a look at Figure 14-4, where you will see a sample environment file.

Section 1 sets the shell options. The **ignoreeof** option requires us to use a **logout** or **exit** command to log out. By trapping the **eof** signal, we keep ourselves from logging out accidentally by pressing **^D** one too many times. (With Bash, you can set the **IGNOREEOF** environment variable instead of using the shell option.) The second shell option sets Emacs for our command line editor. Strictly speaking, you don't need to set this option, as Emacs is the default. However, I like to set it explicitly as a reminder. Finally, we set the **noclobber** option to protect us from accidentally deleting the contents of a file when we redirect standard output. (Chapter 7: trapping the **eof** signal; Chapter 12: shell options, command line editing; Chapter 15: redirecting standard output.)

Section 2 sets the aliases. They include an abbreviation for the **alias** and **date** commands; several variations of the **ls** command; the **del** alias to help us avoid deleting the wrong files; and the **r** and **h** aliases to help us use the history list. (Chapter 8: **date**; Chapter 12: history list, aliases; Chapter 24: **ls**.)

Section 3 is reserved for any shell functions we may want to define. A function allows you to create your own customized commands by writing a small program. Learning to

```
# ===========================================
# Bourne Shell family: Sample environment file
# ===========================================

# 1. Shell options
set -o ignoreeof
set -o emacs
set -o noclobber

# 2. Aliases
alias a=alias
alias d=date
alias del='fc -s ls=rm'
alias h=history
alias l='ls -F'
alias la='ls -a'
alias ll='ls -l'
alias r='fc -s'

#3. Functions
# functions go here
```

FIGURE 14-4: Bourne Shell family: Sample environment file
The environment file is executed automatically whenever a new shell starts. Here is a sample environment file suitable for Bash or the Korn shell. Use this file as a template and adapt it for your own use. See text for details.

write such programs is beyond the scope of this book. However, if you do use functions, this is the place to define them.

C-SHELL FAMILY: SAMPLE INITIALIZATION FILES

In this section, we will discuss two sample initialization files for the C-Shell family (C-Shell and Tcsh). What you are about to read here will tie together everything you have learned in the last three chapters. My intention is to explain the contents of these sample files so you can adapt them for your own use by making whatever changes and additions are necessary to serve your needs.

We'll start with the environment file in Figure 14-5. I will remind you that this is the file that is executed automatically whenever a new shell starts. With the C-Shell, this file is named .cshrc. With the Tcsh, it can be named either .tcshrc or .cshrc. After discussing the environment file, we will move on to Figure 14-6, which contains a sample login file: the file that is executed whenever you log in. With both shells, this file is named .login.

We are starting with the environment file because, in the C-Shell family, it is run first, before the login file. (With the Bourne shell family, the login file is run first.)

```
# =======================================
# C-Shell family: Sample environment file
# =======================================

# 1. Shell variables
set filec  # only necessary for C-Shell
set history = 50
set ignoreeof
set noclobber
set path = (${path} ${HOME}/bin)
set savehist = 30

# 2A. Shell prompt - C-Shell
set prompt = "($PWD) `basename ${SHELL}` [\!]% "
alias cd 'cd \!* && set prompt = "($PWD) `basename ${SHELL}` [\\!]% "'

# 2B. Shell prompt - Tcsh
set prompt = "`basename ${SHELL}` [\!]> "
set rprompt = "(%~)"

# 3. Aliases
alias a alias
alias d date
alias del 'rm \!ls:*'
alias h history
alias l 'ls -F'
alias la 'ls -a'
alias ll 'ls -l'
```

FIGURE 14-5: C-Shell family: Sample environment file

The environment file is executed automatically whenever a new shell starts. Here is a sample environment file suitable for the C-Shell or the Tcsh. Use this file as a template and adapt it for your own use. See text for details.

By now, you should understand most of the commands, variables and options used in the sample files. I'll go over each section for you and, for reference, I'll tell you the chapter in which you can find more information should you need it.

The job of the environment file is to recreate whatever is lost when a new shell is started: shell options, the shell prompt, and aliases.

Section 1 defines the shell variables. We set the size of the history list, add a specific directory to the end of the search path, and turn on file completion. (With the Tcsh, file completion is turned on by default. With the C-Shell, however, it is not, so if you want filename completion, you must set the **filec** variable.) We also set **ignoreeof** to trap the **eof** signal. This forces us to use the **logout** command to log out, which keeps us from logging out accidentally by pressing **^D** one too many times. We also set **noclobber** to protect us from accidentally deleting the contents of a file when we redirect standard output. Finally, we set **savehist** to save the history list when we log out. (Chapter 7: trapping the **eof** signal; Chapter 12: variables; Chapter 13: history list, search path, autocompletion; Chapter 15: redirecting standard output.)

```
# ==================================
# C-Shell family: sample login file
# ==================================

# 1. Environment variables
setenv PAGER less
setenv VISUAL vi

# 2. Command line editor - Tcsh
bindkey -e

# 3. File creation mask
umask 077

# 4. Terminal settings (for remote host only)
stty erase ^H
# stty erase ^?

# 5. Display welcome message
echo "Welcome Harley."
echo "Today is `date`."
echo

# 6. System information
echo "Last three logins:"; last `whoami` | head -3
echo
echo "Current users: `users`"
echo
echo "System uptime:"; uptime
echo
```

FIGURE 14-6: C-Shell family: Sample login file

The login file is executed automatically each time you log in. Here is a sample login file suitable for the C-Shell or the Tcsh. Use this file as a template and adapt it for your own use. See text for details.

Sections 2A and 2B define the shell prompt by setting the **prompt** shell variable. Section 2A is for the C-Shell; section 2B is for the Tcsh. Use either 2A or 2B, but not both. You will notice that the C-Shell prompt contains the name of the working directory. Because this quantity is not updated automatically, we define an alias that will reset the shell prompt whenever we use the **cd** (change directory) command. This is not necessary for the Tcsh. With the Tcsh, we set the right-hand prompt (**rprompt**) to display the name of the working directory. (Chapter 12: variables; Chapter 13: shell prompt.)

Section 3 sets the aliases. They include an abbreviation for the **alias** and **date** commands; several variations of the **ls** command; the **del** alias to help us avoid deleting the wrong files; and the **r** and **h** aliases to help us use the history list. (Chapter 8: **date**; Chapter 12: history list, aliases; Chapter 24: **ls**.)

With the C-Shell family, the login file is simpler than the environment file, because the environment file does most of the work. (This is the opposite of the Bourne shell family.) Take a look at Figure 14-6, where you will see a sample login file.

Section 1 of the login file defines the environment variables. We set the default paging program to **less** and the default text editor to **vi**. (Chapter 12: variables; Chapter 21: paging programs.)

Section 2 sets Emacs for our command line editor. Strictly speaking, you don't need to set this option, as Emacs is the default. However, I like to set it explicitly as a reminder. Since the C-Shell does not support command line editing, we only need this section for the Tcsh. (Chapter 12: command line editing, **bindkey**.)

Section 3 sets the file creation mask to control the default permissions for newly created files (Chapter 25: file permissions, **umask**).

Section 4 is used only for login files on a remote host. You do not need this section when you are using Unix or Linux on your own computer. The **stty** command sets the key mapping for the **erase** signal. I have given you two possible commands. Use whichever one works best with your keyboard. (Chapter 7: **erase** signal, **stty**.)

Section 5 displays a welcome message. You can change this to whatever you want. (Chapter 8: **date**; Chapter 12: **echo**, command substitution.)

Section 6 displays interesting information about the system. (Chapter 4: **last**; Chapter 8: **whoami**, **users**, **uptime**; Chapter 12: **echo**, command substitution; Chapter 15: pipeline; Chapter 16: **head**.)

CHAPTER 14 EXERCISES

REVIEW QUESTIONS

1. What is an initialization file? Name the two types of initialization files. What is a logout file?

2. What is a dotfile? What is an **rc** file?

3. What is a login shell? What is a non-login shell? Why is the distinction important?

4. You have a list of favorite aliases you like to use, so you decide to put the definitions in one of your initialization files. Which file will they go in, the login file or the environment file? Why? What else goes in this file?

APPLYING YOUR KNOWLEDGE

1. Look carefully in your home directory to see if you already have a login file and an environment file. (You can use the command **ls -a** to list your dotfiles.) If so, take a look at what is inside each file. (Either use the **less** command or open the files in your text editor.)

2. Create (or modify) a login file for yourself using the sample file in either Figure 14-3 or 14-6 as a template. If you have an existing file, save a copy under a different name as soon as you open it within your text editor, before you make any modifications. That way, if you make a mistake, you will be able to change back to the original version.

3. Create (or modify) an environment file for yourself using the sample file in either Figure 14-4 or 14-5 as a template. If you have an existing file, make a backup copy as described in the previous exercise.

4. Create a logout file for yourself. If you are not sure what to put in it, use the **echo** command to say goodbye to yourself. The name you use for this file depends on which shell you are using (see Figure 14-1). If you are using the Korn shell, you will have to trap the exit signal (explained in the chapter and in Figure 14-3).

FOR FURTHER THOUGHT

1. The POSIX standard mandates that a shell should support a login file and an environment file, but not necessarily a logout file. This implies that the logout file is less important than the other two files. Why should this be the case?

2. On many systems, when a new account is created the new userid will automatically be given a default login file and, sometimes, a default environment file. Why is this a good idea? Would you advise a new user to modify these files or leave them alone?

# CHAPTER 15

STANDARD I/O,
REDIRECTION AND PIPES

From the beginning, the Unix command line has always had a certain something that makes it different from other operating systems. That "something" is what we might call the Unix toolbox: the large variety of programs that are a part of every Unix and Linux system, and the simple, elegant ways in which you can use them.

In this chapter, I will explain the philosophy behind the Unix toolbox. I will then show you how to combine basic building blocks into powerful tools of your own. In Chapter 16, we will survey the most important of these programs, to introduce you to the resources available for your day-to-day work. By the time you finish these two chapters, you will be on your way to developing the most interesting and enjoyable computer skills you will ever use.

THE UNIX PHILOSOPHY

In the 1960s, the Bell Labs researchers who would become the first Unix developers were working on an operating system called Multics (see Chapter 1). One of the problems with Multics was that it was too unwieldy. The Multics design team had tried to make their system do too many things in order to please too many people. When Unix was designed — at first, in 1969, by only two people — the developers felt strongly that it was important to avoid the complexity of Multics and other such operating systems.

Thus, they developed a Spartan attitude in which economy of expression was paramount. Each program, they reasoned, should be a single tool with, perhaps, a few basic options. A program should do only one thing, but should do it well. If you needed to perform a complex task, you should — whenever possible — do so by combining existing tools, not by writing new programs.

For example, virtually all Unix programs generate some type of output. When a program displays a large amount of output, the data may come so fast that most of it will scroll off the screen before you can read it. One solution is to require that every program be able to display output one screenful at a time when necessary. This is just the type of solution that the original Unix developers wanted to avoid. Why should all programs need to incorporate the same functionality? Couldn't there be a simpler way to ensure that output is presented to users in a way that is easy for them to read?

For that matter, why should every program you run have to know where its output was going? Sometimes you want output to be displayed on the screen; other times you want to save it in a file. There may even be times when you want to send output to another program for more processing.

For these reasons, the Unix designers built a single tool whose job was to display data, one screenful at a time. This tool was called **more**, because after displaying a screenful of data, the program displayed the prompt **--More--** to let the user know there was more data.

The tool was simple to use. A user would read one screenful of data and then press <Space> to display the next screen. When the user was finished, he would type **q** to quit.

Once **more** was available, programmers could stop worrying about how the output of their programs would be displayed. If you were a programmer, you knew that whenever a user running your program found himself with a lot of output, he would simply send it to **more**. (You'll learn how to do this later in the chapter.) If you were a user, you knew that, no matter how many programs you might ever use, you only needed to learn how to use one output display tool.

This approach has three important advantages, even today. First, when you design a Unix tool, you can keep it simple. For example, you do not have to endow every new program with the ability to display data one screenful at a time: there is already a tool to do that. Similarly, there are also tools to sort output, remove certain columns, delete lines that do not contain specific patterns, and on and on (see Chapter 16). Since these tools are available to all Unix users, you don't have to include such functionality in your own programs.

This leads us to the second advantage. Because each tool need only do one thing, you can, as a programmer, concentrate your effort. When you are designing, say, a program to search for specific patterns in a data file, you can make it the best possible pattern searching program; when you are designing a sorting program, you can make it the best possible sorting program; and so on.

The third advantage is ease of use. As a user, once you learn the commands to control the standard screen display tool, you know how to control the output for *any* program.

Thus, in two sentences, I can summarize the Unix philosophy as follows:

- Each program or command should be a tool that does only one thing and does it well.
- When you need a new tool, it is better to combine existing tools than to write new ones.

We sometimes describe this philosophy as:

- "Small is beautiful" or "Less is more".

THE NEW UNIX PHILOSOPHY

Since Unix is well into its fourth decade, it makes sense to ask if the Unix philosophy has, in the long run, proven to be successful. The answer is, yes and no.

To a large extent, the Unix philosophy is still intact. As you will see in Chapter 16, there are a great many single-purpose tools, which are easy to combine as the need arises.

Moreover, because the original Unix developers designed the system so well, programs that are over 30 years old can, today, work seamlessly with programs that are brand new. Compare this to the world of Windows or the Macintosh.

However, the original philosophy has proven inadequate in three important ways. First, too many people could not resist creating alternative versions of the basic tools. This means that you must sometimes learn how to use more than one tool to do the same job.

For example, over the years, there have been three screen display programs in common use: **more**, **pg** and **less**. These days, most people use **less**, which is the most powerful (and most complex) of the three programs. However, **more** is simpler to use, and you will find it on all systems, so you really should know how to use it. My guess is that, one day, you will log in to a system that uses **more** to display output and, if you only know **less**, you will be confused. On the other hand, just understanding **more** is not good enough because, on many systems, **less** is the default (and **less** is a better program). The bottom line: you need to learn how to use at least two different screen display programs.

The second way in which the Unix philosophy was inadequate had to do with the growing needs of users. The idea that small is beautiful has a lot of appeal, but as users grew more sophisticated and their needs grew more demanding, it became clear that simple tools were often not enough.

For instance, the original Unix text editor was **ed**. (The name, which stands for "editor", is pronounced as two separate letters, "ee-dee"). **ed** was designed to be used with terminals that printed output on paper. The **ed** program had relatively few commands; it was simple to use and could be learned quickly. If you had used Unix in the early days, you would have found **ed** to be an unadorned, unpretentious tool: it did one thing (text editing) and it did it well*.

As editors go, **ed** was, at best, mildly sophisticated. Within a few years, however, terminals were improved and the needs of Unix users became more demanding. To respond to those needs, programmers developed new editors. In fact, over the years, literally tens of different text editors were developed.

For mainstream users, **ed** was replaced by a program called **ex**. (The name, which stands for "extended editor" is pronounced as two separate letters, "ee-ex".) Then, **ex** itself was extended to create **vi** ("visual editor", pronounced "vee-eye"). As an alternative to the **ed**/**ex**/**vi** family, an entirely different editing system called Emacs was developed.

Today, **vi** and Emacs are the most popular Unix text editors, but no one would ever accuse them of being simple and unadorned. Indeed, **vi** (Chapter 22) and Emacs are extremely complex.

The third way in which the original Unix philosophy has proved inadequate has to do with a basic limitation of the CLI (command line interface). As you know, the CLI is text-based. This means it cannot handle graphics and pictures, or files that do not contain plain text, such as spreadsheets or word processor documents.

Most command-line programs read and write text, which is why such programs are able to work together: they all use the same type of data. However, this means that when you want to use other types of data — non-textual data — you must use other types of programs. This is why, as we discussed in Chapters 5 and 6, you must learn how to use *both* the CLI and GUI environments.

---

*The **ed** editor is still available on all Unix and Linux systems. Give it a try when you get a moment. Start by reading the man page (**man ed**).

For these reasons, you must approach the learning of Unix carefully. In 1979, when Unix was only a decade old, the original design was still intact, and you could learn most everything about all the common commands. Today, there is so much more Unix to learn, you can't possibly know it all, or even most of it. This means you must be selective about which programs and tools you want to learn. Moreover, as you teach yourself how to use a tool, you must be selective about which options and commands you want to master.

As you read the next two chapters, there is something important I want you to remember. By all means, you should work in front of your computer as you read, and enter new commands as you encounter them. This is how you learn to use Unix. However, I want you to do more than just memorize details. As you read and as you experiment, I want you to develop a sense of perspective. Every now and then, take a moment to pull back and ask yourself, "Where does the tool I am learning right now fit into the big picture?"

My goal for you is that, in time, you will come to appreciate what we might call the new Unix philosophy:

• "Small is beautiful, except when it isn't."

> **HINT**
>
> Whenever you learn how to use a new program, do not feel as if you must memorize every detail. Rather, just answer three questions:
>
> 1. What can this program do for me?
> 2. What are the basic details? That is, what works for most people most of the time?
> 3. Where can I look for more help when I need it?

STANDARD INPUT, STANDARD OUTPUT AND STANDARD ERROR

If there is one single idea that is central to using Unix effectively, it is the concept of standard input and output. Understand this one idea, and you are one giant step closer to becoming a Unix master.

The basic idea is simple: Every text-based program should be able to accept input from any source and write output to any target.

For instance, say you have a program that sorts lines of text. You should have your choice of typing the text at the keyboard, reading it from an existing file, or even using the output of another program. Similarly, the **sort** program should be able to display its output on the screen, write it to a file, or send it to another program for more processing.

Using such a system has two wonderful advantages. First, as a user, you have enormous flexibility. When you run a program, you can define the input and output (I/O) as you see fit, which means you only have to learn one program for each task. For example, the same program that sorts a small amount of data and displays it on the screen, can also sort a large amount of data and save it to a file.

The second advantage to doing I/O in this way is that it makes creating new tools a lot easier. When you write a program, you can depend on Unix to handle the input and output for you, which means you don't need to worry about all the variations. Instead, you can concentrate on the design and programming of your tool.

The crucial idea here is that the source of input and the target of output are not specified by the programmer. Rather, he or she writes the program to read and write in a general way. Later, *at the time the program runs*, the shell connects the program to whatever input and output the user wants to use*.

To implement this idea, the developers of Unix designed a general way to read data called STANDARD INPUT and two general ways to write data called STANDARD OUTPUT and STANDARD ERROR. The reason there are two different output targets is that standard output is used for regular output, and standard error is used for error messages. Collectively, we refer to these facilities as STANDARD I/O (pronounced "standard eye-oh").

In practice, we often speak of these three terms informally as if they were actual objects. Thus, we might say, "To save the output of a program, write standard output to a file." What we really mean is, "To save the output of a program, tell the shell to set the output target to be a file."

Understanding the concepts of standard input, standard output, and standard error are crucial to using Unix well. Moreover, these same concepts are also used to control I/O with other programming languages, such as C and C++.

> **HINT**
>
> You will often see standard input, standard output, and standard error abbreviated as STDIN, STDOUT and STDERR. When we use these abbreviations in conversation, we pronounce them as "standard in", "standard out", and "standard error".
>
> For example, if you were creating some documentation, you might write, "The **sort** program reads from stdin, and writes to stdout and stderr." If you were reading this sentence to an audience, you would pronounce the abbreviations as follows: "The **sort** program reads from standard in, and writes to standard out and standard error."

REDIRECTING STANDARD OUTPUT

When you log in, the shell automatically sets standard input to the keyboard, and standard output and standard error to the screen. This means that, by default, most programs will read from the keyboard and write to the screen.

However — and here's where the power of Unix comes in — every time you enter a command, you can tell the shell to reset standard input, standard output or standard error for the duration of the command.

In effect, you can tell the shell: "I want to run the **sort** command and save the output to a file called **names**. So for this command only, I want you to write standard output to that file. After the command is over, I want you to reset standard output back to my screen."

Here is how it works: If you want the output of a command to go to the screen, you don't have to do anything. This is automatic.

If you want the output of a command to go to a file, type **>** (greater-than) followed by the name of the file, at the end of the command. For example:

---

*Historically, the idea of using abstract I/O devices was developed to allow programmers to write programs that were independent of specific hardware. Can you see how, philosophically, this idea is related to the layers of abstraction we discussed in Chapter 5, and to the terminal description databases (Termcap and Terminfo) we discussed in Chapter 7?

```
sort > names
```

This command will write its output to a file called **names**. The use of a **>** character is apt, because it looks like an arrow showing the path of the output.

When you write output to a file in this way, the file may or may not already exist. If the file does not exist, the shell will create it for you automatically. In our example, the shell will create a file called **names**.

If the file already exists, its contents will be replaced, so you must be careful. For instance, if the file **names** already exists, the original contents will be lost permanently.

In some cases, this is fine, because you do want to replace the contents of the file, perhaps with newer information. In other cases, you may not want to lose what is in the file. Rather, you want to add new data to what is already there. To do so use **>>**, two greater-than characters in a row. This tells the shell to append any new data to the end of an existing file. Thus, consider the command:

```
sort >> names
```

If the file **names** does not exist, the shell will create it. If it does exist, the new data will be appended to the end of the file. Nothing will be lost.

When we send standard output to a file, we say that we REDIRECT it. Thus, in the previous two examples, we redirect standard output to a file called **names**.

Now you can see why there are two types of output: standard output and standard error. If you redirect the standard output to a file, you won't miss the error messages, as they will still be displayed on your monitor.

When you redirect output, it is up to you to be careful, so you do not lose valuable data. There are two ways to do so. First, every time you redirect output to a file, think carefully: Do you want to replace the current contents of the file? If so, use **>**. Or, would you rather append new data to the end of the file. If that is the case, use **>>**.

Second, as a safeguard, you can tell the shell to never replace the contents of an existing file. You do this by setting the **noclobber** option (Bash, Korn shell) or the **noclobber** shell variable (C-Shell, Tcsh). We'll discuss this in the next section.

PREVENTING FILES FROM BEING REPLACED OR CREATED BY REDIRECTION

In the previous section, I explained that when you redirect standard output to a file, any data that already exists in the file will be lost. I also explained that when you use **>>** to append output to a file, the file will be created if it does not already exist.

There may be times when you do not want the shell to make such assumptions on your behalf. For example, say you have a file called **names** that contains 5,000 lines of data. You want to append the output of a **sort** command to the end of this file. In other words, you want to enter the command:

```
sort >> names
```

However, you make a mistake and accidentally enter:

```
sort > names
```

What happens? All of your original data is wiped out. Moreover, it is wiped out *quickly*. Even if you notice the error the moment you press <Return>, and even if you instantly press **^C** to abort the program (by sending the **intr** signal; see Chapter 7), it is too late. The data in the file is gone forever.

This is why. As soon as you press <Return>, the shell gets everything ready for the **sort** program by deleting the contents of your target file. Since the shell is a lot faster than you, by the time you abort the program the target file is already empty.

To prevent such catastrophes, you can tell the shell not to replace an existing file when you use **>** to redirect output. In addition, with the C-Shell family, you can also tell the shell not to create a new file when you use **>>** to append data. This ensures that no files are replaced or created by accident.

To have the shell take such precautions on your behalf, you use what we might call the **noclobber** facility. With the Bourne shell family (Bash, Korn shell), you set the **noclobber** shell option:

```
set -o noclobber
```

To unset this option, use:

```
set +o noclobber
```

With the C-Shell family (C-Shell, Tcsh), you set the **noclobber** shell variable:

```
set noclobber
```

To unset this variable, use:

```
unset noclobber
```

(See Chapter 12 for a discussion of options and variables; see Appendix G for a summary.)

Once **noclobber** is set, you have built-in protection. For example, let's say you already have a file called **names** and you enter:

```
sort > names
```

You will see an error message telling you that the file **names** already exists. Here is such a message from Bash:

```
bash: names: cannot overwrite existing file
```

Here is the equivalent message from the Tcsh:

```
names: File exists.
```

In both cases, the shell has refused to carry out the command, and your file is safe.

What if you really want to replace the file? In such cases, it is possible to override **noclobber** temporarily. With a Bourne shell, you use **>|** instead of **>**:

```
sort >| names
```

With a C-Shell, you use **>!** instead of **>**:

```
sort >! names
```

Using **>|** or **>!** instead of **>** tells the shell to redirect standard output even if the file exists.

As we discussed earlier, you can append data to a file by redirecting standard output with **>>** instead of **>**. In both cases, if the output file does not exist, the shell will create it. However, if you are *appending* data, it would seem likely that you expect the file to already exist. Thus, if you use **>>** and the file does not exist, you are probably making a mistake. Can **noclobber** help you here?

Not with a Bourne shell. If you append data with Bash or the Korn shell and the **noclobber** option is set, it's business as usual. The C-Shell and Tcsh know better. They will tell you that the file does not exist, and refuse to carry out the command.

For example, say you are a C-Shell or Tcsh user; the **noclobber** shell variable is set; and you have a file named **addresses**, to which you want to append data. You enter the command:

```
sort >> address
```

You will see an error message:

```
address: No such file or directory
```

At which point you will probably say, "Oh, I should have typed **addresses**, not **address**. Thank you, Mr. C-Shell."

Of course, there may be occasions when you are appending data to a file, and you really do want to override **noclobber**. For example, you are a C-Shell user and, for safety, you have set **noclobber**. You want to sort a file named **input** and append the data to a file named **output**.

If **output** doesn't exist, you want to create it. The importaznt thing is, if **output** does exist, you don't want to lose what is already in it, which is why you are appending (**>>**), not replacing (**>**). If **noclobber** wasn't set, you would use:

```
sort >> output
```

Since **noclobber** is set, you must override it. To do so, just use **>>!** instead of **>>**:

```
sort >>! output
```

This will override the automatic check for this one command only.

REDIRECTING STANDARD INPUT

By default, standard input is set to the keyboard. This means that, when you run a program that needs to read data, the program expects you to enter the data by typing it, one line at a time. When you are finished entering data, you press **^D** (<Ctrl-D>) to send the **eof** signal (see Chapter 7). Pressing **^D** indicates that there is no more data.

Here is an example you can try for yourself. Enter:

```
sort
```

The **sort** program is now waiting for you to enter data from standard input (the keyboard). Type as many lines as you want. For example, you might enter:

```
Harley
Casey
Weedly
Linda
Melissa
```

After you have pressed <Return> on the last line, press **^D** to send the **eof** signal. The **sort** program will now sort all the data alphabetically and write it to standard output. By default this is the screen, so you will see:

```
Casey
Harley
Linda
Melissa
Weedly
```

There will be many times, however, when you want to redirect standard input to read data from a file, rather than from the keyboard. Simply type **<** (less-than), followed by the name of the file, at the end of the command.

For example, to sort the data contained in a file called **names**, use the command:

```
sort < names
```

As you can see, the **<** character is a good choice as it looks like an arrow showing the path of the input.

Here is an example you can try for yourself. As I mentioned in Chapter 11, the basic information about each userid is contained in the file **/etc/passwd**. You can display a sorted version of this file by entering the command:

```
sort < /etc/passwd
```

As you might imagine, it is possible to redirect both standard input and standard output at the same time, and this is done frequently. Consider the following example:

```
sort < rawdata > report
```

This command reads data from a file named **rawdata**, sorts it, and writes the output to a file called **report**.

FILE DESCRIPTORS; REDIRECTING STANDARD ERROR WITH THE BOURNE SHELL FAMILY

Although the following discussion is oriented towards the Bourne shell family, we will be talking about important ideas regarding Unix I/O. For that reason, I'd like you to read this entire section, regardless of which shell you happen to be using right now.

As I explained earlier, the shell provides two different output targets: standard output and standard error. Standard output is used for regular output; standard error is used for error messages. By default, both types of output are displayed on the screen. However, you can separate the two output streams should the need arise.

If you choose to separate the output streams, you have a lot of flexibility. For example, you can redirect standard output to a file, where it will be saved. At the same time, you can leave standard error alone, so you won't miss any error messages (which will be displayed on the screen). Alternatively, you can redirect standard output to one file and standard error to another file. Or you can redirect both types of output to the same file.

Alternatively, you can send standard output or standard error (or both) to another program for further processing. I'll show you how to do that later in the chapter when we discuss pipelines.

The syntax for redirecting standard error is different for the two shell families. We'll talk about the Bourne shell family first, and then move on to the C-Shell family. To prepare you, however, I need to take a moment to explain one aspect of how Unix handles I/O.

Within a Unix process, every input source and every output target is identified by a unique number called a FILE DESCRIPTOR. For example, a process might read data from file #8 and write data to file #6. When you write programs, you use file descriptors to control the I/O, one for each file you want to use.

Within the Bourne shell family, the official syntax for redirecting input or output is to use the number of a file descriptor followed by **<** (less-than) or **>** (greater-than). For example, let's say a program named **calculate** is designed to write output to a file with file descriptor 8. You could run the program and redirect its output to a file named **results** by using the command:

```
calculate 8> results
```

By default, Unix provides every process with three pre-defined file descriptors, and most of the time that is all you will need. The default file descriptors are 0 for standard input, 1 for standard output, and 2 for standard error.

Thus, within the Bourne shell family, the syntax for redirecting standard input is to use **0<** followed by the name of the input file. For example:

command **0<** *inputfile*

where *command* is a command, and *inputfile* is the name of a file.

The syntax for redirecting standard output and standard error are similar. For standard output:

command **1>** *outputfile*

For standard error:

command **2>** *errorfile*

where *command* is a command, and *outputfile* and *errorfile* are the names of files.

As a convenience, if you leave out the **0** when you redirect input, the shell assumes you are referring to standard input. Thus, the following two commands are equivalent:

```
sort 0< rawdata
sort < rawdata
```

Similarly, if you leave out the **1** when you redirect output, the shell assumes you are referring to standard output. Thus, the following two commands are also equivalent:

```
sort 1> results
sort > results
```

Of course, you can use more than one redirection in the same command. In the following examples, the **sort** command reads its input from a file named **rawdata**, writes its output to a file named **results**, and writes any error messages to a file named **errors**:

```
sort 0< rawdata 1> results 2> errors
sort < rawdata > results 2> errors
```

Notice that you can leave out the file descriptor only for standard input and standard output. With standard error, you must include the **2**. This is shown in the following simple example, in which standard error is redirected to a file named **errors**:

```
sort 2> errors
```

When you redirect standard error, it doesn't affect standard input or standard output. In this case, standard input still comes from the keyboard, and standard output still goes to the monitor.

As with all redirection, when you write standard error to a file that already exists, the new data will replace the existing contents of the file. In our last example, the contents of the file **errors** would be lost.

If you want to append new output to the end of a file, just use **2>>** instead of **2>**. For example:

```
sort 2>> errors
```

Redirecting standard error with the C-Shell family is a bit more complicated. Before we get to it, I need to take a moment to discuss an important facility called subshells. Even if you don't use the C-Shell or Tcsh, I want you to read the next section, as subshells are important for everyone.

SUBSHELLS

TTo understand the concept of a subshell, you need to know a bit about Unix processes. In Chapter 26, we will discuss the topic in great detail. For now, here is a quick summary.

A PROCESS is a program that is loaded into memory and ready to run, along with the program's data and the information needed to keep track of that program. When a process needs to start another process, it creates a duplicate process. The original is called the PARENT; the duplicate is called the CHILD.

The child starts running and the parent waits for the child to die (that is, to finish). Once the child dies, the parent then wakes up, regains control and starts running again, at which time the child vanishes.

To relate this to your minute-to-minute work, think about what happens when you enter a command. The shell parses the command and figures out whether it is an internal command (one that is built-in to the shell) or an external command (a separate program). When you enter a builtin command, the shell interprets it directly within its own process. There is no need to create a new process.

When you enter an external command, the shell finds the appropriate program and runs it as a new process. When the program terminates, the shell regains control and waits for you to enter another command. In this case, the shell is the parent, and the program it runs on your behalf is the child.

Consider what happens when you start a brand new shell for yourself. For instance, if you are using Bash and you enter the **bash** command (or if you are using the C-Shell, and you enter the **csh** command, and so on).

The original shell (the parent) starts a new shell (the child). Whenever a shell starts another shell, we call the second shell a SUBSHELL. Thus, we can say that, whenever you start a new shell (by entering **bash** or **ksh** or **csh** or **tcsh**), you cause a subshell to be created. Whatever commands you now enter will be interpreted by the subshell. To end the subshell, you press **^D** to send the **eof** signal (see Chapter 7). At this point, the parent shell regains control. Now, whatever commands you enter are interpreted by the original shell.

When a subshell is created, it inherits the environment of the parent (see Chapter 12). However, any changes the subshell makes to the environment are *not* passed back to the parent. Thus, if a subshell modifies or creates environment variables, the changes do not affect the original shell.

This means that, within a subshell, you can do whatever you want without affecting the parent shell. This capability is so handy, that Unix gives you two ways to use subshells.

First, as I mentioned above, you can enter a command to start a brand new shell explicitly. For example, if you are using Bash, you would enter **bash**. You can now do whatever you want without affecting the original shell. For instance, if you were to change an environment variable or a shell option, the change would disappear as soon as you entered **^D**; that is, the moment that the new shell dies and the original shell regains control.

There will be times when you want to run a small group of commands, or even a single command, in a subshell without having to deal with a whole new shell. Unix has a special facility for such cases: just enclose the commands in parentheses. That tells the shell to run the commands in a subshell.

For example, to run the **date** command in subshell, you would use:

```
(date)
```

Of course, there is no reason to run **date** in a subshell. Here, however, is a more realistic example using directories.

In Chapter 24, we will discuss directories, which are used to contain files. You can create as many directories as you want and, as you work, you can move from one directory to another. At any time, the directory in which you are currently working is called your working directory.

Let's say you have two directories named **documents** and **spreadsheets**, and you are currently working in the **documents** directory. You want to change to the **spreadsheets** directory and run a program named **calculate**. Before you can run the program, you need to set the environment variable **DATA** to the name of a file that contains certain raw data. In this case, the file is named **statistics**. Once the program has run, you need to restore **DATA** to its previous value, and change back to the **documents** directory. (In other words, you need to reset the environment to its previous state.)

One way to do this is start a new shell, then change your working directory, change the value of **DATA**, and run the **calculate** program. Once this is all done, you can exit the shell by pressing **^D**. When the new shell ends and the old shell regains control, your working directory and the variable **DATA** will be in their original state.

Here is what it looks like, assuming you use Bash for your shell. (The **cd** command, which we will meet in Chapter 24, changes your working directory. Don't worry about the syntax for now.)

```
bash
cd ../spreadsheets
export DATA=statistics
calculate
^D
```

Here is an easier way, using parentheses:

```
(cd ../spreadsheets; export DATA=statistics; calculate)
```

When you use a subshell in this way, you don't have to worry about starting or stopping a new shell. It is done for you automatically. Moreover, within the subshell, you can do anything you want to the environment without having permanent effects. For example, you can change your working directory, create or modify environment variables, create or modify shell variables, change shell options, and so on.

You will sometimes see the commands within the parentheses called a GROUPING, especially when you are reading documentation for the C-Shell family. In our example, for instance, we used a grouping of three commands. The most common reason to use a grouping and a subshell is to prevent the **cd** (change directory) command from affecting the current shell. The general format is:

```
(cd directory; command)
```

REDIRECTING STANDARD ERROR WITH THE C-SHELL FAMILY

Within the Bourne shell family, redirecting standard error is straightforward. You use **2>** followed by the name of a file. With the C-Shell family (C-Shell, Tcsh), redirecting standard error is not as simple, because of an interesting limitation, which I'll get to in a moment.

With the C-Shell family, the basic syntax for redirecting standard error is:

command **>&** *outputfile*

where *command* is a command, and *outputfile* is the name of a file.

For example, if you are using the C-Shell or Tcsh, the following command redirects standard error to a file named **output**:

```
sort >& output
```

If you want to append the output to the end of an existing file, use **>>&** instead of **>&**. In the following example, the output is appended to a file named **output**:

```
sort >>& output
```

If you have set the **noclobber** shell variable (explained earlier in the chapter) and you want to override it temporarily, use **>&!** instead of **>&**. For example:

```
sort >&! output
```

In this example, the contents of the file will be replaced, even if **noclobber** is set.

So what is the limitation I mentioned? When you use **>&** or **>$!**, the shell redirects *both* standard output and standard error. In fact, within the C-Shell family, there is no simple way to redirect standard error all by itself. Thus, in the last example, both the standard output and standard error are redirected to a file named **output**.

It happens that there is a way to redirect standard error separately from standard output. However, in order to do it, you need to know how to use subshells (explained in the previous section). The syntax is:

(*command* **>** *outputfile***)** **>&** *errorfile*

where *command* is a command, and *outputfile* and *errorfile* are the names of files.

For example, say you want to use **sort** with standard output redirected to a file named **output**, and standard error redirected to a file named **errors**. You would use:

```
(sort > output) >& errors
```

In this case, **sort** runs in a subshell and, within that subshell, standard output is redirected. Outside the subshell, what is left of the output — standard error — is redirected to a different file. The net effect is to redirect each type of output to its own file.

Of course, if you want, you can append the output by using **>>** and **>>&**. For example, to append standard output to a file named **output**, and append standard error to a file named **errors**, use a command like the following:

```
(sort >> output) >>& errors
```

COMBINING STANDARD OUTPUT AND STANDARD ERROR

All shells allow you to redirect standard output and standard error. But what if you want to redirect both standard output and standard error to the same place?

With the C-Shell family, this is easy, because when you use **>&** (replace) or **>>&** (append), the shell automatically combines both output streams. For example, in the following C-Shell commands, both standard output and standard error are redirected to a file named **output**:

```
sort >& output
sort >>& output
```

With the Bourne shell family, the scenario is more complicated. We'll talk about the details, and then I'll show you a shortcut that you can use with Bash.

The basic idea is to redirect one type of output to a file, and then redirect the other type of output to the same place. The syntax to do so is:

command x> outputfile y>&x

where *command* is a command, *x* and *y* are file descriptors, and *outputfile* is the name of a file.

For example, in the following **sort** command, standard output (file descriptor 1) is redirected to a file named **output**. Then standard error (file descriptor 2) is redirected to the same place as file descriptor 1. The overall effect is to send both regular output and error messages to the same file:

```
sort 1> output 2>&1
```

Since, file descriptor 1 is the default for redirected output, you can leave out the first instance of the number 1:

```
sort > output 2>&1
```

Before we move on, I'd like to talk about an interesting mistake that is easy to make. What happens if you reverse the order of the redirections?

```
sort  2>&1 > output
```

Although this looks almost the same as the example above, it won't work. Here is why:

The instruction **2>&1** tells the shell to send the output of file descriptor 2 (standard error) to the same place as the output of file descriptor 1 (standard output). However, in this case, the instruction is given to the shell *before* standard output is redirected. Thus, when the shell processes **2>&1**, standard output is still being sent to the monitor (by default). This means that standard error ends up being redirected to the monitor, which is where it was going in the first place.

The net result is that standard error goes to the monitor, while standard output goes to a file. (Take a moment to think about this, until it makes sense.)

To continue, what if you want to redirect both standard output and standard error, but you want to *append* the output to a file? Just use **>>** instead of **>**:

```
sort >> output 2>&1
```

In this case, using **>>** causes both standard output and standard error to be appended to the file named **output**.

You might ask, is it possible to combine both types of output by starting with standard error? That is, can you redirect standard error to a file and then send standard output to the same place? The answer is yes:

```
sort 2> output 1>&2
sort 2>> output 1>&2
```

The commands are different from the earlier examples, but they have the same effect.

As you can see, the Bourne shell family makes combining two output streams complicated. Can it not be made simpler? Why not just send both standard output and standard error to the same file directly? For example:

```
sort > output 2> output
```

Although this looks as if it might work, it won't, because, if you redirect to the same file twice in one command, one of the redirections will obliterate the other one.

And now the shortcut. You can use the above technique with all members of the Bourne shell family, in particular, with Bash and the Korn shell. With Bash, however, you can also use either **&>** or **>&** (choose the one you like best) to redirect both standard input and standard error at the same time:

```
sort &> output
sort >& output
```

This allows you to avoid having to remember the more complicated pattern. However, if you want to redirect both standard output and standard error and append the output, you will need to use the pattern we discussed above:

```
sort >> output 2>&1
```

By now, if you are normal, you are probably getting a bit confused. Don't worry. Everything we have been discussing in the last few sections is summarized in Figures 15-1 and 15-2 (later in the chapter). My experience is that, with a bit of practice, you'll find the rules for redirection easy to remember.

THROWING AWAY OUTPUT

Why would you want to throw away output?

Occasionally, you will run a program because it performs a specific action, but you don't really care about the output. Other times, you might want to see the regular output, but you don't care about error messages. In the first case, you would throw away standard output; in the second case, you would throw away standard error.

To do so, all you have to do is redirect the output and send it to a special file named **/dev/null**. (The name is pronounced "slash-dev-slash-null", although you will sometimes hear "dev-null".) The name **/dev/null** will make sense after you read about the Unix file system in Chapter 23. The important thing about **/dev/null** is that anything you send to it disappears forever*. When Unix people gather, you will sometimes hear **/dev/null** referred to, whimsically, as the BIT BUCKET.

For example, let's say you have a program named **update** that reads and modifies a large number of data files. As it does its work, **update** displays statistics about what is happening. If you don't want to see the statistics, just redirect standard output to **/dev/null**:

```
update > /dev/null
```

Similarly, if you want to see the regular output, but not any error messages, you can redirect standard error. With the Bourne shell family (Bash, Korn shell), you would use:

```
update 2> /dev/null
```

With the C-Shell family (C-Shell, Tcsh) you would use:

```
update >& /dev/null
```

As I explained earlier, the above C-Shell command redirects both standard output and standard error, effectively throwing away all the output. You can do the same with the Bourne shell family as follows:

```
update > /dev/null 2>&1
```

So what do you do if you are using a C-Shell and you want to throw away the standard error, but not the standard output? You can use a technique we discussed earlier when we talked about how to redirect standard error and standard output to different files. In that case, we ran the command in a subshell as follows:

```
(update > output) >& errors
```

Doing so allowed us to separate the two output streams. Using the same construction, we can throw away standard error by redirecting it to the **/dev/null**. At the same time, we can preserve the standard output by redirecting it to **/dev/tty**:

```
(update > /dev/tty) >& /dev/null
```

The special file **/dev/tty** represents the terminal. We'll discuss the details in Chapter 23. For now, all you need to know is that, when you send output to **/dev/tty**, it goes to the monitor. In this way, we can make the C-Shell and Tcsh send standard output to the monitor while throwing away standard error.**

---

*Said a widower during a lull,
"My late wife was exceedingly dull.
If I killed her, they'd trail me
And catch me and jail me,
So I sent her to /dev/null."

**If you are thinking, "We shouldn't have to go to such trouble to do something so simple," you are right. This is certainly a failing of the C-Shell family. Still, it's cool that we can do it.

REDIRECTION: SUMMARIES AND EXPERIMENTING

Redirecting standard input, standard output, and standard error is straightforward. The variations, however, can be confusing. Still, my goal is that you should become familiar with all the variations — for both shell families — which will take a bit of practice. To make it easier, I can help you in two ways.

First, for reference, Figures 15-1 and 15-2 contain summaries of all the redirection metacharacters. Figure 15-1 is for the Bourne shell family; Figure 15-2 is for the C-Shell family. Within these summaries you will see all the features we have covered so far. You will also see a reference to piping. This refers to using the output of one program as the input to another program, which we discuss in the next section.

The second bit of help I have for you is in the form of an example you can use to experiment. In order to experiment with standard output and standard error, you will need a simple command that generates both regular output as well as an error message. The best such command I have found is a variation of **ls**.

The **ls** (list) command displays information about files, and we will meet it formally in Chapter 24. With the **-l** (long) option, **ls** displays information about files.

The idea is to use **ls -l** to display information about two files, **a** and **b**. File **a** will exist, but file **b** will not. Thus, we will see two types of output: standard output will display information about file **a**; standard error will display an error message saying that file **b** does not exist. You can then use this sample command to practice redirecting standard output and standard error.

Before we can start, we must create file **a**. To do that, we use the **touch** command. We'll talk about **touch** in Chapter 25. For now, all you need to know is that if you use **touch** with a file that does not exist, it will create an empty file with that name. Thus, if a file named **a** does not exist, you can create one by using:

```
touch a
```

We can now use **ls** to display information about both **a** (which exists) and **b** (which doesn't exist):

```
ls -l a b
```

Here is some typical output:

```
b: No such file or directory
-rw-------    1 harley staff  0  Jun 17 13:42 a
```

The first line is standard error. It consists of an error message telling us that file **b** does not exist. The second line is standard output. It contains the information about file **a**. (Notice that the file name is at the end of the line.) Don't worry about the details. We'll talk about them in Chapter 24.

We are now ready to use our sample command to experiment. Take a look at Figures 15-1 and 15-2, and choose something to practice. As an example, let's redirect standard output to a file named **output**:

```
ls -l a b > output
```

When you run this command, you will not see standard output, as it has been sent to the file **output**. However, you will see standard error:

```
b: No such file or directory
```

To check the contents of **output**, use the **cat** command. (We'll talk about **cat** in Chapter 16.)

```
cat output
```

In this case, **cat** will display the contents of **output**, the standard output from the previous command:

```
-rw-------   1 harley staff   0   Jun 17 13:42 a
```

Here is one more example. You are using Bash and you want to practice redirecting standard output and standard error to two different files:

```
ls -l a b > output 2> errors
```

Since all the output was redirected, you won't see anything on your screen. To check standard output, use:

```
cat output
```

METACHARACTERS	ACTION
<	Redirect stdin (same as **0<**)
>	Redirect stdout (same as **1>**)
>|	Redirect stdout; force overwrite
>>	Append stdout (same as **1>>**)
2>	Redirect stderr
2>>	Append stderr
2&>1	Redirect stderr to stdout
>& or &>	Redirect stdout+stderr (Bash only)
|	Pipe stdout to another command
2>&1 |	Pipe stdout+stderr to another command

FIGURE 15-1: Bourne Shell family: Redirection of standard I/O

Most command-line programs use standard I/O for input and output. Input comes from standard input (stdin); regular output goes to standard output (stdout); error messages go to standard error (stderr).

With the Bourne Shell family, you control standard I/O by using file descriptors (stdin=0, stdout=1; stderr=2) with various metacharacters. In cases where there is no ambiguity, you can leave out the file descriptor. To prevent the accidental overwriting of an existing file, set the **noclobber** *shell option. If* **noclobber** *is set, you can force overwriting by using* **>\|** *. See text for details.*

METACHARACTERS	ACTION
<	Redirect stdin
>	Redirect stdout
>!	Redirect stdout; force overwrite
>&	Redirect stdout+stderr
>&!	Redirect stdout+stderr; force overwrite
>>	Append stdout
>>!	Append stdout; force file creation
>>&	Append stdout+stderr
>>&!	Append stdout+stderr; force file creation
|	Pipe stdout to another command
|&	Pipe stdout+stderr to another command

FIGURE 15-2: C-Shell family: Redirection of standard I/O

*With the C-Shell family, you control standard I/O by using various metacharacters. To prevent the accidental overwriting of an existing file or the creation of a new file, set the **noclobber** shell variable. If **noclobber** is set, you can force overwriting or file creation by using a ! character. Note that, unlike the bourne shell family (Figure 15-1), there is no simple way to redirect stderr without also redirecting stdout. See text for details.*

To check standard error, use:

`cat errors`

As you are experimenting, you can delete a file by using the **rm** (remove) command. For example, to delete the files **output** and **errors**, use:

`rm output errors`

When you are finished experimenting, you can delete the file **a** by using:

`rm a`

Now that you have a good sample command (**ls -l a b**) and you know how to display the contents of a short file (**cat** *filename*), it's time to practice.

My suggestion is to create at least one example for each type of output redirection in Figures 15-1 and 15-2*. Although it will take a while to work through the list, once you finish you will know more about redirection than 99 $^{44}/_{100}$ percent of the Unix users in the world.

---

*Yes, I want you to practice with at least one shell from each of the two shell families. If you are not sure which shells to choose, use Bash and the Tcsh.

If you normally use Bash, try the examples, then enter the **tcsh** command to start a Tcsh shell, then try the examples again. If you normally use the Tcsh, use that shell first, and then enter the **bash** command to start a Bash shell.

Regardless of which shell you happen to use right now, you never know what the future will bring. I want you to understand the basic shell concepts — environment variables, shell variables, options, and redirection — for any shell you may be called upon to use.

HINT

To experiment with redirection, we used a variation of the **ls** command:

```
ls -l a b > output
ls -l a b > output 2> errors
```

To make your experiments easier, you can create an alias with a simple name for this command (see Chapter 13). With a Bourne shell (Bash, Korn shell), you might use:

```
alias x='ls -l a b'
```

With a C-Shell (C-Shell, Tcsh):

```
alias x 'ls -l a b'
```

Once you have such an alias, your test commands become a lot simpler:

```
x > output
x > output 2> errors
x >& output
```

This is a technique worth remembering.

PIPELINES

Earlier in the chapter, when we discussed the Unix philosophy, I explained that one goal of the early Unix developers was to build small tools, each of which would do one thing well. Their intention was that, when a user was faced with a problem that could not be solved by one tool, he or she would be able to put together a set of tools to do the job.

For example, let's say you work for the government and you have three large files that contain information about all the smart people in the country. Within each file, there is one line of information per person, including that person's name. Your problem is to find out how many such people are named Harley.

If you were to give this problem to an experienced Unix person, he would know exactly what to do. First, he would use the **cat** (catenate) command to combine the files. Then he would use the **grep** command to extract all the lines that contain the word **Harley**. Finally, he will use the **wc** (word count) command with the **-l** (line count) option, to count the number of lines.

Let's take a look at how we might put together such a solution based on what we have discussed so far. We will use redirection to store the intermediate results in temporary files, which we delete when the work is done. Skipping lightly over the details of how these commands work (we will discuss them later in the book), here are the commands to do the job. To help you understand what is happening, I have added a few comments:

```
cat file1 file2 file3 > tempfile1    # combine files
grep Harley < tempfile1 > tempfile2  # extract lines
wc -l < tempfile2                    # count lines
rm tempfile1 tempfile2               # delete temp files
```

Take a look at this carefully. Before we move on, make sure that you understand how, by redirecting standard output and standard input, we are able to pass data from one program to another by saving it in temporary files.

The sequence of commands used above will work. However, there is a drawback: the glue that holds everything together — redirection using temporary files — makes the solution difficult to understand. Moreover, too much complexity makes it easy to make a mistake.

In order to make such solutions simpler, the shell allows you to create a sequence of commands such that the standard output from one program is sent automatically to the standard input of the next program. When you do so, the connection between two programs is called a PIPE, and the sequence itself is called a PIPELINE.

To create a pipeline, you type the commands you want to use separated by the | (vertical bar) character (the pipe symbol). As an example, the previous set of four commands can be replaced by a single pipeline:

```
cat file1 file2 file3 | grep Harley | wc -l
```

To understand a pipeline, you read the command line from left to right. Each time you see a pipe symbol, you imagine the standard output of one program becoming the standard input of the next program.

The reason pipelines are so simple is that the shell takes care of all the details, so you don't have to use temporary files. In our example, the shell automatically connects the standard output of **cat** to the standard input of **grep**, and the standard output of **grep** to the standard input of **wc**.

With the Bourne shell family, you can combine standard output and standard error and send them both to another program. The syntax is:

command1 **2>&1** | *command2*

where *command1* and *command2* are commands.

In the following example, both standard output and standard error of the **ls** command are sent to the **sort** command:

```
ls -l file1 file2 2>&1 | sort
```

With the C-Shell family, the syntax is:

command1 **|&** *command2*

For example:

```
ls -l file1 file2 |& sort
```

When we talk about pipelines, we often use the word PIPE as a verb, to refer to the sending of data from one program to another. For instance, in the first example, we piped the output of **cat** to **grep**, and we piped the output of **grep** to **wc**. In the second example, we piped standard output and standard error of **ls** to **sort**.

When you think about an example such as the ones above, it's easy to imagine an image of a pipeline: data goes in one end and comes out the other end. However, a better metaphor is to think of an assembly line. The raw data goes in at one end. It is then processed by one program after another until it emerges, in finished form, at the other end.

When you create a pipeline, you must use programs that are written to read text from standard input and write text to standard output. We call such programs "filters", and there are many of them. We will talk about the most important filters in Chapters 16-19. If you are a programmer, you can create your own tools by writing filters of your own.

In practice, you will find that most of your pipelines use only two or three commands in a row. By far, the most common use for a pipeline is to pipe the output of some command to **less** (see Chapter 21), in order to display the output of the command one screenful at a time. For example, to display a calendar for 2008, you can use:

```
cal 2008 | less
```

(The **cal** program is explained in Chapter 8.)

One of the basic skills in mastering the art of Unix is learning when and how to solve a problem by combining programs into a pipeline. When you create a pipeline, you can use as many filters as you need, and you will sometimes see pipelines consisting of five or six or more programs put together in an ingenious manner. Indeed, when it comes to constructing pipelines, you are limited only by your intelligence and your knowledge of filters*.

HINT

When you use a command that uses a pipe or that redirects standard I/O, it is not necessary to put spaces around the <, > or | characters. However, it is a good idea to use such spaces. For example, instead of:

```
ls -l a b >output 2>errors
cat f1 f2 f3|grep Harley|wc -l
```

It is better to use:

```
ls -l a b > output 2> errors
cat f1 f2 f3 | grep Harley | wc -l
```

Using spaces in this way minimizes the chances of a typing error and makes your commands easier to understand. This is especially important when you are writing shell scripts.

SPLITTING A PIPELINE: tee

There may be times when you want the output of a program to go to two places at once. For example, you may want to send output to both a file and to another program at the same time. To show you what I mean, consider the following example:

```
cat names1 names2 names3 | grep Harley
```

The purpose of this pipeline is to display all the lines in the files **names1**, **names2** and **names3** that contain the word "Harley". (The details: **cat** combines the three files;

---

*This should give no cause for concern. After you read Chapters 16-19, you will understand how to use the most important filters. Moreover, as one of my readers, you are obviously of above average intelligence.

grep extracts all the lines that contain the characters "Harley". These two commands are discussed in Chapters 16 and 19 respectively.)

Let's say you want to save a copy of the combined files. In other words, you want to send the output of **cat** to a file *and* you want to send it to **grep** at the same time.

To do so, you use the **tee** command. The purpose of **tee** is to read data from standard input and send a copy of it to both standard output and to a file. The syntax is:

tee [**-a**] *file...*

where *file* is the name of the file where you want to send the data.

Normally, you would use **tee** with a single file name, for example:

```
cat names1 names2 names3 | tee masterlist | grep Harley
```

In this example, the output of **cat** is saved in a file called **masterlist**. At the same time, the output is also piped to **grep**.

When you use **tee**, you can save more than one copy of the output by specifying more than one file name. For example, in the following pipeline, **tee** copies the output of **cat** to two files, **d1** and **d2**:

```
cat names1 names2 names3 | tee d1 d2 | grep Harley
```

If the file you name in a **tee** command does not exist, **tee** will create it for you. However, you must be careful, because if the file already exists, **tee** will overwrite it and the original contents will be lost.

If you want **tee** to append data to the end of a file instead of replacing the file, use the **-a** (append) option. For example:

```
cat names1 names2 names3 | tee -a backup | grep Harley
```

This command saves the output of **cat** to a file named **backup**. If **backup** already exists, nothing will be lost because the output will be appended to the end of the file.

The **tee** command is especially handy at the end of a pipeline when you want to look at the output of a command *and* save it to a file at the same time. For example, let's say you want to use the **who** command (Chapter 8) to display information about the userids that are currently logged in to your system. However, you not only want to display the information, you also want to save it to a file **status**. One way to do the job is by using two separate commands:

```
who
who > status
```

However, by using **tee**, you can do it all at once:

```
who | tee status
```

Pay particular attention to this pattern: I want you to remember it:

command | **tee** *file*

Notice that you don't have to use another program after **tee**. This is because **tee** sends its output to standard output which, by default, is the screen.

In our example, **tee** reads the output of **who** from standard input and writes it to both the file **status** and to the screen. If you find that the output is too long, you can pipe it to **less** to display it one screenful at a time:

```
who | tee status | less
```

WHAT'S IN A NAME?

---

tee

In the world of plumbing, a "tee" connector joins two pipes in a straight line, while providing for an additional outlet that diverts water at a right angle. For example, you can use a tee to allow water to flow from left to right, as well as downwards. The actual connector looks like an uppercase "T".

When you use the Unix **tee** command, you can imagine data flowing from left to right as it moves from one program to another. At the same time, a copy of the data is sent down the stem of the "tee" into a file.

THE IMPORTANCE OF PIPELINES

On October 11, 1964, Doug McIlroy, a Bell Labs researcher wrote a 10-page internal memo in which he offered a number of suggestions and ideas. The last page of the memo contained a summary of his thoughts. It begins:

"To put my strongest concerns into a nutshell:

"We should have some ways of connecting programs like [a] garden hose — screw in another segment when it becomes necessary to massage data in another way..."

In retrospect, we can see that McIlroy was saying that it should be easy to put together programs to solve whatever problem might be at hand. As important as the idea was, it did not bear fruit until well over half a decade later.

By the early 1970s, the original Unix project was well underway at Bell Labs (see Chapter 2). At the time, McIlroy was a manager in the research department in which Unix was born. He was making important contributions to a variety of research areas, including some aspects of Unix. For example, it was McIlroy who demanded that Unix manual pages be short and accurate.

McIlroy had been promoting his ideas regarding the flow of input and output for some time. It wasn't until 1972, however, that Ken Thompson (see Chapter 2) finally added pipelines to Unix. In order to add the pipe facility, Thompson was forced to modify most of the existing programs to change the source of input from files to standard input.

Once this was done and a suitable notation was devised, pipelines became an integral part of Unix, and users became more creative than anyone had expected. According to McIlroy, the morning after the changes were made, "...we had this orgy of one liners. Everybody had a one liner. Look at this, look at that..."

In fact, the implementation of pipelines was the catalyst that gave rise to the Unix philosophy. As McIlroy remembers, "...Everybody started putting forth the Unix philosophy. Write programs that do one thing and do it well. Write programs to work together. Write programs that handle text streams, because that is a universal interface..."

Today, well over thirty years later, the Unix pipe facility is basically the same as it was in 1972: a remarkable achievement. Indeed, it is pipelines and standard I/O that, in large part, make the Unix command line interface so powerful. For this reason, I encourage you to take the time to learn how to use pipelines well and to practice integrating them into your day-to-day work whenever you get the chance.

To help you start your journey on the Unix version of the yellow-brick road, I have devoted Chapters 16-19 to filters, the raw materials out of which you can fashion ingenious solutions to practical problems.

Before we move on to talk about filters, however, there is one last topic I want to cover: conditional execution.

CONDITIONAL EXECUTION

There will be times when you will want to execute a command only if a previous command has finished successfully. To do so, use the syntax:

command1 **&&** *command2*

At other times, you will want to execute a command only if a previous command has *not* finished successfully. The syntax in this case is:

command1 **||** *command2*

This idea — executing a command only if a previous command has succeeded or failed — is called CONDITIONAL EXECUTION.

Conditional execution is mostly used within shell scripts. However, from time to time, it can come in handy when you are entering commands. Here are some examples.

Let's say you have a file named **people** that contains information about various people. You want to sort the contents of **people** and save the output to a file named **contacts**. However, you only want to do so if **people** contains the name "Harley" somewhere in the file.

To start, how can we see if a file contains the name "Harley"? We use the **grep** command (see Chapter 19) to display all the lines in the file that contain "Harley". The command is:

```
grep Harley people
```

If **grep** is successful, it will display the lines that contain "Harley" on standard output. If **grep** fails, it will remain silent. In our case, if **grep** is successful, we then want to run the command:

```
sort people > contacts
```

If **grep** is unsuccessful, we don't want to do anything.

Here is a command line that uses conditional execution to do the job:

```
grep Harley people && sort people > contacts
```

Although this command line works, it leaves us with a tiny problem. If **grep** finds any lines in the file that meet our criteria, it will display them on the screen. Most of the time this would make sense but, in this case, we don't really want to see any output. All we want to do is run **grep** and test whether or not it was successful.

The solution is to throw away the output of **grep** by redirecting it to **/dev/null**:

```
grep Harley people > /dev/null && sort people > contacts
```

Occasionally, you will want to execute a command only if a previous command fails. For example, suppose you want to run a program named **update** that works on its own for several minutes doing something or other. If **update** finishes successfully, all is well. If not, you would like to know about it. The following command displays a warning message, but only if **update** fails:

```
update || echo "The update program failed."
```

> **HINT**
>
> If you ever need to abort a pipeline that is running, just press **^C** to send the **intr** signal (see Chapter 7).
>
> This is a good way to regain control when one of the programs in the pipeline has stopped, because it is waiting for input.

CHAPTER 15 EXERCISES

REVIEW QUESTIONS

1. Summarize the Unix philosophy.

2. In Chapter 10, I gave you three questions to ask yourself each time you learn the syntax for a new program: What does the command do? How do I use the options? How do I use the arguments? Similarly, what are the three questions you should ask (and answer) whenever you start to learn a new program?

3. Collectively, the term "standard I/O" refers to standard input, standard output, and standard error. Define these three terms. What are their abbreviations? What does it mean to redirect standard I/O? Show how to redirect all three types of standard I/O.

4. What is a pipeline? What metacharacter do you use to separate the components of a pipeline? What program would you use at the end of a pipeline to display output one screenful at a time?

5. What program do you use to save a copy of data as it passes through a pipeline?

APPLYING YOUR KNOWLEDGE

1. Show how to redirect the standard output of the **date** command to a file named **currentdate**.

2. The following pipeline counts the number of userids that are currently logged into the system. (The **wc -w** command counts words; see Chapter 18.)

   ```
   users | wc -w
   ```

   Without changing the output of the pipeline, modify the command to save a copy of the output of **users** to a file named **userlist**.

3. The password file (**/etc/passwd**) contains one line for each userid registered with the system. Create a single pipeline to sort the lines of the password file, save them to a file called **userids**, and then display the number of userids on the system.

4. In the following pipeline, the **find** command (explained in Chapter 25) searches all the directories under **/etc** looking for files owned by userid **root**. The names of all such files are then written to standard output, one per line. The output of **find** is piped to **wc -l** to count the lines:

   ```
   find /etc -type f -user root -print | wc -l
   ```

   As **find** does its work, it will generate various error messages you don't want to see. Your goal is to rewrite the pipeline to throw away the error messages without affecting the rest of the output. Show how to do this for the Bourne Shell family. For extra credit, see if you can devise a way to do it for the C-Shell family. (Hint: Use a subshell within a subshell.)

FOR FURTHER THOUGHT

1. An important part of the Unix philosophy is that, when you need a new tool, it is better to combine existing tools than to write new ones. What happens when you try to apply this guideline to GUI-based tools. Is that good or bad?

2. With the Bourne shell family, it is simple to redirect standard output and standard error separately. This makes it easy to save or discard error messages selectively. With the C-Shell family, separating the two types of output is much more complex. How important is this? The C-Shell was designed by Bill Joy, a brilliant programmer in his day. Why do you think he created such a complicated system?

3. As a general rule, the world of computers changes quickly. Why do you think so many of the basic Unix design principles work so well even though they were created over 30 years ago?

# CHAPTER 16

FILTERS:
INTRODUCTION AND BASIC OPERATIONS

In Chapter 15, we discussed how the Unix philosophy led to the development of many programs, each of which was a tool designed to do one thing well. We also talked about how to redirect input and output, and how to create pipelines in which data is passed from one program to the next.

In the next four chapters (16, 17, 18 and 19), we will continue the discussion by taking a look at a number of very useful Unix programs called "filters". (I'll give you the exact definition soon.) Using these programs with the techniques we discussed in Chapter 15, you will be able to build flexible, customized solutions to solve a wide variety of problems.

We'll start our discussion by talking about some general topics to help you understand the importance of filters and how they are used. We will then move on to discuss the most important Unix filters. Although some of the filters are related, they are independent tools that do not have to be learned in a particular order. If you want to learn about one specific filter, you can jump right to that section. However, if you have the time, I'd prefer that you read all four chapters in order, from beginning to end, as I will be developing various important ideas along the way. If you want to see a list of the filters before we start, take a look at Figure 16-1, which you will find later in this chapter.

In Chapter 20, we will discuss a very important facility called regular expressions, which are used to specify patterns. Regular expressions can increase the power of filters significantly, so you should consider the next four chapters and Chapter 20 as being complementary.

VARIATIONS OF COMMANDS AND OPTIONS

The purpose of Chapters 16, 17, 18 and 19 is to discuss the basic Unix filters. All of these programs are available with most versions of Unix and Linux. If one of the programs is not available on your system, it may be because the program is not installed by default and you need to install a particular package. For example, with some Linux distributions, you won't be able to use the **strings** program (Chapter 19), unless you have installed the **binutils** (binary file utilities) package.

As you know, the details of a particular program can vary from one system to another. In this chapter, I will describe the GNU version of each command. Since Linux and FreeBSD use the GNU utilities (see Chapter 2), if you are a Linux or FreeBSD user, what you read in these four chapters should work unchanged on your system. If you use another type of Unix, there may be differences, but they will be small.

For example, later in this chapter, I will discuss three options you can use with the **cat** command. If you use Linux or FreeBSD, these options will work exactly as I show you. If you use Solaris, one of the options (**-s**) has a different meaning.

As we discuss each filter, I will introduce you to the most important options for that program. You should understand that most programs will have other options we will not discuss. In fact, almost all the GNU utilities have a *lot* of options, many more than you will normally need.

As you read this chapter, please remember that, whenever you want to learn about a program, you can read the definitive documentation for *your* system by using the **man** command to access the online manual and, if you are using the GNU utilities, the **info** command to access the Info system. (This is all explained in Chapter 9.) In particular, you can use the **man** command to display a list of all the options available with a specific command. For example, to learn about the **cat** command (discussed in this chapter), you can use:

```
man cat
info cat
```

Before we start, let me mention two more points that apply to the GNU utilities (used with Linux and FreeBSD). First, as we discussed in Chapter 10, most of the GNU utilities have two types of options. There are short options, consisting of a dash (hyphen) followed by a single character, and long options consisting of two dashes followed by a word. In Chapter 10, we called these the "dash" and "dash-dash" options, because that is how most people talk about them.

As a general rule, the most important options are the short ones. In most cases, the long options are either synonyms for shorter options or more esoteric options you probably won't need. For this reason, in this book, I generally only talk about the short options.

However, there is one long option you should remember. With the GNU utilities, most commands recognize an option named **--help**. You can use this option to display the syntax for almost any command, including a summary of the command's options. For example, to display the syntax and the options for the **cat** command, you can use:

```
cat --help
```

FILTERS

In Chapter 15, you saw how a series of programs can be used in sequence to create a pipeline, almost like an assembly line. Consider, for example, the following command, in which data passes through four programs in sequence: **cat**, **grep**, **sort** and **less**.

```
cat new old extra | grep Harley | sort | less
```

In this pipeline, we combine three files named **new**, **old** and **extra** (using **cat**), extract all the lines that contain **Harley** (using **grep**), and then sort these results (using **sort**). We then use **less** to display the final output one screenful at a time.

Don't worry about the details of how to use **cat**, **grep** and **sort**. We'll talk about all that later. For now, all I want is for you to appreciate how useful a program can be if it is designed so that it can be used within a pipeline.

We call such programs filters. For example, **cat**, **grep** and **sort** are all filters. Such programs read data, perform some operation on the data, and then write the results. More precisely, a FILTER is any program that reads and writes textual data, one line at a time, reading from standard input and writing to standard output. As a general rule, most filters are designed as tools, to do one thing well.

Interestingly enough, the first and last programs in a pipeline do not have to be filters. In our example, for instance, we use **less** to display the output of **sort**. We will discuss **less** in detail in Chapter 21. For now, I'll tell you that when **less** displays output, it allows you to look at all the data one screenful at a time, scroll backwards and forwards, search for a specific pattern, and so on. Clearly, **less** does not write to standard output one line at a time, which means it is not a filter.

Similarly, the first command in this particular pipeline, **cat** (which combines files), does not read from the standard input. Although **cat** can be used as a filter, in this situation it reads its input from files, not from standard input. Thus, in our example, **cat** is not a filter.

HINT

When you find yourself creating a specific pipeline to use over and over, you can define it permanently by creating an alias in your environment file. (See Chapter 14.) This will allow you to use the pipeline whenever you want, without having to type it every time.

SHOULD YOU CREATE YOUR OWN FILTERS?

If you are a programmer, it is not hard to make your own filters. All you have to do is write a program or shell script that reads and writes textual data, one line at a time, using standard I/O. Any program that does this is a filter and, hence, can be used in a pipeline.

Before you run off to design your own programs, however, let me remind you that every Unix and Linux system comes with hundreds of programs, many of which are filters. Indeed, over the last thirty-five years, some of the smartest programmers in history have been creating and perfecting Unix filters.

This means that, if you think of a great idea for a new filter, chances are someone else had the same idea a long time ago and the filter already exists. In fact, most of the tools we will discuss in this chapter are over thirty years old! Thus, when you have a problem, it behooves you to find out what is already available, before you take the time to write your own program. That is why I spent so much time teaching you about the online manual and the Info system (Chapter 9), as well as the **man**, **whatis**, **apropos** and **info** commands (also Chapter 9).

The art of using Unix well does not necessarily lie in being able to write programs to create new tools, although that certainly is handy. For most people, using Unix well means being able to solve problems by putting together tools that already exist.

THE PROBLEM SOLVING PROCESS

If you watch an experienced Unix person use filters to build a pipeline, the technique looks mysterious. Out of nowhere, it seems, he or she will know exactly which filters to use, and exactly how to combine them in just the right way. Eventually, you will be able to do the same. All it takes is knowledge and practice. At first, however, it helps to break down the process into a series of steps, so let's take a moment to do just that.

Your goal is to figure out how to solve the problem at hand by combining a number of filters into a single pipeline. If necessary, you can use more than one command line, or even a simple shell script containing a list of commands. However, the smartest Unix people solve most of their problems with a single command line, so start with that as your goal.

Right now, there isn't a lot you can do until you actually learn how to use some of the Unix filters. So as you read this section, think of it as general-advice-that-will-eventually-make-sense-to-you. What I am about to explain is a roadmap that shows you where you will be going. Concentrate on the general ideas and, later, when you get stuck, you can unstick yourself by coming back and reading this section again.

So: you have a problem you want to solve using filters and a pipeline. How do you go about doing so? Here are the steps.

1. Frame the problem.

Start by thinking. Find a quiet place, close your eyes, and think about how you can break your problem into parts, each of which can be carried out by a separate program. At this point, you don't need to know which tools you will be using to perform the various tasks. All you need to do is think.

When experienced Unix people think about a problem, they turn it over in their mind, looking at it from different points of view, until they find something that looks like it might work. Then they look for the tools to do the job. Then they experiment, to see how it works. If you watch them work, you will notice they *never* get frustrated. (Take a moment to think about that.)

2. Choose your tools.

There are hundreds of Unix programs — many of which are filters — and, to use Unix well, you need to know which programs are the best for whatever problem you happen to encounter. This, of course, sounds impossible. How can you memorize the function of hundreds of programs, let alone the details?

Actually, you will find that most Unix problems can be solved by selecting filters from a relatively small toolbox of around thirty programs. Over the years, these are the programs that have proven to be the most versatile and the most useful, and these are the programs we will be discussing in the next four chapters. For reference, Figure 16-1 (later in this chapter) contains a list of these important filters.

3. Talk to other people.

Once you have thought about how to frame your problem and you have an idea what tools you might use, look for people you can ask for suggestions. It's true that you should read the manual before you ask for help (see Chapter 9) but, traditionally, Unix has always been taught by word of mouth. To mature as a Unix person, you must see how other, more experienced people solve problems.

4. Select options.

Once you have studied your problem and chosen your tools, you should take a few moments to look at the documentation in the online manual (Chapter 9). Do this for each program you are thinking of using. Your goal is to check out the options, looking for the ones that are relevant to what you are trying to do.

It will always be the case that you can safely ignore most options. However, it is always a good idea to at least skim the description of the options in case there is one you need for this particular problem. Otherwise, you run the risk of doing a lot of extra work because you didn't know that a particular option was available. The smartest, most knowledgeable people I know check the online manual several times a day.

> **HINT**
>
> When it comes to solving problems using redirection, filters and pipelines, the three most important skills are thinking, RTFMing*, and asking other people for their opinions.

THE SIMPLEST POSSIBLE FILTER: `cat`

A filter reads from standard input one line at a time, does something, and then writes the results to standard output one line at a time. What would be the simplest possible filter? The one that does nothing at all.

The name of this filter is **cat** (you will see why in a moment), and all it does is copy data from standard input to standard output, without doing anything special or changing the data in any way.

Here is a simple example you can perform for yourself. Enter the command:

```
cat
```

The **cat** program will start and wait for data from standard input. Since, by default, standard input is the keyboard, **cat** is waiting for you to type something.

Type whatever you want. At the end of each line, press the <Return> key. Each time you press <Return>, the line you have just typed is sent to **cat**, which will copy it to the standard output, by default, your screen. The result is that each line you type is displayed twice, once when you type it, and once by **cat**. For example:

```
this is line 1
this is line 1
```

---

*RTFM is explained in the glossary and in Chapter 9.

```
this is line 2
this is line 2
```

When you are finished, press **^D** (<Ctrl-D>), the **eof** key. This tells Unix that there is no more input (see Chapter 7). The **cat** command will end, and you will be returned to a shell prompt.

By now, you are probably asking, what use is a filter that does nothing? Actually, there are several uses and they are all important.

Since **cat** doesn't do anything, there is no point using it within a pipeline. (Take a moment to think about this until it makes sense.) However, **cat** can be handy all by itself when you combine it with I/O redirection. It can also be useful at the beginning of a pipeline when you need to combine more than one file. Here are some examples.

The first use of **cat** is to combine it with redirection to create a small file quickly. Consider the following command:

```
cat > data
```

The standard input (by default) is the keyboard, but the standard output has been redirected to a file named **data**. Thus, every line that you type is copied directly to this file as soon as you press the <Return> key. You can type as many lines as you want and, when you are finished, you can tell **cat** there is no more data by pressing **^D**.

If the file **data** does not already exist, Unix will create it for you. If the file does exist, its contents will be replaced. In this way, you can use **cat** to create a new file, or replace the contents of an existing file. Experienced users do this a lot, when all they want to do is create or replace a small file.

The reason I say a "small file" is that the moment you press <Return>, the line you just typed is copied to standard output. If you want to change the line, you have to stop **cat**, restart it, and type everything all over again.

I find that using **cat** in this way is a great way to create or replace a small file quickly, say 4-5 lines at most. Using **cat** is faster (and more fun) than starting a text editor, such as **vi** or Emacs, typing the text, and then stopping the text editor. Of course, it is easy to make mistakes so, if I want to type more than 5 lines, I'll use an editor, which lets me make changes as I type.

The second use for **cat** is to append a small number of lines to an existing file. To do this, you use **>>** to redirect the standard output, for example:

```
cat >> data
```

Now, whatever you type is appended to the file **data**. (As I explained in Chapter 15, when you redirect output with **>>**, the shell appends the output.)

The third use for **cat** is to display a short file. Simply redirect the standard input to the file you want to display. For example:

```
cat < data
```

In this case, the input comes from the file **data**, and the output goes to the screen (by default). In other words, you have just displayed the file **data**. Of course, if the file is longer than the size of your screen, some of the lines will scroll off the screen before you can read it. In such cases, you would not use **cat** to display the file; you would use **less** (Chapter 21) to display the file one screenful at a time.

The fourth use for **cat** is to display the last part of any file. Let's say you use the previous command to display the file named **data**. If **data** is a short file that will fit on the screen, all is well. However, if **data** is longer than the size of the monitor, all but the last part will scroll off the screen. Usually, this will happen fast and all you will be left with is the last part of the file — as much as will fit on your screen — which is exactly what you want.

If you'd like to try this for yourself, you can use **cat** to display one of the configuration files I discussed in Chapter 6. For example, try this command:

```
cat < /etc/profile
```

Notice how, when you display a long file, **cat** leaves you looking at the last part of it.

As a convenience, if you leave out the **<** character, **cat** will read directly from the file. (We'll talk about this in the next section.) So, if you want to experiment with the configuration files from Chapter 6, the commands to use are:

```
cat /boot/grub/menu.lst
cat /etc/hosts
cat /etc/inittab
cat /etc/passwd
cat /etc/profile
cat /etc/samba/smb.conf
```

(Notes: 1. If you are not using Linux, your system may not have all of these files. 2. On most systems, you will need to be superuser to display the **menu.lst** file.)

As you experiment with these commands, you will see that, if the file is short, **cat** will show it all to you quickly. If the file is long, most of the file will scroll by so quickly you won't be able to read it. What you will see, as we discussed, is the last part of the file (as much as will fit on your screen).

Later in the chapter, we will meet another program, called **tail**, which can be used to display the end of a file quickly. Much of the time, **tail** works better than **cat**. However, in some cases, **cat** is actually a better choice. This is because **tail** displays the number of lines you specify, with 10 being the default; **cat** shows you as many lines as will fit on your screen. To see what I mean, try using **tail** on some of the files listed above. For example:

```
tail /etc/profile
```

Moving on, the fifth use of **cat** is to copy a file by redirecting both the standard input and output. For example, to copy the file **data** to another file named **newdata**, enter:

```
cat < data > newdata
```

Of course, Unix has a better command to use for copying files. It's called **cp**, and we'll talk about it in Chapter 25. However, it is interesting to know that **cat** can do the job if it needs to.

There is even more that **cat** can do, which we'll get to in the next section. Before we do, let's take a moment to reflect on something truly remarkable. We started with the simplest possible filter, **cat**, a filter that — by definition — does nothing. However, by using **cat** with I/O redirection, we were able to make it sit up and perform a variety of tricks. (This is all summarized in Figure 16-2, later in the chapter.)

Putting **cat** through its paces in this way provides us with a good example of the elegance of Unix. What seems like a simple concept — that data should flow from standard input to standard output — turns out to bear fruit in so many unexpected ways. Look how much we can do with a filter that does nothing. Imagine what is yet to come!

> **HINT**
>
> Part of the charm of Unix is, all of a sudden, having a great insight and saying to yourself, "So *that's* why they did it that way."

INCREASING THE POWER OF FILTERS

By making one significant change to a filter, it is possible to increase its usefulness enormously. The enhancement is to be able to specify the names of one or more input files.

As you know, the strict definition of a filter requires it to read its data from the standard input. If you want to read data from a file, you must redirect the standard input from that file, for example:

```
cat < data
```

However, what if we also had the option of reading from a file whose name we could specify as an argument? For example:

```
cat data
```

This is indeed the case with **cat**, and the last two commands are equivalent. Thus, to display a short file quickly, all you need to do is type **cat** followed by the name of a file, such as in the last example. Experienced Unix users often use **cat** in this way, as a quick way to display a short file. (For longer files, you would use **less**; see Chapter 21.)

At first, such a small change — leaving out the **<** character — seems insignificant, but this is not the case. It is true that we have made the command line simpler, which is convenient, but there is a price to pay. The **cat** program itself must now be more complex. It not only must be able to read from the standard input, it must also be able to read from *any* file. Moreover, by extending the power of **cat**, we have lost some of the beauty and simplicity of a pure filter.

Nevertheless, many filters are extended in just this way, not because it makes it easy to read from one file, but because it makes it possible to read from *multiple* files. For example, here is an abbreviated version of the syntax for the **cat** command:

```
cat [file...]
```

where *file* is the name of a file from which **cat** will read its input.

Notice the three dots after the *file* argument. This means that you can specify more than one file name. (See Chapter 10 for an explanation of command syntax.)

Thus — and here is the important point — in extending the power of **cat** to read from any file, we have also allowed it to read from more than one file. When we specify more than one file for input, **cat** will read all the data from each of the files in turn. As it reads, it will write each line of text, in the order it was encountered, to the standard output. This means we can use **cat** to combine the contents of as many files as we want.

This is a very important concept, so take a moment to consider the following examples carefully:

```
cat name address phone
cat name address phone > info
cat name address phone | sort
```

The first example combines the contents of multiple files (**name**, **address** and **phone**) and displays it on your screen; the second example combines the same files and writes the data to another file (**info**); the third example pipes the data to a program (**sort**) for further processing.

As I mentioned, many other filters, not just **cat**, can also read input from multiple files. Technically, this is not necessary. If we want to operate on data from more than one file, we can collect the data with **cat** and then pipe it to whichever filter we want. For example, let's say we wanted to combine the data from three files and then sort it. There is no need for **sort** to be able to read from multiple files. All we need to do is combine the data using **cat**, and then pipe it to **sort**:

```
cat name address phone | sort
```

This is appealing in one sense. By extending **cat** to read from files as well as standard input, we have lost some of the elegance of the overall design. However, by using **cat** to feed other filters, we can at least retain the purity of the other filters.

However, as in many aspects of life, utility has won out over beauty and purity. It is just too much trouble to combine files with **cat** every time we want to send such data to a filter. Thus, most filters allow us to specify multiple file names as arguments.

For example, the following three commands all sort the data from more than one file. The first command displays the output on your screen; the second command saves the output to a file; the third command pipes the output to another program for further processing. (Don't worry about the details for now.)

```
sort name address phone
sort name address phone > info
sort name address phone | grep Harley
```

At this point, I'd like you to consider the following philosophical question. By definition, a filter must read its data from standard input. Does this mean that a program that can read its data from a file is not really a filter?

There are two possible answers, both of which are acceptable. First, we can decide that when a program like **cat** or **sort** reads from standard input, it is acting like a filter, but when it reads from a file, it is not acting as a filter. This approach maintains the purity of the system. However, it also means that a great many programs may or may not be filters, depending on how they are used.

Alternatively, we can broaden the definition of a filter to allow it to read from either standard input or from a file. This definition is practical, but it sacrifices some of the beauty of the original design.

A LIST OF THE MOST USEFUL FILTERS

At this point, we have discussed the basic ideas related to filters. In the rest of the chapter — and in Chapters 17, 18 and 19 — I will discuss a variety of different filters, one after another. As a preview, Figure 16-1 shows a list of what I consider to be the most useful Unix filters.

Regardless of which type of Unix or Linux you are using, you will find that most of what you read in these four chapters will work on your system. This is because the basic details of the filters we will be covering are the same from one system to another. Indeed, most of these filters have worked the same way for over thirty years!

Before we continue, though, let me remind you that, at any time, you can check the definitive reference for how a program works on *your* system by using the **man** command to display the man page for that program. If you are using the GNU utilities — which is the case with Linux and FreeBSD — (see Chapter 2) you can use the **info** command to access the Info system. For example:

```
man cat
info cat
```

With most of the GNU utilities, you can display the syntax of a command and a summary of its options by using the **--help** option. For example:

```
cat --help
```

For a discussion of how to use **man** and **info**, see Chapter 9. For a discussion of syntax, see Chapter 10.

COMBINING FILES: cat

Related filters: **rev**, **split**, **tac**

The **cat** program copies data, unchanged, to the standard output. The data can come from the standard input or from one or more files. The syntax is:

```
cat [-bns] [file...]
```

where *file* is the name of a file.

We have already covered several ways in which you can use the **cat** program. However, by far, the most important use for **cat** is to combine multiple files. Here are some typical examples that combine three files. Of course, you can use as many files as you want.

FILTER	CHAPTER	SEE ALSO	PURPOSE
awk	—	perl	Programming language: manipulate text
cat	16	split, tac, rev	Combine files; copy standard input to standard output
colrm	16	cut, join, paste	Delete specified columns of data
comm	17	cmp, diff, sdiff	Compare two sorted files, show differences
cmp	17	comm, diff, sdiff	Compare two files
cut	17	colrm, join, paste	Extract specified columns/fields of data
diff	17	cmp, comm, sdiff	Compare two files, show differences
expand	18	unexpand	Change tabs to spaces
fold	18	fmt, pr	Format long lines into shorter lines
fmt	18	fold, pr	Format paragraphs to make them look nice
grep	19	look, strings	Select lines containing a specified pattern
head	16	tail	Select lines from beginning of data
join	19	colrm, cut, paste	Combine columns of data, based on common fields
look	19	grep	Select lines that begin with a specified pattern
nl	18	wc	Create line numbers
paste	17	colrm, cut, join	Combine columns of data
perl	—	awk	Prog. language: manipulate text, files, processes
pr	18	fold, fmt	Format text into pages or columns
rev	16	cat, tac	Reverse order of characters in each line of data
sdiff	17	cmp, comm, diff	Compare two files, show differences
sed	19	tr	Non-interactive text editing
sort	19	tsort, uniq	Sort data; check if data is sorted
split	16	cat	Split a large file into smaller files
strings	19	grep	Search for character strings in binary files
tac	16	cat, rev	Combine files while reversing order of lines of text
tail	16	head	Select lines from end of data
tr	19	sed	Change or delete selected characters
tsort	19	sort	Create a total ordering from partial orderings
unexpand	18	expand	Change spaces to tabs
uniq	19	sort	Select duplicate/unique lines
wc	18	nl	Count lines, words and characters

FIGURE 16-1: The Most Useful Unix Filters

This table shows the most important Unix filters, most of which are over thirty years old. You can solve many different types of problems using the filters from this list. Most often, you will need only a single filter; you will rarely need more than four.

awk *and* **perl** *are complex programming languages you can use to write programs to act as filters within a pipeline. For more information, start with the online manual (***man awk***,* **man perl***), and then look on the Web, where you will find a great deal of information.*

```
cat name address phone
cat name address phone > info
cat name address phone | sort
```

These patterns are worth memorizing, as you will use them a lot. For reference, they are summarized in Figure 16-2.

In the first example, **cat** reads and combines the contents of three files (in this case, **name**, **address** and **phone**), and displays the output on your screen. Normally, you would only use such a command if the files were so short that the combined output would not scroll off the screen. More likely, you would pipe the output to **less** (Chapter 21) to display the output one screenful at a time. For example:

```
cat name address phone | less
```

The second example combines the same three files, but redirects standard output to another file (in this case, **info**). If the file does not exist, the shell will create it. If the file does exist, it will be replaced, which means that the data originally in the file will be lost forever. (See Chapter 15 for a discussion of redirection and file replacement.)

The third example combines the same files and pipes the output to another program for further processing, in this case, **sort** (Chapter 19).

When you use **cat** to combine, there is a common mistake you must be sure to avoid: do not redirect output to one of the input files. For example, say you want to *append* the contents of **address** and **phone** to the file **name**. You might think, all you have to do is combine all three files and save the result in **name**:

```
cat name address phone > name
```

SYNTAX	PURPOSE
cat > *file*	Read from keyboard, create new file or replace existing file
cat >> *file*	Read from keyboard, append to existing file
cat < *file*	Display an existing file
cat *file*	Display an existing file
cat < *file1* > *file2*	Copy a file
cat *file1 file2 file3* | **less**	Combine multiple files, display one screenful at a time
cat *file1 file2 file3* > *file4*	Combine multiple files, save output in a different file
cat *file1 file2 file3* | *program*	Combine multiple files, pipe output to another program

FIGURE 16-2: The Many Uses of the **cat** Program

*The **cat** program is the simplest possible filter. It reads from standard input and writes to standard output without modifying the data. In spite of its simplicity, **cat** can perform a surprising number of tasks, which are summarized in the table. The power of such a simple filter comes from the richness of the Unix I/O redirection and pipeline capabilities.*

*Most of the time, **cat** is used to combine files, either to be displayed (by piping the output to **less**), to be saved in another file (by redirecting standard output to that file), or to be piped to another program for further processing. See text for details.*

This will not work, because of the way the shell handles redirection. Before a program can redirect standard output to a file, the shell must make sure that the file exists and is empty. In this case, if **name** does not exist, the shell will create it. If **name** does exist, the shell will empty it. In our example, by the time **cat** is ready to read from **name**, the file is already empty.

When you enter a command like the one above, you will see a message similar to:

```
cat: name: input file is output file
```

It looks like a warning message but, actually, it is already too late. Even pressing **^C** (to abort the command) won't do any good. By the time you see this message, the contents of **name** have been deleted.

The safe way to append the contents of **address** and **phone** to the file **name** is to use:

```
cat address phone >> name
```

Notice we do not use our output file as an input file. Rather, we append the contents of all the other files to the output file.

To conclude our discussion of **cat**, here are the most useful options:

- The **-n** (number) option will place a line number in front of each line.

- The **-b** (blank) option is used with **-n** and tells **cat** not to number blank lines.

- The **-s** (squeeze) option replaces more than one consecutive blank line with a single blank line.

WHAT'S IN A NAME?

---

cat
The main use of the **cat** program is to combine the contents of multiple files into a single output stream. For this reason, it would be natural to assume that **cat** stands for "concatenate". Actually, this is not the case.

The name **cat** comes from the archaic word "catenate", which means "to join in a chain". As all classically educated Unix users know, *catena* is the Latin word for chain.

SPLITTING FILES: `split`

Related filters: `cat`

We have just discussed how to use **cat** to combine two or more files into one large file. What if you want to do the opposite: split a large file into smaller files? To do so, you use the **split** program. The syntax is:

split [-d] [-a *num*] [-l *lines*] [*file* [*prefix*]]

where *num* is the number of characters or digits to use as a suffix when creating file names; *lines* is the maximum number of lines for each new file; *file* is the name of an input file; and *prefix* is a name to use when creating file names.

The **split** program was developed in the early 1970s, when large text files could create problems. In those days disk storage was limited and processors were slow.* Today, large hard disks are ubiquitous, and computers are extremely fast. As a result, we rarely have problems storing and manipulating large text files. Still, there will be times when you will want to break a large file into pieces and, when you do, **split** can save you a lot of time. For example, you may want to email a very large file to someone whose email account has a limit on the size of received messages.

By default, **split** creates files that are 1,000 lines long. For example, say that you have a file named **data** with 57,984 lines, which you want to break into smaller files. You would use the command:

```
split data
```

This creates 58 new files: 57 files containing 1,000 lines each, and 1 last file containing the remaining 984 lines.

If you want to change the maximum size of the files, use the **-l** (lines) option. For example, to split the file **data** (with 57,984 lines) into files containing 5,000 lines, you would use:

```
split -l 5000 data
```

This command creates 12 new files: 11 files containing 5,000 lines (55,000 lines in all), and 1 last file containing 2,984 lines (the remainder).

HINT

When you use options that require large numbers, you do not type a comma (or, in Europe, a period) to break the number into groups of three. For example, you would use:

```
split -l 5000 data
```

You would not use:

```
split -l 5,000 data
```

If you do use a comma, it will cause a syntax mistake and you will get an error message such as:

```
split: 5,000: invalid number of lines
```

By now you are probably wondering, what are the names of all these new files? If **split** is going to create files automatically, it should use names that make sense. However, it must also be careful not to replace any of your existing files accidentally.

By default, **split** uses names that start with the letter **x**, followed by a 2-character suffix. The suffixes are **aa**, **ab**, **ac**, **ad**, and so on. For instance, in the last example, where **split** created 12 new files, the names (by default) would be:

---

*In 1976, when I was a first-year graduate student working with Unix, I wrote a C program to mathematically manipulate the data in a file that, by today's standards, was relatively small. At the time, however, the file was considered large, and the computer did not have nearly enough memory to hold all the data. As a result, my program had to be very complex, as it had to be able to process data in small pieces, which were swapped in and out of memory as necessary.

```
xaa  xab  xac  xad  xae  xaf  xag  xah  xai  xaj  xak  xal
```

If **split** requires more than 26 files, the names after **xaz** are **xba**, **xbb**, **xbc**, and so on. Since there are 26 letters in the alphabet, this allows for up to 676 (26x26) new file names, **xaa** through **xzz**.

If you don't like these names, there are two ways to change them. First, if you use the **-d** (digits) option, **split** uses 2-digit numbers starting with **00** at the end of the file name, rather than a 2-letter suffix. For example, the following command uses the same file **data** (containing 57,984 lines) we used above:

```
split -d -l 5000 data
```

The 12 new files are named:

```
x00  x01  x02  x03  x04  x05  x06  x07  x08  x09  x10  x11
```

If you don't want your file names to start with **x**, you can specify your own name to be used as a prefix, for example:

```
split -d -l 5000 data harley
```

The new files are named:

```
harley00  harley01  harley02  harley03  harley04  harley05
harley06  harley07  harley08  harley09  harley10  harley11
```

When you use **split** with the **-d** option, you can create up to 100 files (10x10), using the suffixes **00** to **99**. Without **-d**, you can create up to 676 files (26x26), using the suffixes **aa** to **zz**. If you need more files, you can use the **-a** option followed by the number of digits or characters you want in the suffix. For example:

```
split -d -a 3 data
```

The new file names will use 3-digit suffixes:

```
x000  x001  x002  x003...
```

Similarly, you can use **-a** without the **-d** option:

```
split -a 3 data
```

In this case, the new file names use 3-letter suffixes:

```
xaaa  xaab  xaac  xaad...
```

In this way, you can use **split** to break up very large input files without running out of file names.

By default, **split** creates 1,000-line files. However, as I mentioned, you can create any size files you want, even small ones. Here is a typical, everyday example I am sure you can relate to.

You are working for a powerful U.S. senator who is running for President of the United States. It is two weeks before the election and the campaign is suffering. The senator is desperate and, because you know Unix, you are promoted to be the new Chief of Staff.

Your first day on the job, you are given a very large text file, named **supporters**, in which each line contains the name and phone number of a potential voter. Your job is to organize volunteers around the country to call all the people on the list and urge them to vote for your candidate. You decide there is only enough time for each volunteer to call 40 people. You log into your Unix system and enter the command:

```
split -d -l 40 supporters voter
```

You now have a set of files, named **voter00**, **voter01**, **voter02**, and so on. Each of these files (except, possibly, the last one) contains exactly 40 names. You order your staff to email each volunteer one file, along with instructions to call all 40 names on his or her list.

Because of your hard work and superior Unix skills, your candidate is elected. Within a week, you are appointed to a position of great power and influence.

COMBINING FILES WHILE REVERSING LINES: tac

Related filters: **cat**, **rev**

As we have discussed, **cat** is the most basic of all the filters, as well as one of the most useful filters. The **tac** program is similar to **cat** with one major difference: **tac** reverses the order of the lines of text before writing them to standard output. (The name **tac** is **cat** spelled backwards.)

The syntax for **tac** is:

tac [*file...*]

Like **cat**, **tac** reads from standard input and writes to standard output, and **tac** can combine input files. For instance, you have a file named **log**. You want to reverse the order of all the lines in **log** and write the results to a new file named **reverse-log**. The command to use is:

```
tac log > reverse-log
```

For example, let's say **log** contains:

```
Oct 01: event 1 took place
Oct 02: event 2 took place
Oct 03: event 3 took place
Oct 04: event 4 took place
```

After running the **tac** command above, **reverse-log** would contain:

```
Oct 04: event 4 took place
Oct 03: event 3 took place
Oct 02: event 2 took place
Oct 01: event 1 took place
```

At this point, you might be wondering if **tac** is nothing more than a curiosity. Perhaps it was written simply because someone thought the name was cute (being **cat** backwards). However, would you ever actually need this program?

The answer is you don't need **tac** all that often. However, when you do need it, it is invaluable. For example, say you have a program that writes notes to a log file (a common occurrence). The oldest notes will be at the beginning of the file; the newest notes will be at the end of the file. The file, which is named **log**, is now 5,000 lines long, and you want to display the notes from newest to oldest.

Without **tac**, there is no simple way to display the lines of a long file in reverse order. With **tac**, it's easy. Just use **tac** to reverse the lines and pipe the output to **less** (Chapter 21):

```
tac log | less
```

If you need to combine files, you can do that as well, for example:

```
tac log1 log2 log3 | less
```

This command reverses the lines in three files, combines them, and then pipes the output to **less**.

REVERSING THE ORDER OF CHARACTERS: rev

Related filters: **cat**, **tac**

The **tac** program reverses the lines within a file, but what if you want to reverse the characters within each line? In such cases, you use **rev**. The syntax is **rev**:

rev [*file...*]

where *file* is the name of a file.

Here is an example. You have a file named **data** that contains:

```
12345
abcde
AxAxA
```

You enter:

```
rev data
```

The output is:

```
54321
edcba
AxAxA
```

Suppose you want to reverse the order of the characters in each line *and* reverse the lines in the file. Just pipe the output of **rev** to **tac**, for example:

```
rev data | tac
```

The output is:

```
AxAxA
edcba
54321
```

What do you think would happen if you used **tac** first?

```
tac data | rev
```

To complete this section, let's consider one more example. You have a file named **pattern** that contains the following 4 lines:

```
   X
  XX
 XXX
XXXX
```

Consider the output from the following four commands (the **$** is the shell prompt):

```
$cat pattern
   X
  XX
 XXX
XXXX

$tac pattern
XXXX
 XXX
  XX
   X

$rev pattern
X
XX
XXX
XXXX

$rev pattern | tac
XXXX
XXX
XX
X
```

Does it all make sense to you?

SELECT LINES FROM THE BEGINNING OR END OF DATA: `head, tail`

When you have more data than you can understand easily, there are two programs that allow you to select part of the data quickly: **head** selects lines from the beginning of the data; **tail** selects lines from the end of the data.

Most of the time, you will use **head** and **tail** to display the beginning or end of a file. For this reason, I will defer the principal discussion of these commands until Chapter 21, where we will talk about the file display commands. In this section, I will show you how to use **head** and **tail** as filters within a pipeline.

When you use **head** and **tail** as filters, the syntax is simple:

head [-n *lines*]
tail [-n *lines*]

where *lines* is the number of lines you want to select. (In Chapter 21, we will use a more complex syntax.)

By default, both **head** and **tail** select 10 lines of data. For example, let's say you have a program called **calculate** that generates many lines of data. To display the first 10 lines, you would use:

```
calculate | head
```

To display the last 10 lines, you would use:

```
calculate | tail
```

If you want to select a different number of lines, use a hyphen (-) followed by that number. For example, to select 15 lines, you would use:

```
calculate | head -n 15
calculate | tail -n 15
```

You will often use **head** and **tail** at the end of a complex pipeline to select part of the data generated by the previous commands. For example, you have four files: **data1**, **data2**, **data3** and **data4**. You want to combine the contents of the files, sort everything, and then display the first and last 20 lines.

To combine the files, you use the **cat** program (discussed earlier in the chapter). To perform the sort, you use the **sort** program (Chapter 19):

```
cat data1 data2 data3 data4 | sort | head -n 20
cat data1 data2 data3 data4 | sort | tail -n 20
```

Sometimes you will want to send the output of **head** or **tail** to another filter. For example, in the following pipeline, we use **head** to select 300 lines from the beginning of the **sort** output, which we then send to **less** (Chapter 21) to be displayed one screenful at a time:

```
cat data1 data2 data3 data4 | sort | head -n 300 | less
```

Similarly, it is often handy to save the output of **head** or **tail** to a file. The following example selects the last 10 lines of output and saves it to a file named **most-recent**:

```
cat data1 data2 data3 data4 | sort | tail > most-recent
```

HINT

Originally, **head** and **tail** did not require you to use the **-n** option; you could simply type a hyphen followed by a number. For example, the following commands all display 15 lines of output:

```
calculate | head -n 15
calculate | tail -n 15
calculate | head -15
calculate | tail -15
```

Officially, modern versions of **head** and **tail** are supposed to require the **-n** option, which is why I have included it. However, most versions of Unix and Linux will accept both types of syntax so — as long as your mother isn't watching — you can usually leave out the **-n**.

DELETING COLUMNS OF DATA: `colrm`

Related filters: **cut**, **paste**

The **colrm** ("column remove") program reads from the standard input, deletes specified columns of data, and then writes the remaining data to the standard output. The syntax is:

colrm [*startcol* [*endcol*]]

where *startcol* and *endcol* specify the starting and ending range of the columns to be removed. Numbering starts with column 1.

Here is an example: You are a tenured professor at a college in California, and you need a list of grades for all the students in your PE 201 class ("Intermediate Surfing"). This list should not show the students' names.

You have a master data file, named **students**, which contains one line of information about each student. Each line has a student number, a name, the final exam grade, and the course grade:

```
012-34-5678   Ambercrombie, Al    95%   A
123-45-6789   Barton, Barbara     65%   C
234-56-7890   Canby, Charles      77%   B
345-67-8901   Danfield, Deann     82%   B
```

To construct the list of grades, you need to remove the names, which are in columns 14 through 30, inclusive. Use the command:

```
colrm 14 30 < students
```

The output is:

```
012-34-5678    95%   A
123-45-6789    65%   C
234-56-7890    77%   B
345-67-8901    82%   B
```

As a quick review of piping and redirection, let me show you two more examples. First, if the list happens to be very long, you can pipe it to **less**, to display the data one screenful at a time:

```
colrm 14 30 < students | less
```

Second, if you want to save the output, you can redirect it to a file:

```
colrm 14 30 < students > grades
```

If you specify only a starting column, **colrm** will remove all the columns from that point to the end of the line. For example:

```
colrm 14 < students
```

displays:

```
012-34-5678
123-45-6789
234-56-7890
345-67-8901
```

If you specify neither a starting nor ending column, **colrm** will delete nothing.

CHAPTER 16 EXERCISES

REVIEW QUESTIONS

1. What is a filter? Why are filters so important?

2. You need to solve a difficult problem using filters and a pipeline. What four steps should you follow? What are the three most important skills you need?

3. Why is **cat** the simplest possible filter? In spite of its simplicity, **cat** can be used for a variety of purposes. Name four.

4. What is the difference between **tac** and **rev**?

APPLYING YOUR KNOWLEDGE

1. A scientist ran an experiment that generated data that accumulated in a sequence of files: **data1**, **data2**, **data3**, **data4** and **data5**. He wants to know how many lines of data he has altogether. The command **wc -l** reads from standard input and counts the number of lines. How would you use this command to count the total number of lines in the five files?

2. You have a text file named **important**. What commands would you use to display the contents of this file in the following four different ways? (a) As is. (b) Reverse the order of the lines. (c) Reverse the order of the characters within each line. (d) Reverse both the lines and characters. For (b), (c), and (d), which command performs the opposite transformation? How would you test this?

3. In Chapter 6, we discussed the Linux program **dmesg**, which displays the messages generated when the system was booted. Typically, there are a great many such messages. What command would you use to display the last 25 boot messages?

FOR FURTHER THOUGHT

1. Figure 16-1 lists the most important Unix filters. Not counting **awk** and **perl**, which are programming languages, there are 19 different filters in the list. For most problems, you will need only a single filter; you will rarely need more than four. Why do you think this is the case? Can you think of any tools that, in your opinion, are missing from the list?

2. The **split** program was developed in the early 1970s, when large text files could create problems, because disk space was relatively slow storage and very expensive. Today, disks are fast and cheap. Do we still need a program like **split**? Why?

CHAPTER 17
FILTERS: COMPARING AND EXTRACTING

In Chapter 16, we spent a lot of time talking about filters: programs that read and write textual data one line at a time, reading from standard input and writing to standard output. One of the observations that came out of our discussion was that, as a general rule, filters are designed as tools whose job is to do one thing and do it well. In the next three chapters, we will talk about many specific filters and, as you read and think about the examples, you will find this observation to be particularly important.

In this chapter, we will be discussing filters that are designed to compare files and to extract parts of files. At first, you might think these are dull topics, and I don't blame you. After all, there are enough details in this chapter to choke a good-sized horse. As you read the details, however, and as you start to see the intelligence of the design behind the filters, you will come to appreciate how interesting they actually are. In fact, the filters we will be discussing in this chapter are not only interesting, but they are among the most useful and important programs in the Unix toolbox.

COMPARING FILES

Over the years, Unix programmers have created a variety of tools to help you answer the questions: Do two files contain the exact same data? If not, how does the data differ from one file to the next? Comparing two files is more complicated than you might think, because there are various ways to compare and to display the results.

In the next few sections, we will discuss the most important of these tools. In particular, I'll explain what they do, what types of files they compare, and which of their options are the most useful. Along the way, I'll show you examples and give you important tips. My goal is simple: whenever the need to compare files arises, you should be able to analyze the situation quickly, decide which program and which options to use, and be able to interpret the results.

Figure 17-1 summarizes the most important file comparison programs (the ones we will be covering). For completeness, I have also included related programs for sorting and selecting data from files. We will discuss these programs in Chapter 19.

FILTER	PURPOSE	CHAPTER	TYPE OF FILES	NUMBER OF FILES
cmp	Compare two files	17	binary or text	Two
comm	Compare two sorted files, show differences	17	text: sorted	Two
diff	Compare two files, show differences	17	text	Two
sdiff	Compare two files, show differences	17	text	Two
cut	Extract specified columns/fields of data	17	text	One or more
paste	Combine columns of data	17	text	One or more
sort	Sort data	19	text	One or more
uniq	Select duplicate/unique lines	19	text: sorted	One
grep	Select lines containing specified pattern	19	text	One or more
look	Select lines beginning with specified pattern	19	text: sorted	One

FIGURE 17-1: Programs to compare, sort, and select data from files

Unix has a variety of programs to compare files, the most important of which are **comm**, **cmp**, **diff**, *and* **sdiff** *(which can be thought of as a variation of* **diff***). Closely related are the programs that sort files (***sort***), select lines of text (***uniq***), and extract parts of a file (***cut***, ***grep***, ***look***).*

This table summarizes these programs by showing the type of data they use (binary or text; sorted or unsorted), the number of files they use; and their primary purpose. See text for details. (The sorting and selecting programs are discussed in Chapter 19. Binary and text files are discussed in Chapters 19 and 23.)

COMPARING ANY TWO FILES: cmp

Related filters: **comm, diff, sdiff**

You use **cmp** in only one situation: to see if two files are identical. The syntax is:

cmp *file1 file2*

where *file1* and *file2* are the names of files.

The **cmp** program compares the two files, one byte at a time, to see if they are the same. If the corresponding bytes in both files are exactly the same, the files are identical, in which case **cmp** does not do anything. (No news is good news.) If the files are not identical, **cmp** displays a suitable message.

For example, let's say you have two versions of a program: **calculate-1.0** and **calculate-backup**. You want to see if they are exactly the same. Use:

```
cmp calculate-1.0 calculate-backup
```

If the files are the same, you will see nothing. If the files don't match, you will see a message similar to the following:

```
calculate-1.0 calculate-backup differ: byte 31, line 4
```

As you can see in Figure 17-1, there are several other programs you can use to compare files (**comm, diff, diff3** and **sdiff**). All of these programs work with text files.

That is, they expect lines of text: data in which each line contains zero or more regular characters (letters, numbers, punctuation, whitespace) ending with a newline.

Since **cmp** compares files one byte at a time, it doesn't care what type of data the files contain. Thus, you can use **cmp** to compare any type of file, text or binary. For instance, the example above compared two binary files that contain executable programs. You could also compare two music files, two pictures, two word processing documents, and so on. (We will discuss text files and binary files in Chapters 19 and 23.)

COMPARING SORTED TEXT FILES: comm

Related filters: **cmp**, **diff**, **sdiff**

The **comm** program compares two sorted text files, line by line. You use **comm** when you have two similar files, and you want to find the differences. The syntax is:

comm [**-123**] *file1 file2*

where *file1* and *file2* are the names of sorted text files.

The nice thing about **comm** is that it allows you to visualize the differences in the two files. It does so by displaying its output in three columns: the first column contains the lines that are only in the first file; the second column contains the lines that are only in the second file; the third column contains the lines that are in both files. Let me show you an example.

Two close friends, Frick and Frack*, are wondering how many other friends they have in common. They each make a list of their own friends, type the list into a file, and then use the **sort** command (Chapter 19) to sort the file. They then use **comm** to compare the two files.

The sorted list of Frick's friends is in a file called **frick**:

```
Alison Wonderland
Barbara Seville
Ben Dover
Chuck Wagon
Noah Peel
```

The sorted list of Frack's friends is in a file called **frack**:

```
Alison Wonderland
Barbara Seville
Candy Barr
Chuck Wagon
Noah Peel
Sue Perficial
```

---

*Frick and Frack were the stage names of two well-known comedy ice skaters, Werner Groebli and Hans Mauch. Groebli and Mauch came to the United States from their native Switzerland in 1937 and, for decades, performed widely as part of the original Ice Follies. Their most famous trick was the "cantilever spread-eagle" (look for photos on the Web).

Frick and Frack compare the two lists by using the command:

```
comm frick frack
```

The output is:

```
        Alison Wonderland
        Barbara Seville
Ben Dover
    Candy Barr
        Chuck Wagon
        Noah Peel
    Sue Perficial
```

Notice the three columns. The first column has only one name (Ben Dover). This shows that there is only one line that is unique to the first file (**frick**). The second column has two names (Candy Barr, Sue Perficial). This shows that there are two lines that are unique to the second file (**frack**). The third column has four names (Alison Wonderland, Barbara Seville, Chuck Wagon, Noah Peel). This shows that there are four lines that are in both files. Thus, Frick and Frack conclude they have four friends in common.

In this example, the files are small — between them, Frick and Frack have a total of seven friends — and you are probably wondering why they bother to create two files, sort them, run the **comm** command, and interpret the output. Wouldn't it be easier for Frick and Frack to ask one another: Do you know Alison? Do you know Barbara? and so on.

The answer is of course it would, but this is a contrived example. What if you were working with sorted files that had hundreds or thousands of lines — customer records or statistical data or a long list of songs for your MP3 player? In such cases, it would be virtually impossible to compare the lists by hand. You must have a program like **comm**.

Indeed, **comm** is especially useful when you have two versions of a sorted file that vary slightly — perhaps because of a small mistake — and you want to find that variation. For example, say that you have two very long sorted lists of numbers. Somewhere in the lists, there is a place where the numbers do not agree. You use **comm** to compare the files and, in the middle of the output, you see:

```
        01023331
        01023340
        01023356
01023361
    01023362
        01023378
        01023391
        01023401
```

This shows you the exact place where the two files don't match.

To give you control over the output, **comm** allows you to suppress the output of the first, second or third columns by using the **-1**, **-2** and **-3** options respectively. In our last example, for instance, you could use **-3** to suppress the third column, which would eliminate all the unnecessary output:

```
01023361
    01023362
```

Now, all you see are the lines that differ, which is all you want to see. Imagine how much time this saves you if the files contained several thousand numbers.

If you want to suppress more than one column, just combine the options. For example, consider the lists of friends of Frick and Frack we discussed above. Let's say Frack wants to display only those people who are his friends and not Frack's friends. All he has to do is suppress the first and third columns:

comm -13 frick frack

The output shows only those lines that are unique to the second file:

Candy Barr
Sue Perficial

HINT

The most common reason why **comm** does not work as expected is that the input files are not sorted.

If you need to compare two files but you don't want to sort the lines — say, because it will mix up the data — you cannot use **comm**. Instead, you should use **diff** (discussed later in the chapter). This is the case when you compare different versions of the source code for a program.

COMPARING UNSORTED TEXT FILES: `diff`

Related filters: **cmp**, **comm**, **sdiff**

The **comm** program will show you, visually, how two text files differ. However, **comm** has two limitations. First, the input files must be sorted which, in many cases, is not possible. For example, say you have two different versions of a long file, such as a computer program or an essay, and you want to know how they differ. Since the lines of a program or an essay aren't sorted, you can't use **comm**. Of course, you could sort the files first, but then the output wouldn't make any sense: you might find the differences, but you would lose the context.

Moreover, the output of **comm** is fine when you are comparing small- or even medium-sized files, but it can be confusing when you are working with large files. Again, it's a matter of context. When you compare large files, it is important that the output show you not only the differences, but their locations, and do so in a way that makes it easy to find the lines that differ.

The **diff** program is designed to overcome these limitations. Thus, you use **diff** when you want to (1) compare unsorted files or, (2) compare large files. More generally, **diff** can be used to find the differences in any type of work in which incremental additions, deletions or changes are made from time to time. For instance, for many years, programmers have used **diff** (or tools like **diff**) to track the changes between versions of a program as the program is modified.

Before we start, I must warn you that the output of **diff** will look a bit cryptic until you get used to it. However, you *will* get used to it. Regardless, **diff** is a powerful and useful program, and it is important that you learn how to use it, especially if you are a programmer.

The syntax for **diff** is as follows:

diff [**-bBiqswy**] [**-c**|**-C***lines*|**-u**|**-U***lines*] *file1 file2*

where *file1* and *file2* are the names of text files, and *lines* is a number of lines of context to show.

When you compare two files that are identical, **diff** will display no output (similar to **cmp**). If the files are not the same, **diff** will, by default, display a set of instructions that, if followed, would change the first file into the second file. Here is an example.

We have two files. The file **old-names** contains:

```
Gene Pool
Will Power
Paig Turner
Mark Mywords
```

The file **new-names** contains:

```
Gene Pool
Will Power
Paige Turner
Mark Mywords
```

You will notice that the only difference is the spelling of "Paige" in the third line. To compare the files, we use:

```
diff old-names new-names
```

The output is:

```
3c3
< Paig Turner
---
> Paige Turner
```

As I explained, the goal of **diff** is to display the instructions you would need to follow to change the first file into the second file. The syntax of the instructions is simple but terse, and it can take a bit of practice to understand it. However, I do want you to become familiar with these types of instructions, because they are a standard part of the Unix culture. In fact, you will encounter this type of syntax a variety of situations, not just when using **diff**.

The output of **diff** uses three different 1-character instructions: **c** (change), **d** (delete), and **a** (append)*. In the example above, you see only a single **c** instruction. This means that, to turn the first file into the second, you only need to make one modification, a simple change.

To the left and right of each **c**, **d** or **a** character, you will see a list of line numbers. There may be a single line number (such as the **3** above), or there may be a sequence of lines (such as **16,18**). The numbers to the left refer to lines in the first file; the numbers to the right refer to lines in the second file. In our example, the instruction **3c3** tells us to change line 3 of the first file to line 3 of the second file.

Whenever **diff** requires a change, it shows you the actual lines from each file. Lines from the first file are marked by a **<** (less-than) character. Lines from the second file are marked by a **>** (greater-than) character. For readability, the two sets of lines are separated by a line consisting of several hyphens (**---**).

Let's consider another example in which **old-names** contains:

```
Gene Pool
Paige Turner
Mark Mywords
```

And **new-names** contains:

```
Gene Pool
Will Power
Paige Turner
Mark Mywords
```

In this case, the only difference is that the first file does not contain the name "Will Power". When you use **diff** with these two files, the output is:

```
1a2
> Will Power
```

This tells you how to change the first file into the second. All you need to do is append a single line to the first file. Specifically, you would append line 2 of the second file after line 1 of the first file. Notice that **diff** shows you the actual line that needs to be appended. The **>** character tells you that this line is from the second file.

Now, consider a third example in which **old-names** contains:

```
Gene Pool
Will Power
Paige Turner
Mark Mywords
```

---

*Why these three instructions? With two files that are reasonably similar to one another, you can always turn one into the other by some combination of change, delete, and append operations. Take a moment to think about this until it makes sense to you.

And **new-names** contains:

```
Gene Pool
Will Power
Paige Turner
```

The difference here is that the second file does not contain the name "Mark Mywords". When you use **diff**, the output is:

```
4d3
< Mark Mywords
```

In this case, **diff** is telling you that, to turn the first file into the second, you need to delete line 4 from the first file. Again, the actual line is displayed. The **<** character tells you the line is from the first file. (Remember, the goal of **diff** is to tell you how to turn the first file into the second file.)

Note: Within a **d** command, you can generally ignore the number after the **d** (in this case, **3**). It shows you where **diff** found a difference in the second file.

To finish this part of the discussion, let me show you how **diff** works with a more realistic example. Consider the following two files, each of which contains some code from a Perl script. (Don't worry about what the code does; just concentrate on the output of the **diff** command.) The first file, **command-1.01.pl**, contains:

```
# Check for illegal content
# in order to prevent spam
# If the address contains a URL, abort
  if ($required{"address"} =~ m/(http):\/\// ) {
  $error_count += 1;
  }
```

The second file, **command-1.02.pl**, contains:

```
# If the address contains a URL, abort
  if ($required{"address"} =~ m/(http|https|ftp):\/\// ) {
  $error_count += 1;
  &error_exit ("No URLs allowed");
  }
```

The following **diff** command compares the two files:

```
diff command-1.01.pl command-1.02.pl
```

The output is:

```
1,2d0
< # Check for illegal content
< # in order to prevent spam
4c2
```

```
<  if ($required{"address"} =~ m/(http):\/\// ) {
---
>  if ($required{"address"} =~ m/(http|https|ftp):\/\// ) {
5a4
>  &error_exit ("No URLs allowed");
```

There are two ways to interpret this output. Literally, it tells us what instructions to follow to turn the first file into the second:

• Delete lines 1 and 2 from the first file.

• Change line 4 in the first file to line 2 from the second file.

• Append line 4 from the second file after line 5 in the first file.

A better way to interpret the output is to be able to read it and — in an instant — understand how the two files are different in a way that makes sense to you. This, of course, is why you are learning to use **diff** in the first place. The key is being able to read **c** (change), **d** (delete), and **a** (append) commands and instantly grasp their significance. As you can imagine, this takes practice. However, in time, you will be able to read and understand such output quickly and easily.

OPTIONS TO USE WITH diff

The **diff** program is complicated: it has a large number of options and a variety of ways in which it can generate output. In this section and the next, I'll discuss the most important options. For the full details, see the man page for your system (**man diff**).

The first few options tell **diff** to ignore certain differences when comparing. The **-i** (case insensitive) option tells **diff** to ignore any differences between upper- and lowercase letters. For example, when you use **-i**, **diff** considers the following three lines to be the same:

```
This is a BIG test.
this is a big test.
THIS IS A BIG TEST.
```

The **-w** and **-b** options allow you to control how **diff** works with whitespace (spaces and tabs). These options are handy when you have data that is formatted with spaces or tabs that you want to ignore. The **-w** (whitespace) option ignores **all** whitespace. For example, with **-w**, the following two lines are considered to be the same.

```
XX
X    X
```

The **-b** option is similar, but it doesn't ignore all whitespace; it only ignores differences in the amount of whitespace. For example, if you use **-b**, the above two lines would *not* be considered the same because the second line has whitespace, but the first does not. However, the following two lines would be the same:

```
X   X
X       X
```

This is because the two lines both have whitespace; they differ only in the amount of whitespace. The distinction between **-w** and **-b** is subtle, so if you have a whitespace problem and you are confused, try both options and see which works best with your particular data.

The **-B** (blank lines) option tells **diff** to ignore all blank lines. For example, let's say you have two files that contain different versions of an essay you have written. You want to compare them, but one copy is single-spaced, while the other is double-spaced. If you use the **-B** option, **diff** will ignore the blank lines and look only at the lines of text.

The rest of the **diff** options control how **diff** displays its results. The **-q** (quiet) option tells **diff** to leave out the details when two files are not the same. For example, if you compare two files, **frick** and **frack**, that are different, and you use **-q**, all you will see is:

```
Files frick and frack differ
```

As such, comparing two files with **diff   -q** is, essentially, the same as using **cmp** (discussed earlier in the chapter). The biggest difference is that **diff** only compares text files, while **cmp** works with any type of file.

As I mentioned earlier, when **diff** finds that two files are the same, it does not display anything. This is common with many Unix programs: when they have nothing to say, they say nothing. However, there may be times when you want an explicit notice that two files are identical. In such cases, you can use the **-s** (same) option. For example, if you compare the two files **frick** and **frack** and they are the same, you would normally see nothing. If you use **-s**, however, you will see:

```
Files frick and frack are identical
```

OUTPUT FORMATS WHEN COMPARING FILES: diff, sdiff

As we discussed earlier, when **diff** compares two files, the default output consists of instructions (**c**, **d**, **a**) along with line numbers. These instructions, if followed, will turn the first file into the second file. This type of output has the advantage of being terse and, once you get used to it, it actually is readable. In my experience, this is all you need most of the time.

The disadvantage of the default format, however, is that by the time you get used to it, you have made irreversible changes in the gray matter of your brain. The biggest problem is that when you read the output, there is very little context. All you see are some line numbers along with the lines to be changed. For this reason, **diff** has three options (**-c**, **-u** and **-y**) that will produce more readable types of output. In addition, there is another program, **sdiff**, that will compare two files side-by-side. Here are the details.

Using **diff** with the **-c** (context) option will show you the differences between two files in a format that is less terse and more understandable than the default output.

Instead of instructions and line numbers, **diff** will show you the actual lines that differ, as well as two extra lines above and below. Here is an example.

You have two files to compare. The first file, **smart-friends** contains:

```
Alba Tross
Dee Compose
Pat D. Bunnie
Phil Harmonic
```

The second file, **rich-friends**, contains:

```
Alba Tross
Dee Compose
Mick Stup
Pat D. Bunnie
```

First, let's compare the two files in the regular manner:

```
diff smart-friends rich-friends
```

The output is terse, but somewhat cryptic:

```
2a3
> Mick Stup
4d4
< Phil Harmonic
```

Now, let's use the **-c** option:

```
diff -c smart-friends rich-friends
```

The output is much longer, but easier to understand:

```
*** smart-friends     2009-02-14 15:33:50.000000000 -0700
--- rich-friends      2009-02-14 15:34:04.000000000 -0700
***************
*** 1,4 ****
  Alba Tross
  Dee Compose
  Pat D. Bunnie
- Phil Harmonic
--- 1,4 ----
  Alba Tross
  Dee Compose
+ Mick Stup
  Pat D. Bunnie
```

The top two lines give you information about the files. The first file is marked by ***** (star) characters; the second file is marked by **-<**(hyphen) characters. Following these lines, you see an excerpt from each file, showing exactly what needs to be changed to make the files identical.

Although this format is easier to understand than the default output, it has an obvious disadvantage: because **diff** displays excerpts from both files, there is duplicate text, making for a lot of output. When you consider that our example compared only two short files with simple differences, you can imagine how long the output would be if you compared two large files with many differences. In such cases, the **-c** output is much more verbose than the default format.

As a compromise, you can use the **-u** (unified output) option. This produces output similar to **-c** without repeating duplicate lines. For example, when you use:

```
diff -u smart-friends rich-friends
```

The output is:

```
--- smart-friends     2009-02-14 15:33:50.000000000 -0700
+++ rich-friends      2009-02-14 15:34:04.000000000 -0700
@@ -1,4 +1,4 @@
 Alba Tross
 Dee Compose
+Mick Stup
 Pat D. Bunnie
-Phil Harmonic
```

The final output option generates a side-by-side format, in which each line of the first file is displayed next to the corresponding line in the second file. To use this format, use **-y**:

```
diff -y smart-friends rich-friends
```

HINT

By default, when you use **diff** with **-c** or **-u**, the output shows two lines of context above and below every difference.

If you want to display a different number of context lines, you can do so by using **-C** (uppercase "C") instead of **-c**, and **-U** (uppercase "U") instead of **-u**. Use **-C** or **-U** followed by the number of extra lines you want, for example:

```
diff -C5 file1 file2
diff -U3 file1 file2
```

The side-by-side output looks like this:

```
Alba Tross          Alba Tross
Dee Compose         Dee Compose
                  > Mick Stup
Pat D. Bunnie       Pat D. Bunnie
Phil Harmonic     <
```

You can see the advantage of this type of output: it is very easy to see differences. For instance, in our example, it is obvious that three names are common to both files, (Alba, Dee and Pat), one name is only in the second file (Mick), and one name is only in the first file (Phil). The disadvantage, of course, is that, with a long file, you get a lot of output.

If you like this type of output, there is a special-purpose program, **sdiff** (side-by-side **diff**), you can use instead of **diff -y**. For example, the following two commands produce the same output:

```
diff -y smart-friends rich-friends
sdiff smart-friends rich-friends
```

When it is necessary to do a side-by-side comparison, many people prefer to use **sdiff**, because it has a lot of specialized options, which affords a great deal of control. The syntax for **sdiff** is:

```
sdiff [-bBilsW] [-w columns] file1 file2
```

where *file1* and *file2* are the names of text files, and **columns** is the width of the columns.

Using **sdiff** is straightforward. For example, to compare the two files from our example we would use:

```
sdiff smart-friends rich-friends
```

The output is:

```
Alba Tross        Alba Tross
Dee Compose       Dee Compose
                > Mick Stup
Pat D. Bunnie     Pat D. Bunnie
Phil Harmonic   <
```

As I mentioned, **sdiff** has a lot of options. We'll take a look at the most important ones, some of which are the same as the **diff** options. To read about the rest of the options, take a look at the man page on your system (**man sdiff**).

To start, there are several options that allow you to reduce the amount of unnecessary output. First, the **-l** (lowercase "L") option displays only the left column wherever the two files have common lines. For example, if you use:

```
sdiff -l smart-friends rich-friends
```

The output is:

```
Alba Tross        (
Dee Compose       (
                > Mick Stup
Pat D. Bunnie     (
Phil Harmonic   <
```

The **-s** (same) option reduces the output even further: it tells **sdiff** not to display any lines that are the same in both files. For example:

```
sdiff -s smart-friends rich-friends
```

The output is minimal and easy to understand:

```
                > Mick Stup
Phil Harmonic   <
```

When you work with files that have short lines (as in our example), you will often find that the default columns used by **sdiff** are too wide. When this happens, you can use the **-w** option to change the width of the columns. Just use **-w** followed by the number of characters you want in each column. For example:

```
sdiff -w 30 smart-friends rich-friends
```

Of course, you can combine more than one option. My favorite strategy is to start with the **-s** and **-w 30** options. For example:

```
sdiff -s -w 30 smart-friends rich-friends
```

Once I see the output, I adjust the width of the column to suit my data.

Finally, there are four options similar to those used with **diff**. The **-i** option ignores differences between upper- and lowercase letters; **-W** ignores all whitespace; **-b** ignores differences in the amount of whitespace; and **-B** ignores blank lines. (Note that **sdiff** uses **-W**, while **diff** uses **-w**. The difference is for historical reasons and has never been changed.)

DIFFS AND PATCHES

Over the years, **diff** has been a very important tool, used by programmers to keep track of different versions of their programs. For example, let's say you are a programmer and you are working on a C program named Foo. The current version is 2.0; it is stored in the file **foo-2.0.c**. Right now, you are working on version 2.1, which is stored in **foo-2.1.c**. Once version 2.1 is finished, you can capture the changes by running the following command:

```
diff foo-2.0.c foo-2.1.c > foo-diff-2.1
```

The output file (**foo-diff-2.1**) now contains a list of instructions that, when followed, will turn **foo-2.0.c** into **foo-2.1.c**.

In general, a list of instructions that will change one file into another is called a DIFF. Thus, we can say that **foo-diff-2.1** contains the diff that changes **foo-2.0.c** into **foo-2.1.c**.

Programmers create diffs for two reasons: to save storage space when backing up their work, and to distribute changes to other people.

Suppose Foo is a very large program. It would be prudent to make a backup of *every* version, but that would take up a lot of storage space. Instead, you back up a full copy of the base version (**foobar-2.0.c**). From then on, you only need to back up the diffs, which are small: **foo-diff-2.1**, **foo-diff-2.2**, and so on. (When you get to 3.0, you can save another full copy.)

Let's say you are at version 2.7 when a catastrophic event causes you to lose the original files. To restore them from the backup, you start by copying the base file, **foo-2.0.c**. You then use the first diff to recreate **foo-2.1.c**, the second diff to recreate **foo-2.2-c**, and so on, up to **foo-2.7.c**. In other words, by backing up a base copy and a series of diffs, you can recreate all the different versions of your program. In fact, using this technique, you can back up different versions of anything stored in a text file: a story, an essay, a sales presentation, and so on.

When you use a diff in this way — to recreate one file from another — we say that you APPLY the diff. The program that is used to apply diffs is called **patch** (the details of which are beyond the scope of this book). In our example, you would recreate the lost files by copying the base version and all the diffs from the backup, and then using **patch** to apply one diff after another.

The second way in which programmers use diffs is to distribute changes to their programs. For example, let's say a lot of people have the source code of version 2.0 of your Foo program. It took each person a while to download and install the program, but now they have it. What do you do when you are ready to distribute version 2.1?

You could ask everyone to download the entire new program. However, that would take a long time. Instead, you need only distribute the diff, which is small. To change to version 2.1, all your users need to do is use **patch** to apply the diff. If, for some reason, they have a problem with the new version, they can use **patch** to un-apply the diff, and go back to version 2.0.

When programmers use a diff in this way, it is often referred to as a PATCH. Thus, in our example, we would say that you distributed a patch for version 2.1, and your users used the **patch** program to apply the patch.

The advantage of distributing changes in the form of diffs is that it is much, much faster to update software by applying patches than by downloading and installing brand new versions. Indeed, in the early days of the Internet, when downloading was extremely slow, the only practical way to update large programs was by distributing patches that users would then apply on their own.

In the early days of Unix, it was common for programmers to use **diff** and **patch** to maintain, back up, and distribute their programs. However, for a long time, there have been much better systems to automate such tasks, and relatively few programmers use **diff** and **patch** directly. Instead, they work with a sophisticated VERSION CONTROL SYSTEM, sometimes referred to as SOURCE CODE CONTROL SYSTEM (SCCS) or REVISION CONTROL SYSTEM (RCS). Such systems are commonly used by software developers and engineers to manage the development of large programs, documents, blueprints, and so on. In fact, without modern version control systems, it would be impossible for large teams of people to work together on creative projects.

However, regardless of the degree of sophistication, all version control systems rely on the fundamental concepts of creating, distributing and applying diffs. This is why it is important that you understand the basic ideas.

WHAT'S IN A NAME?

Diff

The word diff comes from the **diff** program, which is used to compare two files. Among Unix people, it is common to use "diff" as both a noun and a verb.

For example, you might hear someone say, "Send me your diffs for the Foo program," meaning, "Send me the files that contain the updates for the Foo program."

You will also hear people use diff as a verb: "If you want to see the changes I made to your news article, just diff the two files."

EXTRACTING COLUMNS OF DATA: cut

Related filters: **colrm**, **join**, **paste**

The **cut** program is a filter that extracts specified columns of data and throws away everything else. (This is the opposite of **colrm**, which deletes specified columns of data, and saves everything else.)

The **cut** program has a great deal of flexibility. You can extract either specific columns of each line or delimited portions of each line (called fields). If you are a database expert, you can consider **cut** as implementing the projection of a relation. (If you are not a database expert, don't worry; your life is still complete.)

In this section, I will concentrate on how to use **cut** to extract columns of data. In the next section, we'll talk about how to extract fields of data.

The syntax of **cut** (when you are extracting columns) is:

cut -c *list* [*file...*]

where *list* is a list of columns to extract, and *file* is the name of an input file.

You use the list to tell **cut** which columns of data you want to extract. Specify one or more column numbers, separated by commas. Do not put any spaces within the list. For example, to extract column 10 only, use **10**. To extract columns 1, 8 and 10, use **1,8,10**.

You can also specify a range of column numbers by joining the beginning and end of the range with a hyphen. For example, to extract columns 10 through 15, use **10-15**. To extract columns 1, 8, and 10 through 15, use **1,8,10-15**.

Here is an example of how to use **cut**. Say that you have a file named **info** that contains information about a group of people. Each line contains data pertaining to one person. In particular, columns 14-30 contain a name and columns 42-49 contain a phone number. Here is the sample data:

```
012-34-5678   Ambercrombie, Al   01/01/72   555-1111
123-45-6789   Barton, Barbara    02/02/73   555-2222
```

```
234-56-7890   Canby, Charles     03/03/74   555-3333
345-67-8901   Danfield, Deann    04/04/75   555-4444
```

To display the names only, use:

```
cut -c 14-30 info
```

You will see:

```
Ambercrombie, Al
Barton, Barbara
Canby, Charles
Danfield, Deann
```

To display the names and phone numbers, use:

```
cut -c 14-30,42-49 info
```

You will see:

```
Ambercrombie, Al 555-1111
Barton, Barbara  555-2222
Canby, Charles   555-3333
Danfield, Deann  555-4444
```

If you like, you can leave out the space after **-c**. In fact, most people do just that. Thus, the following command is equivalent to the last one:

```
cut -c14-30,42-49 info
```

Returning to our example, you can save the information by redirecting standard output to a file, for example:

```
cut -c 14-30,42-49 info > phonelist
```

The **cut** program is handy to use in a pipeline. Here is an example. You share a multiuser Linux computer, and you want to make a list of the userids that are currently logged into the system. Since some userids may be logged in more than once, you want to show how many times each userid is logged in.

Start with **who** (Chapter 8). This command will generate a report with one line for each userid that is logged in. Here is a typical sample:

```
harley    console Jul  8 10:30
casey     ttyp1   Jul 12 17:46
weedly    ttyp4   Jul 12 21:22
harley    ttyp0   Jul 12 16:45
linda     ttyp3   Jul 12 17:41
```

As you can see, the userid is displayed in columns 1 through 8. Thus, we can extract the userids by using:

```
who | cut -c 1-8
```

The output is:

```
harley
casey
weedly
harley
linda
```

Now, let's do more. Let's sort the list of userids using **sort**, and count the number of duplications using **uniq -c**. (Both **sort** and **uniq** are explained in Chapter 19.) Putting the whole thing together, we have:

```
who | cut -c 1-8 | sort | uniq -c
```

(Notice that there is no problem using options within a pipeline.) The output is:

```
1 casey
2 harley
1 linda
1 weedly
```

As an interesting variation of this pipeline, let us ask the question: How can we display the names of all userids who are logged in exactly twice? The solution is to search the output of **uniq** for all the lines that contain "2"*. You can do so using **grep** (Chapter 19):

```
who | cut -c 1-8 | sort | uniq -c | grep "2"
```

The output is:

```
2 harley
```

> **HINT**
>
> To rearrange the columns of a table, use **cut** followed by **paste**.

RECORDS, FIELDS AND DELIMITERS; EXTRACTING FIELDS OF DATA: cut

In the last section, I showed you how to use the **cut** program to extract specified columns of data. However, **cut** has another use: it can extract fields of data. In order to understand how this works, we need to discuss a few basic ideas.

Consider two different files. The first file contains the following lines:

```
Ambercrombie  Al       123
Barton        Barbara  234
```

---

*Strictly speaking, this **grep** command will find any lines that contain the character "2". For example, if someone is logged in 12 times or 20 times that will be found as well. A better solution, which uses the techniques that we will discuss in Chapter 20, is to use the command **grep "\<2\>"**. This will find only those lines that contain "2" all by itself.

```
Canby          Charles    345
Danfield       Deann      456
```

The second file contains:

```
Ambercrombie:Al:123
Barton:Barbara:234
Canby:Charles:345
Danfield:Deann:456
```

In both files, each line contains a last name, a first name, and an identification number, in fact, the same information. However, there is a big difference between the files.

The first file is easy for a person to read, because the information is lined up nicely in columns. The second file is more suitable for a *program* to read, because of the : (colon) characters that separate the three parts of each line. Using the terminology we discussed in Chapter 12, we can call the first file human-readable and the second file machine-readable.

You will often encounter machine-readable files, similar to our second example, when you work with data that is designed to be processed by a program. With such data, each line is referred to as a RECORD; the separate parts of each line are called FIELDS; and the characters that act as separators are DELIMITERS. In our example, there are 4 records, each of which has 3 fields (last name, first name, identification number). Within each record, the delimiters are colons.

Of course, delimiters aren't always colons. In principle, any character that does not appear in the actual data can be used as a delimiter. The most common delimiters are commas, spaces, tabs and whitespace (that is, a combination of tabs and spaces).

Commas, in fact, are used so frequently as delimiters that there is a special name to describe data which is delimited by commas. Such data is said to be stored in CSV ("comma-separated value") format*.

Perhaps the most interesting example of a machine-readable file that uses delimiters is the Unix password file (**/etc/passwd**), which we discussed in Chapter 11. The password file contains one line for each userid on the system. Within each line, the various fields are separated by : characters. If a field is empty, you will see two : characters in a row.

To take a look at the password file on your system, use one of the following commands**:

---

*Until the last few years, CSV format was the most popular storage format for data that might need to be exchanged between programs, particularly with spreadsheet programs such as Microsoft Excel. Today, XML (Extensible Markup Language) is more widely used, because it works with many types of data. CSV format, although it is easy to understand, is much more limited as it can only be used with plain text.

For reference (in case you ever need it), here is my version of a comprehensive, technical definition of CSV format:

"CSV format is used to store textual data organized into records, each of which ends with a newline character (or return-newline with Windows). Within each record, fields are delimited by commas. Any whitespace (spaces or tabs) before or after fields is ignored. A field may be enclosed by double quotes, which are ignored. A field *must* be enclosed in double quotes if it contains commas, double quotes or newlines, or if it starts or ends with spaces or tabs. Within a field, a double quote character is represented by two double quotes in a row."

In old versions of Unix, passwords (encrypted, of course) were kept in the password file, hence the name. With modern Unix, the actual passwords are not kept in this file. As we discussed in Chapter 11, for security reasons the encrypted passwords are stored in a different file (/etc/shadow**) called the shadow file.

```
cat /etc/passwd
less /etc/passwd
```

Now that we have laid the groundwork, let me show you how to use the **cut** program to extract fields from the lines of a file. The syntax is:

cut **-c** *list* [*file...*]
cut **-f** *list* [**-d** *delimiter*] [**-s**] [*file...*]

where *list* is a list of fields to extract, *delimiter* is the delimiter used to separate fields, and *file* is the name of an input file.

The list of fields uses the same format as when you use the **-c** option. You specify one or more numbers, separated by commas. Do not put any spaces within the list. For example, to extract field 10 only, use **10**. To extract fields 1, 8 and 10, use **1,8,10**.

You can also specify a range of fields joining the beginning and end of the range with a hyphen. For example, to extract fields 10 through 15, use **10-15**. To extract fields 1, 8, and 10 through 15, use **1,8,10-15**.

Here is an example. Within the password file (**/etc/passwd**), the first field in each line is the userid. Suppose you want to see a list of all the userids registered with the system. Remembering that this file uses a **:** for a delimiter, all you need to do is extract the first field from each line in the password file. The command is:

```
cut -f 1 -d ':' /etc/passwd
```

If you want to sort the list, just pipe the output to **sort** (Chapter 19):

```
cut -f 1 -d ':' /etc/passwd | sort
```

The following example extracts fields number 1, 3, 4 and 5 from the same file:

```
cut -f 1,3-5 -d ':' /etc/passwd | sort
```

You will notice that I have quoted the delimiter (the **:**). This is a good habit in order to make sure that the delimiter is not interpreted incorrectly when the shell parses the command. In this case, it would have been okay to leave out the quotes, but if your delimiter is a space, tab or a metacharacter, you must quote it.

What happens if **cut** encounters a line that does not contain any delimiters? By default, such lines are simply passed through and will be written to standard output. If you want to throw away such lines, you can use the **-s** (suppress) option.

One last point. As with the **-c** option we discussed in the last section, you can leave out the space after **-f** and **-d**. Thus, the following commands are equivalent to our last two examples:

```
cut -f1 -d':' /etc/passwd | sort
cut -f1,3-5 -d':' /etc/passwd | sort
```

Most experienced Unix people leave out the spaces.

HINT

When you want to extract fields from a file that has both delimiters and fixed width columns, you can use either **cut -d** or **cut -c**. In such cases, you will find that working with delimiters (**-d**) is a better choice as it is less prone to error.

COMBINING COLUMNS OF DATA: `paste`

Related filters: `colrm`, `cut`, `join`

The **paste** program combines columns of data. This program has a great deal of flexibility. You can combine several files, each of which has a single column of data, into one large table. You can also combine consecutive lines of data to build multiple columns. In this section, I will concentrate on the most useful feature of **paste**: combining separate files. If you want more details on what **paste** can do for you, check the man page (**man paste**).

The syntax of the **paste** program is:

paste [**-d** *char...*] [*file...*]

where *char* is a character to be used as a separator, and *file* is the name of an input file.

You use **paste** to combine columns of data into one large table. If you want, you can save the table in a file by redirecting standard output. Here is an example. You have four files named **idnumber**, **name**, **birthday** and **phone**. The contents of the files are as follows.

The file **idnumber**:

```
012-34-5678
123-45-6789
234-56-7890
345-67-8901
```

The file **name**:

```
Ambercromby, Al
Barton, Barbara
Canby, Charles
Danfield, Deann
```

The file **birthday**:

```
01/01/85
02/02/86
03/03/87
04/04/88
```

And finally, the file **phone**:

```
555-1111
555-2222
555-3333
555-4444
```

You want to build one large file named **info** that combines all this data into a single table. Within the table, the data from each file should be put into its own column. The command to use is:

```
paste idnumber name birthday phone > info
```

The contents of **info** are:

```
012-34-5678     Ambercromby, Al 01/01/85          555-1111
123-45-6789     Barton, Barbara 02/02/86          555-2222
234-56-7890     Canby, Charles  03/03/87          555-3333
345-67-8901     Danfield, Deann 04/04/88          555-4444
```

You will notice that the output is spaced a bit oddly. That is because, by default, **paste** puts a tab character between each column entry, and Unix assumes that tabs are set every 8 positions, starting with position 1. In other words, Unix assumes that tabs are set at positions 1, 9, 17, 25 and so on. (We will discuss the details of how Unix uses tabs in Chapter 18.)

To tell **paste** to use a different (non-tab) character between columns, use the **-d** (delimiter) option followed by an alternative character in single quotes. For example, to create the same table with a space between columns, use:

```
paste -d ' ' idnumber name birthday phone
```

Now your output looks like this:

```
012-34-5678 Ambercromby, Al 01/01/72 555-1111
123-45-6789 Barton, Barbara 02/02/73 555-2222
234-56-7890 Canby, Charles 03/03/74 555-3333
345-67-8901 Danfield, Deann 04/04/75 555-4444
```

If you specify more than one delimiter, **paste** will use each one in turn, repeating if necessary. For example, the following command specifies two different delimiters, a **|** (vertical bar) and a **%** (percent sign).

```
paste -d '|%' idnumber name birthday phone
```

The output is:

```
012-34-5678|Ambercromby, Al%01/01/85|555-1111
123-45-6789|Barton, Barbara%02/02/86|555-2222
234-56-7890|Canby, Charles%03/03/87|555-3333
345-67-8901|Danfield, Deann%04/04/88|555-4444
```

HINT

Think of **paste** as being similar to **cat**. The difference is that **paste** combines data horizontally, while **cat** combines data vertically.

Using **cut** and **paste** in sequence, you can change the order of columns in a table. For example, say that you have a file named **pizza** containing information about four different pizzas you are going to make for a party:

```
mushrooms regular sausage
olives    thin    pepperoni
onions    thick   meatball
tomato    pan     liver
```

You want to change the order of the first and second columns. First, save each column to a separate file:

```
cut -c 1-9 pizza > vegetables
cut -c 11-17 pizza > crust
cut -c 19-27 pizza > meat
```

Now combine the three columns into a single table, specifying the order that you want:

```
paste -d ' ' crust vegetables meat > pizza
```

Since this is a short file, you can display it using **cat** (see the discussion in Chapter 16).

```
cat pizza
```

The data now looks like this:

```
regular mushrooms sausage
thin    olives    pepperoni
thick   onions    meatball
pan     tomato    liver
```

(Of course, this is a small, contrived example, but think how important this technique would be if you had to interchange columns in a file with hundreds or thousands of lines.)

Once you have made the changes you want, there are two things left to do. First, use the **rm** program (Chapter 25) to delete the three temporary files:

```
rm crust vegetables meat
```

Second, see if you can think of someone to invite to the party who is willing to eat a liver and tomato pizza.

CHAPTER 17 EXERCISES

REVIEW QUESTIONS

1. There are ten important Unix programs to compare, sort and select data from files. What are the ten programs? Why are there so many programs?

2. By default, the **comm** program compares two files and generates three columns of output. Explain the purpose of each column. How do you suppress a specific column?

3. Both the **diff** and **sdiff** programs compare files. When do you use **diff** and when do you use **sdiff**?

4. You are given a large text file. Which program would you use to select: a) duplicate lines, b) unique lines, c) lines containing a specific pattern, d) lines beginning with a specific pattern, e) columns of data?

APPLYING YOUR KNOWLEDGE

1. You are interested in comparing favorite foods with your two friends Claude and Eustace. Create three files named: **me**, **claude**, **eustace**. Each of the files contains five lines in sorted order, each of which has the name of a food. Using only two Unix commands, display a list of those foods that appear in all three lists. Hint: You may need to create a temporary file.

2. The **comm** program is used to compare sorted files; the **diff** program compares unsorted files. Give three examples of types of data which you would compare using **comm**. Give three examples of types of data where you would use **diff**. Are there any instances where either program would work?

3. Each line of the Unix password file (**/etc/passwd**) contains information about a userid. Within the line, the various fields of data are delimited by **:** (colon) characters. One of the fields contains the name of the shell for that userid. Use the following command to display and study the format of the password file on your system:

```
less /etc/password
```

(From within less, you can press <Space> to display the page down and **q** to quit.) What command would you use to read the password file and display a list of the various shells used on your system? How would you sort the output to make it more readable? How would you eliminate duplications?

4. CSV format (comma-separated value format) describes a file containing machine-readable data in which fields are separated by commas. You have five files — **data1**, **data2**, **data3**, **data4**, and **data5** — each of which contains a single column

of data. What command would you use to put the five columns together into one CSV-formatted file named **csvdata**? What happens if one of the files has fewer lines in it than the other files?

FOR FURTHER THOUGHT

1. The purpose of the **diff** program is to highlight differences by displaying terse instructions for turning the first file into the second file. Create two files named **a** and **b**. Compare the output of the following commands:

```
diff a b
diff b a
```

What patterns do you notice?

2. Why is the output of the **diff** command so compact? Should it be easier to understand?

3. You are given a text file with 10,000 lines. The file contains two columns of data, and you must change the order of the columns. You can do so quickly and accurately by using the **cut** and **paste** commands. Suppose you did not have these commands? Using *any* other tools at your disposal, how might you accomplish the job? Consider using a text editor, word processor, a spreadsheet program, writing a program of your own, and so on. Is there anything you can think of that is easier than the Unix **cut** and **paste** programs? Why is this? What qualities do the programs in this chapter have that make them so useful?

CHAPTER 18
FILTERS: COUNTING AND FORMATTING

This is the third of four chapters (16-19) in which we discuss filters: programs that read and write textual data, one line at a time, reading from standard input and writing to standard output. In this chapter, we will talk about how to manipulate text. In particular, I'll show you how to work with line numbers; how to count lines, words and characters; and how to format text in a variety of useful ways.

Along the way, we'll digress a bit so I can cover several very interesting topics, including how Unix handles tabs and spaces, and why you will often see 80-character lines in text files: a story that is a lot more interesting than you might think.

CREATING LINE NUMBERS: nl

Related filters: **nl**

The **nl** filter provides a simple but useful service: it inserts line numbers into text. The syntax is:

nl [**-v** *start*] [**-i** *increment*] [**-b a**] [**-n ln|rn|rz**] [*file...*]

where *start* is the starting number, *increment* is the increment, and *file* is the name of a file.

The *nl* program comes in handy in two situations. First, when you want to insert permanent line numbers into some data, which you will then save. Second, when you want to insert temporary line numbers into the output of a command to make the output easier to understand. Let's start with a simple, but useful example.

You are going on a blind date, and you want to be sure to make a good impression. To prepare for the date, you create a file named **books** containing a list of your favorite books:

```
Crime and Punishment
The Complete Works of Shakespeare
Pride and Prejudice
Harley Hahn's Internet Yellow Pages
Harley Hahn's Internet Insecurity
Harley Hahn's Internet Advisor
```

To number the list, you can use the command:

```
nl books
```

The output is:

```
1  Crime and Punishment
2  The Complete Works of Shakespeare
3  Pride and Prejudice
4  Harley Hahn's Internet Yellow Pages
5  Harley Hahn's Internet Insecurity
6  Harley Hahn's Internet Advisor
```

This looks good, so you save the numbered list by redirecting the standard output to a file named **best-books**:

```
nl books > best-books
```

You now have a list of favorite books, complete with line numbers, with which to impress your date.

The **nl** program is an old one, dating back to the early days of Unix. Traditionally, **nl** is used to insert line numbers into text before printing. For example, let's say you have two files of scientific data: **measurements1** and **measurements2**. You want to print all the data and, to help you interpret it, you want to number each line on the printout. However, you don't want to change the original data.

The strategy is to use **nl** to number the lines and then redirect the output to the **lpr** program, which sends the data to your default printer. (The two principal Unix programs to print files are **lp** and **lpr**.)

```
nl measurements1 measurements2 | lpr
```

In this way, you create temporary numbers that are used once and then thrown away.

In the early days of Unix, terminals printed their output on paper, which was slow, and it was common to send data to a real printer, which could print a lot faster than a terminal. Today, it usually makes more sense to display data on your screen. In this case, all you need to do is pipe the output of **nl** to **less** (Chapter 21), which will display the output one screenful at a time:

```
nl measurements1 measurements2 | less
```

Again, the original data is not changed. When you use **nl**, line numbers are always temporary, unless you save the output to a file.

By default, **nl** generates the numbers 1, 2, 3, and so on, which is fine. If the need arises, however, there are a few options you can use to control the numbering. You can change the starting number by using the **-v** option, and change the increment by using the **-i** option. To show you how it works, here are some examples using a file called **data** that contains several lines of text.

The first example starts numbering at 100:

```
nl -v 100 data
```

The output is:

```
100   First line of text.
101   Second line of text.
102   Third line of text.
103   Fourth line of text.
```

The next example starts numbering at 1 (the default) with an increment of 5:

```
nl -i 5 data
```

The output is:

```
 1   First line of text.
 6   Second line of text.
11   Third line of text.
16   Fourth line of text.
```

The third example uses both options to start numbering at 100 with an increment of 5:

```
nl -i 5 -v 100 data
```

The output is:

```
100   First line of text.
105   Second line of text.
110   Third line of text.
115   Fourth line of text.
```

In addition to **-v** and **-i**, the **nl** program has a variety of formatting options. However, there are only two you are likely to need. First, by default, if your data has blank lines, **nl** will not number them. To force **nl** to number all lines, use the **-b** (body numbering) option followed by the letter **a** (all lines):

```
nl -b a file
```

The **-b** option has other variations, but they are rarely used. Second, you can control the format of the numbers by using the **-n** (number format) option followed by a code:

ln = left-justified, no leading zeros
rn = right-justified, no leading zeros
rz = right-justified, leading zeros

Here is an example:

```
nl -v 100 -i 5 -b a -n rz file
```

This command generates numbers starting with 100, using an increment of 5. All lines are numbered, even blank lines, and the numbers are right-justified with leading zeros.

COUNTING LINES, WORDS AND CHARACTERS: wc

Related filters: **nl**

The **wc** (word count) program counts lines, words and characters. The data may come from another program or from one or more files. The syntax is simple:

wc [**-clLw**] [*file...*]

where *file* is the name of a file.

The **wc** program is *very* useful, in fact, more useful than you might realize at first. This is because you can use **wc** within a pipeline to analyze textual output from any program you want. For example, let's say you want to know how many files are in a particular directory. You can count all the files by hand, or you can generate a list and then pipe it to **wc** to count the lines for you. (I'll show you an example in a moment.)

Let's start with the basics. By default, the output of **wc** consists of three numbers: the number of lines, words and characters in the data. For example, **wc** might report that a file contains exactly 2 lines, 13 words and 71 characters.

When input comes from a file, **wc** will write the file name after the three numbers. If you specify more than one file, **wc** will display one line of output for each file, and an extra line showing the total count — lines, words and characters — for all the files put together.

Here is the example. You are writing a romantic poem for your sweetheart for Valentine's Day. This is all you have written so far:

There was a young man from Nantucket,
Whose girlfriend had told him to

To count the lines, words and characters in the poem, use:

wc poem

The output is:

2 13 71 poem

In other words, the file has 2 lines, 13 words and 71 characters. If you forget which number is which, just remember: Lines, Words, Characters. (If you are a man, you can remember the acronym LWC, "Look at Women Carefully".)

Here are the technical details:

- A "character" is a letter, number, punctuation symbol, space, tab or newline.

- A "word" is an unbroken sequence of characters, delimited by spaces, tabs or newlines.

- A "line" is a sequence of characters ending with a newline. (The newline character is discussed in Chapter 7.)

As I mentioned, if you specify more than one file at a time, **wc** will also show you total statistics. For example:

```
wc poem message story
```

Here is some typical output*:

```
 2   13    71 poem
15   61   447 message
43  552  3050 story
60  626  3568 total
```

By convention, output is always displayed in the following order: number of lines, number of words, number of characters. If you do not want all three numbers, you can use the options: **-l** counts lines, **-w** counts words, and **-c** counts characters. When you use options, **wc** displays only the numbers you ask for. For example, to see only the number of lines in the file **story**, use:

```
wc -l story
```

The output is:

```
43 story
```

To see how many words and characters are in the file **message**, use:

```
wc -wc message
```

The output is:

```
61 447 message
```

The **-c** (character), **-l** (line), and **-w** (word) options have been part of the **wc** command for decades and can be used with any type of Unix or Linux. With Linux, there is also another option, **-L**. This option displays the length of the longest line in the input. For example, let's say you are planning a big party, and you need a list to give to the bouncers of all the people who are not allowed entry. You have created the file **do-not-admit**, with the following four lines:

```
Britney
Paris
Nicole
Lindsay
```

To display the length of the longest line in this file, you would use:

```
wc -L do-not-admit
```

In this case, the first and fourth lines have 7 characters, so the output is:

```
7 do-not-admit
```

---

*These files contain real-life data. The poem is the sample poem we used above; the message is an email message from my editor, dated February 16, 2006, asking when the book would be done; and the story is "Late One Night", written by me, which you can find on my Web site **www.harley.com**.

The **-L** option comes in handy when you need to decide if a file needs some type of formatting. For example, if a file has any lines longer than, say, 70 characters, you might use **fmt** to format the text before sending it to **pr** to prepare for printing (explained later in the chapter).

As you gain experience, you will find that there are two main ways to use **wc**. First, there are times when you need a quick measure of the size of a file. For example, let's say you email a text file to someone. The file is important, and you want to double-check that it arrived intact. Run the **wc** command on the original file. Then tell the recipient to run **wc** on the other file. If the two sets of results match, you can feel confident the file arrived intact. Similarly, suppose you are writing an essay that must be at least 2,000 words. From time to time, you can use **wc -w** to see how close you are getting to your target.

The second use for **wc** is different, but just as important: you can pipe the output of a command to **wc** and check how many lines of text were generated. Because many programs generate one item of information per line, you can, by counting the lines, know how much information was produced. Here are two examples.

First, the **ls** program (Chapter 24) lists the names of files in a directory. For example, the following command displays the names of all the files in the **/etc** directory. (We will discuss directories in Chapter 24.)

```
ls /etc
```

The **ls** program has many options. However, there is no option for counting the number of files. To do so, you pipe the output of **ls** to **wc**. Thus, to count the number of files in the **/etc** directory, you use:

```
ls /etc | wc -l
```

(Try it on your system.)

Here is the second example. In Chapter 8, I showed you how to use **who** to find out which userids are logged in to your system. To display the *number* of userids* logged in, all you have to do is count the lines of output of the **who** command:

```
who | wc -l
```

If you want to get fancy, you can combine this last pipeline with the **echo** program (Chapter 12) and command substitution (Chapter 13) to display a message showing the number of userids currently logged in:

```
echo "There are `who | wc -l` userids logged in right now."
```

For example, if 5 people are logged in, you will see:

```
There are 5 userids logged in right now.
```

If you share a multiuser system, this is an interesting command to put in your login file (see Chapter 14).

---

*A userid ("user-eye-dee") is not a person. It is a name used to log in to a Unix system. As we discussed in Chapter 4, Unix knows only about userids, not users.

HOW UNIX USES TABS

When you look at your keyboard, you see a <Tab> key. This key is a holdover from the days when tabs were used on typewriters. Although we don't use tabs anymore, we still use the <Tab> key, and Unix still uses tab settings. To understand why, let's take a moment and travel back in time to the days when typewriters were the dominant form of life in the office machine community.

The word "tab" is an abbreviation for "tabulate", which means to organize information into a table. The <Tab> keys on the old typewriters were designed to help line up information in columns and to indent text at the beginning of paragraphs. Here is an example showing how it used to work.

You are using an old typewriter, and you want to type a table with three columns. The columns should line up at positions 1, 15 and 25. To prepare, you set two small mechanical markers, called TAB STOPS at positions 15 and 25.

Once this is done, pressing the <Tab> key will cause the carriage to move horizontally to the next tab stop. For example, if you are at position 8 and you press <Tab>, the carriage will move to position 15. If you are at position 19, and you press <Tab>, the carriage will move to position 25. Thus, setting the tab stops in this way gives you an easy way to jump directly to positions 15 and 25 without having to press the <Space> bar repeatedly (and without having to back up if you go too far).

You are now ready to type your table. To start, you put in a piece of paper and position the carriage at the beginning of the line. You type the information for the first column and then press the <Tab> key. This causes the carriage to move to position 15. You type the information for the second column and press <Tab> again. The carriage now moves to position 25. You then type the information for the third column. You are now finished typing the first row of your table. You press the carriage return lever all the way to left, which moves the carriage to the beginning of the next line, leaving you ready to type the next row.

Although the original Unix terminals (see Chapter 7) were not typewriters, they did print on paper and they were able to jump horizontally when they encountered a tab character. For this reason, Unix was designed so that whenever a terminal encountered a tab character, it would act like a typewriter by moving the cursor to the next tab stop on the current line — and, to this day, that is still the case. Unix terminals "display" a tab character by moving the cursor forward to the next tab stop.

By default, Unix assumes that there are tab stops every 8 characters, starting with position 1. Thus, the default Unix tab positions are 1, 9, 17, 25, 33, and so on. When you are typing text and you press the <Tab> key, Unix inserts an invisible tab character. Later, when you look at the text, your terminal will "display" the tab character by creating enough horizontal space to jump to the next tab stop, just like the <Tab> key on an old typewriter.

Consider this example. You have a one-line file containing the letter "A", a tab character, the letters "BBBBB", another tab character, and the letters "CCC:

A<Tab>**BBBBB**<Tab>**CCC**

If you use the **cat** command to display this file, you will see:

A   **BBBB**   **CCC**

The **A** is at position 1. The **BBBB** starts at position 9, and the **CCC** starts at position 17.

Of course, you can't see the tabs: they look like empty space. Thus, as far as your eye is concerned, the gap between the letters might as well be space characters, which are also invisible. For instance, in the example above, when you look at the output of the **cat** command, you can't tell if the empty space between **A** and **BBBB** is (in this case) 1 tab or 7 spaces.

So, the question arises: when you want to indent text or align data into columns, which is better to use, tabs or spaces? This question has been debated for a long time by programmers, because they use empty space to indent control-flow constructs (if-then-else, while loops, and so on).

Some programmers prefer to use tabs for indentation, because they are simpler. For example, each time you press <Tab>, it inserts a single tab character which automatically indents the text to the position of the next tab stop. If you use spaces, you need to press the <Space> bar multiple times, in order to line up the text by hand.

In addition, tabs are also more flexible than spaces. For example, if you want to change the amount of indentation you see on your screen, you need only change the tab stop settings within your text editor program. If you use spaces, you have to go to each line in the program and add or delete actual space characters.

Other programmers argue for using spaces for indentation. Tabs, they say, are clumsy to use because the amount of space they generate varies. A single tab character, they point out, can represent 1 to 8 positions of empty space depending on its location within the line. When you use spaces, what you use is exactly what you get: type 4 spaces, and you get 4 spaces.

Moreover, although it is true you can adjust the tab stop settings within most text editors, much of the time you will be stuck with the default: positions 1, 9, 17, 25, and so on. This much spacing is too much, as it creates large indentations, making the text hard to read. By using real spaces, you can indent 2 or 3 or 4 positions — whatever you want — and it will work exactly the way you want, no matter what text editor or other programs you use.

Of course, the need to create horizontal spacing applies to more than computer programs. Whenever you work with any type of text that requires indentation or that is organized into columns, you must choose whether to use tabs or spaces.

I can't tell you what to use, because everyone has a preference as to what he or she likes best. Over time, you will figure out which choice one works better for you. (Personally, I prefer spaces to tabs.)* What I can tell you is that — whichever choice you end up making — there are two Unix programs to make your life easier (**expand** and **unexpand**), which we will cover in a moment. First, however, we need to discuss a more fundamental question.

---

*When I write programs, I indent 4 positions. When I write HTML (Web pages), I indent 2 positions.

VISUALIZING TABS AND SPACES

When you work with a file that contains tabs and spaces, a problem arises. Since tabs and spaces are invisible, how can you tell where they are?

This can be important when you are working with programs like **expand** and **unexpand** (which we will discuss in the next two sections). The **expand** program changes tabs into spaces; **unexpand** changes spaces into tabs. If you can't see the tabs and spaces, how do you know the commands did what you wanted them to do?

The simplest solution is to view the file from within a text editor or word processor that lets you turn on an option to view invisible characters. There are two choices.

With the **vi** editor (Chapter 22), the command to use is:

```
:set list
```

Spaces will still be invisible, but tabs will show up as **^I**, the control character that represents a tab in the ASCII code. To turn off the option, use:

```
:set nolist
```

If you know how to use **vi**, this is an excellent solution to the problem: quick and easy. In fact, this is how I look at whitespace in files.

If you don't know **vi**, you can use the Nano or Pico editors, which I mentioned in Chapter 14. (They are basically the same editor; Nano is the GNU version of Pico.) Within Nano/Pico, you view spaces and tabs by pressing <Esc>**P** (that is, press the <Esc> key, then press the <P> key). This turns on "Whitespace display mode". To turn it off, just press <Esc>**P** a second time.

Before you can use <Esc>**P**, however, you must add the following line to your Nano/Pico initialization file, either **.nanorc** or **.picorc** respectively (see Chapter 14):

```
set whitespace "xy"
```

where *x* is the character you want to indicate a tab, and *y* is the character you want to indicate a space.

For example, if you want a tab to show up as a **+** (plus) character, and a space to show up as a **|** (vertical bar) character, put the following line in your Nano/Pico initialization file:

```
set whitespace "+|"
```

Using **vi** or Nano/Pico to view spaces and tabs works well. Unfortunately, **vi** is complicated (as you will see in Chapter 22), and it will take you a long time to learn how to use it well. Nano/Pico is a lot simpler but, like **vi**, it does take time to learn.

So what about the very simple GUI-based editors, Kedit and Gedit, we discussed in Chapter 14? As I mentioned, these editors are easy to use. However, they are not very powerful. In particular, they do not allow you to view invisible characters, so let's forget about them for now.

If your system has Open Office, a collection of open source office applications, there is another solution. The Open Office word processor makes it easy to view tabs and spaces within a file. Just pull down the View menu and select "Nonprinting Characters". You turn off the feature the same way. Simple and easy.

Aside from viewing a file in a text editor or word processor, there is a way to check the effects of **expand** or **unexpand** indirectly. You can use the **wc -c** command (discussed earlier in the chapter) to display the number of characters in the file.

Since each tab is a single character, when you use **expand** to change tabs to spaces within a file, the number of characters in the file will increase. Similarly, when you use **unexpand** to change spaces to tabs, the number of characters in the file will decrease. Although using **wc -c** won't show you the invisible characters, it will give you an indication as to whether or not **expand** or **unexpand** worked.

CHANGING TABS TO SPACES: expand

Related filters: **unexpand**

As we discussed earlier in the chapter, when you need to indent text or align data into columns, you can use either tabs or spaces. The choice is yours. Regardless of your preference, however, there will be times when you will find yourself working with data that has tabs, which you need to change into spaces. Similarly, there will be times when you have data with spaces, which you need to change into tabs. In such cases, you can use the **expand** program to change tabs to spaces, and the **unexpand** program to change spaces to tabs. Let's start with **expand**.

The syntax is:

expand [**-i**] [**-t** *size* | **-t** *list*] [*file...*]

where *size* is the size of fixed-width tabs, **list** is a list of tab stops, and **file** is the name of a file.

The **expand** program changes all the tabs in the input file to spaces, while maintaining the same alignment as the original text. By default, **expand** uses the Unix convention that tab stops are set for every 8 positions: 1, 9, 17, 25, 33, and so on. Thus, each tab in the input will be replaced by 1 to 8 spaces in the output. (Think about that until it makes sense.)

As an example, consider the following file named **animals**, which contains data organized into columns. When you display **animals**, you see the following:

```
kitten  cat
puppy   dog
lamb    sheep
nerd    programmer
```

As you can see, the file contains four lines of data. What you can't see is that each line consists of two words separated by a tab:

```
kitten<Tab>cat
puppy<Tab>dog
lamb<Tab>sheep
nerd<Tab>programmer
```

(I have used the designation <Tab> to represent a single tab character.)

The following command expands each tab to the appropriate number of spaces, saving the output in a file named **animals-expanded**:

```
expand animals > animals-expanded
```

The new file now contains the following:

kitten<Space><Space>**cat**
puppy<Space><Space><Space>**dog**
lamb<Space><Space><Space><Space>**sheep**
nerd<Space><Space><Space><Space>**programmer**

(I have used the designation <Space> to represent a single space character.)

If you display the new file using **cat** or **less**, it will look the same as the original file. However, if you use a text editor or word processor to view the invisible characters (as I described in the previous section), you will see that all the tabs have been changed to spaces. More specifically, within each line, **expand** has removed the tab and inserted enough spaces so the following word starts at the next tab stop, in this case, position 9.

As I mentioned, **expand** uses the Unix default by assuming that there are 8 positions between each tab stop. You can change this with the **-t** (tab stop) option. There are two variations. First, if all the tab stops are the same distance apart, use **-t** followed by that number.

For example, let's say you have a large file named **data** that contains some tabs. You want to expand the tabs into spaces and save the output in the file **data-new**. However, you want the tab stops to be set at every 4 characters, rather than every 8 characters; that is, you want: 1, 5, 9, 13, and so on. Use the command:

```
expand -t 4 data > data-new
```

Using this notation, we can say that **-t 8** would be the same as the Unix default, tab stops at every 8 positions; **-t 4** creates tab stops at every 4 positions.

The **-t** has a second variation. If you want the tab stops to be at specific positions, you can specify a list with more than one number, separated by commas. Within the list, numbering starts at 0. That is, **0** refers to the first position on the line; **1** refers to the second position on the line; and so on. For example, to set tab stops at positions 8, 16, 22 and 57, you would use:

```
expand -t 7,15,21,56 data > data-new
```

Finally, there is an option to use when you want to expand tabs, but only at the beginning of a line. In such cases, use the **-i** (initial) option, for example:

```
expand -i -t 4 data > data-new
```

This command expands tabs, but only at the beginning of a line. All other tabs are left alone. In this case, because of the **-t** option, the tab stops are considered to be at positions 1, 5, 9, and so on.

> **HINT**
>
> The **expand** program is useful for pre-processing text files with tabs before sending the files to a program that expects columns to line up exactly.
>
> For example, the following pipeline replaces all the tabs in a file named **statistics**, which has tab stops at every 4 positions. After the tabs are replaced, the first 15 characters of each line are extracted, and the result is sorted:
>
> ```
> expand -t 4 statistics | cut -c 1-15 | sort
> ```

CHANGING SPACES TO TABS: unexpand

Related filters: **expand**

To change spaces to tabs, you use the **unexpand** program. The syntax is:

unexpand [**-a**] [**-t** *size* | **-t** *list*] [*file...*]

where *size* is the size of fixed-width tabs, **list** is a list of tab stops, and **file** is the name of a file.

The **unexpand** program works as you would expect, like **expand** in reverse, replacing spaces with tabs in such a way that the original alignment of the data is maintained.

As with **expand**, the default tab settings are every 8 positions: 1, 9, 17, and so on. To change this, you use the same two forms of the **-t** option as with **expand**: a fixed interval (such as **-t 4**; every 4 positions), or a list of tab stops (such as **-t 7,15,21,56**). If you use a list, numbering starts at 0. That is, **0** refers to the first position on the line; **1** refers to the second position on the line; and so on.

One important difference between **expand** and **unexpand** is that, by default, **unexpand** only replaces spaces at the beginning of a line. This is because, most of the time, you would only use **unexpand** with lines that are indented. You would probably not want to replace spaces in the middle of a line. If, however, you do want to override this default, you can use the **-a** (all) option. This tells unexpand to replace all spaces, even those that are not at the beginning of a line.

As an example, let's say that you are a student at a prestigious West Coast university, majoring in Contemporary American Culture. You have just attended a lecture about Mickey Mouse, during which you have taken careful notes. When you get home, you use a text editor to type your notes into a file named **rough-notes**. It happens that, when you indent lines, your text editor inserts 4 spaces for each level of indentation:

```
Mickey Mouse (1928-)
    Major figure in American culture
    Girlfriend is Minnie Mouse
        (Why same last name, if they are not married?)
    Did not speak until 9th film; The Karnival Kid, 1929
        First words were "Hot Dogs"
For exam, be sure I am able to:
```

```
    Compare Mickey to President Roosevelt & Elvis Presley
    Contrast Mickey with Hamlet (both tortured souls)
```

You want to change all the initial spaces to tabs and save the data in a file called **mickey**. The command to use is:

```
unexpand -t 4 rough-notes > mickey
```

Once you run this command, the file **mickey** contains:

```
Mickey Mouse (1928-)
<Tab>Major figure in American culture
<Tab>Girlfriend is Minnie Mouse
<Tab><Tab>(Why same last name, if they are not married?)
<Tab>Did not speak until 9th film; The Karnival Kid, 1929
<Tab>First words were "Hot Dogs"
For exam, be sure I am able to:
<Tab>Compare Mickey to President Roosevelt & Elvis Presley
<Tab>Contrast Mickey with Hamlet (both tortured souls?)
```

(I have used the designation <Tab> to represent a single tab character.)

FORMATTING LINES: `fold`

Related filters: **fmt**, **pr**

With this section, we begin a discussion of three programs that reformat text to make it easy to read or make it suitable for printing. The **fold** program works with lines; the **fmt** program works with paragraphs; and the **pr** program works with pages and columns. We'll start with **fold**.

The **fold** program performs one simple task: it breaks long lines into shorter lines. If you have a file with overly long lines, **fold** is wonderful. In an instant, it can break the lines according to your specifications, a task that would otherwise take you a great deal of time to do by hand. The syntax for **fold** is:

fold [-s] [-w *width*] [*file...*]

where **width** is the maximum width of the new lines, and **file** is the name of a file.

By default, **fold** breaks lines at position 80. There is a reason for this: in the 1970s, when Unix was developed, 80 was considered to be a round number with respect to lines of text (see the next section). These days, most people don't want text that wide, and 80 is usually too long. To change the width, use the **-w** (width) option, followed by the maximum line size you want. For example, to read data from a file named **long-lines**, reformat it into lines that are no longer than 40 characters, and save the output in a file named **short-lines**, you would use:

```
fold -w 40 long-lines > short-lines
```

When **fold** breaks a line, all it does is insert a return character (see Chapter 7) in the appropriate place, making two lines out of one. Here is an example to show you how it works. You have a file named **alphabet**, which has two lines as follows:

```
abcdefghijklmnopqrstuvwxyz
ABCDEFGHIJKLMNOPQRSTUVWXYZ
```

Each line is 26 characters long. The following command breaks the lines in half, by inserting a return after the 13th character:

```
fold -w 13 alphabet
```

The output is:

```
abcdefghijklm
nopqrstuvwxyz
ABCDEFGHIJKLM
NOPQRSTUVWXYZ
```

When used in this manner, **fold** breaks each long line at its maximum length. For instance, in the last example, **fold** broke the lines at exactly 13 characters. This is fine when you have data that will not be distorted by such changes. However, most of the time, you will want to reformat lines that contain words and, with this type of text, you won't want **fold** breaking a line in the middle of a word.

For example, most word processors store every paragraph as a single long line. When text is stored in this way, the only breaks come *between* paragraphs. Suppose you have copied the following text from a word processor, so that what you see below is actually one very long line:

```
"Man cannot survive except through his mind.  But the mind
is an attribute of the individual.  There is no such thing
as a collective brain.  The man who thinks must think and
act on his own."
```

You want to format this paragraph into 40-character lines. To do so, you use the command:

```
fold -w 40 speech
```

However, **fold** breaks the lines at *exactly* 40 characters, which means that some of the lines are broken in the middle of words:

```
"Man cannot survive except through his m
ind.  But the mind is an attribute of th
e individual.  There is no such thing as
 a collective brain.  The man who thinks
 must think and act on his own."
```

Instead, you use the **-s** option to tell **fold** not to break words:

```
fold -s -w 40 speech
```

The output is:

```
"Man cannot survive except through his
mind.  But the mind is an attribute of
the individual.  There is no such thing
as a collective brain.  The man who
thinks must think and act on his own."
```

Although the right margin is a bit ragged, the words are kept intact. If you want to save the formatted text, just redirect the output:

```
fold -s -w 40 speech > speech-formatted
```

> **HINT**
>
> With some programs, you will find yourself using the same options every time you use the program. To streamline your work, you can define an alias that includes the options (see Chapter 13), so you won't need to type them every time.
>
> As an example, let's say you always use **fold** with **-s -w 40**. You can put one of the following alias definitions in your environment file (see Chapter 14). The first definition is for the Bourne Shell family; the second is for the C-Shell family:
>
> ```
> alias fold="fold -s -w 40"
> alias fold "fold -s -w 40"
> ```
>
> Now, whenever you use **fold**, you will automatically get the -s -w 40 options.
>
> If, from time to time, you want to run **fold** without **-s -w 40**, you can (as we discussed in Chapter 13) suspend the alias temporarily by typing a \ (backslash) character in front of the command name. For example, if you want to use **fold** with **-w 60** instead of **-s w 40**, you can use the command:
>
> ```
> \fold -w 60 long-text > short-text
> ```
>
> To run **fold** with no options, use:
>
> ```
> \fold long-text > short-text
> ```

THE 80-CHARACTER LINE

For many years, programmers have used 80 characters per line of text, and terminals have displayed 80 characters per line of output. With the advent of GUIs, which allow you to resize windows dynamically, the magic number 80 pops up less often as an exact line length. Nevertheless, it is still the case that many Unix programs use a default of 80 characters/line, for example:

- The **fold** program (which we discussed in the previous section) breaks lines, by default, at position 80.

- If you look closely at pages in the online Unix manual (Chapter 9), you can see that they are formatted for an 80-character line.

- When you use a terminal emulator program (Chapter 3), the default line width is usually 80 characters.

Why should this be the case? What's so special about 80 characters/line? Here's the story.

In 1879, the American inventor Herman Hollerith (1860-1929) was working on a system to handle the information for the upcoming U.S. census of 1880. He borrowed an idea from the weaving industry which, since the early part of the 19th century, had been using large cards with holes to control automated looms. Hollerith adapted this idea and developed a system in which census data was stored on punched cards, one card per person. Hollerith designed the cards to be the same size as U.S. banknotes*, which allowed him to use existing currency equipment — such as filling bins — to process the cards. The cards, which came to be known as PUNCH CARDS, had 20 columns, which was later expanded to 45 columns.

Hollerith's system proved to be so useful that, in 1896, he founded the Tabulating Machine Company (TMC) to manufacture his own machines. In 1911, TMC merged with two other companies — the Computing Scale Company of America and International Time Recording Company — to form the Computing Tabulating Recording Company (CTR). In addition to tabulators and punch cards, CTR also manufactured commercial scales, industrial time recorders, and meat and cheese slicers. In 1924, CTR formally changed its name to International Business Machines (IBM).

By 1929, IBM's technology had advanced to the point where they were able to increase the number of columns on punch cards. Using this new technology, the IBM punch card — which, as you remember, was the size of the old dollar bill — was just large enough to hold 80 columns, each of which could store a single character. Thus, when the first IBM computers were developed in the late 1950s, they used punch cards that stored 80 characters/card. As a result, programs and data were stored as 80-character lines and, within a short time, this became the de facto standard.

By the 1980s, punch cards were phased out as programmers began to use terminals and, later, personal computers. However, the 80-character standard persisted, as both terminals and PCs used screens that displayed 80 characters per line, this being what programmers (and programs) expected. It was during this era that Unix was developed, so it was only natural the 80-character line would be incorporated into the Unix culture.

Now you understand why — over 25 years later, and in spite of the popularity of GUIs — the 80-character line survives in various nooks and crannies within the world of Unix.

FORMATTING PARAGRAPHS: `fmt`

Related filters: **`fold`**, **`pr`**

The **`fmt`** program formats paragraphs. The goal is to join the lines within a paragraph so as to make the paragraph as short and compact as possible, without changing the content or the whitespace. In other words, **`fmt`** makes text look nice.

---

*In 1862, the U.S. government issued its very first banknote, a $1 bill that measured 7 3/8 inches x 3 1/8 inches. This was the size of the banknotes in Hollerith's time and, hence, the size of his punch cards. In 1929, the government reduced the dimensions of banknotes by about 20 percent, to 6 1/8 inches x 2 5/8 inches, the size which is used today.

The syntax is:

fmt [**-su**] [**-w** *width*] [*file...*]

where *width* is the maximum width of a line, and *file* is the name of a file.

When **fmt** reads text, it assumes that paragraphs are separated by blank lines. Thus, a "paragraph" is one or more contiguous lines of text, not containing a blank line. The **fmt** program works by reading and formatting one paragraph at a time according to the following rules:

- Line width: Make each line as long as possible, but no longer than a specific length. By default, the maximum line width is 75 characters, although you can change it with the **-w** option. To do so, use **-w** followed by the line width you want, for example, **-w 50**.

- Sentences: Whenever possible, break lines at the end of sentences. Avoid breaking lines after the first word of a sentence or before the last word of a sentence.

- Whitespace: Preserve all indentations, spaces between words, and blank lines. This can be modified by using the **-u** option (see below).

- Tabs: Expand all tabs into spaces as the text is read and insert new tabs, as appropriate, into the final output.

As an example, let's say you have a file named **secret-raw**, which contains the following three paragraphs of text. Notice that the lines are not formatted evenly:

```
As we all know, real
success comes slowly and
is due to a number of different factors all coming
together
over a period of years.

Although there
is no real shortcut, there is a secret: a secret so
powerful that you can use it to
open doors that might otherwise be closed, and to
influence
people to help you time and again. In fact, I would
go as far as to say that this is the secret that has
a lot to do with my success.

The secret is simple...
```

You want to format the text using a line length of 50 characters and save the result in a file named **secret-formatted**. The command to do so is:

```
fmt -w 50 secret-raw > secret-formatted
```

The contents of **secret-formatted** are now as follows:

```
As we all know, real success comes slowly and is
due to a number of different factors all coming
together over a period of years.

Although there is no real shortcut, there is a
secret: a secret so powerful that you can use it
to open doors that might otherwise be closed,
and to influence people to help you time and
again. In fact, I would go as far as to say
that this is the secret that has a lot to do
with my success.

The secret is simple...*
```

The **fmt** program has several other options, but only two are important. The **-u** (uniform spacing) option tells **fmt** to decrease white space so that there is no more than a single space between words, and no more than two spaces at the end of a sentence, a style called FRENCH SPACING**. For example, the file **joke** contains the following text:

```
A man walks  into a  drug store and goes up to   the
pharmacist. "Do you sell talcum powder?" asks
the   man.  "Certainly,"  says
the pharmacist, "just walk
this way."   "If I could walk  that  way," says the
man,       "I wouldn't need   talcum      powder."
```

You format this with:

```
fmt -u -w 50 joke
```

The output is:

```
A man walks into a drug store and goes up to the
pharmacist. "Do you sell talcum powder?" asks
the man.  "Certainly," says the pharmacist, "just
walk this way."  "If I could walk that way,"
says the man, "I wouldn't need talcum powder."
```

Notice there is only a single space at the end of the first sentence. This is because there was only one space in the original file, and **fmt** does not add spaces, it only removes them.

---

*This example is taken from an essay entitled "The Secret of My Success". If you want to read the entire essay, you can find it on my Web site **www.harley.com**.

**With French spacing, sentences are followed by two spaces instead of one. This style is generally used with monospaced fonts, where all the characters are the same width. With such fonts, it helps the eye to have an extra space at the end of a sentence.

The two principal Unix text editors, **vi** and Emacs, both recognize French spacing, which allows them to detect where sentences begin and end. This allows **vi** and Emacs to work with sentences as complete units. For example, you can delete two sentences, change a single sentence, jump back three sentences, and so on. For this reason, many Unix people form the habit of using two spaces after a sentence. (I do, even when I type email.)

The final option, **-s** (split only), tells **fmt** to split long lines, but not to join short lines. Use this option when you are working with text that has formatting you want to preserve, for example, when you are writing a computer program.

THE OLDEN DAYS OF PRINTING

In the next two sections, we are going to discuss **pr**, a program that was created in the early days of Unix, the 1970s. This was a time when printers were so expensive that no one had his own and **pr** was designed to prepare files for printing in a shared environment. However, as you will see, **pr** has important capabilities that — printing aside — are useful in their own right for formatting text.

Before we cover these topics, though, I want to take a moment to lay the foundation by describing what it was like to print files in the early days of Unix.

Because printers were expensive, they were almost always shared by a group of people. Whenever a user wanted to print a file, he would enter the appropriate commands on his terminal to format and print the file. Or he might run a program that generated printed output. Each request for printing was called a "print job" and, each time a print job was generated, it was put into the "print queue" to wait its turn. In this way, one print job after another would be generated, stored and, ultimately, printed.

The actual printer would be in a computer room, a common area used by many people, usually programmers. Output was printed on continuous, fan-fold computer paper, and the output of a single print job was called a "printout". As printouts accumulated, someone — often an "operator", working in the computer room — would separate the printouts by tearing the paper at a perforation. He would then put each printout in a bin, where it would be picked up later by the person who initiated the print request.

Because of how the system was organized, there had to be a way for the operator to be able to take a stack of printed paper and divide it into separate print jobs. The **pr** program was designed to meet the needs of both the user and the operator by offering two services. First, **pr** would format the text into pages; second, **pr** would make sure that each page had its own header, margin and page number. In that way, printed output would not only look nice (for the user), it would be easy to organize (for the operator).

Today, many people think of the **pr** program as being only for printing, which is a mistake. True, **pr** can still do what it was designed to do: prepare output to be sent to a printer (hence the name **pr**). This is still a useful function, and we will discuss these aspects of **pr** in the next section.

However, **pr** can do a lot more for you than simply break text into pages and generate headers, margins and line numbers. It can format text in several very useful ways, especially when you learn how to combine **pr** with **fold** and **fmt**. For example, you can use **pr** to arrange text from a single file into columns. You can also merge text from multiple files, each file having its own column. So once we finish talking about the basic functions of **pr**, I'll show you how to use it in ways that have nothing to do with printing and everything to do with being efficient and clever.

FORMATTING TEXT INTO PAGES: `pr`

Related filters: **fold**, **fmt**

The primary function of **pr** is to format text into pages suitable for printing. The **pr** program can also format text into columns, as well as merge text from multiple files, which we will talk about in the next section. The basic syntax for **pr** is below:

pr [-dt] [+*beg*[:*end*]] [-h *text*] [-l *n*] [-o *margin*] [-W *width*] [*file...*]

where *beg* is the first page to format, and *end* is the last page to format; *text* is text for the middle of the header; *n* is the number of lines per page; *margin* is the size of the left margin; *width* is width of the output; and *file* is the name of a file.

It is common to use **pr** as part of a pipeline to format text before it is sent to a printer. For example, let's say you have a program named **calculate** that generates data which you want to print. The following pipeline sends the output of **calculate** to **pr** to be formatted, and then to **lpr** to be printed. (The two principal Unix programs to print files are **lp** and **lpr**.)

```
calculate | pr | lpr
```

Here is a similar example. You want to combine, format and print the contents of three files:

```
cat data1 data2 data3 | pr | lpr
```

By default, **pr** formats a page by inserting a header at the top, a margin on the left, and a trailer at the bottom. Both the header and trailer take up five lines. The left margin and the trailer are just for spacing, so they are blank. The header, however, contains information on its middle line: the date and time the file was last modified, the name of the file, and the page number. (These details can vary slightly depending on the version of **pr** you are using.) As an example, here is a typical header. Leaving out the blank lines, this is what you might see if you formatted a file named **logfile**:

```
2008-12-21 10:30              logfile                    Page 1
```

The **pr** program assumes pages have 66 lines. This is because old printers used 11-inch paper and printed 6 lines/inch. The header (at the top) and the trailer (at the bottom) each take up 5 lines, which leaves 56 lines/page for single-spaced text. When **pr** creates pages, it processes page 1, page 2, page 3, and so on until all the data is formatted.

If you want to test **pr** and see how it works, an easy way is to format a file and send the output to **less** (Chapter 21). This will allow you to look at the formatted output one screenful at a time. For example, let's say you are taking a class and you have written an essay, which you have stored in a file named **essay**. To take a look at how **pr** would format the text, you can use:

```
pr essay | less
```

If you like what you see, you can then send it to the printer:

```
pr essay | lpr
```

Or, you can save it to a file:

```
pr essay > essay-formatted
```

If your essay was originally written using a word processor, it will have very long lines. This is because word processors store each paragraph as one long line*. In this case, you can first break the lines appropriately by using **fold -s** or **fmt**, whichever works best with your particular text:

```
fmt essay | pr | less
fold -s essay | pr | less
```

Almost all of the time, you will find that, when you use **pr** to format pages for printing, the defaults are just fine. However, if the need arises, you can change them by using several options. The most commonly used option is **-d**, which tells **pr** to use double-spaced text.

Consider the following example, which formats and prints the text file **essay**. This simple pipeline starts by using **fmt** to format the lines of the file. The output of **fmt** is sent to **pr**, where it is formatted into pages with double-spaced text. The output of **pr** is then sent to the printer:

```
fmt essay | pr -d | lpr
```

The result is a spiffy, double-spaced, printed copy of your essay, suitable for editing or for submitting to your teacher. Note that **-d** does not modify the original text: all it does is specify what type of spacing to use when the text is formatted into pages. The original file — **essay** in this case — is left unchanged.

If you want to control which pages are formatted, use the syntax:

pr +*begin*[:*end*]

where *begin* is the first page to format, and *end* is the last page to format.

For example, to skip pages 1 and 2 — that is, to start from page 3 and continue to the end of the file — use:

```
fmt essay | pr -d +3 | lpr
```

---

*Word processing documents are stored in a special binary format. Almost all Unix filters, however, assume that data is stored as text. Thus, if you want to work with a word processing document using the Unix programs in this chapter, you must first save the document as plain text from within the word processor program. For instance, in the examples above, the file **essay** is the plain text version of a word processing document named **essay.doc**.

To format and print pages 3 through 6 only, use:

```
fmt essay | pr -d +3:6 | lpr
```

If you want to specify the text for the middle part of the header, use the **-h** option, for example:

```
fmt essay | pr -h "My Essay by Harley" | lpr
```

To change the total number of lines per page, use **-l**, followed by a number. For example, say you want only 40 lines of *text* per page. Counting the header (5 lines) and the trailer (also 5 lines) you need a total of 50 lines/page:

```
fmt essay | pr -l 50 | lpr
```

To eliminate the header, use the **-t** option. When you use **-t**, there will be no breaks between pages, which means all the lines will be used for text. This is useful when you are formatting text you do not want to print. For example, you might want to change single-spaced text into double-spaced text. The following command formats the contents of **essay**, double-spaced with no headers, and saves the output to a file named **essay-double-spaced**:

```
fmt essay | pr -t -d > essay-double-spaced
```

By default, **pr** does not insert a left margin. This is fine because, most likely, your printer will be set up to create margins automatically. However, if you want to add an extra left margin of your own, use the **-o** (offset) option, followed by the size of the extra margin in spaces. In addition, you can change the width of the output (the default is 72 characters), by using the **-W** option. (Note the uppercase **W**.) When you use **-W**, lines that are too long are truncated, so you must be careful not to lose text. The following is a particularly useful example that illustrates how you might use these two options.

  If you are a student, you know there are times when you need your essays to be a bit longer. For example, you might have an 8-page essay, but your teacher has asked for a 10-page essay. Of course, you could rework your notes, do more research, and rewrite the essay. Or, you could simply print the essay double-spaced with wide margins.*

  The following example formats the contents of the file **essay** using double-spaced pages, with a line width of 50 characters, and a left margin of 5 spaces; that is, 45 characters of text per line. The result is an essay that looks significantly longer than it really is:

```
fmt -w 45 essay | pr -d -o 5 -W 50 | lpr
```

If you want to check the output before you print it, use:

```
fmt -w 45 essay | pr -d -o 5 -W 50 | less
```

Note: It is necessary to use the option **-w 45** with **fmt** because, by default, **fmt** produces lines that are 72 characters long. However, in this case, we have asked **pr** to limit the output to 45 characters of text per line. Thus, we need to make sure none of the lines are

---

*You did not read this here.

longer than 45 characters: otherwise, they would be truncated. As an alternative to **fmt**, you could use the **fold -s** program, which yields similar formatting:

```
fold -s -w 45 essay | pr -d -o 5 -W 50 | lpr
```

> **HINT**
>
> Both **fold** and **fmt** can be used to format lines of text. How do you know which one to use?
>
> The **fold** program does only one thing: break lines. By default, **fold** breaks lines at a specific column. However, with the **-s** option, **fold** breaks lines between words. This leaves the text a bit ragged on the right, but preserves the words.
>
> The **fmt** program formats paragraphs. Like **fold**, **fmt** breaks long lines. However, unlike **fold**, **fmt** will also join together short lines.
>
> Thus, if you need to break lines at a specific point, you use **fold**. If you need to format text that contains short lines, you use **fmt**. That much is clear.
>
> But what about when you need to break lines at word boundaries and the text is already formatted? In that case, you can use either **fold -s** or **fmt**. Note: These two commands will sometimes yield slightly different output, so try both and see which one works best with your particular data.

> **HINT**
>
> When you pre-process text with **fold** or **fmt** before sending it to **pr**, it is wise to specify the exact line width you want, because the three programs have different defaults:
>
> • **fold**: 80 characters/line
> • **fmt**: 75 characters/line
> • **pr**: 72 characters/line

FORMATTING TEXT INTO COLUMNS: pr

As we discussed in the previous section, the purpose of **pr** is to format text into pages suitable for printing. In addition to the simple formatting we have discussed, **pr** can also format text into columns. The input data can come from a single file or from several files.

When you use **pr** to create columns, the syntax is as follows:

pr [**-mt**] [*-columns*] [**-l** *lines*] [**-W** *width*] [*file...*]

where *columns* is the number of output columns, *lines* is the number of lines per page, *width* is the width of the output, and *file* in the name of a file.

Let's start with a single file. To specify the number of output columns, use a - (hyphen) character followed by a number. For example, for two columns, use **-2**. To control the length of the columns, use the **-l** option. Here is a typical example.

You are an undergraduate student at a small, but prestigious liberal arts college. Your academic advisor believes you will have a better chance of being accepted to medical school if you participate in extracurricular activities, so you join the Anti-Mayonnaise Society. As part of your duties, you agree to work on the newsletter. You have just finished writing an article on why mayonnaise is bad. You have saved the article, as plain text, to a file named **article**.

Before you can import the article into your newsletter program, you need to format the text into two columns, with a page length of 48 lines. The following pipeline will do the job. Note the use of **fmt** to format the text into 35-character lines before sending it to **pr**:

```
fmt -w 35 article | pr -2 -l 48 > article-columns
```

The formatted text you need is now stored in a file named **article-columns**.

Where did the number 35 come from? When you use **pr** the default line width is 72. There will be at least one space at the end of each of the two columns, which leaves a maximum of 70 characters of text. Divide this by two to get a maximum of 35 characters/column. (If you use the **-W** option to change the line width, you must change your calculations accordingly.)

> **HINT**
>
> When you format text into columns, **pr** will blindly truncate lines that are too long. Thus, if your text contains lines that are longer than the column width, you must break the lines using **fold -s** or **fmt** before you send the text to **pr**.

By default, **pr** aligns columns using tabs, not spaces. If you would rather have spaces, all you have to do is use the **expand** program (discussed earlier in the chapter) to change the tabs into spaces. For example, the following command line pipes the output of **pr** to **expand** before saving the data:

```
fmt -w 35 article | pr -2 -l 40 | expand > article-columns
```

If you examine the output of this command carefully, you will see that the alignment is maintained by using spaces, not tabs. (For help in visualizing tabs and spaces within text, see the discussion earlier in the chapter.)

The final use for **pr** is to format multiple files into separate columns. Use the **-m** (merge) option, and **pr** will output each file in its own column. For example, to format three files into three separate columns, use:

```
pr -m file1 file2 file3
```

When you format three files in this way, the maximum width of each column is, by default, 23 characters.* If the input files contain lines longer than the column width, **pr** will truncate the lines. To avoid this, you must format the text before sending it to **pr**. Here is an example.

You are preparing a newsletter, and you have written three news stories, which you have saved in the files **n1**, **n2** and **n3**. You want to use **pr** to format the stories into three

---

*The default line width is 72 characters. At the end of each column, there will be at least one space. Since we are creating three columns, subtract 3 from 72 to get a maximum of 69 characters of text. Dividing by 3 gives us a maximum of 23 characters/column.

columns, one per story, all on a single page. Before you use **pr**, you must use **fold -s** or **fmt** to format the text so that none of the lines are longer than 23 characters. The following commands do the work, saving the output in three files **f1**, **f2** and **f3**:

```
fmt -w 23 n1 > f1
fmt -w 23 n2 > f2
fmt -w 23 n3 > f3
```

You can now use **pr** to format the three articles, each in its own column:

```
pr -m f1 f2 f3 > formatted-articles
```

When you merge multiple files in this way, it is often handy to use **-t** to get rid of the headers:

```
pr -mt f1 f2 f3 > formatted-articles
```

This will give you long, continuous columns of text without interruptions.

CHAPTER 18 EXERCISES

REVIEW QUESTIONS

1. What are the three principal options of the **wc** program, and what does each one do? What is it about **wc** that makes it such a useful tool? When you use **wc**, what is the definition of a "line"?

2. When you use tabs with Unix, what are the default tab positions?

3. The **fold**, **fmt** and **pr** programs can all be used to reformat text. What are principal differences between these programs?

4. The **fold**, **fmt** and **pr** programs have different default line lengths. What are they?

APPLYING YOUR KNOWLEDGE

1. Use the command **less /etc/passwd** to look at the password file on your system. Notice that the file contains one line per userid, and that each line contains a number of fields, separated by : characters. The first field is the userid. Create a pipeline that generates a sorted, numbered list of all the userids on your system. Hint: use **cut** (Chapter 17), then **sort**, then **nl**.

2. The command **ls** displays a list of all the files in your working directory (except dotfiles). Create a pipeline that counts the number of files. Hint: use **ls**, then **wc**

with the appropriate option. Next, create a command that displays output like the following (where *xx* is the number of files):

I have *xx* **files in my working directory.**

Hint: Use **echo** (Chapter 12) with command substitution (Chapter 13), making use of the pipeline you just created.

3. Go to a Web site of your choice, and copy some text into the clipboard. From the Unix command line, use the **cat** program to create a file named **webtext**:

cat > webtext

Paste in the text and press **^D**. (Copy and paste is discussed in Chapter 6.) You now have a file containing the text from the Web site. Create a pipeline that formats this text into 40 character lines, changing multiple spaces to single spaces. At the end of the pipeline, display the text one screenful at a time.

4. Using the **webtext** file from the last example, format the text into pages with two columns, suitable for printing. Each column should be 30 characters wide, and the pages should be 20 lines long. The columns should be created with spaces, not tabs. Display the formatted output one screenful at a time. Once you are satisfied that the output is correct, save it to a file named **columns**.

FOR FURTHER THOUGHT

1. As we discussed in the chapter, 80-column lines were used widely in the world of computing because, in the 1950s, the first IBM computers used punch cards, which could hold 80 characters per card. The number 80 was mere serendipity, as the size of the punch card was taken from the size of the old U.S. dollar bill. This is an example of how old technology influences new technology.

In a similar manner, when IBM introduced the PC in 1981, the keyboard design was based on the standard typewriter, which used the so-called QWERTY layout (named after the six keys at the top left). It is widely accepted that the QWERTY layout is a poor one, as the most important keys are in particularly awkward locations. Although there exist much better keyboard layouts, the QWERTY keyboard is still the standard. Why do you think old technology has such a strong influence on new technology. Why is this bad? Why is this good? (When you get a moment, look up the Dvorak layout on the Internet. I have been using such a keyboard for years, and I would never switch back.)

CHAPTER 19

FILTERS: SELECTING, SORTING, COMBINING, AND CHANGING

In this chapter, we conclude our discussion of filters by talking about the most interesting and powerful filters in the Unix toolbox: the programs that select data, sort data, combine data, and change data. These programs are so useful, it behooves us to take the time to discuss them at length.

As you know, powerful programs can take a long time to learn, and that is certainly the case with the filters we will be discussing in this chapter. In fact, these programs are so powerful, you will probably never master all the nuances.

That's okay. I'll make sure you understand the basics, and I'll show you a great many examples. Over time, as your skills and your needs develop, you can check the online manual for more advanced details, and you can use the Web and Usenet to look for help from other people. Most important, whenever you get a chance to talk to a Unix geek in person, get him or her to show you their favorite tricks using the filters in this chapter. That is the very best way to learn Unix.

This is the last of four chapters devoted to filters (Chapters 16-19). In Chapter 20, we will discuss regular expressions, which are used to specify patterns. Regular expressions increase the power of filters and in Chapter 20, you will find many examples that pertain to the filters in this chapter, particularly **grep**, perhaps the most important filter of them all.

SELECTING LINES THAT CONTAIN A SPECIFIC PATTERN: grep

Related filters: **look**, **strings**

The **grep** program reads from standard input or from a file, and extracts all the lines that contain a specified pattern, writing the lines to standard output. For example, you might use **grep** to search 10 long files for all the lines that contain the characters "Harley". Or, you might use the **sort** program (discussed later in the chapter) to sort a large amount of data, and then pipe that data to **grep** to extract all the lines that start with the word "note".

Aside from searching for specific strings of characters, you can use **grep** with what we call "regular expressions" to search for patterns. When you do so, **grep** becomes a *very* powerful tool. In fact, regular expressions are so important, we will discuss them separately in Chapter 20, where you will see a lot of examples using **grep**. (In fact, as you will see in a moment, the **re** in the name **grep** stands for "regular expression".)

The syntax for **grep** is:

```
grep [-cilLnrsvwx] pattern [file...]
```

where *pattern* is the pattern to search for, and *file* is the name of an input file.

Here is a simple example. Most Unix systems keep the basic information about each userid in a file named **/etc/passwd** (see Chapter 11). There is one line of information for each userid . To display the information about your userid, use **grep** to search the file for that pattern. For example, to display information about userid **harley**, use the command:

```
grep harley /etc/passwd
```

If **grep** does not find any lines that match the specified pattern, there will be no output or warning message. Like most Unix commands, **grep** is terse. When there is nothing to say, **grep** says nothing. (Wouldn't it be nice if everyone you knew had the same philosophy?)

When you specify a pattern that contains punctuation or special characters, you should quote them so the shell will interpret the command properly. (See Chapter 13 for a discussion of quoting.) For example, to search a file named **info** for all the lines that contain a colon followed by a space, use the command:

```
grep ': ' info
```

WHAT'S IN A NAME?

grep
In the early 1970s, the text editor that was used with the earliest versions of Unix was called **ed**. Within **ed**, there was a command that would search a file for all the lines that contained a specified pattern, and then print those lines on the terminal. (In those days, Unix users used terminals that printed output on paper.)

This command was named **g**, for global, because it was able to search an entire file. When you used **g** to print all the lines that contained a pattern, the syntax was:

g/*re*/p

where **g** stands for "global"; *re* is a regular expression that describes the pattern you want to search for; and **p** stands for "print".

It is from this serendipitous abbreviation that the name **grep** was taken. In other words, **grep** stands for:

• *Global*: Indicating that **grep** searches through all of the input data.
• *Regular Expression*: Showing that **grep** can search for any pattern that can be expressed as a regular expression (discussed in Chapter 20).
• *Print*: Once **grep** finds what you want, it prints (displays) it for you. As we discussed in Chapter 7, for historical reasons, we often use "print" to mean "display".

(*continue485d...*) Among Unix people, it is common to use "grep" as a verb, in both a technical and non-technical sense. Thus, you might hear someone say, "I lost your address, so I had to grep all my files to find your phone number." Or, "I grepped my living room twice, but I can't find the book you lent me."

As useful as **grep** is for searching individual files, where it really comes into its own is in a pipeline. This is because **grep** can quickly reduce a large amount of raw data into a small amount of useful information. This is a very important capability that makes **grep** one of the most important programs in the Unix toolbox. Ask any experienced Unix person, and you will find that he or she would not want to live without **grep**. It will take time for you to appreciate the power of this wonderful program, but we can start with a few simple examples.

When you share a multiuser system with other people, you can use the **w** program (Chapter 8) to display information about all the users and what they are doing. Here is some sample output:

```
8:44pm up 9 days, 7:02, 5 users, load: 0.11, 0.02, 0.00
User      tty       login@ idle    JCPU   PCPU  what
tammy     ttyp0    Wed10am 4days   42:41  37:56  -bash
harley    ttyp1     5:47pm         15:11         w
linda     ttyp3     5:41pm   10    2:16     13  -tcsh
casey     ttyp4     4:45pm          1:40   0:36  vi dogstuff
weedly    ttyp5     9:22am 1:40     20       1  gcc catprog.c
```

Say that you want to display all the users who logged in during the afternoon or evening. You can search for lines of output that contain the pattern "pm". Use the pipeline:

```
w -h | grep pm
```

(Notice that I used **w** with the **-h** option. This suppresses the header, that is, the first two lines.) Using the above data, the output of the previous command would be:

```
harley    ttyp1     5:47pm         15:11         w
linda     ttyp3     5:41pm   10    2:16     13  -tcsh
casey     ttyp4     4:45pm          1:40   0:36  vi dogstuff
```

Suppose we want to display only the userids of the people who logged in during the afternoon and evening. All we have to do is pipe the output of **grep** to **cut** (Chapter 17) and extract the first 8 columns of data:

```
w -h | grep pm | cut -c1-8
```

The output is:

```
harley
linda
casey
```

What about sorting the output? Just pipe it to **sort** (discussed later in the chapter):

```
w -h | grep pm | cut -c1-8 | sort
```

The output is:

```
casey
harley
linda
```

THE MOST IMPORTANT grep OPTIONS

The **grep** program has many options of which I will discuss the most important. To start, the **-c** (count) option displays the number of lines that have been extracted, rather than the lines themselves. Here is an example.

As we will discuss in Chapter 23, the Unix file system uses directories, which are similar to (but not the same as) the folders used with Windows and the Macintosh. A directory can contain both ordinary files and other directories, called subdirectories. For example, a directory might contain 20 files and 3 subdirectories.

As you will see in Chapter 24, you use the **ls** command to display the names of the files and subdirectories contained in a particular directory. For example, the following command displays the contents of the directory named **/etc**. (The name **/etc** will make sense once you read Chapter 23.)

```
ls /etc
```

If you run this command on your system, you will see that **/etc** contains a lot of entries. To see which entries are subdirectories, use the **-F** option:

```
ls -F /etc
```

When you use this option, **ls** appends a **/** (slash) character to the end of all subdirectory names. For example, let's say that, within the output, you see:

```
motd
rc.d/
```

This means that **motd** is an ordinary file, and **rc.d** is a subdirectory.

Suppose you want to count the number of subdirectories in the **/etc** directory. All you have to do is pipe the output of **ls -F*** to **grep -c**, and count the slashes:

```
ls -F /etc | grep -c "/"
```

On my system, the output is:

```
92
```

---

*By default, **ls** lists multiple names on each line, to make the output more compact. However, when you pipe the output to another program, **ls** displays each name on a separate line. If you want to simulate this, use the **-1** (the number 1) option, for example:

```
ls -1 /etc
```

By the way, if you want to count the total entries in a directory, just pipe the output of **ls** to **wc -l** (Chapter 18), for example:

```
ls /etc | wc -l
```

On my system, there are 242 entries in the **/etc** directory.

The next option, **-i**, tells **grep** to ignore the difference between lower- and uppercase letters when making a comparison. For example, let's say a file named **food-costs** contains the following five lines:

```
pizza $25.00
tuna $3.50
Pizza $23.50
PIZZA $21.00
vegetables $18.30
```

The following command finds all the lines that contain "pizza". Notice that, according to the syntax for **grep**, the pattern comes before the file name:

```
grep pizza food-costs
```

The output consists of a single line:

```
pizza $25.00
```

To ignore differences in case, use **-i**:

```
grep -i pizza food-costs
```

This time, the output contains three lines:

```
pizza $25.00
Pizza $23.50
PIZZA $21.00
```

> **HINT**
>
> The **-i** (ignore) options tell **grep** to ignore differences between upper- and lower case. Later in the chapter, we will discuss two other programs, **look** and **sort**, that have a similar option. However, with these two programs, you use **-f** (fold) instead of **-i**. Don't be confused.
>
> (The word "fold" is a technical term indicating that upper- and lowercase letters should be treated the same. We'll talk about it later.)

Moving on, there will be times when you will want to know the location of the selected lines within the data stream. To do so, you use the **-n** option. This tells **grep** to write a relative line number in front of each line of output. (Your data does not have to contain the numbers; **grep** will count the lines for you as it processes the input.) As an example, consider the following command that uses both the **-i** and **-n** options with the file **food-costs** listed above:

```
grep -in pizza food-costs
```

The output is:

```
1:pizza $25.00
3:Pizza $23.50
4:PIZZA $21.00
```

The **-n** option is useful when you need to pin down the exact location of certain lines within a large file. For example, let's say you want to modify all the lines that contain a specific pattern. Once you use **grep -n** to find the locations of those lines, you can use a text editor to jump directly to where you want to make the changes.

The next option, **-l** (list filenames), is useful when you want to search more than one file for a particular pattern. When you use **-l**, **grep** does not display the lines that contain the pattern. Instead, **grep** writes the names of files in which such lines were found.

For example, say you have three files, **names**, **oldnames** and **newnames**. The file **names** happens to contain "harley"; the file **newnames** contains "Harley"; and the file **oldnames** contains neither. To see which files contain the pattern "Harley", you would use:

```
grep -l Harley names oldnames newnames
```

The output is:

```
newnames
```

Now add in the **-i** option to ignore differences in case:

```
grep -il Harley names oldnames newnames
```

The output is now:

```
names
newnames
```

The **-L** (uppercase "L") option does the opposite of **-l**. It shows you the files that do *not* contain a match. In our example, to list the files that do not contain the pattern "Harley", you would use:

```
grep -L Harley names oldnames newnames
```

The output is:

```
names
oldnames
```

The next option, **-w**, specifies that you want to search only for complete words. For example, say you have a file named **memo** that contains the following lines:

```
We must, of course, make sure that all the
data is now correct before we publish it.
I thought you would know this.
```

You want to display all the lines that contain the word "now". If you enter:

`grep now memo`

you will see:

```
data is now correct before we publish it.
I thought you would know this.
```

This is because **grep** selected both "now" and "know". However, if you enter:

`grep -w now memo`

You will see only the output you want:

```
data is now correct before we publish it.
```

The **-v** (reverse) option selects all the lines that do *not* contain the specified pattern. This is an especially useful option that you will find yourself using a great deal. As an example, let's say you are a student and you have a file named **homework** to keep track of your assignments. This file contains one line for each assignment. Once you have finished an assignment, you mark it "DONE". For example:

```
Math: problems 12-10 to 12-33, due Monday
Basket Weaving: make a 6-inch basket, DONE
Psychology: essay on Animal Existentialism, due end of term
Surfing: catch at least 10 waves, DONE
```

To list all the assignments that are not yet finished, enter:

`grep -v DONE homework`

The output is:

```
Math: problems 12-10 to 12-33, due Monday
Psychology: essay on Animal Existentialism, due end of term
```

If you want to see the number of assignments that are not finished, combine **-c** with **-v**:

`grep -cv DONE homework`

In this case, the output is:

```
2
```

On occasion, you may want to find the lines in which the search pattern consists of the entire line. To do so, use the **-x** option. For example, say the file **names** contains the lines:

```
Harley
Harley Hahn
My friend is Harley.
My other friend is Linda.
Harley
```

If you want to find all the lines that contain "Harley", use:

`grep Harley names`

If you want to find only those lines in which "Harley" is the entire line, use the **-x** option:

`grep -x Harley names`

In this case, **grep** will select only the first and last lines.

To search an entire directory tree (see Chapter 23), use the **-r** (recursive) option. For example, let's say you want to search for the word "initialize" within all the files in the directory named **admin**, including all subdirectories, all files in those subdirectories, and so on. You would use:

`grep -r initialize admin`

When you use **-r** on large directory trees, you will often see error messages telling you that **grep** cannot read certain files, either because the files don't exist or because you don't have permission to read them. (We will discuss file permissions in Chapter 25.) Typically, you will see one of the following two messages:

```
No such file or directory
Permission denied
```

If you don't want to see such messages, use the **-s** (suppress) option. For example, say you are logged in as superuser, and you want to search all the files on the system for the words "shutdown now".

As we will discuss in Chapter 23, the designation **/** refers to the root (main) directory of the entire file system. Thus, if we start from the **/** directory and use the **-r** (recursive) option, **grep** will search the entire file system. The command is:

`grep -rs / 'shutdown now'`

Notice I quoted the search pattern because it contains a space. (Quoting is explained in Chapter 13.)

VARIATIONS OF grep: fgrep, egrep

In the olden days (the 1970s and 1980s), it was common for people to use two other versions of **grep**: **fgrep** and **egrep**.

The **fgrep** program is a fast version of **grep** that searches only for "fixed-character" strings. (Hence the name **fgrep**.) This means that **fgrep** does not allow the use of regular expressions for matching patterns. When computers were slow and memory was limited, **fgrep** was more efficient than **grep** as long as you didn't need regular expressions. Today, computers are fast and have lots of memory, so there is no need to use **fgrep**. I mention it only for historical reasons.

The **egrep** program is an extended version of **grep**. (Hence the name **egrep**.) The original **grep** allowed only "basic regular expressions". The **egrep** program, which came later, supported the more powerful "extended regular expressions". We'll discuss the differences in Chapter 20. For now, all you need to know is that extended regular expressions are better, and you should always use them when you have a choice.

Modern Unix systems allow you to use extended regular expressions by using either **egrep** or **grep -E**. However, most experienced Unix users would rather type **grep**. The solution is to create an alias (see Chapter 13) to change **grep** to either **egrep** or **grep -E**. With the Bourne shell family, you would use one of the following commands:

```
alias grep='egrep'
alias grep='grep -E'
```

With the C-Shell family, you would use one of these commands:

```
alias grep 'egrep'
alias grep 'grep -E'
```

Once you define such an alias, you can type **grep** and get the full functionality of extended regular expressions. To make such a change permanent, all you need to do is put the appropriate **alias** command into your environment file (see Chapter 14). Indeed, this is such a useful alias that I suggest you take a moment right now and add it to your environment file. In fact, when you get to Chapter 20, I will assume you are using extended regular expressions.

Note: If you use Solaris (from Sun Microsystems), the version of **egrep** you want is in a special directory named **/usr/xpg4/bin/***, which means you must use different aliases. The examples below are only for Solaris. The first one is for the Bourne Shell family; the second is for the C-Shell family:

```
alias grep='/usr/xpg4/bin/egrep'
alias grep '/usr/xpg4/bin/egrep'
```

SELECTING LINES BEGINNING WITH A SPECIFIC PATTERN: look

Related filters: **grep**

The **look** program searches data that is in alphabetical order and finds all the lines that begin with a specified pattern.

There are two ways to use **look**. You can use sorted data from one or more files, or you can have **look** search a dictionary file (explained in the next section).

When you use **look** to search one or more files, the syntax is:

look [**-df**] *pattern file*...

where *pattern* is the pattern to search for, and *file* is the name of a file.

Here is an example. You are a student at a school where, every term, all the students evaluate their professors. This term, you are in charge of the project. You have a large file called **evaluations**, which contains a summary of the evaluations for over a hundred

---

*The name **xpg4** stands for "X/Open Portability Guide, Issue 4", an old (1992) standard for how Unix systems should behave. The programs in this directory have been modified to behave in accordance with the XPG4 standard.

professors. The data is in alphabetical order. Each line of the file contains a ranking (A, B, C, D or F), followed by two spaces, followed by the name of a professor. For example:

```
A   William Wisenheimer
C   Peter Pedant
F   Norman Knowitall
```

Your job is to create five lists to post on a Web site. The lists should contain the names of the professors who received an A rating, a B rating, and so on. Since the data is in alphabetical order, you can create the first list (the A professors) by using **look** to select all the lines of the file that begin with **A**:

```
look A evaluations
```

Although this command will do the job, we can improve upon it. As I mentioned, each line in the data file begins with a single-letter ranking, followed by two spaces. Once you have the names you want, you can use **colrm** (Chapter 16) to remove the first three characters of each line. The following examples do just that for each of the rankings: they select the appropriate lines from the data file, use **colrm** to remove the first three characters from each line, and then redirect the output to a file:

```
look A evaluations | colrm 1 3 > a-professors
look B evaluations | colrm 1 3 > b-professors
look C evaluations | colrm 1 3 > c-professors
look D evaluations | colrm 1 3 > d-professors
look F evaluations | colrm 1 3 > f-professors
```

Unlike the other programs covered in this chapter, **look** cannot read from the standard input; it must take its input from one or more files. This means that, strictly speaking, **look** is not a filter.

The reason for this restriction is that, with standard input, a program can read only one line at a time. However, **look** uses a search method called a "binary search" that requires access to all the data at once. For this reason, you cannot use **look** within a pipeline, although you can use it at the beginning of a pipeline.

When you have multiple steps, the best strategy is to prepare your data, save it in a file, and then use **look** to search the file. For example, let's say the four files **frosh**, **soph**, **junior** and **senior** contain the raw, unsorted evaluation data as described above. Before you can use **look** to search the data, you must combine and sort the contents of the four files and save the output in a new file, for example:

```
sort frosh soph junior senior > evaluations
look A evaluations
```

We will discuss the **sort** program later in the chapter. At that time, you will learn about two particular options that are relevant to **look**. The **-d** (dictionary) option tells **sort** to consider only letters and numbers. You use **-d** when you want **look** to ignore punctuation and other special characters. The **-f** (fold) option tells **sort** to ignore differences between upper- and lowercase letters. For example, when you use **-f**, "Harley" and "harley" are considered the same.

If you use either of these **sort** options to prepare data, you must use the same options with **look**, so **look** will know what type of data to expect. For example:

```
sort -df frosh soph junior senior > evaluations
look -df A evaluations
```

WHEN DO YOU USE look AND WHEN DO YOU USE grep?

Both **look** and **grep** select lines from text files based on a specified pattern. For this reason, it makes sense to ask, when do you use **look** and when do you use **grep**?

Similar questions arise in many situations, because Unix often offers more than one way to solve a problem. For this reason, it is important to be able to analyze your options wisely, so as to pick the best tool for the job at hand. As an example, let us compare **look** and **grep**.

The **look** program is limited in three important ways. First, it requires sorted input; second, it can read only from a file, not from standard input; third, it can only search for patterns at the beginning of a line. However, within the scope of these limitations, **look** has two advantages: it is simple to use and it is very fast.

The **grep** program is a lot more flexible: it does not require sorted input; it can read either from a file or from standard input (which means you can use it in the middle of a pipeline); and it can search for a pattern anywhere, not just at the beginning of a line.

Moreover, **grep** allows "regular expressions", which enable you to specify generalized patterns, not just simple characters. For example, you can search for "the letters **har**, followed by one or more characters, followed by the letters **ley**, followed by zero or more numbers". (Regular expressions are very powerful, and we will talk about them in detail in Chapter 20.)

By using regular expressions, it is possible to make **grep** do anything **look** can do. However, **grep** will be slower, and the syntax is more awkward.

So here is my advice: Whenever you need to select lines from a file, ask yourself if **look** can do the job. If so, use it, because **look** is fast and simple. If **look** can't do the job, (which will be most of the time), use **grep**. As a general rule, you should always use the simplest possible solution to solve a problem.

But what about speed? I mentioned that **look** is faster than **grep**. How important is that? In the early days of Unix, speed was an important consideration, as Unix systems were shared with other users and computers were relatively slow. When you selected lines of text from a very large file, you could actually notice the difference between **look** and **grep**.

Today, however, virtually all Unix systems run on computers which, for practical purposes, are blindingly fast. Thus, the speed at which Unix executes a single command — at least for the commands in this chapter — is irrelevant. For instance, any example in this chapter will run so quickly as to seem instantaneous. More specifically, if you compare a **look** command to the equivalent **grep** command, there is no way you are going to notice the difference in speed.

So my advice is to choose your tools based on simplicity and ease of use, not on tiny differences in speed or efficiency. This is especially important when you are writing programs, including shell scripts. If a program or script is too slow, it is usually possible to find one or two bottlenecks and speed them up. However, if a program is unnecessarily complex or difficult to use, it will, in the long run, waste a lot of *your* time, which is far more valuable than computer time.

HINT

Whenever you have a choice of tools, use the *simplest* one that will do the job.

FINDING ALL THE WORDS THAT BEGIN WITH A SPECIFIC PATTERN: look

I mentioned earlier that you can use **look** to search a dictionary file. You do so when you want to find all the words that begin with a specific pattern, for example, all the words that begin with the letters "simult". When you use **look** in this way, the syntax is simple:

look *pattern*

where *pattern* is the pattern to search for.

The "dictionary file" is not an actual dictionary. It is a long, comprehensive list of words, which has existed since the early versions of Unix. (Of course, the list has been updated over the years.) The words in the dictionary file are in alphabetical order, one word per line, which makes it easy to search the file using **look**.

The dictionary file was originally created to use with a program named **spell**, which provided a crude way to spellcheck documents. The job of **spell** was to display a list of all the words within a document that were not in the dictionary file. In the olden days, **spell** could save you a lot of time by finding possible spelling mistakes.

Today, there are much better spellcheck tools and **spell** is rarely used; indeed, you won't even find it on most Linux or Unix systems. Instead, people use either the spellcheck feature within their word processor or, with text files, an interactive program called **aspell**, which is one of the GNU utilities. If you want to try **aspell**, use:

aspell -c *file*

where *file* is the name of a file containing plain text. The **-c** option indicates that you want to check the spelling of the words in the file.

Although **spell** is not used anymore, the dictionary file still exists, and you can use it in a variety of ways. In particular, you can use the **look** program to find all the words that begin with a specific pattern. This comes in handy when you are having trouble spelling a word. For example, say that you want to type the word "simultaneous", but you are not sure how to spell it. Enter:

look simult

You will see a list similar to the following:

```
simultaneity
simultaneous
simultaneously
simultaneousness
simulty
```

It is now a simple task to pick out the correct word and — if you wish — to copy and paste it from one window to another. (See Chapter 6 for instructions on how to copy and paste.)

We'll talk about the dictionary file again in Chapter 20, at which time I'll show you where to find the actual file on your system, and how to use it to help solve word puzzles.

(By the way, a "simulty" is a private grudge or quarrel.)

HINT

When you are working with the **vi** text editor (see Chapter 22), you can display a list of words by using **:r!** to issue a quick **look** command. For example:

```
:r !look simult
```

This command inserts all the words that begin with "simult" into your editing buffer. You can now choose the word you want and delete all the others.

SORTING DATA: sort

Related filters: **tsort, uniq**

The **sort** program can perform two related tasks: sorting data, and checking to see if data is already sorted. We'll start with the basics. The syntax for sorting data is:

sort [**-dfnru**] [**-o** *outfile*] [*infile...*]

where *outfile* is the name of a file to hold the output, and *infile* is the name of a file that contains input.

The **sort** program has a great deal of flexibility. You can compare either entire lines or selected portions of each line (fields). The simplest way to use **sort** is to sort a single file, compare entire lines, and display the results on your screen. As an example, let's say you have a file called **names** that contains the following four lines:

```
Barbara
Al
Dave
Charles
```

To sort this data and display the results, enter:

sort names

You will see:

```
Al
Barbara
Charles
Dave
```

To save the sorted data to a file named **masterfile**, you can redirect the standard output:

```
sort names > masterfile
```

This last example saves the sorted data in a new file. However, there will be many times when you want to save the data in the same file. That is, you will want to replace a file with the same data in sorted order. Unfortunately, you cannot use a command that redirects the output to the input file:

```
sort names > names
```

You will recall I explained, in Chapter 15, that when you redirect the standard output, the shell sets up the output file before running the command. In this case, since **names** is the output file, the shell will empty it before running the **sort** command. Thus, by the time **sort** is ready to read its input, **names** will be empty. Thus, the result of entering this command would be to silently wipe out the contents of your input file (unless you have set the **noclobber** shell variable; see Chapter 15).

For this reason, **sort** provides a special option to allow you to save your output to any file you want. Use **-o** (output) followed by the name of your output file. If the output file is the same as one of your input files, **sort** will make sure to protect your data. Thus, to sort a file and save the output in the same file, use a command like the following:

```
sort -o names names
```

In this case, the original data in **names** will be preserved until the **sort** is complete. The output will then be written to the file.

To sort data from more than one file, just specify more than one input file name. For example, to sort the combined contents of the files **oldnames**, **names** and **extranames**, and save the output in the file **masterfile**, use:

```
sort oldnames names extranames > masterfile
```

To sort these same files while saving the output in **names** (one of the input files), use:

```
sort -o names oldnames names extranames
```

The **sort** program is often used as part of a pipeline to process data that has been produced by another program. The following example combines two files, extracts only those lines that contain the characters "Harley", sorts those lines, and then sends the output to **less** to be displayed:

```
cat newnames oldnames | grep Harley | sort | less
```

By default, **sort** looks at the entire line when it sorts data. However, if you want, you can tell **sort** to examine only one or more fields, that is, parts of each line. (We discussed the concept of fields in Chapter 17, when we talked about the **cut** program.) The options that allow you to use fields with **sort** afford a great deal of control. However, they are very complex, and I won't go into the details here. If you ever find yourself needing to sort with fields, you will find the details in the Info file (**info sort**). If your system doesn't have Info files (see Chapter 9), the details will be in the man page instead (**man sort**).

CONTROLLING THE ORDER IN WHICH DATA IS SORTED: sort -dfn

There are a number of options you can use to control how the **sort** program works

The **-d** (dictionary) looks only at letters, numerals and whitespace (spaces and tabs). Use this option when your data contains characters that will get in the way of the sorting process, for example, as punctuation.

The **-f** (fold) option treats lowercase letters as if they were uppercase. Use this option when you want to ignore the distinctions between upper- and lowercase letters. For example, when you use **-f**, the words **harley** and **Harley** are considered to be the same as **HARLEY**. (The term "fold" is explained below.)

The **-n** (numeric) option recognizes numbers at the beginning of a line or a field and sorts them numerically. Such numbers may include leading spaces, negative signs and decimal points. Use this option to tell **sort** that you are using numeric data. For example, let's say you want to sort:

```
11
2
1
20
10
```

If you use **sort** with no options, the output is:

```
1
10
11
2
20
```

If you use **sort -n**, you get:

```
1
2
10
11
20
```

The **-r** (reverse) option sorts the data in reverse order. For example, if you sort the data in the last example using **sort -nr**, the output is:

```
20
11
10
2
1
```

In my experience, you will find yourself using the **-r** option a lot more than you might think. This is because it is useful to be able to list information in reverse alphabetical order or reverse numeric order.

The final option, **-u** (unique), tells **sort** to check for identical lines and suppress all but one. For example, let's say you use **sort -u** to sort the following data:

```
Barbara
Al
Barbara
Barbara
Dave
```

The output is:

```
Al
Barbara
Dave
```

HINT

As an alternative to sort **-u**, you can use **uniq** (discussed later in the chapter). The **uniq** program is simpler but, unlike **sort**, it does not let you work with specific fields should that be necessary.

WHAT'S IN A NAME?

Fold

There are a variety of Unix programs that have an option to ignore the differences between upper- and lowercase letters. Sometimes, the option is called **-i**, for "ignore", which only makes sense. Much of the time, however, the option is **-f**, which stands for FOLD: a technical term indicating that lowercase letters are to be treated as if they were uppercase, or vice versa, without changing the original data. (The use of the term "fold" in this way has nothing to do with the **fold** program, so don't be confused.)

The term "fold" is most often used as an adjective: "To make **sort** case insensitive, use the fold option." At times, however, you will see "fold" used as a verb: "When you use the **-f** option, **sort** folds lowercase letters into uppercase."

Here is something interesting: the original version of the Unix **sort** program folded uppercase letters into lowercase. That is, when you used **-f**, **sort** treated all letters as if they were lowercase. Modern versions of **sort** fold lowercase into uppercase. That is, they treat all letters as if they were uppercase. Is the difference significant? The answer is sometimes, as you will see when we discuss collating sequences.

No one knows the origin of the term "fold", so feel free to make up your own metaphor.

CHECKING IF DATA IS SORTED: `sort -c`

As I mentioned earlier, **sort** can perform two related tasks: sorting data, and checking to see if data is already sorted. In this section, we'll talk about checking data. When you **sort** in this way, the syntax is:

sort -c[u] [*file*]

where *file* is the name of a file.

The **-c** (check) option tells **sort** that you don't want to sort the data, you only want to know if it is already sorted. For example, to see if the data within the file **names** is sorted, you would use:

sort -c names

If the data is sorted, **sort** will display nothing. (No news is good news.) If the data is not sorted, **sort** will display a message, for example:

sort: names:5: disorder: Polly Ester

In this case, the message means that the data in **names** is not sorted (that is, there is "disorder"), starting with line 5, which contains the data **Polly Ester**.

You can use **sort -c** within a pipeline to check data that has been written to standard output by another program. For example, let's say you have a program named **poetry-generator** that generates a large amount of output. The output is supposed to be sorted, but you suspect there may be a problem, so you check it with **sort -c**:

poetry-generator | sort -c

If you combine **-c** with the **-u** (unique) option, **sort** will check your data in two ways at the same time. While it is looking for unsorted data, it will also look for consecutive lines that are the same. You use **-cu** when you want to ensure (1) your data is sorted, and (2) all the lines are unique. For example, the file **friends** contains the following data:

```
Al Packa
Max Out
Patty Cake
Patty Cake
Shirley U. Jest
```

You enter:

sort -cu friends

Although the data is sorted, **sort** detects a duplicate line:

sort: friends:4: disorder: Patty Cake

THE ASCII CODE; COLLATING SEQUENCES

Suppose you use the **sort** program to sort the following data. What will the output be?

```
zzz
ZZZ
bbb
BBB
aaa
AAA
```

On some systems, you will get:

```
AAA
BBB
ZZZ
aaa
bbb
zzz
```

On other systems, you will get:

```
AAA
aaa
BBB
bbb
ZZZ
zzz
```

How can this be? In the early days of Unix, there was just one way of organizing characters. Today, this is not the case, and the results you see when you run **sort** depend on how characters are organized on *your* particular system. Here is the story.

Before the 1990s, the character encoding used by Unix (and most computer systems) was the ASCII CODE, often referred to as ASCII. The name stands for "American Standard Code for Information Interchange".

TYPE OF UNIX	COMMAND TO DISPLAY ASCII CODE PAGE
Linux	`man ascii`
FreeBSD	`less /usr/share/misc/ascii`
Solaris	`less /usr/pub/ascii`

FIGURE 19-1: Displaying the ASCII code

You will find a summary of the ASCII code in Appendix D of this book. For online reference, most Unix systems have a handy page containing the entire ASCII code. Traditionally, this page was stored in a file named **ascii** *in the directory* **/usr/pub/**. *In recent years, the Unix file system has been reorganized on some systems, and the ASCII reference file has been moved to* **/usr/share/misc**. *On other systems, the file has been converted to a page within the online manual. Thus, the way in which you display the ASCII reference page depends on the system you are using.*

The ASCII code was created in 1967. It specifies a 7-bit pattern for every character, 128 in all. These bit patterns range from **0000000** (0 in decimal) to **1111111** (127 in decimal). For this reason, the 128 ASCII characters are numbered from 0 to 127.

The 128 characters that comprise the ASCII code consist of 33 "control characters" and 95 "printable characters". The control characters were discussed in Chapter 7. The printable characters, shown below, are the 52 letters of the alphabet (26 uppercase, 26 lowercase), 10 numbers, 32 punctuation symbols, and the space character (listed first below):

```
 !"#$%&'()*+,-./0123456789:;<=>?
@ABCDEFGHIJKLMNOPQRSTUVWXYZ[\]^_
`abcdefghijklmnopqrstuvwxyz{|}~
```

The order of the printable characters is the order in which I have listed them. They range from character #32 (space) to character #126 (tilde). (Remember, numbering starts at 0, so the space is actually the 33rd character.) For reference, Appendix D contains a table of the entire ASCII code. You may want to take a moment and look at it now.

For practical purposes, it is convenient to consider the tab to be a printable character even though, strictly speaking, it is actually a control character. The tab is character #9, which places it before the other printable characters. Thus, I offer the following definition: the 96 PRINTABLE CHARACTERS are the tab, space, punctuation symbols, numbers, and letters.

As a convenience, most Unix systems have a reference page showing the ASCII code to allow you to look at it quickly whenever you want. Unfortunately, the ASCII reference page is not standardized, so the way in which you display it depends on which system you are using. See Figure 19-1 for the details.

With respect to a character coding scheme, the order in which the characters are organized is called the COLLATING SEQUENCE. The collating sequence is used whenever you need to put characters in order, for example, when you use the **sort** program or when you use a range within a regular expression (discussed in Chapter 20).

With the ASCII code, the collating sequence is simply the order in which the characters appear in the code. This is summarized in Figure 19-2. For a more detailed reference, see Appendix D.

It is important to be familiar with the ASCII code collating sequence, as it is used by default on many Unix systems and programming languages. Although you don't have to memorize the entire ASCII code, you do need to memorize three basic principles:

* Spaces come before numbers.
* Numbers come before uppercase letters.
* Uppercase letters come before lowercase letters.

Here is an example. Assume that your system uses the ASCII collating sequence. You use the **sort** program to sort the following data (in which the third line starts with a space):

```
hello
Hello
 hello
1hello
:hello
```

NUMBERS	CHARACTERS
0-31	control characters (including tab)
32	space character
33-47	symbols: ! " # $ % & ' ( ) * + , - . /
48-57	numbers: 0 1 2 3 4 5 6 7 8 9
58-64	more symbols: : ; < = > ? @
65-90	uppercase letters: A B C ... Z
91-96	more symbols: [\ ] ^ _ `
97-122	lowercase letters: a b c ... z
123-126	more symbols: {	} ~
127	null control character (del)

FIGURE 19-2: **The order of characters in the ASCII code**

The ASCII code defines the 128 basic characters used by Unix systems. Within the ASCII code, the characters are numbered 0 through 127. The table in this figure summarizes the order of the characters, which is important when you use a program like **sort**. *For example, when you sort text, a space comes before "%" (percent), which comes before the number "3", which comes before the letter "A", and so on. For a more detailed reference, see Appendix D.*

The output is:

```
 hello
1hello
:hello
Hello
hello
```

> **HINT**
>
> When it comes to the order of characters in the ASCII code, all you need to memorize is: Space, Numbers, Uppercase letters, and Lowercase letters, in that order. Just remember "SNUL".*

LOCALES AND COLLATING SEQUENCES

In the early days of Unix, everyone used the ASCII code and that was that. However, ASCII is based on English and, as the use of Unix, Linux and the Internet spread throughout the world, it became necessary to devise a system that would work with a large number of languages and a variety of cultural conventions.

---

*If you have trouble remembering the acronym SNUL, let me show you a memory trick used by many smart people. All you need to do is relate the item you want to remember to your everyday life.

For example, let's say you are a mathematician specializing in difference calculus, and you happen to be working with fourth order difference equations satisfied by those Laguerre-Hahn polynomials that are orthogonal on special non-uniform lattices. To remember SNUL, you would just think of "special non-uniform lattices".

See how easy it is to be smart?

In the 1990s, a new system was developed, based on the idea of a "locale", part of the POSIX 1003.2 standard. (POSIX is discussed in Chapters 11 and 16.) A LOCALE is a technical specification describing the language and conventions that should be used when communicating with a user from a particular culture. The intention is that a user can choose whichever locale he wants, and the programs he runs will communicate with him accordingly. For example, if a user chooses the American English locale, his programs should display messages in English, write dates in the format "month-day-year", use "$" as a currency symbol, and so on.

Within Unix, your locale is defined by a set of environment variables that identify your language, your date format, your time format, your currency symbol, and other cultural conventions. Whenever a program needs to know your preferences, all it has to do is look at the appropriate environment variables. In particular, there is an environment variable named **LC_COLLATE** that specifies which collating sequence you want to use. (The variables all have default values, which you can change if you want.)

To display the current value of all the locale variables on your system — including **LC_COLLATE** — you use the **locale** command:

```
locale
```

If you are wondering which locales are supported on your system, you can display them all by using the **-a** (all) option:

```
locale -a
```

In the United States, Unix systems default to one of two locales. The two locales are basically the same, but have different collating sequences, which means that when you run a program such as **sort**, your results can vary depending on which locale is being used.

Since many people are unaware of locales, even experienced programmers can be perplexed when they change from one Unix system to another and, all of a sudden, programs like **sort** do not behave "properly". For this reason, I am going to take a moment to discuss the two American locales and explain what you need to know about them. If you live outside the U.S., the ideas will still apply, but the details will be different.

The first American locale is based on the ASCII code. This locale has two names. It is known as either the **C** locale (named after the C programming language) or the **POSIX** locale; you can use whichever name you want. The second American locale is based on American English, and is named **en_US** although you will see variations of this name.

The **C** locale was designed for compatibility, in order to preserve the conventions used by old-time programs (and old-time programmers). The **en_US** locale was designed to fit into a modern international framework in which American English is only one of many different languages.

As I mentioned, both these locales are the same except for the collating sequence. The **C** locale uses the ASCII collating sequence in which uppercase letters come before lowercase letters: **ABC...XYZabc...z**. This pattern is called the C COLLATING SEQUENCE, because it is used by the C programming language.

The **en_US** locale uses a different collating sequence in which the lowercase letters and uppercase letters are grouped in pairs: **aAbBcCdD...zZ**. This pattern is more natural, as it organizes words and characters in the same order as you would find in a dictionary. For this reason, this pattern is called the DICTIONARY COLLATING SEQUENCE.

Until the end of the 1990s, all Unix systems used the C collating sequence, based on the ASCII code, and this is still the case with the systems that use the **C/POSIX** locale. Today, however, some Unix systems, including a few Linux distributions, are designed to have a more international flavor. As such, they use the **en_US** locale and the dictionary collating sequence.

Can you see a possible source of confusion? Whenever you run a program that depends on the order of upper- and lowercase letters, the output is affected by your collating sequence. Thus, you can get different results depending on which locale your system uses by default. This may happen, for example, when you use the **sort** program, or when you use certain types of regular expressions called "character classes" (see Chapter 20).

For reference, Figure 19-3 shows the two collating sequences. Notice that there are significant differences, not only in the order of the letters, but in the order of the punctuation symbols.

As an example of how your choice of locale can make a difference, consider what happens when you sort the following data (in which the third line starts with a space):

```
hello
Hello
 hello
1hello
:hello
```

With the **C** locale (C collating sequence), the output is:

```
 hello
1hello
:hello
Hello
hello
```

With the **en_US** locale (dictionary collating sequence), the output is:

```
 hello
:hello
1hello
hello
Hello
```

So which locale should you use? In my experience, if you use the **en_US** locale, you will eventually encounter unexpected problems that will be difficult to track down. For example, as we will discuss in Chapter 25, you use the **rm** (remove) program to delete files. Let's say you want to delete all your files whose names begin with an uppercase letter. The traditional Unix command to use is:

```
rm [A-Z]*
```

This will work fine if you are using the **C** locale. However, if you are using the **en_US** locale, you will end up deleting all the files whose names begin with any upper- or lowercase letter, except the letter **a**. (Don't worry about the details; they will be explained in Chapter 20.)*

My advice is to set your default to be the **C** locale, because it uses the traditional ASCII collating sequence. In the long run, this will create fewer problems than using the **en_US**

C LOCALE: C COLLATING SEQUENCE	
space character	•
symbols	! " # $ % & ` ( ) * + , - . /
numbers	0 1 2 3 4 5 6 7 8 9
more symbols	: ; < = > ? @
uppercase letters	A B C D E F G H I J K L M N O P Q R S T U V W X Y Z
more symbols	[\ ] ^ _ `
lowercase letters	a b c d e f g h i j k l m n o p q r s t u v w x y z
more symbols	{ | } ~

en_US LOCALE: DICTIONARY COLLATING SEQUENCE	
symbols	` ^ ~ < = > |
space character	•
more symbols	_ - , ; : ! ? / . ' " ( ) [ ] { } @ $ * \ & # % +
numbers	0 1 2 3 4 5 6 7 8 9
letters	a A b B c C d D e E f F g G h H i I j J k K l L m M n N o O p P q Q r R s S t T u U v V w W x X y Y z Z

FIGURE 19-3: Collating sequences for the C and **en_US** locales

*In the United States, Unix and Linux systems use one of two locales: **C/POSIX** based on the ASCII code, or **en_US** based on American English. The following two charts show the collating sequences for each of these locales. In the C collating sequence (used with the **C** locale), the numbers, lowercase letters, and uppercase letters are separated by symbols. In the dictionary collating sequence (used with the **en_US** locale), all the symbols come at the beginning, followed by the numbers and letters.*

*Note: In both charts, I have used a dot (•) to indicate the **space** character.*

---

*There are lots of situations in which the **C** locale works better than the **en_US** locale. Here is another one: You are writing a C or C++ program. In your directory, you have files containing code with names that have all lowercase letters, such as **program1.c**, **program2.cpp**, **data.h**, and so on. You also have extra files with names that begin with an uppercase letter, such as **Makefile**, **RCS**, **README**. When you list the contents of the directory using the **ls** program (Chapter 24), all the "uppercase" files will be listed first, separating the extra files from the code files.

locale and the dictionary collating sequence. In fact, as you read this book, I assume that you are using the **C** locale.

So how do you specify your locale? The first step is to determine which collating sequence is the default on your system. If the **C** locale is already the default on your system, fine. If not, you need to change it.

One way to determine your default collating sequence is to enter the **locale** command and check the value of the **LC_COLLATE** environment variable. Is it **C** or **POSIX**? Or is it some variation of **en_US**?

Another way to determine your default collating sequence is to perform the following short test. Create a small file named **data** using the command:

```
cat > data
```

Type the following three lines and then press **^D** to end the command:

```
AAA
[]
aaa
```

Now sort the contents of the file:

```
sort data
```

If you are using the **C/POSIX** locale, the output will be sorted using the C (ASCII) collating sequence:

```
AAA
[]
aaa
```

If you are using the **en_US** locale, the output will be sorted using the dictionary collating sequence:

```
[]
aaa
AAA
```

Before you continue, take a moment to look at the collating sequences in Figure 19-3 and make sure these examples make sense to you.

If your Unix system uses the **C** or **POSIX** locale by default, you don't need to do anything. (However, please read through the rest of this section, as one day, you will encounter this problem on another system.)

If your system uses the **en_US** locale, you need to change the **LC_COLLATE** environment variable to either **C** or **POSIX**. Either of the following commands will do the job with the Bourne Shell family:

```
export LC_COLLATE=C
export LC_COLLATE=POSIX
```

With the C-Shell family, you would use:

```
setenv LC_COLLATE C
setenv LC_COLLATE POSIX
```

To make the change permanent, all you need to do is put one of these commands into your login file. (Environment variables are discussed in Chapter 12; the login file is discussed in Chapter 14.) For the rest of this book, I will assume that you are, indeed, using the C collating sequence so, if you are not, put the appropriate command in your login file right now.

HINT

From time to time, you may want to run a single program with a collating sequence that is different from the default. To do so, you can use a subshell to change the value of **LC_COLLATE** temporarily while you run the program. (We discuss subshells in Chapter 15.)

For example, let's say you are using the **C** locale, and you want to run the **sort** program using the **en_US** (dictionary) collating sequence. You can use:

```
(export LC_COLLATE=en_US; sort data)
```

When you run the program in this way, the change you make to **LC_COLLATE** is temporary, because it exists only within the subshell.

FINDING DUPLICATE LINES: `uniq`

Related filters: **sort**

Unix has a number of specialized filters designed to work with sorted data. The most useful of such filters is **uniq**, which examines data line by line, looking for consecutive, duplicate lines.

The **uniq** program can perform four different tasks:

- Eliminate duplicate lines
- Select duplicate lines
- Select unique lines
- Count the number of duplicate lines

The syntax is:

uniq [**-cdu**] [*infile* [*outfile*]]

where *infile* is the name of an input file, and *outfile* is the name of an output file.

Let's start with a simple example. The file **data** contains the following lines:

```
Al
Al
Barbara
Barbara
Charles
```

(Remember, because input for **uniq** must be sorted, duplicate lines will be consecutive.) You want a list of all the lines in the file with no duplications. The command to use is:

```
uniq data
```

The output is straightforward:

```
Al
Barbara
Charles
```

If you want to save the output to another file, say, **processed-data**, you can specify its name as part of the command:

```
uniq data processed-data
```

To see only the duplicate lines, use the **-d** option:

```
uniq -d data
```

Using our sample file, the output is:

```
Al
Barbara
```

To see only the unique (non-duplicate) lines, use **-u**:

```
uniq -u data
```

In our sample, there is only one such line:

```
Charles
```

Question: What do you think happens if you use both **-d** and **-u** at the same time? (Try it and see.)

To count how many times each line appears, use the **-c** option:

```
uniq -c data
```

With our sample, the output is:

```
2 Al
2 Barbara
1 Charles
```

So far, our example has been simple. The real power of **uniq** comes when you use it within a pipeline. For example, it is common to combine and sort several files, and then pipe the output to **uniq**, as in the following two examples:

```
sort file1 file2 file3 | uniq
cat file1 file2 file3 | sort | uniq
```

> **HINT**
>
> If you are using **uniq** without options, you have an alternative. You can use **sort -u** instead. For example, the following three commands all have the same effect:
>
> **sort -u** *file1 file2 file3*
> **sort** *file1 file2 file3* | **uniq**
> **cat** *file1 file2 file3* | **sort** | **uniq**
>
> (See the discussion on **sort -u** earlier in the chapter.)

Here is a real-life example to show you how powerful such constructions can be.

Ashley is a student at a large Southern California school. During the upcoming winter break, her cousin Jessica will be coming to visit from the East Coast, where she goes to a small, progressive liberal arts school. Jessica wants to meet guys, but she is very picky: she only likes very smart guys who are athletic.

It happens that Ashley is on her sorority's Ethics Committee, which gives her access to the student/academic database (don't ask). Using her special status, Ashley logs into the system and creates two files. The first file, **math237**, contains the names of all the male students taking Math 237 (Advanced Calculus). The second file, **pe35**, contains the names of all the male students taking Physical Education 35 (Surfing Appreciation).

Ashley's idea is to make a list of possible dates for Jessica by finding all the guys who are taking both courses. Because the files are too large to compare by hand, Ashley (who is both beautiful *and* smart) uses Unix. Specifically, she uses the **uniq** program with the **-d** option, saving the output to a file named **possible-guys**:

```
sort math237 pe35 | uniq -d > possible-guys
```

Ashley then emails the list to Jessica, who is able to check out the guys on Myspace before her trip.

> **HINT**
>
> You must always make sure that input to **uniq** is sorted. If not, **uniq** will not be able to detect the duplications. The results will not be what you expect, but there will be no error message to warn you that something has gone wrong.*

MERGING SORTED DATA FROM TWO FILES: `join`

Related filters: **colrm**, **cut**, **paste**

Of all the specialized Unix filters designed to work with sorted data, the most interesting is **join**, which combines two sorted files based on the values of a particular field. The syntax is:

join [**-i**] [**-a1**|**-v1**] [**-a2**|**-v2**] [**-1** *field1*] [**-2** *field2*] *file1 file2*

---

*This is one time where — even for Ashley and Jessica — a "sorted" affair is considered to be a good thing.

where *field1* and *field2* are numbers referring to specific fields; and *file1* and *file2* are the names of files containing sorted data.

Before we get to the details, I'd like to show you an example. Let's say you have two sorted files containing information about various people, each of whom has a unique identification number. Within the first file, called **names**, each line contains an ID number followed by a first name and last name:

```
111  Hugh Mungus
222  Stew Pendous
333  Mick Stup
444  Mel Collie
```

In the second file, **phone**, each line contains an ID number followed by a phone number:

```
111  101-555-1111
222  202-555-2222
333  303-555-3333
444  404-555-4444
```

The **join** program allows you to the combine the two files, based on their common values, in this case, the ID number:

```
join names phone
```

The output is:

```
111  Hugh Mungus 101-555-1111
222  Stew Pendous 202-555-2222
333  Mick Stup 303-555-3333
444  Melon Collie 404-555-4444
```

When **join** reads its input, it ignores leading whitespace, that is, spaces or tabs at the beginning of a line. For example, the following two lines are considered the same:

```
111  Hugh Mungus 101-555-1111
   111  Hugh Mungus 101-555-1111
```

Before we discuss the details of the **join** program, I'd like to take a moment to go over some terminology. In Chapter 17, we discussed fields and delimiters. When you have a file in which every line contains a data record, each separate item within the line is called a field. In our example, each line in the file **names** contains three fields: an ID number, a first name and last name. The file **phone** contains two fields: an ID number and a phone number.

Within each line, the characters that separate fields are called delimiters. In our example, the delimiters are spaces, although you will often see tabs and commas used in this way. By default, **join** assumes that each pair of fields is separated by whitespace, that is, by one or more spaces or tabs.

When we combine two sets of data based on matching fields, it is called a JOIN. (The name comes from database theory.) The specific field used for the match is called the

JOIN FIELD. By default, `join` assumes that the join field is the first field of each file but, as you will see in a moment, this can be changed.

To create a join, the program looks for pairs of lines, one from each file, that contain the same value in their join field. For each pair, `join` generates an output line consisting of three parts: the common join field value, the rest of line from the first file, and the rest of the line from the second file.

As an example, consider the first line in each of the two files above. The join field has the value **111**. Thus, the first line of output consists of **111**, a space, **Hugh**, a space, **Mungus**, a space, and **101-555-1111**. (By default, `join` uses a single space to separate fields in the output.)

In the example above, every line in the first file matches a line in the second file. However, this might not always be the case. For example, consider the following files. You are making a list of your friends' birthdays and their favorite gifts. The first file, **birthdays**, contains two fields: first name and birthday:

```
Al         May-10-1987
Barbara    Feb-2-1992
Dave       Apr-8-1990
Frances    Oct-15-1991
George     Jan-17-1992
```

The second file, **gifts**, also contains two fields: first name and favorite gift:

```
Al         money
Barbara    chocolate
Charles    music
Dave       books
Edward     camera
```

In this case, you have birthday information and gift information for Al, Barbara and Dave. However, you do not have gift information for Frances and George, and you do not have birthday information for Edward. Consider what happens when you use `join`:

```
join birthdays gifts
```

Because only three lines have matching join fields (the lines for Al, Barbara and Dave), there are only three lines of output:

```
Al May-10-1987 money
Barbara Feb-2-1992 chocolate
Dave Apr-8-1990 books
```

However, suppose you want to see all the people with birthday information, even if they do not have gift information. You can use the **-a** (all) option, followed by a **1**:

```
join -a1 birthdays gifts
```

This tells `join` to output all the names in file #1, even if there is no gift information:

```
Al May-10-1987 money
Barbara Feb-2-1992 chocolate
Dave Apr-8-1990 books
Frances Oct-15-1991
George Jan-17-1992
```

Similarly, if you want to see all the people with gift information (from file #2), even if they do not have birthday information, you can use **–a2**:

```
join -a2 birthdays gifts
```

The output is:

```
Al May-10-1987 money
Barbara Feb-2-1992 chocolate
Charles music
Dave Apr-8-1990 books
Edward camera
```

To list all the names from both files, use both options:

```
join -a1 -a2 birthdays gifts
```

he output is:

```
Al May-10-1987 money
Barbara Feb-2-1992 chocolate
Charles music
Dave Apr-8-1990 books
Edward camera
Frances Oct-15-1991
George Jan-17-1992
```

When you use **join** in the regular way (without the **–a** option) as we did in our first example, the result is called an INNER JOIN. (The term comes from database theory.) With an inner join, the output comes only from lines where the join field matched.

When you use either **–a1** or **–a2**, the output includes lines in which the join field did not match. We call this an OUTER JOIN.

I won't go into the details because a discussion of database theory, however interesting, is beyond the scope of this book. All I want you to remember is that, if you work with what are called "relational databases", the distinction between inner and outer joins is important.

To continue, if you want to see only those lines that *don't* match, you can use the **–v1** or **–v2** (reverse) options. When you use **–v1**, **join** outputs only those lines from file #1 that don't match, leaving out all the matches. For example:

```
join -v1 birthdays gifts
```

The output is:

```
Frances Oct-15-1991
George Jan-17-1992
```

When you use **-v2**, you get only those lines from file #2 that don't match:

```
join -v2 birthdays gifts
```

The output is:

```
Charles music
Edward camera
```

Of course, you can use both options to get all the lines from both files that don't match:

```
join -v1 -v2 birthdays gifts
```

The output is now:

```
Charles music
Edward camera
Frances Oct-15-1991
George Jan-17-1992
```

Because **join** depends on its data being sorted, there are several options to help you control the sorting requirements. First, you can use the *-i* (ignore) option to tell **join** to ignore any differences between upper and lower case. For example, when you use this option, **CHARLES** is treated the same as **Charles**.

HINT

You will often use **sort** to prepare data for **join**. Remember: With **sort**, you ignore differences in upper and lower case by using the **-f** (fold) option. With **join**, you use the **-i** (ignore) option. (See the discussion on "fold" earlier in the chapter.)

I mentioned earlier that **join** assumes the join field is the first field of each file. You can specify that you want to use different join fields by using the **-1** and **-2** options.

To change the join field for file #1, use **-1** followed by the number of the field you want to use. For example, the following command joins two files, **data** and **statistics** using the 3rd field of file #1 and (by default) the 1st field of file #2:

```
join -1 3 data statistics
```

To change the join field for file #2, use the **-2** option. For example, the following command joins the same two files using 3rd field of file #1 and the 4th field of file #2

```
join -1 3 -2 4 data statistics
```

To conclude our discussion, I would like to remind you that, because **join** works with sorted data, the results you get may depend on your locale and your collating sequences, that is, on the value of the **LC_COLLATE** environment variable. (See the discussion about locales earlier in the chapter.)

> **HINT**
>
> The most common mistake in using **join** is forgetting to sort the two input files. If one or both of the files are not sorted properly with respect to the join fields, you will see either no output or partial output, and there will be no error message to warn you that something has gone wrong.

CREATE A TOTAL ORDERING FROM PARTIAL ORDERINGS: `tsort`

Related filters: **sort**

Consider the following problem. You are planning your evening activities, and you have a number of constraints:

* You must clean the dishes before you can watch TV.
* You must eat before you clean the dishes.
* You must shop before you can cook dinner.
* You must shop before you can put away the food.
* You must put away the food before you can cook dinner.
* You must cook dinner before you can eat it.
* You must put away the food before you can watch TV.

As you can see, this is a bit confusing. What you need is a master list that specifies when each activity should be done, such that all of the constraints are satisfied.

In mathematical terms, each of these constraints is called a PARTIAL ORDERING, because they specify the order of some (both not all) of the activities. In our example, each of the partial orderings specifies the order of two activities. Should you be able to construct a master list, it would be a TOTAL ORDERING, because it would specify the order of *all* of the activities.

The job of the **tsort** program is to analyze a set of partial orderings, each of which represents a single constraint, and calculate a total ordering that satisfies all the constraints. The syntax is simple:

tsort [*file*]

where *file* is the name of a file.

Each line of input must consist of a pair of character strings separated by whitespace (spaces or tabs), such that each pair represents a partial ordering. For example, let's say that the file **activities** contains the following data:

```
clean-dishes watch-TV
eat clean-dishes
shop cook
shop put-away-food
put-away-food cook
cook eat
put-away-food watch-TV
```

Notice that each line in the file consists of two character strings separated by whitespace (in this case, a single space). Each line represents a partial ordering that matches one of the constraints listed above. For example, the first line says that you must clean the dishes before you can watch TV; the second line says you must eat before you can clean the dishes; and so on.

The **tsort** program will turn the set of partial orderings into a single total ordering. Use the command:

```
tsort activities
```

The output is:

```
shop
put-away-food
cook
eat
clean-dishes
watch-TV
```

Thus, the solution to the problem is:
1. Shop.
2. Put away your food.
3. Cook dinner.
4. Eat dinner.
5. Clean the dishes.
6. Watch TV.

In general, any set of partial orderings can be combined into a total ordering, as long as there are no loops. For example, consider the following partial orderings:

```
study watch-TV
watch-TV study
```

There can be no total ordering, because you can't study before you watch TV, if you insist on watching TV before you study (although many people try). If you were to send this data to **tsort**, it would display an error message telling you the input contains a loop.

WHAT'S IN A NAME?

tsort
Mathematically, it is possible to represent a set of partial orderings using what is called a "directed graph". If there are no loops, it is called a "directed acyclic graph" or DAG. For example, a tree (see Chapter 9) is a DAG.

Once you have a DAG, you can create a total ordering out of the partial orderings by sorting the elements of the graph based on their relative positions, rather than their values. In fact, this is how **tsort** does its job (although we don't need to worry about the details).

In mathematics, we use the word "topological" to describe properties that depend on relative positions. Thus, **tsort** stands for "topological sort".

SEARCHING FOR CHARACTER STRINGS IN BINARY FILES: `strings`

Related filters: **grep**

To use the **strings** program, you need to understand the difference between text files and binary files. Consider the following three definitions:

1. There are 96 printable characters: tab, space, punctuation symbols, numbers, and letters. Any sequence of printable characters is called a CHARACTER STRING or, more informally, a STRING. For example, "Harley" is a string of length 6. (We discussed printable characters earlier in the chapter.)

2. A file that contains only printable characters (with a newline character at the end of each line) is called a TEXT FILE or ASCII FILE. For the most part, Unix filters are designed to work with text files. Indeed, within this chapter, all the sample files are text files.

3. A BINARY FILE is any non-empty file that is not a text file, that is, any file that contains at least some non-textual data. Some common examples of binary files are executable programs, object files, images, sound files, video files, word processing documents, spreadsheets and databases.

If you are a programmer, you will work with executable programs and object files ("pieces" of programs), all of which are binary files. If you could look inside an executable program or an object file, most of what you would see would be encoded machine instructions, which look like meaningless gibberish. However, most programs do contain some recognizable character strings such as error messages, help information, and so on.

The **strings** program was created as a tool for programmers to display character strings that are embedded within executable programs and object files. For example, there used to be a custom that programmers would insert a character string into every program showing the version of that program. This allowed anyone to use **strings** to extract the version of a program from the program itself.

Today, programmers and users have better ways to keep track of such information[*] and the **strings** program is not used much. Still, *you* can use it, just for fun, to look "inside" any type of binary file. Although there is rarely a practical reason for doing so, it is cool to check out binary files for hidden messages. The syntax is:

strings [-*length*] [*file...*]

where **length** is the minimum length character string to display, and **file** is the name of a file, most often a pathname.

As an example, let's say you want to look inside the **sort** program. To start, you use the **whereis** program to find the pathname — that is, the exact location — of the file that contains the program. (We'll discuss pathnames and **whereis** in Chapter 24, so don't worry about the details for now.) The command to use is:

---

[*]As we discussed in Chapter 10, most of the GNU utilities (used with Linux and FreeBSD) support the **--version** option to display version information.

```
whereis sort
```

Typical output would be:

```
sort: /usr/bin/sort /usr/share/man/man1/sort.1.gz
```

The output shows us the exact locations of the program and its man page. We are only interested in the program, so to use **strings** to look inside the **sort** program, we use:

```
strings /usr/bin/sort
```

Such commands usually generate a lot of output. There are, however, three things you can do to make the output more manageable.

First, by default, **strings** will only extract character strings that are at least 4 characters long. The idea is to eliminate short, meaningless sequences of characters. Even so, you are likely to see a great many spurious character strings. However, you can eliminate a lot of them by specifying a longer minimum length. To do so, you use an option consisting of hyphen (**-**) followed by a number. For example, to specify that you only want to see strings that are at least 7 characters long (a good number), you would use:

```
strings -7 /usr/bin/sort
```

Next, you can sort the output and remove duplicate lines. To do so, just pipe the output to **sort -iu** (discussed earlier in the chapter):

```
strings -7 /usr/bin/sort | sort -iu
```

Finally, if there is so much output that it scrolls off your screen before you can read it, you can use **less** (Chapter 21) to display the output one screenful at a time:

```
strings -7 /usr/bin/sort | sort -iu | less
```

If the idea of looking inside programs for hidden messages appeals to you, here is an easy way to use **strings** to explore a variety of programs. The most important Unix utilities are stored in the two directories **/bin** and **/usr/bin**. (We will discuss this in Chapter 23.) Let's say you want to look inside some of the programs in these directories. To start, enter either of the following two **cd** (change directory) commands. This will change your "working directory" to whichever directory you choose:

```
cd /bin
cd /usr/bin
```

Now use the **ls** (list) program to display a list of all the files in that directory:

```
ls
```

All of these files are programs, and you can use **strings** to look at any of them. Moreover, because the files are in your working directory, you don't have to specify the entire pathname. In this case, the file name by itself is enough. For example, if your working directory is **/bin**, where the **date** program resides, you can look inside the **date** program by using the command:

```
strings -7 date | sort -iu | less
```

In this way, you can look for hidden character strings inside the most important Unix utilities. Once you are finished experimenting, enter the command:

```
cd
```

This will change your working directory back to your home directory (explained in Chapter 23).

TRANSLATING CHARACTERS: tr

Related filters: **sed**

The **tr** (translate) program can perform three different operations on characters. First, it can change characters to other characters. For example, you might change lowercase characters to uppercase characters, or tabs to spaces. Or, you might change every instance of the number "0" to the letter "X". When you do this, we say that you TRANSLATE the characters.

Second, you can specify that if a translated character occurs more than once in a row, it should be replaced by only a single character. For example, you might replace one or more numbers in a row by the letter "X". Or, you might replace multiple spaces by a single space. When you make such a change, we say that you SQUEEZE the characters.

Finally, **tr** can delete specified characters. For example, you might delete all the tabs in a file. Or, you might delete all the characters that are not letters or numbers.

In the next few sections, we will examine each of these operations in turn. Before we start, however, let's take a look at the syntax:

```
tr [-cds] [set1 [set2]]
```

where *set1* and *set2* are sets of characters*.

Notice that the syntax does not let you specify a file name, either for input or output. This is because **tr** is a pure filter that reads only from standard input and writes only to standard output. If you want to read from a file, you must redirect standard input; if you want to write to a file (to save the output), you must redirect standard output. This will make sense when you see the examples. (Redirection is explained in Chapter 15.)

The basic operation performed by the **tr** program is translation. You specify two sets of characters. As **tr** reads the data, it looks for characters in the first set. Whenever **tr** finds such characters, it replaces them with corresponding characters from the second set. For example, say you have a file named **old**. You want to change all the "a" characters to "A". The command to do so is:

```
tr a A < old
```

---

*If you are using Solaris, you should use the Berkeley Unix version of **tr**. Such programs are stored in the directory **/usr/ucb**, so all you have to do is make sure this directory is at the beginning of your search path. (The name **ucb** stands for University of California, Berkeley.)

We discuss Berkeley Unix in Chapter 2, and the search path is in Chapter 13.

To save the output, just redirect it to a file, for example:

```
tr a A < old > new
```

By defining longer sets of characters, you can replace more than one character at the same time. The following command looks for and makes three different replacements: "a" is replaced by "A"; "b" is replaced by "B"; and "c" is replaced by "C".

```
tr abc ABC < old > new
```

If the second set of characters is shorter than the first, the last character in the second set is duplicated. For example, the following two commands are equivalent:

```
tr abcde Ax < old > new
tr abcde Axxxx < old > new
```

They both replace "a" with "A", and the other four characters ("b", "c", "d", "e") with "x".

When you specify characters that have special meaning to the shell, you must quote them (see Chapter 13) to tell the shell to treat the characters literally. You can use either single or double quotes although, in most cases, single quotes work best. However, if you are quoting only a single character, it is easier to use a backslash (again, see Chapter 13).

As a general rule, it is a good idea to quote all characters that are not numbers or letters. For example, let's say you want to change all the colons, semicolons and question marks to periods. You would use:

```
tr ':;?' \. < old > new
```

Much of the power of **tr** comes from its ability to work with ranges of characters. Consider, for example, the following command which changes all uppercase letters to lowercase. (What you see below is one long line.)

```
tr ABCDEFGHIJKLMNOPQRSTUVWXYZ
   abcdefghijklmnopqrstuvwxyz < old > new
```

The correspondence between upper- and lowercase letters is clear. However, it's a bother to have to type the entire alphabet twice. Instead, you can use hyphen (–) to define a range of characters, according to the following syntax:

start–end

where *start* is the first character in the range, and *end* is the last character in the range.

For example, the previous example can be rewritten as follows:

```
tr A-Z a-z < old > new
```

A range can be any set of characters you want, as long as they form a consecutive sequence within the collating sequence you are using. (Collating sequences are discussed earlier in the chapter.) For example, the following command implements a secret code you might use to encode numeric data. The digits 0 through 9 are replaced by the first nine letters of the alphabet, A through I, respectively. For example, **375** is replaced by **CGE**.

```
tr 0-9 A-I < old > new
```

As a convenience, there are several abbreviations you can use instead of ranges. These abbreviations are called "predefined character classes", and we will discuss them in detail in Chapter 20 when we talk about regular expressions. For now, all you need to know is that you can use **[:lower:]** instead of **a-z**, **[:upper:]** instead of **A-Z**, and **[:digit:]** instead of **0-9**. For example, the following two commands are equivalent:

```
tr A-Z a-z < old > new
tr [:upper:] [:lower:] < old > new
```

As are these two commands:

```
tr 0-9 A-I < old > new
tr [:digit:] A-I < old > new
```

(Note that the square brackets and colons are part of the name.)

For practical purposes, these three predefined character classes are the ones you are most likely to use with the **tr** program. However, there are more predefined character classes available if you need them. You will find the full list in Figure 20-3 in Chapter 20.

> **HINT**
>
> Compared to other filters, **tr** is unusual in that it does not allow you to specify the names of an input file or output file directly. To read from a file, you must redirect standard input; to write to a file, you must redirect standard output. For this reason, the most common mistake beginners make with **tr** is to forget the redirection. For example, the following commands will not work:
>
> ```
> tr abc ABC old
> tr abc ABC old new
> ```
>
> Linux will display a vague message telling you that there is an "extra operand". Other types of Unix will display messages that are even less helpful. For this reason, you may, one day, find yourself spending a lot of time trying to figure out why your **tr** commands don't work.
>
> The solution is to never forget: When you use **tr** with files, you *always* need redirection:
>
> ```
> tr abc ABC < old
> tr abc ABC < old > new
> ```

TRANSLATING UNPRINTABLE CHARACTERS

So far, all our examples have been straightforward. Still, they were a bit contrived. After all, how many times in your life will you need to change colons, semicolons and question marks to periods? Or change the letters "abc" to "ABC? Or use a secret code that changes numbers to letters? Traditionally, the **tr** program has been used for more esoteric translations, often involving non-printable characters. Here is a typical example to give you an idea.

In Chapter 7, I explained that, within a text file, Unix marks the end of each line by a newline (**^J**) character* and Windows uses a return followed by a newline (**^M^J**). Old versions of the Macintosh operating system, up to OS 9, used a return (**^M**) character**.

Suppose you have a text file that came from an old Macintosh. Within the file, the end of each line is marked by a return. Before you can use the file with Unix, you need to change all the returns to newlines. This is easy with **tr**. However, in order to do so, you need a way to represent both the newline and return characters. You have two choices.

First, you can use special codes that are recognized by the **tr** program: **\r** for a return, and **\n** for newline. Alternatively, you can use a **** (backslash) character followed by the 3-digit octal value for the character. In this case, **\015** for return, and **\012** for newline. For reference, Figure 19-4 shows the special codes and octal values you are most likely to use with **tr**.

The octal values are simply the base 8[†] number of the character within the ASCII code. For reference, you will find the octal values for the entire ASCII code in Appendix D.

Let us consider, then, how to use **tr** to change returns to newlines. Let's say we have a text file named **macfile** in which each line ends with a return. We want to change all the returns to newlines and save the output in a file named **unixfile**. Either of the following commands will do the job:

CODE	CTRL KEY	OCTAL CODE	NAME
\b	^H	\010	backspace
\t	^I	\011	tab
\n	^J	\012	newline/linefeed
\r	^M	\015	return
\\	–	–	backslash

FIGURE 19-4: Codes used by the **tr** program to represent control characters

The **tr** *program is used to translate (change) specific characters into other characters. To specify non-printable characters, you can either use a special code, or a backslash (/) followed by the 3-digit octal (base 8) value of the character. (You will find the octal values for all the characters in the ASCII code in Appendix D.)*

This table shows the special codes and octal values for the four most commonly used control characters. There are others, but you are unlikely to need them with **tr***.*

Note: Since the backslash is used an escape character (see Chapter 13), if you want to specify an actual backslash, you must use two in a row.

---

*As we discussed in Chapter 7, when Unix people write the names of control keys, they often use ^ as an abbreviation for "Ctrl". Thus, **^J** refers to <Ctrl-J>.

For many years, the Macintosh operating system (Mac OS) used **^M to mark the end of a line of text. As I mentioned, this was the case up to OS 9. In 2001, OS 9 was replaced by OS X, which is based on Unix. Like other Unix-based systems, OS X uses **^J** to mark the end of a line of text.

[†]In general, we count in base 10 (decimal), using the 10 digits 0 through 9. When we use computers, however, there are three other bases that are important:
- Base 2 (binary): uses 2 digits, 0-1
- Base 8 (octal): uses 8 digits, 0-7
- Base 16 (hexadecimal): uses 16 digits, 0-9 and A-F

We will talk about these number systems in Chapter 21.

```
tr '\r' '\n' < macfile > unixfile
tr '\015' '\012' < macfile > unixfile
```

As you can see, using these codes is simple once you understand how they work. For example, the following two commands change all the tabs in the file **olddata** to spaces, saving the output in **newdata***:

```
tr '\t' ' ' < olddata > newdata
tr '\011' ' ' < olddata > newdata
```

TRANSLATING CHARACTERS: ADVANCED TOPICS

So far, we have discussed how to use **tr** for straightforward substitutions, where one character is replaced by another character. We will now turn our attention to more advanced topics. Before we do, here is a reminder of syntax we will be using:

tr [**-cds**] [*set1* [*set2*]]

where *set1* and *set2* are sets of characters.

The **-s** option tells **tr** that multiple consecutive characters from the first set should be replaced by a single character. As I mentioned earlier, when we do this, we say that we squeeze the characters. Here is an example.

The following two commands replace any digit (0-9) with the uppercase letter "X". The input is read from a file named **olddata**, and the output is written to a file named **newdata**:

```
tr [:digit:] X < olddata > newdata
tr 0-9 X < olddata > newdata
```

Now these commands replace *each* occurrence of a digit with an "X". For example, the 6-digit number **120357** would be changed to **XXXXXX**. Let's say, however, you want to change all multi-digit numbers, no matter long they are, into a single "X". You would use the **-s** option:

```
tr -s [:digit:] X < olddata > newdata
tr -s 0-9 X < olddata > newdata
```

This tells **tr** to squeeze all multi-digit numbers into a single character. For example, the number **120357** is now changed to **X**.

Here is a useful example in which we squeeze multiple characters, without actually changing the character. You want to replace consecutive spaces with a single space. The solution is to replace a space with a space, while squeezing out the extras:

```
tr -s ' ' ' ' < olddata > newdata
```

---

*When you change tabs to spaces, or spaces to tabs, it is often better to use **expand** and **unexpand** (Chapter 18). These two programs were designed specifically to make such changes and, hence, offer more flexibility.

The next option, **-d**, deletes the characters you specify. As such, when you use **-d**, you define only one set of characters. For example, to delete all the left and right parentheses, use:

```
tr -d '()' < olddata > newdata
```

To delete all numbers, use either of the commands:

```
tr -d [:digit:] < olddata > newdata
tr -d 0-9 < olddata > newdata
```

The final option, **-c**, is the most complex and the most powerful. This option tells **tr** to match all the characters that are *not* in the first set*. For example, the following command replaces all characters except a space or a newline with an "X":

```
tr -c ' \n' X < olddata > newdata
```

The effect of this command is to preserve the "image" of the text, without the meaning. For instance, let's say the file **olddata** contains:

```
"Do you really think you were designed to spend most of
your waking hours working in an office and going to
meetings?" — Harley Hahn
```

The previous command will generate:

```
XX XXX XXXXXX XXXXX XXX XXXX XXXXXXXX XX XXXXX XXXX XX
XXXX XXXXXX XXXXX XXXXXXX XX XX XXXXXX XXX XXXXX XX
XXXXXXXXX X XXXXXX XXXX
```

To finish the discussion of **tr**, here is an interesting example in which we combine the **-c** (complement) and **-s** (squeeze) options to count unique words. Let's say you have written two history essays, stored in text files named **greek** and **roman**. You want to count the unique words found in both files. The strategy is as follows:

1. Use **cat** to combine the files.
2. Use **tr** to place each word on a separate line.
3. Use **sort** to sort the lines and eliminate duplications.
4. Use **wc** to count the remaining lines.

To place each word on a separate line (step 2), all we need to do is use **tr** to replace every character that is not part of a word with a newline. For example, let's say we have the words:

```
As you can see
```

---

*The name **-c** stands for "complement", a mathematical term. In set theory, the complement of a set refers to all the elements that are *not* part of the set. For example, with respect to the integers, the complement of the set of all even numbers is the set of all odd numbers. With respect to all the uppercase letters, the complement of the set {ABCDWXYZ} is the set {EFGHIJKLMNOPQRSTUV}.

This would change to:

```
As
you
can
see
```

To keep things simple, we will say words are constructed from a set of 53 different characters: 26 uppercase letters, 26 lowercase letters, and the apostrophe (that is, the single quote). The following three commands — choose the one you like — will do the job:

```
tr -cs [:alpha:]\' "\n"
tr -cs [:upper:][:lower:]\' "\n"
tr -cs A-Za-z\' "\n"
```

The **-c** option changes the characters that are *not* in the first set; and the **-s** option squeezes out repeated characters. The net effect is to replace all characters that are not a letter or an apostrophe with a newline.

Once you have isolated the words, one per line, it is a simple matter to sort them. Just use the **sort** program with **-u** (unique) to eliminate duplicate lines, and **-f** (fold) to ignore differences between upper and lower case. You can then use **wc -l** to count the number of lines. Here, then, is the complete pipeline:

```
cat greek roman | tr -cs [:alpha:]\' "\n" | sort -fu | wc -l
```

More generally:

```
cat file1... | tr -cs [:alpha:]\' "\n" | sort -fu | wc -l
```

In this way, a single Unix pipeline can count how many unique words are contained in a set of input files. If you want to save the list of words, all you need to do is redirect the output of the **sort** program:

```
cat file1... | tr -cs [:alpha:]\' "\n" | sort -fu > file
```

NON-INTERACTIVE TEXT EDITING: sed

A text editor is a program that enables you to perform operations on lines of text. Typically, you can insert, delete, make changes, search, and so on. The two most important Unix text editors are **vi** (which we will discuss in Chapter 22), and Emacs. There are also several other, less important, but simpler text editors which we discussed in Chapter 14: **kedit**, **gedit**, Pico and Nano.

The common characteristic of all these programs is that they are interactive. That is, you work with them by opening a file and then entering commands, one after another until you are done. In this section, I am going to introduce you to a text editor called **sed**, which is *non-interactive*.

With a non-interactive text editor, you compose your commands ahead of time. You then send the commands to the program, which carries them out automatically. Using a non-interactive text editor allows you to automate a large variety of tasks that, otherwise, you would have to carry out by hand.

You can use **sed** in two ways. First, you can have **sed** read its input from a file. This allows you to make changes in an existing file automatically. For example, you might want to read a file and change all the occurrences of "harley" to "Harley".

Second, you can use **sed** as a filter in a pipeline. This allows you to edit the output of a program. It also allows you to pipe the output of **sed** to yet another program for further processing.

Before we get started, here is a bit of terminology. When you think of data being sent from one program to another in a pipeline, it conjures up the metaphor of water running along a path. For this reason, when data flows from one program to another, we call it a STREAM. More specifically, when data is read by a program, we call the data an INPUT STREAM. When data is written by a program, we call the data an OUTPUT STREAM.

Of all the filters we have discussed, **sed** is, by far, the most powerful. This is because **sed** is more than a single-purpose program. It is actually an interpreter for a portable, shell-independent language designed to perform text transformations on a stream of data. Hence the name **sed** is an abbreviation of "stream editor".

A full discussion of everything that **sed** can do is beyond the scope of this book. However, the most useful operation you can perform with **sed** is to make simple substitutions, so that is what I will teach you. Still, I am leaving out a lot, so when you get a spare moment, look on the Web for a **sed** tutorial to learn more. If you need a reference, check the man page on your system (**man sed**).

The syntax to use **sed** in this way is:

sed [**-i**] *command* | **-e** *command...* [*file...*]

where *command* is a **sed** command, and *file* is the name of an input file.

To show you what it looks like to use **sed**, here is a typical example in which we change every occurrence of "harley" to "Harley". The input comes from a text file named **names**; the output is written to a file named **newnames**:

```
sed 's/harley/Harley/g' names > newnames
```

I'll explain the details of the actual command in a moment. First, though, we need to talk about input and output files.

The **sed** program reads one line at a time from the data stream, processing all the data from beginning to end, according to a 3-step procedure:

1. Read a line from the input stream.
2. Execute the specified commands, making changes as necessary to the line.
3. Write the line to the output stream.

By default, **sed** writes its output to standard output, which means **sed** does not change the input file. In some cases this is fine, because you don't want to change the original file; you want to redirect standard output to another file. You can see this in the example above. The input comes from **names**, and the output goes to **newnames**. The file **names** is left untouched.

Most of the time, however, you *do* want to change the original file. To do so, you must use the **-i** (in-place) option. This causes **sed** to save its output to a temporary file. Once all the data is processed successfully, **sed** copies the temporary file to the original file. The net effect is to change the original file, but only if **sed** finishes without an error. Here is a typical **sed** command using **-i**:

```
sed -i 's/harley/Harley/g' names
```

In this case, **sed** modifies the input file **names** by changing all occurrence of "harley" to "Harley".*

When you use **sed -i**, you must be careful. The changes you make to the input file are permanent, and there is no "undo" command.

> **HINT**
>
> Before you use **sed** to change a file, it is a good idea to preview the changes by running the program without the **-i** option. For example:
>
> ```
> sed 's/xx/XXX/g' file | less
> ```
>
> This allows you to look at the output, and see if it is what you expected. If so, you can rerun the command with **-i** to make the changes*:
>
> ```
> sed -i 's/xx/XXX/g' file
> ```

USING sed FOR SUBSTITUTIONS

Related filters: **tr**

The power of **sed** comes from the operations you can have it perform. The most important operation is substitution, for which you use the **s** command. There are two forms of the syntax:

[**/***address*|*pattern***/**]**s/***search***/***replacement***/**[**g**]

where *address* is the address of one or more lines within the input stream, *pattern* is a character string, **search** is a regular expression, and *replacement* is the replacement text.

In its simplest form, you use the substitute command by specifying a search string and a replacement string. For example:

---

*The **-i** option is available only with the GNU version of **sed**. If your system does not use the GNU utilities — for example, if you use Solaris — you cannot use **-i**. Instead, to use **sed** to change a file, you must save the output to a temporary file. You then use the **cp** (copy) program to copy the temporary file to the original file, and the **rm** (remove) program to delete the temporary file. For example:
```
sed 's/harley/Harley/g' names > temp
cp temp names
rm temp
```
In other words, you must do by hand what the **-i** option does for you automatically.

**There is a general Unix principle that says, before you make important permanent changes, preview them if possible. We used a similar strategy in Chapter 13 with the history list and with aliases. Both times, we discussed how to avoid deleting the wrong files accidentally by previewing the results before performing the actual deletion.
This principle is so important that I want you to remember it forever or until you die (whichever comes first).

```
s/harley/Harley/
```

This command tells **sed** to search each line of the input stream for the character string "harley". If the string is found, change it to "Harley". By default, **sed** changes only the first occurrence of the search string on each line. For example, let's say the following line is part of the input stream:

```
I like harley.  harley is smart.  harley is great.
```

The above command will change this line to:

```
I like Harley.  harley is smart.  harley is great.
```

If you want to change all occurrences of the search string, type the suffix **g** (for global) at the end of the command:

```
s/harley/Harley/g
```

In our example, adding the **g** causes the original line to be changed to:

```
I like Harley.  Harley is smart.  Harley is great.
```

In my experience, when you use **sed** to make a substitution, you usually want to use **g** to change all the occurrences of the search string, not just the first one in each line. This is why I have included the **g** suffix in all our examples.

So far, we have searched only for simple character strings. However, you can make your search a lot more powerful by using what is called a "regular expression" (often abbreviated as "regex"). Using a regular expression allows you to specify a pattern, which gives you more flexibility. However, regexes can be complex, and it will take you awhile to learn how to use them well.

I won't go into the details of using regular expressions now. In fact, they are so complicated — and so powerful — that I have devoted an entire chapter to them, Chapter 20. Once you have read that chapter, I want you to come back to this section and spend some time experimenting with regular expressions and **sed**. (Be sure to use the handy reference tables in Figures 20-1, 20-2 and 20-3.)

For now, I'll show you just two examples that use regular expressions with **sed**. To start, let's say you have a file named **calendar** that contains information about your plans for the next several months. You want to change all occurrences of the string "mon" or "Mon" to the word "Monday. Here is a command that makes the change by using a regular expression:

```
sed -i 's/[mM]on/Monday/g' calendar
```

To understand this command, all you need to know is that, within a regular expression, the notation **[...]** matches any single element within the brackets, in this case, either an "m" or an "M". Thus, the search string is either "mon" or "Mon".

This second example is a bit trickier. Earlier in the chapter, when we discussed the **tr** program, we talked about how Unix, Windows, and the Macintosh all use different characters to mark the end of a line of text. Unix uses a newline (**^J**); Windows uses a return followed by a newline (**^M^J**); and the Macintosh uses a return (**^M**). (These characters are discussed in detail in Chapter 7.)

During the discussion, I showed you how to convert a text file in Macintosh format to Unix format. You do so by using **tr** to change all the returns to newlines:

```
tr '\r' '\n' < macfile > unixfile
```

But what do you do if you have a text file in Windows format and you want to use the file with Unix? In other words, how do you change the "return newline" at the end of each line of text to a simple newline? You can't use **tr**, because you need to change two characters (**^M^J**)into one (**^J**); **tr** can only change one character into another character.

We can, however, use **sed**, because **sed** can change anything into anything. To create the command, we use the fact that the return character (**^M**) will be at the end of the line, just before the newline (**^J**). All we need to do is find and delete the **^M**.

Here are two commands that will do the conversion. The first command reads its input from a file named **winfile**, and writes the output to a file named **unixfile**. The second command uses **-i** to change the original file itself:

```
sed 's/.$//' winfile > unixfile
sed -i 's/.$//' winfile
```

So how does this work? Within a regular expression, a **.** (dot) character matches any single character; the **$** (dollar sign) character matches the end of a line. Thus, the search string **.$** refers to the character just before the newline.

Look carefully at the replacement string. Notice that it is empty. This tells **sed** to change the search string to nothing. That is, we are telling **sed** to delete the search string. This has the effect of removing the spurious return character from each line in the file.

If you have never used regular expressions before, I don't expect you to feel completely comfortable with the last several commands. However, I promise you, by the time you finish Chapter 20, these examples, and others like them, will be very easy to understand.

HINT

To delete a character string with **sed**, you search for the string and replace it with nothing.

This is an important technique to remember, as you can use it with any program that allows search and replace operations. (In fact, you will often use this technique within a text editor.)

TELLING sed TO OPERATE ONLY ON SPECIFIC LINES

By default, **sed** performs its operations on every line in the data stream. To change this, you can preface your command with an "address". This tells **sed** to operate only on the lines with that address. An address has the following syntax:

```
number[,number] | /regex/
```

where *number* is a line number, and *regex* is a regular expression.

In its simplest form, an address is a single line number. For example, the following command changes only the 5th line of the data stream:

```
sed '5s/harley/Harley/g' names
```

To specify a range of lines, separate the two line numbers with a comma. For example, the following command changes lines 5 through 10:

```
sed '5,10s/harley/Harley/g' names
```

As a convenience, you can designate the last line of the data stream by the **$** (dollar sign) character. For example, to change only the last line of the data stream, you would use:

```
sed '$s/harley/Harley/g' names
```

To change lines 5 through the last line, you would use:

```
sed '5,$s/harley/Harley/g' names
```

As an alternative to specifying line numbers, you can use a regular expression or a character string* enclosed in **/** (slash) characters. This tells **sed** to process only those lines that contain the specified pattern. For example, to make a change to only those lines that contain the string "OK", you would use:

```
sed '/OK/s/harley/Harley/g' names
```

Here is a more complex example. The following command changes only those lines that contain 2 digits in a row:

```
sed '/[0-9][0-9]/s/harley/Harley/g' names
```

(The notation **[0-9]** refers to a single digit from 0 to 9. See Chapter 20 for the details.)

USING VERY LONG sed COMMANDS

As I mentioned earlier, **sed** is actually an interpreter for a text-manipulation programming language. As such, you can write programs — consisting of as many **sed** commands as you want — which you can store in files and run whenever you want.

To do so, you identify the program file by using the **-f** command. For example, to run the **sed** program stored in a file named **instructions**, using data from a file named **input**, you would use:

```
sed -f instructions input
```

The use of **sed** to write programs, alas, is beyond the scope of this book. In this chapter, we are concentrating on how to use **sed** as a filter. Nevertheless, there will be times when you will want **sed** to perform several operations, in effect, to run a tiny program. When this need arises, you can specify as many **sed** commands as you want, as long as you precede each one by the **-e** (editing command) option. Here is an example.

---

*As we will discuss in Chapter 20, character strings are considered to be regular expressions.

You have a file named **calendar** in which you keep your schedule. Within the file, you have various abbreviations you would like to expand. In particular, you want to change "mon" to "Monday". The command to use is:

```
sed -i 's/mon/Monday/g' calendar
```

However, you also want to change "tue" to "Tuesday". This requires two separate **sed** commands, both of which must be preceded by the **-e** option:

```
sed -i -e 's/mon/Monday/g' -e 's/tue/Tuesday/g' calendar
```

By now, you can see the pattern. You are going to need seven separate **sed** commands, one for each day of the week. This, however, will require a *very* long command line.

As we discussed in Chapter 13, the best way to enter a very long command is to break it onto multiple lines. All you have to do is type a \ (backslash) before you press the <Return> key. The backslash quotes the newline, which allows you to break the command onto more than one line.

As an example, here is a long **sed** command that changes the abbreviations for all seven days of the week. Notice that all the lines, except the last one, are continued. What you see here is, in reality, one very long command line:

```
sed -i \
-e 's/mon/Monday/g' \
-e 's/tue/Tuesday/g' \
-e 's/wed/Wednesday/g' \
-e 's/thu/Thursday/g' \
-e 's/fri/Friday/g' \
-e 's/sat/Saturday/g' \
-e 's/sun/Sunday/g' \
calendar
```

HINT

When you type \<Return> to continue a line, most shells display a special prompt, called the SECONDARY PROMPT, to indicate that a command is being continued.

Within the Bourne Shell family (Bash, Korn Shell), the default secondary prompt is a **>** (greater-than) character. You can change the secondary prompt by modifying the **PS2** shell variable (although most people don't).

Within the C-Shell family, only the Tcsh has a secondary prompt. By default, it is a **?** (question mark). You can change the secondary prompt by modifying the **prompt2** shell variable.

(The commands to modify shell variables are explained in Chapter 12. Putting such commands in one of your initialization files is discussed in Chapter 14.)

C H A P T E R   1 9   E X E R C I S E S

REVIEW QUESTIONS

1. Of all the filters, **grep** is the most important. What does **grep** do? Why is it especially useful in a pipeline? Explain the meaning of the following options: **-c, -i, -l, -L, -n, -r, -s, -v, -w** and **-x**.

2. What two tasks can the **sort** program perform? Explain the meaning of the following options: **-d, -f, -n, -o, -r** and **-u**. Why is the **-o** option necessary?

3. What is a collating sequence? What is a locale? What is the connection between the two?

4. What four tasks can the **uniq** program perform?

5. What three tasks can the **tr** program perform? When using **tr**, what special codes do you use to represent: backspace, tab, newline/linefeed, return and backslash.

APPLYING YOUR KNOWLEDGE

1. As we will discuss in Chapter 23, the **/etc** directory is used to hold configuration files (explained in Chapter 6). Create a command that looks through all the files in the **/etc** directory, searching for lines that contain the word "root". The output should be displayed one screenful at a time. Hint: To specify the file names, use the pattern **/etc/***.

    Searching through the files in the **/etc** directory will generate a few spurious error messages. Create a second version of the command that suppresses all such messages.

2. Someone bets you that, without using a dictionary, you can't find more than 5 English words that begin with the letters "book". You are, however, allowed a single Unix command. What command should you use?

3. You are running an online dating service for your school. You have three files containing user registrations: **reg1**, **reg2** and **reg3**. Within these files, each line contains information about a single person (no pun intended).

    Create a pipeline that processes all three files, selecting only those lines that contain the word "female" or "male" (your choice). After eliminating all duplications, the results should be saved in a file named **prospects**.

    Once this is done, create a second pipeline that displays a list of all the people (male or female) who have registered more than once. Hint: Look for duplicate lines within the files.

4. You have a text file named **data**. Create a pipeline that displays all instances of double words, for example, "hello hello". (Assume that a "word" consists of consecutive upper- or lowercase letters.) Hint: First create a list of all the words, one per line. Then pipe the output to a program that searches for consecutive identical lines.

FOR FURTHER THOUGHT

1. In an earlier question, I observed that **grep** is the most important filter, and I asked you to explain why it is especially useful in a pipeline. Considering your answer to that question, what is it about the nature of human beings that makes **grep** seem so powerful and useful?

2. Originally, Unix was based on American English and American data processing standards (such as the ASCII code). With the development of internationalization tools and standards (such as locales), Unix can now be used by people from a variety of cultures. Such users are able to interact with Unix in their own languages using their own data processing conventions. What are some of the tradeoffs in expanding Unix in this way? List three advantages and three disadvantages.

3. In this chapter, we talked about the **tr** and **sed** programs in detail. As you can see, both of these programs can be very useful. However, they are complex tools that require a lot of time and effort to master. For some people, this is not a problem. For many other people, however, taking the time to learn how to use a complex tool well is an uncomfortable experience. Why do you think this is so? Should all tools be designed to be easy to learn?

4. Comment on the following statement: There is no program in the entire Unix toolbox that can't be mastered in less time than it takes to learn how to play the piano well.

CHAPTER 20
REGULAR EXPRESSIONS

Regular expressions are used to specify patterns of characters. The most common use for regular expressions is to search for strings of characters. As such, regular expressions are often used in search-and-replace operations.

As a tool, regular expressions are so useful and so powerful that, literally, there are entire books and Web sites devoted to the topic. Certainly, mastering the art of using regular expressions is one of the most important things you can do to become proficient with Unix.

It is possible to create regular expressions that are very complex. However, most of the time, the regular expressions you require will be simple and straightforward, so all you need to do is learn a few simple rules and then practice, practice, practice. The goal of this chapter is to get you started.

Note: Before we start, there is one thing I want to mention. Within this chapter, I will be showing you a great many examples using the **grep** command (Chapter 19). If you find that some of the regular expression features don't work with your version of **grep**, you may have to use **egrep** or **grep -E** instead. In such cases, you can set up an alias to use one of these variations automatically. You will find the details in Chapter 19, as part of the discussion of **grep** and **egrep**. The reasons for this will be clear when we talk about extended and basic regular expressions later in the chapter.

INTRODUCING REGULAR EXPRESSIONS

Within this chapter, I will be showing you examples of regular expressions using the **grep** command, which we discussed in Chapter 19. Although these are convenient examples, you should know that regular expressions can be used with many different Unix programs, such as the **vi** and Emacs text editors, **less**, **sed**, and many more. In addition, regular expressions can be used with many programming languages, such as Awk, C, C++, C#, Java, Perl, PHP, Python, Ruby, Tcl and VB.NET.

The concepts I will be teaching you are typical of regular expressions in general. Once you master the basic rules, all you will ever need to learn are a few variations as the need arises. Although the more esoteric features of regular expressions can vary from one program to another — for example, Perl has a whole set of advanced features — the basic ideas are always the same. If you ever have a problem, all you have to do is check the documentation for the program you are using.

A REGULAR EXPRESSION, often abbreviated as REGEX or RE, is a compact way of specifying a pattern of characters. For example, consider the following set of the three character strings:

harley1   harley2   harley3

As a regular expression, you could represent this set of patterns as **harley[123]**.

Here is another example. You want to describe the set of character strings consisting of the uppercase letter "H", followed by any number of lowercase letters, followed by the lowercase letter "y". The regular expression to use is **H[[:lower:]]*y**.

As you can see, the power of regular expressions comes from using metacharacters and abbreviations that have special meanings. We will discuss the details in the following sections. For reference, the syntax for using regular expressions is summarized in Figures 20-1, 20-2 and 20-3. Take a moment to skim them now, and you can refer back to them, as necessary, as you read the rest of the chapter.

THE ORIGIN OF REGULAR EXPRESSIONS

The term "regular expression" comes from computer science and refers to a set of rules for specifying patterns. The name comes from the work of the eminent American mathematician and computer scientist Stephen Kleene (1909–1994). (His name is pronounced "Klej-nee".)

In the early 1940s, two neuroscientists, Walter Pitts and Warren McCulloch developed a mathematical model of how they believed neurons (nerve cells) worked. As part of their

METACHARACTER	MEANING
.	match any single character except **newline**
^	anchor: match the beginning of a line
$	anchor: match the end of a line
\<	anchor: match the beginning of a word
\>	anchor: match the end of a word
[*list*]	character class: match any character in *list*
[^*list*]	character class: match any character not in *list*
( )	group: treat as a single unit
I	alternation: match one of the choices
\	quote: interpret a metacharacter literally

FIGURE 20-1: Regular expressions: Basic matching

A regular expression is a compact way of specifying a pattern of characters. Within a regular expression, ordinary characters match themselves, and certain metacharacters have a special meaning. This table shows the metacharacters that are used to carry out the basic pattern matching functions.

model, they used very simple, imaginary machines, called automata. In the mid-1950s, Kleene developed a way of describing automata mathematically using what he called "regular sets": sets that could be described using a small number of simple properties. Kleene then created a simple notation, which he called regular expressions, that could be used to describe such sets.

In 1966, Ken Thompson — the programmer who would later develop Unix — joined Bell Labs. One of the first things he did was to program a version of the QED text editor, which he had used at U.C. Berkeley. Thompson extended QED significantly, adding, among other features, a pattern-matching facility that used an enhanced form of Kleene's regular expressions. Until that time, text editors could only search for exact character strings. Now, using regular expressions, the QED editor could search for patterns as well.

OPERATOR	MEANING
*	match zero or more times
+	match one or more times
?	match zero or one times
{n}	bound: match n times
{n,}	bound: match n or more times
{0,m}	bound: match m or fewer times
{,m}	bound: match m or fewer times
{n,m}	bound: match n to m times

FIGURE 20-2: Regular expressions: Repetition operators
Within a regular expression, the following metacharacters, called repetition operators, can be used to match multiple instances of specific characters.
Note: Some programs do not support { ,m} because it is not standard.

CLASS	MEANING	SIMILAR TO...
[:lower:]	lowercase letters	a-z
[:upper:]	uppercase letters	A-Z
[:alpha:]	upper- and lowercase letters	A-Za-z
[:alnum:]	upper- and lowercase letters, numbers	A-Za-z0-9
[:digit:]	numbers	0-9
[:punct:]	punctuation characters	—
[:blank:]	space or Tab (whitespace)	—

FIGURE 20-3: Regular expressions: Predefined character classes
Regular expressions can contain character classes to define a set of characters. For convenience, there are a number of predefined character classes you can use as abbreviations. This table shows the most important ones. Note that the brackets and colons are part of the name.
The rightmost column shows ranges that are equivalent to some of the predefined character classes. You can use these ranges instead of the class names if your system uses the C collating sequence. To ensure that this is the case, you can set the environment variable LC_COLLATE to the value C. (See text for details.)

In 1969, Thompson created the first, primitive version of Unix (see Chapters 1 and 2). Not long afterwards, he wrote the first Unix editor, **ed** (pronounced "ee-dee"), which he designed to use a simplified form of regular expressions less powerful than those he had used with QED. The **ed** program was part of what was called UNIX Version 1, which was released in 1971.

The popularity of **ed** led to the use of regular expressions with **grep** and, later, with many other Unix programs. Today, regular expressions are used widely, not only within Unix, but throughout the world of computing. (Interestingly enough, the features Thompson left out when he wrote **ed** have now been added back in.)

> **HINT**
>
> The next time you are at a Unix party and people start talking about regular expressions, you can casually remark that they correspond to Type 3 Grammars within the Chomsky hierarchy. Once you have everyone's attention, you can then explain that it is possible to construct a simple mapping between any regular expression and an NFA (nondeterministic finite automaton), because every regular expression has finite length and, thus, a finite number of operators.
>
> Within moments, you will be the most popular person in the room.*

BASIC AND EXTENDED REGULAR EXPRESSIONS

This section is a reference and, on your first reading, it may be a bit confusing. Don't worry. Later, after you have read the rest of the chapter and practiced a bit, everything will make sense.

As we discussed in the previous section, regular expressions became part of Unix when Ken Thompson created the **ed** text editor, which was released with UNIX Version 1 in 1971. The original regular expression facility was useful, but limited, and over the years, it has been extended significantly. This has given rise to a variety of regex systems of varying complexity, which can be confusing to beginners.

For practical purposes, you only need to remember a few fundamental ideas. I'd like to take a moment to discuss these ideas now, so you won't have a problem later on when you practice with the examples in this chapter.

Unix supports two major variations of regular expressions: a modern version and an older, obsolete version. The modern version is the EXTENDED REGULAR EXPRESSION or ERE. It is the current standard, and is part of the overall IEEE 1003.2 standard (part of POSIX; see Chapter 11).

The older version is the BASIC REGULAR EXPRESSION or BRE. It is a more primitive type of regular expression that was used for many years, until it was replaced by the 1003.2 standardization. Basic regular expressions are less powerful than extended regular expressions, and have a slightly more confusing syntax. For these reasons, BREs are now considered obsolete. They are retained only for compatibility with older programs.

In this chapter, I will be teaching you extended regular expressions, the default for modern Unix and Linux systems. However, from time to time, you will encounter an old

---

*Well, it's always worked for me.

program that accepts only basic regular expressions. In such cases, I want you to know what you are doing, so here are a few words of explanation.

The two commands most likely to give you a problem are **grep** and **sed** (both of which are covered in Chapter 19). To see what type of regular expressions they support on your system, check your man pages:

```
man grep
man sed
```

If your system uses the GNU utilities — which is the case with Linux and FreeBSD — you will find that some commands have been updated to offer a **-E** option, which allows you to use extended regular expressions. For example, this is the case with **grep**. In general, you can check if a command offers the **-E** option, either by looking at its man page, or by using the **--help** option to display its syntax (discussed in Chapter 10).

HINT

With Linux and FreeBSD, some commands offer a **-E** option to allow you to use extended regular expressions. Since extended regexes are always preferable, you should get in the habit of using **-E**.

If you use such a command regularly, you can create an alias to force **-E** to be used automatically. For an example of how to do this, see the discussion of **grep** and **egrep** in Chapter 19.

Even though extended regular expressions are the modern standard, and even though some programs offer the **-E** option, there will be times when you have no choice but to use basic regular expressions. For example, you may want to use an older program that, on your system, only supports basic regular expressions. (The most common example of this is **sed**.)

In such cases, it behooves you to know what to do, so I'm going to take a moment to explain the difference between basic and extended regular expressions. Of course, this discussion is a bit premature, because we haven't, as yet, talked about the technical details of regexes. However, as I mentioned earlier, if there's anything you don't understand on first reading, you will later, when you come back to it.

As I mentioned earlier in the chapter, the power of regular expressions comes from using metacharacters that have special meanings. We will spend a lot of time in this chapter talking about how to use these metacharacters. (For reference, they are summarized in Figures 20-1, 20-2 and 20-3.)

The chief difference between basic and extended regular expressions is that, with basic regexes, certain metacharacters cannot be used and others must be quoted with a backslash. (Quoting is discussed in Chapter 13.) The metacharacters that cannot be used are the question mark, plus sign, and vertical bar:

```
?  +  |
```

The metacharacters that must be escaped are the brace brackets and parentheses:

```
{  }  (  )
```

EXTENDED REGEX	BASIC REGEX	MEANING
{ }	\{ \}	define a bound (brace brackets)
( )	\(\)	define a group (parentheses)
?	\{0,1\}	match zero or one times
+	\{1,\}	match one or more times
|	—	alternation: match one of the choices
[:*name*:]	—	predefined character class

FIGURE 20-4: Extended and basic regular expressions

The modern standard for regular expressions is the extended regular expression (ERE), defined as part of the 1003.2 POSIX standard. The extended regular expression replaces the older basic regular expression (BRE). Whenever you have a choice, you should use EREs.

For reference, this table shows the limitations of basic regular expressions, which can be summarized as follows:

1. *Brace brackets must be quoted with a backslash.*
2. *Parentheses must be quoted with a backslash.*
3. *You can't use ?, but it can be simulated with \{0,1\}.*
4. *You can't use +, but it can be simulated with \{1,\}.*
5. *You can't use | (vertical bar).*
6. *You can't use predefined character classes.*

For reference, I have summarized these limitations in Figure 20-4. This summary won't mean much the first time you look at it, but it will make sense by the time you finish the chapter.

MATCHING LINES AND WORDS

As I explained earlier, a regular expression (or regex) is a compact way of specifying a pattern of characters. To create a regular expression, you put together ordinary characters and metacharacters according to certain rules. You then use the regex to search for the character strings you want to find.

When a regular expression corresponds to a particular string of characters, we say that it MATCHES the string. For example, the regex **harley[123]** matches any one of **harley1**, **harley2** or **harley3**. For now, you don't need to worry about the details, except to realize that **harley** and **123** are ordinary characters, and [and] are metacharacters. Another way of saying this is that, within the regular expression, **harley** and **123** match themselves, while the [and] (bracket) characters have a special meaning. Eventually, you will learn all the metacharacters and their special meanings.

In this section, we'll cover certain metacharacters, called ANCHORS, that are used to match locations at the beginning or end of a character string. For example, the regex **harley$** matches the string **harley**, but only if it comes at the end of a line. This is because **$** is a metacharacter that acts as an anchor by matching the end of a line. (Don't worry about the details for now.)

To begin our adventures with regular expressions, we will start with the basic rule: All ordinary characters, such as letters and numbers, match themselves. Here are a few examples, to show you how it works.

Let's say that you have a file named **data** that contains the following four lines:

```
Harley is smart
Harley
I like Harley
the dog likes the cat
```

You want to use **grep** to find all the lines that contain "Harley" anywhere in the line. You would use:

```
grep Harley data
```

In this case, **Harley** is actually a regular expression that will cause **grep** to select lines 1, 2 and 3, but not line 4:

```
Harley is smart
Harley
I like Harley
```

This is nothing new, but it does show how, within a regular expression, an **H** matches an "H", an **a** matches an "a", an **r** matches an "r", and so on. All regexes derive from this basic idea.

To expand the power of regular expressions, you can use anchors to specify the location of the pattern for which you are looking. The ^ (circumflex) metacharacter is an anchor that matches the beginning of a line. Thus, to search for only those lines that start with "Harley", you would use:

```
grep '^Harley' data
```

In our example, this command would select lines 1 and 2, but not 3 or 4 (because they don't start with "Harley"):

```
Harley is smart
Harley
```

You will notice that, in the last command, I have quoted the regular expression. You should do this whenever you are using a regex that contains metacharacters, to ensure that the shell will leave these characters alone and pass them on to your program (in this case, **grep**). If you are not sure if you need to quote the regular expression, go ahead and do it anyway. It can't cause a problem.

You will notice that, to be safe, I used strong quotes (single quotes) rather than weak quotes (double quotes). This ensures that all metacharacters, not just some of them, will be quoted properly. (If you need to review the difference between strong quotes and weak quotes, see Chapter 13.)

The anchor to match the end of a line is the **$** (dollar) metacharacter. For example, to search for only those lines that end with "Harley", you would use:

```
grep 'Harley$' data
```

In our example, this would select only lines 2 and 3:

```
Harley
I like Harley
```

You can combine ^ and $ in the same regular expression as long as what you are doing makes sense. For example, to search for all the lines that consist entirely of "Harley", you would use both anchors:

```
grep '^Harley$' data
```

In our example, this would select line 2:

```
Harley
```

Using both anchors with nothing in between is an easy way to look for empty lines. For example, the following command counts all the empty lines in the file **data**:

```
grep '^$' data | wc -l
```

In a similar fashion, there are anchors you can use to match the beginning or end of a word, or both. To match the beginning of a word, you use the 2-character combination **\<**. To match the end of a word, you use **\>**.

For example, say you want to search a file named **data** for all the lines that contain the letters "kn", but only if they occur at the beginning of a word. You would use:

```
grep '\<kn' data
```

To find the letters "ow", but only at the end of a word, use:

```
grep 'ow\>' data
```

To search for complete words, use both **\<** and **\>**. For example, to search for "know", but only as a complete word, use:

```
grep '\<know\>' data
```

This command would select the line:

```
I know who you are, and I saw what you did.
```

But it would not select the line:

```
Who knows what evil lurks in the hearts of men?
```

As a convenience, on systems that use the GNU utilities — such as Linux and FreeBSD — you can use **\b** as an alternate anchor to take the place of both **\<** and **\>**. For example, the following commands are equivalent:

```
grep '\<know\>' data
grep '\bknow\b' data
```

You can think of **\b** as meaning "boundary marker".

It is up to you to choose which word-boundary anchors you like better. I use **\<** and **\>** because, to my eye, they are easier to see. However, many people prefer **\b**, because it is easier to type, and you can use the same anchor at the beginning and end of a word.

When we use regular expressions, the definition of a "word" is more flexible than in English. Within a regex, a WORD is a self-contained, contiguous sequence of characters consisting of letters, numbers, or _ (underscore) characters. Thus, within a regex, all of the following are considered to be words:

fussbudget   Weedly   1952   error_code_5

This same definition holds within many Unix programs. For example, **grep** uses this definition when you use the **-w** option to match complete words.

HINT

When you use **grep** to look for complete words, it is often easier to use the **-w** (word) option than it is to use multiple instances of **\<** and **\>**, or **\b**.

For example, the following three commands are equivalent:

```
grep -w 'cat' data
grep '\<cat\>' data
grep '\bcat\b' data
```

MATCHING CHARACTERS; CHARACTER CLASSES

Within a regular expression, the metacharacter **.** (dot) matches any single character except newline. (In Unix, a newline marks the end of a line; see Chapter 7.)

For example, say you want to search a file named **data** for all the lines that contain the following pattern: the letters "Har", followed by any two characters, followed by the letter "y". You would use the command:

grep 'Har..y' data

This command would find lines that contain, for example:

harley   harxxy   harlly   har12y

You will find the **.** metacharacter to be very useful, and you will use it a lot. Nevertheless, there will be times when you will want to be more specific: a **.** will match *any* character, but you may want to match particular characters. For example, you might want to search for an uppercase "H" followed by either "a" or "A". In such cases, you can specify the characters you want to find by placing them within square brackets **[ ]**. Such a construction is called a CHARACTER CLASS.

For example, to search the file **data** for all lines that contain the letter "H", followed by either "a" or "A", you would use:

grep 'H[aA]' data

Before moving on, I want to make an important point. Strictly speaking, the character class does not include the brackets. For example, in the previous command, the character class is **aA**, not **[aA]**. Although the brackets are required when you use a character class, they are not considered to be part of the character class itself. This distinction will be important later when we talk about special abbreviations called "predefined character classes".

To continue, here is an example that uses more than one character class in the same regular expression. This following command searches for lines that contain the word "license", even if it is misspelled by mixing up the "c" and the "s":

```
grep 'li[cs]en[cs]e' data
```

A more useful command uses **\<** and **\>** or **\b** to match only whole words:

```
grep '\<li[cs]en[cs]e\>' data
grep '\bli[cs]en[cs]e\b' data
```

Those two commands will match any of the following:

```
licence   license   lisence   lisense
```

PREDEFINED CHARACTER CLASSES; RANGES

Some sets of characters are so common, they are given names to make them easy to use. These sets are called PREDEFINED CHARACTER CLASSES, and you can see them in Figure 20-3, earlier in the chapter. (Stop and take a look now, before you continue, because I want you to be familiar with the various names and what they mean.)

Using predefined character classes is straightforward except for one odd rule: the brackets are actually part of the name. Thus, when you use them, you must include a second set of brackets to maintain the proper syntax. (You will remember, earlier, I told you that when you use a character class, the outer brackets are *not* part of the class.)

For example, the following command uses **grep** to find all the lines in the file named **data** that contain the number 21 followed by a single lower- or uppercase letter:

```
grep '21[[:alpha:]]' data
```

The next command finds all the lines that contain two uppercase letters in a row, followed by a single digit, followed by one lowercase letter:

```
grep '[[:upper:]][[:upper:]][[:digit:]][[:lower:]]' data
```

Aside from predefined character classes, there is another way to specify a set of letters or numbers. You can use a RANGE of characters, where the first and last characters are separated by a hyphen. For example, to search for all the lines of the file **data** that contain a number from 3 to 7, you can use:

```
grep '[3-7]' data
```

The range **0-9** means the same as **[:digit:]**. For example, to search for lines that contain an uppercase "X", followed by any two digits, you can use either of these commands:

```
grep 'X[0-9][0-9]' data
grep 'X[[:digit:]][[:digit:]]' data
```

To conclude this section, let us consider one more situation: you want to match characters that are *not* within a particular character class. You can do so simply by putting a ^ (circumflex) metacharacter after the initial left bracket. In this context, the ^ acts as a negation operator.

For example, the following command searches a file named **data** for all the lines that contain the letter "X", as long as it is not followed by "a" or "o":

```
grep 'X[^ao]' data
```

The following two commands search for all the lines that contain at least one non-alphabetic character:

```
grep '[^A-Za-z]' data
grep '[^[:alpha:]]' data
```

> **HINT**
>
> The trick to understanding a complex regular expression is to remember that each character class — no matter how complex it might look — represents only a single character.

LOCALES AND COLLATING SEQUENCES: `locale`; THE ASCII CODE

At this point, you might be wondering if you can use other ranges instead of predefined character classes. For example, could you use **a-z** instead of **[:lower:]**? Similarly, could you use **A-Z** instead of **[:upper:]**; or **A-Za-z** instead of **[:alpha:]**; or **a-zA-Z0-9** instead of **[:alnum:]**?

The answer is maybe. On some systems it will work; on others it won't. Before I can explain to you why this is the case, we need to talk about the idea of "locales".

When you write **0-9**, it is an abbreviation for **0123...9**, which only makes sense. However, when you write **a-z**, it does not necessarily mean **abcd...z**. This is because the order of the alphabet on your particular system depends on what is called your "locale", which can vary from one system to another.

Why should this be the case? Before the 1990s, the character encoding used by Unix (and most computer systems) was the ASCII CODE, often referred to as ASCII. The name stands for "American Standard Code for Information Interchange".

The ASCII code was created in 1967. It specifies a 7-bit pattern for every character, 128 in all. These bit patterns range from 0000000 (0 in decimal) to 1111111 (127 in decimal). The ASCII code includes all the control characters we discussed in Chapter 7, as well as 56 printable characters: the letters of the alphabet, numbers and punctuation. The printable characters are as follows. (Note that the first character is a space.)

```
 !"#$%&'()*+,-./0123456789:;<=>?
@ABCDEFGHIJKLMNOPQRSTUVWXYZ[\]^_
`abcdefghijklmnopqrstuvwxyz{|}~
```

The order of the printable characters is the order in which I have listed them above. They range from character #32 (space) to character #126 (tilde). For reference, you can see a chart of the entire ASCII code in Appendix D. (Take a moment to look at it now.)

As a convenience, most Unix systems have a reference page that contains the ASCII code. This is handy, as it allows you to look at the code quickly whenever you want. Unfortunately, the ASCII code page is not standardized, so the way in which you display it depends on which system you are using. See Figure 20-5 for the details.

As we discussed in Chapter 19, within a character coding scheme, the order in which the characters are organized is called a collating sequence. The collating sequence is used whenever you need to put characters in order, for example, when you sort data or when you use a range within a regular expression.

When you use Unix or Linux, the collating sequence your system will use depends on your locale. The concept of a locale is part of the POSIX 1003.2 standard, which we discussed in Chapter 11 and Chapter 19. As I explained in Chapter 19, your locale — which is set by an environment variable — tells your programs which language conventions you want to use. This enables anyone in the world to choose a locale to match his or her local language.

On some Unix systems, the locale is set so that the default collating sequence matches the order of the characters in the ASCII code. In particular, as you can see above, all the uppercase letters are grouped together, and they come before the lowercase letters. This sequence is called the C collating sequence (Chapter 19), because it is used by the C programming language.

With other Unix systems, including many Linux systems, the locale is set in such a way that the default collating sequence groups the upper- and lowercase letters in pairs: **AaBbCcDd...Zz**. The advantage of this collating sequence is that it is easy to search for words or characters in the same order as you would find them in a dictionary. Thus, it is called the dictionary collating sequence (Chapter 19).

With regular expressions, you can run into problems because Unix expands **a-z** and **A-Z** according to whichever collating sequence is used on your system.

If you are using the C collating sequence, all the uppercase letters are in a single group, as are all the lowercase letters. This means that, when you specify all the upper- or lowercase letters, you can use ranges instead of predefined character classes: **A-Z** instead

TYPE OF UNIX	COMMAND TO DISPLAY ASCII CODE PAGE
Linux	`man ascii`
FreeBSD	`less /usr/share/misc/ascii`
Solaris	`less /usr/pub/ascii`

FIGURE 20-5: Displaying the ASCII code

You will find a summary of the ASCII code in Appendix D of this book. For online reference, most Unix systems have a handy page containing the entire ASCII code. Traditionally, this page was stored in a file named **ascii** *in the directory* **/usr/pub/**. *In recent years, the Unix file system has been reorganized on some systems, and the ASCII reference file has been moved to* **/usr/share/misc**. *On other systems, the file has been converted to a page within the online manual. Thus, the way in which you display the ASCII reference page depends on the system you are using.*

of [:upper:]; **a-z** instead of [:lower:]; **A-Za-z** instead of [:alpha:]; and **A-Za-z0-9** instead of [:alnum:]. You can see this in Figure 20-3.

If you are using the dictionary collating sequence, the letters will be in a different order: **AaBbCcDd...Zz**. This means that the ranges will work differently. For example, **a-z** would represent **aBbCc...YyZz**. Notice that the uppercase "A" is missing. (Can you see why?) Similarly, **A-Z** would represent **AaBbCc...YyZ**. Notice the lowercase "z" is missing.

As an example, let's say you want to search the file **data** for all the lines that contain an upper- or lowercase letter from "A" to "E". If your locale uses the C collating sequence, you would use:

```
grep '[A-Ea-e]' data
```

In this case, the regex is equivalent to **ABCDEabcde**, and it is what most experienced Unix users would expect. However, if your locale uses the dictionary collating sequence you would use:

```
grep '[A-e]' data
```

Traditionally, Unix has used the C collating sequence, and many veteran Unix users assume that **a-z** always refers to the lowercase letters (only), and **A-Z** always refers to the uppercase letters (only). However, this is a poor assumption, as some types of Unix, including many Linux distributions, use the dictionary collating sequence by default, not the C collating sequence. However, regardless of which collating sequence happens to be the default for your locale, there is a way to ensure it is the C collating sequence, which is what most Unix users prefer.

First, you need to determine which collating sequence is the default on your system. To do so, create a short file named **data** using the command:

```
cat > data
```

Type the following two lines and then press **^D** to end the command:

```
A
a
```

Now type the following command:

```
grep '[a-z]' data
```

If the output consists of both lines of the file (**A** and **a**), you are using the dictionary collating sequence. If the output consists of only the **a** line, you are using the C collating sequence. (Why is this?)

If your system uses the C collating sequence, you don't need to do anything. However, please read through the rest of this section, as one day, you will encounter this problem on another system.

If your system uses the dictionary collating sequence, you will probably want to change to the C collating sequence. To do this, you set an environment variable named

LC_COLLATE to either **C** or **POSIX**. Either of the following commands will do the job with the Bourne Shell family:

```
export LC_COLLATE=C
export LC_COLLATE=POSIX
```

With the C-Shell family, you would use either of the following:

```
setenv LC_COLLATE C
setenv LC_COLLATE POSIX
```

To make the change permanent, all you need to do is put one of these commands into your login file. (The login file is discussed in Chapter 14; environment variables are discussed in Chapter 12.)

Once your system uses the C collating sequence, you can substitute the appropriate ranges for the predefined character classes, as shown in Figure 20-3. For the rest of this chapter, I will assume that you are, indeed, using the C collating sequence (so, if you are not, put the appropriate command in your login file right now).

To display information about locales on your system, you can use the **locale** command. The syntax is:

```
locale [-a]
```

Your locale is maintained by setting a number of standard global variables, including **LC_COLLATE**. To see the current value of these variables, enter the command by itself:

```
locale
```

To display a list of all the available locales on your system, use the **-a** (all) option:

```
locale -a
```

USING RANGES AND PREDEFINED CHARACTER CLASSES

Once you make sure you are using the C collating sequence (as described in the previous section) you have some flexibility. When you want to match all the upper- or lowercase letters, you can use either a predefined character class or a range.

For example, the following two commands both search a file named **data** for all the lines that contain the letter "H", followed by any lowercase letter from "a" to "z". For example, "Ha", "Hb", "Hc", and so on:

```
grep 'H[[:lower:]]' data
grep 'H[a-z]' data
```

The next two commands search for all the lines that contain a single upper- or lowercase letter, followed by a single digit, followed by a lowercase letter:

```
grep '[A-Za-z][0-9][a-z]' data
grep '[[:alpha:]][[:digit:]][[:lower:]]' data
```

Here is a more complex example that searches for Canadian postal codes. These codes have the format "letter number letter space number letter number", where all the letters are uppercase, for example, **M5P 3G4**. Take a moment to analyze both these commands until you understand them completely:

```
grep '[A-Z][0-9][A-Z] [0-9][A-Z][0-9]' data
grep '[[:upper:]][[:digit:]][[:upper:]] [[:digit:]][[:
upper:]][[:digit:]]' data
```

The choice of which type of character class to use — a range or a predefined name — is up to you. Many old-time Unix users prefer to use ranges, because that's what they learned. Moreover, ranges are easier to type than names, which require colons and extra brackets. (See the previous example.)

However, names are more readable, which makes them better to use in shell scripts. Also, names are designed to always work properly, regardless of your locale or your language, so they are more portable. For example, say you are working with text that contains non-English characters, such as "é" (an "e" with an acute accent). By using **[:lower:]**, you will be sure to pick up the "é". This might not be the case if you used **a-z**.

REPETITION OPERATORS

Within a regular expression, a single character (such as **A**) or a character class (such as **A-Za-z** or **[:alpha:]**) matches only one character. To match more than one character at a time, you use a REPETITION OPERATOR.

The most useful repetition operator is the ***** (star) metacharacter. A ***** matches zero or more occurrences of the preceding character. (See Chapter 10 for a discussion of the idea of "zero or more".) For example, let's say you want to search a file named **data** for all the lines that contain the uppercase letter "H", followed by zero or more lowercase letters. You can use either of the following commands:

```
grep 'H[a-z]*' data
grep 'H[[:lower:]]*' data
```

These commands will find patterns like:

```
H   Har   Harley   Harmonica   Harpoon   HarDeeHarHar
```

The most common combination is to use a **.** (dot) followed by a *****. This will match zero or more occurrences of any character. For example, the following command searches for lines that contain "error" followed by zero or more characters, followed by "code":

```
grep 'error.*code' data
```

As an example, this command would select the following lines:

```
Be sure to document the error code.
Don't make an error while you are writing code.
Remember that errorcode #5 means "Too many parentheses".
```

The following example searches for lines that contain a colon, followed by zero or more occurrences of any other characters, followed by another colon:

```
grep ':.*:' data
```

At times, you may want to match one or more characters, rather than zero or more. To do so, use the **+** (plus) metacharacter instead of *****. For example, the following commands search the file **data** and select any lines that contain the letters "variable" followed by one or more numbers:

```
grep 'variable[0-9]+' data
grep 'variable[[:digit:]]+' data
```

These commands would select any of the following lines:

```
You can use variable1 if you want.
error in variable3x
address12, variable12 and number12
```

They would not select the lines:

```
Remember to use variable 1, 2 or 3.
variableX3 is the one to use
The next thing to do is set Variable417.
```

What if you want to match either an uppercase "V" or lowercase "v" at the beginning of the pattern? Just change the first letter to a character class:

```
grep '[vV]ariable[0-9]+' data
```

The next repetition operator is the **?** (question mark) metacharacter. This allows you to match either zero or one instance of something. Another way to say this is that a **?** makes something optional. For example, let's say you want to find all the lines in the file **data** that contain the word "color" (American spelling) or "colour" (British spelling). You can use:

```
grep 'colou?r' data
```

The final repetition operators let you specify as many occurrences as you want by using brace brackets to create what is called a BOUND. There are four different types of bounds. They are:

{*n*}	match exactly *n* times
{*n*,}	match *n* or more times
{,*m*}	match *m* or fewer times *[non-standard]*
{*n*,*m*}	match *n* to *m* times

Note: The third construction **{,*m*}** is not part of the POSIX 1003.2 standard, and will not work with some programs.

Here are some examples. The first example matches exactly 3 digits; the second matches at least 3 digits; the third matches 5 or fewer digits; the final example matches 3 to 5 digits.

```
[0-9]{3}
[0-9]{3,}
[0-9]{,5}
[0-9]{3,5}
```

To show you how you might use a bound with **grep**, the following command finds all the lines in a file named **data** that contain either 2- or 3-digit numbers. Notice the use of **\<** and **\>** to match complete numbers:

```
grep '\<[0-9]{2,3}\>' data
```

So far, we have used repetition operators with only single characters. You can use them with multiple characters if you enclose the characters in parentheses. Such a pattern is called a GROUP. By creating a group, you can treat a sequence of characters as a single unit. For example, to match the letters "xyz" 5 times in a row, you can use either of the following regular expressions:

```
xyzxyzxyzxyzxyz
(xyz){5}
```

The last repetition operator, the **|** (vertical bar) character, allows us to use alternation. That is, we can match either one thing or another. For example, say we want to search a file for all the lines that contain any of the following words:

```
cat   dog   bird   hamster
```

Using alternation, it's easy:

```
grep 'cat|dog|bird|hamster' data
```

Obviously, this is a powerful tool. However, in this case, can you see a problem? We are searching for character strings, not complete words. Thus, the above command would also find lines that contain words like "concatenate" or "dogmatic". To find only complete words, we need to explicitly match word boundaries:

```
grep '\<(cat|dog|bird|hamster)\>' data
```

Notice the use of the parenthesis to create a group. This allows us to treat the entire pattern as a single unit. Take a moment to think about this until it makes sense.

To finish this section, I will explain one last metacharacter. As you know, metacharacters have special meaning within a regular expression. The question arises: What if you want to match one of these characters? For example, what if you want to match an actual ***** (star), **.** (dot) or **|** (vertical bar) character?

The answer is you can quote the character with a \ (backslash). This changes it from a metacharacter to a regular character, so it will be interpreted literally. For example, to search the file **data** for all the lines that contain a "$" character, use:

```
grep '\$' data
```

If you want to search for a backslash character itself, just use two backslashes in a row. For example, to find all the lines that contain the characters "*", followed by any number of characters, followed by one or more letters, followed by "$", use:

```
grep '\\\*.*[A-Za-z]+\$' data
```

HOW TO UNDERSTAND A COMPLEX REGULAR EXPRESSION

Once you understand the rules, most regular expressions are easy to write. However, they can be hard to read, especially if they are lengthy. In fact, experienced Unix people often have trouble understanding regular expressions they themselves have written*. Here is a simple technique I have developed over the years to help understand otherwise cryptic regexes.

When you encounter a regular expression that gives you trouble, write it on a piece of paper. Then break the regex into parts, writing the parts vertically, one above the other. Take each part in turn and write its meaning on the same line. For example, consider the regex:

```
\\\*.*[A-Za-z]+\$
```

We can break this down as follows:

```
        \\      →   a \ (backslash) character
        \*      →   a * (star) character
        .*      →   any number of other characters
 [A-Za-z]+      →   one or more upper- or lowercase letters
        \$      →   a $ (dollar) character
```

When you analyze a regular expression in this way, you are, in effect, parsing it, similar to what your program does when it processes the command. With a little practice, you will find that even the most complex regexes become understandable.

SOLVING THREE INTERESTING PUZZLES; THE DICTIONARY FILE

To conclude our discussion, I will show you three interesting puzzles that we will solve using regular expressions. To solve the first two puzzles, we will use a file that, in itself, is interesting, the DICTIONARY FILE.

The dictionary file, which has been included with Unix from the very beginning, contains a very long list of English words, including most of the words commonly found in a concise dictionary. Each word is on a line by itself and the lines are in alphabetical order, which makes the file easy to search. Once you get used to using the dictionary file

---

*Thus, the old riddle, "If God can do anything, can he create a regular expression even he can't understand?"
No doubt this was what Thomas Aquinas was referring to when he wrote in *The Summa Theologica*: "There may be doubt as to the precise meaning of the word 'all' when we say that God can do all things."

imaginatively, you will be able to do all kinds of amazing things. Some Unix commands, such as **look** (discussed in Chapter 19) use the dictionary file to do their work.

The name of the dictionary file is **words**. In the early versions of Unix, the **words** file was stored in a directory named **/usr/dict**. In recent years, however, the Unix file structure has been reorganized and, on most modern systems — including Linux and FreeBSD — the **words** file is stored in a directory named **/usr/share/dict**. On a few systems, such as Solaris, the file is stored in **/usr/share/lib/dict**. Thus, the pathname of the dictionary file may vary from one system to another. (We'll talk about the Unix file system and pathnames in Chapter 23.)

For reference, here are the most likely places you will find the dictionary file:

```
/usr/share/dict/words
/usr/dict/words
/usr/share/lib/dict/words
```

In the examples below, I will use the first pathname, which is the most common. If this name doesn't work for you, try one of the others.

To start, here is a simple puzzle. What are all the English words that begin with "qu" and end with "y". To solve this puzzle, all we need to do is grep* the dictionary file using the following regular expression:

```
grep '^qu[a-z]+y$' /usr/share/dict/words
```

To understand this regular expression, we will use the technique I mentioned earlier. We will break the regex into parts and write the parts vertically, one above the other. The breakdown of the regular expression is as follows:

^	→	beginning of line
qu	→	the letters "qu"
[a-z]+	→	one or more lowercase letters
y	→	the letter "y"
$	→	end of line

Remember that each line of the dictionary file contains only a single word. Thus, we start our search at the beginning of a line and finish it at the end of a line.

The next puzzle is an old one. Find a common English word that contains all five vowels — a, e, i, o, u — in that order. The letters do not have to be adjacent, but they must be in alphabetical order. That is, "a" must come before "e", which must come before "i", and so on.

To solve the puzzle, we can grep the dictionary file for any words that contain the letter "a", followed by zero or more lowercase letters, followed by "e", followed by zero or more lowercase letters, and so on. This time, let's start by writing down the various parts, which we will then put together. This is often a useful technique, when you are creating a complicated regular expression:

---

*As I mentioned in Chapter 19, the word "grep" is often used as a verb.

a	→	the letter "a"
[a-z]*	→	zero or more lowercase letters
e	→	the letter "e"
[a-z]*	→	zero or more lowercase letters
i	→	the letter "i"
[a-z]*	→	zero or more lowercase letters
o	→	the letter "o"
[a-z]*	→	zero or more lowercase letters
u	→	the letter "u"

Thus, the full command is:

```
grep 'a[a-z]*e[a-z]*i[a-z]*o[a-z]*u' /usr/share/dict/words
```

To avoid undue suspense, I will tell you now that you should find a number of words, most of them obscure. However, there are only three such words that are common. They are*:

```
adventitious
facetious
sacrilegious
```

Our last puzzle involves a search of the Unix file system for historical artifacts. Many of the original Unix commands were two letters long: the text editor was **ed**, the copy program was **cp**, and so on. Let us find all such commands.

To solve the puzzle, you need to know that the very oldest Unix programs reside in the **/bin** directory. To list all the files in this directory, we use the **ls** command (discussed in Chapter 24):

```
ls /bin
```

To analyze the output of **ls**, we can pipe it to **grep**. When we do this, **ls** will automatically place each name on a separate line, because the output is going to a filter. Using **grep**, we can then search for lines that consist of only two lowercase letters. The full pipeline is as follows:

```
ls /bin | grep '^[a-z]{2}$'
```

On some systems, **grep** will not return the results you want, because it will not recognize the brace brackets as being metacharacters. If this happens to you, you have two choices. You can use **egrep** instead:

```
ls /bin | egrep '^[a-z]{2}$'
```

Or, you can eliminate the need for brace brackets. Simply repeat the character class, and you won't need to use a bound:

```
ls /bin | grep '^[a-z][a-z]$'
```

---

*Strictly speaking, there are six vowels in English: a, e, i, o, u and (sometimes) y. If you want words that contain all six vowels, just turn these three words into adverbs: "adventitiously", "facetiously" and "sacrilegiously".

Try these commands on your system, and see what you find. When you see a name and you want to find out more about the command, just look it up in the online manual (Chapter 9). For example:

```
man ed cp
```

Aside from the files you will find in **/bin**, there are other old Unix commands in **/usr/bin**. To search this directory for 2-character command names, just modify the previous command slightly.

```
ls /usr/bin | grep '^[a-z]{2}$'
```

To count how many such commands there are, use **grep** with the **-c** (count) option:

```
ls /bin | grep -c '^[a-z]{2}$'
ls /usr/bin | grep -c '^[a-z]{2}$'
```

Note: When you look in **/usr/bin**, you may find some 2-character commands that are not old. To see if a command dates from the early days of Unix, check its man page.

CHAPTER 20 EXERCISES

REVIEW QUESTIONS

1. What is a regular expression? What are two common abbreviations for "regular expression"?

2. Within a regular expression, explain what the following metacharacters match: **.**, **^**, **$**, **\<**, **\>**, [*list*], [^*list*]. Explain what the following repetition operators match: *****, **+**, **?**, {*n*}.

3. For each of the following predefined character classes, give the definition and specify the equivalent range: **[:lower:]**, **[:upper:]**, **[:alpha:]**, **[:digit:]** and **[:alnum:]**. For example, **[:lower:]** represents all the lowercase numbers; the equivalent range is **a-z**.

4. By default, your system uses the dictionary collating sequence, but you want to use the C collating sequence. How do you make the change? What command would you use for the Bourne Shell family? For the C-Shell family? In which initialization file would you put such a command?

APPLYING YOUR KNOWLEDGE

1. Create regular expressions to match:

- "hello"
- the word "hello"
- either the word "hello" or the word "Hello"
- "hello" at the beginning of a line
- "hello" at the end of a line
- a line consisting only of "hello"

Use **grep** to test your answers.

2. Using repetition operators, create regular expressions to match:

- "start", followed by 0 or more numbers, followed by "end"
- "start", followed by 1 or more numbers, followed by "end"
- "start", followed by 0 or 1 number, followed by "end"
- "start", followed by exactly 3 numbers, followed by "end"

Use **grep** to test your answers. Hint: Make sure **grep** is using extended (not basic) regular expressions.

3. As we discussed in Chapter 20, the following two commands find all the lines in the file **data** that contain at least one non-alphabetic character:

```
grep '[^A-Za-z]' data
grep '[^[:alpha:]]' data
```

What command would you use to find all the lines that do not contain even a single alphabetic character?

4. Within the Usenet global discussion group system, freedom of expression is very important. However, it is also important that people should be able to avoid offensive postings if they so desire. The solution is to encode potentially offensive text in a way that it looks like gibberish to the casual observer. However, the encoded text can be decoded easily by anyone who chooses.

The system used for the coding is called Rot-13. It works as follows. Each letter of the alphabet is replaced by the letter 13 places later in the alphabet, wrapping back to the beginning if necessary:

```
A → N        N → A
B → O        O → B
C → P        P → C
D → Q...     Q → D...
```

Create a single command that reads from a file named **input**, encodes the text using Rot-13, and writes the encoded text to standard output. Then create a command that reads encoded Rot-13 data and converts it back to ordinary text. Test your solutions by creating a text file named **input**, encoding it and then decoding it.

FOR FURTHER THOUGHT

1. The term "regular expression" comes from an abstract computer science concept. Is it a good idea or a bad idea to use such names? Would it make much difference if the term "regular expression" was replaced by a more straightforward name, such as "pattern matching expression" or "pattern matcher"? Why?

2. With the introduction of locales to support internationalization, regular expression patterns that worked for years stopped working on some systems. In particular, regular expressions that depended on the traditional C collating sequence, do not always work with the dictionary collating sequence. In most cases, the solution is to use predefined character classes instead of ranges. For example, you should use **[:lower:]** instead of **a-z**. (See Figure 20-3 for the full set.) What do you think of this arrangement? Give three reasons why the old system was better. Give three reasons why the new system is better.

C H A P T E R 2 1
DISPLAYING FILES

With all the time we spend using computers, it is important to remind ourselves that the main product of our effort is almost always some type of output: text, numbers, graphics, sound, photos, video, or some other data. When you use the Unix command-line programs we discuss in this book, the output is usually text, either displayed on your monitor as it is generated, or saved in a file.

For this reason, Unix has always had a variety of programs that allow you to display textual data, either from the output of a program or from a file. In this chapter, we will discuss the programs you use to display the contents of files. We'll start with text files and then move on to binary files.

Throughout the discussion, my goals for you are twofold. First, whenever you need to display data from a file, I want you to be able to analyze the situation and choose the best program to do the job. Second, regardless of which program you decide to use, I want you to be familiar enough with it to handle most everyday tasks competently.

To start our discussion, I'll take you on a survey of the Unix programs used to display files. I'll introduce you to each program, explain what it does, and explain when to use it. You and I will then discuss each program in turn, at which time I will fill in the details. By far, the most important such program is **less**. (I'll explain the name later.) For this reason, we will spend the most time on this very useful and practical program.

As we discuss the various programs, we're going to detour a bit to cover two interesting topics. First, I'm going to describe the two different ways in which text-based programs can handle your input, "cooked mode" and "raw mode". Second, I'm going to introduce you to the binary, octal and hexadecimal number systems, concepts that you must understand when you display binary files.

Throughout this chapter, we will discuss how to display "files" even though, strictly speaking, I have not yet explained what a file actually is. In Chapter 23, we will discuss the Unix file system in detail. At that time, I will give you an exact, technical definition of a Unix file. For now, we'll just use the intuitive idea that a file is something with a name that contains information. For example, you might display a file named **essay** that contains the text of an essay you have written.

One more idea before we start: When people talk about "displaying" a file, it refers to displaying the *contents* of the file. For example, if I write "The following command displays the file **essay**," it means "The following command displays the contents of the file **essay**." This is a subtle, but important point, so make sure you understand it.

SURVEY OF PROGRAMS USED TO DISPLAY FILES

Unix has a variety of programs you can use to display files. In this section, we'll survey the programs, so you will have an overall view of what's available. Later in the chapter, we'll talk about each program in detail.

To start, there are programs whose only purpose is to display textual data one screenful at a time. Such a program is called a PAGER. The name comes from the fact that, in the early days of Unix, users had terminals that printed output on paper. Thus, to look at a file, you would print it on paper, one page a time. Nowadays, of course, to look at a file, you display it on your monitor one screenful at a time. Still, the programs that do the job are called "pagers".

In general, there are two ways to use a pager. First, as we discussed in Chapter 15, you can use a pager at the end of a pipeline to display output from another program. We have seen many such examples in previous chapters, for example:

```
cat newnames oldnames | grep Harley | sort | less
colrm 14 30 < students | less
```

In the first pipeline, we combine the contents of two files, grep the data for all the lines that contain the string "Harley", and send the results to **less** to be displayed. In the second example, we read data from a file, remove columns 14 through 30 from each line of data and, again, send the results to **less** to be displayed.

The other way to use a pager is to have it display the contents of a file, one screenful at a time. For example, the following command uses **less** to examine the contents of the Unix password file (described in Chapter 11):

```
less /etc/passwd
```

You can look at any text file in this manner, simply by typing **less** followed by the name of the file. (We'll discuss options, syntax and other details later in the chapter.)

Although **less** is the principal Unix pager, there are two other such programs you may hear about, **more** and **pg**. You will remember from our discussion in Chapter 2 that, in the 1980s, there were two main branches of Unix, System V developed at AT&T, and BSD developed at U.C. Berkeley. The **pg** program was the default System V pager; **more** was the default BSD pager. Today, both of these programs are obsolete having been replaced by **less**.

On rare occasions, you may have to use **more**. For this reason, we will talk about it a bit, so if you ever encounter it, you'll know what to do. The **pg** program, for the most part, is gone and buried, and there is no need for us to discuss it. I only mention it here for historical reasons: if you see the name, you'll at least know what it is.

Aside from using a pager, you can also display a file by using the **cat** program. As we discussed in Chapter 16, the principal use of **cat** is to combine the contents of multiple files. However, **cat** can also be used to display a file quickly, for example:

```
cat /etc/passwd
```

Since **cat** displays the entire file at once (not one screenful at a time), you would use it only when a file is short enough to fit on your screen without scrolling. Most of the time, it makes more sense to use **less**.

In most cases, you use **less** or **cat** when you want to look at an entire file. If you want to display only part of a file, there are three other programs you can use: **head**, to display the beginning of a file; **tail**, to display the end of a file; and **grep**, to display all the lines that contain (or don't contain) a particular pattern.

In Chapter 16, we discussed how to use **head** and **tail** as filters within a pipeline. In this chapter, I'll show you how to use them with files. In Chapter 19, we talked about **grep** in detail, and in Chapter 20, I showed you a lot of examples. For this reason, we won't need to discuss **grep** in this chapter. (However, I do want to mention it.)

The next group of programs you can use to display files are the text editors. A text editor allows you to look at any part of a file, search for patterns, move back and forth within the file, and so on. It also allows you to edit (make changes to) the file. Thus, you use a text editor to display a file when you want to make changes at the same time, or when you want to use special editor commands to move around the file. Otherwise you would use a pager.

In Chapter 14, I mentioned several text editors that are widely available on Unix and Linux systems: **kedit**, **gedit**, Pico, Nano, **vi** and Emacs. Any of these editors will allow you to display and change files. However, **vi** and Emacs are, by far, the most powerful tools (and the hardest to learn). The only editor we will talk about in detail in this book is **vi**, which we will discuss in Chapter 22.

From time to time, you may want to use a text editor to examine a file that is so important you don't want to make any changes accidentally. To do so, you can run the editor in what is called "read-only" mode, which means you can look at the file, but you cannot make any changes.

To start **vi** in read-only mode, you use the **-R** option. For example, any user can look at the Unix password file (Chapter 11), but you are not allowed to modify it unless you are superuser. Thus, to use **vi** to look at the password file without being able to edit it, you would use:

```
vi -R /etc/passwd
```

As a convenience, you can use **view** as a synonym for **vi -R**:

```
view /etc/passwd
```

Even if you are logged in as superuser, you will often choose to use **vi -R** or **view** to look at a very important system file. This ensures that you don't change it accidentally. (We'll discuss this more in Chapter 22.)

PROGRAM	PURPOSE	CHAPTER
`less`	Pager: display one screenful at a time	21
`more`	Pager (obsolete, used with BSD)	21
`pg`	Pager (obsolete, used with System V)	—
`cat`	Display entire file, no paging	16
`head`	Display first part of file	16, 21
`tail`	Display last part of file	16, 21
`grep`	Display lines containing/not containing specific pattern	19, 20
`vi`	Text editor: display and edit file	21
`view, vi -R`	Read-only text editor: display but don't allow changes to file	22
`hexdump`	Display binary (non-text) files	21
`od`	Display binary (non-text) files	21

FIGURE 21-1: Programs to display files

*Unix and Linux have a large variety of tools you can use to display all or part of a file. This summary shows the most important such tools, along with the chapters in which they are discussed. At the very least, you should be competent with **less**, **cat**, **head**, **tail**, and **grep** to display text files. You should also know how to use **vi**, as it is the principal Unix text editor. If you are a programmer, you should be familiar with either **hexdump** or **od**, so you can display binary files.*

The programs we have discussed so far all work with text files, that is, files that contain lines of characters. However, there are many different types of non-text files, called binary files, and from time to time, you may need to look inside such files. The final two programs I want to mention — **hexdump** and **od** — are used to display files that contain binary data.

For example, say you are writing a program that sends binary output to a file. Each time you run the program, you need to look inside the file to check on the output. That is where **hexdump** or **od** come in handy. We'll talk about the details later in the chapter. As a quick example, either of the following Linux commands lets you look inside the file containing the **grep** program. (Don't worry about the options for now. We'll discuss them later.)

```
hexdump -C /bin/grep | less
od -Ax -tx1z /bin/grep | less
```

For reference, Figure 21-1 contains a summary of the programs we have discussed in our survey. As you look at the summary, please take a moment to appreciate how many Unix tools there are to display files, each with its own characteristics and uses.

INTRODUCTION TO `less`: STARTING, STOPPING, HELP

The **less** program is a pager. That is, it displays data, one screenful at a time. When you start **less**, there are many options to choose from and, once it is running, there are many commands you can use. However, you will rarely need so much complexity. In this chapter, we will concentrate on the basic options and features you are likely to use on a day-to-day basis. For a description of the more esoteric options and commands we won't be covering, see the manual page and the Info page:

```
man less
info less
```

(The online manual and the Info system are discussed in Chapter 9.)

The basic syntax to use **less** is as follows:

less [**-cCEFmMsX**] [**+***command*] [**-x***tab*] [*file...*]

where *command* is a command for **less** to execute automatically; *tab* is the tab spacing you want to use; *file* is the name of a file.

Most of the time, you will not need any options. All you will do is specify one or more files to display, for example:

```
less information
less names addresses
```

You can use **less** to display any text file you have permission to read, including a system file or a file belonging to another userid. (We discuss file permissions in Chapter 25.) As an example, the following command displays a well-known system file, the Termcap file we discussed in Chapter 7:

```
less /etc/termcap
```

The Termcap file contains technical descriptions of all the different types of terminals. Although Termcap has been mostly replaced* by a newer system called Terminfo (see Chapter 7), this file is an excellent example to use when practicing with **less**, so if you want to follow along as you read this chapter, you can enter the above command whenever you want.

Before displaying anything, **less** will clear the screen. (You can suppress this by using the **-X** option.) When **less** starts, it displays the first screenful of data, whatever fits on your monitor or within your window. At the bottom left-hand corner of the screen, you will see a prompt. The initial prompt shows you the name of the file being displayed. Depending on how your system is configured, you may also see other information. For example:

```
/etc/termcap lines 1-33/18956 0%
```

In this case, we are looking at lines 1 through 33 of the file **/etc/termcap**. The top line on the screen is the first line of the file (0%). Subsequent prompts will update the line numbers and percentage.

On some systems, the default is for **less** to display a much simpler prompt without the line numbers and percentage. If this is the case on your system, the first prompt will show only the file name, for example:

```
/etc/termcap
```

Subsequent prompts will be even simpler; all you will see is a colon:

```
:
```

---

*Although the Terminfo system is preferred (see Chapter 7), Termcap is still used by some programs, including **less** itself.

On such systems, you can display extra information in the prompt by using the **–M** option (discussed later in the chapter.)

HINT

For ambitious fanatics with a lot of extra time, **less** offers more flexibility for customizing the prompt than any other pager in the history of the world. (See the man page for details.)

Once you see the prompt, you can enter a command. In a moment, we'll talk about the various commands, of which there are many. For now, I'll just mention the most common command, which is simply to press the <Space> bar. This tells **less** to display the next screenful of data. Thus, you can read an entire file, one screenful at a time, from beginning to end, simply by pressing <Space>.

When you reach the end of the file, **less** changes the prompt to:

```
(END)
```

If you want to quit, you can press **q** at any time. You don't have to wait until the end of the file. Thus, to look at a file, all you need to do is start **less**, press <Space> until you see as much as you want, and then press **q** to quit.

As a quick exercise, try this. Enter one of the following commands to display the Termcap file:

```
less /etc/termcap
less -m /etc/termcap
```

You will see the first screenful of data. Press <Space> a few times, moving down through the file, one screenful at a time. When you get tired of looking at an endless list of cryptic, obsolete terminal descriptions, press **q** to quit.

HINT

When you use **less** to display a file, there are many commands you can use while you are looking at a file. The most important command is **h** (help). At any time, you can press **h** to display a summary of all the commands.

The best way to learn about **less** is to press **h**, see what is available and experiment.

THE STORY OF `less` AND `more`

As I explained earlier in the chapter, the original Unix pagers were **more** (used with BSD) and **pg** (used with System V). You will sometimes hear that the name **less** was chosen as a wry joke. Since **less** is much more powerful than **more**, the joke is that "**less** is more". It's plausible, but not true. Here is the real story.

The original Unix pager, **more**, was a simple program used to display data one screenful at a time. The name **more** came from the fact that, after each screenful, the program would display a prompt with the word "More":

```
--More--
```

The **more** program was useful, but it had serious limitations. The most important limitation was that **more** could only display data from start to finish: it could not back up.

In 1983, a programmer named Mark Nudelman was working at a company called Integrated Office Systems. The company produced Unix software that could create very large log files containing transaction information and error messages. Some of the files were so large that the current version of the **vi** text editor was not able to read them. Thus, Nudelman and the other programmers were forced to use **more** to examine the files when they wanted to look for errors.

However, there was a problem. Whenever a programmer found an error message in a log file, there was no way to back up to see what caused the problem, that is, the transactions immediately preceding the error. The programmers often complained about this problem. As Nudelman explained to me:

"A group of engineers were standing around a terminal in the lab using **more** to look at a log file. We found a line indicating an error and, as usual, we had to determine the line number of the error. Then we had to quit **more**, restart it, and move forward to a point several lines before the error to see what led up to the error. Someone complained about this cumbersome process. Someone else said "We need a backwards **more**." A third person said "Yeah, we need LESS!", which got a chuckle from everyone.

Thinking about the problem, it occurred to Nudelman that it wouldn't be too hard to create a pager that could back up. In late 1983, he wrote such a program, which he indeed called **less**. At first, **less** was used only within the company. However, after enhancing the program, Nudelman felt comfortable making it available to the outside world, which he did in May 1985.

Nudelman released **less** as open source software, which enabled many other people to help him improve the program. Over the years, **less** became more and more powerful and so popular with Unix users that it eventually reached the point where it replaced both **more** and **pg** (the other popular Unix pager). Today, **less** is the most widely used Unix pager in the world and is distributed as part of the GNU utilities (see Chapter 2).

Interesting note: Most programs are released with version numbers such as 1.0, 1.01, 1.2, 2.0 and so on. Nudelman used a simpler system. From the very beginning, he gave each new version of **less** its own number: 1, 2, 3, 4 and so on. Thus, as I write this, the **less** program I am using is version 394.

USING less

As you read a file with **less**, there are a great many commands you can use. For reference, the most important commands are summarized in Figure 21-2. For a more comprehensive summary, you can press **h** (help) from within **less**, or you can enter the following command from the shell prompt:

```
less --help
```

When you display the comprehensive summary, you will see there are many more commands than you will ever need. For example, there are five different ways to move forward (that is, down) by one line, five different ways to move backward (up) by one line, five different ways to quit the program, and so on. Don't be intimidated. You only need to know the commands in Figure 21-2.

The best strategy is to start with the three commands I mentioned earlier: <Space> to page through the file, **h** for help, and **q** to quit. Once you feel comfortable with these three, teach yourself the rest of the commands in Figure 21-1, one at a time, until you have memorized them all. Just work your way down the list from top to bottom. (I chose the order carefully and, yes, you do need to memorize them all.)

BASIC COMMANDS	
h	display help information
<Space>	go forward one screenful
q	quit the program
ADVANCED COMMANDS	
g	go to first line
G	go to last line
=	display current line number and file name
<Return>	go forward one line
n<Return>	go forward *n* lines
b	go backward one screenful
y	go backward one line
*n***y**	go backward *n* lines
d	go forward (down) a half screenful
u	go backward (up) a half screenful
<Down>	go forward one line
<Up>	go forward one line
<PageUp>	go backward (up) one screenful
<PageDown>	go forward (down) one screenful
*n***g**	go to line *n*
*n***p**	go to line *n*% through the file
/*pattern*	search forward for the specified pattern
?*pattern*	search backward for the specified pattern
n	repeat search: same direction
N	repeat search: opposite direction
!*command*	execute the specified shell command
v	start **vi** editor using current file
-*option*	change specified *option*
_*option*	display current value of *option*

FIGURE 21-2: `less`: Summary of the Most Useful Commands

If you need a file on which to practice, use the Termcap file I mentioned earlier in the chapter. The following command will get you started:

```
less -m /etc/termcap
```

(It helps to use the **-m** option when you are practicing, so the prompt will show your position in the file.)

USING less TO SEARCH WITHIN A FILE

Most of the commands in Figure 21-2 are straightforward. However, I do want to say a few words about the search commands. When you want to search for a pattern, you use either **/** (search forward) or **?** (search backward), followed by a pattern. The pattern can be a simple character string or a regular expression (described in Chapter 20). After typing **/** or **?**, followed by the pattern, you need to press <Return> to let **less** know you are finished.

Here are some examples. To search forward in the file for the next occurrence of "buffer", use:

```
/buffer
```

To search backward for the same pattern, use:

```
?buffer
```

Searches are case sensitive, so you will get different results if you search for "Buffer":

```
/Buffer
```

If you want to use case insensitive searching, you can start **less** with the **-I** option (described later in the chapter), for example:

```
less -Im /etc/termcap
```

When you start **less** in this way, searching for "buffer" would produce the same result as searching for "Buffer" or "BUFFER".

If you want to turn the **-I** option off and on while you are reading a file, you can use the **-I** command from within **less**. To display the current state of this option, use the **_I** command. (Changing and displaying options from within **less** is described later in the chapter.)

If you want to perform more searches, you can use regular expressions. For example, let's say you want to search for any string that contains "buf", followed by zero or more lowercase letters. You can use:

```
/buf[:lower:]*
?buf[:lower:]*
```

(For a detailed explanation of regular expressions, including many examples, see Chapter 20.)

Once you have entered a search command, you can repeat it by using the **n** (next) command. This performs the exact same search in the same direction. To repeat the same search in the opposite direction, use **N**.

Whenever you search for a pattern, **less** will highlight that pattern wherever it appears in the file. Thus, once you search for something, it is easy to see all such occurrences as you page through the file. The highlighting will persist until you enter another search.

> **HINT**
>
> Once you have learned how to use the **vi** editor, the **less** commands will make more sense since many of the commands are taken directly from **vi**. This is because virtually all experienced Unix people are familiar with **vi**, so using the same commands with **less** makes a lot of sense.

> **HINT**
>
> If you have too much spare time on your hands, you can use the **lesskey** command to change the keys used by **less**. For details, see the **lesskey** man page.

RAW AND COOKED MODE

Before we continue our discussion, I want to take a moment to talk about a few important I/O (input/output) concepts that will help you better understand how **less** and similar programs work. Let's start with a definition.

A DEVICE DRIVER or, more simply, a DRIVER, is a program that provides an interface between the operating system and a particular type of device, usually some type of hardware. When you use the Unix text-based CLI (command line interface), the driver that controls your terminal is called a TERMINAL DRIVER.

Unlike some other drivers, terminal drivers must provide for an interactive user interface, which requires special preprocessing and postprocessing of the data. To meet this need, terminal drivers use what is called a LINE DISCIPLINE.

Unix has two main line disciplines, CANONICAL MODE and RAW MODE. The details are horribly technical, but the basic idea is that, in canonical mode, the characters you type are accumulated in a buffer (storage area), and nothing is sent to the program until you press the <Return> key. In raw mode (also known as NONCANONICAL MODE), each character is passed directly to the program as soon as you press a key. When you read Unix documentation, you will often see canonical mode referred to as COOKED MODE. (This is, of course, an amusing metaphor, "cooked" being the opposite of "raw".)

When a programmer creates a program, he can use whichever line discipline he wants. Raw mode gives the programmer full control over the user's working environment. The **less** program, for example, works in raw mode, which allows it to take over the command line and the screen completely, displaying lines and processing characters according to its needs.

This is why whenever you press a key, **less** is able to respond instantly; it does not need you to press <Return>. Thus, you simply press the <Space> bar and **less** displays more data; you press **b** and **less** moves backwards in the file; you press **q** and the program quits. You will find many other programs that work in raw mode, such as the text editors **vi** and Emacs.

In canonical (cooked) mode, a program is sent whole lines, not individual characters. This releases the programmer from having to process each character as it is generated. It also allows you to make changes in the line before the line is processed. For example, you can use <Backspace> or <Delete> to make corrections before you press <Return>. When you use the shell, for example, you are working in canonical mode: nothing is sent until you press <Return>.

Virtually all interactive text-based programs use either canonical mode or raw mode. However, there is a third line discipline you may hear about, even though it is not used much anymore.

CBREAK MODE is a variation of raw mode. Most input is sent directly to the program, just like raw mode. However, a few very important keys are handled directly by the terminal driver. These keys (which we discussed in Chapter 7) are the ones that send the five special signals: **intr** (**^C**), **quit** (**^**), **susp** (**^Z**), **stop** (**^S**), and **start** (**^Q**). Cbreak mode, then, is mostly raw with a bit of cooking. In the olden days, it was sometimes referred to whimsically, as "rare mode".

OPTIONS TO USE WITH `less`

When you start **less**, there are a large number of options you can use, most of which can be safely ignored*. For practical purposes, you can consider **less** to have the following syntax:

less [*-cCEFmMs*] [*+command*] [*-xtab*] [*file...*]

where *command* is a command for **less** to execute automatically, *tab* is the tab spacing you want to use, and *file* is the name of a file.

The three most useful options are **-s**, **-c** and **-m**. The **-s** (squeeze) option replaces multiple blank lines with a single blank line. This is useful for condensing output in which multiple blank lines are not meaningful. Of course, no changes are made to the original file.

The **-c** (clear) option tells **less** to display each new screenful of data from the top down. Without **-c**, new lines scroll up from the bottom line of the screen. Some people find that long files are easier to read with **-c**. The **-C** (uppercase "C") option is similar to **-c** except that the entire screen is cleared before new data is written. You will have to try both options for yourself and see what you prefer.

The name **-m** refers to **more**, the original BSD pager I mentioned earlier. The **more** prompt displays a percentage, showing how far down the user is in the file. When **less** was developed, it was given a very simple prompt, a colon. However, the **-m** option was included for people who were used to **more** and wanted the more verbose prompt.

---

*In fact, **less** is one of those odd commands, like **ls** (see Chapter 24), that has more options than there are letters in the alphabet. It's hard to explain why, but I suspect it has something to do with an overactive thyroid.

The **-m** option makes the prompt look like the **more** prompt by showing the percentage of the file that has been displayed. For example, let's say you display the Termcap file (see the discussion earlier in the chapter) using **-m**:

```
less -m /etc/termcap
```

After moving down a certain distance you see the prompt:

```
40%
```

This indicates you are now 40 percent of the way through the file. (By the way, you can jump directly to this location by using the command **40p**. See Figure 21-2.)

The **-M** (uppercase "M") option makes the prompt show even more information: you will see the name of the file and the line number, as well as the percentage that has been displayed. For example, if you use:

```
less -M /etc/termcap
```

A typical prompt would look like this:

```
/etc/termcap lines 7532-7572/18956 40%
```

The line numbers refer to the range of lines being displayed, in this case, lines 7,532 to 7,572 (out of 18,956).

One of my favorite options is **-E** (end). This tells **less** to quit automatically when the end of the file has been displayed. When you use **-E**, you don't have to press **q** to quit the program. This is convenient when you know you only want to read through a file once without looking backward.

The **-F** (finish automatically) option tells less to quit automatically if the entire file can be displayed at once. Again, this keeps you from having to press **q** to quit the program. In my experience, **-F** works best with very short files, while **-E** works best with long files. To see how this works, let's create a very short file named **friends**. To start, enter the command:

```
cat > friends
```

Now type the names of five or six friends, one per line. When you are finished, press **^D** to send the **eof** signal to end the program. (We discuss **^D** in Chapter 7.) Now, compare the following two commands. Notice that with the second command, you don't have to press **q** to quit the program.

```
less friends
less -F friends
```

The **+** (plus sign) option allows you to specify where **less** will start to display data. Whatever appears after the **+** will be executed as an initial command. For example, to display the Termcap file with the initial position at the end of the file, use:

```
less +G /etc/termcap
```

To display the same file, starting with a search for the word "buffer", use:

```
less +/buffer /etc/termcap
```

To start at a particular line, use **+g** (go to) preceeded by the line number. For example, to start at line 37, use:

```
less +37g /etc/termcap
```

As a convenience, **less** allows you to leave out the **g**. Thus, the following two commands both start at line 37:

```
less +37g /etc/termcap
less +37 /etc/termcap
```

The **-I** (ignore case) option tells **less** to ignore differences in upper- and lowercase when you search for patterns. By default, **less** is case sensitive. For example, "the" is not the same as "The". However, when you use **-I**, you get the same results searching for "the", "The" or "THE".

The **-N** (number) option is useful when you want to see line numbers in the output. When you use this option, **less** numbers each line, much like the **nl** command (Chapter 18). For instance, the following two examples generate similar output:

```
less -N file
nl file | less
```

In both cases, of course, the actual file is not changed.

There are two important differences between using **nl** and **less -N**. First, **less** numbers lines in only one way: 1, 2, 3 and so on. The **nl** command has a variety of options that allow you a great deal of flexibility in how the line numbers should be generated. You can choose the starting number, the increment, and so on (see Chapter 18). Second, **less** numbers all lines, even blank ones. By default, **nl** does not number blank lines unless you use the **-b a** option.

Finally, the **-x** option followed by a number tells **less** to set the tabs at the specified regular interval. This controls the spacing for data that contains tab characters. For example, to display a program named **foo.c** with the tabs set to every 4 spaces, use:

```
less -x4 foo.c
```

As with most Unix programs, the default tab setting is every 8 spaces (see Chapter 18).

If you want to change an option on the fly while you are viewing a file, use the **-** (hyphen) command followed by the new option. This acts like an on/off toggle switch. For example, to turn on the **-M** option (to display a verbose prompt) while you are looking at a file, type:

```
-M
```

To turn off the option, just enter the command again.

To display the current value of an option, use an _ (underscore) followed by the option. For example, to check how the prompt is set, use:

_M

Here is another example. You have started **less** without the **-I** option and, as you are looking at the file, you decide you want to do a case insensitive search. All you need to do is type:

-I

After entering your search command, you type **-I** again to turn off the option. If you do this a few times, it's easy to lose track. So, at any time, you can check the status of the option, by typing:

_I

This is a handy pattern to remember.

> **HINT**
>
> When you are new to **less** and you want to learn how to use the various options, you can use the - (change option) and _ (display option) commands to experiment while you are displaying a file.
>
> This is especially useful if you want to learn how to use the **-P** option (which we did not discuss) to change the prompt. You can make a change to the prompt, and see the result immediately.

WHEN TO USE less AND WHEN TO USE cat

As we discussed earlier in the chapter, you can use both **less** and **cat** to display files. With **less**, the file is displayed one screenful at a time; with **cat** the entire file is displayed all at once. If you expect a file to be longer than the size of your screen, it is best to use **less**. If you use **cat**, most of the file will scroll off your screen faster than you can read it. However, what if the file is small?

If you use **cat** to display a small file — one that is short enough to fit on your screen — the data is displayed quickly, and that is that. Using **less** is inconvenient for two reasons. First, **less** will clear the screen, erasing any previous output. Second, you will have to press **q** to quit the program, which is irritating when all you want to do is display a few lines quickly.

You can, of course, use less with the **-F** (finish automatically) option, which causes the program to quit automatically if the entire file can be displayed at once. For example, let's say that **data** is a very small file. You can display it quickly by using the command:

```
less -F data
```

In fact, you can even specify that **less** should use the **-F** option by default. (You do this by setting the **LESS** environment variable, explained later in the chapter.) Once you set this variable, you won't have to type **-F**, and the following two commands are more or less equivalent (assuming **data** is a very small file):

```
less data
cat data
```

However, if you watch experienced Unix people, you will see that they always use **cat** to display short files; they never use **less**. Why is this?

There are four reasons. First, as I mentioned, **less** clears the screen, which erases the previous output. This can be inconvenient. Second it is faster to type "cat" than "less". Third, the name **cat** is a lot cuter than the name **less**. Finally, using **cat** in this way is how Unix people distinguish themselves from the crowd.

These might seem like insignificant reasons, but Unix people like their work to be smooth, fast and fun. So if you want to look like a real Unix person and not a clueless goober, use **cat** when the file is very small, and **less** otherwise.

USING ENVIRONMENT VARIABLES TO CUSTOMIZE YOUR PAGER

As we discussed in Chapter 15, the Unix philosophy says that each tool should do only one thing and do it well. Thus, the Unix pagers (**less**, **more**, **pg**) were all designed to provide only one service: to display data one screenful at a time. If another program requires this functionality, the program does not have to provide the service itself. Instead, it uses a pager.

The most common example occurs when you use the **man** program (Chapter 9) to access the online Unix manual. The **man** program does not actually display the text of the page. Rather, it calls upon a pager to show you the page, one screenful at a time.

The question arises, which pager will **man** and other programs use? You might think that, because **less** is the most popular pager, any program that needs such a tool will automatically use **less**. This is often the case, but not always. On some systems, for example, the **man** program, by default, will use **more** to display man pages. This can be irritating because, as we discussed earlier, **more** is not nearly as powerful as **less**.

However, you *can* specify your default pager. All you have to do is set an environment variable named **PAGER** to the name of the pager you want to use. For example, the following commands set **less** as your default pager. The first command is for the Bourne Shell family (Bash, Korn Shell). The second command is for the C-Shell family (C-Shell, Tcsh).

```
export PAGER=less
setenv PAGER less
```

To make the change permanent, all you need to do is put the appropriate command in your login file. (Environment variables are discussed in Chapter 12; the login file is discussed in Chapter 14.)

Once you set the **PAGER** environment variable in this way, all programs that require an external pager will use **less**. Even if **less** already seems to be the preferred pager for your system, it is a good idea to set **PAGER** in your login file. This will override any other defaults explicitly, ensuring that no matter how your system happens to be set up, you will be in control.

Aside from **PAGER**, there is another environment variable you can use for further customization. You can set the variable **LESS** to the options you want to use every time the program starts. For example, let's say you always want to use **less** with the options **-CFMs** (discussed earlier in the chapter). The following commands set the variable **LESS** appropriately. (The first command is for the Bourne Shell family. The second command is for the C-Shell family.)

```
export LESS='-CFMs'
setenv LESS '-CFMs'
```

Again, this is a command to put in your login file. Once you do, **less** will always start with these particular options. This will be the case whether you run **less** yourself or whether another program, such as **man** runs it on your behalf.

If you ever find yourself using the **more** program (say, on a system that does not have **less**), you can specify automatic options in the same way by setting the **MORE** environment variable. For example, the following commands specify that **more** should always start with the **-cs** options. (The first command is for the Bourne Shell family; the second is for the C-Shell family.)

```
export MORE='-cs'
setenv MORE '-cs'
```

Once again, all you need to do is put the appropriate command in your login file to make your preferences permanent.

> **HINT**
>
> The **less** program actually looks at 30 different environment variables, which allows for an enormous amount of flexibility.
>
> The most important variable is **LESS**, the one variable we have discussed. If you are curious as to what the other variables do, take a look at the **less** man page.

DISPLAYING MULTIPLE FILES WITH less

Anything you can do with **less** using a single file, you can also do with multiple files. In particular, you can move back and forth from one file to another, and you can search for patterns in more than one file at the same time. For reference, Figure 21-3 contains a summary of the relevant commands.

To work with multiple files, all you have to do is specify more than one file name on the command line. For example, the following command tells **less** that you want to work with three different files:

```
less data example memo
```

At any time, you see only one file, which we call the CURRENT FILE. However, **less** maintains a list of all your files and, whenever you want, you can move from one file to another. You can also add files to the list or delete files from the list as the need arises.

When **less** starts, the current file is the first one in the list. In the above example, the current file would be **data**. To move forward within the list, you use the **:n** (next) command. For example, if you are reading **data** and you type **:n**, you will change to **example**, which will become the new current file. If you type **:n** again, the current file will change to **memo**.

Similarly, you can move backwards within the list by using the **:p** (previous) command, and you can jump to the beginning of the list by using the **:x** command. For example, if you are reading **memo** and you type **:p**, the current file will change to **example**. If you type **:x** instead, the current file will change to **data**.

To display the name of the current file, type **:f**. This is a synonym for the **=** command (see Figure 21-2). At this time, you may want to take a moment and practice these three commands before you move on.

One of the most powerful features of **less** is that it allows you to search for a pattern in more than one file. Here is how it works.

As we discussed earlier in the chapter, you use the **/** command to search forwards within a file and **?** to search backwards. After using either of these commands, you can type **n** to search again in the same direction or **N** to search again in the opposite direction.

For example, let's say you enter the command:

/buffer

This performs a forward search within the current file for the string "buffer". Once **less** has found it, you can jump forward to the next occurrence of "buffer" by typing **n**. Or, you can jump backward to the previous occurrence by typing **N**.

When you are working with more than one file, you have an option: instead of using **/** or **?**, you can use **/*** or **?***. When you search in this way, **less** treats the entire list as if it were one large file. For example, let's say you start **less** with the command above:

:n	change to next file in list
:p	change to previous file in list
:x	change to first file in list
:e	insert a new file into the list
:d	delete current file from the list
:f	display name of current file (same as **=**)
=	display name of current file
/*pattern	search forward for specified pattern
?*pattern	search backward for specified pattern

FIGURE 21-3: less: Commands to Use With Multiple Files

```
less data example memo
```

The current file is **data**, and the list of files is:

```
data example memo
```

You type the command **:n**, which moves you within the list to the second file, **example**. You then type **50p** (50 percent), which moves you to the middle of **example**. You now enter the following command to search forward for the string "buffer".

```
/*buffer
```

This command starts from the current position in **example** and searches forward for "buffer". Once the search is complete, you can press **n** to repeat the search moving forward. If you press **n** repeatedly, **less** would normally stop at the end of the file. However, since you used **/*** instead of **/**, **less** will move to the next file in the list automatically (in this case, **memo**) and continue the search.

Similarly, if you press **N** repeatedly to search backwards, when **less** gets to the beginning of the current file (**example**), it will move to the end of the previous file automatically (**data**) and continue the search.

The same idea applies when you use **?*** instead of **?** to perform a backwards search. The ***** tells **less** to ignore file boundaries when you use **n** or **N** commands.

In addition to **:n**, **:p**, **:x**, **/*** and **?***, **less** has two more commands to help you work with multiple files. These commands allow you to insert and delete files from the list.

To insert a file, you type **:e** (examine) followed by one or more file names. The new files will be inserted into the list directly after the current file. The first such file will then become the new current file. For example, let's say the list of files is:

```
data example memo
```

The current file happens to be **example**. You enter the following command to insert three files into the list:

```
:e a1 a2 a3
```

The list becomes:

```
data example a1 a2 a3 memo
```

The current file is now **a1**.

To delete the current file from the list, you use the **:d** (delete) command. (Of course, **less** does not delete the actual file.) For example, if you are working with the list above, and you type **:d**, the current file (**a1**) is deleted from the list:

```
data example a2 a3 memo
```

The previous file (**example**) becomes the new current file.

At first, these commands can be a bit confusing, especially because there is no way to display the actual list so you can see what's what. When you work with multiple files, you'll need to keep the sequence of files in your head. Still, when you want to display more than one file or search through more than one file, you will find these commands to be surprisingly practical, so they are worth learning.

DISPLAYING A FILE USING more

As we discussed earlier in the chapter, the early pagers **more** and **pg** have been replaced by the more powerful program **less**. Although you will probably never see **pg**, you will run into **more** from time to time. For example, you may have to use a system that does not have **less**, and you will have to use **more**. Or you may use a system in which the default pager is **more**, and you may find yourself using it accidentally.* In such cases, it behooves you to know a bit about the program so, in this section, I'll go over the basics for you.

The syntax for **more** is:

more [-cs] [*file...*]

where *file* is the name of a file.

The **more** program displays data one screenful at a time. After each screen is written, you will see a prompt at the bottom left corner of the screen. The prompt looks like this:

--More--(40%)

(Hence the name **more**.)

At the end of the prompt is a number in parentheses. This shows you how much of the data has been displayed. In our example, the prompt shows that you are 40 percent of the way through the file.

The simplest way to use **more** is to specify a single file name. For example:

more filename

If the data fits on a single screen, it will be displayed all at once and **more** will quit automatically. Otherwise, the data will be displayed, one screenful at a time, with the prompt at the bottom.

Once you see the prompt, you can enter a command. The most common command is simply to press the <Space> bar, which displays the next screenful of data. You can press <Space> repeatedly to page through the entire file. After displaying the last screenful of data, **more** will quit automatically.

The most common use for **more** is to display the output of a pipeline, for example:

cat newnames oldnames | grep Harley | sort | more
ls -l | more

When you use **more** in a pipeline, the prompt will not show the percentage:

--More--

This is because **more** displays the data as it arrives, so it has no idea how much there will be.

---

*This is the case on Solaris systems. When you use the **man** command to display a man page, the default pager is **more**. If you use such a system regularly, you can make **less** your default pager by setting the **PAGER** environment variable. See the discussion earlier in the chapter.

When **more** pauses, there are a variety of commands you can use. Like **less**, **more** works in raw mode (explained earlier in the chapter), so when you type single-character commands, you do not have to press <Return>. As you might expect, the most important command is **h** (help), which displays a comprehensive command summary.

For the most part, you can think of **more** as a less powerful version of **less**. For reference, the most important **more** commands are summarized in Figure 21-4. For a comprehensive summary, see the **more** man page (**man more**).

As I mentioned, you can move forward one screenful by pressing <Space>. Alternatively, you can press **d** (down) to move forward a half screenful, or <Return> to move forward one line. To move backward one screenful, press **b**. (Note: The **b** command only works when you are reading a file. Within a pipeline, you can't go backwards because **more** does not save the data.)

To search for a pattern, type **/** followed by the pattern, followed by <Return>. If you want, you can use a regular expression (see Chapter 20). When **more** finds the pattern, it will display two lines before that location so you can see the line in context. To repeat the previous search, enter **/** without a pattern, that is, **/**<Return>.

When you start **more**, the two most useful options are **-s** and **-c**. The **-s** (squeeze) option replaces multiple blank lines with a single blank line. You can use this option to condense output in which multiple blank lines are not meaningful. Of course, this does not affect the original file.

The **-c** (clear) option tells **more** to display each new screenful of data from the top down. Each line is cleared before it is replaced. Without **-c**, new lines scroll up from the bottom line of the screen. Some people find that long files are easier to read with **-c**. You will have to try it for yourself.

BASIC COMMANDS	
h	display help information
<Space>	go forward one screenful
q	quit the program
ADVANCED COMMANDS	
=	display current line number
<Return>	go forward one line
d	go forward (down) a half screenful
f	go forward one screenful
b	go backward one screenful
/pattern	search forward for the specified pattern
/	repeat last search
!command	execute the specified shell command
v	start **vi** editor using current file

Figure 21-4: **more**: Useful Commands

DISPLAYING THE BEGINNING OF A FILE: `head`

In Chapter 16, we discussed how to use **head** as a filter within a pipeline to select lines from the beginning of a stream of data. In this section, I'll show you how to use **head** on its own, to display the beginning of a file. When you use **head** in this way, the syntax is:

head [**-n** *lines*] [*file...*]

where *lines* is the number of lines you want to display, and *file* is the name of a file. By default, **head** will display the first 10 lines of a file. This is useful when you want to get a quick look at a file to check its contents. For example, to display the first 10 lines of a file named **information**, use:

```
head information
```

If you want to display a different number of lines, specify that number using the **-n** option. For example, to display the first 20 lines of the same file, use:

```
head -n 20 information
```

> **HINT**
>
> Originally, **head** and **tail** (discussed next) did not require you to use the **-n** option; you could simply type a hyphen followed by a number. For example, the following commands all display 15 lines of output:
>
> ```
> calculate | head -n 15
> calculate | head -15
>
> calculate | tail -n 15
> calculate | tail -15
> ```
>
> Officially, modern versions of **head** and **tail** are supposed to require the **-n** option, which is why I have included it. However, most versions of Unix and Linux will accept both types of syntax and, if you watch experienced Unix people, you will find that they often leave out the **-n**.

DISPLAYING THE END OF A FILE: `tail`

To display the end of a file, you use the **tail** command. The syntax is:

tail [**-n** [**+**]*lines*] [*file...*]

where *lines* is the number of lines you want to display, and *file* is the name of a file.

By default, **tail** will display the last 10 lines of a file. For example, to display the last 10 lines of a file named **information**, use:

```
tail information
```

To display a different number of lines, use the **-n** option followed by a number. For example, to display the last 20 lines of the file **information**, use:

```
tail -n 20 information
```

Strictly speaking, you must type the **-n** option. However, as I explained in the previous section, you can usually get away with leaving it out. Instead, you can simply type a – (hyphen) followed by the number of lines you want to display. Thus, the following two lines are equivalent:

```
tail -n 20 information
tail -20 information
```

If you put a **+** (plus sign) character before the number, **tail** displays from that line number to the end of the file. For example, to display from line **35** to the end of the file, use:

```
tail -n +35 information.
```

In this case, don't leave out the **-n** to ensure that **tail** does not interpret the number as a file name.

WATCHING THE END OF A GROWING FILE: tail -f

The **tail** command has a special option that allows you to watch a file grow, line by line. This option comes in handy when you must wait for data to be written to a file. For example, you might want to monitor a program that writes one line at a time to the end of a file. Or, if you are a system administrator, you might want to keep an eye on a log file to which important messages are written from time to time.

To run **tail** in this way, you use the **-f** option. The syntax is:

```
tail -f [-n [+]lines] [file...]
```

where *lines* is the number of lines you want to display, and *file* is the name of a file. (The *lines* argument is described in the previous section.)

The **-f** option tells **tail** not to stop when it reaches the end of the file. Instead, **tail** waits indefinitely and displays more output as the file grows. (The name **-f** stands for "follow".)

For example, let's say that over the next few minutes, a particular program will be adding output to the end of a file named **results**. You want to follow the progress of this program. Enter:

```
tail -f results
```

As soon as you enter the command, **tail** will display the last 10 lines of the file. The program will then wait, monitoring the file for new data. As new lines are added, **tail** will display them for you automatically.

When you use **tail -f**, it waits for new input indefinitely; the program will not stop by itself. To stop it, you must press **^C** (the **intr** key; see Chapter 7). This can present a small problem because, until you stop **tail**, you won't be able to enter more commands. There are two ways to handle the situation.

First, you can run `tail  -f` in the background (see Chapter 26) by using an **&** (ampersand) character at the end of the command.

```
tail -f results &
```

When you run `tail` in the background, it can run unattended as long as you want without tying up your terminal. Moreover, because `tail` is running in the same window or virtual console in which you are working, you will instantly see any new output. The disadvantage is that the output of `tail` will be mixed in with the output of whatever other programs you run, which can be confusing.

Note: When you run a program in the background, you can't stop it by pressing **^C**. Instead, you need to use the `kill` command. (The details are explained in Chapter 26.)

An alternative way to use `tail  -f` is to run it in its own terminal window or virtual console (see Chapter 6). If you do this, once `tail` begins you can leave it alone, do your work in a second window or virtual console, and check back with `tail` whenever you want. Using two windows or consoles in this way not only allows you to run other commands while `tail` is running, but it also keeps the output of `tail` separate. The only drawback is that you must remember to keep an eye on the window or console where `tail` is running.

If you would like to practice using `tail  -f`, here is an experiment to try. To start, open two terminal windows (see Chapter 6). In the first window, use the `cat` command to create a small file named **example**:

```
cat > example
```

Type 4-5 lines and then press **^D** to end the input and stop the command. (Using `cat` to create a small file is explained in Chapter 16; using **^D**, the **eof** key, is explained in Chapter 7.)

In the second terminal window, enter the following `tail` command:

```
tail -f example
```

The `tail` program will list the last 10 lines of **example** and then wait for new input. Now return to the first window and add some more lines to the file. The easiest way to do this is to append the data using **>>** (see Chapter 16). Enter the command:

```
cat >> example
```

Now type as many lines as you want, pressing <Return> at the end of each line. Notice that, each time you type a line in the first window, the line shows up in the second window as output from `tail`.

When you are finished experimenting, press **^D** in the first window to tell `cat` there is no more input. Then press **^C** in the second window to stop `tail`.

If you look back at the syntax for using `tail  -f`, you will see that you can specify more than one file name. This is because `tail` can monitor multiple files at the same time and alert you when any one of them receives new data. If you would like to experiment, set up two terminal windows as in our last example. In the first window, use `cat` to create two small files as described above:

```
cat > file1
cat > file2
```

In the second window, run the following command:

```
tail -f file1 file2
```

Now return to the first window and use the following commands in turn to add lines to one of the two files:

```
cat >> file1
cat >> file2
```

Notice that each time you use **cat** (in the first window) to add lines to one of the files, **tail** (in the second window) shows you the name of the file followed by the new lines.

BINARY, OCTAL AND HEXADECIMAL

To conclude this chapter, we are going to talk about two commands, **od** and **hexdump**, that are used to display data from binary files. To interpret the output of these commands, you will need to understand the binary, octal and hexadecimal number systems. So, before we move on, let's take a moment to discuss these very important concepts.

Although these three number systems are very important to computer science and computer programming, a detailed discussion is, unfortunately, beyond the scope of this book. In this section, I'll cover the basic ideas to get you started. If you have your heart set on becoming a computer person, my advice is to spend some time on your own, studying these topics in detail.

Most of the time, we use numbers composed of the 10 digits, 0 through 9. As such, our everyday numbers are composed of powers of 10: 1, 10, 100, 1000, and so on. We call such numbers DECIMAL NUMBERS. For example, the decimal number 19,563 is actually:

$$(1 \text{x} 10{,}000) + (9 \text{x} 1{,}000) + (5 \text{x} 100) + (6 \text{x} 10) + (3 \text{x} 1)$$

Or, using exponents:

$$(1 \text{x} 10^4) + (9 \text{x} 10^3) + (5 \text{x} 10^2) + (6 \text{x} 10^1) + (3 \text{x} 10^0)$$

We refer to this system as BASE 10 or the DECIMAL SYSTEM. The name comes from the idea that all numbers are constructed from 10 different digits. In the world of computers, there are three other bases that are actually more important than base 10:

• Base 2 (binary): uses 2 digits, 0-1
• Base 8 (octal): uses 8 digits, 0-7
• Base 16 (hexadecimal): uses 16 digits, 0-9 A-F

The importance of these systems comes from the way computer data is stored. This is because all data is organized into sequences of electrical traces that, conceptually, are considered to be either off or on. This is true for any type of data, whether it resides in computer memory (such as RAM or ROM) or stored on disks, CDs, DVDs, flash memory, or other devices.

As a shorthand notation, we represent "off" by the number 0, and "on" by the number 1. In this way, any data item, no matter how long or short, can be considered to be a pattern of 0s and 1s. Indeed, in a technical sense, this is how computer scientists think of data: as long streams of 0s and 1s.

Here are a few simple examples. Within the ASCII code, the letter "m" is represented by the pattern:

01101101

The word "mellow" is represented as:

011011010110010101101100011011000110111101110111

(For a discussion of the ASCII code, see Chapter 19 and 20. For a table showing the details of the code, see Appendix D.)

The ASCII code is used only to represent individual characters. When it comes to working with numerical values, we use a variety of different systems. Without going into the details, here is how the number 3.14159 would be represented using a system called "single precision floating-point":

01000000010010010000111111010000

If these examples seem a bit confusing, don't worry. The details are very complex and not important right now. What is important is that you should understand that, to a computer scientist, all data — no matter what type or how much — is stored as long sequences of 0s and 1s. For this reason, it is important to learn how to work with numbers consisting only of 0s and 1s, which we call BINARY NUMBERS.

In computer science, a single 0 or 1 that is stored as data is called a a BIT ("binary digit"); 8 bits in a row is called a BYTE. For instance, the previous example contains a binary number consisting of 32 bits or 8 bytes of data. We refer to this system as BASE 2 or the BINARY SYSTEM. The name reminds us that, in base 2, all numbers are constructed from only two different digits: 0 and 1.

If you are a beginner, the advantages of base 2 will not be obvious, and binary numbers will look meaningless. However, once you get some experience, you will see that binary numbers directly reflect the underlying reality of how data is stored. This is why, in many cases, using binary numbers offers a significant advantage over using base 10 numbers. However, there is a problem: binary numbers are difficult to use because they take up a lot of room, and because they are unwieldy and confusing to the eye.

As a compromise, there are two ways to represent binary numbers in a more compact fashion without losing the direct connection to the underlying data. They are called "base 8" and "base 16". Before I can explain how they work, I want to take a quick diversion to show you how to count in base 2.

In base 10, we start counting from 0 until we run out of digits. We then add 1 to the digit on the left and start again at 0. For example, we start with 0 and count 1, 2, 3, 4, 5, 6, 7, 8, 9, at which point we run out of digits. The next number is 10. We continue 11, 12, 13, 14, 15, 16, 17, 18, 19, and then go to 20. And so on.

Base 2 (in fact, all bases) work the same way. The only difference is in how far we can go before we run out of digits. In base 2, we have only 2 digits: 0 and 1. We start counting at 0, and then move to 1, at which point we run out of digits. So the next number is 10. Then 11, 100, 101, 110, 111, 1000 and so on. In other words:

0 (base 10) = 0 (base 2)
1 (base 10) = 1 (base 2)
2 (base 10) = 10 (base 2)
3 (base 10) = 11 (base 2)
4 (base 10) = 100 (base 2)
5 (base 10) = 101 (base 2), and so on.

DECIMAL (BASE 10)	BINARY (BASE 2)	OCTAL (BASE 8)	HEXADECIMAL (BASE 16)
0	0	0	0
1	1	1	1
2	10	2	2
3	11	3	3
4	100	4	4
5	101	5	5
6	110	6	6
7	111	7	7
8	1000	10	8
9	1001	11	9
10	1010	12	A
11	1011	13	B
12	1100	14	C
13	1101	15	D
14	1110	16	E
15	1111	17	F
16	10000	20	10
17	10001	21	11
18	10010	22	12
19	10011	23	13
20	10100	24	14

FIGURE 21-5: Decimal, Binary, Octal and Hexadecimal Equivalents

In regular life, we use decimal (base 10) numbers. With computers, data is stored in a form that is best reflected using binary (base 2) numbers. Such data can be written in a more compact form by using either octal (base 8) or hexadecimal (base 16) numbers. (See text for details.)

This table shows the equivalent ways of representing the decimal numbers 0 through 20 in binary, octal and hexadecimal. Can you see the patterns? Do they make sense to you?

Take a look at Figure 21-5 where you will see the decimal numbers 0 through 20, along with their base 2 equivalents. (For now, you can ignore the other two columns.)

BASE 8 is also called OCTAL. With this base, we have 8 digits, 0 through 7, so we count as follows: 0, 1, 2, 3, 4, 5, 6, 7, 10, 11, 12, and so on.

BASE 16, also called HEXADECIMAL or HEX, works in a similar fashion using 16 digits. Of course, if we confine ourselves to regular digits, we only have 10 of them: 0 through 9. To count in base 16, we need 6 more digits, so we use the symbols A, B, C, D, E and F. Thus, in base 16, we count as follows: 0, 1, 2, 3, 4, 5, 6, 7, 8, 9, A, B, C, D, E, F, 10, 11, 12, and so on.

OCTAL (BASE 8)	BINARY (BASE 2)
0	000
1	001
2	010
3	011
4	100
5	101
6	110
7	111

FIGURE 21-6: Octal and Binary Equivalents

Every combination of three base 2 digits (bits) can be represented by a single octal digit. Similarly, each octal digit corresponds to a specific pattern of 3 bits.

Take another look at Figure 21-5. By now, all four columns should be starting to make sense. Of course, this may all be new to you, and I don't expect you to feel comfortable with three new ways of counting right away. However, the time will come when it will all seem easy. For example, an experienced programmer can look at the binary number "1101" and instantly think: 13 decimal. Or he can look at the base 8 number "20" and instantly think: 16 decimal. Or he can look at the base 10 number "13" and instantly think: D in hexadecimal. One day it will be just as easy for you; it's not really that hard once you practice.*

So why is all this so important? The answer lies in Figure 21-6. Suppose you ask the question, how many different 3-bit binary numbers are there? The answer is 8, from 000 to 111 (when you include leading zeros). In Figure 21-6, you can see that each of these 8 values corresponds to a specific octal number. For example, 000 (binary) equals 0 (octal); 101 (binary) equals 5 (octal); and so on. This means that any pattern of 3 bits (binary digits) can be represented by a single octal digit. Conversely, any octal digit corresponds to a specific pattern of 3 bits.

This is an extremely important concept, so let's take a moment to make sure you understand it. As an example, consider the binary representation of "mellow" we looked at earlier:

`011011010110010101101100011011000110111101110111`

Here we have 48 bits. Let's divide them into groups of three:

*When I was an undergraduate student at the University of Waterloo (Canada), I worked as a systems programmer for the university computing center. This was in the days of IBM mainframe computers when it was especially important for system programmers to be comfortable with hexadecimal arithmetic. Most of us could add in base 16, and a few people could subtract. For more complicated calculations, of course, we used calculators. My supervisor, however, was an amazing fellow. His name was Romney White, and he could actually multiply in base 16. Romney was the only person I ever met who was able to do this.

Today, by the way, Romney works at IBM, where he is an expert in using Linux on mainframes. When you have a moment, look him up on the Web. (Search for: "romney white" + "linux".)

```
011 011 010 110 010 101 101 100
011 011 000 110 111 101 110 111
```

Using the table in Figure 21-6, we can replace each set of 3 bits with its equivalent octal number. That is, we replace 011 with 3, 010 with 2, and so on:

```
3 3 2 6 2 5 5 4 3 3 0 6 7 5 6 7
```

Removing the spaces, we have:

```
3326255433067567
```

Notice how much more compact octal is than binary. However, because each octal digit corresponds to exactly 3 bits (binary digits), we have retained all the information exactly. Why does this work out so nicely? It's because 8 is an exact power of 3. In particular, $8 = 2^3$. Thus, each digit in base 8 corresponds to 3 digits in base 2.

At this point, you may be wondering, could we represent long strings of bits even more compactly, if we use a number system based on a higher power of 2? The answer is yes. The value of 2^4 is 16, and we can do even better than base 8 by using base 16 (hexadecimal). This is because each hexadecimal digit can represent 4 bits. You can see this in Figure 21-7.

To see how this works, consider once again, the 48-bit binary representation of "mellow":

```
011011010110010101101100011011000110111101110111
```

To start, let's divide the bits into groups of four:

```
0110 1101 0110 0101 0110 1100 0110 1100 0110 1111 0111 0111
```

Using the table in Figure 21-7, we replace each group of 4 bits by its hexadecimal equivalent:

```
6 D 6 5 6 C 6 C 6 F 7 7
```

Removing the spaces, we have:

```
6D656C6C6F77
```

Thus, the following three values are all equivalent. The first in binary (base 2), the second in octal (base 8), and the third in hexadecimal (base 16):

```
011011010110010101101100011011000110111101110111
3326255433067567
6D656C6C6F77
```

What does this all mean? Because we can represent binary data using either octal characters (3 bits per character) or hexadecimal characters (4 bits per character), we can display the raw contents of any binary file by representing the data as long sequences of either octal or hex numbers. And that, in fact, is what I am going to show you how to do when we discuss the **hexdump** and **od** commands. Before we do, however, we need to discuss just one more topic.

READING AND WRITING BINARY, OCTAL AND HEXADECIMAL

What do you think of when you see the number 101? Most people would say "one hundred and one". However, as a computer person, you might wonder: how do I know I am looking at a base 10 number? Perhaps "101" refers to a base 2 (binary) number, in which case its decimal value would be 5:

$$(1x2^2) + (0x2^1) + (1x2^0) = 4 + 0 + 1 = 5$$

Or perhaps it's base 8 (octal), giving it a value of 65 decimal:

$$(1x8^2) + (0x8^1) + (1x8^0) = 64 + 0 + 1 = 65$$

Or could it be base 16 (hexadecimal), with a value of 257 decimal?

$$(1x16^2) + (0x16^1) + (1x16^0) = 256 + 0 + 1 = 257$$

You can see the problem. Moreover, if you want to speak about the number 101, how would you pronounce it? If you knew it was decimal, you would talk about it in the regular way. But what if it is binary or octal or hex? It doesn't make sense to call it as "one hundred and one".

Within mathematics, we use subscripts to indicate bases. For example, 101_{16} means "101 base 16"; 101_8 means "101 base 8"; 101_2 means "101 base 2". When you don't see a subscript, you know you are looking at a base 10 number.

With computers, we don't have subscripts. Instead, the most common convention is to use a prefix consisting of the digit 0 followed by a letter to indicate the base. The prefix 0x means "base 16" (hex); 0o means "base 8" (octal); 0b means "base 2" (binary). For example, you might see 0x101, 0o101 or 0b101. Sometimes, we indicate octal in a different way, by using a single (otherwise unnecessary) leading 0, such as 0101. You can see these conventions illustrated in Figure 21-8.

I realize that, at first, all this may be a bit confusing. However, most of the time the type of number being used is clear from context. Indeed, you can often guess a base just by looking at a number. For example, if you see 110101011010, it's a good bet you are looking at a binary number. If you see a number like 45A6FC0, you know you are looking at a hex number, because only hexadecimal uses the digits A-F.

HEXADECIMAL (BASE 16)	BINARY (BASE 2)
0	0000
1	0001
2	0010
3	0011
4	0100
5	0101
6	0110
7	0111
8	1000
9	1001
A	1010
B	1011
C	1100
D	1101
E	1110
F	1111

FIGURE 21-7: Hexadecimal and Binary Equivalents

Every combination of four base 2 digits (bits) can be represented by a single hexadecimal digit. Similarly, each hexadecimal digit corresponds to a specific pattern of 4 bits.

MEANING	MATHEMATICS	COMPUTERS	PRONUNCIATION
101 base 10	101	101	"one hundred and one"
101 base 16	101_{16}	0x101	"hex one-zero-one"
101 base 8	101_8	0101 or 0o101	"octal one-zero-one"
101 base 2	101_2	0b101	"binary one-zero-one"

FIGURE 21-8: Conventions for Indicating Hexadecimal, Octal, and Binary Numbers

When we work with non-decimal number systems, we need written and spoken conventions to indicate the base of a number. In mathematics, we use subscripts when writing such numbers. With computers we don't have subscripts, so we usually use a special prefix. When we talk about non-decimal numbers, we pronounce each digit separately.

With hex numbers, you will see both upper- and lowercase letters used as digits. For example, the two numbers 0x45A6FC0, 0x45a6fc0 are the same. Most people, however, prefer to use uppercase digits, as they are easier to read.

When we speak about numbers, the rules are simple. When we refer to decimal numbers, we speak about them in the usual way. For example, 101 base 10 is referred to as "one hundred and one"; 3,056 is "three thousand and fifty-six".

With other bases, we simply say the names of the digits. Sometimes we mention the base. For example, if we want to talk about 101 base 16, we say "one-zero-one base 16" or "hex-one-zero-one"; 3,056 base 16 is "three-zero-five-six base 16" or "hex three-zero-five-six".

Similarly, 101 base 8 is "one-zero-one base 8" or "octal one-zero-one"; and 101 base 2 is "one-zero-one base 2", "binary one-zero-one", or something similar. You can see these pronunciations illustrated in Figure 21-8.

WHY WE USE HEXADECIMAL RATHER THAN OCTAL

In Chapter 7, we talked about the type of technology that was used to create computer memory in the olden days. In particular, I mentioned that, in the 1950s and into the 1960s, memory was made from tiny magnetic cores. For this reason, the word CORE became a synonym for memory.

In those days, debugging a program was difficult, especially when the program aborted unexpectedly. To help with such problems, a programmer could instruct the operating system to print the contents of the memory used by a program at the moment it aborted. The programmer could then study the printed data and try to figure out what happened. As I explained in Chapter 7, such data was called a CORE DUMP, and it took a lot of skill to interpret. Today, the expression "core dump" is still used, but you will sometimes see the term MEMORY DUMP or DUMP used instead.

In the early 1970s when Unix was developed, debugging could be very difficult, and programmers often had to save and examine dumps. Although technology had evolved — magnetic cores had been replaced by semiconductors — memory was still referred to as core, and a copy of the contents of memory was still called a core dump. Thus, when Unix saved the contents of memory to a file for later examination, the file was called a CORE FILE, and the default name for such a file was **core**.

Thus, from the very beginning, Unix programmers had a need to examine core files. To meet this need, the Unix developers created a program to display the contents of a core file as octal (base 8) digits. This program was named **od** ("octal dump") and, over the years, it has proven to be an especially useful program. Even today, using **od** is one of the best ways we have to look at binary data.

As we discussed in the previous section, binary data can be represented as either octal numbers, using 3 bits per digit, or hexadecimal numbers, using 4 bits per digit. Octal is relatively easy to learn because it uses digits that are already familiar to us (0 through 7). Hexadecimal, on the other hand, requires 16 digits, 6 of which (A, B, C, D, E, F) are not part of our everyday culture. As such, hex is a lot more difficult to learn than octal. Nevertheless, hexadecimal is used much more than octal. There are three reasons for this.

First, hex is significantly more compact than octal. (To be precise, hex is $^4/_3$ times more compact than octal.) If you want to display bits, it takes a lot fewer hex characters to do the job than octal characters.

The second reason hex is more popular has to do with how bits are used. Computer processors organize bits into fundamental units called WORDS, the size of a word depending on the design of the processor. Since the mid-1960s, most processors have used 16-bit or 32-bit words; today, it is common to find processors that use 64-bit words. In the 1950s and 1960s, however, many computers, especially scientific computers, used 24-bit or 36-bit words.

With a 24-bit or 36-bit word, it is possible to use either octal or hex, because 24 and 36 are divisible by both 3 and 4. Since octal was simpler, it was used widely in the 1950s and 1960s.

With 16-bit, 32-bit or 64-bit words, it is difficult to use octal, because 16, 32 and 64 are not divisible by 3. It is, however, possible to use hexadecimal, because 16, 32 and 64 are all divisible by 4. For this reason, since the 1970s, hex has been used more and more, and octal has been used less and less.

The third reason why hexadecimal is used so widely is that, although it is harder to learn than octal, once you learn it, it is easy to *use*. For this reason, even the earliest versions of **od** came with an option to display data in hexadecimal.

As I mentioned earlier, the venerable **od** program has been around for years, in fact, since the beginning of Unix. However, in 1992, another such program, called **hexdump**, was written for BSD (Berkeley Unix; see Chapter 2). Today, **hexdump** is widely available, not only on BSD systems, such as FreeBSD, but as part of many Linux distributions.

Most experienced Unix people tend to pick a favorite, either **od** or **hexdump**, and use one or the other. For this reason, I am going to show you how to use both of them, so you can see which one you like best.

DISPLAYING BINARY FILES: hexdump, od

The original use for both **hexdump** and **od** (octal dump) was to look at memory dumps contained in core files. By examining a dump, a programmer could track down bugs that would otherwise be elusive. Today, there are much better debugging tools, and programmers rarely look at core files manually. However, **hexdump** and **od** are still useful, as they can display any type of binary data in a readable format. Indeed, these two programs are the primary text-based tools used to look inside binary files.

Since either of these programs will do the job, I'll show you how to use both of them. You can then do some experimenting and see which one you prefer. The biggest difference between the two programs is that **hexdump**, by default, displays data in hexadecimal, while **od**, which is older, defaults to octal. Thus, if you use **od**, you will have to remember the specific options that generate hex output.

Another consideration is that **od** is available on all Unix systems, while **hexdump** is not. For example, if you use Solaris, you may not have **hexdump**. For this reason, if you work with binary files and you prefer **hexdump**, you should still know a bit about **od**, in case you have to use it one day.

Before we get into the syntax, let's take a look at some typical output. In Figure 21-9, you see a portion of the binary data in the file that holds the **ls** program. (The **ls** program is used to list file names. We will talk about it in Chapter 24.)

When you examine data within a file, there will be times when you need to know the exact location of what you are looking at. When you use **less** to look at a text file, it's easy to figure out where you are. At any time, you can use the **=** (equals sign) command to display the current line number. Alternatively, you can use the **-M** option to show the current line number in the prompt, or you can use the **-N** option to display a number to the left of every line.

With a binary file, there are no lines, so line numbers are not meaningful. Instead, we mark each location within the file by an OFFSET, a number that tells you how many bytes you are from the beginning of the file. The first byte has offset 0; the second byte has offset 1; and so on.

Take a look at the sample data in Figure 21-9. The offset — which is not part of the data — is in the left-hand column. In our example, all the numbers are in hexadecimal, so the offset of the first byte of data is 0x120 (that is, hex 120) or 288 in decimal. Thus, the first byte of data in our example is the 289th byte in the file. (Remember, offsets start at 0.)

The first row of output contains 16 bytes. Thus, the offsets run from 0x120 to 0x12F. The second row starts at offset 0x130. To the right of each offset the 16 bytes per line are displayed in two different formats. In the middle column are hex digits, grouped in bytes.

OFFSET	HEXADECIMAL		ASCII
000120	00 00 00 00 00 00 00 00	00 00 00 00 06 00 00 00	|................|
000130	04 00 00 00 2f 6c 69 62	2f 6c 64 2d 6c 69 6e 75	|..../lib/ld-linu|
000140	78 2e 73 6f 2e 32 00 00	04 00 00 00 10 00 00 00	|x.so.2..........|
000150	01 00 00 00 47 4e 55 00	00 00 00 00 02 00 00 00	|....GNU.........|
000160	06 00 00 00 09 00 00 00	61 00 00 00 76 00 00 00	|........a...v...|
000170	00 00 00 00 4c 00 00 00	4b 00 00 00 3f 00 00 00	|....L...K...?...|

FIGURE 21-9: Sample binary data displayed as hexadecimal and ASCII

You can use the **hexdump** *or* **od** *commands to display binary data. Here is a sample of such data displayed in canonical format; that is, with the offset in hexadecimal on the left, the data in hex in the middle, and the same data as ASCII characters on the right. This particular example was taken from the file that contains the GNU/Linux* **ls** *program.*

(Remember, one byte = 8 bits = 2 hex digits.) On the right, the same data is displayed as ASCII characters.

Within most binary files, you will notice that some bytes contain actual ASCII characters. It is easy to identify these bytes by looking at the rightmost column. In our example, you can see the strings **/lib/ld-linux.so.2** and **GNU**. By convention, bytes that do not correspond to printable ASCII characters are indicated by a . (period) character. You can see many such bytes in our example.

Most bytes in a binary file are not characters; they are machine instructions, numeric data, and so on. You can tell this by looking in the rightmost column, where you will see mostly . markers, with a sprinkling of random characters. In our example, the first line and last two lines contain all non-ASCII data. A few bytes do contain values that happen to correspond to characters, but this is coincidental and not meaningful.

The way in which data is displayed in Figure 21-9 is called CANONICAL FORMAT. This format, used for binary data that is displayed or printed, consists of 16 bytes per line. To the left of each line is the offset in hexadecimal. In the middle are the actual bytes, also in hexadecimal. On the right are the ASCII equivalents.

Both **hexhdump** and **od** are able to display binary in many different formats. In fact, both commands support a large variety of options that give you enormous control over how data is displayed. Most of the time, however, it is best to use the canonical format. For that reason, in our discussion of these commands, I will show you which options to use to produce this type of output. If you need information about the other variations, you can find it on the respective man pages.

We'll start with **hexdump** because it is simpler to use. To use **hexdump** to display a binary file in canonical format, the syntax is simple:

hexdump -C [*file...*]

where *file* is the name of a file.

The **hexdump** program has many options that allow you to control output. However, there is an important shortcut: if you use the **-C** (canonical) option, **hexdump** will automatically use the appropriate combination of options so as to produce canonical output.

Here is an example. Let's say you want to look inside the binary file that contains the **ls** program. To start, you use the **whereis** program to find the pathname — that is, the exact location — of the file. (We'll discuss pathnames and **whereis** in Chapter 24, so don't worry about the details for now.) The command to use is:

whereis ls

Typical output would be:

ls: /bin/ls /usr/share/man/man1/ls.1.gz

The output shows us the exact locations of the program and its man page. We are only interested in the program, so we use the first pathname:

```
hexdump -C /bin/ls | less
```

This command displays the contents of the entire file in canonical format. That's all there is to it.

If you want to limit the amount of data being displayed, there are two more options you can use. The **-s** (skip over) option allows you to set the initial offset by specifying how many bytes to skip at the beginning of the file. For example, to display data starting from offset 0x120 (hex 120) use:

```
hexdump -C -s 0x120 /bin/ls | less
```

To limit the amount of output, you use the **-n** (number of bytes) option. The following command starts at offset 0x120 and displays 96 bytes of data (that is, 6 lines of output). In this case, the amount of output is so small, we don't need to pipe it to **less**:

```
hexdump -C -s 0x120 -n 96 /bin/ls
```

This, by the way, is the exact command that generated the output for Figure 21-9.

Incorporating these two options into the syntax, we can define a more comprehensive specification for **hexdump**:

```
hexdump -C [-s offset] [-n length] [file...]
```

where *file* is the name of a file, *offset* is the number of bytes to skip over at the beginning of the file, and *length* is the number of bytes to display. Note: **offset** can be in any base, but **length** must be a decimal number. (No one knows why; make up your own reason.)

HINT

With FreeBSD, you can use the command **hd** as an alias for **hexdump -C**. Thus, on a FreeBSD system, the following two commands are equivalent:

```
hd /bin/ls
hexdump -C /bin/ls
```

If you would like to use this handy command on a different system, all you need to do is create an alias of your own, using one of the following commands. The first one is for the Bourne Shell family; the second is for the C-Shell family:

```
alias hd='hexdump -C'
alias hd 'hexdump -C'
```

To make the alias permanent, put the appropriate command into your environment file. (Aliases are discussed in Chapter 13; the environment file is discussed in Chapter 14.)

To use **od** to display a binary file in canonical format, the syntax is:

```
od -Ax -tx1z [file...]
```

where *file* is the name of a file.

The **-A** (address) option allows you to specify which number system to use for the offset values. For canonical output, you specify **x**, which displays the offsets in hexadecimal.

The **-t** (type of format) option controls how the data is to be displayed. For canonical output, you specify **x1**, which displays the data in hex one byte at a time, and **z**, which displays ASCII equivalents at the end of each line. For a full list of format codes, see the man page (**man od**) or the info file (**info od**).

(Note: This syntax is for the GNU version of **od**, such as you will find with Linux. If you are using a system that does not have the GNU utilities, the command will be more primitive. In particular, you won't be able to use the **z** format code. Check your man page for details.)

As an example, the following **od** command is equivalent to our original **hexdump** command. It displays the contents of the **ls** file in canonical format:

```
od -Ax -tx1z /bin/ls | less
```

If you want to limit the amount of data being displayed, there are two more options you can use. The **-j** (jump over) option specifies how many bytes to skip at the beginning of the file. For example, to start displaying data from offset 0x120 (hex 120) use:

```
od -Ax -tx1z -j 0x120 /bin/ls | less
```

To limit the amount of output, use the **-N** (number of bytes) option. The following command starts at offset 0x120 and displays 96 bytes (6 lines of output). In this case, the amount of output is so small, we don't need to pipe it to **less**:

```
od -Ax -tx1z -j 0x120 -N 96 /bin/ls
```

This command generates output similar to what you see in Figure 21-9.

Incorporating these two options into the syntax, we can define a more comprehensive syntax for **od**:

```
od -Ax -tx1z [-j offset] [-N length] [file...]
```

where *file* is the name of a file; *offset* is number of bytes to skip over at the beginning of the file; and *length* is the number of bytes to display, in decimal, hex or octal.

HINT

The syntax for **od** is complex and awkward. However, you can simplify by creating an alias to specify the options that produce output in canonical format. The following commands will do the job. The first command is for the Bourne Shell family; the second is for the C-Shell family:

```
alias od='od -Ax -tx1z'
alias od 'od -Ax -tx1z'
```

Once you have such an alias, whenever you type **od**, you will automatically get the output you want. To make the alias permanent, put one of these commands into your environment file. (Aliases are discussed in Chapter 13; the environment file is discussed in Chapter 14.)

WHAT'S IN A NAME?

Canonical

Earlier in the chapter, when we discussed how interactive text-based programs handle input, I talked about canonical mode and non-canonical mode. In this section, I mentioned that a certain format for binary output is called canonical output. Computer scientists use "canonical" differently from the regular English meaning, so you should understand the distinction.

In general English, the word "canonical" is related to the idea of a canon, a collection of official rules governing the members of a Christian church. Canonical describes something that follows the rules of the canon. Thus, one might refer to the canonical practices of the Catholic Church.

In mathematics, the same term has a more exact and streamlined meaning. It refers to the simplest, most important way of expressing a mathematical idea. For example, high school students are taught the canonical formula for finding the roots of a quadratic equation.

Computer scientists borrowed the term from mathematics and, in doing so, they relaxed the meaning significantly. In computer science, CANONICAL refers to the most common, conventional way of doing something. For example, in our discussion of the **od** and **hexdump** commands, we talked about the canonical format for displaying binary data. There is nothing magical about this format. However, it works well, it has been used for well over four decades, and it is what people expect, so it is canonical.

WHY DOES SO MUCH COMPUTER TERMINOLOGY COME FROM MATHEMATICS?

As you learn more and more computer science, you will notice that much of the terminology is derived from mathematics. As an example, the word "canonical" — which we used in two different ways in this chapter — comes from a similar mathematical term. You might be wondering why so much computer terminology comes from mathematics. There are several reasons.

Early computer science was developed in the 1950s and 1960s from mathematical theory created in the 1930s and 1940s. In particular, the mathematical foundations of computer science came from the work of Alan Turing (1912-1954), John von Neumann (1903-1957), Alonzo Church (1903-1995) and, to a lesser extent, Kurt Gödel (1906-1978).

During the 1950s and 1960s, almost all computer scientists were mathematicians. Indeed, computer science was considered to be a branch of mathematics(*). It was only natural, then, for pioneers to draw upon terminology from their own fields to describe new ideas.

Over the years, as computer science developed, it required a great deal of analysis and formalization. As with other sciences, the necessary techniques and insight were taken from mathematics which, having been studied and formalized for over 2,000 years, was rich in such tools. (This is why the great German mathematician and scientist Carl Friedrich Gauss referred to mathematics as "The Queen of Sciences".) Even today, computer scientists and programmers in need of abstraction and logical reasoning borrow heavily from mathematics. As they do, it is common for them to modify mathematical terms to suit their own needs.

*At the school where I did my undergraduate work — the University of Waterloo, Canada — the Department of Computer Science was (and still is) part of the Faculty of Mathematics. Indeed, my undergraduate degree is actually a Bachelor of Mathematics with a major in Computer Science.

CHAPTER 21 EXERCISES

REVIEW QUESTIONS

1. Which programs do you use to display a text file one screenful at a time? An entire text file all at once? The first part of a text file? The last part of a text file? A binary file?

2. As you are using **less** to display a file, which commands do you use to perform the following actions? Go forward one screenful; go backward one screenful; go to the first line; go to the last line; search forward; search backward; display help; quit the program.

3. You can use **less** to display more than one file, for example:

```
less file1 file2 file3 file4 file5
```

As you are reading, which commands do you use to perform the following actions? Change to the next file; change to the previous file; change to the first file; delete the current file from the list. Which commands do you use to search forward and search backward within all the files?

4. What command would you use to watch the end of a growing file?

5. When you display a binary file, what is canonical format? How do you display a file in canonical format using **hexdump**? Using **od**?

APPLYING YOUR KNOWLEDGE

1. Check the value of your PAGER environment variable. If it is not set to **less**, do so now. Display the man page (Chapter 9) for the **less** program itself. Perform the following operations:

   • Display help information. Page down to the end of help, one screenful at a time. Take a moment to read each screen. Quit help.
   • Search forward for "help". Search again. Search again. Then search backward.
   • Go to the end of the man page.
   • Go backward one screenful.
   • Go to line 100.
   • Display the current line number.
   • Go to the line 20 percent of the way through the man page.
   • Display the current line number.
   • Go to the beginning of the man page.
   • Quit.

2. You want to use **less** to display the contents of the file **list**, which contains many lines of text. Along with the text, you also want to see line numbers. However, there are no line numbers within the text, and you do not want to change the original file in any way. How would you do this using **nl** and **less**? How would you do it using only **less**? Is there any advantage to using **nl**?

3. Convert the following binary (base 2) number to octal (base 8), hexadecimal (base 16), and decimal (base 10). You must show your work.

   1111101000100101

4. Use the **strings** command (Chapter 19) to look for character strings within the binary file **/bin/ls**. Select one string and use **hexdump** or **od** to find the exact position of that string in the file.

FOR FURTHER THOUGHT

1. You want to use **less** to search through five different files, looking for a particular sequence of words. The obvious solution is to use **less** as follows:

   ```
   less file1 file2 file3 file4 file5
   ```

   However, this requires you to keep track of and manipulate five different files. Instead you might first combine the files into one large file:

   ```
   cat file1 file2 file3 file4 file5 | less
   ```

   Will this make your job easier or harder? Why?

2. In the text, we discussed four numbers systems: decimal (base 10), binary (base 2), octal (base 8) and hexadecimal (base 16). In principle, any positive whole number can be used as a base. Consider base 12, also called DUODECIMAL. In base 12 we use the digits 0 through 9. For the extra two digits, we use A and B. Thus, in base 12, we count as follows: 0, 1, 2, 3, 4, 5, 6, 7, 8, 9, A, B, 10, 11, 12, and so on. The number 22 in base 10 equals 1A in base 12.

   What important advantages does base 12 have over base 10? Hint: How many factors does 12 have compared to 10? How does this simplify calculations? Would our culture be better off if we used base 12 instead of base 10?

   In spite of its advantages, we don't use base 12 with computers. Most of the time we use base 16, which is much more complicated. Why is this?

   By the way, if you have ever read the *Lord of the Rings* books by J.R.R. Tolkein, you will be interested to know that the Elvish languages use a duodecimal number system.

CHAPTER 22
THE vi TEXT EDITOR

A TEXT EDITOR — often referred to as an EDITOR — is a program used to create and modify text files. When you use such a program to modify a file, we say that you EDIT the file.

It is important that you learn how to use a Unix editor well, as you will need it whenever you want to work with plain text. If you are a programmer, you will need an editor to write your programs. For non-programming tasks, you will need an editor to create and modify configuration files, shell scripts, initialization files, Web pages, simple documents, and so on; in fact, you will need an editor when you work with any file that contains text.

Unlike a word processor, an editor works only with plain text, that is, data consisting of printable characters: letters, numbers, punctuation, spaces and tabs (see Chapter 19). As a general rule, editors use one simple monospaced font. Thus, you do not use an editor when you want to prepare a document that has more than one font, or that uses various font sizes, colors, italics, boldface or other attributes. For such work, you use a word processor.

In this chapter, we will cover **vi**, the most important of the Unix editors. Although I will not be able to explain everything — that would take at least several chapters — I will show you most of what you need to know most of the time. (Note: the name **vi** is pronounced as two separate letters: "vee-eye".)

Throughout this chapter, we will be talking about editing "files" even though, strictly speaking, I have not yet explained what a file actually is. I'll do that in Chapter 23, when we discuss the Unix file system. For now, we'll just use the intuitive idea that a file has a name and contains information. For example, you might use **vi** to edit a file named **essay**, which contains the text of an essay you have written.

When you first learn **vi**, it will seem awkward. There is no getting around that. If you feel frustrated, remember that, at one time, everyone has felt the same way. However, once you become experienced, everything will make sense, and **vi** will seem natural and easy to use. This suggests the following hint which, in Chapter 1, we applied to Unix in general:

HINT

vi is easy to use, but difficult to learn.

WHY IS **vi** SO IMPORTANT?

There are many different Unix/Linux text editors, including the simple ones we discussed in Chapter 14 (**kedit**, **gedit**, Pico and Nano). However, the two principal Unix text editors are **vi** and Emacs, both of which have been around for a long time. They are powerful, mature, full-featured programs, by far, the mostly widely used editors. Either one of them will meet your needs.

The **vi** and Emacs editors are vastly different from one another and, as you might expect, it is common to find people disagreeing about which one is better. Indeed, the Unix community has been arguing the question for many years. The truth is **vi** and Emacs represent totally different ways of approaching the activity of text editing. As such, there are **vi** people and there are Emacs people and, when it comes to editing, they see the world differently. Eventually, when you become experienced enough, you yourself will have to make a choice: will you be a **vi** person or an Emacs person?

For now, all you need to understand is that **vi** and Emacs are very complex, and they both take a long time to learn. In this chapter, I will teach you how to use **vi** because it is the more important of the two editors. Later, you can teach yourself Emacs if you so desire.

Regardless of which program you end up choosing for your primary editor, you *must* learn **vi**. The reason is that, unlike any other editor, **vi** is ubiquitous. It has been used by so many people for so long that you will find it on almost every Unix and Linux system in the world. More formally, **vi** is part of the two principal Unix specifications: POSIX (see Chapter 11) and the Single Unix Specification (the standards that must be met to call something "Unix"). Thus, by definition, **vi** must be available on every Unix system, no matter how esoteric. This means that, once you know how to use **vi**, you will be able to edit text on any Unix or Linux system you may encounter, which means you will always be able to edit a configuration file, create an initialization file, or write a simple shell script.

This is particularly important when you work within an environment that provides limited tools. For example, if you have problems with your system and you boot from a rescue disk, you will probably find that **vi** is the only available text editor. Similarly, **vi** is often the only editor available on embedded systems (computerized devices such as mobile phones, DVD players, appliances, and so on).

Personally, I have been using Unix since 1976, and I have never seen a system that did not have **vi**.* Indeed, the **vi** editor is used so widely and is so important that, if you ever apply for a job working with Unix or Linux, it will be assumed that you know **vi**.

A QUICK HISTORY OF **vi**

The **vi** editor was created by Bill Joy, while he was a graduate student at U.C. Berkeley in the late 1970s (Figure 22-1). Joy, an astonishingly skillful programmer, was one of the most prolific and important contributors during the early days of Unix (see Chapter

---

*Some Linux distributions do not automatically install either **vi** or Emacs. The most common reason is that the creators of the distributions did not want to take sides in the never-ending **vi**/Emacs debate. As an alternative, one of the simpler text editors, such as Nano (see Chapter 14) will be installed by default. Rest assured, if you ever encounter such a system, it is very easy to install **vi**.

---

2). In addition to **vi**, Joy was also responsible for the original BSD (Berkeley Unix), the C-Shell, and the first robust implementation of TCP/IP, the protocols that support the Internet. In 1982, he co-founded Sun Microsystems, where he contributed significantly to the development of NFS (Network File System) and the SPARC microprocessor architecture. To understand how, in the late 1970s, Joy came to write **vi** as a grad student, it is necessary to go back to the early days of Unix.

The first important Unix editor was **ed** (pronounced as two separate letters, "ee-dee"). It was written at Bell Labs in 1971 by Ken Thompson, one of the two original creators of Unix (the other being Dennis Ritchie; see Chapters 1 and 2). The **ed** editor was a LINE-ORIENTED EDITOR or LINE EDITOR, which meant that it worked with numbered lines of text. For example, you might enter a command to print lines 100 though 150, or to delete line 17. Such an approach was necessary because of the slowness and limited capabilities of the early terminals (described in Chapter 3).

In the fall of 1975, Bill Joy moved from the University of Michigan In the fall of 1975, Bill Joy left the University of Michigan to become a graduate computer science student at U.C. Berkeley. He had planned to study computing theory, which is quite mathematical. His work, however, led him into programming and, serendipitously, to Unix. The reason was that Ken Thompson happened to be at Berkeley at the same time.

Thompson, who was taking a sabbatical from Bell Labs, had decided to spend a year at Berkeley, his alma mater, as a visiting professor. He arrived at a time when the Berkeley Computer Science department had just acquired a brand new PDP 11/70 minicomputer.

Photo courtesy of Kirk McKusick

FIGURE 22-1: Bill Joy and Dennis Ritchie

In the late 1970s, Bill Joy (right) was a graduate student at U.C. Berkeley. During that time, Joy created the **vi** *editor and the C- Shell, and put together the very first version of BSD (Berkeley Unix).*

In this photo, taken in June 1984 at a Usenix conference in Snowbird, Utah, Joy is shown with Dennis Ritchie (left), co-developer of the original Unix operating system (see Chapter 3). By the time this photo was taken, BSD, along with **vi** *and the C-Shell, were used widely around the world. The round button on Joy's left sleeve (on your right) reads "The Joy of Unix".*

Working with two students, Thompson installed the latest version of Unix (Version 6) on the new computer. He then installed a Pascal system to run under Unix. (Pascal is a programming language, created in 1970 by the Swiss computer scientist, Niklaus Wirth, to teach structured programming.)

Joy and another student, Charles Haley, were intrigued with Thompson's Pascal implementation, and they decided to use it to work on general context-free parsing algorithms (methods used to analyze the structure of source programs). Joy and Haley soon found, however, that the Pascal system had significant limitations. They started to fix the problems, which brought them smack up against the primitive **ed** editor.

Joy and Haley found **ed** so frustrating, they decided to create a better editor. At the time, another visitor, George Coulouris from Queen Mary College (London), had brought his own software to Berkeley: in this case, an editor called **em** ("ee-em"). Coulouris had created **em** as a backward compatible replacement for **ed**. He chose the name **em** to mean "editor for mortals" (the idea being that **ed** was not fit for regular human beings). Joy and Haley took parts of **em** and put them into **ed** to create a hybrid, which they named **en** ("ee-en").

The **en** editor was far from perfect. Both Joy and Haley spent a lot of time working on it, creating one new version after another. Eventually, they came up with something that worked reasonably well, which they called **ex** ("ee-ex"). Compared to **ed**, **ex** was a vastly improved editor. Still, it was a line-oriented editor, the type of program that was appropriate for very old terminals and slow modems.

FIGURE 22-2: The Lear Siegler ADM-3A terminal

*It is a well-known principle that software enhancements are often driven by new hardware. This was the case in 1976, when Bill Joy developed the **vi** text editor. The older line-oriented editors, such as **ed** and **ex**, were designed for use with primitive line-oriented terminals. However, Joy had access to a new screen-oriented terminal, the Lear Siegler ADM-3A. The advanced capabilities of this terminal inspired Joy to create **vi**, a screen-oriented editor. See text for details.*

But now it was 1976, and Joy and Haley had access to a newer type of terminal, the Lear Siegler ADM-3A. The ADM-3A was much more sophisticated than the old Teletype ASR33 on which **ed** had been developed at Bell Labs (see Chapter 3). Where an ASR33 printed output on paper, one line at a time, the ADM-3A had a monitor and was able to display text anywhere on the screen. You can see a photo of an Lear Siegler ADM-3A in Figure 22-2. Compare this to the photo of the Teletype ASR33 in Chapter 3.

To take advantage of the increased capabilities of the ADM-3A, Joy enhanced **ex** by creating a separate screen-oriented interface, which he called **vi** ("vee-eye"). The new **vi** editor supported all of the **ex** commands as well as a large number of new commands that allowed the use of the full screen. For example, unlike the older line-oriented editors, **vi** allowed you to jump visually from one place to another as you edited a file. You could also insert, modify or delete text anywhere you wanted without having to worry about line numbers. In this way, **vi** was a SCREEN-ORIENTED EDITOR or SCREEN EDITOR.

To this day, the **vi** editor is still based on an amalgam of screen-oriented commands and line-oriented commands. Thus, as you learn **vi**, you must teach yourself two different types of commands. As you might expect, this means it can take awhile to learn how to use **vi** well. Still, as you will see, being able to edit your data in two different ways at the same time makes for a particularly powerful tool.

Interestingly enough, **vi** and **ex** are actually the same program. If you start the program in the usual way, using the **vi** command, you see the screen-oriented interface. If you start the program with the **ex** command, you get the older line-oriented interface.

WHAT'S IN A NAME?

ed, ex, vi
In the early days of Unix, many commands were given short, two-letter names. The convention was to pronounce these names as two separate letters. For example, **ed** is "ee-dee"; **ex** is "ee-ex"; and **vi** is "vee-eye". It is incorrect to pronounce **vi** as a single syllable "vie".

The meaning of the name **ed** is simple: it stands for "editor".

The name **ex** is less straightforward. Many people think it was chosen to mean "extended editor". In one sense, this is true, as **ex** greatly extended the power of **ed**. Although the details are a bit fuzzy, the name was actually a continuation of the pattern **ed**... **en**... **ex**. Charles Haley, the co-author of **ex** explained it to me thus: "I think there was an **en**. I don't remember an **eo**. I think we went from **en** to "e-whatever" or **ex**. Bill Joy made a similar comment once in an interview: "I don't know if there was an **eo** or an **ep**, but finally there was **ex**. I remember **en**, but I don't know how it got to **ex**."

If you are interested in seeing which two-letter command names are still in use, look at the end of Chapter 20, where I show how to use the **grep** program to find these names on your own system. If you have a few moments, you might look up these commands in the online manual: you will find some forgotten gems.

Regardless, when Joy extended **ex** by adding screen-oriented commands, he chose a new 2-character name, **vi**, meaning "visual editor".

There were two practical reasons why so many commands were given such small names. First, smart people tend to prefer short, easy-to-use abbreviations. Second, the old terminals were agonizingly slow, and it was convenient to use short command names that were easy to type correctly.

VIM: AN ALTERNATIVE TO `vi`

The **vi** editor was created by Bill Joy in 1976 and distributed as part of 2BSD (the second version of Berkeley Unix) in mid-1978. Eventually, the editor became so popular that AT&T included it in System V, making **vi** the de facto Unix editor. Over the years, many people worked on **vi**, as the responsibility for maintaining it passed from Joy to other programmers. With so many people using and modifying the program, you would expect **vi** to be enhanced, as indeed it was. Until 1992, however, the enhancements were relatively minor.

This was because Joy's original design was so good that, for a long time, there was no pressing need for major improvements. Indeed, to this day, when you use **vi**, what you see in front of you is almost exactly what BSD users were using in the late 1970s. This is not to say that **vi** cannot be improved. It's just that such changes would be so fundamental as to turn **vi** into a significantly different program.

In fact, that is exactly what happened. In the late 1980s, an open source **vi**-clone named STvi (often written as STevie) was created for non-Unix systems. In 1988, a Dutch programmer named Bram Moolenaar took STvi and used it to create a new program he called VIM, the name meaning "**vi** imitation". For several years, Moolenaar worked on Vim, fixing bugs and adding new features until, in 1992, he released the first Unix version of the program. By now, there were so many enhancements, that Moolenaar changed the meaning of the name. Although the program was still called Vim, Moolenaar declared that, from now on, the name should stand for "**vi** improved".

Throughout the 1990s, Vim grew in popularity, particularly within the more geeky part of the Linux community: the programmers, system administrators, network managers, and so on. By the early 2000s, Vim was so popular that it became the editor of choice for most such users and, by 2005, many Linux distributions had replaced **vi** with Vim. Indeed, if you are using Linux right now, chances are that your system has only Vim and not **vi**. If so, when you enter the **vi** command or when you display the **vi** man page (**man vi**), what you will get will be Vim, not **vi**. This is not the case for most non-Linux systems. In fact, with many types of Unix, it is likely that your system will not have Vim unless you have installed it yourself.

In this chapter, we will not talk much about Vim. Rather, we will cover standard **vi**: the canonical program that has been the text editing workhorse for so many years. I have chosen to do this for two reasons.

First, Vim is not really a new version of **vi** or even an extension of **vi**. Vim is a completely different program that is backward compatible with **vi**. The distinction is important. When you run Vim, you are using an editor that has many sophisticated features that do not exist in **vi**. Of course, because Vim is backwards compatible, you can use all the standard **vi** commands. However, the new features that Vim offers are so far-reaching that they make using Vim a much different experience than using **vi**.

As difficult as **vi** can be for beginners, Vim can be more difficult, because it requires you to learn, not only all the **vi** and **ex** commands, but all the additional Vim commands. Moreover, when you use the special features of Vim, your minute-to-minute strategies for solving problems are significantly different from when you use **vi**. For this reason, if you want to learn Vim, the best strategy is to learn **vi** first.

Although this sounds complicated, it actually isn't. Because Vim is crafted so artfully, you can use it exactly as if it were `vi`. Later, once you are comfortable with `vi`, you can expand your horizons and teach yourself how to take full advantage of Vim's power. To help you, at the end of the chapter I will take a few moments to talk about the extra features Vim has to offer and to show you how to get started.

The second reason we are going to concentrate on standard `vi` is that it *is* a standard. No matter what type of Unix or Linux you use, no matter how small your system, `vi` is the only comprehensive text editor that is likely to be available. As such, even if your personal editor-of-choice is Vim, Emacs, Nano, Pico, or something else, using `vi` is a basic skill you need to master.

> **HINT**
>
> How do you know if your system uses Vim instead of `vi`? Enter the command to display the `vi` man page:
>
> `man vi`
>
> If you see the Vim man page, you know your system uses Vim instead of `vi`.

STARTING `vi`

To start `vi`, the basic syntax is:

`vi` `[-rR]` [*file...*]

where *file* is the name of a file you want to edit.

The `vi` program is very complex and, as you might imagine, it has many options. Most of the time, however, you won't need any of them. Indeed, under normal circumstances, you only need to know about two options, `-r` and `-R`, both of which we'll talk about later in the chapter.

To use `vi` to edit an existing file, just specify the name of the file, for example:

`vi essay`

To create a new file, you have two choices. First, you can specify a file name. If the file does not exist, `vi` will create it for you. For example, to use `vi` to create a brand new file named **message**, you would use:

`vi message`

Alternatively, you can create an empty file by entering the `vi` command by itself without a file name:

`vi`

This tells `vi` to create a new file without a name. You can specify the name later, when it comes time to save your data.

STARTING VIM: `vim`

As we discussed earlier, on some systems, especially Linux systems, **vi** has been replaced by Vim. If this is the case on your system, my goal is for you to use Vim as if it were **vi**. Later, once you are comfortable with **vi**, you can teach yourself how to use the extended features offered by Vim. (We'll talk about this more at the end of the chapter.)

For now, all you have to know is how to start Vim so it acts like **vi**. In general, starting Vim is just like starting **vi**. If you specify the name of an existing file, Vim will open it for you. If the file does not exist, Vim will create it for you. If you don't specify a file name, Vim will create an empty file that you can name later, when you save your work. The basic syntax is:

vim -C [**-rR**] [*file...*]

The **-r** and **-R** options work the same way as with **vi**: we'll talk about them later in the chapter. For now, the only option I want to talk about is **-C**. Within both **vi** and Vim, there are many internal settings you can use to affect the behavior of the program. When you start Vim with **-C**, it changes the settings so as to make Vim act as much like **vi** as possible. When you use Vim in this way, we say that it runs in COMPATIBILITY MODE**. Until you have mastered **vi** and are ready to switch to the full Vim, it is a good idea to always start Vim in compatibility mode. For example:

```
vim -C essay
vim -C
```

The first command tells Vim you want to work with a file named **essay**. If the file exists, Vim will open it for you; if not, Vim will create it. The second command tells Vim to create a brand new, unnamed file. This is the command to use when you want to create a new file but you haven't yet decided what to name it.

If Vim has replaced **vi** on your system, the **vi** command will have the same effect as the **vim** command. On such systems, the following two commands are equivalent to the previous commands:

```
vi -C essay
vi -C
```

*As we discussed in Chapter 7, it is a Unix convention to write the ^ (circumflex) character as an abbreviation for <Ctrl>. Thus, **^G** refers to the single character <Ctrl-G>.

On some systems, Vim will not start in compatibility mode when you use the **-C option. If this is the case on your system, you can force Vim into compatibility mode by turning on the **compatible** option in your Vim initialization file (explained later in the chapter).

Whenever you start Vim without specifying a file name, the program will display some helpful information (see Figure 22-3). This information is only for your convenience. Vim will remove it as soon as you begin to enter data.

HINT

Here is a simple test you can run to see if your system uses Vim instead of **vi**. Enter the **vi** command with no file name:

```
vi
```

If you see a mostly empty screen, you are using standard **vi**. If you see the special help information shown in Figure 22-3, you are using Vim. (Once you have run the test, quit the program by typing **:q**, a colon followed by a lowercase "q".)

HINT

To use Vim as if it were **vi**, you start the program in compatibility mode by using the **-C** option. For convenience, you can create an alias using one of the following commands. The first command is for the Bourne shell family (Bash, Korn Shell); the second is for the C-Shell family (Tcsh, C-Shell):

```
alias vi="vim -C"
alias vi "vim -C"
```

To make the alias permanent, put the command in your environment file (see Chapter 14). Once you do this, you can use the **vi** command to run Vim in compatibility mode, and the **vim** command to run Vim in its native mode.

```
                    VIM - Vi IMproved

                      version 7.0.42
                   by Bram Moolenaar et al.
              Modified by <bugzilla@redhat.com>
          Vim is open source and freely distributable

                  Sponsor Vim development!
        type  :help sponsor<Enter>     for information

        type  :q<Enter>                to exit
        type  :help<Enter>  or  <F1>   for on-line help
        type  :help version7<Enter>    for version info

              Running in Vi compatible mode
        type  :set nocp<Enter>         for Vim defaults
        type  :help cp-default<Enter>  for info on this
```

FIGURE 22-3: Vim Startup Screen

When you start Vim without specifying the name of a file, you will see a startup screen with helpful information. The information is displayed for your convenience: it will disappear as soon as you begin to enter data.

COMMAND MODE AND INPUT MODE

As you work with **vi**, your data is kept in a storage area called an EDITING BUFFER. When you tell **vi** that you want to edit a file, **vi** copies the contents of the file to the editing buffer, so you work with a copy of your data, not with the original. Understanding the editing buffer is crucial to using **vi**, so hold on to the concept as you continue reading.

Take a moment to think about what it is like to use a word processor. You can move the cursor to any place you want and just start typing. When you need to move from one place to another within the file, you can use your mouse or the special navigation keys on your keyboard. With a PC, these would be <PageUp>, <PageDown>, <Home>, <End>, and the cursor control (arrow) keys. When you need to use a command, you select an item from a pull-down menu or use a special key combination.

In 1976, when Bill Joy was developing **vi**, terminals did not have navigation keys. Nor did they support GUIs with a mouse, pull-down menus, function keys, or even an <Alt> key. There were only the letters of the alphabet, the numbers, punctuation, and a few miscellaneous keys such as <Shift>, <Ctrl>, <Return> and <Esc>. Without a mouse or navigation keys, there was no simple way to move the cursor from one position to another. Without pull-down menus or special keys, it was not obvious how the user might specify commands, such as insert, change, delete, copy or paste.

The solution Joy chose was to design **vi** to work in two different modes. In COMMAND MODE, whichever keys you type are interpreted as commands. For example, in command mode, the single letter **x** is the command to delete a character; the combination **dd** is the command to delete an entire line. There are many such 1- and 2-character commands and, in order to master **vi**, you are going to have to learn many of them. This may sound difficult but, with a bit of practice, the **vi** commands are actually quite easy to use.

The second mode is INPUT MODE. In this mode, everything you type is inserted directly into the editing buffer. For example, in input mode, if you type "Hello Harley", these 12 characters are inserted into the editing buffer. If you press the **x** key, an "x" is inserted; if you press **dd**, the letters "dd" are inserted.

The beauty of this system is that it does not require anything special, such as navigation keys or a mouse. As such, you can use **vi** with any type of terminal, even over a remote connection. The only special keys you need are <Ctrl> and <Esc>, which were available on every terminal in general use in the late 1970s.

Of course, for the system to work, there must be a way to switch from command mode to input mode and back again. When **vi** starts, you are in command mode. To change to input mode, you use one of several commands (which you will learn in due course). Once you are in input mode, changing back to command mode is easy: just press the <Esc> (Escape) key. If you are already in command mode and you press <Esc>, **vi** will beep.

If you are wondering why the <Esc> key was chosen for this task, take a look at Figure 22-4: a drawing of the keyboard layout of the ADM-3A terminal taken from the ADM-3A Operators Manual. As we discussed earlier, this was the terminal Bill Joy was using when he developed **vi**. Notice the position of the <Esc> key on the left side of the keyboard, just above the <Ctrl> key. This is a good location for such an important key, as it is easy to reach with the fourth or fifth finger of your left hand.

Now, take a look at your own keyboard. Notice that the <Esc> key has been moved to a much less convenient location, the very top left-hand corner of the keyboard. The old position of the <Esc> key was where your <Tab> key is right now, just above the <Caps Lock> key. Take a moment to compare what it is like to press the <Tab> key compared to the <Esc> key. When Bill Joy picked <Esc> as the means of changing from input mode to command mode, the key was easy to reach, which made changing modes fast and easy. Now pressing the <Esc> key requires a long, awkward stretch, making it slower and less comfortable to change modes. Such is life.

To continue, at first it will seem strange to have to change to a special mode just to start typing data. Don't worry. When it comes to **vi**, practice not only makes perfect, but it also brings a kind of comfort and ease that lets you work as fast as you can type. If you are a touch typist, you will find that **vi** is very easy to use once you have memorized the basic commands, as you will be able to do anything you want without taking your hands off the keyboard.

To give you a feeling for what it is like to work with modes, consider the following scenario. (Don't worry about the details. We'll discuss them later in the chapter.) You want to add some data to the middle of a file named **schedule**. To run **vi**, you enter the command:

```
vi schedule
```

As **vi** starts, it does three things. First, it copies the contents of **schedule** to the editing buffer. Next, it positions the cursor at the beginning of the first line of the buffer. Finally, it puts you in command mode.

You begin by using the appropriate commands to move the cursor to the place where you want to add the new data. You then type a command to change to input mode and start typing. At this point, everything you type is inserted directly into the editing buffer. When you are finished typing, you press <Esc> to change back to command mode. You then save the contents of the editing buffer back to the original file and quit the program.

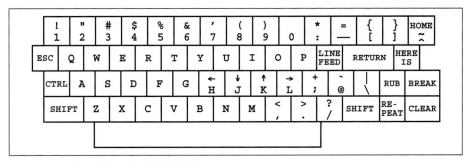

FIGURE 22-4: Keyboard layout of the ADM-3A terminal

A drawing of the keyboard layout of the Lear Siegler ADM-3A terminal, taken from the ADM-3A Operators Manual. This is the type of terminal Bill Joy used to develop the **vi** *text editor. The convenient location of the <Esc> key is one reason why Joy chose it as the means of changing from input mode to command mode. See text for details.*

> **HINT**
>
> Notice that, although it is **vi** that changes from one mode to another, it is common to talk as if it were you, the user, who were making the change. For example, I might say "There are many commands you can use when you are in command mode." Or, "To add text to the editing buffer, you must first change to input mode."
>
> When it comes to computers, this way of speaking is very common. This is because sentient beings tend to identify with their tools more than they like to admit.

KNOWING WHAT MODE YOU ARE IN

Traditionally, **vi** did not do anything to tell you what mode you were in. You were just expected to know. I realize this sounds terribly confusing but, actually, it isn't. Once you have some experience, your mind will keep track of what is happening and, from moment to moment, you will just know what mode you are in.

If you ever do lose your way, remember this: if you are in command mode and you press <Esc>, **vi** will beep at you. Thus, if you are not sure what mode you are in, just press <Esc> twice. This is guaranteed to leave you in command mode and to beep at least once. (Because if you are in input mode, the first <Esc> will change to command mode, and the second <Esc> will beep. If you are already in command mode, both <Esc>s will beep.)

Still, you might ask, why doesn't **vi** do something to show you what mode you are in? Actually, some versions of **vi** will help you in this way, if you set an internal option named **showmode**. (We'll talk about **vi** options later in the chapter.) The command to use is:

```
:set showmode
```

Once you set this option, **vi** will display a message on the bottom line of the screen showing the current mode. (The actual message can vary from one version of **vi** to another, but you won't have any trouble figuring it out.) If you decide that you always want to set **showmode**, you can place the command in your **vi** initialization file, so the option will be set automatically whenever you start **vi**. (We'll discuss initialization files later in the chapter.)

If you are a Vim user, you don't even have to set an option. By default, whenever you enter input mode, Vim will display the following reminder in the bottom left-hand corner of the screen:

```
-- INSERT --
```

As nice as it might be to see a visual reminder, the truth is, it just isn't necessary. As I mentioned earlier, once you get used to **vi** and you have some experience switching from command mode to input mode and back again, you will always know what mode you are in. For this reason, most experienced **vi** users do not even bother to set the **showmode** option, even if it is available. They don't really need it and — after a little practice — neither will you.

> **HINT**
>
> No matter how smart you are, **vi** will make you smarter.

STARTING vi AS A READ-ONLY EDITOR: view, vi -R

There may be times when you want to use **vi** to look at an important file that should not be changed. There are two ways to do this. First, you can start the program with the **-R** (read-only) option. This tells **vi** that you do not want to save data back into the original file. (This option works with both **vi** and Vim.) Second, you can start the program by using the **view** command.

There is really no difference between **vi** **-R** and **view**. You can use whichever is easier to remember. Thus, the following two commands are equivalent:

```
vi -R importantfile
view importantfile
```

Both commands start **vi** using a file named **importantfile** for reading only. Using **vi** in this way protects you from accidentally modifying important data.

You may be wondering, why would anyone would want to use **vi** to work with a file that cannot be changed? If all you want to do is display the file, why not simply use **less** (Chapter 21)? The answer is that **vi** is very powerful and when it comes to displaying a file, many people prefer to use the **vi** commands instead of **less**. Once you master **vi**, you will feel the same way, especially when you need to examine large, complex files.

RECOVERING DATA AFTER A SYSTEM FAILURE

Once in a while, it may happen that the system will go down or you will lose your connection while you are in the middle of editing a file. If so, **vi** will usually make it possible for you to recover your data.

You will remember that, when you use **vi**, the data you are editing is kept in the editing buffer. From time to time, **vi** saves the contents of the editing buffer to a temporary file. Normally, **vi** deletes this file when you are finished editing. However, if the program terminates abnormally, the temporary file will still exist, and you can use it to recover your data.

To recover a file, start **vi** with the **-r** (recover) option:

```
vi -r
```

This will show you all the files that are available for recovery. You can now restart **vi** using **-r** followed by the name of the file. For example:

```
vi -r test.c
```

This will recover your file, hopefully leaving you where you were when the system went down. Note: Be careful not to confuse the **-r** (recover) option with the **-R** (read-only) option.

> **HINT**
>
> Vim maintains an excellent recovery facility by saving your editing buffer in a SWAP FILE, stored in the same directory as the file you are editing. (We'll discuss directories in Chapters 23 and 24.) The swap file is updated automatically each time you type 200 characters or whenever you have not typed anything for four seconds.
>
> To recover a file, you must use the **rm** command (see Chapter 25) to delete the swap file; Vim will not do it for you.
>
> The name of the swap file consists of a **.** (dot), followed by the name of the original file, followed by **.swp**. For example, if you are editing a program called **test.c**, the swap file will be **.test.c.swp**. If you do not delete the swap file, the next time you edit the original file, Vim will create a new swap file with a slightly different name, for example, **.test.c.swo**.

STOPPING **vi**

There are two ways to stop **vi**. Most of the time, you will want to save your work and quit. However, if you accidentally mess up the data, you may want to quit without saving in order to preserve the original contents of the file. In either case, you must be in command mode to enter a quit command. If you are in input mode, you must first press <Esc> to change to command mode.

To save your work and then quit, the command is **ZZ**. (I'll explain the name in a moment.) Hold down the <Shift> key and press <Z> twice. You do not need to press <Return>:

ZZ

To quit without saving your work, the command is **:q!**. After you type this command, you do need to press <Return>:

:q!<Return>

Before you use the **:q!** command, think at least twice. Once you quit without saving your data, there is no way to get it back.

Later in the chapter, I'll explain why the second command starts with a colon and why you need to press <Return>. Rest assured, it all makes sense. (**ZZ** is a **vi** command; **:q!** is an **ex** command.) For now, all I will mention is that in Unix, the **!** (bang) character is sometimes used to indicate that you want to override some type of automatic check. In the case of **:q!**, the **!** tells **vi** not to check if you have saved your data.

> **HINT**
>
> If you use Vim, it is possible to get stuck in limbo if you mistype the **:q!** command. The reason is that, with Vim, typing **q** is the signal to record a macro. (We'll talk about macros later in the chapter.) If this happens to you, you'll see the message "recording" on the bottom line of your window. Don't panic. To stop the macro recording facility, all you have to do is type **q** (for quit) until the message goes away.

WHAT'S IN A NAME?

ZZ

It makes sense that there should be a quick way to save your work and stop **vi**, but why **ZZ**?

Let's say the command had a simpler name such as **s** (for "save"). That would be convenient, but what would happen if you thought you were in command mode, and you were really in input mode? You would start typing data and, before you knew it, you would type an "s" and stop the program.

The name **ZZ** was chosen because, although it is easy to type, it is unlikely you would ever type it by accident.

HOW vi USES THE SCREEN

At this point, I'd like to take a moment to discuss a few short topics related to how **vi** uses the screen. The bottom line of the screen is called the COMMAND LINE. This line is used by **vi** in two different ways: to display messages and to display certain commands as you type them (see the next section). All the other lines on the screen are used to display data.

If your editing buffer contains only a small amount of data, there may not be enough lines to fill up the screen. For example, say that your terminal or window contains 25 lines. The bottom line is the command line, leaving 24 lines to display data. Let's say the editing buffer contains only 10 lines of data. It would be confusing if **vi** displayed 14 empty lines as being blank. After all, you might actually have blank lines as part of your data.

Instead, **vi** marks the beginning of each empty line with a ~ (tilde) character. You can see an example of this in Figure 22-5. As you add new lines to the editing buffer, they will take up more and more of the screen, and the tildes will disappear.

Most of the time, the data you edit with **vi** will consist of plain text: characters, letters, numbers, punctuation and so on. However, if the need arises, you can insert control characters (see Chapter 7) into the editing buffer. To do so, press **^V** followed by the control character you want to enter. For example, if you want to type an actual **^C** character, press **^V^C**. If you actually want to enter a **^V**, type **^V^V**.

When **vi** displays control characters, you will see a **^** character followed by a letter, for example, **^C**. Remember that you are looking at a single character, even though it takes up two spaces on your screen.

As I explained in Chapter 18, the tab character is **^I**. The **vi** editor, like Unix in general, assumes that tabs are set for every 8 positions. (You can change the positioning, but most people don't bother.) If you insert a tab in the editing buffer, you will not see **^I**. Rather, **vi** displays as many spaces as necessary to make it look as if your data is aligned according to the tab. This is just for your convenience: the extra spaces do not really exist. In reality, there is only one single character (**^I**) for each tab.

Finally, if at any time your screen becomes garbled — for instance, if you are working remotely and there is noise on the line — you can tell **vi** to redisplay all the lines on your screen by pressing **^L**.

```
1.  This window has 25 lines.
2.  The bottom line is the command line.
3.  The other 24 lines are used to display data.
4.
5.
6.
7.  Below are 17 empty lines, marked with tildes.
~
~
~
~
~
~
~
~
~
~
~
~
~
~
~
~
~
"harley" [New file]
```

FIGURE 22-5: How **vi** Displays Empty Lines

The bottom line on your screen, the command line, is used by **vi** *in two ways: to display messages and to display certain commands as they are being typed. All other lines are used to display data.*

When the editing buffer does not contain enough data to fill up all the lines, **vi** *marks the empty lines by displaying ~ (tilde) characters. In this example, you can see 17 empty lines, each of which is marked by a single tilde. As more lines of data are inserted into the editing buffer, the empty lines will be used and the tildes will disappear.*

USING **vi** AND **ex** COMMANDS

I explained earlier that **vi** and **ex** are really different faces of the same program. This means that as you use **vi**, you have access to both the **vi** and **ex** commands.

Most **vi** commands are one or two letters. For example, to move the cursor forward one word, you use the **w** command. (Just type "w" in command mode.) To delete the current line, you use the **dd** command. (Just type "dd".) Since **vi** commands are so short, they are not echoed as you type.

With most **vi** commands, you do not press <Return>. For example, as soon as you type "w", the cursor moves forward one word. As soon as you type "dd", the current line

KEY	PURPOSE
\<Backspace>/\<Delete>	erase the last character typed
^W	erase the last word typed
^X/^U	erase the entire line

FIGURE 22-6: Keys to Use to Make Corrections While Using vi

*As you are typing with the **vi** editor, there are three standard Unix keys you can use to make corrections. See Chapter 7 for details.*

disappears. If you make a mistake and type a bad **vi** command, you will hear a beep. However, there will not be an error message. (What would be the point?)

The **ex** commands are longer and more complex than the **vi** commands. For this reason, they are echoed on the command line as you type. All **ex** commands start with : (colon). For example, the following command deletes lines 1 through 5:

`:1,5d`

This next command changes all occurrences of "harley" to "Harley". (Don't worry about the details for now.)

`:%s/harley/Harley/g`

As soon as you type the initial colon, **vi** moves the cursor to the command line (the bottom line of your screen). As you type the command, each character is echoed. When you finish typing the command, you must press \<Return>.

If you make a mistake before you press \<Return>, you have two choices. First, you can press \<Esc> to cancel the command completely. Or you can correct the command using the special keys shown in Figure 22-6 (see Chapter 7 for details). You can also use these same keys in input mode to make corrections as you type.

On some systems, when you make a correction, the cursor will move backwards, but the characters will not be erased from the screen. For example, say that you enter:

`:1,5del`

Before you press \<Return>, you realize that you did not need to type "el" at the end of the command. So, you press \<Backspace> twice. The cursor moves back two positions, but you still see the two characters. Don't worry about it: they are gone. Just press \<Return>.

A STRATEGY FOR LEARNING **vi** COMMANDS

The **vi** editor has a large variety of commands. For convenience, we can group them as follows:

• Commands to move the cursor
• Commands to enter input mode
• Commands to make changes

My goal is for you to learn enough commands from each group so that you are able to form moment-to-moment strategies to carry out any editing task you require. Here is an example to show you what I mean. As you work, the cursor shows your current position within the editing buffer. To insert new data into the buffer, you would use the following strategy:

1. Make sure you are in command mode.
2. Move the cursor to the place at which you want to insert the data.
3. Change to input mode.
4. Enter the data.
5. Press <Esc> to change back to command mode.

Once you learn the basic **vi** commands, you will find that there are a variety of ways to implement any particular strategy. How you choose to do it depends on the specific situation and your level of skill.

One thing that may surprise you is the large number of commands **vi** has to offer. For example, there are 12 different commands just to enter input mode; in command mode, there are 40 different commands just to move the cursor (and these are just the *simple* cursor commands).

As you might guess, no one **needs** to know 12 ways to enter input mode or 40 ways to move the cursor. However, I do want you to learn as many **vi** commands as possible because, believe it or not, that is what makes **vi** so easy to use.

For example, let's say you want to move from the top left corner of the screen to a position halfway down the screen and several words to the right. You could move the cursor one position at a time, which would be slow and awkward. But if you knew all 40 cursor movement commands, you could choose the best ones for the situation and, by typing just three or four keys, you could instantly move the cursor to the exact location you want.

In this chapter, I will cover all the basic **vi** and **ex** commands. For a more comprehensive reference, you can use Appendix C, which contains a summary of all the important commands. My advice is to keep teaching yourself until you know all the commands in Appendix C. From time to time, take a moment to teach yourself a new command; then practice it. All the commands are useful, and they are all worth practicing. As you read the rest of the chapter, I want you to work in front of your computer and follow along. As we discuss each new command, I want you to take some time to experiment with it.

Finally, near the end of the book, you will find a special **vi** index, just for this chapter. This is the place to look when you want to find a **vi**-related topic. (Take a moment right now to find the index.)

> **HINT**
>
> The art of using **vi** well is being able to select the best commands to carry out a task as simply and as quickly as possible.

CREATING A PRACTICE FILE

As you read this chapter, you will need a text file to practice editing. You can create one by using either of the following commands:

```
cp /etc/passwd temp
man vi > temp
```

The first command creates a small file by copying the system password file. The second command creates a large file by copying the **vi** man page. (The **cp** command is explained in Chapter 25; the password file in Chapter 11, the online manual in Chapter 9, and the redirection of standard output using **>** in Chapter 15.)

Both of these commands will leave you with a file named **temp**, which you can use for practice. Once you have such a file, you can edit it by entering the command:

```
vi temp
```

When you are finished, you can remove (delete) the file by using the command:

```
rm temp
```

(The **rm** command is explained in Chapter 25.)

MOVING THE CURSOR

At all times, the cursor is on one of the lines on your screen. This line is called the CURRENT LINE. Within the current line, the cursor will be on or under one particular character, called the CURRENT CHARACTER. Many of the **vi** commands perform an action on either the current line or the current character. For example, the **x** command deletes the current character; the **dd** command deletes the current line.

Whenever you move the cursor, the new position becomes the current character. Similarly, if you move the cursor to a new line, that line becomes the current line. Whenever you move the cursor to a line that is not currently on the screen, **vi** will display a different part of the editing buffer, so that the new current line is visible. In other words, to jump from one part of the editing buffer to another, you simply move the cursor.

Within **vi**, there are many different commands that move the cursor, which means there are many different ways to jump from one place to another within the editing buffer. My goal is to teach you most of these commands. Then, whenever you need to jump to a different part of the editing buffer, you will be able to figure out which sequence of commands will work best. Before long, choosing the fastest cursor movement commands will become second nature.

In some cases, there are several ways to make the exact same cursor movements. For example, there are three different commands to move the cursor one position to the left. In such cases, there is no need to learn all of the equivalent commands. Just pick the one you like the best and practice it. Now, let's get started.

To move the cursor one position, you have a lot of choices. The best commands to use are **h**, **j**, **k** and **l**. They work as follows:

h   move cursor one position left
j   move cursor one position down
k   move cursor one position up
l   move cursor one position right

Why such an odd choice of keys? There are two reasons. First, if you are a touch typist, these four keys will be close to the fingers of your right hand on the home row, making it very easy to move the cursor. (Take a look at your keyboard.)

Second, as we discussed earlier in the chapter, **vi** was developed in 1976 by Bill Joy using an ADM-3A terminal. Take a look at Figure 22-7 where you will see a close-up photo of an ADM-3A keyboard showing these four keys. Notice the arrows above the letters. The ADM-3A was designed to use these four keys as cursor control keys, so it was natural for Joy to use them the same way.

If you are a touch typist, using H, J, K and L to move the cursor is especially convenient. However, there are other keys you can use that are easier to remember. If your keyboard has cursor control keys (arrow keys), you can use those. (I will call them <Left>, <Down>, <Up> and <Right>.) You can also use <Backspace> to move left and the <Space> bar to move right.

<Left>   move cursor one position left
<Down>   move cursor one position down
<Up>   move cursor one position up
<Right>   move cursor one position right
<Backspace> move cursor one position left
<Space>   move cursor one position right

Another way to move up and down is to use the – (minus) and + (plus) commands. Pressing – moves to the beginning of the previous line; pressing + moves to the beginning of the next line. As an alternative, pressing <Return> also moves to the beginning of the next line.

–   move cursor to beginning of previous line
+   move cursor to beginning of next line
<Return> move cursor to beginning of next line

FIGURE 22-7: The H, J, K and L keys on the ADM-3A terminal

When Bill Joy developed vi *in 1976, he was using a Lear Siegler ADM-3A terminal. With this terminal, the keys for H, J, K and L were used—not only to type letters—but to control the cursor (notice the arrows). For this reason, Joy used these same four keys to move the cursor within* vi. *See text for details.*

Within the current line, the **0** (number zero) command moves to the beginning of the line; the **$** (dollar sign) command moves to the end of the line. If the current line is indented, you can use the **^** (circumflex) to move to the first character in the line that is not a space or tab.

0	move cursor to beginning of current line
$	move cursor to end of current line
^	move cursor to first non-space/tab in current line

Aside from moving the cursor by character or by line, there are several commands you can use to move from word to word. (Within **vi**, a WORD is a string of letters, numbers, or underscore characters.) To move forward, use the **w** or **e** commands. The **w** command moves to the first character of the next word; **e** moves to the last character (end) of the current word. To move backwards, use **b** to move to the first character in the previous word. You will find that using **w**, **e** or **b** is often a fast way to move the cursor exactly where you want, saving a lot of keystrokes.

w	move cursor forward to first character of next word
e	move cursor forward to last character of current word
b	move cursor backward to first character of current word

All three commands stop at each punctuation character, which is okay if your data does not contain many such characters. However, if your data has a lot of punctuation, moving in this way is necessarily slow. Instead, you can use the **W**, **E** and **B** commands. These work the same way except they recognize only spaces and newlines as ending a word.

W	same as **w**; ignore punctuation
E	same as **e**; ignore punctuation
B	same as **b**; ignore punctuation

For example, say that the cursor is at the beginning of the following line:

This is an (important) test; don't forget to study.

If you press **w** several times, you will stop at each parenthesis, the semicolon, the apostrophe (single quote), as well as at the beginning of each word. That is, you will have to press **w** 13 times to reach the last word of the line. If you use **W**, you will stop only after each space. You will have to press **W** only 8 times to reach the last word of the line. (This would be a good time to take a moment to try these commands for yourself.)

For larger movements, the parentheses commands jump from sentence to sentence:

)	move forward to next sentence
(	move backward to previous sentence

Similarly, the brace bracket commands jump from paragraph to paragraph:

}	move forward to next paragraph
{	move backward to previous paragraph

Again, these are commands you should try for yourself to make sure you understand exactly how they work. As you do, notice how handy it is being able to jump around by word, sentence and paragraph. Then take a moment to consider the following question: English prose is built from words, sentences and paragraphs. Why is it that, except for **vi**, almost no other text editors and no word processors allow you to work directly with words, sentences and paragraphs?

Within **vi**, the official definition of a SENTENCE is a string of characters, ending in a period, comma, question mark or exclamation mark, followed by at least *two* spaces or a newline character. (The newline character marks the end of a line; see Chapter 7.)

In other words, for **vi** to recognize a sentence, it must either be followed by two spaces or be at the end of the line. The reason for this requirement is that using two spaces allows **vi** to distinguish sentences from words (which are separated by single spaces). Consider the following example, which consists of two sentences, separated by a period and two spaces:

```
Meet me at the Shell Tower at 6pm.  Is this okay with you?
```

A PARAGRAPH is defined as a section of text that starts and ends in a blank line. In other words, putting a tab at the beginning of a line is not enough to indicate a new paragraph.

> **HINT**
>
> In general, it behooves you to form the habit of typing two spaces between sentences and a blank line between paragraphs. This will do three things:
>
> First, your writing will be easier to read.
>
> Second, when you use **vi**, it will be easy to move from one sentence to another (using **(** and **)**) and to move from one paragraph to another (using **{** and **}**).
>
> Third, if you send text to someone who may need to edit it, that person will find your text a lot easier to manipulate. For example, let's say you email a message to someone who is polite enough to edit your text when he replies. It is a lot easier for him to delete whole sentences or paragraphs if the original message was formatted nicely. This may seem like a minor point, but it really isn't.
>
> Prediction: Once you are comfortable with **vi**, you will find yourself annoyed at people who use only a single space between sentences when they write plain text.

There will be times when you will want to make a large move from one part of your screen to another. To start such a move, you can use the **H**, **M** or **L** commands. They jump to the top, middle or bottom of your screen respectively ("high", "middle" and "low").

H   move cursor to top line of screen
M   move cursor to middle line of screen
L   move cursor to last line of screen

In general, the art of moving the cursor is to get to where you want in as few keystrokes as possible. Here is an example. Say that your cursor is on the top line of the screen. The last line of data on the screen contains:

```
today if you can.  Otherwise give me a call.
```

You want to move to the "c" in "call" so you can insert the word "phone".

You could press <Down> many times to move to the line you want, and then press <Right> many times to move to the word you want. However, you can do the whole thing in three keystrokes:

```
L$b
```

1. Move cursor to last line of screen (**L**).
2. Move cursor to end of that line (**$**).
3. Move cursor to beginning of previous word (**b**).

To increase the power of the cursor movement commands, you can repeat a movement by typing a number, called a REPEAT COUNT, before the command. For example, to move forward 10 words, type:

```
10w
```

Notice you do not put a space after the number. Here are two more examples. To move down 50 lines, type any of the following commands:

```
50j
50<Down>
50+
50<Return>
```

To move back three paragraphs, use a repeat count with the **{** (left brace) command:

```
3{
```

As a general rule, you can use a repeat count with any **vi** command, as long as doing so makes sense.

> **HINT**
>
> Whenever you need to move the cursor from one place to another, challenge yourself to do it in as few keystrokes as possible*.

MOVING THROUGH THE EDITING BUFFER

At all times, **vi** displays as much of the editing buffer as will fit on your screen. When you work with a large amount of text, you will be able to see only part of it at once. For example, if your terminal or window has 25 lines, **vi** will be able to display only 24 lines of text at a time. (Remember, **vi** does not display text on the bottom line of the screen, which is used as the command line.) When you want to see another part of the text, you will need to move the cursor to that location within the editing buffer. There are several commands you can use.

---

*This may help you work your way through college. Hang around the Student Center with your laptop, betting people that you can move the **vi** cursor from one point to another faster than anyone else. Start by using a lot of short movement commands like <Up> and <Down>. After you have lost a few bets and the odds increase, you can clean up by using **H**, **M** and **L**, followed by sentence and word commands with a repeat count.

First, you can use the **^F** (forward) command to move down one screenful. (Remember, **^F** refers to <Ctrl-F>.) The opposite command is **^B** (backward), which moves up one screenful. There are also two variations: **^D** moves down a half screenful, and **^U** moves up a half screenful. You use **^F** and **^B** when you want to move through the file quickly. You use **^D** and **^U** when you want to make smaller jumps.

^F   move down (forward) one screenful
^B   move up (back) one screenful
^D   move down a half screenful
^U   move up a half screenful

As a general rule, if you type a number in front of a cursor movement command, the number acts as a repeat count. For example, to move down 6 screenfuls all at once, type:

```
6^F
```

To move up 10 screenfuls, use:

```
10^B
```

Since you can use **^F** and **^B** to jump a long distance in this manner, you do not need to be able to use a repeat count with the **^D** and **^U** commands. Thus, when you type a number in front of **^D** or **^U**, the number has a different meaning: it sets the number of lines that both of these commands should jump. For example, consider the following commands:

```
10^D
10^U
```

Either of these commands tells **vi** to jump 10 lines *and* all subsequent **^D** and **^U** commands should also jump 10 lines (until you reset the count). If you'd like, you can set the number of lines to a large amount. For example, if you want to jump 100 lines at a time, use either:

```
100^D
100^U
```

Until you change this number, all **^D** and **^U** commands will jump 100 lines.

JUMPING TO A PREVIOUS LOCATION

There will be many times when you will move the cursor a long way and, a moment later, want to move it back. Sometimes, such a move is deliberate. For instance, you might jump to the end of the editing buffer, add a single line, and then want to return to what you were doing. The situation can also arise accidentally, when you make a mistake and suddenly find yourself a long way from where you were working.

In such cases, you can return to your previous location by using the `` ` ` `` command (that is, by typing two backquotes in a row). To test this command, start **vi** with a large file. Then use the **G** command with a repeat count to jump to line 10:

```
10G
```

Now move to the 8th character on the line by using the **l** (lowercase "l") command:

8l

Next, use the **G** command to jump to the end of the editing buffer by typing:

G

To return to your previous location (the 8th character in line 10), type two backquotes in a row:

` `

A variation of this command is to use **' '** (two single quotes) instead of two backquotes. This jumps to the beginning of the line, rather than within the line. To test this, move the cursor again to the 8th position in line 10, and then jump to the end of the file:

10G
8l
G

Now, type two single quotes in a row:

' '

Notice the cursor is at the beginning of the line.

A more powerful version of this command allows you to mark any line with an invisible name. You can then use that name to jump to the line whenever you want. To mark a line in this way, type **m** followed by a single letter. The letter is now the name of that line. For example, to mark the current line with the name "a", type:

ma

To jump to a marked line, type a **`** (backquote) or **'** (single quote) followed by the name of the line, for example:

`a
'a

The first command (backquote) jumps to the exact position within the marked line. The second command (single quote) jumps to the beginning of the marked line.

HINT

When you mark a line, you can use any letter you want. In principle, this allows you to mark up to 26 lines (**a** through **z**). In practice, you will rarely need to mark more than one or two lines at a time. The easiest way to mark one line is to type **mm**. You can then jump to this line by typing **'m**. (If you use two marks, use **ma** and **mz**.)

Once you get used to typing these combinations, it will become second nature for you to mark a line, move the cursor to do something else, and then jump back to the original line, all without taking your hands off the keyboard. (Take a moment to appreciate the power of **vi**.)

SEARCHING FOR A PATTERN

One way to move around the editing buffer is to jump to a line that contains a particular pattern. To do so, you use the **/** (slash) and **?** (question mark) commands.

As soon as you press the <**/**> key, **vi** will display a **/** character on the command line (at the bottom of the screen). You can now type any pattern you want and press <Return>. This tells **vi** to search for the next occurrence of that pattern. If you want to search again for the same pattern, just type **/** again and press <Return>.

Here is an example. You are editing a list of people to whom you want to send money, and you wish to find the next occurrence of the pattern "Harley". Type:

```
/Harley
```

Now press <Return>. The cursor will jump to the next line that contains the pattern. To repeat the search and jump once more, type a slash by itself, followed by <Return>:

```
/
```

Since you did not specify a new pattern, **vi** assumes you want to use the same one as the previous **/** command.

By default, **vi** searches are case sensitive. Thus, the following two commands are not the same:

```
/Harley
/harley
```

When **vi** looks for a pattern, it starts from the cursor location and searches forward. If it gets to the end of the editing buffer, **vi** wraps around to the beginning. In this way, **vi** can search the entire editing buffer, regardless of your starting location.

To search backwards, you use the **?** command. For example:

```
?Harley
```

This works the same as **/** except that **vi** searches backwards. Once you use **?** to specify a pattern, you can search backwards for the same pattern again by using **?** by itself:

```
?
```

If **vi** gets to the beginning of the editing buffer, it will wrap around to the end and continue to search backwards. In this way, **vi** can search through the entire editing buffer backwards.

Once you have specified a pattern with **/** or **?**, there are two convenient ways to continue searching for the same pattern. The **n** (next) command searches in the same direction as the original command. The **N** (uppercase "N") command searches in the opposite direction. For example, say that you have just entered the command:

```
/Harley
```

You now want to find the next occurrence of the same pattern. All you have to do is press **n**. (Do not press <Return>.) This is the same as if you had entered **/**<Return> with no pattern. To search repeatedly for the same pattern, press **n** as many times as you want. If you press **N**, **vi** will repeat the same search backwards. As with the other search commands, **n** and **N** will wrap around the end (or beginning) of the editing buffer if necessary.

The exact meaning of **n** and **N** depends on your initial search direction. For example, say that you enter a backwards search command:

?Harley

Pressing **n** will repeat the search backwards (the same direction). Pressing **N** will repeat the search forwards (the opposite direction).

HINT

Although the **/** and **?** search commands were developed for **vi**, you will find them used with other programs. For example, you can use the exact same commands while displaying a file with **less** (see Chapter 21).

For flexibility, you can use a regular expression (regex) to specify a pattern. (Regular expressions are discussed in detail in Chapter 20; you can look there for a lot of examples.) For reference, Figure 22-8 shows the various metacharacters that have special meanings within a regular expression.

Here are a few examples showing the power of using a regex. To search for the next occurrence of an "H", followed by any two characters, use:

/H..

To search for an "H" followed by any two lowercase characters, use:

/H[a-z][a-z]

To search for an "H", followed by zero or more lowercase characters, followed by "y", use:

/H[a-z]*y

METACHARACTER	MEANING
.	match any single character except newline
^	anchor: match the beginning of a line
$	anchor: match the end of a line
\<	anchor: match the beginning of a word
\>	anchor: match the end of a word
[*list*]	character class: match any character in *list*
[^*list*]	character class: match any character not in *list*
\	quote: interpret a metacharacter literally

FIGURE 22-8: Using regular expressions when searching with vi

When you use the **/** *and* **?** *commands to search with* **vi***, you can increase the power of the search by using a regex for the search pattern. For reference, here are the most useful metacharacters you can use with such expressions. For details, see Chapter 20.*

To search for the next line that begins with "Harley", use:

```
/^Harley
```

To summarize:

/ *regex*	search forward for specified regex
/	repeat forward search for previous regex
? *regex*	search backward for specified regex
?	repeat backward search for previous regex
n	repeat last / or ? command, same direction
N	repeat last / or ? command, opposite direction

USING LINE NUMBERS

Internally, **vi** keeps track of each line in the editing buffer by assigning it a line number. If you would like to see these numbers, you turn on the **number** option. (We'll talk about **vi** options later in the chapter.) The command to use is:

```
:set number
```

For example, say that you are using **vi** to write your Applied Philosophy dissertation. The editing buffer contains:

```
I have a little shadow that goes
in and out with me,
And what can be the use of him
is more than I can see.
```

If you enter the command :**set number**, you will see:

```
1  I have a little shadow that goes
2  in and out with me,
3  And what can be the use of him
4  is more than I can see.
```

It is important to realize that the numbers are not really part of your data. They are only there for your convenience. If you want to get rid of the numbers, you can turn off the **number** option as follows:

```
:set nonumber
```

If line numbers are turned off, you can check where you are in the file by pressing **^G**. This displays the name of the file along with your position in the file.

There are two important uses for line numbers. First, as you will see later, you can use them with many of the **ex** commands. Second, you can use the **G** (go to) command to jump to a specific line. Simply type the number of the line, followed by **G**. Do not type a space or press <Return>. For example, to jump to line 100, type:

```
100G
```

To jump to the beginning of the editing buffer, type **1G**. With newer versions of **vi**, you can use **gg** as a synonym for **1G**.

Alternatively, you can jump to a specific line by typing **:** (colon), followed by a line number, followed by <Return>. Here are some examples. The first command jumps to line 1; the second command jumps to line 100; the last command jumps to the end of the file. (When you specify line numbers, the **$** character stands for the last line in the file.)

```
:1
:100
:$
```

Here is a summary of all the variations:

*n*G	jump to line number **n**
1G	jump to first line in editing buffer
gg	jump to first line in editing buffer
G	jump to last line in editing buffer
:*n*	jump to line number *n*
:1	jump to first line in editing buffer
:$	jump to last line in editing buffer

You will find **G** and **1G** (or **gg**) particularly useful, so take a moment and memorize them right now.

INSERTING TEXT

As we discussed earlier in the chapter, you must type a command to change to input mode in order to insert text into the editing buffer. When you are finished inserting text, you press <Esc> to leave input mode and return to command mode. (Remember: When you press <Esc> in command mode, **vi** will beep. If you are not sure what mode you are in, press <Esc> twice. When you hear the beep, you will know you are in command mode.)

There are twelve commands to change to input mode. Half of these commands are for entering new data; the other half are for replacing existing text. Of course, you will ask, why do you need so many different commands just to change to input mode? The answer is that each command opens the editing buffer in a different place. Thus, when you want to insert data, you can choose whichever command works the best in the current situation. Here are the commands:

i	change to input mode: insert before cursor position
a	change to input mode: insert after cursor position
I	change to input mode: insert at start of current line
A	change to input mode: insert at end of current line
o	change to input mode: open below current line
O	change to input mode: open above current line

To see how this works, let's say you are editing a term paper for your Advanced Classical Music class. You are writing about famous lyrics* and the current line happens to be:

For a dime you can see Kankakee or Paree

The cursor is under the letter "K" and you are in command mode. If you type **i**, you will change to input mode. As you type, the data will be inserted before the "K". The letters to the right will be moved over to make room. For example, say that you type:

iAAA<Esc>

(The <Esc> returns you to command mode.) The current line would look like:

For a dime you can see AAAKankakee or Paree

Now, instead, suppose you had pressed **a** to change to input mode. In this case, the data would be inserted *after* the "K". So, let's say you start with the original line and type:

aBBB<Esc>

The current line would now look like:

For a dime you can see KBBBankakee or Paree

> **HINT**
>
> To remember the difference between the **i** and **a** commands, think of **i**=insert, **a**=append.

By using the **I** (uppercase "I") and **A** (uppercase "A") commands, you can insert data at the beginning or end of the current line, respectively. For example, let's say you start with the original line and type:

ICCC<Esc>

The current line would look like:

CCCFor a dime you can see Kankakee or Paree

If the current line is indented using spaces or tabs, **vi** will do the intelligent thing and start inserting after the indentation.

Now, let's say you started with the original line and typed:

ADDD<Esc>

The data you typed is appended to the end of the line. The current line looks like:

For a dime you can see Kankakee or PareeDDD

Finally, to insert below the current line, use the **o** (lowercase letter "o") command. To insert above the current line, use the **O** (uppercase "O") command. In either case, **vi** will open a brand new line for you.

*The line is taken from the 1939 song "Lydia the Tattooed Lady", written by Harold Arlen and Yip Harburg. Over the years, the song was popularized by Groucho Marx, who loved to sing it at the drop of a hat (and sometimes even without the hat).

> **HINT**
>
> To remember the difference between the o and O commands, remember two things:
>   First, the letter "o" stands for "open".
>   Second, imagine that the command name is a balloon filled with helium. The larger balloon, O, floats higher, above the current line. The small balloon, o, floats lower, below the current line.

As you work in input mode, there are two things I want you to remember. As we discussed earlier in the chapter:

- You can use the keys listed in Figure 22-6 to correct mistakes without having to leave input mode: <Backspace> (or <Delete>) to erase a character, ^W to erase a word, and ^X (or ^U) to erase an entire line.

- You can insert a control character by prefacing it with ^V; for example, to enter a backspace, type ^V^H. On the screen, you will see ^H, even though it is a single character.

As I explained earlier, there are many commands to move the cursor. In particular, the ^ (circumflex) command moves to the beginning of the current line (after any indentation); the $ (dollar sign) command moves to the end of the current line. Thus, if you want to insert data at the beginning of the current line, you can type ^ followed by i, instead of I. Similarly, you can insert at the end of the line by using $a instead of A.

Here then, is a wonderful illustration of the beauty of the design of vi. By learning a few extra commands, you can often type one character (I or A) instead of two (^i or $a). If you are a beginner, this may not seem like much, but after just a few days with vi, you will see that anything that saves keystrokes used for common operations is a real convenience. Of course, you do have to learn the extra commands, which is why I say that vi is easy to use, but difficult to learn.

If you are used to editing with a mouse, do not scoff at vi's older, command-oriented design. I urge you to take some time to learn all the important vi commands. Once you do, you will be pleased at how easy it is to edit data without having to take your hands off the keyboard to move a mouse or to press special keys. Moreover, you will find that using vi's powerful cursor movement commands is a lot easier and a lot faster than using a mouse to click on a scroll bar*.

> **HINT**
>
> Tools that are simple enough to use on the first day will feel clunky and awkward after the first month.

---

*You can judge how quickly someone's mind works by noticing how he or she uses a mouse. The faster the flow of ideas (it's called "ideaphoria") the more likely the person is to prefer the keyboard to the mouse. As a general rule, people with high ideaphoria do not like to move their hands away from the keyboard, because it would slow them down.

Have you ever watched someone read a Web page? People with high ideaphoria will press the <PageUp>, <PageDown> or <Space> keys. People with low ideaphoria will use the mouse to move the scroll bar up and down.

CHANGING TEXT

In the last section, we looked at commands that change to input mode so you can insert data into the editing buffer. In this section, we will examine how to change data that is already in the editing buffer. First, I will discuss seven **vi** commands. All but one of these replace data by changing to input mode. Let's start with the one command that does not change to input mode.

To replace a single character by another character, type **r** followed by the new character. For example, let's say that you are writing one of your professors a letter explaining why you were not able to finish your term paper. You are in command mode, and the current line is:

```
would mean missing The Sopranos rerun.   I gm sure you
```

You notice that the word "gm" is wrong. Move the cursor to the "g" and type:

```
ra
```

The current line now looks like:

```
would mean missing The Sopranos rerun.   I am sure you
```

Since you changed only one character, there was no need to enter input mode.

Suppose, however, you want to replace more than one character by overwriting. Move to where you want to start the replacement and type **R** (uppercase "R"). You will change to input mode and each character you type will replace one character on the current line. When you are finished, press <Esc> to return to command mode. Here is an example. The current line is as you left it above. You move the cursor to the "T" in "The" and type:

```
RMa's funeral<Esc>
```

The current line is now:

```
would mean missing Ma's funeral.   I am sure you
```

When you use the **R** command to replace text, **vi** will not move off the current line. Thus, if you type past the end of the line, **vi** will simply append the extra characters to the end of the line.

Sometimes, you will want to replace one or more characters with data that is not exactly the same size. There are a number of commands you can use. The **s** (substitute) command allows you to replace a single character with many characters. In our example, move the cursor to the **a** in "Ma" and type:

```
s
```

The **a** will change to a **$**, and you will be in input mode. You will see:

```
would mean missing M$'s funeral.   I am sure you
```

The **$** shows you which character is being replaced. Type as much as you want and press <Esc> when you are done. Let's say you type:

other<Esc>

The current line is now:

would mean missing Mother's funeral.   I am sure you

The **C** (uppercase "C") command is a variation of this type of change. It allows you to replace all the characters from the cursor to the end of the line. In our example, say that you move to the "I" and type:

C

You will change to input mode and the last character to be replaced is marked with a **$**:

would mean missing Mother's funeral.   I am sure you$

The current character is the "I". Type what you want and press <Esc>. Let's say you type:

We all hoped that<Esc>

The current line becomes:

would mean missing Mother's funeral.   We all hoped that

Sometimes the easiest thing to do is replace an entire line. There are two commands that will do the job: **S** or **cc**. Just move to the line you want to replace and type either of these commands. You will be in input mode. When you press <Esc>, whatever you typed will replace the entire line.

Why are there two identical commands whose names look so different? Many of the **vi** command names follow a pattern. There are names with one lowercase letter, two lowercase letters, or one uppercase letter. According to this pattern, both **S** and **cc** should be the command to replace an entire line. Thus, you can use whichever one makes more sense. (If you can't see the pattern right now, don't worry. Wait until you learn some more commands.)

The final **vi** command to replace data is extremely useful. This command is **c** followed by one of the commands to move the cursor. Once again, you will be put into input mode. This time, whatever you type will replace everything from the cursor up to the position indicated by the move command. This can be a tad confusing, so here are a few examples. Say that the current line is:

would mean missing Mother's funeral.   We all hoped that

The cursor is at the "M". You want to replace the entire word "Mother" with "my dog". Type:

cw

This changes to input mode and marks the last character to be replaced with a **$**. You will see:

would mean missing Mothe$'s funeral.   We all hoped that

You now type:

my dog<Esc>

The current line becomes:

would mean missing my dog's funeral. We all hoped that

Thus, the combination **cw** allows you to change a single word. You can use **c** with any of the cursor movement commands that are single characters. If you want, you can also use a repeat count. For example, the command **c5w** replaces 5 words. The command **c4b** replaces from the current position back 4 words. The command **c (** replaces back to the beginning of the sentence. The command **c }** replaces to the end of the paragraph. To replace 6 paragraphs, move to the beginning of the first paragraph and type **c6 }**.

The following summary shows the **vi** replacement commands:

r   replace exactly 1 character (does not enter input mode)
R   replace by typing over
s   replace 1 character by insertion
C   replace from cursor to end of line by insertion
cc replace entire current line by insertion
S   replace entire current line by insertion
c*move***   replace from cursor to *move* by insertion

REPLACING TEXT

As we discussed earlier, when you use **vi**, you have access to both the **vi** (screen-oriented) commands and the older **ex** (line-oriented) commands. So far, most of the commands we have talked about have been **vi** commands. With this section, we begin to cover the **ex** commands.

All **ex** commands begin with a : (colon) character. Whenever you type a colon at the beginning of a command, **vi** immediately displays it on the command line (at the bottom of the screen). As you type the rest of the command it is echoed on this line (which is why it is called the command line). As you will see, **ex** commands are longer and more complex than **vi** commands. For this reason, **vi** echoes them as you type so you can see what you are doing. The only **vi** commands that are long and complex are the search commands (**/** and **?**), which is why they too are displayed on the command line.

To replace a particular pattern, you use the **ex** command **:s** (substitute). The syntax is:

:s/*pattern***/***replace***/**

where *pattern* is the pattern you want to replace, and *replace* is the replacement text. For example, to replace "UNIX" with "Linux" on the current line, use:

:s/UNIX/Linux/

Using **:s** in this way will replace only the first occurrence of the pattern on the current line. To replace all occurrences, you would type the letter **g** (global) at the end of the command. For instance, to change all occurrences of "UNIX" to "Linux" on the current line, you would use:

`:s/UNIX/Linux/g`

If you want **vi** to ask your permission before making the change, add **c** (confirm) to the end of the command:

`:s/UNIX/Linux/c`

Of course, you can combine both **g** and **c**:

`:s/UNIX/Linux/cg`

When you use the **c** modifier, **vi** will display the line that contains the pattern. It will point out the location of the pattern and then wait for a decision. If you want to make the replacement, type **y** (for yes) and then press <Return>. Otherwise, type **n**<Return> (for no) or simply press <Return> by itself. (If you don't specify "y" or "n", **vi** will prudently assume you don't want to make the change.)

To delete a pattern, simply replace it with nothing. For example, to remove all the occurrences of "UNIX" on the current line, use:

`:s/UNIX//g`

As a convenience, if you do not use a **c** or a **g** at the end of the command, you can omit the final **/** character. As an example, the following two commands are equivalent:

`:s/UNIX/Linux/`
`:s/UNIX/Linux`

There are two important variations of the **:s** command. First, you can specify a particular line number after the colon. This tells **vi** to perform the substitution on that particular line. For example, to change the first occurrence of "UNIX" to "Linux" on line 57, use:

`:57s/UNIX/Linux/`

(Reminder: Use **:set number** to display line numbers; **:set nonumber** to not display line numbers.)

Instead of a single line number, you can indicate a range by separating two line numbers with a comma. For example, to make the same replacement on lines 57 through 60, use:

`:57,60s/UNIX/Linux/`

In this case, **vi** will replace the first occurrence of the specified pattern on each line in the range.

Most of the time, you won't use specific line numbers. However, there are three special symbols that make this form of the command particularly useful. The **.** (period) stands for the current line, and the **$** (dollar sign) stands for the last line in the editing buffer. Thus, the following command replaces all occurrences of "UNIX" with "Linux", from the current line to the end of the editing buffer:

```
:.,$s/UNIX/Linux/g
```

To make the same change from the beginning of the editing buffer (line 1) to the current line, use:

```
:1,.s/UNIX/Linux/g
```

The third special symbol is **%** (the percent sign), which stands for all the lines in the editing buffer. Thus, to change every occurrence of "UNIX" to "Linux" on every line in the editing buffer, use:

```
:%s/UNIX/Linux/g
```

This is the same as making the substitution from line 1 to line **$** (the end of the editing buffer):

```
:1,$/UNIX/Linux/g
```

Using **%** is a lot more convenient than typing **1,$**, so be sure to remember this handy abbreviation: you will use it a lot.

From time to time, you will want **vi** to ask for confirmation before each substitution. This allows you to control which instances of the pattern are replaced. As we discussed, all you need to do is use the **c** (confirm) modifier, for example.

```
:%s/UNIX/Linux/cg
```

When you use such a command, you can stop part way through by pressing **^C** (the **intr** key). This aborts the entire command, not just the current substitution.

For reference, here is a summary of the **:s** command:

:s/*pattern***/***replace***/**	substitute, current line
:*line***/***pattern***/***replace***/**	substitute, specified line
:*line***,***lines***/***pattern***/***replace***/**	substitute, specified range
:%s/*pattern***/***replace***/**	substitute, all lines

At the end of the command, you can use **c** to tell **vi** to ask for confirmation, and **g** (global) to replace all occurrences on each line. To specify a line number, you can use an actual number, a **.** (period) for the current line, or **$** (dollar sign) for the last line in the editing buffer. The number **1** represents the first line in the editing buffer.

DELETING TEXT

There are several ways to delete data from the editing buffer, using both **vi** and **ex** commands. The **vi** commands are as follows:

x	delete character at cursor
X	delete character to left of cursor
D	delete from cursor to end of line
d*move*	delete from cursor to *move*
dd	delete the entire current line

In addition, there are two variations of an **ex** command:

| : *line***d** | delete specified line |
| : *line* , *line***d** | delete specified range |

Regardless of which command you use, you can undo any deletion by using the undo commands, **u** and **U** (discussed in the next section). Remember this: it may save your life one day.

The simplest delete command is **x** (lowercase "x"). It deletes the character at the current cursor position. For example, say you are writing a letter to your parents telling them all about life at school. The current line of the editing buffer contains:

```
I love heiQnous paWrties and avoid the library as a rule
```

You notice that there is a mistake in the third word. You move the cursor to the "Q" and type:

x

The current line is now:

```
I love heinous paWrties and avoid the library as a rule
```

The **X** (uppercase "X") command deletes a single character to the left of the cursor. For example, in the line above, you notice there is another mistake in the fourth word. You move to the "r" and press:

X

The current line is now:

```
I love heinous parties and avoid the library as a rule
```

The **D** (uppercase "D") command deletes from the cursor to the end of the line. For example, say that you move to the space following the word "library" and type:

D

The current line becomes:

```
I love heinous parties and avoid the library
```

The next deletion command, **d** (lowercase "d") is followed by a cursor movement command. This deletes text from the cursor to the position indicated by the move command. This is similar to the **c** (change) command we discussed earlier. Here are some examples:

dw	delete 1 word
d10w	delete 10 words
d10W	delete 10 words (ignore punctuation)
db	delete backwards, 1 word
d2)	delete 2 sentences
d5}	delete 5 paragraphs

There are two especially useful ways to use the **d** command. First, to delete all the lines from the current line to the end of the editing buffer, use **dG**.

Second, to delete all the lines from the current line to the beginning of the editing buffer, use either **dgg** or **d1G**. (As I mentioned earlier, the **gg** command does not work with older versions of **vi**.)

To continue with our example, the current line is still:

`I love heinous parties and avoid the library`

You move to the beginning of the word "heinous" and delete 4 words by typing:

`d4w`

The current line becomes:

`I love the library`

The final **vi** deletion command is **dd**. This deletes the entire current line. If you want to delete more than one line, use a repeat count in front of the command. For example, to delete a single line, use:

`dd`

To delete 10 lines, use:

`10dd`

At times, you will find it more convenient to delete using line numbers. To do so, you use the **ex** command **:d**. To use the **:d** command, you specify either a single line number or a range (two numbers separated by a comma). For example, to delete line 50, use:

`:50d`

To delete lines 50 through 60, use:

`:50,60d`

(Reminder: To display line numbers use **:set number**; to turn off line numbers, use **:set nonumber**.)

As with the other **ex** commands, the symbol **.** (period) stands for the current line and **$** (dollar sign) stands for the last line in the editing buffer. Thus, to delete from the beginning of the editing buffer to the current line, use:

`:1,.d`

This has the same effect as **dgg** or **d1G**. To delete from the current line to the end of the editing buffer, use:

`:.,$d`

This has the same effect as **dG**. To delete the entire editing buffer, use either of the following commands:

```
:1,$d
:%d
```

Remember that **%** stands for all the lines in the editing buffer.

UNDOING OR REPEATING A CHANGE

Once you start making substitutions and deletions, it becomes important to be able to undo your changes. For instance, say you want to change all the occurrences of the word "advertisement" to "ad". You decide to enter:

```
:%s/advertisement/ad/g
```

However, you accidentally make a typing mistake, leaving out the second "d":

```
:%s/advertisement/a/g
```

You have just replaced all occurrences of "advertisement" with the letter "a". However, you can't fix the problem by changing all the "a"s to "ad" because there are "a"s all over the place. You could use the **:q!** command and quit without saving your work (if you were working with an existing file), but then you would lose all your changes for the entire editing session. Is there anything you can do?

Here is a similar situation. You want to delete 10 lines, but instead of typing **10dd** you type **100dd**. You have just deleted 100 lines. Is there any way to get them back?

The answer to both questions is yes. There are two commands you can use to undo changes, as well as a command to repeat the last change:

u   undo last command that modified the editing buffer
U   restore current line
.   repeat last command that modified the editing buffer

The **u** (lowercase "u") command will undo the last command that changed the editing buffer: an insertion, a substitution, a change or a deletion. In both our examples, all you would have to do is type **u** and the substitution/deletion would be nullified. If, after pressing **u**, you decide that you really did want the change, simply press **u** again. The **u** command can undo itself. (If only the rest of life were that simple.)*

The **U** (uppercase "U") command will undo all the changes you made to the *current* line since you last moved to it. For example, let's say you move the cursor to a particular line and make a lot of changes without leaving that line. Unfortunately, you make a big mess of it, so much so that all you want is for the line to be just as it was when you moved to it. Simply type **U** and the line will be restored to its original content. If, after pressing **U**, you don't like the results, you can undo it with the **u** (lowercase "u") command.

---

*Life is only that simple with **vi**. With Vim, pressing **u** more than once in a row undoes previous commands, one at a time. Of course, in many cases, this might be exactly what you want.

The **U** command will undo as many changes as necessary, all at once, to restore the current line. However, **U** will only work as long as you stay on the line. As soon as you move the cursor to a new line, the **U** command will apply to that line, and there is no easy way to restore the old line.

In addition to **u** and **U**, there is another important command that involves the last change to the editing buffer. It is the **.** (dot) command. You use it to repeat the last command that modified the editing buffer. This command can be very useful, so let's take a look at an example.

Say that you want to insert the name "Mxyzptlk" at several different places in the editing buffer. This is a difficult name to spell, and it is a bother to have to type it more than once, so here's the smart way to do it. Move to the place where you want to make the first insertion and type:

iMxyzptlk<Esc>

You have inserted the name into the editing buffer. Now, move to the next place where you want to make the same insertion and type:

.

The exact same insertion will be repeated for you. You can use the **.** command as many times as you want. Be careful though: as soon as you make another change, even a tiny one-character deletion, the effect of the **.** command will change as well.

RECOVERING DELETIONS

Whenever you delete one or more lines of text, **vi** saves the deletion in a special storage area called a NUMBERED BUFFER. There are 9 such buffers, numbered 1 through 9. At any time, you can insert the contents of a numbered buffer into the editing buffer. To do so, type a **"** (double-quote) followed by the number of the buffer, followed by a **p** or **P** (put) command. (Reminder: When you are working with lines, the **p** command inserts below the current line; the **P** command inserts above the current line.)

For example, to insert the contents of buffer #1 below the current line, you would use:

"1p

To insert the contents of buffer #2 above the current line, you would use:

"2P

In this way, you can recall and insert any of your last 9 deletions. Let's say, for example, you have made several deletions and you want to restore one of them. However, you can't remember which one it was.

Start by typing **"1p**. If that doesn't give you the text you want, type **u** to undo the insert and try **"2p**. If that doesn't work, type **u** to undo the insert and try **"3p**. Keep going until you get what you want. The sequence would look like this:

`"1pu"2pu"3pu`...

This in itself is pretty cool. However, **`vi`** can do more. After you undo the first insertion, if you use the `.` (dot) command to repeat the insertion, **`vi`** will automatically increase the buffer number by 1. This means, instead of using the above sequence, you can use:

`"1pu.u.u`...

To test this, use **`vi`** to create a file that contains the following five lines:

```
111
222
333
444
555
```

Type **`1G`** or **`gg`** to jump to the first line. Then type **`dd`** five times in a row to delete each line separately. Now try the recovery sequence above and watch what happens.

Reminder: The numbered buffers only store deleted lines, not parts of a line or individual characters. For example, if you use **`10dd`** to delete 10 lines, the deletion is saved in a numbered buffer. If you use **`5x`** to delete 5 characters, however, the deletion is not saved in this way.

MOVING TEXT

The **`vi`** editor has a special facility that enables you to move or copy text from one place to another. In this section, we'll talk about moving. In the next section, we'll talk about copying.

At all times, **`vi`** keeps a copy of your last deletion in a storage area called the UNNAMED BUFFER. At any time, you can copy the contents of the unnamed buffer to the editing buffer by using the **`p`** and **`P`** (put) commands. (The reason this storage area is called the unnamed buffer is that there are other, similar storage areas which have names.)

The **`p`** (lowercase "p") command inserts the contents of the unnamed buffer after the current position of the cursor. For example, say that the current line contains:

`This good is a sentence.`

You move to the "g" and delete one word.

`dw`

As you do, that word is copied to the unnamed buffer. The current line now looks like this:

`This is a sentence.`

Now you move to the space after "a" and type:

`p`

The contents of the unnamed buffer is inserted to the right of the cursor. The current line becomes:

This is a good sentence.

Here is an example that uses the **P** (uppercase "P") command. Say that the current line contains:

This is right now.

You move to the space before the word "right" and type:

de

This erases up to the end of the word and leaves you with:

This is now.

Now move to the period at the end of the line and type:

P

The deletion is inserted to the left of the cursor. The current line becomes:

This is now right.

It is important to understand that the unnamed buffer can only hold one thing at a time. For example, let's say you have just deleted 1,000 lines of text. A copy of the text is stored in the unnamed buffer. If you want, you can insert it somewhere else in the editing buffer. Now, you delete a single character. The 1,000 lines of text are flushed from the unnamed buffer. If you use the **p** command now, you will get your last deletion, that is, the single character.

To continue, consider, for a moment, the combination **xp**. The **x** command deletes the character at the current cursor position. The **p** command inserts the deletion to the right of the cursor. The net result is to transpose two characters. For example, say that the current line is:

I ma never mixed up.

You move to the first "m" and type:

xp

The current line is now:

I am never mixed up.

Another important combination is **deep**, which you can use to transpose two words. Here is an example. Say that the current line contains:

I am mixed never up.

Move to the space before the word "mixed". (Take care to move to the space before the word, not to the first letter of the word.) Now type:

deep

The **de** command deletes the space and the following word, after which the current line looks like:

I am never up.

The second **e** command moves forward to the end of the next word. The **p** then inserts the deletion after the cursor. The net result is:

I am never mixed up.

In this way, you have used **deep** to transpose two words. Take a moment right now to memorize this combination, so you can type it quickly when you need it.

Whenever you delete whole lines, **p** and **P** will insert whole lines. The **p** command will insert below the current line; **P** will insert above the current line. For example, let's say you want to move 10 lines from one place to another. To start, move the cursor to the first line of text. Then use the **dd** command with a repeat count to delete 10 lines:

10dd

These lines are deleted from the editing buffer and copied to the unnamed buffer. Now move the cursor to the line under which you want to make the insertion and type:

p

Consider, now, what happens when you type **ddp**. The **dd** command deletes the current line. The next line becomes the new current line. The **p** inserts the deletion below the new current line. The net result is to transpose two lines. (Try it.)

To summarize:

p	copy last deletion; insert after/below cursor
P	copy last deletion; insert before/above cursor
xp	transpose two characters
deep	transpose two words (start cursor to left of first word)
ddp	transpose two lines

COPYING TEXT

Copying text from one location to another is a three-step process. First, you use the **y**, **yy** or **Y** commands to copy text from the editing buffer to the unnamed buffer without deleting the original text. Second, you move the cursor to wherever you want to insert the text. Finally, you use **p** or **P** to perform the insertion.

When you copy text to the unnamed buffer without deleting it, we say that you YANK the text. (Hence the names **y**, **yy** and **Y**.) The **y** and **yy** commands work the same as **d** and **dd**, except they yank instead of delete. Here are some examples:

yw	yank 1 word
y10w	yank 10 words
y10W	yank 10 words (ignore punctuation)
yb	yank backwards, 1 word
y2)	yank 2 sentences
y5}	yank 5 paragraphs
yy	yank 1 line
10yy	yank 10 lines

Let's say that you want to copy 5 paragraphs from one place to another. To start, move the cursor to the beginning of the first paragraph. Next, yank the 5 paragraphs into the unnamed buffer without deleting the text:

y5}

Now move the cursor to the line under which you want to make the insertion and insert the text:

p

For convenience, you can use **Y** as a synonym for **yy**. Thus, the following commands both yank 10 lines into the unnamed buffer:

10yy
10Y

Notice something interesting. The **y** command is analogous to **d** in that they both copy text to the unnamed buffer, from the current character to the end of a cursor move. (The only difference is that **d** deletes and **y** yanks.) Similarly, **yy** is analogous to **dd** in that they delete/yank entire lines.

The **Y** command, however, does not work the same as **D**. The **Y** command yanks entire lines. The **D** command deletes from the current character to the end of the line. If you want to yank from the current character to the end of the line, you must use **y$**. To yank from the current character to the beginning of the line, you would use **y0**.

HINT

Whenever you delete or yank text, the text remains in the unnamed buffer until you enter another delete or yank command. Thus, you can use the **p** or **P** commands to insert the same text, over and over, into different locations within the editing buffer.

CHANGING THE CASE OF LETTERS

The **vi** editor has a specific command to change letters from lowercase to uppercase or from uppercase to lowercase. The command is a **~** (tilde). Simply move the cursor to the letter you want to change and press:

~

The ~ causes **vi** to change the case of the current character and then advance the cursor one position. For example, say that the current line contains:

```
"By Jove," he said, "that's a CAPITAL idea."
```

The cursor is at the "C". You press ~. The current line now looks like:

```
"By Jove," he said, "that's a cAPITAL idea."
```

The cursor is now at the "A". Since, ~ moves the cursor one position to the right, you can type ~ repeatedly to change a sequence of letters. In our example, you can change the rest of the word to lowercase by typing six more tilde characters:

```
~~~~~~
```

The current line becomes:

```
"By Jove," he said, "that's a capital idea."
```

If you type ~ when the cursor is at a character that is not a letter, such as a punctuation symbol, **vi** will advance the cursor, but will not make a change. Thus, it is safe to "tilde" your way across a vast distance, as **vi** will simply skip over the non-alphabetic characters. To make this easy, you can put a repeat count in front of this command. For example, to change the case of a 7-letter word, move the cursor to the beginning of the word and type:

```
7~
```

The case of the entire word will be changed, leaving the cursor one position past the end of the word.

Note: With some versions of **vi**, the ~ command will not move past the end of the current line, even when you use a large repeat count, such as **100~**. Other versions of **vi** will process as many characters as you specify, even across multiple lines. When you have a spare moment, you may want to experiment with your version of **vi** to see whether or not the ~ command will move past the end of a line.

SETTING OPTIONS

Like most complex Unix programs, **vi** supports a number of OPTIONS that enable you to control various aspects of its operation. When you start **vi**, each option is given a default value. If you want to change a particular aspect of how **vi** behaves, you can set the value of the appropriate option by using the **:set** command. There are two forms of the syntax, as there are two different types of options:

```
:set [no]option...
:set option[=value]...
```

where *option* is the name of an option, and **value** is the value the option should have.

In most cases, the default values will work just fine (which is why they are the defaults). However, from time to time, you may want to make changes. We have already done this three times in this chapter. First, we used the **showmode** option to tell **vi** to display a reminder whenever we are in input mode. The command we used was:

`:set showmode`

The second option we used was **number** to display line numbers:

`:set number`

Finally, we used **nonumber** to turn off the numbering:

`:set nonumber`

There are two types of **vi** options. The first type are SWITCHES, which are either off or on. The options I just mentioned are all switches. To turn on a switch, you use its name. To turn off a switch, you type "no" in front of the name. For example:

`:set showmode`
`:set noshowmode`
`:set number`
`:set nonumber`

The second type of options, VARIABLES, contain a value. For instance, the **tabstop** variable sets the tab spacing. By default, **tabstop** is set to 8, which means that tabs are expanded to every 8th position (in common with Unix in general; see Chapter 18). If you want the tabs to expand to, say, every 4th position, you would set the **tabstop** variable to 4:

`:set tabstop=4`

As a convenience, it is possible to set more than one option within the same command, for example:

`:set showmode nonumber tabstop=4`

The actual options that are available depend on which version of **vi** you are using. As you would expect, newer versions have more options. Typically, standard **vi** has about 40 or so options, of which 16 are important. Vim has more than 340 options, almost all of which you never need. For reference, Figure 22-9 shows the important **vi** options.

As you can see from the two figures, almost all options have abbreviations. For your convenience, you can use these abbreviations instead of typing the full name. For example, the following two commands are equivalent:

`:set showmode nonumber tabstop=4`
`:set smd nonu ts=4`

HINT

To set options automatically each time you start **vi**, place the appropriate `:set` commands in an initialization file (discussed later in the chapter).

SWITCH	ABBR.	DEFAULT	MEANING
`autoindent`	`ai`	off	with **wrapmargin**: indent to match line above/below
`autowrite`	`aw`	off	if text has been modified, save before changing files
`errorbells`	`eb`	off	beep when displaying an error message
`exrc`	`ex`	off	look for an initialization file in current directory
`ignorecase`	`ic`	off	ignore case when searching
`list`	—	off	show tabs as `^I`; end of line as `$`
`number`	`nu`	off	display line numbers
`readonly`	`ro`	off	do not allow contents of editing buffer to be changed
`showmatch`	`sm`	off	input mode: show matching `()`, `{}`, or `[]`
`showmode`	`smd`	off	display a reminder when in input mode
`wrapscan`	`ws`	off	when searching, wrap around end/beginning of file
`writeany`	`wa`	off	allow write to any file without needing `!` to override

VARIABLE	ABBR.	DEFAULT	MEANING
`lines`	—	24	number of lines of text (window/screen size - 1)
`shiftwidth`	`sw`	8	number of spaces to use with **autoindent**
`tabstop`	`ts`	8	tab spacing
`wrapmargin`	`wm`	0	position from right margin to start wrapping (0=off)

FIGURE 22-9: `vi` Options: Switches and Variables

*You can control various aspects of **vi** by using two different types of options: switches (off or on), and variables (store a value). These two lists show the most useful switches and variables, along with their abbreviations, default values, and meaning.*

DISPLAYING OPTIONS

To display the values of one or more options, you use a variation of the `:set` command. The syntax is:

`:set` [*option*[`?`]... | `all`]

where *option* is the name of an option.

To display the value of all options, use:

`:set all`

Using this command is the best way to see a list of all the options supported by your version of **vi**. To display the value of a single option, type the name of the option followed by a `?` (question mark). For example:

`:set number?`
`:set showmode?`
`:set wrapmargin?`

As a convenience, it is possible to display the value of more than one option name in a single command:

```
:set number? showmode? wrapmargin?
```

Finally, to display the values of only those options that have been changed from their default values, use `:set` by itself:

```
:set
```

When you use this last command, you may see options you don't remember changing. This is because every system has a number of initialization files that are read by **vi** when it starts. One of these files is under your control, and you can use it to set up your working environment to suit your needs. (We'll talk about this later in the chapter.) The other initialization files are either created automatically when **vi** is installed or are set up by your system administrator. Typically, these files will contain commands to modify the values of certain options, which will then show up in the list of options having non-default values.

BREAKING LINES AUTOMATICALLY AS YOU TYPE

When you type a document, you need to break the text into lines. One way to do this is to press <Return> at the end of each line. As I explained in Chapter 7, pressing <Return> generates a newline character, which marks the end of a line. This works fine for small amounts of text, but if you are doing a lot of typing, it's more convenient to let **vi** break the lines for you automatically. To do this, you set the **wrapmargin** (**wm**) option. The syntax is:

```
:set wrapmargin=n
```

where n is the number of positions from the right margin where you want lines to start breaking. For convenience, you can use the abbreviation **wm** instead of the full name.

The **wrapmargin** option only affects input mode. When you set **wrapmargin** to a number greater than 0, it causes **vi** to break a line into two as you are typing when the line extends within that many characters of the right margin. For example, to tell **vi** to break your lines automatically when they get within 6 characters of the right margin, use either of the following commands:

```
:set wrapmargin=6
:set wm=6
```

If you want the longest possible lines, use a value of 1:

```
:set wm=1
```

To turn off automatic line breaking, set **wm** to **0**:

```
:set wm=0
```

If you are working with indented text, you can turn on the **autoindent** (**ai**) option:

```
:set autoindent
```

This tells **vi** to match the indentation to the line above or below the line you are typing.

Automatic line breaking only affects text as you type it. To reformat existing text, you can use either the **r** and **J** commands (see the next section) or the **fmt** command from Chapter 18 (discussed later in the chapter).

> **HINT**
>
> If you set **wrapmargin** to anything smaller than 6, there will be very little space at the end of each line, which makes it awkward to make corrections. In my experience, the best setting for **wrapmargin** is between 6 and 10, which leaves plenty of room for small changes.

BREAKING AND JOINING LINES

There will be many times when you want to break long lines into two or join short lines together. For example:

```
This line is much too long and must be broken into two.
```

You want to break this line after the word "and". The easiest way is to move the cursor to the space following "and" and type:

r<Return>

Using the **r** command replaces a single character with another character. In this case, the **r** command replaces the space with a newline, effectively breaking the line.

If you have lines that are too short, you can combine them by moving the cursor to the first line and type **J** (uppercase "J"). This combines the current line and the next line into one long line. When **vi** joins lines, it automatically inserts spaces in the appropriate places, a single space between words and a double space at the end of a sentence. (Isn't that nice?)

To join more than two lines at the same time, put a repeat count before the **J** command. Here is an example. Your editing buffer contains the following lines:

```
This sentence
is short.
This sentence is also short.
```

Move the cursor to the first line and type:

3J

The result is:

```
This sentence is short.  This sentence is also short.
```

> **HINT**
>
> The **r** and **J** commands are useful for making small adjustments. However, when you need to reformat anything longer than 5-6 lines of text, it is usually better to use the **fmt** command as explained later in the chapter.

COPYING AND MOVING LINES

There will be many times when you will find it convenient to copy or move lines by using line numbers. For these operations, you use the **ex** commands :**co** (copy) and :**m** (move). Both commands use the same format. The only difference is that :**m** deletes the original lines and :**co** does not.

To use these commands, you specify a single line number or a range of line numbers before the command name. These are the lines to be copied or moved. After the command name, you specify the target line number. The new lines will be inserted below the target line. The syntax is:

$x[,y]$:**co**z
$x[,y]$:**m**z

where x, y and z are line numbers.

The source lines (**x**, or **x** through **y**) are copied or moved, and inserted below the target line (**z**). Here are some examples:

:**5co10**	copy line 5, insert below line 10
:**4,8co20**	copy lines 4 through 8, insert below line 20
:**5m10**	move line 5, insert below line 10
:**4,8m20**	move lines 4 through 8, insert below line 20

(Reminder: To display line numbers use :**set number**; to turn off line numbers, use :**set nonumber**.)

As with other **ex** commands, you can use a . (period) to refer to the current line and a **$** (dollar sign) to refer to the last line in the editing buffer. For example, the following command moves lines 1 through the current line to the end of the editing buffer:

:**1,.m$**

You can also use line 0 (zero) to refer to the beginning of the editing buffer. For example, the following command moves from the current line through the last line to the beginning of the editing buffer:

:**.,$m0**

These last two commands are interesting. They both swap the top and bottom parts of the editing buffer. However, there is a subtle difference. With the first command, the current line ends up at the bottom of the editing buffer. With the second command, the current line ends up on top. (Take a moment to think about this.)

ENTERING SHELL COMMANDS

There are several ways to use regular shell commands without having to stop **vi**. First, you can enter a command by typing : **!** followed by the command. This tells **vi** to send the command to the shell to be executed. When the command finishes, control will be returned to **vi**. For example, to display the time and date, enter:

`:!date`

After the command is finished, you will see a message. The message will vary depending on your version of **vi**. Here are the most likely ones:

```
Press ENTER or type command to continue
[Hit return to continue]
Press any key to continue
```

At this point, simply press <Return> and you will be back in **vi**. To repeat the most recent shell command — regardless of how long it has been since you entered it — use:

`:!!`

For example, if the last shell command you entered was **date**, you can display the time and date once again by using `:!!`.

To insert the output of a shell command directly into the editing buffer, you can use the `:r!` command. We'll talk about this command in the next section, where you will find some examples.

From time to time, you will want to enter more than one shell command. You can do so by starting a new shell. There are two ways to do this. First, you can use the `:sh` command:

`:sh`

This will pause **vi** and start a new copy of your default shell. You can now enter as many commands as you want. When you are finished with the shell, stop it by pressing ^D or by entering the **exit** command. You will be returned to **vi**.

Alternatively, you can start a new shell by running an actual command. For example, to start a new Bash shell, run the **bash** program:

`:!bash`

To start a new Tcsh shell, use:

`:!tcsh`

(The various shells are discussed in Chapter 11.) As with `:sh`, when you end the shell, you will be returned to **vi**. This technique is handy when, for some reason, you want to use a non-default shell. For example, say that you normally use Bash but, just this once, you want to test something by running the Tcsh. All you have to do is use the command `:!tcsh`.

To summarize:

`:!`*command*	pause **vi**, execute shell command
`:!!`	pause **vi**, execute previous shell command
`:sh`	pause **vi**, start a new (default) shell
`:!bash`	pause **vi**, start a new Bash shell
`:!tcsh`	pause **vi**, start a new Tcsh shell

INSERTING DATA FROM A FILE INTO THE EDITING BUFFER

To read data from an existing file into the editing buffer, you use the `:r` command. The syntax is:

`:[line]r file`

where *line* is a line number and *file* is the name of a file.

The `:r` command reads the contents of the file and inserts it into the editing buffer *after* the specified line. For example, the following command inserts the contents of the file **info** after line 10:

`:10r info`

To refer to the beginning of the editing buffer, use line 0 (zero). For example, to insert the contents of **info** at the beginning of the editing buffer, use:

`:0r info`

To refer to the end of the editing buffer, use `$`. For example, to insert the contents of **info** at the end of the editing buffer, use:

`:$r info`

If you omit the line number, **vi** will insert the new data after the current line. This is probably the most useful form of the `:r` command. You simply move the cursor to where you want to insert the new data and enter the `:r` command. For example, let's say you want to insert the contents of the file **info** at the end of the current paragraph. Use the `}` (right brace) command to jump to the end of the paragraph, then insert the data:

```
}
:r info
```

INSERTING THE OUTPUT OF A SHELL COMMAND INTO THE EDITING BUFFER

There is a variation of the `:r` command that is especially useful. If, instead of a file name, you type an `!` (exclamation mark) followed by the name of a program, **vi** will execute the program and insert its output into the editing buffer. Here is an example. The **ls** program displays a list of the files in your working directory (see Chapter 24). To insert such a list after the current line, enter:

`:r !ls`

As a second example, here is how you would insert the current time and date above the first line of the editing buffer:

`:0r !date`

To complete our discussion of `:r`, here is a wonderful time-saving idea that illustrates the power of this command. In Chapter 19, we discussed how to use the **look** command to help with spelling. For example, say that you want to use the word "ascetic", but you are not quite sure how to spell it. You can use **look** to display possible words from the dictionary file:

```
look asc
```

Below is some typical output. A quick perusal of the list shows the exact word you want (in the 5th line):

```
ascend
ascendant
ascent
ascertain
ascetic
ascribe
ascription
```

Let's say you are working with **vi**, typing into the editing buffer, and you get to the point where you want to insert this particular word into the text. Press <Esc> to change from input mode to command mode, and then enter the command:

```
:r !look asc
```

The output of the **look** command will be inserted after the current line (the last line you typed). Look at the list and delete all words you don't want. In this case, you would delete all but the 5th word. (If you don't want any of the words, you can use the **u** command to undo insertion.) Once you have deleted all but the correct word, move up to the last line you typed and type:

```
J
```

This will join the new word onto the end of the line. Finally, to return to input mode, ready to insert text at the end of the line, type:

```
A
```

This allows you to append data to the end of the current line. You are now back in business: continue typing.

At first, a sequence of commands such as the one above may seem a bit complex. Actually, once you get used to it, it's quite simple. Moreover, you can do the entire thing without taking your hands off from the keyboard. Try it: it's way cool.

Here is a summary of the **:r** command:

:line**r** *file*	insert contents of *file* after specified line
:**r** *file*	insert contents of *file* after current line
:line**r** !*program*	insert output of *program* after specified line
:**r** !*program*	insert output of *program* after current line

---

HINT

If you don't like the result of a `:r` or `:r!` command, you can reverse it with the **u** (undo) command.

USING A PROGRAM TO PROCESS DATA: `fmt`

The `!` and `!!` (exclamation mark) commands will send lines from the editing buffer to another program. The output of the program will replace the original lines. For example, you can replace a set of lines with the same data in sorted order. Here is how it works.

Move to the line where you want to start. Type the number of lines you want to process, followed by `!!` (two exclamation marks), followed by the name of a program, followed by <Return>. For example, say that you have 5 lines that contain the following data, which you want to sort. (The **sort** program is discussed in Chapter 19.)

```
entertain
balloon
anaconda
dairy
coin
```

Move to the first line and enter:

```
5!!sort
```

Once you type the second `!`, **vi** will move the cursor to the command line and display a `!` character. You can now type any shell command directly on the command line. If necessary, you can press <Backspace> (or <Delete>) to make corrections before you press <Return>. In our example, the original 5 lines will be replaced by:

```
anaconda
balloon
coin
dairy
entertain
```

If you don't like the results, as always, you can undo the change by using the **u** command.

Here is another example you will find especially useful. In Chapter 18, we discussed the **fmt** (format) program. This program reformats the text into lines that are (by default) no longer than 75 characters. While doing so, **fmt** preserves spaces at the beginning of lines, spaces between words, and blank lines. In other words, **fmt** will make your text look nice without changing the paragraph breaks.

The **fmt** program is useful for formatting all or part of your editing buffer when you are creating documents. Once you know how to use **fmt**, you don't have to worry so much about line breaks as you are entering or modifying your data, because you can always fix them later. As an example, the following command will format 10 lines, starting from the current line:

```
10!!fmt
```

So far, all our examples have used the **!!** (double explanation mark) command. The **!** (single exclamation mark) command works in much the same way, except that it gives you more flexibility in specifying the range of input lines.

Type **!** followed by a command to move the cursor, followed by the name of a program. All the lines from the current line to the end of the cursor move will be sent to the program for processing. For example, let's say you want to format the text from the current line to the end of the paragraph. Remembering that the **}** (right brace bracket) command moves the cursor to the end of the paragraph, you would use:

```
!}fmt
```

Later in the chapter, I'll show you how to make this command especially easy to use. (See the section on macros.)

Moving on, here is an easy way to format the entire editing buffer. Jump to the first line of the editing buffer by typing **gg** or **1G**. Then enter:

```
!Gfmt
```

(Remember, the **G** command jumps to the end of the editing buffer.) Similarly, you could sort the entire editing buffer by using **gg** or **1G** followed by:

```
!Gsort
```

To summarize:

n!!*program*	execute *program* on *n* lines
!*move program*	execute *program* from current line through *move*

WRITING DATA TO A FILE

When you stop **vi** using the **ZZ** command, it automatically saves your data. However, there are several commands you can use to write data to a file whenever you want. These commands are important as they allow you to back up your data from time to time without quitting **vi**. They also allow you to save data to a different file. The commands are:

:w	write data to original file
:w *file*	write data to a new file
:w! *file*	overwrite an existing file
:w>> *file*	append data to specified file

The **:w** command writes the contents of the editing buffer to the original file, replacing the current contents of the file. For example, let's say you start **vi** by entering the command:

```
vi memo
```

The contents of the file **memo** are copied to the editing buffer. No matter how many changes you make to the editing buffer, the original file **memo** is not changed. This is important as it allows you to quit without changing your file (by using the `:q!` command). However, at any time, you can copy the contents of the editing buffer to the original file by entering:

`:w`

Normally, you don't need to do this unless you are going to use the `:e` command to start editing a new file (see below). However, if you have made a lot of changes, you might want to take a moment and save them to the original file. This will protect you against losing your work if something goes wrong.

If you specify the name of a file after the `:w` command, **vi** writes the data to that file. For example, to save the contents of the editing buffer to a file named **extra**, enter:

`:w extra`

If the file does not already exist, **vi** will create it. If the file does exist, **vi** will display a warning message. Here are two typical messages:

```
File exists - use "w! extra" to overwrite
File exists (add ! to override)
```

If you really do want to overwrite the file, you must use `:w!` instead:

`:w! extra`

To append data to the end of an existing file, type **>>** (two greater-than signs) after the command name. For example:

`:w>> extra`

Using **>>** preserves the old data. Notice the similarity to the **>>** notation used to append standard output to an existing file (see Chapter 15).

If you want to write only certain lines from the editing buffer, you can specify them in the usual manner. For example, to write line 10 to a file named **save** (replacing the contents of **save**), enter:

`:10w save`

To append lines 10 through 20 to the file named **save**, use:

`:10,20w>> save`

Earlier in the chapter, I explained that there were two ways to quit **vi**. To save your data and quit, you use the command **ZZ**; to quit without saving, you use `:q!`. Actually, there is a third way. As long as you have already used the `:w` command to save your data, you can quit by using `:q`. As a convenience, you can combine these two commands:

`:wq`

Thus, the combination `:wq` has the same effect as **ZZ**.

CHANGING TO A NEW FILE

When you start **vi**, you can specify the name of the file you want to edit. For example, to edit a file named **memo**, you would enter:

```
vi memo
```

If you decide to edit a different file, you do not have to quit and restart the program. To change to a new file, use the `:e` command, followed by the name of the file. For example, to edit a file named **document**, enter:

```
:e document
```

When you start editing a new file, the previous contents of the editing buffer are lost, so be sure to use the `:w` command first to save your data. When you use the `:e` command, **vi** will check to see if you have saved your data. If there is unsaved data, **vi** will not let you change to a new file. If you would like to override this protection, use the `:e!` command. For example, say that you start **vi** using the command:

```
vi memo
```

The contents of **memo** are copied to the editing buffer. As it happens, you make so many mistakes that you would rather just start over. The last thing you want to do is save the contents of the editing buffer back to the original file. Just enter:

```
:e!
```

You are now editing a copy of the original **memo** file: the previous changes have been thrown away. To summarize:

`:e` *file*	edit the specified file
`:e`	reedit the current file, omit automatic check
`:e!` *file*	edit the specified file, omit automatic check

USING ABBREVIATIONS

To create abbreviations for frequently used words or expressions, you use the `:ab` (abbreviate) command. The syntax is:

```
:ab [short long]
```

where *short* is an abbreviation and *long* is the replacement for that abbreviation.

Here is an example. You are working on a resumé for a summer job, and you find it tiresome to type "exceptionally gifted" over and over. Instead, you can establish an abbreviation, say, "eg". Type `:ab`, followed by the short form, followed by the long form:

```
:ab eg exceptionally gifted
```

From now on, whenever you are in input mode and you type **eg** as a separate word, **vi** will automatically replace it with "exceptionally gifted". Notice that the substitution only takes places when "eg" is a word on its own; **vi** is smart enough not to replace "eg" within another word, such as "egotistical".

To remove an abbreviation, use the **:una** (un-abbreviate) command. The syntax is:

:una *short*

where *short* is an abbreviation. Simply type **:una** followed by the name of the short form you wish to remove. For example:

:una eg

At any time, you can see a list of all your abbreviations by entering the **:ab** command by itself:

:ab

> **HINT**
>
> To define abbreviations automatically each time you start **vi**, place the appropriate **:ab** commands in your initialization file (discussed later in the chapter).

MACROS

As we discussed in the previous section, the **:ab** command enables you to create abbreviations to use in input mode. Instead of typing the same text over and over, you can use an abbreviation. Analogously, the **:map** command enables you to create one-character abbreviations that are used in command mode. In effect, this allows you to create your own customized one-character commands, which are called MACROS. The syntax is:

:map [*x commands*]

where *x* is a single character, and *commands* is a sequence of **vi** or **ex** commands.

Here is an example of a simple macro. Earlier in the chapter (in the section on moving text), I showed you how to transpose two words: move the cursor to the space in front of the first word and type **deep**. To make this more convenient, you can define a macro:

:map K deep

Now, to transpose any two words, all you have to do is move the cursor to the space in front of the first word and press **K**.

By definition, macro names must be a single character. If you use a name that already has a meaning, the character will lose that meaning. For example, earlier in the chapter, we talked about the **x** (lower case "x") and **X** (uppercase "X") commands. The **x** command deletes the current character (the character to which the cursor is pointing); **X** deletes the character to the left of the cursor. Consider the following macro definition:

:map X dd

This command creates a macro named **X** (uppercase "X") that deletes the current line. Once you define this macro, the regular **X** command is lost. Still, you may not mind. If you rarely use the command, you might find it convenient to type **X** to delete a line.

Usually, however, it is a good idea not to replace regular commands. This raises the question: which characters are *not* used by **vi** or Vim? Very few, actually. As you can see from Figure 22-10, there are only 14 characters not used by **vi**. Vim is even more extreme: the only common characters it doesn't use as command names are **^K** and **** (backslash). This is not as much of a restriction as you might think, as there are several Vim commands you will probably not need, so it's safe to replace them. These characters are also listed in Figure 22-10.

In a real sense, macros are tiny programs. As with all programming tools, there are far more details than you will ever need, so I won't go into all the fine points.* Instead, I'll show you a few more useful macros to give you an idea of what they can do for you.

As we discussed earlier in the chapter, the **G** command moves the cursor to the end of the editing buffer. The **1G** (go to line 1) command moves to the beginning of the buffer. With some versions of **vi** (and with Vim), you can use **gg** instead of **1G**. If your version of **vi** doesn't support **gg**, however, it is handy to have a simple command to take its place. Consider the following:

```
:map g 1G
```

vi: CHARACTERS TO USE AS MACRO NAMES					
Letters	g	K	q	v	V	Z
Punctuation	@	#	*	\		
Ctrl characters	^A	^K	^O	^W	^X	

VIM: CHARACTERS TO USE AS MACRO NAMES					
Letters	K	q	v	V		
Punctuation	@	\				
Ctrl characters	^@	^A	^K	^O	^T	^X

Figure 22-10: Characters to use as vi and Vim macro names

The :map command allows you to create a macro, an abbreviation for a sequence of vi or ex commands. A macro name must be a single character. If you choose a name that already has a meaning as a command, that meaning will be lost. The first table shows those characters that are not used as vi commands and, hence, are safe to use as macro names.

With Vim, virtually all characters are used as command names. Nevertheless, some commands are used so infrequently, there is no reason not to replace them. These characters are shown in the second table.

---

*If you learn enough tricks and take enough time, you can write very complex **vi** macros. For example, there are people who have written macros to solve the Towers of Hanoi problem and to emulate a Turing Machine (two classical computer science problems). If you like this sort of thing, you should know that Vim comes with much more sophisticated tools than standard **vi**. With Vim, you can record, replay and modify macros. You can also write programs using a full-fledged scripting facility. For more information, search the Web for "vim macros" and "vim scripting".

This command defines a macro named **g** that expands to the command **1G**. Now, when you want to zoom around the editing buffer, you can type **g** (lowercase "g") to jump to the beginning and **G** (uppercase "G") to jump to the end.

Here is another, more complicated macro. Let's say you are writing a program in a language such as C or C++ in which comments are enclosed by **/*** and ***/**, for example:

```
/*  This line is a comment */
```

The following macro creates a comment out of an ordinary line by inserting **/*** at the beginning of the line, and ***/** at the end of the line:

```
:map * I/* ^V<Esc>A */^V<Esc>
```

Let's take this macro apart. Following **:map**, you see a ***** (star) character. This will be the name of the macro.

Next come the commands. To begin, we use **I** to enter input mode at the beginning of the line. Then we type **/*** followed by a space. At this point, we need to press the <Esc> key to quit input mode. To insert an <Esc> code into the macro, we type **^V**<Esc>. (As we discussed earlier in the chapter, **^V** [Ctrl-V] tells **vi** that the next key is to be taken literally.)

Next we use the **A** (append) command to enter input mode at the end of the line. We then type a space, followed by **/***. To quit input mode, we use another <Esc>.

If you enter the above command for yourself, you will see that the <Esc> code is displayed as **^[**. In other words, what you will see on your screen will be:

```
:map * I/* ^[A */^[
```

This is because the <Esc> code is actually **^[**, in the same way that a backspace is **^H** (see Chapter 7), and a tab is **^I**.

Some versions of **vi** allow you to assign a macro to the function keys <F1> through <F10>. To do so, you refer to the function key by typing a **#** character followed by a number: 1=F1, 2=F2... 0=F10. For example, this following command creates a macro assigned to the <F1> key:

```
:map #1 :set all
```

At any time, you can display a list of all your macros by using the **:map** command by itself:

```
:map
```

To remove a macro, use the **:unmap** command. The syntax is:

```
:unmap x
```

where *x* is the name of a macro. For example:

```
:unmap g
:unmap #1
```

INITIALIZATION FILES: `.exrc`, `.vimrc`

When **vi** or Vim starts, it looks for an initialization file in your home directory. If such a file exists, the program will read it and execute any **ex** commands that it finds. This allows you to initialize your working environment automatically. (The home directory is discussed in Chapter 23, initialization files in Chapter 14.)

With **vi**, the initialization file is named `.exrc` (pronounced "dot-E-X-R-C"). With Vim, the file is named `.vimrc` ("dot-vim-R-C")*. As we discussed in Chapter 14, the initial `.` (dot) indicates that these are hidden files; the "rc" designation stands for "run commands".

Creating a **vi** initialization file is straightforward: just insert the **ex** commands you want to be executed automatically each time you start **vi**. In particular, you should include all the `:set` (option), `:ab` (abbreviation), and `:map` (macro) commands you use regularly. You can also use run shell commands by using the `:!` command.

As **vi** reads the initialization file, lines that begin with a `"` (double quote) character are ignored, which means you can use such lines for comments. Similarly, spaces and tabs at the beginning of a line are also ignored, allowing you to indent lines for readability.** Finally, **vi** assumes that everything it reads is an **ex** command, so you do not need to start any of the commands with a colon.

To illustrate these ideas, Figure 22-11 contains a sample initialization file you can use with **vi** or Vim.

Section 1 sets options as follows:

autoindent: (Input mode) When using **wrapmargin** for automatic indentation, match the indentation to the line above or below.

compatible: (Vim only) Forces Vim to run in **vi**-compatible mode. Use this if Vim does not run in **vi** mode, even when you use the **-C** option.

exrc: When starting, look for a second initialization file in the current directory (explained in the next section).

ignorecase: When searching, ignore differences between upper and lower case (very handy).

showmatch: (Input mode) When you type a closing parenthesis, bracket or brace, highlight the matching opening parenthesis, bracket or brace.

showmode: Display a reminder when you are in input mode.

wrapmargin: Specify how close to the end of a line the text should be to trigger automatic indentation.

---

*Vim will first look for a `.vimrc`. If this file does not exist, it will then look for a `.exrc` file. Thus, if you have both files, only the `.vimrc` file will be read.

Some versions of **vi (and Vim) will also ignore blank lines in an initialization file, which lets you make your file even easier to read. If your version of **vi** does not allow blank lines and you use them, you will see a non-specific error message, such as: "Error detected in `.exrc`."

Chapter 22

Section 2 creates the abbreviations. This is a good place to specify shortcuts for tricky words, HTML tags, programming keywords, and so on.

Section 3 defines the macros. As we discussed earlier in the chapter, macros can be complex (especially with Vim). The sample macros here are mostly straightforward. However, I do want to make two comments.

First, if your version of **vi** supports the **gg** command, you don't need the **g** macro.

Second, the macro that uses the <F5> function key (**#5**) ends with a **^M** character — the carriage return code — to simulate your pressing the <Return> key. Note this is a single control character, not two separate characters. When you type this line into the initialization file, you must press **^V**<Return> or **^V^M** to insert an actual **^M**.

Section 4 contains shell commands. I have used a single command line to show you how it works. In this case, I have used the **date** command (Chapter 8) to display the time and date. The **sleep** command pauses for the specified number of seconds (in this case, 2).

If your initialization file contains a bad command, **vi** will display an error message and quit executing the file at that point. Although **vi** will start properly, the rest of the

```
" ================================
" Sample vi/Vim initialization file
" ================================
"
" 1. Options
    set autoindent
    set compatible
    set ignorecase
    set showmatch
    set showmode
    set wrapmargin=6
"
" 2. Abbreviations
    ab eg exceptionally gifted
    ab h Harley
"
" 3. Macros
    map K deep
    map X dd
    map g 1G
    map #5 {!}fmt^M
"
" 4. Shell commands
    !date; sleep 2
```

FIGURE 22-11: **vi**/Vim sample initialization file

When you start **vi** *or Vim, the program looks for an initialization file in your home directory. Here is a sample file you can use as a template to create your own initialization file. See text for details.*

initialization commands in the file will not be processed. Vim is more forgiving: it will display an error message, ask you to press <Enter>, and then continue with the next command in the file.

USING TWO INITIALIZATION FILES

For situations in which you need extra customization, it is possible to use an extra initialization file. Before I can explain how it works, I need to briefly mention a couple of ideas we will be discussing in Chapter 24.

When a userid is created, it is given its own directory, called a "home directory". Within your home directory, you can create as many subdirectories as you need. Each time you log in, you start work in your home directory. However, it is easy to change from one directory to another as you work. At any time, the directory you are currently using is called your "working directory".

When you run **vi** or Vim, it starts by executing the initialization file in your home directory. It then checks the status of the **exrc** option. If this option is turned on, the program looks in your current directory for a *second* initialization file to execute (assuming your current directory is different from your home directory). In this way, you can organize your files into subdirectories, each of which has its very own initialization file.

For example, let's say you are currently working on three projects: an essay, a program, and a Web page. The files for these projects are kept in three separate directories named **essay**, **program** and **webpage**. In each directory, you create a customized **.exrc** or **.vimrc** file that contains the options, abbreviations and macros you want to use when you edit files for that particular project.

You are working in the **program** directory and you want to edit a file named **test.c**. You enter the command:

```
vi test.c
```

As soon as **vi** starts, it looks for an initialization file in your home directory. Once the commands in this file are executed, **vi** checks the **exrc** option. If it is turned on, **vi** looks for a second initialization file in the **program** directory (your current directory). In this way, you are able to customize your working environment in a way that is suitable for editing programs.

LEARNING TO USE VIM

At the beginning of the chapter, we talked about Vim, a complex text editor that is backward compatible with **vi**. Vim was created in 1988 by the Dutch programmer Bram Moolenaar as an "improved" version of a **vi** clone. Since then, Vim has been extended enormously, with hundreds of new features. At the same time, Vim has become so popular that, on many Unix and Linux systems, it takes the place of **vi**. Although you can run Vim in "**vi**-compatible" mode, it is much more than an improved version of **vi**. Vim is a very sophisticated editor in its own right, significantly different from **vi**.

The truth is, Vim is so complex that it is impossible for anyone to teach it to you. You must learn it on your own. However, when you start, you will find an immediate problem: the Vim documentation is not at all suitable for beginners. The solution is to start by learning **vi**. Once you understand **vi**, you will have some context. You can then teach yourself Vim by adding to your knowledge a bit at a time. This is one reason why, in this chapter, we have concentrated on **vi**, not Vim. (The other reason is that **vi** is ubiquitous, while Vim is not available on many Unix systems.)

So, if you want to learn Vim, here is my advice. Start by reading this chapter and practicing until you feel you have mastered **vi**. That should take you at least a month or two. During this time, you will run Vim in **vi**-compatible mode. (The instructions for doing so can be found earlier in the chapter.) Later, you can turn off compatible mode and start using Vim in its own right.

My guess is you have used many programs — especially GUI-based programs — that you were able to pick up on the fly as you were using them. Vim is different. Vim is something you must teach yourself and, to do so, you *must* read the documentation.* Start by running the following command from the shell prompt:

```
vimtutor
```

This will display a tutorial that summarizes the basic commands (most of which you will have already learned from this chapter). When you are finished, type `:q`.

Next, start Vim and take a look at the online help by entering, in turn, each of the following commands. (Again, you can type `:q` to quit.)

```
:help
:help user-manual
:help differences
```

If you find reading the documentation in this way tedious (as I do), read it online. You can find what you need at **www.vim.org**. (Hunt around until you find the Vim "User Manual".)

Please don't let my comments discourage you. Vim is an amazing program and, if you feel so inclined, you should definitely learn it. To inspire you, Figure 22-12 contains a summary of the most important enhancements offered by Vim. As you build on your knowledge of **vi** to learn Vim, my advice is to learn how to use the various features in the order you see them in the figure.

IT'S ALWAYS SOMETHING

To close the chapter, I'd like to tell you a true story, illustrating the type of wistfulness expressed by the American poet John Greenleaf Whittier (1807–1892) in his poem *Maud Muller* when he wrote:

> For of all sad words of tongue or pen,
> The saddest are these: "It might have been!"

As you can see in Figure 22-12, one of the important enhancements offered by Vim is "screen splitting", the ability to split your screen into horizontal or vertical

---

*If you ask another person to teach you Vim, you will just end up confused, and he or she will end up frustrated. Don't say I didn't warn you.

windows. This is a powerful tool in that it allows you to view more than one file at the same time.

Interestingly enough, way back in 1978 at U.C. Berkeley, Bill Joy (the creator of `vi`) was planning to put that exact feature into an early version of the program. Here is the story in his own words, from a 1984 interview in *Unix Review* magazine:

> *"What actually happened was that I was in the process of adding multi-windows to `vi` when we installed our VAX [computer], which would have been in December of '78. We didn't have any backups and the tape drive broke. I continued to work even without being able to do backups — and then the source code got scrunched and I didn't have a complete listing.*
>
> *"I had almost rewritten all of the display code for windows, and that was when I gave up. After that, I went back to the previous version and just documented the code, finished the manual, and closed it off. If that scrunch had not happened, `vi` would have multiple windows. And I might have put in some programmability, but I don't know."*

It happened that, at the time, the American philosopher Roseanne Roseannadanna was visiting the Berkeley Unix lab. When Joy told her what happened she remarked, "Well Bill, it's just like my old Daddy used to tell me, 'Roseanne Roseannadanna, if it's not one thing, it's another.'"

Vim is a highly sophisticated text editor with a great many enhancements over standard `vi`. Here is a summary of the most important such features. The best way to learn Vim, is to start by mastering `vi`. Then teach yourself how to use the enhancements in the order I have listed them.

- Extensive online help.

- Screen splitting: You can split the screen into horizontal and vertical windows, each of which can hold its own file.

- Multi-level undo.

- Mouse support.

- GUI support.

- Command line history.

- Command line completion.

- Filename completion.

- Search history.

- Syntax highlighting: Use color to show the syntax for many different types of files.

- Highlighting: Select text, either lines or blocks, then operate on that text.

- Multiple buffers.

- Macro support: tools to record, modify and run macros.

- Built-in scripting language: Create scripts of your own; share scripts written by other people (available for free on the Internet).

- Autocommands: Execute pre-defined commands automatically.

FIGURE 22-12: Vim: Enhancements over standard `vi`

CHAPTER 22 EXERCISES

REVIEW QUESTIONS

1. How do you start **vi** when you want to: Edit a file named **document**? Edit a brand new file? Open a file named **document** in read-only mode? How do you start Vim in **vi**-compatibility mode?

2. How do you quit **vi** if you have already saved your work? How do you save your work and then quit? How do you quit without saving?

3. As you work with **vi**, your data is kept in a storage area. What is this storage area called? The **vi** editor operates in two principle modes: command mode and input mode. Describe each mode. How do you change from command mode to insert mode? How do you change from insert mode to command mode?

4. Specify the best command to move the cursor to each of the following destinations. Whenever possible, use alphabetic keys.

   • One position left, down, up, right
   • Beginning of current line
   • End of current line
   • Beginning of previous line
   • Beginning of next line
   • Forward one word
   • Backward one word
   • Forward to next sentence
   • Backward to previous sentence
   • Forward to next paragraph
   • Backward to previous paragraph
   • Top line of the screen
   • Middle line of the screen
   • Bottom line of the screen
   • Beginning of editing buffer
   • End of editing buffer
   • Down one screenful
   • Up one screenful
   • Down a half screenful
   • Up a half screenful

5. Within command mode, how do you:

   • Undo the last command that modified the editing buffer.
   • Restore the current line to what it was when you moved to it.
   • Repeat the last command that modified the editing buffer.

APPLYING YOUR KNOWLEDGE

1. Start **vi** and create a brand new empty file named **temp**. Insert the following lines into the file:

   ```
   one   1
   two   2
   three 3
   four  4
   five  5
   ```

   Use a single **vi** command to save your work and quit.

2. Start **vi** to edit the file **temp** from the previous question.

   Using **vi** commands only: Move lines 2 through 4 to be after line 5. Undo the move.

   Using **vi** commands only: Copy lines 2 through 4 to the top of the editing buffer. Undo the change. At this point, the editing buffer should look like it did when you started. Quit without saving.

3. Start **vi** to edit the file **temp** from the previous question.

   Using **ex** commands where possible: Move lines 2 through 4 to be after line 5. Undo the change.

   Using **ex** commands where possible: Copy lines 2 through 4 to the top of the editing buffer. Undo the change. At this point, the editing buffer should look like it did when you started. Quit without saving.

   Compare the **vi** commands you used in Exercise #2 with the **ex** commands you used in Exercise #3. What advantages did the **ex** commands have?

4. Start **vi** to edit the file **temp** from Exercise #1. Insert the date and time at the bottom of the editing buffer. Where is the cursor? Why?

   Without first moving the cursor, use a single command to sort all lines in the editing buffer in reverse alphabetical order. Quit without saving.

FOR FURTHER THOUGHT

1. Once you are comfortable with the **vi** editor, you will find it to be quick, powerful, and easy to use. However, **vi** is a very complex program that takes a lot of effort to master. The backward compatible replacement, Vim, is even more powerful, more complex, and even harder to learn. Considering that **vi** is well over 30 years old and is so difficult to learn, why do you think it is still so popular in the Unix community?

   Do you see a future in which complex tasks will be carried out exclusively by easy-to-use tools, or will there always be a need for programs like **vi**?

2. Broadly speaking, **vi** has two different types of commands: screen-oriented **vi** commands and line-oriented ex commands. The two types of commands are completely different from one another and, indeed, were developed for different types of hardware. Nevertheless, they combine nicely to create a powerful editing environment. Why is this? What does this tell you about the types of tools we should be designing for smart people?

CHAPTER 23
THE UNIX FILESYSTEM

In the next three chapters, we will talk about the Unix filesystem, the part of the operating system that serves you and your programs by storing and organizing all the data on your system. In this chapter, we will cover the basic concepts. We will then discuss the details of using directories in Chapter 24 and using files in Chapter 25.

The goal of this chapter is to answer three key questions. First, what is a Unix file? As you might imagine, a file can be a repository of data stored on a disk. However, as you will see, there is a lot more to it than that. The second question involves organization. It is common for a Unix system to have hundreds of thousands of files. How can so many items be organized in a way that makes sense and is easy to understand? Finally, how is it possible for a single unified system to offer transparent support of many different types of data storage devices?

The discussion begins with a simple question that has a surprisingly complex answer: What is a file?

WHAT IS A FILE?

In the olden days, before computers, the term "file" referred to a collection of papers. Typically, files were kept in cardboard folders, which were organized and stored in filing cabinets. Today, most data is computerized, and the definition of a file has changed appropriately. In its simplest sense, a file is a collection of data that has been given a name*. Most of the time, files are stored on digital media: hard disks, CDs, DVDs, floppy disks, flash drives, memory cards, and so on.

Within Unix, the definition of a file is much broader. A FILE is any source, with a name, from which data can be read; or any target, with a name, to which data can be written. Thus, when you use Unix or Linux, the term "file" refers not only to a repository of data like a disk file, but to any physical device. For example, a keyboard can be accessed as a file (a source of input), as can a monitor (an output target). There are also files that have no physical presence whatsoever, but accept input or generate output in order to provide specific services.

---

*A Unix file can actually have more than one name. We'll talk about this idea in Chapter 25 when we discuss links.

Defining a file in this way — with such generality — is of enormous importance: it means that Unix programs can use simple procedures to read from any input source and write to any output target. For example, most Unix programs are designed to read from standard input and write to standard output (see Chapters 18 and 19). From the programmer's point of view, I/O (input/output) is easy, because reading and writing data can be implemented in a simple, standard way, regardless of where the actual data is coming from or going to. From the user's point of view, there is a great deal of flexibility, because he can specify the input source and output target at the moment he runs the program.

As you might imagine, the internal details of the Unix filesystem — or any filesystem — are complex. In this chapter, we will cover the basic concepts and, by the time we finish, you will find that the Unix filesystem is a thing of compelling beauty: the type of beauty you find only in complex systems in which everything makes sense.

TYPES OF FILES

There are many different types of Unix files, but they all fall into three categories: ordinary files, directories, and pseudo files. Within the world of pseudo files, there are three particular types that are the most common: special files, named pipes, and proc files. In this section, we'll take a quick tour of the most important types of files. In the following sections, we'll discuss each type of file in more detail.

An ORDINARY FILE or a REGULAR FILE is what most people think of when they use the word "file". Ordinary files contain data and reside on some type of storage device, such as a hard disk, CD, DVD, flash drive, memory card, or floppy disk. As such, ordinary files are the type of files you work with most of the time. For example, when you write a shell script using a text editor, both the shell script and the editor program itself are stored in ordinary files.

As we discussed in Chapter 19, there are, broadly speaking, two types of ordinary files: text files and binary files. Text files contain lines of data consisting of printable characters (letters, numbers, punctuation symbols, spaces, tabs) with a newline character at the end of each line. Text files are used to store textual data: plain data, shell scripts, source programs, configuration files, HTML files, and so on.

Binary files contain non-textual data, the type of data that makes sense only when executed or when interpreted by a program. Common examples are executable programs, object files, images, music files, video files, word processing documents, spreadsheets, databases, and so on. For example, a text editor program would be a binary file. The file you edit would be a text file.

Since almost all the files you will encounter are ordinary files, it is crucial that you learn basic file manipulation skills. Specifically, you must learn how to create, copy, move, rename, and delete such files. We will discuss these topics in detail in Chapter 25.

The second type of file is a DIRECTORY. Like an ordinary file, a directory resides on some type of storage device. Directories, however, do not hold regular data. They are used to organize and access other files. Conceptually, a directory "contains" other files. For example, you might have a directory named **vacation** within which you keep all the files having to do with your upcoming trip to Syldavia.

A directory can also contain other directories. This allows you to organize your files into a hierarchical system. As you will see later in the chapter, the entire Unix filesystem is organized as one large hierarchical tree with directories inside of directories inside of directories. Within your part of the tree, you can create and delete directories as you see fit. In this way, you can organize your files as you wish and make changes as your needs change.

(You will recall that, in Chapter 9, during our discussion of the Info system, we talked about trees. Formally, a TREE is a data structure formed by a set of nodes, leaves, and branches, organized in such a way that there is, at most, one branch between any two nodes.)

You will sometimes see the term FOLDER used instead of the word "directory", especially when you use GUI tools. The terminology comes from the Windows and Macintosh worlds, as both these systems use folders to organize files. A Windows folder is a lot like a Unix directory, but not as powerful. A Macintosh folder *is* a Unix directory, because OS X, the Mac operating system, runs on top of Unix (see Chapter 2).

The last type of file is a PSEUDO FILE. Unlike ordinary files and directories, pseudo files are not used to store data. For this reason, the files themselves do not take up any room, although they are considered to be part of the filesystem and are organized into directories. The purpose of a pseudo file is to provide a service that is accessed in the same way that a regular file is accessed. In most cases, a pseudo file is used to access a service provided by the kernel, the central part of the operating system (see Chapter 2).

The most important type of pseudo file is the SPECIAL FILE, sometimes called a DEVICE FILE. A special file is an internal representation of a physical device. For example, your keyboard, your monitor, a printer, a disk drive — in fact, every device in your computer or on your network — can all be accessed as special files.

The next type of pseudo file is a NAMED PIPE. A named pipe is an extension of the pipe facility we discussed in Chapter 15. As such, it enables you to connect the output of one program to the input of another.

Finally, a PROC FILE allows you to access information residing within the kernel. In a few specific cases, you can even use proc files to change data within the kernel. (Obviously, this should be done only by very knowledgeable people.) Originally, these files were created to furnish information about processes as they are running, hence the name "proc".

WHAT'S IN A NAME?

File
When you see or hear the word "file", you must decide, by context, what it means. Sometimes it refers to any type of file; sometimes it refers only to files that contain data, that is, ordinary files.

For example, suppose you read the sentence, "The `ls` program lists the names of all the files in a directory." In this case, the word "file" refers to any type of file: an ordinary file, a directory, a special file, a named pipe, or a virtual file. All five types of files can be found in a directory and, hence, listed with the `ls` program.

However, let's say you read, "To compare one file to another, use the `cmp` program." In this case, "file" refers to an ordinary file, as that is the only type of file that contains data that can be compared.

DIRECTORIES AND SUBDIRECTORIES

We use directories to organize files into a hierarchical tree-like system. To do so, we collect files together into groups and store each group in its own directory. Since directories are themselves files, a directory can contain other directories, which creates the hierarchy.

Here is an example. You are a student at a prestigious West Coast university and you are taking three classes — History, Literature and Surfing — for which you have written a number of essays. To organize all this work, you make a directory called **essays** (don't worry about the details for now). Within this directory, you create three more directories, **history**, **literature** and **surfing**, to hold your essays. Each essay is stored in a text file that has a descriptive name. Figure 23-1 shows a diagram of what it all looks like. Notice that the diagram looks like an upside-down tree.

A PARENT DIRECTORY is one that contains other directories. A SUBDIRECTORY or CHILD DIRECTORY is a directory that lies within another directory. In Figure 23-1, **essays** is a parent directory that contains three subdirectories: **history**, **literature** and **surfing**.

It is common to talk about directories as if they actually contain other files. For example, we might say that **essays** contains three subdirectories and **literature** contains four ordinary files. Indeed, you might imagine that if you could look inside the **literature** directory, you would see the four files. Actually, all files are stored as separate entities. A directory does not hold the actual files. It merely contains the information Unix needs to locate the files.

You, however, don't need to worry about the details, as Unix maintains the internal workings of the entire filesystem automatically. All you have to do is learn how to use the appropriate programs, and Unix will do whatever you want: make a directory, remove a directory, move a directory, list the contents of a directory, and so on. We'll cover these programs in Chapter 24.

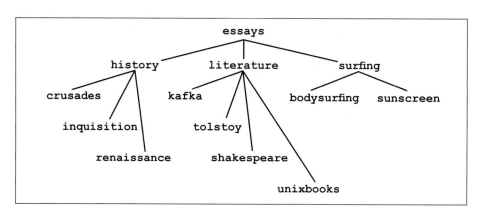

FIGURE 23-1: An example of organizing with directories

To organize files, we use parent directories and subdirectories to create a hierarchical tree. In this example, the parent directory **essays** *contains three subdirectories—***history**, **literature** *and* **surfing**—*each of which contains ordinary files. See text for details.*

SPECIAL FILES

Special files are pseudo files that represent physical devices. Unix keeps all the special files in the **/dev** (device) directory. (We'll talk about the slash at the beginning of the name later in the chapter.) To display the names of the special files on your system, use the **ls** program (Chapter 24) as follows:

```
ls /dev | less
```

You will see many names, most of which you will rarely need to use. This is because, for the most part, special files are used by system programs, not users. Still, there are a few special files that are interesting to know about. I have listed these files in Figure 23-2, and we will discuss them in three different groups: hardware, terminals, and pseudo-devices.

If you are interested in understanding the names of other special files, there is an official master list that can help you. To find this list, search on the Web for "LANANA Linux Device List". (LANANA stands for "Linux Assigned Names and Numbers Authority".) As the name implies, this list is specifically for Linux. However, most of the important special files have similar names on all Unix systems, so the list is useful even if you don't use Linux.

HARDWARE	
/dev/fd0	floppy disk
/dev/hda	hard disk
/dev/hda1	hard disk: partition 1
/dev/sda	SCSI hard disk
/dev/sda1	SCSI hard disk: partition 1
/dev/sda1	USB flash memory card (see text)
/dev/lp0	printer
/dev/usb/lp0	USB printer
TERMINALS	
/dev/tty	current terminal
/dev/tty1	console / virtual console
/dev/pts/0	pseudo terminal
/dev/ttyp0	pseudo terminal
PSEUDO-DEVICES	
/dev/null	discard output, input returns nothing (**eof**)
/dev/zero	discard output; input returns nulls (**0s**)
/dev/random	random number generator
/dev/urandom	random number generator

FIGURE 23-2: The most interesting special files

Special files are pseudo files that are used to represent devices. Such files are mostly used by system programs. Although you will rarely use special files directly, there are a few that are interesting to know about. See text for details.

SPECIAL FILES FOR HARDWARE

All devices connected to the computer are accessible via special files. Let's start with the most straightforward devices, the ones that represent actual hardware. As you can see in Figure 23-2, the file **/dev/fd0** represents a floppy disk drive. The number at the end of a device name refers to a specific device. In this case, **/dev/fd0** refers to the first floppy disk drive. (Computer programmers often start counting at zero.) If there is a second floppy drive, it would be **/dev/fd1**, and so on. Similarly, **/dev/lp0** corresponds to the first printer.

Hard disks are handled a bit differently. The first IDE hard disk is referred to as **/dev/hda**, the second is **/dev/hdb**, and so on. Hard drives are organized into one or more PARTITIONS, which act as separate devices. The first partition of the first hard disk is referred to as **/dev/hda1**. If there is a second partition, it is **/dev/hda2**. SCSI and SATA hard drives have their own names. The first SCSI or SATA drive is **/dev/sda**, the second is **/dev/sdb**, and so on. Again, partitions are numbered, so the first partition on the first SCSI or SATA drive would be **/dev/sda1**.

The SCSI designations are sometimes used for other types of devices as well. A common example is USB flash memory, which is treated as if it were a removable SCSI disk. For this reason, the name of the special file for flash memory will be named **/dev/sda1** or something similar.

SPECIAL FILES FOR TERMINALS: tty

In Figure 23-2 you will notice several different special files that represent terminals. Here is why. In the olden days, terminals were separate physical devices that were connected to a host computer (see Chapter 3). Such terminals were represented by special files named **/dev/tty1**, **/dev/tty2**, and so on. (As I explained in Chapter 7, the abbreviation TTY is a synonym for terminal. This is because the very first Unix terminals were Teletype machines, which were referred to as TTYs.)

The **/dev/tty** naming convention is still used today for terminals that act like hardware devices. In particular, this is the case when you run Unix in single-user mode. Your keyboard and monitor (the console) act as a built-in text-based terminal. The special file that represents this terminal is **/dev/tty1**. Similarly, when you use a virtual console within a desktop environment (see Chapter 6), it too acts like an actual terminal. By default, Linux supports six such consoles, which are represented by the special files **/dev/tty1** through **/dev/tty6**.

Everything is different; however, when you use a GUI to run a terminal emulation program within a window. Because there isn't an actual terminal, Unix creates what we call a PSEUDO TERMINAL or PTY to simulate a terminal. PTYs are used when you open a terminal window within a GUI (Chapter 6), and when you connect to a remote Unix host (Chapter 3). In both cases, the PTY acts as your terminal.

It happens that there are two different systems for creating pseudo terminals, so you will see two types of names. If your version of Unix uses the first system, the special files that represent pseudo terminals will have names like **/dev/ttyp0** and **/dev/ttyp1**. If you use the other system, the names will be **/dev/pts/1**, **/dev/pts/2**, and so on. You can see both types of names in Figure 23-2.

At any time, you can display the name of your terminal by using the **tty** program. For example, let's say you are working at virtual terminal #3. You enter:

```
tty
```

The output is:

```
/dev/tty3
```

For convenience, the special file **/dev/tty** represents whichever terminal you are currently using. For example, if you are using virtual console #3, **/dev/tty** is the same as **/dev/tty3**.

Here is an example of how you can use a special file. As you will see in Chapter 25, you use the **cp** program to make a copy of a file. In Chapter 11, we talked about the password file, **/etc/passwd**. Let's say you want to make a copy of the password file and call the copy **myfile**. The command to do so is:

```
cp /etc/passwd myfile
```

That only makes sense. Now consider the following command:

```
cp /etc/passwd /dev/tty
```

This copies the password file to your terminal. The effect is to display the contents of the file on your monitor. Try it — then take a moment to think about what happened.

SPECIAL FILES FOR PSEUDO-DEVICES

The last type of special file we will discuss is the PSEUDO-DEVICE. A pseudo-device is a file that acts as an input source or output target, but does not correspond to an actual device, either real or emulated. The two most useful pseudo-devices are the NULL FILE and the ZERO FILE. The null file is **/dev/null**; the zero file is **/dev/zero**. Any output that is written to these devices is thrown away. For this reason, these files are sometimes referred to whimsically as "bit buckets".

We discussed the null file in detail in Chapter 15. Here is an example from that chapter. Let's say you have a program named **update** that reads and modifies a large number of data files. As it does its work, **update** displays statistics about what is happening. If you don't want to see the statistics, you can redirect standard output to either of the bit buckets:

```
update > /dev/null
update > /dev/zero
```

If you want to experiment, here is a quick example you can try for yourself right now. Enter the command:

```
cat /etc/passwd
```

You will see the contents of the password file. Now, redirect the output of the **cat** command to either the null file or the zero file. Notice that the output vanishes:

```
cat /etc/passwd > /dev/null
cat /etc/passwd > /dev/zero
```

When it comes to output, the two bit buckets work the same. The only difference is what happens when they are used for input. When a program reads from **/dev/null**, no matter how many bytes of input are requested, the result is always an **eof** signal (see Chapter 7). In other words, reading from **/dev/null** returns nothing.

When a program reads from **/dev/zero**, the file generates as many bytes as are requested. However, they all have the value **0** (the number zero). In Unix, this value is considered to be the NULL CHARACTER or, more simply, a NULL. As strange as it seems, a constant source of null characters can be useful. For instance, for security reasons, it is often necessary to wipe out the contents of a file or an entire disk. In such cases, you can overwrite the existing data with nulls simply by copying as many bytes as necessary from **/dev/zero** to the output target.

(The terminology is a bit confusing: the null file returns nothing, while the zero file returns nulls. Such is life.)

Below is an example in which we use **dd** to create a brand new file completely filled with null characters. (The **dd** program is a powerful I/O tool, which I won't explain in detail. If you want more information, see the online manual.)

```
dd if=/dev/zero of=temp bs=100 count=1
```

In this example, **if** is the input file; **of** is the output file; **bs** is the block size; and **count** is the number of blocks. Thus, we copy a 100-byte block of data from **/dev/zero** to a file named **temp**.

If you want to experiment with this example, run the **dd** command and then display the contents of **temp** with the **hexdump** or **od** programs (Chapter 21). When you are finished, you can remove **temp** by using the **rm** program (Chapter 25).

The final two pseudo-devices, **/dev/random** and **/dev/urandom**, are used to generate random numbers. Thus, whenever a program needs a random number, all it has to do is read from one of these files.

It may be that you are one of those odd people who do not use random numbers much in your personal life. If so, you may wonder why they are important. The answer is that mathematicians and scientists use such numbers to create models of natural processes that involve chance. When used in this way, an unlimited, easy-to-use source of random numbers is invaluable. (If this sort of thing interests you, read a bit about "stochastic processes".) Random numbers are also used by programs that generate cryptographic keys for encrypting data.

TECHNICAL HINT

Unix and Linux provide two different special files to generate random numbers: **/dev/random** and **/dev/urandom**. The difference is subtle, but important, when complete randomness is essential.

Computerized random number generators gather "environmental noise" and store it in an "entropy pool". The bits in the entropy pool are then used to generate random numbers. If the entropy pool runs out, the **/dev/random** file will stop and wait for more noise to be gathered. This ensures complete randomness for crucial operations, such as creating cryptographic keys. However, at times, there can be a delay if it is necessary to wait for the entropy pool to fill.

The **/dev/urandom** file, on the other hand, will never stop generating numbers even when the entropy pool is low (**u** stands for "unlimited). Instead, some of the old bits will be reused. In theory, data that is encrypted using low-entropy random numbers is slightly more susceptible to attack. In practice, it doesn't make much difference, because no one actually knows how to take advantage of such a tiny theoretical deficiency*. Still, if you are paranoid, using **random** instead of **urandom** may help you sleep better. If not, **urandom** will work just fine, and it will never make you wait.

NAMED PIPES: `mkfifo`

A named pipe is a pseudo file used to create a special type of pipe facility. In this way, named pipes act as an extension to the regular pipe facility we discussed in Chapter 15. Before I show you how they work, let's take a quick look at a regular pipeline. The following command extracts all the lines in the system password file that contain the characters "bash". The data is then piped to the **wc** program (Chapter 18) to count the number of lines:

```
grep bash /etc/passwd | wc -l
```

When we use a pipe in this way, it does not have a specific name: it is created automatically and it exists only while the two processes are running. For this reason, we call it an ANONYMOUS PIPE.

A named pipe is similar to an anonymous pipe in that they both connect the output of one process to the input of another. However, there are two important differences. First, you must create a named pipe explicitly. Second, a named pipe does not cease to exist when the two processes end; it exists until it is deleted. Thus, once you create a named pipe, you can use it again and again.

You will often see a named pipe referred to as a FIFO (pronounced "fie-foe"), an abbreviation for "first-in, first-out". This is a computer science term used to describe a data structure in which elements are retrieved in the same order they went in. More formally, such a data structure is called a QUEUE.**

---

*At least in the non-classified literature.

**Compare to a stack (see Chapters 8 and 24), a data structure in which elements are stored and retrieved in a LIFO ("last in, first out") manner.

To create a named pipe, you use the **mkfifo** (make FIFO) program. The syntax is:

mkfifo [**-m mode**] *pipe*

where **mode** is a file mode of the type used with the **chmod** program, and **pipe** is the name of the pipe you want to create. (We'll discuss file modes in Chapter 25 when we talk about **chmod**; for now, you can ignore the **-m** option.)

Most of the time, named pipes are used by programmers to facilitate the exchange of data between two processes, an operation called INTERPROCESS COMMUNICATION or IPC. In such cases, a program will create, use, and then delete named pipes as necessary. Using the **mkfifo** program, you can create a named pipe by hand from the command line. It isn't done much, but let me show you an example, so you can experiment on your own to get a feeling for how it all works.

In order to do the experiment, you will need to open two terminal windows or use two virtual consoles. Then type the following command into the first terminal window. This command uses **mkfifo** to create a named pipe called **fifotest**:

mkfifo fifotest

Now, let's send some input to the pipe. In the same window, enter the following command to grep the system password file for lines containing "bash" and redirect the output to **fifotest**:

grep bash /etc/passwd > fifotest

Now move to the second terminal window or virtual console. Enter the following command to read the data from the named pipe and count the number of lines. As soon as you enter the command, the **wc** program reads from the named pipe and displays its output.

wc -l < fifotest

Once you are finished with the named pipe, you can delete it. To do so, you use the **rm** (remove) program:

rm fifotest

Obviously, this was a contrived example. After all, we accomplished the very same thing a moment ago with a single line:

cat /etc/passwd | wc -l

However, now that you understand how named pipes work, think about how valuable they might be to a programmer whose work requires interprocess communication. All he has to do is have a program create a named pipe, which can then be used as often as necessary to pass data from one process to another. Once the work is done, the program can remove the pipe. Simple, easy and dependable, with no need to create intermediate files to hold transient data.

PROC FILES

Proc files are pseudo files that provide a simple way to examine many types of system information, directly from the kernel, without having to use complicated programs to ferret out the data. The original proc filesystem was developed to extract information about processes*, hence the name "proc".

All proc files are kept in the **/proc** directory. Within this directory, you will find a subdirectory for each process on the system. The names of the subdirectories are simply the process IDs of the various processes. (As we will discuss in Chapter 26, each process has a unique identification number called a "process ID".) For example, let's say that right now, one of the processes on your system is #1952. Information about that process can be found in pseudo files within the **/proc/1952** directory.

The idea for the **/proc** directory was taken from the Plan 9 operating system**, a research project that ran from the mid-1980s to 2002. The Plan 9 project was established at Bell Labs by the same group that created Unix, C and C++. One of the basic concepts in Plan 9 was that all system interfaces should be considered part of the filesystem. In particular, information about processes was to be found in the **/proc** directory. Although Plan 9 was not a success, the idea of accessing many types of information as files was compelling and, in time, was widely adopted by the Unix and Linux communities.

Linux, however, not only adopted **/proc**, but expanded it enormously. Modern Linux systems use this directory to hold many other pseudo files, affording access to a large variety of kernel data. In fact, if you are superuser, it is even possible to change some of the Linux kernel values by writing to a proc file. (Don't try it.) Figure 23-3 shows the most interesting proc files used by Linux. You can display the information in these files in the same way as you would display the contents of an ordinary text file. For example, to display information about your processor, use either of the following commands:

```
cat /proc/cpuinfo
less /proc/cpuinfo
```

Normally, you will never need to look at a proc file unless you are a system administrator. For the most part, proc files are used only by programs that need highly technical information from the kernel. For example, in Chapter 26, we will discuss the **ps** (process status) program that shows you information about the processes on your system. The **ps** program gathers the data it needs by reading the appropriate proc files.

---

*As I mentioned in Chapter 6, the idea of a process is fundamental to Unix. Indeed, within a Unix system, every object is represented by either a file or a process. In simple terms, files hold data or allow access to resources; processes are programs that are executing.

A more precise definition of a process (also from Chapter 6) is a program that is loaded into memory and ready to run, along with the program's data and the information needed to keep track of the program.

**The name Plan 9 came from an extremely hokey science fiction movie *Plan 9 From Outer Space*, generally considered to be the worst movie ever made. Why would a group of highly skilled, visionary computer scientists name a major project after such a movie? All I can say is that it's a geek joke.

PROC FILE	INFORMATION ABOUT...
`/proc/`*xxx*`/`	process #*xxx*
`/proc/cmdline`	kernel options
`/proc/cpuinfo`	processor
`/proc/devices`	devices
`/proc/diskstats`	logical disk devices
`/proc/filesystems`	filesystems
`/proc/meminfo`	memory management
`/proc/modules`	kernel modules
`/proc/mounts`	mounted devices, mount points
`/proc/partitions`	disk partitions
`/proc/scsi`	SCSI and RAID devices
`/proc/swaps`	swap partitions
`/proc/uptime`	times (in seconds) that kernel: has been running, has been in idle mode
`/proc/version`	version of kernel, distribution, `gcc` compiler (used to build kernel)

FIGURE 23-3: The most interesting Linux proc files

Proc files are pseudo files that are used to access kernel information. Such files are mostly used by system programs. Although you will rarely use proc files directly, there are a few that are interesting to know about. See text for details.

There is one particularly intriguing proc file that I did not list in Figure 23-3: **/proc/kcore**. This file represents the actual physical memory of your computer. You can display its size by using the **ls** program with the **-l** option (see Chapter 24):

```
ls -l /proc/kcore
```

The file will look huge; in fact, it will be the same size as all the memory (RAM) in your computer. Remember, though, this is a pseudo file: it doesn't really take up space.

> **HINT**
>
> Linux users: I encourage you to explore the proc files on your system. Looking inside these files can teach you a lot about how your system is configured and how things works. To avoid trouble, make sure you are *not* superuser, even if you are just looking.

THE TREE-STRUCTURED FILESYSTEM; THE FILESYSTEM HIERARCHY STANDARD

In the next few sections, we will talk about the Unix filesystem and how it is organized. In our discussions, I will use the standard Linux filesystem as an example. The details can vary from one Unix system to another, so it is possible that your system will be a bit different from what you read here. The basic ideas, however, including most of the directory names, will be the same.

A typical Unix system contains well over 100,000 files(*) stored in directories and subdirectories. All these files are organized into a FILESYSTEM in which directories are organized into a tree structure based on a single main directory called the "root directory". The job of a filesystem is to store and organize data, and to provide access to the data to users and programs. You can see a diagram of a filesystem organization in Figure 23-4. The root directory is — directly or indirectly — the parent of all other directories in the system.

The first time you look at the organization of the Unix filesystem, it can be a bit intimidating. After all, the names are strange and mysterious, and very little makes sense. However, like most of the Unix world, once you understand the patterns and how they work, the Unix filesystem is easy to understand. Later in the chapter, we'll go over the subdirectories in Figure 23-4, one at a time. At the time, I'll explain how they are used and what the names mean.

Before we start, however, I'd like to take a moment to talk about how the Unix filesystem came to be organized in this way. As we discussed in Chapter 2, the first Unix system was developed in the early 1970s at Bell Labs. Figure 23-5 shows the structure of the original Unix system, which was designed as a hierarchical tree structure. Don't worry about the names, they will all make sense later. All I want you to notice is that the original filesystem looks very much like a subset of the current filesystem (Figure 23-4).

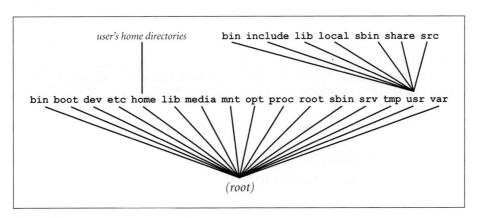

FIGURE 23-4: The standard Linux filesystem

Unix and Linux systems contain a very large number of files—at least 100,000 to 200,000—organized into a tree-structured set of directories and subdirectories. This example shows the skeleton of the standard Linux filesystem.

The sample you see here follows the Filesystem Hierarchy Standard (described later in the chapter). As you can see, the root (main) directory contains 16 subdirectories, each of which has its own subdirectories, sub-subdirectories, and so on. The diagram also shows 7 subdirectories that are commonly found within the /usr directory.

---

*No, I am not exaggerating. Some basic Unix systems come with over 200,000 files. To estimate the number of files and directories on your system, run the following command as superuser:

```
ls -R / | wc -l
```

As Unix evolved over the years, the organization of the filesystem was changed to reflect the needs and preferences of the various Unix developers. Although the basic format stayed the same, the details differed from one version of Unix to another. This created a certain amount of confusion, especially when users moved between System V Unix and BSD (see Chapter 2). In the 1990s, the confusion increased when the creators of various Linux distributions began to introduce their own variations.

In August 1993, a group of Linux users formed a small organization to develop a standard Linux directory structure. The first such standard was released in February 1994. In early 1995, the group expanded their goal when members of the BSD community joined the effort. From then on, they would devote themselves to creating a standard filesystem organization for all Unix systems, not just Linux. The new system was called the FILESYSTEM HIERARCHY STANDARD or FHS. Of course, since there are no Unix police, the standard is voluntary. Still, many Unix and Linux developers have chosen to adopt most of the FHS.

Although many Unix systems differ from the FHS in some respects, it is a well thought-out plan, and it does capture the essence of how modern Unix and Linux filesystems are organized. If you understand the FHS, you will find it easy to work with any other Unix system you may encounter. For this reason, as we discuss the details of the Unix filesystem, I will use the FHS as a model. If you want to see what the basic FHS looks like, take a look at Figure 23-4.

> **HINT**
>
> As you can see in Figure 23-4, all directories except the root directory lie within another directory. Thus, technically speaking, all directories except the root directory are subdirectories.
>
> In day-to-day speech, however, we usually just talk about directories. For example, we might refer to the "**/bin** directory". It is only when we want to emphasize that a particular directory lies within another directory, that we use the term "subdirectory", for example, "**/bin** is a subdirectory of the root directory."

THE ROOT DIRECTORY; SUBDIRECTORIES

From the very beginning, the Unix filesystem has been organized as a tree. In Chapter 9, we discussed trees as abstract data structures and, at the time, I explained that the main node of a tree is called the root (see Chapter 9 for the details). For this reason, we call the main directory of the Unix filesystem the ROOT DIRECTORY.

Since the root directory is so important, its name must often be specified as part of a command. It would be tiresome to always have to type the letters "root". Instead, we indicate the root directory by a single **/** (slash). Here is a simple example to show how it works. To list the files in a specific directory, you use the **ls** program (Chapter 24). Just type **ls** followed by the name of the directory. The command to list all the files in the root directory is:

```
ls /
```

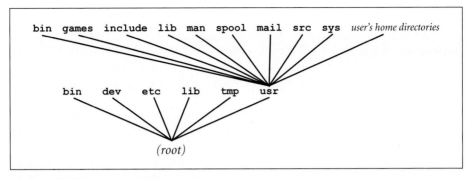

FIGURE 23-5: The original Unix filesystem

From the beginning, the Unix filesystem organized files using directories and subdirectories. This diagram shows the tree-structure used by the original Unix system in the early 1970s. Notice that the tree looks, more or less, like a subset of the current filesystem (Figure 23-4).

When you specify the name of a directory or file that lies within the root directory, you write a **/** followed by the name. For example, within the root directory, there is a subdirectory named **bin**. To list all the files in this directory, you use the command:

```
ls /bin
```

Formally, this means "the directory named **bin** that lies within the **/** (root) directory".

To indicate that a directory or file lies within another directory, separate the names with a **/**. For example, within the **/bin** directory, you will find the file that contains the **ls** program itself. The formal name for this file is **/bin/ls**. Similarly, within the **/etc** directory, you will find the Unix password file, **passwd** (see Chapter 11). The formal name for this file is **/etc/passwd**.

When we talk about such names, we pronounce the **/** character as "slash". Thus, the name **/bin/ls** is pronounced "slash-bin-slash-L-S".

HINT

Until you get used to the nomenclature, the use of the **/** character can be confusing. This is because **/** has two meanings that have nothing to do with one another.

At the beginning of a file name, **/** stands for the root directory. Within a file name, **/** acts as a delimiter. (Take a moment to think about it.)

WHAT'S IN A NAME?

root

In Chapter 4, I explained that, to become superuser, you log in with a userid of **root**. Now you can see where the name comes from: the superuser userid is named after the root directory, the most important directory in the filesystem.

MOUNTING A FILESYSTEM: `mount, umount`

In a Unix filesystem, hundreds of thousands of files are organized into a very large tree, the base of which is the root directory. In most cases, all the files are not stored on the same physical device. Rather, they are stored on a number of different devices, including multiple disk partitions. (As I explained earlier, each disk partition is considered a separate device.)

Every storage device has its own local filesystem, with directories and subdirectories organized into a tree in the standard Unix manner. Before a local filesystem can be accessed, however, its tree must be attached to the main tree. This is done by connecting the root directory of the smaller filesystem to a specific directory in the main filesystem. When we connect a smaller filesystem in this way, we say that we MOUNT it. The directory in the main tree to which the filesystem is attached is called the MOUNT POINT. Finally, when we disconnect a filesystem, we say that we UNMOUNT it.

Each time a Unix system starts, a number of local filesystems are mounted automatically as part of the startup process. Thus, by the time a system is running and ready to use, the main filesystem has already been augmented by several other filesystems.

From time to time, you may have to mount a device manually. To do so, you use the **mount** program. To unmount a device, you use **umount**. As a general precaution, only the superuser is allowed to mount a filesystem. However, for convenience, some systems are configured to allow ordinary users to mount certain pre-set devices, such as CDs or DVDs.

Here is an example of a mount command. In this example, we mount the floppy drive filesystem found on device **/dev/fd0**, attaching it to the main tree at the location **/media/floppy**:

```
mount /dev/fd0 /media/floppy
```

The effect of this command is to enable users to access the files on the floppy via the **/media/floppy** directory.

Mounting and unmounting are system administration tasks that require superuser status, so I won't go into the details. Instead, I will refer you to the online manual (**man mount**). As an ordinary user, however, you can display a list of all the filesystems currently mounted on your system, by entering a **mount** command by itself:

```
mount
```

Broadly speaking, there are two types of storage devices. FIXED MEDIA, such as hard drives, are attached to the computer permanently. REMOVABLE MEDIA can be changed while the system is running: CDs, DVDs, floppy disks, tapes, flash drives, memory cards, and so on. At the system level, the distinction is important because if there is a chance that a filesystem might literally disappear, Unix must make sure that it is managed appropriately. For example, before you can be allowed to eject a CD, Unix must ensure that any pending output operations are complete.

For this reason, the Filesystem Hierarchy Standard mandates specific directories to use mounting filesystems. For fixed media that are not mounted elsewhere (such as extra hard disks), the directory is **/mnt**; for removable media, the directory is **/media**.

WHAT'S IN A NAME?

Mount, Unmount

In the early days of Unix (circa 1970), disk drives were large, expensive devices that, by today's standards, held relatively small amounts of data (40 megabytes at best). Unlike modern hard drives, which are complete units, the older disk drives used removable "disk packs", each of which had its own filesystem.

Whenever a user needed to change a disk pack, the system administrator had to physically unmount the current disk pack and mount the new one. This is why, even today, we talk about "mounting" and "unmounting" a filesystem. When we use the **mount** program, we are performing the software equivalent of mounting a disk pack in a drive.

A TOUR OF THE ROOT DIRECTORY

The fastest way to cultivate a basic understanding of the filesystem on your computer is to look in the root directory and examine all the subdirectories. These directories form the backbone of the entire system. As such, they are sometimes referred to as TOP-LEVEL DIRECTORIES.

Figure 23-6 summarizes the standard contents of the root directory as specified by the Filesystem Hierarchy Standard (FHS) we discussed earlier in the chapter. Although the details vary from one Unix system to another, all modern filesystems can be considered variations of the FHS. Thus, once you understand the FHS, you will be able to make sense out of any Unix filesystem you happen to encounter.

Our goal here is to start with the root directory and work our way through the list of top-level directories. As we discuss each directory, you can check it out on your system by using the **ls** program (Chapter 24). For example, to display the contents of the **/bin** directory, use one of the following commands:

```
ls /bin
ls -l /bin
```

When you use **ls** with no options, you will see only file names. If you use the **-l** (long) option, you will see extra details. If there is too much output, and it scrolls by too fast, you can display it one screenful at a time by piping it to **less** (Chapter 21):

```
ls -l / | less
ls -l /bin | less
```

Root directory: The root directory is the base of the entire filesystem. On many Unix systems, the root directory will contain only subdirectories. On some systems, you will find one ordinary file, the kernel. (See the discussion under **/boot** below.

/bin: This directory holds the most important system programs, the basic tools an administrator would need to work on the system in single-user mode (see Chapter 6). These tools are all executable programs which, as we discussed earlier in the chapter, are binary files. Hence the name **bin**, a place for binary files. More simply, you can think of this directory as a storage bin for programs. Some of the programs in this directory are also used by regular users.

/boot: This is the place where the system stores all the files needed as part of the boot process (discussed in Chapter 2). The kernel must be either in this directory or in the root directory. The kernel is easy to recognize: just enter the following commands and look for a very large file with a strange name:

```
ls -l /boot | less
ls -l / | less
```

If you have updated your system, you will find more than one version of the kernel. In most cases, the one in use is the latest one, which you can identify by looking at the name. (The version number will be part of the name.)

DIRECTORY	CONTENTS
/	Root directory
/bin	Essential programs
/boot	Files required when booting system
/dev	Device files
/etc	Configuration files
/home	Users' home directories
/lib	Essential shared libraries, kernel modules
/lost+found	Damaged files that have been recovered by **fsck**
/media	Mount point for removable media
/mnt	Mount point for fixed media not mounted elsewhere
/opt	Third-party applications ("optional software")
/proc	Proc files
/root	Home directory for root (superuser)
/sbin	Essential system administration programs run by superuser
/srv	Data for services provided by local system
/tmp	Temporary files
/usr	Secondary filesystem used for static data
/var	Secondary filesystem used for variable data

FIGURE 23-6: Contents of the root directory

The skeleton of the Unix filesystem is created by the top-level directories, that is, the subdirectories of the root directory. Here is a list of all the top-level directories mandated by the Filesystem Hierarchy Standard (FHS). Since some Unix and Linux systems do not follow the FHS exactly, you will find variations from what you see here. Still, you can use this list as a starting point from which to understand your own system.

/dev: Within this directory, you will find all the special files. Most special files represent physical devices; a few represent pseudo-devices. (See this discussion earlier in the chapter.) This directory also contains a program named **MAKEDEV**, which is used to create new special files.

/etc: This directory contains configuration files. As we discussed in Chapter 6, a configuration file is a text file that is processed when a program starts, containing commands or information that affects the operation of the program. Configuration files are similar, in spirit, to the **rc** files we discussed in Chapter 14.

/home: When your Unix account was created (see Chapter 4), you were given a "home directory" along with your userid. Your home directory is the place to store all your personal files and directories. The name of your home directory is the same as your userid. Thus, if you are lucky enough to have the userid **harley**, your home directory will be **/home/harley**. We'll talk about home directories in detail later in the chapter. With one exception, all home directories reside in **/home**. The exception is the superuser's home directory, which is **/root** (see below).

/lib: When programs run, they often call upon LIBRARIES, pre-existing modules of data and code. Unix provides a large number of libraries to enable programs to access services offered by the operating system. This directory contains the essential libraries and kernel modules necessary to run the programs in **/bin** and **/sbin**.

/lost+found: If Unix is not shut down properly, files that are only partially written may be damaged. The next time Unix starts, a special program called **fsck** (filesystem check) will be run to examine the filesystem and fix any problems. If corrupt files are found, **fsck** will rescue them and move them to the **/lost+found** directory. The system administrator can then look at the recovered files and dispose of them appropriately.

/media: This is the mount point for removable media, such as CDs, DVDs, floppy disks, flash drives, memory cards, and so on. (See the discussion on mounting filesystems earlier in the chapter.)

/mnt: This is the mount point for fixed media that are not mounted elsewhere, such as extra hard disks. At one time, this was the only mount directory, so you will often see people mount removable media here. Unless you want your life to ultimately be exposed as a total sham, do not emulate such people: removable media belong in the **/media** directory.

/opt: This directory is the place for third-party applications to install themselves. (The name **/opt** stands for "optional software".) Within **/opt**, each application has a subdirectory it can organize as it sees fit. This gives application developers a designated location to install their software without having to worry about the requirements of how a particular filesystem might be organized. The subdirectories in **/opt** are either named after the company or the application. To keep things orderly, there are official lists of names maintained by LANANA (the Linux Assigned Names and Numbers Authority discussed earlier in the chapter). If you want to look at the lists, search on the Web for "LSB Provider Names" or "LSB Package Names". (LSB stands for "Linux Standard Base".)

/root: This is the home directory for the superuser, that is, for userid **root**. All other home directories are in **/home** (see above).

/sbin: The name **/sbin** stands for "system binaries". This directory holds programs that are used for system administration. As a general rule, the programs in this directory must be run as superuser.

/srv: This directory is reserved for data that is related to locally offered services (hence the name **/srv**). Typical services that might store data here are cgi, Web, ftp, cvs, rsync, and so on.

/tmp: This directory is used for temporary storage. Anybody is allowed to store files in this directory. Eventually, however, the contents of **/tmp** will be removed automatically. For this reason, programs will generally use this directory only to hold files that are needed for a short time.

/usr: This directory is the root of a secondary filesystem that contains important subdirectories of its own. The purpose of **/usr** is to hold STATIC DATA, data that does not change without system administrator intervention. By its nature, static data does not change over time. This allows **/usr** to reside on its own device, possibly a read-only device like a CD-ROM. In the olden days, **/usr** was the directory in which users' home directories were kept. Now that **/usr** is used only for static data, home directories — which do change — are kept in **/home** (see above).

/var: The name of this directory means "variable". Like **/usr**, this directory is the root of a secondary filesystem that contains important subdirectories of its own. The difference is that, where **/usr** holds static data, **/var** holds VARIABLE DATA, data that, by its nature, is expected to change over time:log files (that keep track of what is happening on the system), print files, email messages, and so on. Like **/usr**, the **/var** filesystem often resides on its own device. Separating the static data from the variable data in this way makes the system easier to manage. For example, a system administrator can create a backup system that saves the variable files separately (and more often) than the static files.

WHAT'S IN A NAME?

dev, etc, lib, mnt, opt, src, srv, tmp, usr, var
There is a Unix tradition to use 3-letter names for the top-level directories of the filesystem. The reason is that such names are short and easy to type. However, when we talk, these names can be awkward to pronounce. For this reason, each 3-letter name has a preferred pronunciation.
dev: "dev"
etc: "et-cetera" or "et-see"
lib: "libe" (to rhyme with "vibe")
mnt: "mount"
opt: "opt"
src: "source"

(*cont'd...*)
srv: "serv"
tmp: "temp"
usr: "user"
var: "var" (to rhyme with "jar")

As a general rule, if you are talking about something Unix-related and you come across a name with a missing letter or two, put it in when you pronounce the name. For example, the name of the **/etc/passwd** file is pronounced "slash et-cetera slash password". The file **/usr/lib/X11** is pronounced "slash user slash libe slash x-eleven"

You will sometimes hear people say that **etc** stands for "extended tool chest", or that **usr** means "Unix system resources", and so on. None of these stories are true. All of these names are abbreviations, not acronyms.

A TOUR OF THE /usr DIRECTORY

As we discussed earlier, the **/usr** and **/var** directories are mount points for separate filesystems that are integrated into the main filesystem. The **/usr** filesystem is for static data; **/var** is for variable data. Both these directories hold system data, as opposed to user data, which is kept in the **/home** directory.

In addition, both these directories contain a number of standard subdirectories. However, the **/var** filesystem is more for system administrators, so it's not that important to ordinary users. The **/usr** filesystem, on the other hand, is much more interesting. It contains files that are useful to regular users and to programmers. For this reason, I'll take you on a short tour of **/usr**, showing you the most important subdirectories as described in the Filesystem Hierarchy Standard. For reference, Figure 23-7 contains a summary of these directories. As we discussed earlier, you may notice some differences between the standard layout and your system.

DIRECTORY	CONTENTS
/usr/bin	Non-essential programs (most user programs)
/usr/include	Header files for C programs
/usr/lib	Non-essential shared libraries
/usr/local	Locally installed programs
/usr/sbin	Non-essential system administration programs run by superuser
/usr/share	Shared system data
/usr/src	Source code (for reference only)

FIGURE 23-7: Contents of the /usr directory

*The **/usr** directory is the mount point for a secondary filesystem that contains static data of interest to users and programmers. Here are the most important subdirectories you will find within this directory, according to the Filesystem Hierarchy Standard. See text for details.*

/usr/bin: Like its namesake in the root directory (**/bin**), this directory contains executable programs. This directory contains many more programs than **/bin**. In fact, **/usr/bin** is the home of most of the executable programs on the system. On one of my Linux systems, for example, **/bin** has only 100 programs, while **/usr/bin** has 2,084 programs.

/usr/games/: This is my favorite directory in the entire Unix filesystem (except, perhaps, **/home/harley**). As the name implies, this directory contains games. It also contains a variety of diversions and educational programs. In the olden days, **/usr/games** was filled with all kinds of interesting, enjoyable programs. My favorite game was **adventure**, and my favorite diversion was **fortune**. If you look around the Internet, you can still find these programs — and a lot more — and you can download and install them on your own system. (While you are at it, see if you can find "Hunt the Wumpus".) Today, alas, most of the games are gone, which is a terrible shame. Some Unix systems have only a few games; some have none whatsoever. It's almost as if too many people have forgotten that Unix is supposed to be *fun*.

/usr/include/: This is the storage area for include files used by C and C++ programmers. An INCLUDE FILE, sometimes called a HEADER FILE, contains source code that any programmer may use as required. A typical include file has definitions of subroutines, data structures, variables, constants, and so on. We use the name "include file" because, within C, the **#include** statement is used to incorporate such files into a program. The name "header file" refers to the fact that such files are typically included at the very beginning (head) of a program. Include files are given names that have an extension of **.h**, for example, **ioctl.h** and **stdio.h**.

/usr/lib: Like its analog **/lib**, this directory holds libraries, pre-existing modules of data and code used by programs to access services offered by the operating system.

/usr/local: This directory is for the system administrator to use as he or she sees fit to support local users. This is where you will find local programs and documentation. A typical use of this directory is to create a subdirectory, **/usr/local/bin**, to hold programs that are not part of the main system. Putting software here ensures it will not be overwritten when the system is updated.

/usr/sbin: Like **/sbin**, this directory contains system programs used by the administrator. Conceptually, **/usr/sbin** is to **/sbin**, as **/usr/bin** is to **/bin** (see discussion of **/usr/bin** above).

/usr/share: There are a great many files containing static data — documentation, fonts, icons, and so on — that need to be shared among users and programs. The **/usr/share** directory has a large number of subdirectories used to hold such files. For example, in Chapter 20 we talked about the dictionary file. On many systems this file can be found at **/usr/share/dict/words**. The most interesting shared files are the ones that contain the online documentation we discussed in Chapter 9. The Unix manual is stored in **/usr/share/man**; the Info system is stored in **/usr/share/info**.

/usr/src: The name **src** stands for "source code". In this directory, you will find subdirectories containing system source code, generally for reference only. On many Linux systems, you can find the source code for the kernel in **/usr/src/linux**.

/usr/X11: This directory holds the large number of files and directories used by X Window (the GUI-support system; see Chapter 5). On some systems, this directory is named **/usr/X11R7** or (if the system is old) **/usr/X11R6**.

WHY IS THERE MORE THAN ONE DIRECTORY FOR PROGRAMS?

As we have discussed, two different directories are used to hold general-use executable programs: **/bin** and **/usr/bin**. You might be wondering, why does Unix have two such directories? Why not simply store all the programs in one directory? The answer is the two **bin** directories are a historical legacy.

In the early 1970s, the first few versions of Unix were developed at Bell Labs on a PDP 11/45 minicomputer (see Chapter 2). The particular PDP 11/45 used by the Unix developers had two data storage devices. The primary device was a fixed-head disk, often called a drum. The drum was relatively quick, because the read-write head did not move as the disk rotated. However, data storage was limited to less than 3 megabytes.

The secondary device was a regular disk called an RP03. The read-write head on the RP03 disk moved back and forth from one track to another, which allowed it to store much more data, up to 40 megabytes. However, because of the moving head, the disk was a lot slower than the drum.

In order to accommodate multiple storage devices on a single computer, the Unix developers used a design in which each device had its own filesystem. The main device (the drum) held what was called the root filesystem; the secondary device (the disk) held what was called the **usr** filesystem.

Ideally, it would have been nice to keep the entire Unix system on the drum, as it was a lot faster than the disk. However, there just wasn't enough room. Instead, the Unix developers divided all the files into two groups. The first group consisted of the files that were necessary for the startup process and for running the bare-bones operating system. These files were stored on the drum in the root filesystem. The rest of the files were stored on the disk in the **usr** filesystem.

At startup, Unix would boot from the drum. This gave the operating system immediate access to the essential files in the root filesystem. Once Unix was up and running, it would mount the **usr** filesystem, which made it possible to access the rest of the files.

Each of the two filesystems had a **bin** directory to hold executable programs. The root filesystem had **/bin**, and the **usr** filesystem had **/usr/bin**. During the startup process, before the **usr** filesystem was mounted, Unix only had access to the relatively small storage area of the root filesystem. For this reason, essential programs were stored in **/bin**; other programs were stored in **/usr/bin**. Similarly, library files were divided into two directories, **/lib** and **/usr/lib**, and temporary files were kept in **/tmp** and **/usr/tmp**. In all cases, the root filesystem held only the most important files, the files necessary for booting and troubleshooting. Everything else went in the **usr** filesystem.

GENERAL-USE PROGRAMS	
`/bin`	Essential programs
`/usr/bin`	Non-essential programs
`/usr/local/bin`	Locally installed programs
SYSTEM ADMINISTRATION PROGRAMS	
`/sbin`	Essential system administration programs run by superuser
`/usr/sbin`	Non-essential system administration programs run by superuser
`/usr/local/sbin`	Locally installed system programs
THIRD-PARTY APPLICATIONS	
`/opt/`*xxx*	Static data for application *xxx*; includes programs
`/var/opt/`*xxx*	Variable data for application *xxx*

FIGURE 23-8: Directories that hold program files

The Unix filesystem has a number of different locations for program files. General-use programs are stored in directories with the name **bin** *("binary files"). System administration programs are stored in directories named* **sbin** *("system binaries"). Large third-party applications are stored in directories named* **opt** *("optional software"). Programs are further categorized as being either essential or non-essential. Essential programs are necessary to start the system or perform crucial system administration. Everything else is non-essential.*

The details you see here are based on the Filesystem Hierarchy Standard. Your system may differ somewhat.

Today, storage devices are fast, inexpensive, and hold large amounts of data. For the most part, there is no compelling reason to divide the core of Unix into more than one filesystem stored on multiple devices. Indeed, some Unix systems put all the general-use binary files in one large directory. Still, many Unix systems do use separate filesystems combined into a large tree. We will discuss the reasons for such a design later in the chapter, when we talk about the virtual filesystem.

As a general rule, modern Unix systems distinguish between three types of software: general-use programs that might be used by anyone; system administration programs used only by the superuser; and large, third-party application programs that require many files and directories. As we discussed earlier in the chapter, the three different types of programs are stored in their own directories. For reference, Figure 23-8 summarizes the various locations where you will find Unix program files.

HOME DIRECTORIES

With so many system directories chock-full of important files, it is clear that we need an orderly system to control where users store their personal files. Of course, people as intelligent as you and I wouldn't make a mess of things if we were allowed to, say, store our own personal programs in the **/bin** directory, or our own personal data files in **/etc**. But for the most part, we can't have the hoi polloi putting their files, willy-nilly, wherever they want — we need organization.

The solution is to give each user his own HOME DIRECTORY, a directory in which he can do whatever he wants. When your Unix account was created (see Chapter 4), a home directory was created for you. The name of your home directory is kept in the password file (Chapter 11) and when you log in, the system automatically places you in this directory. (The idea of being "in" a directory will make more sense after you have read Chapter 24.) Within your home directory, you can store files and create other subdirectories as you see fit. Indeed, many people have large elaborate tree structures of their own, all under the auspices of their own home directory.

The Filesystem Hierarchy Standard suggests that home directories be created in the **/home** directory. On small systems, the name of a home directory is simply the name of the userid, for example, **/home/harley**, **/home/linda**, and so on. On large systems with many userids, there may be an extra level of subdirectories to organize the home directories into categories. For example, at a university, home directories may be placed within subdirectories named **undergrad**, **grad**, **professors** and **staff**. At a real estate company, you might see **agents**, **managers** and **admin**. You get the idea.

The only userid whose home directory is *not* under **/home** is the superuser's (**root**). Because the administrator must always be able to control the system, the superuser's home directory must be available at all times, even when the system is booting or when it is running in single-user mode (see Chapter 6). On many systems, the **/home** directory is in a secondary filesystem, which is not available until it is mounted. The **/root** directory, on the other hand, is always part of the root filesystem and, thus, is always available.

Each time you log in, the environment variable **HOME** is set to the name of your home directory. Thus, one way to display the name of your home directory is to use the **echo** program to display the value of the **HOME** variable:

```
echo $HOME
```

(The **echo** program simply displays the values of its arguments. It is discussed, along with environment variables, in Chapter 12.)

As a shortcut, the symbol ~ (tilde) can be used as an abbreviation for your home directory. For example, you can display the name of your home directory by using:

```
echo ~
```

Whatever its name, the important thing about your home directory is that it is yours to use as you see fit. One of the first things you should do is create a **bin** subdirectory to store your own personal programs and shell scripts. You can then place the name of this directory — for example, **/home/harley/bin** — in your search path.

(The search path is a list of directories stored in the **PATH** environment variable. Whenever you enter the name of a program that is not built into the shell, Unix looks in the directories specified in your search path to find the appropriate program to execute. See Chapter 13 for the details.)

Figure 23-9 shows a typical directory structure based on the home directory of **/home/harley**. This home directory has three subdirectories: **bin**, **essays** and **games**. The **essays** directory has three subdirectories of its own: **history**,

literature and **surfing**. All of these directories contain files which are not shown in the diagram. As you will see in Chapter 24, making and removing subdirectories is easy. Thus, it is a simple matter to enlarge or prune your directory tree as your needs change.

The **/home** directory is part of the Filesystem Hierarchy Standard, and is widely used on Linux systems. If you use another type of Unix, however, you may find your home directory in a different place. The classical setup — used for many years — was to put home directories in the **/usr** directory. For example, the home directory for userid **harley** would be **/usr/harley**. Other systems use **/u**, **/user** (with an "e"), **/var/home** or **/export/home**. For reference, here are examples of home directory locations you might see on different systems:

```
/usr/harley
/u/harley
/user/harley
/var/home/harley
/export/home/harley
```

On large systems, especially those where files are stored on a network, the exact location of the home directories may be more involved; much depends on how the system administrator has decided to organize the filesystem. For example, I have an account on one computer where my home directory is sub-sub-sub-sub-subdirectory:

/usr/local/psa/home/vhosts/harley

> **HINT**
>
> On any system, you can find out the location of your home directory by entering either of the following commands:
>
> ```
> echo $HOME
> echo ~
> ```

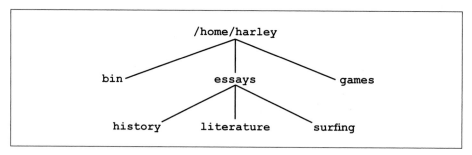

FIGURE 23-9: A typical home directory-based tree structure

Every userid is assigned a home directory. According to the Filesystem Hierarchy Standard, home directories should be in the /home directory, although you will find variations (see text).

Within your home directory, you can create and remove subdirectories according to your needs. This example shows a typical home directory with three subdirectories, one of which has three subdirectories of its own. All six subdirectories contain files, although they are not shown in the diagram.

THE VIRTUAL FILE SYSTEM

In this chapter, you and I have covered a lot of material. To the extent that you care about such things, the details will be more or less interesting. However, there is a lot more to this forest than the leaves on the trees. The Unix filesystem was created by a few very smart people and, over the years, enhanced through the efforts of a great many experienced programmers and system administrators. The end-product is not only utilitarian, but beautiful.

In this section, I want to help you appreciate, not only the usefulness of the system, but its beauty. To do so, I'm going to explain how multiple filesystems residing on a variety of different storage devices are combined into one large tree-structured arrangement.

Earlier in the chapter, I explained that every storage device has its own local filesystem, with directories and subdirectories organized into a tree in the standard Unix manner. Before you can access such a filesystem, it must be connected to the main filesystem, a process we call mounting. In technical terms, we mount a filesystem by connecting its root directory to a mount point, a directory within the main filesystem.

I want you to notice that when we talk about these ideas, we use the word "filesystem" in two different ways. Don't be confused. First, there is the "Unix filesystem", the large, all-inclusive structure that contains every file and every directory in the entire system. Second, there are the smaller, individual "device filesystems" that reside on the various storage devices. The Unix filesystem is created by connecting the smaller device filesystems into one large structure.

To explain how it all works, I need to start at the beginning by answering the question, what happens when the system boots? When you turn on your computer, a complicated series of events are set into motion called the boot process (described in Chapter 2). After the power-on self-test, a special program called the boot loader takes control and reads data from the BOOT DEVICE in order to load the operating system into memory. In most cases, the boot device is a partition on a local hard drive. However, it can also be a network device, a CD, a flash drive, and so on.

Within the data on the boot device lies the initial Unix filesystem called the ROOT FILESYSTEM. The root filesystem, which is mounted automatically, holds all the programs and data files necessary to start Unix. It also contains the tools a system administrator would need should something go wrong. As such, the root filesystem contains, at minimum, the following directories (which are discussed earlier in the chapter):

`/bin /boot /dev /etc /lib /root /sbin /tmp`

Once the root filesystem is mounted and the kernel has been started, other device filesystems are mounted automatically. The information about such filesystems is kept in a configuration file, **`/etc/fstab`***, which can be modified by the system administrator. (The name stands for "file system table".) To look at the file on your system, use the command:

`less /etc/fstab`

---

*On Solaris, the file is named **`/etc/vfstab`**.

The root filesystem is always stored on the boot device. However, there are three other filesystems that may reside on separate devices: **usr**, **var** and **home**. If these filesystems are on their own devices, they are connected to the Unix filesystem by attaching them to the appropriate subdirectories. The **usr** filesystem is mounted at **/usr**; the **var** filesystem is mounted at **/var**; and so on. This is all done automatically so, by the time you see the login prompt, everything has been mounted and the Unix filesystem is up and running.

Each device uses a filesystem appropriate for that type of device. A partition on a hard drive uses a filesystem suitable for a hard drive; a CD-ROM uses a filesystem suitable for CD-ROMs, and so on. As you would imagine, the details involved in reading and writing data vary significantly depending on the type of device. They vary depending on whether the filesystem is local (on your computer) or remote (on a network). Finally, some filesystems — such as **procfs** for proc files — use pseudo files, which do not reside on storage devices. For reference, Figure 23-10 contains a list of the filesystems you are most likely to encounter.

The significant differences among the various filesystems raise an important question. Consider the following two **cp** (copy) commands:

```
cp /media/cd/essays/freddy-the-pig /home/harley/essays
cp /proc/cpuinfo /home/harley/
```

We'll talk about **cp** in Chapter 25. For now, all I want you to appreciate is that the first command copies a file from a directory on a CD, to a directory on a hard disk partition. The second command copies information from a pseudo file (which is generated by the kernel) to a file on a hard disk partition. In both cases, you just enter a simple command, so who takes care of the details?

The details are handled by a special facility called the VIRTUAL FILE SYSTEM or VFS. The VFS is an API (application program interface) that acts as a middleman between your programs and the various filesystems. Whenever a program requires an I/O operation, it sends a request to the virtual file system. The VFS locates the appropriate filesystem and communicates with it by instructing the device driver to perform the I/O. In this way, the VFS allows you and your programs to work with a single, uniform tree-structure (the Unix filesystem) even though, in reality, the data comes from a variety of separate heterogeneous filesystems.

In our first example, data must be read from the CD. The **cp** program issues a read request, which is handled by the virtual file system. The VFS sends its own request to the CD filesystem. The CD filesystem sends the appropriate commands to the CD device driver, which reads the data. In this way, neither you nor your programs need to know any of the details. As far as you are concerned, the Unix filesystem exists exactly as you imagine it and works exactly the way you want it to work.

Can you see the beauty? At one end of every file operation, the virtual file system talks to you in your language. At the other end, the VFS talks to the various device filesystems in their own languages. As a result, you and your programs are able to interact with any of the filesystems without having to communicate with them directly.

DISK-BASED FILESYSTEMS	
ext3	third extended filesystem (Linux)
ext4	fourth extended filesystem (Linux)
FAT32	32-bit File Allocation Table filesystem (Microsoft Windows)
HFS+	Hierarchical File System (Macintosh)
ISO 9660	ISO 9660 standard filesystem (CD-ROMs)
NTFS	NT filesystem (Microsoft Windows)
UDF	Universal Disk Format filesystem (rewritable CDs & DVDs)
UFS2	Unix File System (BSD, Solaris)
NETWORK FILESYSTEMS	
NFS	Network File System (used widely)
SMB	Server Message Block (Windows networks)
SPECIAL-PURPOSE FILESYSTEMS	
devpts	device interface for pseudo terminals (PTYs)
procfs	proc files filesystem
sysfs	system data filesystem (devices & drivers)
tmpfs	temporary storage filesystem

FIGURE 23-10: The most common filesystems

For reference, here are the most common filesystems you will encounter when using a Unix or Linux system. Disk-based filesystems store data on hard disks, CDs, DVDs or other devices; network filesystems support the sharing of resources over a network; special-purpose filesystems provide access to system resources, such as pseudo files.

Now consider another question. Whenever a new type of filesystem is developed (say, for a new device), how can it be made to work with Unix? The answer is conceptually simple. All the developers of the new device have to do is teach the new filesystem to speak "VFS" language. This enables the filesystem to join the world of Unix, where it will fit in seamlessly.

Here is the beautiful part: No matter when you learned Unix — 35 years ago or 35 minutes ago — the Unix filesystem looks and works the same way. Moreover, as new devices and better filesystems are developed over the years, they are integrated into your world smoothly and easily. This is the reason why an operating system that was designed at a time when students were wearing love beads and protesting the war, still works well at a time when students are wearing mobile phones and protesting the war.

And what about the future? We don't know what kind of strange new devices and information sources will become available in the years to come. After all, when it comes to technology, no one can make promises. What I *can* promise you, however, is that no matter what new technology comes along, it will work with Unix. And I can also promise you that, years from now, you will be teaching Unix to your children*.

---

*So save this book.

CHAPTER 23 EXERCISES

REVIEW QUESTIONS

1. What is a Unix file? What are the three main types of files? Describe each type.

2. Explain the difference between a text file and a binary file. Give three examples of each.

3. What is the Filesystem Hierarchy Standard or FHS? Within the FHS, briefly describe the contents of (1) the root directory (**/**); (2) the following top-level directories: **/bin, /boot, /dev, /etc, /home, /lib, /sbin, /tmp, /usr** and **/var**.

4. Within the FHS, which directories contain general-use programs? Which directories contain system administration programs?

5. What is a home directory? Within the FHS, where do you find the home directories? What is the only userid whose home directory is in a different place? Why?

Suppose your userid is **weedly** and you are an undergraduate student at a large university. Give two likely names for your home directory.

APPLYING YOUR KNOWLEDGE

1. The following command will list all the subdirectories of the root directory:

```
ls -F / | grep '/'
```

Use this command to look at the names of the top-level directories on your system. Compare what you see to the basic layout of the Filesystem Hierarchy Standard. What are the differences?

2. As we will discuss in Chapter 24, you can use the **cd** to change from one directory to another, and **ls** to list the contents of a directory. For example, to change to the **/bin** directory and list its contents, you can use:

```
cd /bin; ls
```

Explore *your* system and find out where the following files are stored:

- Users' home directories
- General-use programs (the Unix utilities)
- System administration programs
- Special files
- Configuration files
- Man pages
- Kernel
- Files required when booting the system

Hint: You may find the **whereis** program useful (see Chapter 25).

3. Enter the following command:

```
cp /dev/tty tempfile
```

Type several lines of text and then press **^D**. What did you just do? How did it work? Hint: To clean up after yourself, you should enter the following command to remove (delete) the file named **tempfile**:

```
rm tempfile
```

FOR FURTHER THOUGHT

1. Unix defines a "file" a very general way. Give three advantages to such a system. Give three disadvantages.

2. There is no uniformity as to how closely Unix systems must follow the Filesystem Hierarchy Standard. Some systems stick fairly close to the ideal; others are significantly different. Would it be a good or a bad idea to require all Unix systems to use the same basic filesystem hierarchy? Discuss the advantages and the disadvantages.

WORKING WITH DIRECTORIES

This is the second of three chapters explaining the Unix filesystem. In Chapter 23, we discussed the filesystem as a whole: how it is organized into a tree-like hierarchy of directories and subdirectories, how the various parts of the filesystem are used, and the types of files you will encounter as you use Unix.

Within this overall hierarchy, each user is assigned a home directory to organize as he or she sees fit. In order to work with your part of the tree, as well as the filesystem as a whole, you need to be able to navigate quickly and easily from one directory to another. You also need to be able to organize your files by creating, deleting, moving and renaming subdirectories as needed. Finally, you need to be able to look inside the various directories, so you can work with the files and subdirectories therein.

In this chapter, you will learn all the fundamental skills necessary to work with directories. In Chapter 25, we will conclude our discussion by looking at the commands that work with regular files.

PATHNAMES AND YOUR WORKING DIRECTORY

In Chapter 23, we discussed how to write the full name for a file. Start with a **/** (slash), which stands for the root directory. Then write the names of all the directories you have to pass through to get to the file, following each name with a **/**. Finally, write the name of the file. Here is an example:

/usr/share/dict/words

In this case, the file **words** lies in the **dict** directory, which lies in the **share** directory, which lies in the **usr** directory, which lies in the root directory.

When we write the name of a file in this way, we describe the path through the directory tree from the root directory to the file in question. To do so, we specify a sequence of directories separated by **/** characters. This description is called a PATHNAME or a PATH. What you see above is an example of a pathname.

If the very last part of a pathname is the name of an ordinary file, we call it a FILENAME or, less often, a BASENAME. In our example, **words** is a filename.

Here is another example of a pathname. Let's say your userid is **harley** and your home directory is **/home/harley** (see Chapter 23). You have a file named **memo** that you want to edit using the **vi** text editor (Chapter 22). To start **vi**, you enter the command:

```
vi /home/harley/memo
```

Sometime later, you decide to edit another file, **document**. You enter:

```
vi /home/harley/document
```

In these examples, the pathnames are:

```
/home/harley/memo
/home/harley/document
```

The filenames are:

```
memo
document
```

As you might imagine, typing a full pathname every time you want to access a file is tiresome and prone to error. As a convenience, Unix allows you to designate one directory at a time as your WORKING DIRECTORY (also known as your CURRENT DIRECTORY). Whenever you want to use a file in your working directory, you need only type the filename; you do not need to specify the entire path. For example, if you were to tell Unix that you want to work in the directory **/home/harley** (I won't go into the details just yet), the following commands would be equivalent:

```
vi /home/harley/memo
vi memo
```

The rule is as follows: When you use a name that starts with a **/**, Unix assumes it is a full pathname, starting from the root directory. This is the case in the first command. When you use a filename only, Unix assumes you are referring to a file in your working directory. This is the case in the second command. (Once you have experience, this rule will make a lot of sense.)

Each time you log in, Unix automatically sets your working directory to be your home directory*, which is a convenient place to start work. As you work, you can change your working directory whenever you want by using the **cd** (change directory) command, which we will discuss later in the chapter. During a work session, it is common to change your working directory from time to time, depending on what you are doing. However, it does not matter where you end up. The next time you log in, you will start, once again, in your home directory.

Here is how I want you to think of it. Imagine the Unix filesystem as a very large tree. The trunk of the tree is the root directory, and all the other directories are branches of the tree. For example, the directories **/home** and **/bin** are branches off the root. The

---

*How does Unix know the name of your home directory? The pathname of each userid's home directory is stored in the Unix password file, **/etc/passwd**, described in Chapter 11.

directory **/home/harley** is a branch off **/home**. At any time, you are sitting on some branch in the tree. That is your working directory.

The moment you log in, you find yourself sitting on the branch of the tree that represents your home directory. To move to another branch of the tree, all you need to do is change your working directory. Thus, you can think of the **cd** command as a magic carpet that instantly moves you from one branch of the tree to another.

ABSOLUTE AND RELATIVE PATHNAMES

A pathname or path describes a location in the file tree by listing a sequence of directories separated by **/** (slash) characters. If the sequence starts from the root directory, we call it an ABSOLUTE PATHNAME. If the sequence starts from your working directory we call it a RELATIVE PATHNAME.

To illustrate the differences, I'll use the directory tree in Figure 24-1. This tree shows subdirectories belonging to userid **harley**, whose home directory is **/home/harley**. (Remember from Chapter 4, Unix files are owned by userids, not users.)

Within the home directory, we have two subdirectories, **bin** and **essays**. In keeping with the Unix tradition, the files in the **bin** directory contain executable programs and scripts (see Chapter 23). In this case, there are two such programs, **funky** and **spacewar**. The **essays** subdirectory contains two subdirectories of its own, **history** and **literature**. Each of these directories contains two ordinary files. When userid **harley** logs in, the working directory is automatically set to be the home directory **/home/harley**. Let's take a look at how we might specify the names of the various files.

Let's say we want to use a command in which we need to refer to the **bin** directory. Unix assumes that any name that begins with a **/** is an absolute pathname. That is, it shows the full path to the file, starting from the root directory. If a name does not begin with a **/**, Unix assumes that it is relative pathname. That is, it describes a path starting from the working directory.

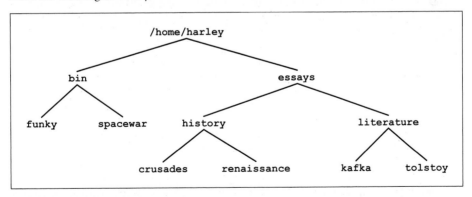

FIGURE 24-1: A sample directory tree

Within the home directory for userid **harley**, *there are two subdirectories:* **bin** *and* **essays**. *The first subdirectory contains two ordinary files. The second subdirectory has two subdirectories of its own, each of which contains two ordinary files. This small tree-structure is used within the text to illustrate the difference between absolute and relative pathnames.*

We can refer to the **bin** directory in two ways. First, the absolute pathname is:

`/home/harley/bin`

Alternatively, since the working directory is **/home/harley**, it is a lot simpler to use the relative pathname:

`bin`

Here is another example using the same working directory. We want to enter a command for which we need to specify the name of the **tolstoy** file in the **literature** directory. The absolute pathname is:

`/home/harley/essays/literature/tolstoy`

Again, the relative pathname is shorter:

`essays/literature/tolstoy`

Here is one final example. Let's say we want to do a lot of work with the files **kafka** and **tolstoy**. It is inconvenient to refer to these files using the absolute pathnames:

`/home/harley/essays/literature/kafka`
`/home/harley/essays/literature/tolstoy`

However, it is only a bit more convenient to use relative pathnames:

`essays/literature/kafka`
`essays/literature/tolstoy`

The best thing to do is to change the working directory to be:

`/home/harley/essays/literature`

(I will show you how to do this in a moment.) Once we change the working directory, we can refer to the files more simply as:

`kafka`
`tolstoy`

Think of the working directory as a base of operations you can change whenever you want. When you log in, you start out in your home directory, but you can change to any directory you want, whenever you want. The idea is to choose your working directory, so as to make filenames as simple as possible and easy to type.

Throughout this book, you will find many examples in which I use filenames such as:

`vi kafka`

Now you understand that, in such cases, I am actually using relative pathnames. In this example, the command starts the **vi** text editor using the file named **kafka** in the working directory. Of course, when necessary, you can always use a full pathname:

`vi /home/harley/essays/literature/kafka`

I want you to remember this idea whenever you use a program whose syntax requires you to specify the name of a file. In such cases, you can use either an absolute pathname or a relative pathname.

HINT

It is a fundamental rule of Unix that whenever you can use an ordinary filename, you can, instead, use a pathname.

THREE HANDY PATHNAME ABBREVIATIONS: . .   .   ~

Unix provides three handy pathname abbreviations. The first is two periods in a row, pronounced "dot-dot":

```
. .
```

When you use `. .` in a pathname, it refers to the parent directory.

To illustrate how this works, let us refer to the sample directory tree in Figure 24-1. Within the home directory **/home/harley**, there are two subdirectories, **bin** and **essays**. The **bin** directory contains two files. The **essays** subdirectory contains two subdirectories of its own, **history** and **literature**. Each of these directories contains two files. Say that you set the working directory to:

```
/home/harley/essays/literature
```

(To do so, you would use the **cd** command, which we will discuss later in the chapter.) Once your working directory is changed in this way, you can refer to the two files in this directory as **kafka** and **tolstoy** (using relative pathnames). At this point, the specification `. .` refers to the parent directory, that is:

```
/home/harley/essays
```

Let's say you want to refer to the file **crusades** within the **history** directory. One way is to type the entire absolute pathname:

```
/home/harley/essays/history/crusades
```

An easier way is to use the abbreviation `. .` to stand for the parent directory:

```
. ./history/crusades
```

When you use `. .`, it is the same as the name of the parent directory, so the above pathname is equivalent to the absolute pathname.

You can use the `. .` more than once to move "up" more than one level. For example, from the same working directory, let's say you want to refer to the **bin** directory. You could use the absolute pathname:

```
/home/harley/bin
```

Alternatively, you can use the `. .` abbreviation twice:

`../../bin`

The first parent directory is:

`/home/harley/essays`

The second parent directory (the grandparent) is:

`/home/harley`

Here is another example. You want to refer to the **funky** file within the **bin** directory. The absolute pathname is:

`/home/harley/bin/funky`

Starting from the same working directory, you can use:

`../../bin/funky`

Here is one last example, which is a bit extreme. (Read slowly to make sure you understand it.) Your working directory is:

`/home/harley/essays/literature`

To refer to the root directory of the entire filesystem, you can use `..` four times:

`../../../..`

Similarly, you can refer to the **/etc** directory as:

`../../../../etc`

Of course, you would probably never use these examples, as it is a lot easier to type **/** and **/etc**. The `..` abbreviation is most useful when you want to refer to directories near your working directory, without having to actually change your working directory.

The second pathname abbreviation is a single period, usually referred to as "dot":

`.`

A single `.` refers to the working directory itself. For example, let's say the working directory is:

`/home/harley/essays/literature`

The following three specifications all refer to the same file:

```
/home/harley/essays/literature/kafka
./kafka
kafka
```

Certainly, it is a lot easier to type `.` than the full name of the working directory. But, as you can see, you don't really need to specify any directory name. As long as a name does not begin with a **/**, Unix will assume that any pathname is relative to your working directory. This principle is important enough that I want to embody it in the form of a hint:

You might ask, why would you ever need to use a single . abbreviation? There are certain situations in which you must specify an absolute pathname. In such cases, you can use the . abbreviation for the name of your working directory. The idea is to avoid typing a long pathname, not only out of laziness (although that is a good idea), but to make it less likely you will make a spelling mistake. (As I am sure you know by now, it is far too easy to make spelling mistakes when typing Unix commands.)

Here is an example. Let's say you have written a program called **plugh**. (I will leave it to your imagination as to what this program might do.) The program is in the directory **/home/harley/adventure** which, at this moment, is your working directory. Normally, you would run a program by entering its name:

```
plugh
```

However, Unix can only run a program if it can find it. In most cases, this means that the file that holds the program should reside in one of the directories in your search path (see Chapter 13). In our example, the directory containing the program is not in your search path. However, Unix can always find and run a program if you specify the absolute pathname. Thus, you can run the **plugh** program by typing:

```
/home/harley/adventure/plugh
```

However, since the program lies in your working directory, you have an easier alternative. Use the . abbreviation:

```
./plugh
```

Be sure you understand that .. and . are abbreviations. As our example illustrates, when you start a name with .. or . you are really specifying a full pathname. Unix is just helping you with the typing.

The third pathname abbreviation is the ~ (tilde). You can use this symbol at the beginning of a pathname to stand for your home directory. For example, to use the **ls** program to list the names of all the files in your home directory, you can use:

```
ls ~
```

To list the files in the subdirectory **bin** that lies within your home directory, you can use:

```
ls ~/bin
```

To refer to another userid's home directory, you can use a ~ followed by the userid. For example, to list the files in the home directory of userid **weedly**, you would use:

```
ls ~weedly
```

Let's say that **weedly** has a **bin** directory of his own and, within that **bin** directory, there is a program named **mouse**. To run the program, you must type the absolute pathname. You have two choices:

```
/home/weedly/bin/mouse
~weedly/bin/mouse
```

These last few examples raise an important question. Can any user look at other people's files and run their programs? For that matter, can a user change someone else's files?

The answer is that all files (including directories) have "permissions". The permissions for a file dictate who can look at and modify the file. On many systems, the default is to let users look at other people's files, but not to modify them or run them. However, file permissions are under the control of the owner of the file. Thus, every Unix user can restrict or allow access to his files as he sees fit. We will discuss these issues in Chapter 25.

TECHNICAL HINT

There are three standard abbreviations you can use when specifying a pathname: . (current directory), . . (parent directory), and ~ (home directory). Although they seem similar, they are not implemented in the same way.

The names . and . . are actual directory entries, created automatically by the filesystem. Every directory in the system contains these two entries.

The name ~ is an abstraction provided by the shell, to make it convenient to refer to your home directory.

MOVING AROUND THE DIRECTORY TREE: cd, pwd

To display the name of your working directory, use the **pwd** (print working directory) command. The syntax is easy:

```
pwd
```

To change your working directory, you use the **cd** (change directory) command. The syntax is:

```
cd [-LP] [directory | -]
```

where *directory* is the name of the directory to which you want to change.

If you enter the command without a directory name, **cd** will, by default, change to your home directory. If you enter the command with – (dash) instead of a directory name, **cd** will change to the previous directory. The **-L** and **-P** options have to do with symbolic links, which we will cover in Chapter 25.

As a general rule, when a Unix name is short and has no vowels, we pronounce its name as separate letters. For example, the **ls** command is pronounced "L-S". Similarly, the **pwd** and **cd** commands are pronounced "P-W-D" and "C-D".

Of all the Unix tools, **cd** and **pwd** are among the most useful. You will find yourself using them a lot, so read this section carefully. Here are some examples of how to use the

cd command. When you practice using your own examples, remember to use the **pwd** command from time to time to check where you are.

To change your working directory to **/home/harley/essays**, use:

`cd /home/harley/essays`

To change to **/bin**, use:

`cd /bin`

To change to **/** (the root directory) use:

`cd /`

For convenience, you can use relative pathnames as well as abbreviations. For example, say that your working directory is currently **/home/harley**. Within this directory, you have two subdirectories, **bin** and **essays**. To change to **bin** (that is, **/home/harley/bin**), simply enter:

`cd bin`

Because the directory name **bin** does not start with a **/**, Unix assumes it is a relative pathname, based on your working directory. Here is another example. Again, your working directory is **/home/harley**. This time you want to change to:

`/home/harley/essays/history`

Using a relative pathname, you can enter:

`cd essays/history`

When you use the **cd** command without a directory name, it changes your working directory to your home directory:

`cd`

Using **cd** in this way is the fastest way to return home when you are exploring a distant branch of the filesystem and you have lost your way.* For example, say that your working directory happens to be **/etc/local/programs**. You want to move to the **bin** directory within your home directory. Just enter:

`cd`
`cd bin`

The first command changes to your home directory. The second command changes to the **bin** directory within your home directory. To make it more convenient, recall that you can enter more than one command on the same line by separating the commands with a semicolon (see Chapter 10). Thus, no matter where you are in the filesystem, you can move to your own personal **bin** directory by entering:

---

*Alternatively, if you happen to be wearing a pair of ruby slippers, you can tap your heels together three times and repeat "There's no place like home."

```
cd; cd bin
```

Here are some examples showing how to use two standard pathname abbreviations we discussed earlier. We'll start with `..`, the abbreviation for the parent directory. Let's say that your working directory is:

```
/home/harley/essays/history
```

To change to the parent directory, **/home/harley/essays**, just go up one level in the tree:

```
cd ..
```

From the original working directory, you could use the following command to change to **/home/harley/essays/literature** by using:

```
cd ../literature
```

To go up more than one level, use the `..` abbreviation more than once. For example, from the original working directory, you could change to **/home/harley/bin** by using:

```
cd ../../bin
```

Question: What happens if you are in the root directory and you enter:

```
cd ..
```

Answer: Nothing will happen. Your working directory will not change, and you will not see an error message. Why? Because Unix considers the parent directory of the root directory to be the root directory itself.* For example, as odd as it seems, the following two pathnames refer to the same file:

```
/etc/passwd
/../../../etc/passwd
```

The other useful abbreviation is `~` (tilde) which, as we discussed, stands for the name of your home directory. Thus, the following two command lines have the same effect: they both set your working directory to the **bin** subdirectory of your home directory:

```
cd; cd bin
cd ~/bin
```

The first command makes the change in two steps; the second command does it all at once.

At times, you will find yourself switching back and forth between two directories. In such cases, **cd** has a special abbreviation to make life easier. If you type – (dash) instead of a directory name, **cd** will change to the last directory you visited. At the same time, **cd** will display the name of the new directory, so you will know where you are.

Here is an example you can try for yourself. To start, use **cd** to change to the **/etc** directory and the **pwd** to confirm the change:

---

*An assumption that has important theological implications.

```
cd /etc; pwd
```

Now change to **/usr/bin**:

```
cd /usr/bin; pwd
```

Finally, enter **cd** with a – character.

```
cd -
```

You are now back in **/etc**.

HINT

At any time, you can find out where you are in the tree by using **pwd** to display the name of your working directory. However, there are two alternatives.

First, it is possible to display the name of your working directory in your shell prompt. As you change from one directory to another, your prompt updates automatically to show you where you are. The details are covered in Chapter 13.

Second, most GUI-based terminal windows display the name of your working directory in the title bar (at the top of the window). Take a moment to see if this is the case with your system.

WHAT'S IN A NAME?

pwd, cd

In Chapter 3, we discussed how the early Unix developers used teletype terminals that printed output on paper. Over the years, Unix has retained the convention of using the word "print" to mean "to display information". Thus, the name **pwd** stands for "print working directory", even though it has been a long time since anyone actually printed the name of their working directory on paper.

If you hang around Unix geeks, you will often hear them use **cd** as a verb. (When they do, the name **cd** is pronounced as two letters "C-D".) For example, someone might say, "To find the basic Unix tools, just C-D to the **/bin** directory and look around." This is consistent with the metaphor in which we imagine ourselves sitting on a branch of a tree, and we use **cd** to move to another branch and **pwd** to remind us where we are.

MAKING A NEW DIRECTORY: mkdir

To make a directory, you use the **mkdir** program. The syntax is:

mkdir [**-p**] *directory...*

where *directory* is the name of a directory you want to make.

Using this program is straightforward. You can name a new directory anything you want as long as you follow a few simple rules. I will go over the rules in Chapter 25 when I talk about naming files. (Remember, as I explained in Chapter 23, directories are really files.) Basically, you can use letters, numbers, and those punctuation symbols that do not have a special meaning. However, most of the time, your life will be easier if you stick to lowercase letters only.

Here is an example. To create a directory named **extra**, within your working directory, use:

```
mkdir extra
```

When you specify a directory name, you can use either an absolute or relative pathname, as well as the standard abbreviations. As an example, let's say that you want to create the directory tree in Figure 24-2 (the directories I used as examples earlier in the chapter.) Within your home directory, you want to make two subdirectories, **bin** and **essays**. Within the **essays** directory, you want two more subdirectories, **history** and **literature**.

To start, make sure that you are in your home directory:

```
cd
```

Now, make the first two subdirectories:

```
mkdir bin essays
```

Next, change to the **essays** directory and make the final two subdirectories:

```
cd essays
mkdir history literature
```

To illustrate the various ways to specify pathnames, let's take a look at two more ways to create the same directories. First, you could have done the whole thing without leaving the home directory:

```
cd
mkdir bin essays essays/history essays/literature
```

The first command changes to the home directory. The second command specifies all four names, relative to your working directory. In the following example, we don't even bother changing to the home directory:

```
mkdir ~/bin ~/essays ~/essays/history ~/essays/literature
```

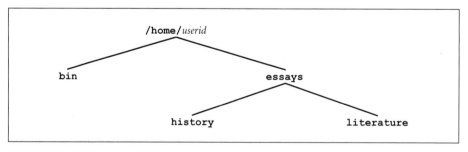

FIGURE 24-2: Making a sample directory tree

*To make a new directory, you use the **mkdir** program. Here is a sample directory tree that is created by using sample **mkdir** commands (see text for details). This tree consists of two subdirectories, **bin** and **essays**, within the home directory. The bin directory has two subdirectories of its own, **history** and **literature**.*

Remember, the **~** (tilde) character is an abbreviation for your home directory.

There are times when it is handy to use the **..** abbreviation to indicate a parent directory. For example, say that you have changed to the **essays** directory:

```
cd ~/essays
```

You now decide to create a subdirectory named **extra** within the **bin** directory. Since the **bin** and **essays** have the same parent (the home directory), you can use:

```
mkdir ../bin/extra
```

When you create a directory, Unix makes you follow two sensible rules. First, within a directory, you cannot create two subdirectories with the same name. For example, you cannot have two directories named **~/essays/history**. (How would you tell them apart?) However, you can have two directories with the same name if they are in different parent directories. For example:

```
~/essays/history
~/homework/history
```

The second rule is that, by default, you cannot make a subdirectory if its parent directory does not exist. For example, you cannot make **~/homework/history** unless you have already made **~/homework**. When you specify more than one directory within a single command, **mkdir** will create the directories in the order you specify. Thus, the following command will work, because you are telling **mkdir** to create the **homework** directory before it creates the **history** directory:

```
mkdir ~/homework ~/homework/history
```

However, the next command will not work, because you can't create a subdirectory before you create the parent directory:

```
mkdir ~/homework/history ~/homework
```

Recall for a moment our analogy comparing the filesystem to a tree. The main trunk is the root directory, and each branch is a subdirectory. The two rules merely say:

1. You cannot create two identical branches.
2. You cannot create a new branch that has nowhere to attach to the tree.

For convenience, you can override the second restriction by using the **-p** (make parent) option. This tells **mkdir** to create all the necessary parent directories automatically. For example, let's say you are researching how the early Romans used Unix, and you need to create the following directory structure to hold your files:

```
~/essays/history/roman/unix/research
```

You can't create the **research** directory unless **unix** exists; you can't create **unix** unless **roman** exists; and so on. Thus, if none of the directories exists, you would have to use a sequence of five commands to create the full structure:

```
mkdir ~/essays
mkdir ~/essays/history
mkdir ~/essays/history/roman
mkdir ~/essays/history/roman/unix
mkdir ~/essays/history/roman/unix/research
```

However, if you use **-p**, you can create everything with a single command:

mkdir -p ~/essays/history/roman/unix/research

> ### HINT
>
> When it comes to filenames, Unix is case sensitive, which means it distinguishes between upper- and lowercase (see Chapter 4). For example, the following three directory names are considered to be different:
>
> **bin**
> **Bin**
> **BIN**
>
> We'll talk about naming files in Chapter 25. For now, let me give you the following advice. When it comes to naming directories, unless you have a really good reason, use only lowercase letters. If you want to break up words, use a − (dash) or _ (underscore), for example:
>
> **backups-january**
> **backups_january**
>
> It is possible to use spaces within a directory name if you enclose the entire name in quotes. Don't do it, however. It only leads to trouble.

REMOVING A DIRECTORY: rmdir

To remove (delete) a directory, use the **rmdir** program. The syntax is straightforward:

rmdir [**-p**] *directory...*

where *directory* is the directory that you want to remove.

For example, to remove the directory **extra** from within the working directory, use:

rmdir extra

When you use **rmdir**, you can specify one or more directory names using absolute or relative pathnames. You can also use the standard abbreviations: **. .** for the parent directory, and **~** (tilde) for the home directory.

Let's take a look at some examples using the sample directory tree we built in the previous section. (See Figure 24-2.) Within the home directory, we have two subdirectories, **bin** and **essays**. Within the **essays** directory, we have two more subdirectories, **history** and **literature**. Say that you want to delete all four of these directories. There are several ways to do the job. First, move to the **essays** directory:

cd ~/essays

From here, you can delete the two subdirectories:

rmdir history literature

Next, move to the parent directory (the home directory):

cd ..

Remove the two main subdirectories:

rmdir bin essays

An alternate method would be to move to the home directory and remove all four subdirectories in one command:

cd
rmdir essays/history essays/literature essays bin

As a final example, you could do all the work without moving to the home directory:

rmdir ~/essays/history ~/essays/literature ~/essays ~/bin

When you remove a directory, Unix makes you follow two sensible rules. First, as a safeguard, you cannot remove a directory unless it is empty. (A directory is not empty if it contains a subdirectory or a file.)

Here is a real life example. It is late Sunday night, and you are working in the computer lab using Linux to complete a special project. Your home directory contains two subdirectories, **data** and **olddata**. The **data** directory contains 100 important files. The **olddata** directory is empty. You decide to remove the **olddata** directory. However, just as you enter the command, a meteorite smashes through the window hitting one of the geeks who is sitting beside you. In the confusion, you accidentally type:

rmdir data

Fortunately, Unix is prepared for just such an eventuality. You see the message:

rmdir: data: Directory not empty

Thanks to the built-in safeguard, your **data** directory is left untouched.

If you want to remove a sequence of empty directories all at once, you can do so by using the **-p** (delete parent) option*. This tells **rmdir** to remove all the necessary parent directories automatically. For example, let's say you have the following directory structure, and that all the directories are empty.

~/essays/history/roman/unix/research

You want to remove all five subdirectories. Without the **-p** option, you would have to start from the innermost subdirectory and work your way up the tree:

---

*Sometimes called the Oedipus option.

```
cd
rmdir essays/history/roman/unix/research
rmdir essays/history/roman/unix
rmdir essays/history/roman
rmdir essays/history
rmdir essays
```

With the **-p** option, however, you can change to your home directory and do the whole thing at once:

```
cd
rmdir -p essays/history/roman/unix/research
```

None of these commands will work if the directories are not empty. As I mentioned, this is for your protection. There will be rare occasions, however, when you really do want to remove a directory that is not empty. To do so, you can use the **rm** program with the **-r** option. Using **rm -r** will remove all subdirectories and their contents, so you must be *very* careful. We will discuss the **rm** program in Chapter 25, so I will defer the details until then.

A moment ago, I mentioned that there are two rules imposed by **rmdir**. First, you cannot remove a directory unless it is empty. The second rule is that you cannot remove any directory that lies between your working directory and the root directory. For example, say that your working directory is:

/home/harley/essays/literature

You cannot remove the **essays** directory or the **harley** directory, because they lie between you and the root directory. However, you can remove the directory:

/home/harley/essays/history

That is, you can use the command:

```
rmdir ../history
```

After all, the **history** directory does not lie between you and the root directory. If you want to remove **essays**, you must first move closer to the root directory, say to **/home/harley**. Now you can remove the directory:

```
cd /home/harley
rmdir essays/history essays/literature essays
```

Question: Your working directory is **/etc**. Can you remove a subdirectory that lies within your home directory?

Answer: Yes, because your working directory (**/etc**) does not lie between the root directory and the directory you want to remove.

To remember this rule, just recall our analogy to a real tree. The trunk is the root directory. Each branch is a subdirectory. At any time, you are sitting on some branch that is your working directory. Removing a directory is like sawing off a branch of the tree.

The restriction on removing directories simply states that you cannot saw off a branch that is holding up the one you are sitting on.

> **HINT**
>
> It is possible to remove your working directory. This is like cutting off the branch of the tree that you are sitting on. Probably Unix shouldn't let you do this, but it does.
>
> Removing your working directory will only cause you trouble. Don't do it.*

MOVING OR RENAMING A DIRECTORY: mv

To move or rename a directory, use the **mv** program. The syntax is:

mv *directory target*

where *directory* is the directory you want to move or rename, and *target* is the target or new name.

You use the **mv** program to "move" a directory from one place to another. If the new location is in the same directory, you have, in effect, renamed the original directory. That is why I say that **mv** both moves and renames.

Let me show you a few examples. You have a directory named **data** in your working directory, and you want to change its name to **extra**. Assuming that a directory named **extra** does not already exist in the same directory, you can use the command:

```
mv data extra
```

The directory that used to be named **data** is now named **extra**.

If the target directory does exist, **mv** will move the original directory into the target. For example, say that you have the following two directories:

```
/home/harley/data
/home/harley/storage
```

You want to move the **data** directory to the **storage** directory. Use:

```
mv /home/harley/data /home/harley/storage
```

Of course, if your working directory is **/home/harley**, you can simplify the command:

```
mv data storage
```

The pathname of the **data** directory is now:

```
/home/harley/storage/data
```

When **mv** moves a directory, it also moves all the files and subdirectories that lie within that directory. For example, say that, before the move, you had a file named **document** within the **data** directory. Its absolute pathname was:

---

*Even though I told you not to do it, I know you're going to do it just to see what happens. When you do, be sure to use a temporary subdirectory. Don't remove your home directory, or you really will be in trouble.

`/home/harley/data/document`

After the move, the absolute pathname becomes:

`/home/harley/storage/data/document`

If you had subdirectories — perhaps even a whole subtree — under **data**, they are moved as well. Thus, you can use the **mv** program for three purposes:

1. Rename a directory.
2. Move a directory.
3. Move an entire directory tree.

The **mv** program can be used to move or rename ordinary files, as well as directories. We will discuss how to do so in Chapter 25.

USING THE DIRECTORY STACK: `pushd`, `popd`, `dirs`

*In Chapter 13, I explained that there are two types of Unix commands. External commands are separate programs. Builtin (or internal) commands are interpreted directly by the shell and are available only if your shell supports them. In this section, I am going to show you how to use three builtin commands, **pushd**, **popd** and **dirs**. These commands are available with Bash, the Tcsh and the C-Shell, but not with the Korn Shell.*

At this point, we have covered the fundamental operations you need to work with directories. You know how to create, delete, move and rename. You also know how to change your working directory and display its name. What we have yet to cover are the many variations of the very important **ls** program, the tool that enables us to look inside a directory and see what's there. Before we move on to **ls**, however, I'd like to take a moment to show you an advanced technique that will help you move around the tree from one directory to another.

In Chapter 8, we talked about the idea of data structures, entities that are used to store and retrieve data according to a set of precise rules. So far, we have discussed three different data structures: the stack (Chapter 8), the queue (Chapter 23), and the tree (Chapters 9 and 23). We are about to use the stack again, so let's have a quick review.

A STACK is a data structure in which elements are stored and retrieved one at a time such that, at any time, the next data element to be retrieved is the last element that was stored. This arrangement is sometimes referred to as LIFO or "last-in first-out". When you store a data element, we say that you PUSH it onto the stack. The most recently pushed data element is said to be at the TOP of the stack. When you retrieve a data element from the top of the stack, we say that you POP the element off the stack. Informally, you can think of a stack as being similar to a spring-loaded column of plates in a cafeteria. The plates are pushed onto the "stack", one at a time. When you want a plate, you pop the top one off the stack. You have no access to any of the other plates.

The shell provides a similar facility to hold directory names. At any time, you can use the **pushd** command to push the name of a directory onto the DIRECTORY STACK. Later, you can use the **popd** command to pop a name off the stack. At any time, you can display the contents of the stack by using the **dirs** command. The syntax for these commands is as follows:

pushd [*directory* | **+***n*]
popd [**+***n*]
dirs [**-c**] [**-l**] [**-v**]

where **directory** is the name of a directory, and **n** is an identifier. Note: when you use options with **dirs**, you must keep them separate. For example, you can use **dirs -l -v**, but not **dirs -lv**.

In this section, we will cover the most important ways to use these three commands. There are a few more esoteric variations, which you can read about in the online manual. (Look on the man page that describes the builtin commands for your shell.) For reference, Figure 24-3 summarizes the commands we will be covering.

Learning how to use the directory stack takes a bit of practice, but it is worth the effort. Once you master the details, you will be able to zip around the filesystem like a VIP with a backstage pass running around a rock concert. The trick is to remember one simple rule:

At all times, the top of the stack holds the name of your working directory.

Whenever you change your working directory, the top of the stack changes automatically. Conversely, whenever you change the top of the stack, your working directory changes automatically. (Think about this for a moment, before you move on.)

Here are some examples. Start by using **cd** to change to the **/etc** directory. Use **pwd** to confirm the change:

cd /etc; pwd

Now display the contents of the stack. To do so, use the **dirs** command with the **-v** (verbose) option. This option tells **dirs** to display each element on the stack on a separate line with a line number. The top of the stack is line #0.

COMMAND	ACTION
dirs	display names: home directory shows as ~
dirs -l	display names: home directory shows as full pathname
dirs -v	display names: one per line, with numeric identifiers
pushd *directory*	change working directory: push *directory* onto stack
pushd +*n*	change working directory: move directory #*n* to top of stack
popd	change working directory: pop top of stack
popd +*n*	remove directory #*n* from stack
dirs -c	remove all names in stack except working directory

FIGURE 24-3: Directory stack commands

The directory stack is an advanced tool that enables you to maintain a list of directories and, whenever you want, change your working directory to a directory in the list.

At all times, the name at the top of the stack is your working directory. Changing this name automatically changes your working directory. Similarly, changing your working directory automatically changes the top name on the stack. You control the stack by pushing names onto it, popping names off it, or selecting a name to move to the top. Each of these operations changes the top of the stack, thereby changing your working directory. See text for details.

```
dirs -v
```

The output is:

```
0   /etc
```

Change to the **/usr** directory, and display the stack again:

```
cd /usr; dirs -v
```

Notice that the top of the stack has changed to point to your new working directory:

```
0   /usr
```

Now, use **pushd** to push three new directory names onto the stack. You must do this as three separate commands. Then use **dirs** to display the stack:

```
pushd /lib
pushd /var
pushd /etc
dirs -v
```

The output is:

```
0   /etc
1   /var
2   /lib
3   /usr
```

The stack now contains four directory names. Now display your working directory:

```
pwd
```

The output is:

```
/etc
```

Notice that you didn't have to change your working directory explicitly. Whenever the top of the stack (#0) changes, your working directory changes automatically.*

Next, use **popd** to pop a single name off the stack. Then display the stack and your working directory:

```
popd
dirs -v
pwd
```

The output of the **dirs** command is:

---

*You may have heard of the legendary magician Harry Houdini (1874–1926). Houdini used to perform a mystifying mind-reading trick in which he would guess someoe's working directory without using the **pwd** command. The secret? When no one was looking, Houdini would use the **dirs** command and sneak a peek at the top of the stack.

```
0   /var
1   /lib
2   /usr
```

The output of the **pwd** command is:

```
/var
```

The **popd** command popped **/etc** off the stack, which brought **/var** to the top of the stack. The instant this happened, **/var** became your working directory. We confirmed this by using **pwd**.

If you look back at the syntax, you will see that there are several options you can use with **dirs**. With no options, **dirs** will display the directory stack in a compressed format with all the names on a single line. If any of the names involve your home directory, **dirs** will represent it with a ~ (tilde) character. With the **-l** (long) option, **dirs** displays the full name of your home directory. Finally, with the **-v** (verbose) option, **dirs** displays one name per line with line numbers. To experiment, push your home directory onto the stack. Then try each of the variations:

```
pushd ~
dirs
dirs -l
dirs -v
dirs -l -v
```

The **dirs** command has one more option, but it has nothing to do with displaying names. The **-c** (clear) option empties the stack. Use this option when you want to clear out the stack and start fresh. To experiment, use **dirs** **-c** (to clear the stack) followed by **dirs** **-v** (to display the stack). Before you enter these commands, see if you can answer the question: Will the second command show an empty stack?

```
dirs -c
dirs -v
```

The answer is you will never see a completely empty stack. This is because the top of the stack is the name of your working directory. Since you always have a working directory, the directory stack must always have at least one name on it.

At this point, I can imagine you are thinking that all of this is interesting (or dull, depending on your point of view), but what good is it? How often, I hear you say, am I going to want to push directory names onto a stack and then pop them off, one at a time, just so I can change my working directory? Why not just use **cd**?

If you are thinking along these lines, you are correct. Most of the time, only the real geeks use the directory stack.* Indeed, if all you want to do is switch back and forth between two directories, you can use **cd** **-** (described earlier in the chapter). Why should you learn more arcane commands and spend time messing around with a stack?

The reason I am teaching you all this is that there is one aspect of the stack that is extremely useful: you can use the **pushd** command to jump into the middle of the stack and "push" a directory name to the top. The moment you do, you change your working directory.

It sounds complicated, but it isn't: it's quick, easy, and very powerful. Here is an example to show you how it works. Start by entering the following commands:

```
cd
dirs -c
pushd /lib
pushd /var
pushd /etc
dirs -v
```

The **cd** command changes to your home directory. The **dirs -c** command clears the stack. At this point, the stack is empty except for your working directory (which is ~, your home directory). The next three **pushd** commands push directory names onto the stack. The final **dirs** command displays the contents of the stack. The output of this command is:

```
0   /etc
1   /var
2   /lib
3   ~
```

There are now four names on the stack, and your working directory is the top one, **/etc** (#0). Let's say you have been working for a while in **/etc** and you want to change to **/lib** (#2). Just enter **pushd**, followed by a **+** (plus) character and the number **2**:

```
pushd +2
```

This tells the shell to move the #2 directory (**/lib**) to the top of the stack (#0). The moment **/lib** becomes #0, it also becomes your working directory. The net effect is to select the #2 directory from the middle of the stack and make it your working directory. At this point, if you use **dirs -v** to display the directory stack, it will look like this:

```
0   /lib
1   ~
2   /etc
3   /var
```

How did this happen? When you push a directory to the top, the directories above it are not lost. Instead, they are moved down the stack. In this case, when you moved directory #2 up to the top, directories #0 and #1 were rotated down towards the bottom.

---

*If you should happen to be someone who uses the directory stack a lot, you should know that I am using the word "geek" in the kindest possible sense.

I have to admit, this example is contrived. After all, there's no point entering commands to build a directory stack, display the stack contents, and then push names to the top, when you can do the same thing by typing a simple command like:

```
cd /lib
```

However, what if the directories had longer names? For example, let's say you are in your home directory **/home/harley**. You now enter the following **pushd** commands to push four very long names onto the directory stack:

```
pushd /home/harley/source/current/calculate/source/2-1.05
pushd /usr/include/linux/nfsd
pushd /home/harley/archive/calculate/source/1-0.31
pushd /usr/share/dict/
```

If you were going to do a lot of work with these directories, it would be a real bother to have to type the names over and over. Instead, you can push them on the stack once. Then, whenever you want, you can push whichever name you want to the top of the stack. For example, let's say you are working in the **dict** directory. After a while, you want to change to the **nfsd** directory. First display the stack to see what number you should push to the top:

```
dirs -l -v
```

The output is:

```
0   /usr/share/dict
1   /home/harley/archive/calculate/source/1-0.31
2   /usr/include/linux/nfsd
3   /home/harley/source/current/calculate/source/2-1.05
4   /home/harley
```

All you need to do is push directory #2 to the top of the stack:

```
pushd +2
```

Later, when you need to change to another directory, just display the directory stack again and push another name to the top. (It is important to display the stack each time, as the numbers change whenever you push.)

Deleting and adding to the directory stack is easy. To delete a name from the stack, use **popd** followed by the number. To add a name to the stack, use **pushd** as described earlier. For example, to remove name #2 from the stack, use:

```
popd +2
```

To push **/home/weedly/bin** onto the stack, use:

```
pushd /home/weedly/bin
```

Something to ponder: In Chapter 13, when we discussed the history list, I showed you how to display a list of commands and then refer to a particular command by its event number.

Can you see the similarity to using the directory stack? You display a list of directories and then refer to a particular directory by its number. (This similarity is not an accident.)

To finish this section, let me show you something totally cool. To make it easy to work with the directory stack, you can create aliases (see Chapter 13) for **dirs -v** and **pushd**. The following commands will do the job for Bash. (Remember, the Korn shell does not support the directory stack.)

```
alias d='dirs -v'
alias p=pushd
```

For the C-Shell family, you would use:

```
alias d 'dirs -v'
alias p pushd
```

Once you define these aliases, using the directory stack is simple. To display the stack, just enter:

```
d
```

To change your working directory by pushing a new name onto the stack, use a command like:

```
p /usr/lib
```

To change your working directory by pushing an existing name to the top of the stack, use a command like:

```
p +4
```

If you have a moment right now, type in these aliases and experiment a bit. As you enter the directory names, be sure to use autocompletion (see Chapter 13) to keep your typing to a minimum. If you want the aliases to be permanent, just put them in your environment file (Chapter 14). For reference, the commands we have discussed in this section are summarized in Figure 24-3.

> **HINT**
>
> If you plan on using the same set of directories over and over, put the appropriate **pushd** commands in your login file (see Chapter 14). That way, each time you log in, your directory stack will be built for you automatically.

THE MOST IMPORTANT PROGRAM OF ALL: ls

Of all the Unix tools, the most important is the **ls** program (pronounced "L-S"), used to display information about the contents of a directory. Why is **ls** so important? To answer this question, we need to consider the fundamental nature of Unix.

As I mentioned in Chapter 6, every object within a Unix system is either a file or a process. In simple terms, files hold data or allow access to resources; processes are programs that are executing. When you use Unix, we call you a user. However, Unix itself does not know about users; Unix only knows about userids (see Chapter 4). Indeed, inside a Unix system, only userids have a real identity. Thus, it is userids, not users, that log in, log out, own files, run programs, send email, and so on.

For this reason, every Unix system has an inside and an outside, with a clear boundary between the two. The inside consists of all the files and processes, along with the userids that inhabit the ghostly environment. The outside is you, the user. The boundary is defined by the physical interfaces: your keyboard, mouse, monitor, speakers, and so on. Although the brains of the operation are inside you (the user), *you* can't enter the Unix environment. Thus, you have no way of sensing directly what exists on the inside and what is happening.

To be sure, you are in charge, and your userid acts as your official representative. However, when you come right down to it you are flying blind, like a pilot in a fog who must depend on his or her instruments. You can't see any of the files or any of the processes. You can't even see your userid. The best you can do is enter commands and interpret the output. For this reason, the most important tools are the ones that act as your ears and eyes, the programs that display information about files and processes. To do so, these tools help you answer the questions: "What is there?" and "What is happening?"

In Chapter 26, I will show you how to check on the status of your processes. (The principal tool we will be using is the **ps** program.) However, as important as processes are, most of the time you just let them do their job. Most of your effort is spent thinking about and manipulating files. Since files reside in directories, the tools that enable you to look inside a directory are particularly important and, by far, the most useful of these tools is **ls**.

And that is why, out of the hundreds of command-line programs that come with every Unix and Linux system, **ls** is the most important program of them all.

LISTING THE CONTENTS OF A DIRECTORY: `ls -CrR1`

To display information about the contents of a directory, you use the **ls** (list files) program. You will find that **ls** is one of the most frequently used Unix programs. As such, it has many options to control its output. For example, on one of my Linux systems, **ls** has 59 options. (That is not a misprint.) Non-Linux systems will have fewer options but even so, you will usually find more than 30.

Obviously, no program actually *needs* 30 options, let alone 59. In our discussion, I will teach you the most important options. For more information, you can always look at the online manual (**man ls**). In this section, I am going to introduce the **ls** program and discuss the basic options. In the following sections, we will discuss the more advanced features of **ls**, at which time I will describe some of the more complex options.

Considering only the most important options, the syntax for the **ls** program is:

`ls [-aCdFglrRs1] [name...]`

where *name* is the name of a directory or file.

Before we move on, take a moment to look at the options and notice **-l** (the lowercase letter "l") and **-1** (the number "1"). These are two different options, so don't confuse them. The **-l** (letter l) option is used a lot; the **-1** (number 1) option is used rarely.

The default behavior of **ls** is to display an alphabetical list of names of files in a directory. For example, to list the files in the **/bin** directory, use:

```
ls /bin
```

If you want to look at the contents of more than one directory, you can specify more than one name. For example, to list the files in the **/bin** and the **/etc** directories, use:

```
ls /bin /etc
```

If you don't specify a directory, **ls** will — by default — display the files in your working directory. Thus, to see the files in your working directory, just enter:

```
ls
```

This two-letter word is the most frequently used command in the world of Unix.

As we discussed earlier, the **.** (dot) character is an abbreviation for the working directory. Thus, the following two commands are equivalent:

```
ls
ls .
```

More useful is the **. .** abbreviation, which stands for the parent directory. Thus, to list the files in the parent of the working directory, you would use:

```
ls ..
```

As you would expect, you can use **. .** more than once to move up the tree as many times as you want. For example, to list the files in the parent directory of the parent directory of the working directory, use:

```
ls ../..
```

When **ls** sends its output to a terminal (which is usually the case), the output will be organized into columns. The number of columns will be chosen automatically so the names fit well on your screen or window. For example, here are the first seven lines of output of a directory listing of the **/bin** directory. (On this particular system, the actual output was 20 lines.)

awk	dmesg	kill	ping	stty
bash	echo	ksh	ps	su
cat	ed	ln	pwd	tcsh
chmod	egrep	login	rm	touch
cp	env	ls	rmdir	umount
cut	ex	mkdir	sed	uname
date	false	more	sort	vi
.	.	.	.	.
.	.	.	.	.
.	.	.	.	.

Notice that the filenames are arranged alphabetically by column. That is, you read down, not across. As I explained in Chapter 23, the **/bin** directory contains many of the standard Unix programs, so the names in this directory should look familiar.

When you redirect the output of **ls** to a file or to a pipeline, **ls** writes only one filename per line. This makes it easy to process the output of **ls** with another program. (Redirection and pipelines are explained in Chapter 15.) A common example is:

```
ls | wc -l
```

The **wc -l** command counts the number of lines of input it receives. Thus, this combination of **ls** and **wc** tells you how many files you have in your working directory.

If, for some reason, you want to force **ls** to write columns to a file or pipeline, use the **-C** option (uppercase "C"), for example:

```
ls -C | less
```

If you want to force **ls** to write one line per filename to your terminal (instead of columns), use the **1** option (the number "1"):

```
ls -1
```

By default, **ls** displays filenames in alphabetical order. (More precisely, **ls** uses the order of the characters within the collating sequence for your locale. See the discussion later in the chapter.) If you want to display the names in reverse order, use the **-r** (lowercase "r") option:

```
ls -r
```

The last **ls** option we will discuss in this section is **-R** which stands for "recursive" (explained in a moment). This option tells **ls** to list information about all the subdirectories and files that reside — directly or indirectly — within the directory you name. In other words, **ls -R** displays information about an entire directory tree.

For example, let's say you want to take a look at all the files and subdirectories created by the users on your system. Just display all the descendants of the **/home** directory:

```
ls -R /home
```

Similarly, to list all the descendents of your working directory, you would use:

```
ls -R
```

Such listings tend to be very long, so you will probably want to pipe the output to **less** to display one screenful at a time. Because the output is going to a pipeline, you must include the **-C** option if you want columns:

```
ls -CR /home | less
ls -CR | less
```

When you want to use **-R**, remember that there is also a **-r** (reverse) option, so be sure to type carefully.

WHAT'S IN A NAME?

Recursive

In computer science, a RECURSIVE data structure is one that is built up from smaller data structures of the same type. Directory trees are recursive because they contain other, smaller trees.

Some directory tools, such as **ls**, have an option to process an entire directory tree, that is, all the subdirectories and files descending from a specific directory. Because such trees are considered to be recursive, the options that process them are usually named **-r** or **-R**.

COLLATING SEQUENCES, LOCALES AND ls

Earlier in the chapter, I mentioned that the default behavior of **ls** is to display an alphabetical list of names of files in a directory. The statement seems straightforward but, actually, it is not. This is because the definition of "alphabetical order" is not the same on all systems. It all depends on your collating sequence which, in turn, is defined by your locale.

As we discussed in Chapter 19, a locale is a technical specification describing the language and conventions to be used when communicating with a user from a particular culture. For example, your locale might be set to American English, British English, Dutch, Spanish, and so on. For our purposes, the most important aspect of your locale is that it defines your collating sequence, the order in which characters are sorted (explained in Chapter 19.)

The default locale for your system was set at the time your system was installed. If you use American English, your locale will be either the **C** (**POSIX**) locale based on the ASCII code, or the **en_US** locale, part of a newer international system. To check your locale, you can use the **locale** command. This will show you the value of various environment variables. The one you want to look at is **LC_COLLATE**, which specifies the name of your collating sequence, because it is your collating sequence that determines the meaning of "alphabetical order" on your system.

The **C** locale uses the same collating sequence as the ASCII code. In particular, all the uppercase letters are grouped together and all the lowercase letters are grouped together, with uppercase coming first: **ABCDEF...abcdef...** We call this the C collating sequence, because it is used with the C programming language.

The **en_US** locale, however, uses the dictionary collating sequence, in which uppercase is mixed with lowercase: **aAbBcCdDeEfF...**

When you list files with **ls**, the order in which they are displayed depends on your collating sequence. For example, let's say you have 6 files named **A**, **a**, **B**, **b**, **C** and **c**. If your locale is **C** and you list the files with **ls**, you will see:

```
A   B   C   a   b   c
```

If your locale is **en_US**, you will see:

```
a   A   b   B   c   C
```

Although this might seem like a small deal, it isn't. Your life will be easier if you use the **C** locale. You will see an important example of this later in the chapter when we discuss wildcards. So, here is what I want you to do.

Take a moment right now and enter the **locale** command. This will show you the environment variables that define your locale. If the **LC_COLLATE** variable is set to **C** or **POSIX**, that is fine. If it is set to **en_US**, I want you to change it permanently to **C**. (This is what I do on my systems.) All you have to do is add the appropriate command to your login file. The first command is for the Bourne Shell family (Bash, Korn Shell); the second command is for the C-Shell family (C-Shell, Tcsh):

```
export LC_COLLATE=C
setenv LC_COLLATE C
```

See Chapter 19 for detailed information about locales and collating sequence; see Chapter 14 for a discussion of the login file.

CHECKING FILE TYPES, PART I: ls -F

You will often want to know what types of files a directory contains. In such cases, you have three choices. You can use **ls** with the **-F** option; you can use **ls** with the **--color** option (Linux only); and you can use the **file** command. In the next three sections, we will discuss each of these techniques in turn.

When you use **ls** with the **-F** (flag) option, it displays a FLAG after the names of certain types of files. These flags are summarized in Figure 24-4. The most important are **/** (slash), which indicates a directory, and ***** (star), which indicates an executable file (such as a program or a script). In most cases, there will not be a flag. This indicates an ordinary, non-executable file.

For example, say that your working directory contains a directory named **documents**, text files named **memo** and **essay**, a program (binary file) named **spacewar**, and a named pipe **tunnel**. To display the names of the files with flags, you would use:

```
ls -F
```

The output is:

```
documents/  essay  memo  spacewar*  tunnel|
```

FLAG	MEANING
none	ordinary file: non-executable
*	ordinary file: executable
/	directory
@	symbolic link (discussed in Chapter 25)
		named pipe/FIFO (discussed in Chapter 23)

FIGURE 24-4: Flags displayed by the `ls -F` command

CHECKING FILE TYPES, PART II: `ls --color`

If you use Linux, you have an alternative to `-F`. You can use the `--color` option to use colors to indicate the various file types.* (We discussed options that start with `--` in Chapter 10.) The syntax is as follows:

`ls --color[=always|=auto|=never]` [*name...*]

where *name* is the name of a directory or file.

When `--color` is turned on, `ls` uses colors to indicate the various types of files. For example, the following command displays the names of the files in your working directory:

`ls --color`

When you use the `--color` option, there are three variations. The first variation is `--color=always`, which is the default. If you like, you can also use **yes** or **force**. Thus, the following four commands are equivalent. They all tell `ls` to use color to indicate the various types of files.

```
ls --color
ls --color=always
ls --color=yes
ls --color=force
```

The second variation is `--color=never`. This tells `ls` not to use color. You would use this if, for some reason, color is turned on and you want to turn it off. If you like, you can also use **no** or **none**. Thus, the following three commands all tell `ls` not to use color:

```
ls --color=never
ls --color=no
ls --color=none
```

At this point, you are probably wondering, why are there so many ways of making what is, essentially, a yes or no choice? The answer is that the programmers who added color support to `ls` decided that users should be able to specify either **never** or **always**, or **yes** or **no**. The other two values, **force** and **none**, were added for compatibility with other versions of `ls`.**

Normally, the special codes that create the color are mixed in with the output. This works okay when it is displayed on your monitor, but can look like gibberish when you send the output to a pipe or save it to a file. To avoid this, you can use the final variation of the `--color` option by setting it to **auto**. This tells `ls` to use colors only when the

---

*With FreeBSD-based systems, including OS X (Macintosh), you can use the `-G` option in a similar way.

**In Chapter 2, I explained that Linux is open source software, which means that anyone can look at (or even modify) the source code. It happens that the variations for the `--color` option are not well documented. However, I was able to figure out the nuances by reading the source code for the `ls` program.

If you are ever really stuck trying to understand how a program works and the documentation is inadequate or confusing, remember that nothing is magic. If you can understand even a little C, try reading the source code. It's not that hard to get the gist of what is happening, and reading other people's code is one of the best ways to improve your own programming.

output is going to a terminal. If you like, you can also use **tty** or **if-tty**. Thus, the following three commands are equivalent:

```
ls --color=auto
ls --color=tty
ls --color=if-tty
```

To see this for yourself, try the following two commands. The first command forces the use of color, which generates special codes that look like gibberish when viewed within **less**. The second command detects that the output is not going to a terminal, so it does not generate the color codes, avoiding the problem with **less**.

```
ls --color=yes /bin | less
ls --color=auto /bin | less
```

Similarly, if color is on, you will want to turn it off when you save the output to a file:

```
ls --color=auto > filelist
```

Many people like to display colors every time they use **ls**. Indeed, it is so common that, on some systems, an alias for **ls** is created automatically with the **--color** option turned on. If you are a Linux user and you always see colors when you use **ls**, even if you do not specify **--color**, chances are you are using an alias without knowing it.

To check if this is the case, you can tell the shell to ignore any aliases by typing a \ (backslash) command before the command (see Chapter 13). If the output is now devoid of color, you can conclude you were using an alias.

```
\ls
```

If you want to turn off the color permanently, just create an alias of your own as a replacement, for example:

```
alias ls='ls --color=no'
```

```
alias ls 'ls --color=no'
```

The first alias is for the Bourne Shell family: Bash, Korn Shell; the second is for the C-Shell family: Tcsh, C-Shell. To make the alias permanent, put it in your environment file. (For help with aliases, see Chapter 13. To read about the environment file, see Chapter 14.)

If you want to turn on color permanently, use one of the following aliases instead in your environment file:

```
alias ls='ls --color=yes'
```

```
alias ls 'ls --color=yes'
```

Personally, I like flags better than colors, so I suggest that you use **-F** as well as **--color**:

```
alias ls='ls -F --color=yes'
alias ls 'ls -F --color=yes'
```

> **HINT**
>
> When you use **ls** with the **--color** option, a variety of different colors are used to indicate different types of files. These colors are set by an environment variable called **LS_COLORS**. You can customize the colors by changing this variable. If this sounds like fun to you, start by reading about the **dircolors** program:
>
> ```
> man dircolors
> info dircolors
> ```
>
> The idea is to use **dircolors** to generate a command that will set **LS_COLORS** the way you want. You can then put this command in your environment file.

CHECKING FILE TYPES, PART III: file

So far, we have discussed two ways to find out what types of files a directory contains. You can use **ls** with **-F** to display a flag after the file name, or you can use **ls** with **--color** to use colors to indicate different file types (or both). A much more sophisticated way to check file types is by using the **file** command, which knows about several thousand different types of files. The syntax is:

file [*name...*]

where *name* is the name of a file or directory. There are a large number of options, but you won't need them. (If you are curious, see the man page.)

Using **file** is straightforward. Simply specify the name of one or more files or directories, for example:

```
file /etc/passwd /bin / ~/elmo.c /bin/ls
```

Here is some typical output:

```
/etc/passwd:          ASCII text
/bin:                 directory
/:                    directory
/home/harley/elmo.c:  ASCII C program text
/bin/ls:              ELF 32-bit LSB executable, Intel 80386
                      version 1 (SYSV), for GNU/Linux 2.6.9,
                      dynamically linked (uses shared libs),
                      stripped
```

The output for the first four files is easy to understand. The first file (the password file) contains plain ASCII text. The second and third files are directories. The fourth file contains C source code. The last file is an executable program. As such, **file** gives us a lot of technical information, which is useful to programmers and system administrators. In case you are interested, here is what it all means.

ELF: Executable and Linking Format, a standard file format for executable files.

32-bit: The word size.

LSB: Compiled with Least Significant Byte word ordering, used with x86 processors.

executable: An executable file.

Intel 80386: Processor architecture for which the file was compiled.

version 1 (SYSV): The version of the internal file format.

GNU/Linux 2.6.9: The version of the operating system and kernel under which the program was compiled.

dynamically linked (uses shared libs): Uses shared libraries, not statically linked.

stripped: Executable file has had the symbol table removed. This is done by the **strip** program in order to reduce the size of the executable file.

In our example, we had two directories, **/bin** and **/** (the root directory). Notice that **file** gave us information about the directory itself. If you want **file** to analyze the files within a directory, you need to specify their names. To specify all the files in a directory, you use what are called "wildcards". We will discuss wildcards later in the chapter. For now, let me give you an example. The following command uses **file** to analyze all the files in the **/etc** directory. Because the output is rather long, we display it one screenful at a time by piping it to **less**:

```
file /etc/* | less
```

KEEPING TRACK OF YOUR DISK SPACE USAGE: ls -hs, du, df, quota

There are three programs you can use to find out how much disk space your files use: **ls -s**, **du** and **quota**. We'll discuss each one in turn.

The first program is **ls** with the **-s** (size) option. This tells **ls** to preface each filename with its size in kilobytes. If you specify a directory name, **ls** will also show a total for the entire directory. Here is an example:

```
ls -s /bin
```

Below is some of the output from this command. (The actual output was 21 lines.)

```
total 8176
   4 awk      12 dmesg     16 kill      40 ping      48 stty
 712 bash     28 echo    1156 ksh       88 ps        32 su
  28 cat      60 ed        35 ln        28 pwd      352 tcsh
  44 chmod     4 egrep     32 login     48 rm        48 touch
  76 cp       24 env      100 ls        24 rmdir     72 umount
  40 cut       4 ex        36 mkdir     60 sed       24 uname
  54 date     24 false     36 more      64 sort     592 vi
    .           .           .           .            .
    .           .           .           .            .
    .           .           .           .            .
```

On the top line, you can see that the total space used by all the files in the directory is 8,176 kilobytes. The other lines show how much space the various files require. The **cat** file, for example, uses 28 kilobytes. With Linux, you can use the **-h** (human-readable) option to display the units along with the numbers. For example:

```
ls -sh /bin/cat
```

The output is:

```
28K /bin/cat
```

The next program you can use to display file size is **du** (disk usage). The syntax is:

```
du [-achs] [name...]
```

where *name* is the name of a directory or file.

When you specify the name of one or more files, **du** will show you the amount of storage used by those files. Here is an example that displays the size of the password file (described in Chapter 11):

```
du /etc/passwd
```

On most systems, the output will be shown as 1K units. For example, the following output tells you that the password file takes up 8K bytes of disk space:

```
8        /etc/passwd
```

To display the units along with the number, use the **-h** (human-readable) option:

```
du -h /etc/passwd
```

This changes the output to:

```
8.0K    /etc/passwd
```

You might be wondering, why does the password file — which is a usually small file — use 8K of disk space. After all, 8K can hold up to 8,192 (8 x 1024) characters, a lot more than the data within the password file. It happens that, for this particular filesystem, storage space on the disk is allotted in chunks of 8K. Thus, even though the file is small, it takes up 8K on the disk. (See the discussion on allocation units later in the chapter.)

As I mentioned, most versions of **du** display output in terms of 1K units. Some systems, however, use 512-byte units. (The unit size is documented on the **du** man page.) This is the case, for instance, with Solaris. On such systems, there will usually be a **-k** option to force **du** to use 1K units. For example, on a Solaris system, you can use either of the following commands to use 1K units to display the disk space used by the password file:

```
du -k /etc/passwd
du -hk /etc/passwd
```

So far, we have used **du** to display the disk space used by specific files. Most often, however, **du** is used to find out how much space is used by all the files in a particular directory tree. If you do not specify a name, **du** will assume you want your working directory. For example, the following command starts from your working directory and displays the name of each subdirectory, sub-subdirectory, sub-sub-subdirectory, and so on. Beside each name **du** shows the total disk space taken up by the files in that directory. At the very end there is a grand total. (Because the output is lengthy, I have piped it to **less** to display one screenful at a time.)

```
du -h | less
```

To see how much disk space is used by all your files, specify your home directory:

```
du -h ~ | less
```

The following commands show how much disk space is used by all the files under **/usr/bin** and all the files under **/etc**:

```
du -h /usr/bin /etc | less
```

If you use the **-s** (sum) option, **du** will display only the total, which cuts out a lot of extraneous output. This is, in my opinion, the most useful way to use **du**. Here are two examples. The first example displays the total disk space used by your personal files (starting from your home directory):

```
du -hs ~
```

The second example does the same for the **/usr/bin**, **/bin**, and **/etc** directories. The first command is for the Bourne Shell family (Bash, Korn Shell). The second command is for the C-Shell family (Tcsh, C-Shell).

```
du -hs /usr/bin /bin /etc 2> /dev/null
(du -hs /usr/bin /bin /etc > /dev/tty) >& /dev/null
```

These commands are a bit complicated, so let's take a moment to discuss them. You will notice that I have thrown away the standard error by redirecting it to the bit bucket (see Chapter 15). I did this because, as **du** processes the directories, it may find subdirectories it does not have permission to read. Each time this happens, **du** will display an error message. Throwing away standard error keeps these messages from being displayed.

The exact method used to redirect standard error depends on which shell you are using. Hence, there is one command for the Bourne Shell family and another command for the C-Shell family. (All the details are explained in Chapter 15.)

Moving on, the **-c** (count) option displays a grand total at the end of the output. This option is most useful when combined with **-s** and **-h**. Here is an example. Once again, the first command is for the Bourne Shell family; the second is for the C-Shell family:

```
du -csh /usr/bin /bin /etc 2> /dev/null
(du -csh /usr/bin /bin /etc > /dev/tty) >& /dev/null
```

This combination of options (**-csh**) is particularly easy to remember because, coincidently, it happens to be the name of the C-Shell program.

Finally, if you use the **-a** (all) option, **du** shows the size of every directory and file it processes. This can make for a very long listing, but it gives you an exact description of how your disk space is being used. For example, to display all the information about disk storage for your personal files, specify your home directory:

```
du -ah ~ | less
```

The next disk storage program is **df**. (The name stands for "disk free-space"). This program shows you how much disk space is used by each filesystem, and how much is available. The **df** program has various options but, generally, you won't need them. The only option I want to mention is **-h**, which displays human-readable output by using storage units of kilobytes, megabytes and gigabytes instead of blocks. Try each of these commands on your system and see which you prefer:

```
df
df -h
```

Here is some typical Linux output from the first command. In this example, the root file system (**/**), which contains almost all the data on the system, has used only 9% of its allocated space. A smaller filesystem, **/boot**, has used 16% of its space.

```
Filesystem     1K-blocks      Used   Available   Use%
/dev/hda1       36947496    312446    31915940    9%  /
/dev/hdd1          99043     14385       79544   16%  /boot
tmpfs             192816         0      192816    0%  /dev/shm
```

So you can compare, here is the output from the second command:

```
Filesystem     Size    Used  Available  Use%
/dev/hda1       36G    3.0G        31G    9%  /
/dev/hdd1       97M     15M        78M   16%  /boot
tmpfs          189M       0       189M    0%  /dev/shm
```

The final disk storage program is **quota**. If you share a Unix or Linux system, there is a good chance your system administrator has imposed a quota on how much disk space each userid is allowed to use. If you exceed your quota, you will not be allowed to use any more disk file space until you delete some files.

If your system has such a quota, you can use the **quota** program to check on your usage and limits:

```
quota
```

To display extra information, use the **-v** (verbose) option:

```
quota -v
```

Note: The four programs **ls -s**, **du**, **df** and **quota** estimate storage usage in different ways, so don't be surprised if the numbers vary somewhat.

HINT

If you are using a shared system, it is important to remember that you are *sharing*. From time to time, use **du** to see how much disk space you are using. If you have files that you do not need, especially large files, be considerate and remove them.

Don't think of it as being forced to live within your quota. Think of it as being a good neighbor.

HOW BIG IS A FILE? BLOCKS AND ALLOCATION UNITS: dumpe2fs

Disk storage is measured in kilobytes, megabytes and gigabytes. One KILOBYTE (1K) is 1,024 (2^{10}) bytes; one MEGABYTE is 1,048,576 (2^{20}) bytes; one GIGABYTE is 1,073,741,824 (2^{30}) bytes. Within a text file, one byte holds a single character. For example, 100 characters require 100 bytes of disk storage.

We have already discussed how to use **ls -s** and **du** to display the amount of disk space used by a file. Before we move on, there is an important point I want you to understand. The amount of disk space used by a file is not the same as the amount of data in the file. Here is why.

Within a filesystem, space is allotted in fixed-size chunks called BLOCKS, which are either 512 bytes, 1K, 2K or 4K depending on the filesystem. The minimum amount of space that can be allocated for a file is a single block. Let's consider a filesystem that uses 1K (1024-byte) blocks. (This is typical for Linux.) A file that contains only 1 byte of data requires a full block. If the file grows to become a single byte larger than one block, it will require a second block. Thus, a file containing up to 1024 bytes of data will require 1 block. A file containing 1025 bytes of data will require 2 blocks.

Question: How many blocks will a 1,000,000-byte file require?

Answer: Assuming the block size is 1024 bytes, 1,000,000 divided by 1024 is a bit less than 976.6. Thus, a 1,000,000-byte file will take up 977 blocks. (This works out to 1,000,448 bytes.)

So far, we have talked about how data is organized within a filesystem. But what happens when the files are written to a disk or other storage medium? For reasons of efficiency, disk storage space is also allotted in fixed-size chunks, which are called ALLOCATION UNITS or CLUSTERS. The size of an allocation unit depends on the filesystem and the storage device. For example, on one of my Linux systems, the block size is 1K. However, disk allocation units are 8K. Thus, a file that requires a single byte actually takes up 8K of disk space.

Question: A file contains 8,500 bytes of data. How many blocks does it require? How much disk space will it take up?

Answer: The file contains 8500/1024 = 8.3K bytes of data. Assuming the block size is 1K, the file will require 9 blocks. Assuming disk space is allotted in allocation units of 8K, the file will take up 2 allocation units, or 16K bytes of disk space.

How do you determine the size of a block and an allocation unit on your system? We'll start with allocation units because the method is simpler. Our strategy is to create a very tiny file and then see how much space it takes up on the disk. This will be the size of a single allocation unit.

The first step is to create a very small file. The following commands will do the job:

```
cat > temp
X
^D
```

To start, enter the **cat** command (Chapter 16) to read input from the keyboard and redirect it to a file named **temp**. Note: If **temp** does not exist, the shell will create it for you. If **temp** already exists, the shell will replace it.

Next, type a line that consists of a single character. In this case, I typed the letter "X" and pressed <Return>. This data will be written to the file **temp**.

Finally, press **^D** (Ctrl-D) to indicate the end of the data by sending the **eof** signal (see Chapter 7). We now have a very small text file consisting of two characters: an "X", followed by a newline.

Enter the **ls -l** command (explained later in the chapter) to display the amount of data contained in the file:

```
ls -l temp
```

The output is:

```
-rw-rw-r-- 1 harley staff 2 Aug 10 11:45 temp
```

The file size is displayed just before the date. As you can see, the file contains 2 bytes of data. Now use the **du** program (discussed earlier in the chapter) to see how much disk space the file takes up:

```
du -h temp
```

Here is the output:

```
8.0K    temp
```

As you can see, in our example, the sample file takes up 8K of storage space on the disk, even though it contains only 2 bytes of data. Thus, we can conclude that the allocation unit for this system is 8K.

To conclude our experiment, use the **rm** program (Chapter 25) to remove the temporary file:

```
rm temp
```

Finding the block size for the filesystem is tricky. Although some file programs, such as **df**, will display a "block size", this is not the official block size of the filesystem: it is just a convenient unit used by the program. The exact method for finding the definitive block size depends on which operating system you are using. With Linux, you use the **dumpe2fs** program; with Solaris, you use **fstyp -v**; and with FreeBSD, you use

dumpfs. As an example, I'll show you how it works with Linux. (If you need more details on any of these programs, check with the online manual.)

As I explained above, all the data within a filesystem is organized into blocks. One of the blocks, called the SUPERBLOCK, is a special data area that holds crucial information about the filesystem itself. With Linux, you can examine the contents of the superblock by using the **dumpe2fs** program. In particular, it is possible to display the block size used by the filesystem. Here is how to do it.

1. Find out the name of the special file that represents the file system, for example, **/dev/hda1**. To do so, you can use the **df** command (discussed earlier in the chapter).

2. To run **dumpe2fs**, you must be superuser. Use the **su** command to change to superuser (see Chapter 6).

3. Enter the **dumpe2fs** command, followed by the name of the special file. This command will display a lot of data from the superblock. The number you want is on a line that contains the string "Block size". So all you have to do is run the **dumpe2fs** command and grep the output for "Block size". Here is an example:

```
dumpe2fs /dev/hda1 | grep "Block size"
```

Note: If the shell can't find the **dumpe2fs** program, you will have to specify the full pathname. The program will be in **/sbin**:

```
/sbin/dumpe2fs /dev/hda1 | grep "Block size"
```

Here is some sample output. In this case, you can see that the filesystem block size is 1K (1024 bytes):

```
Block size: 1024
```

If you want to take a minute to look at all the information from the superblock, pipe the output of **dumpe2fs** to **less**:

```
dumpe2fs /dev/hda1 | less
```

When you are finished, use the **exit** command to log out as superuser (see Chapter 6).

GLOBBING WITH WILDCARDS

Whenever you type a command that uses filenames as arguments, you can specify multiple filenames by using certain metacharacters referred to as WILDCARDS. As you may remember from Chapter 13, a metacharacter is any character that is interpreted by the shell as having a special meaning. Wildcards have a special meaning when you use them within a filename. Here is an example.

Let's say you want to list the names of all the files in your working directory that start with the letter "h". You can use:

```
ls h*
```

In this example, the ***** (star) is a metacharacter that matches any sequence of zero or more characters.

At first glance, wildcards look a lot like the regular expression metacharacters we discussed in Chapter 20. In fact, wildcards are simpler. Moreover, they are used for only one purpose: to match a set of filenames when you type a command. Figure 24-5 shows the basic wildcards and their meanings. Before you move on, take a moment and compare this table with the ones that summarize regular expressions in Chapter 20.

When you use a wildcard, the shell interprets the pattern and replaces it with the appropriate filenames before running the command. For example, let's say you enter:

```
ls h*
```

The shell replaces **h*** with all the filenames in your working directory that begin with the letter **h**. Then the shell runs the **ls** command. For instance, let's say your working directory contains the following six files:

```
a  data-old  data-new  harley  h1  h2  z
```

If you enter the command above, the shell changes it to:

```
ls h1 h2 harley
```

You can, of course, use more than one pattern in the same command:

```
ls h* data*
```

In our example, the shell would change the command to:

```
ls h1 h2 harley data-old data-new
```

Using wildcards to specify files is known formally by different names, depending on which shell you are using. With Bash, it is called PATHNAME EXPANSION; with the Korn shell, it is called FILENAME GENERATION; with the C-Shell and Tcsh, it is called FILENAME SUBSTITUTION. When the shell performs the actual substitution, it is called GLOBBING. Sometimes, the word GLOB is used as a verb, as in, "Unless you set the **noglob** variable, the C-Shell globs automatically."

SYMBOL	MEANING
*	match any sequence of zero or more characters
?	match any single character
[*list*]	match any character in *list*
[^*list*]	match any character not in *list*
{*string1* | *string2*...}	match one of the specified strings

FIGURE 24-5: Summary of wildcards used to specify filenames

Whenever you type a command that uses filenames as arguments, you can use wildcards to match multiple filenames. This table shows the various wildcards and how they are used. Note: When you type a pathname, you cannot match a / character; it must be typed explicitly.

As I mentioned, when wildcards are globbed by the shell, the wildcards are changed to actual filenames before the arguments are passed to the program. If you use a pattern that does not match any files, the shell will display an appropriate message. For example, let's say your working directory contains the files listed above, and you enter the following command:

`ls v*`

This command lists all the files that begin with the letter "v". Since there are no such files, `ls` displays an error message:

`ls: v*: No such file or directory`

Now that you understand the main concepts, let's cover the wildcards in detail, one at a time. The most important wildcard, `*` (star), matches zero or more characters. The `*` wildcard will match any character except `/` (slash) which, as you know, is used as a delimiter within pathnames. (If you want to specify a `/`, you must type it yourself.) For example, the following wildcard specifications match patterns as indicated:

`Ha*`   filenames that begin with "Ha"
`Ha*y`   filenames that begin with "Ha" and end with "y"
`Ha*l*y`   filenames that begin with "Ha", contain an "l", and end with "y"

The `?` (question mark) wildcard matches any single character except `/`. For example:

`d?`   2-character filenames that begin with "d"
`??`   any 2-character filenames
`?*y`   filenames with at least 2 characters, ending with "y"

You can specify a list of characters by using `[` and `]` (square brackets) to enclose the list. This represents a single instance of any of the specified characters. For example:

`spacewar.[co]`   either "spacewar.c" or "spacewar.o"
`[Hh]*`   filenames that begin with either "H" or "h"

To match any character that is not in a list, put a `^` (circumflex) at the beginning of the list. For example, the following command displays the names of all the files in your working directory that do not begin with the letters "H" or "h":

`ls [^Hh]*`

Within square brackets, you can specify a range of characters by using a `-` (dash). For example, the pattern `[0-9]` matches any of the digits 0 through 9. Using a range with letters works the same way, but you must be careful: ranges of letters are expanded according to the collating sequence that is used with your locale. (See the discussion earlier in the chapter.) Consider the following two examples:

`[a-z]*`   filenames that begin with a lowercase letter
`[a-zA-Z]*[0-9]`   filenames that begin with an upper- or lowercase letter and end with a numeral

If you are using the C collating sequence (**C** locale), the order of the letters is **ABCDEF**... **abcdef**... Thus, the examples above will work the way you expect. However, if you use the dictionary collating sequence (**en_US** locale), the examples will not work properly because the order of the letters is **aAbBcCdDeEfF**...**zZ**.

More specifically, with the C collating sequence, **[a-z]** matches any of the lowercase letters, which is what you would want. With the dictionary collating sequence, **[a-z]** matches any of the upper- or lowercase letters except "Z", not at all what you want. Similarly, with the C collating sequence, **[A-Z]** matches any of the uppercase letters. With the dictionary collating sequence, **[A-Z]** matches any upper- or lowercase letter except "a", again not what you want.

For this reason, I strongly suggest you use the C collating sequence, not the dictionary collating. To do so, you must make sure the LC_COLLATE environment variable is set to **C** not **en_US**. (There are instructions earlier in the chapter.)

If, for some reason, you do decide to stick with the dictionary collating sequence, you won't be able to use **[a-z]** or **[A-Z]** as wildcards. However, there are several predefined character classes you can use instead. I have listed the most important ones in Figure 24-6. For a detailed discussion of predefined character classes, see Chapter 20.

Here is an example. You want to display the names of the very oldest Unix programs. Most of these names consist of two lowercase letters, like **ls** and **rm**. The best places to look for such programs are **/bin** and **/usr/bin** (see Chapter 23). If you use the **C** locale, you can use the following command. Try it on your system and see what you find.

```
ls /bin/[a-z][a-z] /usr/bin/[a-z][a-z]
```

If you use the **en_US** locale, you will get spurious results if there happen to be any 2-letter names that contain an uppercase letter. In this case, the correct command would be:

```
ls /bin/[[:lower:]][[:lower:]] /usr/bin/[[:lower:]][[:lower:]]
```

You can see why I recommend always using the C collating sequence.

So far, we have talked about the three different types of wildcards we use with filename expansion: ***** to match zero or more characters, **?** to match any single character, and **[ ]**

CLASS	MEANING	SIMILAR TO...
[[:lower:]]	lowercase letters	[a-z]
[[:upper:]]	uppercase letters	[A-Z]
[[:digit:]]	digits	[0-9]
[[:alnum:]]	upper- and lowercase letters, numbers	[A-Za-z0-9]
[[:alpha:]]	upper- and lowercase letters	[A-Za-z]

FIGURE 24-6: Wildcards: Predefined character classes

Wildcards can use ranges to match any character from a specific set. The most common ranges are **[a-z]** *to match a lowercase letter, and* **[A-Z]** *to match an uppercase letter. As explained in the text, these ranges work with the* **C** *locale, but not with the* **en_US** *locale. As an alternative, you can use predefined character classes, the most important of which are listed in this table. For more details, see Chapter 20.*

to define a list. The final wildcard pattern we need to discuss allows you to specify more than one character string and then match each of the strings in turn. To do so, you use **{** and **}** (brace brackets) to enclose a list of patterns, separated by commas. For example:

```
{harley,weedly}
```

Important: Do not put spaces before or after the commas.

When you use brace brackets in this way, it tells the shell to form a separate filename using each pattern in turn. We call this BRACE EXPANSION. Brace expansion is available only with Bash, the Tcsh and the C-Shell (not with the Korn Shell or the FreeBSD Shell). When a command is processed, brace expansion is done before filename expansion.

Here is an example. Say that you want to list the names of all the files in the directories **/home/harley**, **/home/weedly** and **/home/tln**. You could specify all three directory names explicitly:

```
ls /home/harley /home/weedly /home/tln
```

With brace expansion, the command is simpler:

```
ls /home/{harley,weedly,tln}
```

Here is a second example. You want to combine the contents of the files **olddata1**, **olddata2**, **olddata3**, **newdata1**, **newdata2** and **newdata3**, and store the output in a new file named **master**. Use any of the following commands:

```
cat olddata1 olddata2 olddata3 newdata1 newdata2 newdata3 > master
cat {old,new}data{1,2,3} > master
cat {old,new}data[1-3] > master
```

(The **cat** program, which combines files, is discussed in Chapter 16. The **>** character, which redirects the standard output, is discussed in Chapter 15.)

Brace expansion is important because it can be used in two ways. First, as you have seen, it will match a set of files that have common names. Second, when you are creating new files, it can also be used to describe file names that do not exist. For example, let's say your home directory contains a subdirectory named **work**. The following two **mkdir** commands both create four new subdirectories in the **work** directory. Notice how convenient it is to use brace expansion:

```
mkdir ~/work/essays ~/work/photos ~/work/bin ~/work/music
mkdir ~/work/{essays,photos,bin,music}
```

One last example. In Chapter 25, you will learn how to use the **touch** command to create empty files quickly. Let's say you want to create the following five new files:

```
dataold   datanew   databackup   datamaster   datafinal
```

Using brace expansion, the command is:

```
touch data{old,new,backup,master,final}
```

WHAT'S IN A NAME?

Wildcard, Globbing

The term "wildcard" comes from poker and other card games in which certain cards are designated as being "wild". In a poker game, wild cards can take on a variety of different values.

"Globbing" refers to expanding a pattern with wildcards into a list of filenames. The term "glob" dates back to the very first Unix shell, even before the Bourne Shell (see Chapter 11). At the time, wildcard expansion was performed by a separate program (**/etc/glob**) called by the shell. No one knows why the program was named **glob**, so you can make up your own reason.

Within the Unix community, the idea of globbing is so common that the idea of globbing is used by geeks in everyday discourse. For example, say that one geek text messages to another geek, "Which is your favorite Star Trek show, ST:TOS, ST:TNG or ST:DS9?" The second geek might reply, "I don't watch ST:*".

In a similar vein, you will sometimes see the name UN*X used to represent any type of Unix or Linux. This dates back to the 1970s, when AT&T was claiming that UNIX was a registered trademark, and no one could use the name without their permission. For example, the AT&T lawyers said that UNIX was an adjective, not a noun and that one must never refer to "UNIX", only "the UNIX operating system". In response to such silliness, many Unix geeks started to write UN*X to refer to any type of Unix.

DOT FILES (HIDDEN FILES): `ls -a`

By default, the **ls** program will not display any filenames that begin with a . (dot) character. Thus, if you use a file that you don't want to see each time you use **ls**, all you have to do is give it a name that begins with a dot. As we discussed in Chapter 14, such files are called DOTFILES or HIDDEN FILES. Most of the time, dotfiles are used by programs to hold configuration data or initialization commands. For example, all shells use dotfiles, as does the **vi**/Vim editor (see Figure 24-7).

To display the names of hidden files, you use **ls** with the **-a** (all files) option. For example, to see the names of your hidden files, change to your home directory and use **ls -a**:

```
cd
ls -a
```

Most likely, you will also see some directory names that start with a dot. Such directories are also hidden and you will not see them with **ls** unless you use the **-a** option.

When you use **-a**, you see *all* your files. Unfortunately, there is no option to display only dotfiles. However, by using wildcards, you can restrict the list of filenames to show only the dotfiles. For example, the following command displays the names of all the files in the working directory whose names begin with a . followed by a letter:

```
ls .[a-zA-Z]*
```

The following command is a bit complex but much more useful. It also displays dotfiles. However, it omits both . and .. as well as the contents of any hidden directories:

```
ls -d .??*
```

FILENAME	USE
`.bash_login`	Login file: Bash
`.bash_logout`	Logout file: Bash
`.bash_profile`	Login file: Bash
`.bashrc`	Environment file: Bash
`.cshrc`	Environment file: C-Shell, Tcsh
`.exrc`	Initialization file: **vi**, Vim
`.history`	History file: Bash, Korn Shell, C-Shell, Tcsh
`.login`	Login file: C-Shell, Tcsh
`.logout`	Logout file: C-Shell, Tcsh
`.profile`	Login file: Bash, Korn Shell, Bourne Shell
`.tcshrc`	Environment file: Tcsh
`.vimrc`	Initialization file: Vim

FIGURE 24-7: Dotfiles used by the shells and by vi/Vim

*Any file whose name begins with a . (dot) is called a dotfile or a hidden file. The **ls** program does not display the names of dotfiles unless you use the **-a** option.*

*Dotfiles are most often used by programs to hold configuration data or initialization commands. Here, as examples, are the dotfiles used by the various shells and by the **vi**/Vim text editor.*

Figure 24-7 lists the names of the standard dotfiles we have already covered (Chapter 14 for the shell, Chapter 22 for **vi** and Vim). These are files that, one day, you may want to change. Most likely you will find a lot of other dotfiles in your home directory. Unless you know what you are doing, however, you should leave them alone.

HINT

Many of the dotfiles in your home directory are important. Before you edit one of these files, it is a good idea to make a copy. To do so, use the **cp** program (Chapter 25), for example:

```
cp .bash_profile .bash_profile.bak
```

If you accidentally ruin the file, you will be able to restore it. To do so, use the **mv** command (also Chapter 25), for example:

```
mv .bash_profile.bak .bash_profile
```

LONG DIRECTORY LISTINGS: `ls -dhltu`

When you use the **ls** program, there are several options that will display a variety of information along with the names. The most useful of these options is **-l**, which stands for "long listing":

```
ls -l
```

If the listing is so long that it scrolls off your screen, you can pipe it to **less**:

```
ls -l | less
```

Here is some sample output, which we will analyze:

```
total 32
-rw-rw-r--  1 harley staff  2255 Apr  2 21:52 application
drwxrwxr-x  2 harley staff  4096 Oct  5 11:40 bin
drwxrwxr-x  2 harley staff  4096 Oct  5 11:41 music
-rw-rw-r--  1 harley staff   663 Sep 26 20:03 partylist
```

On the far right you see the names of four files: **application**, **bin**, **music** and **partylist**. On the far left, at the beginning of the line, there is a one-letter indicator showing you the type of file. We'll talk more about this in a moment. For now, I'll mention that a **-** (dash) indicates a regular file; a **d** indicates a directory. Thus, **application** and **partylist** are regular files; **bin** and **music** are directories.

To the left of the filenames there is a time and date. This is called the MODIFICATION TIME. It shows when the file was last changed. In our example, the file **application** was last changed on April 2 at 9:52 PM. (Remember, Unix uses a 24-hour clock; see Chapter 8 and Appendix F.)

As an alternative, you can use **-u** with **-l** to display the ACCESS TIME instead of the modification time. The access time shows the last time the file was read. For example:

```
ls -lu application
```

The output is below. As you can see from the output above, the file **application** was last changed on April 2 at 9:52 PM. However, as you can see from the output below, the file was last read on April 11 at 3:45 PM:

```
-rw-rw-r--  1 harley staff  2255 Apr 11 15:45 application
```

If you want to display the files sorted by time, use the **-t** option:

```
ls -lt
ls -ltu
```

Here is the output from the first command, displaying the files from newest (most recently modified) to oldest (least recently modified):

```
total 32
drwxrwxr-x  2 harley staff  4096 Oct  5 11:41 music
drwxrwxr-x  2 harley staff  4096 Oct  5 11:40 bin
-rw-rw-r--  1 harley staff   663 Sep 26 20:03 partylist
-rw-rw-r--  1 harley staff  2255 Apr  2 21:52 application
```

If you combine **-t** with the **-r** (reverse) option, **ls** displays the files from oldest to newest:

```
ls -lrt
ls -lrtu
```

For example:

```
total 32
-rw-rw-r--   1 harley staff   2255 Apr  2 21:52 application
-rw-rw-r--   1 harley staff    663 Sep 26 20:03 partylist
drwxrwxr-x   2 harley staff   4096 Oct  5 11:40 bin
drwxrwxr-x   2 harley staff   4096 Oct  5 11:41 music
```

HINT

Let's say your working directory has a great many files, and you want to display information about the most recently modified files. The easiest way is to display the files in reverse, time-sorted order:

```
ls -lrt
```

To display the most recently accessed files, use:

```
ls -lrtu
```

Because you are working in a large directory, most of the file names will scroll off the screen. However, it doesn't matter, because all you care about is the last few lines.

Returning to our discussion, at the very top of the listing, **ls** shows the total number of filesystem blocks used by all the files being listed. In this case, the two files and two directories use a total of 32 blocks. (For an explanation of filesystem blocks, see the discussion earlier in the chapter.)

To the left of the date, you see the size of each file in bytes. If the file is a text file, each byte will hold a single character of data. For example, the file **partylist** is a text file that contains 663 characters, including the newline at the end of each line of text. Similarly, the file **application** contains 2,255 bytes of data, including newlines. It is important to realize that the number you see here shows the actual amount of data contained in the file, not the amount of storage space taken up by the file. If you want to find out how much space the file occupies, you must use the **du** or **ls -s** commands, discussed earlier in the chapter.

By default, **ls** displays file sizes in bytes, which can be confusing when the numbers are large. To display larger numbers in units of kilobytes (K) or megabytes (M), use the **-h** (human-readable) option:

```
ls -hl
```

For example, the following output shows the same files as above:

```
total 32
-rw-rw-r--   1 harley staff   2.3K Apr  2 21:52 application
drwxrwxr-x   2 harley staff   4.0K Oct  5 11:40 bin
drwxrwxr-x   2 harley staff   4.0K Oct  5 11:41 music
-rw-rw-r--   1 harley staff    663 Sep 26 20:03 partylist
```

Notice that the two directories each use 4,096 bytes, which is exactly 4K. This is because this particular system uses allocation units of 4K, and every directory starts out with a minimum of 1 allocation unit. (Allocation units are discussed earlier in the chapter.) It is important to remember that the number 4K refers to the size of the directory itself, not the contents of the directory. Although we often talk about a directory as if it "contains" a number of files, it's only a metaphor. Directories take up only a small amount of storage space because they contain information *about* files, not the files themselves.

At the far left of each line, the first character shows you the type of file. There are several possibilities, which are summarized in Figure 24-8. As I mentioned, the most important characters are **–** (dash) which indicates an ordinary file and **d** which indicates a directory. Although the **–** character identifies an ordinary file, it doesn't tell you anything about the file. If you want more information, you can use the **file** command (described earlier in the chapter). For example, in the listing above you can see that **partylist** is an ordinary file. If you want more information, enter:

file partylist

The output is:

partylist: ASCII text

Returning to the file indicators, the less common characters are **l** (lowercase letter "l") for a symbolic link (Chapter 25), **p** for a named pipe (Chapter 23), and **b** and **c** for special files (Chapter 23). When it comes to special files, Unix distinguishes between two types of devices. Devices such as terminals that process one byte of data at a time are called CHARACTER DEVICES. Devices such as disks that process a fixed number of bytes at a time are called BLOCK DEVICES. The letter **c** identifies special files that represent character devices; **b** identifies special files that represent block devices.

To the left of the file size are two names, the userid and group of the owner of the file and the group to which that userid belongs. In our example, all the files are owned by userid **harley**, which is in the group named **staff**. (Some versions of Unix do not show the group unless you use the **-g** option.) To the left of the userid is a number that

INDICATOR	MEANING
–	ordinary file
d	directory
l	symbolic link
b	special file (block device)
c	special file (character device)
p	named pipe/FIFO

FIGURE 24-8: File type indicators used by `ls -l`

When you use **ls** *with the* **-l** *(long listing) option, information about each file is displayed on a separate line. At the far left of the line,* **ls** *displays a single character indicating the type of file. Here is a list of the most important indicators.*

shows how many links there are to this file. Finally, the string of nine characters at the far left (just to the right of the initial character) shows the file permissions. We will discuss these four concepts — file ownership, groups, links, and permissions — in Chapter 25, at which time we will look at the output of the **ls -l** program in more detail.

When you specify the name of a directory, **ls** lists information about the files in that directory. For example, to display a long listing about all the files in the **/bin** directory, you would use:

```
ls -l /bin | less
```

If you want information about the directory itself, use the **-d** (directory) option. This tells **ls** to consider directories as files in their own right. For example, to display information about the **/bin** directory itself, not the contents of **/bin**, you would use:

```
ls -dl /bin
```

Here is some sample output:

```
drwxr-xr-x 2 root root 4096 Dec 21 2008 /bin
```

This is a handy option to remember when you are listing a number of files, some of which are directories, and **ls** displays unwanted information about the contents of every directory. When you use **-d**, it tells **ls** not to look inside any of the directories.

The information displayed by the **-l** option can be used in many imaginative ways by piping the output to a filter (see Chapters 16-19). Here are two examples to give you some ideas. To list the names of all the files that were last modified in September, you can use:

```
ls -l | grep Sep
```

To count how many files were last modified in September, use:

```
ls -l | grep Sep | wc -l
```

USEFUL ALIASES FOR USING ls

The **ls** program is used *a lot*. Indeed, as I mentioned earlier, I consider **ls** to be the most useful program in the entire Unix toolbox. For this reason, it is common to define aliases to make it easy to use **ls** with the most commonly used options. Once you find aliases you like, you can make them permanent by putting them in your environment file. (For a detailed discussion of aliases, see Chapter 13; for information about the environment file, see Chapter 14.)

There are two types of aliases you can use with **ls**. First, there are aliases that redefine **ls** itself. For example, let's say that, whenever you use **ls**, you always want the **-F** and **--color** options. Just use one of the following aliases. The first one is for the Bourne shell family; the second one is for the C-Shell family:

```
alias ls='ls -F --color=auto'
alias ls 'ls -F --color=auto'
```

The second type of alias makes up a new name for a particular variation of **ls**. Here are the aliases for the Bourne Shell family:

```
alias ll='ls -l'
alias la='ls -a'
alias lla='ls -la'
alias ldot='ls -d .??*'
```

For the C-Shell family:

```
alias ll   'ls -l'
alias la   'ls -a'
alias lla 'ls -la'
alias ldot 'ls -d .??*'
```

These aliases make it easy to display a long listing (**ll**), a list of all files (**la**), a long listing of all files (**lla**), and a listing of only dotfiles (**ldot**). For example, once you have defined the **ll** alias, you can display a long listing of the **/bin** directory by using:

```
ll /bin
```

To display a long listing of your working directory, including dotfiles, use:

```
lla
```

To display only your dotfiles, use:

```
ldot
```

My suggestion is to put these aliases in your environment file and spend some time using them. Once you get used to these aliases, you won't want to do without them.

DISPLAYING A DIRECTORY TREE: tree

If you use Linux, there is a powerful tool called **tree** that will draw you a picture of any part of the filesystem. The syntax is:

tree [**-adfFilrst**] [**-L level**] [*directory...*]

where *level* is the depth to descend into the tree, and *directory* is the name of a directory.

To see how it works, list the tree for the entire filesystem. Because the tree will be huge, you will need to pipe it to **less**. When you get tired of reading, press **q** to quit.

```
tree / | less
```

Most of the time, you would use **tree** to visualize your own files. To display your part of the filesystem, use:

```
tree ~ | less
```

Here is some typical output:

```
/home/harley
|-- bin
|   |-- funky
|   `-- spacewar
`-- essays
    |-- history
    |   |-- crusades
    |   `-- renaissance
    `-- literature
        |-- kafka
        `-- tolstoy
```

In this example, the home directory has two subdirectories, **bin** and **essays**. The **bin** directory contains two files. The **essays** directory contains two subdirectories of its own, **history** and **literature**, both of which contain two files.

The **tree** program has a lot of options. I'll explain the most important ones, so you can experiment. To start, some of the options are the same as we use with **ls**. The **-a** option displays all files, including dotfiles; **-s** displays the size of each file as well as the name; **-F** displays a flag showing the type of file; **-r** sorts the output in reverse order; **-t** sorts the output by modification time.

In addition, **tree** has its own options. The most useful is **-d** which displays directories only, for example:

tree -d ~ | less

Using the same tree structure as above, the output is:

```
/home/harley
|-- bin
`-- essays
    |-- history
    `-- literature
4 directories
```

The **-f** option displays full pathnames, for example:

tree -df ~ | less

The sample output is:

```
/home/harley
|-- /home/harley/bin
`-- /home/harley/essays
    |-- /home/harley/history
    `-- /home/harley/literature
4 directories
```

The **-i** option omits the indentation lines. This is useful when you want to collect a set of pathnames:

```
tree -dfi ~ | less
```

The sample output is:

```
/home/harley
/home/harley/bin
/home/harley/essays
/home/harley/history
/home/harley/literature
4 directories
```

To limit the depth of the tree, you can use the **-L** (limit) option, followed by a number. This tells **tree** to only descend that many levels into the tree, for example:

```
tree -d -L 2 /home
```

Finally, the **-l** option tells **tree** to follow all symbolic links (see Chapter 25) as if they were real directories.

To conclude this section, here is an example of how you can use **tree** to find all the directories named **bin** in the entire filesystem. The idea is to start from the root directory (**/**), limit the search to directories only (**-d**), display full pathnames (**-f**), omit indentation lines (-i), and then send the output to **grep** (Chapter 19) to select only those lines that end with **/bin**. The command is:

```
tree -dif / | grep '/bin$'
```

Here is some sample output:

```
/bin
/home/harley/bin
/usr/bin
/usr/local/bin
/usr/X11R6/bin
```

FILE MANAGERS

In this chapter, we have discussed the basic operations you can use with directories: creating, deleting, moving and renaming. We have also discussed how to change your working directory and how to use **ls** to display the contents of a directory in various ways. In Chapter 25, we will cover analogous topics with respect to ordinary files. In particular, I will show you how to create, copy, rename, move and delete files, and how to use **ls** to display information about files.

In both chapters, we use text-based commands that we enter at the shell prompt, the standard Unix CLI (command-line interface) we first discussed in Chapter 6. As powerful as the directory and file commands are, there is an alternative I want you to know about.

Instead of typing commands, you can use a FILE MANAGER, a program designed to help you manipulate directories and files.

File managers use the entire screen or window to display a list of files and directories. By pressing various keys, you can perform any of the common operations quickly and easily. Each file manager works in its own way, so I won't go into the details: you will have to teach yourself. Typically, it can take awhile to master a file manager, but once you do, using it becomes second nature. To start, read the built-in help information.

The classic file manager was the Norton Commander, an extremely popular tool, first written in 1986 by programmer John Socha for the old DOS operating system. Over the years, the dual-panel design developed by Socha has been cloned and extended many times. If you are a Windows user, you probably have some experience with a different type of design, as implemented by Windows Explorer, the default Windows file manager.

In general, we can divide file managers into two families, GUI-based and text based. The GUI-based file managers are designed to be used with a graphical desktop environment, such as Gnome or KDE (see Chapter 5). Most desktop environments come with a default file manager: for Gnome, it is Nautilus; for KDE it is Konqueror (see Figure 24-9). However, there are a variety of other graphical file managers available for free if you want more choice. The text-based file managers are for use within a text-based environment, for example, when you use a virtual console (Chapter 6) or when you access a remote Unix host with a terminal emulator (Chapter 3).

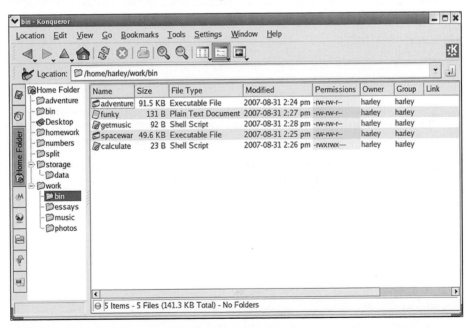

FIGURE 24-9: An example of a file manager

A file manager is a program that helps you manipulate files and directories. Using a file manager is an alternative to typing directory and file commands at the command line. Here is a screenshot of Konqueror, the default file manager for the KDE desktop environment.

For reference, here is a list of selected file managers you may wish to try.

Graphical File Managers:
- File Runner
- Gentoo
- Nautilus (comes with Gnome)
- Konqueror (comes with KDE)
- XFE [X File Explorer]

Text-Based File Managers:
- FDclone (Japanese clone of FD, a DOS file manager)
- Midnight Commander (clone of the classic Norton Commander)
- Vifm (file manager based on **vi** commands)

Finally, there is one more tool I want to mention. You can use the Vim text editor (Chapter 22) to perform file operations. Just start Vim with the name of a directory, and Vim will let you perform basic operations on the files within that directory. Try it when you get a chance. Note: This feature will not work when you start Vim in compatibility mode, that is, with the **-C** option (see Chapter 22).

CHAPTER 24 EXERCISES

REVIEW QUESTIONS

1. What is a pathname? What is the difference between an absolute pathname and a relative pathname?

2. What is the working directory? What is another name for it? Which command displays the name of your working directory? Can you think of another way to display the same information? Which commands — there are more than one — change your working directory?

   Suppose you want a constant reminder of the name of your working directory. How would you arrange that? Hint: Think about your shell prompt.

3. What program do you use to list the files in a directory? Which options do you use to display:

   - All files, including dotfiles (hidden files)
   - Names in reverse alphabetical order
   - Entire tree, including all subdirectories
   - Flag after each name (**/** = directory)
   - Size of each file, in human readable units
   - Long listing (permissions, owner, and so on)
   - Information about a directory itself, not its contents

   When you look at a directory listing, what do the entries . and .. mean?

4. What is globbing? What are wildcards? What are the five different wildcards? What does each one match? How is globbing different from using regular expressions?

5. What program do you use to draw a diagram of a directory tree? Which is the most useful option for this program?

APPLYING YOUR KNOWLEDGE

1. Starting from your home directory, using as *few* commands as possible, create the following directories :

```
temp/
temp/books/
temp/books/unix/harley
temp/books/literature/
temp/books/literature/english/
temp/books/literature/english/shakespeare
temp/books/literature/english/shakespeare/hamlet
temp/books/literature/english/shakespeare/macbeth
```

Display a diagram of the directory tree starting from **temp** that shows only directories. (Note: You may not have the program to do this if you are not using Linux.)

2. Starting with the directories from the the last question, using commands that are as *short* as possible, create the following empty files. (Hint: Use the **touch** command to create the files. It is explained in Chapter 25, and there is an example in this chapter.)

- In the **harley** directory: create **notes, questions, answers**.
- In the **english** directory: create **essay, exam-schedule**.
- In the **hamlet** directory: create **quotes**.

Display a diagram of the directory tree starting from **temp** showing all files and directories.

3. Clear the directory stack. Now push the following two directories onto the stack:

```
~/temp/books/unix/harley
~/temp/books/literature/english/
```

Display the contents of the stack so that each element is on a separate line with a line number. Using the stack, change to the **harley** directory.

4. Create two versions of a command to display the access times of all the files in your working directory with a name that consists of the characters "backup", followed by a single character, followed by 2 digits. The first command should use predefined character classes. The second command should use ranges.

FOR FURTHER THOUGHT

1. You are teaching a Unix class, and it is time to explain how to create directories and how to think about the working directory. You have two choices. First, you can explain the concepts abstractly: we create directories as needed, and we use the **cd** command to change the value of the working directory. Alternatively, you can introduce the metaphor of a tree: directories are like branches of a tree, and using **cd** moves us from one branch to another. Which approach do you think is better? Why?

2. To display file types, you can use either **ls -F** and **file**. Why is it necessary to have two such commands?

CHAPTER 25

WORKING WITH FILES

This is the last of three chapters devoted to Unix files. In Chapter 23, we discussed the Unix filesystem in detail. At the time, I explained that there are three types of files: directories, ordinary files, and pseudo files. For day-to-day work, directories and ordinary files are the most important, so I want to make sure you master all the basic skills related to these two types of files. In Chapter 24, we talked about how to use directories. In this chapter, we will discuss the details of working with ordinary files.

Throughout the chapter, when I use the term "file", I am referring to ordinary files. Thus, to be precise, the title of the chapter should actually be "Working With Ordinary Files".

Our plan for the chapter is as follows: first, I will show you how to create, copy, move and rename ordinary files. We will then discuss permissions, the attributes that allow users to share files. From there, we will talk about what goes on behind the scenes, and you will see that manipulating files actually involves working with "links". Finally, I will explain how to search for files and how to process files that have been found in a search. It sounds like a lot — and it is — but I promise, by the time you finish, it will all make sense.

CREATING A FILE: touch

How do you create a file? Strangely enough, you don't. Unix creates files for you as the need arises; you rarely need to create a new file for yourself.

There are three common situations in which a file will be created for you automatically. First, when necessary, many programs will create a file for you automatically. For example, let's say you start the **vi** editor (Chapter 22) by using the command:

```
vi essay
```

This command specifies that you want to edit a file named **essay**. If **essay** does not exist, **vi** will create it for you the first time you save your work. In our example, I used **vi**, but the same principal applies to many other programs as well.

Second, when you redirect output to a file (see Chapter 15), the shell will create the file if it does not already exist. For example, say that you want to save the output of the **ls** command to a file named **listing**. You enter the **ls** command, redirecting the output:

```
ls > listing
```

If **listing** does not already exist, the shell creates it for you.

Finally, when you copy a file, the copy program creates a new file. For example, say that you want to copy the file **data** to a file named **extra**. You enter the following command:

```
cp data extra
```

If the file **extra** does not exist, it will be created automatically. (The **cp** command is explained later in the chapter.)

However, let's say that for some reason *you* want to create a brand new, empty file. What is the easiest way to do it? In Chapter 24, I explained how to use the **mkdir** command to make a new directory. Is there an analogous command to make an ordinary file? The answer is no, but there is a command that has the side effect of creating an empty file. This command is called **touch** and here is how it works.

In Chapter 24, I explained how to display the modification time (**ls -l**) or access time (**ls -lu**) of a file. The modification time is the last time the file was changed; the access time is the last time the file was read. The main purpose of **touch** is to change the modification time and the access time of a file without changing the file. Imagine yourself reaching out and carefully touching the file (hence the name). The syntax is:

touch [**-acm**] [**-t time**] *file...*

where *time* is a time and date in the form **[[YY]YY]MMDDhhmm[.ss]**.

By default, **touch** sets both the modification and the access times to the current time and date. For example, let's say that a file named **essay** was last modified on July 8 at 2:30 PM. You enter:

```
ls -l essay
```

The output is:

```
-rw-------  1 harley staff  4883 Jul  8 14:30 essay
```

It is now 10:30 AM, December 21. You enter:

```
touch essay
```

Now when you enter the same **ls** command you see:

```
-rw-------  1 harley staff  4883 Dec 21 10:30 essay
```

When might you use **touch**? Let's say you are preparing to distribute a set of files — music, software, whatever — and you want them to all have the same time and date. Change to the directory that holds the files and enter:

```
touch *
```

All the files matched by the ***** wildcard (see Chapter 24) now have the same modification time and access time.

If you want to change the modification time only, use the **-m** option. If you want to change the access time only, use **-a**. To use a specific time and date instead of the current time, use **-t** followed by a time in the format **[[YY]YY]MMDDhhmm[.ss]**. Here are two examples. Let's say today is August 31. The first command changes the modification time (only) to 5:29 PM on the current day. The second command changes the access time (only) to December 21, 2008, 10:30 AM:

```
touch -m -t 08311729 file1
touch -a -t 200812211030 file2
```

Realistically, you will rarely have a need to change the modification time or the access time for a file. However, **touch** has one very important side effect: if the file you specify does not exist, **touch** will create it for you. Thus, you can use **touch** to create brand new, empty files whenever you want. For example, to create a file named **newfile**, just enter:

```
touch newfile
```

If you want, you can create more than one new file at a time:

```
touch data1 data2 data3 temp extra
```

When you use **touch** to create a new file, the modification time and access time will be the current time and date. If this doesn't suit you, you can use the options we discussed above to set a specific time as you create the file.

One last option: If you are updating the modification time or access time for a number of files, and you *don't* want **touch** to create any new files, use the **-c** (no create) option. For example, the following command will update the times for the specified files. However, if a file does not exist it will not be created:

```
touch -c backup1 backup2 backup3 backup4
```

> **HINT**
>
> Most of the time, there is no need to use **touch** to create new files, because — as we have discussed — new files are almost always created for you automatically as the need arises.
>
> Where **touch** does come in handy is when you need some temporary files quickly, say, to experiment with file commands. When this happens, using **touch** is the fastest way to create a set of brand new, empty files, for example:
>
> ```
> touch test1 test2 test3
> ```

NAMING A FILE

Unix is liberal with respect to naming files. There are only two basic rules:

1. Filenames can be up to 255 characters long.*

---

*Technically, the maximum size of a filename is set by the filesystem, not by Unix or Linux. Most modern filesystems default to a maximum filename length of 255 characters. However, some filesystems are more flexible. For example, if you are a filesystem nerd, it is easy to modify the **ext2**, **ext3** or **ext4** filesystems to allow up to 1012 characters in a filename.

2. A filename can contain any character except **/** (slash) or the null character.

This only makes sense. As you know from Chapter 24, the **/** character is used as a separator within pathnames so, of course, you can't use it within a filename. The null character is the character consisting of all zero bits (see Chapter 23). This character is used as a string terminator in the C programming language, and you would normally never use it within a filename.

To these two rules, I am going to add a third one of my own.

3. Create filenames that are meaningful to you.

As an example, the name **data** doesn't mean much compared to the more descriptive **chemlab-experiment-2008-12-21**. True, the long name is complicated and takes longer to type, but once you know how to use filename completion (see Chapter 13), you will rarely have to type a complete name. For example, for the long name above, you might be able to type **ch**<Tab> and let the shell complete the name for you.

My advice is to choose meaningful names for all your files at the moment you create them. Otherwise, you will eventually accumulate many files that may or may not contain valuable data. If you are like everyone else, I am sure you think that, one day, you will go through all your files and delete the ones you don't need. However, if you are like everyone else, you will probably never actually do so.*

> **HINT**
>
> The best way to keep junk from accumulating in your directories is to give meaningful names to your files when you create them.

Unix allows you to create filenames that contain all sorts of outlandish characters: backspaces, punctuation, control characters, even spaces and tabs. Obviously, such filenames will cause trouble. For example, what if you use the **ls -l** command to list information about a file named **info;date**:

```
ls -l info;date
```

Unix would interpret the semicolon as separating two commands:

```
ls -l info
date
```

Here is another example. Say that you have a file named **-jokes**. It would be a lot of trouble using the name in a command, for example:

```
ls -jokes
```

Unix would interpret the **-** (hyphen) character as indicating an option.

---

*If you need convincing, just ask yourself, "Right now, how many photos do I have on my computer that, one day, I will sort through?"

Generally speaking, you will run into trouble with any name that contains a character with a special meaning (<, >, |, ! and so on). The best idea is to confine yourself to characters that cannot be misinterpreted. These are shown in Figure 25-1. Hyphens are okay to use, as long as you don't put them at the beginning of the name.

If you ever do end up with a name that contains spaces or other strange characters, you can sometimes make it work by quoting the name. (Quoting is explained in Chapter 13.) Here is a particularly meretricious example:

```
ls -l 'this is a bad filename, but it does work'
ls -l this\ is\ a\ bad\ filename\,\ but\ it\ does\ work
```

To finish this section, I am going to explain three important file naming conventions. First, as we discussed in Chapters 14 and 24, files whose names begin with a . (dot) character are called dotfiles or hidden files. When you use **ls**, such files are listed only if you specify the **-a** (all) option. By convention, we use names that start with a dot only for files that contain configuration data or initialization commands. (Figure 24-5 contains a list of the common dotfiles.)

Second, we often use filenames that end with a dot followed by one or more letters to indicate the type of the file. For example, C source files have names that end in **.c**, such as **myprog.c**; MP3 music files have names that end in **mp3**; files that have been compressed by the **gzip** program have names that end in **.gz**; and so on. In such cases, the suffix is referred to as an EXTENSION. There are literally hundreds of different extensions. Such extensions are convenient as they allow you to use wildcards (see Chapter 24) to refer to a group of files. For example, you can list the names of all the C source files in a directory by using:

```
ls *.c
```

Finally, as you will remember, Unix distinguishes between upper- and lowercase. Thus, the names **info**, **Info** and **INFO** are completely different. A Unix person would simply use **info**. Now, consider the following names that you might use for a directory that contains programs or shell scripts:

a, b, c...	Lowercase letters
A, B, C...	Uppercase letters
0, 1, 2...	Numbers
.	Dot
-	Hyphen
_	Underscore

FIGURE 25-1: Characters that are safe to use in filenames

*Unix allows you to use any characters you want in a filename except a **/** (slash) or a null. However, your life will be a lot easier if you stick to letters, numbers, the dot, the hyphen (but not at the beginning of a name), and the underscore.*

```
Program Files
ProgramFiles
programfiles
program-files
program_files
bin
```

The first name is what Windows uses. As Unix people, we reject the name immediately because it contains a space. The next name has two uppercase letters, which makes it difficult to type, so we reject it as well. But what about the next three names? They contain no spaces or uppercase letters or strange characters. However, for important directories, it's handy to have short, easy names, which is why **bin** gets our vote.

In the world of Unix, we have a convention that names beginning with uppercase letters are reserved for files that are important in some special way. For example, when you download software that comes in the form of a set of files, you will often find a file named **README**. Because uppercase comes before lowercase in the ASCII code (Chapters 19 and 20), such names will come first in the directory listing and will stand out*. For this reason, as a general rule, I recommend that you use only lowercase letters when you name files and directories.

HINT

If you are programmer, you will be tempted, from time to time, to use the filename **test** for a program or shell script you are developing. Don't do it.

It happens that the shell has a builtin command named **test**, which is used to compare values within a shell script. If you name one of your programs **test**, whenever you try to run the program by typing its name, you will get the shell builtin instead. Nothing will seem to happen, and you will end up wasting a lot of your time trying to figure out the problem.

(If you are interested in knowing what **test** does, look it up in the online manual.)

COPYING A FILE: cp

To make a copy of a file, use the **cp** command. The syntax is:

cp [**-ip**] *file1* **file2**

where *file1* is the name of an existing file, and *file2* is the name of the destination file.

Using this command is straightforward. For example, if you have a file named **data** and you want to make a copy named **extra**, use:

cp data extra

Here is another example. You want to make a copy of the system password file (see Chapter 11). The copy should be called **pword** and should be in your home directory. As we discussed in Chapter 24, the ~ character represents your home directory, so you can use:

cp /etc/passwd ~/pword

---

*If you are using the **C** locale. This will not be the case if you are using the **en_US** locale (see Chapter 19).

If the destination file does not exist, **cp** will create it. If the destination file already exists, **cp** will replace it. When this happens, there is no way to get back the data that has been replaced. Consider the first example:

```
cp data extra
```

If the file **extra** does not exist, it will be created. However, if the file **extra** did exist, it would be replaced. When this happens, the data in the original file is lost forever; there is no way to get it back. (Read the last sentence again.)

To append data to the end of a file, you do not use **cp**. Rather, you use the **cat** program and redirect the output (see Chapter 16). For example, the following command appends the contents of **data** to the end of **extra**. In this case, the original contents of **extra** *are* preserved.

```
cat data >> extra
```

Since **cp** can easily wipe out the contents of a file, if you want to be extra careful, you can use the **-i** (interactive) option:

```
cp -i data extra
```

The **-i** option tells **cp** to ask your permission before replacing a file that already exists. For example, you might see:

```
cp: overwrite extra (yes/no)?
```

If you respond with anything that starts with "y" or "Y" (for "yes"), **cp** will replace the file. If you type any other answer — such as pressing the <Return> key — **cp** will not make the replacement.

The only other option I want you to know about is **-p** (preserve). This option gives the destination file the same modification time, access time, and permissions as the source file. (We will discuss permissions later in the chapter.)

COPYING FILES TO A DIFFERENT DIRECTORY: cp

The **cp** command can be used to copy one or more files to a different directory. The syntax is:

cp [**-ip**] *file... directory*

where *file* is the name of an existing file, and *directory* is the name of an existing directory. The **-i** (interactive) and **-p** (preserve) options work as described in the previous section.

Here is an example. To copy the file **data** to a directory named **backups**, use:

```
cp data backups
```

To copy the three files **data1**, **data2** and **data3** to the **backups** directory, use:

```
cp data1 data2 data3 backups
```

Here is one more example, a little more complicated. Your working directory is **/home/harley/work/bin**. You want to copy the file **adventure** from the directory **/home/harley/bin** to the working directory. To refer to source directory, we use **../../bin**; to refer to the working directory, we use a **.** by itself. The command is:

```
cp ../../bin/adventure .
```

HINT

You can often use wildcards to specify more than one filename (see Chapter 24.) For example, to copy the three files **data1**, **data2** and **data3** to the **backups** directory, you can use:

```
cp data[123] backups
```

If there are no other files whose names begin with **data**, you can use:

```
cp data* backups
```

If there are no other files whose names begin with d, you can use:

```
cp d* backups
```

COPYING A DIRECTORY TO ANOTHER DIRECTORY: cp -r

You can use **cp** to copy a directory and all of its files to another directory by using the **-r** option. The syntax is:

cp -r [**-ip**] *directory1... directory2*

where *directory1* is the name of an existing directory, and *directory2* is the name of the destination directory. The **-i** (interactive) and **-p** (preserve) options work as described earlier in the chapter. The **-r** (recursive) option tells **cp** to copy an entire subtree.

Here is an example. Say that, within your working directory, you have two subdirectories: **essays** and **backups**. Within the **essays** directory, you have many files and subdirectories. You enter:

```
cp -r essays backups
```

A copy of essays, including all its files and subdirectories, is now in **backups**. When you use **-r**, the **cp** command creates new directories automatically as needed.

HINT

To copy all the files in a directory use **cp** with the ***** wildcard (see Chapter 24), for example:

```
cp documents/* backups
```

To copy the directory itself including all its files and subdirectories, use **cp** with the **-r** option, for example:

```
cp -r documents backups
```

MOVING A FILE: mv

To move a file to a different directory, use the **mv** (move) command. The syntax is:

mv [**-if**] *file... directory*

where *file* is the name of an existing file, and *directory* is the name of the target directory.

The **mv** command will move one or more files to an existing directory. (To create a directory, use the **mkdir** command, explained in Chapter 24.) Here are two examples. The first command moves a file named **data** to a directory named **archive**:

```
mv data archive
```

You must be careful. If a directory named **archive** does not exist, **mv** will think you want to rename the file (see below). The next example moves three files, **data1**, **data2** and **data3**, to the **archive** directory:

```
mv data1 data2 data3 archive
```

As with most file commands, you can use a wildcard specification. For example, the last command can be abbreviated to:

```
mv data[123] archive
```

If the target to which you move a file already exists, the source file will replace the target file. In such cases, the original contents of the target file will be lost and there is no way to get it back, so be careful. If you want to be cautious about losing data, use the **-i** (interactive) option. For example:

```
mv -i data archive
```

This tells **mv** to ask your permission before replacing a file that already exists. If you type an answer that begins with the letter y or Y (for "yes"), **mv** will replace the file. If you type any other answer — such as pressing the <Return> key — **mv** will not make the replacement. In this example, **mv** would ask your permission before replacing a file named **archive/data**.

The opposite option is **-f** (force). This forces **mv** to replace a file without checking with you. The **-f** option will override the **-i** option as well as restrictions imposed by file permissions (explained later in the chapter). Use **-f** with care and only when you know exactly what you are doing.

RENAMING A FILE OR DIRECTORY: mv

To rename a file or directory, use the **mv** (move) command. The syntax is:

mv [**-if**] *oldname newname*

where oldname is the name of an existing file or directory, and *newname* is the new name. The **-i** (interactive) and **-f** (force) options work as described in the last section.

Renaming a file or directory is straightforward. For example, to rename a file from **unimportant** to **important**, use:

```
mv unimportant important
```

If the target (in this case, **important**) already exists, it will be replaced. All the data in the original target will be lost, and there is no way to get it back, so be careful. You can use the **-i** and **-f** options, described in the last section, to control the replacement: **-i** tells **mv** to ask you before replacing a file; **-f** forces the replacement no matter what.

As you might expect, you can use **mv** to rename and move at the same time. For example, say that **incomplete** is a file and **archive** is a directory. The following command moves **incomplete** to the directory **archive** (which must already exist). As part of the move, the file will be renamed to **complete**:

```
mv incomplete archive/complete
```

Finally, consider what happens if you use **mv** with a directory named **old** as follows:

```
mv old new
```

If there is no directory named **new**, the **old** directory will be renamed **new**. However, if there is a directory named **new**, the old directory will be moved to become a subdirectory of **new**. (Take a moment to think about this.)

DELETING A FILE: rm

To delete a file, use the **rm** (remove) command. The syntax is:

```
rm [-fir] file...
```

where *file* is the name of a file you want to delete.

(Notice that the name of this command is "remove", not "delete". This will make sense when we talk about links later in the chapter.)

To delete a file, just specify its name. Here are some examples. The first command deletes a file named **data** in your working directory. The second command deletes a file named **essay** in your home directory. The next command deletes a file named **spacewar** in the directory named **bin**, which lies in your working directory.

```
rm data
rm ~/essay
rm bin/spacewar
```

As with all file commands, you can use wildcard specifications (see Chapter 24). Here are two examples. The first command deletes the files **data1**, **data2** and **data3** in the working directory. The second command deletes all the files in your working directory, except dotfiles. (Obviously, this is a very powerful command, so do *not* experiment with it.)

```
rm data[123]
rm *
```

Once you delete a file, it is gone for good. There is no way to get back an erased file, so be careful.

When you use **rm** with a wildcard specification, it is a good idea to test it first with an **ls** command to see what files are matched. Here is an example. You want to delete the files **data.backup**, **data.old** and **data.extra**. You are thinking about using the wildcard specification **data*** which would match all files whose names begin with **data**. However, to be prudent, you check this specification by entering:

```
ls data*
```

The output is:

```
data.backup    data.extra    data.important    data.old
```

You see that you had forgotten about the file **data.important**. If you had used **rm** with **data*** you would have lost this file. Instead, you can use:

```
rm data.[beo]*
```

This will match only those files you really want to delete.

HINT

Before you use **rm** with a wildcard specification, test it first with **ls** to confirm which files will be matched.

HOW TO KEEP FROM DELETING THE WRONG FILES: rm -if

As I mentioned in the previous section, it is a good idea to check a wildcard pattern with **ls** before you use it with an **rm** command. However, even if you check the pattern with **ls**, you might still type it incorrectly when you enter the **rm** command. Here is a foolproof way to solve the problem.

In Chapter 13, in our discussion of aliases, I showed you how to define an alias named **del**, which runs the **rm** command using the same arguments as the preceding **ls** command. For the Bourne shell family (Bash, Korn shell), the command to define this alias is:

```
alias del='fc -s ls=rm'
```

For the C-Shell family (Tcsh, C-Shell), the command is:

```
alias del 'rm \!ls:*'
```

(The details are explained in Chapter 13.) To define the **del** alias permanently, just put the appropriate command in your environment file (Chapter 14). Once the alias is defined, it is easy to use. To start, enter an **ls** command with the wildcard specification that describes the files you want to delete. For example:

```
ls data.[beo]*
```

Take a look at the list of files. If they are really the ones you want to delete, enter:

```
del
```

This will execute the **rm** command using the filenames from the previous **ls** command. If the list of files is not what you want, try changing the pattern.

A handy alternative is to use the **-i** (interactive) option. This tells **rm** to ask your permission before deleting each file. For example, you can enter:

```
rm -i data*
```

The **rm** program will display a message for each file, asking your permission to proceed, for example:

```
rm: remove regular file `data.backup'?
```

If you type a response that begins with "y" or "Y" (for "yes"), **rm** will delete the file. If you type any other answer — such as pressing the <Return> key — **rm** will leave the file alone.

It is common for people to create an alias that automatically inserts the **-i** option every time they use the **rm** command. Here are the aliases. The first one is for the Bourne Shell family; the second one is for the C-Shell family:

```
alias rm='rm -i'
alias rm 'rm -i'
```

Some system administrators put such an alias in the system-wide environment file, thinking they are doing their users a favor.

This practice is to be deplored for two reasons. First, Unix was designed to be terse and exact. Having to type "y" each time you want to delete a file slows down your thought processes. Using an automatic **-i** option makes for sloppy thinking because users come to depend on it.

If you feel like arguing the point, think about this: it is true that, during the first week, a new user who is not used to the **rm** command may accidentally delete one or two files, and he won't get them back. However, the experience is an important one, and it won't be long before he will learn to use the command carefully. I believe that, in the long run, developing your skills is always the better alternative to being coddled. The truth is in spite of the potential power of **rm**, experienced Unix users rarely delete files by accident, because they have formed good habits.

The second reason I don't want you to use the **-i** option automatically is that, eventually, you will use more than one Unix or Linux system. If you become used to a slow, awkward, ask-me-before-you-delete-each-file **rm** command, you will forget that most Unix systems do not work that way. One day, you will find yourself on a different system, and it will be all too easy to make a catastrophic mistake. Your fingers have a memory, and once you get used to typing **rm** instead of **rm -i**, it is a difficult habit to unlearn.

For this reason, if you really must create an alias for **rm -i**, give it a different name, for example:

```
alias erase='rm -i'
alias erase 'rm -i'
```

One final point. Later in the chapter, we will discuss file permissions. At that time, you will see that there are three types of permissions: read, write and execute. I won't go into the details now except to say that without write permission, you are not allowed to delete a file. If you try to delete a file for which you do not have write permission, **rm** will ask your permission to override the protection mechanism.

For example, say that the file **data.important** has file permissions of **400**. (The "400" will make sense later. Basically, it means that you have read permission, but not write or execute permission.) You enter:

```
rm data.important
```

You will see the question:

```
rm: remove write-protected regular file `data.important'?
```

If you type a response that begins with "y" or "Y" (for "yes"), **rm** will delete the file. If you type any other answer — such as pressing the <Return> key — **rm** will leave the file alone. If you are careful, you can tell **rm** to perform the deletion without asking permission — regardless of file permissions — by using the **-f** (force) option:

```
rm -f data.important
```

On some systems, **-f** will also override the **-i** option.

HINT

When you delete files with **rm**, the **-f** (force) option will override file permissions and (on some systems) the **-i** option. For this reason, only use **-f** when you are sure you know what you are doing.

DELETING AN ENTIRE DIRECTORY TREE: rm -r

To delete an entire directory tree, use the **rm** command with the **-r** (recursive) option and specify the name of a directory. This tells **rm** to delete not only the directory, but all the files and subdirectories that lie within the directory. For example, let's say you have a directory named **extra**. Within this directory are a number of files and subdirectories. Within each subdirectory are still more files and subdirectories. To delete everything all at once, enter:

```
rm -r extra
```

Here is another example, deceptively simple, yet powerful. To delete everything under your working directory, use:

```
rm -r *
```

Obviously, **rm** **-r** can be a dangerous command, so if you have the tiniest doubt that you know what you are doing, **-r** is a good option to forget about. At the very least, think about using **-i** (interactive) option at the same time. This tells **rm** to ask permission before deleting each file and directory, for example:

```
rm -ir extra
```

To delete an entire directory tree quickly and quietly, regardless of file permissions, you can use the **-f** option:

```
rm -fr extra
```

Remember, on some systems, **-f** will also override the **-i** option, so please be careful.

> **HINT**
>
> Before using **rm** with the **-r** option to delete an entire directory tree, always take a moment and use **pwd** to display your working directory. Imagine what the following command would do if you were in the wrong directory:
>
> ```
> rm -rf *
> ```

To conclude the discussion of the **rm** command, let's take a quick look at how easy it is to wipe out all your files. Say that your home directory contains many subdirectories, the result of months of hard work. You want to delete all the files and directories under the **extra** directory.

As it happens, you are not in your home directory. What you should do is change to your home directory and then enter the **rm** command:

```
cd
rm -fr extra
```

However, you think to yourself, "There is no point in typing two commands. I can do the whole thing in a single command." You intend to enter:

```
rm -fr ~/extra
```

(Remember, as we discussed in Chapter 24, the ~, tilde, character represents your home directory.) It happens, however, that you are in a hurry, you accidentally type a space before the slash:

```
rm -fr ~ /extra
```

In effect, you have entered a command to delete all the files in two directory trees: ~ (your home directory) and **/extra**.

Once you press <Return>, don't even bother trying to hit **^C** or <Delete> (whichever is your **intr** key) to abort the command. The computer is so much faster than you, there is no way to catch a runaway **rm** command. By the time you realize what has happened, all your files are gone, including your dotfiles. (I tested this command so you don't have to: just believe me.)

As we discussed in Chapter 4, when you log in as **root**, you become superuser. As superuser, you are able to do just about anything, including deleting any file or directory in the entire system. What do you think would happen if you logged in as superuser and entered the following command?

```
rm -fr /
```

(Don't try this at home unless you have a note from your mother.)

TECHNICAL HINT

You must be especially careful when you use **rm -fr** with variables. For example, let's say you have a shell script that uses the variables **$HOME** and **$FILE** (see Chapter 12) as follows:

```
rm -fr $HOME/$FILE
```

If for some reason, neither of the variables is defined, the command becomes:

```
rm -fr /
```

At best, you will delete all your own files, including all your (hidden) dotfiles. If you run the script as superuser, you will cause a catastrophe. Adding the **-i** option won't help because, as I explained earlier, on many systems **-f** overrides **-i**.

IS IT POSSIBLE TO RESTORE A FILE THAT HAS BEEN DELETED?

No.

FILE PERMISSIONS

Unix maintains a set of FILE PERMISSIONS (often called PERMISSIONS) for each file. These permissions control which userids can access the file and in what way. There are three types of permissions: READ PERMISSION, WRITE PERMISSION and EXECUTE PERMISSION. The three permissions are independent of one another. For example, your userid might have read and write permission for a particular file, but not execute permission for the file. It is important to understand that permissions are associated with userids, not users. For example, if someone were to log in with your userid, he or she would have the same access to your files as you do.

The exact meaning of file permissions depends on the type of file. For ordinary files, the meaning of the permissions is straightforward: read permission enables a userid to read the file. Write permission enables a userid to write to the file. Execute permission enables a userid to execute the file. Of course, it makes no sense to try to execute a file unless it is executable. As a general rule, a file is executable if it is a program or a script of some type. A shell script, for example, contains commands to be executed by the shell.

The three types of permissions are distinct, but they do work together. For example, in order to edit a file, you need both read and write permission. In order to run a shell script, you need both read and execute permission.

As you will see later in the chapter, you are able to set and change the permissions for your own files. You do so for two reasons:

• To restrict access by other users

Restricting which userids may access your files provides security for your data in a straightforward manner.

• To guard against your own errors

If you want to protect a file from being deleted accidentally, you can make sure that there is no write permission for the file. Many commands that replace or delete data will ask for confirmation before changing a file that does not have write permission. (This is the case for the **rm** and **mv** commands we discussed earlier in the chapter.)

With directories, permissions have somewhat different meanings than with ordinary files. Read permission enables a userid to read the names in the directory. Write permission enables a userid to make changes to the directory (create, move, copy, delete). Execute permission enables a userid to search the directory.

If you have read permission only, you can list the names in a directory, but that is all. Unless you have execute permission, you cannot, for example, check the size of a file, look in a subdirectory, or use the **cd** command to change the directory.

Consider the following unusual combination. What would it mean if you had write and execute permission for a directory, but not read permission? You would be able to access and modify the directory without being able to read it. Thus, you could not list the contents but, if you knew the name of a file, you could delete it.

For reference, Figure 25-2 contains a summary of file permissions as they apply to ordinary files and directories.

ORDINARY FILE	
Read	Read from the file
Write	Write to the file
Execute	Execute the file
DIRECTORY	
Read	Read the directory
Write	Create, move, copy or delete entries
Execute	Search the directory

FIGURE 25-2: Summary of file permissions

File permissions control which userids can access a file. Every file has three sets of permissions: for the owner, for the group, and for everyone else. Each set of permissions has three components: read permission, write permission, and execute permission. The meanings of these permissions are somewhat different for ordinary files than for directories.

HINT

When you first learn about the directory permissions, they may seem a bit confusing. Later in this chapter, you will learn that a directory entry contains only a filename and a pointer to the file, not the actual file itself.

Once you understand this, the directory permissions will make perfect sense. Read permission means you can read directory entries. Write permission means you can change directory entries. Execute permission means you can use directory entries.

SETUID

Within your Unix system, you do not exist. You log in as a particular userid, and you run programs to do your bidding. As a person who lives in the outside world, your role is limited to furnishing input and reading output. It is your programs that do the real work. For example, to sort data, you use the **sort** program; to rename a file, you use the **mv** program; to display a file, you use **less**; and so on.

As a general rule (with one exception, which we'll discuss in a moment) whenever you run a program, that program runs under the auspices of your userid. This means that your programs have the exact same privileges as your userid. For example, let's say your userid does not have read permission for a file named **secrets**. You want to see what's in the file, so you enter:

```
less secrets
```

Since your userid cannot read the file, the programs you call upon to do your work cannot read the file either. As a result, you see the message:

```
secrets: Permission denied
```

If you really want to see inside the **secrets** file, you have three choices. First, you can change its file permissions (I'll explain how to do so later in the chapter). Second, you can log in with a userid that already has read permission for that file. Third, if you know the **root** password, you can log in as superuser, which allows you to bypass virtually all restrictions.

In other words — unless you are superuser — your programs are bound by the restrictions of your userid, with one exception. There are times when it is necessary for a regular userid to run a program with special privileges. To make this possible, there is a special file permission setting that allows other userids to access a file as if they were the owner (creator) of the file. This special permission is called SETUID (pronounced "set U-I-D") or SUID. The name stands for "set userid".

In most cases, setuid is used to allow regular userids to run selected programs that are owned by **root**. This means that no matter which userid runs the program, it executes with **root** privileges. This enables the program to perform tasks that could normally be done only by the superuser. For example, to change your password, you use the **passwd** program. However, to change your password, the program must modify the password file and the shadow file (see Chapter 11) which requires superuser privileges. For this reason, the **passwd** program itself is stored in a file that is owned by **root** and has setuid turned on.

How can you tell that a file has the setiud file permission? When you display a long listing, you will see the letter "s" instead of "x" as one of the file permissions. For example, you enter:

```
ls -l /usr/bin/passwd
```

This displays a long listing for **passwd** program. The output is:

```
-r-s--x--x  1 root root  21944 Feb 12 2007 /usr/bin/passwd
```

The "s" in the file permissions (4th character from the left) indicates the setuid permission. The "s" replaces what would otherwise be an "x".

Obviously, such permissions can be a security risk. After all, a program running amok with superuser privileges can be used to hack into a system or cause damage. Thus, the use of setuid is strictly controlled. As a general rule, setuid is used only to allow regular userids to run a program with temporary privileges in order to perform a specific task.

HOW UNIX MAINTAINS FILE PERMISSIONS: id, groups

The programmers at Bell Labs who created the first Unix system (see Chapter 1) organized file permissions in a way that is still in use today. At the time Unix was developed, people at Bell Labs worked in small groups that shared programs and documents. For this reason, the Unix developers created three categories: the user, the user's work group, and everyone on the system. They then designed Unix so as to maintain three sets of permissions for each file. Here is how it works.

The userid that creates the file becomes the OWNER of the file. The owner is the only userid that can change the permissions for a file*. The first set of file permissions describe how the owner may access the file. Each userid belongs to a group (explained below). The second set of permissions apply to all other userids that are in the same group as the owner. The third set of permissions apply to the rest of the userids on the system. This means that, for each of your files and directories, you can assign separate read, write and execute permissions for yourself, for the people in your work group, and for everyone else.

Here is an example. You are working with a group of people developing a program. The file that contains the program resides in one of your personal directories. You might set up the file permissions so that both you and your group have read, write and execute permission, while all the other users on the system have only read and execute permission. This means that, while anyone can run the program, only you or members of your group can change it.

Here is another example. You have a document that you don't want anyone else to see. Just give yourself read and write permission, and give no permissions to your group or to everyone else.**

---

* The only exception is that the superuser, who can do virtually anything, can change the permissions for any file. If necessary, the superuser can also change the owner and group of a file by using the **chown** and **chgrp** commands respectively.

**Remember, however, you can't hide anything from the superuser.

It is important to understand that the permissions for "everyone" do not include you or the members of your group. Imagine a strange situation in which you give read permission for a file to everyone, but no permissions to your group. Members of your group will not be able to read the file. However, everyone else will. In addition, if there are users on your network who have access to your filesystem, they too fall in the category of "everyone", even if they don't have an account on your particular system.

So who is in your group? When your system administrator created your account, he or she also assigned you to a GROUP. Just as each user has a name called a userid, each group has a name called a GROUPID (pronounced "group-I-D"). The list of all the groupids in your system is kept in the file **/etc/group**, which you are free to examine at any time:

```
less /etc/group
```

The name of your group is kept in the password file **/etc/passwd** (described in Chapter 11), along with your userid, the name of your home directory, and other information. The easiest way to display your userid and groupid is to use the **id** command. (Just type the name by itself with no options.)

The **id** command is particularly handy in one very specific circumstance. You are doing some system administration work and, from time to time, you need to change from your own userid to **root** (superuser) and back again. If you become confused and you can't remember which userid you are using, you can always enter the **id** command. (This happens to me several times a month.)

Question: Suppose a system administrator is walking through a computer lab, and he sees a machine someone has left logged into a Unix system. What does he do?

Answer: The first thing he does is enter the **id** command to see who is logged in. He makes a note of the userid — so he can talk to the user — and then logs out by typing **exit**.

In the early days of Unix, each userid could belong only to one group. Modern Unix systems, however, allow users to belong to multiple groups at the same time. For each userid, the group that is listed in the password file is called the PRIMARY GROUP. If the userid belongs to any other groups, they are called SUPPLEMENTARY GROUPS. There are two ways in which you can display a list of all the groups to which your userid belongs. First, you can use the **id** program (with Solaris, you must use **id -a**):

```
id
```

Here is some sample output:

```
uid=500(harley) gid=500(staff) groups=500(staff),502(admin)
```

In this case, userid **harley** belongs to two groups: the primary group **staff**, and one supplementary group **admin**.

Another way to display all your groups is to use the **groups** program. The syntax is:

```
groups [userid...]
```

where *userid* is a userid.

By default, **groups** displays the names of the groups to which the current userid belongs. If you specify one or more userids, **groups** will show you to which groups they belong. Try the following two commands on your system. The first one displays all of your groups; the second displays the groups to which the superuser (userid **root**) belongs:

```
groups
groups root
```

How important are groups? In the 1970s, groups were very important. Most Unix users were researchers working in a trustworthy environment that was not connected to an outside network. Placing each userid in a group allowed the researchers to share work and collaborate with their colleagues. Today, however, for regular users, groups are sometimes ignored for two reasons.

First, most people have their own Unix or Linux computer, and when you are the only one using a system, there is no one to share with. Second, even on a shared system or a large network, system administrators often do not find it worthwhile to maintain groups that are small enough to be useful. For example, if you are an undergraduate student at a university, your userid might be part of a large group (such as all social science students) with whom sharing would be a meaningless experience.

Having said that, you should know that some organizations do take the trouble to maintain groups in order to share data files or executable programs. For example, at a university, students taking a particular course may be given userids that belong to a group that was set up just for that course. In this way, the teacher can create files that can be accessed only by those students.

> **HINT**
>
> Unless you have an actual need to share files with the other userids in your group, it's better to ignore the group idea altogether. When you set file permissions (explained later in the chapter), just give the "group" the same permissions you give to "everyone".

DISPLAYING FILE PERMISSIONS: ls -l

To display the file permissions for a file, use the **ls** command with the **-l** (long listing) option. The permissions are shown on the left-hand side of the output. To display the permissions for a directory, set the **-d** option along with **-l**. (The **ls** command, along with these options, is explained in Chapter 24.)

Here is an example. You enter the following command to look at the files in your working directory:

```
ls -l
```

The output is:

```
total 109
-rwxrwxrwx 1 harley staff 28672 Sep 5 16:37 program.allusers
-rwxrwx--- 1 harley staff  6864 Sep 5 16:38 program.group
-rwx------ 1 harley staff  4576 Sep 5 16:32 program.owner
-rw-rw-rw- 1 harley staff  7376 Sep 5 16:34 text.allusers
-rw-rw---- 1 harley staff  5532 Sep 5 16:34 text.group
-rw------- 1 harley staff  6454 Sep 5 16:34 text.owner
```

We discussed most of this output in Chapter 24. Briefly, the filename is on the far right. Moving to the left, we see the time and date of the last modification, the size (in bytes), and the group and userid of the owner. In this case, the owner of the files is userid **harley** and the group is **staff**. To the left of the owner is the number of links (which I will discuss later in this chapter). At the far left, the first character of each line is the file type indicator. An ordinary file is marked by –, a hyphen; a directory (there are none in this example) is marked by a **d**.

What we want to focus on here are the 9 characters to the right of the file type indicator. Their meaning is as follows:

r = read permission
w = write permission
x = execute permission
– = permission not granted

To analyze the permissions for a file, simply divide the 9 characters into three sets of 3. From left to right, these sets show the permissions for the owner of the file, the group, and for all other userids on the system. Let's do this for all the files in the example:

Owner	Group	Other	File
rwx	rwx	rwx	program.allusers
rwx	rwx	---	program.group
rwx	---	---	program.owner
rw-	rw-	rw-	text.allusers
rw-	rw-	---	text.group
rw-	---	---	text.owner

We can now see exactly how each permission is assigned. For instance, the file **text.owner** has read and write permissions for the owner, and no permissions for the group or for anyone else.

FILE MODES

Unix uses a compact, three-number code to represent the full set of file permissions. This code is called a FILE MODE or, more simply, a MODE. As an example, the mode for the file **text.owner** in the last example is **600**.

Within a mode, each number stands for one set of permissions. The first number represents the permissions for the userid that owns the file; the second number represents the permissions for the userids in the group; the third number represents the permissions for all the other userids on the system. Using the example I just mentioned, we get:

6 = permissions for owner
0 = permissions for group
0 = permissions for all other userids

Here's how the code works. We start with the following numeric values for the various permissions:

4 = read permission
2 = write permission
1 = execute permission
0 = no permission

For each set of permissions, simply add the appropriate numbers. For example, to indicate read and write permission, add **4** and **2**. Figure 25-3 shows each possible combination along with its numeric value.

Let's do an example. What is the mode for a file in which:

• The owner has read, write and execute permissions?
• The group has read and write permissions?
• All other userids have read permission only?

Owner: read + write + execute	=	4+2+1 =	7
Group: read + write	=	4+2+0 =	6
Other: read	=	4+0+0 =	4

Thus, the mode is **764**. New let's take a look at the examples from the previous section:

Owner	Group	Other	Mode	File
rwx = 7	**rwx** = 7	**rwx** = 7	777	`program.allusers`
rwx = 7	**rwx** = 7	--- = 0	770	`program.group`
rwx = 7	--- = 0	--- = 0	700	`program.owner`
rw- = 6	**rw-** = 6	**rw-** = 6	666	`text.allusers`
rw- = 6	**rw-** = 6	--- = 0	660	`text.group`
rw- = 6	--- = 0	--- = 0	600	`text.owner`

Now, let's do an example going backwards. What does a file mode of **540** mean? Using Figure 25-3, we see:

Owner: **5** = read + execute
Group: **4** = read
Other: **0** = nothing

Thus, the owner can read and execute the file. The group can only read the file. Everyone else has no permissions.

READ	WRITE	EXECUTE	COMPONENTS	TOTAL
—	—	—	0 + 0 + 0	0
—	—	yes	0 + 0 + 1	1
—	yes	—	0 + 2 + 0	2
—	yes	yes	0 + 2 + 1	3
yes	—	—	4 + 0 + 0	4
yes	—	yes	4 + 0 + 1	5
yes	yes	—	4 + 2 + 0	6
yes	yes	yes	4 + 2 + 1	7

FIGURE 25-3: Numeric values for file permission combinations
There are three types of file permissions: read permission, write permission, and execute permission. The value of these permissions are represented by 3 different numbers which are added together as shown in the table. See text for details.

CHANGING FILE PERMISSIONS: chmod

To change the permissions for a file, use the **chmod** (change file mode) command. The syntax is:

chmod *mode file...*

where *mode* is the new file mode, and *file* is the name of a file or directory.

Only the owner or the superuser can change the file mode for a file. As I mentioned earlier, your userid is automatically the owner of every file you create.

Here are some examples of how you might use **chmod**. The first command changes the mode for the specified files to give read and write permission to the owner, and read permission to the group and to everyone else. These permissions are suitable for a file you want to let anyone read, but not modify.

```
chmod 644 essay1 essay2 document
```

The next command gives the owner read, write, and execute permissions, with read and execute permissions for the group and for everyone else. These permissions are suitable for a file that contains a program that you want to let other people execute, but not modify.

```
chmod 755 spacewar
```

In general, it is prudent to restrict permissions unless you have a reason to do otherwise. The following commands show how to set permissions only for the owner, with no permissions for the group or everyone else. First, to set read and write permissions only:

```
chmod 600 homework.text
```

Next, to set read, write, and execute permissions:

```
chmod 700 homework.program
```

When you create a shell script or a program, it will, by default, have only read and write permissions. In order to execute the script, you will have to add execute permission. Use **chmod** 700 (or **chmod** 755 if you want to share).

HINT

To avoid problems, do not give execute permission to a file that is not executable.

HOW UNIX ASSIGNS PERMISSIONS TO A NEW FILE: umask

When Unix creates a new file, it starts with a file mode of:

666: for non-executable ordinary files
777: for executable ordinary files
777: for directories

From this initial mode, Unix subtracts the value of the USER MASK. The user mask is a mode, set by you, showing which permissions you want to *restrict*. To set the user mask, use the **umask** command. The syntax is:

umask [*mode*]

where *mode* specifies which permissions you want to restrict.

It is a good idea to put a **umask** command in your login file, so that your user mask will be set automatically each time you log in. Indeed, you will see a **umask** command in the sample login files I showed you in Chapter 14.

What should your user mask be? Let's consider some examples. To start, let's say you want write permission to be withheld from your group and from everyone else. Use a mode of **022**:

umask 022

This user mask shares your files without letting anyone change them. In most cases, it is prudent to be as private as possible. To do so, you can withhold all permissions — read, write, and execute — from your group and from anyone else. Use a mode of **077**:

umask 077

To display the current value of your user mask, you can enter the **umask** command without a parameter:

umask

Note: **umask** is a builtin command, which means its exact behavior depends on which shell you are using. Some shells do not display leading zeros. For example, if your user mask is **022**, you may see **22**; if your user mask is **002**, you may see **2**. If this is the case with your shell, just pretend the zeros are there.

WIPING OUT THE CONTENTS OF A FILE: shred

As we discussed earlier in the chapter, once you delete a file, there is no way to get it back. However, the actual disk space used by the file is not wiped clean. Rather, it is marked as being available for reuse by the filesystem. Eventually, the disk space will be reused and the old data will be overwritten by new data. On a large, busy Unix system, this can happen within seconds. However, there is no guarantee when this will happen, and sometimes old data can stay hidden in the unused part of a disk for some time. Indeed, there are special "undelete" tools that are able to look at the unused portion of a disk and recover old data.

Moreover, even if data is overwritten, in extreme cases it is possible for data to be recovered, as long as the data has not been overwritten more than once. If you can take a hard disk to a lab with very expensive data recovery equipment, it may be possible to sense traces of the old data on the magnetic surface of the disk.

For the truly paranoid, then, the best way to delete data forever is to destroy the storage media, say, by melting it. This is relatively easy with a CD or floppy disk, but not so easy with a hard disk, especially if you want to wipe out a few files and not the entire disk. So for those rare occasions in which simple file deletion is not enough, the GNU utilities (see Chapter 2) provide a program called **shred**. Although **shred** is not universally available, you will find it on most Linux systems. The syntax is:

shred -fvuz [file...]

where *file* is the name of a file.

The goal of **shred** is to overwrite existing data so many times that even the most expensive data recovery equipment in the world will feel foolish trying to read the magnetic traces. All you need to do is specify the names of one or more files and **shred** does the work automatically. If you add the **-v** (verbose) option, as I like to do, **shred** will display messages as it progresses:

shred -v datafile

By default, **shred** will overwrite the data many times and will leave the file with random data. Random data, of course, is a tipoff that the file has been "shredded". To hide this, you can use the **-z** option, which tells **shred** to finish the job by filling the file with all zeros. Going further, if you want to delete the file after processing, use the **-u** option. Finally, to override restrictive file permissions, you can use the **-f** (force) option.

Here then is the ultimate **shred** command. It will override existing file permissions, wipe out all the data by overwriting it many times, fill the file with all zeros, and delete the remains:

```
shred -fuvz datafile
```

The **shred** program, of course, can only do so much. If a file has been backed up automatically to another system or copied to a mirror site, all the shredding in the world won't get rid of the remote copies. Moreover, **shred** won't work on all filesystems. For example, when you update a file with the ZFS filesystem (developed by Sun Microsystems), the new data is written to a different location on the disk. The old data is not replaced until that particular part of the disk is reused by another file.

THE IDEA OF A LINK: `stat, ls -i`

When Unix creates a file, it does two things. First, it sets aside space on the storage device to store data. Second, it creates a structure called an INDEX NODE or INODE ("I-node") to hold the basic information about the file. The inode contains all the information the filesystem needs to make use of the file. Figure 25-4 contains a summary of what you would find in an inode in a typical Unix filesystem. Ordinary users don't have to know what is in an inode, because the filesystem handles the details automatically. On Linux systems, it is easy to look inside the inode for a particular file by using the **stat** command. Just type **stat** followed by the name of a file:

```
stat filename
```

The filesystem keeps all the inodes in a large table called the INODE TABLE. Within the inode table, each inode is known by a number called the INDEX NUMBER or INUMBER ("I-number"). For example, say that a particular file is described by inode #478515 . We say that the file has an inumber of 478515. To display the inumber for a file, use **ls** with the **-i** option. For example, the following command displays the inumber for the two files named **xyzzy** and **plugh**[*]:

```
ls -i xyzzy plugh
```

The following two commands display inumbers for all the files in the current directory:

```
ls -i
ls -il
```

When we work with directories, we talk as if they actually contain files. For example, you might hear someone say that his **bin** directory contains a file named **spacewar**. However, the directory does not really contain the file. Actually, the directory only contains the name of the file and its inumber. Thus, the contents of a directory is quite small: just a list of names and, for each name, an inumber.

Let's look at an example. What happens when you create a file named **spacewar** in your **bin** directory? First, Unix sets aside storage space on the disk to hold the file. Next, Unix looks in the inode table and finds a free inode. Let's say that it is inode #478515 . Unix fills in the information in the inode that pertains to the new file. Finally, Unix places an entry in the **bin** directory. This entry contains the name **spacewar** along with an

---

[*]When you have a moment, look up these two names on the Internet.

- Length of file in bytes
- Name of device that contains the file
- Userid of owner
- Groupid
- File permissions
- Last modification time
- Last access time
- Last time inode was changed
- Number of links pointing to the file
- Type of file (ordinary, directory, special, symbolic link...)
- Number of blocks allocated to the file

FIGURE 25-4: Contents of an inode (index node)

An index node or inode contains information about a file. Here is a list of the information typically stored in an inode in a Unix filesystem. The exact contents can vary slightly from one filesystem to another.

inumber of 478515 . Whenever a program needs to use the file, it is a simple matter to look up the name in the directory, use the corresponding inumber to find the inode, and then use the information in the inode to access the file.

The connection between a filename and its inode is called a LINK. Conceptually, a link connects a filename with the file itself. This is why — as you can see from Figure 25-4 — the inode does not contain a filename. Indeed, as you will see in a moment, an inode can be referenced by more than one filename.

MULTIPLE LINKS TO THE SAME FILE

One of the most elegant features of the Unix filesystem is that it allows multiple links to the same file. In other words, a file can be known by more than one name. How can this be? The unique identifier of a file is its *inumber*, not its name. Thus, there is no reason why more than one filename cannot reference the same inumber. Here is an example.

Let's say that your home directory is **/home/harley**. Within your home directory, you have a subdirectory called **bin**. You have created a file in the **bin** directory by the name of **spacewar**. It happens that this file has an inumber of 478515 . Using the **ln** command (described later in the chapter), you create another file named **funky** in the same directory, such that it has the same inumber as **spacewar**. Since both **spacewar** and **funky** have the same inumber, they are, essentially, different names for the same file.

Now, let's say you move to your home directory and create another file named **extra**, also with the same inumber. Then you move to the home directory of a friend, **/home/weedly**, and create a fourth file named **myfile**, also with the same inumber. At this point, you still have only one file — the one identified by inumber 478515 — but it has four different names:

```
/home/harley/bin/spacewar
/home/harley/bin/funky
/home/harley/extra
/home/weedly/myfile
```

Why would you want to do this? Once you get used to the idea of links, you will find ample opportunities to use them. The basic idea — which will make more sense as you become more experienced and sophisticated — is that the same file can have different meanings, depending upon the context in which it is being used. For example, it is often handy to allow different users to access the same file under different names.

However, there is a lot more to the ideas behind links. The reason I want you to understand how they work is because it is the links that underlie the operation of the basic file commands: **cp** (copy), **mv** (move), **rm** (remove), and **ln** (link). If all you do is memorize how to use the commands, you will never really understand what is happening, and the rules for using the filesystem will never really make sense.

In a moment we will consider the implications of this statement. Before we do, I want you to consider a question. Let's say that a file has more than one link; that is, the file can be accessed by more than one name. Which of the names is the most important one? Does the original name have any special significance? The answer is that Unix treats all links as equal. It doesn't matter what the original name of the file was. A new link is considered to be just as important as the old one.

Within Unix, files are not controlled by their names or locations. Files are controlled by ownership and permissions.

CREATING A NEW LINK: ln

Whenever you create a file, the filesystem creates a link between the filename and the file automatically. However, there will be times you want to make a new link to an existing file. To do so, you use the **ln** (link) command. There are two forms of this command. First, to make a new link to a single file, use the syntax:

ln *file newname*

where *file* is the name of an existing ordinary file, and *newname* is the name you want to give the link.

For example, let's say you have a file named **spacewar**, and you want to make a new link with the name **funky**, use:

ln spacewar funky

You will end up with two filenames, each of which refers to the same file (that is, to the same inumber). Once a new link is created, it is functionally the same as the original directory entry.

The second way to use **ln** is to make new links for one or more ordinary files and place them in a specified directory. The syntax is:

ln *file... directory*

where *file* the name of an existing ordinary file, and *directory* is the name of the directory in which you want to place the new links.

Here is an example. Your home directory is **/home/harley**. In this directory, you have two files, **data1** and **data2**. Your friend uses the home directory **/home/weedly**. In this directory, he has a subdirectory named **work**. The file permissions for this directory are such that your userid is allowed to create files. You want to make links to your two files and place them in your friend's directory. Use the command:

```
ln /home/harley/data1 /home/harley/data2 /home/weedly/work
```

To simplify the command, you can use wildcards (see Chapter 24):

```
ln /home/harley/data[12] /home/weedly/work
```

Another way to simplify this command is to change to your home directory before entering the **ln** command:

```
cd; ln data[12] /home/weedly/work
```

Once you create these new links, both files have names in two different directories at the same time. To see the number of links for a file, use the **ls -l** command. The number of links is displayed between the file permissions and the userid of the owner. For example, let's say you enter the command:

```
ls -l music videos
```

The output is:

```
-rw------- 1 harley staff  4070 Oct 14 09:50 music
-rwx------ 2 harley staff 81920 Oct 14 09:49 videos
```

You can see that **music** has only one link, while **videos** has two links.

HOW THE BASIC FILE COMMANDS WORK

It is important that you be able to understand the basic file commands in terms of filenames and links. Here are the basic operations:

1. CREATE A FILE; CREATE A DIRECTORY [**mkdir**]

To create a new file or directory, Unix sets aside storage space and builds an inode. Within the appropriate directory, Unix places a new entry using the filename or directory name you specified, along with the inumber of the new inode.

2. COPY A FILE [**cp**]

To copy to an existing file, Unix replaces the contents of the target file with the contents of the source file. No inumbers change. To copy to a file that does not exist, Unix first creates a brand new file with its own inumber. (Remember, the inumber is really what identifies a file.) The contents of the old file are then copied to the new file. After the copy, there

Chapter 25

are two distinct files. The old filename corresponds to the old inumber; the new filename corresponds to the new inumber.

3. RENAME A FILE or MOVE A FILE [**mv**]

To rename or move a file, Unix changes the filename, or moves the directory entry, or both, but keeps the same inumber. This is why the same command (**mv**) is used to rename and move.

4. CREATE A LINK [**ln**]

To create a new link to an existing file, Unix makes a new directory entry using the filename you specify, pointing to the same inumber as the original file. There is now one file and two filenames, and both filenames point to the same inumber.

5. REMOVE A LINK [**rm**, **rmdir**]

When you remove a link, Unix eliminates the connection between the filename and the inumber by removing the directory entry. If there are no more links, Unix deletes the file.

It is important to understand that removing a link is not the same as deleting a file. If there is more than one link to a file, Unix will not delete the file until the last link is removed. In most cases, however, there is only one link to a file, which is why, most of the time, **rm** and **rmdir** act as delete commands.

Here is a simple example to illustrate the ideas we have just discussed. You have a file named **spacewar**. You decide to make a new link to this file and call it **funky**:

```
ln spacewar funky
```

Now you remove **spacewar**:

```
rm spacewar
```

Even though the first filename is gone, the original file still exists. The file itself will not be deleted until the last link (**funky**) is removed.

SYMBOLIC LINKS: ln -s

The type of links we have discussed enable us to have more than one name refer to the same file. However, such links have two limitations. First, you cannot create a link to a directory. Second, you cannot create a link to a file in a different filesystem.

To create a link to a directory or to a file in a different filesystem, you need to create what is called a SYMBOLIC LINK or a SYMLINK. To do so, you use the **ln** program with the **-s** option. A symbolic link does not contain the inumber of a file. Rather, it contains the pathname of the original file. Whenever you access a symbolic link, Unix uses that pathname to find the file. (In this sense, a symbolic link is similar to a Windows shortcut. Windows Vista, by the way, supports actual Unix-like symbolic links.)

When you use **ls -l** to display the long listing for a file that is a symbolic link, you will notice two things. First, the file type indicator (the leftmost character of the output) will be the lowercase letter **l** for "link". Second, the actual symbolic link is shown at the right side of the line. Here is an example from a system in which the file **/bin/sh** is a symbolic link to the file **/bin/bash**. You enter the command:

```
ls -l /bin/sh
```

The output is:

```
lrwxrwxrwx  1 root root 4 Sep 11 2008  /bin/sh -> bash
```

As you can see, this file is only 4 bytes long, just long enough to hold the pathname of the real file (which is 4 characters long). The fact that this is a symbolic link — and not, say, a 4-character ordinary file — is noted in the inode for the file.

If you want to see the long listing for the file itself, you must specify the actual name:

```
ls -l /bin/bash
```

In this case, the output is:

```
-rwxr-xr-x 1 root root 720888 Feb 10 2008  /bin/bash
```

As you can see, this particular file has 720,888 bytes. As you might have guessed from the name, the file holds the program for the Bash shell.

To distinguish between the two types of links, a regular link is sometimes called a HARD LINK, while a symbolic link is sometimes called a SOFT LINK. When we use the word "link" by itself, we mean a hard link.

As we discussed earlier, to display the number of hard links to a file you use the **ls -l** command. There is, however, no way to display how many soft links (symbolic links) there are to a file. This is because the filesystem itself doesn't even know how many such links exist.

Question: What happens if there exists a symbolic link to a file, and you delete the file?

Answer: The symbolic link will not be deleted. In fact, you can still list it with **ls**. However, if you try to use the link, you will get an error message.

USING SYMBOLIC LINKS WITH DIRECTORIES

In Chapter 24, we discussed how to use the builtin commands **cd** to change the working directory and **pwd** to display the name of the working directory. A question arises: How should **cd** and **pwd** behave when a directory name is a symbolic link to another directory? There are two choices. First, the command can consider the symbolic link to be an entity in its own right, a synonym for the actual directory, much like a hard link is for an ordinary file. Alternatively, the link might be nothing more than a stepping stone to the real directory.

With some shells, the **cd** has two options to give you control over such situations. The **-L** (logical) option tells **cd** to treat symbolic links as if they were real directories on their own. The **-P** (physical) option tells **cd** to substitute the real directory for the symbolic one. Here is an example.

To start, within your home directory, create a subdirectory named **extra**. Next, create a symbolic link to this directory and name it **backups**. Finally, display a long listing of the two files:

```
cd
mkdir extra
ln -s extra backups
ls -ld extra backups
```

Here is some sample output:

```
lrwxrwxrwx 1 harley staff    5 Sep 8 17:52 backups -> extra
drwxrwxr-x 2 harley staff 4096 Sep 8 17:52 extra
```

By looking at the first character of each line, we can see that **backups** is a link and extra is a real directory. Notice that **backups** is only 5 bytes long, just long enough to contain the name of the target directory. The **extra** directory, however, is 4,096 bytes long, the block size for this filesystem (see Chapter 24).

Now, consider the command:

```
cd -L backups
```

This changes the working directory to **backups** even though, strictly speaking, **backups** doesn't really exist. What if, instead, we had used the **-P** option?

```
cd -P backups
```

In this case, the shell would have substituted the actual directory for the symbolic link and our working directory would become **extra**. When this happens, we say that the shell FOLLOWS the link.

By default, **cd** assumes **-L**, so you never really have to specify it. However, if you want the shell to follow a symbolic link, you do have to specify **-P**.

The **pwd** (print working directory) command has the same two options that can be applied when you display the name of your working directory. To test this, create the directory and symbolic link above and enter either of the following commands (they are equivalent):

```
cd backups
cd -L backups
```

Now enter the command:

```
pwd -P
```

The **-P** option tells **pwd** to follow the link. The output will look something like this:

```
/home/harley/extra
```

Now enter either of the following commands. As with **cd**, the **-L** option is the default:

```
pwd
pwd -L
```

In this case, **pwd** does not follow the link, so the output is:

```
/home/harley/backups
```

FINDING FILES ASSOCIATED WITH A UNIX COMMAND: whereis

There will be many instances when you want to find a particular file or set of files. At such times, there are three different programs you can use: **whereis**, **locate**, and **find**. In the next several sections, we will cover each program in turn.

The **whereis** program is used to find the files associated with a specific Unix command: binary (executable) files, source files, and documentation files. Rather than search the entire filesystem, **whereis** looks only in those directories in which such files are likely to be found: **/bin**, **/sbin**, **/etc**, **/usr/share/man**, and so on. (See the description of the Filesystem Hierarchy Standard in Chapter 23.)

The syntax for the **whereis** program is:

whereis [**-bms**] *command...*

where *command* is the name of a command.

Let's say you want to find the files associated with the **ls** command. Just enter:

```
whereis ls
```

Here is some typical output (actually, one long line):

```
ls: /bin/ls /usr/share/man/man1p/ls.1p.gz
/usr/share/man/man1/ls.1.gz
```

In this case, we see that the **ls** program itself resides in the file with the pathname **/bin/ls**. This is straightforward. The next two long pathnames show the location of two different man pages in compressed format:

```
/usr/share/man/man1p/ls.1p.gz
/usr/share/man/man1/ls.1.gz
```

(The **.gz** extension indicates that a file has been compressed by the **gzip** program. Such files are uncompressed automatically before they are displayed.)

The two lines above show that the first man page is in section 1p, and the second is in section 1. You can display either of these pages by using the **man** command (see Chapter 9). Since section 1 is the default, you don't have to specify it. However, you do have to specify any other section, such as 1p. Thus, the commands used to display these pages are:

```
man ls
man 1p ls
```

This example illustrates one of the things I like about **whereis**: it will sometimes find man pages you had no idea existed. For example, on the system used to generate the above output, it happens that there are two different man pages for the **ls** program. Indeed, they are different enough that it is worth reading the both. However, if we hadn't checked with **whereis**, we would not have known about the second page.

If you want to limit the output of **whereis**, there are several options you can use. To display only the pathname of the executable file, use the **-b** (binary) option; for files from the online manual, use the **-m** option; and for source files use the **-s** option. Here is an example. The following command displays the pathnames for the executable files for ten different programs:

```
whereis -b chmod cp id ln ls mv rm shred stat touch
```

Try this command on your system and see what you get.

FINDING FILES BY SEARCHING A DATABASE: `locate`

There are two different Unix programs that provide a general "file finding" service: **locate** and **find**. I want you to learn how to use them both. The **find** program is much older and much more difficult to use. However, it is very powerful and is available on every Unix and Linux system. The **locate** program is newer and easy to use, but less powerful than **find**. Moreover, although it comes with most Linux and FreeBSD systems, it is not available on all Unix systems (for example Solaris). In this section, we'll cover **locate**. In the following sections, we'll discuss **find**.

The job of the **locate** program is to search a special database containing the pathnames of all publicly accessible files, looking for all the names that contain a specific pattern. The database is maintained automatically and updated regularly. The syntax for **locate** is:

```
locate [-bcirS] pattern...
```

where *pattern* is the pattern you are looking for in a pathname.

Here is a simple example. You want to find all the files whose pathname contains the characters "test". Since there will probably be many such files, it is a good idea to pipe the output of the command to **less** (Chapter 12) to display the output one screenful at a time:

```
locate test | less
```

Aside from ordinary characters, you can use a regular expression if you include the **-r** option. Within a regular expression, you can use **^** and **$** to anchor the beginning and end of the pathname respectively. (For help with regular expressions, see Chapter 20.)

Here is an interesting example. You want to search your system for photos. One way is to look for files with an extension of either **.jpg** or **.png**, and save the pathnames in a file. You can then browse the file at your leisure. The commands to use are:

```
locate -r '.jpg$' > photos
locate -r '.png$' >> photos
```

The first command redirects its output to the file **photos**. The second command appends its output to the same file. (For a discussion of redirecting output, see Chapter 15.)

Because **locate** often gives you more than you want, it is common to process the output in some way. One of the most powerful combinations is to pipe the output of **locate** to **grep**. For example, let's say you are using a new system and want to find the Unix dictionary file (see Chapter 20). Most likely, this file will contain the letters "dict" as well as the letters "words". To find all such files, use **locate** to find all the files that contain "dict". Then use **grep** to search the output of **locate** for lines that contain "words". The command is:

```
locate dict | grep words
```

Try it on your system and see what you get.

To modify the operation of **locate**, there are several options you can use. First, the **-c** (count) option displays the total number of files that are matched, instead of displaying the actual filenames. For example, if you want to find out how many JPG files are on your system, use the command:

```
locate -cr '.jpg$'
```

The next option is **-i** (ignore case). This tells **locate** to treat upper- and lowercase letters as being the same. For example, if you want to search for all the files whose pathnames contain either "x11" or "X11", you can use either of the following commands:

```
locate x11 X11
locate -i x11
```

If you want, you can combine **-i** with **-r** to use case-insensitive regular expressions. For example, here is how to search for files whose pathnames start with "/usr" and end with "x11" or "X11":

```
locate -ir '^/usr*x11$'
```

You will often find that it is convenient to match only the last part of the pathname, what we have called the filename or basename (see Chapter 24). To do so, use the **-b** option. For example, to find all the files whose basenames contain the letters "temp", use:

```
locate -b temp
```

To find all the files whose name consists only of the letters "temp", use:

```
locate -br '^temp$'
```

Finally, to display information about the **locate** database on your system, use the **-S** (statistics) option:

```
locate -S
```

As you can see, **locate** is easy to use. Just tell it what you want, and **locate** will find it. However, there is one drawback I want to make sure you understand.

I mentioned earlier that **locate** uses a special database that contains the pathnames of all the publicly available files. On a well-run system, this database is updated automatically at regular intervals. However, when you or anyone else creates a new file, it will not appear in the database until the next update. To get around this limitation, you can use **find** (discussed in the next section), because **find** actually searches the directory tree.

FINDING FILES BY SEARCHING A DIRECTORY TREE: find

So far, we have discussed two different tools that find files: **whereis** and **locate**. Both of these programs are fast and easy to use and, most of the time, they should be your first choice when you are searching for a file.

However, there are limitations. The **whereis** program searches only for files associated with a particular program (executable files, source files, documentation files). The **locate** program doesn't actually perform a search. It simply looks for pattern matches in a database that contains the pathnames of all the publicly accessible files on the system. When you want to do a full search on demand, you need to use **find**.

The **find** program is the oldest and most complex of the three programs. Indeed, **find** is one of the most complex Unix tools you will ever use. However, it has three important advantages over the other programs. First, it is *very* powerful: **find** can search for any file, anywhere, according to a large variety of criteria. Second, once **find** has completed a search, it can process the results in several different ways. Finally, unlike **locate**, **find** is available on all Unix and Linux systems, so you can use it on any system you encounter.

The full syntax for **find** is very complicated. In fact, I won't even show it to you. Instead, we'll start with an overview and move ahead one step at a time.

The general idea is that **find** searches one or more directory trees for files that meet certain criteria, according to tests that you specify. Once the search is complete, **find** performs an action on the files it has found. The action can be as simple as displaying the names of the files. The action can also be more complex: **find** can delete the files, display information about them, or pass the files to another command for further processing.

To run **find**, you specify three things (in this order): directory paths, tests, and actions. The general syntax is:

find *path... test... action...*

Once you enter the command, **find** follows a 3-step process:

1. Path: The first thing **find** does is look at each path, examining the entire directory tree it represents, including all subdirectories.

2. Test: For each file **find** encounters, it applies the tests you specified. The goal is to create a list of all the files that meet your criteria.

3. Action: Once the search is complete, **find** carries out the actions you specified on each file in the list.

Consider the following simple example:

```
find /home/harley -name important -print
```

Without going into the details just yet, let's break this command into parts:

Path: `/home/harley`
Test: `-name important`
Action: `-print`

Within this command, we give **find** the following instructions:

1. Path: Starting from **/home/harley**, search all files and subdirectories.

2. Test: For each file, apply the test **-name important**. (The meaning of this test is to look for files named **important**.)

3. Action: For each file that passed the test, perform the action **-print** (that is, display the pathname).

So what does the above command do? It displays the pathnames of all the files named **important** within the **/home/harley** directory tree.

Take a moment to reflect on how we analyzed the above command. You will find that any **find** command — no matter how complex — can be analyzed in the same way, by breaking it into three parts: paths, tests, actions. Conversely, when you need to construct a complicated **find** command, you can build it up by thinking about these three parts, one after another.

THE find COMMAND: PATHS

As we have discussed, the general format of the **find** program is:

find *path... test... action...*

As you can see, the beginning of every **find** command consists of one or more paths. These paths show **find** where to search. Specifying paths is straightforward, as you will see from the following examples. (When you read them, realize that these examples do not specify any tests or actions. We'll talk about these topics in a moment.) Most of the time, you will use only a single path so, to start, here is a simple example:

```
find backups
```

In this example, we tell **find** to start with the directory named **backups** and search though all its descendents, both files and subdirectories. As you can see, we have used a relative pathname. You can also use absolute pathnames, a . (dot) for the working directory, or a ~ (tilde) for a home directory. Here are a few more partial commands:

```
find /usr/bin
find /
find .
find ~
find ~weedly
```

The first example tells **find** to start searching from the directory **/usr/bin**. The second example searches from the root directory. (Effectively, this tells **find** to search the entire filesystem.) The next example searches from the working directory. The fourth example searches from the home directory. The final example searches from the home directory for userid **weedly**. (For a complete discussion of how to specify pathnames, see Chapter 24.)

If you want, you can specify more than one path for **file** to search, for example:

```
find /bin /sbin /usr/bin ~harley/bin
```

In this example, **find** will search four separate, directory trees. The search results will be processed together as one long list.

THE find COMMAND: TESTS

We use the **find** program to search one or more directory trees, look for files that meet specified criteria, and then perform certain actions on those files. To define the criteria, we specify one or more TESTS. The general format of the command is:

find *path... test... action...*

So far, learning about **find** has been fairly easy. This is where it gets complicated. In the previous section, we discussed how to specify paths. In this section, we will discuss how to use the various tests to specify which files you want to process. There are many different tests, ranging from simple to arcane. As a reference, I have summarized the most important tests in Figure 25-5.

The **find** program is a very old tool, and the basic tests are the same from one system to another. However, the newer versions of **find** support some tests that are not available on all systems. Figure 25-5 summarize the tests that you can use with the version of **find** that is part of the GNU utilities, the program that comes with Linux (see Chapter 2). If you use a different type of Unix, all the basic tests will work, but some of the more esoteric ones may not be supported. To see a complete list of the available tests for your version of **find**, check the man page on your system (**man find**).

As you can see from Figure 25-5, **find** has a lot of different tests. Eventually, you can learn them all as the need arises. For now, my goal is to make sure you understand the most important tests. By far, the two most important tests are **-type** and **-name**, so we'll start with those.

The **-type** test controls which types of files **find** should look at. The syntax is **-type** followed by a one-letter designation. Most commonly, you will use either **f** for ordinary files or **d** for directories. If necessary, you can also use **b** (block devices), **c** (character devices), **p** (named pipe), or **l** (symbolic link). Here are some examples. (Note: In these examples, I have used the action **-print**, which simply displays the results of the search. We'll discuss other, more complicated actions later in the chapter.)

```
find /etc -type f -print
find /etc -type d -print
find /etc -print
```

All three commands perform a search starting from the **/etc** directory. The first command searches only for ordinary files; the second searches only for directories; the third searches for any type of file.

The **-name** test tells **find** to look for files whose names match a specified pattern. If you want, you can use the standard wildcards *****, **?** and **[ ]** (see Chapter 24). If you do, however, you must quote them, so they are passed to **find** and not interpreted by the shell. Here are some examples. All three commands start searching from the working directory (**.**) and search only for ordinary files (**-type f**):

```
find . -type f -name important -print
find . -type f -name '*.c' -print
find . -type f -name 'data[123]' -print
```

The first command searches for files named **important**. The second command searches for filenames with the extension **.c**, that is, C source files. The third command searches only for files named **data1**, **data2** or **data3**.

FILENAMES	
-name *pattern*	filename contains *pattern*
-iname *pattern*	filename contains *pattern* (case insensitive)
FILE CHARACTERISTICS	
-type [**df**]	type of file: **d** = directory, **f** = ordinary file
-perm *mode*	file permissions are set to **mode**
-user *userid*	owner is *userid*
-group *groupid*	group is *groupid*
-size [**-+**]*n*[**cbkMG**]	size is *n* [chars(bytes), blocks, kilobytes, megabytes, gigabytes]
-empty	empty file (size = 0)
ACCESS TIMES, MODIFICATION TIMES	
-amin [**-+**]*n*	accessed *n* minutes ago
-anewer *file*	accessed more recently than *file*
-atime [**-+**]*n*	accessed *n* days ago
-cmin [**-+**]*n*	status changed *n* minutes ago
-cnewer *file*	status changed more recently than *file*
-ctime [**-+**]*n*	status changed *n* days ago
-mmin [**-+**]*n*	modified *n* minutes ago
-mtime [**-+**]*n*	modified *n* days ago
-newer *file*	modified more recently than *file*

FIGURE 25-5: The find program: Tests

*The **find** program searches directory trees looking for files that meet specific criteria, according to various tests. See text for details.*

Like most of Unix, the **-name** test is case sensitive, that is, it distinguishes between upper- and lowercase. To ignore differences in case, use **-iname** instead. Consider, for instance, the following two examples. Both commands start searching from **/usr** and look only for directories:

```
find /usr -type d -name bin -print
find /usr -type d -iname bin -print
```

The second command looks only for directories named **bin**. The second command uses **-iname**, which means it will match directories named **bin**, **Bin**, **BIN**, and so on.

Aside from names, you can select files based on a variety of other characteristics. We have already seen the **-type** test, which selects a particular type of file, usually **f** for ordinary files or **d** for directories. You can also use **-perm** to search for files with a specific mode, and **-user** or **-group** for files owned by a specific userid or groupid. Consider these three examples, which start searching from your home directory:

```
find ~ -type d -perm 700 -print
find ~ -type f -user harley -print
find ~ -type f -group staff -print
```

The first command searches for directories that have a file mode of **700**. (We discussed permissions and modes earlier in the chapter.) The second command searches for ordinary files owned by userid **harley**. The final command searches for ordinary files whose groupid is **staff**.

You can also search for files according to their size, by using **-size** followed by a specific value. The basic format is a number followed by a one-letter abbreviation. The abbreviations are: **c** for characters (that is, bytes), **b** for 512-byte blocks, **k** for kilobytes, **M** for megabytes, and **G** for gigabytes. Here are two examples, both of which search for ordinary files starting from your home directory:

```
find ~ -type f -size 1b -print
find ~ -type f -size 100c -print
```

The first command searches for files that are exactly 1 block in size. Since this is the minimum size for a file, this command effectively finds all your small files. The second command searches for files containing exactly 100 bytes.

Before we move on, I want to take a moment to explain an important point. When you use a size measured in blocks, kilobytes, megabytes, or gigabytes, **find** assumes you are talking about disk space. This is why **-size 1b** finds all your small files. As we discussed in Chapter 24, the minimum allocation of disk space is 1 block.

When you use a size measured in bytes, **find** assumes you are talking about the actual content of the files, not how much disk space it uses. That is why **-size 100c** looks for files that contain exactly 100 bytes of data. In fact, a file containing 100 bytes of data will be found by both **-size 100c** and **-size 1b**.

Whenever you use **-size**, you can preface the number with either a **-** (minus) or **+** (plus) to mean "less than" or "greater than" respectively. (This is a general rule for all numbers used with tests.) For example, the following command finds all your personal files with a size of less than 10 kilobytes. The second command finds all your files with a size greater than 1 megabyte:

```
find ~ -type f -size -10k -print
find ~ -type f -size +1M -print
```

The final group of tests allow you to search for files based on their access or modification times. The tests are summarized in Figure 25-5, so I won't go over each one in detail. Let me just give you a few examples. Suppose you want to find all of your files that have been modified in the last 30 minutes. Use the **-mmin** test with the value **-30**, for example:

```
find ~ -mmin -30 -print
```

Let's say you want to find files that have not been used for over 180 days. Use **-atime** with the value **+180**:

```
find ~ -atime +180 -print
```

Finally, to find all your files that have been changed in the last 10 minutes, use:

```
find ~ -cmin -10 -print
```

THE find COMMAND: NEGATING A TEST WITH THE ! OPERATOR

When necessary, you can negate a test by preceding it with the **!** (exclamation mark) OPERATOR. To do so, just type **!** before the test. When you use **!**, you must follow two rules. First, you must put a space on each side of the **!** mark, so it can be parsed properly. Second, you must quote the **!**, so it is passed to **find** and not interpreted by the shell. (This is a good habit anytime you want to pass metacharacters to a program.)

As an example, consider the following command that searches from your home directory and displays the names of all ordinary files that have the extension **.jpg**:

```
find ~ -type f -name '*.jpg' -print
```

Suppose, instead, we want to display the names of those files that do **not** have the extension **.jpg**. All we have to do is use the **!** operator to reverse the test:

```
find ~ -type f \! -name '*.jpg' -print
```

You will notice that I used a backslash to quote the **!** operator. If you prefer you can use single quotes instead. (For more information about quoting, see Chapter 13.)

```
find ~ -type f '!' -name '*.jpg' -print
```

When necessary, you can negate more than one test. Just make sure that each test has its own **!** operator. For example, suppose you want to see if you have any files that are neither ordinary files or directories. That is, you want to see if you have any symbolic links, named pipes, special files, and so on. The command to use is:

```
find ~ \! -type f \! -type d -print
```

THE find COMMAND: DEALING WITH FILE PERMISSION ERROR MESSAGES

The **find** program is a great tool for searching through large directory trees. In particular, by starting at **/** (the root directory), you can search the entire filesystem. However, when you search outside your own home directory area, you will find that some directories and files are off-limits, because your userid does not have permission to access them. Each time this happens, **find** will display an error message.

For example, the following command searches the entire filesystem looking for directories named **bin**:

```
find / -type d -name bin -print
```

When you run this command, you will probably see many error messages similar to the following:

```
find: /etc/cron.d: Permission denied
```

In most cases, there is no reason to see these messages, because they don't really help you. In fact, all they do is clutter your output. So how can you get rid of them?

Since error messages are written to standard error (see Chapter 15), you can get rid of the messages by redirecting standard error to **/dev/null**, the bit bucket. With the Bourne Shell family (Bash, Korn shell), this is easy:

```
find / -type d -name bin -print 2> /dev/null
```

With the C-Shell family (C-Shell, Tcsh), it is a bit more complicated, but it can be done:

```
(find / -type d -name bin -print > /dev/tty) >& /dev/null
```

The details are explained in Chapter 15.

THE find COMMAND: ACTIONS

As we have discussed, we use the **find** program to search one or more directory trees, look for files that meet specified criteria, and then perform certain actions on those files. The general format of the command is:

find *path... test... action...*

So far, we have talked about how to specify paths and tests. To conclude our discussion, we will now talk about actions. An ACTION tells **find** what to do with the files it finds. For reference, I have summarized the most important actions in Figure 25-6. (For a complete list, see the **find** man page on your system.)

As you can see, actions start with a **–** (dash) character, just like tests. The most commonly used action is **-print**, which tells **find** to display the pathnames of all the files it has selected. More precisely, **-print** tells **find** to write the list of pathnames to standard output. (Why the name **-print**? As we discussed in Chapter 7, for historical reasons, it is a Unix convention to use the word "print" to mean "display".)

Here is a simple, straightforward example that starts from the working directory and searches for files named **important**:

```
find . -name important -print
```

With most versions of **find**, if you do not specify an action, **-print** is assumed by default. Thus, the following two commands are equivalent:

```
find . -name important -print
find . -name important
```

Similarly, with the GNU version of **find**, if you do not specify a path, the working directory is assumed by default. Thus, if you are a Linux user, the following three commands are equivalent:

ACTIONS	
-print	write pathname to standard output
-fprint *file*	same as **-print**; write output to *file*
-ls	display long directory listing
-fls *file*	same as **-ls**; write output to *file*
-delete	delete file
-exec *command* **{ } \;**	execute *command*, **{ }** indicates matched filenames
-ok *command* **{ } \;**	same as **-exec**, but confirm before running *command*

FIGURE 25-6: The find program: Actions

*The **find** program searches directory trees, looking for files that meet criteria, according to tests that you specify. For each file that is found, **find** performs the actions you specify. See text for details.*

```
find . -name important -print
find . -name important
find -name important
```

Moving on, let me show you a more useful example. You want to search the entire filesystem for music files in MP3 format. To do so, you use **find** to start from the root directory and search for all the ordinary files that have an extension of **.mp3**. Since you will be searching throughout the filesystem, you know that **find** will generate spurious file permission error messages (see the previous section). For this reason, you redirect standard error to the bit bucket. The full command is:

```
find / -type f -name '*.mp3' -print 2> /dev/null
```

If the list of MP3 files is long, most of it will scroll off your screen. If so, you have two choices. First, you can pipe the output to **less** to display one screenful at a time:

```
find / -type f -name '*.mp3' -print 2> /dev/null | less
```

Alternatively, you can save the output in a file, so you can peruse it later at your leisure. To do so, use the **-fprint** action instead of **-print**. The syntax is simple: just type **-fprint** followed by the name of the file. For example, the following command finds the names of all the MP3 files on the system and stores them in a file called **musiclist**:

```
find / -type f -name '*.mp3' -fprint musiclist 2> /dev/null
```

The **-print** action displays pathnames. If you want more information about each file, you can use the **-ls** action instead. This action displays information similar to the **ls** command with the option **-dils**. The formatting is done internally. (**find** doesn't really run the **ls** program.) What you will see is:

• Inode number
• Size in blocks
• File permissions
• Number of hard links
• Owner
• Group
• Size in bytes
• Time of last modification
• Pathname

As an example, the following command searches from your home directory for all files and directories that have been modified in the last 10 minutes. It then uses **-ls** to display information about these files:

```
find ~ -mmin -10 -ls
```

The **-fls** action is similar to **-ls** except that, like **-fprint**, it writes its output to a file. For example, the following command finds all your files that have been modified in the last 10 minutes and writes their pathnames to a file named **recent**:

```
find ~ -mmin -10 -fls recent
```

The next action **-delete** can be very useful. However, it can easily turn around and bite you, so be careful how you use it. The **-delete** action removes the link to every file that has been found in the search. If that link is the only one, the file is deleted (see the discussion on links earlier in the chapter). In other words, using **-delete** is similar to using the **rm** command.

Here is an example. Starting the search from your home directory, you want to remove all the files with the extension **.backup**:

```
find ~ -name '*.backup' -delete
```

Here is a more complex (and more useful) example. The following command removes all the files with the extension **.backup** that have not been accessed for at least 180 days:

```
find ~ -name '*.backup' -atime +180 -delete
```

Using the **-ls** and **-delete** actions is similar to sending the output of a search to the **ls** and **rm** programs respectively. However, **find** offers much more generality: you can send the search output to any program you want by using the **-exec** action. The syntax is:

```
-exec command {} \;
```

where *command* is any command you want, including options and parameters.

Here is how it works. You type **-exec** followed by a command. You can specify any command you want, as well as options and parameters, just as if you were typing it on the command line. Within the command, you use the characters **{}** to represent a pathname found by **find**. To indicate the end of the command, you must end it with a **;** (semicolon). As you can see from the syntax above, the semicolon must be quoted. This ensures that it is passed to **find** and not interpreted by the shell. (Quoting is explained in Chapter 13.)

The **-exec** action is, more than any other feature, what makes **find** so powerful, so it is crucial that you learn how to use it well. To show you how it works, let's start with a trivial example. The command below starts searching from your home directory, looking for all your directories. The results of the search are sent to the **echo** program, one at a time, to be displayed.

```
find ~ -type d -exec echo {} \;
```

With some shells, you will have a problem if you don't quote the brace brackets:

```
find ~ -type d -exec echo '{}' \;
```

As a quick aside, let me remind you that you can quote the semicolon with single quotes instead of a backslash if you want:

```
find ~ -type d -exec echo {} ';'
find ~ -type d -exec echo '{}' ';'
```

An **-exec** action is carried out once for each item that is found during the search. In this case, if there are, say, 26 directories, **find** will execute the **echo** command 26 times. Each time **echo** is executed, the **{ }** characters will be replaced by the pathname of a different directory.

The reason I call the previous command a trivial example is that you don't really need to send pathnames to **echo** to display them. You can use **-print** instead:

```
find ~ -type d -print
```

However, our **-exec** action can be much more powerful. Let's say that, for security reasons, you decide no one but you should be allowed to access your directories. To implement this policy, you need to use **chmod** to set the file permissions for all your directories to **700**. (See the discussion of file permissions earlier in the chapter.) You could type a **chmod** for each directory, which would take a long time. Instead, use **find** to search for your directories and let **-exec** do the work for you:

```
find ~ -type d -exec chmod 700 {} \;
```

One more example. You are using a version of **find** that does not support the **-ls** or **-delete** actions. How can you replace them? Just use **-exec** to run **ls** or **rm**, for example:

```
find ~ -name '*.backup' -exec ls -dils {} \;
find ~ -name '*.backup' -exec rm {} \;
```

For more control, there is a variation of **-exec** that let's you decide which command should be executed. Use **-ok** instead of **-exec**, and you will be asked to confirm each command before it is executed:

```
find ~ -type d -ok chmod 700 {} \;
```

PROCESSING FILES THAT HAVE BEEN FOUND: xargs

When you use **find** to search for files that meet a specific criteria, there are two ways to process what you find. First, you can use the **-exec** action as described in the previous section. This allows you to use any program you want to process each file. However, you must understand that **-exec** generates a separate command for each file. For example, if your search finds 57 files, **-exec** will generate 57 separate commands.

For simple commands that operate on a small number of files, this may be okay. However, when a search yields a large number of files, there is a better alternative. Instead of using **-exec**, you can pipe the output of **find** to a special program designed to work efficiently in such situations. This program, named **xargs** ("X-args"), runs any command you specify using arguments that are passed to it via standard input. The syntax is:

xargs [**-prt**] [**-i**_string_] [_command_ [_argument..._]]

where _command_ is the command you want to run; _string_ is a placeholder; and _argument_ is an argument read from standard input.

Let's start with a simple example. You want to create a list of all your ordinary files showing how much disk space is used by each file. You tell **find** to start from your home directory and search for ordinary files. The output is piped to **xargs** which runs the command **ls -s** (Chapter 24) to display the size of each file. The whole thing looks like this:

```
find ~ -type f | xargs ls -s
```

Here is a more complex example that should prove valuable in your everyday life. You are a beautiful, intelligent woman with excellent taste, and you want to phone me to tell me how much you enjoy this book. You remember that, over a year ago, a mutual friend sent you an email message containing my name and number, and that you saved it to a file. You haven't looked at the file since, and you can't even remember its name or what directory it was in. How can you find the phone number?

The solution is to use **find** to compile a list of all your ordinary files that were last modified more than 365 days ago. Pipe the output to **xargs** and use **grep** (Chapter 19) to search all the files for lines containing the character string "Harley Hahn". Here is the command to use:

```
find ~ -type f -mtime +365 | xargs grep "Harley Hahn"
```

In this case, the phone number is found in a file named **important** in your home directory. The output is:

```
/home/linda/important: Harley Hahn (202) 456-1111
```

When you need to process output from **find**, the **echo** command can be surprisingly useful. As you remember from Chapter 12, **echo** evaluates its arguments and writes them to standard output. If you give it a list of pathnames, **echo** outputs one long line containing all the names. This line can then be piped to another program for further processing.

As an example, let's say you want to count how many ordinary files and directories you have. You use two separate commands, one to count the files, the other to count the directories:

```
find ~ -type f | xargs echo | wc -w
find ~ -type d | xargs echo | wc -w
```

Both commands use **find** to search from your home directory. The first command uses **-type f** to search only for ordinary files; the second command uses **-type d** to search only for directories. Both commands pipe the output of **find** to **xargs**, which feeds it to **echo**. The output of the **echo** command is then piped to **wc -w** (Chapter 18) to count the number of words, that is, the number of pathnames.

From time to time, you will want to be able to use the arguments sent to **xargs** more than once in the same command. To do so, you use the **-i** (insert) option. This allows you to use **{ }** as a placeholder that will be replaced with the arguments before the command is run. Let me start with a simple example to show you how it works.

Consider the following two commands, both of which search for ordinary files starting from your working directory:

```
find . -type f | xargs echo
find . -type f | xargs -i echo {} {}
```

In the first command, **echo** writes a single copy of its arguments to standard output. In the second command, **echo** writes two copies of its arguments to standard output. Here is a more useful example that moves all the files in your working directory to another directory, renaming the files as they move.

```
find . -type f | xargs -i mv {} ~/backups/{}.old
```

This command uses **find** to search your working directory for ordinary files. The list of files is piped to **xargs**, which runs an **mv** command (explained earlier in the chapter). The **mv** command moves each file to a subdirectory named **backups**, which lies within your home directory. As part of the move, the extension **.old** is appended to each filename.

Let's say your working directory contains three ordinary files: **a**, **b** and **c**. After the above command is run, the working directory will be empty, and the **backups** directory will contain **a.old**, **b.old** and **c.old**.

If you want to use **-i** but, for some reason, you don't want to use **{}**, you can specify your own placeholder. Just type it directly after the **-i**, for example:

```
find . -type f | xargs -iXX mv XX ~/backups/XX.old
```

When you write such commands, it is possible to create unexpected problems, because you can't see what is happening. If you anticipate a problem, use the **-p** (prompt) option. This tells **xargs** to show you each command as it is generated, and to ask your permission before running it. If you type a reply that begins with "y" or "Y", **xargs** runs the command. If you type any other answer — such as pressing the <Return> key — **xargs** skips the command.

Here is an example you can try for yourself. Use **touch** (explained earlier in the chapter) to create several new files in your working directory:

```
touch a b c d e
```

Now enter the following command to add the extension **.junk** to the end of each of these filenames. Use **-p** so **xargs** will ask your approval for each file:

```
find . -name '[abcde]' | xargs -i -p mv {} {}.junk
```

If you want to see which commands are generated but you don't need to be asked for approval, use **-t**. This causes **xargs** to display each command as it is run. You can think of **-t** as meaning "tell me what you are doing":

```
find . -name '[abcde]' | xargs -i -t mv {} {}.junk
```

Important: Be sure not to group **-i** with any other options. For example, the following command will not work properly, because **xargs** will think that the **p** following **-i** is a placeholder, not an option:

```
find . -name '[abcde]' | xargs -ip mv {} {}.junk
```

The last option I want you to know about is **-r**. By default, **xargs** always runs the specified command at least once. The **-r** option tells **xargs** not to run the command if there are no input arguments. For example, the following command searches your working directory and displays a long listing of any files that are empty:

```
find . -empty | xargs ls -l
```

Suppose, however, there are no empty files. The **ls -l** command will run with no arguments. This will produce a long listing of the entire directory, which is not what you want. The solution is to use the **-r** option:

```
find . -empty | xargs -r ls -l
```

Now **xargs** will only run the **ls** command if there are arguments.

As you can see, connecting **find** and **xargs** is an easy way to build powerful tools. However, I don't want to give you the impression that **xargs** is only used with **find**. In fact, **xargs** can be used with any program that can supply it with character strings to use as arguments. Here are some examples.

You are writing a shell script, and you want to use **whoami** (Chapter 8) to display the current userid, and **date** (also Chapter 8) to display the time and date. To make it look nice, you want all the output to be on a single line:

```
(whoami; date) | xargs
```

You have a file, **filenames**, that contains the names of a number of files. You want to use **cat** (Chapter 16) to combine all the data in these files and save the output to a file named **master**:

```
xargs cat < filenames > master
```

Finally, you want to move all the C source files in your current directory to a subdirectory named **archive**. First, create the subdirectory if it does not already exist:

```
mkdir archive
```

Now use **ls** and **xargs** to list and move all the files that have an extension of **.c**. I have included the **-t** option, so **xargs** will show you each command as it is executed:

0p7   0p7

CHAPTER 25 EXERCISES

REVIEW QUESTIONS

1. Which command do you use to create a brand new, empty file? Why do you rarely need to use this command? Give three common situations in which a file would be created for you automatically.

2. Examine each of the following character strings and decide whether or not it would make a good filename. If not, explain why.

```
data-backup-02      Data Backup 02
data_backup_02      Data;Backup,02
DataBackup02        databackup20
DATABACKUP02        data/backup/20
```

3. What are file permissions? What are the two main uses for file permissions? Which program is used to set or change file permissions? What are the three types of file permissions? For each type, explain what it means when applied (a) to an ordinary file (b) to a directory.

4. What is a link? What is a symbolic link? What is a hard link and a soft link? How do you create a link? How do you create a symbolic link?

5. Which three programs are used to find a file or a set of files? When would you use each one?

APPLYING YOUR KNOWLEDGE

1. Within your home directory, create a directory named **temp** and change to it. Within this directory, create two subdirectories named **days** and **months**. Within each directory, create two files named **file1** and **file2**. Hint: Use a subshell (see Chapter 15) to change the working directory and create the files.

   Once all the files are created, use the **tree** program (Chapter 24) to display a diagram of the directory tree showing both directories and files. If your system doesn't have **tree**, use **ls -R** instead.

2. Continuing from the previous exercise:

   Within the **days** directory, rename **file1** to **monday** and rename **file2** to **tuesday**. Then copy **monday** to **friday**. Within the **months** directory, rename **file1** to **december** and **file2** to **july**.

   Move back to **temp** and use **tree** to display another diagram of the directory tree. If your system doesn't have **tree**, use **ls -R** instead.

Create a link from **december** to **april**. Create a symbolic link from **december** to **may**. Display a long listing of the **months** directory. What do you notice?

To clean up, use a single command to delete the **temp** directory, all its subdirectories, and all the files in those directories. Use one final command to confirm that **temp** no longer exists.

3. Use a text editor to create a file named **green**. Within the file, enter the line:

    `I am a smart person.`

    Save your work and quit the editor.

    Create a link to the file **green** and call it **blue**. Display a long listing of **green** and **blue** and make a note of their modification times.

    Wait 3 minutes, then use the text editor to edit the file **green**. Change the one line of text to:

    `I am a very smart person.`

    Save your work and quit the editor.

    Display a long listing of **green** and **blue**. Why do they both have the same (updated) modification time even though you only edited one file? What would have happened if you had changed **blue** instead of **green**?

4. You are setting up a Web site in which all the HTML files are in subdirectories of a directory named **httpdocs** in your home directory. Use a pipeline to find all the files with the extension **.html** and change their permissions to the following:

    Owner: read + write
    Group: nothing
    Other: read

FOR FURTHER THOUGHT

1. Most GUI-based file managers maintain a "trash" folder to store deleted files, so they can be recovered if necessary. With such systems, a file is not gone for good until it is deleted from the "trash". Why do the Unix text-based tools not offer such a service?

2. Imagine going back in a time machine to 1976, when I first started to use Unix. You find me and ask for a tour of the Unix system I am using. To your surprise, you see files, directories, subdirectories, a working directory, a home directory, special files, links, inodes, permissions, and so on. You also see all the standard commands: **ls**, **mkdir**, **pwd**, **cd**, **chmod**, **cp**, **rm**, **mv**, **ln** and **find**. Indeed, you notice that virtually every idea and tool you learned about in this chapter was developed more than thirty years ago.

What is it about the basic design of the Unix filesystem that has enabled it to survive for so long and still be so useful? Is this unusual in the world of computing?

3. The **find** program is a powerful tool, but very complicated. Imagine a GUI-based version of the program that enables you to choose options from a large drop-down list, enter file patterns into a form, select various tests from a menu, and so on. Would such a program be be easier to use than the standard text-based version? Could a GUI version of **find** replace the text-based version?

PROCESSES AND JOB CONTROL

Within Unix, every object is represented by either a file or a process. In simple terms, a file is an input source or output target, while a process is a program that is executing. Files offer access to data; processes make things happen.

It is very important that you have a firm understanding of both files and processes. We discussed files in detail in Chapters 23, 24 and 25. In this chapter, we will cover processes and the related topic of job control. To do so, we will consider several key questions. Where do processes come from? How are they managed by the system? How do you control your own processes?

As you read this chapter, much of what we have discussed throughout the book will come together in a way that will bring you a great deal of satisfaction. Once you understand processes and how they are managed, you will appreciate the richness of Unix, and how its various parts interact to form a complex, elegant system.

HOW THE KERNEL MANAGES PROCESSES

In Chapter 6, we discussed the idea of a process, a program that is executing. More precisely, a PROCESS is a program that is loaded into memory and ready to run, along with the program's data and the information needed to keep track of the program. All processes are managed by the kernel, the central part of the operating system. The details, as you can imagine, are complex, so let me offer you a summary.

When a process is created, the kernel assigns it a unique identification number called a PROCESS ID or PID (pronounced as three separate letters, "P-I-D"). To keep track of all the processes in the system, the kernel maintains a PROCESS TABLE, indexed by PID, containing one entry for each process. Along with the PID, each entry in the table contains the information necessary to describe and manage the process.

Does this arrangement sound familiar? It should, because it is similar to the system of inumbers and inodes we discussed in Chapter 25. As you will remember, every file has a unique identification number called its inumber, which is used as an index into the inode table. Each inode contains the information necessary to describe and manage a particular file. Thus, the process table is similar to the inode table. Analogously, a process ID corresponds to an inumber, while an entry in the process table corresponds to an inode.

A small Unix system can easily have over 100 processes running at the same time. Some of them, of course, are programs run by the users. Most processes, however, are started automatically to perform tasks in the background. On a large system, there can be hundreds or even thousands of processes all needing to share the system's resources: processors, memory, I/O devices, network connections, and so on. In order to manage such a complex workload, the kernel provides a sophisticated scheduling service, sometimes referred to as the SCHEDULER.

At all times, the scheduler maintains a list of all the processes waiting to execute. Using a complicated algorithm, the scheduler chooses one process at a time, and gives it a chance to run for a short interval called a TIME SLICE. (On a multiprocessor system, the scheduler will choose more than one process at a time.)

When we talk about concepts such as time slices, we often refer to processing time as CPU TIME. This term dates back to the olden days — before modern single-chip processors — when the bulk of the computation was performed by a central processing unit or CPU.

A typical time slice consists of about 10 milliseconds (10 thousandths of a second) of CPU time. Once the time slice is over, the process goes back on the scheduling list and another process is started. In this way, every process, eventually, is given enough CPU time to complete its work. Although a time slice isn't very long by human standards, modern processors are very, very fast and 10 milliseconds is actually long enough to execute tens of thousands of instructions. (Think about that for a moment.)

Each time a process finishes its time slice, the kernel needs to put the process on hold. However, this must be done in such a way that, later, when the process is restarted, it is able to continue exactly where it left off. To make this possible, the kernel saves data for every process that is interrupted. For example, the kernel will save the location of the next instruction to be executed within the program, a copy of the environment, and so on.

FORKING TILL YOU DIE

So how are processes created? With one notable exception (discussed later in the chapter), every process is created by another process. Here is how the system works.

As we discussed in Chapter 2, the kernel is the core of the operating system. As such, the kernel provides essential services to processes, specifically:

- Memory management (virtual memory management, including paging)
- Process management (process creation, termination, scheduling)
- Interprocess communication (local, network)
- Input/output (via device drivers, programs that perform the actual communications with physical devices)
- File management
- Security and access control
- Network access (such as TCP/IP)

When a process needs the kernel to perform a service, it sends the request by using a SYSTEM CALL. For example, a process would use a system call to initiate an I/O operation. When you write programs, the exact method of using a system call depends on your programming language. In a C program, for example, you would use a function from a standard library. Unix systems typically have between 200-300 system calls, and part of becoming a programmer is learning how to use them, at least the most important ones.

The most important system calls are the ones used for process control and I/O (see Figure 26-1). Specifically, the system calls used to create and use processes are **fork**, **exec**, **wait**, and **exit**.

The **fork** system call creates a copy of the current process. Once this happens, we call the original process the PARENT PROCESS or, more simply, the PARENT. The new process, which is an exact copy of the parent, is called the CHILD PROCESS or the CHILD. The **wait** system call forces a process to pause until another process has finished executing. The **exec** system call changes the program that a process is running. And, finally, the **exit** system call terminates a process. To make it easy to talk about these concepts, we often use the words FORK, EXEC, WAIT and EXIT as verbs. For example, you might read, "When a process forks, it results in two identical processes."

What is amazing is that, by using only these four basic system calls (with a few minor variations we can ignore), Unix processes are able to coordinate the elaborate interaction that takes place between you, the shell, and the programs you choose to run. To illustrate how it works, let's consider what happens when you enter a command at the shell prompt.

As you know (from Chapter 11), the shell is a program that acts as a user interface and script interpreter. It is the shell that enables you to enter commands and, indirectly, to access the services of the kernel. Although the shell is important, once it is running

SYSTEM CALL	PURPOSE
fork	create a copy of the current process
wait	wait for another process to finish executing
exec	execute a new program within the current process
exit	terminate the current process
kill	send a signal to another process
open	open a file for reading or writing
read	read data from a file
write	write data to a file
close	close a file

FIGURE 26-1: Commonly used system calls

*Many important tasks can be performed only by the kernel. When a process needs to perform one of these tasks, it must use a system call to send a request to the kernel to do the job. Unix/Linux systems generally have 200-300 different system calls. The most commonly used system calls are the ones used for process control (**fork**, **wait**, **exec**, **exit** and **kill**), and file I/O (**open**, **read**, **write** and **close**).*

it is just another process, one of many in the system. Like all processes, the shell has its own PID (process ID) and its own entry in the process table. In fact, at any time, you can display the PID of the current shell by displaying the value of a special shell variable with the odd name of **$** (dollar sign):

```
echo $$
```

(See Chapter 12 for a discussion of shell variables.)

As we discussed in Chapter 13, there are two types of commands: internal and external. Internal or builtin commands are interpreted directly by the shell, so there is no need to create a new process. External commands, however, require the shell to run a separate program. As such, whenever you want to run an external command, the shell must create a new process. Here is how it works.

The first thing the shell does is use the **fork** system call to create a brand new process. The original process becomes the parent, and the new process is the child. As soon as the forking is done, two things happen. First, the child uses the **exec** system call to change itself from a process running the shell into a process running the external program. Second, the parent uses the **wait** system call to pause itself until the child is finished executing.

Eventually, the external program finishes, at which time the child process uses the **exit** system call to stop itself. Whenever a process stops permanently, for whatever reason, we say that the process DIES or TERMINATES. In fact, as you will see later in the chapter, when we stop a process deliberately, we say that we "kill" it.

Whenever a process dies, all the resources it was using — memory, files, and so on — are deallocated, so they can be used by other processes. At this point, the defunct process is referred to as a ZOMBIE. Although a zombie is dead and is no longer a real process, it still retains its entry in the process table. This is because the entry contains data about the recently departed child that may be of interest to the parent.

Immediately after a child turns into a zombie, the parent — which has been waiting patiently for that child to die — is woken up by the kernel. The parent now has an opportunity to look at the zombie's entry in the process table to see how things turned out. The kernel then removes the entry from that table, effectively extinguishing the last remnant of the child's short, but useful life.

To illustrate the procedure, let's consider what happens when you enter a command to run the **vi** text editor. The first thing the shell does is fork to create a child process, identical to itself. It then begins waiting for the child to die.* At the same instant, the child uses **exec** to change from a process running the shell to a process running **vi**. What you notice is that, an instant after you enter the **vi** command, the shell prompt is replaced by the **vi** program.

When you finish working with **vi** you quit the program. This kills the child process that has been running **vi** and turns it into a zombie. The death of the child causes the kernel to wake up the parent. This, in turn, causes the zombie to be removed from the process table. At the same time, the original process returns to where it was. What you notice is that, an instant after you stop the **vi** program, you see a new shell prompt.

---

*Unix programming is not for the faint of heart.

ORPHANS AND ABANDONED PROCESSES

You might ask, what if a parent forks and then dies unexpectedly, leaving the child all alone? The child, of course, keeps executing but it is now considered to be an ORPHAN. An orphan can still do its job, but when it dies there is no parent to wake up. As a result, the dead child — now in the form of a zombie — is stuck in limbo.

In the olden days, an orphaned zombie would stay in the process table forever or until the system was rebooted (whichever came first). On modern Unix systems, orphaned processes are automatically adopted by process #1, the **init** process (discussed later in the chapter). In this way, whenever an orphan dies, **init**, acting *in loco parentis* is able to swoop down and — without a trace of hesitation — initiate the steps that will lead to the destruction of the the zombie.

A similar situation arises when a parent creates a child, but does not have the good manners to wait for the child to die. Later, when the child dies and turns into a zombie, the neglectful parent has left the poor zombie — like Mariana in the Moated Grange* — saying to itself, "My life is dreary, he cometh not, I am aweary, aweary, I would that I were dead!"

Fortunately, this is an uncommon event. In fact, such occurrences generally happen only when a program has a bug that allows the program to create a child without waiting for the child to die. Interestingly enough, if one of your own programs inadvertently creates an immortal zombie in this manner, there is no direct way for you to get rid of it. After all, how can you kill something that is already dead?

To get rid of an abandoned child that has become a zombie, you can use the **kill** program (described later in the chapter) to terminate the *parent*. Once the parent dies, the zombie becomes an orphan, which will automatically be adopted by the **init** process. In due course, **init** will fulfil its destiny as a responsible step-parent by driving the final stake through the heart of the zombie.

Is Unix programming cool or what?

DISTINGUISHING BETWEEN PARENT AND CHILD

Earlier in the chapter, I explained that the shell executes an external command by forking to create a child process. The child process then execs to run the command, while the parent waits for the child to terminate.

As we discussed, forking results in two identical processes: the original (the parent) and the copy (the child). But one process has to wait and the other has to run a program. If the parent and child are identical, how does the parent know it's the parent, and how does the child know it's the child? In other words, how do they each know what to do?

The answer is when the **fork** system call has finished its work, it passes a numeric value, called a RETURN VALUE, to both the parent and the child process. The return value for the child is set to 0 (zero). The return value for the parent is set to the process ID of the newly created child. Thus, after a fork operation is complete, a process can tell if it is the parent or the child simply by checking the return value. If the return value is greater than zero, the process knows it is the parent. If the return value is 0, the process knows it is the child.

*See the poem "Mariana in the Moated Grange" by Alfred Tennyson.

So what happens when you run an external command? After the shell forks, there are two identical shells. One is the parent; the other is the child but, at first, they don't know which is which. To figure it out, each process checks the return value it received from **fork**. The shell with the positive return value knows it is the parent, so it uses the **wait** system call to pause itself. The shell with the zero return value knows it is the child, so it uses the **exec** system call to run the external program. (Like all tricks, it doesn't look like magic once you understand how it is done.)

THE VERY FIRST PROCESS: init

In the next section, we will begin to take a look at the day-to-day programs and techniques you will use to control your processes. Before we do, however, I want to digress for a moment to discuss a very interesting observation. If processes are created by forking, every child process must have a parent. But then, that parent must have a parent of its own, and so on. Indeed, if you trace the generations back far enough, you come to the conclusion that, somewhere, there must have been a very first process.

That conclusion is correct. Every Unix system has a process that — at least indirectly — is the parent of all the other processes in the system. The details can vary from one type of Unix to another, but all I want is for you to understand the general idea. I'll describe how it works with Linux.

In Chapter 2, we talked about the boot procedure, the complex set of steps that starts the operating system . Towards the end of the boot procedure, the kernel creates a special process "by hand", that is, without forking. This process is given a PID (process ID) of 0. For reasons I will explain in a moment, process #0 is referred to as the IDLE PROCESS.

After performing some important functions — such as initializing the data structures needed by the kernel — the idle process forks, creating process #1. The idle process then execs to run a very simple program that is essentially an infinite loop doing nothing. (Hence, the name "idle process".) The idea is that, whenever there are no processes waiting to execute, the scheduler will run the idle process. By the time process #0 has metamorphosized into the idle process, it has served its purpose and, effectively, has vanished. Indeed, if you use the **ps** command (discussed later) to display the status of process #0, the kernel will deny that the process even exists.

But what of process #1? It carries out the rest of the steps that are necessary to set up the kernel and finish the boot procedure. For this reason, it is called the INIT PROCESS, and the actual program itself is named **init**. Specifically, the init process opens the system console (see Chapter 3) and mounts the root filesystem (see Chapter 23). It then runs the shell script contained in the file **/etc/inittab**. In doing so, **init** forks multiple times to create the basic processes necessary for running the system (such as setting the runlevel; see Chapter 6) and enabling users to login. In doing so, **init** becomes the ancestor of all the other processes in the system.*

---

*Process #0, the idle process, forks to create process #1, the init process. Thus, strictly speaking, the ultimate ancestor of all processes is actually process #0. However, once process #0 finishes its job, it effectively disappears. Thus, we can say that process #1 is the only *living* ancestor of all the processes in the system.

In fact, if a process were ever to become interested in genealogy, it would not be able to trace its roots past process #1, because processes are not allowed to read the source code for the kernel.

Unlike the idle process (#0), the init process (#1) never stops running. In fact, it is the first process in the process table, and it stays there until the system is shut down. Even after the system has booted, **init** is still called upon to perform important actions from time to time. For example, as we have already discussed, when a parent process dies before its child, the child becomes an orphan. The **init** program automatically adopts all orphans to make sure their deaths are handled properly.

Later in the chapter, when we discuss the **ps** (process status) command, I will show you how to display the process IDs of both a process and its parents. You will see that if you trace the ancestry of any process in the system far enough, it will always lead you back to process #1.

FOREGROUND AND BACKGROUND PROCESSES

When you run a program, the input and output is usually connected to your terminal. For text-based programs, input comes from your keyboard, and output goes to your monitor. This only make sense because most of the programs you will use need to interact with you in order to do their job.

Some programs, however, can run by themselves without tying up your terminal. For example, let's say you want to use a program to read a very large amount of data from a file, sort that data, and then write the output to another file. There is no reason why such a program can't work on its own without your intervention.

As we have discussed, whenever you enter a command to run a program, the shell waits for the program to finish before asking you to enter another command. However, if you were using the sorting program I described above, there would be no need to wait for it to finish. You could enter the command to start the program and then move right along to the next command, leaving the program to run on its own.

To do this, all you have to do is type an **&** (ampersand) character at the end of the command. This tells the shell that the program you are running should execute all by itself. For example, say the command to run the sorting program is as follows:

```
sort < bigfile > results
```

If you enter this exact command, the shell will launch the program and wait until the program finishes executing. It is only when the program is done that the shell will display a prompt to tell you that it is waiting for a new command. However, it works differently when you enter the command with an **&** at the end:

```
sort < bigfile > results &
```

In this case, the shell does not wait for the program to finish. As soon as the program starts, the shell regains control and displays a new prompt. This means you can enter another command without waiting for the first program to finish.

When the shell waits for a program to finish before prompting you to enter a new command, we say the process is running in the FOREGROUND. When the shell starts a program, but then leaves it to run on its own, we say the process is running in the BACKGROUND. In the first example, we ran the **sort** program in the foreground. In the second example, we ran **sort** in the background by typing an **&** character at the end of the command.

As I explained in Chapter 15, most Unix programs are designed to read input from standard input (stdin) and write output to standard output (stdout). Error messages are written to standard error (stderr). When you run a program from the shell prompt, stdin is connected to your keyboard, and stdout and stderr are connected to your monitor. If you want to change this, you can redirect stdin, stout and stderr at the time you run the program.

Reading from the keyboard and writing to the monitor works fine when you run a process in the foreground. However, when you run a program in the background, the process executes on its own to allow you to enter another command. What happens, then, if a background process tries to read or write to standard I/O? The answer is the input is disconnected, but the output connections do not change.

This has two important implications. First, if a process running in the background tries to read from stdin, there will be nothing there and the process will pause indefinitely, waiting for input. The process wants to read, and it is going to wait and wait and wait until you give it something to read. In such cases, the only thing you can do is use the **fg** command to move the process to the foreground (discussed later). This allows you to interact with the process and give it what it wants.

Second, if a process running in the background writes to either stdout or stderr, the output will show up on your monitor. However, since you are probably working on something else, the output will be mixed in with whatever else you are doing, which can be confusing and distracting.

CREATING A DELAY: `sleep`

In order to demonstrate how background output can get mixed up with foreground output, I have a short experiment for you. In this experiment, we are going to run a sequence of two commands in the background. The first command will create a delay; the second command will then write some output to the terminal. In the meantime (during the delay), we will start another program in the foreground. You will then see what happens when a background process writes its output to the screen while you are working in the foreground.

Before we get started, I want to tell you about the tool we will use to create the delay. We will be using a program named **sleep**. The syntax is:

sleep *interval*[**s**|**m**|**h**|**d**]

where *interval* is the length of the delay.

Using **sleep** is straightforward. Just specify the length of the delay you want in seconds. For example, to pause for 5 seconds, use:

sleep 5

If you enter this command at your terminal, it will seem as if nothing is happening. However, 5 seconds later, the program will finish and you will see a new shell prompt.

With Linux or any other system that uses the GNU utilities (see Chapter 2), you can specify a one-letter modifier after the interval: **s** for seconds (the default), **m** for minutes; **h** for hours, and **d** for days. For example:

```
sleep 5
sleep 5s
sleep 5m
sleep 5h
sleep 5d
```

The first two commands pause for 5 seconds. The next three commands pause for 5 minutes, 5 hours, and 5 days respectively.

Most often, we use **sleep** within a shell script to create a specific delay. For example, let's say Program A writes data to a file that is needed by Program B. You may need to write a shell script to make sure the data file exists before you run Program B. Within the script, you use **sleep** to create, say, a 5 minute delay within a loop. Every 5 minutes, your script checks to see if the file exists. If not, it waits for another 5 minutes and tries again. Eventually, when the file is detected, the script moves on and runs Program B.

At the command line, **sleep** is useful when you want to wait a specified amount of time before running a command, which is what we will be doing. To run the experiment, I want you to enter the following two command lines quickly, one right after the other:

```
(sleep 20; cat /etc/passwd) &
vi /etc/termcap
```

The first command runs in the background. It pauses for 20 seconds and then copies the contents of the password file (Chapter 11) to your terminal. The second command runs in the foreground. It uses the **vi** text editor (Chapter 22) to look at the Termcap file (Chapter 7).

After you enter the second command and **vi** has started, wait a short time and you will see the contents of the password file splattered all over your screen. Now you can appreciate how irritating it is when a background process writes its output to your terminal when you are working on something else.

The moral? Don't run programs in the background if they are going to read or write from the terminal.

(Within **vi**: To redraw the screen, press **^L**. This is a handy command to remember for just such occasions. To quit, type **:q** and then press <Return>.)

A program is a candidate to run as a background process only if it does not need to run interactively; that is, if it does not need to read from your keyboard or write to your screen. Consider our earlier example:

```
sort < bigfile > results &
```

In this case, we can run the program in the background because it gets its input from one file (**bigfile**) and writes its output to another file (**results**).

Interestingly enough, the shell will allow you to run *any* program in the background; all you have to do is put an **&** character at the end of the command. So be thoughtful. Don't, for instance, run **vi**, **less** or other such programs in the background.

HINT

If you accidentally run an interactive program in the background, you can terminate it by using the **kill** command, discussed later in the chapter.

TECHNICAL HINT

Compiling a source program is a great activity to run in the background. For example, let's say you are using the **gcc** compiler to compile a C program named **myprog.c**. Just make sure to redirect the standard error to a file, and everything will work fine. The first command below does the job for the Bourne shell family (Bash, Korn Shell). The second command is for the C-Shell family (Tcsh, C-Shell):

```
gcc myprog.c 2> errors &
gcc myprog.c >& errors &
```

Another common situation occurs when you need to build a program that uses a makefile. For example, say you have downloaded a program named **game**. After unpacking the files, you can use **make** to build the program in the background:

```
make game > makeoutput 2> makeerrors &
```

In both cases, the shell will display a message for you when the program has finished.

JOB CONTROL

In the early 1970s, the first Unix shells offered very little in the way of process control. When a user ran a program, the resulting process used the terminal for standard input, standard output, and standard error. Until that process finished, the user was unable to enter any more commands. If it became necessary to terminate the process before it finished on its own, the user could press either **^C** to send the **intr** signal or **^** to send the **quit** signal (see Chapter 7). The only difference was that **quit** would generate a core dump for debugging.

Alternatively, a user could type an **&** (ampersand) character at the end of the command line to run the program as an ASYNCHRONOUS PROCESS. An asynchronous process had two defining characteristics. First, by default, standard input would be connected to the empty file **/dev/null**. Second, because the process was running on its own without any input from the user, it would not respond to the **intr** or **quit** signals.

Today, we have GUIs, terminal windows, and virtual consoles, which make it easy to run more than one program at the same time. In the 1970s, however, being able to create asynchronous processes was very important, as it enabled users to start programs that would run by themselves without tying up the terminal. For example, if you had a long source program to compile, you could use an asynchronous process to do the job. Once the process started, your terminal would be free, so you wouldn't have to stop working. Of course, if the asynchronous process got into trouble, you would not be able to terminate it with ^C or ^/. Instead, you would have to use the **kill** command (covered later in the chapter).

As we discussed in Chapter 11, the original Bourne Shell was created in 1976 by Steven Bourne at Bell Labs. This shell was part of AT&T Unix and it supported asynchronous processes, which is all there was until 1978 when Bill Joy, a graduate student at U.C. Berkeley, created a brand new shell, which he called the C-Shell (see Chapter 11). As part of the C-Shell, Joy included support for a new capability called JOB CONTROL. (Joy also added several other important new features, such as aliases and command history.)

Job control made it possible to run multiple processes: one in the foreground, the rest in the background. Within the C-Shell, a user could pause any process and restart it as needed. He could also move processes between the foreground and background, suspend (pause) them, and display their status. Joy included the C-Shell in BSD (Berkeley Unix), and job control proved to be one of the shell's most popular features. Even so, AT&T Unix did not get job control for four more years, until David Korn included it in the first Korn Shell in 1982. Today, job control is supported by every important Unix shell.

The essential feature of job control is that every command you enter is considered to be a JOB identified by a unique JOB NUMBER also referred to as a JOB ID (pronounced "job-I-D"). To control and manipulate your jobs, you use the job id along with a variety of commands, variables, terminal settings, shell variables, and shell options. For reference, these tools are summarized in Figure 26-2.

Within the Bourne Shell family (Bash, Korn Shell), job control is enabled when the **monitor** option is set. This is the default for interactive shells, but it can be turned off by unsetting the option (see Chapter 12). With the C-Shell family (Tcsh, C-Shell), job control is always turned on for interactive shells.

It is natural to wonder, how is a job different from a process? For practical purposes, the two concepts are similar, and you will often see people use the terms "job" and "process" interchangeably. Strictly speaking, however, there is a difference. A process is a program that is executing or ready to execute. A job refers to all the processes that are necessary to interpret an entire command line. Where processes are controlled by the kernel, jobs are controlled by the shell, and in the same way that the kernel uses the process table to keep track of processes, the shell uses a JOB TABLE to keep track of jobs.

As an example, let's say you enter the following simple command to display the time and date:

```
date
```

This command generates a single process, with its own process ID, and a single job with its own job ID. As the job runs, there will be one new entry in the process table and one new entry in the jobs table. Now consider the following more complicated command lines. The first uses a pipeline consisting of four different programs. The second executes four different programs in sequence:

```
who | cut -c 1-8 | sort | uniq -c
date; who; uptime; cal 12 2008
```

Each of these command lines generates four different processes, one for each program, and each process has its own process ID. However, the entire pipeline — no matter how many processes it might require — is considered to be a single job, with a single job ID. While the job is running, there will be four entries in the process table, but only a single entry in the job table.

JOB CONTROL COMMANDS	
`jobs`	display list of jobs
`ps`	display list of processes
`fg`	move job to foreground
`bg`	move job to background
`suspend`	suspend the current shell
`^Z`	suspend the current foreground job
`kill`	send signal to job; by default, terminate job

VARIABLES	
`echo $$`	display PID of current shell
`echo $!`	display PID of the last command you moved to the background

TERMINAL SETTINGS	
`stty tostop`	suspend background jobs that try to write to the terminal
`stty -tostop`	turn off **tostop**

SHELL OPTIONS: BASH, KORN SHELL	
`set -o monitor`	enable job control
`set +o nomonitor`	turn off **monitor**
`set -o notify`	notify immediately when background jobs finish
`set +o nonotify`	turn off **notify**

SHELL VARIABLES: TCSH, C-SHELL	
`set listjobs`	list all jobs whenever a job is suspended (Tcsh only)
`set listjobs long`	**listjobs** with a long listing (Tcsh only)
`set notify`	notify immediately when background jobs finish
`set nonotify`	turn off **notify**

FIGURE 26-2: Job control: Tools

Job control is a feature supported by the shell that enables you to run multiple jobs, one in the foreground, the rest in the background. You can selectively suspend (pause) jobs, restart them, move them between the foreground and background, and display their status. To do so, you use a variety of commands, variables, terminal settings, shell variables, and shell options.

At any time, you can display a list of all your processes by using the **ps** (process status) command. Similarly, you can display a list of your jobs by using the **jobs** command. We'll discuss the details later in the chapter.

RUNNING A JOB IN THE BACKGROUND

To run a job in the background, you type an **&** character at the end of the command. For example, the following command runs the **ls** program in the background, with the output redirected to a file named **temp**:

```
ls > temp &
```

Each time you run a job in the background, the shell displays the job number and the process ID. The shell assigns the job numbers itself, starting from 1. For example, if you create 4 jobs, they will be assigned job numbers 1, 2, 3 and 4. The kernel assigns the process ID, which is, in most cases, a multi-digit number.

As an example, let's say you entered the command above. The shell displays the following:

```
[1] 4003
```

This means that job number #1 has just been started, with a process ID of 4003. If your job consists of a pipeline with more than one program, the process ID you see will be that of the last program in the pipeline. For example, let's say you enter:

```
who | cut -c 1-8 | sort | uniq -c &
```

The shell displays the following:

```
[2] 4354
```

This tells you that you have started job #2 and that the process id of the last program **uniq**) is 4354.

Since background jobs run by themselves, there is no easy way for you to keep track of their progress. For this reason, the shell sends you a short status message whenever a background job finishes. For example, when the job in our first example finishes, the shell will display a message similar to the following:

```
[1]   Done    ls > temp
```

This message notifies you that job #1 has just finished.

If you are waiting for a particular background job to finish, such notifications are important. However, it would be irritating if the shell displayed status messages willy-nilly when you were in the middle of doing something else, such as editing a file or reading a man page. For this reason, when a background job ends, the shell does not notify you immediately. Instead, it waits until it is time to display the next shell prompt. This prevents the status message from interfering with the output from another program.

If you do not want to wait for such messages, there is a setting you can change to force the shell to notify you the instant a background job finishes, regardless of what else you might be doing. With the Bourne shell family (Bash, Korn Shell), you set the **notify** option:

```
set -o notify
```

To unset this option, use:

```
set +o notify
```

With the C-Shell family (Tcsh, C-Shell), you set the **notify** variable:

```
set notify
```

To unset this variable, use:

```
unset notify
```

For a discussion of how to use shell options and shell variables, see Chapter 12. If you want to make the setting permanent, just place the appropriate command in your environment file (Chapter 14).

SUSPENDING A JOB: fg

At any time, every job is in one of three STATES: running in the foreground; running in the background; or paused, waiting for a signal to resume execution. To pause a foreground job, you press **^Z** (Ctrl-Z). As described in Chapter 7, this sends the **susp** signal, which causes the process to pause. When you pause a process in this way, we say that you SUSPEND it or STOP it.

The terminology can be a bit misleading, so let's take a moment to discuss it. The term "stop" refers to a temporary pause. Indeed, as you will see, a stopped job can be restarted. Thus, when you press **^Z** it merely pauses the job. If you want to halt a process permanently, you must press **^C** or use the **kill** command (both of which are discussed later in the chapter).

When you stop a program, the shell puts it on hold and displays a new shell prompt. You can now enter as many commands as you like. When you want to resume working with the suspended program, you move it back to the foreground by using the **fg** command. Using **^Z** and **fg** in this way enables you to suspend a program, enter some commands, and then return to the original program whenever you want. Here is a typical example of how you might make use of this facility.

You are using the **vi** text editor to write a shell script. Within the script, you want to use the **cal** command to display a calendar, but you are not sure about the syntax. You suspend **vi**, display the man page for **cal**, find out what you want, and then return to **vi** exactly where you left off. Here is how you do it. To start, enter the following command to run **vi**:

```
vi script
```

You are now editing a file named **script**. Pretend you have typed several lines of the script and you need to find out about the **cal** program. To suspend **vi**, press **^Z**:

^Z

The shell pauses **vi** and displays an informative message:

```
[3]+  Stopped     vi script
```

In this case, the message tells you that **vi**, job #3, is now suspended. You are now at the shell prompt. Enter the command to display the man page for **cal**:

man cal

Look around for a bit, and then press **q** to quit. You will see the shell prompt. You can now restart **vi** by moving it back into the foreground:

fg

You are now back in **vi**, exactly where you left off. (When you want to quit **vi**, type **:q** and press <Return>.)

HINT

If you are working and, all of a sudden, your program stops and you see a message like "Stopped" or "Suspended", it means you have accidentally pressed ^Z.

When this happens, all you have to do is enter **fg**, and your program will come back to life.

When you suspend a job, the process is paused indefinitely. This can create a problem if you try to log out, because you will have suspended jobs waiting around. The rule is, when you log out, all suspended jobs are terminated automatically. In most cases, this would be a mistake. So if you try to log out and you have suspended jobs, the shell will display a warning message. Here are some examples:

```
There are suspended jobs.
You have stopped jobs.
```

If you try to logout and you see such a message, use **fg** to move the suspended job into the foreground and quit the program properly. If you have more than one suspended job, you must repeat the procedure for each one. This will prevent you from losing data accidentally.

On occasion, you may be completely sure that you want to log out even though you have one or more suspended jobs. If so, all you have to do is try to log out a second time. Since the shell has already warned you once, it will assume you know what you are doing, and you will be allowed to log out without a warning. Remember, though, that logging out in this way will terminate all your suspended jobs; they will not be waiting for you the next time you log in.

HINT FOR TCSH USERS

When you suspend a job with the Tcsh, the shell displays only a short message "Suspended" with no other information. However, if you set the **listjobs** variable, the Tcsh will display a list of all your jobs whenever any job is suspended. The command to use is:

```
set listjobs
```

If you give **listjobs** a value of **long**, the Tcsh will display a "long" listing that also shows each job's process ID:

```
set listjobs=long
```

My suggestion is to put this command in your environment file (see Chapter 14) to make the setting permanent.

SUSPENDING A SHELL: suspend

Pressing **^Z** will suspend whichever job is running in the foreground. However, there is one process it will not suspend: your current shell. If you want to pause your shell, you'll need to use the **suspend** command. The syntax is:

suspend [-**f**]

Why would you want to suspend a shell? Here is an example. As we discussed in Chapter 4, when you have your own Unix or Linux system, you must do your own system administration. Let's say you are logged in under your own userid, and you need to do something that requires being superuser, so you use **su** (Chapter 6) to start a new shell in which you are **root**. After you have been working for a while, you realize that you need to do something quick under your own userid. It would be bothersome to stop the superuser shell and have to restart it later, because you would lose track of your working directory, any variable changes, and so on. Instead, you can enter:

suspend

This pauses the current shell — the one in which you are superuser — and returns you to the previous shell in which you were logged in under your regular userid. When you are ready to go back to being superuser to finish your admin work, you can use the **fg** command to move your superuser shell back to the foreground:

fg

Here is another example. Let's say you use Bash as your default shell, but you want to experiment with the Tcsh. You enter the following command to start a new shell:

tcsh

At any time, you can use **suspend** to pause the Tcsh and return to Bash. Later, you can use **fg** to resume your work with the Tcsh.

The only restriction on suspending shells is that, by default, you are not allowed to suspend your login shell. This prevents you from putting yourself in limbo by stopping your main shell. In certain circumstances, however, you may actually want to pause a login shell. For example, when you start a superuser shell by using **su** – instead of **su**, it creates a login shell (see Chapter 6). If you want to suspend the new shell, you must use the **-f** (force) option:

```
suspend -f
```

This tells **suspend** to pause the current shell, regardless of whether or not it happens to be a login shell.

JOB CONTROL VS. MULTIPLE WINDOWS

In Chapter 6, we discussed a variety of ways in which you can run more than one program at a time when you are using Unix or Linux on your own computer. First, you can use multiple virtual consoles, each of which supports a completely separate work session. Second, within the GUI, you can open as many terminal windows as you want, each of which has its own CLI (command line interface) with its own shell. Finally, some terminal window programs allow you to have multiple tabs within the same window, with each tab having its own shell.

With so much flexibility, why do you need to be able to suspend processes and run programs in the background? Why not just run every program in its own window and do without job control? There are several important answers to this question.

First, your work will be a lot slower if you need to switch to a different virtual console, window, or tab every time you begin a new task. In many cases, it is a lot less cumbersome to simply pause what you are doing, enter a few commands, and then return to your original task.

Second, when you use multiple windows, you have a lot more visual elements on your screen, which can slow you down. Moreover, windows need to be managed: moved, resized, iconized, maximized, and so on. Using job control makes your life a lot simpler by reducing the mental and visual clutter.

Third, it often happens that the commands you use within a short period of time are related to a specific task or problem. In such cases, it is handy to be able to recall previous commands from your history list (see Chapter 13). When you use separate windows, the history list in one window is not accessible from another window.

Finally, there will be times when you will use a terminal emulator to access a remote host (see Chapter 3), especially if you are a system administrator. In such cases, you will have only a single CLI connected to the remote host. You will not have a GUI with multiple windows or several virtual consoles. If you are not skillful at using job control, you will only be able to run one program at a time, which will be frustrating.

As a general rule, when you need to switch between completely unrelated tasks — especially tasks that require a full screen — it makes sense to use multiple windows or separate virtual consoles. In most other cases, however, you will find that job control works better and faster.

DISPLAYING A LIST OF YOUR JOBS: `jobs`

At any time, you can display a list of all your jobs by using the **jobs** command. The syntax is:

```
jobs [-l]
```

In most cases, all you need to do is enter the command name by itself:

```
jobs
```

Here is some sample output in which you can see three suspended jobs (#1, #3, #4) and one job running in the background (#2):

```
[1]   Stopped    vim document
[2]   Running    make game >makeoutput 2>makeerrors &
[3]-  Stopped    less /etc/passwd
[4]+  Stopped    man cal
```

If you would like to see the process ID as well as the job number and command name, use the **-l** (long listing) option:

```
jobs -l
```

For example:

```
[1]   2288 Stopped    vim document
[2]   2290 Running    make game >makeoutput 2>makeerrors &
[3]-  2291 Stopped    less /etc/passwd
[4]+  2319 Stopped    man cal
```

Notice that in both listings, one of the jobs is flagged with a **+** (plus sign) character. This is called the "current job". Another job is flagged with a **−** (minus sign) character. This is the "previous job".

These designations are used by the various commands that manipulate jobs. If you don't specify a job number, such commands will, by default, act upon the current job. (You will see this when we discuss the **fg** and **bg** commands.) In most cases, the CURRENT JOB is the one that was most recently suspended. The PREVIOUS JOB is the next one in line. In our example, the current job is #4 and the previous job is #3.

If there are no suspended jobs, the current job will be the one that was most recently moved to the background. For example, let's say you enter the **jobs** command and you see the following:

```
[2]   Running    make game >makeoutput 2>makeerrors &
[6]-  Running    calculate data1 data2 &
[7]+  Running    gcc program.c &
```

In this case, there are no suspended jobs. However, there are three jobs running in the background. The current job is #7. The previous job is #6.

MOVING A JOB TO THE FOREGROUND: `fg`

To move a job to the foreground you use the **fg** command. There are three variations of the syntax:

fg
fg %[*job*]
%[*job*]

where *job* identifies a particular job.

Although the syntax looks confusing, it's actually quite simple, as you will see. The simplest form of the command is to enter **fg** by itself:

fg

This tells the shell to restart the current job, the one that is flagged with a **+** character when you use the **jobs** command. For example, let's say you use the **jobs** command and the output is:

```
[1]    2288 Stopped     vim document
[2]    2290 Running     make game >makeoutput 2>makeerrors &
[3]-   2291 Stopped     less /etc/passwd
[4]+   2319 Stopped     man cal
```

The current job is #4, which is suspended. If you enter the **fg** command by itself, it restarts job #4 by moving it to the foreground.

Let's say that, in another situation, you enter the **jobs** command again and the output is:

```
[2]    Running     make game >makeoutput 2>makeerrors &
[6]-   Running     calculate data1 data2 &
[7]+   Running     gcc program.c &
```

In this case, the current job is #7, which is running in the background. If you enter **fg** by itself, it will move job #7 from the background to the foreground. This allows you to interact with the program.

To move a job that is not the current job, you must identify it explicitly. There are several ways to do so, which are summarized in Figure 26-3.

Most of the time, the easiest way to specify a job is to use a **%** (percent) character, followed by a job number. For example, to move job number **1** into the foreground, you would use:

fg %1

You can also specify a job by referring to the name of the command. For example, if you want to restart the job that was running the command **make game**, you can use:

fg %make

Actually, you only need to specify enough of the command to distinguish it from all the other jobs. If there are no other commands that begin with the letter "m", you could use:

```
fg %m
```

An alternative is to use `%?` followed by part of the command. For example, another way to move the **make game** command to the foreground is to use:

```
fg %?game
```

As I mentioned, if you use the **fg** command without specifying a particular job, **fg** will move the current job into the foreground. (This is the job that is marked with a **+** character when you use the **jobs** command.) Alternatively, you can use either `%` or `%+` to refer to the current job. Thus, the following three commands are equivalent:

```
fg
fg %
fg %+
```

Similarly, you can use `%-` to refer to the previous job:

```
fg %-
```

This is the job that is marked with a **-** (minus sign) when you use the **jobs** command.

As a convenience, some shells (Bash, Tcsh, C-Shell) will assume that you are using the **fg** command if you simply enter a job specification that begins with a `%` character. For example, let's say that job number **2** is the command **vim document** and that no other jobs use similar names. All of the following commands will have the same effect:

> **HINT**
>
> To switch back and forth between two jobs quickly, use:
>
> ```
> fg %-
> ```
>
> Once you get used to this command, you will use it a lot.

JOB NUMBER	MEANING
`%%`	current job
`%+`	current job
`%-`	previous job
`%n`	job #n
`%name`	job with specified command name
`%?name`	job with *name* anywhere within the command

FIGURE 26-3: Job control: Specifying a job

To use a job control command, you must specify one or more jobs. You can refer to the jobs in several different ways: as the current job, as the previous job, using a particular job number, or using all or part of the command name.

```
%2
fg %2
fg %vim
fg %?docu
```

In each case, the shell will move job number **2** into the foreground.

With some shells, there is one final abbreviation that you can use: a command consisting of nothing but the single character **%** will tell the shell to move the current job to the foreground. Thus the following four commands are equivalent:

```
%
fg
fg %
fg %+
```

Have you noticed something interesting? If you type a job specification all by itself, the shell will assume you want to use the **fg** command. Thus, **fg** is the only command in which the command name itself is optional. Remember this interesting bit of trivia; someday it will help you win friends and influence people.

HINT

Although our examples showed several jobs suspended at the same time, you will usually pause only a single job, do something else, and then return to what you were doing.

In such cases, job control is very simple. To suspend a job, you press **^Z**. To restart the job, you enter either **fg** or (if your shell supports it) **%**.

MOVING A JOB TO THE BACKGROUND: bg

To move a job to the background, you use the **bg** command. The syntax is:

bg [%*job*...]

where *job* identifies a particular job.

To specify a job, you follow the same rules as with the **fg** command. In particular, you can use the variations in Figure 26-3. For instance, to move job number **2** into the background, you would use:

bg %2

If you'd like, you can move more than one job to the background at the same time, for example:

bg %2 %5 %6

To move the current job into the background, use the command name by itself, without a job specification:

bg

As you might imagine, you will use the **fg** command more often than the **bg** command. But there is one important situation when **bg** comes in handy. Say that you enter a command that seems to be taking a long time. If the program is not interactive, you can suspend it and move it to the background. For example, let's say that you want to use **make** to build a program named **game**, so you enter the command:

```
make game > makeoutput 2> makeerrors
```

After waiting awhile, you realize this could take a long time. Since **make** does not need anything from you, there is no point in tying up your terminal. Simply press **^Z** to suspend the job; then enter **bg** to move the job to the background. Your terminal is now free.

HINT

The **bg** command is useful when you intend to run a program in the background but forget to type the **&** character when you entered the command. As a result, the job starts running in the foreground.

Just suspend the job by pressing **^Z**, and then use the **bg** command to move the job into the background.

LEARNING TO USE THE ps PROGRAM

To display information about processes, you use the **ps** (process status) program. The **ps** program is a useful tool that can help you find a particular PID (process ID), check on what your processes are doing, and give you an overview of everything that is happening on the system. Unfortunately, **ps** has so many confusing and obtuse options that the mere reading of the man page is likely to cause permanent damage to your orbitofrontal cortex.

There are several reasons for this situation. First, as we discussed in Chapter 2, in the 1980s there were two principal branches of Unix: the official UNIX (from AT&T) and unofficial BSD (from U.C. Berkeley). UNIX and BSD each had their own version of **ps**, and each version had its own options. Over time, both types of **ps** became well-known and widely used.

As a result, many modern versions of **ps** support *both* types of options, which we refer to as the UNIX OPTIONS and the BSD OPTIONS. This is the case with Linux, for example. Thus, with the Linux version of **ps**, you can use either the UNIX or BSD options, whichever you prefer. From time to time, however, you will encounter versions of **ps** that support only the UNIX options or only the BSD options. Since you never know when you will be called upon to use such a system, you must be familiar with both types of options.

Second, **ps** is a powerful tool that is used by system administrators and advanced programmers for various types of analysis. As such, there are a lot of technical options that are not really necessary for everyday use. Still, they are available and, when you read the man page, the descriptions can be confusing.

Third, if you have a system that uses the GNU utilities — such as Linux (see Chapter 2) — you will find that **ps** supports, not only the UNIX options and BSD options, but an extra set of GNU-only options. Most of the time, however, you can ignore these options.

Finally, to add to the confusion, you will sometimes see the UNIX options referred to as POSIX OPTIONS or STANDARD OPTIONS. This is because they are used as the basis for the POSIX version of **ps**. (POSIX is a large-scale project, started in the 1990s, with the aim of standardizing Unix; see Chapter 11).

By now, it should be clear that, in order to make sense out of all this, we will need a plan, so here it is.

Although **ps** has many, many options, very few of them are necessary for everyday work. My plan is to teach you the minimum you need to know to use both the UNIX options and the BSD options. We will ignore all of the esoteric options, including the GNU-only ones. Should you ever need any of the other options, you can, of course, simply check with the **ps** man page on your system (**man ps**) to see what is available.

THE ps PROGRAM: BASIC SKILLS

To display information about processes, you use the **ps** (process status) program. As we just discussed, **ps** has a great many options that can be divided into three groups: UNIX, BSD and GNU-only. I will teach you how to use the most important UNIX and BSD options, which is all you will normally need.

When it comes to **ps** options, there is an interesting tradition. The UNIX options are preceded by a dash in the regular manner, but the BSD options do not have a dash. Remember this when you are reading the man page: if an option has a dash, it is a UNIX option; if not, it is a BSD option. I will maintain this tradition within our discussion.

If your version of **ps** supports both the UNIX and BSD options, you can use whichever ones you prefer. In fact, experienced users will sometimes use one set of options and sometimes use the other, whatever happens to be best for the problem at hand. However, let me give you a warning. Don't mix the two types of options in the same command: it can cause subtle problems.

To start, here is the basic syntax to use **ps** with UNIX options:

ps [**-aefFly**] [**-p** *pid*] [**-u** *userid*]

And here is the syntax to use with BSD options:

ps [**ajluvx**] [**p** *pid*] [**U** *userid*]

In both cases, *pid* is a process ID, and *userid* is a userid.

Rather than go through each option separately, I have summarized everything you need to know in several tables. Figure 26-4 contains the information you need to use **ps** with UNIX options. Figure 26-5 shows what you need for BSD options. Take a moment to look through both these figures. At first, it may look a bit confusing, but after you get used to it, everything will make sense.

Let's say that all you want to see is basic information about all the processes running under your userid from your terminal. In this case, you need only enter the command name by itself:

ps

Here is some typical output using the UNIX version of **ps**:

```
  PID  TTY        TIME  CMD
 2262  tty1   00:00:00  bash
11728  tty1   00:00:00  ps
```

Here is the same output using the BSD version of **ps**:

```
  PID  TT  STAT     TIME  COMMAND
50384  p1  Ss    0:00.02  -sh (sh)
72883  p1  R+    0:00.00  ps
```

In general, **ps** displays a table in which each row contains information about one process. In the UNIX example above, we see information about two processes, #2262 and #11728. In the BSD example, we see information about processes #50384 and #72883.

Each column of the table contains a specific type of information. There are a variety of different columns you will see depending on which options you use. As a reference, Figure 26-6 shows the most common column headings. Let's use the information in this figure to decode the information in our examples.

Which processes are displayed?	
ps	processes associated with your userid and your terminal
ps -a	processes associated with any userid and a terminal
ps -e	all processes (includes daemons)
ps -p *pid*	process with process ID *pid*
ps -u *userid*	processes associated with specified *userid*

Which data columns are displayed?	
ps	`PID TTY TIME CMD`
ps -f	`UID PID PPID C TTY TIME CMD`
ps -F	`UID PID PPID C SZ RSS STIME TTY TIME CMD`
ps -l	`F S UID PID PPID C PRI NI ADDR SZ WCHAN TTY TIME CMD`
ps -ly	`S UID PID PPID C PRI NI RSS SZ WCHAN TTY TIME CMD`

Particularly Useful Combinations	
ps	display your own processes
ps -ef	display all user processes, full output
ps -a	display all non-daemon processes
ps -t -	display all daemons (only)

FIGURE 26-4: The **ps** program: UNIX options

The **ps** *(process status) program displays information about the processes that are running on your system. There are two sets of options you can use: UNIX options and BSD options. Here is a summary of the most important UNIX options.*

Starting with the UNIX example, we see there are four columns labeled **PID**, **TTY**, **TIME** and **CMD**. Looking up these names in Figure 26-6, we see the following:

PID: process ID
TTY: name of controlling terminal
TIME: cumulative CPU time
CMD: name of command being executed

Thus, we can see that process #2262 is controlled by terminal **tty1**, has taken virtually no CPU time, and is running Bash. The information for process #11728 is pretty much the same. The only difference is that this process is running the **ps** command. What you see in this example is the minimum you see, because there are always at least two processes: your shell and the **ps** program itself. The **ps** process does not live long, however. In fact, it dies as soon as its output is displayed.

Now let us analyze the BSD example the same way. Looking at the output, we see five columns labeled **PID**, **TT**, **STAT**, **TIME** and **COMMAND**. Checking with Figure 26-6, we see the following:

PID: process ID
TT: name of controlling terminal

Which processes are displayed?	
ps	processes associated with your userid and your terminal
ps a	processes associated with any userid and a terminal
ps ax	all processes (includes daemons)
ps p *pid*	process with process ID *pid*
ps U *userid*	processes associated with *userid*

Which data columns are displayed?	
ps	PID TT STAT TIME COMMAND
ps j	USER PID PPID PGID SESS JOBC STAT TT TIME COMMAND
ps l	UID PID PPID CPU PRI NI VSZ RSS WCHAN STAT TT TIME COMMAND
ps u	USER PID %CPU %MEM VSZ RSS TT STAT STARTED TIME COMMAND
ps v	PID STAT TIME SL RE PAGEIN VSZ RSS LIM TSIZ %CPU %MEM COMMAND

Particularly Useful Combinations	
ps	display your own processes
ps ax	display all processes
ps aux	display all processes, full output

FIGURE 26-5: The ps program: BSD options

*The **ps** (process status) program displays information about the processes that are running on your system. There are two sets of options you can use: UNIX options and BSD options. Here is a summary of the most important BSD options.*

STAT: state code (O,R,S,T,Z)
TIME: cumulative CPU time
COMMAND: full command being executed

In general, the output of the BSD version of **ps** is straightforward, except for the **STAT** column, which we will get to in a moment.

Before we leave this section, I want to show you a small but interesting variation: when you use BSD options, **ps** displays abbreviated terminal names. Take a moment to look carefully at the **TT** column in the example above. Notice that you see only two characters, in this case **p1**. The full name of this terminal is actually **ttyp1**. (Terminal names are discussed in Chapter 23.)

FIGURE 26-6: The **ps** program: Column headings

*The **ps** (process status) program displays information about processes. The information is organized into columns, each of which has a heading. Because the headings are abbreviations, they can be a bit cryptic.*

For reference, here are the column headings you are likely to encounter using the basic options described in Figures 26-4 and 26-5.

Most of the time, you will probably ignore the more esoteric columns. Still, I have explained them all in case you are curious. As you can see, the headings used by the UNIX options differ from those used by the BSD options. For the meaning of the state codes, see Figure 26-7.

BSD HEADINGS	MEANING
%CPU	percentage of CPU (processor) usage
%MEM	percentage of real memory usage
CMD	name of command being executed
COMMAND	full command being executed
CPU	short-term CPU usage (scheduling)
JOBC	job control count
LIM	memory-use limit
NI	nice number, for setting priority
PAGEIN	total page faults (memory management)
PGID	process group number
PID	process ID
PPID	parent's process ID
PRI	scheduling priority
RE	memory residency time in seconds
RSS	resident set size (memory management)
SESS	session pointer
SL	sleep time in seconds
STARTED	time started
STAT	state code (O,R,S,T,Z)
TIME	cumulative CPU time
TSIZ	text size in kilobytes
TT	abbreviated name of controlling terminal
TTY	full name of controlling terminal
UID	userid
USER	user name
VSZ	virtual size in kilobytes
WCHAN	wait channel

UNIX HEADINGS	MEANING
ADDR	virtual address within process table
C	processor utilization (obsolete)
CMD	name of command being executed
F	flags associated with the process
NI	nice number, for setting priority
PID	process ID
PPID	parent's process ID
PRI	priority (higher number = lower priority)
RSS	resident set size (memory management)
S	state code (D,R,S,T,Z)
STIME	cumulative system time
SZ	size in physical pages (memory management)
TIME	cumulative CPU time
TTY	full name of controlling terminal
UID	userid
WCHAN	wait channel

THE ps PROGRAM: CHOOSING OPTIONS

The best approach to using **ps** is to start by asking two questions: Which processes am I interested in? What information do I want to see about each process? Once you decide what you need, all you need to do is use Figure 26-4 (for UNIX) or Figure 26-5 (for BSD) to choose the appropriate options.

For example, let's say you want to see the process ID of every process running on the system, as well as the process ID of all the parents. Let's do UNIX first. To start, we ask ourselves, which option will display all the processes on the system? From Figure 26-4, we see that this is the **-e** (everything) option.

Next, we must find the option that will display the process ID for each process and its parent. Checking with Figure 26-6, we see that the column headings we want are **PID** and **PPID**. Going back to Figure 26-4, we look for options that will show these two headings. All four choices will do the job, so let's use **-f** (full output) because it displays the least amount of output.

Putting it all together, we have figured out how to display the process ID for every process in the system as well as all the parents:

```
ps -ef
```

Most likely, this command will generate a lot of lines, so it is a good idea to pipe the output to **less** (Chapter 21) to display one screenful at a time:

```
ps -ef | less
```

Now let's do the same analysis for the BSD version of **ps**. To start, we look at Figure 26-5 to see which option will display all the processes in the system. The answer is **ax**. Next, we look for the options that will display the parent's process ID. We have two choices, **j** and **l**. Let's choose **j** because it generates less output. Thus, the BSD version of the command we want is:

```
ps ajx | less
```

As an exercise, let's see what it takes to trace the parentage of one of our processes as far back as possible. To start, we will use a UNIX version of **ps** to display our current processes:

```
ps
```

The output is:

```
    PID TTY          TIME CMD
  12175 tty2     00:00:00 bash
  12218 tty2     00:00:00 ps
```

Our goal is to trace the parentage of the shell, process #12175. To start, we ask the question, what option will display information about one specific process? Looking at Figure 26-4, we see that we can use **-p** followed by a process ID. Next we ask, which option will display the parent's process ID? The answer is **-f**. Thus, to start our search, we use the command:

ps -f -p 12175

The output is:

```
UID         PID  PPID  C  STIME  TTY        TIME  CMD
harley    12175  1879  0  14:14  tty1   00:00:00  -bash
```

From this we can see that the parent of process #12175 is process #1879. Let us repeat the same command with the new process ID:

ps -f -p 1879

The output is:

```
UID        PID  PPID  C  STIME  TTY       TIME  CMD
root      1879     1  0  09:36  ?     00:00:00  login -- harley
```

Notice that the parent of process #1879 is process #1. This is the init process we discussed earlier in the chapter.

Before we move on, there are two interesting points I wish to draw to your attention. First, notice the **?** character in the **TTY** column. This indicates that the process does not have a controlling terminal. We call such processes "daemons", and we will talk about them later in the chapter. Second, we see that process #1879 is running the **login** program under the auspices of userid **root**. This is because **login** is the program that enables users to log in to the system. You may remember that, in Chapter 4, we used the same program to log out and leave the terminal ready for a new user.

To finish our search for the ultimate parent, let us display information about process #1:

ps -f -p 1

The output is:

```
UID        PID  PPID  C  STIME  TTY       TIME  CMD
root         1     0  0  09:34  ?     00:00:01  init [5]
```

We have reached the end of our genealogical journey. As we discussed earlier in the chapter, the parent of process #1 (the init process) is process #0 (the idle process). Notice, by the way, that process #1 ran the **init** command to boot the system into runlevel 5 (multiuser mode with a GUI). We discuss runlevels in Chapter 6.

THE ps PROGRAM: STATES

Let us now conclude our discussion of the **ps** command by talking about states. As we discussed earlier in the chapter, processes are generally in one of three states: running in the foreground; running in the background; or suspended, waiting for a signal to resume execution. There are also other less common variations, such as the zombie state, when a process has died but its parent is not waiting for it.

To look at the state of a process, you use **ps** to display the **S** column (with UNIX options) or the STAT column (with BSD options). Let's start with the UNIX version. Checking with Figure 26-4, we see that the UNIX options that display the **S** column are **-l** and **-ly**. We'll use **-ly** because it displays less output. Thus, to display a list of all your processes including their state, you would use:

```
ps -ly
```

Here is some typical output from a Linux system:

```
S UID   PID PPID C PRI NI RSS  SZ WCHAN  TTY      TIME CMD
S 500 8175 1879 0  75  0 464 112 wait   tty1 00:00:00 bash
T 500 8885 8175 0  75  0 996 366 finish tty1 00:00:00 vim
R 500 9067 8175 2  78  0 996 077 -      tty1 00:00:02 find
R 500 9069 8175 0  78  0 800 034 -      tty1 00:00:00 ps
```

The state is described by the one-letter code in the **S** column. The meanings of the codes are explained in Figure 26-7. In this case, we can see that the first process in the list, process #8175 (the shell), has a state code of **S**. This means it is waiting for something to finish. (In particular, it is waiting for the child process #90682, the **ps** program itself.)

The second process, #8885, has a state code of **T**, which means it is suspended. In this case, the **vim** editor was running in the foreground, when it was suspended by pressing **^Z**. (This procedure is described earlier in the chapter.)

The third process, #9067, has a state code of **R**. This means it is running. In fact, it is a **find** command (Chapter 25) that is running in the background.

Finally, the last process is the **ps** program itself. It also has a state code of **R**, because it too is running — in this case, in the foreground. It is this process that has displayed the output you are reading. In fact, by the time you see the output, the process has already terminated, and the shell process (#8175) has regained control.

Before we leave this example, I would like to point out something interesting. By looking at the PIDs and PPIDs, you can see that the shell is the parent of all the other processes. (This should make sense to you.)

Now let's discuss how to check states with BSD options. To start, take a look at Figure 26-6. The heading we want to display is **STAT**. Now look at Figure 26-5. Notice that all the variations of **ps** display the **STAT** column, including **ps** by itself with no options. If you are using a pure BSD system, all you need to use is:

```
ps
```

If you are using a mixed system (as is the case with Linux), you will have to force BSD output by using one of the BSD options. My suggestion is to choose **j** because it generates the least amount of output:

```
ps j
```

Here is some typical output, using the plain **ps** command on a FreeBSD system. (With the **j** option, the output would be similar but with more columns.)

```
  PID  TT  STAT  TIME      COMMAND
52496  p0  Ss    0:00.02   -sh (sh)
52563  p0  T     0:00.02   vi test
54123  p0  Z     0:00.00   (sh)
52717  p0  D     0:00.12   find / -name harley -print
52725  p0  R+    0:00.00   ps
```

The first process, #52496, is the shell.* Notice that the STAT column has more than one character. The first character is the state code. The second character gives esoteric technical information we can safely ignore. (If you are interested, see the man page.) In this case,

LINUX, FREEBSD	
D	Uninterruptible sleep: waiting for an event to complete (usually I/O; D="disk")
I	Idle: sleeping for longer than 20 seconds (FreeBSD only)
R	Running or runnable (runnable = waiting in the run queue)
S	Interruptible sleep: waiting for an event to complete
T	Suspended: either by a job control signal or because it is being traced
Z	Zombie: terminated, parent not waiting

SOLARIS	
O	Running: currently executing (O="onproc")
R	Runnable: waiting in the run queue
S	Sleeping: waiting for an event to complete (usually I/O)
T	Suspended: either by a job control signal or because it is being traced
Z	Zombie: terminated, parent not waiting

FIGURE 26-7: The ps program: Process state codes

With certain options, the ps command displays a column of data indicating the state of each process. With the UNIX options, the column is labeled S, and contains a single-character code. With the BSD options, the column is labeled STAT and contains a similar code, sometimes followed by 1-3 other, less important characters. Here are the meanings of the codes, which vary slightly from one system to another.

---

*As you will remember from Chapter 11, the name of the old Bourne shell was **sh**. You might be wondering, is this a Bourne shell? The answer is no; the Bourne shell has not been used for years. It happens that the FreeBSD shell is also named **sh**.

the state code is **S**. Looking this up in Figure 26-7, we see that the process is waiting for something to finish. Specifically, it is waiting for a child process, #52725, the **ps** program.

The second process, #52563, has a state code of **T**, meaning it is suspended. In this case, **vi** was suspended by pressing **^Z**.

The third process, #54123, is an old shell with a state code of **Z**, which means it is a zombie. This is an unusual finding. Somehow, the process managed to die while its parent was not waiting for it. (See the discussion on zombies earlier in the chapter.)

The fourth process, #52717, is a **find** program running in the background. It has a state code of **D**, indicating that it is waiting for an I/O event to complete (in this case, reading from the disk). This makes sense, as **find** does a lot of I/O. You must remember, however that whenever you use **ps**, you are looking at an instantaneous snapshot. As it happened, we caught **find** when it was waiting for I/O. We might just as easily have found it running, in which case the state code would have been **R**.

Finally, the last process, #52725, is the **ps** program itself. It has a state code of **R**, because it is running in the foreground.

Before we leave this example, let me draw your attention to an interesting point. If you look at the rightmost column, **COMMAND**, you will see that it displays the entire command being executed. This column is only available with the BSD options. With the UNIX options, all you will ever see is the **CMD** column, which only shows the name, not the full command.*

HINT

If you are using a system like Linux that supports both the UNIX and BSD options, you can pick the options that best serve your needs. For example, let's say you want to display a list of processes along with the full command (**COMMAND**), not the command name (**CMD**). If you have access to BSD options, you can use:

```
ps j
```

There is no easy way to do this using only UNIX options. (Yay for BSD!)

HINT FOR PARANOIDS

On a multiuser system, you can amuse yourself by using **ps** to snoop on what other people are doing. In particular, when you use BSD options, you can look in the **COMMAND** column and see the full commands that other users have entered. (If your system doesn't support BSD options, you can do the same thing with the **w** program; see Chapter 8.)

At first this will seem like harmless fun, until you realize that everyone else on the system can see what *you* are doing as well.

So be careful. If you are a guy, what do you think the system administrator or your girlfriend** would think if they were to snoop on you and see that, for the last hour, you have been working with the command **vi pornography-list**?

---

* With Solaris, the **CMD** column does show the full command.
**You need to be even more careful if your girlfriend *is* the system administrator.

MONITORING SYSTEM PROCESSES: `top`, `prstat`

To look at your own processes, you can use the **ps** command. However, what if you want to examine the system as a whole? To be sure, **ps** has options that will display a large variety of information about all the processes on the system. However, **ps** has a major limitation: it shows you a static snapshot of the processes, how they looked at a particular instant in time. Because processes are dynamic, this limitation becomes important when you need to watch how the various processes are changing from moment to moment. In such cases, you can use the **top** program to display overall system statistics updated every few seconds, as well as information about the most important processes as they change in real time.

The name of the program comes from the fact that it shows you the "top" processes, that is, the ones that are using the most CPU time. The syntax for using **top** is a bit complicated and can vary slightly from one system to another. Here is the basic syntax that you would use with Linux. With other systems, the options will vary, so you will have to check your online manual.

top [**-d** *delay*] [**-n** *count*] [**-p** *pid*[,*pid*]...]

where *delay* is the refresh interval in seconds; **count** is the total number of times to refresh; and **pid** is a process ID.

The **top** program is available with most Linux and BSD systems. If your system does not have **top**, there will usually be an equivalent program. For example, with Solaris, you can use **prstat** instead. Because the options can vary depending on your version of **top**, it is worth a moment of your time to check with the man page on your system.

To watch how **top** works, enter the command by itself:

```
top
```

To quit the program at any time, press **q** or **^C**.

Like **less** and **vi**, **top** works in raw mode (see Chapter 21). This allows it to take over the command line and screen completely, displaying lines and changing characters as necessary. As an example, take a look at Figure 26-8, where you see an abbreviated example of some typical output.

The output can be divided into two parts. The top five lines show information about the system as a whole. In our example, the top line shows the time (9:10 AM), how long the system has been running (14 hours and 50 minutes), and the number of users (7). There is also a wealth of other, more technical information showing statistics about processes, CPU time, real memory (memory), and virtual memory (swap space).

Below the system information, you see data describing the various processes, one process per line, listed in order of CPU usage. In our example, the system is quiet. In fact, **top** itself is the top process.

The **top** program is powerful because it automatically refreshes the statistics at regular intervals. The default interval varies depending on your version of **top**. For example, on one of my Linux systems, the default is 3 seconds; on my FreeBSD system, it is 2 seconds; on my Solaris system (using **prstat**), it is 5 seconds. To change the refresh rate, use the **-d** (delay) option. For example, to tell **top** to refresh itself every second, you would use:

```
top -d 1
```

Some versions of **top** allow you to enter even shorter intervals. If your system supports it, try running with a very fast refresh rate, such as:

```
top -d 0.1
```

On a busy system, this makes for a fascinating display.*

Because **top** works in raw mode, you can type various commands as the program runs. The most important command is **q**, which quits the program. The next most important command is **h** (help) or **?**, which displays a summary of all the commands. A third command — not always documented — is the <Space> key. This forces **top** to refresh the display at that moment. Pressing <Space> is useful when you have chosen a slow refresh rate, and you need an instant update. I won't go over all the commands here, as they are very technical. However, when you have a moment, press **h** and see what is available with your version of **top**.

For extra control, there are two other options you can use. By default, **top** refreshes indefinitely. The **-n** option let's you tell **top** to refresh only a certain number of times. For example, to refresh the display 6 times, once every 10 seconds, you would use:

```
top -d 10 -n 6
```

In this case, the program will run for only 60 seconds.

```
top - 9:10:24 up 14:50, 7 users, load average: 0.32,0.17,0.05
Tasks: 97 total, 1 running, 92 sleeping, 4 stopped, 0 zombie
Cpu(s): 1.7% us, 2.0% sy, 0.0% ni, 96.4% id, 0.0% wa
Mem: 385632k total, 287164k used, 98468k free, 41268k buffer
Swap: 786424k total, 0k used, 786424k free, 156016k cached

  PID USER      PR NI VIRT  RES  SHR S %CPU %MEM  TIME+  COMMAND
 4016 harley    16  0 2124  992  780 R  1.3  0.3 0:00.35 top
 3274 harley    15  0 7980 1808 1324 S  0.3  0.5 0:01.14 sshd
    1 root      16  0 1996  680  588 S  0.0  0.2 0:01.67 init
    2 root      34 19    0    0    0 S  0.0  0.0 0:00.00 ksoftirqd
    3 root      RT  0    0    0    0 S  0.0  0.0 0:00.00 watchdg
    4 root      10 -5    0    0    0 S  0.0  0.0 0:00.00 events
    5 root      10 -5    0    0    0 S  0.0  0.0 0:00.01 khelper
    6 root      11 -5    0    0    0 S  0.0  0.0 0:00.00 kthread
    8 root      10 -5    0    0    0 S  0.0  0.0 0:00.02 kblockd
   11 root      10 -5    0    0    0 S  0.0  0.0 0:00.00 khubd
```

FIGURE 26-8: The **top** program

*The **top** program is used to display dynamic information about the "top" processes on the system, that is, the processes that are using the most CPU time. What you see here is an abbreviated example of the type of output **top** displays. The output is updated at regular intervals. As **top** executes, you can type commands to control its behavior. For help press **h**; to quit press **q** or ^C.*

*Tip for guys: If you have a hot date you are eager to impress, invite her back to your place and have her sit in front of your computer. Then log into a busy Unix or Linux system and run **top** with a refresh rate of 1 second or less. If that doesn't impress her, nothing will.

To display information about a specific process, use **-p** followed by the process ID, for example:

```
top -p 3274
```

To specify more than one process ID, separate them with commas. For example, the following command uses a refresh rate of 1 second and displays information about processes #1 through #5:

```
top -d 1 -p 1,2,3,4,5
```

In general, **top** is used more by system administrators and programmers than by regular users. Typically, an admin will use **top** for performance monitoring. For example, he may want to see how a new application is doing on a server, or he may want to evaluate two different database programs to see which one works more efficiently. Programmers will often use **top** to test how a program performs under various workloads.

You will find that **ps** suits your needs more often than **top**. However, in certain situations, **top** can be invaluable. For example, if you are using a system that, all of a sudden, becomes abnormally slow, you can use **top** to find out what is happening.

DISPLAYING A PROCESS TREE: `pstree`, `ptree`

So far, we have discussed two important tools you can use to display information about processes: **ps** to look at static information, and **top** to look at dynamic information. A third tool, **pstree**, is useful when you want to understand the relationships between processes.

Earlier in the chapter, I explained that every process (except the very first one) is created by another process. When this happens, the original process is called the parent; the newly created process is called the child. Whenever a new process is created, it is given an identification number called a process ID or PID.

Towards the end of the startup procedure, the kernel creates the very first process, the idle process, which is given a PID of #0. After performing a number of tasks, the idle process creates the second process, the init process, which is given a PID of #1. The idle process then goes into a permanent sleep (hence the name).

The job of the init process is to create a variety of other processes. Most of these third-generation processes are daemons (I'll explain the name later in the chapter), whose job is to wait for something to happen and then react appropriately. In particular, there are daemons that do nothing but wait for users to log in. When a user is ready to log in, the daemon creates another process to handle the task. The login daemon then creates another process to run the user's shell. Finally, whenever the shell needs to execute a program for the user, the shell creates yet another process to carry out the job.

Although this arrangement seems complicated, it can be simplified enormously by making one simple observation: every process (except the first one) has a single parent. Thus, it is possible to imagine all the processes in the system arranged into a large, tree-structured hierarchy with the init process at the root of the tree. We call such data structures PROCESS TREES, and we use them to show the connections between parent processes and their children.

You can display a diagram of any part of the system process tree by using the **pstree** program. For example, you can display the entire process tree, starting from the init process. Or, you can display a subtree based on a specific PID or userid. The syntax to use is:

pstree [-aAcGnpu] [*pid* | *userid*]

where **pid** is a process ID, and **userid** is a userid.

The **pstree** program is available with most Unix systems. If your system does not have **pstree**, there will sometimes be an equivalent program. For example, with Solaris, you can use **ptree** instead. (See the online manual for the details.) On other systems, the **ps** command has special options to display process trees. You can try **ps f** or **ps -H**, although the output won't be as good as with **pstree**.

To see how **pstree** works, start by entering the command without any options. By default, **pstree** draws the process tree for the entire system, starting with the init process. This generates a lot of lines, so it is a good idea to pipe the output to **less** (Chapter 21) to display one screenful at a time:

pstree | less

Here is an abbreviated example showing the first eight lines of output on a Linux system. Notice that the root of the tree — the init process — is at the top of the diagram:

```
init-+-apmd
     |-and
     |-automount
     |-crond
     |-cups-config-dae
     |-cupsd
     |-2*[dbus-daemon---{dbus-daemon}]
     |-dbus-launch
```

As you look at this process tree, I want you to notice several things. First, at each level, the tree is sorted alphabetically by process name. This is the default, which you can change using the **-n** option (see below).

Next, notice the notation **2*** in the second to last line. This means that the there are two identical subtrees. Using such notation allows **pstree** to create a more compact diagram. If you want **pstree** to expand all subtrees, even the identical ones, use the **-c** (do not compact) option.

Finally, you can see that **pstree** uses plain ASCII characters to draw the branches of the tree. With some terminals, **pstree** will use special line drawing characters instead. This enables it to draw continuous lines. If for some reason your output doesn't look right, you can use **-A** to force the use of ASCII characters or **-G** to force the use of line drawing characters. Take a moment to experiment and see which type of output looks best on your system:

```
pstree -A | less
pstree -G | less
```

Aside from the display options, there are options that enable you to control which information is displayed. My two favorite options are **-p**, which displays the PID of each process, and **-n**, which sorts the tree by PID, instead of by process name:

```
pstree -np
```

Here are the first eight lines of the output using these options. We see that the process tree starts with process #1 (the init process). This process has a number of children: process #2, #3, #4, #5, #6, and so on. Process #6 has children of its own: #8, #11, #13, #80, and so on.

```
init(1)-+-ksoftirqd(2)
        |-watchdog(3)
        |-events(4)
        |-khelper(5)
        |-kthread(6)-+-kblockd(8)
        |            |-khubd(11)
        |            |-kseriod(13)
        |            |-pdflush(80)
```

By default, **pstree** draws the entire process tree starting from the root, that is, starting from process #1. There will be times, however, when you will be most interested in parts of the tree. In such cases, there are two ways you can limit the output. If you specify a PID, **pstree** will display the subtree descended from that particular process.

Here is an example. You use Bash for your shell. From the shell, you have two processes in the background: **make** and **gcc**. You also have two processes that are suspended: **vim** and **man**. You want to display a process tree showing only these processes. To start, you use **ps** or **echo $$** to find out the PID of your shell. It happens to be #2146. You then enter the following command:

```
pstree -p 2146
```

Here is the output:

```
bash-+-gcc(4252)
     |-pstree(4281)
     |-make(4276)
     |-man(4285)---sh(4295)---less(4301)
     `-vim(4249)
```

Notice that **man** has created a child process to run a new shell (#4295), which has created another child process (#4301) to run **less**. This is because **man** calls upon **less** to display its output.

The second way in which you can restrict the range of the process tree is to specify a userid instead of a PID. When you do this, **pstree** displays only those processes that are running under the auspices of that userid, for example:

```
pstree -p harley
```

The last two options I want to mention are used to show extra information along with the process name. The **-a** (all) option displays the entire command line for each process, not just the name of the program. The **-u** (userid change) option marks the transition whenever a child process runs under a different userid than its parent.

THINKING ABOUT HOW UNIX ORGANIZES PROCESSES AND FILES: fuser

Before we move on, I want to take a moment and ask you to think about the similarities between how Unix organizes processes and files.

Both processes and files can be thought of as existing within hierarchical trees with the root at the top. The root of the process tree is process #1 (the init process). The root of the file tree is the root directory (see Chapter 23). Within the process tree, every process has a single parent process above it. Within the file tree, every subdirectory has a single parent directory above it. To display the file tree, we use the **tree** program (Chapter 24). To display the process tree, we use the **pstree** program.

With a little more thought, we can find even more similarities. Every process is identified by a unique number called a process ID. Every file is identified by a unique number called an inumber. Internally, Unix keeps track of processes by using a process table, indexed by process ID. Within the process table, each entry contains information about a single process. Similarly, Unix keeps track of files by using an inode table, indexed by inumber. Within the inode table, each entry (the inode) contains information about a single file.

However, for a very good reason, this is about as far as we can push the analogy. Why? Because there is a fundamental difference between processes and files. Processes are dynamic: at every instant, the data that describes them is changing. Files are comparatively static.

For example, to display information about files, we use the **ls** program (Chapters 24 and 25), which simply looks in the inode table for its data. To display information about processes, we use the **ps** and **top** programs, and gathering information about processes is trickier. To be sure, some basic data can be found in the process table. However, most of the dynamic information must come from the kernel itself, and obtaining such information is not as simple as looking in a table.

In order to procure the data they need to do their jobs, both **ps** and **top** must use a type of pseudo file called a proc file (see Chapter 23). Within the **/proc** directory, every process is represented by its own proc file. When a program needs information about a process, it reads from that process' proc file. This, in turn, triggers a request to the kernel to supply the necessary data. The whole thing happens so quickly that it doesn't occur to you that finding process information is more complicated than finding file information.

You might be wondering, are there any tools that bridge the gap between processes and files? Yes, there are. One of the most interesting is **fuser**, a system administration tool that lists all the processes that are using a specific file. For example, let's say you enter the following command to run the **find** program (Chapter 25) to search for files named **foo**. Notice that the program is run in the background, and that it redirects the standard output to a file named **bar***:

---

*See Chapter 9 for a discussion of the names **foo** and **bar**.

```
find / -name foo -print > bar 2>/dev/null &
```

When the program starts, the shell displays the following message, showing you the job ID (3) and the process id (3739):

```
[3] 3739
```

Since standard output is redirected to **bar**, you know that this particular file will be in use while the program is running. To check this, you enter the command:

fuser bar

Here is the output:

bar: 3739

As you can see, the file **bar** is in use by process #3739. In this way, **fuser** provides an interesting example of how a single tool can gather information about both processes and files at the same time.

If you try experimenting with **fuser**, you may run into a problem that is worth discussing. The **fuser** program is meant to be used by system administrators. For this reason, it is commonly stored with other such tools in one of the admin directories, such as **/sbin** (see Chapter 23). However, unless you are logged in as superuser, it is unlikely that the admin directories will be in your search path. This means that, when you type in the **fuser** command, the shell will not be able to find the program.

When you encounter such a problem, simply use **whereis** (Chapter 25) to find the location of **fuser** on your system. For example:

whereis fuser

Here is some typical output:

fuser: /sbin/fuser /usr/share/man/man1/fuser.1.gz

In this case, the first path is the location of the program; the second path is the location of the man page. To run **fuser**, all you need to do is show the shell where to find the program:

/sbin/fuser bar

This is the technique to use when you want to run a program whose directory is not in your search path.

KILLING A PROCESS: kill

The **kill** program has two uses: to terminate a process and to send a signal to a process. In this section, we'll talk about termination. In the next section, we'll discuss the more general topic of signals.

As a rule, programs run until they finish on their own or until you tell them to quit. You can usually stop a program prematurely by pressing **^C** to send the **intr** signal (see Chapter 7), or by typing a quit command. However, these methods won't always work.

For instance, on occasion, a program will freeze and stop responding to the keyboard. In such cases, pressing ^C or typing a quit command will not work. A similar problem arises when you want to terminate a program running in the background. Because background processes don't read from the keyboard, there is no way to reach the program directly.

In such cases, you can terminate a program by using the **kill** program. When you terminate a program in this way, we say that you KILL it. The syntax to use is:

kill [-9] *pid...* | *jobid...*

where *pid* or *jobid* identifies the process.

Most of the time, you will want to kill a single process. First you will use **ps** or **jobs** to find the process ID or job ID of the process you want to kill. Then you will use **kill** to carry out the actual termination. Consider the following example. You have entered the command below to run the **make** program in the background:

```
make game > makeoutput 2> makeerrors &
```

Some time later, you decide to kill the process. The first step is to find out the process ID. You enter:

```
ps
```

The output is:

```
PID TTY          TIME CMD
2146 tty2     00:00:00 bash
5505 tty2     00:00:00 make
5534 tty2     00:00:00 ps
```

The process ID you want is **5505**. To kill this process, you enter:

```
kill 5505
```

The shell will kill the process and display a message, for example:

```
[2]   Terminated   make game >makeoutput 2>makeerrors
```

This means the process that was running the program **make game** has been killed. The number at the beginning of the line means that the process was job #2.

An alternative way to list your processes is to use the **jobs -l** command. Let's say you had used the following command instead of **ps**:

```
jobs -l
```

Here is what you would have seen:

```
[2]-  5505 Running     make game >makeoutput 2>makeerrors &
```

Again, you could use the command **kill 5505** to kill the **make** process. However, there is an alternative. You can specify a job number in the same manner as when you use the **fg** and **bg** commands (see Figure 26-3). Thus, in this case, any of the following commands would work:

```
kill 5505
kill %-
kill %2
kill %make
kill %?game
```

Here is another common situation. A foreground process becomes so unresponsive, you can't stop it no matter what you type, including **^C**. You have two choices. First, you can try pressing **^Z** to suspend the process. If this is successful, you can then use **ps** or **jobs** to find the process and terminate it with **kill**.

Alternatively, you can open up a new terminal window and use **ps -u** or **ps U** to list all the processes running under your userid. You can then identify the runaway process and terminate it with **kill**. In fact, this is sometimes the only way to kill a process that is off by itself in deep space.

If you are using a remote Unix host, you have a third choice. If all else fails, simply disconnect from the host. On some systems, when your connection drops, the kernel automatically kills all your processes. Of course, this will kill any other programs that may be running.

Whenever you kill a process with children, it has the side effect of killing the children. Thus, you can kill an entire group of related processes simply by finding and killing the original parent. (In Unix, family ties run deep.)

When **^C** or a quit command doesn't work, **kill** will usually do the job. However, on occasion, even **kill** will fail. In such cases, there is a variation that always works: specify the option **-9** as part of the command. This sends the "sure kill" signal **9** (which we will discuss in the next section). For example:

```
kill -9 5505
kill -9 %2
```

Sending signal **9** will always work. However, it should be your last choice, because it kills too quickly. Using **kill -9** does not allow the process to release any resources it may be using. For example, the process may not be able to close files (which may result in data loss), release memory, and so on. Using **kill -9** can also result in abandoned child processes, which will not be able to die properly. (See the discussion on orphans earlier in the chapter.)

Although the kernel will usually clean up the mess, it is smart to try all the other techniques before resorting to drastic measures.

SENDING A SIGNAL TO A PROCESS: `kill`

As we have just discussed, you can use the **kill** program to terminate a process that is otherwise unreachable. However, **kill** is not merely a termination tool. It is actually a powerful program that can send any signal to any process. When used in this way, the more general form of the syntax is:

kill [*-signal*] *pid...|jobid...*

where *signal* is the type of signal you want to send, and *pid* or *jobid* identifies a process, as discussed in the previous section.

In Chapter 23, we encountered the concept of interprocess communication or IPC, the exchanging of data between two processes. At the time, we were discussing the use of named pipes as a means of sending data from one process to another. The purpose of the **kill** program is to support a different type of IPC, specifically, the sending of a very simple message called a SIGNAL. A signal is nothing more than a number that is sent to a process to let it know that some type of event has occurred. It is up to the process to recognize the signal and do something. When a process does this, we say that it TRAPS the signal.

In Chapter 7, we encountered signals during our discussion of several of the special key combinations, such as **^C** and **^Z**. When you press one of these keys, it sends a signal to the current foreground process. For example, when you press **^C**, it sends signal **2**.

There are a large variety of signals used within Unix, most of which are of interest only to system programmers. For reference, Figure 26-9 contains a list of the most commonly used signals. Notice that each signal is known by a number, as well as a standardized name and abbreviation (both of which should be typed in uppercase letters).

In general, the signal numbers for **HUP**, **INT**, **KILL** and **TERM** are the same on all systems. However, the other signal numbers can vary from one type of Unix to another. For this reason, it is a good habit to use the names or abbreviations — which are always the same — rather than numbers. The chart in Figure 26-9 shows the signal numbers that are used with Linux.

If you would like to see the full list of signals supported by your system, enter the **kill** command with the **-l** (list) option:

```
kill -l
```

If this option does not work on your system, you can look for an include file (see Chapter 23) named **signal.h** and display its contents. One of the following commands will do the job.

```
locate signal.h
find / -name 'signal.h' -print 2> /dev/null
```

The **kill** program lets you specify any signal you want. For example, let's say you want to suspend job %2, which is running in the background. Simply send it the **STOP** signal:

```
kill -STOP %2
```

If you do not specify a signal, **kill** will, by default, send the **TERM** signal. Thus, the following commands (all acting upon process **3662**) are equivalent:

```
kill 3662
kill -15 3662
kill -TERM 3662
kill -SIGTERM 3662
```

As I mentioned, there are many different signals, and the purpose of the `kill` command is to send one specific signal to a particular process. In this sense, it might have been better to name the command `signal`. However, by default, `kill` sends the **TERM** signal, which has the effect of killing the process, and this is why the command is called `kill`. Indeed, most people use `kill` only for killing processes and not for sending other signals.

For security reasons, a regular userid can send signals only to its own processes. The superuser, however, is allowed to send signals to any process on the system. This means that, if you are using your own system and you become stuck with a process that just won't die, you can always change to superuser and use `kill` to put the process out of its misery. Be very careful, though, superuser + `kill` is a highly lethal combination that can get you into a lot of trouble if you don't know exactly what you are doing.

SETTING THE PRIORITY FOR A PROCESS: `nice`

At the beginning of the chapter, I explained that even a small Unix system can have over a hundred processes running at the same time. A large system can have thousands of processes, all of which need to share the system's resources: processors, memory, I/O devices, network connections, and so on. In order to manage such a complex workload, the kernel uses a sophisticated subsystem called the scheduler, whose job is to allot resources dynamically among the various processes.

In making such moment-to-moment decisions, the scheduler considers a variety of different values associated with each process. One of the more important values is the PRIORITY, an indication of how much precedence a process should be given over other processes. The priority is set by a number of factors, which are generally beyond the reach of individual users. This only makes sense for two reasons.

First, managing processes efficiently is a very complex operation, and the scheduler can do it much better and much faster than a human being, even an experienced system administrator. Second, if it were possible to manipulate priorities, it would be far too

NUM.	NAME	ABBREV.	DESCRIPTION
1	SIGHUP	HUP	Hang-up: sent to processes when you log out or if your terminal disconnects
2	SIGINT	INT	Interrupt: sent when you press ^C
9	SIGKILL	KILL	Kill: immediate termination; cannot be trapped by a process
15	SIGTERM	TERM	Terminate: request to terminate; can be trapped by a process
18	SIGCONT	CONT	Continue: resume suspended process; sent by **fg** or **bg**
19	SIGSTOP	STOP	Stop (suspend): sent when you press ^Z

FIGURE 26-9: Signals

Signals are used as a simple, but important form of interprocess control. This list shows the most commonly used signals, along with their names. When you use **kill** *to send a signal to a process, you can specify the signal using its number, its name, or its abbreviation. If you use a name or abbreviation, be sure to type uppercase letters. Some of the numbers vary from one type of system to another so, as a general rule, it is best to use names or abbreviations, which are standardized. The signal numbers shown here are the ones used with Linux.*

tempting for users to raise the priorities of their own programs at the expense of other users and the system itself.

In certain situations, however, you may want to do the opposite. That is, you may want to **lower** the priority of one of your programs. Typically, this will happen when you are running a non-interactive program that requires a relatively large amount of CPU time over an extended period. In such cases, you might as well be a nice person and run the program in the background at a low priority. After all, you won't notice if the program takes a bit longer to finish, and running it with a low priority allows the scheduler to give precedence to other programs, making the system more responsive and efficient.

To run programs at a lower priority you use a tool called **nice**. (Can you see where the name comes from?) The syntax is:

nice [**-n** *adjustment*] *command*

where *adjustment* is a numeric value, and *command* is the command you want to run.

The simplest way to use **nice** is simply to type the name in front of a command you plan on running in the background, for example:

nice gcc myprogram.c &

That's all there is to it. When you start a program in this way, **nice** will cause it to run at a reduced priority. However, **nice** will not automatically run the program in the background. You will need to do that yourself by typing an **&** character at the end of the command.

Which types of programs should you use with **nice**? In general, any program that can run in the background and which uses a large amount of CPU time. Traditional uses for **nice** are for programs that compile a large amount of source code, that make (put together) software packages, or that perform complex mathematical computations. For example, if you share a multiuser system and you are testing a program that calculates the 1,000,000th digit of pi, you definitely want to run it with as low a priority as possible.

When it comes to using **nice**, there are two caveats of which you should be aware. First, you can use **nice** only with self-contained programs that run on their own. For example, you can use **nice** with external commands and shell scripts. However, you cannot lower the priority of builtin shell commands (internal commands), pipelines, or compound commands.

The second consideration is that you should use **nice** only with programs that run in the background. Although it is possible to lower the priority of a foreground program, it doesn't make sense to do so. After all, when a program runs in the foreground, you want it to be able to respond to you as quickly as possible.

In most cases, it will suffice to use **nice** in the way I have described. On occasion, however, you may want to have more control over how much the priority is lowered. To do so, you can use the **-n** option followed by a value called the NICE NUMBER or NICENESS. On most systems, you can specify a nice number of 0 to 19. The higher the nice number, the lower the priority of the program (which means the nicer you are as a user).

When you run a program in the regular way (without **nice**), the program is given a niceness of 0. This is considered to be normal priority. When you use **nice** without the

-n option, it defaults to a niceness of 10, right in the middle of the range. Most of the time, that is all you need. However, you can specify your own value if necessary.

For example, let's say you have a program called **calculate** that spends hours and hours performing complex mathematical calculations. To be a nice guy, you decide to run the program in the background with as low a priority as possible. You can use a command like the following:

```
nice -n 19 calculate > outputfile 2> errorfile &
```

By now, you are probably wondering, if a high nice number will lower the priority of a program, will a low nice number raise the priority? The answer is yes, but only if you are superuser. As superuser you are allowed to specify a negative number between -20 and -1. For example, to run a very special program with as high a priority as possible, change to superuser and enter the command:

```
nice -n -20 specialprogram
```

As you might imagine, setting a negative nice number is something you would rarely need to do. Indeed, most of the time, you are better off letting the scheduler manage the system on its own.

> **HINT**
>
> When you share a multiuser system, it is a good habit to use **nice** to run CPU intensive programs in the background at a low priority. This keeps such programs from slowing down the system for other users.
>
> However, **nice** can also come in handy on a single-user system. When you force your most demanding background programs to run at a low priority, you prevent them from slowing down your own moment-to-moment work.
>
> (In other words, being nice always pays off.)

CHANGING THE PRIORITY OF AN EXISTING PROCESS: renice

On occasion, you may find yourself waiting a long time for a program that is running in the foreground, when it occurs to you that it would make more sense for the program to be running in the background at a low priority. In such cases, all you have to do is press ^Z to suspend the process, use **bg** to move it to the background, and then lower its priority. To lower the priority of an existing process, you use **renice**. The syntax is:

renice *niceness* **-p** *processid*

where *niceness* is a nice number, and *processid* is a process ID.

As we discussed in the previous section, a higher nice number means a lower priority. When you use **renice** as a regular user, you are only allowed to increase the nice number for a process, not lower it. That is, you can lower the priority of a process, but not raise it. In addition, as a reasonable precaution, regular users can only change the niceness for their own processes. (Can you see why?) These limitations, however, do not apply to the superuser.

Here is an example of how you might use **renice**. You enter the following command to run a program that calculates the 1,000,000th digit of pi:

```
picalculate > outputfile 2&> errorfile
```

After watching your program do nothing for a while, it occurs to you that you might as well run it in the background. At the same time, it would be a good idea to lower the priority as much as possible. First, press **^Z** to suspend the foreground process. You see a message like the following:

```
[1]+  Stopped     picalculate >outputfile 2>errorfile
```

This tells you that the process, job #1, is suspended. You can now use **bg** to move the process to the background:

```
bg %1
```

You then see the following message, which tells you that the program is running in the background:

```
[1]+ picalculate >outputfile 2>errorfile &
```

Next, use **ps** to find out the process ID:

```
ps
```

The output is:

```
 PID TTY        TIME CMD
4052 tty1   00:00:00 bash
4089 tty1   00:00:00 picalculate
4105 tty1   00:00:00 ps
```

Finally, use **renice** to give the process the highest possible niceness, thereby lowering its priority as much as possible:

```
renice 19 -p 4089
```

You will see the following confirmation message:

```
4089: old priority 0, new priority 19
```

HINT

If your system seems bogged down for no apparent reason, you can use **top** to see if there are any non-interactive processes taking a lot of CPU time. If so, you can consider using **renice** to lower the priority of the processes. (Warning: Don't muck around with processes you don't understand.)

DAEMONS

How many processes do you think are running on your system right now? It is easy to find out. Just use the **ps** program with the appropriate options to list every process, one per line, and then pipe the output to **wc -l** (Chapter 18) to count the lines.

Here are two commands that will do the job. The first command uses **ps** with UNIX options. The second uses the BSD options:

```
ps -e | wc -l
ps ax | wc -l
```

As a test, I ran these commands on three different Unix systems. First, I checked a Solaris system, which I accessed over the Internet. Absolutely no one else was using the system and nothing else was running on it. Next, I checked a Linux system sitting next to me. It was running a full GUI-based desktop environment, and no one else but me was using the system. Finally, I checked a FreeBSD system that acts as a medium-sized Web server and database server.

Here is what I found. Not counting the **ps** program itself, the small Solaris system was running 46 processes; the small Linux system was running 95 processes; and the medium FreeBSD system was running 133 processes. Remarkably, these are all relatively small numbers. It is not unusual for a good-sized Unix system to be running hundreds or even thousands of processes at the same time.

Obviously, most of these processes are not programs run by users. So what are they? The answer is they are DAEMONS, programs that run in the background, completely disconnected from any terminal, in order to provide a service. (With Microsoft Windows, the same type of functionality is provided by programs called "services".) Typically, a daemon will wait silently in the background for something to happen: an event, a request, an interrupt, a specific time interval, etc. When the trigger occurs, the daemon swings into action, doing whatever is necessary to carry out its job.

Daemons carry out a great many tasks that are necessary to run the system. For reference, I have listed some of the more interesting daemons in Figure 26-10. Although you will find a few daemons (such as **init**) on most Unix systems, there is a fair bit of variation. To find the daemons on your system, use **ps** and look in the output for a **?** character in the **TTY** column. This indicates that the process is not controlled by a terminal.

The best command to use is the variation of **ps** that displays all the processes that are not controlled by a terminal:

```
ps -t - | less
```

If this command does not work on your system, try the following:

```
ps -e | grep '?' | less
```

Most daemons are created automatically during the last part of the boot sequence. In some cases, the processes are created by the init process (process #1). In other cases, the processes are created by parents that terminate themselves, turning the daemons into orphans. As you may remember from our discussion earlier in the chapter, all orphans are adopted by the init process. Thus, one way or the other, most daemons end up as children of process #1. For this reason, one definition of a daemon is any background process without a controlling terminal, whose parent's process ID is #1.

If you are using a Linux system, take a moment to look in the **/etc/rc.d/init.d** directory. Here you will find a large number of shell scripts, each of which is used to start, stop or restart a particular daemon.

DAEMON	PURPOSE
`init`	Ancestor of all other processes; adopts orphans
`apache`	Apache Web server
`atd`	Runs jobs queued by the **at** program
`crond`	Manages execution of prescheduled jobs (**cron** service)
`cupsd`	Print scheduler (CUPS=Common Unix Printing System)
`dhcpd`	Dynamically configure TCP/IP information for clients (DHCP)
`ftpd`	FTP server (FTP=File Transfer Protocol)
`gated`	Gateway routing for networks
`httpd`	Web server
`inetd`	Internet services
`kerneld`	Loads and unloads kernel modules as needed
`kudzu`	Detects and configures new/changed hardware during boot
`lpd`	Print spooling (line printer daemon)
`mysql`	MySQL database server
`named`	Internet DNS name service (DNS=Domain Name System)
`nfsd`	Network file access (NFS=Network File System)
`ntpd`	Time synchronization (NTP=Network Time Protocol)
`rpcbind`	Remote procedure calls (RPC)
`routed`	Manage network routing tables
`sched`	Another name for **swapper**
`sendmail`	SMTP server (email)
`smbd`	File sharing & printing services for Windows clients (Samba)
`sshd`	SSH (secure shell) connections
`swapper`	Copies data from memory to swap space to reclaim physical memory
`syncd`	Synchronizes file systems with contents of system memory
`syslogd`	Collects various system messages (system logger)
`xinetd`	Internet services (replacement for **inetd**)

FIGURE 26-10: Daemons

A daemon is a process that runs silently in the background, disconnected from any terminal, in order to provide a service. Unix systems typically have many daemons, each waiting to perform its job as needed. Here is a list of interesting daemons you will find on many systems. Notice that many of the names end with the letter "d".

WHAT'S IN A NAME?

Daemon

Daemons are processes that provide services by running silently in the background, disconnected from any terminal. Although the name is pronounced "dee-mon", the correctly spelling is "daemon".

You may occasionally read that the name stands for "Disk and Executing Monitor", a term from the old DEC 10 and 20 computers. However, this explanation was made up after the fact. The name "daemon" was first used by MIT programmers who worked on CTSS (Compatible Time-sharing System), developed in 1963. They coined the term to refer to what were called "dragons" by other programmers who worked on ITS (Incompatible Time-sharing System).

CTSS and ITS were both ancestors to Unix. ITS was an important, though strange, operating system that developed a cult following at MIT. As CTSS and ITS programmers migrated from MIT to Bell Labs (the birthplace of Unix), the idea of daemons traveled with them.

So why the name "daemon"? One story is that the name comes from "Maxwell's demon", an imaginary creature devised by the Scottish physicist James Maxwell (1831-1879) for a thought experiment related to the second law of thermodynamics. You can believe this or not. (I don't.)

Regardless of the origin, nobody knows why we use the British variation of the spelling. In Celtic mythology, a daemon is usually good or neutral, merely a spirit or inspiration. A demon, however, is always an evil entity. Perhaps there is a lesson here somewhere.

THE END OF THE LAST CHAPTER

I would like to thank you for spending so much time with me talking about Unix and Linux. I wrote this book in order to make Unix accessible to intelligent people and, to the extent that I have helped you, I am grateful for the opportunity.

Unix has traditionally attracted the most talented computer users and programmers, for whom working on Unix was a labor of love. One reason Unix is so wonderful, is that most of it was designed before the men in suits sat up and took notice. That is why Unix works so well and why it is so elegant; the basic Unix philosophy was developed long before the business and marketing people started trying to make money from it. As we discussed in Chapter 2, in the 1990s, this philosophy was transplanted to the Linux Project and to the open source community, with wonderful results.

You may remember my observing that Unix is not easy to learn, but it is easy to use. By now, you will realize what this means: that it is more important for a tool to be designed well for a smart person, than it is for the tool to be easy enough to be used on the first day by someone whose biggest intellectual challenge in life is downloading a ringtone.

You have my word that every moment you spend learning and using Unix will repay you generously. I can't be by your side as you work, but you do have this book, and I have put in a great deal of effort to provide you with the very best Unix companion I could.

Although I may be irreverent at times — indeed, whenever I am able to make a joke that my editors can't catch — I would like to take a moment to wish you the very best. As you read and re-read this book, please remember: I am on *your* side.

Harley Hahn

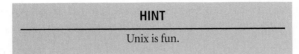

HINT
Unix is fun.

CHAPTER 26 EXERCISES

REVIEW QUESTIONS

1. What is a process? What part of the operating system manages processes? Define the following terms: process ID, parent process, child process, fork and exec.

2. What is a job? What part of the operating system manages jobs? What is job control?

   What is the difference between running a job in the foreground and running a job in the background? How do you run a job in the foreground? How do you run a job in the background? How do you move a job from the foreground to the background?

3. The **ps** (process status) program is used to display information about processes. What are the two types of options you can use with this program? For each type of option, which commands would you use to display information about:

   • Your current processes
   • Process #120357
   • All the processes running on the system
   • Processes associated with userid **weedly**

4. You are a system administrator. One of your systems seems to be bogging down and your job is to figure out why. To start, you want to take a look at various processes running on the system and how they are changing from moment to moment. Which program will you use? Specify the command that will run this program with an automatic update every 5 seconds.

5. What is the difference between killing a process and stopping a process? How do you kill a process? How do you stop a process?

6. You have started a program named **foobar** that is running amok. What steps would you take to kill it? If **foobar** does not respond, what do you do?

EXERCISES

1. Enter a command line that pauses for 5 seconds and then displays the message "I am smart." Wait for 5 seconds to make sure it works.

   Now change the delay to 30 seconds, and re-enter the command line. This time, before the 30 seconds are up, press **^C**. What happens? Why?

2. You have just logged into a Unix system over the Internet using your userid, which is
weedly. You enter the command **ps** **-f** command and see:

```
UID          PID  PPID  C STIME TTY          TIME CMD
weedly      2282  2281  0 15:31 pts/3    00:00:00 -bash
weedly      2547  2282  0 16:13 pts/3    00:00:00 ps -f
```

Everything looks fine. Just out of curiosity, you decide to check on the rest of the
system, so you enter the command **ps** **-af**. Among the output lines, you see:

```
weedly      2522  2436  0 16:09 pts/4   00:00:00 vim secret
```

Someone else is logged in using your userid! What do you do?

3. Create a pipeline to count the number of daemons on your system. Then create a
second pipeline to display a sorted list of all the daemons. You should display the
names of the daemons only and nothing else.

FOR FURTHER THOUGHT

1. Using the **kill** command to kill processes is more complicated than it needs to be.
Describe a simpler way to provide the same functionality.

2. Why are there two different types of options for **ps**? Is this good or bad?

APPENDIX A
SUMMARY OF UNIX COMMANDS COVERED IN THIS BOOK

This appendix summarizes the 143 Unix commands discussed in this book. At the end of each name, the designation [*X*] indicates the chapter in which the command is discussed.

See Appendix B for a summary of commands organized into categories.

! [13]	Reexecute command from the history list
!! [13]	Reexecute last command from the history list
& [26]	Run a program in the background
^^ [13]	Substitute/reexecute last command from history list
^Z [26]	Suspend (pause) a foreground process
alias [13]	Create/display aliases
apropos [9]	Display command names based on keyword search
bash [11]	Bash shell
bc [8]	Arbitrary-precision, easy-to-use calculator
bg [26]	Move job to the background
bindkey [13]	Set command-line editing mode
cal [8]	Display a calendar
calendar [8]	Display current reminders from **calendar** file
cat [16]	Combine files; copy standard input to standard output
cd [24]	Change your working directory
chmod [25]	Change file permissions for files or directories
chsh [11]	Change your default shell
cmp [17]	Compare two files
colrm [16]	Delete specified columns of data
comm [17]	Compare two sorted files, show differences
cp [25]	Copy files; copy directories
csh [11]	C-Shell
cut [17]	Extract specified columns/fields of data

date [8]	Display the time and date
dc [8]	Arbitrary-precision, stack-based calculator
df [24]	Display disk space used/available for filesystems
diff [17]	Compare two files, show differences
dirs [24]	Display/clear contents of the directory stack
dmesg [6]	Display boot messages (Linux)
du [24]	Display amount of disk storage used by files
dumpe2fs [24]	Display filesystem information from superblock
echo [12]	Write arguments to standard output
env [12]	Display environment variables
exit [4]	Exit a shell
expand [18]	Change tabs to spaces
export [12]	Export shell variables to the environment
fc [13]	Display/reexecute commands from the history list
fg [26]	Move job to the foreground
file [24]	Analyze type of file
find [25]	Search for files in a directory tree; process results
fmt [18, 22]	Format paragraphs to make them look nice
fold [18]	Format long lines into shorter lines
fuser [26]	Identify processes that are using specific files
grep [19]	Select lines containing a specified pattern
groups [25]	Display the groups to which a userid belongs
head [16,21]	Select lines from beginning of data
hexdump [21]	Display binary (non-text) files
history [13]	Display commands from the history list
hostname [8]	Display the name of your system
id [25]	Display current userid and groupid
info [9]	Display file from the Info reference system
init [6]	Change to another runlevel
jobs [26]	Display information about jobs
join [19]	Combine columns of data based on common fields
kill [26]	Terminate a process; send a signal to a process
ksh [11]	Korn shell
last [4]	Check the last time userid has logged in
leave [8]	Display reminder at a specified time
less [21]	Pager: display data, one screenful at a time
ln [25]	Create a new link to a file
locate [25]	Search for files
lock [8]	Temporarily lock your terminal
login [4]	Terminate a login shell and initiate a new login

Chapter references are indicated by the numbers in brackets.

logout [4]	Terminate a login shell
look [19]	Select lines that begin with a specified pattern
ls [24, 25]	Display various types of information about files
man [9]	Display pages from the online Unix reference manual
mkdir [24]	Create a directory
mkfifo [23]	Create a named pipe
more [21]	Pager: display data, one screenful at a time
mount [23]	Mount a filesystem
mv [24, 25]	Move or rename files or directories
nice [26]	Run a program using specified scheduling priority
nl [18]	Add line numbers to text
od [21]	Display binary (non-text) files
passwd [4]	Change your login password
paste [17]	Combine columns of data
popd [24]	Change working directory; pop name off directory stack
pr [18]	Format text into pages or columns
print [12]	Write arguments to standard output
printenv [12]	Display environment variables
prstat [26]	Display dynamic information about processes
ps [26]	Display information about processes
pstree [26]	Display diagram of a process tree
ptree [26]	Display diagram of a process tree
pushd [24]	Change working directory; push name on directory stack
pwd [24]	Display pathname of your working directory
quota [8, 24]	Display your system resource quotas
reboot [6]	Reboot the computer
renice [26]	Change scheduling priority of a running program
rev [16]	Reverse order of characters in each line of data
rm [25]	Delete files or directories
rmdir [24]	Remove an empty directory
sdiff [17]	Compare two files, show differences
sed [19]	Non-interactive text editing
set [12]	Set/display shell options and shell variables
setenv [12]	Set/display environment variables
sh [11]	Bourne shell
shred [25]	Delete a file securely
shutdown [6]	Shutdown the computer
sleep [26]	Delay for a specified interval
sort [19]	Sort data; check if data is sorted
split [16]	Split a large file into smaller files

Chapter references are indicated by the numbers in brackets.

stat [25]	Display information from an inode
strings [19]	Search for character strings in binary files
stty [7]	Set/display operating options for your terminal
su [6]	Change to superuser or another userid
sudo [6]	Run a single command as superuser
suspend [26]	Suspend (pause) a shell
tac [16]	Combine files while reversing order of lines of text
tail [16, 21]	Select lines from end of data
tcsh [11]	Tcsh shell
tee [15]	Copy standard input to a file and to standard output
top [26]	Display data about the most CPU-intensive processes
touch [25]	Update access/modification times of file; create file
tr [19]	Change or delete selected characters
tree [24]	Display a diagram of a directory tree
tsort [19]	Create a total ordering from partial orderings
tty [23]	Display name of the special file for your terminal
type [8]	Locate a command: display its pathname or alias
umask [25]	Set file mode mask for file creation
umount [23]	Unmount a filesystem
unalias [13]	Delete aliases
uname [8]	Display the name of your operating system
unexpand [18]	Change spaces to tabs
uniq [19]	Remove adjacent repeated lines in a text file
unset [12]	Delete shell variables
unsetenv [12]	Unset environment variables
uptime [8]	Display how long your system has been up
users [8]	Display userids that are currently logged in
vi [22]	**vi** text editor
view [22]	Start **vi** text editor in read-only mode
vim [22]	Vim text editor
w [8]	Display info about userids and active processes
wc [18]	Count lines, words and characters
whatis [9]	Display one-line summary of specified command
whence [8]	Locate a command: display its pathname or alias
whereis [25]	Find files associated with a command
which [8]	Locate a command: display its pathname or alias
who [8]	Display info about currently logged in userids
whoami [8]	Display the userid that is currently logged in
xargs	Run command using arguments from standard input
xman [9]	GUI-based: display pages from online reference manual

Chapter references are indicated by the numbers in brackets.

SUMMARY OF UNIX COMMANDS
COVERED IN THIS BOOK

This appendix summarizes the 143 Unix commands discussed in this book, organized into categories. At the end of each name, the designation [X] indicates the chapter in which the command is discussed. See Appendix A for a summary of commands in alphabetical order. The categories are:

Building Blocks	Files	System Tools
Command Tools	Filesystems	Terminals
Comparing Files	Logging In and Out	Text Formatting
Directories	Processes and Job Control	Tools
Displaying Data	Shells	Users and Userids
Documentation	Selecting Data	Variables
Editing		

BUILDING BLOCKS

cat [16]	Combine files; copy standard input to standard output
tee [15]	Copy standard input to a file and to standard output
xargs [25]	Run command using arguments from standard input

COMMAND TOOLS

alias [13]	Create/display aliases
type [8]	Locate a command: display its pathname or alias
unalias [13]	Delete aliases
whence [8]	Locate a command: display its pathname or alias
which [8]	Locate a command: display its pathname or alias

COMPARING FILES

cmp [17]	Compare two files
comm [17]	Compare two sorted files, show differences
diff [17]	Compare two files, show differences
sdiff [17]	Compare two files, show differences

DIRECTORIES

cd [24]	Change your working directory
chmod [25]	Change file permissions for files or directories
dirs [24]	Display/clear contents of the directory stack
du [24]	Display amount of disk storage used by files
file [24]	Analyze type of file
ls [24, 25]	Display various types of information about files
mkdir [24]	Create a directory
mv [24,25]	Move or rename files or directories
popd [24]	Change working directory; pop name off directory stack
pushd [24]	Change working directory; push name on directory stack
pwd [24]	Display pathname of your working directory
rm [25]	Delete files or directories
rmdir [24]	Remove an empty directory
tree [24]	Display a diagram of a directory tree

DISPLAYING DATA

cat [16]	Combine files; copy standard input to standard output
echo [12]	Write arguments to standard output
head [16, 21]	Select lines from beginning of data
hexdump [21]	Display binary (non-text) files
less [21]	Pager: display data, one screenful at a time
more [21]	Pager: display data, one screenful at a time
od [21]	Display binary (non-text) files
print [12]	Write arguments to standard output
tail [16, 21]	Select lines from end of data

DOCUMENTATION

apropos [9]	Display command names based on keyword search
info [9]	Display file from the Info reference system
man [9]	Display pages from the online Unix reference manual
whatis [9]	Display one-line summary of specified command
xman [9]	GUI-based: display pages from online reference manual

EDITING

sed [19]	Non-interactive text editing
vi [22]	**vi** text editor
view [22]	Start **vi** text editor in read-only mode
vim [22]	Vim text editor

FILES

chmod [25]	Change file permissions for file or directory
cp [25]	Copy files; copy directories

Chapter references are indicated by the numbers in brackets.

du [24]	Display amount of disk storage used by files
find [25]	Search for files in a directory tree; process results
ln [25]	Create a new link to a file
locate [25]	Search for files
ls [24, 25]	Display various types of information about files
mkfifo [23]	Create a named pipe
mv [24, 25]	Move or rename files or directories
rm [25]	Delete files or directories
shred [25]	Delete a file securely
stat [25]	Display information from an inode
touch [25]	Update access/modification times of file; create file
umask [25]	Set file mode mask for file creation
whence [8]	Locate a command: display its pathname or alias
whereis [25]	Find files associated with a command

FILESYSTEMS

df [24]	Display disk space used/available for filesystems
dumpe2fs [24]	Display filesystem information from superblock
mount [23]	Mount a filesystem
umount [23]	Unmount a filesystem

LOGGING IN AND OUT

login [4]	Terminate a login shell and initiate a new login
logout [4]	Terminate a login shell
passwd [4]	Change your login password

PROCESSES AND JOB CONTROL

& [26]	Run a program in the background
^Z [26]	Suspend (pause) a foreground process
fg [26]	Move job to the foreground
suspend [26]	Suspend (pause) a shell
jobs [26]	Display information about jobs
bg [26]	Move job to the background
ps [26]	Display information about processes
top [26]	Display data about the most CPU-intensive processes
prstat [26]	Display dynamic information about processes
pstree [26]	Display diagram of a process tree
ptree [26]	Display diagram of a process tree
fuser [26]	Identify processes that are using specific files
kill [26]	Terminate a process; send a signal to a process
nice [26]	Run a program using specified scheduling priority
renice [26]	Change scheduling priority of a running program

Chapter references are indicated by the numbers in brackets.

SHELLS

! [13]	Reexecute command from the history list
!! [13]	Reexecute last command from the history list
^^ [13]	Substitute/reexecute last command from history list
bash [11]	Bash shell
bindkey [13]	Set command-line editing mode
chsh [11]	Change your default shell
csh [11]	C-Shell
exit [4]	Exit a shell
fc [13]	Display/reexecute commands from the history list
history [13]	Display commands from the history list
ksh [11]	Korn shell
sh [11]	Bourne shell
tcsh [11]	Tcsh shell

SELECTING DATA

cut [17]	Extract specified columns/fields of data
grep [19]	Select lines containing a specified pattern
head [16, 21]	Select lines from beginning of data
look [19]	Select lines that begin with a specified pattern
strings [19]	Search for character strings in binary files
tail [16, 21]	Select lines from end of data

SYSTEM TOOLS

dmesg [6]	Display boot messages (Linux)
hostname [8]	Display the name of your system
init [6]	Change to another runlevel
reboot [6]	Reboot the computer
shutdown [6]	Shutdown the computer
su [6]	Change to superuser or another userid
sudo [6]	Run a single command as superuser
uname [8]	Display the name of your operating system
uptime [8]	Display how long your system has been up

TERMINALS

lock [8]	Temporarily lock your terminal
stty [7]	Set/display operating options for your terminal
tty [23]	Display name of the special file for your terminal

Chapter references are indicated by the numbers in brackets.

TEXT FORMATTING

colrm [16]	Delete specified columns of data
expand [18]	Change tabs to spaces
fmt [18, 22]	Format paragraphs to make them look nice
fold [18]	Format long lines into shorter lines
join [19]	Combine columns of data based on common fields
nl [18]	Add line numbers to text
paste [17]	Combine columns of data
pr [18]	Format text into pages or columns
rev [16]	Reverse order of characters in each line of data
sed [19]	Non-interactive text editing
split [16]	Split a large file into smaller files
tac [16]	Combine files while reversing order of lines of text
tr [19]	Change or delete selected characters
unexpand [18]	Change spaces to tabs
uniq [19]	Remove adjacent repeated lines in a text file

TOOLS

bc [8]	Arbitrary-precision, easy-to-use calculator
cal [8]	Display a calendar
calendar [8]	Display current reminders from **calendar** file
date [8]	Display the time and date
dc [8]	Arbitrary-precision, stack-based calculator
leave [8]	Display reminder at a specified time
sleep [26]	Delay for a specified interval
sort [19]	Sort data; check if data is sorted
tsort [19]	Create a total ordering from partial orderings
wc [18]	Count lines, words and characters

USERS AND USERIDS

groups [25]	Display the groups to which a userid belongs
id [25]	Display current userid and groupid
last [4]	Check the last time userid has logged in
quota [8, 24]	Display your system resource quotas
users [8]	Display userids that are currently logged in
w [8]	Display info about userids and active processes
who [8]	Display info about currently logged in userids
whoami [8]	Display the userid that is currently logged in

Chapter references are indicated by the numbers in brackets.

VARIABLES

echo [12]	Write arguments to standard output
env [12]	Display environment variables
export [12]	Export shell variables to the environment
print [12]	Write arguments to standard output
printenv [12]	Display environment variables
set [12]	Set/display shell options and shell variables
setenv [12]	Set/display environment variables
unset [12]	Delete shell variables
unsetenv [12]	Unset environment variables

Chapter references are indicated by the numbers in brackets.

APPENDIX C
SUMMARY OF vi COMMANDS

This appendix contains a summary of all the **vi** commands covered in this book. For more information, see Chapter 22 in which I discuss **vi** in detail.

STARTING

vi *file*	Start **vi**, edit specified file
vi -R *file*	Start **vi** read-only, edit specified file
view *file*	Start **vi** read-only, edit specified file
vim *file*	Start Vim, edit specified file.
vim -C *file*	Start **vi** in compatibility mode

STOPPING

:q!	Stop without saving data
ZZ	Save data and stop
:wq	Save data and stop
:x	Save data and stop

RECOVERING AFTER SYSTEM FAILURE

vi -r	Display names of files that can be recovered
vi -r *file*	Start **vi**, recover specified file

KEYS TO USE TO MAKE CORRECTIONS

<Backspace>/<Delete>	Erase the last character typed
^W	Erase the last word typed
^X/^U	Erase the entire line

CONTROLLING THE DISPLAY

^L	Redisplay the current screen
:set number	Display internal line numbers
:set nonumber	Do not display internal line numbers

MOVING THE CURSOR

h	Move cursor one position left
j	Move cursor one position down
k	Move cursor one position up
l	Move cursor one position right
<Left>	Move cursor one position left
<Down>	Move cursor one position down
<Up>	Move cursor one position up
<Right>	Move cursor one position right
<Backspace>	Move cursor one position left
<Space>	Move cursor one position right
–	Move cursor to beginning of previous line
+	Move cursor to beginning of next line
<Return>	Move cursor to beginning of next line
0	Move cursor to beginning of current line
$	Move cursor to end of current line
^	Move cursor to first non-space/tab in current line
w	Move cursor forward to first character of next word
e	Move cursor forward to last character of next word
b	Move cursor backward to first character of previous word
W	Same as **w**; ignore punctuation
E	Same as **e**; ignore punctuation
B	Same as **b**; ignore punctuation
)	Move forward to next sentence beginning
(	Move backward to previous sentence beginning
}	Move forward to next paragraph beginning
{	Move backward to previous paragraph beginning
H	Move cursor to top line
M	Move cursor to middle line
L	Move cursor to last line

MOVING THROUGH THE EDITING BUFFER

^F	Move down (forwards) one screenful
^B	Move up (backwards) one screenful
n^F	Move down n screenfuls
n^B	Move up n screenfuls
^D	Move down a half screenful
^U	Move up a half screenful
n^D	Move down n lines
n^U	Move up n lines

SEARCHING FOR A PATTERN

/*regex*	Search forward for specified regular expression
/	Repeat forward search for previous pattern
?*regex*	Sarch backward for specified regular expression
?	Repeat backward search for previous pattern
n	Repeat last / or ? command, same direction
N	Repeat last / or ? command, opposite direction

SPECIAL CHARACTERS TO USE IN REGULAR EXPRESSIONS

.	Match any single character except newline
*	Match zero or more of the preceding characters
^	Match the beginning of a line
$	Match the end of a line
\<	Match the beginning of a word
\>	Match the end of a word
[ ]	Match one of the enclosed characters
[^]	Match any character that is not enclosed
\	Interpret the following symbol literally

LINE NUMBERS

*n*G	Jump to line number *n*
1G	Jump to first line in editing buffer
gg	Jump to first line in editing buffer
G	Jump to last line in editing buffer
:map g 1G	Define macro so **g** will be the same as **1G**
:*n*	Jump to line number *n*
:1	Jump to first line in editing buffer
:$	Jump to last line in editing buffer

INSERTING

i	Change to insert mode: insert before cursor position
a	Change to insert mode: insert after cursor position
I	Change to insert mode: insert at start of current line
A	Change to insert mode: insert at end of current line
o	Change to insert mode: open below current line
O	Change to insert mode: open above current line
\<Escape\>	Leave insert mode, change to command mode

MAKING CHANGES

r	Replace exactly 1 character (do not enter input mode)
R	Replace by typing over
s	Replace 1 character by insertion
C	Replace from cursor to end of line by insertion
cc	Replace entire current line by insertion
S	Replace entire current line by insertion
c*move*	Replace from cursor to *move* by insertion
~	Change the case of a letter

REPLACING A PATTERN

:s/*pattern*/*replace*/	Substitute, current line
:*line***s**/*pattern*/*replace*/	Substitute, specified line
:*line*,*line***s**/*pattern*/*replace*/	Substitute, specified range
:%s/*pattern*/*replace*/	Substitute, all lines

At the end of a command, use c to ask for confirmation, and g (global) to replace all occurrences on each line. To specify a line number, you can use an actual number, a . (period) for the current line, or $ (dollar sign) for the last line in the editing buffer. The number 1 represents the first line in the editing buffer.

UNDOING OR REPEATING A CHANGE

u	Undo last command that modified the editing buffer
U	Restore current line
.	Repeat last command that modified the editing buffer

BREAKING AND JOINING LINES

r<Return>	Break current line into two (replace character with newline)
J	Join current line and next line into one long line
:set wm=*n*	Auto line break within *n* positions of right margin

DELETING

x	Delete character at cursor
X	Delete character to left of cursor
D	Delete from cursor to end of line
dd	Delete the entire current line
d*move*	Delete from cursor to *move*
dG	Delete from current line to end of editing buffer
d1G	Delete from current line to start of editing buffer
*line***d**	Delete specified line
:*line*,*line***d**	Delete specified range

DELETING: USEFUL COMBINATIONS

dw	delete 1 word
d*n***w**	delete *n* words
d*n***W**	delete *n* words (ignore punctuation)
db	delete backward, 1 word
d*n***)**	delete *n* sentences
d*n***}**	delete *n* paragraphs
dG	delete from current line to end of editing buffer
dgg	delete from current line to start of editing buffer
d1G	delete from current line to start of editing buffer

COPYING THE LAST DELETION

p	copy buffer; insert after/below cursor
P	copy buffer; insert before/above cursor
xp	transpose two characters
deep	transpose two words (start to the left of first word)
ddp	transpose two lines
"1pu.u.u...	recall one deletion after another

COPYING AND MOVING LINES

:*line***co***target*	copy specified line; insert below target
:*line*,*line***co***target*	copy specified range; insert below target
:*line***m***target*	move specified line; insert below target
:*line*,*line***m***target*	move specified range; insert below target

YANKING

y*move*	yank from cursor to *move*
yy	yank the entire current line

YANKING: USEFUL COMBINATIONS

yw	yank 1 word
y*n***w**	yank *n* words
y*n***W**	yank *n* words (ignore punctuation)
yb	yank backward, 1 word
y*n***)**	yank *n* sentences
y*n***}**	yank *n* paragraphs
yG	yank from current line to end of editing buffer
ygg	yank from current line to start of editing buffer
y1G	yank from current line to start of editing buffer

EXECUTING SHELL COMMANDS

`:!`*command*	pause **vi**, execute specified shell command
`:!!` pause **vi**,	execute previous shell command
`:sh`	pause **vi**, start a shell
`:!csh`	pause **vi**, start a new C-Shell

READING DATA INTO EDITING BUFFER

`:`*line*`r` *file*	insert contents of *file* after specified line
`:r` *file*	insert contents of *file* after current line
`:`*line*`r !`*command*	insert output of *command* after specified line
`:r !`*command*	insert output of *command* after current line
`:r !look` *pattern*	insert words that begin with specified pattern

USING SHELL COMMANDS TO PROCESS DATA

n`!!`*command*	execute *command* on *n* lines
`!`*move command*	execute *command* from cursor to *move*
`!`*move* `fmt`	format lines from cursor to *move*

WRITING DATA

`:w`	write data to original file
`:w` *file*	write data to specified file
`:w>>` *file*	append data to specified file

CHANGING THE FILE WHILE EDITING

`:e` *file*	edit the specified file
`:e!` *file*	edit the specified file, omit automatic check

ABBREVIATIONS

`:ab` *short long*	set *short* as an abbreviation for *long*
`:ab`	display current abbreviations
`:una` *short*	cancel abbreviation *short*

APPENDIX D
THE ASCII CODE

Before the 1990s, the character encoding used by Unix (and most computer systems) was the ASCII CODE, often referred to as ASCII. The name stands for "American Standard Code for Information Interchange".

The ASCII code was created in 1967. It specifies a 7-bit pattern for every character, 128 in all. These bit patterns range from 0000000 (0 in decimal) to 1111111 (127 in decimal). For this reason, the 128 ASCII characters are numbered from 0 to 127.

The 128 characters that comprise the ASCII code consist of 33 "control characters" and 95 "printable characters". The control characters are discussed in see Chapter 7. The printable characters, shown below, are the 52 letters of the alphabet (26 uppercase, 26 lowercase), 10 numbers, 32 punctuation symbols, and the space character (listed first below):

```
 !"#$%&'()*+,-./0123456789:;<=>?
@ABCDEFGHIJKLMNOPQRSTUVWXYZ[\]^_
`abcdefghijklmnopqrstuvwxyz{|}~
```

As a convenience, most Unix systems have a reference page showing the ASCII code to allow you to look at it quickly whenever you want. Unfortunately, the ASCII reference page is not standardized, so the way in which you display it depends on which system you are using. You can see the details in Figure 19-1 or Figure 20-5.

CHARACTER	DECIMAL	HEX	OCTAL	BINARY	
	0	00	000	0000 0000	(null)
Ctrl-A	1	01	001	0000 0001	
Ctrl-B	2	02	002	0000 0010	
Ctrl-C	3	03	003	0000 0011	
Ctrl-D	4	04	004	0000 0100	
Ctrl-E	5	05	005	0000 0101	
Ctrl-F	6	06	006	0000 0110	
Ctrl-G	7	07	007	0000 0111	(beep)
Ctrl-H	8	08	010	0000 1000	**backspace**
Ctrl-I	9	09	011	0000 1001	**tab**
Ctrl-J	10	0A	012	0000 1010	
Ctrl-K	11	0B	013	0000 1011	
Ctrl-L	12	0C	014	0000 1100	
Ctrl-M	13	0D	015	0000 1101	**return**
Ctrl-N	14	0E	016	0000 1110	
Ctrl-O	15	0F	017	0000 1111	
Ctrl-P	16	10	020	0001 0000	
Ctrl-Q	17	11	021	0001 0001	
Ctrl-R	18	12	022	0001 0010	
Ctrl-S	19	13	023	0001 0011	
Ctrl-T	20	14	024	0001 0100	
Ctrl-U	21	15	025	0001 0101	
Ctrl-V	22	16	026	0001 0110	
Ctrl-W	23	17	027	0001 0111	
Ctrl-X	24	18	030	0001 1000	
Ctrl-Y	25	19	031	0001 1001	
Ctrl-Z	26	1A	032	0001 1010	
Ctrl-[	27	1B	033	0001 1011	**escape**
Ctrl-\	28	1C	034	0001 1100	
Ctrl-]	29	1D	035	0001 1101	
Ctrl-^	30	1E	036	0001 1110	
Ctrl-_	31	1F	037	0001 1111	

CHARACTER	DECIMAL	HEX	OCTAL	BINARY	
(space)	32	20	040	0010 0000	**space**
!	33	21	041	0010 0001	(exclamation mark)
"	34	22	042	0010 0010	(double quote)
#	35	23	043	0010 0011	(number sign)
$	36	24	044	0010 0100	(dollar sign)
%	37	25	045	0010 0101	(percent sign)
&	38	26	046	0010 0110	(ampersand)
'	39	27	047	0010 0111	(single quote)
(	40	28	050	0010 1000	(left parenthesis)
)	41	29	051	0010 1001	(right parenthesis)
*	42	2A	052	0010 1010	(asterisk)
+	43	2B	053	0010 1011	(plus)
,	44	2C	054	0010 1100	(comma)
–	45	2D	055	0010 1101	(minus/hyphen)
.	46	2E	056	0010 1110	(period)
/	47	2F	057	0010 1111	(slash)
0	48	30	060	0011 0000	
1	49	31	061	0011 0001	
2	50	32	062	0011 0010	
3	51	33	063	0011 0011	
4	52	34	064	0011 0100	
5	53	35	065	0011 0101	
6	54	36	066	0011 0110	
7	55	37	067	0011 0111	
8	56	38	070	0011 1000	
9	57	39	071	0011 1001	
:	58	3A	072	0011 1010	(colon)
;	59	3B	073	0011 1011	(semicolon)
<	60	3C	074	0011 1100	(less than)
=	61	3D	075	0011 1101	(equals)
>	62	3E	076	0011 1110	(greater than)
?	63	3F	077	0011 1111	(question mark)

CHARACTER	DECIMAL	HEX	OCTAL	BINARY	
@	64	40	100	0100 0000	(at sign)
A	65	41	101	0100 0001	
B	66	42	102	0100 0010	
C	67	43	103	0100 0011	
D	68	44	104	0100 0100	
E	69	45	105	0100 0101	
F	70	46	106	0100 0110	
G	71	47	107	0100 0111	
H	72	48	110	0100 1000	
I	73	49	111	0100 1001	
J	74	4A	112	0100 1010	
K	75	4B	113	0100 1011	
L	76	4C	114	0100 1100	
M	77	4D	115	0100 1101	
N	78	4E	116	0100 1110	
O	79	4F	117	0100 1111	
P	80	50	120	0101 0000	
Q	81	51	121	0101 0001	
R	82	52	122	0101 0010	
S	83	53	123	0101 0011	
T	84	54	124	0101 0100	
U	85	55	125	0101 0101	
V	86	56	126	0101 0110	
W	87	57	127	0101 0111	
X	88	58	130	0101 1000	
Y	89	59	131	0101 1001	
Z	90	5A	132	0101 1010	
[	91	5B	133	0101 1011	(left square bracket)
\	92	5C	134	0101 1100	(backslash)
]	93	5D	135	0101 1101	(right square bracket)
^	94	5E	136	0101 1110	(circumflex)
_	95	5F	137	0101 1111	(underscore)

CHARACTER	DECIMAL	HEX	OCTAL	BINARY	
`	96	60	140	0110 0000	(backquote)
a	97	61	141	0110 0001	
b	98	62	142	0110 0010	
c	99	63	143	0110 0011	
d	100	64	144	0110 0100	
e	101	65	145	0110 0101	
f	102	66	146	0110 0110	
g	103	67	147	0110 0111	
h	104	68	150	0110 1000	
i	105	69	151	0110 1001	
j	106	6A	152	0110 1010	
k	107	6B	153	0110 1011	
l	108	6C	154	0110 1100	
m	109	6D	155	0110 1101	
n	110	6E	156	0110 1110	
o	111	6F	157	0110 1111	
p	112	70	160	0111 0000	
q	113	71	161	0111 0001	
r	114	72	162	0111 0010	
s	115	73	163	0111 0011	
t	116	74	164	0111 0100	
u	117	75	165	0111 0101	
v	118	76	166	0111 0110	
w	119	77	167	0111 0111	
x	120	78	170	0111 1000	
y	121	79	171	0111 1001	
z	122	7A	172	0111 1010	
{	123	7B	173	0111 1011	(left brace bracket)
		124	7C	174	0111 1100	(vertical bar)
}	125	7D	175	0111 1101	(right brace bracket)
~	126	7E	176	0111 1110	(tilde)
	127	7F	177	0111 1111	del

WHAT TO DO IF YOU FORGET THE ROOT PASSWORD

When you use your own Unix system, you are the system administrator, which means there is no one to help you if something goes wrong.

So what do you do if you forget the **root** (superuser) password?

Here are the steps to follow to solve this problem for a typical Linux system. The actual details may vary a bit from one system to another, but what you read here should work with most modern Linux distributions.

I won't explain all of the commands in detail, because that would take us into the realm of system administration, which is beyond the scope of this book. If there is a command you don't understand, just look it up in the online manual or ask someone for help.

If you have **sudo** privileges (see Chapter 6), you may be able to change the **root** password quickly by using the command:

```
sudo passwd root
```

You will find that more elaborate measures are necessary if you don't have **sudo** privileges, or if your system is configured in such a way that **sudo** will not let you change the **root** password.

The general strategy is to take control of the computer by booting from a live Linux CD. Then mount the main (root) file system that resides on your hard disk. Once this is done, you can use the mount point as the root of the file system, and then change the **root** password with the standard **passwd** program.

1. Boot Linux from a live CD.

2. Press <Crtl-Alt-F1> to get to a command line.

3. Change to superuser:

    ```
    sudo su
    ```

4. Start the partition table editor:

```
parted
```

(If your system does not have **parted**, you'll have to use another partition editor such as **fdisk**, **cfdisk** or **sfdisk**.)

5. Within **parted**, display the partitions on your primary hard disk:

```
print
```

6. Write down the device name for the hard disk that contains your Linux system, for example, **/dev/hda** or **/dev/sda**.

7. Write down the number of the main Linux partition, for example, partition number 2.

If you are not sure which is the root partition, look for a file system type of **ext3**, **ext2**, **reiserfs** or **xfs**. If there is more than one such partition, write down all their numbers.

8. Stop the **parted** program:

```
quit
```

You should now be back at the shell prompt.

9. Create a mount point for the file system that resides on the hard disk. (In this example, I will call it **harley**):

```
mkdir /mnt/harley
```

10. Mount the root file system from the hard disk by using the device name and partition number you got from **parted**. For example, if your device name was **/dev/hda** and your partition was number 2, you would use the command:

```
mount /dev/hda2 /mnt/harley
```

If, in step 7, you found more than one possible partition, choose one of them. If it doesn't work, you can try another.

11. Confirm that you have mounted the root partition. To test this, see if the shadow file (**/etc/shadow**) — the file that contains the passwords — lies in that partition:

```
ls /mnt/harley/etc/shadow
```

If the password file isn't there, you have not mounted the root partition. Go back to step 10 and try a different partition. Continue until you have successfully mounted the root partition.

12. Change the **root** password on the hard disk system.

There are various ways to do this. The simplest strategy is to run the **passwd** command using the new mount point as the root of the file system. This can be done with one simple command:

```
chroot /mnt/harley passwd
```

This **chroot** (change root) command means: "Change the root of the file tree temporarily to **/mnt/harley**, and then execute the command **passwd**."

Since you are in superuser mode, the **passwd** command will change the **root** password. And since the file system root is temporarily **/mnt/harley**, the password file that will be used is the one on the hard disk (**/mnt/harley/etc/shadow**).

In this way, you are able to change the **root** password for the system on the hard disk.

13. Remove the CD, reboot from the hard disk, and test to make sure the password was changed correctly.

WHAT'S IN A NAME?

Root

Within Unix, the name "root" has four different meanings:

• The userid of the superuser.
• The name of the directory that is the starting point of the Unix file tree.
• The name of the main Unix file system.
• The name of the disk partition that contains the root file system.

Notice that, within the short set of instructions in this appendix, we have managed to use the word "root" in all four ways.

That is, we mounted the <u>root</u> file system that resides in the <u>root</u> partition, in order to make the mount point the <u>root</u> of the Unix file tree so we could change the <u>root</u> password.

Unix and the Internet are used around the world, and times must be expressed carefully, especially within the headers of email messages and Usenet articles.

In general, both Unix and the Internet use a 24-hour clock. For example, within the header of an email message, you might see 20:50 instead of 8:50 PM. If you are not used to a 24-hour clock, use the conversion information below.

Conversion between the 24-hour time system and the AM/PM time system.			
(midnight)	12:00 AM = 00:00	12:00 PM = 12:00	(noon)
	1:00 AM = 01:00	1:00 PM = 13:00	
	2:00 AM = 02:00	2:00 PM = 14:00	
	3:00 AM = 03:00	3:00 PM = 15:00	
	4:00 AM = 04:00	4:00 PM = 16:00	
	5:00 AM = 05:00	5:00 PM = 17:00	
	6:00 AM = 06:00	6:00 PM = 18:00	
	7:00 AM = 07:00	7:00 PM = 19:00	
	8:00 AM = 08:00	8:00 PM = 20:00	
	9:00 AM = 09:00	9:00 PM = 21:00	
	10:00 AM = 10:00	10:00 PM = 22:00	
	11:00 AM = 11:00	11:00 PM = 23:00	

Whenever your programs need to know the time, date, or time zone, they get the information from settings that are maintained by Unix. For example, when you send a mail message, your mail program puts the date, time, and time zone on the message.

To ensure that the time and date are always correct, most Unix systems use a program to synchronize the computer's clock with an exact time source on the Internet. This program runs in the background, checking the time and date automatically at regular intervals, and making corrections as necessary*. Although the time checking is automatic, you do need to make sure your time zone is set correctly. Normally, this is done when you install Unix.

In practice, you will see time zone information expressed in three different ways. First, when you see a specific time, you may also see an abbreviation for the local time zone. For example, here is the output from a **date** command (see Chapter 8) that shows a time of 8:50 PM, Pacific Daylight Time (PDT):

```
$ date
Sun Dec 21 20:50:17 PDT 2008
```

Another way you might see this same information is with the time converted to UTC (Coordinated Universal Time), also referred to as GMT (Greenwich Mean Time) or UT (Universal Time)**. (In case you are not familiar with UTC, I explain it below.)

UTC is considered to be a universal time. It is expected that everyone who uses the Internet should be able to translate UTC times into his or her own local time. If you are not sure how to do this, the tables in Figures F-1 and F-2 will help you.

You will often see UTC/GMT/UT times in an email message or Usenet article, even when the message or article did not originate in the UTC time zone. The conversion is done automatically by the software. As an example, here is the same time as the one

ABBREVIATION	TIME ZONE	DIFFERENCE FROM UTC
UTC	Coordinated Universal Time	0
GMT	Greenwich Mean Time	same as **UTC**
UT	Universal Time	same as **UTC**
EST	Eastern Standard Time	-5 hours
EDT	Eastern Daylight Time	-4 hours
CST	Central Standard Time	-6 hours
CDT	Central Daylight Time	-5 hours
MST	Mountain Standard Time	-7 hours
MDT	Mountain Daylight Time	-6 hours
PST	Pacific Standard Time	-8 hours
PDT	Pacific Daylight Time	-7 hours

FIGURE F-1: U.S. Time Zones in Relation to UTC

Most parts of the U.S. change to Daylight Saving Time on the second Sunday in March. The change back to Standard Time is on the first Sunday in November.

---

*Time-checking is carried out using a system called NTP or Network Time Protocol. The purpose of NTP is to synchronize computer clocks with a reference clock. The reference clock can be on the same network or on the Internet.

The program that does the work is **ntpd**, a daemon that runs in the background. Some systems use a program called **ntpdate**, which is not a daemon. **ntpd** does a better job at time synchronization and, eventually, it will replace **ntpdate**. For this reason, the use of **ntpdate** is deprecated. Similarly, an older program called **rdate** is also deprecated in favor of **ntpd**.

**There are technical differences between UTC, GMT and UT. However, for practical purposes, you can consider them the same.

above specified as UTC. To display the current time in this format, use **date** with the **-u** option:

```
$ date -u
Sun Dec 21 03:50:17 UTC 2008
```

Notice how, in this example, the UTC time is 3:50 AM one day later. This is because UTC is 7 hours ahead of PDT. For reference, Figure F-1 summarizes the time zones used in the U.S. and how they compare to UTC. Figure F-2 does the same for the European and Indian time zones[*].

One last way in which you may see time specified is as a local time followed by the difference in hours from UTC. Here is an example taken from an email header. The format is a bit different from that of the **date** command.

```
Date: Sun, 21 Dec 2008 20:50:17 -0700
```

This header line shows the same time, 8:50 PM, and indicates that the local time zone is -7 hours different from UTC.

Once you understand how time zones differ from UTC, you can use the tables in Figures F-2 and F-3 to convert local times and calculate time zone differences. Here are some examples.

ABBREVIATION	TIME ZONE	DIFFERENCE FROM UTC
UTC	Coordinated Universal Time	0
GMT	Greenwich Mean Time	same as **UTC**
UT	Universal Time	same as **UTC**
WET	Western European Time	same as **UTC**
WEST	Western European Summer Time	+1 hour
BST	British Summer Time	+1 hour
IST	Irish Summer Time	+1 hour
CET	Central European Time	+1 hour
CEST	Central European Summer Time	+2 hours
EET	Eastern European Time	+2 hour
EEST	Eastern European Summer Time	+3 hours
IST	India Standard Time	+5.5 hours

FIGURE F-2: European and Indian time zones in relation to UTC

In most places, the change to Summer Time is made on the last Sunday in March. The change back to regular time is made on the last Sunday in October.

---

[*]Time zone information is actually much more complicated than you might think. The information in these tables covers only a small number of the world's time zones.

To keep track of all such data, Unix systems use a standard reference known as the **tz** or **zoneinfo** database. This database is sometimes called the Olson database, named after the American programmer Arthur David Olson, who started compiling time zone information in the mid-1980s.

You live in New York and it is summer. You get an email message with the time 17:55 UTC. What is this in your local time?

In the summer, New York uses EDT (Eastern Daylight Time). Checking with the tables, you see the difference between UTC and EDT is -4 hours. Thus, 17:55 UTC is 13:55 EDT, or 1:55 PM New York time.

You live in California and you have a friend in Germany. How many hours is he ahead of you?

Assume it is winter. California uses PST (Pacific Standard Time), and Germany uses CET (Central European Time). From the tables, the difference between UTC and PST is -8 hours. The difference between UTC and CET is +1 hours. Thus, your friend is 9 hours ahead of you.

In the summer, PST changes to PDT, and CET changes to CEST. However, the difference between the two time zones does not change, and your friend is still 9 hours ahead of you.

You work at a technically advanced Internet company on the U.S. West coast. You are the manager of the Foobar department, and you have to arrange a weekly telephone meeting with the programmers, who work in Bangalore, India, and the Vice President of Information Confusion, who works in New York. What is the best time to have the meeting?

To start, let's assume it is winter. The U.S. West Coast uses PST, New York uses EST, and India uses IST (India Standard Time). According to the tables, the difference between PST and UTC is -8 hours. The difference between EST and UTC is -5 hours. The difference between IST and UTC is +5.5 hours. This means that India is 10.5 hours ahead of New York and 13.5 hours ahead of the U.S. West Coast. For example, midnight on the West Coast is 1:30 PM in India.

Let's say that you can induce the programmers to come in early and talk to you at 7:30 AM their time. In New York, it will be 9:00 PM the previous day. On the West Coast, it will be 6:00 PM the previous day. This is a good fit, so you set up your weekly meeting at 6:00 PM Monday on the West Coast, 9:00 PM Monday in New York, and 7:30 AM Tuesday morning in India.

In the summer, PST moves ahead 1 hour to PDT, and EST moves ahead 1 hour to EDT. Indian time doesn't change. Looking at the tables and recalculating, we see that, during the summer, India is only 9.5 hours ahead of New York and 12.5 hours ahead of the West Coast. Thus, if you keep the same times for the West Coast and New York, the programmers don't have to show up until 8:30 AM, which lets them sleep in for an extra hour.

WHAT'S IN A NAME?

UTC, UT, GMT

Greenwich (pronounced "Gren-itch"), a borough of London, was the home of the Royal Observatory from 1675-1985. It was at this observatory that our modern system of timekeeping and longitude was developed. For this reason, the imaginary north- south line that runs through the observatory is designated as 0 degrees longitude.

(*continued...*) In 1884, the time at Greenwich was adopted as the global standard used to determine all the time zones around the world. This global standard time is called Greenwich Mean Time or GMT. (In this context, the word "mean" refers to average.) GMT is used widely on the Internet, and is sometimes referred to by the newer, more official name of UT (Universal Time).

In addition to UT, you will see another name, UTC (Coordinated Universal Time). UTC is the official value of Universal Time as calculated by the U.S. National Bureau of Standards and the U.S. Naval Observatory.

You might wonder why the abbreviation for Coordinated Universal Time is UTC, not CUT.

UTC was adopted as an official international standard in 1970. The work was done by a group of experts within the International Telecommunication Union. When it came time to name the new standard, the group had a problem.

In English, the abbreviation for Coordinated Universal Time would be CUT. But in French, the name is *Temps Universel Coordonné*, and the abbreviation would be TUC. The group of experts wanted the same abbreviation to be used everywhere, but they couldn't agree on whether it should be CUT or TUC. The compromise was to use UTC. Although the abbreviation is inexact in both English and French, it had the enormous advantage of keeping the peace.

(Not too many people know this, but now you do.)

A P P E N D I X   G
SHELL OPTIONS
AND SHELL VARIABLES

Every shell supports a variety of ways for you to control its behavior. The Bourne Shell family (Bash, Korn Shell) uses shell options; the C-Shell family (Tcsh, C-Shell) uses both shell options and shell variables. This appendix summarizes these options and variables.

For a detailed discussion of both shell options and shell variables, see Chapter 12.

BOURNE SHELL FAMILY

The Bourne Shell family uses a large number of options to control the behavior of the shell. In particular, interactive shells require different options than non-interactive shells. (In fact, this is what makes them interactive.) There are two ways to specify such options. First, they may be invoked in the standard manner by specifying options on the command line when the shell is started. This is the case for non-interactive shells that are run automatically, and for interactive shells that you yourself start by entering a command. For example:

```
bash -vx
```

(By the way, these two options are particularly useful when you are testing or debugging a shell script.)

Within an interactive shell — that is, at the shell prompt — you can turn options on or off as you wish. To set (turn on) an option, use the **set -o** command. To unset (turn off) an option, use the **set +o** command. When you use these commands, you specify the long name for the option, not its abbreviation. For example:

```
set -o verbose
set +o xtrace
```

To display the current state of all the options, use either command by itself:

```
set -o
set +o
```

SHELLS	OPTION	LONG NAME	MEANING
B K	-a	allexport	Export all subsequently defined variables and functions
• K		bgnice	Run background jobs at lower priority
B •	-B	braceexpand	Enable brace expansion
B K	-c	—	Read commands from string argument
B K	-E	emacs	Command line editor: Emacs mode; turns off **vi** mode
B K	-e	errexit	If a command fails, abort and exit script
B K	-h	hashall	Hash (remember) locations of commands as they are found
B •	-H	histexpand	Enable **!** style history substitution
B •		history	Enable command history
B K	-I	ignoreeof	Ignore **eof** signal **^D**; use exit to quit shell (see Chapter 7)
B K	-k	keyword	Place all keyword arguments in the environment
• K		markdirs	When globbing, append **/** to directory names
B K	-m	monitor	Job control: enable
B K	-C	noclobber	Do not allow redirected output to replace a file
B K	-n	noexec	Debug: read commands, check syntax, but do not execute
B K	-f	noglob	Disable globbing (expansion of filenames)
• K		nolog	Do not save function definitions in history file
B K	-b	notify	Job control: notify immediately when background jobs finish
B K	-u	nounset	Treat using an unset variable as an error
B K	-t	onecmd	Read and execute one command, then exit
B •		posix	Conform to POSIX standard
B •	-p	privileged	Use privileged mode to run a script or start a shell
B •	-r	—	Start shell in restricted mode
• K	-s	—	Sort positional parameters
• K		trackall	Aliases: substitute full pathnames for commands
B K	-v	verbose	Debug: echo each command to stderr (standard error)
B K	-V	vi	Command line editor: **vi** mode; turns off Emacs mode
• K		viraw	In **vi** mode: process each character as it is typed
B K	-x	xtrace	Debug: as command executes, echo to stderr (that is, trace)

FIGURE G-1: Bourne Shell family: Shell options

This table summarizes the important shell options available with the Bourne Shell family. The leftmost column shows which shells support each option: B = Bash; K = Korn Shell. A dot indicates that a shell does not support that option. Note that some options, such as **bgnice**, *have a long name but not a short option name. For more information, see the man page for your particular shell.*

Notes: (1) Although Bash supports the **emacs** *and* **vi** *options, it does not use* **-E** *and* **-V**. *(2) The Korn shell uses* **-h** *and* **-t**, *but does not support the long names* **hashall** *and* **onecmd**.

The **-o** variation prints human-readable output; **+o** prints output suitable for a script. (Try them.)

In all, the Bourne Shell family uses a great many shell options. In most cases, you will not need to change them, because the defaults will work just fine. For reference, however, the table in Figure G-1 summarizes the shell options for Bash and the Korn Shell. Not all options are available with all shells, so be sure to look at the leftmost column, which shows you which shells support each option.

With Bash, there are extra options available to control a variety of features. To set and unset these options, you use the **shopt** ("shell options") command. The **shopt** options are so esoteric that you are unlikely to need them. If you have a moment, though, and you'd like to take a look at them, see the **shopt** man page.

> **HINT**
>
> The best place to read about the Bash **shopt** options is the Bash man page. To find the relevant discussion, search for "shopt".

C-SHELL FAMILY

The C-Shell family also uses options to control the behavior of the shell. These options are summarized in Figure G-2. If you compare the options in Figure G-2 with those in Figure G-1, you will notice that most of the C-Shell options are also used by the Bourne Shell family. However, there is an important difference.

SHELLS	OPTION	SHELL VARIABLE	MEANING
C T	-c		Read commands from string argument; compare to **-s**
· T	-d		Load directory stack from **.cshdirs** file
C T	-e		If a command fails, abort and exit script
C T	-i		Interactive mode (affects prompts, error handling, etc.)
C T	-n		Debug: read commands, check syntax, but do not execute
C T	-s		Read commands from stdin (standard input); compare to **-c**
C T	-t		Read and execute one command, then exit
C T	-v	verbose	Debug: print each command, after history substitution only
C T	-V	verbose	Debug: set **verbose** before reading **.tcshc/.cshrc** file
C T	-x	echo	Debug: echo each command, after *all* substitutions
C T	-X	echo	Debug: set **echo** before reading **.tcshc/.cshrc** file

FIGURE G-2: C-Shell family: Shell options

This table summarizes the important shell options available with C-Shell family. The leftmost column shows which shells support each option: C = C-Shell; T = Tcsh. A dot indicates that a shell does not support that option. For more information, see the man page for your particular shell.

Note: The **-v** *and* **-V** *options work by setting the* **verbose** *shell variable. The* **-x** *and* **-X** *options work by setting the* **echo** *shell variable.*

In the Bourne Shell family the behavior of the shell is controlled entirely by options, of which there are three types: regular command-line options (such as **-v**), "long name" options used with the **set +o** command, and the large number of extra options used only with the Bash **shopt** command.

Although the C-Shell family does use a small number of command-line options (Figure G-2), for the most part, the behavior of a shell is controlled by shell variables. This is one of the important differences between C-Shell family and the Bourne Shell family, and is explained in detail in Chapter 12. For reference, Figure G-3 contains a summary of the shell variables used by the C-Shell and Tcsh.

SHELLS	SHELL VARIABLE	MEANING
• T	addsuffix	Autocomplete: append **/** (slash) after directory names
• T	ampm	Show times in 12-hour AM/PM format
• T	autocorrect	Spell-correct: invoke spell-word editor before completion attempt
• T	autoexpand	Autocomplete: invoke expand-history editor before completion attempt
• T	autolist	Autocomplete: when completion fails, list remaining choices
• T	autologout	Time (in minutes) until auto-logout, if you don't type a command
C T	cdpath	Directories to be searched by **cd**, **chdir**, **popd**
• T	color	Cause **ls-F** command to use color
• T	complete	Autocomplete: **igncase**=ignore case; **enhance**=also **. -** are separators
• T	correct	Spell-correct: **cmd**=command; **all**=entire line; **complete**=complete instead
C T	cwd	Your current working directory (compare to **owd**)
C T	echo	Debug: echo each command, after all substitutions
• T	echo_style	**echo** command: **bsd** (support **-n**); **sysv** (support **** escape); **both**; **none**
• T	edit	Command line editor: enable
C T	fignore	Autocomplete: suffixes to ignore
C •	filec	Autocomplete: enable (always on with Tcsh)
• T	group	Current groupid
C T	hardpaths	Directory stack: resolve pathnames to contain no symbolic links
C T	history	Command history: number of lines in history list
C T	home	Your home directory
C T	ignoreeof	Do not quit shell upon **eof** signal (**^D**)
• T	implicitcd	Typing directory name by itself means change to that directory
• T	inputmode	Command line editor: set initial mode at start of line, **insert** or overwrite

FIGURE G-3: C-Shell family: Shell variables (continued on next page)

This table summarizes the important shell variables used with the C-Shell family to control the behavior of the shell. The leftmost column shows which shells support each option: C = C-Shell; T = Tcsh. A dot indicates that a shell does not support that option.

For more information, see the man page for your shell. For information about autocompletion, spell-correction, or command line editing, see the Tcsh man page. For a detailed discussion of shell variables, see Chapter 12.

SHELLS	SHELL VARIABLE	MEANING
• T	`listjobs`	Job control: list all jobs whenever a job is suspended; `long` = long format
• T	`loginsh`	Set to indicate a login shell
C T	`mail`	List of files to check for new email
• T	`matchbeep`	Autocomplete: make a sound; `ambiguous`, `notunique`, `never`, `nomatch`
C T	`nobeep`	Autocomplete: never make a sound
C T	`noclobber`	Do not allow redirected output to replace a file
C T	`noglob`	Globbing (filename expansion): disable
C T	`notify`	Job control: notify immediately when background jobs finished
• T	`owd`	Your most recent [old] working directory (compare to `cwd`)
C T	`path`	Directories to search for programs
C T	`prompt`	Your shell prompt (customize by changing this variable)
• T	`pushdsilent`	Directory stack: `pushd` and `popd` do not list directory stack
• T	`pushdtohome`	Directory stack: `pushd` without arguments assumes home directory (like `cd`)
• T	`recexact`	Autocomplete: match exact match even if longer match is possible
• T	`rmstar`	Force user to confirm before executing `rm *` (remove all files)
• T	`rprompt`	When prompting, string to print on right side of screen (hint: set `to %/`)
• T	`savedirs`	Directory stack: before logout, save directory stack
C T	`savehist`	Command history: before logout, save this number of lines in history list
C T	`shell`	Pathname of your login shell
C T	`term`	Type of terminal you are using
C T	`user`	Current userid
C T	`verbose`	Debug: echo each command, after history substitution only
• T	`visiblebell`	Use a screen flash instead of an audible sound

FIGURE G-3: C-Shell family: Shell variables (continued from previous page)

GLOSSARY

This glossary contains definitions for the 622 technical terms explained in this book. After each definition, the number in square brackets indicates the chapter in which the term is discussed.

A

absolute pathname A pathname in which the full name of every directory is specified, from the root directory to the actual file. [24]

accelerator key Within a GUI, a key combination using the <Alt> key that acts as a shortcut for clicking on an item. For example, when you are working within a window, you can usually pull down the File menu by using the accelerator key <Alt-F>. [6]

access time With respect to a file, the last time the file was read. To display the access time for a file, you use the **ls** program with the **-lu** options. Compare to **modification time**. [24]

account Permission to use a Unix system, including a bona fide userid and password, as well as restrictions as to how that userid may use the system. [4]

action When using the **find** program to search for files, an instruction specifying what to do with the results of a search. For example, the action **-print** writes the results of a search to standard output. See also **test** and **operator**. [25]

active window Within a GUI, the window that currently has the focus. Whatever you type on the keyboard is used as input for the program running in the active window. [6]

admin Synonym for **system administrator**. [4]

alias Within the shell, a user-defined name given to a command or to a list of commands. The most common uses for an alias are to act as an abbreviation or as a customized variation of a command. [13]

allocation unit With respect to a Unix filesystem on a hard disk or other medium, the fundamental unit of storage allocation. The allocation unit size depends on the nature of the disk and is typically a multiple of the filesystem block size. Compare to **block**. [24]

alphanumeric Describes data that consists only of letters (alpha) or numbers (numeric). Punctuation is not alphanumeric. [13]

anchor Within a regular expression, one of several metacharacters (**^**, **$**, **\\<**, **\\>**) used to match locations at the beginning or end of a character string. [20]

anonymous pipe Same as **pipe**. [23]

apply (a diff) To follow the instructions contained in a diff, to recreate one file from another. Typically, one would apply a diff to recreate a later version of a file from an earlier version. See also **diff** and **patch**. [17]

argument   When you type a command, items on the command line, usually coming after any options, that are used to pass information to the program you want to run. For example, in the command **ls -l datafile**, **-l** is an option and **datafile** is an argument. See also **option**. [10]

ASCII   Same as **ASCII code**. [19]

ASCII code   Often abbreviated as ASCII. A standardized character encoding system, created in 1967 and modified in later years, in which character data is represented as bits. Each character is stored in a single byte (8 bits). Within a byte, the leftmost bit is ignored; the other 7 bits form a pattern of 0s and 1s that represents the particular character. In all, the ASCII code contains 128 distinct bit patterns ranging from **0000000** to **1111111**. For reference, the full ASCII code is shown in Appendix D. See also **printable characters**. [19] [20]

ASCII file   Same as **text file**. [19]

asynchronous process   With respect to the very oldest Unix shells (before job control), a process that runs on its own without any input from the user. With the development of job control, asynchronous processes were replaced by background processes. See also **job control** and **background process**. [26]

autocompletion   Within the shell, a feature that helps the user enter commands by automatically completing words. There are several types of autocompletion: **command completion**, **filename completion**, **variable completion**, **userid completion** and **hostname completion**. [13]

B

back door   A secret facility, used by a hacker to access a system or control a program surreptitiously. [13]

background process   A process for which the shell does not wait to complete before displaying the next shell prompt. We say that such processes run "in the background". Compare to **foreground process**. [26]

backwards compatible   Describes a program that supports the features of an older program. For example, the Tcsh is backwards compatible with the older C-Shell; Bash and the Korn Shell are backwards compatible with the older Bourne Shell. [11]

bang   The exclamation mark (**!**) character. A bang is often used to change the mode of what you are doing, for example, to pause the current program and send a command to the shell. [9]

bang character   See **bang**. [9]

bar   A meaningless word, used to represent an unnamed item during a discussion or exposition. The word "bar" is usually used along with "foo" to refer to two unnamed items. The convention is to use "foo" for the first item and "bar" for the second item. For example, you might hear someone ask the question, "I have two files, foo and bar. How can I copy all the lines in foo that contain a particular pattern to end of bar?" See also **foo** and **foobar**. [9]

base 2   Same as **binary system**. [21]

base 8   Same as **octal**. [21]

Chapter references are indicated by the numbers in brackets.

base 10   Same as **decimal system**. [21]

base 12   Same as **duodecimal**. [21]

base 16   Same as **hexadecimal**. [21]

basename   Synonym for **filename**. [24]

Bash   The most important member of the Bourne shell family, originally created by Brian Fox, in 1987, under the auspices of the Free Software Foundation. The name Bash stands for "Bourne-again shell". Bash is used widely, being the default shell on virtually all Linux systems. The name of the Bash program is `bash`. See also **Bourne shell family**. [11]

basic regular expression   Sometimes abbreviated as BRE. An old type of regular expression, used for many years, now replaced by extended regular expressions. Compared to the more modern extended regular expressions, basic regular expressions, BREs are less powerful and have a slightly more confusing syntax. For these reasons, they are considered obsolete, retained only for compatibility with older programs. Compare to **extended regular expression**. See also **regular expression**. [20]

binary digit   One of the two digits 0 and 1 used in the binary system. See also **bit** and **binary system**. [21]

binary file   A file containing non-textual data that makes sense only when read by a program. Common examples of binary files are executable programs, object files, images, music files, video files, word processing documents, spreadsheets and databases. Compare to `text` file. [19]

binary number   A number expressed by using the binary system, that is base 2. See also **binary system**. [21]

binary system   Same as base 2. A number system, based on powers of 2, in which numbers are constructed using the 2 digits 0 and 1. See also **octal**, **decimal system**, **duodecimal** and **hexadecimal**. [21]

bit   The basic element of data storage, containing a single element that is always in one of two states. The custom is to speak of a bit as containing either a 0 or a 1. A bit that contains a 0 is said to be "off". A bit that contains a 1 is said to be "on". The term `bit` is a contraction of "binary digit". See also **byte**, **binary system** and **binary digit**. [21]

bit bucket   A whimsical name for any file with the characteristic that all output written to the file is thrown away. There are two bit buckets: the null file (`/dev/null`) and the zero file (`/dev/zero`). Both are pseudo-files, a type of special file. See also **null file**, **zero file**, and **pseudo-file**. [15]

block   With respect to a Unix filesystem, the fundamental unit of storage allocation within the filesystem itself, usually 512 bytes, 1K, 2K or 4K. A typical Linux filesystem uses 1K blocks. Compare to **allocation unit**. [24]

block device   A device such as a disk that when reading or writing, processes a fixed number of bytes at a time. In the output of the `ls -l` command, a character device is indicated by the symbol **b**. Compare to **character device**. [24]

boot   To take control of a computer and perform such initializations as are necessary, whenever the computer starts or restarts. See also **boot loader** and **boot device**. [2]

Chapter references are indicated by the numbers in brackets.

boot device The device from which the boot loader reads the data necessary to start the operating system. In most cases, the boot device is a partition on a local hard drive. However, it can also be a network device, a CD, a flash drive, and so on. See also **boot** and **boot loader**. [23]

boot loader A small program that takes control when you start or restart your computer in order to load enough software for the operating system to start. With a dual boot or multi-boot system, the boot loader allows you to choose which operating system you want to use. The most common Linux boot loaders are GRUB and LILO. See also **boot** and (boot loader. [2]

bound [20] Within a regular expression, a specification, used within the { } repetition operator, to match the desired character a specific number of times. For example, within the repetition operator {3,5}, the bound 3,5 specifies a match of 3 to 5 times. See also **repetition operator**.

Bourne shell The first widely used Unix shell, originally developed in 1976 by Steven Bourne, a researcher at Bell Labs. Although the Bourne Shell has been updated over the years, it is rarely used today, as it lacks the advanced features of the modern shells. The name of the Bourne shell program is **sh**. See also **Bourne shell family**. [11]

Bourne shell family The shells whose principle characteristics are based on the Bourne Shell and the Bourne shell programming language. The most important members of the Bourne shell family are Bash, the Korn shell, the Zsh, the Pdksh, and the FreeBSD shell. The Bourne shell itself is rarely used today. [11]

brace expansion With Bash, the C-Shell or Tcsh, the facility that enables you to use braces to enclose a set of character strings, which are used to match or generate filenames containing each of the strings in turn. See also **pathname expansion**. [24]

branch Within a tree (data structure), a path that joins one node to another. Corresponds to an edge in a graph. See also **tree**. [9]

browser A client program, such as Internet Explorer or Firefox, used to access the Web as well as other Internet facilities, such as mail, Usenet and anonymous FTP. For most people, a browser acts as the primary interface to the Internet. [3]

BSD An operating system developed at the University of California at Berkeley, originally based on AT&T UNIX. The name BSD stands for "Berkeley Software Distribution". The first version of BSD, later referred to as 1BSD, was distributed in 1977. In the 1980s, BSD was one of the two main branches of Unix; the other was **System V**. [2]

BSD options With respect to the **ps** (process status) command, those options that are derived from the 1980s version of **ps** that was part of BSD (Berkeley Unix). BSD options do not start with a dash. Compare to **UNIX options**. [26]

builtin Within the shell, a command that is interpreted by the shell directly. Same as **builtin command** and **internal command**. [13]

builtin command Same as **builtin**. [13]

byte A unit of data storage, 8 consecutive bits. One byte can hold a single ASCII character. See also **bit** and **binary system**. [21]

Chapter references are indicated by the numbers in brackets.

C

C collating sequence The collating sequence, based on the ASCII code, used by the **C** (**POSIX**) locale; named after the C programming language. Within the C collating sequence, uppercase letters come before lowercase letters (**ABC... XYZabc...xyz**). Compare to **dictionary collating sequence**. See also **ASCII code**, **collating sequence** and **locale**. [19]

C-Shell A shell developed in 1978 by Bill Joy, a graduate student at U.C. Berkeley. Pronounced "see-shell". The C-Shell programming language is based on the language C (hence the name). In its time, the C-Shell was used widely and became one of the most important shells of all time. Today, most C-Shell users prefer the more powerful Tcsh. The name of the C-Shell program is **csh**. See also **Tcsh** and **C-Shell family**. [11]

C-Shell family The shells whose principal characteristics are based on the C-Shell, in particular, the C-Shell programming language. The most widely used members of the C-Shell family are the Tcsh and the C-Shell itself. [11]

canonical
  1. In mathematics, the simplest, most important way of expressing an idea. [21]
  2. In computer science, the most common, conventional way of doing something. [21]

canonical format With respect to binary data being displayed or printed, a commonly used format consisting of 16 bytes per line. To the left of each line is the offset in hexadecimal. In the middle are the actual bytes, also in hexadecimal. On the right are the ASCII equivalents. The command **hexdump -C** displays binary data in canonical format. [21]

canonical mode A line discipline in which characters typed as input to a program are not sent to the program immediately. Rather, the characters are accumulated in a buffer (storage area) and are sent only when the user presses the <Return> key. Compare to **raw mode** and **cbreak mode**. See also **line discipline**. [21]

carriage return
  1. A special character used to control the operation of an output device, indicating that the cursor or print position should move to the beginning of the line. In the ASCII code, the carriage return character has the value 13 in decimal, or 0D in hexadecimal. [4]
  2. On an old Teletype ASR33, the operation in which the print head is moved to the beginning of the line. [4]
  3. On a manual typewriter, the lever used to return the carriage (the cylinder on which the paper is held) to the far left position. [4]

case sensitive Describes a program or operating system that distinguishes between upper- and lowercase letters. [4]

cbreak mode A variation of raw mode, a line discipline in which most input is sent directly to the program, except a few very important characters that are handled directly by the terminal driver (**^C**, **^**, **^Z**, **^S** and **^Q**). Compare to **canonical mode** and **raw made**. See also **line discipline**. [21]

Chapter references are indicated by the numbers in brackets.

CDE A desktop environment based on the Motif window manager, developed in the early 1990s as a large, multi-company effort in collaboration with the Open Group. CDE is an abbreviation for Common Desktop Environment. [5]

character class With respect to regular expressions, an element, beginning and ending with square brackets, containing a set of characters, for example, **[ABCDE]**. A character class is used to match any single character within the set. See also **predefined character class** and **range**. [20]

character device A device, such as a terminal, that when reading or writing, processes data one byte at a time. In the output of the **ls -l** command, a character device is indicated by the symbol **c**. Compare to **block device**. [24]

character string A sequence of plain-text characters, consisting only of letters, numbers or punctuation. [12] More strictly, a sequence of printable characters. [19] Same as **string**. See also **printable character**.

character terminal A terminal that displays only characters (text): letters, numbers, punctuation and so on. Same as **text-based terminal**. [3]

child Same as **child process**. [15] [26]

child directory Same as **subdirectory**. [23]

child process A process that has been started by another process. The new process is the child; the original process is the parent. See also **parent process**. [15] [26]

chording When using a mouse or other pointing device, pressing two or more buttons at the same time. [6]

CLI Abbreviation for "command line interface". A text-based interface in which the user types commands that are interpreted by the shell. Compare to **GUI**. [6]

click When using a mouse or other pointing device, to press a button. [6]

client A program that requests a service from a server. [3]

clipboard Within a GUI, an invisible storage area used to hold data that has been copied or cut; such data can be pasted into a window. The data in the clipboard is changed only when it is replaced by new data. The contents of the clipboard are lost when you close the GUI (by shutting down, logging off, or rebooting). [6]

close Within a GUI, to stop the program running in a window, causing the window to disappear. [6]

close button Within a GUI, a small rectangle, usually in the top right-hand corner of the window, that, when clicked, closes the window. [6]

cluster Synonym for **allocation unit**. [24]

code Synonym for source code. [2]

collating sequence Describes the order in which characters are placed when sorted. In modern versions of Unix or Linux, the collating sequence depends on the choice of locale. See also **locale**. [19]

command completion A type of autocompletion that completes a partially typed command at the beginning of a line. Command completion is available with Bash and the Tcsh. See also **autocompletion**. [13]

Chapter references are indicated by the numbers in brackets.

command line

1. When entering a Unix command: the entire line that you type before you press the <Return> key. [6]
2. When using the **vi** editor: the bottom line of the screen, upon which certain commands are echoed as they are typed. [22]

command line editing   Within the shell, a powerful facility that allows you to use a large variety of commands to manipulate what you type on the command line, including the ability to use the the history list and autocompletion. Command line editing is available with Bash, the Korn Shell, and the Tcsh. It is used in either **Emacs mode** or **vi** mode. [13]

command line interface   See **CLI**. [6]

command mode   When using the **vi** text editor, a mode in which the characters you type are interpreted as commands. Compare to **insert mode**. [22]

command processor   A program that reads and interprets commands entered at the terminal or read from a file. The shell is a command processor. [11]

command substitution   Within the shell, to specify that the output of one command is to be inserted into another command, which is then executed. To use command substitution, you enclose the first command in backquote (`) characters. [13]

command syntax   Same as **syntax**. [10]

comment   Within a program, a line that is ignored. Comments are used by programmers to insert notes into a program, in order to provide documentation for the programmer and for anyone else who may read the program. Within a shell script, comments start with the **#** (hash) character. [14]

compatibility mode   When using the Vim text editor, a mode in which Vim works as much as possible like the **vi** text editor. [22]

conditional execution   Within the shell, a facility that allows the execution of a command only if a previous command has, as specified by the user, either succeeded or failed. [15]

configuration file   A file whose contents is read by a program at the time the program starts. Typically, a configuration file contains commands or information that affect the operation of the program. [6]

console   The terminal, considered to be part of the host computer, that is used to administer the system. [3]

context menu   Within a GUI, a pop-up menu containing a list of actions that relate to an object. Typically, you cause a pop-up menu to appear by right-clicking on the object. [6]

cooked mode   Same as **canonical mode**. [21]

copy   Within a GUI, to copy data from a window to the clipboard without changing the original data. [6]

copyleft   A legal principle, originally applied to free software, that gives anyone permission to run a program, copy the program, modify the program, and distribute modified versions, as long as they do not add restrictions of their own. The first implementation of copyleft was the GPL (GNU General Public License). [2]

Chapter references are indicated by the numbers in brackets.

core

1. Originally, a tiny, round, hollow magnetic device used in core memory. [7] [21]
2. More generally, a synonym for computer memory. [7] [21]

core dump In the 1960s and 1970s: a printout of the contents of the memory used by a program that had aborted. A core dump could take up many pages of paper and took great skill to interpret. [7]

core file A file (named **core**) that is generated automatically when a program aborts. A core file, which contains a copy of the contents of memory at the moment the program aborted, can be analyzed by a programmer in order to figure out what went wrong. [7] [21]

core memory An obsolete type of computer memory, first introduced in 1952, constructed from a large number of tiny, round, hollow magnetic devices (cores) arranged in a lattice with several electrical wires running through each core. By changing the current in the wires, it was possible to modify the magnetic properties of individual cores to be either "off" or "on", allowing for the storage and retrieval of binary data. [7] [21]

CPU The processor, the main component of a computer. For example, the amount of processor time used by a program is called CPU time. In the early days of mainframe computers, the term CPU was an acronym standing for "central processing unit". [8]

CPU time The amount of time a process has executed on the processor. See also **time slice**. [26]

cracker A person who deliberately tries to break into a computer system with the purpose of doing things that people in authority do not want him to do. [4]

CSV (comma-separated value) format Describes a file containing machine-readable data in which fields are separated by commas, that is, in which the delimiters are commas. See also **delimiters**, **record** and **field**. [17]

current character When using the **vi** text editor, the character at which the cursor is currently positioned. Many **vi** commands perform an action on the current character. See also **current line**. [22]

current directory Synonym for **working directory**. The default directory, used when entering Unix commands. The current directory is set by the **cd** (change directory) command; the name is displayed by the **pwd** (print working directory) command. [24]

current file When using the pager **less**, the file currently being viewed. [21]

current job With respect to job control, the job that was most recently suspended or, if there are no suspended jobs, most recently moved to the background. Certain job control commands act upon the current job by default. See also **job**, **job control** and **previous job**. [26]

current line When using the **vi** text editor, the line on which the cursor is currently positioned. Many **vi** commands perform an action on the current line. See also **current character**. [22]

cut Within a GUI, to copy data from a window to the clipboard. As part of the operation, the original data is deleted from the window. [6]

Chapter references are indicated by the numbers in brackets.

D

daemon A program that runs in the background, completely disconnected from any terminal, in order to provide a service. (With Microsoft Windows, the same type of functionality is provided by a "service".) [26]

data structure In computer science, any well-defined method of organizing data such that there exist algorithms for storing, retrieving, modifying, and searching the data. The most common types of data structures are lists, linked lists, associative arrays, hash tables, stacks, queues, deques (double-ended queues), as well as a variety of tree-based structures. See also **queue, stack** and **tree**. [8]

decimal number A number expressed by using the decimal system. See also **decimal system**. [21]

decimal system Same as base 10. A number system, based on powers of 10, in which numbers are constructed using the 10 digits 0, 1, 2, 3, 4, 5, 6, 7, 8 and 9. See also **binary system, octal** and **hexadecimal**. [21]

default An assumed value that will be used when an particular item is not specified. [10]

del A character that, on some Unix systems, is used instead of a backspace (`^H`) to erase a single character. You will sometimes see the `del` character represented by the two characters `^?`. Within the ASCII code, the `del` character has a value of 127 in decimal or 7F in hexadecimal. [7]

delimiter Within a file containing machine-readable data, designated characters that separate adjacent fields. Data in which commas are used as delimiters is said to be in CSV (comma-separated value) format. See also **CSV format, field** and **record**. [17]

desktop Within a GUI, the overall visual space in which you work. More generally, the abstract environment in which you organize your work. Desktop environments, such as KDE and Gnome, allow you to use more than one desktop, only one of which is visible at a time. (Within Gnome, desktops are called "workspaces".) [6]

desktop environment A GUI-based system that provides a working environment whose purpose is to help the user carry out the complex cognitive tasks associated with using a computer. Sometimes called a desktop manager. In the Linux world, the two most widely used desktop environments are KDE and Gnome. See also **KDE** and **Gnome**. [5]

desktop manager Same as **desktop environment**. [5]

destructive backspace The type of backspace that occurs when the cursor moves back and characters are erased. This is what happens when you press the <Backspace> key. Compare to **non-destructive backspace**. [7]

device driver A program that acts as the interface between the operating system and a particular type of device, usually some type of hardware. Same as **driver**. [2] [21]

device file Same as **special file**. [23]

dictionary collating sequence The collating sequence used by the `en_US` locale, in which uppercase letters and lowercase letters are grouped in pairs (`AaBbCcDd... Zz`). Compare to **C collating sequence**. See also **collating sequence** and **locale**. [19]

Chapter references are indicated by the numbers in brackets.

dictionary file A file, included with Unix, that contains a very long list of English words, including most of the words commonly found in a concise dictionary. Each word is on a line by itself and the lines are in alphabetical order, making the file easy to search. The dictionary file is available to any user; it is also used by the **look** command and by the (now obsolete) **spell** command. [20]

die With respect to a process, to stop running. Same as **terminate**. [26]

diff A list of simple editing instructions that, when followed, change one file into another. See also **apply** and **patch**. [17]

directory One of the three types of Unix files; a file that resides on a storage device, used to organize and access other files. Conceptually, a directory "contains" other files. Compare to **ordinary file** and **pseudo file**. See also **file**. [23]

Directory Node Within the Info system, a special node that contains a list of links to the major topics. The directory node acts as the main menu for the entire Info system. [9]

directory stack A stack, maintained by the shell to store directory names that can be used to change the working directory. See also **stack**. [24]

distribution A particular version of a Linux system. [2]

distro Abbreviation for **distribution**. [2]

dotfile A file whose name begins with a `.` (dot) character. When the **ls** command lists filenames, dotfiles are not listed unless requested specifically by using the **-a** (all files) option. Same as **hidden file**. [14] [24]

double-click When using a mouse or other pointing device, to press a button twice in rapid succession. [6]

drag Within a GUI, to move a graphical object. To do so, you use your mouse to point to the object. You then hold down a mouse button, move the mouse (which moves the object to a new location), and then release the button. [6]

driver Same as **device driver**. [2] [21]

dual boot Describes a computer that is set up to boot one of two different operating systems, as chosen by the user during the startup process. [2]

dump Same as **core dump**. [21]

duodecimal Same as base 12. A number system, based on powers of 12, in which numbers are constructed using the 12 digits 0, 1, 2, 3, 4, 5, 6, 7, 8, 9, A and B. See also **binary system**, **octal**, **decimal system**, **duodecimal** and **hexadecimal**. [21]

E

echo To display a character on the monitor that corresponds to a key that has been pressed by a user. For example, when you press the <A> key, Unix echoes the letter "A". [3]

edit (verb) To use a text editor to modify the contents of a file. [22]

editing buffer When using the **vi** text editor, a storage area containing the data you are currently editing. [22]

editor Same as **text editor**. [22]

Emacs mode Within the shell, a mode used with command line editing in which the editing commands are the same ones as are used with the Emacs text editor. See also **command line editing** and **vi mode**. [13]

Chapter references are indicated by the numbers in brackets.

emulate   To cause a computer to act like a different device. To use your computer to connect to a Unix host, you run a program (for example, **ssh**) that emulates a terminal. [3]

environment   When using the shell, a table of variables that is copied and made available to all child processes, that is, to any program started by that shell. [12]

environment file   A type of initialization file that runs whenever a new shell starts. See also **login file**, **initialization file** and **logout file**. [14]

environment variable   Within the shell, a variable that is stored in the environment. Because the environment is inherited by all child processes, environment variables can be thought of as global variables. However, they are not strictly global, because changes made by the child are not propagated back to the parent. See also **shell variable**, **global variable** and **local variable**. [7] [12]

escape
1. When a program is in a specific mode, to do something that changes the program to a different mode. For example, within the **vi** editor, you press the <Esc> key to escape from insert mode to command mode. [13]
2. Within the shell, a synonym for **quote**. For example, in the command **echo** hello\; **goodbye**, we say that the backslash escapes the semicolon. [13]

escape character   When using a program, a key that, when pressed, changes the program from one mode to another. [13]

event   Within the shell, a command that has been stored in the history list. [13]

event number   Within the shell, a number that identifies an event (a command that has been stored in the history list). [13]

exec   With respect to a process, to change the program that the process is running. See also **fork**, **wait** and **exit**. [26]

execute   To follow the instructions contained in a program. Same as **run**. [2]

execute permission   A type of file permission that allows the executing of a file or the searching of a directory. Compare to **read permission** and **write permission**. See also **file permission**. [25]

exit   With respect to a process, to stop running. See also **fork**, **exec** and **wait**. [26]

export   Within the Bourne shell family (Bash, Korn shell), to cause a variable to become part of the environment, thereby making the variable accessible to child processes. [12]

extended regular expression   Sometimes abbreviated as ERE. A type of regular expression that offers more powerful features than the older, traditional Unix regular expressions (basic regular expressions). EREs are considered to be the current standard, part of the IEEE 1003.2 (POSIX) specification. Compare to **basic regular expression**. See also **regular expression**. [20]

extension   An optional part of a filename, at the end of the name, following a . (dot) character. For example, the filename **foobar.c** has the extension **c**. Extensions enable users, and sometimes programs, to identify the type of file. [25]

external command   Within the shell, a command that is interpreted by running a separate program. Compare to **internal command**. [13]

Chapter references are indicated by the numbers in brackets.

F

field   Within a file containing machine-readable data, a specific part of a record. See also **record**. [17]

FIFO

1. Abbreviation for "first-in, first out". Describes a data structure, such as a queue, in which elements are retrieved in the same order in which they went in. Compare to **LIFO**. See also **queue** and **stack**. [23]

2. A synonym for **named pipe**, pronounced "fie-foe". [23]

file

1. Any source, with a name, from which data can be read; any target, with a name, to which data can be written. There are three types of files: **ordinary file**, **directory**, and **pseudo file**. [23]

2. A synonym for ordinary file. [23]

file descriptor   Within a Unix process, a unique number that identifies an input source or an output target. By default, standard input uses file descriptor **0**; standard output uses **1**; and standard error uses **2**. [15]

file manager   A program that helps you manipulate files and directories. Using a file manager is an alternative to typing directory and file commands at the command line. The default file manager for the KDE desktop environment is Konqueror; the default file manager for Gnome is Nautilus. [24]

file mode   A three-number octal value, for example 755, that describes three sets of file permissions: **read permission**, **write permission**, and **execute permission**. The first number describes the permissions for the **owner**. The second number describes the permissions for the **group**. The third number describes the permissions for all userids. [25]

file permissions   One of three types of authorizations (read, write and execute) that specifies how a file may be accessed. See also **read permission**, **write permission**, and **execute permission**. [25]

filename   The very last part of a pathname, the actual name of a file. [24]

filename completion   A type of autocompletion that completes a partially typed filename. Filename completion is available with Bash, the Korn Shell, the C-Shell, and the Tcsh. See also **autocompletion**. [13]

filename generation   Within the Korn Shell and Bourne Shell, the facility that implements globbing, that is, the replacing of wildcard patterns by matching filenames. Within Bash, this same facility is referred to as pathname expansion; within the C-Shell and Tcsh, it is called filename substitution. See also **wildcard** and **globbing**. [24]

filename substitution   Within the C-Shell or Tcsh, the facility that implements globbing, that is, the replacing of wildcard patterns by matching filenames. Within Bash, this same facility is referred to as pathname expansion; within the Korn Shell and Bourne Shell, it is called filename generation. See also **wildcard**, **globbing** and **brace expansion**. [24]

Chapter references are indicated by the numbers in brackets.

filesystem

1. The Unix filesystem: a hierarchical tree-structure based on a single main directory (the root directory), containing all the files on a Unix system, including files from disk-based filesystems, network filesystems, and special-purpose filesystems. See also **root directory** and **tree**. [23]

2. Device filesystem: a hierarchical tree-structure containing the files stored on a specific device or disk partition. [23]

filesystem hierarchy standard A standard that describes how a Unix system should organize its directories, in particular, the top-level directories and selected second-level directories. Abbreviated as FHS. [23]

filter Any program that reads and writes textual data, one line at a time, reading from standard input and writing to standard output. As a general rule, most filters are designed as tools, to do one thing well. [16]

fixed media Describes storage devices that are attached to a computer permanently, for example, hard drives. Compare to **removable media**. [23]

flag

1. A synonym for **option**. [10]

2. When using the **ls** (list files) program with the **-F** option, a single character displayed at the end of a filename to indicate the type of file. The various flags are **/** (directory), ***** (executable file), **@** (symbolic link), and **|** (named pipe/FIFO). The absence of a flag indicates an ordinary, non-executable file. [24]

focus Within a GUI, the indication of which window is active. Once a window has the focus, whatever you type on the keyboard is used as input for the program running in that window. [6]

fold

1. As an adjective, describes the idea that lowercase letters are to be treated as if they were uppercase, or vice versa. For example, "The **sort** command has a fold option **-f**." [19]

2. As a verb, the act of treating lowercase letters as if they were uppercase, or vice versa. For example, "The **-f** option tells **sort** to fold lowercase letters into uppercase." [19]

folder When using a GUI-based tool, a synonym for **directory**. Otherwise, not used with Unix (unless you want to sound like a clueless goober). [23]

follow When using a symbolic link, to refer to the name of the directory contained in the link. See **symbolic link**. [25]

foo A meaningless word, used to represent an unnamed item during a discussion or exposition. When a second unnamed item must be discussed, it is often referred to as "bar". For example, you might hear someone ask the question, "I have two files, foo and bar. How can I copy all the lines in foo that contain a particular pattern to the end of bar?" See also **bar** and **foobar**. [9]

Chapter references are indicated by the numbers in brackets.

foobar A meaningless word, used to represent an unnamed item during a discussion or exposition. "Foobar" is often used to represent some type of pattern. For example, you might see the following question posted to a Usenet discussion group: "How do I remove a file named "`-foobar`"?" See also **foo** and **bar**. [9]

foreground process A process that must finish before the shell can display the next shell prompt. We say that such a process runs "in the foreground". Compare to **background process**. [26]

fork With respect to a process, to create a copy of the process. The original process is called the **parent process**; the new process is called the **child process**. See also **exec**, **wait** and **exit**. [26]

free software Software that can legally be examined, modified, shared and distributed by anyone. [2]

Free Software Foundation An organization, started in 1985 by Richard Stallman and a small group of programmers, devoted to the creation and distribution of free software; home of the GNU project. [2]

FreeBSD shell A member of the Bourne shell family, the default shell for the FreeBSD operating system. The name of the FreeBSD shell program is `sh`. See also **Bourne shell family**. [11]

french spacing Within typography, the use of two spaces (rather than one) at the end of each sentence. The practice is based on the use of monospaced fonts, such as the ones originally used with typewriters. [18]

FSF Abbreviation for **Free Software Foundation**. [2]

G

General Public License Same as **GPL**. [2]

gigabyte A unit of storage measurement, $2^{30} = 1,073,741,824$ bytes. Abbreviated as G or GB. See also **kilobyte** and **megabyte**. [24]

glob (verb) The act of **globbing**. [24]

global variable A variable whose value is available outside of the scope in which it was created. See also **local variable**, **shell variable** and **environment variable**. [12]

globbing An operation in which a wildcard pattern is replaced by a list of matching filenames, typically within a command that is processed by the shell. See also **wildcard** and **pathname expansion**. [24]

Gnome A widely used, free desktop environment. The Gnome Project was founded in August 1997 by two programmers, Miguel de Icaza and Federico Mena. Their goal was to create an alternative to KDE that could be distributed under a more liberal license. Compare to **KDE**. See also **desktop environment**. [5]

GNU The name of the Free Software Foundation's project to develop an entire Unix-like operating system independent of commercial software, to be distributed as free software. GNU is a whimsical name, a recursive acronym standing for "GNU's not Unix". See also **Free Software Foundation** and (free software. [2]

Chapter references are indicated by the numbers in brackets.

GNU Manifesto An essay, written by Richard Stallman, the principal founder of the Free Software Foundation, in which he explained his reasons for promoting the idea of free software. The GNU Manifesto was first published in the March 1985 issue of *Dr. Dobb's Journal of Software Tools*. [2]

GPL Abbreviation for General Public License. A legal license, first used in 1989 by the Free Software Foundation, to implement the idea of copyleft as applied to free software. The GPL allows allow anyone to run a program, copy the program, modify the program, and distribute modified versions, as long as they do not add restrictions of their own. [2]

graphical user interface See **GUI**. [5]

graphics terminal A terminal that displays, not only characters, but anything that can be drawn on the screen using small dots: pictures, geometric shapes, shading, lines, colors, and so on. [3]

group
1. A set of userids that share common file permissions. Groups make it easy for people who work together to read, write or execute each other's files. The name of a group is called its groupid (pronounced "group-I-D"). See also **groupid**, **primary group**, **supplementary group** and **file mode**. [25]
2. Within a regular expression, a sequence of characters within parentheses, treated as a single unit, often before a repetition operator, for example, **(xyz){5}**. In this case, the group **(xyz)**, combined with the repetition operator **{5}**, matches the character string "xyz" 5 times in a row. [20]

groupid The name of a group used for sharing file permissions. Pronounced "group-I-D". See also **group**. [25]

grouping Within the shell, especially the C-Shell, a list of commands, typed within parentheses, that are to be executed by a subshell. [15]

GUI Abbreviation for "graphical user interface"; pronounced either "gooey" or as three separate letters "G-U-I". A system that allows you to interact with a computer by using a pointing device (usually a mouse) and a keyboard to manipulate windows, icons, menus and other graphical elements. Compare to **CLI**. [5]

H

hack To put forth a massive amount of nerd-like effort, often programming. [4]

hacker A person who hacks. [4]

hard link Synonym for **link**. Used to distinguish between a regular link (hard link) and a symbolic link (soft link). [25]

hardware The physical components of a computer: keyboard, monitor, mouse, disk drives, processor, memory, and so on. [2]

header file Same as **include file**. [23]

headless system A computer that runs on its own, without direct input from a human being. A typical headless system would be a server, with no monitor, keyboard or mouse. When necessary the server can be controlled via a network connection. [3]

Chapter references are indicated by the numbers in brackets.

hex Same as **hexadecimal**. [21]

hexadecimal Same as base 16. A number system, based on powers of 16, in which numbers are constructed using the 16 digits 0, 1, 2, 3, 4, 5, 6, 7, 8, 9, A, B, C, D, E and F. Often abbreviated as hex. See also **binary system**, **octal**, **decimal system** and **duodecimal**. [21]

hidden file A file whose name begins with a **.** (dot) character. When the **ls** command lists filenames, hidden files are not listed unless requested specifically by using the **-a** (all files) option. Same as **dotfile**. [14] [24]

history list Within the shell, a list of the commands that have been entered. A user can access the history list in a variety of ways — the details depend on the shell being used — in order to recall previous commands, which can then be modified and reentered. Some shells allow the user to set the size of the history list and to specify whether or not the list should be saved when the user logs out. [13]

hold When using a mouse or other pointing device, to press a button and keep it down while performing an action, such as moving a window. [6]

home directory The directory designated to hold the files for a particular userid. Whenever you log in, your current directory is automatically set to be your home directory. [23]

host A computer that runs Unix. Users use a terminal to connect to the host. [3]

hostname completion A type of autocompletion that completes a partially typed computer name, when a word begins with an **@** (at) character. The word to be completed must be the name of a computer on the local network. Hostname completion is available with Bash. See also **autocompletion**. [13]

human-readable With respect to a program, describes output that is designed to be particularly easy for a person to read. Compare to **machine-readable**. [12]

I

icon Within a GUI, a small picture that represents an object, such as a window, program or file. [6]

iconify Same as **minimize**. [6]

idle process Process #0, the original process, created as part of the boot sequence. The idle process performs a number of initialization functions, creates process #1 (the init process), and then runs a very simple program that is essentially an infinite loop doing nothing. (Hence, the name "idle process".) See also **boot** and **init process**. [26]

idle time When using the CLI (command line interface), the length of time since the user has pressed a key. [8]

include file A file containing C or C++ source code that can be inserted into a program as required. A typical include file has definitions of subroutines, data structures, variables, constants, and so on. Also called a **header file**. [23]

index node Same as **inode**. [25]

index number Same as **inumber**. [25]

infix notation Arithmetical notation in which an operator is placed in between the operands, for example, "5 + 7". Compare to **prefix notation** and **postfix notation**. [8]

Info A help system, derived from Emacs and separate from the online Unix manual, used to document the GNU utilities. [9]

Chapter references are indicated by the numbers in brackets.

Info file   Within the Info system, a file containing the documentation for one topic. [9]

inherit   With respect to a child process, to be given access to a copy of a variable that was part of the environment of the parent process. [12]

init process   Process #1, created by the process #0 (the idle process). The ancestor of all other processes on the system. The init process completes the last part of boot sequence. Among other tasks, it starts the system in a particular runlevel. The init process also adopts all orphan processes to make sure they are handled properly. See also **boot**, **idle process**, **runlevel** and **orphan**. [26]

initialization file   A file that contains commands to be executed whenever a user logs in or whenever a new shell starts. There are two types of initialization files: A **login file** runs whenever a user logs in; an **environment file** runs whenever a new shell starts. See also **logout file**. [14]

inner join   A type of join in which the output includes only those lines in which the join field matches. Compare to **outer join**. See also **field**, **join** and **join field**. [19]

inode   Abbreviation for index node, pronounced "eye-node". Within a filesystem, a structure that holds the basic information about a file. See also **inode table**, **inumber**, and **link**. [25]

inode table   A table containing all the inodes in a filesystem. Each inode describes a single file, identified by its inumber. See also **inode** and **inumber**. [25]

input mode   When using the **vi** text editor, a mode in which the characters you type are inserted into the editing buffer. Compare to **command mode**. [22]

input stream   Data read by a program. Compare to **output stream**. See also **stream**. [19]

interactive   Describes a program that communicates with a person. When you run an interactive program, the input comes from your keyboard or your mouse, and the output is sent to your monitor. [12]

interactive shell   A shell that provides the interface for a user working at a terminal. [12]

interface   The part of a machine that provides a way for the user to interact with the machine. For example, with a desktop computer, the interface consists of the monitor, the keyboard, the mouse, the speakers and, possibly, a microphone and webcam. [3]

internal command   Within the shell, a command that is interpreted by the shell directly. Same as **builtin command** and **builtin**. Compare to **external command**. [13]

interprocess communication   The exchange of data between two processes. Abbreviated as IPC. See also **signal**. [23]

inumber   Abbreviation for index number, pronounced "eye-number". Within a filesystem, a number that identifies a particular inode (index node) within the table of inodes. See also **inode**, **inode table**, and **link**. [25]

J

job   Within the shell, the internal representation of a command that is currently running or suspended. In most cases, a job corresponds to a single process. However, with a pipeline or a compound command, a job corresponds to multiple processes. Jobs are controlled by the shell, unlike processes, which are managed by the kernel. See also **job control**, **job number** and **job table**. Compare to **process**. [26]

Chapter references are indicated by the numbers in brackets.

job control   A facility, supported by the kernel and implemented by the shell, enabling a user to run multiple processes, one in the foreground, the rest in the background. With job control one can move processes between the foreground and background, suspend (pause) them, and display their status. See also **job**, **job number** and **job table**. [26]

job ID   Same as **job number**. [26]

job number   A unique number, assigned by the shell, that identifies a particular job. Sometimes referred to as a job number. Job numbers start from 1 and count up. See also **job**, **job control** and **job table**. Compare to **process ID**. [26]

job table   A table, maintained by the shell, used to keep track of all the jobs started by each userid. The job table contains one entry per process, indexed by job ID. Each entry in the table contains the information necessary to describe and manage a particular job. See also **job**, **job control** and **job ID**. Compare to **process table**. [26]

join   Combining two sets of data based on matching fields. See also **field**, **join field**, **inner join** and **outer join**. [19]

join field   When creating a join, the field used to match two sets of data. See also **field**, **join**, **inner join** and **outer join**. [19]

K

KDE   A widely used, free desktop environment. The KDE Project was founded in October 1996 by Matthias Ettrich, a German student. His goal was to create a complete, integrated, graphical working environment; in fact, the first modern desktop environment. Compare to **Gnome**. See also **desktop environment**. [5]

kernel   The central part of an operating system that is always running in order to provide essential services as they are needed. [2]

keyword   Within the shell, one of several builtin commands that are used to control the flow within a shell script. For example, with Bash: `case`, `for`, `function`, `if`, `select`, `time` and `while`. [13]

kill   To terminate a process permanently. Under normal circumstances, a foreground process can be killed by pressing `^C` or (for programs that run in raw mode) by typing a quit command. Compare to **suspend**. [12]

kilobyte   A unit of storage measurement, $2^{10} = 1{,}024$ bytes. Abbreviated as K or KB. See also **gigabyte** and **megabyte**. [24]

Korn shell   A member of the Bourne shell family, developed as a replacement for the Bourne shell in 1982 by David Korn, a researcher at Bell Labs. The name of the Korn shell program is `ksh`. See also **Pdksh** and **Bourne shell family**. [11]

L

lag   When using a remote Unix system, a noticeable delay between the time you press a key or move your mouse and the time you notice the result of your action. [3]

layers of abstraction   A model in which a large overall goal is defined in terms of layers, which are visualized as being stacked from the bottom up, one on top of the next. Each layer provides services to the layer above and requests services from the layer below, with no other interactions. [5]

Chapter references are indicated by the numbers in brackets.

leaf   Within a tree (data structure), a node that has only one connection; that is, a node at the end of a branch. See also **tree**. [9]

left button   On a mouse or other pointing device, the button that, when the mouse is on your right, is the leftmost button. See also **right button** and **middle button**. [6]

left-click   When using a mouse or other pointing device, to press the left button. [6]

library   A pre-existing module of data and code, usually used to enable programs to access services offered by the operating system. [23]

LIFO   Abbreviation for "last in, first out". Describes a data structure, such as a stack, in which elements are retrieved in the opposite order to which they went in. Compare to **FIFO**. See also **stack** and **queue**. [8] [24]

line discipline   A facility used by a terminal driver to provide the preprocessing and postprocessing necessary for an interactive interface. See also **canonical mode** and **raw mode**. [21]

line editor   Same as **line-oriented editor**. [22]

line-oriented editor   A text editor that numbers lines of text and uses commands based on these numbers. Same as line editor. Compare to **screen-oriented editor**. [22]

linefeed
1. A special character used to control the operation of an output device, indicating that the cursor or print position should move down one line. Within Unix, the linefeed character is called a newline and is used to indicate the end of a line of text. When sent to a terminal, a linefeed causes the cursor to move down one line. Within the ASCII code, the linefeed character is **^J** (Ctrl-J), with a value of 10 in decimal or 0A in hexadecimal. See also **newline** and **return**. [4] [7]
2. On an old Teletype ASR33, the operation in which the print head is moved down one line. [4]

link
1. Abbreviation for index number, pronounced "eye-number". Within a filesystem, a number that identifies a particular inode (index node) within the table of inodes. See also **inode** and **link**. [25]
2. Within the Info system, a facility that lets you jump from one node to another node. [9]

Linus's Law   "Given enough eyeballs, all bugs are shallow." In other words, when a vast number of people test and read new code, it does not take long to find the bugs. Linus' Law was coined by Eric Raymond in his essay "The Cathedral and the Bazaar". The name was chosen to honor Linus Torvalds, the founder of the Linux kernel project. [2]

Linux
1. Any Unix-like kernel created by the Linux project. The project to develop such kernels was started in 1991 by Linus Torvalds. [2]
2. More generally, any operating system based on a Linux kernel. More generally, any operating system based on a Linux kernel. Such operating systems are sometimes referred to as GNU/Linux, to indicate that a Linux kernel is combined with the GNU utilities. [2]

Chapter references are indicated by the numbers in brackets.

live CD A CD that has been made bootable, containing everything necessary to run a full operating system. When you boot from a live CD, you bypass the hard disk, allowing you to use an operating system without having to install it on your system. [2]

local Describes a variable that exists only within the scope in which the variable was created. For example, shell variables are local to the shell in which they exist. [12]

local variable A variable that exists only within the scope in which it was created. For example, within the shell, a variable that is not part of the environment is a local variable. See also **global variable**, **shell variable** and **environment variable**. [12]

locale A technical specification describing the language and conventions that should be used when communicating with a user from a particular culture. The intention is that a user can choose whichever locale he wants, and the programs he runs will communicate with him accordingly. For users of American English, the default locale is either the **C** (**POSIX**) locale based on the ASCII code; or the **en_US** locale, part of a newer international system. [19]

log in To initiate a Unix work session. [4]

log out To terminate a Unix work session. [4]

login Describes the process of logging in. [4]

login file A type of initialization file that runs whenever a user logs in. See also **environment file**, **initialization file** and **logout file**. [14]

login shell The shell that starts automatically when you log in. See also **non-login shell**. [11] [14]

logout Describes the process of logging out. [4]

logout file A file that contains commands that are executed whenever a user logs out. See also **initialization file**, **login file** and **environment file**. [14]

lowercase Describes small letters, "a" to "z". [4]

M

machine-readable With respect to a program, describes output that is formatted so as to be suitable for processing by another program. Such output may be difficult for a person to read. Compare to **human-readable**. [12]

macro When using the **vi** text editor, a one-character abbreviation for a command. [22]

mail server A computer that provides the service of sending and receiving email for various clients. [3]

mainframe computer A large, expensive computer, typically used by institutions — such as governments, universities and companies — that can afford a staff of programmers and administrators. The name "mainframe" was coined in the early 1970s to distinguish the older, large computers from the new minicomputers. [3]

man page Within the online manual, the documentation for a single topic. By tradition, the documentation for each topic is referred to as a "page", even though it might be large enough to fill many printed pages. Same as **page**. See **online manual**. [9]

(the) Manual Same as the **online manual**. When Unix users refer to "the Manual", they always mean the online manual. [9]

Chapter references are indicated by the numbers in brackets.

map To create a mapping. [7]

mapped Expresses the idea that a mapping exists between two objects. For example, the <Ctrl-C> character is mapped onto the `intr` signal. Thus, when you press <Ctrl-C>, it has the effect of sending the `intr` signal. [7]

mapping An equivalence between two objects. For example, if we say that A is mapped onto B, it means that, when we use A, it is the same as using B. [7]

match With respect to a regular expression, to correspond to a particular character string. [20]

maximize Within a GUI, to expand a window to its largest possible size. [6]

maximize button Within a GUI, a small rectangle, usually in the top right-hand corner of the window, that, when clicked, maximizes the window. [6]

megabyte A unit of storage measurement, $2^{20} = 1,048,576$ bytes. Abbreviated as M or MB. See also **kilobyte** and **gigabyte**. [24]

memory dump Same as **core dump**. [21]

menu A list of items from which you can make a selection. Within a GUI, there are two types of menus: **pull-down menus** (more common) and **pop-up menus** (less common). [6]

menu bar Within a GUI, a menu consisting of a horizontal list of words near the top of a window. [6]

metacharacters Within the shell, a character that has a special, non-literal meaning. [13]

microkernel A kernel consisting of a relatively small program that calls upon other programs, called servers, to perform much of its work. By their nature, microkernels are somewhat inefficient. However, because of their modular structure, they are easier to maintain and customize than other types of kernels. Compare to **monolithic kernel**. [2]

middle button On a mouse or other pointing device, the middle button. Although almost all mice have left and right buttons, many do not have a middle button. See also **right button** and **left button**. [6]

middle-click When using a mouse or other pointing device, to press the middle button. [6]

minicomputer Any of the relatively small and inexpensive computers that were manufactured in the 1970s and 1980s. Until personal computers became available in the 1980s, most Unix systems ran on minicomputers. Compare to **mainframe**. [3]

minimize Within a GUI, to cause a window to vanish from the main part of the screen. To restore a window that has been minimized, you click on its icon within the taskbar. [6]

minimize button Within a GUI, a small rectangle, usually in the top right-hand corner of the window, that, when clicked, minimizes the window. [6]

mode
  1. A particular state of a program or a device. For example, you can use Unix in text mode (using the CLI) or graphics mode (using a GUI). Similarly, when you use the `vi` editor, you are, at any time, either in command mode or insert mode. [6] [13]
  2. Same as **file mode**. [25]

Chapter references are indicated by the numbers in brackets.

modification time With respect to a file, the last time the file was changed. To display the modification time for a file, you use the **ls** program with the **-l** option. Compare to **access time**. [24]

modifier key On a keyboard, a key that can be held down while pressing another key, for example, <Shift>, <Ctrl> and <Alt>. [7]

monolithic kernel A kernel consisting of a single, relatively large program that performs all its operations internally. Monolithic kernels are efficient, but can be unwieldy, which makes them difficult to design and maintain. Compare to **microkernel**. [2]

mount (verb) To enable access to a filesystem residing on a device by connecting the device filesystem to the main Unix filesystem. To mount a filesystem, you use the **mount** command. The directory to which the device filesystem is attached is called the **mount point**. See also **unmount**) and **filesystem**. [23]

mount point The directory within the Unix filesystem to which a device filesystem is connected (that is, mounted). See also **mount**) **and filesystem**. [23]

multi-boot Describes a computer that is set up to boot one of a number of different operating systems, as chosen by the user during the startup process. [2]

multiprogramming The old name for multitasking. Describes an operating system that can execute more than one program at a time. [3]

multitasking Describes an operating system that can execute more than one program at a time. [2]

multiuser Describes an operating system that can support more than one user at a time. [2]

N

name An identifier used to refer to a variable. [12]

named pipe A type of pseudo file used to connect the output of one program to the input of a second program. Unlike an anonymous pipe (regular pipe), a named pipe is created explicitly and exists until it is deleted. Thus, a named pipe can be used repeatedly. Also called a **FIFO** ("fie-foe"). Compare to **pipe**. See also **pseudo file**. [23]

newline The Unix name for the linefeed character. Within text, a newline character is used to indicate the end of a line. When sent to a terminal, a newline causes the cursor to move down one line. Within the ASCII code, the newline character is **^J** (Ctrl-J), with a value of 10 in decimal or 0A in hexadecimal. [7]

News (the) Synonym for **Usenet**. [3]

news server A server that stores Usenet articles and makes them available to users via newsreader programs. [3]

newsgroup A Usenet discussion group. [3]

newsreader A client program used to access the Usenet system of discussion groups. [3]

nice number A number used to modify the priority of a process. The higher the nice number, the lower the priority. In most cases, the nice number of a process is changed by either the **nice** or **renice** command in order to lower the priority of the process. [26]

Chapter references are indicated by the numbers in brackets.

niceness Synonym for **nice number**. [26]

node

1. Within a tree (data structure), a fork in a path. Corresponds to a vertex in a graph. See **tree**. [9]

2. Within the Info system, a section that contains information about one specific topic. [9]

non-destructive backspace The type of backspace that occurs when the cursor moves back but nothing is changed. This is what happens when you press the <Left> arrow key. [7]

non-interactive Describes a program that runs independently of a person. For example, a non-interactive program might read its input from a file and write its output to another file. [12]

non-interactive shell A shell that is running a shell script. [12]

non-login shell Any interactive shell that was not started at the time the user logged in. See also **login shell**. [14]

noncanonical mode Same as **raw mode**. [21]

null Describes a variable that has no value. [12]

null character Also called a null. The character consisting of all **0** bits, that is, the numeric value **0**. See also **zero file**. [23]

null file The pseudo-file **/dev/null**. When the null file is used as an output target, it throws away all input. When used as an input source, it always returns the **eof** signal (that is, nothing). The null file is one of the two **bit buckets**, the other being the **zero file**. See also **pseudo-file**. [23]

numbered buffer When using the **vi** text editor, one of 9 storage areas (numbered 1 through 9) used to store and retrieve data. See also **unnamed buffer**. [22]

O

octal Same as base 8. A number system, based on powers of 8, in which numbers are constructed using the 8 digits 0, 1, 2, 3, 4, 5, 6, and 7. See also **binary system**, **decimal system**, **duodecimal** and (hexadecimal system. [21]

offset The location within a file of a particular byte, the first byte having offset 0. [21]

one or more Indicates that you must use at least one of something. For example, the syntax for a command might allow you to specify one or more file names. This means that you must use at least one name. Compare to **zero or more**. [10]

online

1. In an older sense, describes the idea of being connected to a specific computer system. For example, when you connect to a remote Unix host, you are online. [9]

2. Describes an Internet resource or service, for example, online banking. [9]

3. Describes a person who is currently using the Internet, for example, "Linda is online right now." [9]

4. Describes a situation that exists only because of the Internet, for example, an online relationship. [9]

Chapter references are indicated by the numbers in brackets.

online manual A collection of information, available to all Unix users at all times, containing documentation about commands and important system facilities. The online manual is divided into sections, each of which contains many entries (called pages) that document a single topic. You can access the online manual by using the **man** command or, with a GUI, by using **xman**. Alternatively, you can find many versions of the online manual on the Web. There is longstanding tradition that users should check the online manual before asking for help. See **RTFM**. When Unix users refer to "the Manual", they always mean the online manual. [9]

Open Software Foundation An organization, formed in May 1988 by eight Unix vendors (including IBM, DEC and HP), for the purpose of creating their own "standard" Unix. Abbreviated as OSF. Compare to **Unix International**. [5]

open source movement A loosely organized international social movement among programmers, based on the willingness to work together on free software. [2]

open source software
1. Software whose source code is freely distributed, often with the software itself. [2]
2. Synonym for **free software**. [2]

operating system A complex master control program whose principal function is to make efficient use of the hardware. The operating system acts as the primary interface to the hardware for both users and programs. [2]

operator When using the **find** program, an instruction used to group together or modify tests. For example, the **!** operator negates the meaning of a test. See also **test** and **action**. [25]

option
1. When entering a Unix command: an optional part of a command, almost always prefaced with **-** or **--** (one or two hyphens), that specifies how you want the command to execute. For example, you might enter the command **ls -l**. This is the **ls** command with the **-l** option. In conversation, the **-** character is usually pronounced "dash", even though it is actually a hyphen or minus sign (depending on your point of view). If you were to talk about the last example, you would say that you used the **ls** command with the "dash L" option. See also **argument**. [10]
2. When using the **vi** text editor: a setting that enables you to control a specific aspect of the program's operation. There are two types of **vi** options: **switch** and **variable**. [22]

ordinary file One of the three types of Unix files. Same as **regular file**. A file that contains data and resides on a storage device, such as a hard disk, CD, DVD, flash drive, memory card, or floppy disk. As such, ordinary files are the type of files you work with most of the time. Compare to **directory** and **pseudo file**. See also **file**. [23]

orphan A child process whose parent has terminated. See also **die** and **zombie**. On most system, orphans are adopted by process #1, the init process, so they can be processed properly. See also **init process**. [26]

OSF Abbreviation for **Open Software Foundation**. [5]

Chapter references are indicated by the numbers in brackets.

outer join   A type of join in which the output also includes the lines in which the join field does not not match. Compare to **inner join**. See also **field**, **join** and **join field**. [19]

output stream   Data that is written by a program. Compare to **input stream**. See also **stream**. [19]

owner   With respect to a file, the userid that controls the file's permissions. By default, the userid that created the file is the owner. However, the owner can be changed with the **chown** program. [25]

P

page   Within the online manual, the documentation for a single topic. By tradition, the documentation for each topic is referred to as a "page", even though it might be large enough to fill many printed pages. Same as **man page**. See **online manual**. [9]

pager   A program that displays text data from a file or a pipeline, one screenful at a time. [21]

paragraph   When using the **vi** text editor, a section of text that starts and ends in a blank line. Various **vi** commands act upon paragraphs when moving the cursor or modifying text. See also **word** and **sentence**. [22]

parent   Same as **parent process**. [15] [26]

parent directory   A directory that contains another directory. A directory that lies within a parent directory is called a **subdirectory** or **child directory**. See also **directory**. [23]

parent process   A process that starts another process. The original process is the parent; the new process is the child. See also **child process**. [15] [26]

parse   Within the shell, to separate a command into logical components, which can then be analyzed and interpreted. [13]

partial ordering   When ordering elements of a set, a binary relation that orders some, but not all members of the set with respect to one another. Compare to **total ordering**. [19]

partition   On a storage device such as a hard disk, a logically discrete part of the disk on which an operating system or a filesystem can be installed. [2]

partition manager   A program used to manipulate partitions on a disk or similar device. [2]

password   A secret pattern of characters that must be typed as part of the login process to ensure that a user is authorized to use a particular userid. [4]

password aging   A security requirement that forces a user to change his or her password regularly, for example, every 60 days. [4]

password file   A system file, **/etc/passwd**, that contains information about all the userids in the system. Each line in the file contains information about one userid. On old systems, the password file contained the passwords (encoded, of course). On modern systems, the passwords are kept separately in a shadow file. See also **shadow file**. [11]

paste   Within a GUI, to copy data from the clipboard to a window. The data within the clipboard is not changed in any way. [6]

patch   A diff used to modify a program, usually to fix bugs or to enhance the program in some way. See also **apply** and **diff**. [17]

Chapter references are indicated by the numbers in brackets.

path Same as **pathname**. [24]

pathname A description of the location of a file within the directory tree. Same as **path**. See also **absolute pathname** and **relative pathname**. [24]

pathname expansion Within the Bash shell, the facility that implements globbing, that is, the replacing of wildcard patterns by matching filenames. Within the C-Shell and Tcsh, this same facility is referred to as filename substitution; within the Korn Shell and Bourne Shell, it is called filename generation. See also **wildcard**, **globbing** and **brace expansion**. [24]

Pdksh A member of the Bourne shell family, a free, open source version of the Korn shell, originally developed in 1987 by Eric Gisin. Pdksh is an acronym for "public domain Korn shell". The name of the Pdksh program is **ksh**. See also **Korn shell** and **Bourne shell family**. [11]

permission Same as **file permission**. [25]

PID Same as **process ID**. A unique number, assigned by the kernel, that identifies a particular process. Pronounced "P-I-D". See also **process** and **process table**. [26]

pipe
  1. A connection between two consecutive programs in a pipeline, in which the output of one program is used as the input for a second program. Sometimes called an (anonymous pipe. Compare to **named pipe**.
  2. (verb) To send data from one program to another so as to create a pipeline. [15]

pipeline An arrangement in which two or more programs process data in sequence, the output of one program becoming the input to the next program. [15]

pointer Within a GUI, a small, movable image that indicates the position to which the pointing device (mouse) is currently pointing. The shape of the pointer may change, depending on what you are doing and where it is on the screen. [6]

Polish Notation Arithmetical notation in which an operator is placed before the operands, for example, "+ 5 7". Named in honor of Jan Lukasiewicz (1878-1956), a renowned Polish mathematician, logician and philosopher. Same as **prefix notation**. See also **Reverse Polish Notation**. [8]

pop With a stack, to retrieve the data element from the top of the stack (that is, the last element written) while simultaneously removing it from the stack. [8] [24]

pop-up menu Within a GUI, a menu that appears from no apparent location as a result of some action, often a right-click. [6]

port As a verb, to adapt software designed for one computer system to run on another system; "Tammy ported the Foo program from Linux to Windows." As a noun, to refer to such software; "Tammy created the Windows port of the Foo program." [2]

POSIX A project, started under the auspices of the IEEE (Institute of Electrical and Electronics Engineers) in the early 1990s, with the goal of standardizing Unix. Pronounced "pause-ix". The specification for the POSIX shell is described by IEEE standard 1003.2. Most modern shells in the Bourne shell family adhere to this standard. This is not the case for shells in the C-Shell family. [11]

Chapter references are indicated by the numbers in brackets.

POSIX options   Same as UNIX options. [26]

postfix notation   Arithmetical notation in which an operator is placed after the operands, for example, "5 7 +". Also called **Reverse Polish Notation**. Compare to **infix notation** and **prefix notation**. [8]

predefined character class   With respect to regular expressions, a name that can be used instead of a set of characters within a character class. For example, the predefined character class `[:digit:]` can be used instead of `0-9`. See also **character class**. [20]

prefix notation   Arithmetical notation in which an operator is placed before the operands, for example, "+ 5 7". Also called **Polish notation**. Compare to **infix notation** and **postfix notation**. [8]

previous job   With respect to job control, the second most recently suspended job or, if there are no suspended jobs, most recently moved to the background. See also **job**, **job control** and **current job**. [26]

primary group   With respect to a specific userid, the one group that is listed as the userid's group in the system password file. All other groups to which the userid belongs are called supplementary groups. Compare to **supplementary group**. See also **group** and **file mode**. [25]

print   To display information on the terminal. For example, the command to display the name of your working directory is **pwd**: "print working directory". [7]

printable characters   Within a character encoding system, those characters that can be displayed and printed; not control characters. Within the ASCII code, there are 96 printable characters: letters, numbers, punctuation symbols, the space, and (for practical purposes) the tab. See also **ASCII code**. [19]

priority   With respect to scheduling the execution of processes, an indication of how much precedence a process should be given over other processes. The priority of a process is inversely proportional to its nice number. See also **process** and **nice number**. [26]

proc file   A type of pseudo file used to access information residing within the kernel. In a few specific cases, proc files can be used to change data within the kernel. Originally, these files were created to furnish information about processes, hence the name "proc". See also **pseudo file**. [23]

process   A program that is loaded into memory and ready to run, along with the program's data and the information needed to keep track of the program. Processes are controlled by the kernel, unlike jobs, which are controlled by the shell. See also **job**, **process ID** and **process table**. [6] [15] [26]

process ID   A unique number, assigned by the kernel, that identifies a particular process. Often referred to as a PID ("P-I-D"). See also **process** and **process table**. Compare to **job ID**. [26]

process table   A table, maintained by the kernel, used to keep track of all the processes in the system. The process table contains one entry per process, indexed by PID (process ID). Each entry in the table contains the information necessary to describe and manage a particular process. See also **process** and **process ID**. Compare to **job table**. [26]

Chapter references are indicated by the numbers in brackets.

process tree A data structure in the form of a tree-structured hierarchy that shows the connections between parent processes and their children. The process tree for the entire system has the init process at the root of the tree. See also **process**, **parent process**, **child process** and **init process**. [26]

program A list of instructions that, when carried out by a computer, performs a task. [2]

Project Athena A collaboration between researchers at MIT, IBM, and DEC, started in 1984. The goal was to create the first standardized, networked, hardware-independent, graphical operating environment for use by the students at MIT . Project Athena is noteworthy for having created the first version of X Window. [5]

prompt A short message, displayed by a program, indicating that the program is ready to accept input from the keyboard. [4]

pseudo file One of the three types of Unix files. A pseudo file is used to access a service, usually provided by the kernel. Because pseudo files do not store data, they require no disk space. The most important types of pseudo files are **special files**, **named pipes**, and **proc files**. Compare to **ordinary file** and **directory**. See also **file**. [23]

pseudo terminal A simulated terminal used when you open a terminal window within a GUI or when you connect to a remote Unix computer. Abbreviated as PTY. See also **terminal**. Compare to **virtual console**. [23]

pseudo-device A type of special file that acts as an input source or output target but does not correspond to an actual device, either real or emulated. The two most useful pseudo-devices are the **null file** and the **zero file**. See also **special file**. [23]

PTY Abbreviation for **pseudo terminal**. [23]

pull-down menu Within a GUI, a menu that appears when you click on a word or icon. [6]

punch card A type of card, invented by U.S. inventor Herman Hollerith (1860-1929), used to store data that is encoded by holes punched in columns. [18]

push With a stack, to store a data element on the stack. [8] [24]

Q

queue A data structure in which elements are stored and retrieved one at a time, such that elements are retrieved in the same order they were stored. See also **FIFO** ("first-in first-out") and **data structure**. [23]

quote Within the shell, to indicate that certain characters are to be interpreted literally according to certain rules. This is done by placing one or more characters within single quotes (') or double quotes ("), or by placing a backslash (\) before a single character. See also **strong quotes** and **weak quotes**. [13]

R

range With respect to regular expressions, within a character class, a specification for a set of characters that can be ordered. A range consists of the first member of the set, followed by a hyphen, followed by the last member of the set. For example, the range **0-9** specifies the digits **0** through **9**. See also **character class**. [20]

Chapter references are indicated by the numbers in brackets.

raw mode A line discipline in which characters typed as input to a program are sent to the program as soon as the user presses a key. Compare to **canonical mode** and **cbreak made**. See also **line discipline**. [21]

read permission A type of file permission that allows the reading of a file or directory. Compare to **write permission** and **execute permission**. See also **file permission**. [25]

reboot A process that stops Unix and then restarts the computer, effectively stopping and restarting Unix. [6]

record Within a file containing machine-readable data, a line of data. See also **field** and **delimiter**. [17]

recursive

1. Describes an algorithm or program (computer science), or a function (mathematics) that is defined in terms of itself. Informally, describes a name or acronym that can be expanded indefinitely, for example, the recursive acronym GNU stands for "GNU's not Unix". [2]

2. With respect to Unix file commands, describes options that process an entire sub-tree of directories. Such options are usually named **-r** or **-R**. [24]

redirect To redefine the source for standard input or the target for either standard output or standard error. [15]

regex Abbreviation for **regular expression**. [20]

regular expression A specification, based on specific metacharacters and abbreviations, that provides a compact way of unambiguously describing a pattern of characters. Abbreviated as "regex" or, more simply, "re". [20]

regular file Same as **ordinary file). [23]**

relative pathname A pathname that is interpreted in such a way that it starts from the current directory. [24]

removable media Describes storage devices that can be inserted or removed while the system is running; for example, CDs, DVDs, floppy disks, tapes, flash drives, and memory cards. Compare to **fixed media**. [23]

repeat count When using the **vi** text editor, a number, typed before a command, that causes the command to be repeated automatically the specified number of times. For example, the command **dd** deletes the current line. The command **10dd** deletes 10 lines, starting with the current line. [22]

repetition operator Within a regular expression, one of several metacharacters (*****, **+**, **?**, **{ }**) used to match more than one character at a time. See also **bound**. [20]

resize Within a GUI, to change the size of a window. [6]

restart Same as **reboot**. [6]

restore Within a GUI, after a window has been minimized or maximized, to cause the window to regain its original size and position. [6]

return A character that, when sent to a terminal, causes the cursor to move to the beginning of the line. In the ASCII code, the return character has the value 13 in decimal, or 0D in hexadecimal. See also **linefeed** and **newline**. [7]

Chapter references are indicated by the numbers in brackets.

return value   When a program or function calls another program or function, data sent back to the calling program. The **fork** system call sends a zero return value to the child process and a non-zero return value (the process ID of the child) to the parent process. [26]

Reverse Polish Notation   Arithmetical notation in which an operator is placed after the operands, for example, "5 7 +". Often abbreviated as RPN. Named in honor of Jan Lukasiewicz (1878-1956), a renowned Polish mathematician, logician and philosopher. Same as **postfix notation**. [8]

revision control system   A sophisticated system, commonly used by software developers to manage the development of large programs or documents. Same as **source control system**. Generic term is **version control system**. [17]

right buttons   On a mouse or other pointing device, the button that, when the mouse is on your right, is the rightmost button. See also **left button** and **middle button**. [6]

right-click   When using a mouse or other pointing device, to press the right button. [6]

root

　　1. A special userid that affords a user special privileges and great power. To maintain proper security, the **root** password is kept secret, known only to the system administrator. A user who has logged in as **root** is called the superuser. [4]

　　2. Within the Unix filesystem, the main directory. Same as **root directory**. The root directory is, directly or indirectly, the parent directory of all the other directories in the filesystem. [23]

　　3. Within a tree (data structure), the main node from which the tree arises. See **tree**. [9]

root directory   The main directory of the Unix filesystem. The root directory is, directly or indirectly, the parent directory of all the other directories. See also **root** and **filesystem**. [23]

root filesystem   A filesystem stored on the boot device, containing all the programs and data files necessary to start Unix, as well as the tools a system administrator would need should something go wrong. [23]

router   A special-purpose computer that relays data from one network to another. [3]

RPN   Abbreviation for **Reverse Polish Notation**. [8]

RTFM

　　1. Pronounced as four separate letters, "R-T-F-M". Within the Unix culture, RTFM is used as a verb to express the idea that, before asking for help with a problem, one should look for information in the online manual. For example, "Can you help me with the **sort** command? I have RTFM'd but I still can't figure it out." Originally, RTFM was an acronym for "Read the fuckin' manual." Today, RTFM is a valid word in its own right and is the longest verb without vowels in the English language. [9]

　　2. In a more general sense, RTFM is used to express the idea that, before someone asks for assistance, he should try to help himself by reading the appropriate documentation, or by searching for information on the Web and on Usenet. [9]

run   To follow the instructions contained in a program. Same as **execute**. [2]

Chapter references are indicated by the numbers in brackets.

runlevel One of a small number of modes in which Unix can be run, determining which fundamental services are to be provided. More technically, a system software configuration that allows a specified group of processes to exist. See also **init process**. [6]

runtime level Same as **runlevel**. [6]

S

scheduler A service, provided by the kernel, that keeps track of the processes waiting for processor time, in order to decide which process to execute next. [6] [26]

screen editor Same as **screen-oriented editor**. [22]

screen-oriented editor A text editor that allows you to enter, display and manipulate data anywhere on the screen, without having to use commands that require line numbers. Same as screen editor. Compare to **line-oriented editor**. (22)

scroll To move lines on the screen of a terminal, usually up or down, in order to make room for new lines. [7]

search path Within the shell, the list of directories in which the shell looks when it needs to find a program that must be executed. [13]

secondary prompt A special shell prompt used to indicate that a command is being continued onto a new line. See also **shell prompt**. [19]

sentence When using the **vi** text editor, a string of characters, ending in a period, comma, question mark or exclamation mark, followed by at least two spaces or a newline character. Various **vi** commands act upon sentences when moving the cursor or modifying text. See also **word** and **paragraph**. [22]

server
  1. A program that offers a service of some type, usually over a network. The program that requests such services is called a client. [3]
  2. A computer that runs a server program. [3]
  3. A program used by a microkernel to perform specific tasks. [2]

set
  1. Within the shell, to create a variable and, possibly, give it a value. [12]
  2. Within the Bourne shell family (Bash, Korn shell), to turn on an option. See also **unset**. [12]

setuid Often abbreviated as suid (pronounced "S-U-I-D"); stands for "set userid". A special type of file permission used only with files that contain executable programs. When setuid is set, a program executes with the permissions of the owner of the file regardless of which userid runs the program. Setuid is usually used to enable regular userids to run programs owned by **root** that require superuser privileges. [25]

shadow file A system file, **/etc/shadow**, that contains encoded passwords with related data, such as expiration dates. See also **password file**. [11]

shell A program that provides one of the primary interfaces to Unix by acting as a command processor and by interpreting scripts of commands. [2] [11]

Chapter references are indicated by the numbers in brackets.

shell option   Within the Bourne shell family (Bash, Korn shell), a setting that acts as an off/on switch in order to control a particular aspect of the shell's behavior. Within the C-Shell family (C-Shell, Tcsh), shell options are not used. Instead, the behavior of the shell is controlled by setting shell variables. [12]

shell prompt   One or more characters displayed by the shell to indicate that it is ready to accept a new command. See also **secondary prompt**. [4] [13]

shell script   A list of commands, stored in a file, that can be executed by a shell. Most shells have special programming commands designed specifically for use within shell scripts. [11] [12]

shell variable   Within a shell, a local variable that is not part of the environment and, hence, is not accessible to child processes. See also **environment variable**, **local variable** and **global variable**. [12]

shortcut key   Within a GUI, a key or key combination that allows you to initiate a particular action without having to go to the trouble of pulling down a menu and selecting an item. [6]

shutdown   A process that stops Unix and turns off the computer. [6]

signal   A type of interprocess communication in which a simple message, in the form of a number, is sent to a process to let it know that some type of event has occurred. It is up to the process to recognize the signal and do something. When a process does this, we say that it traps the signal. See also **interprocess communication** and **trap**. [26]

single-user mode   Runlevel #1. A runlevel in which only the superuser may log in, usually to perform some type of system maintenance or repair. [6]

Slackware   The first successful Linux distribution, released in July 1993 by Patrick Volkerding. The name "slack" was a whimsical choice, taken from the Church of the SubGenius, a parody religion. Slack refers to the feeling of exhilaration and satisfaction that comes from achieving your personal goals. [2]

soft link   Synonym for **symbolic link**. Used to distinguish between a regular link (hard link) and a symbolic link (soft link). [25]

software   Computer programs of all types. [2]

source   Synonym for **source code**. [2]

source code   A program written in a computer language, readable by a knowledgeable person. To convert a source program into an executable program, it must be translated into machine language. Informally, source code is often referred to as "source". [2]

source control system   A sophisticated system, commonly used by software developers to manage the development of large programs or documents. Same as **revision control system**. Generic term is **version control system**. [17]

special file   A type of pseudo file that provides an internal representation of a physical device. Also called a **device file**. See also **pseudo file**. [23]

squeeze   With respect to programs that modify text (such as `tr`), while performing a translate operation, to treat multiple adjacent identical characters as a single character. For example, replacing multiple spaces in a row by a single space. See also **translate**. [19]

Chapter references are indicated by the numbers in brackets.

stack A data structure in which elements are stored and retrieved one at a time, such that, at any time, the next data element to be retrieved is the last element that was stored. See also **LIFO** ("last-in first out") and **data structure**. [8] [24]

standard error The default target for error messages written by a program. Abbreviated as **stderr**. When a user logs in, the shell automatically sets standard error to be the monitor. Thus, by default, most programs write their error messages to the monitor. See also **standard input**, **standard output** and **standard I/O**. [15]

standard I/O Collectively, refers to **standard input**, **standard output** and **standard error**. Abbreviation for "standard input/output". [15]

standard input The default input source for a program. Abbreviated as **stdin**. When a user logs in, the shell automatically sets standard input to the keyboard. Thus, by default, most programs read their input from the keyboard. See also **standard output**, **standard error** and **standard I/O**. [15]

standard options Same as UNIX options. [26]

standard output The default target for general output written by a program. Abbreviated as **stdout**. When a user logs in, the shell automatically sets standard output to be the monitor. Thus, by default, most programs write their output to the monitor. See also **standard input**, **standard error** and **standard I/O**. [15]

state The current status of a process. At any time, a process is in one of three possible states: running in the foreground; running in the background; or suspended (paused), waiting for a signal to resume execution. See also **foreground process**, **background process** and **suspend**. [26]

static data Within the Unix filesystem, data that does not change without system administrator intervention. Compare to **variable data**. [23]

stderr Abbreviation for **standard error**. [15]

stdin Abbreviation for **standard input**. [15]

stdout Abbreviation for **standard output**. [15]

stop To pause a process temporarily, usually by pressing the **^z** key. Once a process is stopped, it waits for a signal to resume execution. Same as **suspend**. Compare to **kill**. See also **process** and **job control**. [26]

stream Data that is either read by a program (an **input stream**) or written by a program (an **output stream**). [19]

string A sequence of printable characters. Same as **character string**. See also **printable character**. [19]

strong quotes When using the shell, a synonym for single quotes (`'`). Within single quotes, no characters have special meanings. Compare to **weak quotes**. [13]

subdirectory Also called a child directory. A directory that lies within another directory. All directories, except the root directory, can be considered subdirectories. The directory that contains a subdirectory is called the parent directory. See also **directory**. [23]

subshell Any shell that is started from within another shell. [15] [26]

suid Abbreviation for **setuid**. Pronounced "S-U-I-D". [25]

Chapter references are indicated by the numbers in brackets.

superblock Within a Unix filesystem, a special data area that holds crucial information about the filesystem itself. [24]

superuser A user, usually the system administrator, who has logged in using the **root** userid, which affords special privileges. See also **root**. [4]

supplementary group With respect to a specific userid, aside from the userid's primary group, any other group to which the userid belongs. Compare to **primary group**. See also **group** and **file mode**. [25]

suspend To pause a process temporarily, usually by pressing the **^Z** key. Once a process is suspended, it waits for a signal to resume execution. Same as **stop**. Compare to **kill**. See also **process** and **job control**. [26]

swap file When using the **vi** text editor, a copy of the editing buffer that is saved automatically in the same directory in which you are editing. Should your work session be aborted expectedly — say by a system crash — the swap file can be used to recover your data. [22]

switch

1. When entering a Unix command: another name for an option. [10]
2. When using the **vi** text editor: a type of option that is either on or off. Compare to **variable**. See also **option**. [22]

symbolic link Within a filesystem, a type of link that is, literally, the pathname of another file. A symbolic link is sometimes called a soft link to distinguish it from a regular link (hard link). Often referred to as a symlink. Compare to **link**. [25]

symlink Abbreviation for **symbolic link**. [25]

syntax The formal description of how a command should be entered. [10]

sysadmin Synonym for **system administrator**. [4]

system administrator The person who administers and manages a Unix system. Same as **sysadmin**. [4]

system call A facility used by a process to call upon the kernel to provide a service. [12]

system call A facility used by a process to request the kernel to perform a service. [26]

system maintenance mode Obsolete term for **single-user mode**. [6]

system manager Obsolete term for **system administrator**. [4]

System V A version of UNIX developed at AT&T, released in 1983. In the 1980s, System V was one of the two main branches of the Unix; the other was **BSD**. [2]

T

tab stop On a typewriter, a mechanical marker that sets a position where the carriage will stop when the <Tab> key is pressed. [18]

task Within a GUI, a program that is running in a window. [6]

task switching Within a GUI, to change the focus from one window to another, often by using a key combination to cycle through the list of currently running tasks. With most GUIs, the task switching keys are <Alt-Tab> to move forward through the list, and <Alt-Shift-Tab> to move backward through the list. [6]

Chapter references are indicated by the numbers in brackets.

taskbar Within a GUI, a horizontal bar, usually at the bottom of the screen, which contains a representation of each window that is currently active. The representation of a window is usually an icon, possibly with some text. Within Gnome the functionality of the taskbar is provided by the "Window List". [6]

TCO Abbreviation for **total cost of ownership**. [5]

Tcsh A member of the C-Shell family, originally developed in the late 1970s by Ken Greer of Carnegie-Mellon University as a completely free version of the C-Shell. Pronounced "tee-see-shell". The Tcsh is used widely as a powerful, backwards compatible replacement for the traditional C-Shell. The name of the Tcsh program is either **tcsh** or **csh**. See also **C-Shell family**. [11]

Termcap A database, consisting of one large file, that contains technical descriptions of all the different types of terminals. In modern systems, Termcap has been replaced by **Terminfo**. [7]

terminal The hardware used to access a Unix system via a keyboard, a monitor and, possibly, a mouse. A Unix terminal can be a machine designed to be a terminal, or it can be a computer that is running a program to act like (emulate) a terminal. [3]

terminal driver The program that acts as the driver for a terminal. [21]

terminal room In the 1970s and 1980s, a room in which there were a number of terminals connected to a host computer. To use a Unix system, you would go to the terminal room, and wait for a free terminal. [3]

terminal server A special-purpose computer that acts as a switch, connecting terminals to host computers. [3]

terminate With respect to a process, to stop running. Same as **die**. [26]

Terminfo A database, consisting of a collection of files, containing technical descriptions of all the different types of terminals. In modern systems, Terminfo replaces an older database called **Termcap**. [7]

test When using the **find** program, a specification defining the criteria used during the file search. For example, the test **-type f** tells **find** to search only for ordinary files. See also **action** and **operator**. [25]

Texinfo The official documentation system for the GNU project. Texinfo provides a sophisticated set of tools that use a single information file to generate output in a variety of formats: Info format, plain text, HTML, DVI, PDF, XML and Docbook. Most commonly pronounced as "Tekinfo". [9]

text Data that consists of characters: letters, numbers, punctuation, and so on. [3]

text editor A program used to create and modify text files. Often referred to informally as an editor. [22]

text file A file that contains only printable characters, with a newline character at the end of each line. Unix filters are designed to work with text files. Sometimes called an ASCII file. Compare to **binary file**. See also **printable character**. [19]

text-based terminal A terminal that displays only characters (text): letters, numbers, punctuation and so on. Same as **character terminal**. [3]

Chapter references are indicated by the numbers in brackets.

time slice   A very short interval during which a particular process is allowed to use the processor. A typical time slice would be 10 milliseconds (10 thousandths of a second). See also **CPU time**. [6] [26]

time-sharing system   The old name for a multiuser system. Describes an operating system that can support more than one user at a time. [3]

title bar   Within a GUI, the horizontal area at the top of a window that has the name of the program running in the window. [6]

top   Within a stack, the location of the data element that was most recently pushed onto (written to) the stack. [8] [24]

Top Node   Within the Info system, the root of a tree. As a general rule, the Top Node contains a summary of the topic under discussion, as well as a menu showing the topics covered in the file. [9]

top-level directory   Any subdirectory of the root directory. The root directory and the top-level directories form the backbone of the Unix filesystem. See also **root directory** and **filesystem**. [23]

total cost of ownership   A business term, often abbreviated as TCO. An estimate of the total cost of owning and using a machine or a system over its lifetime. To estimate the TCO for a computer, one must consider the cost of hardware, software, upgrades, maintenance, technical support, and training. As a rule of thumb, the TCO of a business PC is 3 to 4 times its purchase price. [5]

total ordering   When ordering elements of a set, a binary relation that orders all the members of the set with respect to one another. Compare to **partial ordering**. [19]

translate   With respect to programs that modify text (such as `tr`), to change every instance of a character to one or more specified characters. See also **squeeze**. [19]

trap   For a program that is executing, to notice and react to a specific signal, especially signals that might abort or otherwise affect the program. [7]

tree   A data structure formed by a set of nodes, leaves, and branches, organized in such a way that there is, at most, one branch between any two nodes. See also **data structure**, **node**, **leaf**, **branch**, **root**. [9]

triple-click   When using a mouse or other pointing device, to press a button three times in rapid succession. [6]

U

UI   Abbreviation for **Unix International**. [5]

Unix
1. Any operating system that meets generally accepted "Unix-like" standards with respect to providing user and programming services. [2]
2. Describes a worldwide culture, based on the Unix operating systems, involving interfaces, shells, programs, languages, conventions and standards. [2]

UNIX   The specific family of operating system products and associated software originally developed by AT&T. Compare to **Unix**. [2]

Chapter references are indicated by the numbers in brackets.

Unix International An organization formed in December 1989 by AT&T, Sun, and several smaller companies, as an alternative to the Open Software Foundation. Abbreviated as UI. [5]

Unix manual Same as the **online manual**. [9]

UNIX options With respect to the **ps** (process status) command, those options that are derived from the 1980s version of **ps** that was part of AT&T UNIX. UNIX options start with a single dash. Compare to **BSD options**. Also called POSIX options and standard options. [26]

unmaximize button Within a GUI, a small rectangle, usually in the top right-hand corner of the window, that, when clicked, will restore a window that was previously maximized. [6]

unmount (verb) To disable access to a filesystem residing on a device by disconnecting it from the main Unix filesystem. To unmount a filesystem, you use the **umount** command. See also **mount** and **filesystem**. [23]

unnamed buffer When using the **vi** text editor, a storage area containing a copy of your last deletion. See also **numbered buffer**. [22]

unset
  1. Within the shell, to delete a variable. [12]
  2. Within the Bourne shell family (Bash, Korn shell), to turn off an option. See also **set**. [12]

uppercase Describes the capital letters, "A" to "Z". [4]

Usenet A worldwide system of discussion groups. [3]

user A person who uses a Unix system in some way. Unix does not know about users: Unix only knows about userids. [4]

user mask A three-number octal value that indicates which file permissions should be withheld from newly created files. [25]

user name completion Same as **userid completion**. [13]

userid A name, registered with a Unix system, that identifies a specific account. Pronounced "user-eye-dee". [4]

userid completion A type of autocompletion that completes a partially typed userid, when a word begins with a ~ (tilde) character. Userid completion is available with Bash, the C-Shell, and the Tcsh. See also **autocompletion**. [13]

utility Any of the hundreds of programs that are distributed with a Unix/Linux operating system. [2]

V

value Data that is stored in the variable. [12]

variable
  1. A quantity, known by a name, that represents a value. [12]
  2. When using the **vi** text editor, an option that contains a value. Compare to **switch**. See also **option**. [22]

Chapter references are indicated by the numbers in brackets.

variable completion A type of autocompletion that completes a partially typed variable name, when a word begins with a **$** (dollar) character. Variable completion is available with Bash and the Tcsh. See also **autocompletion**. [13]

variable data Within the Unix filesystem, data that, by its nature, is expected to change over time; for example, a log file. Compare to **static data**. [23]

version control system Generic name for a sophisticated system, commonly used by software developers and engineers, to manage the development of large programs, documents, blueprints, and so on. When used by programmers, usually referred to as a **source control system** or **revision control system**. [17]

vi A powerful, screen-oriented text editor, part of every Unix system. The **vi** editor is the de facto standard Unix text editor. The name **vi** is pronounced as two separate letters "vee-eye". See also **Vim**. [22]

vi mode Within the shell, a mode used with command line editing in which the editing commands are the same ones as are used with the **vi** text editor. See also **command line editing** and **Emacs mode**. [13]

Vim A very powerful, backward compatible replacement for the **vi** text editor. On many Unix and Linux systems, Vim, by default, takes the place of **vi**. See also **vi**. [22]

virtual console One of several terminal emulation programs running at the same time, each of which supports an independent work session. Within Linux, the most common default configuration offers the user 7 virtual consoles: #1-6 are full-screen, text-based terminals for using a CLI; #7 is a graphics terminal for running a GUI. In such systems, the desktop environment (such as KDE or Gnome) runs within virtual console #7. See also **terminal**. Compare to **pseudo terminal**. [6]

virtual filesystem An API (application program interface) that provides a uniform way for programs to access data regardless of how that data is stored or generated. The virtual filesystem is what makes it possible to organize separate, heterogeneous device filesystems into one large Unix filesystem. Abbreviated as VFS. [23]

visit Within the Info system, to look at the contents of a particular node. [9]

VT100 The most popular Unix terminal of all time, introduced in 1978 by the Digital Equipment Corporation. The VT100 was so popular that it set a permanent standard. Even today, most terminal emulation programs use specifications based on the VT100. [3]

W

wait After a process has forked to create a child process, to pause until the child has finished running. See also **fork**, **exec** and **exit**. [26]

weak quotes When using the shell, a synonym for double quotes ("). Within double quotes, only the three metacharacters **$** (dollar), ` (backquote), and **** (backslash) retain their special meaning. Compare to **strong quotes**. [13]

Web server A computer that stores Web pages and makes them available via a network, usually the Internet. [3]

Chapter references are indicated by the numbers in brackets.

whitespace

    1. With the shell, one or more consecutive spaces or tabs.

    2. With some programs, one or more consecutive spaces, tabs or newlines. [10]

wildcard   When specifying a filename, typically within a Unix command, a metacharacter used to create a pattern that can match multiple files. See also **globbing** and **pathname expansion**. [24]

window   When using a GUI, a bounded region of the screen, usually a rectangle. [5]

window manager   Within a GUI, the program that controls the appearance and characteristics of the graphical elements (windows, buttons, scroll bars, icons, and so on). [5]

window operation menu   Within a GUI, when you are using a window, a pull-down menu containing a list of actions that pertain to the window itself, such as Move, Resize, Minimize, Maximize and Close. To display the Window Operation menu, you click on the tiny icon at the top-left of the window (at the left edge of the title bar). [6]

word

    1. The fundamental unit into which bits are organized and manipulated by a particular processor. Most modern processors use 32-bit or 64-bit words. [21]

    2. When using a regular expression: a self-contained, contiguous sequence of characters consisting of letters, numbers, or underscore characters. [20]

    3. When using the **vi** text editor: a string of letters, numbers, or underscore characters. Various **vi** commands act upon words when moving the cursor or modifying text. See also **sentence** and **paragraph**. [22]

working directory   Also called **current directory**. The default directory, used when entering Unix commands. The working directory is set by the **cd** (change directory) command; the name is displayed by the **pwd** (print working directory) command. [24]

workspace   Within the Gnome desktop environment, a **desktop**. [6]

write permission   A type of file permission. With a file, it allows reading. With a directory, it allows creating, moving, copying or deleting within the directory. Compare to **read permission** and **execute permission**. See also **file permission**. [25]

X

X   Same as **X Window**. [5]

X terminal   Any graphics terminal designed to be used with the X Window system. Today, the X terminal standard is the basis for graphics terminal emulation, in the same way that the VT100 is the basis of character terminal emulation. [3]

X Window   A widely-used system designed to support graphical user interfaces (GUIs). The correct usage of this term is singular, "X Window", not plural, "X Windows". The X Window system is often referred to simply as "X". [5]

Y

yank   (verb) When using the **vi** text editor, to copy text to the unnamed buffer without deleting the text. See also **unnamed buffer**. [22]

Chapter references are indicated by the numbers in brackets.

Z

zero file   The pseudo-file **/dev/zero**. When used as an output target, the zero file throws away all input. When used as an input source, it always returns a null character. The null file is one of the two **bit buckets**, the other being the **zero file**. See also **pseudo-file** and **null character**. [23]

zero or more   Indicates that you can use one or more of something or that you can omit the item entirely. For example, the syntax for a command might allow you to specify zero or more file names. This means that you can specify one or more names, or you can omit the name entirely. Compare to **one or more**. [10]

zombie   A child process that has died, but has not yet been made to vanish by its parent. If the child is an orphan (without a parent), it will remain a zombie until the system does something to cause the child to vanish. See also **die** and **orphan**. [26]

Zsh   A member of the Bourne shell family, a very powerful, complex shell, originally developed in 1990 by Paul Falstad, a student at Princeton University. Zsh is pronounced "zee-shell". The name of the Zsh program is **zsh**. See also **Bourne shell family**. [11]

Chapter references are indicated by the numbers in brackets.

QUICK INDEX
FOR THE vi TEXT EDITOR

For a summary of **vi** *commands, see Appendix C on page 827.*

TOPICS

vi COMMANDS (continued)

n	584-586, 829	U	595, 597-598, 830	y}	831
O	587-589, 829	u	595, 597-598, 830	y1G	831
o	587-589, 829	W	579, 828	yb	831
P	598-599, 599-601, 831	w	574, 579, 828	yG	831
p	598-599, 599-601, 831	X	594, 595, 830	ygg	831
R	590, 592, 830	x	577, 594, 595, 600, 830	yW	831
r	590, 592, 607, 830	xp	831	yw	831
r\<Return\>	830	Y	601-602	yy	601-602, 831
S	591, 592, 830	y	601-602, 831	ZZ	572, 573, 827
s	590, 592, 830	y)	831		

ex COMMANDS

:!	608-609, 832	:help (Vim)	622	:set number	586, 827
:!!	609, 832	:m	608, 831	:set showmode	570
:!csh	832	:map	616-618	:set wm=	830
:$	829	:map g 1G	829	:sh	609, 832
:%s	830	:q!	572, 827	:una	616, 832
:1	829	:r	610-611, 832	:unmap	618
:ab	615-616, 832	:r!	459, 832	:w	613-614, 832
:co	608, 831	:r !look	832	:w>>	832
:d	595, 596	:s	592-594, 830	:wq	827
:e	615, 832	:set	429, 603-606	:x	827
:e!	832	:set nonumber	586, 827		

SPECIAL CHARACTERS

!	612-613, 832	+	578, 828	`	583
!!	612-613, 832	−	578, 828	``	582
"	598-599	.	597-598, 830	{	579, 828
$	579, 828	/	584-586, 829	}	579, 828
' '	583	:	587	~	602-603, 830
(	579, 828	?	584-586, 829	0	579, 828
)	579, 828	^	579, 828		

KEYS

\<Backspace\>	578, 827-828	\<Space\>	578, 828	^U	582, 828
\<Delete\>	827	\<Up\>	578, 828	^V	573
\<Down\>	578, 828	^B	582, 828		
\<Left\>	578, 828	^D	582, 828		
\<Return\>	575, 578, 828	^F	582, 828		
\<Right\>	578, 828	^L	573, 827		

INDEX

Note: There is a special index for the vi text editor on page 891.
For a summary of vi commands, see Appendix C, page 827.

Page numbers followed by n indicate topics found in footnotes.

Page numbers followed by n indicate topics found in footnotes.

Page numbers followed by n indicate topics found in footnotes.

Page numbers followed by n indicate topics found in footnotes.

Page numbers followed by n indicate topics found in footnotes.

Page numbers followed by n indicate topics found in footnotes.

Page numbers followed by n indicate topics found in footnotes.

Page numbers followed by n indicate topics found in footnotes.

Page numbers followed by n indicate topics found in footnotes.

Page numbers followed by n indicate topics found in footnotes.

Page numbers followed by n indicate topics found in footnotes.

Page numbers followed by n indicate topics found in footnotes.

Page numbers followed by n indicate topics found in footnotes.

Page numbers followed by n indicate topics found in footnotes.

Page numbers followed by n indicate topics found in footnotes.

Page numbers followed by n indicate topics found in footnotes.

Page numbers followed by n indicate topics found in footnotes.

M

^M key
    return character   156-157
    sending carriage return signal   155
-m shell option   847
Mach   24
machine-readable output
    defined   870
    human-readable output versus   274-276
macros
    defined   870
    vi text editor   616-618
Mac OS X. See OS X
mail servers   48-49, 870
mail shell variable   850
mainframe computers   39, 870
makefiles, building   776
manual. See online manual
man command   192-193, 202-203, 234, 236, 248,
    286, 374, 382, 819, 822. See also man pages
man -f command   208, 236
man -k command   209, 236
man pages. See also man command
    for builtin commands   210, 286-287
    command syntax in   235
    displaying   193-196
        in separate window   196-197
        as web pages   198-199
    explained   193, 870
    finding   747
    format of   204-208
    referencing in   203
    running shell commands from   197-198
    for shells, displaying   248
map   871
mapped   871
mappings
    defined   132, 871
    for keyboard signals   140
        changing   152-153
        displaying   151-152
    for erase signal   143
margins, setting   442
markdirs shell option   847
Mashey, John   241, 242
match   871
matchbeep shell variable   850
matching in regular expressions
    characters   505-506
    lines   502-505
    words   502-505
mathematics, relationship with computer
    science   556-558
maximize button (window controls)   106, 871
maximizing windows   104-107, 871
Maxwell, James   814
McCulloch, Warren   498
McIlroy, Doug   369

/media directory   645
megabytes   695, 871
memory
    core memory   146-147
    virtual memory   115
memory dump   550, 871
Mena, Federico   84, 89
menus
    defined   871
    usage of, explained   102-104
menu bar   103, 871
merging
    multiple files into columns   444-446
    sorted data   473-477
messages, login   59-61
metacharacters
    escaping   266, 501-502
    explained   277-279, 871
    list of   280
    matching lines/words with regular
        expressions   502-505
    quoting   279-283, 514
    for redirection
        Bourne Shell family   363
        in C-Shell family   364
    in regular expressions   498
    strong quotes and weak quotes   283-284
Metacity window manager   79, 84
Meta key   216
microkernels
    explained   11-12, 871
    Minix as   26
Microsoft Windows. See Windows
middle-clicking   102, 871
middle mouse button   102, 871
minicomputers   39, 871
minimize button (window controls)   106, 871
minimizing windows   104-107, 866, 871
Minix   23-24, 26
MIT, history of X Window   75-76
MIT Artificial Intelligence Lab   15
mkdir command   669-672, 743, 819, 822
mkfifo command   636, 819, 823
-mmin test (find command)   755
/mnt directory   645
modes   98, 281, 871. See also file modes
modification time
    changing   715-717
    defined   704, 872
modifier keys   138-139, 872
modifying
    search path   289-291
    shell prompts   293-294
monitor shell option   274, 847
monolithic kernels
    explained   11-12, 872
    Linux as   26
Moolenaar, Bram   564, 621

Page numbers followed by n indicate topics found in footnotes.

Page numbers followed by n indicate topics found in footnotes.

null file   633, 873
null value   258
numbering lines. See line numbers
number systems
    explained   544-548
    octal versus hexadecimal numbers, popularity
        of   550-551
    reading and writing   549-550
numbers, in options   386

O

obase variable (bc program)   180-182
obscenity case (Jacobellis v. Ohio)   14
octal codes for unprintable characters   485
octal numbers
    explained   544-548, 873
    popularity versus hexadecimal numbers   550-551
    reading and writing   549-550
od command   524, 551-555, 819, 822
offsets   552, 873
-ok action (find command)   760
Olson, Arthur David   843*n*
Olson database   843*n*
olwm (Open Look window manager)   82
onecmd shell option   847
"one or more"   231-232, 873
online   190, 873
online manual   189-190. See also documentation;
        man pages
    explained   192-193, 870, 874, 887
    info command versus   212
    organization of   199-201
    searching for commands   209
OpenBSD   30
    when to use   31
Open Group   13, 86
Open Look window manager   82
Open Office   91
    viewing tabs/spaces   429
Open Software Foundation (OSF)
    defined   13, 874
    formation of   81-82
open source movement   18-19, 874
open source software   16, 874
open system call   769
operating systems
    explained   9-10, 874
    GNU   16
    Unix-like systems, defining   14
Operating Systems: Design and Implementation
        (Tanenbaum)   24
operations, order of   177
operators
    defined   874
    repetition operators, in regular
        expressions   499
/opt directory   645

options. See also shell options
    diff command   403-408
    explained   226-229, 863, 874
    grep command   450-454
    learning   235-237, 374
    less program   531-534
    look command   456-457
    ls command   683-685
    numbers in   386
    ps command
        selecting   793-794
        types of   788-789
    sort command   456-457, 461-462
    tr command   486-488
    vi text editor
        displaying   605-606
        list of   605
        setting   603-604
ordinary files   628, 874
organization of online manual   199-201
organizing files in directories   630. See also
        directories; filesystems
origin of. See history of
original Unix filesystem   641
orphans   771, 874
OSF (Open Software Foundation)
    defined   874
    formation of   81-82
OS X, as based on Unix   4-5, 32
outer joins   476, 875
output. See also standard output
    of background processes, writing to
        screen   774-776
    discarding   360-361
    machine-readable versus human-readable
        274-276
output display, pausing   147-148
output options (diff command)   404-408
output streams   489, 875
overriding noclobber option   351
owd shell variable   850
ownership of files   732, 875

P

-p shell option   847
<PageDown> key   218
pagers. See also less program; more program
    customizing with environment variables   535-536
    explained   194, 522, 875
PAGER environment variable   535
pages
    defined   875
    formatting text into   440-443
<PageUp> key   218
paging programs. See pagers
paper tape in Teletype terminals   142
paragraphs, formatting   436-439

Page numbers followed by n indicate topics found in footnotes.

Page numbers followed by n indicate topics found in footnotes.

Page numbers followed by n indicate topics found in footnotes.

Page numbers followed by n indicate topics found in footnotes.

Index 917

Page numbers followed by n indicate topics found in footnotes.

Page numbers followed by n indicate topics found in footnotes.

Page numbers followed by n indicate topics found in footnotes.

Page numbers followed by n indicate topics found in footnotes.

Page numbers followed by n indicate topics found in footnotes.

Page numbers followed by n indicate topics found in footnotes.

Page numbers followed by n indicate topics found in footnotes.

Page numbers followed by n indicate topics found in footnotes.

Page numbers followed by n indicate topics found in footnotes.